Prepare with The Power of Classroom Practice

Register for **MyEducationLab** today at www.myeducationlab.com

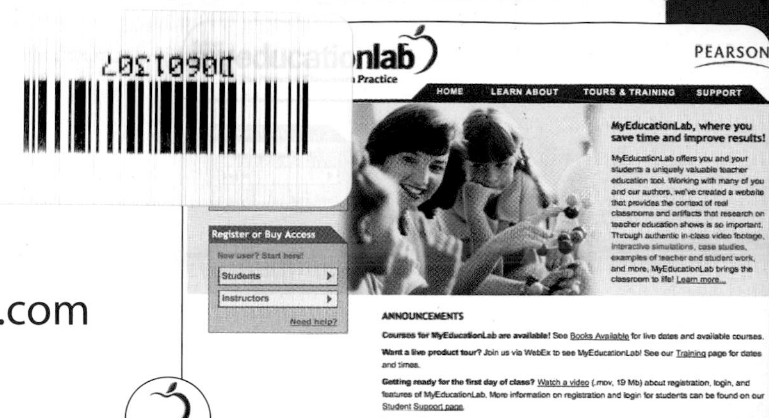

What is MyEducationLab?

MyEducationLab is easy to use and integrate into this book. Wherever you see the MyEducationLab logo in the margins or elsewhere in the text, follow the simple instructions to access the videos, strategies, cases, and artifacts associated with these assignments, activities, and learning units on MyEducationLab. MyEducationLab is organized topically to enhance the coverage of the core concepts discussed in the chapters of your book. For each topic on the course you will find most or all of the following resources:

Students:

- Take **Practice Tests** for each chapter of your text.
  - Completion of each practice test generates a **study plan** that is unique to you.
  - The study plan links to text excerpts, activities with feedback, and videos and other media that can help you master concepts covered in your text.
- Complete **Assignments and Activities** to apply text content to real classroom situations.
- Explore the **Building Teaching Skills and Dispositions** exercises to practice and strengthen the skills that are essential to teaching.

MyEducationLab offers:

- Authentic **classroom video** shows real teachers and students interacting, and helps prepare you for the classroom.
- **Case studies** offer real-life perspectives on common issues and challenges faced in the classroom.
- Authentic student and teacher **classroom artifacts** provide you with the actual types of materials encountered every day by teachers.

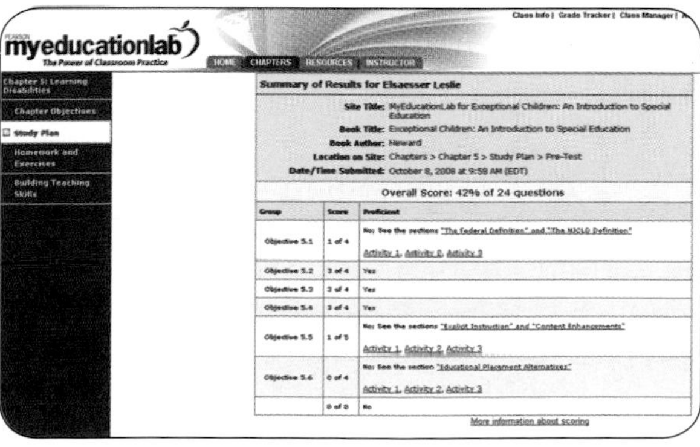

CONNECTION TO NATIONAL STANDARDS: Now it is easier than ever to see how coursework is connected to national standards. Each topic on MyEducationLab lists intended learning outcomes connected to the appropriate national standards. And all of the Assignments and Activities and all of the Building Teaching Skills and Dispositions in MyEducationLab are mapped to the appropriate national standards and learning outcomes.

ASSIGNMENTS AND ACTIVITIES: Designed to save instructors preparation time and enhance student understanding, these assignable exercises show concepts in action (through video, cases, and/or student and teacher artifacts). They help students synthesize and apply concepts and strategies they read about in the book.

BUILDING TEACHING SKILLS AND DISPOSITIONS

These learning units help students practice and strengthen skills that are essential to quality teaching. Students are presented with the core skill or concept and then given an opportunity to practice their understanding of this concept multiple times by watching video footage (or interacting with other media) and then critically analyzing the strategy or skill presented.

STUDY PLAN

A MyEducationLab Study Plan is a multiple choice assessment tied to chapter objectives and supported by study material. A well-designed Study Plan offers multiple opportunities to fully master required course content as identified by the objectives in each chapter:

- **Chapter Objectives** identify the learning outcomes for the chapter and give students targets to shoot for as they read and study.
- **Multiple Choice Assessments** assess mastery of the content. These assessments are mapped to chapter objectives, and students can take the multiple choice quiz as many times as they want. Not only do these quizzes provide overall scores for each objective, but they also explain why responses to particular items are correct or incorrect.
- **Study Material: Review, Practice and Enrichment** give students a deeper understanding of what they do and do not know related to chapter content. This material includes text excerpts, activities that include hints and feedback, and interactive multi-media exercises built around videos, simulations, cases, or classroom artifacts.
- **Flashcards** help students study the definitions of the key terms within each chapter.

GENERAL RESOURCES ON YOUR MYEDUCATIONLAB COURSE

The Resources section on MyEducationLab is designed to help students pass their licensure exams, put together effective portfolios and lesson plans, prepare for and navigate the first year of their teaching careers, and understand key educational standards, policies, and laws. This section includes:

- **Licensure Exams:** Contains guidelines for passing the Praxis exam. **The Practice Test Exam** includes practice multiple-choice questions, case study questions, and video case studies with sample questions.
- **Lesson Plan Builder:** Helps students create and share lesson plans.
- **Licensure and Standards:** Provides links to state licensure standards and national standards.
- **Beginning Your Career:** Educate Offers tips, advice, and valuable information on:
    - o Resume Writing and Interviewing: Expert advice on how to write impressive resumes and prepare for job interviews.
    - o Your First Year of Teaching: Practical tips on setting up a classroom, managing student behavior, and planning for instruction and assessment.
    - o Law and Public Policies: Includes specific directives and requirements educators need to understand under the No Child Left Behind Act and the Individuals with Disabilities Education Improvement Act of 2004.

What if I need help?

We've got you covered 24/7.
There is a wealth of helpful information on the site, under "Tours and Training "and" Support."
Technical support is available 24 hours a day, seven days a week, at http://247pearsoned.custhelp.com.

Visit **www.myeducationlab.com** for a demonstration of this exciting new online teaching resource.

Effective Practices in Early Childhood Education

Building a Foundation

Sue Bredekamp
Early Childhood Education Consultant

Boston Columbus Indianapolis New York San Francisco Upper Saddle River
Amsterdam Cape Town Dubai London Madrid Milan Munich Paris Montreal Toronto
Delhi Mexico City São Paulo Sydney Hong Kong Seoul Singapore Taipei Tokyo

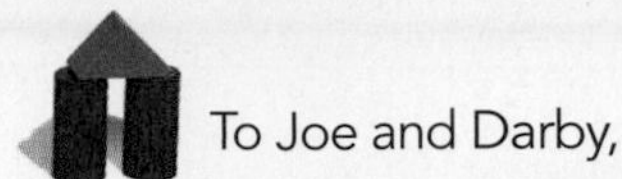

To Joe and Darby,

my two best friends who have been by my side the whole way

Vice President and Editor in Chief: Jeffery W. Johnston
Senior Acquisitions Editor: Julie Peters
Senior Development Editor: Max Effenson Chuck
Editorial Assistant: Tiffany Bitzel
Vice President, Director of Marketing: Quinn Perkson
Marketing Manager: Erica DeLuca
Marketing Assistant: Drew Jameson
Senior Managing Editor: Pamela D. Bennett
Senior Project Manager: Mary Harlan
Senior Operations Supervisor: Matthew Ottenweller
Operations Specialist: Laura Messerly
Senior Art Director: Diane Lorenzo
Text and Cover Design: Rokusek Design
Photo Coordinator: Lori Whitley
Permissions Administrator: Rebecca Savage
Cover Art: Shutterstock
Media Producer: Autumn Benson
Media Project Manager: Rebecca Norsic
Full-Service Project Management: Amy Gehl, S4Carlisle Publishing Services
Composition: S4Carlisle Publishing Services
Printer/Binder: Courier Kendallville, Inc.
Cover Printer: Lehigh-Phoenix Color
Text Font: Minion

Credits and acknowledgments borrowed from other sources and reproduced, with permission, in this textbook appear on appropriate page within text.

Photo Credits: Michael Hall/Corbis RF, p. 7; Frank Siteman, pp. 15, 107, 292, 329, 461; Krista Greco/Merrill, pp. 21, 77 (bottom); Courtesy of Detroit Medical Center, p. 23; Katelyn Metzger/Merrill, pp. 28, 49, 85, 117, 267; Shutterstock, pp. 36 (left), 97, 273; Annie Pickert/AB Merrill, pp. 36 (right), 57, 208, 291, 361, 378, 389, 398, 406, 434 (bottom); Randy Olson/Aurora Photos, Inc., p. 39; Anthony Magnacca/Merrill, pp. 47, 77 (top), 189, 313, 439, 458, 494; Scott Cunningham/Merrill, pp. 51, 77 (center), 88, 484; Courtesy of the Library of Congress, p. 63; Ellen B. Senisi/The Image Works, pp. 65, 161; iStockphoto.com, p. 72; Felicia Martinez/PhotoEdit Inc., p. 73; Michael Newman/PhotoEdit Inc., pp. 86, 258, 349, 400, 476; Will & Deni McIntyre/Photo Researchers, Inc., p. 115; Elizabeth Crews/Elizabeth Crews Photography, pp. 119, 293, 449; The Atelier–Diana Municipal Preschool © Preschools and Infant-Toddler Centers – Istituzione of the Municipality of Reggio Emilia, Italy, from "Advisories," published by Reggio Children, 2002, p. 127; Patrick White/Merrill, p. 133; © Ellen B. Senisi, pp. 139, 157, 167, 169, 240, 332, 335, 341, 368, 369, 375, 390, 397, 413, 416, 473, 487, 491; Richard Hutchings/PhotoEdit Inc., pp. 150, 235, 315; Explorer/Photo Researchers, Inc., p. 170; Mark Burnett/Photo Researchers, Inc., p. 185; Kirk Condyles/The Image Works, p. 201; Nancy Sheehan Photography, pp. 206, 422, 451; BananaStock, pp. 211, 275; Mac H. Brown/Merrill, p. 212; Bob Daemmrich Photography, Inc., pp. 216, 495; George Dodson/PH College, pp. 217, 432; Shirley Zeiberg/PH College, p. 233 (left); Monkey Business Images/Dreamstime, p. 233 (right); Jupiter Unlimited, p. 245; Bill Aron/PhotoEdit Inc., p. 256; Spencer Grant/PhotoEdit Inc., pp. 260, 457; David Mager/Pearson Learning Photo Studio, p. 268; T. Lindfors/Lindfors Photography, pp. 272, 280, 344, 382; Mona Lisa Amas and Shelley Kadota, pp. 298, 303, 308 (all); Adam Jones/Photo Researchers, Inc., p. 300; Ryan McVay/Getty Images, Inc.–Photodisc, pp. 321, 364; Hope Madden/Merrill, p. 330; Jim West/PhotoEdit Inc., p. 384; Silver Burdett Ginn Needham, p. 401; Getty Images, Inc.–Photodisc, p. 409; Photos to Go, p. 418; Robert Brenner/PhotoEdit Inc., p. 429; Laura Dwight/Creative Eye/MIRA.com, p. 434 (top); Nancy Forsyth, pp. 469, 472; Ruth Jenkinson © Dorling Kindersley, p. 475; Trish Gant © Dorling Kindersley, p. 479; Will Hart/PhotoEdit Inc., p. 489; Kathy Kirtland/Merrill, p. 496. All chapter-opening images by Getty, iStockphoto, Jupiter Unlimited, Shutterstock, and SuperStock.

Every effort has been made to provide accurate and current Internet information in this book. However, the Internet and information posted on it are constantly changing, so it is inevitable that some of the Internet addresses listed in this textbook will change.

Library of Congress Cataloging-in-Publication Data

Bredekamp, Sue.
Effective practices in early childhood education : building a foundation / Sue Bredekamp.
p. cm.
Includes bibliographical references and index.
ISBN 978-0-205-51532-5
1. Early childhood education—United States. 2. Child development—United States. I. Title.
LB1140.23.B72 2011
372.210973--dc22
2009039793

10 9 8 7 6 5 4 3 2 1

www.pearsonhighered.com

ISBN 13: 978-0-205-51532-5
ISBN 10: 0-205-51532-0

About the Author

Sue Bredekamp, Ph.D.

Dr. Sue Bredekamp is an early childhood education specialist from Washington, D.C., who serves as a consultant on curriculum, teaching, and professional development for national organizations such as the National Association for the Education of Young Children (NAEYC), the Council for Professional Recognition, and Head Start. From 1981 to 1998, she was director of Accreditation and Professional Development for NAEYC, where she developed and directed a national accreditation system for early childhood programs. She is the editor of NAEYC's highly influential publication, *Developmentally Appropriate Practice in Early Childhood Programs* (1987), and coeditor of the 1997 and 2009 editions.

From 2007 to 2009, Dr. Bredekamp served on the Committee on Early Childhood Mathematics of the National Research Council. She coauthored *Learning to Read and Write: Developmentally Appropriate Practices for Young Children*, the joint position statement of the International Reading Association and NAEYC. She was a consultant for RISE Learning Solutions, producer of distance learning programs for early childhood professional development, and the content developer and on-air faculty for *HeadsUp! Reading*, a distance learning course on early literacy.

Dr. Bredekamp is a frequent keynote speaker and author of numerous books and articles related to standards for professional practice and professional development. Dr. Bredekamp holds a Ph.D. in curriculum and instruction from the University of Maryland. Her professional experience includes teaching and directing programs for children ages 2 through 6, training child care staff at a community college, and serving on the faculty of the Human Development & Childhood Education program at Mount Vernon College in Washington, D.C. She has been a visiting lecturer at Macquarie University in Sydney, Australia; Monash University in Melbourne, Australia; the University of Alaska; and the University of Hawaii.

Contributors

This book represents a collaborative effort, made possible by the invaluable contributions of the expertise and diverse perspectives of the following individuals.

Carol Copple

Carol Copple is director of Publications and Initiatives in Educational Practice at NAEYC. She was on the faculty at Louisiana State University, and at the Educational Testing Service she codeveloped and directed a research-based model for early childhood education. Her publications include *Developmentally Appropriate Practice in Early Childhood Programs*, *Basics of Developmentally Appropriate Practice: An Introduction for Teachers of Children 3 to 6*, and *Educating the Young Thinker: Classroom Strategies for Cognitive Growth.* Dr. Copple contributed most of the *Becoming an Intentional Teacher*, *How Would You Respond?* and *What Works* features in this book as well as invaluable assistance in conceptualizing aspects of the book.

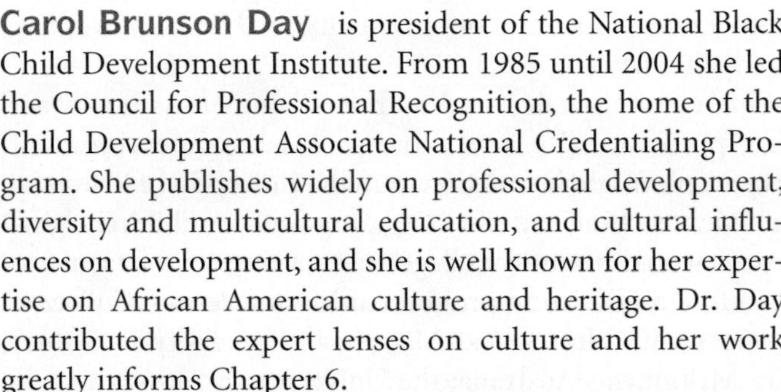

Carol Brunson Day is president of the National Black Child Development Institute. From 1985 until 2004 she led the Council for Professional Recognition, the home of the Child Development Associate National Credentialing Program. She publishes widely on professional development, diversity and multicultural education, and cultural influences on development, and she is well known for her expertise on African American culture and heritage. Dr. Day contributed the expert lenses on culture and her work greatly informs Chapter 6.

Carol Brunson Day

Gail E. Joseph

Gail E. Joseph is the faculty director of the Early Childhood and Family Studies program at the University of Washington and an assistant professor of educational psychology. Her work focuses on teaching young children social–emotional skills and interpersonal problem solving. Dr. Joseph contributed most of the expert lenses on inclusion, as well as much of Chapters 5 and 14. Her real-life classroom examples enliven the book throughout.

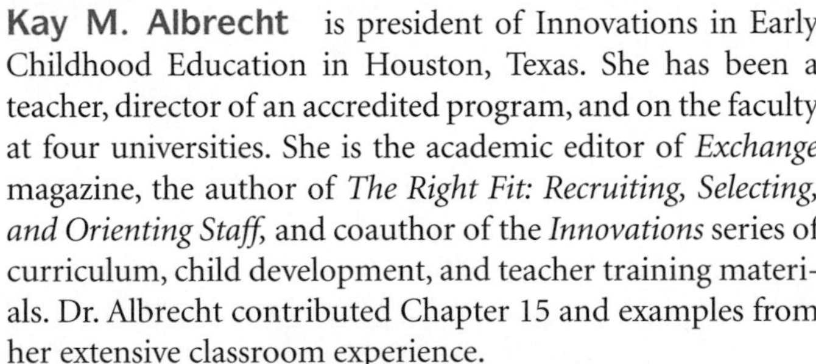

Kay M. Albrecht is president of Innovations in Early Childhood Education in Houston, Texas. She has been a teacher, director of an accredited program, and on the faculty at four universities. She is the academic editor of *Exchange* magazine, the author of *The Right Fit: Recruiting, Selecting, and Orienting Staff,* and coauthor of the *Innovations* series of curriculum, child development, and teacher training materials. Dr. Albrecht contributed Chapter 15 and examples from her extensive classroom experience.

Kay M. Albrecht

Luis A. Hernandez

Luis A. Hernandez is an early childhood education specialist with Training and Technical Assistance Services, Western Kentucky University. He serves on numerous national boards and his expertise includes second language learning, changing demographics and diversity, early literacy, and adult learning. He contributed to the expert lenses on language and cultural diversity.

Foreword

Is it developmentally appropriate or not? In the years since the National Association for the Education of Young Children's position statement on developmentally appropriate practice (DAP) was first released in 1987, this question has been the subject of much discussion and debate. Publication of the position statement arose from the concern that some programs had unrealistic expectations for young children. School reform was a hot-button topic and the notion that early childhood education had a role to play was leading some educators to implement what became known as the *push-down curriculum,* that is, a pedagogy more appropriate for much older children.

Since the publication of the NAEYC position statement, "developmentally appropriate practice" has become synonymous with "quality" for many early childhood educators, while at the same time others have legitimately asked whether it is possible to describe "appropriate practices" given the wide variety of early childhood settings, the diversity of our society, and the competing theoretical/philosophical orientations within the early childhood field. Three issues have fueled this controversy: content knowledge (what should children learn), individual and cultural diversity (how standardized should expectations be), and pedagogy (how should children be taught). This book should help answer these questions and resolve many of these disputes.

Why has developmentally appropriate practice been interpreted so differently? One reason is that some people do not understand that child development is not a curriculum, but a set of principles. In this book, the author, Sue Bredekamp, has shown us how principles and practice go together. She tells us that practices should not be assumed to be good or bad in advance, but must be looked at in context: What do these children need to learn (as determined by teachers, parents, professionals, school districts, etc.), what is their prior knowledge (derived from individual, family, and cultural experience), and what pedagogy is likely to be most effective (different methods for different content areas and for different children)? According to Bredekamp, developmentally appropriate practice does not tell teachers exactly what and how to teach. It provides a set of developmental principles and guidelines, and identifies a variety of learning experiences and evidence-based teaching strategies to respond to those principles.

In this book Bredekamp makes it clear that all children need numerous opportunities to learn about literacy, mathematics, science, social studies, and the arts, as well as self-regulation, positive social skills, and physical development and health. Further, each program should consider what particular children need. She puts to rest the idea that *developmentally appropriate* means that teachers should not intentionally teach preschoolers. On the other hand, she points out the usefulness of teacher-guided play in helping children learn the concepts and skills necessary for school success. According to Bredekamp, teachers must decide what is appropriate for a particular child or group of children at a particular time and place. Many teaching strategies may be responsive to the same principle and good teachers use a range of techniques.

Bredekamp's definition of developmentally appropriate practice challenges teachers to have a store of professional knowledge that includes learning principles, discipline knowledge, positive guidance practices, and an understanding of the cultural background of different children and families to be skilled at planning, teaching, and assessing children. This book will certainly go a long way toward helping prepare new and experienced teachers to master these challenges.

Barbara T. Bowman

Barbara T. Bowman
Irving B. Harris Professor of Child Development
Erikson Institute and Chief Officer
Office of Early Childhood Education
Chicago Public Schools

Preface

After graduating from college with an English degree that prepared me for little more than reading novels and poems, I took a few credit hours of early childhood education and got a job as a preschool teacher in a child care center. I will never forget my first day of teaching. One reason I remember it so well is that it was so long! Feeling completely incompetent, I seriously thought about not going back the next day. Then, I realized that while I had a choice not to return, the children did not. They deserved a better teacher than I was at that time. As a result, I continued teaching, went back to school, and set out to learn as much as possible about child development and how best to teach young children—and I have been learning ever since.

I was motivated to write this book for two reasons. First, I considered what I wish I had known on my first day of teaching. I didn't know much about child development and practically nothing about individual, cultural, and linguistic differences. I had no idea how complex the role of the teacher is. For example, I understood that children learn through play, but I was clueless about what I should be doing while they played. I had no skills for working with families. And the 8-hour child care day loomed very long indeed. I didn't understand that young children are not only capable of but also want to learn engaging, challenging curriculum content. During the next decade, I took courses in early childhood education and continued teaching preschoolers. Gradually, my teaching improved and I came to see how much children benefited as a result. Since then I have devoted my career to learning more about each of these topics, as well as learning from children, and then translating that knowledge for new and experienced teachers.

The second reason I wrote this book is to convey what I have learned over the course of the past 30 years working for professional organizations, most notably the National Association for the Education of Young Children (NAEYC), to develop standards for high-quality early childhood programs and teacher preparation. My work on NAEYC's position statements on developmentally appropriate practice has had the greatest impact on my professional life and thinking. In this book, I "unpack" the concept of *developmentally appropriate practices* for students because an understanding of those principles is the basic framework on which to build early childhood programs and schools for children from birth through age 8.

In addition, my goal is to share what I have learned as NAEYC's vision of developmentally appropriate practice has evolved over time. I have been privileged to participate in numerous discussions and heated debates involving many of the most highly respected researchers and leaders in our field. For instance, collaborating with colleagues in early childhood special education and with scholars of cultural and linguistic diversity has had a significant impact on my world view. These processes taught me how dynamic professions are built on a firm foundation of core knowledge and values, but also how they change in response to new research and varying contexts.

The lessons I have learned permeate this book. In most cases, I explicitly describe current research and its implications for effective teaching and curriculum. But implicit in this book are other things I have come to know: the power of listening to opinions that differ from one's own, the necessity of being open to new knowledge, the benefits of negotiation, the importance of learning from history, the resilience of the enduring values of early childhood education, and the sheer joy of teaching young children.

I, like countless other early childhood educators, joined this profession and stay in it because I firmly believe my work can make a difference in the lives of children and their families. But to make a lasting difference our practices must be effective—they must contribute to children's learning and development. I wrote this book to help accomplish that goal, building on the basic framework of developmentally appropriate practice while emphasizing intentional teaching, challenging and interesting curriculum, and evidence-based, effective practices for a new generation of early childhood educators. Each of these primary goals is discussed on the following pages.

Describes What Effective Teachers Do to Enhance Children's Learning and Development

- This text emphasizes the idea that effective teachers are thoughtful and purposeful in everything they do. Effective teachers have the knowledge to make informed decisions and adapt to individual differences, including those of children with disabilities and special needs.

- Every chapter includes features that bring teaching to life. Most of these features were contributed by Carol Copple, coeditor of NAEYC's *Developmentally Appropriate Practice in Early Childhood Programs.*

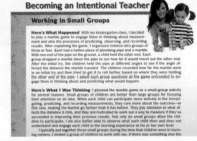

- One of the key themes of the book is intentional teaching. Intentional teachers not only know what to do with children but they also know why they are doing it and can explain the rationale for the decisions they make to other teachers, administrators, and families. To help students understand this concept, **Becoming an Intentional Teacher** features reveal what teachers are thinking in classroom situations and *how* and *why* they select the strategies they do.

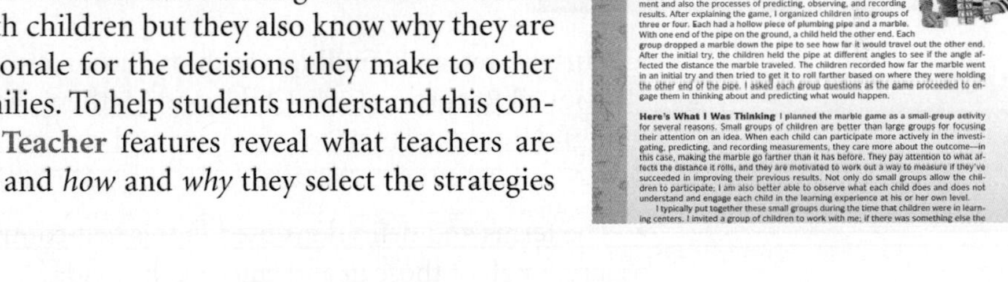

Becoming an Intentional Teacher

Working in Small Groups

Here's What Happened With my kindergarten class, I decided to play a marble game to engage them in thinking about measurement and also the processes of predicting, observing, and recording results. After explaining the game, I organized children into groups of three or four. Each had a hollow piece of plumbing pipe and a marble. With one end of the pipe on the ground, a child held the other end. Each group dropped a marble down the pipe to see how far it would travel out the other end. After the initial try, the children held the pipe at different angles to see if the angle affected the distance the marble traveled. The children recorded how far the marble went in an initial try and then tried to get it to roll farther based on where they were holding the other end of the pipe. I asked each group questions as the game proceeded to engage them in thinking about and predicting what would happen.

Here's What I Was Thinking I planned the marble game as a small-group activity for several reasons. Small groups of children are better than large groups for focusing their attention on an idea. When each child can participate more actively in the investigating, predicting, and recording measurements, they care more about the outcome—in this case, making the marble go farther than it has before. They pay attention to what affects the distance it rolls, and they are motivated to work out a way to measure if they've succeeded in improving their previous results. Not only do small groups allow the children to participate; I am also better able to observe what each child does and does not understand and engage each child in the learning experience at his or her own level.

I typically put together these small groups during the time that children were in learning centers. I invited a group of children to work with me; if there was something else the

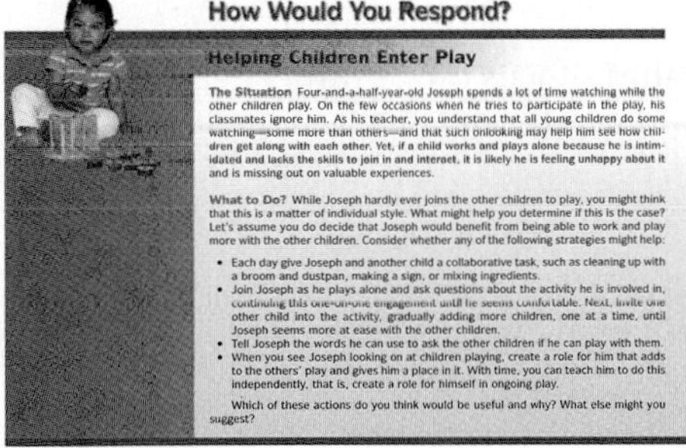

How Would You Respond?

Helping Children Enter Play

The Situation Four-and-a-half-year-old Joseph spends a lot of time watching while the other children play. On the few occasions when he tries to participate in the play, his classmates ignore him. As his teacher, you understand that all young children do some watching—some more than others—and that such onlooking may help him see how children get along with each other. Yet, if a child works and plays alone because he is intimidated and lacks the skills to join in and interact, it is likely he is feeling unhappy about it and is missing out on valuable experiences.

What to Do? While Joseph hardly ever joins the other children to play, you might think that this is a matter of individual style. What might help you determine if this is the case? Let's assume you do decide that Joseph would benefit from being able to work and play more with the other children. Consider whether any of the following strategies might help:

- Each day give Joseph and another child a collaborative task, such as cleaning up with a broom and dustpan, making a sign, or mixing ingredients.
- Join Joseph as he plays alone and ask questions about the activity he is involved in, continuing this one-on-one engagement until he seems comfortable. Next, invite one other child into the activity, gradually adding more children, one at a time, until Joseph seems more at ease with the other children.
- Tell Joseph the words he can use to ask the other children if he can play with them.
- When you see Joseph looking on at children playing, create a role for him that adds to the others' play and gives him a place in it. With time, you can teach him to do this independently, that is, create a role for himself in ongoing play.

Which of these actions do you think would be useful and why? What else might you suggest?

- Effective teachers are informed decision makers. **How Would You Respond?** features engage students in reflection and critical thinking about a complex teaching situation or issue confronting the early childhood field. The scenarios present options to consider. Because there is no one right answer, students can appreciate the complexity of teaching and diverse perspectives.

- Teachers of young children must have a broad repertoire of effective teaching strategies. **Chapter 9, Teaching to Enhance Learning and Development**, is a unique, practical chapter that describes the art and science of teaching young children and focuses on teaching strategies that work.

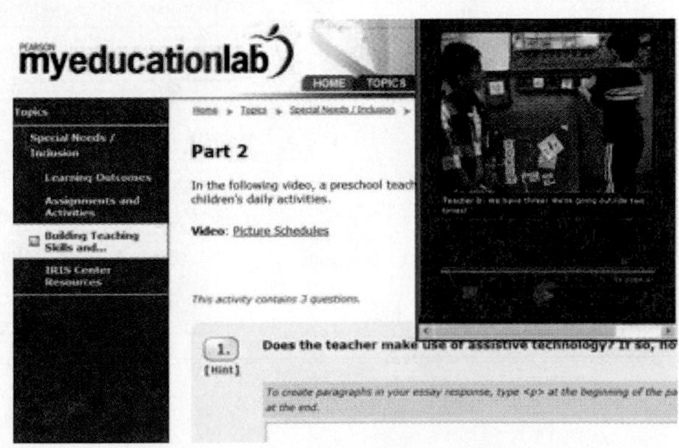

- **Building Teaching Skills and Dispositions** and **Assignments and Activities** on MyEducationLab are assignable exercises in key areas such as planning a culturally responsive curriculum and making decisions about what is developmentally appropriate.

Demonstrates How Current Research Informs Effective Practices

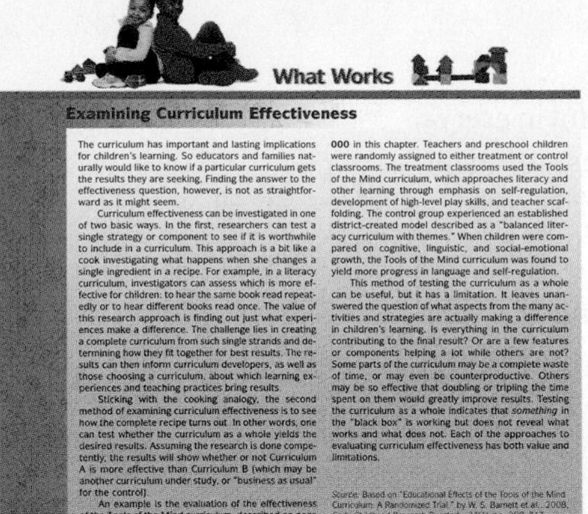

What Works

Examining Curriculum Effectiveness

The curriculum has important and lasting implications for children's learning. So educators and families naturally would like to know if a particular curriculum gets the results they are seeking. Finding the answer to the effectiveness question, however, is not as straightforward as it might seem.

Curriculum effectiveness can be investigated in one of two basic ways. In the first, researchers can test a single strategy or component to see if it is worthwhile to include in a curriculum. This approach is a bit like a cook investigating what happens when she changes a single ingredient in a recipe. For example, in a literacy curriculum, investigators can assess which is more effective for children: to hear the same book read repeatedly or to hear different books read once. The value of this research approach is finding out just what experiences make a difference. The challenge lies in creating a complete curriculum from such single strands and determining how they fit together for best results. The results can then inform curriculum developers, as well as those choosing a curriculum, about which learning experiences and teaching practices bring results.

Sticking with the cooking analogy, the second method of examining curriculum effectiveness is to see how the complete recipe turns out. In other words, one can test whether the curriculum as a whole yields the desired results. Assuming the research is done competently, the results will show whether or not Curriculum A is more effective than Curriculum B (which may be another curriculum under study, or "business as usual" for the control).

An example is the evaluation of the effectiveness of the Tools of the Mind curriculum, described on page 000 in this chapter. Teachers and preschool children were randomly assigned to either treatment or control classrooms. The treatment classrooms used the Tools of the Mind curriculum, which approaches literacy and other learning through emphasis on self-regulation, development of high-level play skills, and teacher scaffolding. The control group experienced an established district-created model described as a "balanced literacy curriculum with themes." When children were compared on cognitive, linguistic, and social-emotional growth, the Tools of the Mind curriculum was found to yield more progress in language and self-regulation.

This method of testing the curriculum as a whole can be useful, but it has a limitation. It leaves unanswered the question of what aspects from the many activities and strategies are actually making a difference in children's learning. Is everything in the curriculum contributing to the final result? Or are a few features or components helping a lot while others are not? Some parts of the curriculum may be a complete waste of time, or may even be counterproductive. Others may be so effective that doubling or tripling the time spent on them would greatly improve results. Testing the curriculum as a whole indicates that *something* in the "black box" is working but does not reveal what works and what does not. Each of the approaches to evaluating curriculum effectiveness has both value and limitations.

Source: Based on "Educational Effects of the Tools of the Mind Curriculum: A Randomized Trial," by W. S. Barnett et al., 2008, *Early Childhood Research Quarterly, 23*(3), pp. 299–313.

- In an era of standards, accountability, and rapid change in the field, the text helps students understand research and the connections between child development, curriculum content, assessment, and intentional teaching.

- **What Works** features present research-based practices in action, including descriptions of demonstrated effective practices such as dialogic reading, teaching mathematics with unit blocks, and how sociodramatic play promotes self-regulation.

- Current research findings, such as those contained in the 2009 National Research Council Report on Early Childhood Mathematics, are brought to life and made meaningful by connections to classroom and community examples.

- The terms and definitions used in this text contribute to establishing a shared vocabulary for all of those in and entering the field.

- **Expert Lens** features focus on culture, linguistic diversity, and including all children. Preeminent professionals in the field—Carol Brunson Day, Gail Joseph, and Luis Hernandez—discuss practice through diverse lenses, expanding the sources of information teachers use to make decisions and helping them look at questions or problems from broader perspectives. Widening the lens with which teachers view their practice is a strategy to move beyond the persistent educational tendency to dichotomize difficult or controversial issues into "either/or" choices and instead move toward "both/and" thinking.

Including All Children

Developmentally Appropriate Practice and Children with Disabilities

A child with a disability acts like a magnifying glass on the developmental appropriateness of an early childhood program. The basic elements of developmentally appropriate practice are necessary for inclusion to succeed. However, the converse is also true. When children with disabilities are included in programs that are not developmentally appropriate, it becomes difficult for the child with special needs—indeed, for all of the children—to make meaningful progress. Compare the experiences of these two young children:

You See? It is adapted from *Brown Bear, Brown Bear* (Martin, 1996), but features pictures of the children in the class, paired with their names. Isaac loves the book, and reads along with the teacher. As the teacher reads each child's names in the story, they get to stand up and move. After the story, it is time for singing. Isaac knows this because circle time happens in a similar routine each day.

The teacher pulls out the "song chart" featuring the pictures and titles of eight different songs. One song is about a train. Isaac loves trains and seems eager to hear the new song. He points to the "Trains on the track." The teacher helps Isaac remove the song card. Isaac holds the card while the children sing. Then Isaac makes the sign for "play" with his hands. The teacher says, "Yes, Isaac it is time for centers." She lets Isaac choose a center first, because she knows it is hard for him to wait. Isaac brings the teacher the song card, and then points to the picture of the water table. His teacher models, "I want to play at the. . . ." Isaac, says, "Water table." His teacher, proud of his increasing verbal skills, gives him a hug and says, "Off you go to the water table." When Isaac's mother picks him up from school, his teacher describes how often he used his words and which friends he played with at center time.

As is clear from Isaac's case, developmentally appropriate practice provides the necessary foundation for successful inclusion. But individually appropriate adaptations are essential for children with disabilities and other special needs.

Culture Lens

Fostering Cultural Continuity

Take a moment to think about what you understand about culture. Do you tend to think about culture only as characteristic of children and families who are "culturally different"? Does the concept of culture only apply to some children? Actually, it is important to remember that *every* child is socialized in a cultural group, and the most important elements influencing children's development are really aspects of their cultural experiences that are often the hardest to observe.

What people sometimes think of as "cultural" are the products that culture produces, such as dress or holiday celebrations. These are the surface features of culture. But culture produces more indiscernible behaviors and attitudes that emerge from the same set of rules as the surface features of culture. These deep structural aspects of culture act as much more powerful influences on children's development than the surface features. For example, if the cultural group believes that women should not be seen by men except for those in the immediate family, a woman's mode of dress will reflect this value. At the same time, this cultural belief will have much farther reaching effects on her behavior and life choices than simply how she dresses. Consider an example in an early childhood classroom:

It is circle time in kindergarten and the children are supposed to bring an object from home that has writing on it. Most of the children eagerly seek their turn, waving their hands widely, and showing off how well they can read the words. Jai has brought something but is clearly not eager to share. The teacher assumes that he can't read the words. So, she doesn't call on him.

As in all developmental domains, culture influences the expression of emotions. Although emotions such as fear, anger, and happiness are part of human interactions in all cultural groups, variations emerge in the way they are expressed. Jai, who is from India, is from a cultural group that avoids drawing too much attention to individuals or expressing emotions too openly. Children from other, more individualistic cultures such as the United States, are generally encouraged to express their feelings openly. These cultural differences account for Jai's behavior and that of the other children in his class more than their reading abilities.

Cultural differences do not mean that one way is right and the other wrong. They simply demonstrate that there is a wide variety of developmental patterns that can be explained best by understanding the cultural context in which development occurs.

Language Lens

Speaking Two Languages

Of 16 children in Pedro Cordero's Head Start classroom, 12 speak Spanish as their home language. Pedro uses both English and Spanish in his interactions with the children. During conversations with individual children, he often speaks Spanish, finding that it helps him get to know the children and build positive relationships with them. During more formal gatherings such as story time or working in a small group, he often speaks English. But he connects new words to real objects or pictures, and he checks children's understanding regularly. Pedro's assistant teacher only speaks English; she and the English-speaking children provide language models for the dual language learners.

In many states in the United States today, the type of teaching Pedro does would be prohibited by law. In the belief that bilingual education harms children, prevents learning English, and hurts academic success, some states have adopted "English-only" laws.

But what does research say about English-only teaching and the children's success in school? Researchers in a large-scale study observed 345 Spanish-speaking children in 161 prekindergarten programs, and asked teachers to rate children's social and behavior skills and the quality of their relationships with them. In the classrooms observed, about two-thirds of the parents said their child did not speak English at home. The study found that when teachers spoke some Spanish, Spanish-speaking children were found to have better social skills than children whose teachers spoke only English.

In addition, children whose teachers spoke some Spanish were less likely to be victims of aggression, bullying, or teasing, and their teachers were more likely to have a positive relationship with them. The amount of Spanish that teachers spoke was significantly related to teachers' ratings of children's assertiveness, attention and task persistence, and ability to get along with other children. On the other hand, the more English interactions children had, the more likely they were to have behavior and learning problems and become easily frustrated.

An important—and seemingly contradictory—finding was that the amount of Spanish spoken in the classroom was not related to a child's English proficiency. In the study, teachers spoke Spanish with Spanish-speaking children only 20% of the time. When speaking directly to Spanish-speaking children, teachers who spoke some Spanish still used English two-thirds of the time. When speaking to a group, teachers tended to use English. When teachers spoke Spanish, however, they had more elaborate conversations with children, a key finding considering the research on the value of extended conversations for vocabulary development.

The researchers concluded that contrary to popular belief, English-only teaching of young children may contribute to the achievement gap, rather than closing it. From the perspective of research, both the Spanish-speaking and English-speaking children in Pedro Cordero's Head Start class should benefit from his approach to teaching.

Sources: Based on "Spanish Speaking Children's Social and Language Development in Pre-Kindergarten Classrooms," by F. Chang, G. Crawford, D. Early, and D. Bryant, 2007, *Journal of Early Education and Development, 18*(2), pp. 243–269; and *Is Public Pre-K Preparing Hispanic Children to Succeed in School?* (Preschool Policy Brief 13), by L. M. Laosa, and P. Ainsworth, 2007, New Brunswick, NJ: National Institute for Early Education Research.

Focuses on Curriculum That Promotes Children's Learning and Development

- The text provides an overview of curriculum so that early childhood teachers understand right from the start that there is content in the curriculum for young children. Many early childhood introductory courses focus on child development. This text includes both child development and curriculum content knowledge, and shows how they are connected.

- Chapters 12 through 15 describe the goals for young children's learning and development that predict success in school and life in language, literacy, and the arts; math, science, and technology; social–emotional learning and social studies; and physical development and health. Each of these chapters includes examples of effective strategies relevant to the specific curriculum area such as how to build social problem-solving skills or ways to promote dual language learning.

- Play is integrated throughout as an effective means to support all domains of development and promote learning in all curriculum areas. Today many people see play as something separate from the rest of the curriculum, making statements such as "We can't let children play because we have to teach literacy" or "We don't have time for outdoor play in primary grades because we have to get children ready for standardized tests." Play should not be treated as a separate part of an early childhood program that can be cut if someone deems it unimportant. Play, in its various forms, is integrally connected to every aspect of children's development, and it builds learning across all areas of the curriculum. Therefore, you will find a discussion of play in every chapter of this book.

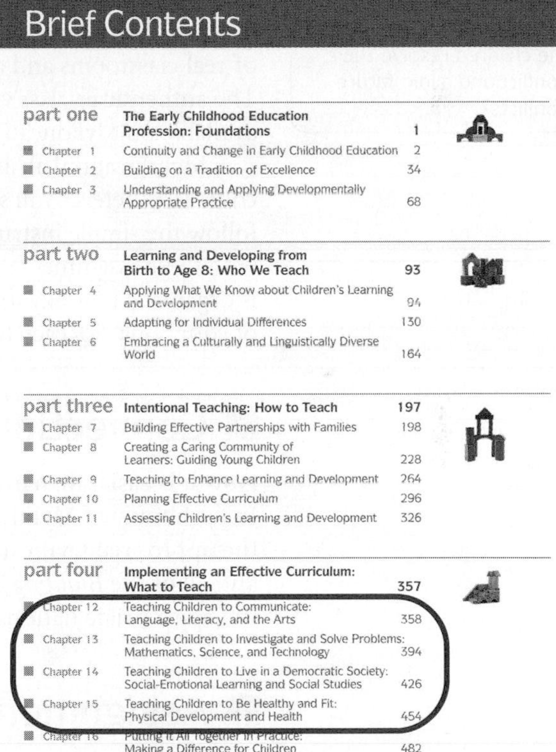

Brief Contents

- The emphasis on implementing effective curriculum reflects current trends, such as the goal of aligning prekindergarten and primary education, new NAEYC accreditation and professional preparation standards, and enhanced expectations for teacher qualifications.

Using MyEducationLab with This Book

MyEducationLab

Go to the Assignments and Activities section of Topic 9: Guiding Children in the MyEducationLab for your course and complete the activity entitled *Peaceful Conflict Resolution*. What are some strategies that this teacher uses to help the children resolve their conflict and avoid future conflicts?

The power of classroom practice.

> Teacher educators who are developing pedagogies for the analysis of teaching and learning contend that analyzing teaching artifacts has three advantages: it enables new teachers time for reflection while still using the real materials of practice; it provides new teachers with experience thinking about and approaching the complexity of the classroom; and in some cases, it can help new teachers and teacher educators develop a shared understanding and common language about teaching. . . . [1]

As Linda Darling-Hammond and her colleagues point out, grounding teacher education in real classrooms—among real teachers and students and among actual examples of students' and teachers' work—is an important, and perhaps even an essential, part of training teachers for the complexities of teaching in today's classrooms. For this reason, we have created a valuable, time-saving website—MyEducationLab—that provides you with the context of real classrooms and artifacts that research on teacher education tells us is so important. The authentic in-class video footage, interactive skill-building exercises, and other resources available on MyEducationLab offer you a uniquely valuable teacher education tool.

MyEducationLab is easy to use and integrate into both your assignments and your courses. Wherever you see the MyEducationLab logo in the margins or elsewhere in the text, follow the simple instructions to access the videos, strategies, cases, and artifacts associated with these assignments, activities, and learning units on MyEducationLab. MyEducationLab is organized topically to enhance the coverage of the core concepts discussed in the chapters of your book. For each topic on the course you will find most or all of the following resources:

Connection to National Standards

Now it is easier than ever to see how your course work is connected to national standards. In each topic of MyEducationLab you will find intended learning outcomes connected to the appropriate national standards for your course. All of the *Assignments and Activities* and all of the *Building Teaching Skills and Dispositions* in MyEducationLab are mapped to the appropriate national standards and learning outcomes as well.

Assignments and Activities

Designed to save instructors preparation time, these assignable exercises show concepts in action (through video, cases, or student and teacher artifacts) and then offer thought-provoking questions that probe your understanding of these concepts or strategies. (Feedback for these assignments is available to the instructor.)

Building Teaching Skills and Dispositions

These learning units help you practice and strengthen skills that are essential to quality teaching. First you are presented with the core skill or concept and then given an opportunity to

[1] Darling-Hammond, I., & Bransford, J., Eds., (2005). *Preparing Teachers for a Changing World*. San Francisco: John Wiley & Sons.

practice your understanding of this concept multiple times by watching video footage (or interacting with other media) and then critically analyzing the strategy or skill presented.

IRIS Center Resources

The IRIS Center at Vanderbilt University (http://iris.peabody.vanderbilt.edu, funded by the U.S. Department of Education's Office of Special Education Programs) develops training enhancement materials for preservice and in-service teachers. The center works with experts from across the country to create challenge-based interactive modules, case study units, and podcasts that provide research-validated information about working with students in inclusive settings. On your MyEducationLab course we have integrated this content where appropriate to enhance the content coverage in your book.

General Resources on Your MyEducationLab Course

The *Resources* section on your MyEducationLab course is designed to help you pass your licensure exam, put together an effective portfolio and lesson plan, prepare for and navigate the first year of your teaching career, and understand key educational standards, policies, and laws. This section includes:

- *Licensure Exams:* Access guidelines for passing the Praxis exam. The *Practice Test Exam* includes practice questions, *Case Histories*, and *Video Case Studies*.
- *Portfolio Builder and Lesson Plan Builder:* Create, update, and share portfolios and lesson plans.
- *Preparing a Portfolio:* Access guidelines for creating a high-quality teaching portfolio that will allow you to practice effective lesson planning.
- *Licensure and Standards:* Link to state licensure standards and national standards.
- *Beginning Your Career:* Educate yourself—access tips, advice, and valuable information on:
  - Résumé Writing and Interviewing: Expert advice on how to write impressive résumés and prepare for job interviews.
  - Your First Year of Teaching: Practical tips to set up your classroom, manage student behavior, and learn to more easily organize for instruction and assessment.
  - Law and Public Policies: Specific directives and requirements you need to understand under the No Child Left Behind Act and the Individuals with Disabilities Education Improvement Act of 2004.
- *Special Education Interactive Timeline:* Build your own detailed timelines based on different facets of the history and evolution of special education.

Book-Specific Resources

The book-specific resources developed for your course include a study plan and video interviews with the author.

Study Plan

A MyEducationLab Study Plan is a multiple-choice assessment tied to chapter objectives, and supported by study material. A well-designed Study Plan offers multiple opportunities to fully master required course content as identified by the objectives in each chapter:

- *Chapter Objectives* identify the learning outcomes for the chapter and give you targets to shoot for as you read and study.

- *Multiple-Choice Assessments* allow you to assess your mastery of the content (tied to each chapter objective) by taking the multiple-choice quiz as many times as needed. Not only do these quizzes provide overall scores for each objective, but they also explain why responses to particular items are correct or incorrect.
- *Study Material: Review, Practice, and Enrichment* gives you a deeper understanding of what you do and do not know related to chapter content. This can be accessed through the *Multiple-Choice Assessment* (after you take a quiz you receive information regarding the chapter content on which you still need practice and review) or through a self-directed method of study. This material includes text excerpts, activities that include hints and feedback, and media assets (video, simulations, cases, etc.).

MyEducationLab

Go to the Book Specific Resources in the MyEducationLab for your course and select Author Interviews in Chapter 1 and watch and listen to the video *Inspiration for Writing Her Book.* Sue Bredekamp describes what inspired her to write this text.

Author Interview

Video interviews with Sue Bredekamp appear in the book-specific resources as well. Margin notes direct you to her videos in Author Interview, where she discusses topics such as why she wrote the book, the behaviors of effective teachers, and the importance of understanding the individual differences in the children you teach.

You have another opportunity to see and hear her in the Professional Perspectives sections in some of the topics of the MyEducationLab for your course. Here Dr. Bredekamp discusses such topics as developmentally appropriate practice, standards for teachers, and the role of culture in children's development.

Visit www.myeducationlab.com for a demonstration of this exciting new online teaching resource.

Instructor Supplements

The following instructor tools supplement, support, and reinforce the content presented throughout the text. All supplements are available for download for instructors who adopt this text. Go to www.pearsonhighered.com, click on "Educators," register for access, and download files. For more information, contact your Pearson representative.

- **Online Instructor's Manual.** The Instructor's Manual provides chapter-by-chapter tools to use in class. Chapter summaries, presentation (lecture) outlines, teaching strategies, in-class activities, and key terms will reinforce key concepts or applications and keep students engaged.
- **Online Test Bank.** These multiple-choice and essay questions tied to each chapter provide students the opportunity to assess their understanding of the chapter content. An answer key is provided.
- **Course Management Content: Electronic Test Banks in Blackboard and WebCT.** The assessment items in the *Online Test Bank* are available in Blackboard and WebCT formats.
- **Online PowerPoint Slides.** Each slide reinforces key concepts and big ideas presented throughout the text.
- **MyTest.** This computerized Test Bank software gives instructors electronic access to *Online Test Bank* items, allowing them to create and customize exams.

Pearson MyTest is a powerful assessment generation program that helps instructors easily create and print quizzes and exams. Questions and tests are authored online, allowing ultimate flexibility and the ability to efficiently create and print assessments anytime, anywhere!

To access Pearson MyTest and your test bank files, simply go to www.pearsonmytest.com to log in, register, or request access.

Features of Pearson MyTest include:

Premium assessment content

- Draw from a rich library of assessments that complement your Pearson textbook and your course's learning objectives.
- Edit questions or tests to fit your specific teaching needs.

Instructor-friendly resources

- Easily create and store your own questions, including images, diagrams, and charts using simple drag-and-drop and Word-like controls.
- Use additional information provided by Pearson, such as the question's difficulty level or learning objective, to help you quickly build your test.

Time-saving enhancements

- Add headers or footers and easily scramble questions and answer choices—all from one simple toolbar.
- Quickly create multiple versions of your test or answer key, and when ready, simply save to MS-Word or PDF format and print!
- Export your exams for import to Blackboard 6.0, CE (WebCT), or Vista (WebCT)!

Acknowledgments

My life has been enriched by many friends, colleagues, and teachers whom I have had the privilege of working with for almost four decades in early childhood education. It is impossible to acknowledge all of them, but this book would not have been possible without the active help and encouragement of the following people:

- Carol Copple, a great collaborator and wonderful friend, whose original vision this book reflects and who never ceases to add value to everything I think and write
- Laura Colker, the most generous of friends and colleagues, for welcoming me to KampCoCo, for sharing her ideas, and for her gracious support ever since
- Max Effenson Chuck, my development editor, for her unwavering positive encouragement and outstanding editing over several years, the best developmental editor that a developmentalist could ever have
- Julie Peters, my editor at Pearson, whose vast knowledge of early childhood teacher education and innovative ideas educated me and shaped this work
- Kelly Villella Canton, for signing me to write this text and for her creative contributions
- The late Carol Seefeldt, who taught the first early childhood course I ever took and mentored me through my dissertation, in hopes that my work reflects her vision
- Marilyn Smith, J. D. Andrews, and Barbara Bowman for personal and professional friendship and guidance
- Artist and future teacher Kia Morawetz and her mom, my great friend Barbara Willer
- Theresa Locke, Mona Lisa Amas, Shelley Kadota, and the children at Hoaliku Drake Preschool, Kamehameha Schools Community-Based Early Childhood Education
- Patty Smith Hill, founder of NANE, whose life and work have inspired my own, and whose vision for early childhood education laid the foundation for NAEYC's commitment to developmentally appropriate practice
- My 21 nieces and nephews, both great and grand, who have enriched my life immeasurably
- Mom and Dad, for their unconditional love throughout my life
- Joe Bredekamp, for his love, understanding, support, and incredible patience throughout life with a crazy person.

I would like to thank all of those who served on our Advisory Council:

Sandra Alber, Oakland University
Jennifer Aldrich, University of Central Missouri
Leanne Alexandrini, Hudson County Community College
Kathy Allen, Blue Ridge Community College
Sheri Anders, Mississippi State University
Karen Anderson, Stonehill College
Janet Arndt, Gordon College
Barb Arnold-Tengesdal, University of Mary
Nancy Beaver, Eastfield College
Melissa Becker, Tarleton State University
Celia Billescas Hilber, Jacksonville State University
Janet Bliss, Colby-Sawyer College
Fredalene Bowers, Indiana University of Pennsylvania
Nancy Cavanaugh, College of Mt. St. Joseph
Basanti Dey Chakraborty, New Jersey City University
Nancy Cheshire, Fairmont State University
Dianna Chiabotti, Napa Valley College

Tausha Clay, Milligan College
Tracy Collins, Texas A&M University
Susan Davies, Ivy Tech Community College
Cynthia DiCarlo, Louisiana State University
Rosanne Dlugosz, Scottsdale Community College
Fran Dulcich, Onondaga Community College
Shaquam Edwards, College of Marin
Miriam Folk, Florida State College at Jacksonville
Jill Gelormino, St. Joseph's College
Sabine Gerhardt, University of Akron
Mike Godfrey, Brigham Young University
Lynda Goldberg, Mohave Community College
Avila Hendricks, Lincoln University
Wendy Jacocks, Southeastern Louisiana University
Candace Jaruszewicz, College of Charleston
Jennifer Johnson, Vance-Granville Community College
Janice Jones, Ohlone College
Alvin Kuest, Great Lakes Christian College
Lisa Lauer, Nicholls State University
Anne Leser, Bowling Green State University, Firelands
Cathy Mebane, Gateway Community College
Kari Merritt, University of Wisconsin–Stout
Mary Mindess, Lesley University
Jo Murphy, Front Range Community College, Westminster
Bridget Murray, Henderson Community College
Barbie Norvell, Coastal Carolina University
Glenda Orgill, Yakima Valley Community College
Carol Ortega, San Jacinto College, Central
Sandra Owen, Cincinnati State Technical and Community College
Elizabeth Persons, Pensacola Junior College
Debra Pierce, Ivy Tech Community College
Stephen Powers, Bronx Community College
Laurie Prusso, Modesto Junior College
Brenda Ragle, Ivy Tech Community College
Juliette Relihan, Salve Regina University
Nancy Self, Texas A&M University
Joan Silver, St. Joseph's College
Anne Slanina, Slippery Rock University
Ruslan Slutsky, University of Toledo
Ro-Jean Straw, York County Community College
Linda Taylor, Ball State University
Kevin Thrasher, Grand Canyon University
Kay Timme, Sam Houston State University
Marilyn Toliver, John A. Logan College
Carmelita Valencia-Daye, Gateway Community College
Herman Walston, Kentucky State University
Cindy Waters, Upper Iowa University
Shawn DiNarda Watters, Mount Union College
Lisa White, Athens Technical College
Julie Williams, Pulaski Technical College
Kathy Ann Wilson, American River College
Diane Wolter, College of Lake County
Andrea Zarate, Hartnell College

I would also like to thank the many reviewers who contributed to the development of this book over several revisions: Jennifer Aldrich, University of Central Missouri; Kathy Allen, Blue Ridge Community College; Sheri Anders, Mississippi State University; Margaret H. Annunziata, Davidson County Community College; Ginny Buckner, Duke University; Cheryl Bulat, Morton College; Virginia Buysse, University of North Carolina; Camille Catlett, University of North Carolina; Tracy Collins, Texas A&M University; Mary Cordell, Navarro College; Cynthia DiCarlo, Louisiana State University; Susannah Dickman, Owensboro Community and Technical College; Rosanne Dlugosz, Scottsdale Community College; Dede Dunst, Mitchell Community College; Tyler Esch, McCook Community College; Linda Espinosa, University of Missouri, Columbia; Miriam Folk, Florida State College at Jacksonville; Priscilla Garcia, Laredo Community College; Heather Garrison, East Stroudsburg University of Pennsylvania; Erin Glenn, College of the Canyons; Caroline M. Hagen, Jamestown College; Nancy Hughes, Plattsburgh State; Sai Jambunathan, New Jersey City University; Jennifer Johnson, Vance-Granville Community College; Lisa M. Lauer, Nicholls State University; Alison Lutton, NAEYC; Cathy Mebane, Gateway Community College; Marlene Morgan, Lee College; Sandra Owen, Cincinnati State Technical and Community College; Christine Peterson, California University of Pennsylvania; Cathy Pollock, Asheville Buncombe Technical and Community College; L. Kathryn Sharp, University of Memphis; Ruslan Slutsky, University of Toledo; Deborah Tertinger, York Technical College; Gwen Walter, Forsyth Technical Community College; Betty Ann Watson, Harding University; Shawn DiNarda Watters, Mount Union College; Lisa White, Athens Technical College; and Pamela J. Winton, University of North Carolina, Chapel Hill.

Sue Bredekamp

Brief Contents

Contents

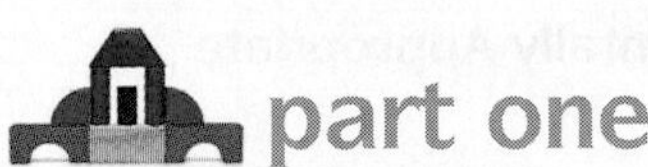 part one

The Early Childhood Education Profession: Foundations 1

■ Chapter 3

part two

■ Chapter 4

Chapter 5

Chapter 6

part three

■ Chapter 9

■ Chapter 10

■ Chapter 11

part four

Special Features

Effective Practices in Early Childhood Education

part one

foundations

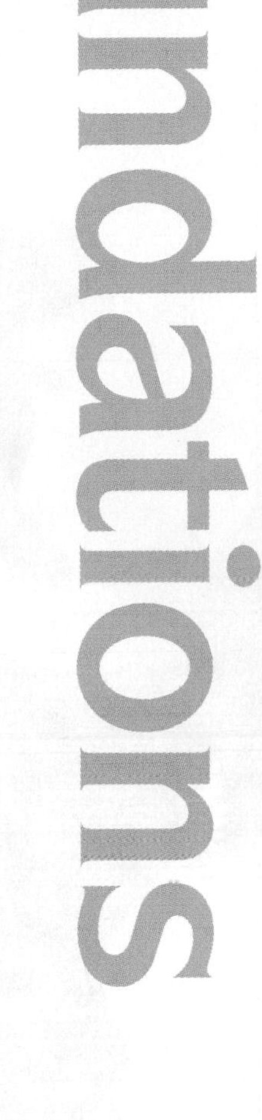

The Early Childhood Education Profession

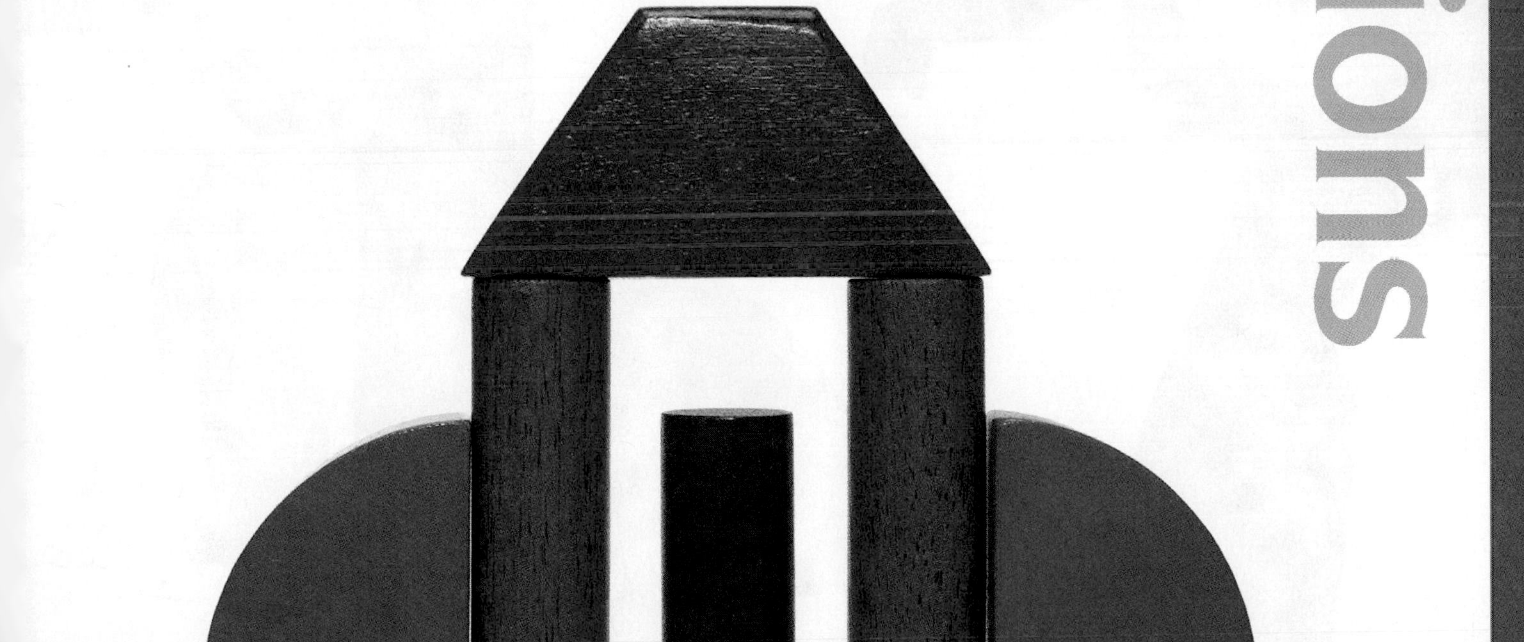

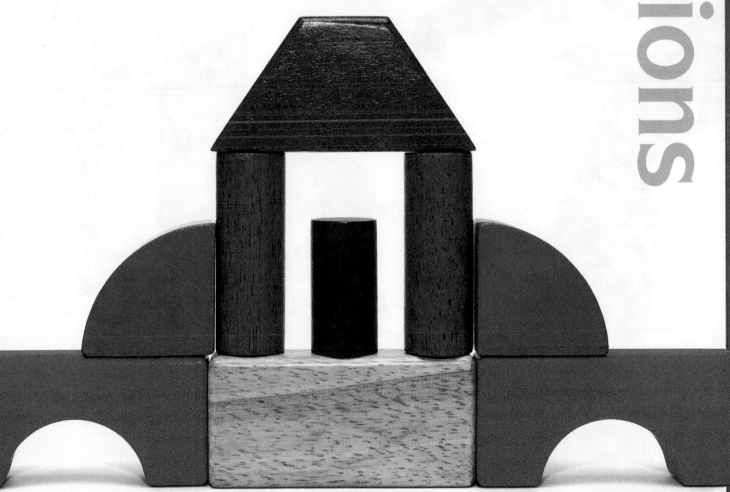

1 Continuity and Change in Early Childhood Education

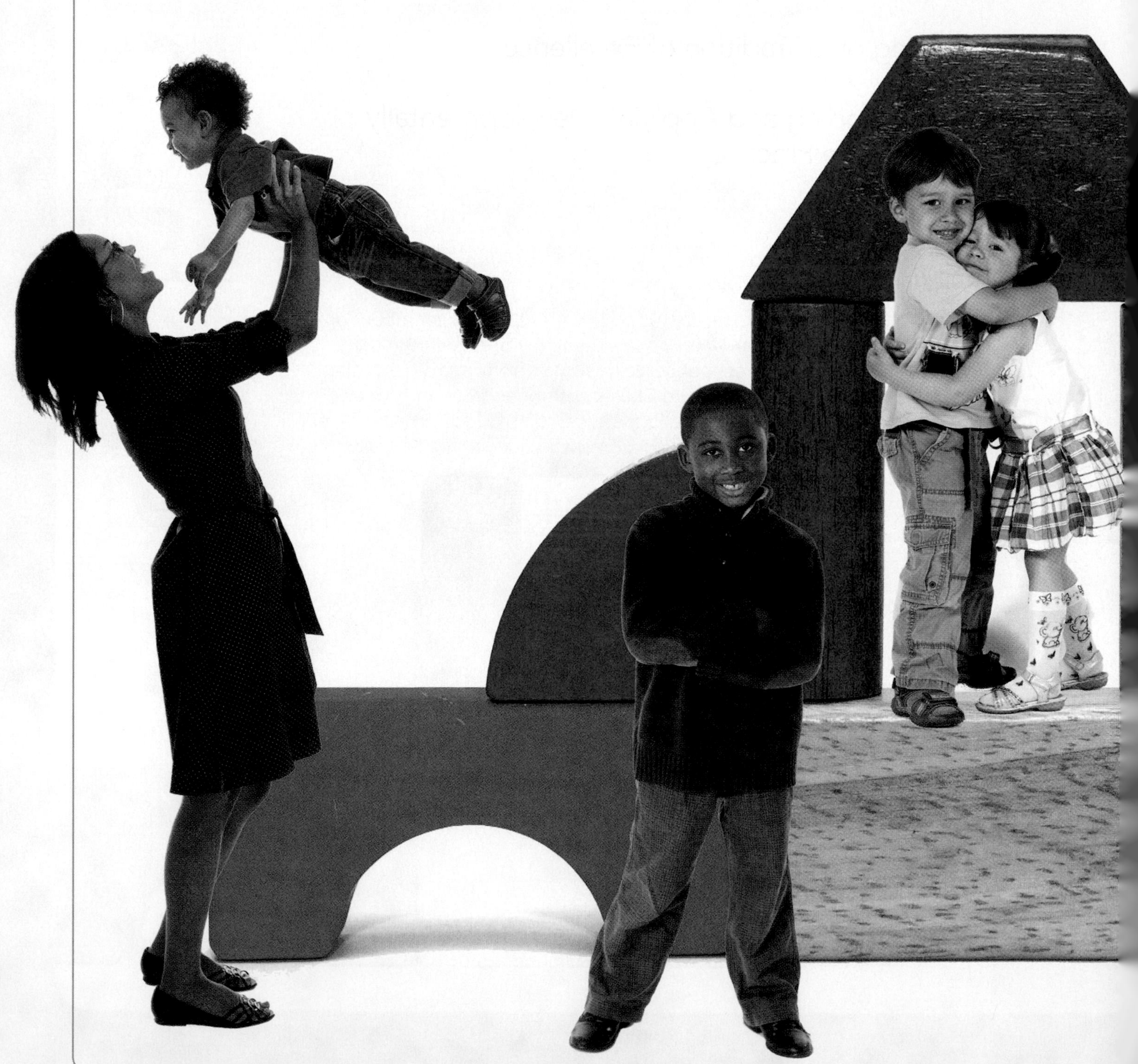

Thinking Ahead

1. What is early childhood education?
2. What are the standards for high-quality early childhood programs and why is quality so important?
3. Why become an early childhood educator? What are the dimensions of intentional, effective teaching?
4. What are the shared values of early childhood professionals as a cultural group?
5. What does research say about the lasting benefits of early childhood education?
6. How can early education promote social justice and help narrow the achievement gap between children from low-income families and their more affluent peers?
7. What are some of the current trends affecting early childhood education?
8. How does early childhood education practice today reflect both continuity and change?

At Cresthaven Primary School, teachers, children, and family members of all generations are viewing children's work and sharing memories during the year-end celebration. This public school serves children from age 3 to grade 3, through a partnership with Reed Child Development Center nearby. The Reed Center provides state-funded preschool classrooms for 3- and 4-year-olds who will attend Cresthaven as well as before- and after-school care and child care for infants and toddlers.

The preschoolers are in awe of the "big school" where they will attend kindergarten and are excited to see their work displayed in the hallway. "Look, Mommy! Here's my painting of the yellow fish," cries 4-year-old Amber as she tugs on her mother's hand. "See where I wrote my name. And here's Brenda's picture. She's my new best friend." Amber's mother smiles and tries to read what her daughter wrote: "I lk fsh." The teacher, Ms. Engels, comes up and says, "Amber knows a lot about writing and letters. She can write her name, and she is starting to write the consonants she hears in words."

For several years, Cresthaven School has been involved with its neighbors in a community garden project. In each class, the teachers connect the larger curriculum—especially science and social studies goals—to aspects of the garden project. Six-year-old Sergio and his grandmother walk down the hall where they find the list of all the meals the kindergartners prepared with the vegetables they harvested. He exclaims, "And tonight, we get to eat strawberries!" Meanwhile, first-grader Mathias quietly explains to some parents, "Me and my friends made this graph. It shows the vegetables the kids liked most." Third-grader Carola describes her class project to her father. "You'll like this, Dad. For social studies, we're figuring out where food comes from and why it costs so much."

The second-grade teacher, Ms. George, gets everyone's attention. "Our class is going to do their PowerPoint presentation of the garden project in 15 minutes." Seven-year-old Kelsey takes 75-year-old Mrs. Carrero by the hand and invites her to see the slide show. The children share most of the food raised in the garden with elderly neighbors such as Mrs. Carrero. "I'll show you the chapter book I can read, too," says Kelsey.

Four-year-old Cooper, who has autism, has been in Ms. Watson's class for 2 years. His mother comes up and quietly whispers to Ms. Watson, "I wanted you to know that Cooper got invited to Martie's birthday party. I never thought that would happen, but he's made more progress here than I ever imagined."

As she's leaving, Nicky's mom stops to thank Isela and Evan, who are finishing their first year of teaching 2-year-olds. They remember their struggles with Nicky's tantrums as he hugs his mom's leg and playfully peeks around at Evan. She says, "I know he is growing up and has to move to preschool, but we are really going to miss you two." ▲

Listening to these children, parents, and teachers, some new to the field and others with many years of experience, reveals the most exciting—as well as challenging—dimensions of early childhood education. Teaching young children is hard work. It takes energy, physical stamina, patience, a sense of humor, and a wide range of knowledge and skill. But early childhood professionals soon discover the rewards of their efforts. Nothing is quite as exciting as making a baby smile and giggle, seeing a toddler's grin as he climbs the stairs on his own, or observing a preschooler's serious look as she comes to the rescue as a pretend firefighter. And what can compete with a first grader's feeling of utter accomplishment that accompanies learning to read?

MyEducationLab

Go to the Book Specific Resources in the MyEducationLab for your course and select Author Interviews in Chapter 1 and watch and listen to the video *Inspiration for Writing Her Book.* Sue Bredekamp describes what inspired her to write this text.

Early childhood education is a rewarding profession for many reasons. We describe the diverse field of early childhood education and discuss its rewards in this chapter. We also discuss why early childhood education is a field "on the rise" and the current trends that present both challenges and opportunities. We also describe how, in a period of rapid change, the early childhood profession continues to be shaped by its enduring values. Above all, early childhood educators enter and stay in the field primarily for one reason—they know that their work makes a difference in the lives of children and families.

What Is Early Childhood Education?

Early childhood education is a highly diverse field that serves children from birth through age 8. During these years, children participate in many different kinds of care and education settings. Regardless of where they work or specific job titles, however, early childhood teachers are **professionals**. This means that they make decisions based on a specialized body of knowledge; continue to learn throughout their careers; and are committed to providing the best care and education possible for every child. The opportunity to make a difference in this exciting field has never been greater, as we discuss next.

Why Early Childhood Education Is a Field on the Rise

Early childhood education benefits greatly from increasing public recognition, respect, and funding. Even in the depths of a serious economic recession in 2009, the federal government set aside billions of dollars for early childhood education as part of the American Recovery and Reinvestment Act, commonly referred to as the "stimulus package."

Politicians on both sides of the aisle in states as diverse as Oklahoma, Georgia, New York, Illinois, Massachusetts, Tennessee, California, and Florida have called for increased funding for prekindergarten programs (Barnett, Epstein, Friedman, Boyd, & Hustadt, 2008). These positive developments reflect growing public recognition of the benefits of early education, especially for children at risk of later school failure, but also for middle-class children. For example, a 2008 poll found that 7 in 10 voters wanted state and local governments to provide prekindergarten for all children (Wilson, 2008).

A growing number of policy makers, parents, and researchers now consider early childhood programs essential for fostering school readiness and long-term success in life (Kirp, 2007). Groups, such as the prestigious Committee for Economic Development, consider early childhood education a necessary investment in the future of our country (Galinsky, 2006). Law enforcement groups support expansion of early childhood education as a crime prevention strategy (Newman et al., 2000). In the words of Nobel Prize–winning economist James Heckman (2006), a powerful advocate for early education:

> We cannot afford to postpone investing in children until they reach school age—a time when it may be too late to make a meaningful difference. Policies that seek to remedy deficits incurred in early years are much more costly than early investments wisely made.

Several factors have contributed to the rise in status of early childhood education. These include an impressive body of research on the positive effects of early childhood programs and concerns about the persistent achievement gap in our schools. Next we examine the overall landscape of the field, including the types of settings where children are served.

MyEducationLab

Go to the Professional Perspectives section in Topic 12: Professionalism/ Ethics in the MyEducationLab for your course and select the video entitled *The Changing Field of Early Childhood Education* and watch and listen to Sue Bredekamp discuss this topic.

early childhood education Education and child care services provided for children from birth through age 8.

professionals Members of an occupational group that make decisions based on a specialized body of knowledge, continue to learn throughout their careers, and are committed to meeting the needs of others.

The Landscape of Early Childhood Education

Although early childhood terminology is not uniform across diverse settings, throughout this text we will use vocabulary that is consistent with that used by the **National Association for the Education of Young Children** (NAEYC) and that we feel best represents the present and future of the field. NAEYC, headquartered in Washington, D.C., is the world's largest professional organization of early childhood educators. Founded in 1926, NAEYC's mission is to act on behalf of the needs, rights, and well-being of young children from birth through age 8.

One way the association achieves its mission is by establishing standards for teacher preparation at the associate, baccalaureate, and graduate-degree levels (Hyson, 2003; NAEYC, 2009b). NAEYC's standards have considerable influence in the field; it is likely that the course you are now taking is designed to address some of the association's teacher education standards. NAEYC (2005b) also administers an accreditation system for high-quality children's programs and provides resources such as publications and conferences to support teachers' continuing professional development.

National Association for the Education of Young Children (NAEYC) The world's largest organization of early childhood educators, whose mission is to act on behalf of the needs and interests of children from birth through age 8. NAEYC establishes standards for teacher preparation and accreditation of early childhood programs.

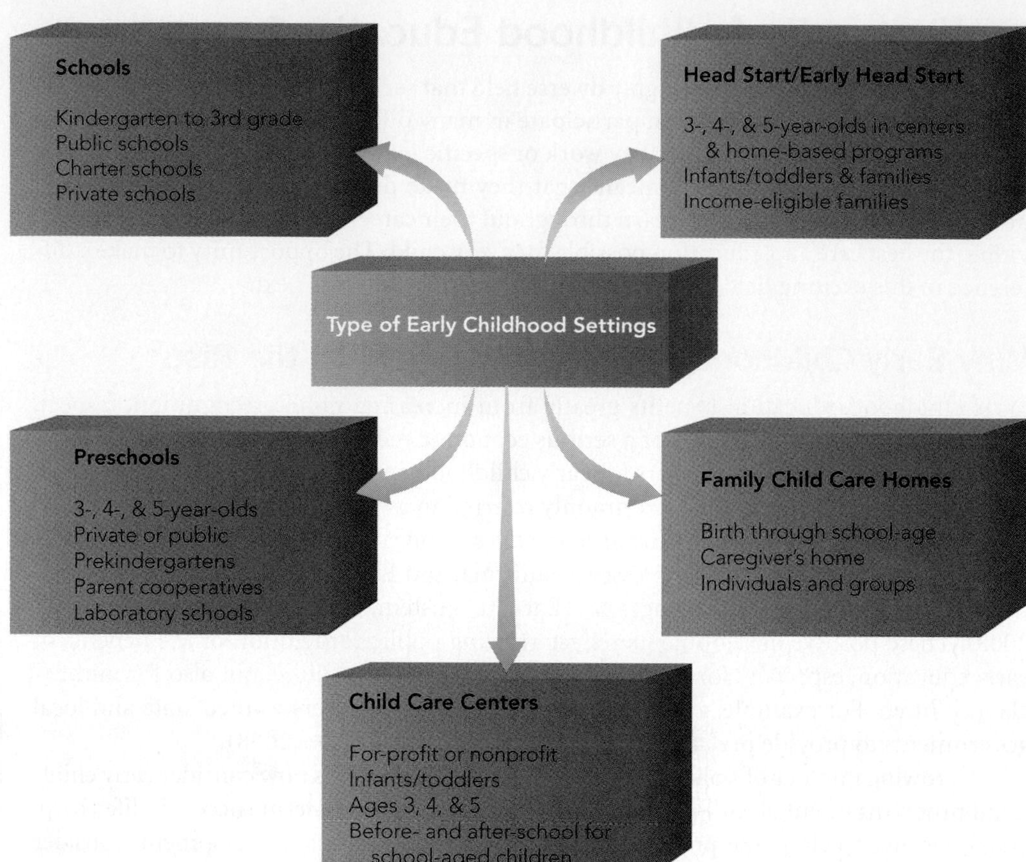

Figure 1.1 Types of Early Childhood Settings

Given NAEYC's definition of the field—birth through age 8—early childhood teachers work with various groups:

1. *Infants and toddlers:* birth to 36 months
2. *Preschoolers:* 3- and 4-year-olds
3. *Kindergartners:* 5- and 6-year-olds
4. *Primary grades 1, 2, and 3:* 6-, 7-, and 8-year-olds.

Because early childhood is defined so broadly, the field encompasses child care centers and homes, preschools, kindergartens, and primary grade schools. Figure 1.1 provides an illustration of the various settings where young children are educated and cared for. Young children are always learning and they always need loving care. Therefore, it is important *not* to distinguish child care from early education, but rather to ensure that all children have access to programs that are both caring and educational, regardless of the length of day or who provides the service.

child care center Group program that provides care and education for young children during the hours that their parents are employed.

family child care home Child care in which caregivers provide care in their own homes for a small group of children, often multi-age groups.

preschool Educational programs serving 3- and 4-year-olds delivered under various sponsorships.

parent cooperative Preschool program owned, operated, and partially staffed by parents.

Child Care

The term *child care* typically refers to care and education provided for young children during the hours that their parents are employed. To accommodate work schedules, child care is usually available for extended hours such as from 7:00 AM to 6:00 PM. In some settings, such as hospital-affiliated child care centers, care is offered for longer hours to accommodate evening, weekend, or even night shift employment.

Child care is typically provided in two types of group programs: **child care centers** and **family child care homes**. In either setting, children's care may be privately funded by parent tuition or publicly subsidized for low-income families. Child care centers usually enroll children from infancy through preschool-age children, and many also offer before- and after-school care for primary grade children. In family child care homes, caregivers provide care in their own homes for a small group of children, often of varying ages. Family child care is the setting of choice for many parents of infants and toddlers because of its home-like atmosphere.

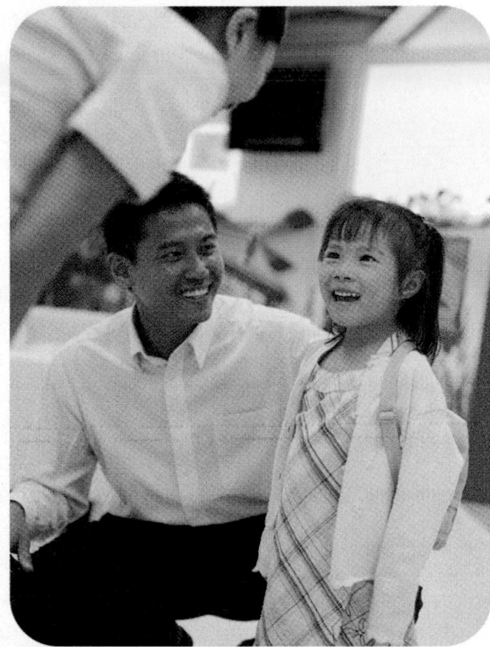

Early childhood education includes child care centers, preschools, prekindergartens, family child care homes, and schools. But every high-quality program provides both loving care and education for young children and support for their families.

Preschool

Preschool programs, as the name implies, serve 3- and 4-year-olds prior to their entrance to kindergarten. Preschool programs may be operated by community organizations or by churches, temples, or other faith-based organizations and also by **parent cooperatives**, which are run and partially staffed by groups of parents. Preschools often operate half-day, although extended hours—the school day—are becoming more common. Some colleges and universities operate **laboratory schools**, which usually serve children of students and faculty and also act as models for student teachers.

Preschools are called by various names, including *nursery schools* and *prekindergartens*. (To further complicate matters, child care centers are also called preschools.) Preschool programs are both privately and publicly funded. Those that are primarily funded by parent tuition tend to serve middle- or upper-income families. Two particular types of preschool are designed primarily for children from low-income families: public prekindergarten and Head Start.

Public Prekindergarten

The term **prekindergarten (pre-K)** usually refers to preschools that are funded by state and local departments of education. Currently, public prekindergarten is in the news media regularly and is the fastest growing sector of the field, with enrollment increasing enormously in recent years. In 1980, 96,000 preschoolers were served in public elementary schools; by 2005, enrollment had increased to more than 1 million children (Barnett & Yarosz, 2007). As of 2008, 43 states provide funding for preschool education (National Center for Children in Poverty, 2009).

The primary purpose of prekindergarten is to improve **school readiness**; that is, to prepare children for kindergarten. Although some state officials narrowly define readiness as literacy and math skills, the early childhood profession uses a multidimensional definition of school readiness (National Education Goals Panel, 1995) that includes children's:

- Physical development, health, and well-being
- Social-emotional development and learning
- Cognitive development and general knowledge such as mathematics and science
- Positive approaches to learning such as curiosity and motivation
- Language development and early literacy skills.

The majority of public prekindergarten programs are designed for children from low-income families or those who are considered at risk for school failure due to conditions such as low levels of maternal education or speaking a language other than English in the home. However, a growing number of people are calling for funding of **universal voluntary prekindergarten**, the goal of which is to make these programs available to families of all income levels who choose to use them, which we discuss later in this chapter.

laboratory school School operated by colleges and universities that usually serves children of students and faculty and also act as models of excellent education for student teachers.

prekindergarten (pre-K) Educational program serving 3- and 4-year-olds, usually in public schools.

school readiness Children's competencies related to success in kindergarten, including physical development, health, and well-being; social–emotional development and learning; cognitive development and general knowledge, such as mathematics and science; positive approaches to learning such as curiosity and motivation; and language development and early literacy skills.

universal voluntary prekindergarten Publicly funded preschool usually for 4-year-olds, but sometimes 3-year-olds; available to any family that chooses to use it.

Head Start

Head Start is a federally funded, national program that promotes school readiness by enhancing the social and cognitive development of children ages 3, 4, and 5. Head Start provides educational, health, nutritional, social, and other services to the nation's poorest children and families whose incomes fall below the official poverty level (Head Start, 2008b). In addition to these comprehensive services, parent involvement is a special focus of the program. Parents volunteer in the classroom and also serve in governance roles, with the goal of empowering families to move out of poverty. In fact, during the 2005–2006 year, 27% of Head Start staff members were parents of current or former Head Start children (Head Start, 2008b). In recent years, Head Start has also focused on promoting the early reading and math skills needed for children's success in school.

Head Start Federally funded, national program that promotes school readiness by enhancing the social and cognitive development of children ages 3, 4, and 5 through providing educational, health, nutritional, social, and other services to the nation's poorest children and families.

Early Head Start Federally funded program serving low-income pregnant mothers, infants, and toddlers that promotes healthy family functioning.

Most Head Start children are served in classroom-based preschool programs, although in rural or remote areas, a home-based option is available. About 12% of Head Start's enrollment is children with disabilities (Head Start, 2008b). The families served by Head Start are highly diverse, as Table 1.1 illustrates. About one-third of the children speak a language other than English at home. In addition, the program has a special focus on serving American Indians, Alaska Natives, and migrant and seasonal workers.

In response to new research on early brain development and concerns that age 4 or even age 3 is too late for services to be effective, the government launched **Early Head Start** in 1995. Early Head Start serves low-income pregnant mothers, infants, and toddlers. It also promotes healthy family functioning. In 2007, there were 650 Early Head Start programs in all 50 states, the District of Columbia, and Puerto Rico (Head Start, 2008b). Rec-

Table 1.1 Head Start Program Statistics

ENROLLMENT	908,412
AGES	
Number of 5-year-olds	3%
Number of 4-year-olds	51%
Number of 3-year-olds	36%
Number under 3 years of age	10%
RACIAL/ETHNIC COMPOSITION	
American Indian/Alaska Native	4.0%
African American	30.1%
White	39.7%
Hispanic/Latino	34.7%
Asian	1.7%
Hawaiian/Pacific Islander	.8%
Biracial/multiracial	4.9%
Unspecified/other	18.8%

Source: From *Head Start Facts,* 2008, Washington, DC: U.S. Department of Health and Human Services. Retrieved December 19, 2008, from http://www.acf.gov/programs/ohs/about/fy2008.htm.

ognizing the positive outcomes produced by Early Head Start (Love et al., 2007), the 2009 government stimulus package increased Early Head Start funding.

Early Intervention and Early Childhood Special Education

Early childhood special education serves children with disabilities or special needs who meet eligibility guidelines that are determined on a state-by-state basis, according to the **Individuals with Disabilities Education Act (IDEA)**. In addition to serving children with identified disabilities, some states provide **early intervention** services for infants and toddlers who are at risk of developmental delay and their families.

Federal legislation enacted during the past three decades has fundamentally changed the way in which early childhood services are organized and delivered to children with disabilities and special needs (Division for Early Childhood & NAEYC, 2009). These children, including children who are at risk for disabilities or who exhibit challenging behaviors, are far more likely to participate in a typical early childhood program than in the past (Sandall, Hemmeter, Smith, & McLean, 2005). This trend, called **inclusion**, is defined and described in the *Including All Children: What Does Inclusion Mean?* feature.

All early childhood educators are likely to work with children with disabilities at some point in their careers. This inevitability broadens what teachers need to know right from the start, and requires that general early childhood teachers develop skills to collaborate with special educators.

early childhood special education Services for children with disabilities or special needs who meet eligibility guidelines that are determined on a state-by-state basis according to the Individuals with Disabilities Education Act.

Individuals with Disabilities Education Act (IDEA) Federal law governing provision of services for children with disabilities and special needs.

early intervention Services for infants and toddlers who are at risk of developmental delay and their families.

inclusion Participation and services for children with disabilities and special needs in programs and settings where their typically developing peers are served.

Including All Children

What Does Inclusion Mean?

Mark and Monique Berger operate a family child care program in their home. Their state permits group homes, such as theirs, to serve 12 children. The licensing agent informs them that they are required by law to serve children with disabilities and special needs. One mother, whose son Barry has cerebral palsy, has inquired about enrolling him in their program. Mark wants to be sure that they abide by the law, but Monique is a little unsure about what it means to include a child with a disability in her child care home.

Although full inclusion of children with disabilities in early childhood programs has been the law of the land for several years, Mark and Monique are not alone in being unsure about what it means. To help them and other professionals like them, the Division for Early Childhood of the Council for Exceptional Children and NAEYC (2009) jointly developed a statement defining early childhood inclusion:

> Early childhood inclusion embodies the values, policies, and practices that support the right of every infant and young child and his or her family, regardless of ability, to participate in a broad range of activities and contexts as full members of families, communities, and society. The desired results of inclusive experiences for children with and without disabilities and their families include a sense of belonging and membership, positive social relationships and friendships, and development and learning to reach their full potential.

The statement describes the key features of high-quality inclusive programs, which are (1) access, (2) participation, and (3) supports.

A defining feature of high-quality early childhood inclusion is *access*, which means providing children with a wide range of learning opportunities, activities, and environments. In inclusive settings, adults also promote belonging, *participation*, and engagement of children with disabilities and their typically developing peers in a variety of intentional or purposeful ways.

Finally, an infrastructure of inclusion *supports* must be in place to ensure a foundation for the efforts of individuals and organizations that provide inclusive services to children and families. For example, Mark and Monique will need access to ongoing professional development and support to acquire the knowledge, skills, and dispositions required to effectively meet Barry's needs and contribute to his development. In addition, specialized services and therapies for Barry will need to be coordinated and integrated with the other activities they offer the children.

Reference: Division for Early Childhood & National Association for the Education of Young Children. (2009). Early childhood inclusion: A joint position statement of the Division for Early Childhood (DEC) and the National Association for the Education of Young Children (NAEYC). Chapel Hill: The University of North Carolina, FPG Child Development Institute. Retrieved August 23, 2009, from http://community.fpg.unc.edu/resources/articles/files/EarlyChildhoodInclusion-04-2009.pdf.

Kindergarten and Primary Grades

Most 5- through 8-year-old children attend public schools, although many attend secular or faith-based private schools funded by parent tuition. Typically considered the first year of formal schooling, **kindergarten** has traditionally been designed for 5-year-olds. However, states establish varying dates for the legal entrance age to kindergarten (Datar, 2003). Most states require that children who are entering kindergarten must have their fifth birthday no later than September 1, although some use July 1. This means that kindergartens enroll many 6-year-olds.

First, second, and third grade are the **primary grade** years of school (6 through 8 years of age). These grades are especially important because during these grades, children are expected to acquire the fundamental abilities of reading and mathematics, along with the foundations of other academic disciplines including social studies, science, the creative arts, technology, and physical education. In first to third grade, children are learning to read; after that, they are expected to read to learn. Therefore, if a good foundation is not laid during the primary years, children are likely to struggle in later years (Juel, 1988). Increasing numbers of school systems are funding **charter schools**. Charter schools are independently operated and have greater flexibility than regular schools for meeting regulations and achieving goals. In school districts where charter schools are an option, parents have a choice of where to send their children.

How Early Childhood Education Is Expanding

Participation in early childhood programs has increased steadily for many decades as more children participate in group programs at younger ages. In 1965, only 60% of 5-year-olds went to kindergarten, whereas today almost 95% do (Barnett & Yarosz, 2007). A similar but steeper growth trend is apparent for younger children. In 1960, only 10% of 3- and 4-year-olds were enrolled in any type of early childhood program. In 2005, two-thirds of 4-year-olds and more than 40% of 3-year-olds participated in a preschool program (Barnett & Yarosz, 2007). Every type of early childhood program has seen growth, including private preschools and child care centers, state-funded prekindergartens, preschool special education, and Head Start (Barnett, 2008).

Growth in Preschool Attendance

Changes in preschool participation are apparent in the findings of the *Early Childhood Longitudinal Study, Birth Cohort* (Jacobson Chernoff, Flanagan, McPhee, & Park, 2007). The study identified the primary setting where 4-year-old children received the most hours of early care and education. Only 20% were in no regular setting outside their home. Almost 60% were in a child care center, preschool, or Head Start center; 13% were cared for by a relative; and 8% were in a home-based, nonrelative care setting, such as a family child care center or care provided by a neighbor or friend.

This study reveals a shift in the way preschool is viewed in the United States. Preschool, rather than kindergarten, is coming to be seen as the first year of school for children (Jacobson Chernoff et al., 2007). The percentage of children who attend center-based preschools is approximately the same whether or not their mothers are employed. This finding indicates that the growth in preschool enrollment is related to increased demand for early education as much as increased need for child care (Barnett & Yarosz, 2007).

Providing Child Care for Working Families

Expansion of the early childhood field is directly related to the increased demand for child care for employed families. A substantial increase in labor force participation of mothers with young children has occurred during the past 30 years, with many women now the primary or sole earner in the family. Currently, almost 63% of women with children under age 6 and 59% of mothers of children under age 3 are in the labor force (National Association of Child Care Resource and Referral Agencies, 2009). An even greater proportion of mothers of school-age children need child care for some hours of the day.

kindergarten Typically considered the first year of formal schooling; serves 5- and 6-year-olds.

primary grades First, second, and third grade; sometimes includes kindergarten.

charter schools Independently operated, publicly funded schools that have greater flexibility than regular schools in meeting regulations and achieving goals.

Recognizing how important good child care is to maintaining a productive workforce, a number of employers now sponsor on-site child care centers or subsidize child care expenses as an employee benefit. Employers find that support for child care reduces absenteeism and turnover (National Child Care Information Center, n.d.).

In addition, the federal government provides child care assistance through **Temporary Assistance for Needy Families (TANF)**. The TANF program, more commonly known as Welfare to Work, provides temporary financial aid, but requires recipients to move into the labor force or schooling, further increasing the demand for child care. In addition, **Child Care and Development Block Grants (CCDBG)** allocate funds to states for low-income working families to purchase their own child care.

The economic crisis that began in 2008 led to increased unemployment, which, in turn, negatively affected enrollments in early childhood programs. In some situations, families removed their children from preschool or child care centers because they could no longer afford or did not need these services. Some employers were seen as being less willing or able to subsidize child care as a benefit. The long-term effects of the economic downturn on early childhood programs remain to be seen. Nevertheless, increased funding for child care and early education at this difficult time in the nation's history is solid evidence of its broad support and recognition of its value.

Access to Early Childhood Education

Despite the overall increase in the number of children attending preschool, access to programs varies considerably depending on family income and other factors. In fact, the children who are most likely to benefit from high-quality programs are the least likely to participate in them. Consider the following statistics:

- Young children who live in poverty are less likely to attend preschool than children from middle-income or higher income families. As illustrated in Figure 1.2, 89% of 4-year-olds whose families earn more than $100,000 are enrolled in preschool, compared to 55% of those who earn $20,000 to $30,000 (Barnett & Yarosz, 2007).
- Head Start and state-funded prekindergarten programs increase the participation rates for low-income families, but only about 60% of income-eligible families have access to Head Start because insufficient slots are available (Barnett & Yarosz, 2007).

Temporary Assistance for Needy Families (TANF) Federally funded program, more commonly known as Welfare to Work, that provides temporary financial aid, but requires recipients to move into the labor force or schooling.

Child Care and Development Block Grants (CCDBG) Federal funds allocated to states for low-income working families to purchase child care.

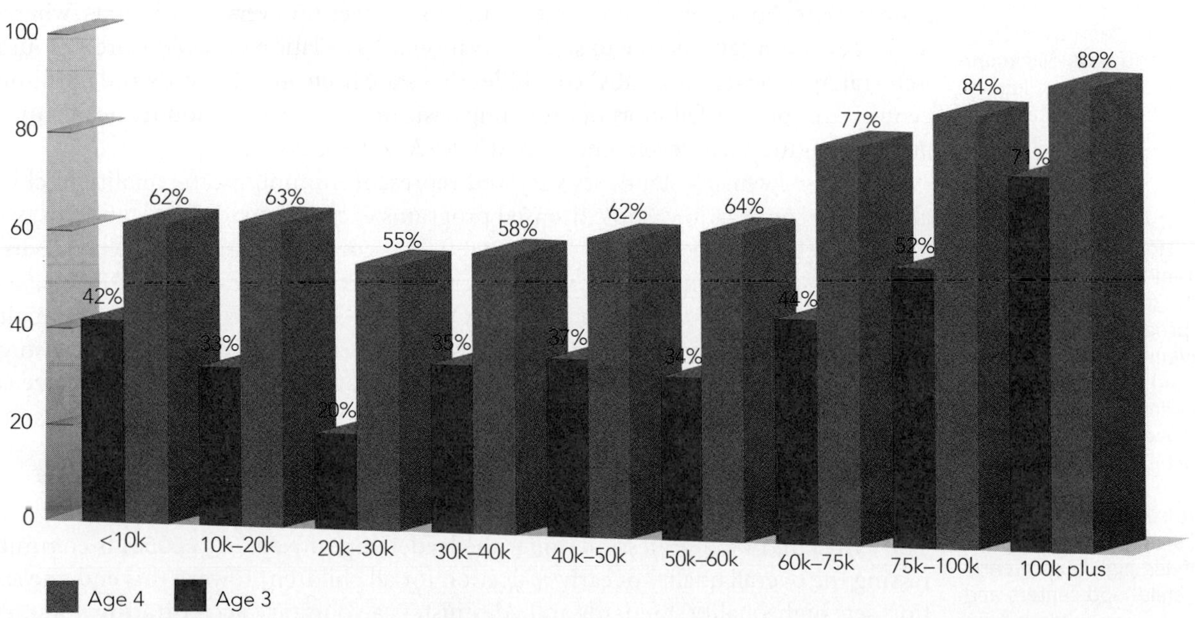

Figure 1.2 Preschool Participation by Income

- Families with moderate incomes above the poverty level face the greatest hurdle because they are not eligible for subsidized programs and cannot afford private ones (Wat, 2008).
- Preschool participation varies considerably depending on the mother's education. In 2005, 87% of children whose mothers had a college education participated in preschool, compared to only 55% of those whose mothers were high school dropouts. Again, the children who need preschool the most—those whose mothers are less likely to provide educational experiences at home—are the least likely to get it.
- Preschool participation also varies by children's ethnicity (Barnett & Yarosz, 2007). In 2005, 75% of 4-year-old African American children attended preschool, whereas 69% of white children did. Hispanic children had the lowest rate of preschool attendance at 59%.

As the field expands, a vital consideration is the quality of the programs children experience, a topic discussed in the next section.

Importance of Quality in Early Childhood Education

Growing attention to early education primarily results from impressive research demonstrating its effectiveness in improving outcomes for children. All of the research that has influenced policy, however, finds that the key ingredient in the effectiveness of early childhood education is the quality of the program for children. But what is quality?

Setting Standards for Quality

Earlier in this chapter, we described different types of early childhood programs. Various kinds of programs must meet different sets of standards, which are intended to determine the program's quality.

Child Care Licensing Standards

Child care centers and in some states, family child care homes, are regulated by each state's **child care licensing standards**. These set minimum requirements for a program to operate legally. Such standards usually establish a minimum number of teachers required per child (teacher/child ratios), teacher qualifications, and health and safety requirements.

These standards, designed to ensure children's protection, vary considerably from state to state. For example, one state requires a teacher for every four infants, whereas another permits a ratio of one to six. The National Association of Child Care Resource and Referral Agencies (NACCRRA) concludes that state licensing standards and monitoring of centers' compliance fall short of providing basic protection for children's health and safety and promoting their development (NACCRRA, 2008b, 2009).

child care licensing standards Minimum requirements, legally established by each state, for a child care program to operate.

quality rating systems (QRS) State-operated systems that evaluate and rate the quality of child care programs according to achievement of benchmarks beyond those required for minimal licensing, such as having more highly qualified teachers or better ratios.

accreditation system NAEYC's voluntary system for identifying high-quality early childhood centers and schools serving children from birth through kindergarten.

Because licensing standards vary and represent minimums, the quality of child care also varies considerably. Some licensed programs exceed the required standards, whereas others barely meet them (NACCRRA, 2009). To address this issue and help parents make informed decisions, many states now operate **quality rating systems (QRS)**, also called *quality rating and improvement systems* (QRIS). These systems rate program quality according to achievement of benchmarks beyond those required for minimal licensing, such as having more highly qualified teachers or better ratios. The state may recognize centers that meet higher standards with more stars and pay higher reimbursement rates for children served. In some states, achieving accreditation is the highest level.

Accreditation Standards

The early childhood profession under the leadership of NAEYC (2005e) is committed to raising the overall quality of early education for all children. Toward this end, the association sets high-quality standards and administers a voluntary **accreditation system** for all types of early childhood centers and schools serving children from birth through kinder-

Table 1.2 NAEYC Early Childhood Program Standards

Standard	Standard Description
1. Relationships	The program promotes positive relationships among all children and adults to encourage each child's sense of individual worth and belonging as a part of a community and to foster each child's ability to contribute as a responsible community member.
2. Curriculum	The program implements a curriculum that is consistent with its goals for children and promotes learning and development in each of the following areas: social, emotional, physical, language, and cognitive.
3. Teaching	The program uses developmentally, culturally, and linguistically appropriate and effective teaching approaches that enhance each child's learning and development in the context of the program's curriculum goals. Teachers purposefully use multiple instructional approaches to optimize children's opportunities for learning.
4. Assessment of children's progress	The program is informed by ongoing systematic, formal, and informal assessment approaches to provide information on children's learning and development. These assessments occur within the context of reciprocal communications with families and with sensitivity to the cultural contexts in which children develop. Assessment results are used to benefit children by informing sound decisions about children, teaching, and program improvement.
5. Health	The program promotes the nutrition and health of children and protects children and staff from illness and injury.
6. Teachers	The program employs and supports a teaching staff that has the educational qualifications, knowledge, and professional commitment necessary to promote children's learning and development and to support families' diverse needs and interests.
7. Families	The program establishes and maintains collaborative relationships with each child's family to foster children's development in all settings. These relationships are sensitive to family composition, language, and culture.
8. Community relationships	The program establishes relationships with and uses the resources of the children's communities to support the achievement of program goals.
9. Physical environment	The program has a safe and healthful environment that provides appropriate and well-maintained indoor and outdoor physical environments. The environment includes facilities, equipment, and materials to facilitate child and staff learning and development.
10. Leadership and management	The program effectively implements policies, procedures, and systems that support stable staff and strong personnel, fiscal, and program management so all children, families, and staff have high-quality experiences. (Includes teacher/child ratios and group sizes.)

Source: From "NAEYC Early Childhood Program Standards and Accreditation Criteria: The Mark of Quality in Early Childhood Education," 2005, Washington, DC: NAEYC.

garten. The standards that programs must achieve to obtain accreditation are listed in Table 1.2. These standards apply to any early childhood program regardless of length of day or sponsorship. NAEYC accreditation standards are designed to answer the question "What is high quality?"

To understand what we mean by *quality*, it is important to see the relationships among the standards rather than to see them as a discrete list. In the accreditation system, the primary focus is on *children* as described in the first five standards: relationships, curriculum, teaching, assessment of children's progress, and health. The other five standards address teachers, partnerships with families and communities, and administration including the physical environment and leadership and management. Meeting these standards establishes a supportive context that makes it possible to achieve and maintain the quality of life for children described in the first five standards.

Military Child Care Act

The largest employer-sponsored child care system in the world is the U.S. military. Its voluntary workforce of men and women depends on the provision of high-quality child care. In 1989, Congress passed the Military Child Care Act to ensure consistently high standards of quality in these programs. The act required that centers seek NAEYC accreditation, and also included provisions for teacher training and a career ladder tying compensation to increased professional development. The Military Child Care Act resulted in significantly improved quality and learning outcomes for children (Zellman & Johansen, 1998). In addition, the military child care system is now seen as a model for all employer-sponsored child care (N. D. Campbell, Appelbaum, Martinson, & Martin, 2000).

Head Start Standards

Head Start Program Performance Standards National standards that establish the level of quality of services provided by every Head Start program.

Quality is also a critically important issue in Head Start, particularly so because it serves the nation's most vulnerable children. Head Start programs are regularly monitored for compliance with the national **Head Start Program Performance Standards** (Head Start, 1998). These standards are similar to accreditation standards, but they also address the comprehensive services that are part of Head Start's mandate.

Measuring Quality in Early Childhood Programs

structural quality Features of an early childhood program, such as maximum group sizes, teacher/child ratios, and teacher qualifications, that are relatively easy to quantify and measure.

process quality The quality of the relationships and interactions among teachers and children, and the appropriateness of the materials, learning experiences, and teaching strategies occurring in an early childhood program.

Early Childhood Environment Rating Scale (ECERS-R) Observational instrument used to rate program quality on a 7-point scale from inadequate to excellent.

Classroom Assessment Scoring System (CLASS) Preschool and elementary classroom observational instrument that focuses on the instructional strategies teachers use to support children's learning and the quality of their relationships with children.

As we can see from examining accreditation standards, the early childhood field defines quality as having two dimensions: structural and process (FPG Child Development Institute, 2008). **Structural quality** includes features such as maximum group sizes, teacher/child ratios, and teacher qualifications, which are relatively easy to quantify and measure. **Process quality**, on the other hand, refers to the quality of the relationships and interactions among teachers and children, and the appropriateness of the materials, learning experiences, and teaching strategies. These features are much more difficult to evaluate, and yet, they are the key aspects of the quality of children's experiences. They describe what life should be like for children in a program, how they should be treated, and how their learning and development should be promoted.

Structural quality and process quality are interconnected. For example, well-qualified teachers are needed to plan and implement an engaging curriculum and teach effectively. Similarly, positive relationships between teachers and children are more likely to be established when the size of the group and ratio of adults to children is relatively small. An age-appropriate, well-equipped, and organized physical environment is needed to protect children's health and safety and to promote active learning.

The most difficult challenge is determining how to measure compliance with quality standards. To see if a program is meeting requirements, it is relatively easy to examine transcripts of teachers or count the number of children in a group. But it is much harder—especially for an outside evaluator—to decide if teachers have positive relationships with each child and family or if they are using effective teaching strategies. These standards can only be assessed by directly observing what goes on in classrooms (FPG Child Development Institute, 2008; NAEYC, 2005e).

To provide consistent ways of measuring quality, researchers have developed observation tools. The most widely used program quality assessment is the **Early Childhood Environment Rating Scale (ECERS-R)** (Harms, Clifford, & Cryer, 2005) with versions for preschool, infant/toddler, family child care, and school-age programs. Another observational measure is the **Classroom Assessment Scoring System (CLASS)** for preschool and primary grades (Pianta, LaParo, & Hamre, 2008). The CLASS focuses on the instructional strategies teachers use and the quality of their relationships with children.

Research shows that how well classrooms and teachers score on these measures predicts how well children score on measures of language, literacy, mathematics, and social–emotional abilities (Early et al., 2005; National Institute of Child Health and Human Development Early Child Care Research Network, 2002; Pianta et al., 2005).

The overall conclusion of all of the research on the effectiveness of early education is that what teachers actually do with children is the most important determinant of the quality of children's experiences and their learning outcomes (LoCasale-Crouch et al., 2007; Pianta et al., 2005). After decades of research on quality in early childhood programs, one thing we know for certain is that teachers matter. If children are to reach their full potentials, then professionals must also, a topic we discuss in the next section.

Why Become an Early Childhood Educator?

Choosing to teach young children, like every career decision, involves weighing many factors. Prospective teachers need to be familiar with what the work entails and the possible career options. Most important, they need to determine whether the demands and rewards of their chosen profession are a good match with their own strengths, dispositions, and personal goals (Colker, 2008).

The Joys of Teaching Young Children

Working with children demands patience and the willingness to care for and about other people's children, even or especially the least lovable of those children. Teaching young children is truly rewarding work, even when it is most challenging (Colker, 2008). Each day brings new discoveries, accomplishments, and joys for children and teachers.

Picture a 4-year-old child. What are the first thoughts that come to mind? Curious? Eager to learn? Excellent early childhood teachers take advantage of young children's deep desire to actively engage with and make sense of the world around them. Recall the sense of satisfaction you felt when you mastered a difficult task such as learning to read or ride a bike. Children, too, gain great pleasure from the sense of mastery that comes from learning something new or overcoming an obstacle.

intentional teachers
Teachers who have a purpose for the decisions they make and can explain that purpose to others.

Another word that comes to mind when thinking of children is *fun*. Yes, good early childhood programs prepare children for later success in school, but they also provide them with joyful learning experiences every day of their young lives. Children should have fun in child care centers and homes, preschools, and schools. They love to be silly, joke, and tease; to sing, move, and dance; to play by themselves and with friends; to know that adults care for them; to wonder about and explore the natural world; and to generally enjoy living. When teachers create a safe and supportive place for children to experience the unique joys of childhood, children will thrive—and their teachers will also.

Intentional teachers are purposeful, but they are also playful. How can teachers keep the fun in childhood while helping children achieve important learning goals?

Becoming an Effective, Intentional Teacher

One overarching theme of this book is that effective early childhood practice requires teachers to be intentional in everything they do. **Intentional teachers** have a purpose for the decisions they make and can explain that purpose to others (Copple & Bredekamp, 2009; Epstein, 2007b). However, we believe that intentional teaching involves much more. Intentional teaching is a multifaceted, multidimensional concept that conveys many of the personal and professional qualities of an early childhood educator.

MyEducationLab

Go to the Book Specific Resources in the MyEducationLab for your course and select Author Interviews in Chapter 1 to watch and listen to the video *What Effective Teachers Do*. How does Sue Bredekamp describe effective teaching?

Dimensions of Intentional Teaching

Consider how well your own aspirations and dispositions fit with our description of the dimensions of intentional teaching. Professional, intentional early childhood teachers exhibit these characteristics:

- *Caring and committed.* They recognize that developing a personal, positive, warm relationship with each child is the foundation for everything they do. Their commitment to children means putting children's needs before their own and recognizing that teaching young children is less a job than a calling.
- *Enthusiastic and engaged.* They genuinely enjoy being with young children however messy or challenging they may be, and share in the excitement of their discoveries. They become energetically and intensely involved in children's activity, whether it means getting down on the floor to play and talk with a baby or thinking through the solution to a problem with a kindergartner.
- *Curious and creative.* They are eager to learn, just as children are. Young children want to learn all sorts of things that teachers themselves may not know—what's inside a bug, why the sky is blue, how an airplane flies. Intentional teachers model an inquisitive attitude. They want to find out along with children, and they approach questions or problems in new, imaginative ways.
- *Respectful and responsive.* They value and treat children, families, and colleagues with dignity and esteem. They respond thoughtfully to diversity in all of its forms: language, culture, race/ethnicity, ability/disability, age, gender, and sexual orientation. They are open and accepting of perspectives that are different from their own.
- *Passionate and patient.* They bring their own emotions and deep interests into their work such as a passion for music, painting, or poetry; a preference for belly laughs or quiet smiles. At the same time, they recognize that children have their own intense feelings that can spill over into anger, frustration, or fits of tears. Intentional teachers respond calmly and thoughtfully, without becoming upset or annoyed themselves.
- *Purposeful and playful.* They have important goals for children—to help them make friends, regulate their emotions, control their bodies, learn to read and write—and they plan carefully to help children achieve their goals. But along the way, they joke and laugh with children, accept silliness, encourage and support play, and make learning itself playful. A sense of humor is a necessity.
- *Focused and flexible.* They are like cameras that can scan the entire classroom and then narrow their attention to meet one child's need or respond to her question or idea. They can be teaching a reading lesson with a specific goal in mind and switch gears when a child starts talking about his brother's illness.
- *Aware and accountable.* They are self-aware; they reflect on and evaluate their own performance; and strive to improve. But their judgments are not made in isolation; they compare their performance to a standard of excellence. Intentional teachers are willing to be accountable; they accept responsibility for their actions.
- *Informed and effective.* They know how children develop and learn; they know how to teach and what to teach. They use research-based teaching practices that lead to positive outcomes for children and help children make sense of the world around them. Intentional teachers also regularly check to see if what they are doing is actually working. Are children making progress toward developmentally appropriate goals?
- *Listening and learning.* They realize that the more they learn about children, the more they need to know. They understand that choosing to teach is choosing to be a lifelong learner. Intentional teachers learn from children every day; they listen to children, and they pay close attention to all of children's cues. They stay up to date about new knowledge and continue to grow as professionals.

MyEducationLab

Go to the Assignments and Activities section of Topic 8: Developmentally Appropriate Practice/ Teaching Strategies in the MyEducationaLab for your course and complete the activity entitled *Implementing Developmentally Appropriate Practice*. Observe and listen to these preschool teachers and note the many dimensions of intentional teaching evident in their work as well as the joys of teaching young children.

For an example of intentional teaching in practice, read the *Becoming an Intentional Teacher: Purposeful and Playful* feature. Now that we have described both the dedication

Becoming an Intentional Teacher

Purposeful and Playful

Here's What Happened We give our preschool children a variety of experiences with voting for their preferences in everyday situations, such as choosing the best name for our guinea pig. On a Monday we told them that in two more days we were going to visit the firehouse, which is about four blocks from the school. Earlier, the teachers had talked about how to get the class there and felt it would be okay either to walk or take the school van.

The children discussed the issue. Some thought walking would be more fun. Jen pointed out that since the walk would take longer, we'd have less time to spend at the firehouse. Mateo, who had just gotten a tricycle for his birthday, exclaimed, "I wish we could ride trikes there!" "Yeah!" several other children agreed. I said, "*I* wish we could fly over there" and flapped my arms like wings. The children laughed at this silly idea. "I wish we could swim there!" James declared, getting into the spirit. And when I asked how else we could get to the firehouse, children came up with even more ways—some serious and some far out of the range of the possible. After we had some fun with this line of thinking, I drew them back to the vote.

Here's What I Was Thinking In our program, we like to involve the children in voting about meaningful issues. When they decide things together rather than having adults determine everything for them, they are learning to participate in decision making as we do in our society. Also, such decision making seems to give them a sense that all of us together function as a community. We think that's very important. They also learn math concepts as we record and compare the votes. The children were quite engaged throughout the experience—in thinking about and expressing the reasons for their preferences and in comparing the votes on each side of the question. When Mateo mentioned the tricycles, I thought it would be interesting and fun to play with ideas of different ways we could—or couldn't—get to our destination. Thinking in a "what if" way is a great mental stretch for children besides being fun.

and the delight that teaching young children entails, we turn to an overview of the job opportunities available in the field.

Career Options for Early Childhood Educators

As the field of early education grows, so do the potential career options and opportunities for early childhood professionals. At the same time, however, the field is experiencing a shortage of qualified teachers (Kagan, Kauerz, & Tarrant, 2008). Even as a large percentage of the current teaching staff is nearing retirement, teacher qualification requirements are being raised in many sectors of the field (Whitebook, 2003).

Because the early childhood field is so diverse and covers such a broad age range, early childhood educators have many possible career choices. Careers tend to fall into two categories:

- Working *with* children involves daily interaction and direct responsibility for children's care and education and includes positions such as classroom teacher or family child care provider.
- Working *for* children involves work that supports children's development and education, whether in proximity to the children, such as being a child care center director, or at a further distance, such as being a teacher education professor.

Over the course of their careers, many early childhood professionals move back and forth between these types of jobs. However, we believe that success in working *for* children is greater if an individual has actually worked *with* children. No one in the early childhood community can do his or her job well without knowing what life is like in an early childhood setting (Colker, 2008). This experience informs decisions at every level.

Working *with* Children

MyEducationLab

Go to the Assignments and Activities section of Topic 5: Program Models in the MyEducationLab for your course and complete the activity entitled *Quality Child Care Settings*. As you watch the video and answer the accompanying questions, consider a career teaching in a child care center and the importance of high quality programs for children.

Early childhood teachers are usually the first to admit that they aren't in this profession for the money. It is the satisfaction they get from working with children that is deeply rewarding. For many of them, the fact that they make an impact on the life of every child they encounter is a powerful incentive and the reason that, once they enter the field, they are there to stay (Colker, 2008).

Early childhood teachers work with different age groups from infancy through primary grade children in a wide range of settings. The qualifications and required certifications for specific jobs will vary, but a broad-based education in the field is necessary preparation. Following are some of the options and opportunities available for interesting and rewarding work:

- *Head Start* teachers can alter the life trajectory of young children and their families who are most in need. They help ensure that children from low-income families receive an excellent education and comprehensive health, nutrition, and other services.
- *Early Head Start* teachers intervene early with mothers and their babies to help set them on a course of healthy development.
- *Child care center* teachers provide loving care and education to children for extended periods of time each day, and help employed parents feel secure about their children's care so they can do their jobs. Careers in child care offer the option of teaching various age groups: infants and toddlers, preschoolers, and school-age children before and/or after school. Although teaching in child care pays less than in other settings, many teachers relish its flexible and creative environment. Conditions also vary by administrative agency; for example, an employer-sponsored child care center may offer more benefits and higher compensation than a community-based one.
- Teachers in *family child care homes* literally open their doors to small groups of children from infancy through school age, providing a home-like atmosphere of care and education. Family child care means being your own boss, but requires administering a small business as well as caring for children.
- *Preschools* vary a great deal—public, private, faith based, and so on—each with its own benefits that will appeal to different teachers' interests and match their goals. A public prekindergarten, for example, may provide better salaries, whereas a private one may be more flexible about curriculum and expectations for children.
- A teacher in a *parent cooperative preschool* has the opportunity to develop particularly close relationships with families but also needs the ability to work with parents as coteachers, an acquired skill.
- Teachers in *public schools* have the option of teaching different age groups from kindergarten through primary grades. Schools are bureaucracies with regulations and an established curriculum and tests, but as professionals, teachers make hundreds of classroom decisions every day. And salaries and benefits in the public schools are the most secure of any sector in early childhood.
- *Early childhood special educators* and *early intervention specialists* are qualified individuals who work with children with special needs in various settings, such as in school systems, Head Start, or child care. Inclusion of children with special needs means that early childhood special educators work closely with regular classroom teachers. In fact, in some states, the same teacher education program prepares teachers for certification in both fields simultaneously.
- *Mentor teacher* is an evolving career option for more experienced, outstanding professionals. It is helpful for new teachers to work with a mentor teacher to improve their skills or to get help for children with particular learning challenges. Mentor teachers

are becoming more common in elementary schools, preschools, and child care programs (Barnett, 2003).

- The need for *bilingual teachers* and those who are qualified to teach dual language learners is growing (National Task Force on Early Childhood Education for Hispanics, 2007). As the population becomes ever more diverse, these qualifications will be useful in any early childhood setting. Read the *Language Lens: Linguistic Diversity in Early Childhood Programs* feature to understand more about this pressing need.

Given the variety of careers available, early childhood teachers have many options. Even when an entire career is spent teaching the same age group in the same workplace, teachers will always encounter new challenges and new experiences. I once asked a former

Language Lens

Linguistic Diversity in Early Childhood Programs

The children in Natalia's kindergarten class, located in a suburb of Washington, D.C., speak 11 different languages. Natalia and two of the children are the only ones whose first language is English. Natalia works hard to create a caring community where all the children comfortably experiment with learning English. She also strives to communicate with the parents. Last year, Natalia's class included speakers of eight languages—some of which were different from those spoken this year.

The number of languages represented in Natalia's classroom may seem extreme, but cultural and linguistic diversity is now the norm in our nation's schools. Between 1996 and 2006, the overall population of children in pre-K through grade 12 only grew by 3.66%, but the number of children whose primary language is not English increased by 57%. In the next 20 years, the biggest single child-related demographic change is predicted to be an increase in English language learners.

The trends are especially apparent in the preschool population. For example, consider these statistics:

- Hispanics now constitute one-fifth of the nation's young children (infants through 8-year-olds) and are projected to be a quarter of all young children in the United States by 2030.
- Only 16% of Head Start programs serve exclusively English-speaking children.
- Almost 3 in10 Head Start children come from families who speak a primary language other than English. Of these families, most speak Spanish (about 85%).
- The remaining language groups are (in order of frequency): East Asian, Middle Eastern/South Asian, European/Slavic, African, Native Central/South American and Native Mexican, Caribbean, Pacific Island, and Native North American and Alaska Native languages—140 in all.
- Although Spanish is overwhelmingly the dominant "second" language in Head Start, it is important to note that Spanish-speaking families are not all alike—they come from a wide variety of countries and cultures.

Many of these children are from immigrant families, but quite a few were born in this country. In the last 35 years, the immigrant population in the United States has tripled to 35 million people in 2005. More than half the immigrants are Latino, and one-quarter are Asian. California, Florida, Illinois, New Jersey, New York, and Texas account for 70% of the immigrant population.

However, the geographic distribution of these families is ever changing. In recent years, states as diverse as Arizona, Arkansas, Colorado, Georgia, Kentucky, Nebraska, Nevada, North Carolina, Utah, and Tennessee have seen rapid immigration growth. According to the National Clearinghouse for English Language Acquisition, 13 states have seen the population of English language learners increase more than 200%, and many small communities have seen immigrant population grow by as much as 600% in the past decade.

In the past, most teachers could safely assume that they would never encounter a language other than English in their entire career. Today, Natalia's experience or something like it is not so very rare.

Sources: Dual Language Learners in the Early Years: Getting Ready to Succeed in School, by K. G. Ballantyne, A. R. Sanderman, and N. McLaughlin, November 2008; Washington, DC: National Clearinghouse for English Language Acquisition, retrieved from http://www.ncela.gwu.edu/resabout/ecell/earlyyears.pdf; *Dual Language Learning: What Does It Take?* (Head Start dual language report), by Head Start, February 2008, Washington, DC: U.S. Department of Health and Human Services; *Shifting Landscape: Immigration Transforms Communities*, by L. A. Maxwell, January 8, 2009, *Education Week, 28*(17), retrieved August 8, 2009, from http://www.cal.org/qualitycounts/

teacher after 40 years of teaching, "Didn't you ever get tired of teaching first grade?" She looked stunned and replied, "Never, because every group was different." Having been a child in her class at one time, I clearly understood what she meant—that every child is different and unique and that being a teacher never loses its fascination.

Working *for* Children

At some point in their careers, all early childhood professionals should work with children in order to understand, firsthand, how educators help shape our young children. However, there are many opportunities for early childhood educators to pursue positions working *for* children. With additional education, specialized training and experience, a background in early childhood can lead to positions such as these:

- *Director* of a child care center or preschool, or school principal (with additional course work in administration)
- *Curriculum developer* for an individual school, network of schools, or publisher
- *Parent educator, home visitor*, or *family services worker* in Head Start, Early Head Start, or another community agency
- *Policy staff* at local/state/federal agencies, associations, and organizations
- *College faculty* teaching teachers and/or conducting research
- *Writer/producer of resources for children* such as children's book author, technology developer, children's museum staff, or media performer

In previous sections, we discussed how the profession defines quality and what it means to be a professional, intentional early childhood teacher. These definitions reflect the profession's core values and beliefs, a topic to which we turn next.

The Culture of Early Childhood Education

A key theme of this book is the important role that culture plays in development and learning. Broadly defined, **culture** is the rules and expectations for behavior of members of a group that are passed on from one generation to the next. These rules determine to a large extent what group members regard as important, and what values shape their actions and judgments.

Like other professional groups, the early childhood profession has its own culture. This culture is transmitted both explicitly and implicitly from more experienced, competent members to new initiates in three ways: through formal education, through on-the-job experiences, and through mentoring in either setting. New teachers may become confused or flustered when the cultural rules transmitted in one setting, such as their college classroom, do not seem to match the expectations for behavior in another, such as their first teaching assignment.

Cultural groups define themselves in many ways, including the language they use, how they identify themselves, the values they share, and their fundamental beliefs. We discuss these topics in the following sections.

Shared Vocabulary

culture The explicit and implicit values, beliefs, rules, and expectations for behavior of members of a group that are passed on from one generation to the next. These rules determine to a large extent what group members regard as important, and what values shape their actions and judgments.

One aspect of early childhood culture is a common vocabulary. Shared language facilitates communication and minimizes misunderstandings within groups. The profession gives particular meaning to terms like *developmentally appropriate*, *play*, *relationships*, *comprehensive services*, *integrated*, or *inclusion* (all of which are defined in this book). Their definitions are tailored to our profession and may not mirror how these words are used in other professions or in everyday life.

An essential part of joining a profession is learning its language. For example, although the larger society uses the term *day care*, within the profession the accepted term is *child care*. We believe that saying *child care* is more respectful of children and a more accurate description of the setting and the job.

Shared Identity

Most professionals feel a sense of belonging to their group. They identify themselves as members of the profession, whether it is as a doctor, a lawyer, or an accountant. In early childhood education, it is often harder to "name" ourselves. The profession itself does not have an agreed-on name (Goffin & Washington, 2007). Among the names it is known by are *early care and education*, *child care*, *early education*, and *early development and learning*. In this book, we refer to the field as *early childhood education*. We prefer this term because it contains the word *child*, which is an ever-present reminder of the primary focus of our work. We also believe that the term encompasses the key elements of caring, development, and learning.

Early childhood educators are members of a profession that shares knowledge, values, and beliefs about children and their work. Meeting with more experienced teachers is one way of becoming a professional. Can you think of others?

Another challenge to establishing a clear identity is what to call the role itself. Infant/toddler teachers and teachers in center-based care are often called *caregivers*. In family child care, adults are called *providers*. But we embrace the term *teacher*, because it is the broadest term, captures most of the job responsibilities, commands society's respect, and is after all what children usually call the adults who care for and educate them no matter what the setting.

Shared Values

The early childhood profession is committed to a core set of values that is deeply rooted in the history of the field. NAEYC (2005b) articulates these core values in its code of ethical conduct:

> We have made a commitment to:
> - Appreciate childhood as a unique and valuable stage of the human life cycle
> - Base our work on knowledge of how children develop and learn
> - Appreciate and support the bond between the child and family
> - Recognize that children are best understood and supported in the context of family, culture (including ethnicity), community, and society
> - Respect the dignity, worth, and uniqueness of each individual (child, family member, and colleague)
> - Respect diversity in children, families, and colleagues
> - Recognize that children and adults achieve their full potential in the context of relationships that are based on trust and respect.

I often take informal polls of teachers during speeches at education conferences. A question I always ask is: "What are your values as an early childhood educator?" Most of the core values just listed are mentioned. Yet there is one that is always stated emphatically and is usually first—play! Early childhood professionals strongly value play as essential for children's development and learning. Because play is so important in early childhood, we will revisit the topic throughout this book. Political and economic forces threaten these values at times, but nevertheless, they endure.

Shared Beliefs

Although early childhood culture shares many beliefs, a few beliefs dominate:

- The strong belief in the potential of all children, regardless of their life circumstances and individual abilities or disabilities.
- The belief in the power of **developmentally appropriate practice** to produce positive results for children. Developmentally appropriate practice is teaching that engages children's interests and adapts for their age, experience, and ability to help them meet challenging and achievable goals.
- The belief that early childhood teachers are professionals who make informed decisions about what is developmentally appropriate for each child in each situation.
- The fundamental belief in the potential of our work to make a real and lasting difference in the world.

Effective Teaching
Effective early childhood educators are intentional in everything they do and know that their work makes a difference in the lives of children and families.

This is the final justification for joining the profession: the opportunity to make a contribution to children's lives. Many professions exist primarily to solve problems. Doctors and nurses treat illnesses. Firefighters put out fires and rescue people. Insurance agents help people recover from losses or catastrophes. The work of early childhood professionals, on the other hand, is to prevent problems from occurring. Our job is to set children on a positive course from the beginning. The proven effectiveness of early intervention when young children face difficulties creates room for optimism and hope.

The Positive Effects of Early Childhood Education

We began this chapter by citing ways that early childhood is a "field on the rise." The positive attention and support the field has garnered is to a large extent the result of an impressive body of research on the importance of the early years and the lasting benefits of early childhood programs.

Brain Research

Among the most exciting achievements in developmental psychology in the past century were new insights into how the brain grows and functions during the earliest years of life. Brain research, which had previously been confined to laboratories, began to be publicized regularly in popular newspapers and magazines beginning in the mid-1990s, and continues to make news regularly (The brain, 2007). Technologies such as positron emission tomography (PET) scans and functional magnetic resonance imagery (fMRI) reveal the inner workings of babies' brains to policy makers, educators, and the public.

Three major conclusions from brain research have significantly lifted the profile of early childhood education—and particularly the importance of experiences in the first 3 years of life (Center on the Developing Child, 2007; Nelson, de Haan, & Thomas, 2006; R. A. Thompson, 2008):

1. Positive experiences in the early years—especially warm, responsive, caring, conversational relationships—literally grow babies' brains.
2. Negative experiences such as prolonged stress, physical or sexual abuse, or exposure to violence can have dire consequences for brain development.
3. Early intervention including intensive early education and comprehensive support services for families—the earlier and more intensive the better—can ameliorate the negative effects.

developmentally appropriate practice
Ways of teaching that engage children's interests and adapt for their age, experience, and ability, to help them meet challenging and achievable learning goals.

Dramatic evidence along with powerful visual images of brain scans has raised awareness of the vital importance of early experiences. For example, a group of researchers in Pittsburgh examined brain scans of maltreated children. They found striking evidence of smaller brain volumes, with more negative effects the earlier the abuse began and the longer it lasted (De Bellis et al., 1999). Findings such as these demonstrate the critical importance of early intervention.

New technologies reveal dramatic differences in the brain development of children who have suffered abuse and neglect (left) compared with those who have had positive early experiences (right). Brain research demonstrates the importance of early childhood education, especially for infants and toddlers.

Research Supporting the Lasting Benefits of Early Childhood Education

A large body of research demonstrates that high-quality early childhood programs can have long-lasting positive consequences for children, especially children from economically disadvantaged backgrounds, and can be cost effective (Barnett, 2008; Galinsky, 2006). Three well-designed longitudinal studies—the Perry Preschool Project, the Abecedarian Early Childhood Intervention Project, and the Chicago Child-Parent Centers—followed children from early childhood into adulthood. The findings of these studies have been singularly influential with policy makers.

The Perry Preschool Project

The Perry Preschool Project, which began in the early1960s in Ypsilanti, Michigan, was one of the first studies to demonstrate the lasting effects of a high-quality preschool education on educational and economic outcomes. (Perry Preschool later became the HighScope Educational Research Foundation.) Researchers found that Perry Preschool graduates were less likely to be assigned to special education or be retained in grade, and had better achievement test scores than children who did not attend preschool (Berrueta-Clement, Schweinhart, Barnett, Epstein, & Weikart, 1984). Preschool participation was also related to less involvement in delinquency and crime, and a higher rate of high school graduation (Schweinhart, Barnes, & Weikart, 1993). At age 40, program participants were significantly more likely to have higher levels of education, be employed, earn higher wages, and own their own homes; they were less likely to be welfare dependent, and had fewer arrests (Schweinhart et al., 2005).

These outcomes benefited not only the participants, but the larger society as well. Economists estimated that for every dollar spent on the program, $17 was returned on the original investment (Schweinhart et al., 2005). This means that Americans saved money in terms of the decreased costs of crime, special education, children repeating a grade in school, and welfare payments, as well as increases in taxes paid by those children who achieve in school and later earn higher incomes.

The Abecedarian Project

The University of North Carolina's Abecedarian Early Childhood Intervention Project demonstrated that intensive early intervention (5 years of full-day, high-quality child care with parent involvement) can greatly enhance the development of children whose mothers have low income and education levels (F. A. Campbell, Ramey, Pungello, Sparling, & Miller-Johnson, 2002; F. A. Campbell et al., 2008). The Abecedarian program produced positive effects on achievement in reading and mathematics throughout elementary and high school. Children who participated were significantly less likely to be retained in grade or placed in special education, and they were more likely to attend a 4-year college and to have a skilled job. Access to free child care improved the mothers' long-term employment opportunities and earnings.

Chicago Child-Parent Centers

Perry Preschool and Abecedarian were relatively small-scale demonstration programs. A third longitudinal study of the Title I federally funded Chicago Child-Parent Centers reached similar positive conclusions with a large-scale, public school program involving more than 1,500 children (Temple & Reynolds, 2007). Since 1985, the Chicago Child-Parent Centers (CPC) have provided preschool and kindergarten for children from low-income families, and family support services with continued intervention in early elementary school.

Children who participated in CPC demonstrated higher school achievement, better social adjustment, less frequent grade retention, lower dropout rates, and lower rates of juvenile arrest (Temple & Reynolds, 2007). The most positive results were for those children who attended preschool and also participated in a follow-up program during elementary school—a finding that supports the movement toward alignment of quality education from preschool through grade 3 (Galinsky, 2006; Reynolds, Magnuson, & Ou, 2006). In addition, a cost–benefit analysis revealed a substantial return on the original investment in the form of reduced crime rates, costs to crime victims, and school remedial services, as well as participants' increased earning capacity (Galinsky, 2006).

The Positive Effects of Head Start, Child Care, and Prekindergarten

Perhaps no other federally funded project has been as thoroughly studied as Head Start over the more than 40 years of its existence. An overall conclusion that can be drawn is that Head Start has positive effects on children's overall development, health and dental care, and preparation for school, including improved literacy skills and social–emotional development (Barnett, 2008; Puma et al., 2005). Although Head Start participation does not close the achievement gap between poor and middle-class children, it does narrow the gap (Zill, Sorongon, Kim, Clark, & Woolverton, 2006).

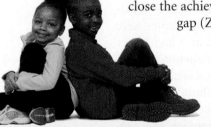

What Works

High-Quality Preschool and School Readiness

As policy makers consider whether to increase funding for Head Start, public prekindergarten, or child care for needy families, they want to know whether these programs are effective. Their first question is usually, "How well do early childhood programs prepare children for school?" In response, a growing body of research provides evidence of the positive effects of early education. Here is one example.

Oklahoma's state-funded prekindergarten program has generated considerable attention. It is universal—that is, available to families of all income levels who choose to enroll their children. It is based in the school system and reaches a higher percentage of 4-year-olds than any other state pre-K program. Although most classes are located in public schools, some classes are located in Head Start and child care programs that meet the same standards for quality.

The Oklahoma program has high standards compared to other states, with lead teachers required to have a B.A. degree and be certified in early childhood education. Notably, prekindergarten teachers earn the same wages and benefits as other public school teachers. Student–teacher ratios are 10 to 1 and class sizes are limited to 20.

An evaluation of the program involving more than 3,000 children found strong positive effects on children's language and cognitive test scores for all of the children regardless of economic status or ethnicity. But the largest gains were for poor children of color, with Hispanic children making the most learning progress followed by African Americans. A similar study comparing Tulsa's (Oklahoma) pre-K program and the Tulsa County Head Start program (which also receives state funds) found that both programs produce substantial improvements in early literacy and math skills.

Sources: The Effects of Oklahoma's Universal Pre-Kindergarten Program on Hispanic Children, by W. T. Gormley, 2008, Washington, DC: Center for Research on Children in the U.S. (CROCUS), Georgetown University, retrieved July 28, 2009, from http://www.crocus.georgetown.edu; "The Effects of Universal Pre-K on Cognitive Development," by W. T. Gormley, T. T. Gayer, D. Phillips, and B. Dawson, 2005, *Developmental Psychology, 41*(6), pp. 872–884.

Child care research consistently finds that children who participate in high-quality programs demonstrate better language and mathematics ability and fewer behavior problems than children in poor quality care (Cost, Quality, and Child Care Outcomes Study Team, 1995; NICHD Early Child Care Research Network, 2002; Peisner-Feinberg et al., 1999). Positive effects are evident for all groups of children, but are greater for children from lower-income families.

Studies such as those described here, and many others like them, prove that high-quality early childhood programs can have positive short- and long-term consequences for young children. Such evidence sways policy makers as they decide how to allocate taxpayer dollars, as we see in the *What Works: High-Quality Preschool and School Readiness* feature. Research is also powerfully connected to another reason early childhood education is a field on the rise—the country's need to close the achievement gap, as addressed in the next section.

Social Justice and Closing the Achievement Gap

One of our nation's greatest challenges is addressing the persistent gap that exists between the school achievement of African American and Latino children and their white peers. The causes for these differences are widely debated, but scholars tend to agree that they result primarily from the fact that race and ethnicity are strongly associated with **socioeconomic status (SES)** in the United States (Neuman, 2008). For example, 34% of African American children and 29% of Latino children are in the lowest socioeconomic level of U.S. citizens compared with less than 10% of white children (Fass & Cauthen, 2008). The fact is that family income is much more closely related to cognitive skills than race or ethnicity (Lee & Burkam, 2002).

In addition, the number of young children growing up poor in our country is increasing, with the largest growth in poverty among children under age 5 and children of color, which could further widen the achievement gap in the future (Fass & Cauthen, 2008; Neuman, 2008). The achievement gap has profound consequences for our nation's future and its ability to compete in a global, highly technological society (Mullis, Martin, & Foy, 2008). Moreover, the potentially devastating effects on the life trajectories of individuals cannot be ignored.

Where the Gap Begins

Differences in children's cognitive ability are substantial right from "the starting gate" (Lee & Burkam, 2002; Magnuson & Waldfogel, 2005). At age 4, children who live below the poverty line are 18 months below what is considered normal for their age group (Klein & Knitzer, 2007). Before kindergarten, children in the lowest socioeconomic group have average cognitive scores that are 60% below those of the most affluent group (Lee & Burkam, 2002; West, Denton, & Germino-Hausken, 2000). Average math achievement is 21% lower for African American children than for white children and 19% lower for Hispanic children.

Inequity in socioeconomic status is the most important predictor of children's cognitive skills. Compared to other factors such as race/ethnicity, family educational expectations, access to quality child care, home reading, computer use, and television viewing habits, poverty accounts for a larger difference in cognitive scores than any other factor by far (Lee & Burkam, 2002).

Schools' Contributions to the Gap

Children from low-income families not only enter kindergarten with fewer cognitive skills than their more affluent peers, but also are more likely to encounter poorer quality elementary schools (Neuman, 2008). School quality is usually measured in terms of higher student achievement, more resources, more qualified teachers, more positive teacher attitudes, and better neighborhood or school conditions (Lee & Burkam, 2002). As a result,

socioeconomic status (SES) Family income level.

the inequalities in cognitive abilities that are present even before kindergarten entry are not eliminated, but rather are magnified by their elementary school experience (Lee & Burkam, 2002).

Children who begin school behind tend to stay behind. By fourth grade, less than one-third of American children read at or above grade level (National Assessment of Education Progress, 2005). Reading achievement at the end of first grade has been found to predict reading skill at the end of fourth grade (Juel, 1988; Juel, Griffith, & Gough, 1986), which subsequently predicts high school graduation. Moreover, deep-seated inequities in communities and schools tend to increase rather than diminish these early achievement gaps over time. As one child advocacy group states, "Our children are not failing to learn. Our schools are failing to teach them effectively" (Foundation for Child Development, 2008, p. 4).

Early Education and Social Justice

As we saw from research cited previously, these initial inequalities can be reduced. Children from low-income families who attend high-quality early childhood programs begin kindergarten with higher achievement, thus providing the potential to narrow the gap at the outset. This research, as well as studies on the effectiveness of services for children with disabilities and special needs, proves that early intervention is less costly, more effective, and more humane than later remediation (Galinsky, 2006; Sandall et al., 2005; Temple & Reynolds, 2007). Children living in poverty, however, are less likely to have access to high-quality programs. Read the *How Would You Respond? Public Support for Early Childhood Education* feature and consider possible strategies to address this problem.

How Would You Respond?

Public Support for Early Childhood Education

The Situation Early childhood education has become a political priority in the United States and increased public funding is becoming more available. However, the amount of money is limited and the ways to use it to improve early childhood programs and to benefit children and families varied.

What to Do? Of the following potential uses of funds for early childhood education, which ones do you think have the best chance of producing positive, lasting results for children? Why do you think they are productive ways to use public dollars?

- Make Early Head Start programs available in more communities.
- Expand the number of children served by Head Start.
- Provide professional development for teachers in child care centers, Head Start, and primary schools who do not have early childhood specialized degrees.
- Provide funds to expand public prekindergarten to serve children of all income levels whose families choose to enroll their children.
- Help states and school districts increase early childhood teacher compensation.
- Provide grants for increased early childhood special education services.
- Forgive college loans for early childhood education majors who agree to teach in low-income communities.

Are there other funding options that you think would be more productive than these?

Improving quality and increasing access to early childhood programs is an important strategy for enhancing social justice in America and improving learning outcomes for all children. These goals can only be addressed, however, in the context of current trends in the field and the nation, which we discuss next.

Current Trends in Early Childhood Education

Early childhood education is literally a field in transition. Major trends affecting the field include the universal prekindergarten movement, more focus on standards and accountability of programs and schools, calls for greater alignment among settings across the full early childhood age span, and increased teacher qualifications. These changes present new challenges, but also opportunities. In the sections that follow, we describe the potential benefits as well as the controversies of each trend. Even a cursory look at these trends reveals that they are interconnected.

Universal Prekindergarten Movement

The early years of the 21st century have seen enormous growth in funding and public support for universal, voluntary prekindergarten for 4-year-olds and even 3-year-olds in some places (Barnett, Epstein, Friedman, Boyd, & Hustadt, 2008b). Head Start and most state prekindergarten programs are targeted to children from low-income families or those considered at risk of school failure. However, a growing number of states, including Georgia, Oklahoma, and Florida, now make preschool education universally available to all 4-year-olds, regardless of family income. Participation in these programs is voluntary, depending on whether families choose to send their children. Other states are moving toward universal services. This trend has contributed to the field's growth; today the number of 4-year-olds in state pre-K programs actually exceeds the number enrolled in Head Start (Barnett, 2008).

Universal prekindergarten is not without controversy, however. Proponents cite research showing that middle-class children benefit from prekindergarten (although the cost of high-quality programs is out of reach for most of these families) (Wat, 2008). There is also some evidence that the language skills of children from low-income families improve when they participate in mixed-income programs (Schechter & Bye, 2007). In contrast, critics believe that limited funds should go to the neediest families (Fuller, 2007). Another concern is the competing need to fund services for infants and toddlers.

The prekindergarten movement has contributed to another trend: greater involvement of public schools in preschool education. In the past, young children rarely encountered a public school before kindergarten, but now the public education system is a major player in the early childhood landscape. As a result, issues that have dominated K–12 education for some time now affect programs for younger children, such as more focus on standards and accountability.

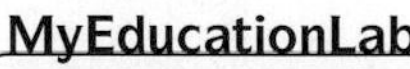

Go to the Professional Perspectives section in Topic 4: Observation/ Assessment in the MyEducationLab for your course and select the video entitled *Setting Standards for Teachers* and watch and listen to Sue Bredekamp discuss this topic.

Standards and Accountability

Since the 1990s, educational systems in the United States have emphasized learning standards—what children should know and be able to do at various ages. As of 2007, for example, 49 states had published early learning standards for preschool children in areas such as language, literacy, and mathematics (Scott-Little, Lesko, Martella, & Milburn, 2007).

At the same time, a strong emphasis on **accountability** has emerged. The concept is that schools and teachers, which are recipients of public dollars, need to be held accountable for children's achieving learning standards. This leads to two related issues: (1) What are teachers to be held accountable for? and (2) How will it be measured?

accountability The process of holding teachers, schools, or programs responsible for meeting a required level of performance.

Current trends in early childhood education include more focus on standards and accountability from prekindergarten through third grade. The overarching goal is to help children become more successful readers and writers.

To hold public schools accountable for eliminating the persistent gaps in achievement between different groups of children, Congress passed the **No Child Left Behind Act (NCLB)** in 2001 (U.S. Department of Education, 2002). The goals of NCLB included strengthening core academic programs (reading and mathematics) so that by 2013–2014, all students would be experiencing high-quality teaching and learning and be at the "proficient" level or above on state tests beginning at third grade. For the first time in history, states were required to report student progress separately by subgroups: the economically disadvantaged, major racial and ethnic groups, special education students, and English language learners.

In addition, NCLB called for highly qualified teachers to implement effective, **scientifically based instructional practices**, ways of teaching that research has demonstrated to improve learning outcomes. NCLB funds were used for large-scale initiatives to improve reading. These efforts led to increased emphasis on particular methods of teaching reading and a stronger focus on early literacy in preschool.

In 2002, a related effort—Good Start, Grow Smart—the government called for early learning standards in literacy, language, and mathematics in Head Start and federally funded programs. The Head Start Child Outcomes Framework (Head Start Bureau, 2003), a comprehensive set of goals for children's learning and development, now guides curriculum in these programs.

No Child Left Behind Act (NCLB) Federal law passed in 2001 to increase school accountability, improve reading and mathematics achievement, and narrow the achievement gap. It emphasizes improved scores on standardized tests beginning in the third grade.

Although the goals of No Child Left Behind—increasing accountability and equity—were worthy, the methods were highly controversial (NAEYC, 2009b). Critics believe that overemphasis on standardized test scores narrows the curriculum to what is tested, does not truly measure all of children's important capabilities, and punishes schools that need the most help (NAEYC, 2009a; Pedulla, 2003). Regardless of the failings of and expected modifications to this specific piece of legislation, accountability is unlikely to go away in the future.

scientifically based instructional practices Curriculum and instructional practices that research has demonstrated improve learning outcomes.

Alignment of Preschool and K–3

A trend that is related to accountability and increased involvement of public schools in early education is the call for better alignment of preschool with K–3 (Reynolds et al., 2006). Traditionally, preschool and K–3 have been two separate worlds with very little communication between them. **Alignment** means that curriculum at the preschool level would lay a foundation for the kindergarten curriculum, which could then build on what children have learned more easily. The idea is to ease transitions for students between schools and school levels and enhance continuity of learning, while also respecting the needs of young children (Bogard & Takanishi, 2005; Foundation for Child Development, 2008; Takanishi & Kauerz, 2008).

Many early childhood educators are concerned that the push for alignment will narrow the curriculum to literacy and mathematics, apply learning standards intended for older children, and lead to inappropriate testing of young children (NAEYC, 2009a). They are especially concerned that schools will eliminate valuable experiences such as play, the arts, and support for social–emotional development. NAEYC (2009a) supports better connected education for preschool and elementary children. At the same time, however, NAEYC stresses that alignment does not mean that preschool children should learn primary grade skills at an earlier age. Rather, curriculum should reflect what children can and should learn at each age, and teachers should know how to help children make progress.

MyEducationLab

Go to the Assignments and Activities section of Topic 5, Program Models in the MyEducationLab for your course and complete the activity entitled *Teaching in the Primary Grades*. How has the current focus on standards and accountability affected both teachers and students? What strategies do effective teachers use to ensure positive school experiences for all children?

Higher Teacher Qualifications

Another related trend is to raise preschool teacher qualifications, with an emphasis on college degrees in early childhood education or child development (NAEYC, 2005e; Whitebook, 2003). Several research reviews have concluded that having bachelor's degree–level teachers with specialized training in early childhood education leads to better outcomes for young children (Barnett, 2003; Bowman, Donovan, & Burns, 2001; Whitebook, 2003). Although some research has not found clear benefits of degrees (Early et al., 2006; LoCasale-Crouch et al., 2007), overall, studies tend to support the fact that the more specialized education teachers have, the better it is for the children they teach.

Head Start's teacher qualifications have incrementally been raised over the years. For many years, teachers were required to have only a **Child Development Associate (CDA) credential.** This competency-based credential requires 120 clock hours of training (which may or may not be credit bearing) and 480 hours of experience with children, plus passing a written test. The Head Start Act of 2009 requires that by 2013, 50% of teachers hold a bachelor's degree, a significant increase in qualifications.

Raising teacher qualifications has the potential to improve quality for children and also compensation and status for teachers. The biggest challenge will be providing adequate funding to increase compensation commensurate with teacher qualifications (Kagan et al., 2008).

An additional concern is the need to maintain a diverse workforce that reflects the population of children served. State prekindergarten programs have a much larger percentage of teachers with bachelor's degrees (73%) than Head Start (36%) or center-based programs (30%) (Kagan et al., 2008). However, Head Start teachers are much more likely to reflect the cultural and linguistic diversity of the community (Head Start, 2008b).

alignment Coordination of the curriculum from one level of education to the next in order to build on what children have already learned and to ease transitions for students between schools and school levels.

Child Development Associate (CDA) credential National competency-based credential for entry-level early childhood educators.

Continuity and Change in Early Childhood Education

As the field expands and changes occur in response to new political and economic realities, many long-time early childhood professionals are concerned that the fundamental values of the field will be lost (Bredekamp, 2008b; NAEYC, 2009a). Development, including development of professions, is characterized by both continuity and change. In this book we describe how the fundamental values of early childhood education can be retained and enhanced (thus, maintaining continuity with the important tenets of the past), while also presenting what is known from new research about effective teaching practices for *all* children. Some ways of thinking and practicing should be cherished and held onto, whereas others may need to be updated or abandoned.

Resolving Contradictions between Enduring Values and Current Trends

We propose that the way to resolve potential contradictions that arise over difficult or controversial issues is to "widen the lens." Widening the lens is a metaphor for expanding the sources of information professionals use to make decisions; gaining insights from diverse perspectives including through the lenses of culture, language, and ability/disability; and looking at questions or problems from broader perspectives. Widening the lens is a strategy to move beyond the tendency to oversimplify complex educational issues into "either/or" choices and to move toward "both/and" thinking.

Embracing *Both/And* Thinking

Widening the lens to consider diverse points of view—*both/and* thinking—is a constructive response to addressing both continuity and change in the field. Table 1.3 offers examples of how this process applies to the field today.

Table 1.3 Continuity and Change in Early Childhood Education

In the Past, Early Childhood Education Tended to Emphasize	Today Early Childhood Education Emphasizes
Processes of how children develop and learn	*Both* the processes of how children develop and learn *and* the content—what they are learning
Inputs—standards (such as licensing or accreditation) that mandate what programs should do	*Both* program standards (inputs) *and* outcomes (early learning standards for what children should know and be able to do)
Quality	*Both* quality *and* accountability
Activities	*Both* coherent curriculum plans *and* links to learning goals
Free play	*Both* child-initiated, developmentally valuable play *and* playful learning
Developmental appropriateness	*Both* effectiveness *and* developmental appropriateness (Are children making learning and developmental progress from the experiences we deem appropriate?)
Observation of children	*Both* observation for many purposes *and* assessment of children's outcomes
Facilitating learning	*Both* intentional teaching *and* positive, supportive relationships
Development, not academics (viewing early childhood education as separate and distinct from what follows in the primary grades)	*Both* viewing learning and development as a continuum from birth to age 8, *and* working toward alignment from pre-K to grade 3
Typical, normative development	*Both* adapting for the individual variation of every child *and* intervention and adaptation for children with disabilities and special needs, as well as children who are advanced

Throughout this text, we will revisit these issues as well as the profession's core values and demonstrate how new research can help teachers effectively put these values into practice. Chapters are devoted to each of the core values: child development and learning, relationships, families, communities, individuality, and cultural diversity. We discuss the overarching value of play in the context of all the key topics in this book.

We began by pointing out that early childhood education is a field on the rise. The profession is expanding, growing in status, and gaining support from policy makers and the general public. A huge body of research supports the importance of the work. It is indeed an exciting time to be an early childhood educator.

Revisiting Cresthaven Child Development Center

We began this chapter by peeking in and eavesdropping on the end-of-the-year event for Cresthaven Primary School and Reed Child Development Center. Now that we have seen the broader picture of the early childhood landscape, the teachers' thoughts and emotions become more meaningful. At this event, we saw the wide range of age groups that early childhood encompasses, as well as some of the diverse settings. In addition, these teachers exemplify fundamentals of intentional teaching.

The collaborative partnership between the school and child care program supports alignment of curriculum from preschool through third grade, and eases transitions for children and families. The garden project is one example of how these teachers connect the curriculum to the larger community, and provide children with meaningful, hands-on learning opportunities. Children, families, and teachers not only celebrated the good times they'd had, but children also demonstrated how much they'd learned through the displays of their work and through technology.

Across the classrooms, we saw the value of communication and responsive relationships among teachers and families. New teachers Isela and Evan have learned that early childhood education is hard work, but have also begun to experience the rewards. Their patience and focus on intentional teaching is paying off for Nicky. Cooper's experience demonstrates the power of inclusion and how it benefits both children with disabilities and their peers. At the end of the day, these teachers go home feeling good about what they've accomplished, but knowing that there is more to learn and new adventures awaiting them tomorrow.

MyEducationLab

To assess your understanding of the different types of early childhood settings and what effective teachers do, go to the Book Specific Resources section in the MyEducationLab for your course, select *Effective Practices in Early Childhood Education*, Chapter 1 of the Study Plan, and then complete the multiple choice questions and activities.

Chapter Summary

- Early childhood education is a diverse field that covers the broad age range of birth through age 8. Teachers work in child care centers and homes, preschools, kindergartens, and primary grade schools.
- The early childhood profession sets standards for high-quality programs for children. The most important determinants of the quality of children's experiences and strongest predictors of positive outcomes are the social and instructional interactions that occur between teachers and children.
- Becoming a professional, intentional early childhood teacher is a challenging and rewarding opportunity. Early childhood education is expanding and is a "field on the rise," benefiting from growing public recognition and support. Many career options are available to work with children or work for children.
- Early childhood professionals are part of a cultural group that shares a vocabulary, an identity, values, and beliefs. These include emphasis on the uniqueness of early childhood, the value of play, the importance of relationships and a sense of community, valuing and teaching each child as an individual, respecting linguistic and cultural diversity, and promoting relationships with families.
- Brain research demonstrates the importance of early experience to later development. A large body of evidence

exists supporting the positive long-term and short-term consequences of high-quality early childhood programs.

- High-quality early childhood education has an important role to play in improving children's school readiness and addressing social justice concerns about closing the achievement gap in our schools.
- New political and economic realities present challenges and opportunities for the field including the universal prekindergarten movement; more focus on standards, accountability, and scientifically based practices; increased teacher qualifications; and calls for greater alignment across the full early childhood age span.
- Early childhood education is a rewarding profession for many reasons, but above all, early childhood educators enter and stay in the field because they know that their work makes a difference in the lives of children and families.

key terms

accountability
accreditation system
alignment
charter schools
Child Care and Development Block Grants (CCDBG)
child care centers
child care licensing standards
Child Development Associate (CDA) credential
Classroom Assessment Scoring System (CLASS)
culture
developmentally appropriate practice
early childhood education
Early Childhood Environment Rating Scale (ECERS-R)
early childhood special education
Early Head Start
early intervention
family child care homes
Head Start
Head Start Program Performance Standards
inclusion
Individuals with Disabilities Education Act (IDEA)
intentional teachers
kindergarten
laboratory school
National Association for the Education of Young Children (NAEYC)
No Child Left Behind Act (NCLB)
parent cooperative
prekindergarten (pre-K)
preschool
primary grade
process quality
professionals
quality rating systems (QRS)
school readiness
scientifically based instructional practices
socioeconomic status (SES)
structural quality
Temporary Assistance for Needy Families (TANF)
universal voluntary prekindergarten

reading & websites

Chenfield, M. B. (2007). *Celebrating young children and their teachers: The Mimi Brodsky Chenfeld Reader.* St. Paul, MN: Redleaf Press.

Feeney, S., Galper, A., & Seefeldt, C. (2009). *Continuing issues in early childhood education* (3rd ed.). Upper Saddle River, NJ: Pearson Merrill.

Harms, T., Clifford, R. M., & Cryer, D. (2005). *Early childhood environment rating scale (ECERS-R),* Rev. ed. New York: Teachers College Press.

Hyson, M. (Ed.). (2003). *Preparing early childhood professionals: NAEYC's standards for programs.* Washington, DC: NAEYC.

National Association for the Education of Young Children (NAEYC)
www.naeyc.org

National Institute for Early Education Research (NIEER)
www.nieer.org

National Resource Center for Health and Safety in Child Care
This site provides access to licensing information for every state.
http://nrc.uchsc.edu/STATES/states.htm

1. Visit several different types of early childhood programs, such as a faith-based preschool, publicly funded or employer-sponsored child care center, a Head Start center, public prekindergarten, or family child care home. Observe the physical environments, activities of the children, and the teacher's behaviors. Reflect on the similarities and differences among the settings. Decide why you think the programs are alike or different.
2. Go to the Pre-K Now website (www.preknow.org) and read current press clippings related to the prekindergarten movement. Reflect on how these trends may be affecting the field, both positively and negatively.
3. Interview several experienced teachers who work in different settings with various age groups. Ask them about their values as early childhood educators. Reflect on how the values of professionals relate to the age group they teach and where they work. Decide if what you learn from practicing professionals is consistent with the discussion of the values of early childhood in this chapter.
4. Review the NAEYC accreditation standards and your own state child care licensing standards. Reflect on the degree to which each set of standards appears to be influenced by the shared values of the profession. Decide if the standards should be revised to better align with those values.
5. Interview several early childhood professionals who have had at least 20 years of experience in the field. Ask them about the various jobs they have had. Reflect on whether they have worked with children and/or for children. Decide what type of a career path would be most appealing to you.

observe, reflect, decide

2 Building on a Tradition of Excellence

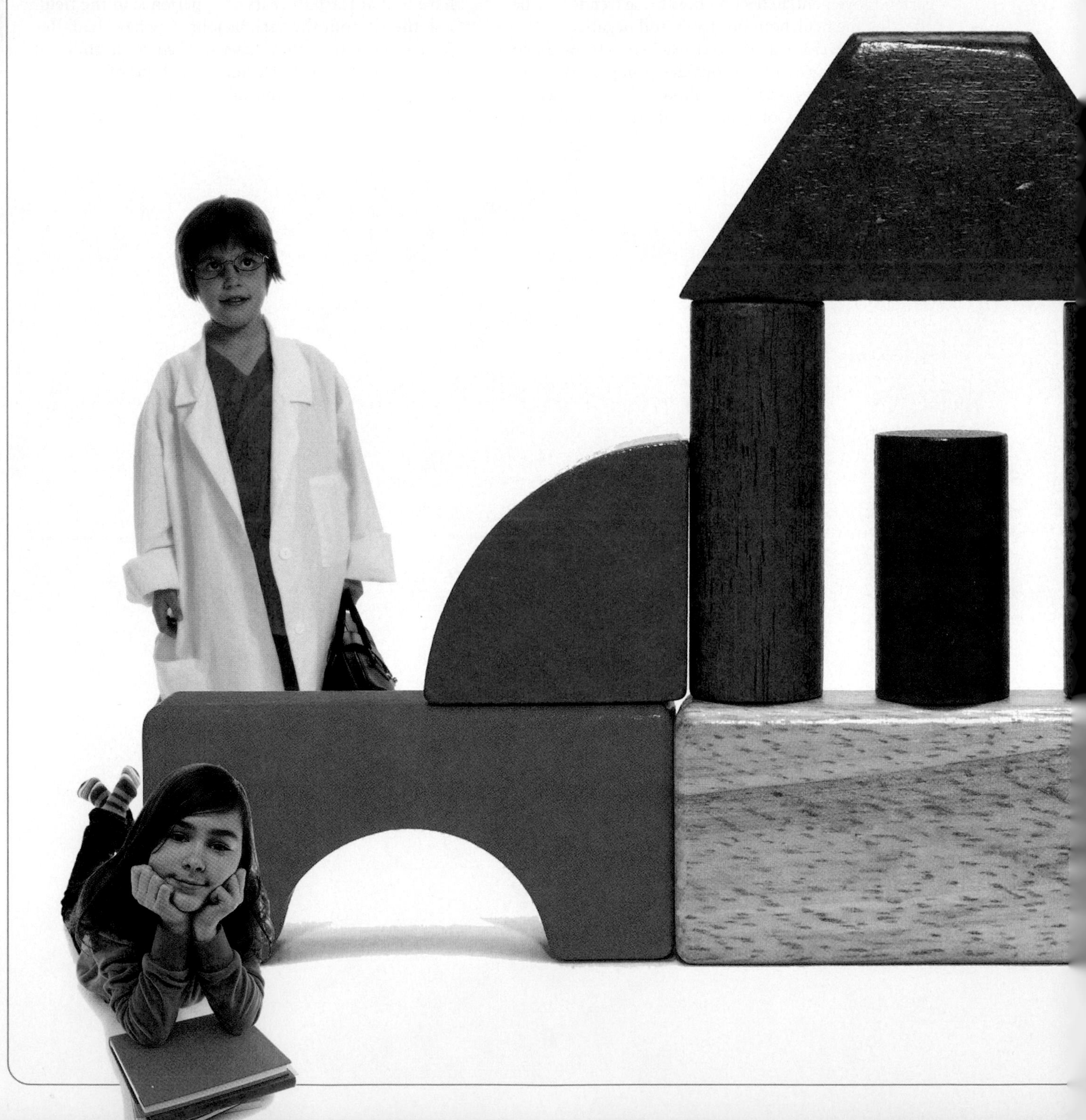

Thinking Ahead

1. Why is it important to learn from the past?
2. How has the view of children changed through history? What effect has the changing view of childhood had on programs and services for children?
3. What were the beliefs of Comenius, Pestalozzi, Froebel, and Montessori and how did they influence early childhood education in the United States?
4. How did the progressive education movement and the work of John Dewey influence early childhood education today?
5. What events and people propelled the kindergarten, nursery school, and child care movements? What roles did Patty Smith Hill and Lucy Sprague Mitchell play in the history of early childhood education?
6. How did trends in early childhood history come together and influence the launch of the national Head Start program?

Grant, Melinda, and Reece are enrolled in an introductory course in early childhood education. Their first assignment is to observe a preschool classroom. The professor says, "I want you to pretend that you are from another planet, or from such a remote part of the earth that you have never seen a preschool classroom before. Observe for one hour and write down exactly what you see there. Don't try to guess what I want you to observe or second-guess yourself, just write what you see."

After completing their observations, Grant, Melinda, and Reece compare notes. Their lists are different in some respects but the following items appear on all three lists: child-sized furniture; one-inch cube blocks; and wooden parquetry blocks in various colors and shapes. They see groups of children building roads and towers with wooden blocks. The classrooms each have a library area with picture books, alphabet books, and stories (each room even has a copy of *Goodnight, Moon* on the bookrack). One class has sandpaper letters. There are also woodworking benches, sand tables, a posted recipe for cooking a snack, and dress-up clothes and props. In all three classes children are actively playing or working with

teachers in small groups. One group had been to visit the firehouse (as evidenced by a chart on the wall recording children's remembrances) and there are firehats and hoses to play with. At snack time in one room, the children sing "Happy Birthday" to their friend.

During class, the professor asks each student to share one thing on his or her list and then for a show of hands to see who else had seen the same thing. There is remarkable uniformity among the observations. The professor explains, "What you observed are traces of the history of early childhood education. Your unfiltered observations are like the first steps archaeologists take in uncovering what has gone before. You may be surprised to find that all these things you observed can be traced back to specific people or events in the history of the field. They were put there and they remain there for a reason. First, we'll find out how they got there in the first place, and the rest of this course will help you understand why they are still there or how practices have changed in the intervening years." ▲

Early childhood educators tend to like stories. We love sharing stories about the enchanting things that young children say and do. We listen to parents' stories about their children. We tell stories about our own childhoods. And, we exchange stories about our teaching—sometimes when we have a bad day, and almost always when we have a very good day. Those good days usually involve seeing an exciting example of a child's developmental progress.

Stories—that is what *history* is—in fact, the two words have the same Latin origin. The goal of this chapter, then, is to tell the story of early childhood education. We begin by describing how studying history is relevant. Next, we describe how the concept of childhood has changed over the course of history. Finally, we tell several stories about major historical movements and how they influence early childhood education practice today. Because parts of these stories occurred simultaneously and overlap, a timeline of major events appears in Table 2.1 on pages 42–45.

Traces of the history of the field of early childhood education can be seen in any preschool classroom today. What in these classroom environments might have been present in a preschool 80 years ago? Why do you think it is still being used?

Learning from the Past

Early childhood education is a field with a long and rich history going back to ancient times. Its history differs from that of education for older children, which has been considered a public responsibility for more than a century, essential to sustaining a democratic society. By contrast, young children's care and education is so closely tied to families that private and public support for early childhood care and education is a very recent phenomenon. In addition, early childhood education is a more interdisciplinary field than elementary education, with historical influences coming from not only child development and education, but also from medicine, psychology, sociology, and other areas. As a result, many historical paths have converged to lead the field to where it is today.

Understanding Current Issues

The history of early childhood education, especially during the past 150 years, reveals that the past and the present are inexorably linked. Most of the issues and controversies we encounter today have been visited in some form in the past. For example, even all those years ago, teachers grappled with questions such as these: What environments and materials should be provided? What are the goals for children's learning and development? How should children be taught? What is the role of the teacher? How should parents be involved? Who is qualified to be a teacher, and how should services be funded? All of these issues have dominated debates about early childhood since its inception and continue to do so.

Rather than assuming that these issues are being encountered for the first time, understanding how they have been resolved in the past can inform current discussions. One reason this is so important is that "the solution to every problem contains the seeds of a new problem" (Bredekamp & Glowacki, 1996). For example, early in the 20th century advocates fought for kindergarten to be part of public schools. Succeeding in doing so eventually meant that kindergarten teachers were able to earn public school salaries and services became available for all children. But this solution also created a new problem—kindergartens became, and still are, more like first grades than like preschools in curriculum expectations and teaching methods. Today's advocates for public prekindergarten need to be aware of this history as they pursue their goals.

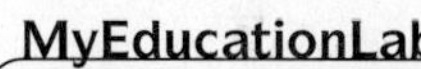

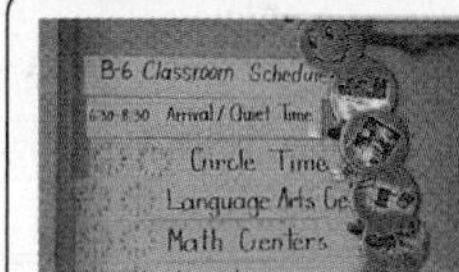

Go to the Assignments and Activities section of Topic 1: History in the MyEducationaLab for your course and complete the activity entitled *Today's Kindergarten Classroom*. As you watch the video and answer the accompanying questions, note how kindergarten has changed over time and what lessons might be learned from this history.

Consider how this phenomenon may be evident in your own life. A problem that many college students face is the high cost of tuition. Students solve this problem in different ways—taking out a loan, working full time or part time while going to school, or choosing a less expensive school. But each of these solutions can lead to a new challenge. The loan needs to be repaid; a full-time job delays graduation; the accessible school may not meet the students' needs. In turn, each of these "problems" leads to a subsequent solution and the process begins anew.

The idea that solving problems creates new challenges can be discouraging; however, it need not be. As long as we are working on solving new problems or challenges, we are making progress. History is composed of such progress in spurts as well as in setbacks. Explore this idea of a cycle of solutions and challenges by reading and discussing the *How Would You Respond? Solutions Create New Problems* feature.

Avoiding Getting Stuck in the Past

Just as it is true that we continue to confront similar questions and challenges as our forebears, it is equally true that responses to these issues need to reflect current knowledge. As we will see, many of the principles and values that guide the field today are remarkably consistent with earlier views (Copple & Bredekamp, 2009). There are also essential differences based on newer research, theories, and realities. Getting stuck in the past can lead to defending past practices simply because we have always done it that way. Knowing why it was "done that way," however, can lead to changing it for the better.

How Would You Respond?

Solutions Create New Problems

The Situation The federal government passes legislation to provide funding to states to make public prekindergarten universally available to all children whose families choose to use it. Many advocates for children are delighted by this unprecedented support for early childhood education. They are especially pleased because it solves the problem of unequal access to preschool education. Previously, the poorest children were eligible for Head Start, but space was not available for all income-eligible children. More affluent families could afford to pay for preschool, but many middle-class and working poor families could not afford to send their children to preschool. Federal funding appears to solve these problems.

What Might Happen? Based on lessons from the past, what new problems might be generated by this solution in relation to each of the following issues?

- Qualifications of teachers
- Enrollments of large numbers of 4-year-olds in public schools
- Funding for every child
- Establishment of learning goals and selection of curriculum models
- The role of parents
- The need for child care among working families
- Impact on other early childhood programs and child care services

What other issues might be raised by the solution of funding universal preschool?

Aspiring to Make a Difference for Children

History is not just the story of events, but the stories of people. The history of early childhood education is replete with inspiring stories of women and men who devoted their lives to improving those of children and families. Many "dauntless women" (Snyder, 1972) contributed in countless ways to early childhood education at a time when women's opportunities for higher education and careers were severely restricted. Similarly, men have been at the forefront of building the profession although children were considered the purview of women.

The stories of these pioneers of early childhood education, who were forward looking in both their thinking and their deeds, serve as inspiration and motivation for current and future professionals. Learning about their lives, the obstacles they faced in their work, and the brilliance of their minds sets a high standard for the rest of us.

Advocating for Change

Understanding the paths history has taken is important if early childhood educators are to be successful in improving services in the future. Even a brief summary of historical underpinnings reveals that change is a constant. For example, at times, services for children have been a priority while at other times (regularly, in fact), they are threatened. The Head Start program is a case in point. In the mid-1960s, Head Start was launched to great fanfare as a means to end poverty in this country, an impossibly unrealistic goal. But over the years, the program has fallen prey to changing public attitudes and funding priorities.

Throughout these years, some advocates have set idealistic goals, which can be inspiring; yet history has taught us that unrealistic goals doom a program to failure. In the intervening years, advocates have made it plain that Head Start plays a key role in empowering poor families to improve their lives and in preparing their children for success in school. However, they also clarify that Head Start is not a cure for the ills of poverty nor is it an inoculation against poor school experiences that follow. To be most effective, advocates for improving Head Start and other early childhood programs and services should use the lessons of successful efforts in the past.

Examining the history of childhood education reveals that there have been significant changes—transformations actually—in how children are viewed. In the sections that follow, we examine the changing view of childhood and its effect on children's lives.

The Changing View of Children

Different periods of history have had differing perspectives on children and the idea of childhood itself (Aries, 1962). These perspectives matter because they have direct implications for how children are treated and what kinds of education they are provided. Different eras in history have tended to view children as miniature adults, born in sin, blank slates, innocent, economic valuables, competent, and as citizens with rights. At times, one or the other of these perspectives has tended to prevail. To some extent, all of these views of children persist to this day. In the sections that follow, each of the perspectives of childhood just mentioned is described, along with the potential positive and negative consequences for children's lives.

Children as Miniature Adults

From the Middle Ages to about the 17th century in Western Europe, children were basically seen as adults on a smaller scale (Aries, 1962). Children dressed like adults, did adult-like work, and even played the same games. In fact, it wasn't until the 15th and 16th centuries that children appeared in paintings wearing specialized children's clothing.

In the 18th century, discovery of smallpox inoculation and better conditions in general reduced the death rate among children, which likely contributed to changes in the idea of childhood (Aries, 1962). Previously, the extremely high infant mortality rate motivated families to produce a large number of children to ensure the survival of a few. Families depended on their children to provide labor to support the family. Therefore, children were not particularly valued as individuals. However, as children's survival became less precarious, so too did their value and the image attached to them.

Today, the image of children as miniature adults is apparent once again in the clothes children wear and the images they are exposed to through the media. Primary-grade girls dress like teenagers or young adults. Concern exists that they are too sexy too soon (Levin & Kilbourne, 2008). Preschoolers engage in team sports previously reserved for older children. Children's toys have been replaced by adult-like video games and computers.

Centuries ago, children were viewed as "miniature adults." Children today are once again dressing like adults, playing adult-type games, and being exposed to adult images through the media at younger and younger ages.

Children in Need of Redemption

The image of the child during the 1300s to 1800s was shaped by the religious belief that children were born in sin and needed redemption. Misbehavior of any kind was considered sinful and punished harshly.

Schools in Europe and America in the 18th and 19th centuries were based on this image of children. Children learned to read from the Bible, recited memorized passages, and were often beaten or ridiculed for errors. Many people today continue to believe that severe punishment is necessary to shape children's moral character.

Children as Blank Slates

English philosopher John Locke (1632–1704) countered the religious argument that children are born with a predetermined sinful nature. Instead, he believed that children are born as *tabula rasa*, blank slates. What gets written on the slates is determined by their experiences in the environment. Locke's view was a step forward because it rejected the notion of inherent sinfulness and strongly emphasized the importance and value of education.

Locke was accurate in assuming that environmental experiences play a major role in children's learning; however, he did not see individual differences in children or how they actively shape their own experiences. Nevertheless, Locke's image of children as blank slates persists. Many schools today still operate on the notion that children are empty vessels that need to be filled, rather than active participants in the process of education.

Children as Innocents

In contrast to Locke's theory as well as the notion of children as sinners in need of redemption, French philosopher Jean-Jacques Rousseau (1712–1778) introduced the Romantic image of the child as innocent. Rousseau's novel *Emile* promoted the idea that children are born good rather than evil, and that they have inherent abilities upon which to build (Wolfe, 2000). He saw the goal of education as building on children's natural goodness to help them achieve their potential.

Rousseau believed that it is important to observe children. He was among the first to propose the concept of stages of development that children pass through, each having its own unique characteristics. He believed that children should not be rushed through stages, nor that one stage was simply preparation for another, a concept that continues to influence practice 150 years later.

Rousseau's image of childhood was a radical departure from the views of his day. Although he did not put these ideas into practice, they influenced many thinkers who followed and continue to have an influence today. Early childhood education has a strong tradition of focusing on the positive in children to develop individual potential.

Children's Economic Value

At various points in history, children's value has been calculated in response to a number of factors. Even today, some consider children to be their parents' property. They were, and still are in some communities, economically necessary to contribute work to the sustenance and care of the family; this includes taking care of other children and parents in old age. In the 19th and early 20th centuries, however, child labor laws limited children's potential economic contributions to family well-being. As children's economic contributions diminished, they began to take on more intrinsic emotional value in the family. For example, insurance companies compensated parents for a child's death or injury not only because of the costs involved and the potential income lost, but also as an attempt to compensate for the emotional loss.

The Competent Child

Scientific study of children beginning in the 20th century led to an alternative view of childhood—the **competent child**—the idea that children are active players in their own development and learning. The more researchers learned about children's competencies beginning at birth, the less plausible it became to see them as blank slates. Brain research in recent decades has further reinforced this image of children's innate competence.

The image of the competent child has had a major impact on early childhood practices and the larger culture. But negative consequences can emanate as well. Producers of videotapes and television and computer programs claim that they can teach a baby to read or produce a future Einstein. In addition, the image of the competent child has contributed to the trend to hurry young children through childhood toward expectations or experiences more appropriate for older children or adults (Elkind, 2001).

MyEducationLab

To observe competence demonstrated by a baby boy, go to the Video Examples section of Topic 4: Child Development/Theories in the MyEducationaLab for your course and watch the video entitled *Intelligence: Infancy*. Reflect on how this observation affects your image of young children.

The Child as a Citizen with Rights

The image of the child throughout history has come almost full circle in its relation to adults. But rather than seeing children as small-scale adults, a present-day development is to view children as citizens who have inalienable rights just as adults do. In a democratic society, rights are implemented as laws such as those that protect children from abuse or prosecution as adults. Similarly, toys and other products used by children must meet safety regulations.

Internationally, the image of a child with rights has gained widespread attention. In 1989, the United Nations Convention on the Rights of the Child (www.unicef.crc) went into effect. It has been ratified by every developed country in the world except Somalia and the United States. The declaration calls for protection of all children from physical, mental, and sexual abuse. One provision states that, although parents have primary responsibility for children's upbringing, states should provide appropriate assistance and support for child care programs. This is one of several provisions that have been politically controversial in this country. Although the United States has not officially endorsed the UN Convention, its mere existence promotes an image of the child as inherently worthy of specific rights.

Images of Childhood Today

Elements of all of these images of childhood are present in children's lives today and influence how they are treated. While our country tends to see children as innocents in need of protection by parents and the government, we also propel them into adult experiences at young ages. Our schools swing back and forth between taking an approach that children are empty vessels or viewing them as inherently competent contributors to their own learning. On the one hand, children are highly valued, and on the other hand, they are abused and neglected.

As we explore the evolution of early childhood practice in the sections that follow, it will become apparent which of these images have had the greater influence on the field. We can only present highlights of the rich history of the field here; for a more complete picture, consult the timeline of major events listed in Table 2.1.

competent child The image of children as active players in their own development and learning.

Table 2.1 Timeline of Major Events in Early Childhood Education

Date	Event in the History of Early Childhood Education
1658	John Amos Comenius publishes *Orbis Pictus*, the first picture book for children.
1690	John Locke proposes that children are born as *tabula rasa*, blank slates, promoting the importance of education and the environment.
1762	Jean-Jacques Rousseau publishes *Emile*, promoting the idea of the natural goodness of children and the need for education to build their inherent potential.
1804	Johann Pestalozzi opens a school based on his philosophy of education. Friedrich Froebel and Robert Owen study with him there.
1825	Robert Owen opens a child care center for mill workers in New Harmony, Indiana, a model community.
1837	Friedrich Froebel, the "father of kindergarten," establishes his first "children's garden" in Germany.
1856	Margarethe Schurz founds the first German-speaking kindergarten in the United States.
1860	Elizabeth Palmer Peabody organizes the first English-speaking kindergarten.
1873	Susan Blow founds the first public school kindergarten in St. Louis, Missouri.
1875	Charities set up day nurseries in immigrant communities.
1892	The International Kindergarten Union is founded.
1895	G. Stanley Hall lectures kindergarten teachers on child development study, beginning the connection between the child study movement and early education.
1896	John and Alice Dewey found the University of Chicago Laboratory School, where they develop and implement progressive education ideas.
1897	The first meeting is held of the National Congress of Mothers, which later becomes the National Parent-Teacher Association (PTA).
1903	The first day nursery for African American children opens in New York City.
1907	Maria Montessori starts *Casa dei Bambini* in Rome, demonstrating the effectiveness of her method with poor children.
1909	The first White House Conference on Children is held. It focuses on mental health and child guidance.
1911	Margaret and Rachel Macmillan found an open-air nursery in London that focuses on children's health and education.
1911	Arnold Gesell begins the Child Study Institute at Yale University.
1912	The U.S. Children's Bureau is established.
1919	The White House Conference on Standards of Child Welfare issues statements that influence child labor laws and maternal and child health programs.
1920	The 19th amendment to the U.S. Constitution grants women the right to vote.
1921	Patty Smith Hill starts a progressive nursery school at Teachers College.
1926	Patty Smith Hill founds the National Committee on Nursery Schools (later NANE) to establish a professional organization for nursery school educators. NANE later becomes NAEYC.
1926	Nursery schools are linked to the study of child development and education. Day nurseries focus on needs of poor and immigrant families.

Table 2.1 Timeline of Major Events in Early Childhood Education

Date	Event in the History of Early Childhood Education
1929	The National Association for Nursery Education (NANE) is formally established with Lois Meek Stoltz as its first president (later becomes NAEYC). *Minimum Essentials of Nursery Education* is its first publication. Merging NANE with IKU is discussed, but doesn't happen.
1930	IKU changes its name to the Association for Childhood Education (later adds *International*).
1931	Local and state licensing of day nurseries begins, but with little consistency or enforcement.
1933	Works Progress Administration (WPA) establishes national nursery schools serving poor children and employing teachers, nurses, and social workers throughout the Great Depression.
1933	George Stoddard, former NANE president, starts the Society for Research in Child Development, separating the child study arm from NANE.
1935	The Social Security Act passes, creating Aid to Dependent Children (welfare program for mothers to care for children), later called Aid to Families with Dependent Children. Becomes Temporary Assistance for Needy Families (TANF) in 1996 welfare reform.
1937	NANE's conference theme is "Safeguarding the Early Years of Childhood." This is the last NANE conference held in the segregated South until 1964. NANE took an early stand on equal rights.
1941	The Lanham Act provides funds for child care during World War II, primarily for mothers serving the war effort. Selected WPA nurseries also receive funding.
1943	Kaiser Shipbuilding, using Lanham Act funds, starts two child care centers for employees, offering high-quality care for children and comprehensive services for families.
1945	NANE cancels its biennial conference because of the war, but publishes the first issue of the *Bulletin*, which later becomes the journal *Young Children*.
1946	UNICEF is established within the United Nations. Federal funding for the Lanham Act is withdrawn after the war ends.
1952	*Ding Dong School*, the first television program for preschoolers, is created by Dr. Frances Horwich (Miss Frances), former NANE president.
1957	Russia launches a satellite, *Sputnik*, sparking intense focus on the quality of American education, especially math and science, and to a lesser extent early education.
1958	The NYC Inter-City Day Care Council becomes the National Committee for the Day Care of Children. In 1968 it becomes the Day Care and Child Development Council, and in 1982 the Child Care Action Campaign, which advocates for quality standards for child care centers and improved staff compensation.
1960	Katherine Whiteside Taylor launches organization that becomes Parent Cooperative Preschools International.
1962	The Perry Preschool Project begins in Ypsilanti, Michigan. Later becomes the HighScope Educational Research Foundation.
1964	The Economic Opportunity Act begins the War on Poverty, which includes Head Start, a comprehensive program for preschoolers of low-income families.
1965	Head Start begins as a summer demonstration program.
1966	Concerned about the quality of Head Start summer training, NAEYC contracts to study and recommend training sites based on faculty and curriculum.
1966	The Children's Television Workshop creates *Sesame Street*, funded by the Ford Foundation, the Carnegie Corporation of New York, and the U.S. Department of Health, Education, and Welfare (HEW; now Health and Human Services).

(continued)

Table 2.1 Timeline of Major Events in Early Childhood Education *(continued)*

Date	Event in the History of Early Childhood Education
1968	The federal government funds the establishment of model preschool programs for children with disabilities (then called *handicapped children*).
1968	The Federal Interagency Day Care Requirements (FIDCR) to set a national standard for child care funding are proposed, but never implemented. (Their demise later becomes impetus for NAEYC to launch its accreditation system.)
1970	The White House Conference on Children endorses the Comprehensive Child Development Act to provide public funding for child care and early education; vetoed by President Richard Nixon in 1971.
1970	The National Black Child Development Institute (NBCDI) is founded.
1971	Stride Rite Corporation in Boston starts the first employer-sponsored child care center.
1973	Marian Wright Edelman founds the Children's Defense Fund. The National Head Start Association is founded. The Division for Early Childhood of the Council for Exceptional Children is formed to focus on young children with special needs.
1974	The Child Abuse Prevention and Treatment Act passes.
1975	The Education for All Handicapped Children Act (P.L. 94–142) is enacted; later amended as the Individuals with Disabilities Education Act (IDEA).
1975	The Head Start Program Performance Standards are promulgated to ensure quality and consistency.
1979	The federally funded National Day Care Study is released, linking higher quality to smaller group sizes and trained staff.
1982	The National Association for Family Day Care is established (later changed to National Association for Family Child Care).
1984	The HighScope Educational Research foundation publishes *Changed Lives: The Effects of the Perry Preschool Project*, documenting the lasting positive consequences and cost effectiveness of high-quality preschool education.
1985	NAEYC launches its national, voluntary accreditation system for child care centers and schools.
1986	Public Law 99–457 establishes early intervention support for children with special needs from birth to age 3 and their families.
1987	NAEYC publishes its position statement on *Developmentally Appropriate Practice in Early Childhood Programs Serving Children from Birth through Age 8,* which is significantly revised in 1997 and again in 2009.
1989	The United Nations Convention on the Rights of the Child is adopted.
1990	The Act for Better Child Care passes, providing funding for Child Care and Development Block Grants to states, the first U.S. law that specifically provides funding for child care support.
1990	The National Education Goals Panel establishes goals for 2000, including "By the year 2000, all children will start school ready to learn," raising public awareness about early childhood education and services.
1992	The Reggio Emilia approach becomes well-known in the United States. The *One Hundred Languages of Children* exhibit tours and delegations visit schools in Reggio Emilia, Italy.
1995	Head Start Reauthorization establishes Early Head Start to serve low-income pregnant women and families with infants and toddlers.
1997	The Individuals with Disabilities Act is reauthorized, strengthening early childhood services.
1997	The *I Am Your Child* public awareness campaign is launched by Rob and Michelle Reiner, disseminating information about brain research and early development.

Table 2.1 Timeline of Major Events in Early Childhood Education

Date	Event in the History of Early Childhood Education
1998	The National Research Council of the National Academy of Sciences releases the very influential report *Preventing Reading Difficulties in Young Children*.
2000–2001	The National Research Council releases *From Neurons to Neighborhoods: The Science of Early Childhood Development* and *Eager to Learn: Educating Our Preschoolers*.
2001	Congress passes the No Child Left Behind Act to increase accountability and equity in public education and focus on evidence-based practices. NCLB funds Reading First for K–3, and Early Reading First for preschool.
2005	NAEYC launches its "reinvented" accreditation system with revised standards and procedures.
2005	The advocacy organization Pre-K Now works with states to significantly increase public awareness and funding for universal, voluntary prekindergarten.
2005	The National Institute for Early Education Research (NIEER) at Rutgers University disseminates research and public information in support of funding for early childhood programs.
2007	The Foundation for Child Development supports age 3 to grade 3 initiative to promote continuity in education of children across this age range.
2007	Congress passes Improving Head Start for School Readiness Act.
2007	National Task Force on Early Childhood Education for Hispanics releases *Para Nuestros Niños: Expanding and Improving Early Education for Hispanic Children in the United States*.
2008	Forty-nine states have Early Learning Standards for preschool children.
2009	National Research Council releases *Mathematics Learning in Early Childhood: Paths to Excellence and Equity*.
2009	American Recovery and Reinvestment Act of 2009 ("stimulus package") includes significant investments in early childhood education.

Source: Based on *NAEYC at 75: Reflections on the Past, Challenges for the Future*, 2001, Washington, DC: NAEYC.

European Influences on American Early Childhood Education

Like much of American history, early education was strongly influenced by western European ideas. It is important to keep in mind, however, that European ideas were not the only, nor necessarily the best, educational concepts in the world. Nevertheless, current practices in the United States strongly reflect these early influences. To consider early childhood history through a broader lens, read the accompanying *Culture Lens: Early Childhood Education through the Lens of Non-Western Culture* feature.

Rousseau's belief in the inherent goodness and potential of children had a strong impact on the educational ideas and practices that followed. Two other thinkers who shared similar views are Comenius and Pestalozzi. Unlike Rousseau, however, both created schools that implemented their vision.

John Amos Comenius

John Amos Comenius (Jan Komensky in his native Czech) (1592–1670) was a minister who wrote about educational reform and directed a school where he could put his ideas into practice. He believed in three key ideas (Wolfe, 2000): (1) Teaching methods needed to be radically changed from punitive approaches to make learning easier, deeper, and

Culture Lens

Early Childhood Education through the Lens of Non-Western Culture

Ideas from non-Western, alternative histories have much to offer early childhood education practices. One contemporary scholar who has written of diverse cultural approaches to educating children is Timothy Reagan (2005). He studies views from Africa, the Aztecs, North American Indians, the Rom, Chinese Confucians, Indian Hindus and Buddhists, and also Islamic traditions.

Consider the African culture where child-rearing practices and education are based on African people's view of the relationship between the physical and spiritual reality (Mbiti, 1992). They believe that understanding children requires understanding their spiritual purpose. Before a child is born, the child is a complete spirit—in some traditions, the child is an ancestor returning. At birth children are celebrated and the community is expected to make room for this child's purpose in the community. Because the spirit has come home to a community, not just to a biological set of parents, it becomes a community responsibility to take care of this child (Bunseki Fu-Kiai & Lukondo-Wamba, 1988; Some, 1999).

According to Dr. Itihari Toure (C. B. Day, personal communication, December 2008):

> The view of the spirit returning for the sake of the community also informs the responsibilities of the child. Child rearing is a collective process and children in different traditions not only have specific family responsibilities but partake in various community traditions as they must retain and transmit the values of the specific community. Biological parents and community members take care of all children. Exposure to various crafts and skills needed for the community to thrive, songs and dances that represent various stages of life, and the countless stories that recall the history of the people are part of the child-rearing experience. . . . When children engage in formal schooling, the motivation is not based on personal achievement alone; there is a desire to bring pride and regard to the community through the personal achievement. This perception of purpose and success comes from a consistent socialization about the value of one's family and community interdependent with the value of oneself. It is often referred to as *Ubunutu* (I am because we are; we are because I am).

Understanding how other cultures rear children brings to light a very important consideration for all educators: Every child is a product of his or her own history. Knowing that other cultures rear their children according to non-Western beliefs deepens and broadens the possibilities for educating children to their full potential, in ways that may resonate with their own historical and cultural realities.

References: Bunseki Fu-Kiai, K. K., & Lukondo-Wamba, A. M. (1988). *Kindezi: The Kongo art of babysitting*. New York: Vantage Press; Mbiti, J. (1992). *African religions and philosophy* (2nd ed.). Portsmouth, NH: Heinemann; Reagan, T. (2005). *Non-Western educational traditions: Indigenous approaches to education thought and practice* (3rd ed.) Mahwah, NJ: Lawrence Erlbaum Associates; Some, S. (1999). *Welcoming spirit home: Ancient African teachings to celebrate children and community*. Novato, CA: New World Library.

more pleasant; (2) teachers should engage children with nature and follow their lead; and (3) children should learn in their own language, rather than Latin.

To accomplish his last goal, Comenius wrote a new kind of book, *Orbis Pictus*, or "the world in pictures." Popular for the next 200 years, this was the first children's picture book or illustrated textbook ever published. It was organized around topics of interest such as birds and plants and included pictures with labels attached. Comenius also wrote the first illustrated alphabet book to teach children to read in their own language.

Some of the educational ideas that Comenius practiced in his school were radical for his time but sound familiar to early childhood educators today. For example, he thought the early years were an extremely important foundation for later learning. He believed that children learn through their senses and need to be active, and he felt that children's interests and firsthand experiences promote learning and memory. Comenius believed that children are born in the image of God, and was vehemently opposed to physical punishment (Wolfe, 2000). Like Rousseau, he identified developmental stages.

Comenius's ideas have endured for centuries. For example, in the 1990s eastern European countries that had been under Communist dictatorship moved toward democracy. One strategy was to reform previously rigid educational systems. With the help of American philanthropy, the International Step by Step Association (www.issa.nl) was founded to develop Head Start–like preschool programs. There was some concern that these "American" ideas—such as child-centered education—would be culturally inappropriate. However, these concerns underestimated the lasting reverence for native son Comenius—who is, after all, the forerunner of much of American early childhood education.

First created more than 400 years ago, picture books remain one of the most popular, valuable, and engaging learning materials in early childhood programs and homes.

Johann Pestalozzi

Johann Pestalozzi (1746–1827) was a Swiss educator who, like Comenius, founded his own school and trained teachers. He believed that all children—including children who lived in poverty—could benefit from education (Nourot, 2005). The field's current views of best practice are remarkably consistent with many of Pestalozzi's ideas about teaching and learning.

Learning and Teaching in Pestalozzi's School

Pestalozzi (1894/2007) described his philosophy in a book titled *How Gertrude Teaches Her Children*. He believed that teachers must study child development. He thought that learning proceeds through stages, with children needing to master skills and knowledge before moving on to the next stage (Wolfe, 2000). Pestalozzi promoted what came to be called the "whole child" point of view—that children's physical, emotional, social, moral, and intellectual development are integrated and united. He called these "the hand, heart, and head."

Other important ideas of Pestalozzi included the notion that children need to discover ideas for themselves through their own activity—a precursor of Piaget's theory of **constructivism**. He rejected punishment and threats as motivators and felt that instead, children are motivated to learn by their interests. Like many early theorists, Pestalozzi viewed development as a natural unfolding or blossoming from within, with teachers acting as gardeners who nurture the process rather than direct it. Although this view is simpler than our understanding of development today, it persisted well into the 20th century.

Impact of Pestalozzi's Work

Pestalozzi's ideas directly influenced schools for young children in the 19th century. Particularly influential was his notion of object lessons—learning from direct observation and sensory experience in the natural world—that begin with the here and now and move beyond (Wolfe, 2000).

A well-known school influenced by Pestalozzi was founded by Robert Owen (1771–1858) as part of his idealized community in Scotland, New Lanark. Owen spread his ideas to America by founding a similar model community in New Harmony, Indiana. Although his experiment did not survive long, the school provided care and education for hundreds of children, from infancy to age 10, whose parents worked in the mills—one of the earliest examples of a child care center.

Friedrich Froebel

Friedrich Froebel (1782–1852) built on Pestalozzi's ideas but extended them to develop a specific curriculum and educational materials. His view of development as a process of natural unfolding is evident in the name of his school, a "garden for children." Froebel is well known as the "father of the kindergarten."

constructivism Learning theory derived from the work of Jean Piaget which assumes that children actively build their knowledge from firsthand experiences in stimulating environments.

Froebel believed in the innate goodness and capacities of children, and saw God's image in them. Like Pestalozzi, he believed that education should be based on children's interests and their active involvement, and that teachers need to understand children's development by directly observing their actions (Wolfe, 2000).

He described stages of development that are similar to those Piaget articulated in the 20th century. He saw infancy (birth to 3 years) as focused on the family and the infant's relationship with the mother. He wrote *Mother Play and Nursery Songs* to assist mothers in their interactions with very young children—something most mothers today take for granted. Froebel's second stage (ages 3 to 7), for which he developed his kindergarten materials, was the focus of most of his work. The third stage (ages 7 to 10) focused on more formal school instruction.

Froebel's Kindergarten

Froebel's metaphor of the children's garden was more than poetry. He strongly believed that children's learning is a process of unfolding from within. He also believed that learning would occur on the child's own timetable and not until the child was ready. Froebel's kindergarten emphasized children's free play, singing, and movement (Nourot, 2005). The materials he developed, which were called **Froebel's occupations and gifts**, were used to guide and structure children's play. As a result, Froebel's view of "free" play was not as free as some interpret today.

The role of the teacher in Froebel's kindergarten was to be like a gardener. Teachers were to observe, nurture, and help but not interfere with the natural growth of the child. They needed to be aware of children's development, however, so they could provide a new challenge as children engaged with the gifts and occupations.

Froebel's Gifts

Froebel's gifts were concrete materials for children to manipulate in specific ways. The first gift was a box of six wooden balls in the colors of the spectrum—red, orange, yellow, green, blue, and violet—plus corresponding strings. Each child could use these materials in many creative ways, but Froebel and his teachers identified more than 100 games to play with this one gift and accompanying songs and rhymes (Wolfe, 2000).

Another gift was a cube that could be divided into eight smaller cubes and put back together to form a whole. Children could play many games with this gift, but it also promoted basic math concepts related to number and geometry. Froebel also invented parquetry blocks—a set of flat, colored, wooden shapes that could be put together to form various designs. Other gifts included sticks and rings made of wire and natural materials such as seeds and pebbles. The same or similar materials are prevalent in early childhood classrooms today where children use them in creative ways, and also to learn mathematics and science.

Froebel's Occupations

In contrast to the gifts, occupations were planned experiences designed to train children's eye–hand coordination and mental activity (Wolfe, 2000). The occupations included activities such as drawing on grid paper, lacing paper strips, weaving mats, folding and cutting paper into designs, constructing with sticks, or making models from cardboard.

Froebel believed that the use of the gifts and occupations engaged children in symbolically representing objects and events in the real world—such as creating a model or drawing a picture of a building. The key role of representation in learning, which Froebel presaged, is now well supported by research.

Froebel's occupations and gifts Invented by Froebel for kindergartners, occupations were planned experiences designed to train children's eye–hand coordination and mental activity, and gifts were concrete materials, many of which influenced later toy development.

Impact of Froebel's Work

Froebel's work had a major impact on education in the United States, leading directly to a large-scale kindergarten movement here. Several teachers and teacher educators who studied Froebel's methods in Europe—"kindergartners" as they were called—transplanted his ideas in this country.

Kindergartens today bear less and less resemblance to Froebel's "children's garden"; today they have become more like formal first grades (Graue, 2006). However, many of his basic ideas are still evident in preschool and child care programs. Although no one actually uses the specific set of gifts and occupations today, they were clearly the prototypes for many of the toys and materials, such as one-inch cube and parquetry blocks, that are pervasive in preschool classrooms. Common activities—constructing models or using natural materials in art and projects—also mirror some of his occupations.

Froebel's work had a direct, significant impact on development of kindergartens in the United States, which we return to later in this chapter. First, we visit another European educator who lived a century later than Froebel, but whose work also stands out for its contributions to the field—Maria Montessori.

Considered the father of the kindergarten, Friedrich Froebel invented special educational materials—called gifts—some of which are still used today, such as small wooden cubes, parquetry blocks, and Lincoln logs.

Maria Montessori

Maria Montessori (1870–1952) was a major figure in the history of early childhood education. A brilliant woman, she was Italy's first female physician. She was nominated for the Nobel Peace Prize, and her face graced the 1,000 Italian lira note until Italy abandoned the lire for the euro. Montessori was, and probably always will be, the only early childhood educator whose face adorned a currency.

History of the Montessori Method

Montesssori's contributions grew out of her work with poor children in a housing project in the slums of Rome. The prevailing opinion was that these children were considered to be mentally deficient. However, Montessori believed that what appeared to be mental retardation was not biologically based, but rather caused by the lack of stimulation in their environments.

In 1907, she started a program for children, ages 4 through 7, called *Casa dei Bambini* (Children's House), and developed a highly successful approach to teaching the children, which revealed that they were not mentally disabled at all. Montessori demonstrated that educating needy children is a less costly and more effective strategy than waiting until they create problems for society. This is the same justification that was used to launch Head Start in the mid-1960s, and it is still the core rationale for much of the current investment in early education.

MyEducationLab

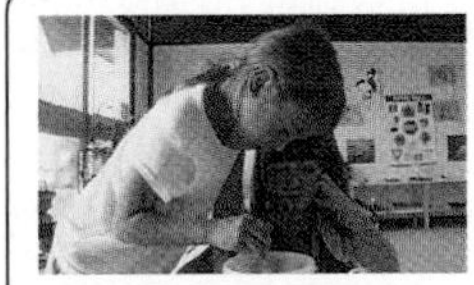

To observe how a Montessori classroom works, go to the Video Examples section of Topic 5: Program Models in the MyEducationaLab for your course and watch the video entitled *Intelligence: Montessori*. What are the key elements of the Montessori Method and what is the role of the teacher in a Montessori classroom?

Key Elements of the Montessori Method

The Montessori method includes several basic elements. In the sections that follow, we briefly describe Montessori's views about children and learning, the environment, and the teacher's role.

Image of Children: The Absorbent Mind. Like other key figures in early childhood history, Montessori (1909/1964) believed that children develop naturally in an organized environment. Her image of the child is the **absorbent mind**—actively learning from sensory experiences. She also believed that children from 4 to 7 years old are internally motivated to interact with the world, and do not need external encouragement or rewards.

absorbent mind Maria Montessori's image of the child as actively learning from sensory experiences.

Where Montessori deviated greatly from others in the field, both at her time and in the present day, was in her opinion of play. Montessori dismissed play as a waste of children's time (Snyder, 1972; Wolfe, 2000). She also minimized the value of social interaction for children's learning. As evidence, children each had an individual small mat to work on and not be disturbed by others.

A Prepared Learning Environment. Montessori believed that poor children deserve high-quality experiences. She also believed that children need an orderly environment that supports their ability to work on and complete tasks independently. Accordingly, she designed classroom environments and materials that demonstrate respect for children. Montessori innovations included child-sized tables and other furnishings, and materials arranged on open shelves for easy access by children.

To facilitate learning and prevent wasted time, she developed educational materials for children to use in prescribed ways. Montessori designed self-correcting learning materials for children, many of which are still commonly used. For example, she created puzzles with little knobs attached to each piece, for very young children to practice the pincer grasp used for writing; and to practice fine motor skills, she invented a cloth board with buttons and buttonholes. Montessori emphasized that there was one right way to use each of her materials. She did not consider her materials to be toys; instead, she viewed them as educational tools. Children were also taught practical life skills such as washing a table and sweeping a floor.

MyEducationLab

Go to the Assignments and Activities section of Topic 1: History in the MyEducationaLab for your course and complete the activity entitled *Montessori Classroom*. As you watch the video and answer the accompanying questions, note how Montessori materials are used today and how these materials have influenced all early childhood classroom.

Montessori's belief in sensory learning extended to academic areas as well, specifically writing, reading, and mathematics. For example, she created sandpaper alphabets so that children could feel the shapes of the letters as a first step toward writing. She thought children should learn to write as a strategy to teach reading. This was an innovative concept for its time (when promoting reading at an early age was not accepted by her peers in early education), and also presaged later understandings of the strong connection between writing and reading in becoming literate.

The Teacher's Role. Montessori's view of the teacher's role is to prepare the environment, observe children, and demonstrate materials but not to interfere with their natural exploration. Although teachers' interactions with children are very intentional in the Montessori method, much of the learning is assumed to occur as children interact with materials. The teacher presents brief individual or small-group lessons, but most of the day children choose their activities. Their choices have limits, however, because the adults arrange those choices.

Impact of Montessori's Work

From 1910 to 1920, interest in Montessori's approach gained popularity in the United States; several elements of her approach remain widely accepted practices today. However, overall interest in her methods soon faded here, primarily due to her unwillingness to adapt her approach to new knowledge and her rejection of key elements of American philosophy, such as the importance of play.

Not until the 1950s was interest in Montessori revived in the United States. In contrast to Montessori's original intent to serve poor children, Montessori schools in the United States have tended to be private, serving a more affluent population. In recent years, however, the approach has been embraced by some magnet and charter public schools. Two Montessori accrediting programs, the Association Montessori Internationale (AMI) and the American Montessori Society (AMS), provide information and teacher training and certification. Today the United States has thousands of Montessori schools. But the brand is not copyrighted, and any school can use it. Therefore, to ensure that a school is true to the Montessori philosophy, it should be accredited by AMI or AMS.

A recent study of a public Montessori school in Milwaukee found that the approach contributed positively to 5-year-olds' literacy, math, and social skills (Lillard, 2005). The researchers also found positive effects on children's creativity and social skills at age 12 (Lillard & Else-Quest, 2006).

Maria Montessori's lasting contribution to the field was her development of Montessori materials and her impact on the organization of early childhood environments. The difference between the Montessori approach and more typical early childhood practice is that Montessori materials are designed very intentionally to help children learn specific skills.

The following sections present three interwoven stories of early childhood education in America—the kindergarten movement, progressive education, and the nursery school movement. These stories are described separately but, in reality, they happened simultaneously and were inextricably connected. A parallel story—the child care movement—was also occurring, but played out differently as you will read later in this chapter.

It is important to note that the following discussion is dominated by white European Americans because their work is most often included in the "official" written history of the field. At the same time, however, similar events were occurring in the African American community. That history is less well known primarily because historical sources are scarce, but also because there is a strong oral rather than written tradition in the African American community (Simpson, n.d.). Nevertheless, records exist that cast light on this significant part of early childhood education history, which we discuss in a later section.

Montessori classrooms are specially designed environments in which children learn by interacting with the materials. What skills might children acquire by working with the Montessori materials depicted here?

The Kindergarten Movement in the United States

The United States provided fertile ground for the growth of Froebel's "children's gardens." In the sections that follow, we describe how the movement began and spread widely and its lasting impact.

Early Days of the Kindergarten Movement

The earliest leaders in the kindergarten movement transplanted Froebel's ideas directly. The first kindergarten in the United States was founded by Margarethe Schurz (1832–1876) in Wisconsin in 1856 (Snyder, 1972). Schurz had studied with Froebel and, upon immigrating to the United States, started a German-speaking school to teach her own and neighbors' children. Later, Schurz met Elizabeth Palmer Peabody (1804–1894) and their encounter was the impetus for the American kindergarten movement.

Elizabeth Peabody was part of a well-known family of social reformers. Her sister, Mary, was married to Horace Mann, considered to be the father of public education in the United States. In Boston, Elizabeth Peabody organized the first English-speaking kindergarten in 1860, and soon after wrote the first American kindergarten textbook for teachers (Snyder, 1972). She understood that teachers needed to be trained in Froebel's philosophy to ensure the quality and integrity of the expanding kindergarten movement. She also traveled widely and became an outspoken advocate for the cause, inspiring new generations of leaders, the most influential of whom was Susan Blow.

Susan Blow's Leadership

Susan Blow (1843–1916) was the major voice in not only expanding the kindergarten movement, but also in fighting to keep it true to Froebel's original vision. Born to a wealthy, socially conscious, and deeply religious family, she considered it necessary to devote her life to a worthy cause. Inspired by Elizabeth Peabody's promotion of kindergarten, Blow visited Froebelian kindergartens in the United States and Germany and became the leading interpreter of the approach at home.

Founding Public Kindergarten

In 1873, with the administrative support of William Harris, a reform-minded school superintendent in St. Louis, Susan Blow founded the first public school kindergarten (Snyder, 1972) in response to Harris's concern that schooling did not begin for children until age 7. Blow was ambivalent about connecting kindergarten to public school fearing that "the formality of the grades would seize kindergarten in its grip" (Snyder, 1972, p. 66). Nevertheless, she worked with Harris for more than a decade launching more than 50 kindergarten classrooms in the district. Teacher training was an essential part of her strategy, with teachers working directly with children in the mornings and attending lectures in the afternoons on topics such as the correct use of Froebel's gifts and occupations—a combination of theory and practicum that continues to this day in teacher education.

Upon Harris's departure from his post, a new school administration was less supportive of Blow's cause and threatened her ideal vision of kindergarten. Subsequently, Blow turned her energy from developing and spreading Froebelian kindergarten ideals to defending them (Snyder, 1972). Blow promoted a rigid application of Froebel's methods and materials (such as using the gifts in narrowly prescribed ways), which was actually antithetical to his more creative vision of kindergarten.

Founding the International Kindergarten Union

In 1892, Blow convened a group of ardent kindergartners from throughout the country and formed the International Kindergarten Union (IKU). (Much later the IKU became the Association for Childhood Education International.) The original mission of the IKU was not just to disseminate information, but to protect the integrity of Froebelian kindergartens. Within two decades, this mission was to come into direct conflict with winds of change that were occurring in the wider educational world, emanating from the progressive education movement, described in the next section.

Progressive Education

The **progressive education movement** was a major effort to reform schooling at all levels to make it more democratic. Its tenets were in direct contrast to the prevailing practices in schools of the time, which emphasized rote memorization, strict conformity, and harsh discipline. The traditional curriculum was limited to the "3 Rs": reading, writing, and arithmetic.

The story of the progressive education movement in the United States is integrally connected to the story of the nursery school movement (or preschool as we now call it). Many principles of developmentally appropriate practice are derived directly from the work of early progressive leaders. Although differences exist between the earlier ideas and current views, the commonalities between the two visions—progressive education and developmentally appropriate practice—are striking. The following sections present the contributions of John Dewey.

John Dewey

progressive education movement Major effort to reform schooling in the early 20th century to make it more democratic and responsive to children's needs. This movement was highly influential on early childhood education and later ideas about developmentally appropriate practice.

John Dewey (1859–1952) was a professor of philosophy first at the University of Chicago and then for 47 years at Teachers College, Columbia University, in New York City. While in Chicago, John and his wife, Alice Chapman Dewey (d. 1927), founded the University of Chicago Laboratory School to implement their philosophy of a humane approach to education. Alice taught at the school, prepared the curriculum, and served as principal. The school, which they ran from 1893 to 1903, became a laboratory for developing and trying out their approach. The University of Chicago Laboratory School still exists; the children of President Barack Obama are two of its most famous recent students.

Principles of Progressive Education

John Dewey (1916) believed that the purpose of education is to ensure the effective functioning of a democratic society. He believed that the traditional approach to schooling could not produce citizen decision makers. He was concerned that in a democratic society, it is "impossible to foretell definitely what civilization will be twenty years from now" (Dewey, 1929, p. 6). Therefore, it is important to teach children to take initiative and use judgment. Dewey (1929) articulated his philosophy in *My Pedagogic Creed*. Let's take a look at some of the principles of progressive education, as described by Dewey in that document.

What Education Is

"Education is the process of living and not preparation for future living" (Dewey, 1929, p. 7). This famous quote of John Dewey summarizes his definition of education and continues to influence early childhood education.

Dewey was a prolific writer whose words still inspire. The titles of his books alone convey his basic ideas about education: *Democracy and Education*, *Education and Experience*, *The School and Society*, *Freedom and Culture*, and *The Child and the Curriculum*. In Dewey's mind, schooling could not be separated from the larger needs of democratic society, and children, rather than subject matter, needed to be at the center of the curriculum.

What the School Is

Dewey (1900) believed that the school is primarily a social institution and should function as a community. The teacher's role is to be a member of the community. Teachers should not directly impose discipline, but rather influence and assist children as they work together.

According to Dewey, teachers and parents should learn from each other—an accepted idea today, but radical for his time. In his school, parents and teachers met regularly to discuss topics such as why children should or should not learn to read at an early age—again, an issue that many educators and parents debate today (Wolfe, 2000).

What the Curriculum Is

Dewey believed that subject matter—reading, writing, geography, history, science—should be introduced to children in ways that they can understand and that involve them in social interaction. He introduced the idea of **integrated curriculum**, now a staple of early childhood education, which addresses learning goals across multiple subjects at the same time. For example, children might learn economics, history, geography, and other subjects by studying the workers in their neighborhood. A tenet of Dewey's philosophy is that teachers should find ways to integrate traditional curriculum into topics of interest to children, such as building a model of the neighborhood. Dewey also brought expressive and constructive activities into the classroom such as cooking, sewing, and woodworking. He felt academic skills should grow out of these activities.

What Teaching Should Be

Dewey (1929) believed that the traditional emphasis on children as passive learners was a "waste of time." He strongly emphasized the importance of teachers observing children and building on their interests. In progressive schools, the role of teachers is to guide or facilitate learning based on what they know about children and to choose the right problems and questions to further children's learning. For example, teachers don't simply teach geography as adults know it; rather, they teach the geography concepts and topics that the child is interested in and capable of learning. This approach, called the **child-centered curriculum**, has been falsely interpreted over the years to mean that children determine the curriculum (Bredekamp & Copple, 1997). Although teachers build curriculum from children's experiences and interests, Dewey felt strongly that teachers needed *both* to know what children are interested in *and* also to know the content that children needed to learn. This *both/and* thinking principle in progressive education has often been lost in translation.

MyEducationLab

To watch how integrated curriculum is used in the classroom, go to the Video Examples section of Topic 7: Curriculum Content Areas in the MyEducationaLab for your course and watch the video entitled *Integrated Curriculum*. Note how key elements of John Dewey's educational approach have influenced early childhood education and continue to be implemented today.

integrated curriculum
Learning plan that addresses goals across multiple areas of the curriculum at the same time.

child-centered curriculum
John Dewey's idea that curriculum should reflect the concepts and topics that the child is interested in and capable of learning.

The Impact of Progressive Education on Schooling

Although progressive education has often been misinterpreted and periodically comes under attack by proponents of more traditional practices, its contributions to American education are profound. Lois Meek Stoltz (1977), the first president of NAEYC and a contemporary of Dewey, eloquently captured the impact:

> I think it is very difficult for people of this generation to realize, or even picture, what the public schools were like in the early 1900s. Children were in their seats all day long. When they rose, they rose to count, "1, 2, 3," they then turned, marched, and went to the cloakroom. Then they did the same thing when they marched out of the school and when they marched in. Everybody read out of the same book at the same time. There was very little consideration for individual differences. (pp. 103–104)
>
> In my opinion, the progressive education movement was the greatest force in America in improving public school education. . . . Much more attention to individual differences took place, and teachers began to let children use their own initiative, much more attention to problem solving and activity. The 20 years—1925 to 1945—really remade public education. (pp. 108–109)

Earlier in this chapter, we talked about how solutions to problems contain the seeds of new problems. Progressive education was a case in point. Giving children more freedom meant that some people interpreted this as chaos, creating a backlash or a new problem. And yet, as Stoltz points out, the efforts overall led to real change in schools—and that change is progress.

Although he was a philosophy professor, Dewey was strongly influenced by the trend in his day toward more scientific approaches in education. This trend, called the *child study movement*, is described in the next section.

The Child Study Movement

As far back as Pestalozzi, educators understood that teaching should be based on direct study of children. Beginning in the late 19th century, G. Stanley Hall (1844–1924) launched the **child study movement**. Hall was interested in understanding individual differences in children through direct observation.

Hall's students went on to develop systematic scientific approaches to studying child development. Arnold Gesell (1880–1961) is famed for launching a child study laboratory at Yale University, called the Gesell Institute. There he observed large samples of children and derived age-related norms for children's growth and development such as by what age children should take their first steps or speak their first words. These norms were considered "universal" and have been widely influential. However, in the late 20th century, Gesell's age-related norms were criticized for understating individual differences and not using diverse samples of children.

Hall was a strong critic of Froebelian kindergarten. He thought that its rigid methodology lacked a scientific basis. Thus, the child study movement played an important role in bringing about changes in the kindergarten movement, and it also contributed in large measure to the growing nursery school movement. We tell this story in the section that follows.

child study movement Early 20th century effort to scientifically observe and systematically document children's individual development under the leadership of G. Stanley Hall and Arnold Gesell.

nursery schools Schools serving children younger than kindergarten age; out-of-date term for preschool or prekindergarten.

The Nursery School Movement

Dewey's laboratory school and his emphasis on child observation reflected his understanding of the need to base education on the study of children. Similarly, other universities launched lab schools to train teachers and study children. Many of these schools served children younger than kindergarten age, and were called **nursery schools**, based on their philosophy of nurturing children's development. Laboratory schools were established for the purposes of research and demonstration of teaching methods, rather than to serve parents or neglected children (Hewes et al., 2001). As a result, many of these programs served middle- and upper-class children of faculty or community members.

The nursery school movement eventually launched the wider field of early childhood education. It grew out of the kindergarten and child study movements through the leadership of two women whose contributions to early childhood education are unparalleled: Patty Smith Hill, founder of NAEYC, and Lucy Sprague Mitchell, founder of Bank Street College. Every early childhood educator should know the stories of these women and their contemporaries, who played seminal roles in laying the foundation of early childhood education as we know it today. We who follow are their direct descendents.

Patty Smith Hill

Patty Smith Hill's life story parallels the early history of early childhood education, with each phase of her life connected to important developments in the field. She was a joyful child, teacher of young children, creator of resources for children, teacher educator, and national leader.

Hill's Early Life Experiences

Patty Smith Hill (1868–1946) was fortunate to have an idyllic childhood. Her father believed that girls should be prepared for a profession, a radical idea at the time. Her mother was also a progressive thinker who had grown up on a plantation and had secretly, and also illegally, taught slaves to read, write, and calculate (Wolfe, 2000). Furthermore, Patty Hill's mother believed that play was essential to childhood. Hill's experiences as a child influenced her views of childhood and education for her entire life.

Work as a Kindergarten Teacher

By the 1880s, the kindergarten movement was under way and Anna Bryan launched a teacher training program in Louisville, Kentucky, where Patty Hill became one of the first students (Snyder, 1972). Hill started her own kindergarten where she encouraged new and creative uses for Froebel's gifts as toys, and constructive materials such as blocks and clay. Her kindergarten evidenced her belief in the value of children's play as a way to learn.

In 1896, Patty Hill and her mentor, Anna Bryan, were among a group of influential kindergarten educators who attended one of G. Stanley Hall's lectures on new knowledge and insights gained from the systematic study of children's development. Hall's severe criticism of the Froebelian approach as unscientific outraged the attendees, all of whom stormed out of the meeting—with the exception of Patty Hill and Anna Bryan (Hewes, 1976). Hill and Bryan stayed and continued to study with Hall, and they developed a new curriculum for teaching young children. Hill's involvement in the child study movement and belief in the importance of the "whole child" caused her to deeply value a multidisciplinary approach to the field, involving physicians, social workers, psychologists, artists, and others with diverse areas of expertise—an aspect of early childhood education that continues to this day.

> **Effective Teaching**
> Observation of children's development throughout history laid the foundation for our understanding of effective early childhood education practices today.

In 1903, Louisville's kindergartens became part of the public schools. Patty Hill was excited about the potential benefits, but feared that key kindergarten practices including parent education, would be lost (Snyder, 1972). She also feared, as others since her have done, that public school kindergarten would push children into early reading, writing, and arithmetic, and away from play.

Patty Hill's vision for kindergarten included three purposes (Hill, [1926]1987, p. 12):

1. The most imperative function is "to minister to the nature and needs of children from 4 to 6 years of age."
2. The kindergarten teacher's second duty is to see the relation of her work to the first-grade curriculum and lay the foundation that children need "without sacrificing the right of the kindergarten child to free, full development on his own level."
3. The third function is to connect kindergarten to the home, to reduce the gap between the two, and to build on the learning that takes place there.

This vision of kindergarten, especially the role of parents, was not just ahead of Hill's time, but one to aspire to today.

Creator of Resources for Children

Patty Hill not only worked with children, but also developed resources for them. Among her creations was a set of wooden blocks that looked like pieces of lumber from which children could build structures large enough for them to play in. She and her musician sister, Mildred, wrote many songs for children, using music as a fun teaching tool. Their most famous song is the well-loved, often-sung "Happy Birthday," although few people know its composers.

Hill also wrote many poems about children's interests, and books to help children learn to read. Much like her mother, Hill was concerned about racial inequality. In the early 1940s, she worked for months on a set of readers showing "fine-looking Negro and dark-skinned" children, but she despaired when no publisher would consider them (Hewes, 1976). She believed that respectful images would help resolve racial prejudices.

Hill's Work as a Teacher Educator

In 1905, Patty Smith Hill joined the faculty of Teachers College in New York, where she stayed for 30 years and was considered a master teacher (Snyder, 1972). She focused her work in the community school, which served the poor children of the neighborhood, as opposed to the campus lab school, which served well-off children of faculty. Hill also studied Montessori's methods and visited Italy, but disagreed with Montessori's disdain for play.

The Dean of Teachers College, James Earl Russell, was famous for bringing together divergent points of view (Snyder, 1972). One of his provocative ideas was to bring Susan Blow to coteach a course on kindergarten methods with Patty Hill. Among the topics they debated were opposing views of work and play. Although students loved their lively debates, eventually it became clear that Hill's point of view was carrying the day (Snyder, 1972).

Hill's Contributions as a National Leader

Patty Hill was active in the IKU and served as its president in 1908. However, her more liberal ideas about kindergarten methods, including her promotion of play and creativity, came into conflict with others' more rigid interpretations of Froebel's ideas.

In 1904, the IKU formed the Committee of Nineteen, a group with varying perspectives on kindergarten practice, to articulate positions and resolve disputes on such topics such as the role of play and the content of the curriculum (Wolfe, 2000). Each year the committee issued a report, and disagreements became more apparent over time. By 1909, differences could not be resolved and three reports were produced: one by Susan Blow, another one by Patty Smith Hill, and a compromise report by Lucy Wheelock (Snyder, 1972). Patty Hill's report was to become the vision for kindergarten practice as we know it today. Nevertheless, the process of debating conflicting points of view, which she embraced, continues to be an essential part of the work of early childhood educators (Bredekamp, 2001).

Patty Hill as a Founder of NAEYC

As nursery schools began to proliferate in the 1920s, Hill was concerned about the lack of standards and curriculum plans and the threat of unqualified people taking leadership positions (Hewes, 1976). In 1926, she formed the National Committee on Nursery Schools, which became the National Association for Nursery Education (NANE). The committee included Lois Meek Stoltz, Arnold Gesell, and Abigail Eliot. Stoltz became the organization's first president.

In the 1960s, NANE changed its name to NAEYC, the National Association for the Education of Young Children. Patty Hill was its first member and her views dominated the work of the nursery school movement during its early years. NANE's first publication in 1929 was *Minimum Essentials for Nursery School Education.* In this tradition, NAEYC has been involved in setting standards ever since (Bredekamp, 2001).

We have chosen to tell the story of Patty Smith Hill in such detail because she lived so many of the historical events that helped define present-day early childhood education. In the next section, we share the story of one of her close colleagues working in progressive education in New York, Caroline Pratt.

Caroline Pratt

Caroline Pratt (1867–1954) attended the kindergarten education program at Teachers College. Like Patty Smith Hill, Pratt rejected the Froebelian kindergarten curriculum. She believed that it was far too structured and did not allow children to play freely or experiment with materials.

Pratt's Educational Philosophy

Pratt focused her energies on studying children directly. Her motto, as well as the title of the book for which she is best known, was "I learn from children" (Wolfe, 2000). She became intrigued by the potential of engaging children with open-ended play equipment and materials.

Like others in the progressive education movement, Pratt looked to education to transform society and worked in settlement houses with poor children. She set up classrooms with her own hand-made blocks and toys, crayons, and paper and observed children's play. Based on her observations, Pratt realized the benefits for children of firsthand experiences and self-directed plans, field trips and pretend play, letting children find answers to their own questions, the relationship of play and intelligence, and the need to nurture children's play (Wolfe, 2000). Pratt also saw an active role for teachers in supporting children's play. These conclusions have all been supported by empirical research in the intervening years.

Inventor of Unit Blocks

Caroline Pratt's most lasting contribution is undoubtedly her design of wooden unit blocks. She admired Patty Hill's blocks but found them difficult for younger children to manipulate. She wanted blocks that would allow children to openly express their ideas about the world. Her blocks are made of natural hardwood, in various three-dimensional shapes, and mathematically precise because each block is a fraction or multiple of the standard unit. For example, the standard unit block is one-half of the next size block, one-quarter of the size after that, and so forth. What Pratt intuitively believed about the value of these tools for children's learning has been proven true by research. For a summary of these benefits of block play, read the *What Works: Caroline Pratt's Unit Blocks* feature.

Pratt created wooden people representing families and community workers to add a pretend element to the block play. She also designed large hollow wooden blocks to encourage large muscle play and for outdoor use. For more than a century, millions of children have enjoyed and learned from these wonderful, creative materials. However, because she did not patent them, Pratt never benefited financially.

The Play School

Caroline Pratt founded The Play School for 4- through 6-year-old children in New York's Greenwich Village in what was then a low-rent area. The name telegraphed the school's purpose and approach. The school's curriculum promoted children's creativity, with a strong focus on the arts and dramatics. Pratt provided children with extensive firsthand experiences in their environment through weekly field trips (Wolfe, 2000), which led to investigations and follow-up activities. For example, after visiting a paper mill, the children delved into an in-depth study of how paper is made.

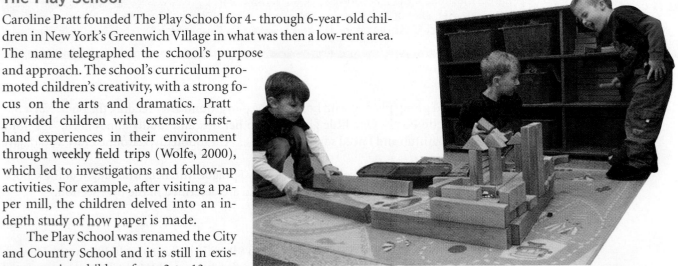

Caroline Pratt's invention of wooden unit blocks was a major contribution to early childhood education that countless children have enjoyed and benefited from. Research continues to uncover new and lasting learning benefits of block play.

The Play School was renamed the City and Country School and it is still in existence serving children from 2 to 13 years of age. A recent message on the school's website (www.cityandcountry.org) told of

What Works

Caroline Pratt's Unit Blocks

Terence and Sam are building tracks for their subway train. "It isn't finished," Terence says. "Let's make the dark part where it's got a roof [the underground]." He starts to lay blocks along the side and then a roof.

"Wait, that's not going to work," Sam worries. "The subway cars can't get in. We need to make it higher for them."

After some trial and error, the boys use taller blocks for the tunnel sides, add a roof and run the train underneath, shouting, "Yay, we did it!"

The wooden unit blocks Terence and Sam are using are among the most popular and highly regarded play and learning materials for young children. In the early 1900s when teacher Caroline Pratt designed these blocks—called *unit blocks* because each block is a fraction or multiple of the standard unit—she was most interested in providing open-ended tools to promote children's creative play. But many learning possibilities emerged. As children built with the blocks, they developed their fine motor skills; classified blocks, ordered by size and measured; explored symmetry, balance, and stability; discovered the mathematical relationships among the blocks (e.g., two small blocks equal one longer block); engaged in pretend play; worked and solved problems together; and did many other things that would contribute to their development and give them hours of pleasure.

Today, researchers agree that unit blocks are indeed valuable learning materials. Because of the spatial and mathematical relationships that exist between the types of unit blocks, researchers studying children's math development and learning have been particularly interested in the effects of block play. Young children's spontaneous activities with blocks do in fact include mathematical play and exploration of spatial relationships. Research suggests that benefits from block play persist over the years.

Evidence also indicates that teachers make a difference in the complexity level of children's constructions and the outcomes of their block play. Children's block structures are more complex when teachers talk with children during their play, saying, for example, "What would happen if . . . ?" or "Sometimes people use a block to join a structure. . . ." And children are especially likely to develop math concepts in block play if teachers introduce math vocabulary and engage children in mathematical thinking related to their play. For example, the teacher might comment, "For your wall you have the blocks standing on their thin edge" or "Hmm, you've run out of the long blocks for your road. What can you do? . . . And how many will you need?" When teachers give voice to thought and extend children's thinking, they enhance the learning potential of an already valuable and much-loved learning material—unit blocks.

Based on *Mathematics Learning in Early Childhood: Paths Toward Excellence and Equity*, by C. T. Cross, T. A. Woods, & H. Schweingruber (Eds.), Committee on Early Childhood Mathematics, and National Research Council, 2009, Washington, DC: National Academies Press.

a 3-year-old group playing with boxes on the playground after reading the book *Not a Box* by Antoinette Portis. One little girl stood on her box and loudly announced, "It's not a box. It's a bathtub and I need some conditioner." Undoubtedly, Caroline Pratt would have loved it.

One of Pratt's closest colleagues was Lucy Sprague Mitchell, who taught at the school. Mitchell's enormous contributions to the field are described in the next section.

Lucy Sprague Mitchell

Lucy Sprague Mitchell (1878–1967) has been identified as a major link between Dewey's progressive education movement of the early 20th century and NAEYC's current concept of high-quality, developmentally appropriate education (P. Greenberg, 1987). Indeed, her life spanned the period from the beginning of John Dewey's work to the birth of Head Start in

1965. In the sections that follow, we describe her early life, educational experiments and her ideas about curriculum, and the important role of Bank Street College, which she founded.

Mitchell's Early Years

Lucy Sprague Mitchell was a brilliant woman who studied at Teachers College with John Dewey and Edward Thorndike, the father of educational measurement and statistical research. Her life's work drew on both of these influences—a progressive philosophy combined with research-based practice. Mitchell focused her work on improving the lives of children through school reform.

The Bureau of Educational Experiments

In 1916, using inherited funds, Mitchell launched the Bureau of Educational Experiments (B.E.E.) to teach teachers and conduct research. The goals of the Bureau of Educational Experiments (Wolfe, 2000) were to:

- Focus on child development rather than learning specific curriculum
- Take a whole-child approach to learning and development
- Observe how children's development is stimulated by experiences and activities
- Focus on scientific measurement of stages of development and establishing norms (representing the influence of Arnold Gesell as well as Thorndike).

Bank Street College

When the bureau moved to 69 Bank Street, its name was changed to Bank Street College of Education. A graduate program in teacher education, Bank Street College played essential roles in the history of early childhood education and continues to do so. We can only mention a few here. Most notably, Mitchell's educational philosophy, as developed through her work at the City and Country School, emphasized children's firsthand experiences and play. Her ideas came to be called the **Bank Street approach**. In this model, children's experiences in the "here and now" provide the launching pad for their learning. These experiences, such as the field trips or projects described earlier, gradually widen children's horizons beyond the here and now. The concept is that curriculum should be based on individual children's development, and that learning occurs through interaction with the environment and other people (Mitchell & David, 1992). The Bank Street approach has been widely influential in early childhood curriculum development, especially in teaching social studies.

One element of the Bank Street approach that has sometimes been underemphasized is the role of the teacher. In Mitchell's words, "We were looking at children learning, and *intentionally* facilitating the process every day" (P. Greenberg, 1987, p. 75). Read the feature *Becoming an Intentional Teacher: Expanding Children's Experience* for an example of the teacher's role in the Bank Street approach.

The Writer's Workshops for Children's Authors

Mitchell herself was a prolific writer and authored a series of children's books. She created a writer's workshop for authors of children's books at Bank Street in 1937, which offered scholarships to ensure racial and socioeconomic diversity. The writer's laboratory was established to help authors better understand children's development and interests, and to promote their use of the rhythms and rhymes of language that are so important and enjoyable for children (Wolfe, 2000). Among the best-known writers who participated in the workshop were Margaret Wise Brown and Ruth Krauss. Brown's books *Goodnight Moon* and *The Runaway Bunny* remain classics, as does *The Carrot Seed* by Krauss.

Near the end of Lucy Sprague Mitchell's life, she was instrumental in numerous national efforts to expand early childhood education beyond laboratory schools and use it for true social reform. She lived to see the Bank Street approach used as the model for the Head Start program, a cornerstone of the war on poverty. Head Start is also known for its emphasis on parent involvement, which was another part of the nursery school movement, described in the next section.

Bank Street approach Originating with Lucy Sprague Mitchell at Bank Street College, a curriculum framework based on individual children's development, emphasizing that learning begins in children's experiences in the immediate environment (here and now).

Becoming an Intentional Teacher

Expanding Children's Experience

Here's What Happened The preschool I work in uses the Bank Street curriculum approach. I was planning to do some cooking with my 4-year-old class, so I wanted them to learn more about where foods come from. In our urban neighborhood, most children have limited experience with growing things; however, there is a community garden that a few of the families participate in, and those children are involved with planting, watching things grow, and eating the produce. In talking with the "garden families" to find out what they grow and what the children do in the garden, I found that the parents were eager to send in a tomato or zucchini from their gardens for the class to see and taste. We did that first, and then made a trip to the garden. After the trip, I encouraged the children to draw and write about what they had seen, and I brought in library books like *The Carrot Seed* (Krauss, 1945) and *Whose Garden Is It?* (Hoberman, 2004) to share with them.

Here's What I Was Thinking When children have little experience with growing things, they eat fruits, vegetables, and other foods without understanding where they come from. Even if an adult tells them, "Tomatoes come from the ground," it doesn't compute. There's a gulf between their experience and what someone tells them or shows them in a book, and this gulf limits their understanding, interest, and willingness to try new foods. Part of what should be happening in preschool, and later in school, is bridging this gulf, and sometimes the best way to do that is with direct hands-on experience. Other children in the group may know about gardening and growing things, but haven't seen pictures representing them or read stories about them, so providing that experience is valuable in the early childhood classroom too.

Parent Cooperative Preschools

As early as 1916, parents organized to start their own nursery schools. In these programs, which are called *parent cooperatives* or *co-ops*, the parents "own" and administer the program. They hire a teacher and take turns volunteering in the classroom as a second staff member. Most parent co-ops throughout the 20th century used a play-based, progressive education–influenced approach.

The number of parent cooperative nursery schools grew rapidly in the 1950s and 1960s, and through the leadership of Katherine Whiteside Taylor an association was formed, Parent Cooperative Preschools International (www.preschools.coop.org). Many key leaders in the field, such as Lilian Katz, were involved in the co-op movement, initially as parents. In recent years, the number of parent cooperative preschools has declined due to the increase of mothers in the workforce. Nevertheless, the movement reinforced the integral role of parents in early childhood education.

In the previous sections, we discussed the interconnected stories of the kindergarten, progressive education, and nursery school movements. Many more outstanding leaders contributed to these efforts than we can describe here. Table 2.1 on pages 42–45 is designed to fill in the chronology. In the next section, we turn to the parallel story of the child care movement.

■ The Child Care Movement

The history of child care in the United States followed a different path from that of kindergarten and preschool. To briefly summarize, kindergartens and preschools grew out of child study, focused on middle-class children, and were associated with education and development. By contrast, child care grew out of social welfare efforts for poor families and focused on the need to support working parents. Consequently, child care became associated with physical care rather than education.

In the later part of the 20th century and into the 21st century, these differences have become less distinct. However, these histories still play out in public policy and attitudes. For example, federal child care funding is part of public assistance for needy families, whereas prekindergarten support comes from state education agencies. In the sections that follow, we describe some of the key events and people involved in the history of the child care movement.

McMillan Sisters

Margaret McMillan (1860–1931) and Rachel McMillan (1859–1917) worked to improve the lives of young children in London and North America during the early 20th century. The purpose of their work was to offer children a temporary alternative to the dreadful living conditions in the London slums, which severely damaged the health of most poor children. Accordingly, they set up a health clinic, a nursery school (they coined the phrase) for children under age 5, and a training school for teachers.

The McMillan sisters developed a model open-air nursery that was unique in emphasizing outdoor play, nutritious food, cleanliness, and rest to promote healthy development. The program was also educational. These centers for working families were called **day nurseries**—the forerunner of present-day child care centers.

The McMillan sisters' work was influential in the United States. Several Americans studied with them in England, including Abigail Eliot (1892–1992), who subsequently imported many of their ideas and founded one of the first nursery schools in the United States in 1922.

As always happens, events in the larger context had a major impact on early childhood education and particularly on the history of child care. These included the Great Depression and World War II.

Works Progress Administration Nurseries

During the Great Depression of the 1930s, the Works Progress Administration (WPA) was established to address the high unemployment rate (25%), as well as to build needed public works throughout the country. One of the WPA programs established in 1933 was the Federal Emergency Relief Nursery Schools. The purpose of the **WPA nurseries**, which were open from 9 AM to 5 PM, was to support the economy by providing jobs for those who worked on the site, and by providing child care to families seeking work (Nourot, 2005). Like the day nurseries of the McMillan sisters, WPA centers focused on promoting physical care and healthy living habits (Nourot, 2005). But in contrast to the McMillan sisters' vision, most WPA centers did not emphasize education.

The WPA nurseries had both positive and negative effects on early childhood education. Because day nurseries served children from poor families, the idea of expanding nursery education to all children was born (Nourot, 2000). However, the rapid expansion of WPA nursery schools meant that teachers were hired with minimal training. This cycle of expanding services without attention to ensuring qualified staff has plagued the child care field throughout its existence. As the Depression ended, so too did the WPA nursery schools. But a major national crisis—World War II—followed shortly, leading to another important chapter in the history of child care.

The Lanham Act

World War II necessitated full deployment of not only men into the armed services but women into the workplace to replace the men and support industry. This massive workforce shift required immediate child care assistance, which the federal government provided in the form of the **Lanham Act**. This legislation funded emergency work-site child care centers, which operated for 10 to 12 hours per day.

day nurseries Programs designed to serve working families in the late 19th and early 20th centuries; the forerunner of present-day child care centers.

WPA nurseries Federal emergency relief nursery schools, funded by the Works Progress Administration (WPA) during the Great Depression, designed to support the economy by providing jobs for those who worked on the site and child care services to families seeking work.

Lanham Act Federal legislation to provide emergency child care and other services for families employed in the war effort during World War II.

One of the most famous centers was located at the Kaiser Shipbuilding company in Oregon. Kaiser was the largest of the Lanham Act centers, operating 24 hours a day all year long. Lois Meek Stoltz was the director, and the manager was Jimmy Hymes, who later became a professor and president of NAEYC. The program, still considered a model, provided health services and nutritious meals for children and mothers, parent education, teacher training, and a play-based educational experience for children.

As happened with the WPA nurseries, the Lanham Act centers ended along with the war. Child care was no longer supported because mothers left the workforce as fathers reentered it. These high-quality centers remain an ideal for working families; yet it wasn't until the 1980s that employer-sponsored child care again became a major sector of the early childhood field.

The stories related thus far of the kindergarten, nursery school, and child care movements were lived and recorded by members of the majority group—white, European Americans. However, African Americans were also part of these stories and have made significant contributions to the history of early childhood education, which we discuss in the next section.

African American Leaders in Early Childhood Education

History is written by those who gain the largest amount of power. Throughout U.S. history, African Americans have been denied power beginning with slavery, when it was illegal to teach slaves to read and write, much less attend school. Once schooling became available, it was legally segregated by race until the 1954 *Brown v. Board of Education* Supreme Court decision banned the practice. But even after desegregation became the law of the land, equal rights and equal educational opportunity for all racial groups were still denied.

Over the centuries of enslavement, a few formal, mostly religious schools provided education for African American children (C. E. Cunningham & Osborn, 1979). By the 1830s, however, such schools were prohibited. Educating slaves was a clandestine and dangerous operation, requiring courage on the part of both teachers and students. We saw earlier how Patty Smith Hill's mother was one of those who took that risk and its effect on her daughter's life choices thereafter.

African American Kindergartens and Teacher Training

After the Civil War, education became the vehicle for advancement of African Americans, propelled by national leaders such as Mary McLeod Bethune (1875–1955), who founded Bethune-Cookman College in 1904, and became an effective voice for civil rights and equal educational opportunity. Between 1865 and 1890, prominent African American institutions of higher education were founded such as Howard University (1867), Hampton University (1868), Tuskegee University (1881), and Spelman College (1881). These and other historically black colleges and universities (HBCUs) made important contributions to the study of child development, then usually housed in Home Economics departments (C. E. Cunningham & Osborn, 1979).

Early childhood education was seen as an important foundation for future advancement. Many HBCUs operated teacher education programs and laboratory schools (Osborn, 1991). These programs reflected the prevailing philosophies of Pestalozzi, Froebel, and later Dewey and G. Stanley Hall. By 1873, Hampton Institute (now University) in Virginia had a kindergarten teacher training program and a children's school that was influenced by Montessori's ideas about children learning practical skills (C. E. Cunningham & Osborn, 1979). Tuskegee in Alabama offered training for parents in child-rearing methods. In the early 1900s, Howard University in Washington, D.C., awarded degrees in kindergarten education, and Atlanta University operated a Froebelian kindergarten and an elementary and high school for African American students (J. E. Hale, personal communication, February 2009).

The National Association of Colored Women (NACW) was founded in 1896. Its first president, Mary Church Terrell (1863–1954), was a strong supporter of early childhood education. Under her leadership, the NACW helped establish kindergartens for African American children throughout the country (C. E. Cunningham & Osborn, 1979).

Historically black colleges and universities have played important roles in the study of child development and the education of future generations of teachers. Although not well known, the contributions of African American early childhood educators have been significant in the field's history.

African Americans and the Nursery School Movement

In 1927, five years after Abigail Eliot started the first nursery school in the United States, Dorothy Howard founded the "first Black nursery school" in Washington, D.C., which she operated for more than 50 years and served children of professional families (Simpson, n.d., p. 262). Spelman College in Atlanta opened the first laboratory school in an African American college in 1930, under the direction of Pearlie Reed (C. E. Cunningham & Osborn, 1979). This school used the "whole-child" philosophy of the larger nursery school movement. Still in operation, the school is named for Marian Wright Edelman, founder and president of the Children's Defense Fund, the nation's premier children's advocacy organization (www.spelman.edu).

From 1929 to 1969, Oneida Cockrell (1900–1970) directed the Rosenwald-Garden Apartment Nursery School and Kindergarten in Chicago (Simpson, n.d.). This program became a model for children's centers in urban apartment dwellings, and also served children with disabilities early on. Cockrell participated in the White House Conference on Children and Youth in 1950. Cockrell also taught at the University of Chicago laboratory school.

Spelman College produced many future early childhood luminaries. Its first graduate student, Ida Jones Curry, became head of teacher training at Hampton Institute in 1932 (C. E. Cunningham & Osborn, 1979). Curry worked with the McMillan sisters for a time in London, and was a leader in NANE.

Among Curry's students at Hampton was Evangeline Ward (1920–1985), who made significant contributions to the field (Simpson, n.d.). Ward was president of NAEYC from 1970 to 1974, and not only was she the first African American president of the organization but also the only president to ever serve two terms. In the mid-1970s, Ward (1977) was the first to take on the challenge of developing a code of ethics for the profession. She was also the first executive director of the Child Development Associate (CDA) national credentialing program.

Many other African American early childhood leaders played major roles in the field's history. Space does not permit citing all of their accomplishments. At a time when their educational opportunity was severely limited, these professionals overcame huge obstacles to earn doctoral degrees at major national and international universities, to educate and mentor future generations of teachers, and to voluntarily serve in professional organizations. The harvest of their work is still being reaped, but was essential as the field expanded exponentially with the launch of Head Start in the mid-1960s, which brought together the strands of early childhood history.

■ Head Start: Bringing the Stories Together

The Civil Rights movement of the 1960s brought about real change in virtually every aspect of society. Early childhood education was no exception. In response to the call for

MyEducationLab

Go to the Assignments and Activities section of Topic 3: Family/Community in the MyEducationLab for your course and complete the activity entitled *Head Start*. How does Head Start today reflect the lessons learned from early childhood history?

equal opportunity in this country, President Lyndon Johnson launched the War on Poverty. One of the cornerstones of this far-reaching effort, and the only one that still exists, was the Head Start program. Head Start represents a coming together of the nursery school movement, which had previously served middle-class families, and the child care movement, which originated to serve the indigent and working poor. The following sections describe how the key elements of Head Start reflect the lessons learned from early childhood history.

A Comprehensive Program

Just like Patty Smith Hill, Maria Montessori, the McMillan sisters, and so many others, the framers of Head Start believed in serving the whole child. Early childhood education has long been a multidisciplinary field. Head Start reflects this history as a comprehensive program providing health, mental health, social services, and parent involvement, in addition to education.

Head Start was also a pioneer in fully including children with disabilities, who must constitute 10% of the population served. This mandate harkens back to the lessons learned from Montessori about the benefits of early intervention. Early education for all children with disabilities is a relatively recent phenomenon. For an overview of its history, see the lens on *Including All Children: Early Childhood Special Education in Historical Perspective.*

An Educational Program

The educational model for the Head Start program is the nursery school, specifically the Bank Street model (P. Greenberg, 1987). Over the years, Head Start's educational program has changed as new knowledge about learning and teaching has emerged. But its core is developmentally appropriate practice, with its foundation going as far back as Comenius and Pestalozzi.

Including All Children

Early Childhood Special Education in Historical Perspective

When I first met my neighbor Clark—a large, friendly man about my age—I was struck by his delightful sense of humor and love of fishing and television. Even a brief encounter with Clark revealed that he had an intellectual disability, but spending time with him was always great fun. One day, while reading a book on my porch, I spied Clark watching me. When I asked him to join me, he replied, "I'd like to read a book." An older neighbor who'd known Clark since he was a child later explained, "Clark started school like all the other kids, back in the mid-1950s, but after a few days, they sent him home. They said, 'It didn't work out.'" Clark never returned to school.

If Clark had been born today, he would probably be diagnosed as having mild mental retardation. His life experience would have been quite different due to major changes in special education services. In the latter part of the 20th century, parents of children with disabilities who were unable to obtain services, formed organizations such as the Association for Retarded Children (ARC) and United Cerebral Palsy and also started preschools. With the advocacy of parents, special educators, and other professionals, public laws began to change. In 1972, the government mandated that 10% of Head Start's student population be children with special needs.

By far the most important event in the history of special education was passage of Public Law 94-142, the Education for All Handicapped Children Act of 1975, which was renamed the Individuals with Disabilities Education Act (IDEA) in 1990. This law established standards for how public schools must serve children with disabilities, from ages 3 to 21. A few years later, Public Law 99-457 extended services to children from birth to 3 years of age with emphasis on the role of families in early intervention. In addition, the Americans with Disabilities (ADA) Act of 1990 requires that programs be accessible for persons with disabilities, and prohibits child care centers from discriminating on the basis of disability.

The history of special education goes back to well before Maria Montessori demonstrated the power of early intervention to change children's lives. It is the story of many people working together to make a difference on behalf of children like Clark.

Because it was based on the laboratory nursery school model, most Head Start programs were and still are half-day. This is changing as more families need full-day child care, but Head Start has yet to completely merge the child care and nursery school threads of the field.

The rapid launch and expansion of Head Start meant that, like the WPA and Lanham Act centers, a large workforce of teachers was needed on short notice. As a result, minimal training was required for teachers. Efforts to improve staff qualifications as well as compensation have been challenging ever since.

Lessons learned throughout the long history of early childhood education were brought to bear when Head Start was launched in the mid-1960s.

A Parent Involvement Program

A core component of Head Start's mission is parent involvement. Here we see the influence of Lucy Sprague Mitchell and Jimmy Hymes, and the parent cooperative movement. In Head Start, however, parents are not only involved in the classroom; they are also part of the governance of the program, acting in major decision-making roles.

As part of the War on Poverty, Head Start's mandate included hiring parents as teachers and in other positions. At times, as many as one-third of the staff have been parents in the program. As in the case of WPA nurseries, however, hiring parents has presented the challenges of ensuring that the teachers are professionally qualified and created the need for a professional development infrastructure.

The National Laboratory

An important part of Head Start's mission is to act as the national laboratory for the field. In this role, Head Start has funded seminal research and contributed to the development of curriculum and teacher training models. Head Start programs also partner with universities on research projects. In this capacity, Head Start has supplanted the child study laboratory schools of the early 20th century.

Head Start programs are locally administered and controlled. But Head Start has maintained its integrity and consistency despite its national scope because every grantee must meet the Head Start Program Performance Standards. These standards address, at least for Head Start, the recurring questions that confront the early childhood field.

Building on a Tradition of Excellence: Lessons from History

The fundamental questions that have faced the field since its inception continue to dominate the conversation today: How is quality defined in programs for children? What should be the qualifications for teachers and how should they be prepared? What are the goals for children's learning and development? What should be the content of the curriculum and how should it be taught?

Looking back through history, we find that many ideas are revisited: stages of development, active learning, children's interests, sensory learning, positive guidance, image of the child, the teachers' role, and the role of materials and environments. But differences emerge as well. Today we view the teacher's role as more intentional than our predecessors did, and we no longer see children's development as a natural unfolding. Instead, we better understand the interaction of environment and biology. In addition, developmental stages are not rigid as previously assumed. Standards and approaches need to be flexible and changing—based on new knowledge—unlike Maria Montessori and Susan Blow who refused to change their views.

The most basic history lessons that early childhood teachers should never forget include these:

- We all need to learn from children, as did all of the historical figures discussed in this chapter and as Caroline Pratt wisely put it.
- We need to draw on science and the wisdom of experience, as Patty Smith Hill and Lucy Sprague Mitchell modeled for us.
- And as Patty Smith Hill believed, it is always valuable to listen to opposing points of view and learn from them.

Revisiting the College Classroom

MyEducationLab

To assess your understanding of the history of early childhood education, go to the Book Specific Resources section in the MyEducationLab for your course, select *Effective Practices in Early Childhood Education*, Chapter 2 of the Study Plan, and then complete the multiple choice questions and activities.

Take a moment to revisit the classroom observations of the college students in the opening vignette of this chapter. The traces of early childhood history should now be apparent. The students saw Comenius's picture books and alphabet books, evidence of Froebel's gifts in the wooden cube and parquetry blocks, and the legacy of Maria Montessori in the child-sized furniture and sandpaper letters. They also observed children's active play with Caroline Pratt's unit blocks, and Patty Smith Hill's beloved dramatic play. Their firehouse field trips are reminiscent of John Dewey's call for active learning and integrated curriculum, as well as Lucy Sprague Mitchell's Bank Street approach. The woodworking tables and cooking are more evidence of Dewey's influence. Finally, the students saw the lasting contribution of Lucy Sprague Mitchell's writer's workshops in Margaret Wise Brown's *Goodnight Moon*, and the enduring joy of singing Patty Smith Hill's "Happy Birthday" on one child's most special day.

Chapter Summary

- Studying history is valuable because it helps people today understand current issues, avoid getting stuck in the past, aspire to make a difference for children, and advocate for change.
- Different periods of history have had different perspectives on children and childhood, which have implications for how children are treated and what kinds of education they are provided.
- Early education in the United States was strongly influenced by western European ideas, such as those of Comenius, Pestalozzi, Froebel, and Montessori. Although European ideas are not the only, nor necessarily the best, educational concepts in the world, current practices strongly reflect these early influences.
- The kindergarten movement in the United States was based directly on the work of Froebel led by Elizabeth Peabody, Susan Blow, and others who spread his ideas widely through teacher training and founding the International Kindergarten Union.
- The progressive education movement led by John Dewey had a profound impact on education in the United States, especially early childhood education, whose principles of developmentally appropriate practice are congruent with progressive ideas.
- The nursery school movement, which grew out of the child study movement, eventually launched the wider field of early childhood education through the leadership of Patty Smith Hill and Lucy Sprague Mitchell, among many others.
- The child care movement grew out of social welfare efforts for poor families, focused on the need to support working parents, and became associated with physical care rather than education, although this division is changing.
- African Americans played significant roles in the history of early childhood education although their contributions are not well documented.
- The launch of Head Start in the mid-1960s brought together the various strands of early childhood history, which are reflected in its comprehensive services, a Bank Street–based educational program, parent involvement, and its role as a national laboratory.

key terms

absorbent mind
Bank Street approach
child-centered curriculum
child study movement
competent child
constructivism
day nurseries
Froebel's occupations and gifts
integrated curriculum
Lanham Act
nursery schools
progressive education movement
WPA nurseries

reading & websites

Hinitz, B. F. (2009). History of early childhood education in multicultural perspective. In J. L. Roopnarine & J. E. Johnson (Eds.), *Approaches to early childhood education* (5th ed., pp. 3–24). Upper Saddle River, NJ: Merrill/Pearson.

Hirsch, E. (1996). *The block book*. Washington, DC: NAEYC.

NAEYC. (2001). *NAEYC at 75: 1926–2001*. Washington, DC: Author.

Wortham, S. (2002). *Childhood: 1892–2002*. Wheaton, MD: Association for Childhood Education International.

American Montessori Society
amshq.org

Association for Childhood Education International
www.acei.org

International Step by Step Association
www.issa.nl.org

Office of Head Start
http://eclkc.ohs.acf.hhs.gov/hslc

observe, reflect, decide

1. Visit an art gallery or examine an art history textbook. Look for paintings of children dated from the 14th century to the present day. Reflect on what the concept of "childhood" has meant at various points in history as depicted in the paintings. Decide how the image of childhood has changed over time, and what implications that might have for how children are treated.
2. Observe in a Montessori school. Notice the types of materials that are available, how they are used by children, and what teachers are doing while children use the materials. Reflect on how the school's interpretation of the Montessori Method compares to what you have read about Montessori's ideas. How do you think Maria Montessori would have evaluated the classroom you observed?
3. Observe the environment and teaching practices in public school prekindergarten and kindergarten classrooms. Reflect on what Patty Smith Hill might have thought about present-day early childhood programs in public schools. Decide what you think is congruent with her views of education and what is contrary.
4. Visit a toy store or explore the website of a toy company. What kinds of toys are popular with various age groups? How do today's toys reflect the changing images of children and the ideas and contributions of the historical figures in early childhood education described in this chapter?
5. Go to the website of the Office of Head Start and review the Head Start Program Performance Standards. Consider how these standards reflect the coming together of the various stories in early childhood history: the kindergarten, child care, and nursery school movements.

3 Understanding and Applying Developmentally Appropriate Practice

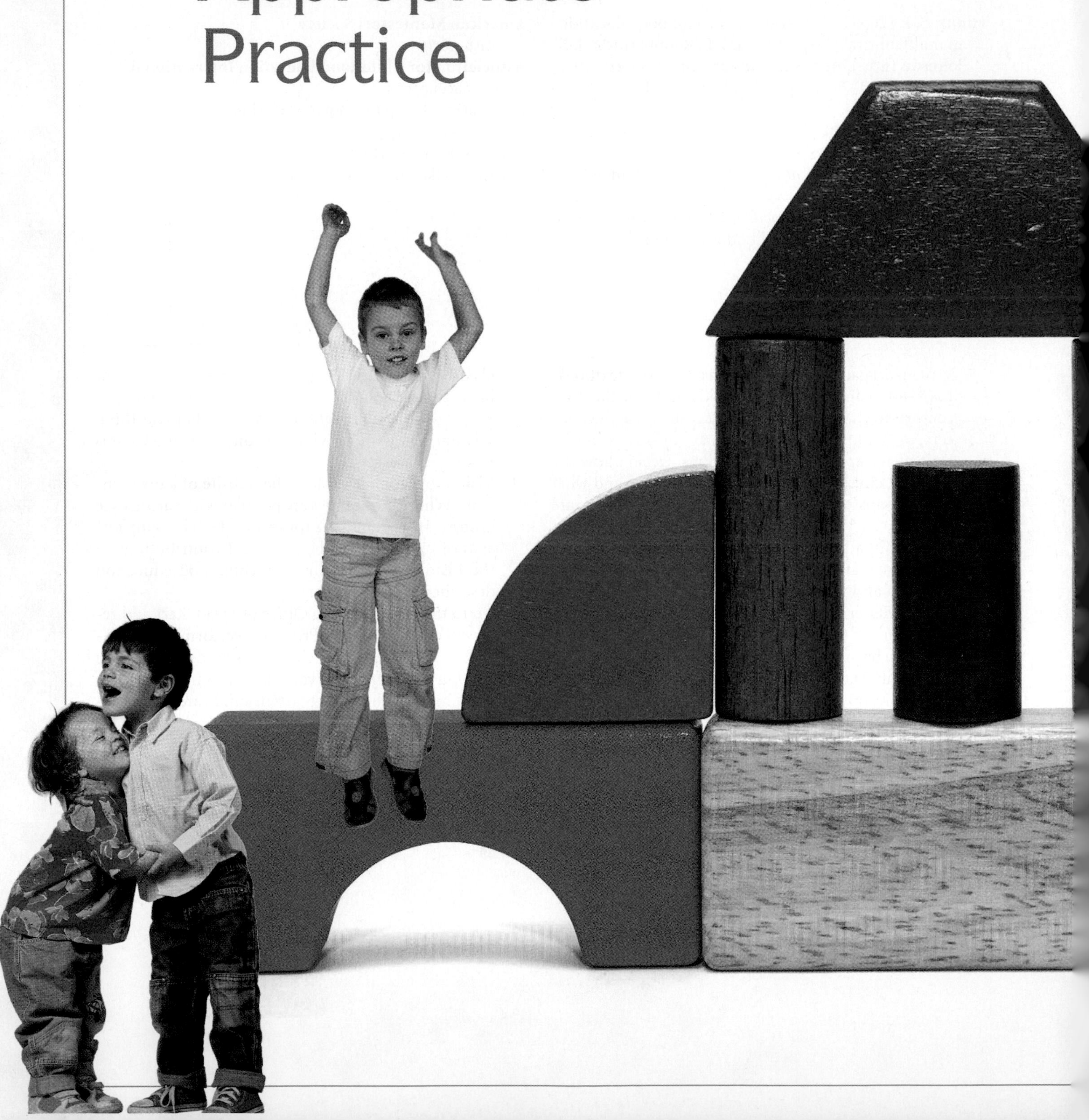

Thinking Ahead

1. What is developmentally appropriate practice?
2. What does it mean to be an intentional teacher?
3. How do teachers make decisions about what is developmentally appropriate for young children?
4. What five tasks make up the role of the early childhood teacher?
5. What does it mean to "widen the lens" when considering issues of practice? Why is this a useful way of thinking?
6. What does research say about developmentally appropriate practice?

Today is Olivia's first day of preschool in her Head Start program at the local elementary school that her older brothers also attend. They have been teasing her about how hard school is and she is a little fearful as well as excited. She hesitantly enters the building clutching the postcard her teacher sent her to welcome her to school. Aware that several of the newly enrolled children and their families speak Spanish at home, Olivia's teacher, Mr. Washington, has arranged for a translator to be present this morning. He has also learned a few key phrases in Spanish himself, including how to say, "I'm sorry, I don't speak Spanish, but Ms. Lopez is here to help."

When Olivia's grandmother arrives at the classroom door, Mr. Washington greets her in Spanish and pulls the translator into the conversation. Olivia's brothers and mother speak English but her grandmother only speaks Spanish. Then Mr. Washington stoops down to Olivia's eye level and greets her warmly with a smile, "I'm so happy that you are here, Olivia. We're going to have lots of fun playing, listening to stories, and making friends." Mr. Washington offers his hand to Olivia and escorts her to a cubby with her name on it where she can store her belongings. "We're going to have some quiet play time while the children are arriving and then we'll eat breakfast

together. Your grandmother says that you like to do puzzles so I'll show you where we keep them," Mr. Washington says. Olivia feels good already because her teacher is so nice and she likes the chairs and tables that are just her size. The puzzles are ones that she can put together all by herself, too. Olivia is already feeling comfortable at school on her first day because her teacher understands and engages in developmentally appropriate practice. ▲

Throughout this book and throughout your studies and work as an early childhood educator, you will hear the term *developmentally appropriate practice*. In this chapter we discuss the evolution of this concept and examine how it is used in the classroom. We also discuss the concept of becoming an intentional teacher. Next, we address the question of how to decide what is developmentally appropriate and the multifaceted role of the early childhood teacher. We also introduce the idea of "widening the lens" as a metaphor for thinking in less polarized ways about best practice.

The concepts addressed in this chapter are part of the foundational knowledge of early childhood education. These topics provide a basic framework for organizing much of your beginning knowledge. A large body of literature exists about child development and its application to early childhood practice (see Copple & Bredekamp, 2009; Gestwicki, 2006; Kostelnik, Soderman, & Whiren, 2006; Spodek & Saracho, 2006). This chapter considers some of this literature, as well as the definition, principles, and guidelines for developmentally appropriate practice as described by the National Association for the Education of Young Children (NAEYC, 2009a).

Defining Developmentally Appropriate Practice

Over time, the phrase *developmentally appropriate practice* (sometimes abbreviated as D.A.P.) has been defined and used in different ways. Its definition has evolved as new research and knowledge have become available.

What Is Developmentally Appropriate Practice?

Developmentally appropriate practice is teaching that is attuned to children's ages, experience, abilities, and interests, and that helps them attain challenging and achievable goals. The foundations of developmentally appropriate practice, as it is defined today, lie in the history of early childhood education. Most fundamental is the premise that teaching young children should be based on what is known about how they develop and learn optimally.

Within the field of developmental psychology, the concept of *developmentally appropriate* has been widely used for more than a century and refers to age-related and individual human variation. Early childhood educators have long used the phrase *developmentally appropriate* to describe materials, learning experiences, or expectations for children of varying ages. For example, during the late 1970s, the federal government charged the Head Start program with helping children acquire basic educational skills. Most early childhood educators agreed that this goal was acceptable if, and only if, the program was implemented in a "developmentally appropriate way" (J. Klein, personal communication, 1980).

developmentally appropriate practice (D.A.P.) Ways of teaching that engage children's interests and adapt for their age, experience, and ability to help them meet challenging and achievable learning goals.

The NAEYC Position Statement on Developmentally Appropriate Practice

The concept of developmentally appropriate practice gained widespread recognition and influence in the mid-1980s when NAEYC published position statements on developmen-

tally appropriate practice (Bredekamp, 1987). A **position statement** is a document that articulates a stance, usually research based, that an organization is taking in response to an issue or a problem. Based on new research, the experience of practitioners, and the changing contexts in which early childhood education occurs, NAEYC revised its statement on developmentally appropriate practice in the mid-1990s (Bredekamp & Copple, 1997), and again in 2009 (NAEYC, 2009a).

NAEYC's current position statement (2009a) describes principles and guidelines for teaching young children from birth through age 8. NAEYC also presents recommended practices for different age groups: infants and toddlers, preschoolers, kindergartners, and children in the primary grades (Copple & Bredekamp, 2009). The position statement is widely used as a summary of the field's best thinking, a defense of its valued practices, and an advocacy tool for improving programs for young children.

MyEducationLab

Go to the Professional Perspectives section in Topic 8: DAP/Teaching Strategies in the MyEducationLab for your course and select the video entitled *NAEYC Position Statement on Developmentally Appropriate Practice* and watch and listen to Sue Bredekamp discuss this topic.

Each revision of the statement is in response to particular trends occurring at the time. In 1986–1987, NAEYC sought to clarify the term to help professionals consistently interpret its standards for early childhood program accreditation. A second motivation at that time was to counter the trend toward "push-down" curriculum in schools, in which content that was previously taught in first grade was being taught in kindergarten or even preschool (Shepard & Smith, 1988). This shift in curriculum expectations led to increasing numbers of children struggling or failing in their earliest school experiences or being judged not ready for kindergarten.

The appropriateness of expectations for children, as well as curriculum and teaching practices, continues to be an issue addressed in each subsequent revision of NAEYC's statement. In addition, the 1997 revision brought more attention to the critical role of culture and language in development, the inclusion of children with disabilities, and the teacher's role as intentional decision maker (Bredekamp, 1997a). The 2009 statement continues these emphases and also responds to current issues such as addressing the achievement gap and alignment from pre-K to grade 3.

Over the years, the position statement has generated controversy, including questions about whether the recommended practices apply equally well to diverse groups of children (e.g., Hyun, 1998; Mallory & New, 1994; New, 2007). In turn, new research and critiques in the literature and in professional forums continue to stimulate productive discussions among early childhood educators about what is best for young children.

MyEducationLab

Go to the Assignments and Activities section of Topic 4: Observation/Assessment in the MyEducationLab for your course and complete the activity entitled *Observing Children in Authentic Contexts*. As you watch the video and answer the accompanying questions, consider how this teacher meets these 3-year-old children where they are and helps them achieve new goals.

Developmentally Appropriate Practice in the Classroom

Developmentally appropriate practice begins with early childhood educators' knowledge of how children learn and develop. Its ultimate goal is to promote the development and enhance the learning of each individual child served. "Developmentally appropriate practice" is used by some as a short-hand term for the value of play or letting children be children, not pushing them to grow up too soon. In fact, these views of developmentally appropriate practice are only partial truths. Developmentally appropriate practice is a term that is used within the early childhood profession to describe the complex work of the early childhood teacher.

Knowing how children learn and develop is essential for teachers of young children. The more they know about and "tune in" to the way children think and learn, the more effective their teaching and the more satisfying their work. To successfully engage in developmentally appropriate practice (Copple & Bredekamp, 2006), teachers need to:

- Meet children where they are, as individuals and as a group.
- Help each child attain challenging and achievable goals that contribute to his or her ongoing development and learning.

position statement A document that articulates a stance, usually research based, that an organization is taking in response to an issue or a problem.

Meeting Children Where They Are

Knowing what children are generally capable of and how they learn, within a given age range, provides teachers with a starting point for planning and organizing a program. But

In developmentally appropriate classrooms, teachers get to know each child as an individual and build a positive relationship. What is this teacher doing to "meet children where they are" as individuals?

such a broad picture is not enough to achieve developmentally appropriate practice. Teachers must go beyond what is "typical"; they must recognize that they will have little success if they try to teach everyone the same way. They must also recognize that if their expectations are too high, children become frustrated; if their expectations are too low, their students will become bored. In either case—teaching only what is "typical" or having unrealistic expectations—children will fail to make learning progress.

Good teachers continually observe children's engagement with materials, activities, and people in order to learn about each child's abilities, interests, and needs. Based on this information, they plan curriculum and adapt their teaching strategies to help children make continued progress. Meeting children where they are might look something like this:

> Nathan only knows a few letters, he does not sit still during story time, and he is significantly behind on many of the kindergarten literacy goals. His teacher knows, however, that all kinds of transportation vehicles fascinate him. On a class visit to the library, she helps Nathan locate several information books on transportation to read with him and have him take home. He especially likes one book about all kinds of trucks. To interest Nathan in learning letters and words, his teacher prints the names of the different trucks on cards for him to match with the pictures. Soon, Nathan is drawing pictures of the trucks and trying to write the words himself.
>
> Four-year-old Jamal speaks Arabic at home and is learning English at school. His teacher often reads to him in a small group, with other children whose home language is not English, using books with limited vocabulary and clear correspondence between the pictures and words. She also uses other cues to aid his understanding. For instance, she uses real objects as props when she introduces new words such as the kinds of food that the *Very Hungry Caterpillar* (Carle, 1969) is eating. She stays in close contact with his parents, communicating through a translator, to learn about the competencies he demonstrates at home, and she encourages the family to talk and read with him in their own language.

These examples demonstrate how teachers meet children where they are by assessing what they already know as well as learning about their interests. At the same time, teachers keep in mind the teaching goals.

Helping Children Reach Challenging and Achievable Goals

Meeting learners where they are is important, but it is just the beginning. As illustrated in the preceding examples, learning is most effective when materials or experiences not only build on what children already know and on what they can do, but also require them to stretch toward new skills and understandings.

Developmentally appropriate goals for a given group of children need to be realistic and attainable for most children within the age range of the group. This means they must be challenging but not so difficult that children fail to achieve them. Further, children need to have plenty of opportunities to practice their newly acquired skills to the point of mastery. Young children often initiate such practice on their own, such as when they repeatedly count the steps they climb or try time and again to balance on one foot.

Once new skills have been mastered, children need new challenges to continue to learn. These new challenges should provide children with a reasonable stretch that is "just

achievable." For example, consider a group of kindergartners learning to play catch. If the teacher consistently throws the ball way over children's heads, they will soon give up in frustration. But if she makes the task too easy—perhaps rolling the ball on the ground—most 5-year-olds would quickly grow bored and call it "baby stuff." Instead, a teacher who is taking into account what is developmentally appropriate will provide just the right amount of challenge for each child. One child will need the ball thrown right into her extended arms, while another who has had more practice will joyfully leap to catch it over her head.

> **Effective Teaching**
> To be developmentally appropriate, teaching practices must be effective—they must contribute to children's ongoing development and learning.

Teaching in a developmentally appropriate way brings together meeting the learner where he or she is and helping children achieve goals. Teachers keep the curriculum's learning goals in mind as they determine where children are and the next steps forward. What is challenging and achievable varies from one child to the next, depending on each child's level of development; prior experiences, knowledge, and skills; and the context within which the learning takes place.

To be developmentally appropriate, teaching practices must be effective—they must *contribute* to children's ongoing development and learning. That is, if children are not learning and progressing toward important outcomes, then the practices and experiences in the program are not developmentally appropriate. To ensure their practices are in fact effective and developmentally appropriate, teachers need to be intentional in everything they do.

Engaging in Intentional Teaching

To be effective in their work, teachers cannot leave important aspects of children's development and learning to chance. In everything early childhood teachers do—from organizing the environment to planning the curriculum to choosing specific teaching strategies or adapting their plans for individual children—effective teachers are **intentional teachers**. Intentional teachers have a purpose for their actions; they make decisions for a reason. The intentional teacher plans carefully in advance, but also has enough knowledge to make thoughtful decisions throughout the day, even during the unplanned, spontaneous "teachable moments" that inevitably arise.

intentional teachers Professionals who have a purpose for the decisions they make and can explain that purpose to others.

Making Purposeful Decisions

Intentional teaching and developmentally appropriate practice go hand in hand. Sometimes in early childhood classrooms where children spend significant periods of time in exploration, play, and activities they choose and pursue independently, uninformed observers may think that the situation is "anything goes." However, if the child is in a program that truly is developmentally appropriate, teachers' intentionality undergirds the entire program and all of the experiences provided. The teacher carefully organizes the environment and selects and arranges the materials to promote children's active engagement, both mental and physical.

Developmentally appropriate teaching practices must be effective. Intentional teachers don't simply assume that play is developmentally appropriate. They support children's play so that it benefits children's development as much as possible.

In planning the learning experiences, the intentional teacher thinks carefully about what will foster children's enthusiasm for learning and enable them to reach important goals in all areas of their development and learning. She regularly observes and assesses children and then uses the information gleaned

MyEducationLab

To observe an example of intentional teaching in first grade, go to the Video Examples section of Topic 7: Curriculum/Content Areas in the MyEducationLab for your course and watch the video entitled *Teaching Reading*. What is this teacher intentionally doing to support children's reading development? Can she explain how and why she makes her decisions about teaching?

to gauge her interactions with the children, both individually and in small groups, to promote ongoing learning and enable children to master new challenges.

Understanding and Explaining Decisions

Intentional teachers are able to explain the rationale for their decisions to administrators, other teachers, and family members. Intentional teachers are also alert to the need to modify plans, recognizing that there will be times when what they have planned doesn't work out. Perhaps the children will master a skill sooner than expected and lose interest in the activity; or, conversely, a task may be beyond the children's current abilities and they become confused or discouraged. In either case, an intentional teacher will have planned for such possibilities and be prepared to modify the learning experience or shift to another strategy that will be more effective in achieving the goal. Consider the following examples of practices, which are generally thought to be developmentally appropriate in light of the additional criteria of intentionality and effectiveness:

> Tiana Carstairs teaches 4-year-olds in a Head Start program. Each day she reads a different Big Book (an oversize picture book with limited text per page) to the class. The children enjoy the readings and respond readily to Tiana's questions about the letters in print or sounds they hear. She also points out concepts of print by tracking the words on the page left to right and noting how to turn the pages. An observer in Tiana's class would undoubtedly view her practice as developmentally appropriate. What the casual observer would miss, however, is that 14 of the 16 children have mastered the concepts of print that Tiana continues to teach. In addition, 4 children already know all the letters.
>
> Rather than use this same teaching strategy every day without reflection, Tiana should regularly assess children's learning so that she continually adds challenge as children achieve new goals. Although the children enjoy the Big Book readings, the limited vocabulary contained in the books is not helping them learn new words. Tiana needs to be more intentional about building vocabulary in this group of children who are already significantly behind in language development. She needs to employ effective practices such as reading more complex stories and information books in small groups and engaging children in conversations about the readings.
>
> Jana Baker teaches in a full-day kindergarten. She believes strongly in the value of play for children's learning and development, and she has been able to preserve time and materials for play in her classroom. In the early days of Jana's career when parents or principals questioned her, she defended play by simply stating that it is developmentally appropriate. But as pressures increased for literacy instruction in kindergarten, Jana found herself thinking more critically about her practice. She observed that during choice time, children's play had become repetitive. Boys built the same roads and towers in the block area. Few children engaged in dramatic play, and those who did pretended to be characters they had seen on TV or in video games. Other children wandered from one activity to another without engagement or sustained interest.
>
> Jana realized that she didn't know enough about play; she couldn't explain clearly why it was valuable for children and didn't know how to enhance children's involvement. After attending workshops and reading professional journals, Jana became aware that there were many missed opportunities for learning in her classroom. She learned ways to help children engage in mature, sustained, sociodramatic play that builds social and emotional skills and language. She introduced board games to help children learn mathematics while cooperating and having fun.
>
> Jana began to see that choice time provided many opportunities for her to engage in one-on-one, extended conversations with children or to build writing, reading, and

math into their play. In short, Jana became intentional in her interactions with children during play and in the kind of play experiences she provided. As a result, play became a more effective teaching and learning experience for the children in her kindergarten.

As we can see in the previous scenarios, intentional teachers continually reflect on their own decisions and gather evidence of how well children are doing. They may discuss their practices with colleagues and children's families. They modify their practices when these are not benefiting children. Read the feature titled *Becoming an Intentional Teacher: What Did You Do Today?* for an example of a teacher's actions and the thinking behind them.

Intentional teaching requires constant decision making. Next we describe what teachers need to consider when making good decisions.

MyEducationLab

Go to the Professional Perspectives section in Topic 8: DAP/Teaching Strategies in the MyEducationLab for your course and select the video entitled *Using Developmentally Appropriate Practice to Bridge the Achievement Gap* and watch and listen to Sue Bredekamp discuss this topic.

Deciding What Is Developmentally Appropriate

Teachers of young children make hundreds of decisions every day: which book to read to what size group, which questions to ask when, how to intervene with a child who is struggling to enter a play situation, and so forth. They must be able to negotiate difficult situations, such as what to do when a child shares a confidential family secret, how much support to give two boys who are trying to fairly divide the blocks, and what intervention to try with a first grader who is significantly behind in reading development. The list goes on and on. Day after day and hour after hour, teachers are called on to determine what is developmentally appropriate.

In many cases, decisions are the result of careful advance consideration and planning. For example, teachers must consider what kinds of learning experiences will be provided to help the group achieve important learning goals. These decisions include planning curriculum so that the learning goals established for the group are achievable and challenging for the children. For instance, although the school district prekindergarten curriculum calls for teaching the alphabet, Ms. Jonas determines which children in her class have not yet achieved this goal and which children have already mastered the alphabet. The curriculum plan as written may be appropriate for many children in the former group, but the latter group can connect letters and sounds and use recognizable letters in their own writing.

MyEducationLab

Go to the Assignments and Activities section of Topic 8: Developmentally Appropriate Practice/ Teaching Strategies in the MyEducationLab for your course and complete the activity entitled *Developmentally Appropriate Programs for Various Ages*. As you watch the videos and answer the accompanying questions, observe how each teacher makes decisions about what is developmentally appropriate for each group of children. What differences do you observe in the learning experiences and teaching strategies for infants/toddlers, preschoolers, and first graders?

Other decisions teachers make include setting up the physical environment, which materials to place where, how to schedule the day, or how to group children for various learning experiences. Ms. Jonas ensures that the alphabet is displayed at children's eye level as a model for children's writing, and that magnetic letters and alphabet puzzles are available for children to manipulate in their work and play. She organizes the daily schedule to ensure that children have ample time to write on their own and, during the day, she works in small groups with children who need extra help learning letters.

Some situations require teachers to make immediate decisions. For instance, suppose a dump truck pulls up outside the preschool window. The teacher may decide to interrupt his prior plans and follow the children's interest by taking them outside to observe the truck unloading the gravel for a new driveway next door. Or he may see that most of the children are engrossed in learning centers and decide not to interrupt. Likewise, if the story a teacher is reading to a group doesn't seem to hold the children's interest, she can readily switch gears and select another book or engage children in an active song.

Primary grade teachers must make numerous short- and long-term decisions as they support children's learning, particularly each child's reading progress. Some teaching decisions have lasting consequences for individual children. For example, identifying a child for special education services or determining a plan to work with a child who is extremely aggressive and disruptive has far-reaching consequences. When making such a decision, the teacher needs to take into consideration many sources of information, observations over time, and the diverse perspectives of family members and other professionals such as special educators or social workers.

Becoming an Intentional Teacher

What Did You Do Today?

Here's What Happened After the 45-minute learning center time in my preschool classroom, I asked each child to tell what he or she had done. A few children just pointed to where they had gone or ran back over there to show me. I thought of these children as the "Pointers." A few others verbally identified the center they had played in, saying something like, "I was in the block area" or just "Blocks," but added nothing about what they were doing there. I'll call them the "Namers." Other children said more about what they had done and sometimes the other children they played with, though their descriptions were often unclear to anyone who hadn't been there ("I tried and tried to get it to stay, but it fell"). This group I'll call the "Detailers." There were variations within these levels, but basically the children fell into these three groups.

After doing this reflection exercise for a few days to be sure I had a good idea of each child's level of responding, I began asking children to reflect in small groups and added some more challenge to help each child move to the next level. For example, in working with children who were Pointers, I had a photo of each center, and I would ask the child to find the center where they had worked. Then I said, "Oh, you worked in the art center, right?" or "Ah, you were building in the block area." I repeated the name of the center several times.

With the Namers, I asked them to tell me what they did in the center they identified. Sometimes I asked a question such as, "What were you building today?" and if I got no response, I added, "Were you building a road, or something else?" I would also say things like "Hmm, let's see, what was I doing? I spent some time watching children in each of the centers, and I took my sick puppy to the veterinarian's office that Mark and Bobbie were running."

With the Detailers, I used a variety of methods. Sometimes I paired two children who responded at similar levels and had them tell each other what they had done in centers that day. Because a child often couldn't follow all of her partner's account, they would ask each other questions like, "What fell? What were you trying to build?"

Here's What I Was Thinking I decided to start this routine—asking the children what they had done in the centers—for two main reasons. First, it helps develop their ability and tendency to reflect, to think about the past—in this case the recent past—rather than the present. At their age, children are increasing in their capacity to think back (or forward to the future) if they have experiences that encourage them to do it. They're very interested in their own activities, so they are more motivated than they might otherwise be. This is also a good way to extend their oral language and communication skills.

I started wherever each individual child was and tried to help each one go a little farther, including the ones who were already saying a lot. They can and should move forward, too. Sometimes I tried using a visual support like the photos of the centers to see if that would help stimulate a little more language. I also modeled both the language, for instance, by repeating the center names, and the practice of thinking back and reflecting on what one has done.

Having pairs of children tell each other things is a useful approach because children want their peers to understand them and will try hard to get their message across. I also model talking and asking questions to get clarification, and the children pick it up and do it themselves. Gradually the more verbal children who at first give a lot of disjointed details get better at giving a coherent account of their activities.

Making Informed Decisions

Large or small, all decisions that teachers make should be informed decisions. NAEYC (2009a) identifies three fundamental considerations that guide teachers in making decisions about what is developmentally appropriate for children:

age appropriate Age-related human characteristics that allow teachers to make general predictions within an age range about what materials, interactions, and experiences will be safe, interesting, challenging, and within reach for children and, thus, likely to best promote their learning and development.

1. *Consider what is known about development and learning of children within a given age range.* Having knowledge of age-related human characteristics allows teachers to make general predictions within an age range about what materials, interactions, and experiences will be safe, interesting, challenging, and within reach for children, and thus likely to best promote their learning and development. This dimension is sometimes called **age appropriate**.
2. *Consider what is known about each child as an individual.* Gathering information about the strengths, interests, and needs of each individual child in the group enables teachers to adapt and be responsive to that individual variation.
3. *Consider what is known about the social and cultural contexts in which children live.* Learning about the values, expectations, and behavioral and linguistic conventions that shape children's lives at home and in their communities allows teachers to create learning environments and experiences that are meaningful, relevant, and respectful for all children and their families.

In each of these three areas, the knowledge to be considered is substantial and changes over time. Intentional teachers make sure to stay informed both through ongoing professional development, which includes gaining information from new research, and through those avenues that will provide necessary information about the children they teach, their families, and their communities. Let's examine each of these areas more closely and see what each contributes to the decisions teachers make.

Consider What Is Known about Child Development and Learning

During early childhood, it is possible to make relatively accurate predictions about children's capabilities based on age ranges. Babies need constant care and careful supervision because they put everything in their mouths. Two-year-olds who have mastered walking waste no time in running headlong into furniture and walls. Preschoolers are fairly good communicators, but need help to keep expanding their vocabulary. Primary grade children are reasonably independent learners when motivated by the topic or activity.

Because children's needs, interests, and abilities differ as they grow and change, developmentally appropriate environments for different age groups will look different. What differences can you see in these classrooms for infants/toddlers (bottom), preschoolers (center), and primary grade children (top)?

Adults—especially parents, family members, and teachers—consider what is developmentally appropriate every day without necessarily recognizing it. For instance, when selecting a toy for 2-year-old Hudson, his aunt chooses a schoolhouse with a handle for carrying. The toy has a label that indicates there are no small parts that can be swallowed. She determines that the toy is manageable for most toddlers whose fine motor skills are limited so they are unlikely to become frustrated. Because the toy is age appropriate, it should hold Hudson's interest. Like most 2-year-olds, Hudson is beginning to engage in pretend play and also loves to carry his toys around with him.

Some characteristics that young children typically demonstrate at various times are common knowledge. For example, when a young panda cub makes his media debut, reporters uniformly observe that he behaves "like a toddler." Readers immediately get the picture even without the description that follows—"He squirmed in the arms of his keepers, climbed and tumbled over a rock pile, and walked through a small stream. He also showed a penchant for putting things in his mouth" (Barker, 2005).

Knowing age-related characteristics helps guide teachers' expectations of children's behavior and abilities, the organization of the environment, and the materials provided. They also guide teacher's planning and affect their interactions with children. For an example of age-appropriate interaction, read the *What Works: Baby Talk* feature.

What Works

Baby Talk

Here's an example of developmentally appropriate practice that works for babies:

> If you are like most adults, your interaction with a baby may sound like a high-pitched voice saying this: "Hi, baby. How are you this morning, baby, baby?" You pause. The infant moves his mouth, waves his arms, or just looks at you intently. And now you say, "Oh, you had a good sleep, did you? Are you ready to have some fun today?" When the baby gurgles, you say, "You are ready, aren't you? Jesse's ready, ready, ready to play!"

Adults (and even older children) talk to babies differently than they do to each other. Researchers have dubbed this special kind of speech *motherese* or *parentese,* and they have observed its use around the world. What's more, they know that babies like it. Infants consistently prefer hearing parentese to adult conversation. In laboratory studies, they show this preference by turning their heads one way to trigger a tape of parentese more often than they turn it the other way to hear a tape of adult-to-adult conversation.

This preference persists when the parentese is in a language the baby doesn't usually hear. In other words, even though infants don't know what the words mean, they prefer speech with the exaggerated intonation of parentese. This rhythmic quality of a voice holds "emotion-identifying" information that infants appear to enjoy. So it makes sense that adults exaggerate the rhythm of the speech they direct toward infants. The higher-pitched sounds, slower tempo, and repetition of parentese may also draw the baby's interest.

The parentese speech pattern is probably not essential for infants' language acquisition, researchers believe, but it does attract their attention and get them to focus on spoken language. It also may draw attention to certain language features that help babies learn. Hearing the exaggerated sounds of parentese may make it easier for them to learn the sounds of their own language. Repeating what the child attempts to say, another characteristic of parentese, may help babies figure out words and even aspects of grammar. So when you're talking with babies, go ahead and do what comes naturally. Pour on the expressive tone of voice and use plenty of repetition. It may sound a little silly to the adult ear, but it sounds good to the baby!

Sources: "Acoustic Determinants of Infant Preference for Motherese Speech," by A. Fernald and P. Kuhl, 1987, *Infant Behavior and Development, 10,* pp. 279–293; "Learning to Speak," by J. L. Locke, 1993, *Journal of Phonetics, 21,* pp. 141–146.

Consider What Is Individually Appropriate

One of the most basic principles of child development is that there are individual differences. In fact, children demonstrate a wide range of variability across every area of development—physical, cognitive, social, and emotional—while remaining within the range of "typical" development.

The development of some children falls outside the range of what's typical in one aspect or another. For example, in some respects, children with disabilities or developmental delays and children who are gifted add further diversity to the range of individual differences. The expert lens feature, *Including All Children: Developmentally Appropriate Practice and Children with Disabilities*, illustrates this point.

Averages or norms never tell more than a small part of the story; far more informative is the range, that is, the large variation of growth or performance across different individuals within the age (Copple & Bredekamp, 2006). Picture a group of 4-year-old children. They range in height from 35 to 46 inches, and in weight from 30 to 55 pounds. One can already skip, while another still takes the stairs two feet at a time. One can read while another knows only a few letters. One converses fluently in two languages, while another has

Including All Children

Developmentally Appropriate Practice and Children with Disabilities

A child with a disability acts like a magnifying glass on the developmental appropriateness of an early childhood program. The basic elements of developmentally appropriate practice are necessary for inclusion to succeed. However, the converse is also true. When children with disabilities are included in programs that are not developmentally appropriate, it becomes difficult for the child with special needs—indeed, for all of the children—to make meaningful progress. Compare the experiences of these two young children:

> Tara, a 4-year-old with autism, is sitting next to her teacher at circle time. The teacher is reading from a small-sized book, and many of the children cannot see the pictures very well, including Tara. Circle time has been in progress for over 20 minutes and many of the children are getting restless. Tara begins rocking back and forth and looking at the door. Without warning, the teacher stops reading the book and tells the children to stand up for a finger play. Tara bolts from the circle and runs to the water table. She begins splashing and yelling. The teacher stops and asks Tara to return to circle. When Tara does not return on her own volition, the assistant teacher physically moves her back to the circle, and a 10-minute struggle ensues. When Tara's father comes to pick her up, the teacher describes "her bad day" and asks him to talk to Tara about listening at school.
>
> Isaac is also 4 years old and also has a diagnosis of autism. He is sitting on a brightly colored carpet square between two of his preschool peers at circle time. His teacher is reading a book the class made called *Friends, Friends, Who Do You See?* It is adapted from *Brown Bear, Brown Bear* (Martin, 1996), but features pictures of the children in the class paired with their names. Isaac loves the book, and reads along with the teacher. As the teacher reads each child's name in the story, he or she stands up and moves. After the story, it is time for singing. Isaac knows this because circle time happens in a similar routine each day.
>
> The teacher pulls out the "song chart" featuring the pictures and titles of eight different songs. One song is about a train. Isaac loves trains and seems eager to hear the new song. He points to the "Trains on the track." The teacher helps Isaac remove the song card. Isaac holds the card while the children sing. Then Isaac makes the sign for "play" with his hands. The teacher says, "Yes, Isaac, it is time for centers." She lets Isaac choose a center first because she knows it is hard for him to wait. Isaac brings the teacher the song card, and then points to the picture of the water table. His teacher models, "I want to play at the. . . ." Isaac says "Water table." His teacher, proud of his increasing verbal skills, gives him a hug and says, "Off you go to the water table." When Isaac's mother picks him up from school, his teacher describes how often he used his words and which friends he played with during center time.

As is clear from Isaac's case, developmentally appropriate practice provides the necessary foundation for successful inclusion. But individually appropriate adaptations are essential for children with disabilities and other special needs.

MyEducationLab

Go to the Assignments and Activities section of Topic 11: Special Needs/Inclusion in the MyEducationLab for your course and complete the activity entitled *The Benefits of Inclusion in an Early Childhood Classroom*. As you watch the video and answer the accompanying questions, consider how developmentally appropriate, inclusive classrooms meet the needs and support the learning of all children.

just mastered talking in complete sentences. One will play for extended periods with two or more friends, while another struggles to play cooperatively for even a short time.

Children also have individual personality traits and preferences, some of which are obvious even in early infancy. Some babies are feisty, while others are more passive. Some children stand back and watch for quite a while before attempting something new, and some plunge right in. Some children talk nonstop, while others cannot be enticed to speak up. One preschooler rides a tricycle with abandon, while another prefers to sit quietly with a puzzle or pegboard. A second grader loves to read and spends all of her free time with a book, while another struggles with reading but looks forward to math because it's her best subject.

The term **individually appropriate** refers to teachers using what they know about the personality, strengths, interests, and abilities of each individual child in the group to adapt for and be responsive to individual variation. Consider, for instance, two tricycle riders: The fearless rider may need more careful supervision to prevent injury, while the warier child may need extra encouragement and support to develop his large motor skills. Similarly, some children will need enriched experiences to accelerate their language development, while a few may need individual support to continue to build on their precocious reading ability. A withdrawn, timid child may need a great deal of emotional support to cope with life's challenges, while another needs help controlling aggression to make friends.

With the individual differences that exist, teachers clearly cannot expect all children in a group to learn the same thing in the same way at the same time. Even when the teacher introduces a concept or reads a book to a whole group, each child will take away something different from the learning experience. Therefore, to help children progress, teachers must continually keep track of what children know and are able to do, what they are struggling with, and what is engaging their interest and meets their needs.

Consider Children's Social and Cultural Contexts

All learning and development occur in and are influenced by social and cultural contexts (Bronfenbrenner, 1979). In fact, *appropriate behavior* is always culturally defined. The cultural contexts a child grows up in begin with the family and extend to include the cultural group or groups with which the family identifies. **Culture** refers to the behaviors, values, and beliefs that a group shares and passes on from one generation to the next. Because children share their cultural context with members of their group, cultural differences are differences between groups rather than individuals. Therefore, cultural variation needs to be considered as well as individual variation in deciding what is developmentally appropriate.

individually appropriate Information about the strengths, interests, abilities, and needs of each individual child in the group that enables teachers to adapt to and be responsive to individual variation.

culture The explicit and implicit values, beliefs, rules, and expectations for behavior of members of a group that are passed on from one generation to the next.

culturally appropriate Applying knowledge of the social and cultural contexts in which children live, which helps teachers build on children's prior knowledge and make experiences meaningful and responsive.

Children learn the values, beliefs, expectations, and habitual patterns of behavior of the social and cultural contexts in their lives. Cultures, for example, have characteristic ways of showing respect; there may be different rules for how to properly greet an older or younger person, a friend, or a stranger. Attitudes about time and personal space vary among cultures, as do the ways to take care of a baby and dress for different occasions. In fact, most of our experiences are filtered through the lenses of our cultural group. We typically learn cultural rules very early and very deeply, so they are not part of our conscious thought.

Social contexts of young children's lives differ in ways such as these: Is the child growing up in a large family, or a family of one or two children? In a single-parent family, a two-parent family, with same-sex parents, or a household that includes extended family members? In an urban, suburban, or rural setting? Has the child been in group care settings from a young age, or is this the first time in a group program? What social and economic resources are available to the family? All of these situations frame the social context and impact children's lives in unique ways.

For young children, what makes sense and how they respond to new experiences are fundamentally shaped by the social and cultural contexts to which they have become accustomed. To ensure that learning experiences are meaningful, relevant, and respectful to children and their families—that is, for those experiences to be **culturally appropriate**—teachers must have some knowledge of the social and cultural contexts in which children live. Such knowledge helps teachers build on children's prior experiences and learning so they can help children progress.

All young children must adjust when they move from the security and familiarity of their homes into schools or early childhood programs. The challenge is greatest, however, for children whose cultural experiences at home differ sharply from those predominating at the school or program. For these children, the transition can be confusing and frightening. Consider a Native American child, whose culture expects children to quietly listen and observe adults, entering a classroom where the teacher expects everyone to speak up. Think of how you feel, at least for a moment, when people around you are speaking a language you don't understand. Even as adults with all of our coping mechanisms intact, we tend to feel uncertain, ignorant, and uncomfortable in environments different from those to which we are accustomed. (Are they talking about us?)

For teachers, being responsive to all social and cultural variation can be challenging. Our own cultural experience is so integral to us that we are rarely aware of it. If we are in the position of power as a teacher, we must be especially careful to be aware of and respectful toward those whose cultural backgrounds and accepted rules for behavior may be different from ours. Most importantly, we must be careful not to assume that our own cultural perspective is superior and make negative judgments based on our cultural variations. An example illustrates the potentially damaging result of such judgments:

> A European American teacher is employed in a school serving a predominantly African American community. One of her principal teaching strategies is questioning. But she finds that her questions are often met with blank stares or disdain from the children and she assumes they don't know the answers. She doesn't realize that within their cultural community, people rarely ask questions that they already know the answers to.

To better accommodate the realities of cultural and linguistic diversity in schools and early childhood programs, teachers today need to work at being especially sensitive and responsive to the perspectives of children and their families that may be different from their own. To broaden your own perspective, read the *Culture Lens: Fostering Cultural Continuity* feature.

Consider All You Know When Making Decisions

The three considerations that teachers must take into account when making decisions—knowledge about children's learning and development, information about individual children, and information about the social and cultural contexts of children's lives—should not be viewed in isolation. All three considerations, in fact, interact with and influence each other; they are always intertwined in shaping children's development and behavior. For example, children all over the world follow a similar developmental pattern when learning language. They all progress from cooing, to babbling, to one-word utterances, to telegraphic speech ("Daddy up"), to short sentences, and finally to more complex sentences. However, a wide range of individual variation exists in language acquisition of children who are roughly the same age, because of both differences in language experience and developmental variation. At age 3, Joey speaks in one-word utterances, whereas his same-age cousin, Michael, expounds in paragraphs. Finally, each child speaks the language, including the dialect, of his or her own cultural group. Six-year-old Amelia speaks English to her mother and Spanish to her father. All of these factors influence children's language development and how teachers think about supporting it optimally for all children.

Now let's look at how the meshing of the three considerations plays out in the decisions of one primary grade teacher:

> Frida Lopez has 22 children in her first-grade class. Her first challenge each year is to get to know the children very well. She spends time meeting with their families, engages in one-on-one conversations with children, observes their behavior and skills throughout the day, and sets up specific tasks to evaluate their skills such as literacy tasks or solving math problems with counters.
>
> As she goes about getting to know her students, she regularly assesses their abilities and interests in relation to what she knows from her study of child development,

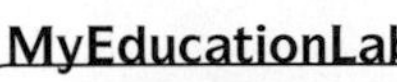

Go to the Assignments and Activities section of Topic 6: Curriculum Planning in the MyEducationLab for your course and complete the activity entitled *Designing Curriculum to Meet the Needs of all Children*. How do these teachers consider all they know in making decisions about what is developmentally appropriate for children?

Culture Lens

Fostering Cultural Continuity

Take a moment to think about what you understand about culture. Do you tend to think about culture only as characteristic of children and families who are "culturally different"? Does the concept of culture only apply to some children? Actually, it is important to remember that *every* child is socialized in a cultural group, and the most important elements influencing children's development are really aspects of their cultural experiences that are often the hardest to observe.

What people sometimes think of as "cultural" are the products that culture produces, such as dress or holiday celebrations. These are the surface features of culture. But culture produces more indiscernible behaviors and attitudes that emerge from the same set of rules as the surface features of culture. These deep structural aspects of culture act as much more powerful influences on children's development than the surface features. For example, if the cultural group believes that women should not be seen by men except for those in the immediate family, a woman's mode of dress will reflect this value. At the same time, this cultural belief will have much farther reaching effects on her behavior and life choices than simply how she dresses. Consider an example in an early childhood classroom:

> It is circle time in kindergarten and the children are supposed to bring an object from home that has writing on it. Most of the children eagerly seek their turn, waving their hands widely, and showing off how well they can read the words. Jai has brought something but is clearly not eager to share. The teacher assumes that he can't read the words. So, she doesn't call on him.

As in all developmental domains, culture influences the expression of emotions. Although emotions such as fear, anger, and happiness are part of human interaction in all cultural groups, variations emerge in the way they are expressed. Jai, who is from India, is from a cultural group that avoids drawing too much attention to individuals or expressing emotions too openly. Children from other, more individualistic cultures such as the United States are generally encouraged to express their feelings openly. These cultural differences account for Jai's behavior and that of the other children in his class more than their reading abilities.

Cultural differences do not mean that one way is right and the other wrong. They simply demonstrate that there is a wide variety of developmental patterns that can be explained best by understanding the cultural context in which development occurs.

> the curriculum goals, and her experiences teaching other 6- and 7-year-olds. She finds that a few children exceed her expectations in reading or social skills, whereas others are significantly behind their peers in some areas. Each child has a unique personality and profile of abilities, and Frida becomes more aware of these.
>
> Neela has Down syndrome, and Frida has already met with her parents and the team of special education professionals who create and implement an individualized educational plan for her. After a few weeks, Frida becomes concerned that another child, Almonzo, might have an undiagnosed language delay. In the case of the six children whose home languages are not ones Frida knows, she recognizes that she must take extra steps to find out about them. Using community volunteers and, in one case, a paid translator, Frida connects with the families of her students to build relationships and to learn what capabilities the children exhibit in their homes and communities.

So we see that in meeting the children, Frida seamlessly draws on her knowledge of child development and learning, as well as her knowledge of them as individuals and members of cultural groups. Precisely because children are so different and their abilities vary so greatly, Frida will need to draw from a wide repertoire of teaching strategies to help them achieve developmentally appropriate goals. Consider the three dimensions of decisions about developmentally appropriate teaching while reading the feature *How Would You Respond? Teacher Decision Making.*

So far we have described the areas of knowledge that teachers consider in making decisions about developmentally appropriate practice—what teachers need to know and think about. Now we turn to the work of the teachers—what do early childhood teachers do? What are the dimensions of practice that describe the teacher's role?

Understanding the Complex Role of the Teacher

According to the NAEYC's (2009a) guidelines for developmentally appropriate practice, the complex job of an early childhood teacher has five interrelated dimensions: (1) creating a caring community of learners, (2) teaching to enhance learning and development, (3) planning curriculum to achieve important goals, (4) assessing children's learning and development, and (5) establishing reciprocal relationships with families. One way to remember these dimensions is to visualize the five points of a star, as depicted in Figure 3.1. Each of the five points is necessary for the star to be complete, and they are all interrelated—take one away and the figure is no longer a star.

It may be helpful, in fact, to think of it as a "mariner's star" (NAEYC, 1998a). Seafaring people use the stars to guide their way, but without considerable knowledge of the stars' positioning and their relation to navigation, mindlessly following a star won't lead to a destination. So it is with the mariner's star of early childhood teaching. Each of the star's points links to a set of guidelines that represent a large body of knowledge about early childhood education. Just as the stars guide seafaring people, the mariner's star helps guide teachers' professional behavior; but without that strong foundation of knowledge, the guidelines themselves have little meaning.

In the following sections, we introduce each aspect of the teacher's role in accordance with NAEYC's guidelines for developmentally appropriate practice. Each of these aspects of the teacher's role is described in a later chapter.

MyEducationLab

Go to the Book Specific Resources in the MyEducationLab for your course and select Author Interviews in Chapter 3 to watch and listen to the video *The Mariner's Star*. What are the five dimensions of the Mariner's Star?

How Would You Respond?

Teacher Decision Making

The Situation Suppose you have recently changed jobs to a new elementary school and the location draws families with a wider range of cultural and language backgrounds than you have worked with previously. There is a modest budget for adding books to the classrooms, and the teachers also plan to make use of the nearby public library. You will be teaching second grade.

What to Do? As you approach the selection of books, which of the following ideas are consistent with the principles of developmentally appropriate practice?

- Avoid books designed for children of third grade or older.
- Focus on books with very few words so that children who don't speak much English will be able to understand and enjoy them.
- Select good books without reference to language or culture.
- Ask families to share stories and help make books in the languages they speak at home to add to the classroom library.
- Take children to the library and let them pick books that interest them.

Do you have other thoughts for improving the school's reading materials?

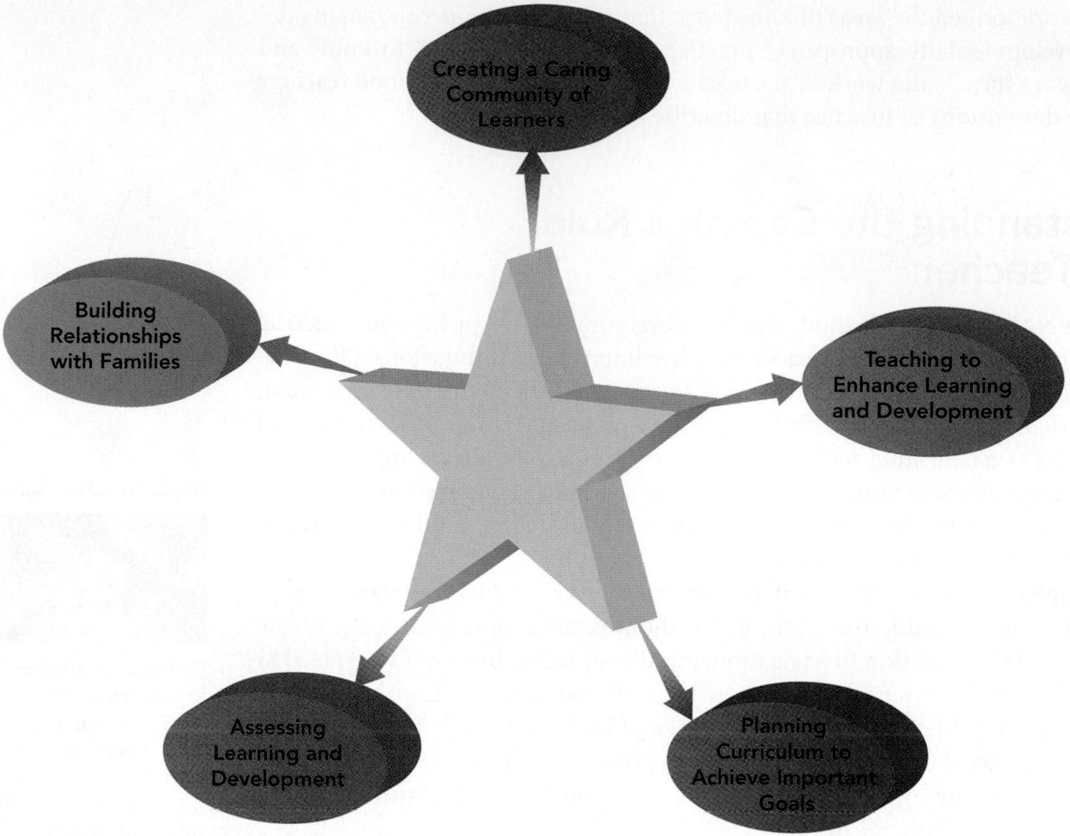

Figure 3.1 Mariner's Star: The Complex Role of the Teacher
Adapted from p. 24 of *Basics of Developmentally Appropriate Practice: An Introduction for Teachers of Children 3 to 6*, by C. Copple and S. Bredekamp, 2006, Washington, DC: NAEYC. Reprinted with permission from the National Association for the Education of Young Children.

Create a Caring Community of Learners

An early childhood setting—whether it serves infants and toddlers, preschoolers, kindergartners, or second graders—needs to be a caring community of learners. The term **caring community of learners** incorporates several key ideas that characterize early childhood education: (1) Children's care and education are equally important; (2) children learn through positive relationships with adults and other children; and (3) the learning context matters, referring to both the indoor and outdoor environments, how the environments are organized, and the materials and equipment they contain.

Children learn when they feel safe and cared for. They thrive in an environment in which they see positive images that reflect their own identity and where they see their own contributions to the community, such as photos of themselves and of their families, as well as seeing their own work displayed. They also see examples throughout the community that reinforce their cultural identity. The messages are clear to each child: You belong here. We care about and support each other. You have important things to contribute to this group. You will thrive here.

caring community of learners A group or classroom in which children and adults engage in warm, positive relationships, treat each other with respect, and learn from and with each other.

The foundation of young children's learning is in positive relationships with other people who are responsive to them. At the same time, the early childhood setting is a learning community where adults and children learn with and from each other. Each child's thinking can build on or challenge that of another. When Josué tells Willa she can't be the doctor because she's a girl, Willa promptly informs him, "I go to Dr. Ashai and she's a lady, so there." Josué has to adjust his concept of *doctor* to include women as well as men.

In a caring community, children acquire the ability to regulate their own emotions and behavior and to make friends. Teachers actively teach children social and emotional skills and engage in individualized interventions for children who persistently demonstrate challenging behaviors such as aggression.

Teach to Enhance Learning and Development

Teaching seems the most obvious aspect of the teacher's role, but it isn't simple at all. Early childhood teachers typically do not conform to the images that come to mind for many adults when they think of "teaching"—the teacher standing in front of a blackboard or at a podium lecturing. Teaching simply looks different in the early childhood setting, and it takes many forms.

Effective early childhood teachers know the children in their group very well. They thoughtfully plan the learning experiences and environment with these children in mind while also keeping in mind the learning goals. They use a variety of teaching strategies to help each child develop and learn. And they guide young children to become socially responsible, self-regulating, contributing members of the community.

Teachers also use various learning contexts such as teacher-guided group work, including both large-group and small-group preplanned experiences, and periods of play and engagement in which children primarily guide their own activity with the support of teachers (Epstein, 2007a; Christie & Roskos, 2006; Siraj-Blatchford, Muttock, Sylva, Gilden, & Bell, 2003). Teachers use various ways of grouping children for learning; they may gather a reading group of similar ability level or organize a group of children with different language abilities to work together on a project. Teachers' behavior needs to vary with the setting as well. In addition, routines such as eating meals and transitioning from one place or activity to another are all potentially valuable learning contexts if teachers use these activities as opportunities for one-on-one conversations with children or to reinforce a learning goal through singing a song or reciting a poem.

curriculum A written plan that describes the goals for children's learning and development, and the learning experiences, materials, and teaching strategies that are used to help children achieve those goals.

scientifically based curriculum Derives from research evidence about what kinds of learning outcomes relate to later achievement, and what types of teaching and learning experiences help children acquire those outcomes. Such a curriculum has been evaluated and its effectiveness demonstrated.

Plan Curriculum to Achieve Important Goals

If developmentally appropriate practice tends to focus on the *how* of teaching, then curriculum is the *what*—the content that children are expected to learn. **Curriculum** is a written plan that describes the knowledge and skills to be taught in the educational program and the learning experiences through which teaching takes place (Copple & Bredekamp, 2006, p. 61).

Currently, there is increased demand for **scientifically based curriculum** that is based on research about important learning goals that predict later achievement, the sequences in which concepts and skills build on each other, and the teaching strategies that have proven effective. Whatever the process through which a curriculum is selected, developed, or planned, to be effective it must be implemented with attention to individual differences and cultural variation among children (NAEYC & National Association of Early Childhood Specialists in State Departments of Education [NAECS/SDE], 2003).

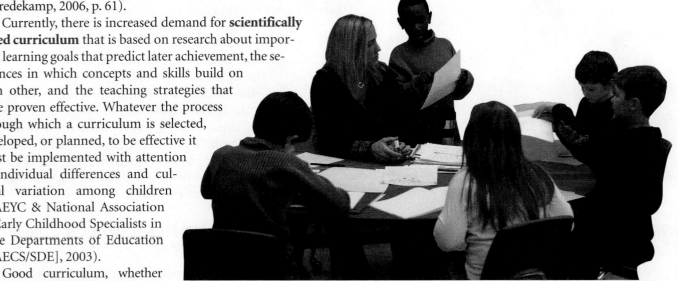

Intentional teachers use every possible opportunity to promote children's learning, including preplanned small-group lessons and conversations during meals, transitions, and routines.

Good curriculum, whether published resources used in school districts or teacher developed, offers teachers flexibility and ways of adapting, often providing many more suggested activities or materials than teachers could possibly use. Thus, they have many further decisions to make. Teachers need to be very familiar with the curriculum plan, especially the key learning and development outcomes for children—that is, what children should know and be able to do as a result of their participation in this program.

Assess Children's Development and Learning

In the current era of educational accountability, assessment is often a controversial topic. However, it is an integral component of developmentally appropriate practice. **Assessment** is the process of observing and documenting the work children do and how they do it as the basis for a variety of educational decisions. Assessment is important because teachers must draw on assessment information about individual children in an ongoing, systematic process to understand children's learning and development.

Children, especially very young children, are moving targets. What they can't do today, they can do tomorrow. What they didn't know or understand yesterday may gradually become clear, or they may have an "Aha!" moment of recognition. Their development may follow a typical though somewhat slower trajectory in one area or they may be in need of intervention for a serious developmental delay. To address any of these situations, teachers must use appropriate, accurate tools to assess children.

Each decision that teachers make about children has consequences. The more important and lasting the consequence, the more vital it is that the decision is based on multiple sources of information, including information from parents.

assessment The ongoing process of gathering evidence of children's learning and development, and then organizing and interpreting the information to make informed decisions about instructional practice.

reciprocal relationship A two-way relationship in which information and power are shared evenly.

Build Relationships with Families and Communities

Young children do not come with résumés; they come with families. NAEYC (2009a) guidelines emphasize the importance of teachers and administrators developing **reciprocal relationships** with children's families. *Reciprocal* refers to a two-way relationship, in which information and power are shared evenly. Such a relationship is based on mutual respect, trust, cooperation, and shared responsibility. A reciprocal relationship requires regular open communication and a willingness to negotiate differences toward shared goals.

We've already seen that in order to teach young children effectively teachers must get to know each child well. The younger the child, the more teachers must rely on family members as key informants about the child's competencies, interests, needs, and cultural experiences. Young children's competencies are not always apparent, especially if they have been acquired in a cultural context that is different from that of the teacher. For example, a child may know colors and basic shapes, and be able to count up to 20 in Russian, yet demonstrate none of this knowledge in English at school. Through a relationship with the parents, however, this teacher can ascertain that she needs to help the child learn the English words for concepts he already knows, rather than teach these concepts. This allows both the teacher and child the opportunity to use what he already knows and move on to other important concepts more efficiently.

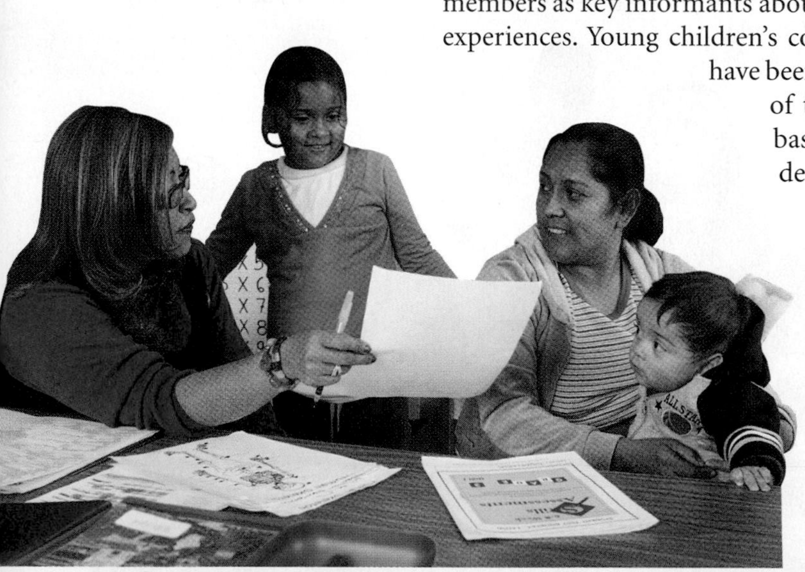

Developmentally appropriate practices are respectful of children's cultural and linguistic backgrounds. Intentional teachers build two-way, reciprocal relationships with families to get to know children as individuals and to understand their cultural context.

Seeing the Teacher's Role in Context

In each aspect of their work, whether creating a caring community, teaching, planning curriculum, assessing, or working with families,

teachers must draw on a broad base of information to make useful decisions. The following example illustrates how the five dimensions of the teacher's role come together during a memorable experience for a beginning teacher:

> Scotty's teacher, Gina, believes him to be the "bad boy" in his preschool class. Gina feels she is constantly correcting what he has done wrong. One day, a fight breaks out in the block corner and a chorus of voices arises, shouting, "Scotty did it!" Gina sighs, not surprised by these events until she remembers that Scotty isn't there that day. She realizes that her focus on Scotty's misdeeds has made him the "bad boy" in everyone's eyes.
>
> Her realization forces Gina to reflect on her own and Scotty's behavior. She realizes that she doesn't really know Scotty, and spends time systematically observing him. Soon she discovers strengths she can help him build on, such as his exceptional fine motor skills, and comes to see that there is much Scotty can do well. She gives him opportunities to use these skills (she allows him to cut up the oranges for snack under her supervision), and finally catches him doing something right for a change. Gina also meets with Scotty's mother so that together they can begin to focus on his positive behavior rather than his missteps. Gradually, Gina notices that Scotty's behavior improves. As a result, both Gina and Scotty's mother begin to enjoy him more. With more support and a sense of accomplishment, he makes friends with several other children.

In making professional decisions, one strategy teachers should always consider is to broaden their own perspective, just as Gina did. They need to take into consideration as many points of view as possible—to "widen the lens" with which they see children, their families, and the educational process.

Widening the Lens: Moving from *Either/Or* to *Both/And* Thinking

Questions of educational practices in the United States are often dichotomized as either/or choices. Is phonics *or* vocabulary more important in learning to read? Should preschool stress social–emotional development *or* cognitive development? Should early childhood programs have child-initiated *or* teacher-directed experience? These either/or choices oversimplify the complex processes of becoming literate or developing the whole child. Either/or thinking assumes that there is one right answer to a complex question. Instead, children would be better served and educators more effective if the questions were addressed with *both/and* thinking. Both/and thinking rejects simplistic answers to complex questions and requires diverse perspectives and several possible correct answers to be considered.

To avoid either/or thinking, it is useful to use the analogy of *widening the lens.* Think of yourself as holding a camera and altering the view by adjusting the lens. Depending on how you adjust the lens, your view and, therefore, your perspective changes. You might zoom in on one child's expression, or you might zoom out to see the whole room arrangement. You could bring even more information into the picture, especially with a video camera, perhaps including the child's friends, extended family, or community. In fact, to engage in developmentally appropriate decision making, teachers must indeed widen their views. Just as the camera lens adjusts to display different views, teachers allow their minds to expand and accommodate several ideas at once.

As we have discussed, children of similar ages are *both* alike *and* different. Likewise, children of the same cultural group share some characteristics but not all. When you widen the lens, you will find that your view broadens and you can incorporate more information. As a result, you are less likely to get stuck in either/or thinking. When you widen the lens through which you look at children, the curriculum, teaching practices, assessment, and families—all aspects of your work—you begin to recognize the complexity and interrelationships among the principles that guide early childhood practice.

Developmentally appropriate classrooms function as caring communities of learners where each child is actively involved and valued, and families are welcomed.

Consider the following example that demonstrates the power of widening the lens. When teachers are willing to look beyond the view they have held, they enhance their effectiveness in their work with children and families, as in the following situation:

> Ms. Grantham is the director of a Head Start program. Several parents complain to her that they aren't seeing worksheets or similar products showing their children's learning coming home in the backpacks or displayed in the classroom. Her program doesn't use worksheets because their philosophy of developmentally appropriate practice is based on children's active engagement. Ms. Grantham believes that worksheets are just busy work for children and don't really teach them anything.
>
> At first, she thinks that the parents are just uninformed about good early childhood education. But she asks a few more questions to better understand their perspective. Ms. Grantham comes to see that both she and the parents want the children to succeed—in the wider view, they are in agreement. And what the families are asking for is evidence that the children are in fact learning and on track to succeed in school.
>
> Reflecting on the parents' legitimate desire, Mrs. Grantham realizes that she could do a much better job of sharing with the families concrete samples of the children's work that show what they are learning. She starts to meet with families regularly about what children are doing and learning. She displays the children's work, describes what they have learned and will be learning next, and what she and the teachers are doing to help build the children's skills and knowledge.

Now it's your turn. What do you see when you widen your lens? Try to think of several examples where widening the lens would help you be a better teacher or improve your relationships with family members, college professors, or work colleagues.

Examining the Research

The basic research question regarding any educational practice is this: Does it work? Is this educational practice effective in helping children achieve important learning outcomes? Because developmentally appropriate practice involves many different teaching behaviors and aspects of classroom organization, research on the broad construct of developmentally appropriate practice is difficult to conduct. However, subsequent chapters present the research base for each dimension of the teacher's role, and area of the curriculum.

Research Reviews

One way of thinking about the research basis for developmentally appropriate practice is to consider the broader early childhood knowledge base about children's learning and development and the specific practices that are effective in promoting it. This knowledge is summarized in major scientific reports such as *Eager to Learn: Educating Our Preschoolers* (Bowman et al., 2001), *From Neurons to Neighborhoods: The Science of Early Childhood Development* (Shonkoff & Phillips, 2000), and *A Science-Based Framework for Early Childhood Policy* (Center on the Developing Child, 2007).

Similarly, a vast amount of evidence demonstrates the lasting positive effects of high-quality early childhood programs (see Barnett, 2008). Although these studies were not designed to evaluate developmentally appropriate practice per se, the practices employed in effective programs were consistent with NAEYC's guidelines. In short, well-grounded research about learning and development, summarized in such reports, is the foundation for NAEYC's work on developmentally appropriate practice and provides solid guidance for early childhood educators.

MyEducationLab

Go to the Video Examples section of Topic 4: Observation/Assessment in the MyEducationLab for your course and watch the video entitled *The Importance of Wonder*. Reflect on the positive effects of this developmentally appropriate preschool program on all aspects of children's development and learning

Research on Elements of Developmentally Appropriate Practice

Some studies examined effects of developmentally appropriate practice in preschool or kindergarten compared to "inappropriate" practices. These studies typically have defined appropriate classrooms as those characterized by child-initiated activity, active learning, problem solving, and positive, warm relationships between teachers and children. On the other hand, inappropriate classrooms are characterized by didactic lessons, heavy reliance on whole-group instruction, and emphasis on seatwork and rote learning. Much of the feedback in such classrooms tends to be teachers' correcting of children.

Effects on Social–Emotional Development

In observing numerous preschool classrooms, Stipek and her colleagues (1998) found that positive affect among teachers and children seemed to go along with developmentally appropriate practice, whereas negative affect was more likely to be found in classrooms using more inappropriate practices. Recent observational research in prekindergarten and primary grade classrooms has also found that positive, warm relationships with teachers that are developmentally appropriate promote both academic success and social skills (Hamre & Pianta, 2005, 2007). Research following children from infancy to age 4 in child care programs also found that high-quality, developmentally appropriate experiences and interactions with teachers contribute positively to children's development (NICHD Early Child Care Research Network, 2003).

Several studies of developmentally appropriate practice looked at children's social or emotional outcomes. For example, studies relating teaching practice to stress behaviors in children found significantly fewer stress-related behaviors in preschool and kindergarten children in more developmentally appropriate classrooms compared to children in less appropriate classrooms (Burts et al., 1992; Hart et al., 1998). Children in less appropriate preschools have also been found to score lower on measures of motivation (Stipek, Feller, Daniels, & Milburn, 1995).

Effects on Learning

A growing body of evidence supports the effectiveness of developmentally appropriate practices in enhancing children's learning (Huffman & Speer, 2000; Siraj-Blatchford et al., 2003). In a study examining the effect of developmentally appropriate practice on the academic achievement of urban kindergarten and first-grade children, children in the more developmentally appropriate classrooms scored higher on measures of letter/word identification and applied problem solving (Huffman & Speer, 2000). Another study found developmentally appropriate practice in Head Start to be positively related to children's school readiness and cognitive development (Bryant, Burchinal, Lau, & Sparling, 1994).

One large-scale, statewide study of prekindergarten in South Carolina evaluated the effects of implementing the HighScope approach, which is congruent with principles of developmentally appropriate practice, on the later academic achievement of economically disadvantaged children (Frede & Barnett, 1992). The researchers found that children's increased academic achievement in first-grade classrooms was related to moderate or high levels of developmentally appropriate practice in prekindergarten. Similarly, Burts et al.

(1993) found that children who attended more developmentally appropriate kindergartens had better reading scores in first grade.

A more recent study demonstrated the effectiveness of building on a developmentally appropriate framework such as HighScope with additional research-based teaching strategies (Bierman et al., 2008), such as those we describe in this book. This Head Start intervention program involved brief lessons on literacy and social skills, "hands-on" activities, and specific teaching strategies designed to promote children's social–emotional competencies, language development, and emergent literacy skills. Materials were also provided to parents to enhance children's development at home. The program significantly improved children's vocabulary, emergent literacy, emotional understanding, social problem solving, social behavior, and learning engagement.

The Future of Developmentally Appropriate Practice

One of the most important functions of NAEYC's work on developmentally appropriate practice has been to further discussion and debate in the field about teaching practices. Given the history of the field, it is likely that this topic will continue to be debated. What aspects are most likely to continue to provoke thought? Undoubtedly the realities of diversity and changing cultural contexts in our country will continue to raise questions about what is culturally as well as developmentally appropriate. Increased demands for accountability and the challenge to close the achievement gap raise the stakes over which practices can be successfully defended. Likewise, debates about what belongs in the curriculum have been a constant and will continue in the future, but are likely to be driven more by research than in the past.

The word *appropriate* is a culturally laden term and thus will continue to provoke controversy. Similarly, it is difficult to counteract the tendency of teachers and other professionals to emphasize "typical development" over individual differences and cultural variations (Graue, Kroeger, & Brown, 2003). After all, the first can be learned by reading books and journals, whereas the latter two require ongoing assessment of children, building relationships with families, and reflecting on how our own cultural perspectives influence our judgments and behavior.

To be developmentally appropriate, practices must contribute to children's learning and development. Therefore, this book focuses on recommended teaching practices, which must be responsive to children's individual development and cultural variation to be deemed appropriate. At the same time, we also focus on whether those practices help children achieve important learning goals. By definition, developmentally appropriate practices should be effective practices. To be effective, teachers must know children, they must know *how* to teach, and they must know *what* to teach. Each of these areas of knowledge must be informed by research. The following equation describes these components of effective, research-based practice.

Effective Practice =
Knowing Children + Knowing How to Teach + Knowing What to Teach

Ultimately, the truest measure of developmentally appropriate practice is seeing children joyfully, physically, and intellectually engaged in meaningful learning about their world and everyone and everything in it (Copple & Bredekamp, 2009).

Revisiting Mr. Washington's Classroom

At the beginning of this chapter we met Olivia, who was somewhat timidly experiencing school for the first time. Having explored the basic premises of developmentally appropriate practice, we can now see Olivia's experience with a more informed eye. Her classroom, with its *age-appropriate* materials, furnishings, and environment, not only made Olivia feel comfortable but also encouraged her involvement. Furthermore, her teacher, Mr. Washington, drew on his knowledge of how children develop and learn by working to establish a warm, positive relationship with Olivia right from the start. He also provided Olivia with a learning experience that would build on what she was already able to do, such as her proficiency with puzzles.

At the same time, Mr. Washington demonstrated the importance of paying attention to what is *individually appropriate*. He made Olivia feel welcome by sending her a personal postcard, designating her cubby with her name, and piquing Olivia's interest in puzzles. Finally, Mr. Washington was *culturally appropriate*—sensitive to the cultural context in which Olivia lives—using his own language attempts and a skilled translator to communicate with and reassure Olivia's grandmother. In so doing, he demonstrated that he values Olivia's family, their language, and cultural background. Taken together, the actions in that brief scenario demonstrate the teacher's broad base of knowledge and bode well for Olivia's successful transition to school.

MyEducationLab

To assess your understanding of developmentally appropriate practice, go to the Book Specific Resources section in the MyEducationLab for your course, select *Effective Practices in Early Childhood Education*, Chapter 3 of the Study Plan, and then complete the multiple choice questions and activities.

Chapter Summary

- Developmentally appropriate practice is teaching that is attuned to children's ages, experience, abilities, and interests, and that helps them attain challenging and achievable goals.
- Intentional teachers have a purpose for everything that they do, are thoughtful and prepared, and can explain the rationale for their decisions and actions to other teachers, administrators, or parents.
- Decisions about developmentally appropriate practice are based on knowledge of child development and learning (what is age appropriate), knowledge about children as individuals, and knowledge of the social and cultural contexts in which children live (what is culturally appropriate).
- The role of the early childhood teacher has five interrelated dimensions: (1) creating a caring community of learners, (2) teaching to enhance learning and development, (3) planning curriculum to meet important goals, (4) assessing children's learning and development, and (5) establishing reciprocal relationships with families.
- "Widening the lens" is a metaphor to help teachers remember to consider diverse perspectives and move beyond *either/or* thinking to *both/and* thinking when solving problems or making decisions about practice.
- Well-grounded research about learning and development is the basis for NAEYC's position statements on developmentally appropriate practice and provides solid guidance for early childhood educators.

key terms

age appropriate
assessment
caring community of learners
culturally appropriate
culture
curriculum
developmentally appropriate practice
individually appropriate
intentional teachers
position statement
reciprocal relationships
scientifically based curriculum

readings & websites

Copple, C., & Bredekamp, S. (2006). *Basics of developmentally appropriate practice: An introduction for teachers of children 3 to 6*. Washington, DC: National Association for the Education of Young Children.

Copple, C., & Bredekamp, S. (Eds.). (2009). *Developmentally appropriate practice in early childhood programs serving children from birth through age 8* (3rd ed.). Washington, DC: National Association for the Education of Young Children.

Kostelnik, M. J., Soderman, A. K., & Whiren, A. P. (2011). *Developmentally appropriate curriculum: Best practices in early childhood education* (5th ed.) Upper Saddle River, NJ: Pearson.

ASCD Whole Child Initiative
www.wholechildeducation.org

National Association for the Education of Young Children
www.naeyc.org/dap

National Institute for Early Education Research
www.nieer.org

Zero to Three—National Center for Infants, Toddlers, and Families
www.zerotothree.org

observe, reflect, decide

1. Observe a group of three or more toddlers in an early childhood classroom and note ways in which they are developmentally similar and ways in which their individuality comes through. Reflect on whether the materials and environment are age appropriate. Decide how well you think the teacher is able to meet the individual needs of very young children in a group.
2. Observe a child with special needs in an inclusive preschool program. Reflect on whether the program is developmentally appropriate as well as individually appropriate for this child. Decide how it might be improved to better serve children with disabilities.
3. Observe in a school or child care center. Look for evidence of the children's cultural and linguistic groups. Reflect on the difficulty of going beyond the outward manifestations of culture to understand the deeper meanings. Decide what you might do as a teacher of children from a cultural group very different from your own.
4. Observe the children in a kindergarten or primary grade classroom. Reflect on whether they appear to be mentally engaged with what is going on, and whether the expectations for their behavior are developmentally appropriate. Decide what you think the teacher could do to better meet the developmental and learning needs of the age group, as well as those of individual children.
5. Reflect on your own experiences as a first, second, or third grader. Can you remember situations in which you felt your teacher understood your individual needs and interests? What did the teacher do? How did it make you feel?

part two

Who We Teach

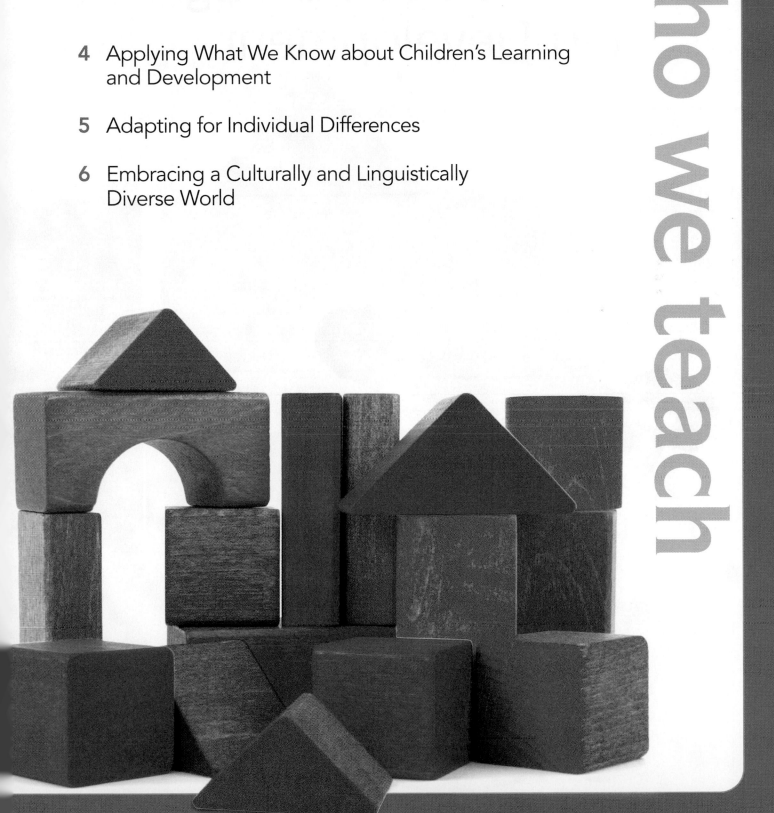

Learning and Developing from Birth to Age 8

4 Applying What We Know about Children's Learning and Development

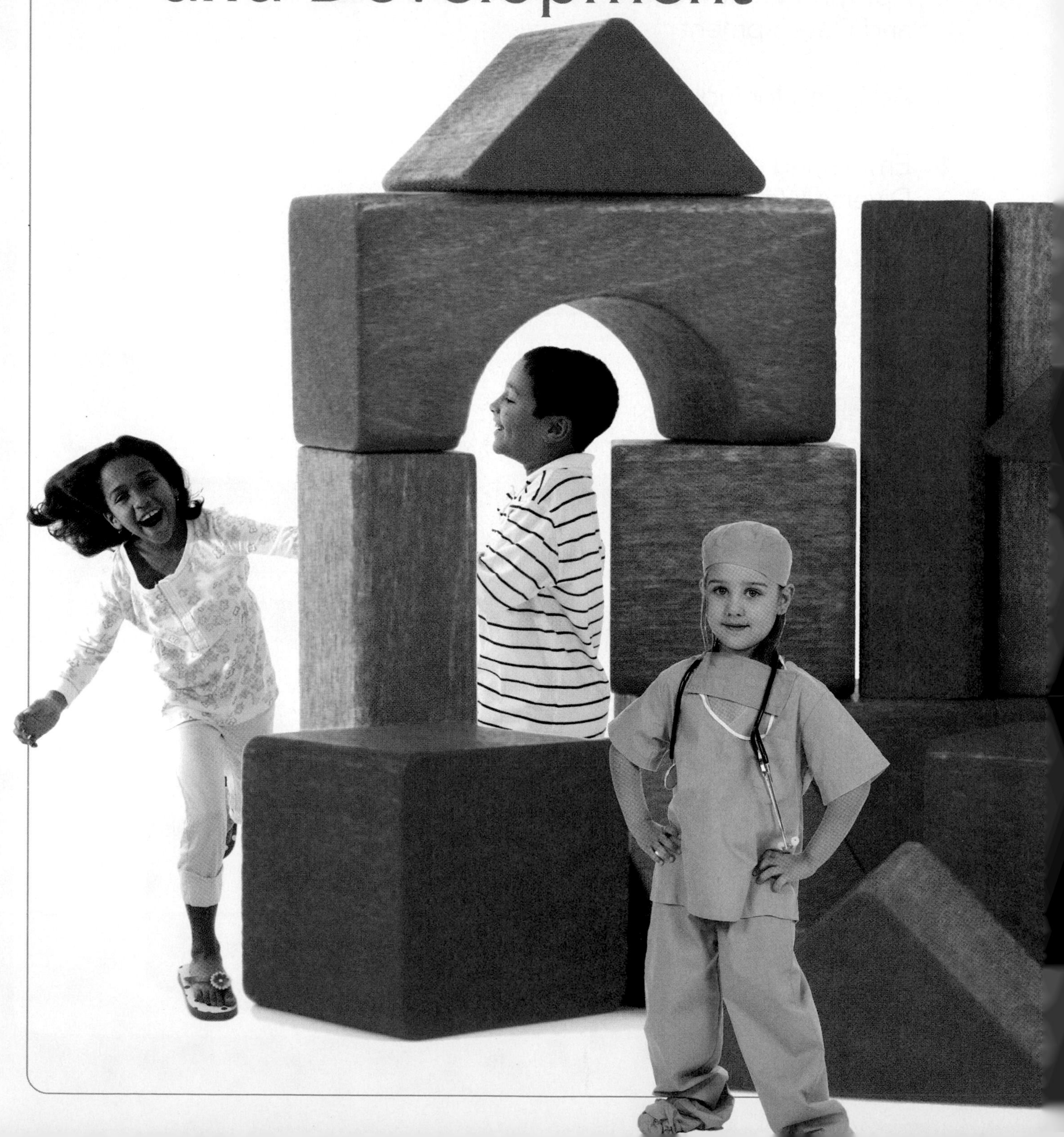

Thinking Ahead

1. What is development? What is learning? How are these processes related?
2. What is a theory? What is the relationship of theory, research, and practice?
3. What do we know about brain development in the early years and what are the implications for practice?
4. What are the key components of the major development theories of Erikson, Maslow, Piaget, and Vygotsky and how do they apply to practice?
5. What are the key components of the major learning theories—behaviorism and social cognitive theory—and how do they apply to practice?
6. What is the role of play in children's development and learning, and how do teachers support it?
7. What principles of practice can be derived from theories of learning and development to inform decisions about effective practice?
8. What is the Reggio Emilia approach to early education, and how is it an example of applying theory to practice, and practice leading theory?

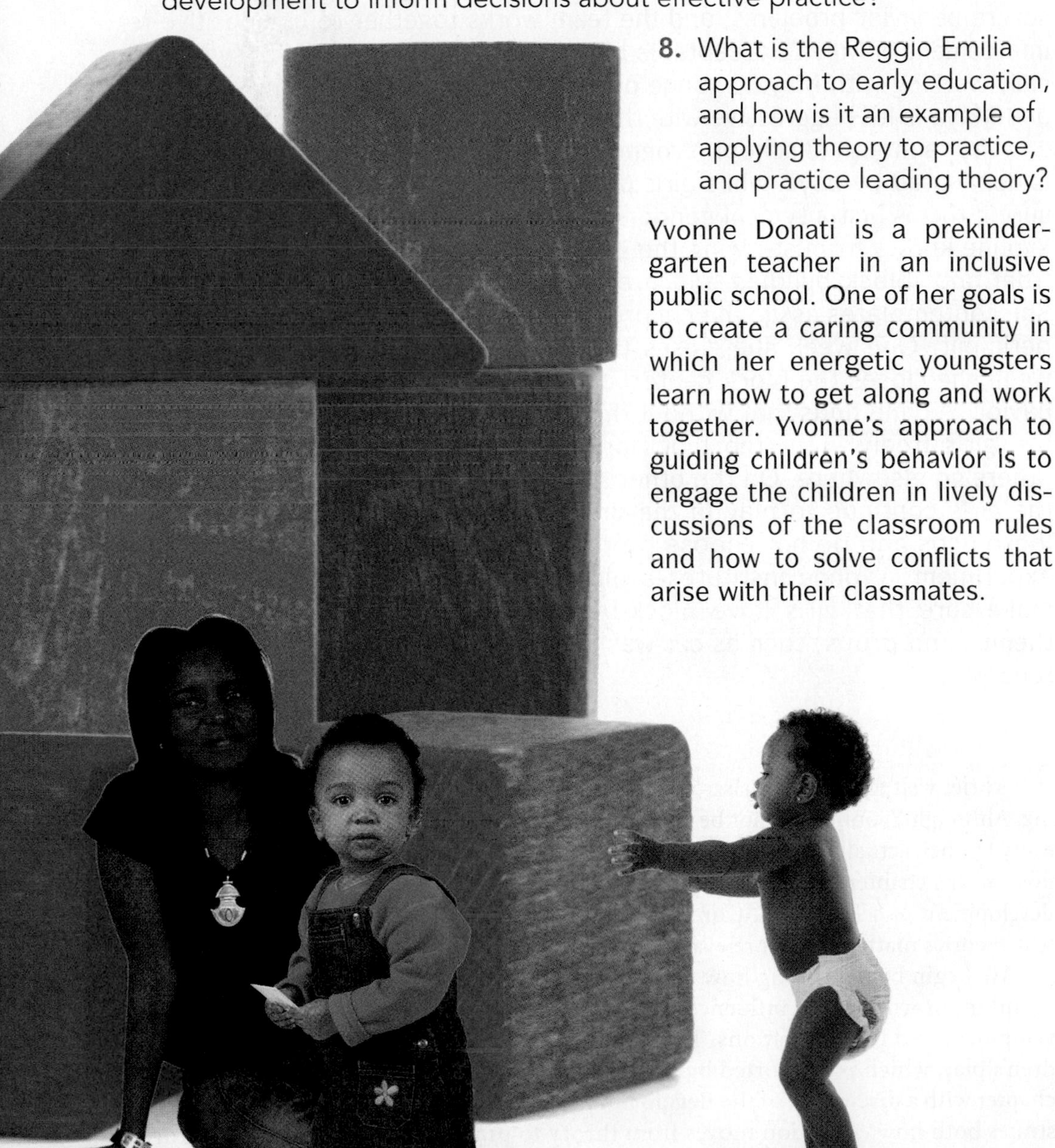

Yvonne Donati is a prekindergarten teacher in an inclusive public school. One of her goals is to create a caring community in which her energetic youngsters learn how to get along and work together. Yvonne's approach to guiding children's behavior is to engage the children in lively discussions of the classroom rules and how to solve conflicts that arise with their classmates.

In planning curriculum, Yvonne draws on the children's interests to integrate literacy instruction with science study of plants or animals, and children often work on small-group projects such as making a terrarium. She and the children have large-group meetings and she sometimes reads to the whole group, but she keeps these periods brief. She tries to find ways to make sure the children are physically active such as doing motions to songs or fingerplays. She also actively engages children's minds, as when she gives clues for the children to guess what object is hidden in a paper bag or take turns figuring out what a new word means in a story.

When children encounter new challenges in their play, Yvonne helps them to come up with their own solutions rather than solving the problem for them. She asks probing questions: "Why do you think your tomato plant didn't grow tall?" "Let's compare your plant and Juana's—why is hers taller?"

Because some children in Yvonne's class have identified disabilities, she regularly meets with the special education team and cooperates in implementing the children's individualized education programs (IEPs). Maya has severe behavior problems, and the team works together to use positive reinforcement of Maya's acceptable behavior. After a few weeks of systematically working with Maya, Yvonne observes that the new strategy is working and Maya is less aggressive with the other children.

After a month of school, Yvonne observes that every day the block area is dominated by boys, while girls prefer the dramatic play center. She isn't sure if this is just a typical gender difference or if there is another reason. Yvonne knows from studying the importance of play that children benefit from both block building and pretend play and that the benefits differ. She contemplates assigning children to areas, but then she designs an experiment. One week she closes the dramatic play center, and the next week she closes the block center, observing and recording children's behavior. Yvonne finds that without the availability of the dramatic play center, girls freely enter the block area; some boys play with them while others go elsewhere. On the other hand, when the block center is closed, the girls continue to play in the dramatic center, but the boys seem at loose ends and do not choose pretend play. Based on the results of her experiment, Yvonne institutes a play planning session each morning to make sure that girls have block-building opportunities. She also adds themes and props, such as car wash props, to interest more boys in pretend play. ▲

This brief visit to Yvonne's classroom reveals several things about her approach to teaching. Although Yvonne may not be fully aware of it, the decisions she makes, like those of every teacher, actually reflect various theories of how children learn and develop. The purpose of this chapter is to help you understand and apply the prevailing theories of child development and learning. At times, both beginning and experienced teachers wonder why theories matter or what relevance theories have to their work.

We begin by describing how theories of child development and learning are most useful in informing and influencing practice. Next, we describe research on brain development and its implications. Then, we discuss the critically important role of children's play, which is supported by all major developmental theories. We conclude the chapter with a discussion of the Reggio Emilia approach because that approach demonstrates both how education moves from theory to practice and how practice can drive theory.

Understanding Development and Learning

Intentional, effective teaching requires that teachers understand how children think and learn, and how best to support their healthy development at various ages in all areas—physical, social, emotional, and cognitive. Both development and learning are complicated processes requiring that teachers not only study research and theory, but also study children themselves.

What Is Development?

If you spend any time with early childhood educators, you are likely to hear that it is important for teachers to understand child development. This is true. But what do they need to know about development and why is it important? To answer these questions, we must first define terms. **Development** is age-related change that results from an interaction between biological maturation and physical and/or social experience.

Development occurs as children grow, adapt, and change in response to various experiences. Consider how language develops. Biology plays a role, with babies all over the world producing similar sounds at about the same age. But language development requires more than maturation. Babies need social interaction with adults and older children who talk to them. As they grow physically and are able to get around on their own, infants and toddlers encounter more examples of language interaction, and their speech starts to take off around age 2 (just as their legs do).

development Age-related change that results from an interaction between biological maturation and a physical and/or social experience; development occurs as children grow, adapt, and change in response to various experiences.

What Is Learning?

By contrast, **learning** is a change in knowledge or skill that results from experience or instruction. Learning and development are not the same things, although they affect each other. Learning is a similar, though not identical, process whether a person is 3 years old or 33. For example, learning to read for a first grader isn't completely different than it is for an older person.

learning A change in knowledge or skill that results from experience or instruction.

Because experience plays a role in both development and learning, there is a close connection between these processes, especially in the early years of life when children are growing and changing so rapidly. Sometimes development leads to learning (Piaget, 1952). For example, when a baby develops the ability to grasp objects and begins to put them in her mouth, she learns a lot about the objects in her world. Some are hard, others soft; some taste good, others don't. In this case, her development fosters her learning. Children's developmental level can also put limitations on what they are capable of learning. For example, preschoolers can do some abstract thinking, but they won't fully understand complex, abstract concepts such as chronological time until they are older.

Learning can also drive development. As children gain more experience in the world and come to understand more complex concepts, their cognitive development is affected. In primary grade children, cognitive development advances significantly as a result of the wide range of experiences school provides.

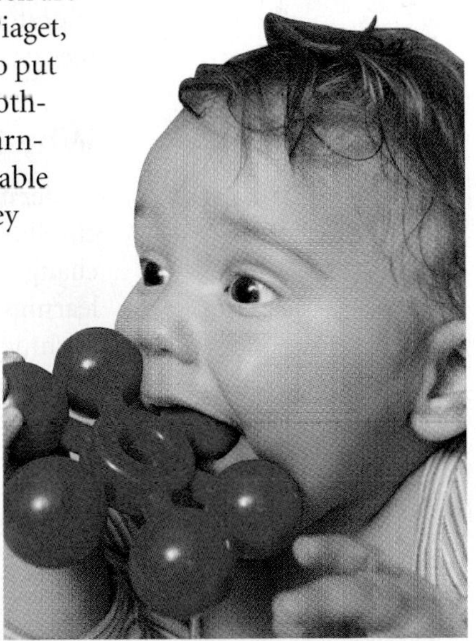

During early childhood, children's development and learning are closely connected. Right from the start, babies put things in their mouths and this teaches them about objects in the world—how they feel and what they do.

The Role of Theory

Centuries ago, human beings thought that the world was flat. No one wanted to venture too far out onto the sea for fear of falling off the edge. Slowly, more people traveled further from shore, and others observed that the tops of arriving ships appeared first and then gradually the rest. If the earth were flat, the entire ship would appear at once. These observations and experiences led to the conclusion that the earth is not flat, but is actually a sphere.

This simple example illustrates the power of theories. A **theory** is an explanation of how information and observations are organized and relate to one another. As we can see, theories are important because they affect how people think and behave. In education, theories of learning and development affect how people treat children, how they structure classroom environments, and how they teach.

MyEducationLab

Go to the Book Specific Resources in the MyEducationLab for your course and select Author Interviews in Chapter 4 to watch and listen to the video *How Research Informs Practice*. How does Sue Bredekamp describe the role of research?

The Relationship between Theory, Research, and Practice

Where do theories come from? Theories usually evolve from research, which can take the form of systematic observations over time or scientifically controlled experiments. In fact, a theory derives from a **hypothesis**, which is a tentative explanation for a phenomenon. The more research is available to support the "truth" of a theory, the more useful the theory becomes in guiding practice. Yvonne had a theory about why girls and boys play differently. She tested and then revised her theory by conducting an informal research study.

When research findings contradict earlier conclusions, theories evolve, are discarded, or are replaced with new ones. In the early part of the 20th century, the prevailing theory of child development was **maturationist.** According to this theory, derived from research by Arnold Gesell (1940; Ames & Ilg, 1979), the sequence of changes in abilities and behavior is largely predetermined by children's biological growth processes rather than their experiences or learning.

Maturation theory led to the notion that teachers needed to wait until children were ready for experiences to be effective. Because it was assumed that children were not ready to read until first grade, few literacy experiences were provided in preschool or kindergarten. Research in the intervening years demonstrated that differences in children's abilities are heavily influenced by their experiences (Shonkoff & Phillips, 2000). As a result, maturationist theory has been displaced by other theories. Nevertheless, maturationist theory continues to influence some practices such as kindergarten "redshirting"—holding children out of kindergarten until they are a year older and presumably more ready to learn.

Theories can also drive the way research is conducted and findings are interpreted. For example, if a theory is assumed to be universally true for all children, then research that supports the theory is assumed to apply to all children. Even if the research has only been conducted with white, middle-class children, the findings are applied to children of color or children of different socioeconomic, linguistic, or cultural backgrounds. As early childhood educators come to understand more about the role of culture in development and learning, theory and research must be more cautiously interpreted through these lenses.

Why Study Child Development and Learning?

Understanding theories of learning and development is particularly important for early childhood teachers for several reasons. During the first 8 years of life, children grow and change more rapidly than at any other period of the life span. As a result, development and learning are more closely connected in early childhood, making the developmental accomplishments and learning that take place at this point critically important foundations for what follows.

Understanding child development and learning helps teachers in many ways, including:

- Setting and evaluating goals that are achievable for most children within a given age range, and that also challenge children to go on learning
- Accurately interpreting children's behavior as predictable for their age or in need of intervention
- Knowing predictable sequences of development and learning to plan curriculum and adapt teaching to accommodate where individual children are in the sequence
- Predicting the kinds of topics and experiences that will be interesting and meaningful to children of different ages
- Using information about typical and atypical development to identify and diagnose potential disabilities or developmental delays in children.

theory An explanation of how information and observations are organized and relate to one another.

hypothesis An assumption about or tentative explanation of a phenomenon.

maturationist Theory of development that assumes that the sequence of changes in abilities and behavior is largely predetermined by children's biological growth processes rather than by their experiences or learning.

In previous sections, we defined and described the relationships between development and learning, and between theory, research, and practice. Teachers have much to learn about these topics, but we begin with the most current area of new knowledge, brain development.

Brain Development and Implications for Practice

Some of the most exciting discoveries about human development ever made have occurred in the past 25 years as advanced technologies have enabled scientists to directly study how the brain grows and changes. Tools such as positron emission tomography (PET) scans and functional magnetic resonance imagery (fMRI) open windows into how the brain functions when people perform different tasks and how the brains of children and adults compare (M. H. Johnson, 2005). An explosion of brain research has captured the imagination of the general public and policy makers, in addition to educators and parents.

A major conclusion of this research is that brain development results from an interaction between what is happening in children's minds and their experiences in the world (Nelson, de Haan, & Thomas, 2006). In other words, learning affects brain development, and brain growth and change affect learning (R. A. Thompson, 2008).

How the Brain Promotes Learning

The brain is the most complex of human organisms, the most important to overall functioning, yet we know the least about it. But we are learning more.

The Physical Brain

The brain is composed of a massive number of nerve cells or **neurons** that receive information through the senses or from other neurons, and then communicate information back to other parts of the body (Nelson et al., 2006). One connection might alert the baby to look at a human face, whereas another might signal a smile in response to mommy's face. These connections that carry information between neurons are called **synapses**.

In utero, the baby's brain undergoes astonishing growth. Neurons are produced at a rapid rate, and they migrate (or move) to the places in the brain where they will develop and be used. They also begin the process of differentiation—specialization for particular functions. The processes of neuron production, migration, and differentiation are mostly directed by genes. However, they are also affected by maternal health, nutrition, and environmental risks, such as alcohol or drug use.

The adult brain has about 100 billion neurons, about the same number that babies have at birth. The major difference between the newborn brain and adult brain, however, is the intricate network of connections (synapses) between the neurons, the brain's wiring system (Gopnik, Meltzoff, & Kuhl, 1999). During the first 2 to 3 years of life, babies' brains overproduce synapses going from about 2,500 at birth to 15,000—many more than adults have. After that, the brain starts **pruning** unnecessary or unused synapses. Throughout life, new synapses are formed and others are pruned away.

Pruning is important because it contributes to efficient brain operation, aids learning and memory, and increases the brain's flexibility, actions that neuroscientists term *plasticity*. **Plasticity** is the brain's ability to develop and change in response to experiences. After pruning, fewer, stronger connections among brain cells strengthen those that remain. This process is similar to pruning a bush that has grown too large; cutting off unneeded branches strengthens those that remain and may mean more blossoms in the future.

The Role of Experience in Brain Development

During early childhood—a period of rapid brain growth—the brain is most receptive and responsive to experience (R. A. Thompson, 2008). Children's relationships with the family

neurons Nerve cells in the brain that receive information through the senses or from other neurons, and then communicate information back to other parts of the body.

synapses Connections in the brain that carry information between neurons.

pruning The process whereby the brain eliminates unnecessary or unused synapses, which contributes to efficient brain operation, aids learning and memory, and increases the brain's flexibility.

plasticity The brain's ability to develop and change in response to experiences.

and community impact brain development, and influence how well the neurological system works. Both positive and negative experiences modify the brain architecture, with the most emotionally intense and most meaningful experiences having the greatest effects (Levitt, 2008). For these reasons, highly stressful experiences during early childhood can have lasting negative consequences (R. A. Thompson, 2008).

Although too little stimulation can lead to poor outcomes, exposing young children to overstimulating environments is not supported by brain research (R. A. Thompson, 2008). Babies and toddlers in particular become stressed when they are overstimulated. They either tune out (usually by going to sleep) or act out (usually by crying). Either way, they aren't learning.

windows of opportunity Periods of time during which human brains are particularly susceptible and responsive to certain types of experience.

Brain research indicates that the years up to age 10 are the prime time for learning. Instead of critical periods, researchers use the term **windows of opportunity** to suggest that there are times in life when the brain is most open to certain types of experiences. One such example is language development in babies as described in the feature *What Works: Babies and Brain Research.*

Young children's brains are much more active, connected, and flexible than adults' (R. A. Thompson, 2008). However, this does not mean, as some people have concluded, that the first few years of life are such a critical period that after age 3 or 5 the window

What Works 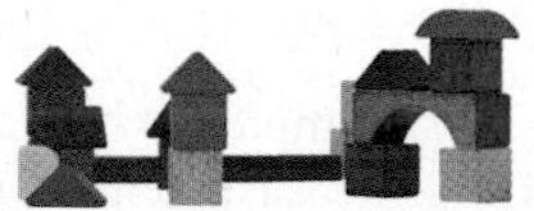

Babies and Brain Research

One of the conclusions from research on brain development is that there are windows of opportunity during which human brains are particularly susceptible and responsive to certain types of experience. One of those windows relates to language development among very young children.

Patricia Kuhl is a leading authority on speech development. She has conducted numerous studies with very young infants to test babies' ability to discriminate the sounds of diverse languages. Surprisingly, Kuhl has found that very young babies are not only able to discriminate the sounds of their own language, but they also respond to different sounds in every language presented to them, including those they had never heard. This means that American babies perked up when new sounds were introduced whether in English, Russian, Chinese, French, Thai, or African languages. Kuhl concluded that babies know much more about language than ever imagined and that they are, in fact, born "citizens of the world" (Gopnik, Meltzoff, & Kuhl, 1999, p. 106).

The next question Kuhl investigated was what would happen after babies were a little older and had more experience hearing the language around them. Kuhl found that 7-month-old Japanese and American babies could discriminate /r/ from /l/ equally well. But at 10 months of age, Japanese babies no longer responded to the change from /r/ to /l/, a phonetic distinction that does not exist in their native language. American babies, on the other hand, not only could make this distinction, but they had actually gotten better at doing so. Apparently, the different language experiences that babies have during that first year of life shape their brains in different ways.

This research supports the value of early exposure for learning a second language. Kuhl and others have found that if children are introduced to a second language between 3 and 7 years of age they are able to speak it like a native—that is, without an accent. After about age 10, however, people who learn another language are never able to speak it like a native speaker. Contrary to this finding, most "foreign" language instruction in U.S. schools doesn't occur until high school, long after this window of opportunity has closed, making learning a new language more difficult.

What brain research tells us is that when babies are born, there is a great deal of neurological capacity in place. But during the first few years of life, the brain changes in major ways in response to experience—the brain learns, especially from human interaction. Which leads to another conclusion: The brain—and the baby, of course—love to learn from other people.

Reference: Gopnik, A., Meltzoff, A. N., & Kuhl, P. K. (1999). *The scientist in the crib: Minds, brains, and how children learn.* New York: William Morrow.

for learning closes. On the contrary, brains remain flexible throughout life, as demonstrated when an 80-year-old learns to knit or a 58-year-old learns Italian.

Implications of Brain Research

Fostering optimal early brain development is foundational for positive outcomes for children. Reviews of brain research (Bransford, Brown, & Cocking, 2000; Nelson et al., 2006; R. A. Thompson, 2008) lead to several conclusions:

- The brain's most significant development occurs before birth, placing great importance on prenatal care.
- Early experiences change and organize the physical structure of the brain.
- Different parts of the brain are more responsive to experiences at different times. There are windows of opportunity for particular types of learning.
- Neglect, abuse, and stress pose serious threats to healthy brain development. Prevention and early intervention become even more important in light of the potentially lasting negative consequences for brain development.
- Brains develop best when children experience loving relationships, play, opportunities to explore their world, interesting and engaging things to learn about, and healthy, safe environments.
- Brain development is integrated; as children get older, the areas within the brain become better connected.

During preschool and the primary grades, considerable growth and change take place in the frontal lobes of the brain, the areas that are responsible for regulating thought and action (Berk, 2006). As a result, the following skills improve considerably during these years: attention, impulse control, planning, reasoning, problem solving, and memory (R. A. Thompson, 2008).

MyEducationLab

Go to the Assignments and Activities section of Topic 2: Child Development/Theories in the MyEducationLab for your course and complete the activity entitled *Development of Infants and Toddlers*. As you watch the video and answer the accompanying questions, reflect on the important brain development that occurs in the first 3 years of life and how high quality early childhood programs support young children's optimum development.

Implications for Practice

Brain research has electrified public interest in early childhood education. Nevertheless, neuroscience provides clearer guidance about the kinds of experiences that harm development rather than those that enrich it (R. A. Thompson, 2008). This reinforces the need to prevent child abuse and neglect and eliminate risk factors such as exposure to toxic substances and poor nutrition. Likewise, evidence from brain research supports the need for Head Start–like comprehensive family services to minimize stress and trauma in children's lives and improve the mental and physical health of caregivers.

At least at the present time, brain research is not precise enough to provide guidance about specific ways to optimize development (R. A. Thompson, 2008). In general, it validates the importance of positive relationships with parents and teachers. And because the areas of the brain that contribute to social-emotional and cognitive development are connected, early childhood programs should focus on both (R. A. Thompson, 2008).

However, we have much less knowledge of specific curricula, products, or teaching practices that enhance brain development (Shonkoff & Phillips, 2000; R. A. Thompson, 2008); therefore, teachers should be wary of products that claim to be based on brain research. It appears that the best course is to use educational practices that have been shown to be effective. Neuroscience is most useful when coupled with the larger body of knowledge about theories of development and learning, which we describe in the sections that follow.

Theories of Child Development

In this section, we present the theories of child development that are influential in early childhood education today. One of the most debated aspects of human development has been whether biology or experience (nature or nurture) plays the bigger role in explaining individual differences. Some theories place greater emphasis on inborn, biologically driven changes, whereas others consider the environment to be the primary influence. Most of the prominent theories, however, reflect the prevailing view that human development is a product of *both* biology/heredity *and* environment/experiences.

Before discussing specific theories, however, it is important to point out that theories are generated in particular social and cultural contexts. Theories are often derived from research conducted with only one population of children—most frequently, white middle-class children. Therefore, despite the frequent claim that theories are "universal" and apply equally well to all children, they need to be evaluated from a broader perspective as described in the *Culture Lens: Seeing Child Development Theory through the Lens of Culture* feature.

As we will see, multiple theories exist because of the various dimensions of development, such as social, emotional, and cognitive. The work of Erik Erikson and Abraham Maslow, which we describe in the sections that follow, has been influential in guiding practice in social and emotional development and motivation to learn. (Another important theory of human development, Urie Bronfenbrenner's ecological theory, is described in the chapter on relationships with families and community.)

Culture Lens

Seeing Child Development Theory through the Lens of Culture

An especially important consideration in evaluating theories is the cultural background of the children and families who participated in the research. For decades, one theory of how parental child rearing affects preschool children's development has been assumed to apply to all children and families (Baumrind, 1971). The theory identifies three parenting styles:

1. **Authoritative.** Loving, nurturing, involved, and sensitive parents who explain their reasons for discipline have children who are motivated to learn and well adjusted socially and emotionally.
2. **Authoritarian.** Restrictive, punishing, rejecting, and controlling parents have children who lack initiative and are inhibited.
3. **Permissive.** Parents who are warm and accepting of children, but minimally involved and laissez-faire about discipline have children with the lowest levels of motivation and achievement.

Authoritative parenting is thought to be the most effective style of child rearing. Most research on the theory, however, has been conducted with Caucasian middle-class families. New research with Head Start families (McWayne, Owsianik, Green, & Fantuzzo, 2008) using culturally familiar language and behaviors identified similar but not identical types of parenting: active-responsive (e.g., tell child "I'm proud" when he tries to be good), passive-permissive (e.g., tell child "I'll punish," but don't), and active-restrictive (e.g., I spank the child when she is disobedient). Research with low-income, urban, African American families found no relationships between these different parenting styles and preschool children's social-emotional skills.

What might account for these contradictory findings between diverse cultural groups? When children grow up in poverty-stricken, dangerous communities and face possible discrimination and prejudice, parents' priorities reflect these conditions. They may express their love by focusing on survival skills and making sure that their children behave maturely and competently in situations where people are biased against them. With these goals in mind, the effectiveness of restrictive parenting makes more sense.

Compared to Caucasian middle-class families, African American childrearing tends to be spread among a number of people in the extended family and community. The mother may be relatively passive and permissive, for example, whereas others in the child's circle such as a grandmother or aunt may be more restrictive or actively responsive.

What can we conclude from revisiting a widely accepted child development theory like Baumrind's parenting framework? Research that leads to a new theory needs to be conducted with diverse populations of children and families. Otherwise, the theory simply can't be said to apply to them. In addition, research needs to be interpreted through a wide lens that considers the social and cultural contexts in which children live—in this case, the realities of life for low-income, urban, African American families.

References: Baumrind, D. (1971). Current patterns of parental authority. *Developmental Psychology, 4,* 1–103; McWayne, C. M., Owsianik, M., Green, L. E., & Fantuzzo, J. W. (2008). Parenting behaviors and preschool children's social and emotional skills: A question of the consequential validity of traditional parenting constructs for low-income African Americans. *Early Childhood Research Quarterly, 23,* 173–192.

Erikson's Psychosocial Theory of Human Development

Psychologist Erik Erikson (1902–1994) was influenced by cultural anthropologists and came to see the importance of culture and social experience in shaping development. Based on extensive investigations conducted with his wife, Joan, Erikson published his seminal book, *Childhood and Society* (1950/1963).

He proposed an eight-stage theory of personal and social development in which at each stage of life an individual confronts a major challenge or "crisis." Successful negotiation of the crisis requires achieving a balance between two possible extremes. If crises are not resolved positively at particular points in the life span, Erikson postulated that later problems will ensue. Table 4.1 provides an overview of Erikson's eight stages, the typical crisis, and successful resolution.

Stages of Personal and Social Development in Early Childhood

Erikson hypothesized the following four stages of psychological and social development in the lives of children. He assumed that mothers and other family members are the principal actors in children's lives during the first three stages. However, children today participate in out-of-home child care from birth. Therefore, teachers also play significant roles in helping young children negotiate these critical life events.

Stage 1: Trust versus mistrust (birth to 18 months). Eight-month-old Martin is standing up in his crib sobbing and bouncing on his chubby legs. His family child care provider, Joanne, comes in and soothingly says, "I can tell you are wet and hungry. Let's change your diaper now." Martin sighs as she picks him up lovingly. Joanne knows Martin well enough to interpret his cries and respond accordingly; in turn, Martin is comforted by the fact that when he cries, Joanne is there for him.

The major task of infants and their caregivers is to develop a sense of trust in the world, a feeling that their needs for food and love will be met. Babies' trust develops

Table 4.1 Erikson's Stages of Personal and Social Development

Stage	Approximate Age	Psychosocial Crisis	Desired Resolution
1	Birth to 18 months	Trust vs. mistrust	Acquiring a sense of security and some control over environment
2	18 months to 3 years	Autonomy vs. doubt	Awareness of growing competence and separateness as human being
3	3 to 6 years	Initiative vs. guilt	Exercising a growing sense of power and ability to act on own without undue risk-taking
4	6 to 12 years	Industry vs. inferiority	Finding satisfaction in school achievement and mastery of new skills
5	12 to 18 years	Identity vs. role confusion	Finding sense of self and building relationships in peer group
6	Young adult	Intimacy vs. isolation	Building close relationships and connections with sexual partners, friends
7	Middle adulthood	Generativity vs. self-absorption	Gaining satisfaction from life's work, nurturing future generations, and caring for others
8	Late adulthood	Integrity vs. despair	Reflecting on life with contentment, facing death without hopelessness

Source: Adapted from "Figure of Erikson's Stages of Personality Development," from *Childhood and Society* by Erik H. Erikson.

through responsive relationships with caregivers. If adults are inconsistent or rejecting, the baby learns that the world is an untrustworthy place and that he has little power to influence what happens to him.

> *Stage 2: Autonomy versus doubt (18 months to 3 years).* Belinda is 22 months old. She has been in the same child care center with the same primary caregiver, Sandy, since she was 5 months old. She and Sandy have a warm, loving relationship. But lately, Belinda has begun to resist just about everything Sandy wants her to do. As soon as Sandy finishes dressing her, Belinda starts pulling off her shoes or shirt. She yells, "I want red shirt." Sandy calmly says, "Okay, you can choose. Do you want your red shirt or your yellow one (the one she is already wearing)?" Belinda pumps up her chest and says, "Yellow one."

Belinda's behavior may seem like a step backward toward infancy, but actually it is evidence of her advancing development. By 18 months, most babies are mobile and are soon able to communicate their wants and needs in words. They begin to separate from primary caregivers, try to do things for themselves, and assert their autonomy with statements like "Me do it!" or "Mine." This desire to break away from caregivers is sometimes called the "terrible twos" because it can lead to power struggles. One minute the child wants to hold onto the adult, and the next minute she wants to push away. But becoming a more autonomous human being is a major task of growing up. If adults are too harsh or restrictive with children at this age, they can feel powerless and doubt their own competence. One effective strategy is giving a toddler a manageable amount of power, such as Sandy did by offering a choice of two shirts.

> *Stage 3: Initiative versus guilt (3 to 6 years).* Donald teaches 4-year-olds. He loves this age group because he finds that most 4-year-olds can do many things on their own, while at the same time expressing their unbridled joy at every new accomplishment. He sets up his classroom and daily schedule to allow for as much choice as possible, while also being available to assist children during these periods of child-initiated activity. Dorcas especially needs his help because her parents have been somewhat overprotective and she is hesitant to try new experiences.

The preschool and kindergarten years are marked for most children by an increasing sense of their own abilities, especially improved motor skills and exploding language capacity. This sense of confidence, at times unwarranted, leads children to initiate their own activities. When children's initiatives are regularly punished or thwarted, they may begin to feel guilty and withdraw. The resolution for negotiating this stage is making sure that encouraging children's initiative and risk-taking is balanced by ensuring their safety.

> *Stage 4: Industry versus inferiority (6 to 12 years).* Melodie's second-grade class is working in small groups on two-digit subtraction problems. One group works feverishly, arguing with each over the correct answers and giving each other high fives when they figure them out. Another group of children is quieter, appearing frustrated and unsure. Looking over at the others, Max says, "We're the dumb group. We'll never do good in math."

During the elementary school years, children's spheres expand, and the opinions of teachers and peers become more important and parents' less so. School work becomes a major part of children's lives, and they begin to find satisfaction in achievement and in mastering new skills. They also begin to compare themselves to others and are more capable of judging their own performance. When children's accomplishments are not up to their standards, they may develop a sense of inferiority.

Erikson emphasized that development does not end during childhood but continues throughout the life span. Adults—students, teachers, and parents—will see themselves in the later stages (see Table 4.1). Understanding the struggles of the later stages—identity versus role confusion, intimacy versus isolation, generativity versus self-absorption, and integrity versus despair—can provide teachers with insight into the behavior of adolescents (who may be parents) and other adults, including parents and colleagues. However, the first four stages are most relevant to the work of early childhood educators.

Implications for Teaching

Erikson's theory has important implications for the social-emotional climates of early childhood programs, as we can see from visiting the Love and Learn Child Care Center. In this center, babies and toddlers have primary caregivers who stay with them for 2 or 3 years so teachers get to know them well and can provide consistent, responsive care. The preschool and kindergarten classes are structured with extended periods of time for children to initiate their own activities within the options that the teacher provides. Teachers encourage children to voice their opinions and ideas. The after-school program provides time, space, and materials for primary grade children to pursue and master hobbies and interests such as photography, computers, painting, sports, and writing stories.

In this book, we advocate a *both/and* approach to many questions regarding early childhood practice. Erikson's theory is an example of this approach because each of the crises that children must negotiate is resolved by achieving a balance between the two poles. Trust is essential, for example, but children also need to develop a healthy sense of caution when interacting with strangers. Similarly, preschool children's initiative should be encouraged, but they also need to learn limits.

Erikson's theory emphasizes the role of the sociocultural context on children's personal and social development, but parts of his theory assume particular cultural perspectives. For example, his emphasis on the singular role of the mother during the first three stages doesn't reflect the value that some cultural groups place on multiple caregivers (see the *Culture Lens* feature on page 102). Nevertheless, Erikson's theory makes a lot of sense to teachers of young children who observe these patterns daily.

Maslow's Self-Actualization Theory

Abraham Maslow (1908–1970) was part of a group of psychologists, called humanists, who studied healthy personality development rather than mental illness, as psychologists had done previously. Maslow (1954) developed **self-actualization theory**, which identifies a hierarchy of needs, as depicted in Figure 4.1, that motivate people's behavior and goals that are necessary for healthy personality development.

Hierarchy of Human Needs

Maslow's hierarchy is a pyramid depicting the relationship between needs and goals. The bottom two layers represent the basic physical needs required to sustain life, such as food, water, and shelter, and the fundamental psychological needs for safety and security. Maslow postulated that unless these needs are met, humans cannot move up the hierarchy to achieve the next goals or growth needs: love and a sense of belonging and then self-esteem. The top of the pyramid represents self-actualization, which is achievement of life's goals in many, individual forms. Goals that contribute to self-actualization are things that make life meaningful and satisfying. Maslow speculated that self-actualization is not achieved by everyone although most people strive for it.

Implications for Practice

Maslow's theory is useful as a framework for understanding how people are motivated. If children are hungry, it follows that they cannot focus their attention on anything else. Similarly, if children are frightened or emotionally insecure, they cannot learn effectively. Meeting children's basic physical needs as well as their need for psychological safety and emotional security is at the heart of good early childhood practice. Consider free school lunch programs and state licensing standards that set requirements for operating a child care center—many of these mandates are designed to protect children's health, safety, and security.

Effective early childhood programs go beyond meeting children's basic needs, however. Their goals include establishing positive, affectionate relationships among children and adults (the need for love and belonging) and building children's competence in all areas and, therefore, their self-esteem. Meeting children's needs and helping them achieve

self-actualization theory Maslow's view that behavior and learning are motivated by a hierarchy of needs.

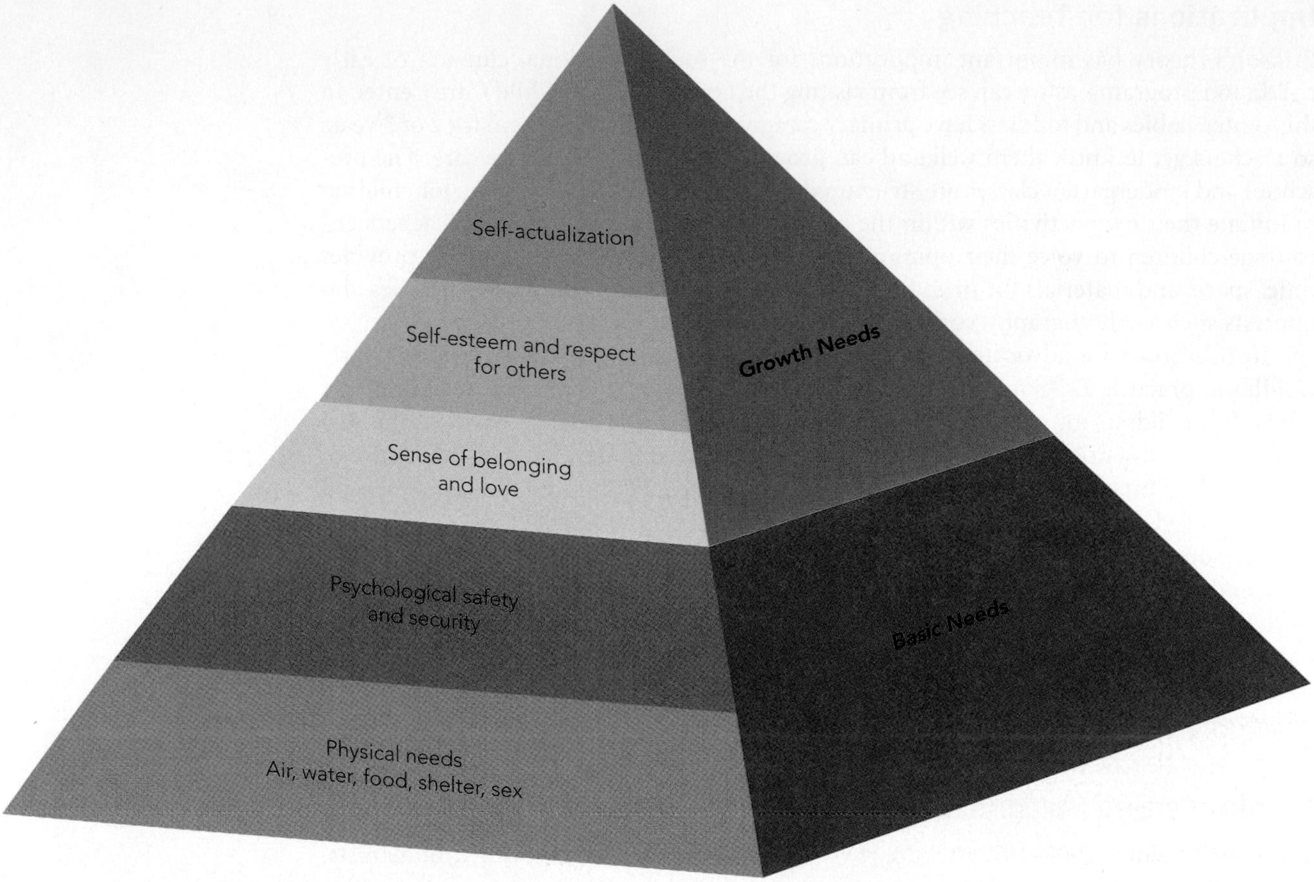

Self-actualization

Self-esteem and respect for others

Sense of belonging and love

Psychological safety and security

Physical needs
Air, water, food, shelter, sex

Growth Needs

Basic Needs

Figure 4.1 Maslow's Hierarchy of Needs

these goals contributes to life satisfaction and successful learning. Although children will not reach the pinnacle of Maslow's hierarchy—self-actualization—the foundations are laid during those early years. Adults might want to consider that a career teaching young children can be a self-actualizing experience, especially for those who find this work meaningful, playful, rewarding, and contributing to a better world.

The theories of both Erikson and Maslow apply primarily to social and personality development and the motivation to learn. Next, we turn to two theorists—Piaget and Vygotsky—whose work applies primarily to cognitive development. Because all domains of development are so integrally connected, however, these theories also have implications for social-emotional development.

Piaget and Cognitive Theory

The cognitive-developmental theory of Jean Piaget (1896–1980) has had enormous impact on the field of early childhood education. Although parts of his theory—particularly the stages of cognitive development—have been criticized, he remains a towering and influential figure decades after his death.

Swiss-born, Piaget spent the greater part of his life observing and listening to children of various ages, beginning with detailed observations of his own three children as infants. Piaget's wife, Valentine, did most of the minute-by-minute, day-by-day observing and recording of the children's behavior beginning at birth using the only tools available at the time, pen and paper (Gopnik et al., 1999).

Several aspects of Piaget's theory readily apply to education. The following sections present key concepts for teachers: constructivism, the process of learning (adaptation), types of knowledge, and the general idea of stages of cognitive development.

Constructivist Learning Theory

Piaget's relatively complex theory can be summed up in a simple sentence: "Children don't think like adults." Einstein called this discovery by Piaget "so simple that only a genius could have thought of it" (Papert, 1999). Piaget believed that children's minds are not empty vessels to be filled with knowledge by adults; instead, children actively try to make sense of their experiences by building or constructing their own knowledge. Piaget's theory of how children learn is called **constructivism**.

From his own perspective as a scientist, Piaget viewed children as little scientists who hypothesize about how the world works, and continually test and refine their own theories (Piaget, 1955). The following example illustrates how Piaget (1930, p. 35) did his work as well as how a young child thinks:

> *Piaget:* Where does the wind come from?
> *Ost (age 4):* From outside.
> *Piaget:* How is it made outside?
> *Ost:* By the motor cars.
> *Piaget:* What else can make the wind?
> *Ost:* Bicycles, trams, carts, dust.
> *Piaget:* What else?
> *Ost:* When you blow, when you sweep.

This dialogue demonstrates Piaget's major idea that children develop their own theories of how the world works. These theories are tested by experience, which subsequently causes the child's theory to be strengthened, changed, or discarded.

constructivism Learning theory derived from the work of Jean Piaget; assumes that children actively build their knowledge from firsthand experiences in stimulating environments.

scheme or **schema** The organization of mental structures people use to think or guide behavior; the structures develop and change with experience.

adaptation The mental process of altering concepts (schemes) in response to experience, which occurs in two ways: through assimilation and accommodation.

assimilation When new information or experience is understood in connection with existing knowledge (schemes).

How Development Occurs: The Process of Adaptation

One way we can tell that children construct their own knowledge is that they come up with their own ideas about or explanations for events. This is one reason why young children can be so enchanting. Five-year-old Pearson arrives at kindergarten one morning and proudly announces to his teacher, "I know what A + A is—B!" Pearson hasn't discovered algebra, but he does apply what he has learned about how numbers work ($1 + 1 = 2$) to the alphabet. However mistaken Pearson is at this point, he is clearly thinking and trying to connect what he is learning to what he already knows.

Piaget believed that all children, like Pearson, have an inborn ability to organize and make sense of their experiences. Piaget coined the term **scheme** or **schema** for the organizing structures people use to think or guide behavior. Schemes develop and change with experience. Toddler Veronica has a big German shepherd dog named Darby. When Veronica meets the Labrador next door, she calls him Darby, too. Her mom responds, "He's a doggie, but his name isn't Darby. It's Milo." Then, Veronica sees a pony at the petting zoo and exclaims with glee, "Doggie!" But when she goes to pet the pony, she realizes he is much taller than either Darby or Milo. Again, her mother clarifies: "No, he has four legs like Darby and Milo, but he's a pony, not a doggie." At home, Veronica's mom shows her books about animals to help her learn their names and characteristics.

Gradually, after many such experiences, Veronica forms an accurate scheme for dogs (including the fact that dogs are not all the same) and another scheme for ponies. **Adaptation** is the process of changing schemes in response to experience. Adaptation occurs in two ways: through assimilation and accommodation. **Assimilation** occurs when new information or experience is understood in connection with an existing scheme. Veronica assimilated her experience with Milo into her scheme for dogs.

As preschoolers play and interact with objects and other people, they construct their own understanding about the world, such as how a kicking motion affects a ball.

By contrast, if the new information doesn't fit within an existing scheme, the child must modify that scheme or construct a new one, a process called **accommodation**. In Veronica's case, the pony couldn't be assimilated into her doggie scheme, so a new scheme for pony had to be created. As Veronica gets older and has many more experiences, she will create different schemes to organize this basic information. Pony will be connected with the general scheme of animals, as well as the narrower scheme of animals you can ride.

When Veronica touched the pony and her mother gave her new information, she experienced **disequilibrium**, which is an imbalance in thinking that occurs when new information or physical experience cannot be understood in terms of what is already known (i.e., cannot be assimilated). Piaget believed that human beings seek equilibrium—we want the world to make sense, so we try to restore balance by creating new schemes or adapting existing ones, the process of **equilibration**.

Piaget theorized that learning depends on this process of adapting schemes through assimilation and accommodation in order to achieve equilibrium. He also believed that to change schemes children need both hands-on physical experience (they need to act on objects) and social interaction with peers and adults who help clarify their thinking. In the case of Veronica, her pony scheme was constructed through her real-life encounter at the zoo, as well as her conversations with her mother.

Types of Knowledge

Another important point of Piaget's theory is that there are different kinds of knowledge. Piaget believed that children's minds develop as the result interactions between experience and biology. But the process is not identical for every type of learning. In fact, Piaget (1952) identified three types of knowledge—physical, logico-mathematical, and social-conventional—which are acquired in different ways.

- **Physical knowledge** is understanding how objects move and function in space—how the physical world works. Two-year-old Evan loves to watch the rubber ball roll down the ramp, and repeats the action over and over. Then he tries using a rubber block. Even though the block is soft like the ball, it doesn't cooperate. Evan's hands-on experience with the ball and block adds to his knowledge of how different objects function in the physical world.
- **Logico-mathematical knowledge** is the relationships that are constructed in our minds between objects or concepts. Unlike physical knowledge, logico-mathematical knowledge is not directly observable. While playing with his ramp, Evan sees that Delia has two small balls and he has one big one. He decides that he wants a second ball. The idea that two balls are more than one ball is an example of logico-mathematical knowledge. Evan created the relationship between the objects in his mind; it does not exist otherwise. He could just as easily have focused on the relationship of size instead of quantity and decided to keep the big ball.
- **Social-conventional knowledge** is the culturally agreed-on names and symbols that need to be transmitted to the learner directly. For example, the letters of the alphabet, number names, and the meaning of the colors on the stoplight are all arbitrary. This kind of knowledge can't be reinvented by every learner. Usually, children hear these words or ideas repeatedly and eventually remember them.

A challenge for teachers is to recognize that different types of knowledge require different types of teaching and learning. Just because social-conventional knowledge is most efficiently learned through instruction does not mean that other types of knowledge can be easily acquired this way. Complex concepts such as counting, which is logico-mathematical knowledge, require much deeper understanding than simply reciting the number names. At the same time, children can't learn to count if they don't know the number sequence, just as they can't learn to read if they don't know the alphabet. Therefore, in constructing their understanding of concepts, children often draw on all three kinds of knowledge.

accommodation When new information or experience doesn't fit within an existing concept (scheme), the child must modify it or construct a new scheme.

disequilibrium An imbalance in thinking that occurs when new information or physical experience cannot be understood in terms of what is already known (cannot be assimilated).

equilibration The process whereby humans try to make sense of new experiences by creating new concepts (schemes) or adapting existing ones.

physical knowledge Understanding how objects move and function in space and how the physical world works.

logico-mathematical knowledge The relationships that are constructed in our minds between objects or concepts.

social-conventional knowledge The culturally agreed-on names and symbols that need to be transmitted to the learner directly.

Table 4.2 Piaget's Stages of Cognitive Development

Stage	Approximate Age	Characteristics
Sensorimotor	Birth to 2 years	Learns through senses and physical movement, gradually moving from reflexes to conscious activity.
Preoperational	2 to 7 years	Develops ability to learn through symbols—language and mental representations of thoughts; thinking is controlled more by perceptions than logic.
Concrete operational	7 to 11 years	Able to think and solve problems more logically, through concrete experience; abstract thinking is limited.
Formal operational	11 years to adulthood	Can think and solve problems abstractly, using symbolic thought and systematic experimentation.

Source: Based on *Educational Psychology: Theory and Practice*, 4th edition, by R. Slavin, 2006, Boston: Pearson Allyn & Bacon.

Cognition and Biology: Stages of Cognitive Development

Piaget believed that biology plays a key role in cognitive development with specific cognitive abilities changing in significant ways as children get older. His theory identifies four stages of cognition, as listed in Table 4.2. Piaget theorized that although the ages were approximate, the order of the stages is fixed and that every child goes through each stage.

Sensorimotor Stage (Birth to Age 2). During the years from birth to about age 2, children learn about the world through a combination of their sensory abilities—sight, hearing, taste, touch, smell—and their motor skills. Newborn and young infants rely on reflexes such as sucking and grasping to build schemes. When baby Sonia grasps her rattle and brings it to her mouth, she finds out lots of things about the rattle—it makes a noise she likes, and it feels hard and cold. Another characteristic of the sensorimotor period is that babies lack **object permanence**, which means that when an object is no longer in their sight, it ceases to exist for them. For example, if Mommy hides the favorite rattle under a blanket, Sonia won't look for it. Then when the blanket is removed, Sonia will inevitably be surprised to find the rattle there.

As children get older and are able to move on their own, crawling and toddling, they use more conscious movements to find out how things work. But their learning occurs through their actions; they don't yet think or plan in advance. Consider 18-month-old Ryan, who stacks his blocks in front of the cabinet door. When he opens the door, the blocks fall over, much to his surprise and dismay. Nevertheless, Ryan keeps stacking and knocking over the blocks, not realizing that if he moved the toys before opening the door, they wouldn't fall down.

Very young children also tend to see everything from their own intellectual and emotional point of view, what Piaget called **egocentrism**. Their experiences, such as shaking the rattle or making milk flow by sucking, convince them that they are the center of their world and can cause events to happen.

By about age 2, young children begin to be able to use symbols such as words, instead of relying on actions and objects to learn about the world, and they move into Piaget's second stage of cognitive development—preoperational.

object permanence A concept that babies lack early in the period of sensorimotor development, so that when an object is no longer in their sight, it ceases to exist for them.

egocentrism The process whereby very young children tend to see everything from their own intellectual and emotional point of view.

Preoperational Stage (Ages 2 to 7). Several major cognitive developments occur during this stage. First, children's language development explodes, which provides symbols that enable children to think (that is, hold a mental representation) of an object or event.

Ryan can now picture the door knocking down his blocks and, therefore, thinks ahead to building in a safer place. As a result of this new thinking ability, children are less dependent on sensorimotor learning, although active learning is still most effective.

Piaget did many classic experiments with preoperational children trying to gauge their ability to solve various prearranged tasks. What he concluded from these studies is that preoperational children rely on their perceptions or intuitions about solutions rather than on logic. For example, at snack time, 4-year-olds Isela and Ruth each have one graham cracker. Isela breaks hers into four pieces and tells Ruth, "Look! I have more crackers than you do!" Nothing her teacher says will convince Ruth that they have the same amount. Ruth is not content until the teacher resignedly breaks her cracker into four pieces as well.

From his observations, Piaget concluded that there are several specific limitations to the thinking of preoperational children. Ruth and Isela's situation demonstrates that they were unable to conserve quantity. **Conservation** is the concept that the quantity of objects or liquids does not change just because their physical appearance is transformed. If Ruth had a tall glass of milk and her teacher poured the milk into a short fat one, no doubt she would think that she has less milk and feel cheated once more. Ruth is unable to reverse the operation of pouring the milk in her mind and figure out that the amount has not changed. The same phenomenon—judging by appearances rather than logic—is observed when preschool children are presented with two equal rows of checkers. After one row is spread out and appears longer, even though no checkers have been added or removed, preoperational children will assume that the spread-out row has more checkers.

Preoperational children also continue to be egocentric, though less so over time. On a trip to a puppet show, a group of 3-year-olds boards a public bus. Martha sits down next to an elderly lady and asks, "Are you going to see the puppets, too?" Still seeing the world from her own point of view, Martha assumes that other people are doing what she's doing and for the same reason.

MyEducationLab

Go to the Assignments and Activities section of Topic 2: Child Development/Theories in the MyEducationLab for your course and complete the activity entitled *Development in the Primary Grades*. As you watch the video and answer the accompanying questions, consider what the boy in the video reveals about the thinking and memory abilities of children at this age.

Concrete Operational Stage (Ages 7 to 11). During the elementary school years, children's thinking becomes more logical, and they are able to solve problems mentally and reverse operations. They are no longer fooled by a conservation problem. Children are capable of carrying out mental actions. Piaget used the word *concrete* to refer to this stage of cognition because this age group is not yet capable of thinking about and fully comprehending complex, abstract concepts such as historical time or death. Instead, they are most successful at solving problems they can directly experience. Piaget believed that abstract reasoning is not possible until the stage of formal observations in adolescence and adulthood, and that some people never reach this stage of cognitive development.

Criticisms of Piaget's Theory

Piaget's theory was first widely disseminated in the United States in the 1970s and had a major impact on views of how children learn and appropriate ways to teach. Parents, toy manufacturers, and publishers were also influenced by Piaget's ideas about the competence of children, leading to an explosion in educational products for babies. However, in the past few decades, critics have questioned some of the fundamental tenets of Piagetian theory.

Research in the intervening years demonstrated that Piaget underestimated children's capabilities to some extent (R. Case & Okamoto, 1996; Gelman, 2000; Gelman & Baillargeon, 1983; Mix, Huttenlocher, & Levine, 2002). For example, researchers have found that under certain circumstances and with clearer directions, younger children have been able to perform tasks Piaget considered impossible (R. Case & Okamoto, 1996), such as taking the perspective of another person (describing what that person is seeing rather than assuming they are seeing what you are seeing). In addition, the inability to conserve quantity does not interfere with some preschool children's learning basic mathematics concepts, as Piaget assumed (Clements & Sarama, 2009).

conservation The understanding that the quantity of objects stays the same regardless of changes in appearance.

Misinterpretations of Piaget's stage theory emphasized the limitations of children's thinking at each stage, which caused some educators to focus more on what children were

not able to do rather than on their developing competencies. For example, mathematics and literacy, which are based on understanding symbols, were often considered too abstract for preoperational children and, therefore, not taught until children were older.

Researchers today agree that a major, though gradual, transformation occurs in children's cognitive abilities around kindergarten age, known as the **5- to 7-year shift** (Berk, 2006; Sameroff & McDonough, 1994). Rather than children passing through sharply drawn stages, both brain development and experience contribute to children's expanded memory and more logical reasoning (Berk, 2006; Bransford et al., 2000).

Contributions of Piagetian Theory to Practice

Despite the criticisms of Piagetian theory, the contributions of his work are enormous. Visit any good-quality early childhood program and you will see evidence of these contributions. Children are actively engaged in learning—not sitting still and listening to a teacher talk most of the time. There are concrete learning materials and children have time to use them on their own. The environment itself is designed to promote learning.

Piaget's work with infants and toddlers significantly affected how we see their competence today. The idea that babies are in the sensorimotor stage of learning led to a whole industry of toys and equipment—mobiles over cribs, noise-making toys that babies control, and board books.

Piaget's method of studying children's thinking—the clinical interview—led to this breakthrough in child development theory and was a major contribution to the field. Read the *Becoming an Intentional Teacher: Interviewing to Uncover Thinking* feature for more about this technique and its benefits.

Einstein's quote on page 107 captures the most lasting contribution of Piaget's work—he changed the way that we view young children and how they learn. Children don't think like adults and they do construct their own understanding. Despite his many lasting contributions, in recent years Piaget's theory has been eclipsed by Vygotsky's theory, discussed in the next section.

Vygotsky and Sociocultural Theory

Lev Vygotsky (1896–1934) was born in Russia the same year as Piaget. Although he died young, he was a prolific writer and after his death his theories were further developed and disseminated by his students. Because his work was not translated into English until 1962, it was unknown in the West until long after his death. The Stalinist regime also suppressed his work in his native country.

Vygotsky's **sociocultural theory** is based on his belief that children learn from social interaction within a cultural context. He emphasized that *what* children learn is determined by the culture in which they grow up, such as when an urban child learns to negotiate dangerous street crossings, while a rural child may learn to milk a cow. In recent years, Vygotsky's views on learning and teaching have become more influential than Piaget's, although the theories are actually complementary (Copple & Bredekamp, 2009).

Vygotsky's Theory of How Development Occurs

Vygotsky viewed development as primarily a continuous process driven by learning. However, at particular ages, the primary learning task differs. Babies learn through their senses and by manipulating objects (similar to Piaget's view). Relationships with adults, who talk and play with babies and often use objects when doing so, drive learning during the first 2 years of life.

From ages 2 to 5, children's development is dominated by their perceptions and reactions. They pay attention to what is interesting and meaningful to them, rather than to what adults prefer. They act and react without prior thinking or reflecting on past actions. For example, when Ms. Broyles says, "It's time to go outside, so put away your toys and get your coats," most 3- and 4-year-olds will run to the door. Much to Ms. Broyle's dismay, they still have this reaction after weeks of school. Vygotsky believed that a major goal

5- to 7-year shift Major transition in cognitive abilities that gradually occurs between 5 and 7 years of age, resulting in increased ability to think logically, self-regulate, and solve problems.

sociocultural theory Vygotsky's theory that children learn from social interaction within a cultural context.

Becoming an Intentional Teacher

Interviewing to Uncover Thinking

Here's What Happened In our preschool classroom, we have lots of hands-on materials for children to learn about geometric shapes. They especially like the attribute blocks, a set of plastic blocks that come in three colors (red, yellow, and blue); five shapes (rectangle, square, triangle, circle, and pentagon), two sizes (big and small), and two widths (thick and thin). I tend to informally observe how children play with the blocks. I see that Lelia accurately names the shapes as she sorts them into separate piles. She clearly understands that a shape doesn't change if the color, size, or width changes.

One of the goals in our preschool curriculum is for children to name and analyze the properties of basic geometric shapes. This means that it isn't enough for children to be able to identify a triangle; they have to know the characteristics of a triangle (it has three angles and three sides). For a more structured observation of her skill, I ask Lelia to find other triangles in the room. Lelia searches around the class and brings me a traffic sign from the block corner and a picture on the cover of a shape book.

I notice that Lelia's examples are all equilateral triangles—ones in which three sides are the same length. To find out what Lelia really knows and is thinking about triangles, I need to talk with her:

Teacher (picking up one of the attribute blocks): "How do you know this is a triangle?"
Lelia (running her finger around the block): "It's got three pointy parts."
Teacher: "What else can you tell me about it?"
Lelia: "It has three straight parts, and it's red."
Teacher (picking up a ramp-shaped unit block): "Is the side of this block a triangle?"
Lelia: "No! It's too squished."

Here's What I Was Thinking Based on my observations of Lelia as she played with the attribute blocks and performed the task I set up for her to find other examples, I felt confident that Lelia could identify and describe the properties of a triangle. However, I know that children's behavior doesn't always reveal what they understand, so I decided to interview Lelia. I set up a discrepant situation by showing her a triangle that did not look exactly like the ones she is used to. Her response made it clear that she, like many other preschoolers, thinks that all triangles have to have sides of equal length. Although I had observed that she can identify shapes and even describe some of their properties, Lelia's concept of triangle is only partially accurate. She doesn't believe that an isosceles triangle (with only two equal-length sides) is really a triangle. This is probably because all of the examples Lelia sees or plays with are equilateral triangles.

After my interview with Lelia, I pull together small groups of children for similar discussions about triangles. Once they all agree that a triangle has "three sides and three points," which I tell them are called "angles," most of them come to the conclusion that there are many more triangles to be found in our classroom than they previously thought.

Although early childhood educators have known the importance of child observation for a century, they have placed less emphasis on interviewing children. Piaget demonstrated that we can't possibly know what children are thinking unless we talk with them, as I intentionally did with Lelia and her classmates.

of preschool is to help children move from such reactive thinking to the ability to think *before* they act (Bodrova & Leong, 2005).

During the preschool years, children need to acquire cognitive and social-emotional competencies that shape their minds for all further learning—language, memory, focused attention, and self-regulation (Bodrova & Leong, 2005). If these important foundations are in place, in the primary grades children acquire the ability to "learn on demand," as Vygotsky

called it. They are more likely to cooperate with the school's agenda—learning to read, calculate, and follow group rules—even when they would rather be doing something else.

According to Vygotsky, cognitive development involves the zone of proximal development, scaffolding, social construction of knowledge, language and other symbol systems, self-regulation, and play. These concepts, discussed in the sections that follow, have important implications for practice.

Zone of Proximal Development

Twenty-month-old Ave is trying desperately to get on the pony riding toy. Her teacher, Khari, observes that she is about to cry in frustration. He could just pick her up and put her on it, but instead he gently lifts her leg so that she gets over the last hurdle herself. Ave gives him a big smile as she pushes off with her feet and makes a circle around the room.

By giving Ave "a leg up," Khari helped her accomplish a goal that she couldn't do on her own, but could achieve with his assistance. Vygotsky (1978) identified this as the **zone of proximal development (ZPD)**—the distance between the actual developmental level an individual has achieved (their independent level of problem solving) and the level of potential development they could achieve with adult guidance or through collaboration with other children. The assistance, guidance, and direction teachers provide children in their ZPD is called **scaffolding**.

Social Construction of Knowledge

Scaffolding does not mean that teachers control or shape learning, as behaviorists believe (see p. 117). Instead, children learn by solving problems collaboratively with the teacher's support or by working with peers, which is called **co-construction** or social construction of knowledge.

> Seven-year-olds Lucrezia and Gloria are drawing a map of their school. Lucrezia is working on the classrooms and Gloria is drawing the entrance area, lunchroom, and offices. They have the following exchange:
>
> *Lucrezia:* You are making them too big. There won't be room for my part.
> *Gloria:* Well, they are bigger. See all the stuff we have to put in.
> *Lucrezia:* But the lunchroom is the biggest. How can we make this work?
>
> Each girl has a different perspective on the problem. As they continue to work on it, they try different solutions, none of them satisfactory to both. Finally, they determine the following:
>
> *Gloria:* We need to figure out how to measure the rooms.
> *Lucrezia:* My brother showed me on the GPS that one inch means one mile. We need to figure out something like that.
>
> They then proceed to address the new problems of finding a way to measure the school and creating a scale for their map.

In this example, peers work collaboratively to construct understanding. They challenge each other's ideas and alter their perspectives as a result. Lucrezia, the more accomplished peer in this scenario, introduces some cultural knowledge—what she has learned about a GPS. In other situations, the teacher plays the role of provocateur, challenging the children's thinking and thus, promoting their learning.

Language and Thought

Because Vygotsky (1962) believed that learning depends on interaction with other people, he also believed that speech is the most important tool for learning. Babies begin by communicating through gestures, as when they learn that holding up their arms means "pick me up." Then they connect sounds and words with their meanings; saying "Da Da" gets a different result than saying "Ma Ma." Language growth during the preschool years enables children to learn through conversation. Speech gradually becomes internalized and used for thinking.

zone of proximal development (ZPD) The distance between the actual developmental level an individual has achieved (her independent level of problem solving) and the level of potential development she could achieve with adult guidance or through collaboration with other children.

scaffolding The assistance, guidance, and direction teachers provide children to help them accomplish a task or learn a skill (within their ZPD) that they could not achieve on their own.

co-construction Children learning by solving problems collaboratively with the teacher's support or by working with peers; also called *social construction of knowledge*.

MyEducationLab

Go to the Building Teaching Skills and Dispositions section of Topic 2: Child Development/Theories in the MyEducationLab for your course and complete the activity entitled *Understanding How Young Children Develop and Learn*. As you watch the video and answer the accompanying questions, what examples do you observe of teaching practices that reflect the theories of development and learning discussed in the text? How do you think young children learn best and what should teachers do to promote their learning?

Think of a situation, such as learning a psychology concept or solving a mathematics problem, which you didn't really understand until you talked about it with someone else or at least stated your ideas out loud. According to Vygotsky, articulating an idea is necessary for real understanding. He described the relationship between language and thought as moving from interpersonal (between people) to intrapersonal (inside the child). Learning begins in conversation between people and then becomes part of an individual's thinking.

Interpersonal understanding or socially constructed knowledge is turned into intrapersonal knowledge through **private speech** (Vygotsky, 1962). For preschool children, private speech can look like thinking out loud. As 3½-year-old Ivor stands in front of the easel contemplating the next color to use, thick paint starts running down the paper. Ivor says, "Whoa, don't do that. I'm gonna get you with my brush," and proceeds to do so. By age 6 or 7, private speech becomes silent and is used for thinking and problem solving.

To summarize, children first use language for conversation. Then, through the vehicle of private speech, they literally use language to talk to themselves and to control their own behavior—that is, for self-regulation.

Self-Regulation

Vygotsky considered the development of self-regulation the primary task of the years before formal school entry. **Self-regulation** is the ability to adapt or control behavior, emotions, and thinking (Bodrova & Leong, 2006). Self-regulation is important for all domains of development, as brain research suggests. The prefrontal cortex is responsible for control over emotions and also for focused attention, planning (thinking ahead), and monitoring cognitive processes, which is called **executive function** (Bodrova & Leong, 2006).

Preschool children's self-regulation ability has been found to predict their academic success in the early grades, more than their intelligence or family background (Blair & Razza, 2007; McClelland, Acock, & Morrison, 2006). By contrast, early problems in self-regulation are strongly related to later problems in school and life (Calkins & Williford, 2009). Teachers or parents may understand self-regulation as "the capacity to control one's impulses both to stop doing something that is unnecessary (even if one wants to continue doing it), and to start doing something that is needed (even if one does not want to do it)" (Boyd, Barnett, Bodrova, Leong, & Gomby, 2005, p. 4). This is why self-regulation is so strongly related to success. Every day preschool teachers require children to stop playing (which they usually want to continue) and start cleaning up (which they don't want to do). Similarly, children in primary grades must attend to the reading lesson when they would rather go outside for recess.

Research supports Vygotsky's theory, which can be applied to working with children with special needs. Read the *Including All Children* feature to see how applying Vygotsky's theory can promote self-regulation in a child with attention deficit/hyperactivity disorder (ADHD).

Play and Vygotsky's Theory

According to Vygotsky (1978), make-believe play is the *leading activity* in children's development from about ages 2 through 5. Play creates a zone of proximal development in which a child behaves "as though he were a head taller than himself" (Vygotsky, 1978, p. 102). When children pretend to be adults—parents, teachers, or workers, as they often do—they use more sophisticated language than usual and model grown-up behavior.

Pretend play in small groups is especially valuable for promoting self-regulation because it is the one activity that requires children to regulate their own behavior, be regulated by others, and regulate others all within the same context (Bodrova & Leong, 2006; Boyd et al., 2003). Picture 5-year-olds playing restaurant. Each child, whether customer, waiter, or cook, has an assigned role and must stick to the script. The customer can't say, "Can I take your order?" That's the waiter's role. If the customer begins serving the food, the play breaks down. The waiter says, "You can't do that. You have to sit down, look at the menu, and eat." The rules have to be renegotiated. The customer may say, "Okay, but I get to be the waiter next." So we see that the customer has to regulate herself (stay in her role and follow the rules), be regulated by others (the waiter), and regulate others (place her order so the waiter can do his job).

private speech The process whereby interpersonal understanding or socially constructed knowledge is turned into intrapersonal knowledge (thinking aloud becomes thinking to oneself).

self-regulation The ability to adapt or control behavior, emotions, and thinking.

executive function The ability to control emotions, focus attention, plan and think ahead, and monitor cognitive processes.

Including All Children

Promoting Self-Regulation in Children with ADHD

Ronnie is really struggling in first grade. He doesn't listen, finish his work, or follow basic directions. He is always fidgeting, getting out of his seat, or playing with his pencil. He becomes easily frustrated and doesn't cooperate with the other children, who don't want to play with him or sit next to him.

The Centers for Disease Control and Prevention (2009) reports that more than 7% of school-age children, like Ronnie, are diagnosed with attention deficit/hyperactivity disorder (ADHD). These children find it much harder than other children to focus their attention or control their impulses and bodies. They are not self-regulated and are likely to have problems in school.

ADHD is linked to heredity and brain functioning. Parents and teachers do not cause ADHD. However, their interactions with children can exacerbate the situation, resulting in poor relationships, severe behavior problems, and low self-esteem. By contrast, positive relationships can prevent or lessen these effects.

Children with ADHD get much more negative than positive feedback. Their parents and teachers tend to direct, command, and offer little praise. In a discouraging cycle, parents and teachers try mightily to control these children's behavior and continue to fail. In fact, having a child with severe ADHD in the classroom can spill over into the teacher's being controlling and negative with all of the children.

Children with ADHD tend to use private speech (talking out loud to themselves) even more than other children of the same age while working on tasks, but what they say is less likely to be task related (Berk & Winsler, 1995). Their private speech may distract them and be less effective in controlling their attention and behavior. They are also less likely to move from speech to thought, which would help them think before they act.

Applying Vygotsky's theory to Ronnie's situation, an early intervention specialist works with his parents and teacher to build his self-regulation. They break tasks into smaller parts that Ronnie can successfully do and gradually turn over control to him. Instead of saying, "Get dressed now, Ronnie!" and becoming frustrated as Ronnie dawdles, his parents aid him with small steps. They prompt him to talk out loud about what he is doing ("Okay, what do you put on first? That's good. Now, what next?") As Ronnie gains control, they encourage him to whisper his answers. Gradually, he mumbles less as he dresses. His teacher uses similar strategies. Over time, Ronnie's behavior and school work improves, and he makes some friends.

None of this change is easy or instant. Children with ADHD require considerable support. Some need medication to curb the most challenging symptoms. But medication alone is insufficient; good teaching is needed.

References: Berk, L. E., & Winsler, A. (1995). *Scaffolding children's learning: Vygotsky and early childhood education.* Washington, DC: NAEYC; Centers for Disease Control and Prevention. (2009). *Summary of health statistics for U.S. children: National Health Interview Survey, 2007*. Retrieved August 16, 2009, from www.cdc.gov/nchs/fastfacts/adhd.htm.

As is evident in the foregoing example, sociodramatic play promotes children's ability to take another person's perspective (Vygotsky, 1977). Assuming a pretend role—being another person for a while—helps children move to another perspective and then back to their own. This ability to take another's perspective—to go beyond egocentrism—is necessary in school where children need to see the perspectives of teachers and other children.

Elena Bodrova, who studied in Russia with Vygotsky's students, and her colleague Deborah Leong developed a Vygotskian curriculum model, *Tools of the Mind* (Bodrova & Leong, 2003, 2007). The model focuses on teachers building self-regulation in children through mature sociodramatic play.

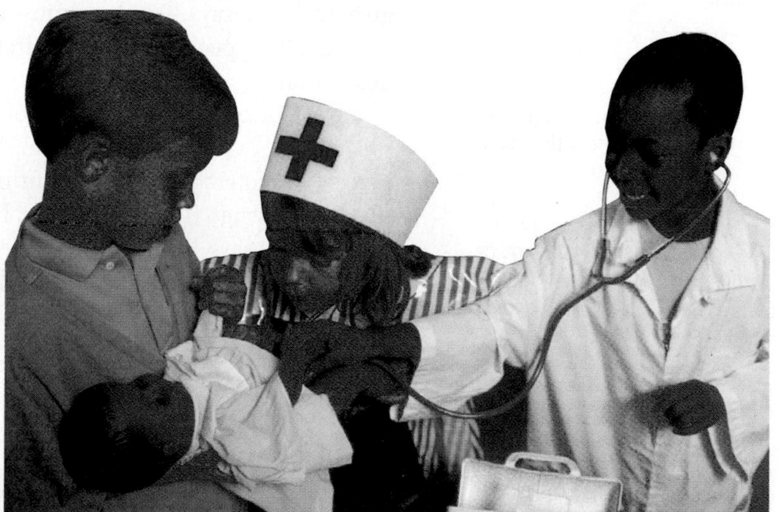

Vygotsky saw play as the leading activity for preschoolers and kindergartners. Sociodramatic play—in which children dress up and play parts in a scenario—builds many skills such as language and self-regulation.

Implications for Practice

Vygotsky's sociocultural theory has many implications for early childhood practice. Teaching in the zone of proximal development requires that children experience a challenging curriculum—

not content that is meant for older children, but content that moves them ahead in thinking and problem solving.

Similarly, the role of the teacher becomes more important than ever, not as controller of the classroom, but as a collaborator with children in constructing their learning. Teachers need to scaffold children's learning, and set up situations where groups of children work together to solve problems and have the freedom to think out loud. During preschool and kindergarten, teachers need to intentionally support mature sociodramatic play to promote self-regulation, a topic we will return to later in this chapter.

In the previous sections we described the developmental theories of Erikson, Maslow, Piaget, and Vygotsky. Erikson's work, as well as that of Maslow, provides insights into children's social and personality development and their motivation. The theories of Piaget and Vygotsky cast considerable light on the processes of cognitive development and have much to teach teachers. In the next section, we turn to descriptions of the most influential theories of learning.

Learning Theories

In contrast to developmental theories, which are linked to age-related changes in children, learning theories are assumed to apply in the same way regardless of the age of the learner. In the following sections, we describe the work of two major learning theorists: B. F. Skinner and Albert Bandura. (Another important theory is Howard Gardner's multiple intelligences, which we discuss in the chapter on individual differences.)

B. F. Skinner and Behaviorism

One of the most influential learning theories of the last half century is **behaviorism** or **behavioral learning.** According to this theory, learning is a change in behavior that is controlled by the consequences, either positive or negative, that follow the behavior. Using pleasant or unpleasant consequences to control behavior is called **operant conditioning**.

Psychologist B. F. Skinner (1904–1980) developed the theory of operant conditioning through systematic experiments. Skinner discovered that he could train rats to press a lever by rewarding them with food. From experiments with animals and people, Skinner developed the core principles of operant conditioning, an example of which follows:

> During center time in her prekindergarten, Nessa Stokes observes as Jemma works to fill in every space on the small pegboard. As Jemma tires and looks as though she will give up, Nessa says, "You've almost filled the whole pegboard, Jemma. It's hard to pick up those little pegs, and fit them in the tiny holes." Jemma smiles proudly and continues her task.
>
> Nessa moves among groups of children, commenting positively on their accomplishments. "Good job, Eduardo. You are putting all the blocks back in the right places." An altercation breaks out in the computer center as Kennedy refuses to give up her seat when it is Dona's turn. Dona says, "Give or you won't be my friend." Nessa steps in and says, "Kennedy, you need to give Dona her turn, or tomorrow you won't get a turn at the computer." Kennedy weighs the consequences briefly, and reluctantly yields the mouse to Dona.

behaviorism or **behavioral learning** Theory that learning is a change in behavior that is controlled by the consequences, either positive or negative, that follow the behavior.

operant conditioning The process of using pleasant or unpleasant consequences to control behavior.

consequences Principle of operant conditioning that behavior changes as a result of what occurs immediately afterward.

reinforcer Consequence—either positive or negative—that increases or strengthens a behavior.

Although Nessa's actions in this brief scenario may seem relatively simple, she is in fact implementing several key principles of operant conditioning.

Operant Conditioning

The most important principle of operant conditioning is that behavior changes as a result of its immediate **consequences.** Positive consequences strengthen the frequency of specific behaviors, while unpleasant consequences decrease the frequency. **Reinforcers** are consequences that increase or strengthen behaviors. There are two kinds of reinforcers: positive and negative.

Positive reinforcement is a reward or pleasant consequence that follows a behavior, causing that behavior to be repeated. In the previous example, Nessa reinforced or rewarded Jemma's efforts with the pegboard with a smile and positive words of encouragement. As a result, Jemma kept working at a difficult task. Similarly, Eduardo continued picking up the blocks after the teacher recognized his effort.

Negative reinforcement also increases the frequency of a desired behavior, but in a different way. A negative reinforcer is an unpleasant consequence that is *avoided* if the person performs a behavior more frequently. For example, an annoying bell or buzzer—a negative reinforcer—signals when the seat belt is still unfastened after a car is started. To avoid the sound, most people fasten the seat belt as soon as they can. In Nessa's classroom, she used negative reinforcement when she told Kennedy that she would sacrifice her next turn on the computer if she didn't give Dona a turn. Dona also used negative reinforcement by threatening to withdraw her friendship. To avoid these negative reinforcers, Kennedy changed her behavior.

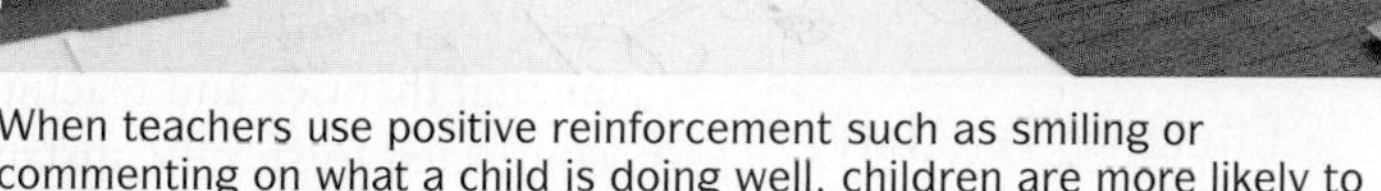

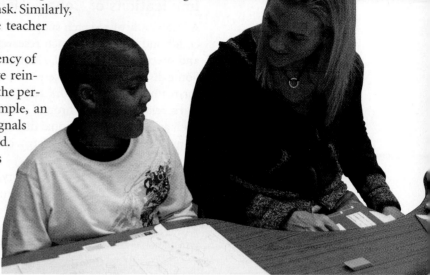

When teachers use positive reinforcement such as smiling or commenting on what a child is doing well, children are more likely to continue to behave in appropriate ways.

Negative reinforcement is sometimes confused with, but is not the same thing as, **punishment**. Punishment is an unpleasant consequence that stops or *decreases* the frequency of a behavior. Many people, teachers as well as parents, think punishments are effective in changing behavior and use them often. However, the problem with punishment is that it may temporarily stop an undesirable behavior, but it does not teach the child what to do instead. As a result, repeated punishment soon becomes ineffective in changing behavior. For example, in Tiffany's first-grade classroom, when children misbehave they get a red card and their name goes on the board, while those who behave well get a green card. But day after day the same children get the red card. Receiving the card—a punishment—does not improve their behavior.

Teachers need to understand that punishment only decreases an undesirable behavior temporarily. To increase a desired behavior, reinforcement is needed. In fact, in some cases, punishment actually serves as a negative reinforcer and increases the behavior. Consider the situation where a first-grade teacher decides to punish a disruptive child by making him miss recess. If the child wants to avoid recess because he doesn't get chosen for a team or is bullied, then removing him from recess is not a punishment but a reward and, thus, will have the opposite effect from the one the teacher intended.

When reinforcers are removed, the conditioned behavior diminishes and eventually disappears, a process called **extinction**.

What to Reinforce: Shaping Behavior

Most human behavior is complex, much more so than that of the hungry rats Skinner studied. Children learn to take turns, follow classroom rules, or ride a bike over time and after many tries, some successful and others not. It would be impossible to wait to reinforce a highly complex behavior until a child performed it well. What if a kindergarten teacher only reinforced a child's writing when the letters were formed perfectly on the line? Many children would give up. Instead, an effective teacher recognizes the child's attempts, each step on the way to mastering writing the letters correctly. Teaching a new skill or behavior by rewarding each step toward the goal is called **shaping**.

Shaping requires the teacher to carefully observe the **successive approximations**—not the actual desired behaviors but each approximate behavior that is closer to the goal. For example, when 3-year-old Lola's scribbles begin to look like (approximate) a circle or straight line, her family child care provider Titia says, "Oh, look, Lola, you made an O like

positive reinforcement A reward or pleasant consequence that follows a behavior, causing that behavior to be repeated.

negative reinforcement An unpleasant consequence that is avoided if the person performs a desired behavior more frequently.

punishment An unpleasant consequence that stops or decreases the frequency of a behavior.

extinction The process whereby a conditioned behavior diminishes and eventually disappears when reinforcers are removed.

shaping Teaching a new skill or behavior by rewarding each step or successive approximation toward the goal.

successive approximations Behaviors that are reinforced (shaped) that are not the actual desired behaviors, but each approximate behavior that is closer to the goal.

in your name." Lola didn't intend to draw an O, but it is likely that Titia's praise will result in Lola producing pages of O's to get more of Titia's positive attention.

Implications of Behaviorism for Practice

A huge body of research supports the effectiveness of principles of behaviorism. In early childhood education, much research has been conducted with children with disabilities and special needs (Sandall, Hemmeter, Smith, & McLean, 2005; Wolery & Wilbers, 1994). Some disabilities, such as cerebral palsy or Down syndrome, affect children's ability to perform functional behaviors (e.g., eating or dressing) that typically developing children learn relatively easily through imitation and repetition. Other children with conditions such as autism or emotional disorders may exhibit challenging behaviors. In these situations, using behavioral learning techniques can be effective, as Yvonne learned in the opening vignette of this chapter.

Behaviorism is a learning theory, not a theory of development. Therefore, the principles apply regardless of the age of the learner. However, as the name implies, the effectiveness of behaviorism is *limited* to teaching or changing observable behaviors. Even with this limitation, the important thing to remember is that behaviorism can be highly effective. At times, the wrong behaviors get reinforced such as when an aggressive child gets what he wants by bullying.

> **Effective Teaching**
> Effective teachers draw on diverse theories to fully understand how best to intentionally support each child's development and learning.

Behaviorism, as epitomized by Skinner's work, is often pitted against developmental theories and teaching approaches. This is usually because behaviorism is connected to specific instructional practices, such as when teachers tell children facts or information and reward their correct answers. Another strong criticism of behaviorism is that overreliance on external rewards undermines children's internal motivation (Kohn, 1999; Reineke, Sonsteng, & Gartrell, 2008). For example, paying children to read books may make them less motivated to read on their own when the payment isn't available.

But effective teaching is not an *either/or* choice between constructivism and behaviorism. These theories each apply best to different phenomena. Behaviorism may work to change observable behaviors; but it does not explain nor is it effective in influencing the less visible, but essential processes of thinking, concept development, and problem solving. To explain this kind of learning, we must look to the theories of Piaget or Vygotsky, as described earlier. Building on the work of behaviorists and bridging the gap between behaviorism and cognitive theory is the work of Albert Bandura, described in the next section.

Albert Bandura and Social Cognitive Theory

Developed by psychologist Albert Bandura (born in 1925), **social cognitive theory** (also called *social learning theory*) is both a behavioral and cognitive theory and, therefore, serves as a bridge between those two views of learning. Whereas Skinner's work emphasized that a person's behavior needs to be directly reinforced to change, Bandura demonstrated that people can learn more efficiently from observing the consequences of another person's behavior. This theory has important implications for classroom teaching.

Bandura theorized that observational learning depends on learners having an image in their mind of the behavior they observed and its consequences—a memory of an event captured in pictures and/or words. This theory explains an important way that children learn—they observe and then model the behaviors they observe. Bandura's emphasis on the importance of a mental image adds a cognitive dimension to the learning theory and separates it from Skinnerian behaviorism.

To test his hypothesis that children would model observed behaviors, Bandura (1973) conducted hundreds of studies. In now famous research, he filmed situations in which kindergartners observed an adult or another child beating up a plastic, inflated clown "Bobo" and being complimented or rewarded for doing so. Then, given the opportunity, the children who watched the demonstration not only beat up Bobo as well, but used the exact same motions and expressions, "Sockeroo!"

social cognitive theory Bandura's theory that people can learn efficiently from observing the consequences of another person's behavior.

Modeling and Observational Learning

The basic principles of social cognitive theory are (1) children learn by **modeling**, that is, imitating the behavior of others, and (2) they can learn vicariously. **Vicarious learning** is based on observing the effects of other people's behavior, rather than experiencing the rewards or punishments directly. Consider the following example of modeling:

> Mr. Evans' group of 3-year-olds is getting louder and louder as they boisterously encourage each other to jump up and down and scream at the top of their lungs. Wanting to scream himself, Mr. Evans chooses instead to tiptoe around the group, take Bettina by the hand, and whisper softly to follow him. One by one, the children stop their jumping and begin imitating Mr. Evans' toe walking. Gradually, their voices quiet as well, in hopes of getting a turn to be the teacher's partner.

modeling Teacher showing children a skill or desirable way of behaving or speaking; also children imitating the behavior of others.

vicarious learning Learning by observing the effects of other people's behavior, rather than experiencing rewards or punishments directly.

self-regulated learning Bandura's theory that people not only learn by modeling the behavior of others, but by observing and evaluating their own.

The children in Mr. Evans' group observed his behavior and saw that Bettina gained his favor by following his lead. According to Bandura (1986), observational learning has four phases:

1. *Attention.* The first step in observational learning is paying attention. Children pay attention to role models who are interesting, novel, or seemingly powerful. This is why action figures on television garner a lot of children's attention. Teachers use many fun and interesting ways to get and hold children's attention, such as talking through a puppet, having them guess what is hidden in a bag, or simply being excited themselves. Mr. Evans surprised the children with the novel behavior of walking on his tiptoes.
2. *Retention.* During this phase of the process, the teacher models the behavior and gives children a chance to practice it. Mr. Evans' goal was to get the children to lower their voices, so he modeled whispering and got the children talking softly.
3. *Reproduction.* The next step is for children to try to reproduce the behavior on their own. Mr. Evans and Bettina step aside from the group, and observe as the other children take their turns whispering and tiptoeing.
4. *Motivation.* Observational learning works because children find that they will be rewarded in some way for imitating the desired behaviors. Such motivation can be based on something that happened in the past or is promised in the future. Or, as in Mr. Evans' class, the potential reward can be vicarious. Seeing Bettina rewarded with the teacher's positive attention encouraged the others to follow her lead.

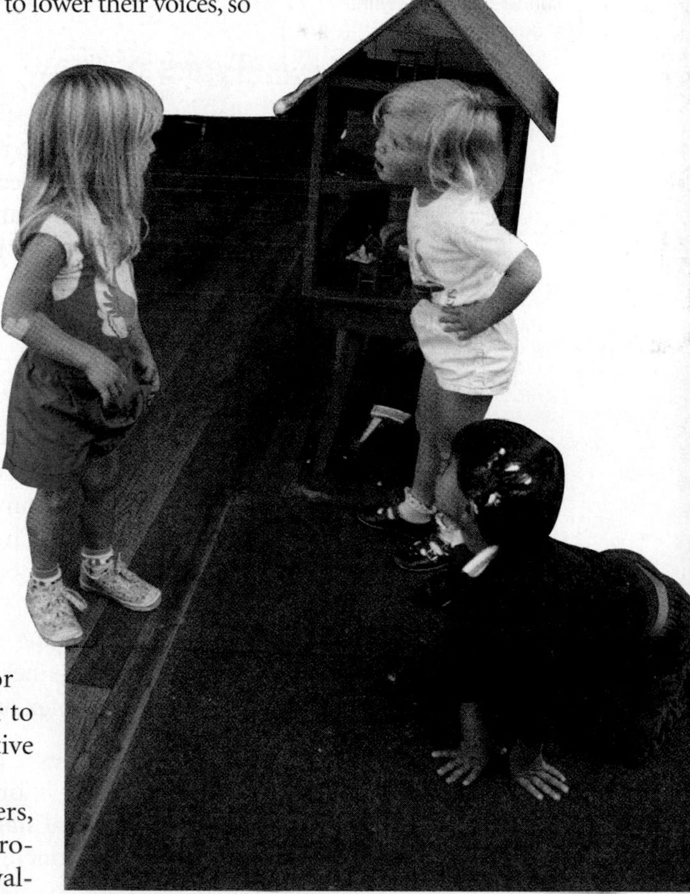
According to Bandura, children learn from watching what other children do and the consequences that follow. What do you think the teacher should do if one of the children is fighting or hurting other people?

Self-Regulated Learning

Bandura's theory goes even further as a cognitive theory in his concept of **self-regulated learning**. Bandura (1997) postulated that people not only learn by modeling the behavior of others, but by observing and evaluating their own. Self-regulated learning requires that individuals have internalized standards and that they have the ability to reflect on their own performance and to reward or punish themselves. Bandura's emphasis on self-regulation is similar to Vygotsky's. Both theories view self-regulation as essential for cognitive and social-emotional development.

These high-level cognitive abilities are developing in preschoolers, but are further along in most primary grade children. Teachers can promote self-regulated learning by engaging children in setting goals, evaluating their own performance, and celebrating their successes. For example, in Ms. Ross's first-grade classroom, children do a lot of writing. Periodically, she sits down with one child to discuss various pieces of work. The child chooses a few to scan into the computer and preserve in a portfolio. When parents come for a conference, the children talk about why they chose this special piece of work.

Children in the primary grades become capable of setting standards for their own behavior and comparing their performance to that of others. Eight-year-old Melissa is unhappy with herself because she watched TV last night instead of studying, and today she got a failing grade on her math quiz.

We have now described the major theories that explain how children develop and learn and their implications for effective teaching. In the following section, we discuss how play contributes to all areas of children's lives.

The Role of Play in Development and Learning

MyEducationLab

Go to the Book Specific Resources in the MyEducationLab for your course and select Author Interviews in Chapter 4 to watch and listen to the video *Play in Development and Learning*. According to Sue Bredekamp, what should teachers understand about play?

Psychologists and educators have studied children's play for a very long time. Despite the large body of research supporting its benefits, however, child-initiated play is becoming less valued and disappearing from children's lives today (Hirsh-Pasek, Golinkoff, Berk, & Singer, 2008; Zigler & Bishop-Josef, 2004). Many factors conspire against play: television and computer use, lack of safe playgrounds, overemphasis on direct teaching of literacy and mathematics, and highly structured activities or lessons such as sports or ballet (Elkind, 2008; Hirsh-Pasek et al., 2008; E. Miller & Almon, 2009).

Early childhood educators deeply value play. But to use play effectively in teaching children, and to advocate for its value, it is important to be clear about what types of play matter and why it is worth defending. In the sections that follow, we describe what play is, how it develops, and how it benefits children.

Types of Play

Play is complex and difficult to define because there are different kinds of play: play with toys, movement play, rough-and-tumble play, make-believe play, and play with games and computers. Most often, *play* is defined as activity that is freely chosen, initiated and controlled by children, and enjoyable. Despite the lack of definitional clarity, most people would say, "You know it when you see it." And more importantly, children know when they are playing.

Different types of play have different benefits for children. Definitions for different types of play follow:

- *Functional play.* Children play with and manipulate objects, such as when a baby shakes a rattle or a toddler bangs a drum.
- *Constructive play.* Children use toys or objects to create something new, such as making a puppet from a sock, a design on a computer screen, or a castle out of Legos.
- *Symbolic play.* Children use one thing to represent or stand for another. Pretend play is a form of symbolic play. A stick becomes a magic wand. A piece of cloth becomes a veil or a cape.
- *Games with rules.* Children follow prescribed rules for playing together toward a common goal. Games include simple ones such as *Candyland* or *Chutes and Ladders*, as well as complex ones such as chess or baseball.

Piaget related types of play to stages of development (Johnson, Christie, & Wardle, 2005). He theorized that functional play dominates the sensorimotor stage (birth to 2 years), and that the preoperational stage (2 to 7 years) is characterized by symbolic and constructive play. Children in the concrete operational stage (7 to 11 years) tend to play games with rules.

How Play Develops

Children's pretend play becomes more complex over time, especially if people play with them and provide props. The following sections describe this sequence.

Functional Play

Babies and toddlers engage in functional play, focusing on objects and then on the people who use the objects with them. Toddlers enjoy repetition and practice as they play, for instance, when a toddler bangs a hammer over and over.

If parents or teachers pretend with young children during functional play, toddlers will begin to pretend too. Ms. Morgan sits next to 2-year-old Hester, picks up a cup, and pretends to drink. "This is delicious tea," she says. Soon Hester takes a cup and says, "Yum." This type of pretense is the foundation for later symbolic play.

Constructive Play

Constructive play begins as functional play and becomes more symbolic as children use objects to create new ones. For example, children act out pretend roles during block building.

Symbolic Play

Play helps build **symbolic representation**—using one thing to mean something else—such as when letters are used to represent sounds or number symbols represent quantities. At first, toddlers use real objects or toys in their pretend play such as picking up the cup and pretending to drink. If adults encourage this type of play, children use other objects in their play. They might pretend that a block is a cup. Finally, children who have lots of experience with pretend play no longer need an object to pretend, using their hands to represent drinking from a cup or stomping their feet and saying, "I'm an elephant." This type of play helps children move from thought that is linked to physical actions to the ability to use words and other symbols to represent concepts (Piaget, 1962; Vygotsky, 1962).

By the time most children turn 4 years old, they begin to develop more complex play with roles and symbolic uses of props. Many preschool- and even kindergarten-age children, however, still play at the toddler level. Bodrova and Leong (2003) define this kind of repetitive, unimaginative play as "immature play" to distinguish it from the "mature play" that is expected of 4- and 5-year-olds. Mature play contributes more to children's development than immature play and promotes self-regulation and other skills (Smilansky & Shefatya, 1990).

MyEducationLab

Go to the Assignments and Activities section of Topic 2: Child Development/Theories in the MyEducationLab for your course and complete the activity entitled *Promoting Children's Play*. As you watch the video and answer the accompanying questions, consider what the children are learning from block building and the teacher's role in their play. How is this play both constructive and symbolic?

Games with Rules

As children move into primary grades, they spend less time in pretend play and more time playing games with rules (e.g., sports and board or computer games). Games require children to follow the established rules; they rarely get a chance to discuss, negotiate, or change the rules—which would contribute to the development of social competence and self-regulation (Bodrova & Leong, 2003). When pretend play is replaced by sports or other organized activities during the preschool years, these important foundational skills might not develop fully (Bodrova & Leong, 2003).

The Benefits of Play

Research demonstrates that play contributes to language development, self-regulation, attention, creativity, problem solving, and social and emotional skills (Berk, Mann, & Ogan, 2006; Bodrova & Leong, 2003; Smilansky & Shefatya, 1990). Play has been found to help prepare children for school (Bowman, Donovan, & Burns, 2001; Shonkoff & Phillips, 2000). Research also links play to children's literacy and mathematics skills (Ginsburg, 2006; Zigler, Singer, & Bishop-Josef, 2004).

Children's play can be enhanced through adult intervention, as in the *Tools of the Mind* curriculum described previously. Sara Smilansky (1968), an Israeli psychologist, conducted seminal studies of play among children living in poverty. She found that they did not engage in the same kind of mature sociodramatic play favored by their middle-class peers and were behind in other areas as well. Smilansky trained children to play in more complex ways—using modeling and other techniques—which significantly improved their language and social and cognitive development, findings that have been replicated with other populations (Smilansky & Shefatya, 1990).

symbolic representation The process of mentally using one thing to stand for something else.

Play and Motivation

Although it is very important for children's development, play is not the only way that children learn, as we have seen from examining several different theories. If so, why is it so important for teachers to defend and use play as a major context for teaching and learning? One reason is that preschool children themselves are intrinsically motivated to play. Play is so enjoyable for children that teachers don't need to coerce or cajole them to participate (Bredekamp, 2004).

In one study (Wiltz & Klein, 2001), preschoolers were asked what they like to do at school. Ninety-eight percent of the children said play was their favorite activity. When asked what they did not like about school, nearly a third of the children said meanness by teachers or peers, and others did not like naptime and time-out. But many also disliked circle time, especially in poorer quality programs where it lasted 30 to 40 minutes and involved repetition of calendar, letters, and numbers. Even in high-quality classrooms where circle time was more interesting and engaging, many children reported disliking it primarily because it takes too long. As one little boy, Don said, "Well, I don't really like . . . you know, like sit in circle and listen . . . I don't like that part [because] I think it's too long for me. I'd rather be playing" (Wiltz & Klein, 2001, p. 225). Considering the many benefits of play and the threats to play for children today, read and reflect on the *How Would You Respond? I'd Rather Be Playing* feature.

How Would You Respond?

I'd Rather Be Playing

The Situation You are a kindergarten teacher who has just started working at a new school. The district recently changed the curriculum to meet state standards and requires a large block of time for language arts, followed by small-group math teaching. Your school only has half-day kindergarten and the new requirements leave no time for play. After a few weeks of school, you are discouraged because you struggle to keep children's attention and find yourself spending your time dealing with serious behavior problems. In your teacher education program and during student teaching, you learned how beneficial play is for 5-year-olds' development and learning.

What to Do? Your principal and the parents expect you to implement the curriculum, and you will be accountable for children's progress in literacy and mathematics. But you also know that if kindergartners aren't self-regulated and have limited social skills, they will struggle academically in later grades. Which of the following actions would meet the needs of children and also the goals of the principal and parents?

- Plan the schedule to include a block of time (about 45 minutes) for small groups of children to engage in sociodramatic play or constructive play. At the same time, have some children work in small groups on math or literacy tasks. Alternate days when children have more time in each activity.
- Limit whole-group times that require prolonged sitting or listening to you.
- Intentionally add opportunities for children to practice self-regulation skills such as planning what and who they will play with.
- Observe the quality and maturity of children's play. Consider whether it is repetitive or chaotic, and how you can make it more productive.
- Observe social relationships and interactions during play. Pair more outgoing children with more reserved children at times to stimulate conversation and build social skills.
- Build literacy and mathematics learning opportunities into play. Be nearby to assist children as they use writing and counting tools for real purposes.
- Prepare a thorough, informed presentation on the value of play, and how you are incorporating it in meeting curriculum goals.
- Regularly assess children's progress on curriculum goals, and evaluate how well your play-based approach is working.

Can you think of other strategies to preserve play in the kindergarten while meeting curriculum goals?

Principles of Child Development and Learning That Inform Developmentally Appropriate Practices

Looking across theories and research, teachers can become confused. As we have seen, theories explain different aspects of children's learning or development, and at times they may seem contradictory. How can teachers make sense of diverse theories? To address these questions, we provide a framework for thinking holistically about development and learning.

NAEYC (2009a) summarizes the research and theory undergirding developmentally appropriate practice in a list of principles. Although these principles do not cover everything teachers need to know about development and learning, they highlight some of the key concepts that have implications for practice. In Table 4.3 the principles are listed and illustrated with a few examples.

In promulgating this list of principles, NAEYC (Copple & Bredekamp, 2009, pp. 10–11) offers several caveats. First, while the list is comprehensive, it is not exhaustive; other principles could be added. In addition, just as all domains of development and learning are interconnected, so too are the principles. For instance, cultural and individual variations are addressed in separate principles, and yet they play a role in all of the other principles. In other words, decisions about applying any given principle should consider children as individuals and as members of cultural groups. Despite these limitations, the principles reflect a solid base of research to guide teachers' decision making.

We conclude with the following discussion of the Reggio Emilia approach to early childhood education. We describe this influential approach here because the it demonstrates both how education moves from theory to practice and how practice can drive theory.

The Reggio Emilia Approach: Theory into Practice and Practice Driving Theory

The internationally known schools of Reggio Emilia, Italy, have been called "the place theory and practice touch like the magic moment when night becomes day" (quoted in Bredekamp, 2008b, p. 49). Since the approach was first introduced in the United States, it has inspired teachers throughout the country and made major contributions to the knowledge base (Edwards, Gandini, & Forman, 1998; Reggio Children & Project Zero, 2001).

The Schools of Reggio Emilia, Italy

The city-run preschools and infant/toddler centers serving children from birth through age 6 originated as a movement among parents following World War II. Founder Loris Malaguzzi was inspired by the parents and committed himself to the continued evolution of the schools until his death in 1994.

Malaguzzi used the metaphor "the hundred languages of children" to connote the complex elements of the approach. First and foremost, the metaphor communicates the inherent genius of every child. Secondly, the "hundred languages" stand for the processes of children's learning as well as how they demonstrate it. In addition, "languages" are various forms of media—drawing, sculpting, writing, photography, video, music, words, numbers, and so on—that are used to promote and display children's understanding of the world. By focusing attention on what children are capable of doing, the Reggio approach has made young children's amazing competence visible to the world.

Reggio Emilia approach Principles of early childhood education practice developed in schools in Reggio Emilia, Italy; emanates from the image of the child rich in potential and as a citizen with rights.

The **Reggio Emilia approach** is not a curriculum, nor is it a model. It draws on several theories in an integrated fashion, but also goes beyond them. For example, a visitor to the schools would see evidence of Vygotskian sociocultural theory in the collaborative project work among small groups of children and also in the co-construction of knowledge between

Table 4.3 Principles of Development and Learning to Guide Practice

Principle of Development and Learning	Implications for Practice	Example
Principle 1: Domains of children's development—physical, social, emotional, and cognitive—are closely related. Development in one domain influences and is influenced by development in other domains.	Curriculum should be comprehensive, addressing development and learning of the whole child.	During a project on caring for pets, 4-year-olds learn science concepts about the physical needs of animals, use language and early literacy skills to tell and write stories about their pets, express their emotions about pets, and use their bodies to act out pet behaviors.
Principle 2: Many aspects of children's learning and development follow well-documented sequences, with later abilities, skills, and knowledge building on those already acquired.	Teachers need to know the predictable, but not rigid, sequences of development and learning so they can assess children accurately and plan for children's continued progress.	Ms. Rodriguez is familiar with the scope and sequence in the first-grade reading curriculum, so she adjusts her expectations and work with children individually and in small groups at their various levels of reading ability.
Principle 3: Development and learning proceed at varying rates from child to child, as well as at uneven rates across different areas of a child's individual functioning.	Teachers need to get to know each child well, regularly observing and assessing each child's abilities, skills, knowledge, and dispositions.	Josh and Jon are both 3 years old, but while Josh is very verbal, Jon is still talking in one-word utterances. However, Jon has excellent fine motor skill that Josh lacks. Their teacher pairs them to play with a pegboard where they each get practice using and improving their language and motor skills.
Principle 4: Development and learning result from a dynamic and continuous interaction of biological maturation and experience.	Teachers recognize that although there are inborn individual differences and limits on children's learning based on maturation, experience plays a large role in children's development. Teachers know the benefits of early intervention for preventing later problems.	Kindergarten teachers explain to parents that the "gift of time"—holding children out of school until they are older—is not a good policy because children will benefit more from the experience of attending school rather than simply waiting to mature.
Principle 5: Early experiences have both cumulative and delayed effects on individual children's development. Optimal periods exist for certain types of development and learning.	Teachers need to know research on the short- and long-term effects of early experience.	In her family child care home, Mrs. Pickett rarely uses TV or videos because they can harm children's long-term attention spans and don't build language the way real conversation does.
Principle 6: Development proceeds toward greater complexity, self-regulation, and symbolic or representational capacities.	Teachers add greater complexity to learning experiences over time. Teachers engage children in conversations about thinking and problem solving.	Recognizing that young children often "think out loud," preschool teachers don't expect or want silent classrooms. They organize play and projects where children can talk about their ideas with each other.
Principle 7: Children develop best when they have secure, consistent relationships with responsive adults and opportunities for positive relationships with peers.	Teachers develop a warm, positive, trusting relationship with each child. Teachers protect the physical health and safety of each child.	At the beginning of the school year, Ms. Vargas conducts a home visit or meets with parents to get to know each child and family. She takes time to talk with each child each day.

Table 4.3 Principles of Development and Learning to Guide Practice

Principle of Development and Learning	Implications for Practice	Example
Principle 8: Development and learning occur in and are influenced by social and cultural contexts.	Teachers recognize that children's competence acquired in their home culture may not be apparent in the school culture. Teachers know that what is meaningful to children varies depending on their culture and language.	Concerned about Marta's language development but not fluent in Spanish herself, Ms. Kamp works with another teacher, Ms. Gonzales, to obtain an accurate assessment of Marta's vocabulary and grammar in her home language, which turns out to be within the normal range.
Principle 9: Always mentally active in seeking to understand the world around them, children learn in a variety of ways; a wide range of teaching strategies and interactions are effective in supporting all of these kinds of learning.	Teachers use a variety of teaching strategies—both teacher-guided and child-guided—to meet the needs of individual children, some of whom need more support than others even in exploration and play. Teachers use a variety of learning contexts—large group, small group, and independent. They individualize teaching from child to child and day to day.	Introducing a new math computer program, Ms. Hayes demonstrates and instructs the children in how to drag the cursor to move the images on the screen. Then the children take turns experimenting with the program to see how they can create their own illustrations for their stories. Ms. Hayes is close by to provide just the right amount of assistance for each child and introduce new words that describe the pictures.
Principle 10: Play is an important vehicle for developing self-regulation as well as promoting language, cognition, and social competence.	Teachers purposefully plan time and materials for children's educationally valuable play. Teachers observe children at play and interact constructively with them.	Ms. Phillips sets up a grocery store in her kindergarten where children engage in counting money, reading labels, making lists, and using vocabulary as they play together. She plays the part of customer to get the play going and model shopping behavior.
Principle 11: Development and learning advance when children are challenged to achieve at a level just beyond their current mastery, and also when they have many opportunities to practice newly acquired skills.	Teachers provide children with a high proportion of experiences at which they can be successful as well as providing them with some experiences that are at the "just achievable" level of challenge to stretch their learning and development.	Mr. Durkin provides ample opportunity for writing in his classroom but observes that many children continue to write their own names but nothing more. He suggests that friends write each other's names and provides name cards as models. The children find this challenge great fun.
Principle 12: Children's experiences shape their motivation and approaches to learning, such as persistence, initiative, and flexibility; in turn, these dispositions and behaviors affect their learning and development.	Teachers draw on and cultivate children's interests to get their attention and keep them engaged in learning. Teachers encourage positive approaches to learning such as curiosity and creativity.	Ms. Elias's kindergartners are bored by the reading workbooks the district provides. So she offers options for children to engage with stories. Children act out the stories, make up movements and songs, or write their own stories—experiences that motivate them to take initiative and persist at challenging tasks.

Source: Based on *Developmentally Appropriate Practice in Early Childhood Programs Serving Children from Birth through Age 8*, revised edition, edited by C. Copple and S. Bredekamp, 2009, Washington, DC: National Association for the Education of Young Children.

teachers and children. In addition, teachers and peers place themselves in zones of proximal development, continually scaffolding each other's learning. Teachers often act as provocateurs for children, deliberately creating what Piaget termed *disequilibrium*, to drive children's learning.

Principles and Values of the Reggio Emilia Approach

The Reggio Emilia approach is based on a set of core values and principles (Gandini, 1993, 2008). A brief summary of its core components follows.

The Image of the Child

The foundation of the Reggio Emilia approach is the *image of the child* as rich in potential, strong, and powerful with rights as a citizen and contributing member of the community. In Reggio, children with special rights (what Americans call *children with special needs*) are given precedence in school enrollment.

Children's Relationships and Interactions

Malaguzzi (1993) called the approach "an education based on relationships." Teachers stay with the same group of children for 3 years and focus on reciprocal relationships among children (often in small groups) and the community.

The Role of Parents

Malaguzzi often said that the school has three protagonists without which schools do not exist: children, teachers, and parents. The active participation of parents is essential to the operation of the schools; parents are deeply involved in the learning activities of the children.

The Role of Space: An Amiable School

The environments convey the message that "this is a place where adults have thought about the quality and the instructive power of space" (Gandini, 2008, p. 25). Americans are struck by the aesthetic beauty of the schools, but each element is designed for a purpose, such as to promote small-group interaction or display evidence of the process of children's learning.

Teachers and Children as Partners in Learning

Teachers do not consider themselves experts who impart knowledge, but rather partners with children in the journey of discovery. They act as a resource to children, asking provocative questions, exploring children's thoughts and hypotheses, and learning along with them.

Curriculum as a Process of Inviting and Sustaining Learning

There is no preset curriculum in Reggio schools. Teachers prepare a declaration of intent about possible learning experiences they will offer to children, but the curriculum emerges from children's interests in topics or questions and their desire to find out more or solve a problem. However, teachers do have goals and plan in advance for possible directions the work will take. They pay careful attention to children and regularly meet to discuss how to further children's involvement and deepen their understanding.

MyEducationLab

To observe the Reggio Emilia approach in action, go to the Video Examples section of Topic 5: Program Models in the MyEducationLab for your course and watch the video entitled *Reggio Emilia*. Which of the principles and values described in your text do you see implemented in this Reggio-inspired school in the United States?

The Many Languages of Children

Each school has a special teacher, called an *atelierista*, who is knowledgeable about the visual arts and works closely with the other teachers and children. Each preschool has an *atelier*, a specially equipped studio or workshop that contains a wide range of materials and resources that are used by children to represent their ideas and thinking and in projects.

In the United States, the Reggio Emilia approach is sometimes erroneously described as an art program. However, the Italians do not see the children's work as art but rather as symbolic representation that is an integral part of learning (see page 121 for a discussion of representation). When children represent the same concept using different media, their understanding deepens. For example, drawing a horse in one dimension conveys a partial

The Reggio Emilia approach to early childhood education has inspired schools in the United States to rethink the environment and children's representational ability. What does a Reggio-inspired learning environment communicate about and to children?

concept of the animal. Constructing a three-dimensional model of a horse in clay requires thinking about how the horse stands up and how it runs.

Learning through Projects

Short- and long-term projects are a major teaching and learning strategy in Reggio schools. Facilitated by teachers, children work in small groups on a topic or a problem of interest to them. Ideas for projects, great and small, grow out of children's experiences or chance encounters. An invitation from the town to design a theater curtain for the opera house led to a lengthy project that included generating artistic designs, making computer models, painting large murals, and exploring cloth production. The project culminated in a celebratory unveiling (Vecchi, 2002).

The Power of Documentation

The growth in children's thinking that occurs through project work is captured in one of the most compelling and unique aspects of the approach: documentation.

As a project proceeds, teachers and the *atelierista* carefully arrange and display transcripts of children's discussions, photographs of them at work, and representations of their thinking and learning in various media (drawings, sculptures, and constructions). These documentations can be interpreted as assessments, but they are more like records of the processes of learning and problem solving in groups of children. What goes on in children's minds cannot be seen, but documentation *makes learning visible* (Reggio Children & Project Zero, 2001). Documentation powerfully communicates the competence of children to parents, community members, and policy makers. Teachers use documentation to help children revisit their experiences, remember and analyze their thinking, and deepen their understanding.

Finally, play is a vital part of Reggio schools, although most written accounts or presentations about Reggio in the United States fail to talk to about play. One must observe in the schools to see that play is as important to the Reggio Emilia approach as it to developmentally appropriate practice.

The Reggio Emilia Approach: Integrating Theory and Practice

One of the most important contributions of Reggio Emilia is the deeper understanding of how *representation* not only reflects what children know and can do, but also changes it. Other practices that have expanded theoretical understandings are the role projects and documentation can play in higher order thinking, and the effectiveness of collaboration and co-construction as teaching and learning strategies. Although these practices are not entirely new to the United States, the quality of implementation in Reggio is beyond what is usually seen here with few exceptions.

The Reggio Emilia approach is deeply rooted in the sociocultural context of its region and town in Italy. Therefore, it cannot be successfully imitated in a different cultural milieu. Instead, American educators can learn from and with Reggio educators as they continue to learn from and with children, and can be inspired by the possibilities inherent in their work.

Revisiting Ms. Donati's Classroom

We began this chapter by visiting Yvonne Donati's classroom. Having examined various theories of learning and their applications, we can see her practices in a clearer light. Yvonne operates from a constructivist perspective. She sees children as active learners and structures her classrooms and plans curriculum accordingly. Yvonne also implements sociocultural theory as she scaffolds children's learning in the zone of proximal development through appropriately timed prompts, questions, and assistance. Yvonne also applies brain research, building positive relationships, and research on play.

Although Yvonne's teaching practices primarily reflect cognitive theories, she also applies principles of operant conditioning—reinforcements to increase positive behaviors. Yvonne discovers that behavioral principles can be particularly effective under certain circumstances, such as when she applies them for a limited period of time in working with Maya's special need.

Finally, Yvonne does some theory building of her own by testing her hypotheses about children's play with an informal research study. Theories are born, grow, or die from research that often begins in informal observations of children such as Yvonne's.

MyEducationLab

To assess your understanding of children's learning and development, go to the Book Specific Resources section in the MyEducationLab for your course, select *Effective Practices in Early Childhood Education*, Chapter 4 of the Study Plan, and then complete the multiple choice questions and activities.

Chapter Summary

- Development is age-related change that occurs as the result of an interaction between biological maturation and physical and/or social experience. Learning is a change in knowledge or skill that results from experience or instruction.
- A theory is an explanation of how information and observations are organized and relate to one another. Theories are important because they affect how people think and behave. In education, theories of learning and development affect how teachers treat children, how they structure environments, and how they teach.
- Early experiences change and organize the physical structure of the brain. Neglect, abuse, and stress pose serious threats to healthy brain development. High-quality, developmentally appropriate early childhood education can contribute to healthy brain development.
- The most influential theories of social-emotional development are Erikson's psychosocial theory and Maslow's hierarchy of needs. The most prominent theories of cognitive development are Piaget's theory of constructivism and Vygotsky's sociocultural theory.
- The most prominent learning theories are B. F. Skinner's theory of behaviorism and Albert Bandura's social cognitive theory.
- Research demonstrates that play contributes to language development, self-regulation, attention, creativity, problem solving, social and emotional skills, and literacy and mathematics skills.
- Effective early childhood education is based on knowledge of child development and learning. NAEYC summarizes the key concepts of that knowledge base in 12 principles that can be used to guide practice.
- The Reggio Emilia approach is an example of how theories can be coherently applied to practice. The Reggio Emilia approach also demonstrates how practice can drive theory.

key terms

accommodation
adaptation
assimilation
behaviorism or behavioral learning
co-construction
consequences
conservation
constructivism
development
disequilibrium
egocentrism
equilibration
executive function
extinction
5- to 7-year shift
hypothesis
learning
logico-mathematical knowledge
maturationist
modeling
negative reinforcement
neurons
object permanence
operant conditioning
physical knowledge
plasticity
positive reinforcement
private speech
pruning
punishment
Reggio Emilia approach
reinforcer
scaffolding
scheme or schema
self-actualization theory
self-regulated learning
self-regulation
shaping
social-conventional knowledge
social cognitive theory
sociocultural theory
successive approximations
symbolic representation
synapses
theory
vicarious learning
windows of opportunity
zone of proximal development (ZPD)

readings & websites

Johnson, J. E., Christie, J. F., & Wardle, F. (2005). *Play, development and early education*. Boston: Pearson.

Roopnarine, J. L., & Johnson, J. E. (Eds.). (2009). *Approaches to early childhood education* (5th ed.). Upper Saddle River, NJ: Pearson.

Wien, C. A. (Ed.). (2008). *Emergent curriculum in the primary classroom: Interpreting the Reggio Emilia approach in schools*. New York: Teachers College Press.

Frank Porter Graham Child Development Institute
www.fpg.nc.edu

Jean Piaget Society for the Study of Knowledge and Development
www.piaget.org/free-books.html

North American Reggio Emilia Alliance (NAREA)
www.narea.org

Reggio Children International Center for the Defense and Promotion of the Rights and Potentials of All Children
www.zerosei.comune.re.it/inter/reggiochildren

observe, reflect, decide

1. Spend a morning in a preschool or primary grade classroom and carefully observe the teacher's behavior. Reflect on whether the teacher's behavior is influenced by a particular theory of development or learning. Decide which theories are more apparent in the learning environment and teaching strategies you observe. Decide how effective the practices appear to be in promoting children's development and learning.
2. Reflect on your own experiences as a student in elementary school. What theory of learning seemed to dominate? Can you remember specific situations where you learned from positive reinforcement or from observing and modeling the behavior of others? Can you remember opportunities to work collaboratively with peers—to *co-construct* understanding? How effective did you find different approaches and in which learning situations?
3. Observe in an inclusive early childhood program. Observe how a child with special needs is included in the classroom and what types of teaching practices are used with the child. Decide if a particular theoretical approach dominates the interactions between the teacher/therapists and the child with a disability and how effective it appears to be.
4. Observe children's play in a preschool classroom. Reflect on how complex the play is and how engaged children are. Do you observe mature sociodramatic play? If so, reflect on how it supports children's self-regulation and other skills. If not, decide what the teacher could do to enhance the children's play.
5. Reflect on Maslow's hierarchy of needs and how people's needs motivate their behavior. Do you know individuals who are struggling to meet their basic needs? How does this affect their lives and choices? What motivates you to pursue your education or particular interests? Envision yourself as self-actualized. What would you be doing?

5 Adapting for Individual Differences

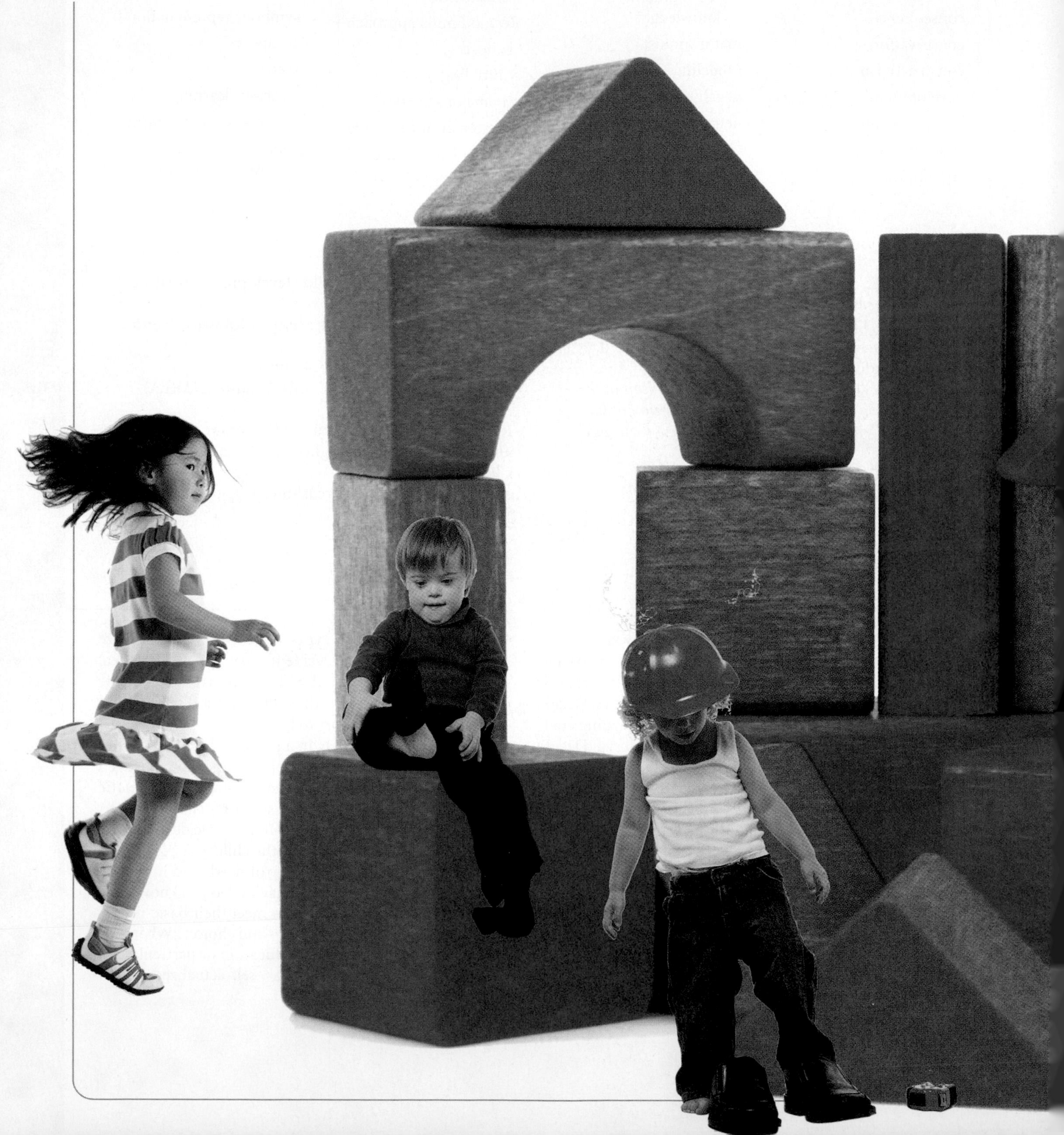

Thinking Ahead

1. What are the types and sources of individual differences among children?
2. What do teachers need to know about individual variation among children and how to accommodate individual differences?
3. What is Gardner's theory of multiple intelligences and what are its implications for practice?
4. What are the Response to Intervention and Recognition & Response models and how do they address individual differences in young children's learning?
5. What practices are required by law for children with disabilities and special needs?
6. What practices for teaching children with special needs are effective for teaching all children?

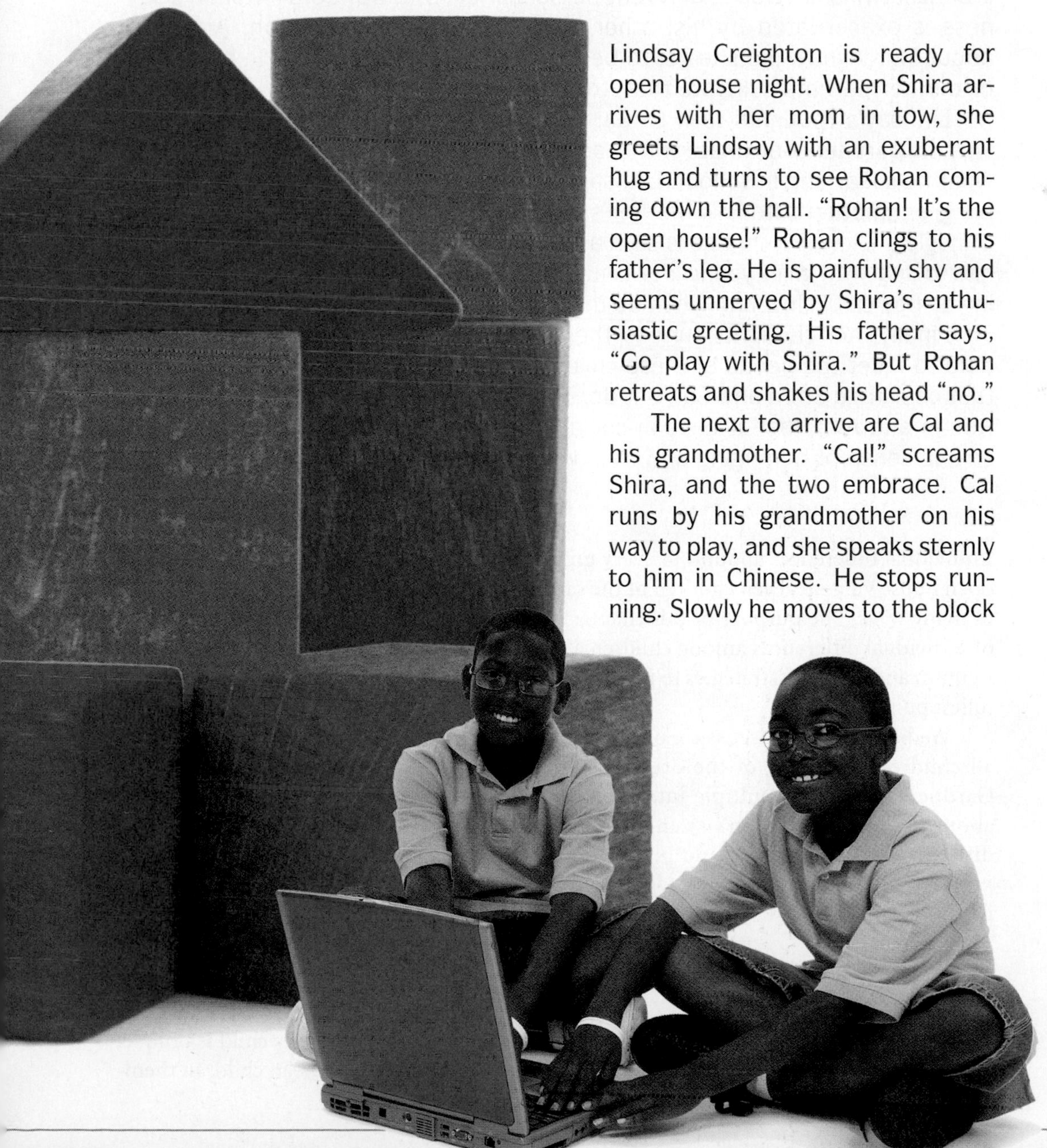

Lindsay Creighton is ready for open house night. When Shira arrives with her mom in tow, she greets Lindsay with an exuberant hug and turns to see Rohan coming down the hall. "Rohan! It's the open house!" Rohan clings to his father's leg. He is painfully shy and seems unnerved by Shira's enthusiastic greeting. His father says, "Go play with Shira." But Rohan retreats and shakes his head "no."

The next to arrive are Cal and his grandmother. "Cal!" screams Shira, and the two embrace. Cal runs by his grandmother on his way to play, and she speaks sternly to him in Chinese. He stops running. Slowly he moves to the block corner with Shira. When she hands him a pink car, Cal sighs, "This is for girls. I need a boy car."

Carter and his parents arrive. Shira says hello to Carter, but then speaks to his parents, "Carter can play if he wants." Carter flaps his arms and repeats a favorite phrase from a children's movie. He moves closer to Shira and grabs her cheeks. His parents intervene and say, "Too close, Carter." Behind Carter and his parents are the twins, Alice and Alexandra. Shira's mom, Beth, greets them, "Hello, Alice. Hello, Alex." Alice rolls her eyes and says, "You got us mixed up again!" Beth apologizes, but the twins' mom says, "Even I get them mixed up sometimes, until they are in a place like this. Just watch. Alice will try to take over, and Alex will stay in a quiet corner until the open house is over." Ruby is the last to arrive. Her father immediately asks Lindsay if any of the food has nuts. When Lindsay says, "No, I made sure," he still asks to see the ingredient labels due to Ruby's severe allergy.

Later, Lindsay reflects on the evening. Although the children are all about the same age, they are so different. She marvels at the fact that even the identical twins have such different personalities. She wonders if Rohan's shyness is exacerbated by his father's insistence on participation. And what about Shira—how did she get to be such a social butterfly? Is it in her genes, or did her parents cultivate that, too?

Lindsay's thoughts turn to Carter, who has autism. She considers how well his parents coordinate with his teacher and other specialists to reinforce what he's learning in school. Lindsay also thinks of 5-year-old Cal, living with his grandmother after his mother's parental rights were revoked as a result of neglect. How is it that he is such a positive and vivacious boy given all he has had to deal with in his young life? Lindsay smiles when she thinks about Cal wanting a "boy car." How and when do these gender stereotypes crystallize?

Finally, her thoughts turn to the challenges she faces. How will she be able to meet the needs of these children? How will she provide experiences that challenge Shira and Cal, but don't overwhelm Carter? How will she make Rohan and Alex feel at ease in social situations? And how will she create a strong sense of belonging and friendship among these children? ▲

Individual differences abound in every group of young children. As is evident from the open house vignette, even children of the same chronological age differ from one another in many ways. The purpose of this chapter is to examine what is known about the range of individual differences among children and how teachers can effectively adapt the curriculum and teaching strategies to help all children participate, develop, and learn to their fullest potential.

We begin with a discussion of the range of individual variation that exists among all children and some of the origins of these differences. Next we describe Howard Gardner's theory of multiple intelligences, which is a useful framework for thinking about individual children's strengths, needs, interests, and abilities. Then we discuss differentiating instruction and present a model for responding to the diverse learning needs of all children. We conclude with a discussion of teaching children with disabilities and special needs.

Individual Differences among Young Children

Anyone who has been a parent or a teacher is aware of the fact that every child is unique. Even people who do not have parenting or teaching experience have been children themselves and are well aware of the fact that we are all different. Try to remember your earliest school experience and picture the children in your class. Were all the boys or girls alike? Did everyone enjoy and excel at the same activities? Did all of your classmates learn at the same pace and in the same way? Was anyone exactly like you? Of course, the answer to all of these questions is "No."

Acknowledging the uniqueness of each child is only the beginning. Effective early childhood teachers understand typical and atypical child development; they also understand the importance of knowing each child as an individual. They use this knowledge to plan and adapt curriculum and to help each child meet important learning goals (NAEYC, 2009a).

Every class of young children is made up of unique individuals. Intentional teachers must find ways to meet the needs of every child while also challenging each one to continue learning.

Why Pay Attention to Individual Differences?

One of the most well-known facts about child development is that there is a wide range of individual variation (Shonkoff & Phillips, 2000). But what does "wide range" mean and what are the implications for teachers? The concept of a range of variation is based on an average; for example, we might say that on average men are 5' 10" tall. This average was calculated based on the heights of a huge number of men. When we consider their heights individually, however, they may range from 4' 8" to 7' 1". Now, consider a range of variation in relation to children's development. On virtually every characteristic we could measure—saying first words, balancing on one foot, knowing the alphabet—the pace and timing of children's performance vary. The average age at which most children master a skill, for example, doesn't tell us much without knowing the range, which gives us a far clearer picture of reality.

In general, teachers need to be cautious about focusing too much on averages. Many aspects of schooling, including the graded structure and power of standardized tests, tend to reflect the assumption that all children will achieve certain skills and knowledge at the same time. As a result, the tendency is for schools to ignore the range of variation and to try to teach all children the same way.

But if we want every child to achieve the same goals, we must treat them and teach them as individuals. Acknowledging that individual differences exist does not mean lowering expectations for some children. In fact, high expectations for children's learning are necessary if they are to succeed. In the sections that follow, we describe some important aspects of variation among children. But first we discuss theories about the origin of individual differences—the question of nature versus nurture.

Where Do Individual Differences Come From?

One of the most enduring debates in psychology is the degree to which development is the product of biology (nature) or environment (nurture). The question is often framed as whether nature or nurture is more influential in determining who we become as individuals. Although we know that physical characteristics are inherited, the genetic markers are less clear when it comes to an individual's behavior, intelligence, and personality. Consider the twins in Lindsay Creighton's classroom at the beginning of this chapter. Is Alice more outgoing and Alex more cautious because these personality traits are not part of the genetic pattern they share? Or does this difference result because their parents encouraged the girls in different ways?

The Influence of Biology on Development

In the past, some psychologists (Jensen, 1980) proposed that people behave as they do because of inborn characteristics. This belief emphasizes the influence of **nature**, the hereditary or

nature The hereditary or genetic contributions to human development.

genetic contributions to human development. Whether we are male or female, have freckles, blonde hair, or a certain type of personality can be influenced by genetic factors.

Nature also refers to the biological and neurological drivers of development. For example, physical growth and advances in motor skills for most humans develop in a predictable sequence. Newborn reflexes soon give rise to voluntary movements and the development of abilities such as rolling over, crawling, walking, and running. Similarly, language development has a biological component. The fact that most infants, regardless of culture, begin to coo and babble at approximately the same ages provides strong evidence that nature indeed affects development.

Whereas some aspects of nature influence a similar course of development for most children, genetics also affects individual differences. For example, most children take their first steps by about 1 year of age, but there is a wide range of variation among individuals. David took his first steps at 7 months, whereas his brother Jeffrey wasn't mobile until 18 months.

The Role of the Environment

Although biology influences individual differences, some scientists (Skinner, 1953, 1968) believe that people behave in certain ways more as a result of their experiences in the environment or because they are taught to do so. This belief stresses the influence of **nurture** on human behavior.

Heredity may play a role in influencing personality traits, but according to the nurture perspective, environmental factors ultimately determine who we become. Parents' discipline methods, for example, might have more influence on their children's behavior than the parents' genetic contributions. Other dimensions of the environment also influence children's development, such as the quality of their child care setting, the family's economic resources, the number of siblings in the home, and the safety of the community.

The Transactional Relationship between Nature and Nurture

Although the *nature versus nurture* debate continues, the current thinking is that "nature and nurture are partners in how developing people interact with the surrounding environment" (Shonkoff & Phillips, 2000, p. 39). The **transactional theory of development** (Sameroff, 1975) explains that development is the result of *both* biology *and* experience and the ways in which they influence each other.

To illustrate how nature and nurture interact, consider the following examples. Myra, a highly verbal and inquisitive 6-year-old, seems to inspire her teacher to engage her in intellectually stimulating projects, such as finding out what causes earthquakes, which in turn further Myra's already accelerated development and learning. By contrast, Alyssa, who is deaf, is withdrawn and rarely joins in activities even though her teacher uses sign language. Alyssa's lack of responsiveness may provoke her teacher to initiate communication with her less often.

Both biology and experience play critical, interrelated roles in children's development. Therefore, the kinds of experiences children have become vitally important, a topic we discuss next.

nurture Environmental factors and experiences that influence human development and behavior.

transactional theory of development Theory that development is the result of both biology and experience and how they influence each other.

risk factors Inherited or experiential conditions that potentially contribute to poor developmental outcomes for children, such as peer rejection, academic failure, juvenile delinquency, and school expulsion.

How Experience Affects Outcomes for Children: Risk or Resilience

According to the transactional theory of development, children's experiences impact their overall development. Accumulation of certain kinds of experiences can place children at risk for negative outcomes. Similarly, if children have repeated positive experiences, their development is likely to be enhanced.

Understanding Risk Factors

Risk factors are inherited or experiential conditions that potentially contribute to negative outcomes for children (Huffman et al., 2001). Among the most frequently identified

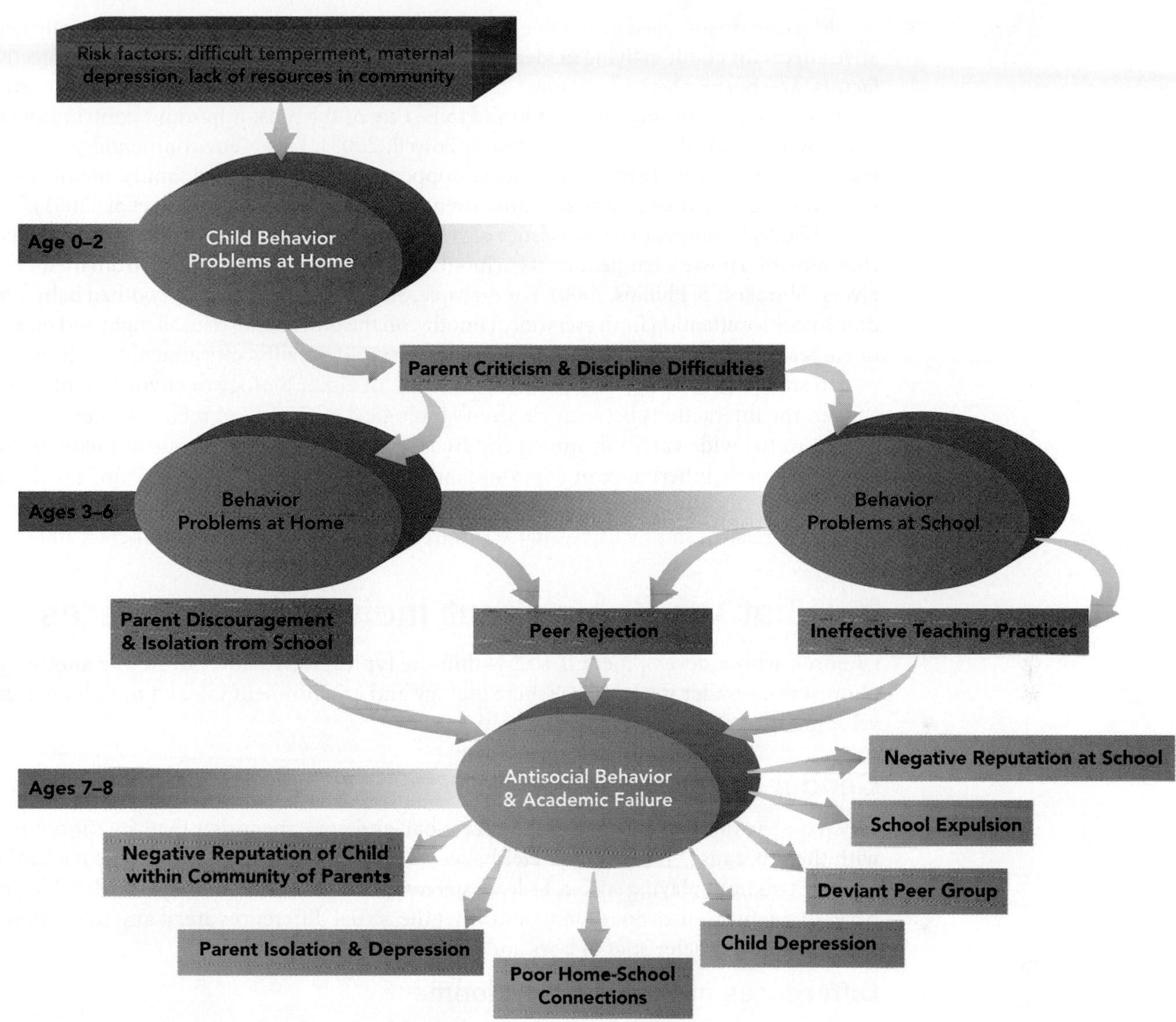

Figure 5.1 Ripple Effect of Multiple Risk Factors
Source: © Carolyn Webster-Stratton. Used with permission of Carolyn Webster-Stratton.

risk factors are living in poverty, living with a single parent, low education level of parents, disability, and child abuse (Huffman et al., 2001). The concept of risk factors has led to the use of the term *children at risk* of school failure.

When risk factors multiply in children's lives, they produce a growing number of poor developmental outcomes—what might be called a *ripple effect.* That is, the more risk factors children have, the more likely they are to experience developmental delays and social or health problems. These conditions, in turn, can lead to a host of poor outcomes such as peer rejection, academic failure, dropping out of school, mental health disorders, or criminal behavior. Figure 5.1 illustrates the potential ripple effect of experiencing multiple risk factors.

Promoting Resilience

Research on children with multiple risk factors demonstrates that exposure to risk and adversity does not necessarily result in negative outcomes for some children (Rutter, 1987; Werner & Smith, 1982). Positive, supportive experiences can mediate risk and help children become resilient. **Resilience** refers to a child's ability to overcome, adapt to, or minimize the damaging effects of adversity.

resilience A child's ability to overcome, adapt to, or minimize the damaging effects of adversity.

Mechanisms—called **protective factors**—exist that may minimize the potentially negative effects for children living in identified high-risk situations. Like risk factors, protective factors are both inherited (nature) and experiential (nurture). A continuous, positive parent–child relationship has been found to be one of the most important contributors to the development of resilience (Masten & Powell, 2003). Other environmental protective factors include a variety of external social supports, such as extended family, membership in a church or spiritual group, and close friends and neighbors (Huffman et al., 2001).

Children's inherent characteristics also contribute to resilience. For example, resilient children often possess temperaments in infancy that elicit positive responses from their caregivers (Shonkoff & Phillips, 2000). For example, Stefano is a happy, easily soothed baby who draws positive attention from everyone. Timothy, on the other hand, cries all night and doesn't nurse readily. His mother begins to feel inadequate and has difficulty attaching to him.

In short, risk and resilience are not the result of either biology or environment alone. Rather, the interactions between children's biological makeup and their experiences contribute to the wide variation among children and families. Teachers must remember that a child's genetic inheritance or environmental circumstances should never limit their expectations of children. In fact, one of the most important sources of resilience in children is positive relationships with teachers (Hamre & Pianta, 2001, Howes & Ritchie, 2002).

What We Know about Individual Differences

Children whose development is well within the typical range differ from one another in many ways. Gender is a key area where biology and environment interact to influence development, as described in the next section.

Gender Differences

When 3-year-old Lucienne receives a soccer ball and goal, she insists that she cannot play with them because "It's for boys." Her belief was reinforced by the fact that the packaging showed two boys playing soccer. Indeed, stereotypes about girls and boys are durable and pervasive, which raises questions about what the actual differences are, if any, in the development and characteristics of boys and girls.

Differences in Physical Development

There is little evidence of gender differences in most domains of development and learning. In some domains, however, the characteristics of females and males have been found to differ. Physically, for example, females are typically more mature at birth and males are more likely to be miscarried, die in infancy, or develop hereditary diseases (Jacklin, 1989). On average, females also reach developmental milestones such as talking earlier than males (Bukatko & Daehler, 2003).

Cognitive Skills

Although there are no significant gender-based differences in overall intelligence, tests of cognitive abilities find some specific differences between girls and boys. Notably, boys demonstrate a slight but consistent advantage in the domain of visual–spatial ability (Halpern & LaMay, 2000; Linn & Peterson, 1985; Voyer, Voyer, & Bryden, 1995). This skill involves the ability to visualize and mentally transform or rotate figures or objects, which relates to success in academic areas such as mathematics, engineering, drawing, and graphics (Khairul & Azniah, 2004).

Some evidence suggests, however, that gender differences in visual–spatial ability are to some extent a product of children's experience (Clements & Sarama, 2008). For example, during the preschool years, boys tend to spend more time than girls doing the kinds of activities that build visual–spatial skills: building with blocks, playing with Legos, and putting puzzles together. When girls engage in such play and teachers make the experience meaningful, such as talking with them about what they are doing or reading a story about shapes, girls perform as well as boys on these visual–spatial tasks (Casey, Erkut, Ceder, & Young, 2008).

protective factors
Mechanisms, both inherited and experiential, that may minimize the potentially negative effects for children living in identified high-risk situations.

Social Behavior

Popular culture suggests that vast differences exist in social behavior between females and males; however, scientific research suggests that few broad gender differences exist in the area of social behaviors (Feingold, 1994; Maccoby, 2002; Maccoby & Jacklin, 1974). There are, however, subtle differences. Boys tend to play in slightly larger groups and their play generally takes up more space (Maccoby, 2002). Girls tend to form more intimate friendships (Dolgin & Kim, 2006), whereas boys' friendships are more geared toward a mutual interest in activities (Erwin, 1998). And even as early as 2 years of age, girls talk more about emotion than boys (Cervantes & Callanan, 1998).

Perhaps the most notable gender difference is that boys are more overtly aggressive than girls beginning in the preschool years. Boys are also more physically active and more likely to engage in rough-and-tumble play (Pelligrini & Smith, 1998). They display more physical aggression, try to dominate peers, and subsequently display more antisocial behaviors than females (Block, 1983; Loeber & Hay, 1997).

Although it is tempting to think these gender differences are innate, the reality is more complicated. Current thinking is that differences in girls' and boys' social behaviors are heavily influenced by the situation (Zakriski, Wright, & Underwood, 2005). Because boys and girls are often observed playing with their same-sex peers, differences between the sexes can appear to be greater than they really are and similarities less obvious (Maccoby, 2002). For example, preschooler Leo gets into frequent fights with his peers and appears to be more aggressive than Johanna. But this difference might have more to do with Leo's rough-and-tumble peer group than any innate tendency to aggressive behavior.

In addition, gender differences in aggression are largely a function of where the behavior occurs and how aggression is defined. The largest sex differences are found in less structured, natural environments such as on the playground. However, if the definition of *aggression* is an attempt to hurt another person through manipulation, gossip, or exclusion from a social group, called *relational aggression*, then girls are found to be more aggressive than boys starting in the preschool years (Bjorkqvist, 1994; Crick, Casas, & Mosher, 1997; Crick & Grotpeter, 1995). If Johanna were to be picked on as often as Leo, she might be perceived as being aggressive, too. There is also the possibility that Johanna would react differently than Leo. Rather than using physical aggression, she would probably resort to relational aggression, such as name-calling or saying, "I won't be your friend."

Gender-Related Expectations

Although gender is a biological trait, much gender-related behavior is learned. From very early ages, children receive messages about what is expected of girls and boys that influence their behavior. By preschool age, children are beginning to firmly establish their gender identity, although they may still think that changing their clothes or activity can affect it. Sex role stereotyping can play a powerful role in the classroom. Consider how you as a teacher might react in the situation described in the *How Would You Respond?* feature.

Among the individual differences that have the greatest significance for teachers are variations in cognitive development and abilities, social and emotional development including temperament, approaches to learning, physical development, and interests. These topics are discussed briefly in the sections that follow.

Individual Differences in Cognitive Development and Abilities

A major contributor to individual differences is variation in language development. Consider the fact that although, on average, babies say their first word at 11 months, the range is from 8 to 14 months (B. Hart & Risley, 1999). In addition, although the average age at which half of what children say is understandable is 19 months, the range is 15 to 30 months (B. Hart & Risley, 1999), making teaching toddlers a challenging task indeed.

As children get older, variation only increases. Observations of 2-year-olds demonstrate that, on average, children produce 134 different words per hour, but the range is

How Would You Respond?

Barbie Play

The Situation Several 5-year-old girls who are very absorbed at home with Barbie dolls, hairstyles, and makeup kits have been engaging in such play in the classroom. Although there are no glamour dolls or beauty items in the classroom, at every opportunity the girls play out fashion, beauty, and dating themes, using whatever materials they can find. Often the theme of the play is how to get a boy's attention or dress up to "look hot."

What to Do? You first will want to give the situation some thought. Might the girls derive any benefits from this type of play? What, if anything, concerns you about it? What would you like to see happen?

You might determine that girl-gets-boy play isn't the kind of activity you would like to see the children engaging in; much like the repetitive war play you see some of the boys engage in, you think it is stereotyped. What would you do?

Here are some ideas to consider:

- Leave the girls alone, hoping that their fascination will run its course.
- Ban this kind of play entirely.
- Try to redirect the girls to other play. (What kind of redirection might be successful?)
- Make remarks aimed at providing balance and perspective to the girls' present ideas. For example, "The teenager who lives next door to me sometimes likes to dress up and fix her hair and nails, and sometimes she likes to wear old jeans and be really comfortable. She plays on the ice hockey team, and she loves to read about dolphins."

Which of these things would you do and why? Which do you think might have unintended and undesirable consequences? What else can you suggest?

18 to 286 words (B. Hart & Risley, 1999). Such wide variation makes it challenging for teachers and parents to determine whether a child's development is just at the slow end of the range or is actually delayed.

By the time children reach kindergarten, their language, literacy, and mathematics abilities vary widely, and the achievement gap is already apparent (Lee & Burkam, 2002; West, Denton, & Germino-Hausken, 2000). However, it is important to remember our earlier caution about averages when thinking about a large group of individuals such as children from low-income families. A wide range of variation exists within this group as well; although many children will be behind, others will not.

Individual Differences in Emotional and Social Development

Social skills and emotional self-regulation are among the most important skills for success in school and life. Positive social skills include the ability to make friends, join in play, and comfort other children in distress (Bowman, Donovan, & Burns, 2001). Children who lack social skills are more likely to be angry and to argue and fight or withdraw from others.

Differences in social and emotional development are often related to temperament differences that may be apparent at birth. **Temperament** is defined as "the pattern of arousal and emotionality that is characteristic of an individual" (Bowman et al., 2001, pp. 93, 96). Temperament includes such characteristics as typical activity level, attention span, and mood (Thomas & Chess, 1984). A key dimension of temperament is how well children adapt and respond to new situations. Recall the twins, Alexandra and Alice, in the chapter-opening vignette. Alice confidently joins in and becomes the life of the party, whereas Alex is fearful and inhibited in the new situation.

temperament The pattern of arousal and emotionality that is characteristic of an individual.

Teachers who understand their children's different temperaments will have more success in developing good relationships with each child. This understanding will help teachers assess how well a child's temperament fits the expectations of a given situation (Bowman et al., 2001). Instead of assuming that an inhibited child has poor social skills or that an uninhibited child is too aggressive or out of control, teachers should adapt to each child's needs. For Alexandra, her teacher will need to help her feel comfortable and secure in new surroundings. Alice, however, may need help adapting to structured routines, controlling her exuberance, and paying attention when needed. Temperament is now thought of as one dimension of a larger topic, approaches to learning, discussed next.

Individual Differences in Approaches to Learning

Early childhood educators are becoming increasingly aware that children's *approaches to learning* are critically important determinants of their success in school (Fantuzzo, Perry, & McDermott, 2004; Hyson, 2008). **Approaches to learning** are "behaviors, tendencies or typical patterns that children use in learning situations" (Hyson, 2008, p. 10). These include both how children feel about learning—their level of enthusiasm, interest, and motivation—and how children engage with learning. Do they pay attention? Do they persist when tasks are challenging or frustrating? If one solution doesn't work out, are they flexible and creative in trying something new?

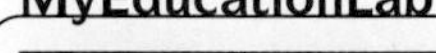

Go to the Book Specific Resources in the MyEducationLab for your course and select Author Interviews in Chapter 5 to watch and listen to the video *Individual Differences*. What does Sue Bredekamp want teachers to know about individual differences?

As with all other aspects of learning and development, there are individual differences in children's approaches to learning, which vary depending on the situation. For example, 7-year-old Wes enjoys taking things apart and putting them together; he will persist for hours working on his simple machines project for science. But during reading class, Wes loses interest and his attention wanders; his reading progress suffers. In response, his teacher brings in several books on machines and Wes's enthusiasm for reading improves.

Even a brief visit to a classroom during choice time reveals the diversity of children's approaches to learning. Dontrelle can play with Legos for an hour. Ivy loves music, especially songs with movements, but wanders from one area to another, never alighting on one activity. Becca prefers painting but is perfectly happy if it is not available. The challenge for teachers is to foster children's positive approaches to learning and build on their strengths to help them acquire new skills and abilities.

Individual Differences in Physical Development

Children of the same chronological age vary considerably in height and weight. Teachers sometimes inaccurately judge children's maturity based on their physical characteristics. For example, boys who are small for their age may be thought to be less mature than taller boys and inaccurately judged not ready for kindergarten. At the same time, taller children, both girls and boys, are often assumed to be older and more capable than they are.

approaches to learning
Behaviors, tendencies, or typical patterns that children use in learning situations that include both how they feel about learning—their level of enthusiasm, interest, and motivation—and how they engage with learning.

Physical development is largely determined by biology; however, experience also plays a role in how physical skills and abilities develop. On average, girls develop fine motor skills earlier than boys, but cultural expectations for girls' behavior may contribute to these differences (Bowman et al., 2001). Girls, for instance, may be given dolls to dress with miniature clothes and shoes that require fine motor skills, and they may be encouraged by teachers or parents to play in a more restricted way than boys. Similarly, because boys may be less adept with pencils or unable to sit still for group time, teachers might think they are less competent. Just as teachers must understand each child's temperament, they must also come to understand each child's physical skills and capabilities in order to provide a wide range of learning opportunities to find the best match.

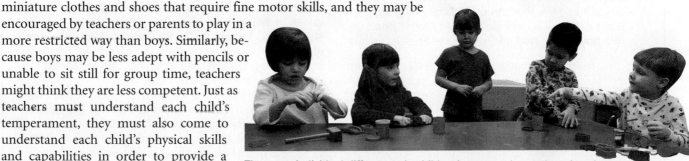

There are individual differences in children's approaches to learning. As you can see, the child in the middle hesitates to join in play, whereas others may be enthusiastic and engaged right from the start.

Seeing Each Child as an Individual

There is a scene in the movie *Mary Poppins* when Ms. Poppins meets her charges, Jane and Michael, for the first time. The star nanny pulls out her "magical measuring tape." The special tape measurer allows her to instantaneously surmise important and unique information about the children that helps her to plan how she will best care for them. While this type of measuring tape does not exist in reality, it illustrates a necessary first step in working with young children: getting to know them.

For teachers to build positive relationships and teach effectively, they need to understand children's preferences, interests, background, and culture. For children, this information is most often accessed by carefully and purposefully observing what they do, and by speaking directly to parents and other caregivers. The task of knowing children is continuous, involving observing and assessing on a regular basis.

Some teachers find it helpful for parents to complete surveys about their child. Items on these surveys include favorite foods, family members, pets, favorite toys or activities,

Culture Lens

The Relationship between Individual Differences and Cultural Differences

Early childhood teachers must respond to both individual differences in children and to cultural differences. Why both? When teachers respond to the individual child, aren't they also responding to the cultural child? The answer is yes and no.

Every child is unique and develops an individual personality as a result of her or his personal history. At the same time, everyone develops some behaviors that are shared with members of his or her cultural group. Because culture is a group characteristic, the rules of a culture are shared by group members and are not unique to individuals. When teachers think only of children as individuals, they risk missing important information about what children have learned about group expectations. Consider this example:

> Edwin comes in from outdoor play crying; he is soaked with water and covered with sand and mud. His teacher, Ms. Amos, starts to undress him to help him get cleaned up and he cries harder. When she tries to help him remove his shoes, he forcefully pulls away. Ms. Amos knows him to be stubborn and tries to coax him into letting her help and consoles him while attempting to undress him, but to no avail. What his teacher doesn't know is that in Edwin's cultural group, you don't get your school clothes dirty, boys don't cry, and boys dress and undress themselves in private.

Had this teacher known more about Edwin's cultural group, she could have responded in a more appropriate way. She might have offered him a change of clothes and let him go to a private place to change himself. On the other hand, what teachers know about group differences when blindly applied to all individuals in a cultural group may be equally inappropriate because individuals within groups differ from one another.

> After the incident with Edwin, Ms. Amos decides to learn more about his cultural background. She talks to colleagues and becomes a more careful observer of Edwin and his family, as well as of other children from his cultural group. One day Edwin's cousin Sammy comes in soaked and covered with sand and mud. Ms. Amos decides not to help him clean up, but offers him a change of clothes. When he takes the clean clothes, returns to the playground, and throws them in the sandbox, his teacher is stunned because she expected him to go in the bathroom and change. Sammy, however, was not at all upset by the wet clothes and enjoyed acting contrary to expectations.

So why did the two boys—both from the same cultural group—behave so differently? Because culture is learned, it can be well learned by some people in the group and less well learned by others. Some families are tradition oriented, others less so. Further, even though families and individuals learn the cultural rules, some people conform to what they have learned, while others don't.

Thus, members of a cultural group will behave differently depending on how deeply embedded they are within the core of a culture. Thinking about differences in behavior in this way helps teachers understand why, for instance, all Japanese people don't always "act Japanese." And it helps teachers avoid stereotyping groups and applying untested assumptions about individuals.

An important thing to remember is that knowing who children are as members of cultural groups provides more information than simply knowing them as individuals. But the most important point is that children are both individuals and cultural beings at the same time and in the same place.

how to tell when their child is upset, certain fears, or other special needs. With this information, teachers can help ensure that children are motivated to get involved, that the content of conversations and level of instruction are relevant, and that they communicate respect for children's families and cultural background.

As we have seen in previous sections, individual differences result from both heredity and experience. A key determinant of children's experience is their culture. For example, cultural groups differ in their views about appropriate behavior for males and females. Cultural differences and individual differences are not the same thing, but they are connected. The *Culture Lens* feature will help you understand the relationship between individual and cultural differences.

The connection between interests and abilities is the foundation of an important theory relevant to individual differences in human beings. This theory of multiple intelligences is described in the section that follows.

Multiple Intelligences and Individual Differences

One of the most useful frameworks for thinking about variation among children is the **theory of multiple intelligences** developed by Howard Gardner (2004). Rather than thinking about intelligence as one score that can be measured by an intelligence test, Gardner identified eight different intelligences, which are listed and described in Table 5.1. Gardner believes that individual children have different profiles of strengths and weaknesses among these intelligences. His theory challenges teachers to think of the many different ways children are intelligent and can demonstrate their competence.

theory of multiple intelligences Theory developed by Howard Gardner that identifies eight different intelligences as opposed to a single score on an intelligence test; this theory is useful for thinking about variation among children and teaching to their strengths.

Gardner (2004) points out that typically schooling only focuses on two of the intelligences: logical/mathematical and linguistic. Consider the fact that college entrance exams

Table 5.1 Gardner's Theory of Multiple Intelligences

Intelligence	Definition	Children's Interests in School and Later Life
Logical/mathematical	Ability to reason, analyze, solve logical problems	Earth, space, and physical sciences; mathematics; computers
Linguistic	Ability to communicate; sensitivity to words and functions of language	Reading, writing, teaching, public speaking
Musical	Ability to produce and appreciate music	Singing, playing instruments, composing and listening to music
Naturalist	Sensitivity to the natural world, plants, and animals	Outdoor play, nature, biology, environmental science, gardening
Spatial	Ability to perceive the visual–spatial world	Visual arts, photography, architecture, graphic design
Bodily/kinesthetic	Ability to control body movements and objects	Dancing, physical education, sports, movement exploration
Interpersonal	Sensitivity to the feelings and desires of others	Making friends, collaborative learning, social studies
Intrapersonal	Awareness of own feelings and strengths	Keeping a diary, reading, writing poetry

Sources: Based on Gardner, 2006, 2000.

MyEducationLab

Go to the Assignments and Activities section of Topic 2: Child Development/Theories in the MyEducationLab for your course and complete the activity entitled *Applying Multiple Intelligences Theory*. As you watch the video and answer the accompanying questions, consider how planning for multiple intelligences helps teachers adapt for individual differences in children?

result in scores for math and verbal ability. When educators only test children's verbal and math abilities, as is often the case, they miss children's strengths in other important areas such as sociability or psychomotor skills. Gardner also believes that attention to the full range of children's capabilities could help more children succeed in school, thus narrowing the achievement gap for children from low-income families and children of color.

What are the implications of Gardner's theory for teachers? Consider the following example of teaching with multiple intelligences in mind. Hanita Blume teaches a mixed-age group of 4- and 5-year-olds. One of the primary goals of the math curriculum is to develop children's concept of number, which includes counting and beginning operations, such as adding and subtracting. The range of ages and experiences among children within her group affects their levels of math ability. She takes these differences into account as well as the fact that each of these children has different capabilities and interests.

Hanita does not try to evaluate individual children's "intelligences." Instead, she plans a variety of learning opportunities to draw on children's strengths and interests to help them all achieve the math goals. Following are some of the learning experiences she provides relevant to each of the multiple intelligences:

- *Logical/mathematical:* Hanita engages children in solving real-world problems with numbers, such as "We have nine children and only five chairs. How many more chairs do we need?"
- *Linguistic:* Hanita reads a counting book in small groups and engages children in counting the objects on each page.
- *Musical:* In large and small groups, Hanita sings counting songs and does fingerplays such as *Five Little Monkeys* to engage children in counting forward and backward.
- *Naturalist:* During outdoor play time, Hanita works with children to make collections of natural objects such as leaves or stones. Children place the objects in categories (large or small, according to color), count the number in each category, and determine which has more or less.
- *Spatial:* Hanita provides many different kinds of blocks and small manipulative toys for children to count and categorize, and talks with them, supplying the counting words for those who need the help.
- *Bodily/kinesthetic:* Hanita engages children in using their bodies to learn the counting sequence and concept of number. Children stomp their feet or clap their hands three times, four times, and so on.
- *Interpersonal:* Hanita organizes small cooperative groups of children to work on math games such as *Chutes and Ladders*, children roll the die, read the number of dots, and count the number of spaces. There is no competition.
- *Intrapersonal:* Hanita works one-on-one with some children in tasks such as calculating attendance, and then asks them to reflect on what they know about counting.

As we can conclude from the example of Hanita's classroom, seeing children as individuals with multiple intelligences does not mean that every child must be taught differently. Instead, individual variation among children requires adapting teaching practices in several ways, that is, differentiating instruction, as discussed next.

The Learning Cycle of Differentiating Instruction

differentiated instruction The creation of multiple paths so that children of different abilities, interests, and learning needs experience equally appropriate ways to achieve important learning goals.

In highly diverse classrooms, teachers need to differentiate instruction so that they create opportunities for all students to learn. **Differentiated instruction** refers to creating multiple paths so that children of different abilities, interests, and learning needs experience equally appropriate ways to achieve important learning goals. *Equally appropriate* does not mean the same or uniform. Nor does differentiated instruction mean that children receive their own assignments or that they receive a private, one-on-one lesson away from others.

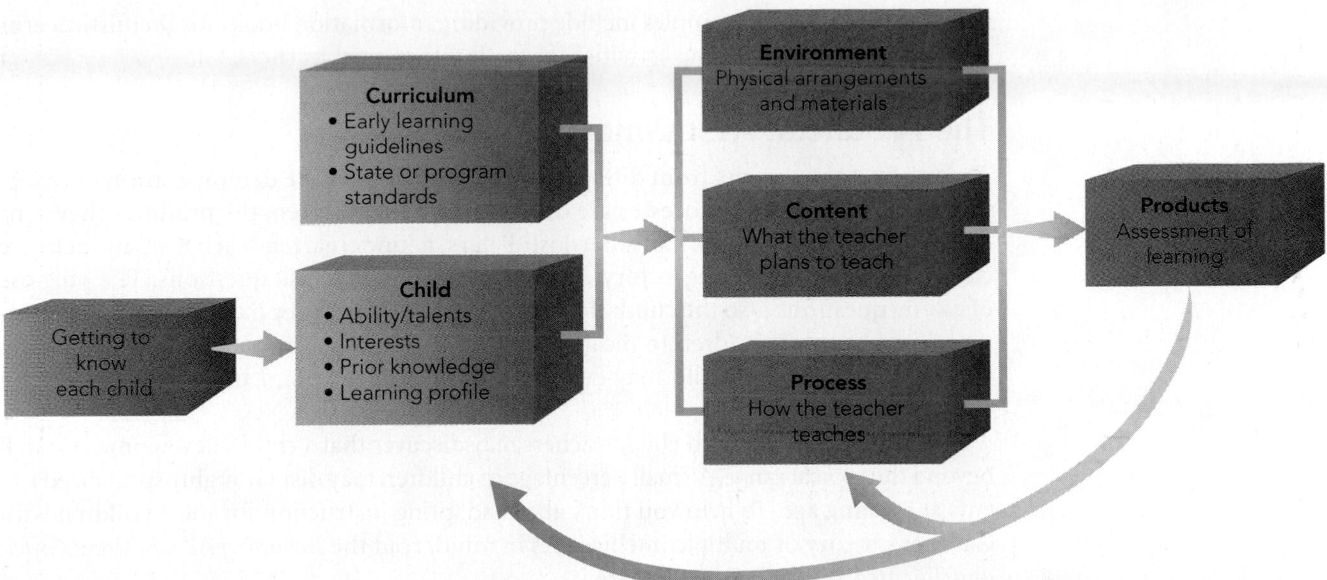

Figure 5.2 Learning Cycle of Differentiated Instruction in the Early Childhood Classroom

Source: Adapted from *Planning for Differentiated Instruction*, by L. Oaksford and L. Jones, 2001, based on ideas from Tomlinson, *The Differentiated Classroom,* 1999, Tallahassee, FL: Leon County Schools. Retrieved August 15, 2009, from www.cast.org/publications/ncac/ncac_diffinstruc.html. Reprinted by permission of Linda Oaksford.

Rather, it means that teachers provide interrelated learning opportunities that help facilitate children's mastery of new skills and content knowledge.

Differentiated instruction is a cyclical process that is illustrated in Figure 5.2. First, teachers must get to know each child in the classroom. They must also know the curriculum. Both of these components influence how teachers plan and differentiate instruction. Planning must take into account the learning environment, the content, the process, and the product, each of which is described next.

Planning the Environment

The environment refers to the overall look and feel of the classroom. A differentiated environment provides various spaces throughout the classroom for learning to occur. For example, soft, cozy spaces allow some children to work alone. Other spaces are designed for intrapersonal learners to work together in small groups. A differentiated environment also provides a variety of materials. For example, a writing center might have sandpaper letters or plastic magnetic letters for tactile learners. Children who learn best while moving may have places to stand and work at tables.

Differentiating Content

Differentiating the content involves meeting children where they are and focusing instruction on what they need to learn next. For example, a child who knows letters can begin to map letter sounds to the alphabet and is also ready to receive instruction on blending letters to make sounds. A child who is already reading words is ready to work on fluency and comprehension.

The Process of Teaching

The process refers to how the teacher provides specific content instruction. The intentional teacher considers the child's abilities and interests when planning content instruction. For example, when teaching science, the teacher provides hands-on tools for children to observe, measure, and record their observations. A computer program is motivating for many children. Other examples include providing information books for linguistic learners and cooperative learning activities for the intrapersonal learners.

The Products: Assessment of Learning

The product that results from differentiated instruction is the demonstration of learning. When content and processes are differentiated for children, the products they produce will be different, too. Consider Josh Peters, a kindergarten teacher in an inclusive classroom. As he is reading a story, he stops occasionally to ask questions. The purpose of asking questions is so the children can demonstrate what they have learned (the product). He asks some children to recall the events of the story and others to predict what will happen next. One child may even be asked to simply point to an illustration of a character in the story.

In getting to know each child, teachers may discover that a child's development is well beyond the typical range. A small percentage of children may display highly specialized talents at a young age. To help you think about adapting instruction for these children with Gardner's theory of multiple intelligences in mind, read the *Including All Children: Gifted and Talented Young Children* feature.

Including All Children

Gifted and Talented Young Children

Melvin's Head Start teacher, Ms. Dell, thinks he is "very precocious." At age 3, he used words like *inspiration*, *nocturnal*, and *actually*. He also exhibited an intense curiosity, asking high-level questions such as, "Where does gasoline come from?"

Melvin's teacher modifies the curriculum to challenge him. She sets up a time for Melvin to visit the Early Head Start room and read to the toddlers. She orders *National Geographic* to satisfy his insatiable curiosity about geography. She is also patient with Melvin's occasional temper tantrums and persistent questioning that would bother most other adults. When it is time to enroll Melvin in kindergarten, Ms. Dell suggests to his mom that she have him evaluated for the school district's Accelerated Learning Program.

Ms. Dell is an exceptional preschool teacher. She understands the importance of recognizing the signs of giftedness in young children—particularly in children from low-income families who are more often considered at risk than gifted—and nurturing the gift so that it may flourish. She also understands that gifted children's development can be uneven, in that they may have great strengths in many areas but still be at age level or below in others. Cognitively gifted children may be very good at articulating social norms and playground rules and the reasons behind them. At the same time, their ability to match actions to words—their social competence—may be at age level. A gifted child may also stand out from peers as different and may struggle to make friends.

What is giftedness? According to the National Association for Gifted Children (NAGC), there is no universally accepted definition; giftedness, intelligence, and talent may look different in different contexts and cultures. Traditionally, giftedness was determined by a high IQ score, but today broader conceptions are used to identify a child as gifted and talented. A child may be gifted in music, drama, or sports, for instance.

One way to identify young gifted children is to focus on a range of behaviors that occur in daily conversation and activities. Some common abilities of gifted 4-, 5-, and 6-year-olds include:

- Curiosity about many things and thoughtful questions
- Solving problems in unique ways and using prior knowledge in new contexts
- Sustained attention span, willingness to persist on challenging tasks, and good memory
- Especially original imagination, wit, and humor
- Keen observation skills and rapid mastery of new learning
- Desire to work independently and take initiative
- Talent in making up stories and an interest in reading

However determined, for their talents to flourish, gifted children need engaging educational experiences and differentiated instruction. When interesting, engaging teaching and learning experiences are provided for all children, the needs of gifted children are more likely to be met in a regular classroom.

Source: Based on information from the National Association for Gifted Children website, www.nagc.org.

Gifted and talented children are on one end of the spectrum; on the other end is a small percentage of children whose skills are considered to be below the typical range. These children may have a developmental delay or disability. In the following sections, we discuss ways of meeting the individual needs of all children, including children whose abilities are outside the expected range.

Responsive Education for Diverse Learners

As we have seen, every early childhood classroom is composed of diverse learners—children of widely varying abilities and interests. In recent years, greater emphasis has been placed on preventing learning problems and intervening earlier for all children, rather than waiting until a child has been identified for special education or labeled as having a learning disability. Comprehensive strategies for identifying and differentiating instruction to meet the individual needs of diverse learners include the Response to Intervention model for primary grade children and the Recognition and Response model for preschoolers.

Response to Intervention

Response to Intervention (**RTI**) is three-tiered comprehensive framework intended to prevent school failure, especially in the areas of reading and mathematics (see Figure 5.3a) (Gersten et al., 2008). Designed to bridge general and special education, this model looks at all students with the goal of preventing learning delays from becoming learning disabilities (Coleman, Roth, & West, 2009). Children with already identified disabilities are expected to be found at all three tiers of the model. For children who show signs of struggling, this model provides additional supports such as more focused time, content, scaffolding, and/or one-on-one attention.

The three tiers of the RTI model include:

1. Research-based curriculum and instruction for all children (typically meets the needs of 80% of the children)
2. Universal screening for learning difficulties, focused instruction, and ongoing progress monitoring for those who are not making expected learning progres (approximately 15% of children)
3. Intensive instructional intervention for those children who need it (approximately 5% of children).

Recently, the principles of RTI have been applied to working with preschool children, as discussed next.

Recognition and Response

Developed by researchers at the Frank Porter Graham (FPG) Child Development Institute (2007b), **Recognition and Response (R&R)**, also called *RTI Pre-K*, is a model for providing high-quality early education and targeted interventions matched to the learning needs of 3- to 5-year-old children. R&R supports children who may not have had sufficient prior opportunity to learn and gives them access to valuable learning experiences as soon as possible. The components of the model (Buysse, Peisner-Feinberg, & Berger, 2008) include:

- *Recognition*, which involves monitoring the learning progress of all children
- *Response*, which provides a core curriculum and intentional teaching for *all* children and targeted interventions for *some* children who need additional supports
- *Collaborative problem solving*, in which teachers, parents, specialists, and others make informed decisions based on assessment results to plan and evaluate instruction and interventions at all tiers.

Figures 5.3a and 5.3b depict the three-tiered RTI and R&R models, respectively. Each tier of the R&R model is described next (Coleman, Buysse, & Neitzel, 2006; Coleman et al., 2009).

Response to Intervention (RTI) A three-tiered framework intended to prevent learning delays in primary grades from becoming learning disabilities.

Recognition and Response (R&R) A three-tiered model, also called *RTI Pre-K*, for providing high-quality early childhood education and targeted interventions matched to the learning needs of 3- to 5-year-old children.

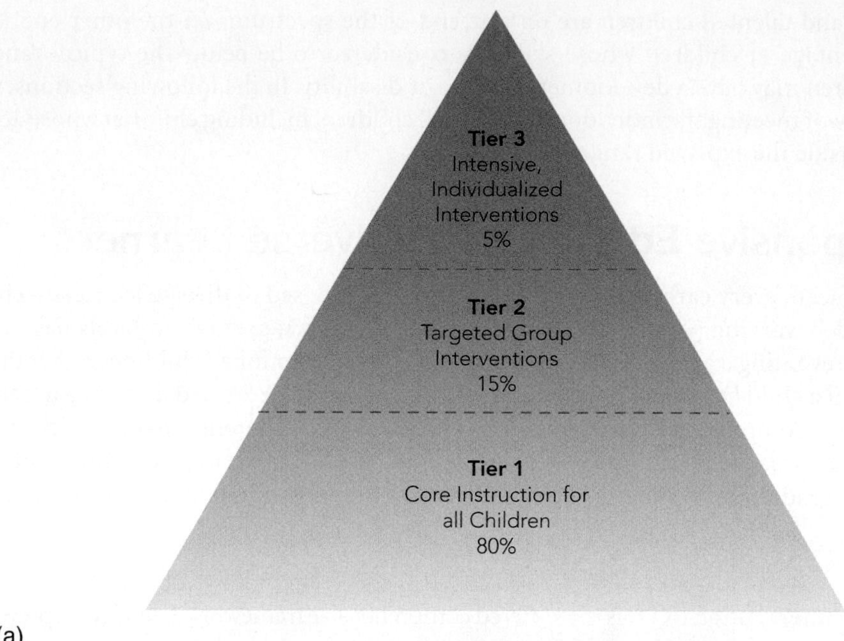

(a)

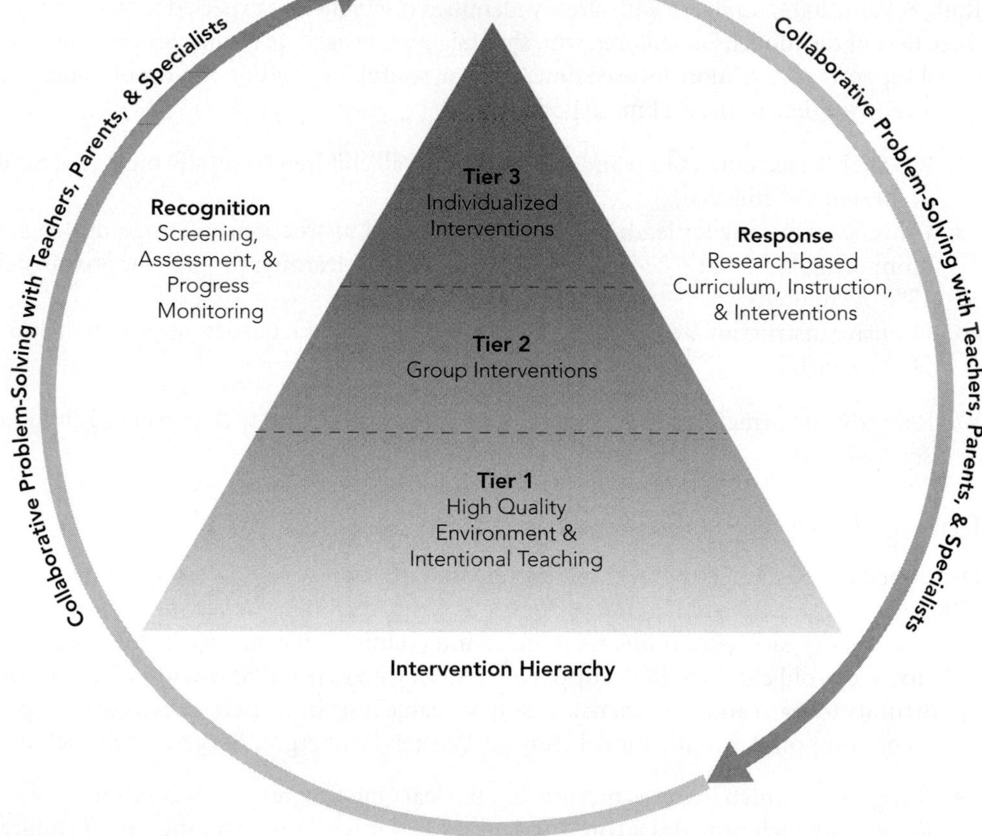

(b)

Figure 5.3 (a) Three-Tiered RTI Model and (b) R&R Model

Source: Part (a): Adapted with permission from the National Association of State Directors of Special Education, 2005. Part (b): "Recognition & Response System for Early Intervening," in *Recognition & Response Implementation Guide,* 2008, Chapel Hill: The University of North Carolina, FPG Child Development Institute.

Tier 1 of the R&R model provides a foundation of high-quality early childhood education for all children, including a comprehensive, evidence-based curriculum and intentional teaching. Tier 1 also involves universal screening, assessment, and monitoring of children's learning progress to obtain information about each child and to determine whether a child would benefit from additional support.

Tier 2 provides developmentally appropriate, large- and small-group interventions for children who need more focused learning experiences. These require relatively minor adjustments to classroom practices (FPG Child Development Institute, 2007b). For example, some children may need regularly scheduled, focused small-group reading to improve vocabulary and other literacy skills. To complement the more explicit activities and build on children's strengths and interests, teachers also embed learning opportunities in daily activities and routines. With these children, teachers monitor their learning progress more frequently and use the information to guide instruction. Parents and family members are included as part of the collaborative problem-solving team.

Tier 3 focuses on the approximately 5% of children who do not make expected progress via the Tier 1 and Tier 2 interventions. At Tier 3, children receive intensive, individualized interventions. These include effective strategies to scaffold children's learning such as prompting and modeling (described later in this chapter), and continued use of everyday activities and routines. Progress monitoring and collaborative problem solving continue to guide decisions about the child.

RTI and Recognition & Response are models that apply to all children. Children who receive Tier 2 and 3 interventions may or may not have previously identified disabilities or special needs. These children may be from low-income families and may be behind their peers at entry to school. Some children who are dual-language learners may also benefit from more individualized instruction.

The value of such prevention/intervention models is becoming more widely recognized. A growing body of research demonstrates the effectiveness of RTI in preventing and addressing learning disabilities (Coleman et al., 2006). As of 2004, the Individuals with Disabilities Education Act (IDEA) permits schools to use special education funds for RTI, which may reduce the number of children who are identified for special education. Nevertheless, there will always be a small percentage of children with identified disabilities and special needs, a topic we discuss next.

Individual Variation Beyond the Typical Range

All teachers must be prepared to work with children who have special learning and developmental needs for several reasons. First, federal laws require that children with special needs be included in classrooms and programs where their typically developing peers are found, and that their learning progress be reported for accountability purposes. Second, effective practices exist that can positively alter the course of children's development and their success in life. Third, many of the strategies proven effective for children with special needs can be equally effective in addressing the individual variation among typically developing children. In short, generalist early childhood educators who are familiar with the expertise of early childhood special education can be more effective teachers of all children.

> **Effective Teaching**
> Early childhood educators who are familiar with the expertise of early childhood special education can be more effective teachers of all children.

To best understand how to work with children with special needs, it is important to understand the language of special education, which we discuss in the first section that follows. In the next section, we introduce several principles that every teacher should know about children with disabilities. Then we describe the laws regulating special education and the benefits of serving children with disabilities in settings with their typically developing peers.

The Language of Early Childhood Special Education

One of the challenges for generalist early childhood educators is learning special education terminology. Because each field tends to have its own vocabulary, communicating effectively across these related fields requires a common vocabulary.

Defining Terms

Children with special needs is a broad term used to describe children who may have multiple risk factors, specialized health care needs such as asthma, mental or emotional health concerns, severe allergies, or physical and/or cognitive disabilities. The more specific term **children with disabilities** refers to children who have been identified as having a specific category of disability, such as autism or cerebral palsy. However, the terms *children with special needs* and *children with disabilities* are often used interchangeably.

Another all-encompassing, though less frequently used, term is **exceptional children**. This term is used to communicate inclusion of gifted and talented children as well as children whose development is below the expected range. In fact, the professional association for special educators is called the **Council for Exceptional Children** (CEC). Early childhood special educators are members of the **Division for Early Childhood** (DEC) of the Council for Exceptional Children. Table 5.2 lists and defines the most common categories of exceptionality.

children with special needs A broad term used to describe children who may have multiple risk factors, specialized health care needs, mental or emotional health concerns, severe allergies, or physical and/or cognitive disabilities.

children with disabilities Children who have been identified as having a specific category of disability, such as autism or cerebral palsy.

exceptional children An all-encompassing term used to communicate inclusion of gifted and talented children as well as children whose development is below the expected range.

Council for Exceptional Children (CEC) The national professional association for special educators.

Division for Early Childhood (DEC) Subdivision of the Council for Exceptional Children that is the national professional organization for early childhood special educators and early intervention specialists.

person-first language Language that recognizes that a child is a child first, whether or not he or she has a disability (e.g., saying "child with special needs" as opposed to "special needs child").

The Use of Person-First Language

A distinguishing characteristic of special educators and advocates for children with disabilities is that they embrace what is called **person-first language**. Person-first language recognizes that a child is a child first, whether or not he or she has a disability. Consider the difference between describing 4-year-old Zain as "a special needs child" or as "a child with special needs." The former phrase emphasizes the disability, whereas the latter communicates that Zain is first and foremost, a child whose special needs are only part of his identity.

By contrast, placing the adjective first modifies the entire noun to which it is referring; this can place undue emphasis on inability. For example, if you hear a traffic reporter describe a "disabled car," you think of a car that cannot be driven at all. Compare this to what you may think when you hear "a car with a flat tire." For similar reasons, we refer to a "child with Down syndrome" or "a child with autism," instead of saying a "Down's child" or "an autistic." A fundamental tenet of inclusion is that children are children regardless of disability status, and the use of person-first language reflects this principle.

Admittedly, using person-first language can sometimes feel cumbersome. But language matters. How we describe people and conditions communicates our attitudes about them. Currently, person-first terms begin with the word *individuals*, thus emphasizing the uniqueness of each person regardless of an identified disability.

What Teachers Should Know about Children with Disabilities

Children with disabilities display a variation in skills beyond what is considered typical; as a result, in many instances, these children qualify for special education services. These services are provided by professionals and therapists who have specialized knowledge about childhood disabilities and disorders. Therefore, it is neither necessary nor reasonable for early childhood educators to know everything about every disorder that might affect a child. Yet, they do need to understand several key principles about children's disabilities (Wolery & Wilbers, 1994):

1. *Children with disabilities are diverse and distinct from one another.* Perhaps the most important determinant of a positive early education experience is teachers' recognition of each child in the program as a distinctive individual. In this regard, all children are considered to have unique skills, interests, dislikes, and talents. Although children with disabilities share similarities with other children, they also have more specialized needs that

Table 5.2 Types of Exceptionality

Category	Definition
Attention deficit/hyperactivity disorder (ADHD)	Diagnosis describing children who display hyperactive behaviors, have difficulty attending to the task at hand, and tend to be impulsive.
Autism spectrum disorders (ASD)	Collective term given to developmental disabilities that impair the way in which individuals interact and communicate with others. ASD includes autism, Asperger's syndrome, and pervasive developmental disorder not otherwise specified (PDD-NOS).
Down syndrome (DS)	Condition in which extra genetic material causes delays in the way a child develops and often leads to mental retardation. Children with DS tend to share certain physical features such as a flat facial profile, an upward slant to the eyes, small ears, a single crease across the center of the palms, and an enlarged tongue.
Cerebral palsy (CP)	Refers to any one of a number of neurological disorders that appear in infancy or early childhood and permanently affect body movement and muscle coordination. The symptoms of this disorder do not worsen over time.
Deafness and hearing impairment	Hearing impairment is defined by IDEA as "an impairment in hearing, whether permanent or fluctuating, that adversely affects a child's educational performance." Deafness is defined as "a hearing impairment that is so severe that the child is impaired in processing linguistic information through hearing, with or without amplification."
Visually impaired or blind	Loss or partial loss of vision.
Mental retardation	Disability characterized by significant limitations both in intellectual functioning and in adaptive behavior as expressed in conceptual, social, and practical adaptive skills.
Developmental delay	Diagnosis describing a child who is behind expectations for his or her age group as measured by appropriate diagnostic instruments and procedures. Occurs in one or more of the following areas: physical development, cognitive development, communication development, social or emotional development, or adaptive development. Children with developmental delays may need special education and related services.
Gifted	Term applied to children with outstanding talent who perform or show potential for performing at remarkably high levels of accomplishment when compared with others of their age, experience, or environment.

children without special needs do not have. As a result, they may require more specialized, individualized instruction. However, it is vitally important for teachers to remember that there is no child for whom disability is the sole defining feature; children are diverse in countless ways including culturally, linguistically, and socioeconomically.

Even with the same diagnosis, such as mental retardation or autism, a great deal of variability exists in the severity of the effects—from mild to moderate to severe. In addition, because each child grows up amid different environmental factors, such as the family's resources or the quality of the child's school, the interaction between the disability and the child's environment plays a key role in the child's development.

2. *Various disorders do not necessarily occur in isolation.* Some children may have more than one disability. For example, a child with a hearing impairment may also have low vision or a seizure disorder. Moreover, some children's primary disability can lead to additional disabilities. For example, a child with a visual impairment may not be able to explore his environment and may develop motor or cognitive delays as well. Early identification and effective intervention can prevent secondary disabilities.

Inclusion means that every teacher must be prepared to work with children with disabilities and special needs in the regular classroom. The first step is for teachers to remember that children with disabilities are children first and, like every child, they are unique.

3. *A diagnosis rarely results in precise educational interventions.* The nature of interventions and therapeutic treatments such as speech and language therapy need to correspond directly to the child's current skills and abilities, the concerns identified by the family, needs and resources, and the influence of specific instructional strategies. Teachers should not assume that a particular diagnosis will automatically respond to a specific intervention (Wolery & Wilbers, 1994).

Although these three principles will help teachers work effectively with children with special needs, all teachers must be familiar with special education laws. These laws are discussed in the next section.

What Teachers Should Know about Legal Requirements for Children with Disabilities

Federal laws govern how special education services are delivered in the United States. First, we describe the legislation generally. Then we discuss in more detail the requirements for individualized planning for children with special needs.

The Individuals with Disabilities Education Act

Many children with disabilities are eligible for early intervention and early childhood special education services. Both early intervention (EI) and early childhood special education (ECSE) are regulated under the Individuals with Disabilities Education Act (IDEA), formerly the Education of the Handicapped Act. Part B of IDEA is a federal program that provides funds to states and local school districts to support education for children with disabilities ages 3 to 21. Part C provides funds for states to support early intervention services for children from birth to age 3. IDEA was designed to provide protections for children to ensure their right to a **free appropriate public education (FAPE)**. The principle of the law is that children with disabilities should not be denied the same opportunities offered to everyone else.

free appropriate public education (FAPE) Education for children with disabilities that is required by IDEA, so that children with disabilities are not denied the same opportunities offered to everyone else.

To receive specially designed instruction, at no cost to parents, to meet the unique needs of a child with a disability, children must meet **eligibility guidelines** according to IDEA. These guidelines are determined on a state-by-state basis. In addition, some states provide early intervention services for infants and toddlers who are at risk of developmental delay and their families. Early intervention is designed to prevent a possible problem rather than to treat an existing one.

eligibility guidelines Guidelines established on a state-by-state basis according to IDEA that determine whether children may receive special education services.

The Individuals with Disabilities Education Improvement Act (IDEIA) was signed into law in December 2007. The most relevant part of the law for early childhood teachers is Section 619 of Part B of IDEA (also known as Early Childhood Special Education), which applies specifically to preschoolers with disabilities. To meet all children's individual needs, the law requires that a team of educators and family members create an individualized education plan for each student.

Individualized Education Programs

When a child meets the disability requirements of the law and is identified as needing special education and related services, school districts are obligated to prepare and implement an **individualized education program (IEP)**, which is designed to meet the unique needs of the child. The IEP is a written plan for services that is developed, reviewed, and revised by an IEP team. Figure 5.4 is a sample IEP. The IEP must contain the following information:

individualized education program (IEP) A written plan designed to meet the unique needs of a child with a disability or special need; it is developed, reviewed, and revised by an IEP team during meetings for each child who is eligible for special education services.

1. A statement of the child's present levels of academic achievement and functional performance.

Student Name: Calvin Chinn **Student ID** 981957925

Measurable Annual Goals and Objectives/Benchmarks

The purpose of the measurable annual goals and objectives/benchmarks is to outline the student's instructional program derived from the present levels of performance and most recent evaluation.

Measurable Annual Goal

Behavior	Baseline to Goal Level	Evaluation Tool for Measuring Progress
Calvin will [X] increase [ ] decrease Cognitive/preacademic skills by expanding his play skills Before or by the anniversary of this IEP	Baseline performance: Activates toys and uses functional actions when supported by an adult Goal level performance: Independent use of functional play skills with a variety of objects	[ ] standardized tests [ ] criterion-referenced tests [X] systematic observation [ ] portfolios [ ] checklists/rating scales [ ] curriculum-based measurement [ ] precision teaching [ ] inventories/surveys [ ] teacher-developed tests

What the child is doing now
What the child will be able to do after intervention

Objective/Benchmark

Behavior	Criterion	Evaluation Tool for Measuring Progress	Timeline
Calvin will independently activate at least 6 different toys during play	3 activations of each toy within one week	[ ] standardized tests [ ] criterion-referenced tests [X] systematic observation [ ] portfolios [ ] checklists/rating scales [ ] curriculum-based measurement [ ] precision teaching [ ] inventories/surveys [ ] teacher-developed tests [ ] rubrics	Initiated: 9/26/2010 Projected date for completion: 12/2010
Behavior	**Criterion**	**Evaluation Tool for Measuring Progress**	**Timeline**
When given a model Calvin will use funtional actions with objects (i.e., use toys for their intended purpose) across four categories: (1) dramatic play props, (2) blocks & building materials, (3) art materials, (4) literacy materials.	4/5 trials for each category within one week	[ ] standardized tests [ ] criterion-referenced tests [X] systematic observation [ ] portfolios [ ] checklists/rating scales [ ] curriculum-based measurement [ ] precision teaching [ ] inventories/surveys [ ] teacher-developed tests [ ] rubrics	Initiated: 12/2010 Projected date for completion: 4/2011
Behavior	**Criterion**	**Evaluation Tool for Measuring Progress**	**Timeline**
Calvin will independently use functional actions with objects (i.e., use toys for their intended purpose) during play acros[s] different areas of the class[room]	3 examples of functional actions per day for two weeks	[ ] standardized tests [ ] criterion-referenced tests [X] systematic observation [ ] portfolios [ ] checklists/rating sc[ales] [ ] curriculum-bas[ed me]asurement	Initiated: 4/2010 Projected date for [c]ompletion: 9/26/2011

What does the behavior look like and under what conditions should it be performed?
How will we know when the objective has been achieved? How will you test?
What tools/method will be used to test the objective? (Should relate directly to the criteria.)
When do you anticipate starting and completing the objective? At least one objective should end on the day the IEP is due.

Figure 5.4 Sample IEP

Source: From Experimental Education Unit, University of Washington.

MyEducationLab

Go to the Assignments and Activities section of Topic 11: Special Needs/ Inclusion in the MyEducationLab for your course and complete the activity entitled *Understanding Inclusion*. What are the legal requirements for serving children with disabilities and special needs? What goals for children are these laws designed to achieve?

2. A statement of measurable annual goals, including academic and functional goals designed to:
   - Meet the child's needs that result from the child's disability to enable the child to be involved in and make progress in the general education curriculum; and
   - Meet each of the child's other educational needs that result from the child's disability.
3. A description of benchmarks or short-term objectives.
4. A description of:
   - How the child's progress toward meeting the annual goals will be measured; and
   - When periodic reports on the progress the child is making toward meeting the annual goals (such as through the use of quarterly or other periodic reports, concurrent with the issuance of report cards) will be provided.
5. A statement of the special education and related services and supplementary aids and services, based on peer-reviewed research to the extent practicable, to be provided to the child, or on behalf of the child.
6. A statement of any individually appropriate accommodations that are necessary to measure the academic achievement and functional performance of the child on state- and district-wide assessments.

The IEP Team

The IEP is developed by a team that consists of educators, experts, and family. By law, the team members must include:

- The child's parent(s) or guardian(s)
- The child's early childhood teacher
- The child's early childhood special education teacher
- A representative of the community program who has certain specific knowledge and qualifications
- An individual who can interpret the instructional implications of evaluation results (this may be one of the other listed members, such as an occupational therapist or speech language pathologist)
- Other individuals, who are chosen at the discretion of the parent or the agency, who have knowledge or special expertise regarding the child, including related services personnel, such as the speech language pathologist or physical therapist, as appropriate.

Early Intervention for Infants and Toddlers

Children from birth to 3 years old who have a developmental delay, a diagnosed condition, or, in some states, who are identified as at risk for developing a developmental delay may qualify for early intervention (EI) services. These children will have an **individualized family service plan (IFSP)**. An IFSP documents and guides the early intervention process for children with disabilities and their families. The IFSP contains information about the services necessary to facilitate a child's development and enhance the family's capacity to facilitate the child's development. Some parents learn that their child has a disability at or even before birth. For these families, hospitals may initiate EI as early as infancy. For other children, developmental delays or disabilities emerge as the child grows. In these cases, a parent, pediatrician, teacher, child care provider, or family friend initially may raise concerns about the child's development.

individualized family service plan (IFSP) Documents and guides the early intervention process for children with disabilities from birth to age 3 and their families; contains information about the services necessary to facilitate a child's development and enhance the family's capacity to facilitate the child's development.

Children with developmental delays enter EI services following some kind of diagnostic testing or developmental evaluation administered in partnership with the family by a team of specialists. Through the IFSP process, family members and service providers work as a team to plan, implement, and evaluate services tailored to the family's unique concerns, priorities, and resources.

According to IDEA, the IFSP, like the IEP, is a written plan that must contain specific information, including:

1. The child's present levels of physical, cognitive, communication, social or emotional, and adaptive development

2. The family's resources, priorities, and concerns relating to enhancing the development of the child with a disability
3. The major outcomes to be achieved for the child and the family; the criteria, procedures, and timelines used to determine progress; and whether modifications or revisions of the outcomes or services are necessary
4. Specific early intervention services necessary to meet the unique needs of the child and the family, including the frequency, intensity, and the method of delivery
5. The environments in which services will be provided, including justification of the extent, if any, to which the services will not be provided in a *natural environment.* The *natural environment* refers to settings that are natural or normal for the child's same age peers without disabilities
6. The projected dates for initiation of services and their anticipated duration
7. The name of the service provider who will be responsible for implementing the plan and coordinating with other agencies and persons
8. Steps to support the child's transition to preschool or other appropriate services.

Differences between IFSPs and IEPs

Unlike the IEP, the IFSP (Bruder, 2001):

- Revolves around the family, because the family is the constant in a child's life.
- Includes outcomes for the family, as opposed to focusing only on the child.
- Includes activities involving multiple agencies to integrate all services into one plan.
- Names a service coordinator to help the family during the development, implementation, and evaluation of the IFSP.
- Involves the notion of natural environments, which create opportunities for learning interventions in everyday routines and activities, rather than only in formal, contrived environments.

The laws that dictate services for children with disabilities and special needs came about for many reasons. These laws reflect research demonstrating the benefits of such services for children with special needs and the larger society. But the laws also reflect underlying values about what life should be like for all children.

Embracing Natural Learning Environments and Inclusion

One of the primary goals of federal laws governing services for children with disabilities is to make sure that these children lead lives that are as similar as possible to those of their typically developing peers. To fully achieve the goals of the law, however, professionals need to understand the rationale and embrace the values that led to the law being passed in the first place.

Benefits of Natural Learning Environments

The law requires that services be delivered in everyday routines, activities, and places where infants, toddlers, and their families would be spending time if the child did not have a disability. These are known as **natural learning environments**. These can be child care centers, parks, a neighbor's house, or the zoo. Natural learning environments are important because for young children, learning occurs most effectively in the contexts where children will need to use the new skill (Dunst, 2001; Dunst, Hamby, Trivette, Raab, & Bruder, 2000).

So what is *not* a natural environment? Places children go because they have a disability, such as hospitals, clinics, and therapy offices, are not optimal places for children to learn new skills. Young children, especially those under age 3, do not easily learn a skill in one setting and transfer it to another.

natural learning environments Settings that are natural or normal for the child's same-age peers without disabilities such as child care centers, parks, a neighbor's house, or the zoo, as opposed to hospitals, clinics, and therapy offices.

Benefits of Inclusion

Inclusion is based on the same principle as natural learning environments—that children with disabilities need to be where their typically developing peers are found. Although most images of inclusion involve school settings like preschool or public schools, inclusion is also important in home and community environments such as parks, recreation, and faith settings. Successful inclusion means that *all* children in the classroom participate, learn, and thrive (DEC & National Association for the Education of Young Children [NAEYC], 2009).

It is important for teachers to understand that inclusion benefits others in addition to the children being served. Table 5.3 lists the benefits of inclusion for five groups of people: children with disabilities, children without disabilities, communities, families of children with disabilities, and families of children without disabilities. In the sections that follow, we describe what teachers need to do for children with special needs if inclusion is to be effective.

Table 5.3 Benefits of Inclusion

Recipient of Benefit	Description of Benefit
Children with disabilities	1. They are spared the effects of separate, segregated education, including the negative effects of labeling and negative attitudes fostered by lack of contact with them. 2. They are provided with competent models that allow them to learn new adaptive skills and/or learn when and how to use their existing skills through imitation. 3. They are provided with competent peers with whom to interact and thereby learn new social and/or communicative skills. 4. They are provided with realistic life experiences that prepare them to live in the community. 5. They are provided with opportunities to develop friendships with typically developing peers. 6. They do as well or better than children in specialized programs, particularly with respect to social development (National Professional Development Center on Inclusion [NPDCI], 2007).
Children without disabilities	1. They are provided with opportunities to learn more realistic and accurate views about individuals with disabilities. 2. They are provided with opportunities to develop positive attitudes toward others who are different from themselves. 3. They are provided with opportunities to learn altruistic behaviors and when and how to use such behaviors. 4. They are provided with models of individuals who successfully achieve despite challenges. 5. They do as well or better than children in specialized programs, particularly with respect to social development (NPDCI, 2007).
Communities	1. They can conserve their early childhood resources by limiting the need for segregated, specialized programs. 2. They can conserve educational resources if children with disabilities who are included in the preschool level continue in regular rather than special education placements during the elementary school years.
Families of children with disabilities	1. They are able to learn about typical development. 2. They may feel less isolated from the remainder of their communities. 3. They may develop relationships with families of typically developing children who can provide them with meaningful support.
Families of children without disabilities	1. They may develop relationships with families who have children with disabilities and thereby make a contribution to them and their communities. 2. They will have opportunities to teach their children about individual differences and about accepting individuals who are different.

Source: Reprinted with permission from *Including Children with Special Needs in Early Childhood Programs*, by M. Wolery and J. Wilbers, 1994, Washington, DC: NAEYC. Reprinted with permission from the National Association for the Education of Young Children.

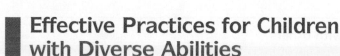

Effective Practices for Children with Diverse Abilities

The spirit of inclusion is to ensure that the individual needs of all children are being met in inclusive settings. Children with disabilities need environments that are "organized and adjusted to minimize the effects of their disabilities and to promote learning of a broad range of skills" (Wolery, Strain, & Bailey, 1992, p. 95). Furthermore, like children without disabilities who are identified for Tier 3 interventions in RTI and R&R systems, children with disabilities may need more intensive, individualized instruction.

Such **specialized instruction** involves teachers matching an individual child's goals and objectives with appropriate teaching methods and materials. In addition, teachers need to decide what amount of assistance each child with special needs requires, provide the assistance, and then determine whether the instruction was effective. Most often, a team of specialists is available to help the early childhood teacher achieve these goals.

MyEducationLab

Go to the Assignments and Activities section of Topic 11: Special Needs/ Inclusion in the MyEducationLab for your course and complete the activity entitled *The Importance of Identification and Early Intervention for Children with Disabilities*. As you watch the video and answer the accompanying questions, reflect on the mother's experience with her premature baby and how early identification and intervention helps both children and their families.

Working on a Team

Working collaboratively with a team is critical to the success of including young children with special needs in the classroom. Each member of the team has different expertise in areas such as early childhood, special education, motor development, and communication development; additionally, all members possess specific knowledge about the particular child. The family's role is to provide information about their child's strengths and needs. They help assess functional skills and develop the IFSP or IEP with the team. They implement intervention strategies at home and in the community and provide critical information about the effectiveness of interventions.

Generally, team meetings focus on helping children with special needs and their families reach their full potential. More specifically, the team meeting is used to (1) identify and prioritize individualized goals, (2) determine if modifications to the environment or curriculum are needed, (3) design specialized instructional strategies, and (4) monitor the child's progress toward the goals.

Assessing Young Children of Diverse Abilities

The effectiveness of individualized instruction for children with disabilities depends in large part on accurately assessing their needs and progress. Throughout this book we address the topic of assessment as related to all children. In this section, we discuss types of assessment that are used in order to best accommodate children with special needs. Assessment types include screening and diagnostic and eligibility assessments, which are used to determine if the child has a developmental delay or disability and is eligible for services. The assessments that are the most relevant to early childhood teachers are the types that are useful for planning what children with special needs should be learning. Approaches that are appropriate for this purpose are curriculum-based assessment and routines-based assessment.

specialized instruction Involves teachers matching an individual child's goals and objectives with appropriate teaching methods and materials, deciding what amount of assistance each child with special needs requires, providing the assistance, and then determining whether the instruction was effective.

Curriculum-Based Assessments

Curriculum-based assessments trace a child's progress along a continuum of functional skills within a developmentally sequenced curriculum organized by developmental domain. **Functional skills** are those that are useful to children in their everyday lives. For example, it is generally useful for children to learn to open doors, turn faucets on and off, use the toilet, and feed themselves. A **developmental domain** is an area of development such as fine and gross motor skills, cognitive abilities, self-help capabilities, and social and communication skills. Curriculum-based assessments serve to link assessment, intervention, and evaluation. Figure 5.5 shows a sample of test items from a frequently used curriculum-based assessment called the *Assessment, Evaluation and Programming System* (AEPS) (Bricker, 2002).

functional skills Skills that are useful to children in their everyday lives.

developmental domain An area of development such as fine and gross motor skills, cognitive abilities, self-help capabilities, and social and communication skills.

A. Interaction with others

1. Interacts with others as play partners
   - 1.1 Responds to others in distress or need
   - 1.2 Establishes and maintains proximity to others
   - 1.3 Takes turns with others
   - 1.4 Initiates greetings to others who are familiar
   - 1.5 Responds to affective initiations from others
2. Initiates cooperative activity
   - 2.1 Joins others in cooperative activity
   - 2.2 Maintains cooperative participation with others
   - 2.3 Shares or exchanges objects
3. Resolves conflicts by selecting effective strategy
   - 3.1 Negotiates to resolve conflicts
   - 3.2 Uses simple strategies to resolve conflict
   - 3.3 Claims and defends possessions

Figure 5.5 Sample Test Items from the AEPS Social Domain

Source: List of AEPS Test Items A: Interactions with Others (p. 191) from *Assessment, Evaluation, and Programming System for Infants and Children (AEPS®)*, edited by D. Bricker, 2002, Baltimore: Paul H. Brookes Publishing Co., Inc.

Following is an example of how curriculum-based assessment using the AEPS is implemented:

> Corwin (age 3½) has experienced an eligibility evaluation for special education based on a recommendation from his pediatrician. According to the multidisciplinary team, he qualifies for early childhood special education because he has a moderate communication and social skills delay. Consequently, Corwin's parents are referred to the local preschool special education program near their house. After his parents observe the inclusive program, they enroll Corwin. During his first week at school, Corwin's teachers use a curriculum-based measure, the AEPS test for 3- to 6-year-olds, to identify his needs and develop functional goals and objectives for his IEP. As illustrated in Figure 5.5, test items on the AEPS are lists of functional skills in developmental sequence. The assessment is conducted within the context of the preschool routines and activities.
>
> When Taiya Stoner, Corwin's teacher, observes him independently perform items that are on the test, these tasks are noted as "mastered" and listed as his current levels of performance on his IEP. For example, Corwin mastered item 3.3, "claims and defends possessions," because he was observed holding onto the toy train when a peer asked for it. He then screamed for the teacher's help when a peer grabbed at the train, which meant he has also mastered item 3.2, "uses simple strategies to resolve conflict." Behaviors he had difficulty displaying or did not display over the course of a few observations were considered targets for intervention, such as "uses verbal or nonverbal strategies to initiate cooperative activities and encourages peers to participate (Corwin moves to sit next to a peer)" and "selects appropriate strategies to negotiate conflict with peers." Taiya suggested these to his parents as goals for his IEP. After his teachers and therapists provide instruction to Corwin on the identified goals, they administer the AEPS again to determine if their guidance was effective and to establish new goals for Corwin.

In this example, all of the steps of the linked system are in place. First, the teachers use the assessment (in this case the AEPS) to determine what the child needs to be taught. Then they teach the skills identified based on the AEPS. Finally, the team reassesses, using the same tool to determine if Corwin is making progress.

Routines-Based Assessment

The second approach for determining goals for a child is called routines-based assessment, which is used to determine which functional skills a child should be taught. For example, Gwynneth's kindergarten teacher, Tamara Calhoun, is asked by the special education teacher to complete a routines-based assessment of Gwynneth's performance throughout the day in order to identify some functional learning goals for her. Tamara lists classroom activities in chronological order, such as arrival, circle time, centers, clean up, snack, and so on. She then observes Gwynneth's behavior during these routines and sets goals to work on with her, such as "Gwynneth will get off bus; walk to the classroom with group; put coat and backpack in cubby." Using routine-based assessment at home, her parents' list includes typical daily routines such as wake up, eat breakfast, and get dressed.

To ensure accurate information as well as follow-through, parents of children with special needs must participate in the assessment process. After the team gathers information to determine the child's functional goals, the next step is to plan for individualized instruction.

Planning Individualized Instructional Strategies

Every early childhood teacher needs a repertoire of teaching strategies to be effective with all children. Sometimes, however, in order to learn new skills, children with special needs require more explicit teaching than typically developing children. In these instances, teachers use strategies that are carefully planned and implemented more frequently throughout the day. Individualized instruction involves identifying specific goals, creating learning opportunities, providing teacher support, reinforcing children's learning, and monitoring their progress.

Identifying Goals for Children

Either of the assessment approaches described previously can be used to determine learning goals. The ECSE teacher on the team can help write objectives that are functional and generative. **Generative skills** are those that can be used across settings, people, events, and objects. For example, one of the skills identified for Damon is "uses two fingers to pick up objects." To be generative, Damon needs to learn to use the skill across settings such as during mealtime to pick up Cheerios, or in the bath to pick up the soap. He also needs to use the skill across objects such as crayons or beads, and under various conditions such as when the items are mushy or hard. If an identified skill is too limited, such as "uses a finger and thumb grasp to put beads into a bottle," it is difficult to create enough learning opportunities to be effective and the skill is less likely to be useful in different situations.

generative skills Skills that can be used across settings, people, events, and objects.

Creating Learning Opportunities

Effective teachers create learning opportunities in daily routines and activities that provide the child with multiple tools for learning a new skill (Rule, 1998). These opportunities may be more focused, but are not essentially different than those provided for every child. One strategy is to introduce unexpected events, as when the teacher says or does something that the child does not anticipate. These events may be funny or interesting things the adult says. For example, when teaching 6-year-old Miguel to use prepositions, his teacher walks over to where he is sitting and sits backwards next to him. Then she asks, "Miguel, where are you?" Miguel, giggling, says, "Right here." His teacher says "Right where? Are you *behind* me or *in front* of me?"

All children have different abilities and interests that teachers can use to help them meet learning goals. With minor adaptations, this teacher provides support for every child to learn early literacy skills.

MyEducationLab

Go to the Building Teaching Skills and Dispositions section of Topic 11: Special Needs/Inclusion in the MyEducationLab for your course and complete the activity entitled *Making Accommodations and Modifications to Promote Inclusive Practices*. As you watch the videos and answer the accompanying questions, what strategies do effective teachers use to help children with disabilities and special needs achieve individualized goals?

Using Helping Strategies

To help children learn skills, teachers use helping strategies called **prompts**. These are gestural, model, physical, pictorial, or verbal clues that elicit responses from children to assist them in using a specific skill (Sandall & Schwartz, 2008):

- *Gestural prompts:* Movements that teachers use to let children know what behavior is expected. For example, when the teacher wants Julia to ask for more raisins, she waits and looks expectantly at Julia until she says, "I want more raisins."
- *Model prompts:* Involves the teacher saying or doing the behavior he wants the child to do. The teacher says "please" and "thank you" when he passes food during lunchtime.
- *Physical prompts:* Gentle touching and guiding of children by the teacher to help the children accomplish a skill. When teaching Larisha to wash her hands, the teacher places her hands over Larisha's hands and helps her to turn on the faucet, get soap, rub her hands together, dry her hands, and turn off the faucet with the towel.
- *Pictorial prompts:* Visual cues that help children accomplish a skill. To help Owen play independently at center time, his teacher places pictures of each center on a piece of construction paper, and Owen refers to a picture when he moves to another activity area.
- *Verbal prompts:* Teacher language strategies that help children accomplish a skill. When it is time for Dushawn to come to the group for story time, his teacher gives him a verbal prompt: "Dushawn, please come sit on your carpet square next to me." This may be enough for Dushawn to learn that he is expected to join the group.

Reinforcing Children's Learning

An essential component of instruction for young children with special needs is that the child receives positive feedback following her performance of the new skill. If so, the child is more likely to try the new skill again.

In educational settings, positive reinforcement can be very simple and natural. **Naturally occurring reinforcers** are consequences that are likely to occur *whenever* the child performs the skill and are, therefore, highly effective. For example, when Raven puts on her coat independently, the teacher says, "Raven, you zipped up your coat all by yourself. Now you can go outside to play." Some examples of naturally occurring reinforcers include using the paint after making a request to do so; playing with friends after asking to join the group; and being acknowledged by a teacher for trying hard at a difficult task.

Monitoring Progress

The effectiveness of instruction depends on the team monitoring the child's progress to determine if the IEP needs modification, or if the child is ready to move on to learning a new skill. Information about children's progress can be collected in many ways. One data collection system used by many teachers is to observe and document the child's learning using a checklist of skills or a rating scale of the child's performance. A rating scale allows the teacher to indicate the level of a child's skill along a continuum. For example, the lowest level might be "child refuses to perform the skill" and the highest "child performs the skill independently," with several steps in between.

All early childhood teachers need to learn how to teach children with special needs in inclusive settings. In addition, when general early childhood educators learn some of the important skills of early childhood special education, they can apply these skills to teaching all children. Read the *Becoming an Intentional Teacher: Individualizing Group Time* feature for an example of applying this special education knowledge with typically developing children.

Providing individualized instruction may seem to be a daunting task for teachers, especially if the group of children is large. To make this task easier, one of the most effective strategies is to use peer-mediated learning. This strategy, described in the *What Works* feature, creates opportunities for peers who are typically developing or who have a particular

prompts Gestural, model, physical, pictorial, or verbal clues that elicit responses from children to assist them in using a specific skill.

naturally occurring reinforcers Consequences that are likely to occur *whenever* the child performs the skill and are, therefore, highly effective.

Becoming an Intentional Teacher

Individualizing Group Time

Here's What Happened Halfway through the kindergarten year, there was a child in my class, Tasha, who continued to have difficulty with large-group instruction times. She would touch the other children, sometimes even leaning her whole body against them and touching their hair or face. She was easily distracted and stood up to look out the windows several times during story time. She also would leave circle time before it finished and wander around.

So, here is what I did. I gave each child a carpet square to use during circle time placing Tasha farthest away from the window, but closest to me. I started circle time with an active movement song. When the children sat down, I gave Tasha a card to hold that had pictures of the expected behaviors when sitting in a large group (keep feet and hands to self; look and listen to the action; raise a quiet hand to ask a question). Tasha and I had made the card together. She drew the pictures and I wrote the words for each reminder. I also used Tasha's favorite puppet, Whiskers, to greet and excuse children at circle time.

Here's What I Was Thinking Tasha is a child who has difficulty attending in large groups and is easily distracted. Young children in general can have difficulty remembering expected behaviors and directions. I also realized that Tasha wasn't as motivated as other children to listen and participate at circle time. At first, I thought that perhaps I should let Tasha wander when she didn't want to be at circle time. But she is already 6 years old and, although she has some difficulties with attention, her parents and I believe that she can be successful at circle time. Starting with an active song helps get some energy out before sitting. The carpet squares help Tasha, and other children, remember where to keep their bodies during circle time. Placing Tasha's seat away from the windows minimizes distractions, and seating her close to me allows for some gentle reminders to pay attention.

I wasn't completely sure that I should single Tasha out by giving her a "reminder card," but then I figured Tasha was already being singled out by her peers as the one who always disrupted their story. I could explain to the children that everyone in the class has their individual needs met, for example, children with allergies, special diets, adaptive pencils, and so on. The reminder card is helping Tasha remember what we all are supposed to be doing at circle time. The card also keeps Tasha's hands busy, making it less likely that she will touch her peers. Beginning and ending circle time with Whiskers, the cat puppet, motivates Tasha to come to circle right away and stay through the end. These easy-to-implement modifications help Tasha to learn more and spend more time with her peers.

set of competencies that another child may be working on to take a peer-to-peer instructional role in promoting learning (Harris, Pretti-Frontczak, & Brown, 2009).

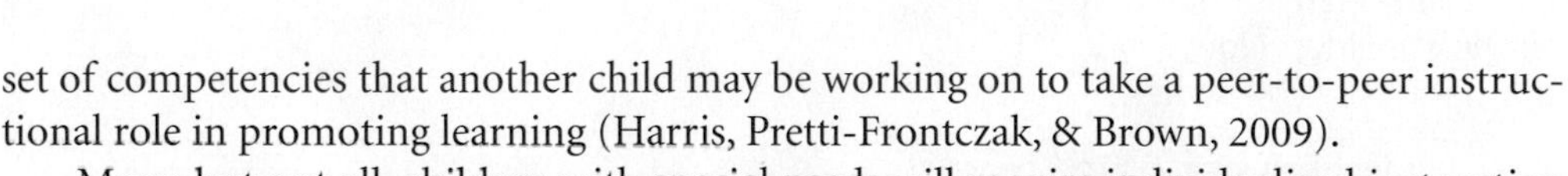

Many, but not all, children with special needs will require individualized instruction to achieve positive learning and developmental outcomes in inclusive programs. But equally important is cultivating a culture of inclusion. A culture of inclusion provides children with and without disabilities a sense of belonging and membership in the peer group (DEC & NAEYC, 2009), as we discuss next.

Fostering Friendships in the Inclusive Classroom

Successful inclusion requires the needs of children with disabilities to be met. Among those important needs is the need for positive social relationships with other children. Indeed,

What Works

Peer-Mediated Learning

Teachers cannot be everywhere at once, so in some inclusive preschools, the teacher can rely on peers to assist children with special needs in learning or practicing some skills. This strategy is called *peer-mediated learning* and has been found to be especially effective in developing social skills in children with disabilities. When the intentional teaching objective is to develop social interaction between children, peers are the most appropriate vehicle. The following example demonstrates how teachers use peer-mediated learning.

> Kathy Edwards, the preschool teacher in an inclusive classroom, pulls aside two socially skilled children, Samantha and Ike, before center time. She asks them if they would like to do some special work today. The two, knowing what this entails, nod with enthusiasm.
>
> "Okay," says Kathy. "Today we are going to practice getting someone's attention to ask if they want to play. What do you think you should do to get someone's attention?"
>
> *Samantha:* "We could say their name."
> *Kathy:* "Yes, we could say their name. But, what if they still don't look at us?"
> *Ike:* "We could tap them on the shoulder and look at their face."
> *Kathy:* "Okay, good. We can say their name and then tap them on the shoulder. Ike, can you show us how you can get my attention?"
>
> Ike moves closer to Kathy and says her name, "Kathy." Kathy pretends not to hear and then Ike taps her shoulder and says her name. Kathy looks and says, "That was great. You got closer, said my name, and tapped me on the shoulder. Now, if you want me to play with you, what would you do next?"
>
> *Samantha:* "You could say 'You want to play?' Or, you could give them a toy."
> *Kathy:* "Yes. You can get a friend's attention, ask if they want to play, and hand them a toy. Samantha, can you pretend to ask me to play?"
>
> Kathy practices a few more times with both Ike and Samantha and then has them practice together. Kathy then says, "Okay, now you can go play. And today, your "buddy" is going to be James. See if you can remember all that we practiced, and ask James to play with you at the train table. Remember that some of our friends don't answer us right away, so we have to keep trying."
>
> Ike and Samantha handily engage James, who has autism, in play at the train table. When Kathy catches their eye, she gives a thumbs-up. Ike and Samantha smile. At the end of the day, Kathy presents Samantha, Ike, and James with a special "Buddy Day" certificate.

To incorporate peers into an individualized program for a child with special needs, the following points are important to keep in mind:

- The peer needs to know how to perform the target skill (i.e., ask to play).
- Many different peers should be incorporated into the learning process. The teacher should choose several peers to be helpers for the child with special needs. Asking the same peer each time could result in buddy burnout.
- Peers need to know that the teacher values their work. Teachers can smile, give a hug or pat, or provide more formal recognition such as getting to do a special activity.
- Avoid calling the peer a "teacher"; this may hinder the development of reciprocal friendships for young children with special needs.

Source: From "Interventions for Young Children with Autism," by P. Strain, I. Schwartz, and E. Bovey, 2007, pp. 253–272, in *Social Competence of Young Children: Risk, Disability & Intervention*, edited by W. H. Brown, S. L. Odom, and S. R. McConnell, Baltimore: Paul H. Brookes Publishing.

early friendships are the most powerful single predictor of long-term adjustment for children with disabilities (Strain & Schwartz, 2001).

Children from ages 3 to 5, especially those with disabilities, may not naturally acquire the skills to function socially with their peers, which can be a barrier to developing friendships. They need teachers to help them. Young children's social relationships involve three main concepts, which occur along a continuum in inclusive settings: friendships, social acceptance, and social rejection (Strain & Schwartz, 2001). More passive than friendship, **social acceptance** occurs when a child is treated as a member of the group; other children play, smile, and sit beside the child throughout the day. By contrast, **social rejection** is when peers do not choose to play with a child or outwardly refuse the child's requests to join in their play.

Intentional teachers foster friendships between children with special needs and their typically developing peers. What are some ways teachers can build positive relationships among children in inclusive classrooms?

Not only are friendships a critical component and predictor of positive mental health, but children develop and learn important social and communication skills in the context of social relationships (Strain & Joseph, 2006; R. A. Thompson, 2002). Therefore, it is critically important that teachers use proven strategies to promote friendships among children with disabilities and their typically developing classmates. Table 5.4 lists types of social skills interventions that have proven effective for children with a variety of disabilities (Vaughn et al., 2003).

Having explored the topic of individual differences among both typically developing children and children with special needs, we now see that teachers can draw on a large body of effective practices to achieve their goals for all children. Successful inclusion of children with disabilities and special needs involves much more than the children's presence in the classroom. Teachers need to get to know all of the children and continually assess their learning and development. They must plan and implement individualized instructional strategies. Most important, teachers must create a classroom climate in which every child is valued and fully included.

Revisiting Ms. Creighton's Classroom

At the beginning of this chapter, we met some of the children in Lindsay Creighton's preschool class and wondered how she could possibly meet the needs of these diverse children. Now that we have explored the topic of adapting for individual differences, we can see how Lindsay successfully teaches all of the children.

Lindsay's study of child development helps her to understand that children's personalities and behaviors are the result of an interaction between their genetic makeup and their experiences in the environment. Therefore, she is aware of how important her work is in helping them achieve their full potential. Lindsay has high goals for each child's learning. But she realizes that because children are unique, she needs to use differentiated instruction to help them achieve the goals.

For Cal, whose grandmother does not speak English, Lindsay works with a translator as well as a team that includes a social worker. For Rohan and Ruby, who both seem painfully shy, Lindsay recognizes that these children are also very different. They each have different interests and abilities. Because Rohan likes quiet activities and playing with one other child, Lindsay encourages him in that direction and he gradually becomes more confident. Ruby is hesitant until she is assured that Lindsay will protect her from an allergic reaction. The other children soon become comfortable with that fact as they say, "Ruby's body was born not liking peanuts." They all embrace the need to protect Ruby's health.

Although at first Lindsay and the other children mix up the twins, Alex and Alice, they soon become aware that each is an individual. Lindsay focuses on working with each girl separately and engaging them in different activities so their uniqueness becomes evident to all. Carter's needs are more severe and specific. Working as a member of his IEP team

social acceptance Occurs when a child is treated as a member of the group; other children play, smile, and sit beside the child throughout the day.

social rejection Occurs when peers choose not to play with a child or outwardly refuse the child's requests to join in their play.

MyEducationLab

To assess your understanding of how to adapt your instruction to accommodate individual differences, go to the Book Specific Resources section in the MyEducationLab for your course, select *Effective Practices in Early Childhood Education,* Chapter 5 of the Study Plan, and then complete the multiple choice questions and activities.

Table 5.4 Strategies for Facilitating Social Relationships in Inclusive Settings

Strategy	Examples
Modeling—Peers and teachers demonstrate specific desired behaviors to children with disabilities.	Assign two children at a time to complete classroom jobs. Make transition times social by pairing children. Carefully select the members of small groups in order to provide peer models for children with disabilities. Read books and have class discussions about friendship, problem solving, and conflict resolution. Use puppets to model specific friendship skills during large-group time.
Play related—Teachers focus on specific play activities intended to help the development of cognition, language, and social functioning.	Plan dramatic play activities with specific roles (e.g., order-taker, customer, cook) and assign the roles. Set up a "Buddy" center during choice time; children play with select toys and games that require two children. Establish "buddy" days; teachers arrange buddies between children with disabilities and typically developing peers. Select and have available materials and equipment that facilitate social interaction (e.g., wagon, rowboat, teeter-totter, board games).
Prompting—Teachers prompt children to display target behaviors.	Provide insufficient materials for a small group art activity and encourage children to problem solve how to do something together or take turns. When children are disengaging from play with one another, prompt them to reverse dramatic play roles. ("How about you be the mom now and she is the baby?")
Rehearsal and practice—Children practice the target behaviors.	Prior to a center time, ask children who they are going to play with or what specific toy or material they are going to share. Provide opportunities to observe and interact with socially competent peers. Teach sociodramatic play sequences at circle time, and allow children to practice the interaction with a puppet, before going to centers.

Source: Based on "Social Skills Interventions for Young Children with Disabilities," by S. Vaughn et al., 2003, *Remedial and Special Education, 24*(1), pp. 2–15.

and supported by his parents, Lindsay becomes more confident in her ability to teach Carter and to help him achieve his individualized goals.

After several months of working with this class, Lindsay decides that adapting for individual variation is the most interesting part of her work. At first, she was concerned when confronted with such diversity. But now, she finds that children's individuality is what makes her days most interesting and unpredictable. As she expands her repertoire of skills for working with diverse children, she finds that seeing individual children's progress is richly rewarding.

Chapter Summary

- Children differ from one another in many ways, including rate and timing of cognitive and language development, social skills and temperament, and interests. The transactional theory of development explains that development is influenced by *both* biology *and* experience, and how they interact with each other.
- Effective early childhood teachers understand the importance of knowing each child as an individual. One of the most useful frameworks for thinking about the variation among children is Gardner's theory of multiple intelligences.
- *Differentiating instruction* means to create multiple paths so that children of different abilities, interests, or learning needs experience equally appropriate ways to achieve important learning goals.

- All teachers need to be prepared to work with children who have special learning and developmental needs because federal law requires it, effective practices exist to alter the course of children's learning, and many of these practices can be used with typically developing children.
- Specialized instruction involves teachers matching an individual child's goals with appropriate teaching methods and materials, deciding what amount of assistance is needed by the child, providing the assistance, and determining whether the instruction was effective. Of equal importance to specialized instruction is cultivating a culture of inclusion, which provides children with disabilities with a sense of belonging and membership in the peer group.

key terms

approaches to learning
children with disabilities
children with special needs
Council for Exceptional Children (CEC)
developmental domain
differentiated instruction
Division for Early Childhood (DEC)
eligibility guidelines
exceptional children
free appropriate public education (FAPE)
functional skills
generative skills
individualized education program (IEP)
individualized family service plan (IFSP)
natural learning environments
naturally occurring reinforcers
nature
nurture
person-first language
prompts
protective factors
Recognition and Response (R&R)
resilience
Response to Intervention (RTI)
risk factors
social acceptance
social rejection
specialized instruction
temperament
theory of multiple intelligences
transactional theory of development

readings & websites

Hyson, M. (2008). *Enthusiastic and engaged learners: Approaches to learning in the early childhood classroom.* New York: Teachers College Press.

Milbourne, S. A., & Campbell, P. H. (2007). *CARA's kit: Creating adaptations for routines and activities.* Philadelphia, PA: Child and Family Studies Research Programs, Thomas Jefferson University. Distributed by Division for Early Childhood, www.de-sped.org.

Sandall, S., & Schwartz, I. (2008). *Building blocks for successful early childhood programs: Strategies for including all children* (2nd ed.). Baltimore: Paul H. Brookes Publishing.

Strain, P. S., & Joseph, G. E. (2006). *You've got to have friends. Young exceptional children monograph series 8: Social emotional development.* Longmont, CO: Sopris West.

Center for Response to Intervention in Early Childhood
www.crtiec.org

Division for Early Childhood of the Council for Exceptional Children (DEC)
www.dec-sped.org

National Professional Development Center on Inclusion
www.npdci.org

Project Zero at Harvard University
www.pz.harvard.edu
Provides resources on Gardner's theory of multiple intelligences

observe, reflect, decide

1. Reflect on Howard Gardner's theory of multiple intelligences and your own abilities and interests. How would you describe your profile of intelligences? In which areas are you stronger? Weaker? How could your schooling and personal life be better matched to your intelligence profile?
2. Reflect on gender differences. How much and which kinds of observed differences between girls and boys do you think are influenced by biology and how much by experience? Do you think teachers should treat all children the same, or should they consider gender differences when working with young children?
3. Visit an infant/toddler program. Observe babies to see if you detect differences in temperament. Do you see differences in teachers' responses based on babies' behavior? Explain. Is there anything you would do differently than those teachers you observed?
4. Visit an inclusive early childhood classroom. Observe the children with special needs. Are they meaningfully engaged in the classroom? Do they seem to have friends? Are they accepted or are they socially rejected? If they are socially rejected, what strategies would you use to try to help them gain acceptance among their peers?
5. Consider a situation in which children in your class come to school dirty, smelly, and wearing the same clothes day after day. Some children may be obese or physically unattractive to you in some way. Reflect on how you would feel about these children and their families. How do you think your feelings might affect your behavior toward them? What could you do about these situations?

6 Embracing a Culturally and Linguistically Diverse World

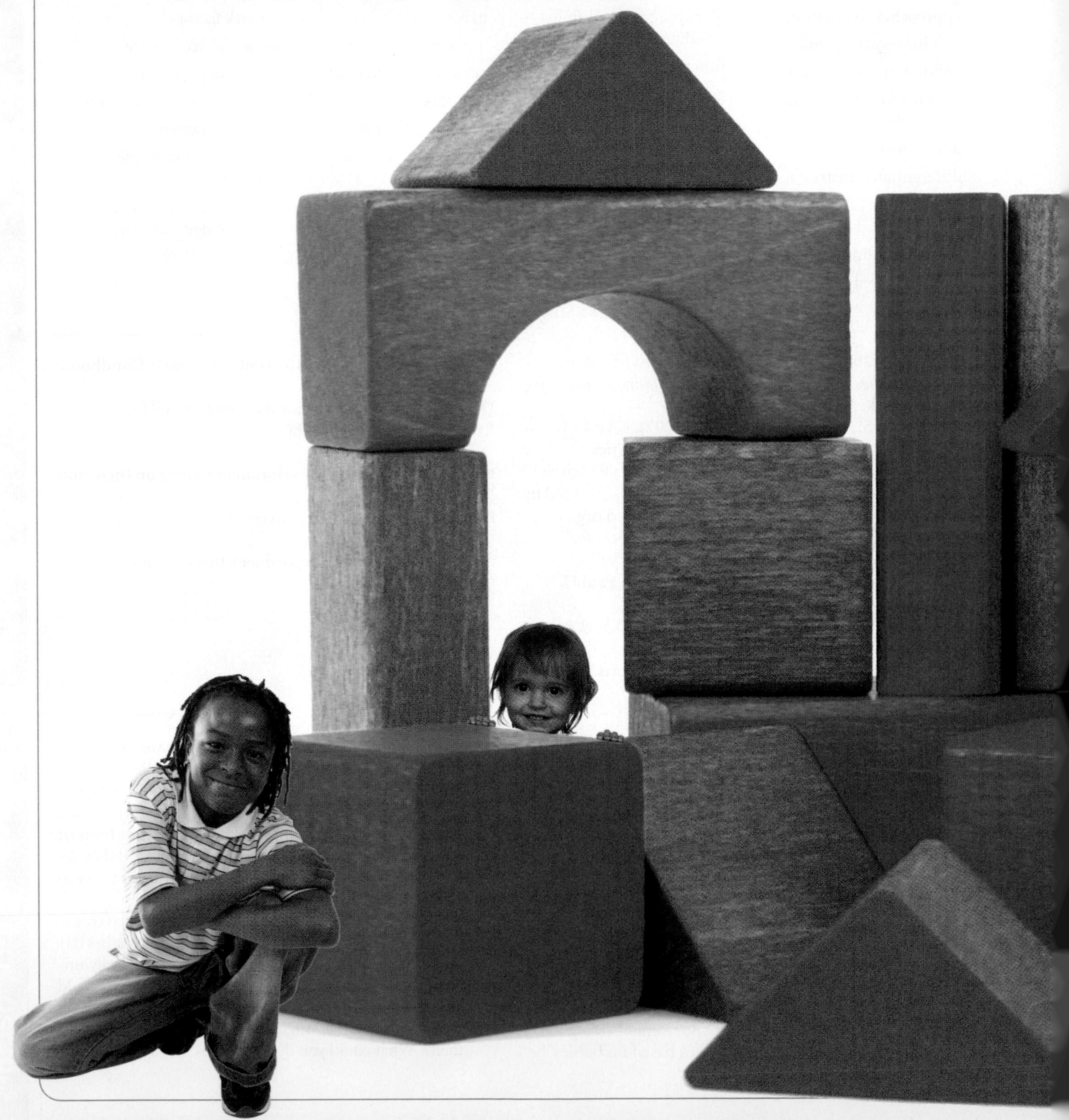

Thinking Ahead

1. What is culture? How do cultural contexts influence children's learning and development?
2. How do the rules for behavior differ among various cultural groups and how are these groups similar?
3. What is your cultural group or groups? How does your cultural background influence your thinking and behavior?
4. Why is it essential for teachers to understand and be sensitive to children's linguistic and cultural diversity?
5. What is cultural competency? What are effective cross-cultural communication strategies?
6. How do teachers resolve contradictions and conflicts that arise in working cross-culturally?
7. What are developmentally appropriate, culturally responsive learning goals that support children's identity, help them learn to value and respect diversity, and counter stereotypes and biases?

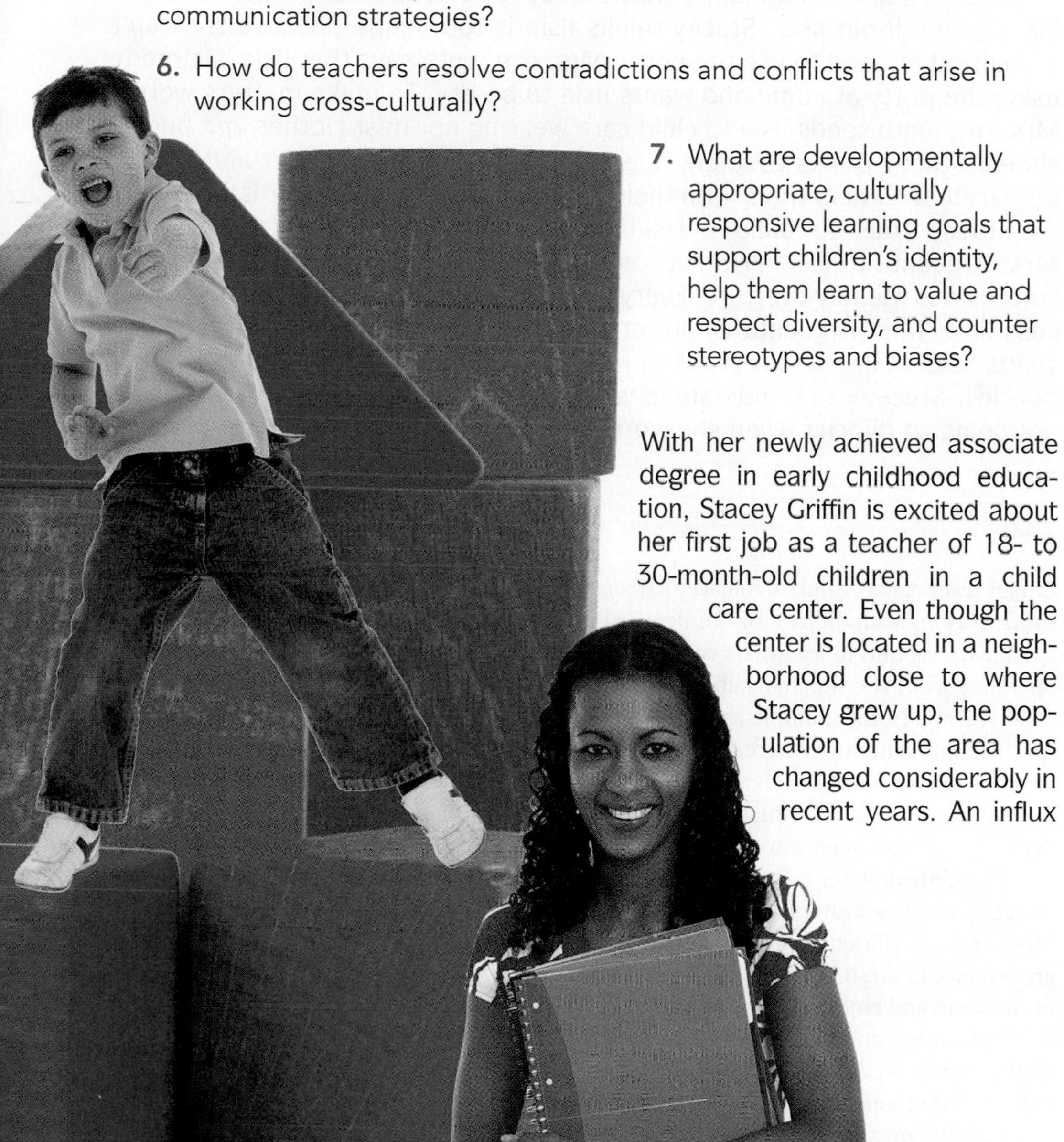

With her newly achieved associate degree in early childhood education, Stacey Griffin is excited about her first job as a teacher of 18- to 30-month-old children in a child care center. Even though the center is located in a neighborhood close to where Stacey grew up, the population of the area has changed considerably in recent years. An influx of immigrants from Latin America is apparent in the number of families with young children who have displaced the elderly, white, European American, long-term residents, as well as in the goods available and language spoken in local markets. Despite these changes, Stacey feels confident that she knows enough about child development and early childhood practice to be a good teacher.

By the end of the first month, however, Stacey is feeling frustrated and less sure of herself. In the mornings, most of the families arrive late. They continue to carry their children into the classroom even though Stacey has informed them (gently, she thinks) that the children are capable of walking on their own and need to practice their developing motor skills. Similarly, she disapproves of the parents' continuing to spoon feed the children rather than giving them finger food that they can manage on their own.

Mrs. Arguenta is unhappy that Stacey isn't cooperating in toilet training 18-month-old Ilsia. Stacey thinks Ilsia is too young because she can't verbalize her need to use the potty. Mrs. Arguenta says that Ilsia is already using the potty at home and wants Ilsia to be dry. To make matters worse, Mrs. Arguenta sends Ilsia to child care wearing her best clothes and buckle shoes. Stacey thinks toddlers need to move about in comfort and should go barefoot to help them with their walking. Besides, the floor is carpeted.

Stacey tries to build a relationship with Mrs. Arguenta. She asks Mrs. Arguenta to call her Stacey instead of Miss Griffin, but Mrs. Arguenta ignores this friendly overture. Every time Stacey tries to meet with her to discuss Ilsia, Mrs. Arguenta is late or doesn't come. One day, Mrs. Arguenta sends Ilsia's 10-year-old sister to pick her up, which is a violation of center policies. Stacey can't understand why Mrs. Arguenta and the other families are being so difficult when she works so hard to communicate with them. ▲

MyEducationLab

Go to the Book Specific Resources in the MyEducationLab for your course and select Author Interviews in Chapter 6 to watch and listen to the video *Embracing Cultural and Linguistic Diversity*. Why did Sue Bredekamp choose to use the word "embracing" ?

Some readers may think that Stacey's struggles as a new teacher are caused by the fact that she is working with difficult or uninterested parents. Others may think that Stacey is too inflexible to respond to legitimate concerns of families. In fact, Stacey and Mrs. Arguenta are operating from two different, albeit equally legitimate, cultural perspectives on appropriate child rearing. In the example above, we see the conflicts almost entirely from Stacey's perspective. But if the story were told from Mrs. Arguenta's view or that of other families, we might question Stacey's skills as a teacher; we might also question her sensitivity to the families' perspectives. In this situation, whatever appears to be happening on the surface, the underlying reality is an encounter between individuals from different cultural contexts.

The United States is becoming increasingly diverse with schools enrolling more children from various cultural and linguistic backgrounds than in the past (Child Trends, 2005). Most early childhood programs already serve children from diverse linguistic and cultural groups or will do so in the future. Therefore, it is more important than ever for teachers to understand and embrace the realities of a culturally and linguistically diverse world.

But culture and its influences are subtle. Moreover, the majority cultural group of the United States—predominantly individuals of Anglo-European descent—tends to define culture and linguistic diversity as issues or challenges to be dealt with or solved. In fact, the word *diverse* means different, which begs the question, "different from what?" The implication is that people whose cultural identity is not white European American or who are not native speakers of English are different from the norm.

In this book, we talk about the realities of culture and language because these forces influence the learning and development of all children. At the same time, we use the verb *embrace* when discussing culture and language to create a classroom climate that is culturally and linguistically supportive and responsive for *all* children. We believe that such a perspective is a precursor to helping all children achieve their full potentials.

In this chapter, we define the term *culture* and identify the basic principles of the role of culture in development and learning. We also describe a framework for thinking about contrasting cultural beliefs, values, and practices. We discuss effective teaching and learning strategies for working with all children, beginning with awareness of one's own cultural perspective.

Understanding Cultural Diversity

The United States has always been a nation of immigrants, its diversity being a hallmark of American society. Recent waves of immigration and higher birth rates among certain groups have made the nation even more diverse. Approximately 41% of the children in the United States are classified by the U.S. Census Bureau as Latino, Asian, or African American/African, and about 20% are children of immigrants (Child Trends, 2005). In many parts of the United States, the majority of children are members of a so-called "minority" group (California Tomorrow, 2007). In the future, however, the concepts of majority and minority status are likely to become confusing if not meaningless.

Given the diversity of children and families served in child care centers and schools, as well as changing demographics, every teacher will work with diverse groups of children and families. Even if differences are not outwardly apparent, individuals differ from one another in many ways: religion, national heritage, language, traditions, and many more. Therefore, all teachers must be committed to making it part of their ongoing education to learn about the diverse populations of their classrooms.

Defining Culture

Culture refers to both explicit and implicit values, beliefs, and patterns of behavior that are passed on from generation to generation (Day, 2005; National Association for the Education of Young Children [NAEYC], 2009a). Culture encompasses customs, rituals, ways of interacting and communicating, and expectations for behaviors, roles, and relationships that are shared by members of a group (Olsen, Bhattacharya, & Scharf, 2007).

culture Explicit and implicit values, beliefs, and patterns of behavior that are passed on from generation to generation; customs, rituals, ways of interacting and communicating, and expectations for behaviors, roles, and relationships that are shared by members of a group.

To understand the concept of culture, it is crucial to understand that culture is a characteristic of *groups*, not an aspect of individual variation. Children learn the values, beliefs, and expectations for behavior from their cultural group. In Chapter 4, we learned how young children are similar to other children of the same age. In Chapter 5, we discussed how each child is unique and different from every other child. In this chapter, we describe how children share similar characteristics with other children of their cultural group. Although each of these three chapters focuses on a distinct principle of development, it is important to recognize that these principles are interrelated. All three of the following statements are equally true:

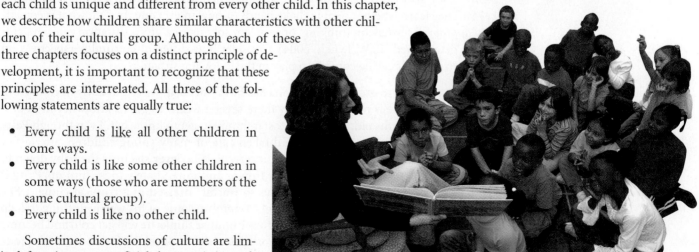

- Every child is like all other children in some ways.
- Every child is like some other children in some ways (those who are members of the same cultural group).
- Every child is like no other child.

Sometimes discussions of culture are limited, focusing on superficial characteristics such as those that can be observed. For example, we judge cultural origin based on the clothing that

The population of young children in the United States is becoming ever more diverse. Effective teachers embrace the realities of cultural and linguistic diversity to help all children reach their full potential.

people wear, the holidays they celebrate, the accents with which they speak, or the music they enjoy. Although these external cues do reveal something about children and their families, they neglect or ignore the deeper structures of culture—the values and rules—that truly influence behavior and decisions.

MyEducationLab

Go to the Professional Perspectives section in Topic 10: Cultural & Linguistic Diversity in the MyEducationLab for your course and select the video entitled *The Role of Culture in Development* and watch and listen to Sue Bredekamp discuss this topic.

The Role of Culture in Development

Why is culture so relevant for early childhood educators? The simplest answer to this question is that culture shapes and influences every child's development and learning (Bronfenbrenner, 1979, 2004; Rogoff, 2003). In fact, all aspects of human life are touched and affected by people's cultural contexts. This includes how people communicate, think, behave, solve problems, and organize communities and governments (E. W. Lynch, 2004).

Although the biological factors that influence maturation are similar for all human beings, culture has a huge influence on how children experience their growth and development—on how they are nurtured (Shonkoff & Phillips, 2000). In general, cultural rules influence how children behave and how they make sense of their experiences.

Culture Influences Behavior

Acculturation is the process whereby children learn expected rules of behavior. From their cultural group, children learn such critical lessons as how to show respect and how to properly greet an older or younger person, a friend, or a stranger (Rogoff, 2003).

Consider the range of child-rearing practices among various cultural groups. Are babies carried on mother's backs or pushed in strollers? Do infants and young children sleep in their parents' bed or down the hall in their own rooms? Do adults respond immediately to a baby's cry or wait to see if the child settles? Are mothers primarily responsible for a baby's care or is that care shared among different members of the extended family? These are only a few examples of the many ways cultural practices begin to shape children's development from the earliest moments of life.

Some cultural rules are explicitly taught, such as "hold the fork in your right hand and the knife in your left" or vice versa. In most countries, mixing up these rules would be of little consequence. By contrast, in Middle Eastern cultures, people eat with their right hand and use their left hand for toileting. Therefore, offering your left hand to someone is interpreted as a grave insult.

Children learn many cultural rules from adults or other children through modeling. From observation, children learn when to smile or look someone in the eye (Gonzalez-Mena, 2008). They also learn when to speak up and when to listen (Ramsey, 2004; Williams, 1994). They learn whether people shake hands or bow in greeting. In fact, what is considered *appropriate* behavior, thinking, or problem solving in a given situation is always culturally determined (E. W. Lynch, 2004). Consider how different cultural perspectives on appropriate child rearing come into play in the following situation:

> Patty Briggs is so excited because she has finally been approved to adopt a child from Costa Rica. She is prepared to stay there several weeks to get to know her little boy, who is 12 months old, and for his foster family to get to know her. Even though Patty has studied child development and taken care of many young children, after a few days in Costa Rica, she starts to feel uncertain. Whenever she puts the baby down to crawl on the floor, the foster mother frowns and immediately picks him up. Patty is concerned because the baby is always so warmly dressed in a tropical climate. She finds that he has diaper rash and wants to remove some of his warm clothing to help him heal. However, it's clear that the foster mother thinks he will get cold and become ill. During the time that Patty is in Costa Rica, she respects the foster mother's mode of caring for the baby, but also treats his diaper rash. After the adoption, she sends photos of him to his foster family to reassure them that he is well cared for (P. Briggs, personal communication, 1990).

acculturation The process whereby children learn expected rules of behavior.

Culture Creates Meaning

Cultural rules determine the meaning attached to particular behaviors. Therefore, teachers need to be aware of how different experiences can carry different meanings for children. Consider the example of physical touch. Touch is an important aspect of human behavior, but different cultural groups attach different interpretations to the same kinds of touch (E. W. Lynch, 2004). In the United States, it is not unusual for opposite-sex couples to hold hands or lock arms as outward signs of affection. In other parts of the world, these behaviors between men and women might not be tolerated. Similarly, in some countries members of the same sex walk arm in arm as a sign of friendship, but in the United States, same-sex public displays of affection are interpreted as a sign of sexual orientation. Accordingly, we see that the same behavior—holding hands or taking someone's arm—means something different depending on the cultural context.

Miscommunication between teachers and parents who are from different cultural groups or who speak different languages can lead to misunderstanding and even conflict. Intentional teachers are aware that families may have different perspectives that need to be heard and respected.

How does this concept affect teachers and children? When the same behaviors mean different things or different behaviors mean the same thing, mixed messages can result, as occurred in Stacey's classroom at the beginning of this chapter. Stacey thinks that using one's first name signals a positive relationship, whereas Mrs. Arguenta interprets it as a sign of disrespect.

How Culture Functions: Principles to Keep in Mind

As you continue your professional journey, you will probably find that the more you learn about culture, the more you need to know. This is not a comfortable position for most educators. While you may think that you should know all the answers, this is not realistic; the most effective stance is to acknowledge what you don't know and remain open to new learning. This will serve you well throughout your teaching career and in all areas of your professional journey.

In the meantime, it is useful to understand several key principles about how culture affects human development. These principles are listed and briefly described here (Day, 2006a, 2006b; Hanson, 2004; C. B. Phillips, 1991).

1. *Everyone has a culture, and is a product of one or more cultural groups.* This first principle is the foundation of all understanding about culture. Accepting this principle requires going beyond respecting diversity to deeper understanding; it requires that European American teachers reject the tendency to see white, European American children as exhibiting *ordinary* behaviors, while thinking about children of other ethnic ancestries as exhibiting *cultural* behaviors (Day, 2006a, 2006b). Members of the majority cultural group in any country tend to have more difficulty recognizing that their cultural background influences their thinking and behavior.

2. *Culture is dynamic.* Culture is not a fixed, static entity. Because it is born of traditions and historical experiences, intervening events can affect and change cultural rules. When groups immigrate, they take aspects of their culture with them; however, as they interact with members of other cultural groups, they may change. Similarly, the cultural traditions in the country of origin may diverge as a result of differing circumstances.

New information and changing political situations may also challenge cultural assumptions, such as appropriate roles for men and women. In the 1960s, for instance, the women's movement and other political events led to rapid shifts in expectations for women and men in America. Similarly, Hillary Clinton's 2008 campaign for president altered perceptions about women as leaders, especially for young girls.

Because culture is dynamic, teachers need to be careful not to make assumptions about students' and families' behaviors based on outdated information or even prior experience with members of a particular group. A teacher might assume, for example, that European

American parents reject gender stereotyping, but change that assumption when several families send in princess costumes for their daughters to play with.

3. *Culture, language, ethnicity, and race are aspects of experience that influence people's beliefs and values.* Culture is only one determinant, albeit a strong one, of people's values, beliefs, and behaviors. **Ethnicity** refers to the shared characteristics and experiences of a group of people, such as nationality, race, history, religion, and language. Ethnicity is usually connected to the geographic origin of a group, as with Greek or Chinese people. Additional factors, including socioeconomic status, education, occupation, ability/disability, sexual orientation, personality, and events in the larger society, influence how people behave and how groups function (E. W. Lynch, 2004).

All of these factors interact to influence the values and behavior of various groups and of individuals within groups. History in particular plays a key role. For example, the history of slavery, racism, and discrimination in the United States and other countries has had a significant, differential effect on people's lives and opportunities and continues to do so. Racism persists as new groups become its target, including Arabic people and immigrants from Spanish-speaking countries. In addition, gay and lesbian people have been and continue to be discriminated against. Although considerable progress has been made toward equality of all groups of Americans, the struggle continues.

4. *Differences within a cultural group may be as great as, or greater than, differences between cultural groups.* Assuming that children who share the same culture or language are all alike is like assuming that all 3-year-olds are alike. Although there are some similarities, there are many differences in their skills, abilities, and behaviors. Likewise, children from the same cultural group share some attitudes, beliefs, and values, but there are many that they do not share. Children from one cultural group are both alike and different from children of another. African American children growing up in low-income, urban areas will share some but not all of the culturally determined behaviors of African American children whose families have been middle class professionals for generations.

Therefore, it is vitally important not to stereotype individuals who are members of particular groups even while learning some of the common practices, values, or beliefs of those groups.

5. *Culture is defined in terms of differences among groups and is complicated by issues of power and status.* Think for a minute about words like *mainstream*, *dominant*, *majority*, and *minority*. In the United States, each of these words is used to describe group differences in relationship to white European Americans. But to members of other cultural groups such as Latinos, Native Americans, or African Americans, European Americans are the diverse group. When one group, such as European Americans, becomes the reference point against which other groups are compared, that group is the one with the most power and privilege in the society (Barrera, Corso & Macpherson, 2003; Delpit, 2006).

ethnicity The shared characteristics and experiences of a group of people, such as nationality, race, history, religion, and language.

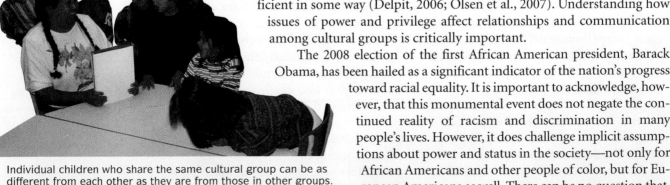

The practices of the cultural group that has the greatest power and status become the standard or norm against which other behaviors are judged (Olsen et al., 2007). Cultural groups that have less status and power are perceived as deficient in some way (Delpit, 2006; Olsen et al., 2007). Understanding how issues of power and privilege affect relationships and communication among cultural groups is critically important.

The 2008 election of the first African American president, Barack Obama, has been hailed as a significant indicator of the nation's progress toward racial equality. It is important to acknowledge, however, that this monumental event does not negate the continued reality of racism and discrimination in many people's lives. However, it does challenge implicit assumptions about power and status in the society—not only for African Americans and other people of color, but for European Americans as well. There can be no question that, to some extent, the face of power has changed.

Individual children who share the same cultural group can be as different from each other as they are from those in other groups. In what ways might these children be similar to each other? How might they differ?

Relationship of Race and Culture

An overview of the principles just discussed reveals that there is a complex relationship between race and culture/ethnicity that knowledgeable teachers need to understand. Because race is a sensitive topic in the United States, the words *culture* and *race* are sometimes inaccurately used synonymously, but they are not the same thing (Wardle, 2008a, 2008c).

Scientists argue that a person's race cannot be determined by examining her or his biological makeup (Wardle, 2008a, 2008b, 2008c). Nevertheless, race is associated with a person's biology and is determined by who their parents are, whereas culture is learned. As evidenced by how census data are collected, racial classifications are real and, for the most part, politically determined (Nieto, 2004; C. B. Phillips, 1994). For example, the same person might be considered racially black in the United States, colored in South Africa, and brown in Brazil. President Barack Obama is almost universally described as African American, despite the fact that he, like more than 6 million other Americans, is biracial or multiracial.

Teachers need to understand that although a very limited number of racial categories, such as Asian or Caucasian, are identified based on skin color and other physical characteristics, hundreds of cultural/ethnic groups exist. Asian peoples include Chinese, Japanese, Koreans, Vietnamese, Hmong, and many others, some of which have been historic enemies (Wardle, 2008a). Similarly, Hispanic is not an actual racial, cultural, or even linguistic group despite its designation as such by census takers. Given these complex realities, the increasing diversity of immigrants, and the growing number of biracial and multiracial children, it is essential that teachers not make assumptions about children and families' racial and cultural identities (Wardle, 2008a).

The most useful strategy is for responsive teachers to create a classroom climate in which it is safe to talk about and notice racial and cultural differences (Lee, Ramsey, & Sweeney, 2008). Reading a book such as *Colors around Me* by Vivian Church can start a conversation about how people with different shades of black skin are a part of the same race because their ancestors originally came from Africa.

In the previous sections, we described principles for understanding culture and how they interrelate. In the next section, we discuss similarities and differences among diverse cultures and how they govern various cultural groups' thinking and behavior.

A Framework for Thinking about Culture

To help you understand the role of culture in the lives of children and families, and your own life, we examine a framework for thinking about values, beliefs, and practices among various cultural groups. In using this framework, it is important that you develop an awareness of similarities and differences among groups (E. W. Lynch, 2004).

Individualistic and Collectivist Cultural Orientations

Different cultural groups have different sets of values and beliefs, but beyond that, they have different ways of connecting with each other and functioning as a group. In some cultural groups, individual members put their needs first before those of the group; other cultures are group-oriented, putting the group's needs before their own individual needs. This framework classifies cultural groups in terms of two general orientations: (1) individualism and (2) collectivism (Gonzalez-Mena, 2008; Greenfield & Cocking, 1994; Welch, 2007; Zepeda, Rothstein-Fisch, Gonzalez-Mena, & Trumbull, 2006).

Individualistic Cultures

The values of **individualistic cultural groups** include focusing on the needs of the individual, independence, self-expression, and personal property and choice. These cultures emphasize the rights of the individual over the rights of the group. With its history of individual rights and focus on personal achievement, this is the dominant cultural orientation in the United States.

individualistic cultural groups Cultural groups that focus on the needs of the individual, independence, self-expression, and personal property and choice.

Picture an individualistic-oriented classroom. All of the children have their own cubbies marked with their names in which to store their belongings. Developing independence in children is an important goal. The children's individual work is displayed and carefully identified. When parents visit, they look carefully to find their child's contribution. The focus on individual children and their accomplishments is evident.

Collectivist Cultures

By contrast, **collectivist cultural groups** focus on the needs of the group rather than on those of the individual. These cultural groups value interdependence, cooperation and mutual assistance, shared property, and social responsibility. Collectivist cultures stress respect for tradition and authority over the rights of the individual. Among cultural groups that exhibit a collectivist orientation are Latinos, Asians, and people in West African and Middle Eastern countries. Because the United States is a nation of immigrants, many cultural groups within this country, as well as Native Americans and African Americans, are oriented more toward collectivism than individualism (Hanson, 2004).

In a collectivist-oriented classroom, children's group work is displayed. A colorful mural representing the contributions of scores of children adorns the entrance to the school. Teachers show parents examples of how children worked together on projects, as well as samples of their children's writing or art.

These two classrooms are described in overly simplistic terms. Most classrooms would evidence both cultural orientations because, in reality they are not polar opposites but rather points on a continuum.

Continuum of Common Cultural Values

Instead of classifying cultural groups as *either* individualistic *or* collectivist, a more useful strategy is to think of values that are common across all cultural groups as varying along a continuum. Such a continuum is depicted in Figure 6.1.

Understanding the Continuum

Individuals within cultural groups vary all along the continuum; families are more or less inclusive, just as they are more or less traditional rather than either traditional or not. In addition, the ends of the continuum can be seen from a *both/and* perspective. For example, in the United States, schools and society emphasize *both* individual achievement *and* cooperation, working together to solve problems, and taking care of those in need.

Consider how misunderstandings can occur when teachers and family members operate from different points on the collectivist and individualist continuum, as in the following example:

> Mr. Wu is late for a team meeting to discuss his son's IEP. The disabilities coordinator, Ms. Armstrong, impatiently taps her foot, repeatedly looks at her watch, and gets more and more irritated as minutes tick by. Ms. Garcia, the classroom teacher, seems less concerned. When Mr. Wu arrives, he doesn't apologize for being late, but he does tell Ms. Garcia that his mother is taking care of his son and she has questions to ask about her grandson. Ms. Garcia understands that Mr. Wu's respect for his mother took precedence over arriving at the meeting on time.
>
> When the meeting ends, Ms. Garcia reviews her notes with Ms. Armstrong. She politely states, "I could see that you were concerned about the meeting running overtime. I know that you are very busy, but I believe that Mr. Wu did not intend to inconvenience us by being late. His greatest priority was to show respect for his mother, and I'm glad he consulted her because with her input we can do a better job of helping her grandson." In this way, Ms. Garcia did not tell Ms. Armstrong that her cultural views are wrong; instead, she clarified her own cultural views and those of Mr. Wu.

collectivist cultural groups Cultural groups that focus on the needs of the group rather than those of the individual.

Continua	Collectivist Cultural Values		Individualistic Cultural Values
Family orientation continuum	***Extended family and kinship networks*** Families live together or in proximity and share responsibilities like childrearing. Older children may assume responsibility for younger ones. Such networks may extend to neighbors and friends as well. Decisions are made in the best interest of the family rather than the individual.	↔	***Small unit families with little reliance on the extended family*** Families consist of parents and children only. They rely less on extended family with regard to day-to-day childrearing.
Interdependence and individuality continuum	***Interdependence*** Families value interdependence. Independence may be seen as selfishness and rejection of the family. Children are encouraged to contribute to the successful functioning of the family rather than to stand out in any particular way.	↔	***Individuality*** Families value individuality and self-expression in children. One of the primary goals is to develop children's self-esteem and independence.
Time continuum	***Time is given*** Individuals view time as given rather than measured. The time needed for a task to be done or for a visit with a friend is more important than the clock.	↔	***Time is measured*** Individuals believe "time is money." They consult clocks and calendars to make sure that time is carefully scheduled and used productively. Wasting time or being late is considered a fault or sign of disrespect.
Tradition and technology continuum	***Tradition oriented*** Groups place more value on reverence for the past, traditions, rituals, and the wisdom of elders. New technologies are suspect. Focusing on youth may be considered unwise and disrespectful to elders.	↔	***Future oriented*** Groups embrace new advances in technology and revere youth as hope for the future.
Ownership continuum	***Broadly defined ownership*** Ownership is shared by the entire family or community. Relationships are more important than objects. If a visitor admires a piece of jewelry or clothing, the wearer may immediately give it as a gift.	↔	***Individual and specific ownership*** Individually owned property is a strong value.
Rights and responsibilities continuum	***Differentiated rights and responsibilities*** Rights and responsibilities are predetermined by gender or age.	↔	***Equal rights and responsibilities*** Individuals share strong belief in personal freedom, equal rights, and equal responsibilities.

Figure 6.1 Collectivist and Individualist Cultural Values

Source: From "Developing Cross-Cultural Competence," by E. W. Lynch, 2004, in *Developing Cross-Cultural Competence: A Guide for Working with Children and Their Families,* 3rd ed., edited by E. W. Lynch and M. J. Hanson, Baltimore: Paul H. Brookes Publishing Co., Inc.

Applying the Continuum in Practice

Conceptualizing variations in cultural values along a continuum helps teachers in several ways: (1) It reduces the tendency to stereotype groups; (2) it reduces the likelihood that differences will be categorized as right or wrong, that is, an *us versus them* mentality; and (3) it has the potential to increase understanding and communication among teachers and families who may differ in their perspectives (E. W. Lynch, 2004). Ultimately, cultures may tend toward one end of the continuum or the other, but the values of most people fall somewhere in between. All cultures value families, for instance, but they define family membership differently.

Following is an example of what might happen during an encounter between members of individualist and collectivist cultural groups:

> To help children feel comfortable in their new surroundings, kindergarten teacher Alisha Watson created a bulletin board to display photos of children's families so that there would be something familiar to the children in the room. She asked for children to bring in pictures of themselves with their siblings and parents, and couldn't understand why some of the families never responded to her request. She thought perhaps families didn't have cameras or didn't want to participate in school activities. In frustration, she finally gave up the idea of the family bulletin board. Alisha never imagined that some parents weren't comfortable limiting the photo to just the immediate family. To many of them the extended family, which includes neighbors and friends, is what matters. One mother was upset that grandparents would not be included, but didn't want to alienate the new teacher.

As we can see, Alisha's concept of "family" represents a more individualistic orientation than that of many families in her classroom. Alisha could have avoided the problem by respecting the families' own definitions of their members.

The continuum of cultural values (E. W. Lynch, 2004) is intended to help you concentrate on common values—how cultural groups are similar as well as different. At the same time, effectively working across cultural groups requires looking inward and analyzing your own cultural perspective, as we describe next.

Understanding Your Own Cultural Perspective

As you read about collectivist and individualistic cultural values, how did you feel? Did you identify with one end of the continua or another? Did you find yourself judging people whose values and practices reflect the other extreme?

Teachers, like all human beings, view the world through their own cultural lenses. To be effective, you will need to overcome any potential biases about children's behavior in order to build on their prior knowledge and current levels of ability, and to help children make sense of their experiences. The first step in accomplishing this goal is to examine your own cultural perspective.

Become Aware of Your Own Cultural Experiences

Begin by reflecting on the origins of your family. Here are some questions to stimulate these reflections (Day, 2005; E. W. Lynch, 2004):

- What stories have you heard about your ancestors or relatives living in other parts of the world?
- How do you identify yourself culturally? Do you feel a connection to your cultural background?
- Do you or does anyone in your family speak a language other than English? What language(s) do you speak?
- Are there rituals, traditions, or holidays that reflect your family's heritage?

- How does your family express affection?
- How do your family members communicate? Are they more likely to listen and think before speaking, or do they jump into conversation eagerly, even talking over one another?
- Can you think of advice or sayings that guided behavior in your family?

Questions like these help you become aware of how your own values, beliefs, and practices affect your behavior. Now think about how your cultural perspective affects your views of appropriate child-rearing practices. Ask yourself the following questions and compare your answers with those of colleagues:

- What are your thoughts regarding infant feeding practices? Should the goal be for children to learn as toddlers how to independently feed themselves? Or do you believe that adults should feed babies as long as possible?
- What do you think are appropriate discipline techniques? Should children be given time-outs, spanked, or lose privileges when they misbehave? Should parents explain their reasoning to children?
- What behaviors are acceptable for girls? For boys?

Finally, examine how your cultural beliefs and biases affect your behavior and emotions. Reflect on these questions:

- Have you ever felt uncomfortable or surprised in another part of the United States or in another country? What was the situation? Perhaps you felt that people invaded your personal space? Or weren't respectful of your time?
- Have you ever felt awkward or embarrassed by something you said or did when you were traveling or among another cultural group? Did you think about why you might have felt that way?
- Have you ever done or said something that was culturally inappropriate? Did your behavior embarrass or offend other people?

Finding yourself in another group and experiencing what it feels like not to be certain of the rules is an excellent way to gain deeper understanding of your cultural views and those of other groups. I (the author) have had many such experiences when speaking about early childhood education throughout the United States and in other countries. I remember specifically telling a story about the struggles I encountered during my early days of teaching. I often said, "I knew that I was smart, but I also knew that I didn't know enough about teaching young children and I had a lot to learn." Much to my surprise (and subsequent embarrassment), I later learned that many audiences were so stunned to hear me call myself smart that they couldn't hear anything else I said! Pointing out individual achievement even with self-deprecating humor is simply not considered appropriate behavior in many groups.

A part of reflecting on your own cultural experience includes comparing your perspective with that of other people. Therefore, the next step is to learn about other cultural groups and how your views and behaviors compare and contrast with theirs.

Learn about the Perspectives of Other Cultural Groups

To fully understand your own cultural perspectives, it is useful to learn as much as possible about how other groups think and respond to different situations and events. This knowledge will help overcome the tendency to impose your values and beliefs on the children that you teach and their families. To learn more about other cultural groups:

- Read widely about children and families of diverse cultures and backgrounds.
- Seek out and read what has been written about diversity by researchers and theorists from a wide variety of cultural backgrounds.
- Identify key informants—family members, community elders, neighborhood leaders—who are willing to talk openly with you about their beliefs, values, and practices. To get as

How Would You Respond?

Demographic Changes in the Classroom

The Situation Since last year, your second-grade class has added a number of Hmong children. In fact, the entire school and the community, a midsized town in Wisconsin, have experienced this influx. You know little about the Hmong students and their cultural backgrounds, although you have heard that they are having more difficulties in school than most of the other Asian immigrant groups. The four Hmong children in your group stick together and do not interact much with you or the other children. To teach the children successfully and to relate well to their families, you realize you need to know more about this population of immigrants.

What to Do? Following is a list of approaches you might consider. What potential problems or limitations, if any, do you see with each approach? Which of these strategies do you think would be most effective?

- Look in the library and online for information about the history and culture of the Hmong people.
- Talk with the children's parents and other family members.
- Send home a survey for each family to complete about their traditions, holidays, and food preferences.
- Talk with older children or adults from the Hmong community who have learned English.
- Talk with people who reside in or near the neighborhoods where the Hmong live in greatest numbers to see if they have gained insight into the cultural rules and values of Hmong people.
- Think about how varied people are in your own culture and recognize there will be such differences among the Hmong children and their families.

What else could you do to be a more effective teacher in this situation?

much accurate information as possible and to avoid stereotyping, don't rely on one person to be your cultural translator.

- Read books and magazines, watch movies, or search websites produced by members of diverse cultural groups.
- If possible, immerse yourself in another culture and experience the discomfort of not knowing exactly what to say or how to behave.
- Most important of all, observe carefully and listen closely to learn how various cultural groups communicate and nurture their young.

At some point in your teaching career, you will find yourself in a situation where cultural knowledge and experience will be essential to your work. Read and discuss the *How Would You Respond? Demographic Changes in the Classroom* feature to explore this probability in more depth.

Now that we have discussed the complex concept of culture and identified several key principles that describe how culture functions in children's development, consider how this knowledge can be applied to the classroom. How will this knowledge inform your teaching?

Teaching in a Culturally and Linguistically Diverse World

Imagine it is the first day of school. Parents who are dropping off their children are using various dialects and languages that you don't recognize. Some of the children are crying and clinging to their parent, while others, it is clear, have been told that crying is not allowed, so they are standing with quivering chins trying to hold it together. You are making the rounds, introducing yourself to the children, trying to get them excited about the day and the upcoming year.

You may have been through this before, as a student teacher working in a culturally diverse classroom, but every year the dynamic and the ethnic mix change. It will be up to you to find a way to communicate with English language learners, to be sensitive to the fact that the English language has many idioms that may be foreign to children who are mastering English, and to be sensitive to each child's home life, whether they live with their parents and siblings; their extended family; or whether they are from a single-parent home. The key is to learn as much as you can about each of the children, to get to know their families, and to always be culturally responsive in the classroom.

Why Does Culture Matter to Teachers?

Children from diverse language and cultural groups and those from low-income families (who are disproportionately linguistically and culturally diverse) are the very children who are not being well served in our nation's schools. In fact, the purpose of No Child Left Behind was to hold schools accountable for educating every child and to close the achievement gap between groups of children.

The underlying causes and remedies for the achievement gap are complex, but part of the solution must be to recognize and build on the competencies that children bring from prior experiences (Barbarin & Crawford, 2006; Bowman & Stott, 1994). To do so requires that teachers acquire cultural understanding. Without such knowledge, at least three problems can occur: (1) teachers can misunderstand children, (2) teachers can inaccurately assess children's competence, and (3) teachers can plan incorrectly to promote children's learning (Barbarin & Crawford, 2006; Bowman, Donovan, & Burns, 2001; Bowman & Stott, 1994; Zepeda et al., 2006).

MyEducationLab

Go to the Assignments and Activities section in Topic 10: Cultural & Linguistic Diversity in the MyEducationLab for your course and complete the activity entitled *Understanding Culture*. As you watch the four videos and answer the accompanying questions, consider why it is so important for teachers to understand children's cultural contexts.

Misunderstanding Children

Failing to understand the influence of children's backgrounds on their development can lead to misunderstanding and miscommunication about children and their families, as the following example illustrates (based on Zepeda et al., 2006):

> In Carey Foster's Head Start class, she tries to promote children's self-concepts and self-esteem by having them make "All about Me" books at the beginning of the year. The children draw pictures and Carey writes down what they say about themselves.
>
> Four-year-old Isela Rodriguez dictates, "My brothers are big and strong and help my mother."
>
> Carey says, "But this book isn't about your brothers. It's about you. Let's say you have brown eyes and you can write your name."
>
> Isela doesn't respond. She feels unsure because she is proud of how her family helps each other, but her teacher doesn't seem to care about that. During the parent open house, Carey proudly displays Isela's book for her mother, who doesn't look impressed. Carey doesn't realize that Isela's mother thinks her daughter is becoming conceited and selfish in this school.

Carey's classroom activity was at odds with the interdependence valued by Isela's family. Most likely, this situation would have turned out better if Carey had been sensitive to Isela's discomfort initially. Instead of taking over for Isela, Carey could have said, "Tell me more about the people in your family." Listening would have helped Carey better understand the values of Isela's family.

One area where cultural groups often differ is how they approach discipline. If teachers are unaware of these differences, they may be ineffective in guiding children's behavior. Furthermore, their methods may prove to be counterproductive. For example, time-out—removing children from the group for misbehavior for a period of time—is a discipline strategy that is widely used by parents and teachers. In general, the strategy is not effective because it simply stops the children's negative behavior temporarily without teaching children what to do instead. Nevertheless, teachers and parents continue to use time-out. Let's consider time-out from a cultural perspective in the following example:

> Mark Temple is a new teacher who is struggling to control his first-grade class for reading instruction. His school is in a close-in suburb of a major city, and some people call it the "little United Nations" because it serves so many cultural groups. Today, Mark is reading a story to the group and Yao cannot keep still. He touches and sits very close to the other children, who pull away and are distracted by his behavior. After several warnings, Mark puts Yao in time-out for the duration of the story. Mark notices that Yao is sitting very quietly with his head bowed and a dejected look on his face, trying hard not to cry. Mark assumes that Yao is sorry for disrupting story time and that the time-out was effective.
>
> Mark's interpretation of Yao's response to his time-out, however, is uninformed. Mark's ignorance of Yao's Chinese cultural values causes him to misunderstand Yao's behavior. Yao loves his school and is excited by the opportunity to sit close to the other children. Being assigned to time-out means being isolated from the group where he feels most comfortable and happy. Yao feels confused, ashamed, and guilty, not because he didn't follow the rules but because he has been separated from the others. Yao is humiliated because he thinks that the group has rejected him.

Inaccurate Assessment of Children

Ignorance of children's culturally determined behavior can lead teachers to make inaccurate assessments of children's competence and ability. Language barriers can also lead to incorrect assessments of children's abilities. Similarly, cultural and linguistic differences can lead to errors in identifying and serving children with disabilities.

Assessing English Language Learners. Assessing the learning of English language learners or children who speak a variation of English requires special tools and expertise. Too many English language learners are judged to be language delayed when they are actually demonstrating typical second language development (Head Start, 2008a). No assumptions about children's competence should be based on measures in a language in which children are not fluent (NAEYC & National Association of Early Childhood Specialists in State Departments of Education, 2003).

An English language learner or a child who speaks a variation of English may have a well-developed vocabulary and understand many concepts, but may not be well understood at school. In such a situation, it can be difficult to accurately assess either the child's competence or his or her needs, as illustrated in the *Language Lens* feature.

Cultural Diversity and Disabilities. One of the biggest mistakes that educators and the general public make is to equate cultural differences with disabilities. The fact is that children with disabilities cross all cultural groups. Likewise, cultural and linguistic diversity impact all dimensions of special education services.

In a classroom of diverse learners, teachers may have a difficult time identifying students who have special needs. In addition, diagnosis and intervention planning for children with disabilities is a challenge when the child is of a different culture or language group than the professionals (Hanson & Lynch, 2004). Read the *Including All Children: Diversity and Disability* feature for an example of these challenges.

Failure to Promote Children's Achievement

Misunderstanding and inaccurate assessment of children's competence can lead to ineffective teaching that does not meet the needs of all students. If children's competence is acquired in a context that does not match that of the teacher or school, several potential problems can arise. Teachers can negatively judge children on the basis of their culturally influenced behaviors. Without accurate assessment, teachers' expectations for children's learning can be too low.

Language Lens

Accurate Assessment of Culturally Diverse Children

Cultural and linguistic diversity are *not* disabilities. However, the intersection between these different abilities can have significant consequences for children and families. The following example illustrates the impact of cultural and linguistic diversity on identification and diagnosis of children's special needs:

> The student body of Rosa Parks Elementary School is about 30% Latino, 30% European American, and 40% African American. Scott James is an African American first-grade teacher. The school's speech therapist, Tess Brooks, is a white, European American. Scott meets with Tess because he is concerned about two students, Reynoldo and Patrizia, who are behind in reading. Both children speak Spanish at home, but speak both English and Spanish at school. While Reynoldo is quite verbal, Patrizia hardly speaks at all. Scott thinks that Reynoldo's reading problem is related to a language delay, but because he doesn't speak Spanish, Scott can't be sure. However, the other children, even the Spanish-speaking children, don't seem to understand Reynoldo very well either. As for Patrizia, Scott thinks she may have an undiagnosed hearing loss.
>
> But Scott's bigger concern is that the screening tools aren't very accurate for assessing language delays in Spanish, and Tess shares his concern. She thinks the best strategy is to get more information from Reynoldo's family about his communication at home. Using an interpreter, Tess and Scott meet with Reynoldo's mother. She is clearly alarmed. She tells the translator that these teachers think Reynoldo is stupid because he doesn't speak English, but she knows that there is nothing wrong with her son.
>
> Scott privately meets with Patrizia's grandmother, again using a translator. Her reaction is different from Reynoldo's mother: "I've been worried, too, because she hardly talks at home either. But I understand her when she talks and so does her brother."

In these situations, Scott and Tess must walk a fine line. They can easily make a mistake. When assessment tools aren't sensitive to language differences, or when professionals do not understand a child's language, they can inaccurately diagnose a delay. In this case, a child may be mislabeled as "delayed," which can negatively affect teachers' and parents' expectations for him. On the other hand, if professionals assume that a language difference is the only cause, they can miss a real problem. The latter error has lasting consequences because the child may not receive needed intervention services.

In the above scenario, Reynoldo's speech problems were real, and not a product of learning a second language. Without an accurate assessment of the problem, Reynoldo did not receive therapy and his language delay worsened. Patrizia, on the other hand, did not have a hearing loss. What her grandmother and Scott thought was a language delay was actually shyness.

Source: Based on *Cross-Cultural Considerations in Early Childhood Special Education* (Technical Report #14), by T. Bennett et al., 2001, Urbana-Champaign, IL: University of Illinois, Culturally and Linguistically Appropriate Services (CLAS). Retrieved August 20, 2009, from http://clas.uiuc.edu/techreport/tech14.html#4b.

If teachers do not recognize what students already know—what they have learned based on prior experiences—teachers cannot help them build on it (Bowman & Stott, 1994). For example, many early childhood programs encourage and expect children to speak up and share stories of their own experience or background. Yet this may not be a task that all students can do. Consider, for instance, that among many Native American tribes, children are expected to listen to older adults rather than speak themselves (Williams, 1994). Tribal stories may be considered sacred and not to be shared with outsiders. If teachers do not understand these diverse communication styles, they may have trouble assessing what children already know.

As we stated earlier, different cultural groups often make different meanings from the same experience. If new learning is to be meaningful, teachers must help children make connections between what they know and are able to do at home and in their community and what is expected in school. Meaningful learning is more likely when teachers focus on the learning goal rather than on the specific means to the goal. For example, if the goal of a first-grade science curriculum is for children to understand life cycles, studying buffalo, which may be familiar to Native American children in the West, is as effective as learning about cows for children in the Midwest.

Misunderstandings, the roots of which are cultural in many cases, can have dire consequences. For example, cultural studies of African American children, boys in particular,

Including All Children

Diversity and Disability

Effective early intervention practices are supposed to be family centered, involving families both in decision making and implementation. However, cultural differences can complicate communication and understanding between families and professionals. These differences can become a challenge in planning intervention strategies for children with disabilities, as the following example illustrates:

> Little Sparrow is a 3-year-old Native American child who was born with Down syndrome. Her family believes that such births are natural and that Little Sparrow's contributions to the community are important, however small. The community's goal is to maintain harmony among everyone. Little Sparrow is enrolled in Head Start on the reservation. Head Start program standards require that they provide early intervention services for children with disabilities. The teachers are members of the tribe, but they must work with the disabilities coordinator, who is not. Together, they help Little Sparrow improve her functional skills such as feeding and toileting, and she is making progress at school.
>
> The disabilities coordinator meets with the family to ensure that they will follow up on the effective strategies at home. But the family seems nonresponsive. They can't understand why the school is so concerned about changing Little Sparrow when they love her just the way she is. And they don't want to single her out for special attention among the other children, which could upset the harmonious relationships in their community.

In this example, we see how a family's cultural perspective can be at odds with professional views. The professionals' intervention goals may not emphasize what is valued by the family, or the intervention may emphasize what they do not value. Such conflicting goals need to be negotiated if children's best interests are to be served.

In the case of Little Sparrow, the teachers worked with the disabilities coordinator to relinquish control of the situation and meet with elders in the community. They described their goals and how they thought that supporting Little Sparrow to do more would benefit everyone, actually bringing more harmony to the group. The elders decided that help for Little Sparrow would be shared by many adults and children in the tribe, and that in turn the little girl would help the others as best she could.

Sources: Based on *Understanding Families: Approaches to Diversity, Disability, and Risk*, by M. J. Hanson and E. W. Lynch, 2004, Baltimore: Paul H. Brookes Publishing; and "Cross-Cultural Conceptions of Child-Rearing: Implications for Reviewing/Evaluating Intervention Practices," by J. T. McCollum, T. Yates, M. Ostrosky, and J. Halle, 2001, Chap. IV in *Cross-Cultural Considerations in Early Childhood Special Education* (Technical Report #14), by T. Bennett et al., 2001, Urbana-Champaign, IL: University of Illinois, Culturally and Linguistically Appropriate Services (CLAS). Retrieved August 20, 2009, from http://clas.uiuc.edu/techreport/tech14.html#4b.

find that on average they tend to be more physically active and emotive than their European American peers (Hale, 1988, 1994). Teachers may incorrectly judge this exuberance as aggression. As a result, the very behavior that is rewarded and expected in their community may be censored by their teachers in school (Hale, 1994). When such negative responses persist, children may become discouraged and, perhaps, more disruptive (Barbarin & Crawford, 2006). Consequently, African American boys are disproportionately represented in special education and more likely to be expelled, even in preschool (Gilliam, 2005; Harry & Klingner, 2005).

In the previous sections, we saw how teachers' lack of cultural understanding can lead to several errors in supporting children's learning and development. In the next section, we focus on the realities of linguistic diversity and its interaction with culture in children's development and learning.

Linguistically Appropriate Practice

The primary goal of this chapter is to encourage you to embrace the realities of cultural and linguistic diversity. Although we have focused much attention on culture, language and culture are inextricably linked (Nieto, 2004). Language is the vehicle through which children make sense of the world.

The Relationship of Language and Culture

Language is a major vehicle for transmitting culture (Nieto, 2004). If a concept does not exist in a culture, there is no need for a word to represent that concept. Consider a language without a word for *privacy*. What would that tell you about the culture's values? Most likely, the cultural group places greater value on the needs and rights of the group than on those of the individual. Also, personal space and private ownership may be less important.

How words are defined and used also reflects cultural differences. For example, in Italian, the same verb, *discutere*, means "to discuss" or "to argue." Picture a group of Italians or Italian Americans all talking at once, with raised voices and many gestures. Arguing is just another form of discussion, and is much less threatening than in societies where English is spoken and where *arguing* has negative connotations.

Similarly, some languages may have many words to distinguish subtle variations in meaning that are important to the group. A large vocabulary for types of snow and ice is essential in the Arctic, but unnecessary in more temperate climates. What if English only had one word for *blue*? How could we communicate clearly without words like *turquoise, navy*, or *periwinkle*? The inextricable link between language and culture means that one cannot be embraced without also embracing the other.

Effective Teaching
Effective teachers work to understand the social and cultural contexts in which children live so that they can accurately assess children's competence and promote their continued learning.

Embracing Linguistic Diversity

The United States has always been a country in which many people are bilingual or multilingual. With increasing numbers of children speaking a language other than English at home, opportunity exists to help these children become bilingual. To do so, it is important that teachers support children's development and maintenance of their home language while helping children acquire proficiency in English. In short, these children are **dual-language learners**—learning two languages at once (Head Start, 2008a).

All children in our society need to acquire English, but they can become proficient without giving up their home language (Genesee, Paradis, & Crago, 2004; Oller & Eilers, 2002; Tabors, 2008). The key is for teachers to support continued development of the home language and to inform parents that if they encourage their children to speak English both in the home and at school at a very early age, their children may lose their home language. Home language loss can harm children's long-term academic achievement (Espinosa, 2010; Oller & Eilers, 2002; Slavin & Cheung, 2005). In addition, if parents do not speak English well and their children lose the home language, serious communication and relationship problems between parents and children are likely to occur (Espinosa, 2007; Wong Filmore, 1991). Therefore, teachers should encourage families to speak to children in whatever language the parent is most comfortable to support children's educational achievement.

In the previous sections, we discussed how educational systems often misunderstand, inaccurately assess, and fail to serve culturally and linguistically diverse children. In the upcoming sections, we look at what kinds of practices are effective for teaching diverse learners.

MyEducationLab

Go to the Assignments and Activities section in Topic 10: Cultural & Linguistic Diversity in the MyEducationLab for your course and complete the activity entitled *Incorporating Children's Culture within Teaching Practices*. How does the teacher incorporate children's home language in the classroom, and promote children's positive identity and achievement?

Effective Practices for Culturally and Linguistically Diverse Children

Helping children achieve their learning potential should be the goal of all educational programs. One strategy is to focus less on what is not working and more on educational success stories. The late Asa Hilliard, proponent of Afrocentric education, called on educators and policy makers to identify and replicate the practices of teachers and schools that produce outstanding results for children of color: high rates of achievement, graduation, and later college attendance (Hilliard, 2006; Ladson-Billings, 1994; Perry, Steel, & Hilliard, 2003).

A body of research demonstrates that taking children's cultural backgrounds into consideration in curriculum and teaching is related to positive learning outcomes for students across age groups. The federally funded Center for Research on Education, Diversity, and

dual-language learner Someone who is learning more than one language at a time.

Excellence (CREDE; formerly the National Center for Research on Cultural Diversity and Second Language Learning) reviewed more than 200 studies to identify successful practices for working with diverse groups. These studies were conducted with elementary school children across many cultural groups: Puerto Ricans, African Americans, Native Hawaiians, Native American Indians, Mexican immigrants, Appalachian urban immigrant whites, Southeast Asian newcomers, Eskimos or Aleuts, and European American gifted and talented children. Based on this research, key principles of effective practice for culturally diverse learners were gleaned (Tharp, Estrada, Dalton, & Yamachuchi, 2000, 2003). These principles, described in Table 6.1, are congruent with several aspects of NAEYC's position on developmentally appropriate practices (Tharp & Entz, 2003; Yamauchi & Kuwahara, 2008).

More research is needed on the relationship of these teaching practices to improved achievement among diverse populations of children. However, research with native Hawaiian children at the Kamehameha School demonstrates the effectiveness of respecting children's cultural context (see the *What Works: Making Education Culturally Compatible* feature).

To accommodate diverse learners, teachers must integrate students' diverse backgrounds into the curriculum. A particular kind of ability is required to successfully use this type of effective practice in the classroom: cultural competence.

Table 6.1 Principles of Effective Teaching for Culturally Diverse Learners

Principle (or Standard)	Definition	Example
1. Joint productive activity	Teachers and students work together toward a common goal. Teachers participate with children in activity.	Teachers and small groups (three to four) of children take a nature walk to collect signs of animal life near their school.
2. Language and literacy development	Teachers incorporate language and literacy learning throughout the day and in all areas of the curriculum.	Teachers engage children in conversation about what they observe. Teachers and children read and write about the life cycles of the animals they observe.
3. Meaningful learning	Teachers connect school learning to children's lives.	Teachers begin with what children or their families know and share about animals in their immediate experience.
4. Challenging learning	Teachers focus on complex thinking.	Teachers pose problems for children to think about, such as what would happen if the trees were cut down and how the problems could be addressed.
5. Instructional conversation	Teachers and children engage in individual and small-group dialogues.	Children are grouped by interest, talk with each other, and meet with the teacher to discuss and share what they have learned and identify new questions.
6. Modeling	Children learn through observation.	Children watch teachers carefully handling a class pet.
7. Student-directed learning	Children generate learning topics and activities.	Children brainstorm questions to investigate and ways to find out answers.

Source: Based on "Research to Practice. Joint Productive Activity: Collaboration That Builds New Understandings," by L. A. Yamauchi and R. H. Kuwahara, 2008, *Young Children*, *63*(6), pp. 34–38.

What Works

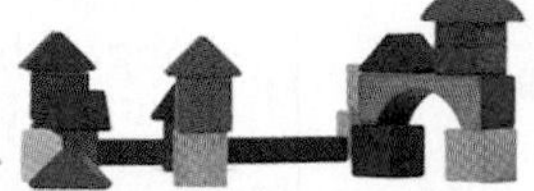

Making Education Culturally Compatible

Education is most effective when it takes into account students' cultural backgrounds. This premise has generated numerous programs and innovations. Among the best documented is the Kamehameha Early Education Program (KEEP), a language arts program designed in the early 1970s to help underachieving native Hawaiian children improve their reading skills. Kamehameha schools were funded by the last surviving member of the Hawaiian royal family, Princess Bernice Pauahi Bishop, to provide an excellent education for native Hawaiian children. KEEP emphasized the importance of making children's educational experiences and their home/community experiences compatible by using the children's native culture as a basis for instructional practices.

KEEP staff determined that Hawaiian children typically turn to their peers and older siblings rather than to adults when in need of assistance. Based on this knowledge, teachers set up peer-learning centers in the classrooms. The idea was to encourage children to help one another with learning tasks and to give them considerable responsibility for their own learning rather than having the teacher tightly control their actions, which would be at odds with Hawaiian culture.

Further, teachers encouraged children to come up with responses cooperatively as opposed to having children speak one at a time, as is typical of most conventional classes. This way of speaking during lessons resembles the rules for participation in *talk story*, a typical way of communicating in Hawaiian culture. Specifically, students build joint responses during story time, either among themselves or together with the teacher. KEEP evaluations demonstrated that Hawaiian children's literacy and language learning gained substantially from the compatibility of the educational approach with their home and community experiences. The study of effective teaching practices for linguistically and culturally diverse students continues at the National Center for Research on Education, Diversity, and Excellence (CREDE) at the University of California, Berkeley (http://crede.berkeley.edu).

Source: Based on "The Effective Instruction of Comprehension: Results and Description of the Kamehameha Early Education Program," by R. G. Tharp, 1982, *Reading Research Quarterly, 17*(4), pp. 503–527.

Becoming Culturally Competent: The Key to Effective Teaching

Conflict may arise in situations where families and teachers do not have an inherent understanding of each other. Consider the following example:

> Decatur Elementary School, which serves a wide range of cultural groups, has a lending library to encourage primary grade children to read at home. After a few weeks, the library is bare because the families don't return the books. The European American teachers make insistent pleas for return of the books. The children begin to feel that their teachers are accusing them of stealing. But the children and their families don't understand; they assumed the books were meant for all the children in the neighborhood.

To resolve a conflict such as this, teachers must be well versed in effective cross-cultural communication. To provide the best education for all children, teachers need to become *culturally competent.*

Cultural Competence

cultural competence The ability to work effectively across cultural groups.

Cultural competence is the ability to work effectively across cultural groups (Olsen et al., 2007, p. 2) and to work respectfully with those who are different from oneself. Cultural

MyEducationLab

Go to the Building Teaching Skills and Dispositions section of Topic 10: Cultural & Linguistic Diversity in the MyEducationLab for your course and complete the activity entitled *Creating Culturally Diverse Environments to Facilitate Children's Development*. As you watch the videos and answer the accompanying questions, consider what teachers need to know and do to effectively teach in a culturally and linguistically diverse world.

competence is not a set of skills, but is instead a way of being—an openness to continual learning (Olsen et al., 2007). Although various characteristics demonstrate cultural competence, several are particularly applicable to teachers in diverse classrooms (E. W. Lynch, 2004; E. W. Lynch & Hanson, 2004). Some characteristics of cultural competence follow along with the ways they apply to the teachers at Decatur Elementary School and the lending library situation:

- *An awareness of their own cultural perspectives.* Teachers reflect on their own feelings about losing the books. They are mystified and a little upset. They invested time and money in the library and can't understand why it failed.
- *Appreciation and respect for individuals from other cultures.* Teachers do not prejudge children and families by their standards, realizing that more collectivist cultural groups view ownership of materials differently than individualistic ones.
- *A belief that cross-cultural interactions should be viewed as learning opportunities rather than challenges.* Teachers decide to find out what might have caused the misunderstanding, rather than giving up in frustration.
- *An ability to identify and use cultural resources.* Teachers seek the advice of leaders in the community to help them understand what happened.
- *An appreciation for the integrity and value of all cultures.* Teachers realize that sharing the books more widely is a valuable although different way of achieving their goal of making reading material available to children.
- *Willingness to continue to try to understand other people's perspectives.* Teachers decide to talk regularly with older children, family, and community members to discuss school happenings.
- *Flexibility and a sense of humor.* Teachers look back and laugh at how naïve their expectations were and how rigid their reactions.
- *Comfort with uncertainty.* The main lesson the teachers learn is that they aren't going to be right all the time; there are no simple answers to complex situations.

This list of competencies is prerequisite for becoming a truly successful teacher.

Cross-Cultural Communication

The foundation of cultural competence is the ability to communicate effectively with members of diverse cultural groups (E. W. Lynch, 2004). To foster good communication, teachers must develop an understanding of how various cultural groups use verbal and nonverbal means of communicating. These communication styles are another example of a cultural continuum such as those described earlier in the chapter. In this case, the continuum extends from high-context cultures to low-context cultures.

Communication in High-Context and Low-Context Cultures

Awareness of different communication styles will help you better appreciate the competence of children whose cultural background is different from your own and avoid misunderstandings in communicating with parents.

high-context culture Culture in which communication relies less on words and more on contextual cues, such as facial expressions, gestures, or other physical clues, to convey meaning.

low-context culture Culture that focuses on direct, logical, precise verbal communication.

Communication among those in **high-context cultures** relies less on words and more on contextual cues, such as facial expressions, gestures, or other physical clues, to convey meaning (E. W. Lynch, 2004). Examples of groups that are more attuned to nonverbal messages include Asian, American Indian, African American, Arab, and Latino groups.

In contrast, **low-context cultures** focus on direct, logical, precise verbal communication (E. W. Lynch, 2004). Low-context cultural groups include European Americans, Germans, and Scandinavians. Members of low-context cultures often become impatient if the speaker does not come to the point quickly or the communication is not direct (E. W. Lynch, 2004). Similarly, low-context communicators may be confused when they miss the meaning of gestures or unstated emotions.

Effective communication across these styles can be challenging. Shirley Brice Heath (1983, 1989) was one of the first to describe the consequences when children of high-context backgrounds encounter low-context schools. Her research identified situations such as the typical sharing time (show-and-tell), during which the teacher asks children what they did over the weekend. A low-context girl might chronologically describe events: "I went to my brother's soccer game. Then we went to McDonald's. Then my grandma came for dinner." This recitation meets the teacher's expectations of a clear, precise account. On the other hand, a high-context girl uses a more narrative, episodic style, which assumes that the listener can fill in the context. "My brother sang a funny song. Here's how it goes." When the child begins to sing, the teacher grows impatient, thinks the little girl's description doesn't make sense, and asks her to sit down. Think of the conflicting messages these children receive about the value of their experiences and their communication.

Difficulty communicating between low-context and high-context groups is not limited to teachers and children. Adults are even more steeped in their culture's ways of behaving than children. Imagine the difficulties that can arise when a high-context teacher attempts to talk to a low-context parent about a child's behavior problem. Or think of involving a high-context parent in creating an IEP for a child with a disability, which requires very accurate communication.

Verbal and Nonverbal Communication

A general description of high- and low-context communication styles only begins to describe the complexity of cross-cultural communication. Virtually every aspect of nonverbal communication can be misinterpreted. Of greater concern is that the failure to understand and respect cultural rules of behavior can offend and insult the very people with whom you are trying to communicate.

A number of nonverbal cues can lead to misunderstandings between people from different cultures. For example, allowing for or not allowing for personal space, when and why we smile, when we make eye contact or touch, and how we use silence and view time are all culturally relevant (Gonzalez-Mena, 2008). We have already discussed some of these, but a few others may be surprising. Consider smiling. Most of us assume that smiling is a universal, human way of communicating and it is. But like other behaviors, it can mean different things to different cultural groups. Russians, for example, smile when they are happy, not just to be friendly (Gonzalez-Mena, 2008). This could account for why Russians are often depicted in American movies as unusually dour. Some Asian groups, on the other hand, smile more often than Americans, even when embarrassed or unhappy (Gonzalez-Mena, 2008).

Silence can communicate volumes, but it is also interpreted through a cultural lens. Some Asian groups pause before speaking as a respectful sign that they are really listening (Gonzalez-Mena, 2008). Some European Americans may interpret such periods of silence to mean that the other person isn't listening or doesn't have anything to say.

A full discussion of the typical ways of communicating among various cultural groups is beyond the scope of this book. Consult the resources listed at the end of this chapter to learn more about the practices, beliefs, values, and communication styles of various groups. As you encounter diverse, changing groups of children, you will need to continually update your knowledge to improve communication and avoid misunderstandings with children and parents.

As we saw in the chapter-opening scenario, contradictions may arise because what professionals think is good for children and what families believe and value might be very different. Finding a middle ground that balances what professionals consider developmentally appropriate practice with what families consider culturally appropriate is paramount to effective teaching.

Culturally competent teachers are able to work effectively across cultural groups. What knowledge and skills do teachers need to be culturally competent?

MyEducationLab

Go to the Professional Perspectives section in Topic 10: Cultural & Linguistic Diversity in the MyEducationLab for your course and select the video entitled *Social and Cultural Contexts* and watch and listen to Sue Bredekamp discuss this topic.

Developmentally and Culturally Appropriate Practice

Just as we are all products of our cultural upbringings, we are also products of our cultural environments, such as our schools, summer programs we might have attended, and jobs we have held. Organizations including schools and child care programs also have their own cultures. When the culture—especially the rules for behavior—of the school or child care center is similar to that of children's families, their adaptation and ability to make sense of experiences is greatly eased. These children implicitly know much of what is expected even though they need to learn specific information such as the classroom routines. On the other hand, when there are cultural differences between the rules imposed at school and those imposed at home, children have greater difficulty adjusting. Not only do they have to learn the curriculum, but they also have to learn the implicit rules of discourse, such as "Respond promptly" or "Even though the teacher knows the answer, he will still expect you to answer the question." In this section, we address the sometimes controversial topic of the congruence of developmentally appropriate and culturally appropriate practices (Bredekamp & Copple, 1997; Hyun, 1998; Mallory & New, 1994; NAEYC, 2009a).

For culturally diverse children to be successful in school, teachers must explicitly teach the rules of behavior that children of the majority culture already know. Lisa Delpit (2006), an African American education professor and recipient of a MacArthur "genius" award, eloquently describes how the school culture is the "culture of power" and children who have access to its rules are more likely to succeed and gain access to the power in society. Delpit further describes how constructivist teaching, such as the developmentally appropriate practices advocated by NAEYC (2009a), may leave children of diverse cultural perspectives at a disadvantage. In her view, constructivism and other progressive education approaches reflect the dominant European American cultural perspective. For children of other cultural backgrounds, success in school may depend on their ability to become *bicultural*, that is, to learn the rules of the school culture while holding on to the rules of the home culture.

Like Delpit, many early childhood educators have questioned the cultural appropriateness of developmentally appropriate practice (Gonzalez-Mena, 2008; Hyun, 1998; Mallory & New, 1994; Sanders, Diehl, & Kyler, 2007). Let's think about this question in terms of what we've learned so far about culture.

The Culture of Early Childhood Education

Previously we presented a framework contrasting individualistic and collectivist cultures. Even a cursory examination of NAEYC's guidelines for developmentally appropriate practice (NAEYC, 2009a) or the association's accreditation standards (NAEYC, 2005e) reveals the degree to which these documents reflect the individualistic cultural orientation. Goals such as promoting independence, self-concept and self-esteem, discovery, and child-initiated activity permeate the standards. Overall, a "child-centered" philosophy underlies the approach.

A clear example of this orientation is the role of play in early childhood education (Zepeda et al., 2006). Children are encouraged to play and explore the environment and materials, and to play with adults and other children. On the other hand, in collectivist cultures, learning is directed by adults and depends more on observation of adults than on play, exploration, and child-chosen activity (Zepeda et al., 2006). In these cultures, objects such as toys are less important than social interaction, and play occurs mostly with siblings and other children. Consider that children from these diverse cultural orientations might gravitate toward peers in a free-flowing preschool classroom, instead of making independent choices of materials as expected by the teacher.

Another standard focuses on the importance of warm, nurturing relationships among teachers and children (NAEYC, 2005f, 2009a). But, the definition of "nurturing" behavior is also culturally influenced. For example, white European Americans might think that African American parents and teachers are harsh in the way they talk to or discipline their children (Hale, 1994). This "harshness" may reflect the need to help children of color navigate in a society that is often hostile to them. Consequently, those who observe this dynamic without this shared cultural perspective may not appreciate the love that is being conveyed. Similarly, African American teachers and parents may value children learning academics more than playing in preschool because they know these skills are essential for their children to succeed in school (Sanders et al., 2007).

The point of this discussion is to acknowledge that the prevailing standards for good practice in early childhood education described throughout this book and taught in most teacher education courses reflect the dominant culture of society. At the same time, these same standards require that programs be responsive to cultural and linguistic diversity. Given the diversity of children and families served today, teachers must help children to become **bicultural**, capable of operating successfully in both their home environment and the culture of the larger world. Accomplishing this goal requires teachers to resolve some of the inevitable contradictions that arise between what is considered developmentally appropriate and what is culturally appropriate.

Resolving Contradictions

As you have seen, when you are caring for and educating other people's children, you are being relied on to do so in a way that adheres to other people's beliefs and values. In the case of infants and toddlers, for example, how feeding, sleeping, dressing, and toileting are handled is not consistent across cultures. Likewise, with preschoolers and elementary grade children, teachers and families may disagree fundamentally on appropriate discipline as well as how and what children should be learning. Resolving these differences is an important part of working with children and families. Read the *Becoming an Intentional Teacher: Responding to Cultural Differences* feature for an example of how one teacher finds the balance between her ideas and family perspectives.

Professionals tend to think they know the right answers to situations that arise in the classroom. Yet in most situations, no one right answer exists. It is true that some practices, such as spanking children, are prohibited by law and others by licensing standards. In these cases, no compromise is possible. But more often, *both/and* solutions are more useful than *either/or* choices when such contradictions occur, as illustrated in the following real-life example (adapted from Bredekamp, 1997a, p. 47):

> Antonia Lopez was director of a program for Mexican American children and families in California. One of the program's primary objectives was to promote cultural congruity. As a relatively collectivist cultural group, Mexican Americans value cooperation over competition and this value was encouraged in the program. Another accepted cultural practice is the giving of gifts to express respect and appreciation.
>
> During the year, an uncomfortable situation arose. Parents began giving teachers gifts, and over time the gifts became more elaborate. The gift-giving escalated into a competition to see who could give the best gift, a direct contradiction of the program's goals. To resolve this dilemma, Antonia and her staff established two rules for dealing with the situation:
>
> Rule 1: You can't accept the gifts.
> Rule 2: You can't reject the gifts.
>
> With these rules in place, the staff had to arrive at an alternative solution. They agreed that rather than teachers' accepting gifts for themselves, gifts would be accepted on behalf of the school. Depending on the gift, it was shared by all the children, or displayed in a place of honor for everyone to appreciate. Soon families' gift-giving became less competitive and moved toward the goal of making the program a better place for everyone.

When teachers and families disagree on what is best for children, remembering Antonia's rules may be a good strategy. If teachers cannot accept the family's position for some

bicultural Capable of operating successfully in both the home environment and the dominant culture of the larger world.

Becoming an Intentional Teacher

Responding to Cultural Differences

Here's What Happened Before the new group of 3-year-olds started in the fall, I let all of the families know that the children were welcome to bring from home any kind of "comfort object" they would like. Emma brought her favorite bear, Cookie. When she went to get him from her cubby at nap time, Cookie was gone, and when she searched for Cookie, she found Linh curled up and ready for her nap, holding the bear. I explained to Linh that the bear was Emma's and gently took him from her and returned him to Emma. After this sequence of events repeated itself for several days, I talked to Linh's mother, Mrs. Pham, and asked for her help in getting her daughter to leave Emma's bear alone. Although her English was pretty good, she looked at me with total incomprehension at this request. During the next few weeks, I talked with a few Vietnamese people who had lived in the community for a while. From our discussions, I saw the part of the picture I had been missing. In the Vietnamese and most other Asian cultures, the idea of individual ownership is not as important as shared ownership and enjoyment of things.

I went back to Linh's mom to give her a sense of how Emma's experiences were different from Linh's. I also talked with Emma's mom about where Linh was coming from on this. At her mother's encouragement, Linh brought in a toy animal that she and her siblings play with at home. After a few weeks, Linh and Emma sometimes would have their animals play together in the dramatic play area.

Here's What I Was Thinking Getting the information from members of the Vietnamese community was very helpful, as was my own research about "collectivistic" cultures. Maybe I could have gotten to this eventually by talking with Linh's mother, but because I didn't understand the basis of her response, I didn't want to risk offending her as a result of my own ignorance. Once I had some understanding of collectivistic and individualistic cultures, I could talk with Mrs. Pham and see if we were communicating clearly. I felt it was important to go beyond just resolving the immediate conflict between the girls.

I also think it is important for the families as well as the children to learn about the differences in cultural values and practices. After all, the Vietnamese children will be experiencing the values predominant in European American culture throughout their lives in the United States, and ultimately the goal is for them to become sufficiently "bicultural" so that they can manage well in both worlds. At the same time, I was impressed with the way the Vietnamese children get along and share toys, which is a goal we have for all 3-year-olds. And the families who are natives to our area need to understand the new people who are joining our community too. In fact, because Linh and Emma are so young, I thought their families might gain more cultural knowledge from this situation than they would.

reason, but they also cannot reject it, then they will have to work toward an alternative solution—one that might better serve everyone's interests.

In the previous sections, we discussed cultural competence and ways of resolving contradictions between cultural and professional practices. In the sections that follow, we discuss how the curriculum for children should be culturally responsive.

Culturally Responsive Learning Goals

Awareness and responsiveness to diversity must be integrated across all areas of curriculum and teachers' relationships with children. Cultural diversity is a reality that drives responsive teaching and learning. In this section, we discuss goals for children's learning and ways of helping children achieve those goals. Culturally responsive teaching is designed to achieve three goals (Day, 2005; Derman-Sparks, 1992):

1. Fostering and supporting children's development and sense of identity within their own cultural group
2. Assisting children to experience and value diversity
3. Fostering children's critical thinking and countering stereotypes and biases (negative expressions toward groups).

Curriculum and teaching practices to help children achieve these goals need to be developmentally appropriate, that is, within the range of what is understandable and achievable for children. Next, we provide examples of age-appropriate expectations for each teaching and learning goal.

Culturally responsive curriculum and teaching promotes children's positive sense of their own identity, valuing of diversity, and critical thinking about stereotyping and bias.

Foster Children's Positive Identity within Their Own Group

As a teacher working with young children, one of your goals is to foster a positive sense of identity and help them develop a sense of self-worth. **Identity** refers to the characteristics that individuals recognize as constituting a sense of self and belonging to a group. Consider how important your own name is—it represents you and is a strong part of your identity. Teachers need to ensure that children's names are spelled and, most importantly, pronounced correctly. Fostering children's identity may also involve their bicultural and/or biracial identity (Wardle, 2008a). Because membership in a cultural/ethnic group has such a strong influence on identity, it is important for teachers to be aware of and support children's connection to their group.

In classrooms with children from multiple cultural or ethnic groups, teachers sometimes try to minimize the differences among students instead of acknowledging them. In an effort to discourage prejudice in the classroom, they may state proudly, "We don't see differences among children. We're color-blind here." Such statements deny the reality that children plainly see and experience. Teachers may think that talking about differences draws unnecessary attention to them and leads to prejudices. But this attitude, although well intentioned, actually has the opposite effect by denying vitally important aspects of children's identity (Derman-Sparks, 1992; Derman-Sparks & Edwards, 2010). Consider how you would feel if your significant other said, "I don't notice that you are a woman (or a man)."

MyEducationLab

Go to the Assignments and Activities section of Topic 10: Cultural & Linguistic Diversity in the MyEducationLab for your course and complete the activity entitled *Supporting Cultural Diversity in the Classroom*. As you watch the video and answer the accompanying questions, consider whether and how reading this book fosters children's positive identity.

One question European American teachers often ask is, "But what if all the children in the class are white?" This question itself reveals the confusion that exists between race and culture in our society because "white" is not a cultural group, and white-skinned people are members of many different cultural groups. In addition, close examination of this question reveals the perspective, discussed earlier in this chapter, that the white, majority group somehow doesn't have a culture (Derman-Sparks & Ramsey, 2006). Thus, it is important to help all children become aware of similarities and differences between themselves and others. Society sends countless messages about the superiority of white European Americans. Therefore, in supporting a positive sense of identity among these children, teachers must avoid contributing to feelings of entitlement and superiority to others who are not of the majority culture.

To foster positive identity, teachers must make an effort to ensure that the learning environment is welcoming to *every* child and reflects the identities and cultures of every child in the class. They can use photos or drawings of children with family members, audiotapes of family member's voices, as well as books, music, and other materials that reflect

identity The collection of characteristics that individuals recognize as constituting their sense of self and belonging to a group.

Table 6.2 Fostering Children's Positive Identity

Developmental Expectations	2- and 3-Year-Olds	4-Year-Olds	5-Year-Olds	6-Year-Olds	7- and 8-Year-Olds
Goal 1: To foster children's positive identity within their own cultural group	• Notice gender, racial, and other physical differences • See themselves as single, unique individuals ("I'm Tristan. You can't be Tristan.") • Do not have gender or racial constancy (think changing clothes may change their gender)	• Begin to see identity as including gender, race, and ethnicity • See themselves as part of family, but not part of larger group(s) • Rapidly absorb the cultural rules and language of home culture, and may think this is how everyone lives • Are vulnerable to effects of bias in society	• Have established fairly firm sense of gender and race identity that is unchanging • Experience increased possibility of being teased or rejected on basis of identity • Are increasingly influenced by prevailing negative stereotypes about themselves	• Have established core sense of identity including gender, race, ethnicity, physical ability or disability • Become more interested in associating with children who are like them (same gender) • Identify with families as member of larger racial or ethnic group • Can suffer damage to identity from effects of bias	• Have developed complex sense of identity, including how all elements of diversity add up to being one person (I am an African American boy, who speaks English and Creole, am Catholic, and like football) • Demonstrate interest in learning about own and other groups through oral history or biographies

Source: Adapted from pp. 118–120 of L. Derman-Sparks (1992). Reaching potentials through antibias, multicultural curriculum. In S. Bredekamp and T. Rosegrant (Eds.), *Reaching Potentials: Appropriate Curriculum and Assessment for Young Children*, Vol. 1. Washington, DC: NAEYC. Reprinted with permission from the National Association for the Education of Young Children.

children's cultural identity in a positive way. Table 6.2 lists developmental expectations to help children achieve the goal of a positive identity.

Experience and Value Diversity

Just as it is important to have a strong sense of self, it is important to value diversity in others. Related goals are the ability to respectfully ask about and comfortably adapt to differences (Derman-Sparks, 1992). The following sections describe how teachers can help children acquire the knowledge and disposition to learn about the similarities and differences among people.

Helping Children Learn about Differences

As our nation's history demonstrates, just exposing children to people of different races, cultures, abilities, or backgrounds is not sufficient to help them learn to value diversity. In fact, simple exposure can actually exacerbate negative reactions (Derman-Sparks, 1992).

Research on inclusion of children with disabilities, for example, finds that teachers need to work with all of the children to help a child with special needs be accepted and included in the group (Sandall, Schwartz, & Joseph, 2001). Preschoolers may think that if they talk to or play with a child in a wheelchair, they won't be able to walk either. Teachers need to actively support positive interactions among children and intervene when negative reactions occur. Teachers shouldn't deny differences with statements such as "He's just like you." Instead, an honest explanation is best: "You and Justin both like to move around the classroom and playground. You walk and run, while Justin uses his wheelchair to get where he wants to go."

Similarly, teachers should not admonish children for noticing differences. A teacher who says "It isn't nice to ask questions about other people" leaves a child without the correct information she or he needs. A child might ask, "Why is Derrick's skin darker than Deion's?" A more helpful explanation might be, "Children usually look like their parents, and Derrick's parents also have dark skin."

Likewise, dismissing children's anxieties or fears about differences may lead to avoidance or contribute to the development of prejudices. Consider the situation where 5-year-old Ariel says, "I don't like Mashiko because she don't speak English." Her teacher responds, "Oh, yes, you do. We're all friends here." Such a patronizing comment may lead Ariel to avoid or dislike Mashiko even more. Instead, the teacher might say, "Mashiko can speak Japanese and she's learning English. Maybe you can help her."

Avoiding Tourist Curriculum

In helping children to understand and value diversity, teachers need to avoid the "tourist curriculum." A **tourist curriculum** (Derman-Sparks & A.B.C. Task Force, 1989) is one in which a culture is visited as though it were an exotic destination where people dress, talk, dance, and eat differently before returning to the "normal" place where we all live. Here are some signs of a tourist curriculum (Derman-Sparks & A.B.C. Task Force, 1989):

- Trivializing by organizing activities around food or holidays
- Tokenism, such as having only one book about any cultural group
- Disconnecting diversity from the rest of the curriculum, such as having a one-week unit on a different culture or only discussing diversity on Martin Luther King Day
- Stereotyping groups, such as only using Native American images from the past or wearing traditional dress
- Misrepresenting groups such as using only books about Africa to teach about African Americans.

Integrating Diversity into the Curriculum

Developing relationships with people from diverse cultural groups and engaging in authentic experiences is the best way to help children experience and value diversity. Such opportunities also help children to understand that their perspective on the world is not necessarily the only or the best, but simply different. It is also important for children to understand that there are many languages in the world and no language is better than others. Regardless of the composition of their class or school, children today are exposed to diversity through the media, for example, seeing an African American president on television or listening to a Latino news anchor. Their wider community may also be more diverse than the immediate neighborhood and serve as a source of study. Table 6.3 lists developmental expectations to help children learn about and value diversity.

Cultural diversity can also be integrated throughout the curriculum. One way to help children experience and learn to value diversity is to teach overriding concepts that cut across cultural groups—we all need shelter, nourishment, friends, families, and exercise, but we meet these needs in various ways. In the primary grades, children begin to study history and the lives of people in their communities and beyond. Through oral histories, and reading biographies and autobiographies, children can learn about their own ethnic group and others.

Building each child's positive identity and helping them appreciate and value diversity lays the foundation for them to think critically about fair treatment of all people. This is the third goal of culturally responsive teaching.

tourist curriculum An approach in which a culture is visited as though it were an exotic destination where people dress, talk, dance, and eat differently before returning to the "normal" place where we all live.

Table 6.3 Assisting Children to Experience and Value Diversity

Developmental Expectations	2- and 3-Year-Olds	4-Year-Olds	5-Year-Olds	6-Year-Olds	7- and 8-Year-Olds
Goal 2: To assist children to experience and value diversity among people	• Notice and ask about other people's physical characteristics • Notice other children's cultural acts ("Makei speaks English and I speak Korean.") • May exhibit discomfort or fear about color differences or physical disabilities	• Increasingly aware of and interested in how they are alike and different from other children • Are influenced by societal norms about behavior ("Girls can't do that.") • May express discomfort based on differences (e.g., "You can't play. You don't speak English.")	• Demonstrate continued interest in racial, ethnic, gender, and ability differences and similarities • Demonstrate heightened awareness of themselves as members of a family • Absorb and use stereotypes to define, tease, or reject other children	• Have absorbed their family's ways of classifying and responding to differences among people • Use prevailing biases against children • Understand how others have an ethnic identity	• Are curious about other people's lives, religion, and traditions • Can begin to appreciate aspects of other cultures beyond surface features like holidays or foods • May feel connected to own group and experience tension or conflict with other children based on race, ethnic identity, or class

Source: Adapted from pp.118–120 of L. Derman-Sparks (1992). Reaching potentials through antibias, multicultural curriculum. In S. Bredekamp and T. Rosegrant (Eds.), *Reaching Potentials: Appropriate Curriculum and Assessment for Young Children*, Vol. 1. Washington, DC: NAEYC. Reprinted with permission from the National Association for the Education of Young Children.

Thinking Critically and Countering Biases and Stereotypes

We live in a society in which great strides toward tolerance, understanding, and acceptance have been made; yet racism, classism, sexism, homophobia, ageism, and other negative expressions of bias and forms of discrimination persist. As a result, children will often experience these biases and at times express them. **Biases** are negative feelings and expressions toward groups or individuals. Understanding bias means recognizing that differences are not problematic, but negative reactions to differences are.

bias Negative feelings and expressions toward groups or individuals.

anti-bias curriculum Curriculum that involves learning experiences and teaching strategies that are specifically designed to counter stereotyping and guard against expressions of bias.

Countering bias and stereotypes is an area in which teachers must be ever vigilant. The early childhood field has embraced the concept of an anti-bias curriculum. An **anti-bias curriculum** includes learning experiences and teaching strategies that are specifically designed to counter the stereotyping of diverse groups and to guard against expressions of bias (Derman-Sparks & Edwards, 2010; York, 2006). To achieve this goal, teachers must review books, videos, games, toys, and other curriculum materials to ensure that they do not perpetuate negative images of any group of people. Teachers must also pay attention to toys or materials that children bring from home.

In addition, teachers need to work with children to establish expectations for behavior that prohibit expressions of bias toward other people to ensure that race, gender, age, sexual orientation, appearance, and ability are never the subject of teasing or ridicule. This is an area where teachers must have a zero tolerance policy. They should intervene immediately when such behavior occurs, reminding children of the rules for how children are treated in the classroom. They also need to offer comfort to the child who is the target of biased behavior: "Yolanda, it was unfair and unkind for Caleb to say you can't play because you have brown skin. Caleb, remember that we treat people fairly in this school."

Following are three important considerations when handling discriminatory or biased behaviors (Derman-Sparks & A.B.C. Task Force, 1989; Derman-Sparks & Edwards, 2010):

1. *Don't ignore.* Teachers need to address any signs of bias head on. Ignoring discriminatory behaviors implies that they are acceptable. Consequently, the victim feels unsafe and the perpetrator feels supported, the opposite of what is desirable. For example, Ms. Eli is busy helping her first graders with math problems—when she hears Jasmine tell Hiroke that he has funny eyes. Ms. Eli contemplates saying nothing. Instead, she quietly says to Jasmine, "Everyone's looks are unique and different. Please remember that negative comments about people's appearance are hurtful and we don't allow that here."
2. *Don't excuse.* Sometimes teachers will avoid an uncomfortable situation by saying things like "He didn't really mean it." Excusing expressions of bias teaches one child that the behavior is okay and the victim of that behavior that he or she will not be protected. Instead, the teacher could have said, "Calling other people names hurts them, but it also makes you look mean and not very smart. If you have bad feelings about someone's behavior, we need to learn better ways for you to express them."
3. *Don't be afraid to intervene.* Fear and ignorance are among the biggest impediments to confronting and eliminating discrimination in our society. Teachers may be afraid that they will say the wrong thing to children, or that parents will be upset if they talk about race, culture, language, or socioeconomic conditions. However, unless they are part of the solution to addressing bias and discrimination in society, teachers must accept the responsibility for being part of the problem. For example, two children in Mr. Pinto's second-grade class are living in a homeless shelter. The children are teased for coming to school each day wearing the same clothes. Mr. Pinto privately arranges for them to receive clothing donations. He also talks with the teasers about their feelings, and finds out that some of the most verbal children are actually afraid of losing their homes, too.

Children's ability to think critically and counter stereotypes and bias vary considerably by age. Table 6.4 provides examples of developmental expectations for different age groups.

The three goals of culturally responsive teaching do not need to be addressed as separate subject areas or topics of study. Instead, these goals should be integrated throughout the learning environment and curriculum and in all aspects of teachers' interactions with children and their families.

Whereas it is true that all children are born ready to learn, it is equally true that their learning takes place within social and cultural contexts. Just as our cultural backgrounds influence our own development, behavior, and learning, developing an understanding of the role of each child's culture should influence what and how we teach young children. Although overall learning goals may be more or less the same across cultures, different teaching strategies may be required to help children achieve those goals.

To build successful relationships with children, you will need to take into account and learn about each child's cultural worlds because their experiences and home language are integral components of their identity. As a teacher, you will need to demonstrate respect and support for children's language and culture. You must also help children make sense of their new experiences in school by making connections to their prior knowledge and

Table 6.4 Fostering Critical Thinking and Countering Stereotypes and Biases

Developmental Expectations	2- and 3-Year-Olds	4-Year-Olds	5-Year-Olds	6-Year-Olds	7- and 8-Year-Olds
Goal 3: To foster children's critical thinking and counter stereotypes and bias	• Are learning to be comfortable with various differences through repeated supportive experiences • Are learning to express their feelings when they want something or are hurt	• Begin to develop the foundation for critical thinking by comparing fair and unfair behaviors and images • Can learn that teasing or rejecting others because of their identity is hurtful • Engage in simple problem solving and conflict resolution for dealing with teasing or rejection of others	• Can begin to think critically about stereotypes • Can begin to think critically about unfair and hurtful behaviors • Can problem solve about how to handle specific unfair behaviors or comments • With adult help, can work with other children to counter bias encountered in daily life (e.g., children compose a letter to request a ramp for their friend's wheelchair)	• Begin to compare correct and incorrect beliefs about groups (e.g., "Some people say men can't be teachers, but Mr. Clements is.") • Use respectful ways of asking about differences • Problem solve conflicts involving bias	• Can think about how their own ideas may reflect prevailing biases • Can use beginning reading skills to learn about stereotypes and biases related to gender, race, ethnicity, disabilities, and class • Engage in group actions to address actual discriminatory situations in their school or community

Source: Adapted from pp.118–120 of L. Derman-Sparks (1992). Reaching potentials through antibias, multicultural curriculum. In S. Bredekamp and T. Rosegrant (Eds.), *Reaching Potentials: Appropriate Curriculum and Assessment for Young Children*, Vol. 1. Washington, DC: NAEYC. Reprinted with permission from the National Association for the Education of Young Children.

experiences obtained in other cultural contexts. Culturally and linguistically appropriate ways of teaching are not "add-ons," they are integral dimensions of developmentally appropriate practice.

Revisiting Ms. Griffin's Classroom

At the beginning of this chapter, we saw how Stacey struggled in her relationship with families during her first year of teaching. Now that we have explored the many ways culture influences thinking and behavior, we can revisit Stacey's situation and see how it could be improved for everyone involved.

Rather than giving up in frustration, Stacey attends a professional conference and takes workshops on cultural and linguistic diversity. This motivates her to do some reading and talking with the more experienced staff members at her center. These experiences cause Stacey to reexamine some of her prior assumptions and, in turn, change some of the ways she teaches.

Her first step is to alter her daily schedule so the beginning of the day is an informal time for her to talk and play with small groups or individual children. Before she calls for a group gathering to sing or tell the children the plans for the day, Stacey waits for all of the children to arrive. This schedule means that she is no longer frustrated if parents bring their children late.

Stacey reflects on the disagreements she has been having with families over carrying and dressing their children. She recognizes that these differences are quite minor. Consequently, she decides not to interfere with close family relationships by imposing her views of what is best for children's development.

Stacey explains to families that she doesn't always have time to feed each child individually, so at times she gives them finger food. In response to parents' concerns, however, she promises that she will help feed the children as much as possible. In general, she finds that once their families leave for the day, the children tend to model each other and function more independently.

In her conflict with Mrs. Arguenta, Stacey realizes that Mrs. Arguenta was showing respect by refusing to call her by her first name. Stacey comes to see that Mrs. Arguenta has a legitimate point of view about teaching Ilsia to use the toilet. She tries using the skills she learned for resolving conflict. She agrees to try Mrs. Arguenta's strategies, while Mrs. Arguenta agrees that they may not be entirely successful because Stacey has a group of children to supervise.

Finally, Stacey explains to Mrs. Arguenta that because of licensing laws, the center can only release a child to an adult; for that reason, they cannot have Ilsia's 10-year-old sister pick her up. This is an issue where compromise is not possible. Mrs. Arguenta presents a list of adult family members who have permission to pick up Ilsia.

As we see from the encounter between Stacey and Mrs. Arguenta, cultural competence and cross-cultural communication are key elements of effective practice in early childhood education.

MyEducationLab

To assess your understanding of how the role of culture influences instruction, go to the Book Specific Resources section in the MyEducationLab for your course, select *Effective Practices in Early Childhood Education*, Chapter 6 of the Study Plan, and then complete the multiple choice questions and activities.

Chapter Summary

- Culture can be defined as the values, beliefs, and patterns of behavior, both explicit and implicit, that are passed on from generation to generation. All learning and development occur in and are influenced by social and cultural contexts.
- A framework for studying culture is to understand that the beliefs, values, and behaviors that characterize cultural groups vary along a continuum from individualistic to collectivist.
- Teachers need to become aware of their own cultural perspectives as the first step toward becoming culturally competent.
- Knowledge of culture is important because without it, teachers can misunderstand children, inaccurately assess children's competence, and/or fail to promote children's learning.
- Cultural competence is the ability to work and communicate effectively, both verbally and nonverbally, with members of diverse cultural groups.
- Given the diversity of children and families served today, teachers must help children to become bicultural, capable of operating successfully in both their home environment and the larger world. Helping children become bicultural requires teachers to resolve some of the inevitable contradictions that arise between what is considered developmentally appropriate and what is culturally appropriate.
- Culturally responsive learning goals for children are to foster and support children's development and sense of identity within their own cultural group, to assist children to experience and value diversity, to foster children's critical thinking, and to counter stereotypes and biases (negative expressions toward groups).

key terms

acculturation
anti-bias curriculum
bias
bicultural
collectivist cultural groups
culture
cultural competence
dual-language learner
ethnicity
high-context culture
identity
individualistic cultural groups
low-context culture
tourist curriculum

readings & websites

Derman-Sparks, L., & Edwards, J. O. (2009). *Anti-bias education: Empowering our children and ourselves.* Washington, DC: NAEYC.

Espinosa, L. M. (2010). *Getting it right for young children from diverse backgrounds: Applying research to improve practice.* Upper Saddle River, NJ: Pearson.

Lynch, E. W., & Hanson, M. J. (Eds.). (2004). *Developing cross-cultural competence: A guide for working with children and their families* (3rd ed.). Baltimore: Paul H. Brookes Publishing.

York, S. (2006). *Roots and wings: Affirming culture in early childhood programs.* Upper Saddle River, NJ: Pearson.

California Tomorrow
www.californiatomorrow.org

Center for the Study of Biracial Children
www.csbchome.org

Multicultural Children's Literature
www.multiculturalchildrenlit.com

National Association for Bilingual Education
www.nabe.org

National Association for Multicultural Education
www.name.org

observe, reflect, decide

1. Reflect on how your own cultural experiences create a lens through which you see and evaluate the world and other people's (especially children's) behavior. Ask yourself questions such as these:
   - How do people in my family and community show respect for elders?
   - How do we care for children?
   - How do we meet and greet new acquaintances?
   - How do we express strong emotions?
   - How do we feel about issues like time and personal space?
2. Put yourself in a situation where you do not understand the language. Visit a bilingual or language-immersion classroom. Rent a foreign language movie or watch a non-English television program. How do you feel in these situations? What clues do you use to try to understand what is being said? Now think about what it would be like to be a young child who is just learning a new language. Think of ways that you can help make that child's world comprehensible.
3. Visit classrooms that represent diverse configurations of children (ethnically diverse, all children of color, and all white). Observe the environment and teachers' behaviors. Reflect on the extent to which teachers are helping children develop a positive identity, value diversity, and think critically about biases.
4. Your program director has put you in charge of organizing an event around holiday time that will involve children and families. She wants the event to celebrate the diversity of students and families in your class, but cautions you that you need to be sensitive to all of the children's backgrounds and family dynamic.
   - What will the event be and when will it be held?
   - What will you have the children do to help you prepare for the event?
   - How can you best celebrate the diversity of the student population in your class without resorting to a "tourist" curriculum?
   - What would you do about a child whose family does not celebrate holidays for religious reasons?

part three

how to teach

Intentional Teaching

7 Building Effective Partnerships with Families

Thinking Ahead

1. What do we know about families today? What is the role of families in children's development? How does the larger context affect family functioning?
2. What are reciprocal relationships between teachers and families, and how are they best developed? What are the elements of family-centered practice?
3. What are effective strategies for maintaining two-way communication with families?
4. How can teachers involve families in their children's care and education?
5. How can teachers build partnerships with families to achieve both their goals and parents' goals for children?

Vilma Suarez has worked as a toddler teacher in an Early Head Start center for 3 years. She loves her job, but her days can be exhausting. Today was one of those days. Before the children even arrived, Vilma had a meeting with the early intervention team to discuss Aiya's individualized family service plan (IFSP). Aiya is deaf, and the team wants Vilma to begin signing with her. Aiya's mother is silent throughout the meeting. She is a new immigrant and feels threatened by this powerful group of professionals. Vilma is patiently working to gain her trust, beginning with sitting by her at the meeting and being available to talk about other things besides Aiya's disability.

When Mrs. Vacaro drops 2-year-old Tomas off, he sobs and clings to her, and Mrs. Vacaro is clearly torn about leaving him. Vilma speaks softly to Tomas and gets his

attention with his favorite stacking toy. Finally, Mrs. Vacaro is able to pry him loose and reluctantly departs. Vilma tries to call her during the day to reassure her, but Mrs. Vacaro attends school and cannot be reached on her cell phone.

The assistant teacher supervises the children's naptime while Vilma conducts a parent conference. The conference is difficult because she has to talk to Mr. Henderson about his son's out-of-control biting. Mr. Henderson angrily says, "Just smack him. That's what I do." Vilma realizes that this situation will have to be negotiated carefully.

At 5:00 PM, when Mrs. Vacaro comes in clearly dreading the worst, Vilma greets her with the news that Tomas had great fun today playing with his friends, ate well, and even said two new words. As Vilma reassures her about how well Tomas is doing, Mrs. Vacaro sighs and fights back tears. She stoops to cuddle Tomas, and Vilma turns to talk with Marcy's grandmother and David's father, who have just arrived.

During her bus ride home, Vilma reflects on her day. She remembers that when she began her career, she was excited about working with very young children. Because she has three children of her own and helped parent her younger siblings, she felt confident working with babies and toddlers and was relieved to have a job where she didn't have to work with adults. Vilma shakes her head, remembering how naïve she was. She now knows that working with children is only one part of her job. Working with their families is the bigger challenge. But doing so is also very rewarding. She understands that by learning from and with families, her contributions to children's lives will last long after they leave her classroom. ▲

Whatever your age, if someone asked you to picture the most important people in your life, it is likely that images of your family members would come to mind. Perhaps you would picture the people you grew up with, or your spouse/partner and children. Some of you might picture both your nuclear family including your siblings and your extended family of cousins, aunts, uncles, and grandparents. Families play essential roles in every aspect of human development through the life span. During early childhood, however, families are the primary context for children's development and learning, with child care and early education settings playing a secondary, albeit critically important, role. Given that these two contexts—families and early childhood programs—are the two main environments in which children develop and learn, it is essential for teachers and parents to work in concert if children are to develop to their fullest potential.

Because young children are inherently connected to their families, early childhood teachers work with children *and* families. The younger the child, the stronger the connection to family and, therefore, the closer the relationship between teacher and parent must be. Most early childhood educators enter the field because of their interest in teaching young children; initially, they may not grasp the importance of developing skills to work with families. In fact, teachers report that working with families is among the areas where they feel least prepared and need the most help (Early & Winton, 2001). Throughout this book, we use the terms *families* and *parents* to mean those people who are primarily responsible for the children you teach whoever they are—parents, stepparents, grandparents, guardians, foster families, or other household members.

This chapter describes how teachers establish reciprocal relationships with families. We begin by painting a picture of today's families, their exquisite diversity, and the challenges they face in providing for their children. Next, we describe the nature of productive, reciprocal partnerships between teachers and the principles of family-centered practice. We describe effective strategies for communicating with families and involving them in their children's education. We also acknowledge that some strategies are not effective in all situations; relationships with families are not always smooth. Therefore, the chapter provides a framework for building partnerships that is effective in resolving the inevitable conflicts that arise when working with families of young children.

Families today come in all shapes and sizes. How would you describe the membership in your family? How does it compare with the family your parents grew up in or that of your grandparents?

Understanding Today's Families

One can hardly read a newspaper or watch a television program today without hearing dire warnings about the state of the American family and the myriad threats it faces. While it is true that families in the early 21st century confront many challenges, it is equally true that the family is and has always been a dynamic, resilient, and effective institution for nurturing and acculturating each new generation.

What is a family? This may seem like a fairly easy question to answer, but it is not. Each of you, no doubt, has your own definition of family based on your own experiences. Throughout your career as a teacher, you will work with children who experience a wide range of family configurations, as discussed next.

Welcoming Diverse Family Types

Louise's child care class consists of fifteen 3- to 5-year-olds. Four of the children live with their mothers and fathers; Blake and Debra are only children, Madeline is the youngest of four, and Stephen is the eldest of three. Five children live with their mothers only, but among them Joseph and Lauren are in shared custody arrangements and split days of the week living with their fathers. Both Joseph and Lauren have stepmothers as well as stepsiblings. Lauren also has a baby half-brother. Of the other three children who live with their mothers, Marin doesn't know her father at all, and Jackson has infrequent contact with his biological father. Jeanine's mom is serving in the military overseas. Marta lives with her two dads who are a gay couple, and Logan lives with his two moms. Kim lives with his parents and siblings and also his paternal grandparents, aunt, and one cousin. David has lived with his grandmother and two brothers since his mother died, and his father is in jail. The diverse family configurations represented in Louise's class are typical of America today: two-parent, single-parent, families of divorce, blended/stepfamilies, extended families, and gay/lesbian families.

Despite statistics and experience to the contrary, many people still think of the family as consisting of two first-time married parents and their biological or adopted children, known as the nuclear family. In looking at how children grow up today, however, as depicted in Figure 7.1, we see that fewer than half of children live in nuclear families. Single-parent families account for 28%, with stepfamilies, also called blended families, representing 16%, and 6% living in extended families. Extended families are defined as a family unit where two or more generations of close family relatives live together in one household. In early childhood programs, conversations and curriculum often focus on children's experiences in their families, but because families today have changed so much, teachers need to be careful not to make assumptions about their students' families.

Contrary to popular belief, there has never been a "typical" or "traditional" family structure in America (Welch, 2007). Various factors contribute to changing family structures over time. For example, until quite recently in history, women died in childbirth at alarming rates, and men also died young in wars or of disease. Therefore, although divorce was less common, many children grew up in single-parent families or blended families. Consider for a moment your own experiences of family, and

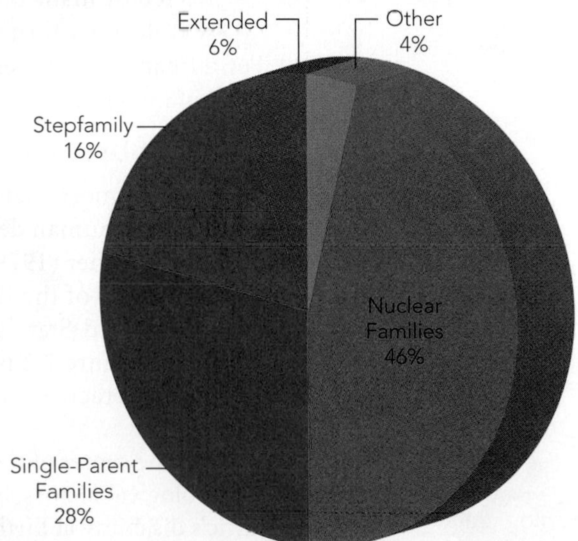

Figure 7.1 Where Children Live
Source: U.S. Census Bureau, 2005.

those of your parents and grandparents. While I grew up in a "traditional" nuclear family of married parents and two children, my father was raised by his widowed father, and my mother had four half-siblings. My husband's father was orphaned and raised by an aunt; his mother was raised by her grandmother.

Regardless of your own family experiences or values, as a teacher you will encounter many different family configurations. The likelihood of successfully working with families will increase if you accept the following assumptions:

- Families are diverse in many ways: composition, culture, religion, economic status, work, mobility, and sexual orientation.
- Families are not good or bad; they are different and unique.
- Families, with rare exceptions, want the best for their children, regardless of the difficult circumstances they may be trying to overcome.
- All families have strengths and resources, hopes and dreams for their children, just as all families face challenges.
- It is not your right to pass judgment on families. You do not need to agree with families at all times, but you cannot reject a child's family and at the same time successfully care for and educate the child.

The more you know about the intricacies of family functioning, the more likely you will be able to put the above assumptions into practice. In the next section, we describe the theoretical perspectives that help explain how families function and change.

Understanding Family Dynamics

Joelynn and Jeff Robeson already have 18-month-old twins when their third child, Eric, is born with spina bifida, a physical disability that requires repeated hospitalizations and considerable care. Just when Joelynn and Jeff are beginning to adjust to the strain on their marriage of caring for three young children, including one with special needs, the factory where Jeff works shuts down and he is out of a job. Suffering from depression and alcohol abuse, Jeff leaves Joelynn without child support, forcing her to seek public assistance. After a while, however, the rules for continuing on public assistance require Joelynn to work full time, and she must leave her three young children in the care of her sister, who also has two preschool-age children. Joelynn suffers from the stresses of trying to care for her children and support them on her minimum wage salary.

As is true for every family, the development of each member of the Robeson family is affected by many different factors, both internal and external to the family. To analyze these factors, we turn to two theoretical perspectives: Bronfenbrenner's ecological theory of human development and family systems theory. Each of these theories, described in the following sections, helps explain family dynamics.

Bronfenbrenner's Ecological Model of Human Development

One of the most useful theories for understanding the influence of social and cultural contexts on human development is the ecological model developed by psychologist Urie Bronfenbrenner (1979, 2004). Bronfenbrenner (1917–2005) was one of the key conceptual founders of the Head Start program. The comprehensive services that are the hallmark of Head Start can be attributed, in part, to the influence of Bronfenbrenner's thinking. Figure 7.2 presents **Bronfenbrenner's ecological model**, which describes the diverse, interactive contexts that influence the development of individuals and families over time.

Bronfenbrenner's ecological model Describes the diverse, interactive contexts that influence the development of individuals and families over time.

At the center of the model is the individual whose development is influenced not only by biological factors, but also by cognition and social interaction. In the Robeson family, Eric's disability at birth is a biological contributor to his development, but other variables also contribute to his individual development and mediate his disability. For example, Eric's personal characteristics, such as his above average intelligence and his lively personality, attract the positive attention of everyone he meets.

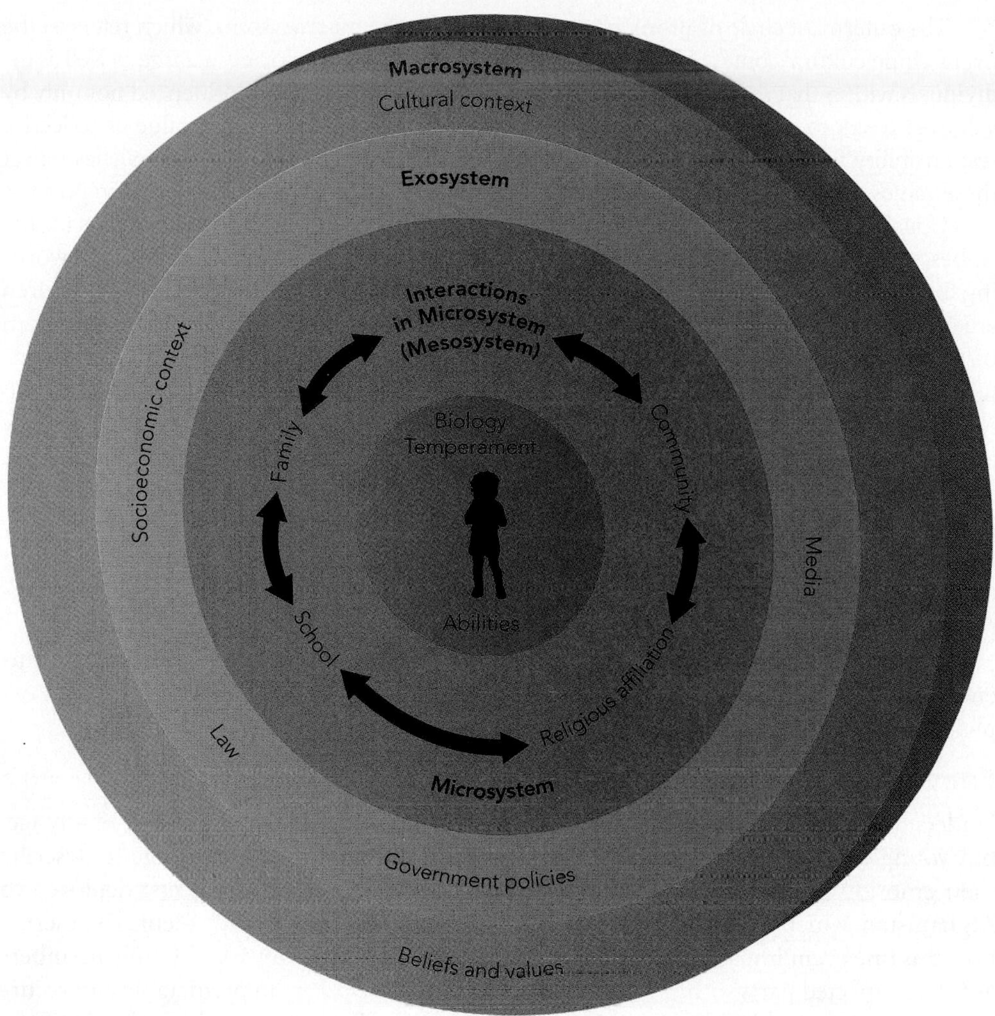

Figure 7.2 Bronfenbrenner's Ecological Model

The environment surrounding an individual from birth and beyond plays significant interactive roles in a child's development. According to Bronfenbrenner, the context closest to the individual, called the **microsystem**, consists of the interactions in which people are most directly involved. These include the family, school and child care programs, religious institutions, and the community. In the Robeson family, Eric was born into a family that was already caring for very young twins. His siblings' existence was part of the context into which he was born, but his birth and his disability dramatically changed the family's context. As a result, a member of the extended family was needed to provide child care; this event is another part of his microsystem. Caring for three additional young children, however, would have profound effects on Eric's aunt's family as well. This is an example of what Bronfenbrenner calls the **mesosystem**—how events that occur within the microsystem interact and affect each other.

The **exosystem** consists of society's larger systems and policies that impact the individual and elements of the microsystem. The exosystem represents all of the various systems that affect the development of human beings over the course of a lifetime. These systems include economics, education, the media, politics, communication, health, and the law. Elements of the exosystem interact to have major consequences for individuals. In the case of the Robeson family, economic factors beyond their control seriously affected the family. The factory closing led to Jeff's unemployment, which eventually led to the family's requiring public assistance. The politics and laws governing eligibility for public support made it necessary for Joelynn to work outside the home and place the children in child care.

microsystem The interactions in which people are most directly involved, including the family, school and child care programs, religious institutions, and the community.

mesosystem How events that occur within the microsystem interact and affect each other.

exosystem Society's larger systems and policies that affect the development of human beings over the course of a lifetime, including economics, education, the media, politics, communication, health, and the law.

The outermost circle of Bronfenbrenner's model is the **macrosystem**, which refers to the overarching cultural context of the values and beliefs that influence society at large as well as individuals within that society. American society, for example, is strongly influenced not only by values of freedom and individual rights and responsibilities, but also by the value of collective responsibility for its neediest members. As a result, our institutions and social policies reflect these values, such as laws regarding provision of public assistance for families living in poverty.

Consider how changes in various elements of the exosystem could alter outcomes for the Robeson family and their children, especially Eric. With Jeff out of work and Joelynn working for minimum wage, the family's income is below poverty level and, therefore, the children are eligible for Early Head Start. This federal program provides child care for children from birth to age 3, early intervention services for Eric, and family support services. The early intervention team helps Joelynn learn how to support Eric's development at home. They put Jeff in touch with mental health counselors to help him deal with his depression, and they also connect him to Alcoholics Anonymous and career retraining. Through the counseling and guidance offered by Early Head Start, Jeff gets a maintenance job in the Head Start program while he attends computer school. Joelynn begins training as a nurse's aide, inspired by her newfound abilities to care for Eric's health. The twins thrive in the social atmosphere at the child care center. The family reunites and its emotional as well as financial security improves. The changes in Eric's family will have lasting benefits for his development as well.

Now that you have seen how various systems external to the family interact to influence the family and children's development, we focus on family systems theory, which explains the internal workings of family dynamics.

Family Systems Theory

Understanding family dynamics is an important aspect of working with children of any age, but young children in particular because they don't always have the language to describe their emotions and needs. Rodney may be angry because his father was just deployed to Afghanistan, which makes his mother sad and nervous and his big sister silent. To describe how this one event impacts the entire family, **family systems theory** views family members as interconnected parts with each member influencing the others in predictable and recurring ways (Christian, 2006; Welch, 2007). Family systems theory focuses on explaining family behavior, that is, why individual family members behave as they do in relation to one another and to those outside the family. Understanding how families function as systems can help teachers serve diverse children and build family partnerships more effectively.

Family systems theory describes some common characteristics of families, including boundaries, roles, rules, hierarchy, climate, and equilibrium (Christian, 2006). Each of these characteristics can be described on a continuum. For example, all families have rules regarding the acceptable behavior of members; some families operate according to strict and inflexible rules, whereas others have few rules or apply rules inconsistently. Table 7.1 presents characteristics of family systems, what they mean, and implications for effective teaching practice. Because each dimension of family functioning is particularly influenced by the cultural beliefs and practices of the family and community, teachers need to view family variability on these dimensions as differences rather than positives or negatives (Christian, 2006).

In the previous sections, we have seen how families influence and are influenced by social, cultural, and political contexts. We have also seen how different families' characteristics influence their behavior toward their children and in relation to teachers and school. In the next section, we describe some of the challenges confronting America's families today.

macrosystem The overarching cultural context of the values and beliefs that influence society at large as well as individuals within that society.

family systems theory Views family members as interconnected parts with each member influencing the others in predictable and recurring ways.

Understanding Family Circumstances and Challenges

Families today face many challenges in providing the best care and education for their children. We regularly hear dire predictions about children *at risk*. This term is widely used although it has no consistent definition and often tends to stigmatize children, families, and/or communities (Moore, 2006). Because families are the most critical setting for children's development, risk factors affecting families such as poverty, single parenthood, and low levels of

Table 7.1 Characteristics of Family Systems

Dimension	Explanation	Implication and Example
Boundaries	Limitations on what or who is considered in or out of the family. Some families are open to new people and new ideas, whereas others tend to be more closed and restrictive. Families at one extreme may share too much information about the private workings of the family, whereas extremely closed families may conceal information such as domestic violence or substance abuse.	Respecting a family's boundaries is an important skill of effective early childhood professionals. When the Robeson family enrolled in the Early Head Start program, the staff found that Joelynn was open to sharing her problems and seeking help, but Jeff at first felt the program was too intrusive into his personal business.
Roles	In every family, individual members have roles—the parts that individuals typically play in relation to others. Most of us readily remember our role in the family. Were you the baby, the peacemaker, or the rescuer?	These roles have powerful lasting effects on development that are often played out in school as well. For example, 7-year-old Deon's parents have addiction problems. From a young age, he has felt responsible for taking care of them and his younger sister. Deon's teacher values his serious attitude toward his work, but wishes that he didn't worry so much about his parents and could be more carefree.
Rules	The standards or traditions that dictate correct behavior in various situations and how we relate to one another. Defining and passing on rules for behavior is the major function of cultural groups; therefore, rules are, by definition, culturally determined.	Differences in teachers' and parents' expectations about rules often require negotiation. Deon's parents think he should act like a man and contribute to the family rather than play outside or spend time with friends.
Hierarchy	The decision making, control, and power within the family, who is in charge, and how power is distributed and used. Like rules, hierarchy is strongly influenced by culture. In some families, parents share responsibility equitably; in others, hierarchy is determined by gender, with fathers and mothers making decisions about different aspects of parenting. In some groups, power is vested in elders. Hierarchies change over time.	Teachers need to be aware of family hierarchy because so many interactions involve decisions, and effective family partnerships and family-centered practice require the sharing of power. In the Robeson family, Jeff was the one in charge during the early years of the marriage, but when he lost his job, power shifted to Joelynn as the breadwinner and single parent.
Climate	The emotional and physical environment in which a child grows up. Emotionally close families can compensate to some extent for threatening physical environments, and the opposite is also true.	The classroom climate needs to be emotionally safe and secure for all children. The Robeson family lived in a physically safe neighborhood, but the tensions between the parents created a hostile emotional climate in the home for a time.
Equilibrium	The sense of balance or consistency that family members experience. Growth and change, both positive and negative, are inevitable aspects of human development, but too much inconsistency creates confusion and resentment.	Teachers can help work with families during times of change to maintain stability and consistency. For example, at the Early Head Start center, the Robeson twins were kept in the same class with the same teachers for 2 years during the period of upheaval in their family. Then the Early Head Start staff worked with the Head Start program to transition the twins smoothly to preschool.

Source: Based on "Understanding Families: Applying Family Systems Theory to Early Childhood Practice," by L. G. Christian, 2006. *Young Children*, *61*(1), pp. 12–20.

parental education (which tend to co-occur) are found to be related to poor outcomes for children (Moore, 2006). Other factors that place families at risk include family dysfunction, abuse, parental mental illness, substance abuse, and illness (Moore, 2006). Community risk factors create challenges for families as well; these include poverty, crime, unemployment, and high levels of teen parenthood (Moore, 2006).

Families at Risk

Among these challenges, the largest risk factor is poverty. Consider, for example, that children living in poverty are less likely to have access to health care. In fact, according to statistics compiled by the Children's Defense Fund (CDF, 2007), 9 million children (one in nine) have no health insurance, even though 87% of these children have a working parent. African American children are twice as likely as white children not to have medical insurance. In addition, homelessness is on the rise; in fact, families with children are the fastest growing group of homeless people (Congressional Research Service, 2005).

In 2004, 13 million American children (one in six) were poor, representing an increase of 12% since 2000 (CDF, 2007). Growing up in poverty is related to many negative outcomes for children including increased likelihood of abuse, neglect, school failure, delinquency, and violence. Child poverty continues to grow despite the fact that most poor children live in working families (CDF, 2007). Moreover, a disproportionate number of children of color live in poverty (CDF, 2007):

- Nearly 1 in 3 American Indian children
- More than 1 in 3 African American children
- Nearly 1 in 3 Latino children
- One in 10 Asian children
- Nearly 1 in 10 white, non-Latino children.

Cumulative risk factors increase the likelihood of poor outcomes. High rates of divorce contribute to child poverty because single parents, particularly single mothers, are more likely to have low incomes. Economic stress also affects two-parent families. Almost 60% of mothers of children under age 5 are in the workforce, which adds the cost of child care for many financially strapped families.

Resilient Families

Despite difficult family circumstances and challenges, it is important to note that poverty, neglect, and discrimination do not necessarily set children up for failure. Families' assets or strengths (i.e., their protective factors) can counter the potential negative effects of risks (Moore, 2006). Although public attention tends to focus on all that is wrong with the American family, compelling evidence exists that many families—including those living in the most difficult circumstances—have inner strengths that counter risk factors and predict positive results for children (Moore, Chalk, Scarpa, & Vandivere, 2002).

Research finds that contemporary families have high levels of important family strengths: closeness, concern, caring, and interaction (Moore et al., 2002). Moreover, a positive, caring relationship with a parent can mitigate many risk factors (Brazelton & Greenspan, 2000; Garbarino, 1995). Similarly, ongoing positive relationships with other adults, especially caregivers and teachers, are important protective factors (Howes & Ritchie, 2002; Hyson, 2004; Pianta & Stuhlman, 2003).

Programs such as Head Start and Early Head Start serve our nation's neediest families. Early childhood teachers work closely with families and can be resources to help strengthen and build resilience in families facing challenges.

Child Trends (2007) finds that about 10% of children growing up in two-parent, low-conflict families have problems, whereas 20% of all other children experience problems. Their conclusion is somewhat contrary to the popular images of at-risk children and families today: Most kids do fine. Some children with highly stable families will have problems; more children whose families experience several risk factors will struggle. The take-away message with regard to risk and protective factors is that there are no guarantees. Poor outcomes are not inevitable for children placed at risk, just as low risk is not a guarantee of success in life. Given the critical role of families in children's development and learning, the simple conclusion is that anything we can do to strengthen families is a good idea (Child Trends, 2007).

One effective strategy for strengthening families is parent education. Parents often need help and child development information to enhance their parenting. Parent education can reduce family risk, increase resilience, and be an especially effective deterrent to child abuse (Child Welfare Information Gateway, 2008).

Because they work directly with families as well as children, early childhood educators have the opportunity as well as the responsibility to strengthen families. In the next section, we address ways teachers can build reciprocal relationships with families toward the goal of achieving better outcomes for all children.

Effective Teaching
Effective partnerships between teachers and families are based on two-way communication and reciprocal relationships.

Building Reciprocal Relationships with Families

In her book on partnerships with parents, Janis Keyser (2006, p. xi) describes her development as an early childhood professional as progressing through three stages of relationship with parents: save the child, save the parents, and drawing on parents' expertise. These stages are identical to my own experience and that of many other early childhood teachers.

Like many others in the early childhood profession, Keyser chose this field because of her love of children. In the earliest days of her practice, when she encountered a child whose needs were great, she entered the first stage: "save the child." Inevitably there would be several children whom she thought if only she could save them from their parents, their lives would be better. She quickly realized the futility of this approach and moved on to the next stage of her development, which she calls "Save the parents." Realizing that it would be impossible to save all of the children from their parents, she determined to fix the parents. She thought that if she taught them everything early childhood professionals know, they would become better parents. Soon, however, she realized that this notion fails to recognize that families bring unique knowledge, experiences, goals, resources, and rich culture to their roles. In fact, she concluded that families add unique value to the knowledge of early childhood teachers. In the final stage of development in her relationships with families, she rejected both goals of saving children and saving parents in favor of drawing on parents' expertise to work in partnerships with families that are in children's best interests.

MyEducationLab

Go to the Book Specific Resources in the MyEducationLab for your course and select Author Interviews in Chapter 7 to watch and listen to the video *Building Relationships with Families*. What does Sue Bredekamp say about the importance of building reciprocal relationships with families?

Keyser's story about her own development as a teacher mirrors how the profession's views of parent–teacher relationships have evolved over time (Powell & Gerde, 2006; Powell & O'Leary, 2009). In the past, and even today in some educational settings, teachers thought that they could care for and educate children almost in spite of their parents. Today, however, the prevailing view of effective practice requires two-way communication, reciprocal relationships, and partnerships between teachers and families (Powell & O'Leary, 2009). Before describing the elements of effective partnerships, we need to clarify the distinct roles of teachers and parents in the lives of young children.

Clarifying Roles of Teachers and Parents

One of the challenges to building effective partnerships for early childhood teachers is that the younger the child in their care, the more blurred the lines become between parenting and teaching. Nevertheless, there are definite distinctions between the roles, as contrasted in Table 7.2. These distinctions help explain why both perspectives are essential in providing high-quality care and education for each child. Moreover, children know the difference

Table 7.2 Contrasting Roles of Teachers and Parents

Teacher's Role in a Child's Life	Parents' Role in Their Child's Life
Relationship is short term.	Relationship lasts a lifetime.
Relationship develops mainly during program hours; responsibilities do not extend beyond.	Bonding begins at birth, some might say even earlier; responsibilities extend 24 hours a day for many years.
Child seldom has teacher's exclusive attention.	Child often has one-on-one time with parents, and shares them only with siblings.
Teacher is *an* important person in the child's life.	Parents are *the* most important people in their child's life.
Teacher tends to be objective about the child's behavior and development.	Parents tend to be emotional and biased about their child's behavior and development.
Teacher is unlikely to know the child's extended family members, neighbors, or friends; Child usually does not know the teacher's family or communities.	Parents are the hub of their child's nuclear family. They link the child to the extended family and various communities.
Teacher is trained in and expected to use professional early childhood knowledge and guidelines more than cultural, social, or personal preferences in interactions with the child.	Parents are not usually trained in child development; they usually follow cultural, social, and personal preferences in raising their child.

Source: From *Relationships, the Heart of Quality Care: Creating Community among Adults in Early Care Settings,* by A. C. Baker and L. A. Manfredi/Petitt, 2004, p. 62, Washington, DC: NAEYC. Reprinted with permission from the National Association for the Education of Young Children.

between their parents and their caregivers and teachers from the earliest ages. The issues have more to do with adults' perceptions than children's perceptions.

reciprocal relationships Two-way relationships in which information and power are shared; based on mutual respect, trust, cooperation, and shared responsibility.

Understanding these different but complementary roles reminds teachers of the important boundaries between their roles and those of parents. Children benefit greatly from the lasting unconditional love of at least one adult, usually a parent (Brazelton & Greenspan, 2000). At the same time, children benefit from the more objective view that teachers can bring when they evaluate the children's needs and strengths. To help all of their students, teachers can draw on their experience from observing many children's development and knowing how to effectively support children's social and academic development in group situations such as that of the school or child care center. By contrast, parents are the most knowledgeable sources of information about their child's development and experience in settings outside the school. Moreover, parents are the most accurate, key informants about children's cultural and linguistic backgrounds. Once teachers are clear about what they and parents bring to the table, the opportunity exists to build reciprocal relationships with families.

Young children are integrally connected to their families. Effective early childhood programs depend on positive relationships between teachers and parents.

Defining Reciprocal Relationships

Reciprocal relationships are two-way relationships in which information and power are shared. Such a relationship can only develop in an atmosphere of mutual respect, trust, cooperation, and shared responsibility. These are the elements of what is now called *family-centered care* or *family-centered practice* (Keyser, 2006).

Family-centered practice is a term that originated in the early childhood special education community. According to special educators, family-centered practice provides resources and supports to families that promote children's development and learning and, at the same time, strengthen the competence of families in their roles. To achieve this goal, professionals may provide parent education and activities to foster parents' competence, confidence, and enjoyment of interactions with their child.

Considerable research documents the benefits of family-centered practice for children and families, especially for children with disabilities and special needs (Sandall, Hemmeter, Smith, & McLean, 2005). The *Including All Children* feature demonstrates the value of family-centered practice for children and their families. Although family-centered practices have been at the heart of early childhood special education, they are also now recognized as essential elements of all high-quality early childhood programs (NAEYC, 2005d).

family-centered practice Providing resources and supports to families that promote children's development and learning and, at the same time, strengthen the competency of families in their role.

Family-centered practice is interpreted slightly differently by general educators than by special educators because the needs of the families they work with are different, and because of the child's specific needs. For general early childhood educators, family-centered practice

Including All Children

Family-Centered Practice

Teachers' skill in using family-centered practices is essential to the success of programs for children with special needs. Family-centered practices reflect the belief that the more time, energy, knowledge, and skills families have, the more likely the child's development will thrive, as we see in the following example.

Jennifer, the family service worker from the Beginnings Child Development Center, works with Carolyn and Bill's son Ben. Three-year-old Ben is diagnosed with language and social skills delays and also demonstrates challenging behaviors. Jennifer visits their home in the evening so Bill can be there. She spies Ben behind a chair, kneels down, and pulls some cars and race track pieces out of her bag. As Ben comes closer, Jennifer tells Bill that he might enjoy playing with his son. Bill moves to the floor and begins assembling the pieces. Jennifer models how to provide a choice of colors to Ben to get him to use his words. "Ben, do you want the red or green car?" Ben eagerly replies, "Red." Before letting him grab it, Jennifer says, "Red . . ." and looks at him expectantly. Ben says, "Red car." Jennifer smiles and gives the car to Ben. She turns to Bill and asks, "Want to try?" She moves aside to let Bill play with Ben.

Then Jennifer gives Carolyn a video she made of Ben during the school trip to the Children's Museum. Jennifer explains that the teachers tried some new "social skill" strategies with Ben. Carolyn didn't go along because during the last field trip Ben's behavior was "out of control." She swears she will not take Ben to community outings until he is older, but she is pleased to see how the teachers were able to support his behavior at the Children's Museum.

Carolyn notices Ben enjoying the cars and comments on how much he is using his words. Jennifer shows Carolyn how she can use a paper towel roll to make a "track" for small cars. Carolyn loves the idea and decides to tape the track to the side of the refrigerator. "This way, he can keep busy and I can supervise him while making dinner." Jennifer is pleased because she knows dinnertime has been very stressful for Ben's family. Jennifer will check back in a couple of days to see how the new ideas are working. As she packs to go, Jennifer gives Bill information about the "dads' support group" he is interested in and gives Carolyn a list of respite care providers.

While Jennifer spends minimal time directly with Ben during this visit, she provides supports to his family that will enable them to be true partners in Ben's development and learning. She provides support and ideas, such as respite care, and teaches the parents how to use intervention techniques in the course of daily routines and activities. Thus, Jennifer increases the likelihood that Ben will receive many hours of intervention—provided by his family rather than only 1 hour provided by the "professional."

A few days later, Jennifer calls to find out how things are going. Bill tells her that he is going to the support group, and that the language strategy is working. When Jennifer asks to speak with Carolyn, Bill tells her Carolyn is not at home—she is at the Children's Museum with Ben.

focuses on building partnerships with families. These partnerships are characterized by several key principles: mutual respect and trust; regular, frequent two-way communication; collaboration, shared decision making, and shared power; and negotiation of conflicts toward win–win solutions (Bredekamp, 1997a; Keyser, 2006).

Mutual trust and respect develop gradually after numerous interactions. Although teachers and parents may initially disagree on certain issues, the goal is to recognize and respect one another's knowledge and expertise (Keyser, 2006). If parents feel respected, they are more likely to share information that teachers need to know.

Collaboration, shared decision making, and shared power can be difficult to negotiate for inexperienced teachers. Many early childhood educators fail to grasp the extent of their actual and perceived power in relationships with families. In addition, cultural differences may be a complicating factor in achieving collaborative decision making. The *Culture Lens* feature describes the challenge and value of sharing power with diverse families.

Differences of opinion and goals are inevitable when working with other people's children. If mutual trust and respect are to be maintained and parents are to continue to be empowered, such conflicts must be negotiated toward win–win solutions (discussed later in this chapter). There are instances, however, when negotiation is not an option, such as in cases of suspected child abuse or neglect. Policies regarding teachers' responsibilities for reporting child abuse should be clearly communicated to families as well as teachers (NAEYC, 2005e).

If you, like many of your colleagues, think early childhood education involves just working with children, you might feel intimidated by the idea of developing reciprocal relationships with families. In the next section, we address the fundamental skill of two-way communication with families.

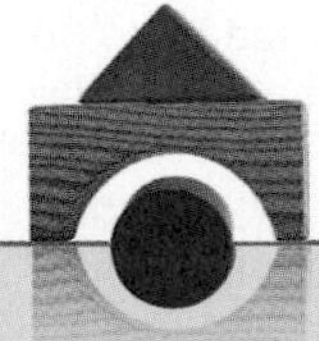

Culture Lens

Sharing Power with Families

One element of effective partnerships with families is shared power between professionals and parents. Sharing power requires that teachers and families communicate openly, negotiate differences of opinion, and be willing to learn and change. The result is that the school changes as well as the family.

Sharing power, however, requires teachers to be culturally sensitive. Teachers (regardless of their own background) must recognize that there are differences in power and status afforded various cultural groups by the larger society, which play out in relationships, as illustrated in the following example.

> Hoyer Elementary School serves a growing population of relatively affluent Spanish-speaking families. The principal and faculty are ethnically diverse, but they all speak only English. The families want the school to offer bilingual education to help their children maintain and improve Spanish. The teachers don't think this is a good idea.

Analyzing the power dynamics of this situation is revealing. The teachers don't realize that they are using their power to make decisions for the parents. They rationalize that the children won't learn English if they hear Spanish at school. They also don't acknowledge that the proposal threatens their power because they don't speak Spanish themselves. By contrast, the families are angry but not surprised that they are powerless to influence the school's decision. They know that anti-immigration feelings in the country create a backlash against speakers of their language.

How could this situation have been better resolved? The teachers admit that they don't want to feel stupid for not speaking Spanish. They open up a dialogue with families and find that the parents want their children to learn English, but not at the expense of their home language. These families know that being bilingual will be a later advantage for their children in the global economy. The conversations continue with both teachers and parents feeling less threatened by the idea. The principal decides to begin by organizing after-school Spanish language activities, and soon they find that English-speaking children also join in.

The idea that parents and teachers should share power can be difficult for both parties, especially when they come from different backgrounds that have uneven power in the larger society. When a decision is needed about some aspect of children's education, teachers may expect parents to rely on their judgment. Parents may be forced to give up their power to the school. A more effective strategy is for teachers and parents to share power to truly provide the best for each student.

■ Communicating with Families

Building relationships with families requires effective communication—one of the biggest challenges teachers face. Before we describe positive ways of communicating with families, we begin with considering some of the most common barriers to effective communication.

Barriers to Effective Communication

Effective communication between teachers and families means more than sharing information; it means developing shared understanding about who the child is, each party's goals, and how to achieve them. Early childhood education covers a broad age span—from birth through age 8. During the earliest years, children are most likely to be served in some form of child care while parents work. At the other end of the age continuum, children are in school and perhaps child care for part of the day. In each of these situations, communication problems can arise.

Communication Problems in Child Care Settings

In child care programs for infants, toddlers, and young preschoolers, deep emotions can consume parents as they leave their children in someone else's care, which can create tension with teachers. Following are examples of typical situations that arise over the care of young children and the feelings they may generate in parents:

- *Competition.* Parents may feel jealous if the child becomes attached to another adult. Three-year-old Madison has been in child care for 1 month. Her mother feels conflicted about it and threatened by the growing relationship between Madison and her teacher. She tells her husband, "I'm afraid Madison loves her teacher more than me. When I left the center, Madison called her teacher 'Mommy' and I cried all the way to work."
- *Guilt and loss.* At times, parents feel a sense of loss over missed experiences. Jacob is 11 months old. His mother is torn between her desire to spend more time with him and her rewarding but demanding career. She worked very hard to earn her law degree, and her job is stressful. At the same time, she feels guilty about neglecting Jacob. She thinks, "I'm going to miss seeing my baby's first steps."
- *Differing child-rearing goals.* Disagreements between parents and teachers, both large and small, are inevitable. Tawanna, who is 4½ years old, enrolled in a new center recently, and her father has concerns about the informality and lack of emphasis on academic skills. He tells his wife, "I don't like Tawanna getting dirty at school. And I want her to learn to read to be ready for school, but they say that's not important yet. And they let the children call them by their first names in that school. I want Tawanna to learn good manners."
- *Power struggles.* Parents may feel that they are losing control over their child's upbringing. Sonya is turning 6, a milestone event in her family. Her grandmother is incensed, however, because she wants to hold a party at school, and the teachers won't let her control it. She tells her friend, "They say I can't send cupcakes for Sonya's birthday because they're not healthy food, but she wants cupcakes and so do I."

These parents' feelings illustrate that sharing their children with other adults is difficult and can be threatening to the close parent–child relationship. When other people have considerable influence over their children's lives, parents can feel powerless.

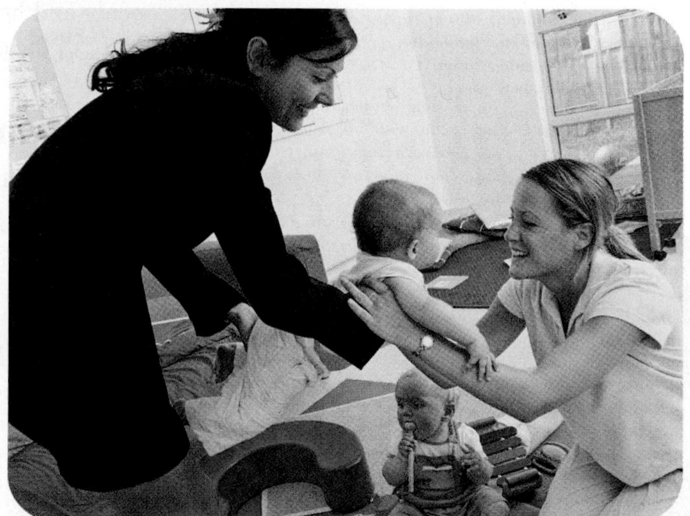

Infant/toddler teachers sometimes find that parents may feel threatened or unsure about sharing their child's care with another person. How can this teacher build a positive relationship that will benefit the baby and the family?

Communication Problems in School

Schools and parents can encounter a number of obstacles in their efforts to communicate. Following are examples of some common barriers to communication:

- *Confusion about regulations and policies.* Parents may lack the information they need about the school's goals, procedures, and policies. For example, Rosemary Hills School has a policy that parents need to be alerted in the middle of first grade about whether their children's reading is below grade level so that an intervention plan can be set up. Shelley's mother becomes very anxious: "It's only January, and the teacher thinks that Shelley will have to stay back in first grade because she's not reading at grade level. I don't want my little girl to flunk, but what can I do?"
- *Lack of flexibility.* The school may not be sensitive to parents' individual needs and concerns. Mr. Jenkins is a concerned father who wants to be involved in his children's education, but he is frustrated: "That school always has meetings and events during the day, but I can't take off work."
- *Lack of attention to individual children.* At times, parents' concerns arise from fears that teachers don't really know and understand their children. Parents may feel that teachers' expectations for their children are too low because of the child's socioeconomic status, disability, or race, as in these examples:
  - Seven-year-old Abigail has Down syndrome. Her two mothers believe that the teachers don't think Abigail can learn, so they don't teach her anything.
  - Ms. Rice tells her mother, "I think that teacher is racist. She assigned all the black boys to the lowest reading group."

Communication problems can arise when parents don't understand how the school functions and how they can influence decisions. They may feel powerless to alter a policy or the teacher's perceptions about their child. Teachers may think they provide adequate information, but if the parent doesn't understand the message, considerable anxiety and confusion may result for the parents and the child as well.

At other times, power struggles can ensue due to conflicting goals. Some families have very high expectations for their children's success in school, so they may pressure teachers and children to ensure academic achievement. The media has started using the term *helicopter parent* to describe parents who "hover over" their children and try to control everything in their lives. Some parents will come forward and complain often, whereas others are too intimidated to voice even the gentlest concerns. To address these communication problems openly and honestly, teachers can use a variety of strategies, discussed next, that will benefit both the child and the family.

Communicating Effectively with Families

Communication is the basis of all relationships. Positive relationships begin when parents feel welcome in the school.

A Welcoming Environment

On entering a school or child care center, parents can usually tell how welcome they are. The environment communicates messages about whether families are expected to be regular participants, infrequent guests, or simple agents of transmittal. Is there a sign greeting children and families? Do teachers greet them at the door? Is there an area where they can gather and visit with each other? Are there adult-sized chairs? Is there a bulletin board stocked with current information? Can parents easily find their children's work and personal space for their belongings?

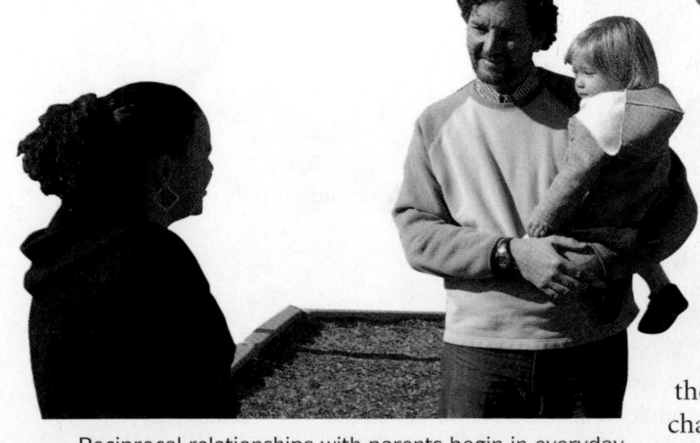

Reciprocal relationships with parents begin in everyday chitchat—casual conversation about children that builds trust and respect.

The physical environment plays an important role in welcoming families. However, face-to-face communication between teachers and parents is more important

Types of Message

Substantive communication is possible and more effective when it is built on a strong base of casual, routine conversation. Think of the messages that teachers need to send to parents as basically two kinds: tennis balls and slippery eggs (NAEYC, 1998).

Picture yourself tossing a tennis ball back and forth from hand to hand. **Tennis ball messages** are easily "tossed" and easily received. These messages help form the foundation of a relationship. Tennis ball messages constitute the everyday chitchat between teachers and parents. This kind of back-and-forth communication helps each party in the relationship to learn and become comfortable with the other's style.

> *Teacher:* Hello, Mr. Watkins, it's good to see Neil back at school today. I hope your family enjoyed the visit with his grandparents.
>
> *Parent:* We had a great time. They live so far away that Neil only sees them a few times a year. They had to leave this morning, so we are all a little down.

Now picture yourself tossing a slippery egg to another person. You would hold the egg carefully and toss it very gingerly, assuming that the other person is prepared to catch it with equal care. If the egg were tossed carelessly or too abruptly, a mess would result. The same is true of **slippery egg messages**. They are more difficult to toss and catch, and must be tossed gently to be sure that the catcher receives the communication as intended (NAEYC, 1998). Even the best of relationships requires slippery egg messages at times. Some relationships seem to consist almost entirely of slippery egg communications. How these messages are sent—the style of communication—determines how well they are received, as we see in the next section.

Communication Styles

There are at least three styles of communication: passive, aggressive, and assertive. **Passive communication** is sensitive to the listener's feelings, but so vague that the message is easily misunderstood. **Aggressive communication** is truthful, but the delivery is hurtful. **Assertive communication**—telling the truth in a thoughtful and considerate way—is the most effective form of communication (NAEYC, 1998).

The goal in sending a slippery egg message—the kind that is difficult to send as well as to receive—is to use assertive communication. Compared to passive or aggressive styles of communication, assertive communication succeeds in delivering the difficult message while also maintaining and perhaps deepening the relationship. These varying styles of communication are described and compared in Table 7.3.

Following is an example of these three communication styles in action. First-grade teacher Julia Sykes is concerned that one of her students, DeShawn Jameson, is not making progress in reading. Julia sets up a meeting with DeShawn's mother to discuss the problem. They chat comfortably for a few minutes, but Ms. Jameson is clearly nervous, anticipating bad news. Here are three ways that Julia might present the situation:

- *Passive communication:* "I know you are worried about how DeShawn is doing in school and so am I. All the children take time to get settled and he'll come around as soon as he's ready." With such a passive statement, Julia demonstrates caring for the parent and child, but fails to convey the seriousness of the situation. Ms. Jameson is confused and a little angry because she doesn't understand why she took off work for this meeting.
- *Aggressive communication:* "We've got a problem with DeShawn. He is so far behind in reading, he'll probably have to repeat first grade." Julia dreaded delivering this bad news, so she blurted it out with little concern for Ms. Jameson's feelings. Ms. Jameson immediately becomes defensive: "What do you mean? Why aren't you teaching him right?"

tennis ball messages Communications that are easily "tossed" and easily received and that help form the foundation of a relationship; they constitute the everyday chitchat between teachers and parents.

slippery egg messages Communications that are difficult to toss (send) and catch (receive), and must be expressed gently to be sure that the catcher receives the communication as intended.

passive communication Speaking in a way that is sensitive to the listener's feelings, but so vague that the message is easily misunderstood.

aggressive communication Speaking the truth in a hurtful way.

assertive communication Telling the truth in a thoughtful and considerate way; considered the most effective form of communication.

Table 7.3 Styles of Communication

	Passive Communication	Aggressive Communication	Assertive Communication
Speaker's Behavior	Speaker cares more about the listener's feelings than about clearly conveying the substance of the message.	Speaker focuses on substance of message with little regard for listener's feelings.	Speaker tells the truth and cares about the listener.
Listener's Response	Listener is emotionally distracted. Not focused on substance of message.	Listener is emotionally distracted. Not focused on substance of message.	Listener is emotionally involved. Responds to substance of message.
Outcome of the Communication	The relationship is damaged. Loss of trust and confusion about expectations result.	The relationship is damaged. Anger, resentment, and unresolved feelings about the balance of power result.	The relationship is strengthened. The possibility exists for dialogue and resolution of both substantive and emotional issues.

Source: Adapted from NAEYC. 1998. *The Leading Edge Workbook: A National Videoconference/Seminar on Developmentally Appropriate Practice in Early Childhood Programs,* "Styles of Communication," p. 22. Unpublished manuscript. Washington, DC: Author. Reprinted with permission from the National Association for the Education of Young Children.

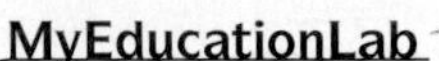

Go to the Assignments and Activities section of Topic 3: Family/Community in the MyEducationLab for your course and complete the activity entitled *Daily Conversations with Families.* How do the teachers in the video use everday conversations to build positive, reciprocal relationships with families?

- *Assertive communication:* "Ms. Jameson, during the first three months of school, I've found that DeShawn isn't making the reading progress that he should be. We don't expect all the children to learn to read at the same time. But I'm concerned that if he falls behind even more, he will really have a hard time catching up. What I'd like to do is have him evaluated by a reading specialist to see if he would benefit from tutoring, which is provided free by the school. I wanted you to come in today so we could talk about how DeShawn is doing at home and what options we have to help him." In this communication, Julia conveys caring for DeShawn and his mother, but she also tells the truth—that there is a problem and there are possible solutions to work on together.

Assertive communication is often effective when working with challenging situations and distraught or angry parents. As the *Becoming an Intentional Teacher* feature reveals, it is important to be open and to really listen to parents' complaints. Teachers use many different vehicles to accomplish clear, honest, regular communication. In the sections that follow, we describe some of these strategies.

Informally Communicating with Children's Families

In programs for infants and toddlers, families and teachers must communicate daily, both morning and evening, to ensure that children receive optimum care. Morning drop-off and afternoon pickup times are good for engaging in the kind of chitchat, or tennis ball back-and-forth, communication that builds relationships between teachers and parents.

For example, "How are you this morning, Ms. Kelly? I can see that Monique doesn't look too happy. Is there something I should know to help her get settled?"

Two-year-old Monique's mom might say, "She wouldn't eat her breakfast and I had to leave or I'd be late for work." "No problem. We'll feed her here, and don't worry or you'll be late," the teacher replies.

In another circumstance, Ms. Kelly looks distraught and responds, "Monique's father left last night and I've been up all night crying."

Here is an entirely different situation, calling for an entirely different response. "I can see you are upset. I'll take Monique now so you can go to work and I'll call to let you know how she's doing. If you would like, we can talk privately later."

Moments of informal conversation are so important for building trust and mutual respect. At the same time, teachers need to make sure that children are supervised during

Becoming an Intentional Teacher

Welcome "Complainers"

Here's What Happened I taught 3- and 4-year-olds in an NAEYC-accredited child care center. Our program was well known in the community as a high-quality center. I taught there for 10 years and we enjoyed good relationships with our families. One mother, Mrs. Mayer, became a constant complainer, however, when her little boy, Noah, kept getting sick. I knew that Noah had asthma, so I wasn't surprised when he missed days at the center. I was surprised, however, by how much Mrs. Mayer blamed me for Noah's repeated illnesses. At first, I tried to explain to her that increased illness is not unusual for children when they are in group care. When my explanation met with resistance, I started to become defensive. In my defense, I assured Mrs. Mayer that our program was licensed and accredited, which means that we meet all required health standards.

One day, when Noah returned after an absence, his mother looked particularly weary. I asked my assistant teacher to take over the group while I spoke with Mrs. Mayer privately. She explained that she had spent the night with Noah in the emergency room. As we talked, I realized that due to Noah's chronic illness, colds and other seemingly innocuous childhood sicknesses are life-threatening experiences. I gave Mrs. Mayer a copy of our center's health policy handbook and asked her to review it and give me feedback. We set up a time to meet again.

Mrs. Mayer came back to me 2 days later with suggestions for ways we could focus everyone's attention on illness prevention. For example, while the staff did a good job of hand washing regularly, we were less attentive to the children's hand washing and we neglected to teach them to cough or sneeze into their elbows. We also acknowledged that, to accommodate parents so they wouldn't have to miss school or work, we often allowed sick children to attend the center when perhaps they should have stayed home.

To address Mrs. Mayer's concerns and to figure out a reasonable solution, I organized staff and parent meetings and asked Mrs. Mayer to speak to both groups. At first, some of the other parents believed that we were making policy changes to accommodate just one child; however, once they heard Noah's story, most parents were sympathetic. Together we agreed to make changes that we would reevaluate after a prescribed amount of time. After a few months, Noah's asthma attacks were much less frequent. In addition, other parents reported that their children were sick less often.

Here's What I Was Thinking Months before school begins, I work hard to build a relationship with my children's families. I make home visits, hold open houses, and write letters or e-mails to families introducing myself and the school—everything I can think of. When Mrs. Mayer began to complain about Noah's getting sick at school, I wondered if she was just a negative person or if she should find another program. As I spoke more with her, I came to realize that her complaints were evidence of her commitment as a parent. In meeting with her, I learned that her experience as the parent of a chronically ill child provided valuable knowledge that we could use in the program. I decided that it wouldn't work if I was the only one who changed health procedures, so I had to get the other parents and staff involved. The outcome was improved health for all the children and for the teachers, too.

these conversations, and that it is clear who is responsible for this duty. Any confidential conversation should be scheduled for another time.

Following are three strategies for ensuring that daily messages are delivered:

- *Information logs.* Daily messages must be relayed about children's eating, sleeping, toileting, signs of change in mood, and changes in developmental status. For example, last night baby Maggie stood up and tried to climb out of her crib—a first in her skill achievement. When her dad drops her off at child care, he needs to let the staff know about Maggie's new skill so they can take steps to prevent accidents and ensure her safety. Given that several different people are responsible for Maggie's care throughout the day, the staff keep written logs about each child's needs and development, and pass them along to each other.

- *Daily notes "About My Day."* This message delivery system is important for all young children, but it is essential for babies and toddlers. Very young children can't communicate for themselves to families and teachers, so daily communication can't be left to chance conversations. Written notes that take little time to complete are essential. Ms. Evans writes a note for 2½-year-old Gabriel's mother: *Gabriel had a hard time waking up from nap this afternoon. He doesn't seem to be sick, but didn't eat as much as usual.*
- *Daily chitchat.* For teachers and parents of preschoolers, regular communication—the daily chitchat—is still important for building and maintaining the relationship. Teachers need to know about events at home that may affect a child, and parents love to hear about interesting or funny things their children have said or done. Teachers should be very careful to keep this informal conversation light and save talking about more difficult issues until private, scheduled times.
- *Weekly updates.* For preschoolers and older children, regular reporting of activities, such as the topic of study or upcoming events, is sufficient, and can be accomplished using weblogs, e-mail alerts, newsletters, or bulletin boards.

Using Technology to Communicate with Families

Technology has transformed all communication in the 21st century. Parents are more accessible than ever because of cell phones and e-mail. Regular communication about program activities and children's progress can be posted electronically. Program websites need to be password secured to limit access.

In thinking about the great potential of technology, it is also important to consider its limitations. Some families may not have access to e-mail or the Internet; others may not have cell phones. Some do not speak or read English. In addition, e-mail may not be entirely private; for this reason, all confidential communications should take place in person. Finally, e-mail and especially instant messaging may foster the use of incorrect grammar and spelling. Teachers should always be careful to ensure accuracy in written communication, electronic or otherwise.

Conferencing with Individual Families

In addition to their everyday, routine communication with families, teachers and parents need to meet for more formal regular conferences. Traditionally, the purpose of parent–teacher conferences has been for teachers to report on children's progress. These conferences are usually a one-way communication, with teachers providing information to parents, who serve as the passive audience. With one-way communications, however, parents might feel as though the teachers are issuing a report card on their parenting.

Formal parent–teacher conferences are important times to communicate about children's progress and potential problems. But for conferences to be effective, teachers need to make parents as comfortable as possible and listen as much as they talk.

More effective conferences promote two-way communication (Keyser, 2006). Teachers not only provide parents with information about their child's progress, but they also listen to what parents say about their child's development and learning. In this setting, parents and teachers have a conversation and ask as well as answer questions.

Because families have diverse needs and schedules, arranging conference times can be tricky. Consider Noreen Hayes, a kindergarten teacher in a large, urban school district. Three months into the school year, she is preparing for her first set of formal family conferences. Because many of the families work two jobs or odd

hours, she is concerned that scheduling conferences will be difficult. To ease the stress for families, she offers a full week of times for them to sign up, including early morning, evening, and weekend hours. To make sure she can accommodate these families, she arranges for community volunteers to provide babysitting and translation services as needed. She also arranges for snacks to be available for parents arriving after work. She organizes the seating arrangement with adult-sized chairs comfortably facing each other. Before conferences, she carefully collects samples of drawings, writing, and photos of projects and other work to share with each child's parents. Consider this scenario:

> When Jillian's mother arrives, looking nervous, Noreen offers her coffee. After they are comfortable, Noreen begins by saying, "Jillian is such a curious little girl. Every day, her questions keep me on my toes. Last week, before we visited the aquarium, she wanted to know how the fish breathe."
>
> Jillian's mother smiles and says, "She drives us crazy with her why, why, why."
>
> "Let me show you some of things she's been learning," Noreen replies, "and how she's discovering ways to get answers to her questions."
>
> When Noreen describes some of the literacy goals, Jillian's mother says, "Oh, I know. At home she is always rhyming words and retelling me the stories you read."
>
> Noreen makes a note about what she's learned from this parent because Jillian has not yet demonstrated these skills at school.

MyEducationLab

Go to the Assignments and Activities section of Topic 3: Family/Community in the MyEducationLab for your course and complete the activity entitled *Parent-Teacher Conference.* Consider all the ways the teacher's behavior makes this an effective parent-teacher conference.

Noreen's conference with Jillian's mother includes many key points to keep in mind when preparing and conducting conferences with families. Table 7.4 summarizes principles for planning and conducting family conferences.

Formal conferences take considerable time to plan and carry out effectively. This time is well spent, however, when it is used to build partnerships and solve problems.

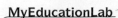

home visiting Visits made by a teacher to the child's home on a regular basis to exchange information with parents.

Communicating Outside the School or Program

Conferences are typically held at school or in the child care center—on the teacher's turf. As a result, a disproportionate amount of power is attributed to the professionals, putting parents at somewhat of a disadvantage. For this reason, teachers should consider other options for meeting with families such as home visiting and meeting on neutral ground.

Home Visiting. **Home visiting**, during which a teacher goes to the child's home on a regular basis to exchange information with parents, has a long tradition in early childhood education. For decades, home visits were required by federally funded programs such as Head Start. In addition, many of the model early childhood programs that demonstrated lasting effects, such as the Perry Preschool Project, and the Abecedarian Project included weekly home visits. Home visits are an excellent way for teachers to establish a more comfortable relationship with families, and children usually love the idea of their teacher visiting them at home.

In recent years, home visits have become less common for several reasons. They are time consuming and teacher union contracts may discourage them. Because today's children often live in less self-contained communities and take transportation to school, home visits become logistically difficult. Teachers may feel unsafe visiting communities where there have been incidents involving violence or drugs. Likewise, some families may be uncomfortable about teachers' visiting for reasons of poverty or differences in language and cultural background.

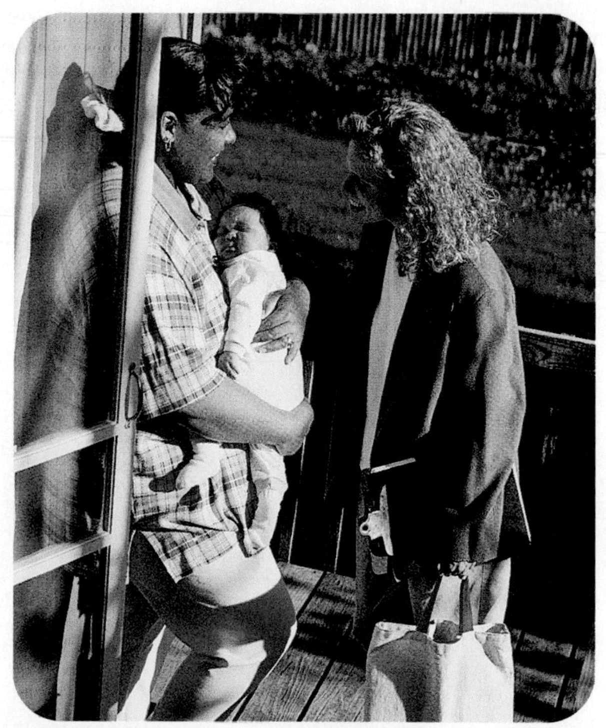

Communicating with families outside of school is an effective way for teachers to build relationships with individual children and their families. What can teachers do during home visits to help achieve that goal?

Despite some of these barriers, when home visits are possible and mutually agreed on, they can be effective in building a

Table 7.4 Planning and Conducting Family Conferences

Principles of Effective Conferences	Strategies for Implementing Conferences
Prepare families in advance.	Notify families in writing about the purpose of the conference. Ask families to think about what goals they have for the conference and for their children, what information they want to share, and what questions they want to ask.
Schedule the conferences at times convenient for both parents and teachers.	Accommodate parents' work schedules as much as possible. Set a specific time limit for the conference, 20 to 30 minutes, so parents can plan accordingly.
Provide appropriate space for the conference.	The space should be private to ensure confidential conversations. The furniture arrangement should communicate openness and comfort; use adult-sized chairs around a table or in front of a desk. There should be no physical barrier between teachers and families, such as a desk that sets up an artificial power relationship.
Collect children's portfolios or samples of their work.	Use examples of children's work as a springboard for discussion.
Plan the conference agenda.	Make sure to include time to talk about children's progress and ask questions of each other.
Always begin on a positive note.	Begin your discussion about the child by sharing a specific comment about the child's strengths, interests, or abilities. An anxious parent can then relax, become less defensive, and be more able to listen and talk freely.
Plan in advance how to deliver a slippery egg message.	When you have difficult information or a problem about the child to discuss, think in advance how you would phrase the concern and what suggestions or solutions you would offer. "Four-year-olds are just learning how to make friends. I have observed that Kenny often plays alone, and sometimes when he tries to join in, he gets aggressive. I thought maybe he could bring something interesting from home to get the other children's attention in a positive way. I'm also going to give him some phrases to say when he wants to play. I wondered if he has had any difficulty like this at home or in the neighborhood, or if you have any ideas for me to help Kenny make friends."
Give and receive information about children's progress.	Use open-ended questions as much as possible. Two-way communication, shared power, and collaborative decision making build true partnerships with families. "Reshia loves the construction center and is learning words for all the tools and road-building equipment. What does she like to talk about at home?"
Set goals together for next steps.	Strive to identify a common goal and create a plan to work together. "I hear you saying that you want Garrett to learn to use the toilet on his own as soon as possible, before the new baby is born. That's a goal we share. But he hasn't shown any interest at the center yet. What's he doing at home? Maybe we could try to be consistent in how we work with him."

Sources: Based on *Families, Schools, and Communities: Building Partnerships for Educating Children*, 3rd edition, by C. Barbour, N. H. Barbour, and P. A. Scully, 2005, Upper Saddle River, NJ: Pearson Merrill Prentice Hall; and *From Parents to Partners: Building a Family-Centered Early Childhood Program,* by J. Keyser, 2006, St. Paul, MN: Redleaf Press.

foundation for a reciprocal relationship. Some guidelines for successful home visits include these:

- *Be available for a home visit.* Let families know that you would like to visit the children at home to make them more comfortable with you and to learn more about their interests. Do not be offended if families decline the opportunity.
- *Set a time for the visit and stick to it.* Visits should last from15 to 30 minutes.
- *Reassure families in advance about the visit's purpose.* Families need to know that you do not expect them to entertain you, feed you, or clean up for your visit. Nevertheless, teachers should be respectful of diverse cultural perspectives; for example, some cultural groups would be hurt or insulted if a guest refused food.
- *Include the child in the visit.* Ask children to share something they like to do at home or in the community.
- *If you take a photo, ask permission first, and perhaps pose the family together at the front door to protect their privacy.* Use a digital camera so the family can see the photo that you will display at school.

MyEducationLab

Go to the Assignments and Activities section of Topic 3: Family/ Community in the MyEducationLab for your course and complete the activity entitled *Home Visits to Connect with Families.* As you read the case study, consider the benefits of home visiting for children and their families.

Meeting on Neutral Ground. Given that home visiting and conferencing at school can be threatening or difficult, some teachers find that meeting families on neutral ground such as a local coffee shop or fast-food restaurant may be the best strategy. Talking in a less formal setting over a cup of coffee, parents and teachers may be more relaxed and able to work out solutions to difficult problems.

Early childhood education is most effective when there is regular two-way communication between families and teachers. Truly effective early childhood programs go beyond communication to active involvement of families in their children's education, a topic addressed in the next section.

Involving Families in Programs and Schools

More than 40 years of research confirms that family involvement has a positive impact on children's achievement in school (Epstein et al., 2002). The benefits of parent involvement are so well established that they are written into public law. For example, the Head Start program requires parent involvement at all levels, from classroom interaction with children to representation on policy-making boards. Special education laws also dictate specific roles for families as decision makers about services for their children. In the sections that follow, we examine research on the benefits of family involvement and then describe ways to involve family members meaningfully in their children's education.

Benefits of Family Involvement

A thorough review of research (Henderson & Mapp, 2002; National Coalition for Parent Involvement in Education [NCPIE], 2006) summarizes the impact of family involvement on children's achievement in school. Students with involved parents, regardless of family income, are more likely to:

- Earn higher grades and score better on achievement tests
- Be promoted
- Attend school regularly
- Have better social skills and adapt well to school
- Benefit from long-term positive consequences such as completing high school and seeking postsecondary education.

Further, research shows that children prosper when families of all income and education levels and of diverse cultural backgrounds support their children's learning at home

MyEducationLab

Go to the Assignments and Activities section of Topic 3: Family/Community in the MyEducationLab for your course and complete the activity entitled *Involving Families: Super Smile Day.* How does the experience such as Super Smile Day provide meaningful involvement for families and the community in an early childhood program?

(NCPIE, 2006). However, white, middle-class families are more likely to be involved in school and to be better informed about how to help their children at home (Swick, Head-Reeves, & Barbarin, 2006). Therefore, schools need to make extra effort to involve all families because this would be an effective way to address the achievement gap between children of color growing up in poverty and their more affluent, white peers (Henderson & Mapp, 2002; Swick et al., 2006).

The benefits of family involvement for children's success in school and life are well documented. Next, we examine some effective strategies for involving parents in early childhood centers and schools.

Providing Opportunities for Meaningful Family Involvement

Research on successful school, family, and community partnerships identified six types of effective family–school involvement (Epstein et al, 2002). These are listed in Table 7.5.

To be successful, the various types of family involvement listed in Table 7.5 require effort on the part of teachers and parents. For instance, volunteering is one of the most common ways of involving parents. Sometimes, however, volunteers are used only to wipe tables, clean playgrounds, or bake cookies for bake sales. These may be necessary tasks, but more meaningful opportunities are available. If the school prepares parents in advance, classroom volunteers can provide one-on-one conversation or small-group reading for young children. If families engage in such learning experiences with children at school, they are more likely to do these things at home with their children.

As we see in Table 7.5, another effective form of family involvement is collaborating with the community. To learn how schools put this research finding into practice, read the *What Works: Building Community Partnerships* feature.

Throughout this chapter, we have discussed the importance of relationships with families. In the next section, we provide a conceptual framework for building partnerships with families and describe specific skills for negotiating conflicts.

Table 7.5 Types of Meaningful Family Involvement

Types of Involvement	Strategies for Involving Families
Type 1: Parent education	Assist families with parenting and child-rearing skills, understanding child development, and providing supportive learning environments at home. Assist schools in understanding families' child-rearing practices and cultural traditions.
Type 2: Communication	Communicate with families about children's progress and experiences in school. Communicate with teachers about children's development and learning observed in the home.
Type 3: Volunteering	Recruit, train, and schedule opportunities to involve families as volunteers in classrooms.
Type 4: Learning at home	Involve families with their children in learning opportunities at home. Provide curriculum-related suggestions and materials.
Type 5: Decision making	Include families as participants in program decisions and advocacy through policy councils, committees, PTA/PTO, and other parent organizations.
Type 6: Collaborating with the community	Coordinate community resources and services for children, families, and the school or program with businesses, agencies, and other groups. Provide services to the community.

Source: From *School, Family, and Community Partnerships: Your Handbook for Action* by J. Epstein et al. Copyright 2002 by Sage Publications Inc. Books. Reproduced with permission of Sage Publications Inc. via Copyright Clearance Center.

What Works

Building Community Partnerships

Just as partnerships between teachers and families contribute to positive outcomes for children, early childhood programs and schools function most effectively when they build reciprocal partnerships in the broader community. For example, a Head Start program, with its comprehensive services for families, may serve as a focal point for positive change in a poverty-stricken community. Likewise, a community organization might adopt a neighborhood school, clean up and equip its playground, or provide literacy volunteers and other services that improve school performance.

Teachers, especially beginning teachers, may feel overwhelmed by the idea of building partnerships with communities in addition to carrying out their other responsibilities. However, community linkages can enhance their work and make it more effective. All communities have unique individuals with talents to share with early childhood programs. A local orchestra might have musicians who are willing to visit and perform for the children. Artists of all kinds can enrich children's experiences with demonstrations and skill instruction. Doctors, nurses, dentists, or hygienists can demonstrate healthy practices for young children. One preschool has an annual Truck Touch as a community experience and fund-raiser in which the nearby International Harvester company loans giant tractor trailers for the children to see and explore under careful supervision. The Truck Touch is open to all children in the community for free, and an accompanying snack bar raises funds for the preschool's library.

Schools can also inform families about child-related events or activities in the community such as concerts, puppet shows, museum exhibits, storytelling, and the like. Connecting families, including siblings, through such community events can help create a network of family support, which is especially helpful for single or teen parents. Such a network can serve as a protective factor for families in communities at risk.

In addition, teachers can use knowledge of the community in planning curriculum. For example, a town has an ongoing project to clean up the environment around a creek area that was once a beaver dam. Each class in the local primary school takes on an aspect of the project and expands its study of ecology over several years.

When early childhood programs fully integrate into the community by inviting community participation in the program and by taking advantage of what the community has to offer, positive outcomes result for everyone involved.

Source: Based on "Effects of a Community Initiative on the Quality of Childcare," by D. Bryant, K. L. Maxwell, and M. Burchinal, 1999, *Early Childhood Research Quarterly, 14*(4), pp. 449–464; and *Families and Community Relationships: A Guide to the NAEYC Early Childhood Program Standards and Related Accreditation Criteria*, 2005. Washington, DC: National Association for the Education of Young Children.

Building Partnerships with Families: A Framework

Denyce Lyons is nearing the end of her first year teaching 4-year-olds in Head Start. She has enjoyed the children, but continues to struggle at times in her relationships with parents. Now she's facing one of the biggest challenges of the year. The program where Denyce works traditionally holds a graduation ceremony, complete with caps, gowns, and diplomas and lengthy performances by the children to mark the year's end. Denyce feels strongly that such programs are not developmentally appropriate. She also thinks they are a waste of time and money that could be used more effectively. When she announces that there will be no graduation ceremony this year, several parents become very angry and go to the director, who threatens to fire Denyce if she doesn't change her mind. Such drastic breakdowns in relationships between teachers and families are all too common in programs for young children. In this section, we

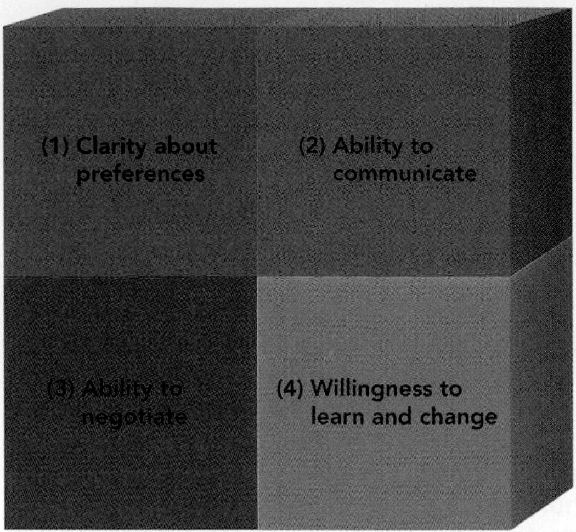

Figure 7.3 Framework for Partnerships with Families

present a framework for building effective partnerships with families. This framework is designed to prevent crises such as Denyce's and to address them when they do arise.

Effective partnerships with families involve four key strategies: clarity about preferences, ability to communicate, ability to negotiate, and willingness to learn and change (NAEYC, 1998). Figure 7.3 presents this partnership model visually. Each of these building blocks of partnership is described in the sections that follow and then used to address Denyce's graduation ceremony dilemma.

Clarifying Preferences

Teachers and families have preferences about all aspects of children's learning and development. Sometimes these preferences are shared. For example, most people prefer that children dress warmly in cold weather. However, in other cases, parents and teachers may have conflicting preferences in their child-rearing practices or educational goals. Areas where teacher and family preferences may be strong and at odds include napping, snacking and meal structure, tasks children should do for themselves, learning to use the toilet and bathroom habits, talking and listening, cleanliness, discipline techniques, roles of girls and boys, and traditions and holidays. There are various sources and reasons for these different preferences:

- Cultural backgrounds
- Personal experiences as members of families both as children and as parents
- Outside influences such as information gained from the media
- Education and training.

Both teachers and parents are influenced by all of these factors. To understand and negotiate these differences, teachers must clarify their preferences and reflect on the sources of their beliefs. Is a strong preference for children learning to feed themselves at an early age the result of studying child development or being the mother of five children? Does a teacher believe that children should take turns based on research about social skills or a cultural judgment about good manners?

Revisiting the Head Start graduation dilemma presented earlier, Denyce needs to reflect on why she feels so strongly about preschool graduation ceremonies. She recalls that one of her professors at the community college stated unequivocally that requiring preschoolers to perform for adults is not developmentally appropriate. Denyce reasons that such events are inappropriate because they last too long, straining children's attention spans and self-control. She also objects to a few children being singled out for "star" treatment. She thinks that valuable class time is spent unproductively in rehearsals and teaching children how to march in line. Upon reflection, Denyce believes that the money spent on props such as caps and gowns would be better used to buy books or other educational materials for the school. Denyce also recognizes that she is worried that the children will misbehave and she will be judged a poor teacher. On closer analysis, Denyce has to admit to herself that she thinks graduating from preschool is not much of an accomplishment and the ceremonial trappings should be saved for greater achievements such as high school graduation.

Communicating Preferences

The next step in building partnerships is communicating with families about preferences. In situations such as Denyce's where a difference of opinion exists, clear and honest communication is vital. Denyce needs to begin by listening to parents' preferences for holding a graduation ceremony. She does this by organizing a meeting to which she invites the dissatisfied families. Rather than beginning with her viewpoint, Denyce encourages parents to air their concerns:

> "We've always had graduations here. My two older kids have their diplomas and I want this for Dedra, too," says one mother.
>
> "We want to have this big party so we can let the kids know how proud we are," says one of the fathers.
>
> After several parents express their feelings, a grandmother sighs and says, "This may be the only graduation I get to go to. My other grandkids dropped out of school."
>
> Having listened carefully and respectfully to each one's concerns, Denyce states her interpretation of what the parents have said. "I think you want me to understand how much you value your children's accomplishments in Head Start, and how important this experience has been for the children and for you. I can tell from your comments that you really value education, and it sounds like you think it's a really important thing to celebrate." Several parents nod, and agree that Denyce's summary reflects their feelings.
>
> Denyce then explains her own concerns about the graduation. "I value the children's learning, too, but I am concerned that spending time getting ready for the ceremony will take away time that the children could be learning skills they'll need in kindergarten. I also think that the money we spend on the graduation could be used for classroom supplies like books that would last longer."

This opportunity to communicate identifies differences in the parents' and Denyce's perspectives. If Denyce continues to insist she is right, the parents will probably feel disrespected and lose power in the relationship. The children will see their parents' anger at the teacher. If the parents "win" and the director forces Denyce to hold graduation, she will do so begrudgingly and the children will sense her lack of commitment. In both cases, whether teachers win and parents lose or parents win and teachers lose, the real losers are the children. The next step to build and maintain a partnership is to negotiate the conflict toward a win–win solution (Fisher, Ury, & Patton, 1992).

Negotiating Successfully

Collaborating and sharing power with families requires negotiation skills. There are certain characteristics of power relationships that determine successful or unsuccessful negotiations. Table 7.6 illustrates these characteristics and shows that neither exercising power

Table 7.6 Understanding Shared Power

Power or Fighting	Shared Power or Negotiation	No Power or Avoidance
Characterized by: Put downs Threats Punishment Arbitrary action	**Characterized by:** Talking about the problem Communicating Seeking solutions	**Characterized by:** Walking away Giving up Holding in feelings and opinions Changing the subject
Gets these results: One winner Doubts and fears Revenge	**Gets these results:** Both sides can win Real solutions All are satisfied	**Gets these results:** Problem is still there No one is satisfied Ongoing discomfort

Source: Adapted from NAEYC. 1998. *The Leading Edge Workbook: A National Videoconference/Seminar on Developmentally Appropriate Practice in Early Childhood Programs,* "Understanding Shared Power," p. 24. Unpublished manuscript. Washington, DC: Author. Reprinted with permission from the National Association for the Education of Young Children.

unilaterally nor avoiding a power struggle results in a positive outcome. Shared power requires win–win negotiation.

The Five-Step Negotiation Process

Successful negotiations that result in a win–win solution to a conflict involve several steps (Fisher et al., 1992). Each step is described next and then illustrated using an example from the conflict over the graduation.

Step 1: Express preferences, interests, and concerns. As a teacher, when you are expressing preferences, it is useful to focus on what you value rather than taking a rigid position. Denyce might have stated her strongly held position: "I'm against graduations for young children because they're developmentally inappropriate." Instead Denyce expressed her preferred value for her students: "I would like to use the money for classroom materials and I don't want to take time away from teaching." Similarly, the families made their interest known by pointing out that they value education and that graduation marks an important milestone in their children's lives.

Step 2: Find common ground. Successful negotiation requires compromise. Sometimes people view compromise as a loss, a sign of weakness, or as giving in. Compromise is actually an effective strategy for achieving a win–win negotiated solution to a conflict. To achieve a satisfactory compromise, parties need to identify their common ground: their fundamental agreements, as well as the areas where they disagree. Denyce and the parents agree on the value of education and their desire to communicate their pride in the children. The areas they don't agree on are wearing caps and gowns and allowing time for rehearsals and a ceremony.

Step 3: Identify areas of flexibility. The next step in the negotiation process is to identify areas of potential flexibility. These might include ways of varying timing, frequency, or quantity. For example, the time designated for preparing for graduation and for the performance are negotiable areas. In addition, the amount of money available and how it is used are areas that could be flexibly negotiated. The parents' expectations of the ceremony could also be negotiable.

Step 4: Brainstorm wins for all. Having identified areas of flexibility, Denyce and the parents can brainstorm possible solutions that would be agreeable to all concerned. One possible solution is having a party for everyone during which the children sing some of the songs and recite some of the poems they have learned this year. Other possibilities include using the money that would have been spent on caps and gowns to buy books for the center, and creating "diplomas" on the computer rather than buying them. Other suggestions are that parents provide refreshments and that all of the children wear white shirts during the party.

Step 5: Try for a while and then reevaluate if necessary. Negotiated solutions should be tried and evaluated to make sure that all parties are satisfied. During and after the "graduation" party, Denyce talked with the parents to get their reactions. Some of the parents still missed the caps and gowns, but they were pleased when the children took such interest and pride in the new books. Several parents thought the program was actually more fun because it was less rehearsed and funnier than previous years. One parent pointed out that he was glad that there weren't any stars of the show and all the children performed the same thing. Perhaps because the program was only 15 minutes long, none of the children misbehaved and all seemed to enjoy themselves, including Denyce. Because some parents didn't like the white shirts and wanted their children to dress up in their best clothes, Denyce agreed to try that idea next year.

The final building block of successful partnerships is the willingness to learn and change, described next.

Demonstrating a Willingness to Learn and Change

We can see from the negotiation between Denyce and the parents in her Head Start classroom that effective partnerships with families depend on the willingness to learn and change. In Denyce's case, she was willing to listen to the parents' concerns respectfully and, as a result, she learned how much they value education for their children and why the graduation ceremony was meaningful for them. On the other hand, the families learned about Denyce's concerns for their children's readiness for kindergarten and, hence, were willing to change their expectations regarding appropriate ways to celebrate the children's achievements. True partnerships occur only when both teachers and families are willing to learn from one other and to grow and change as a result.

The five-step negotiation process outlined here does not involve a quick fix; it requires time and respect for the other parties' interests, strengths, and abilities. Win–win negotiation depends on appreciating the importance of everyone's interests, particularly parents' perceptions about what is important for their children. Denyce could easily have erred by trivializing the parents' desire to see their children "graduate." Instead, she accurately perceived that graduation represented an underlying value of education rather than the actual ceremony. Try out your own negotiation skills with the *How Would You Respond?* feature.

As we have seen, teaching young children requires working with families, which requires good communication and negotiation skills. Throughout this chapter, we examined

How Would You Respond?

Accommodating Parents' and Children's Needs

The Situation A single mother in your program, Ms. James, tells you that it is very important that her 4-year-old daughter, Alison, not take a nap at school. She explains that Alison has an 8-year-old brother, Randall, who is a struggling reader. Ms. James wants her daughter to go to bed promptly at 8:00. Until Alison is asleep, Ms. James cannot spend one-on-one time with her son who needs her help with his schoolwork. When Alison naps during the day, she gets to sleep after 9:00, which is late to begin helping Randall with his reading.

What to Do? Various courses of action are possible in this situation. Which do you think would be most useful and why?

- Try to accommodate the parent's request because she has a right to request what she thinks is best for her family as a whole.
- Compromise by allowing Alison to take a very short nap, waking her up after 10 or 15 minutes. This won't be enough to disrupt her bedtime, yet she can join in the group naptime.
- Tell Ms. James that all children in the program nap if they are tired and you are not willing to keep awake any child who needs rest.
- Talk with Ms. James about ways of involving Alison in the reading routine with her brother. Alison might draw or look at books while her mother is working with Randall. Then, Ms. James or perhaps Randall could read or tell Alison a story before she goes to bed.

Use the steps in negotiating conflicts to identify other strategies that might be useful.

the various aspects of building effective partnerships with families and communities. These include establishing reciprocal relationships, communicating effectively, and negotiating conflicts. We conclude with a return visit to Vilma Suarez's Early Head Start program where we began.

Revisiting Ms. Suarez's Classroom

Now that we have explored the many ways that teachers build effective partnerships with families, we can see how well Vilma Suarez fulfills this important responsibility. She plays a key role in implementing Aiya's IFSP plan, but she also respects and supports Aiya's mother and works to gain her trust. She helps Tomas and Mrs. Vacaro through difficult daily transitions and takes time to communicate with her throughout the day.

Her biggest challenge will be resolving the conflict with Mr. Henderson over his son's biting. She needs to employ all of her skills of effective communication and negotiation. She begins by saying, "Mr. Henderson, I know how upsetting it is when children bite, but the law prohibits hitting children at the center. I would like to talk with you about other ways we can work together on this problem." Thus begins the complex negotiation process that Vilma knows from experience may take one meeting or many.

MyEducationLab

To assess your understanding of how to build effective partnerships with families, go to the Book Specific Resources section in the MyEducationLab for your course, select *Effective Practices in Early Childhood Education,* Chapter 7 of the Study Plan, and then complete the multiple choice questions and activities.

As the families arrive the next morning, Vilma notices that Mrs. Vacaro is even more anxious than she was the night before when she picked up Tomas. Feeling that she has gained Mrs. Vacaro's trust over the many months they have known each other, Vilma carefully asks, "Is everything all right?" Mrs. Vacaro's eyes well up and she whispers, "I'm pregnant again, and I don't have health insurance."

Vilma calmly replies, "Tomas will make a wonderful brother. He's so loving. I'm sure you're feeling a lot of stress. But our Early Head Start program can help you. With your permission, I'll check with the director during the day about the resources we have to offer you and the help we can find in the community. If you have time, we can meet this evening or I'll phone you at home." Mrs. Vacaro exhales with relief and promises to check back at the end of the day. She calls good-bye to Tomas who is already eating his breakfast with the other children.

Chapter Summary

- Families are diverse in many ways: composition, culture, religion, economic status, work, mobility, and sexual orientation.
- Along with reciprocal relationships and partnerships between teachers and families, family-centered practice is characterized by several key principles: mutual respect and trust; regular, frequent two-way communication; collaboration, shared decision making, and shared power; and negotiation of conflicts toward win–win situations.
- Effective two-way communication is the basis for positive relationships with families. Communication strategies include teachers' creating a welcoming environment, informal conversation, sharing important information daily and/or weekly depending on the age of the child, using an assertive communication style especially when discussing delicate issues, conferencing, home visiting, and using technology.
- More than 40 years of research confirms that family involvement in schools and early childhood programs has a positive impact on children's achievement.
- Effective partnerships with families involve four key strategies: clarity about preferences, ability to communicate, ability to negotiate, and willingness to change and learn.

key terms

aggressive communication
assertive communication
Bronfenbrenner's ecological model
exosystem
family-centered practice
family systems theory
home visiting
macrosystem
mesosystem
microsystem
passive communication
reciprocal relationships
slippery egg messages
tennis ball messages

readings & websites

Baker, A. C., & Manfredi/Petitt, L. A. (2004). *Relationships, the heart of quality care: Creating community among adults in early care settings.* Washington, DC: NAEYC.

Barrera, I., & Corso, R. M., with Macpherson, D. (2003). *Skilled dialogue: Strategies for responding to cultural diversity in early childhood.* Baltimore: Paul H. Brookes Publishing.

Hanson, M. J., & Lynch, E. W. (2004). *Understanding families: Approaches to diversity, disability, and risk.* Baltimore: Paul H. Brookes Publishing.

Keyser, J. (2006). *From parents to partners: Building a family-centered early childhood program.* St. Paul, MN: Redleaf Press.

Center for the Improvement of Child Caring/ Center for Effective Parenting
www.ccicparenting.org

Child Trends
www.childtrends.org

National Coalition for Parent Involvement in Education
www.ncpie.org

Office of Head Start, Administration for Children and Families
Provides extensive resources on family and community involvement, including fatherhood and grandparent initiatives.
http://eclkc.ohs.acf.hhs.gov

observe, reflect, decide

1. Reflect on the family you grew up in or the family you live with now. Think about how your family functions in terms of boundaries, climate, roles, and rules. Consider a situation in which the family experienced stress. What impact did that event have on the family dynamics? How did it affect the family's equilibrium? Why and how do changes in family dynamics affect teachers?
2. Visit a child care center or elementary school and observe the physical facility as though you were a parent seeking to enroll your child. How does it make you feel? Is there evidence that families are welcome and expected to be involved?
3. Review the parent involvement section of the Head Start Program Performance Standards (online at http://eclkc.ohs.acf.hhs.gov/hslc). Visit a Head Start program and talk to the teacher about how his or her program implements these standards. What types of family involvement does this program utilize? Are there other ways parents might be involved in the program?
4. Consider a conflict that you have had in your personal or professional life. Think about how you might have applied the five-step negotiation process to the situation. Do you think the outcome would have been more acceptable for everyone involved?
5. As a teacher, you will work with many different kinds of families, including a father with sole custody, gay and lesbian parents, mothers and fathers in the military who are deployed, grandparents parenting grandchildren, parents involved in drug or alcohol abuse or in prison, parents who are much older than you, teenage parents, and so on. Reflect on whether you have personal biases toward any of these types of families. How would your biases potentially affect your teaching? What do you think you should do in such a situation?

8 Creating a Caring Community of Learners: Guiding Young Children

Thinking Ahead

1. What are the elements of a caring community of learners?
2. Why is it important for teachers to create a caring community of learners?
3. How can the Teaching Pyramid model help teachers create a caring community, promote social competence, and address children's challenging behaviors?
4. How do teachers build positive relationships with young children?
5. How do teachers organize the learning environment and daily schedule to enable children to do their best and prevent behavior problems?
6. How do teachers effectively guide children's behavior toward the goal of promoting positive social–emotional development in each child?
7. How do teachers use individualized interventions with children who exhibit persistent challenging behaviors such as biting and bullying?

Today is the first day of school for Sue Brady, a teacher of 20 four-year-olds in a child care center. She and her coteacher, Elly Donahue, are both inexperienced teachers responsible for a group of children for the first time. Sue and Elly spent the last week preparing their classroom. They are a little worried that there are not enough toys to keep children's interest and have requested more from the director. The room has a sink, but it is located in the pathway from the front door to the closet so it is not possible to put the paint easels near it. There is no book rack and the books are stacked on an open shelf, near the blocks. There is one large open area with a rug that they plan to use for group time and block building next to a table for toys. Tables are lined up along the far side of the room.

As soon as the children begin to arrive, things go wrong. Playtime becomes disorganized and the children dump materials all over the floor rather than use them constructively. The teachers give so much attention to the children who are out of control that they neglect the others who are behaving well, such as Edie, who is absorbed in her painting at the easel. Over the course of the day, the teachers' voices become louder as they try to restore order while the noise level in the room becomes almost unbearable. No one cooperates during cleanup time.

At lunch, Ricky blows milk at his friends through his straw and the others soon emulate his skill. Sue asks Paula and Aimee, "Would you like to go outside now?" and they simply say, "No," leaving her unsure about what to do since she can't leave them alone inside. On the playground, Booth punches Elijah hard in the stomach, seemingly for no reason. Furious but feeling totally incompetent, Sue grabs Booth by the arms and repeatedly says, "Say you're sorry!" while Booth just smirks and Elijah cries loudly. Both teachers can't wait for naptime, yet when they turn out the lights, the ensuing chaos becomes overwhelming. Children refuse to stay on their cots, grab toys off the shelves, talk loudly, and make it impossible for even the most exhausted to sleep. Sue will remember this day vividly because it is one of the longest days of her life, and unfortunately the next day will be all too similar. ▲

This glimpse into Sue's classroom is not a fictional account. It is actually what happened to me on my first day of teaching many years ago. I learned very quickly that teaching young children is hard work. I also discovered that there was a lot more that I needed to know to become an effective teacher.

The goal of this chapter is to help ensure that you and the children you teach do not experience days like the one described above. This chapter describes research-based practices—ways of creating a caring community of learners—that make teaching young children more effective and enjoyable. To help you learn how to promote children's social competence and address challenging behaviors, we will describe a conceptual framework—the Teaching Pyramid (Fox, Dunlap, Hemmeter, Joseph, & Strain, 2003; Hemmeter, Ostrosky, & Fox, 2006). Applying this framework will help you create a caring community of learners in which young children thrive. Using these research-based, positive guidance strategies will not prevent all of the challenges you face as a teacher, but it will greatly reduce the bad days and help you become more effective in your work with all children.

Building a Caring Community of Learners

A **caring community of learners** is a group or classroom in which children and adults engage in warm, positive relationships; treat each other with respect; and learn from and with each other. The late Jim Greenman (2005a), one of the foremost experts on children's environments, described early childhood programs as "caring spaces, learning places." This phrase is apt because it emphasizes a fundamental principle of early childhood education: that children's care and education are interrelated.

caring community of learners A group or classroom in which children and adults engage in warm, positive relationships; treat each other with respect; and learn from and with each other.

Wherever children are served, they are always learning and being cared for. In other words, *both/and* thinking is required. High-quality early childhood programs provide *both* nurturing responsive care *and* stimulating, interesting educational experiences. If children's needs for either care or learning are neglected, the program will be ineffective.

Integrating Care and Education

From the earliest moments of life, children's development, who they become, is influenced by the nurturance and care that they receive from adults—first their parents, then members of the extended family and other caregivers. In the next sections, we describe the importance of relationships in the family, and then with teachers.

Attachment Theory

Decades of research on mother–child interactions support the concept that children's ability to learn depends on their developing trusting relationships with caregivers—what is called **attachment theory** (Bowlby, 1969/2000). Much of the research was conducted by Mary Ainsworth and her colleagues (1978). They observed how young children interacted with their mothers when they were brought into a novel or strange situation (such as being presented with new or unusual materials to explore). They identified kinds of attachments between mothers and children that have varying effects on children's development. It is important to note, however, that attachment is influenced by cultural contexts and will look and mean different things to diverse cultural groups.

Secure Attachment. According to attachment theory (Ainsworth et al., 1978; Bowlby, 1969/2000; Scroufe, 1996), when children's caregivers are responsive and sensitive to their needs, children develop **secure attachment relationships** that allow them to venture forth and comfortably explore and learn about the world. Children who are securely attached to their caregivers have a strong foundation not only for building relationships with other people, but also for learning (Watson, 2003). Securely attached children see their caregivers as trustworthy and, in turn, come to see themselves as competent.

What does secure attachment look like? Consider Matthew, a 2½-year-old who enjoys a warm, loving relationship with his mother. When his mother enrolls him in a child care center, she stays with him for almost an hour while he becomes acclimated. At first he clings to her leg and eyes the toys and other children. Gradually, however, he ventures a few steps toward an enticing ramp that the other kids are sliding down, but quickly runs back to his mother. After a few more attempts, he hesitantly joins in the fun by rolling a ball down the incline, all the while seeking regular eye contact with his mother. After a while, he begins to explore the classroom, occasionally returning to her side for reassurance. Matthew's mother is the **secure base** from which to explore his new environment. During the next few days, his mother stays with him for shorter periods of time, until one day he joyfully waves good-bye to her at the door. He no longer needs her actual presence as a physical base from which to explore because he has internalized the sense of trust and confidence that she provides. Teachers can help children make such transitions from the secure attachments of home to child care settings. Read the *Becoming an Intentional Teacher: Easing Separation Woes* feature for a classroom example.

Insecure Attachment. By contrast, some children grow up in families that, for a variety of reasons, are unable or unwilling to provide reasonably consistent, sensitive, responsive care. Mothers or other caregivers may be depressed, ill, or stressed by economic or other conditions that lead them to be neglectful, punitive, or hostile to their young children. Some children grow up in very difficult circumstances in which they may have been abused, neglected, or exposed to drugs and violence. Growing up in such an environment may leave children unable to trust adults to keep them safe, and as a result, they lack social competence. Such *insecurely attached* children may be disruptive in child care centers or schools (Ainsworth et al., 1978).

Various patterns of insecure attachment exist depending on children's experiences, which are related to different patterns of behavior (Ainsworth et al., 1978; Bowlby, 1969/2000). Children who have experienced rejection and insensitivity from adult caregivers may demonstrate **insecure-avoidant attachment**. These children tend to turn away

attachment theory The theory that children's ability to learn depends on their developing trusting relationships with caregivers.

secure attachment relationship A responsive and sensitive relationship with caregivers that allows children to venture forth and comfortably explore and learn about the world.

secure base An attachment figure (mother or caregiver) who serves as an anchor for children to rely on and from which children can safely venture out and explore.

insecure-avoidant attachment Rejection and insensitivity from adult caregivers that causes children to turn away from or avoid adults and not seek their comfort.

Becoming an Intentional Teacher

Easing Separation Woes

Here's What Happened A month before a new group of 1- and 2-year-olds entered our child care center, I contacted the families to learn about the daily routines at home. I encouraged the parents to have the child bring a favorite blanket or toy to the center. I also asked if there were snapshots of family members or maybe a pet that they could share so I could make a little photo book for each child. I suggested to parents that, if possible with their work schedules, children stay for a shorter time for a few days rather than a full day.

On the first day, Sasha's mom whispered to me that she was going to sneak out so her 2-year-old son wouldn't get upset at seeing her go. I told her I thought it would help Sasha if she said goodbye and told him when she would be back.

Here's What I Was Thinking In typical development, usually in the period from 10 months to about 2 years, the child learns that separations from parents are not permanent and begins to be able to deal with time apart. What helps with learning to do this are the child's representational abilities, which are increasing over this period. That's one reason that bringing a favorite thing from home gives children comfort. It reminds the child that home is still a part of his day. Looking at family photos helps with this, too. Starting with a shorter day also allows the child to hold on to the idea that his parent is coming back and then gradually extend that to a longer period.

Parents sometimes want to leave without saying good-bye, and that's understandable. They think the child will be less upset. But what this sneaking away actually does is create mistrust in children. It's better for 1- and 2-year-olds when Mom or Dad tells them, "I'm leaving now and I'll be back right after you have your lunch." I try to reassure the parents not to worry or feel guilty if their child is crying and having difficulty with the separation for a while. It means there's a bond there. During the day, I also try to call or e-mail parents to put their minds at ease.

from or avoid adults and do not seek their comfort; in fact, they may become hostile in order to avoid rejection before it occurs.

Other insecurely attached children who have experienced confusing and inconsistent nurturing from adults are said to be experiencing **insecure-ambivalent/resistant attachment.** Because they are unsure whether adults will be there for them, these children may appear to seek comfort but then reject it when it is offered. They may be irritable and fussy, easily frustrated, and difficult to manage in a group.

insecure-ambivalent/resistant attachment Children's inability to trust adults to keep them safe due to neglect, abuse, or other difficult circumstances that results in a lack of social competence.

In more extreme circumstances, when children have experienced neglect, abuse, or violence in the home, they may exhibit **disorganized/disoriented attachment** (Main & Solomon, 1990). Because their past experiences with adults have left them without secure attachments, they have not developed useful strategies for seeking comfort or attention or for handling difficulties. Their behavior can be very unpredictable and confusing to teachers and negatively affect their ability to learn.

disorganized/disoriented attachment Seen in children who lack secure attachments with adults due to having experienced neglect, abuse, or violence in the home, who have not developed useful strategies for seeking comfort or attention or handling difficulties.

Attachment to Teachers

Although earlier attachment studies focused on mother–child attachment, current research also applies the theory to teacher–child relationships (Howes & Ritchie, 2002; Howes & Smith, 1995; Pianta, 1999; Pianta & Stuhlman, 2003). This research demonstrates that across the full age span of infancy through the primary grades, a caring, sensitive relationship with a teacher is related to both positive social and academic development (Ritchie, Maxwell, & Bredekamp, 2009).

In addition, attachment relationships with parents may not predict attachment relationships with teachers (Howes & Ritchie, 2002). Just as a child who is securely attached to parents may be insecurely attached to teachers, a child who is insecurely attached to parents may develop a secure attachment to a teacher.

Building such relationships with insecurely attached children can be challenging for teachers. These children are those who are most in need of such support if they are to succeed in school and life. While the attachment literature tends to focus on individual relationships between parents or teachers and children, it does not focus on children's roles as members of groups, which we discuss next.

Establishing a Community Where Children Learn Together

Across the age span of birth through age 8, teachers create a caring community by promoting positive interactions among young children (National Association for the Education of Young Children [NAEYC], 2005f, 2009a). Such a community is essential not only for social–emotional development but for learning in every area. What it takes to accomplish this varies, however, depending on the age of the children served.

Infants and Toddlers

Building relationships with babies and toddlers takes time, sensitive touch, talking, and playful learning experiences (Albrecht & Miller, 2001). Teachers create a climate of respect by listening and responding to babies' verbal and nonverbal cues, such as their cries or coos, their facial expressions, and body movements. These behaviors send signals about the baby's wants and needs, such as "I'm hungry" or "I'm bored and want to do something else." When adults respond appropriately to their cues, babies begin to develop a sense of trust and efficacy.

Teachers also model the kind of warmth and caring that they want children to develop. Even very young infants and toddlers demonstrate empathic behaviors toward their peers (Greenspan, 1990). Teachers can promote empathy by labeling children's feelings and helping them comfort one another; for instance, "Claudia is crying because she dropped her binky. Let's give it back to her."

Preschoolers and School-Age Children

As children get older, their awareness of others heightens, and the need for teachers to promote positive interactions among children increases. Teachers set the tone for a harmonious classroom by organizing cooperative learning experiences so that children can play and work

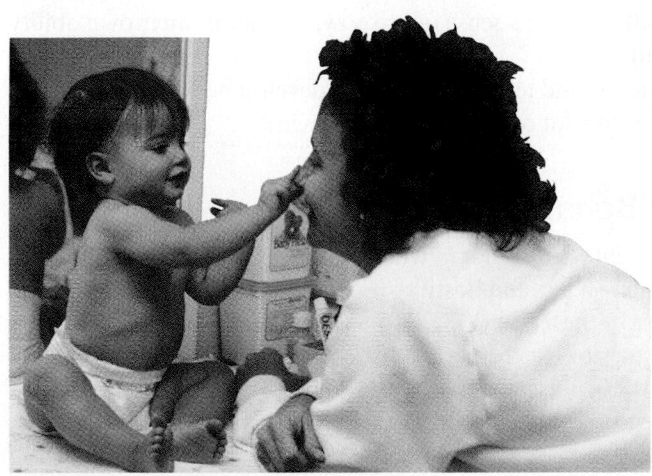

Effective teachers develop warm, responsive, positive relationships with each child. From infancy through primary grades, the quality of teacher–child relationships is related to positive learning and developmental outcomes for children.

together on projects or in small groups. In preschool and even more so in the primary grades, achieving a harmonious classroom involves the entire group working together. To foster such harmony, encouraging children to talk about potential or actual social problems, offer solutions, and reflect on the outcomes during class meetings can be effective (Rightmyer, 2003; Vance & Weaver, 2002).

Vygotsky's theory of learning as a social construction of knowledge emphasizes that much of our understanding occurs as we talk with and listen to other people's ideas. This give and take of conversation and debate with other people plays a major role in learning. Promoting social construction of knowledge requires that children learn, not just as individuals, but also in the context of small and large groups—as part of a community of learners.

The Value of a Caring Community of Learners

Building a caring community of learners requires effort on the part of teachers and children, but the effort pays off in short- and long-term benefits. In the present, the classroom will be a more harmonious, pleasant environment in which children are more likely to learn successfully. In addition, experiencing a caring community helps achieve three essential, long-term goals for children:

1. To develop positive social skills and emotional self-regulation, which are essential tasks during the first 5 to 8 years of life
2. To prevent future social and behavioral difficulties, which is more efficient, effective, and humane than later remediation
3. To build a foundation of learning for later success in school and in life.

Helping Children Develop Positive Social Skills and Emotional Self-Regulation

A major developmental accomplishment of the first 5 years of life is the development of self-regulation in all spheres of behavior. This process begins early as babies learn to regulate their sleeping, crying, and other behavior patterns, and expands during the preschool years to more complex self-regulation. It is during these years that children develop the ability to control emotions, to learn to delay gratification, and to build relationships with other people—all key factors essential for healthy development (Denham, 2006; Shonkoff & Phillips, 2000).

Other important goals of the early years are the development of self-concept and self-esteem. **Self-concept**, which forms rapidly during the preschool years, refers to children's stable perceptions about themselves despite variations in their behavior. Children's **self-esteem**, or perception of their own worth, is also in its formative stages during these years and can be fragile. Similarly, children gradually acquire a sense of **efficacy**, a belief in their own ability to accomplish what they set out to do.

Positive self-concept, self-esteem, and feelings of efficacy develop best as children take initiative and master challenges with a lot of adult encouragement.

Preventing Social and Behavioral Difficulties

self-concept Children's stable perceptions about themselves despite variations in their behavior.

self-esteem Children's perception of their own worth.

efficacy Children's belief in their own ability to accomplish what they set out to do.

Teachers today report a larger percentage of children who exhibit extremely challenging behaviors, such as excessive aggression, anger, and hostility (Fox et al., 2003; McCabe & Frede, 2007). These children take up most of the teacher's attention, yet fail to improve. In worst case scenarios, some of these children may be expelled from child care or preschool, experiencing failure before their educational experiences have even begun (Gilliam, 2005). During the last few decades, since federal laws began requiring child care programs and schools to fully include children with disabilities and special needs, the number of children with challenging behaviors may have increased. Some disabilities such as attention deficit/hyperactivity disorder (ADHD) or autism may adversely affect children's social behavior (Bell, Carr,

Denno, Johnson, & Phillips, 2004). To successfully teach in these increasingly complex classrooms, all teachers must have knowledge of effective, research-based early intervention strategies before they encounter these difficult situations. Children who exhibit persistent challenging behaviors are those most in need of good teaching.

Teachers today report that more children are exhibiting challenging behaviors than in the past. Why might this be true? What might account for this perception?

Building positive social skills and healthy emotional relationships during the early years is more effective than trying to remedy problems later. Research demonstrates that preschool children who are aggressive and those who are neglected or rejected by peers are likely to encounter significant difficulties in school and in life (Ladd, Herald, & Andrews, 2006). Children who fail to develop minimal social competence and, thus, are unable to make friends are at significant risk of dropping out of school, becoming delinquent, or experiencing mental health problems in adolescence or adulthood (Asher, Hymel, & Renshaw, 1984; Parker & Asher, 1987.)

Even when children are 3 or 4 years old, it is possible to observe which children are isolated and do not make friends easily. These children are particularly difficult to handle because even adults do not find them pleasant to be around and may want to avoid them. Yet teachers working with socially isolated children must recognize that these are the children who need their help most. With systematic support and intentional teaching during the preschool years, they can assist children to develop social competence.

If the problems are ignored because teachers are hoping "they'll grow out of it," the problems will only get worse as children get older. Here is an example, of a proactive problem-solving approach:

> Preschool teacher Karen Hagey observed that every time 3½-year-old Marcus tried to push his way into the block corner, the other children shouted, "Get out, Marcus! You can't play." She thought about forcing the children to accept Marcus, but realized that they would resent him and he would be humiliated by her interference. Instead, Karen quietly coached Marcus on strategies for entering play: "Let's sit next to Jason and see if you and I can build a tall tower." Marcus's tower soon eclipsed that of his peers, who started to pay attention to his skill. After a few days of this kind of assistance from Karen, Marcus entered the play area more calmly and Jason said, "Hey, Marcus, help me make my building as tall as me."

Social–Emotional Development and Academic Success

Social competence in the early years is clearly linked to academic success in school (Hamre & Pianta, 2001; Pianta, 1999). Children in preschool and the primary grades perform better on measures of academic achievement, language, and social–emotional development when they have positive, sensitive, trusting relationships with their teachers (Bryant et al., 2005; Pianta et al., 2005). We now have a large body of research to guide teachers in this important work.

The Teaching Pyramid Model for Creating a Caring Community

The Center on Social and Emotional Foundations for Early Learning (www.vanderbilt.edu/csefel) disseminates resources to teachers that translate research on social–emotional development into best practice. The center developed a model—the *Teaching Pyramid*—for promoting social competence and preventing challenging behavior in young children,

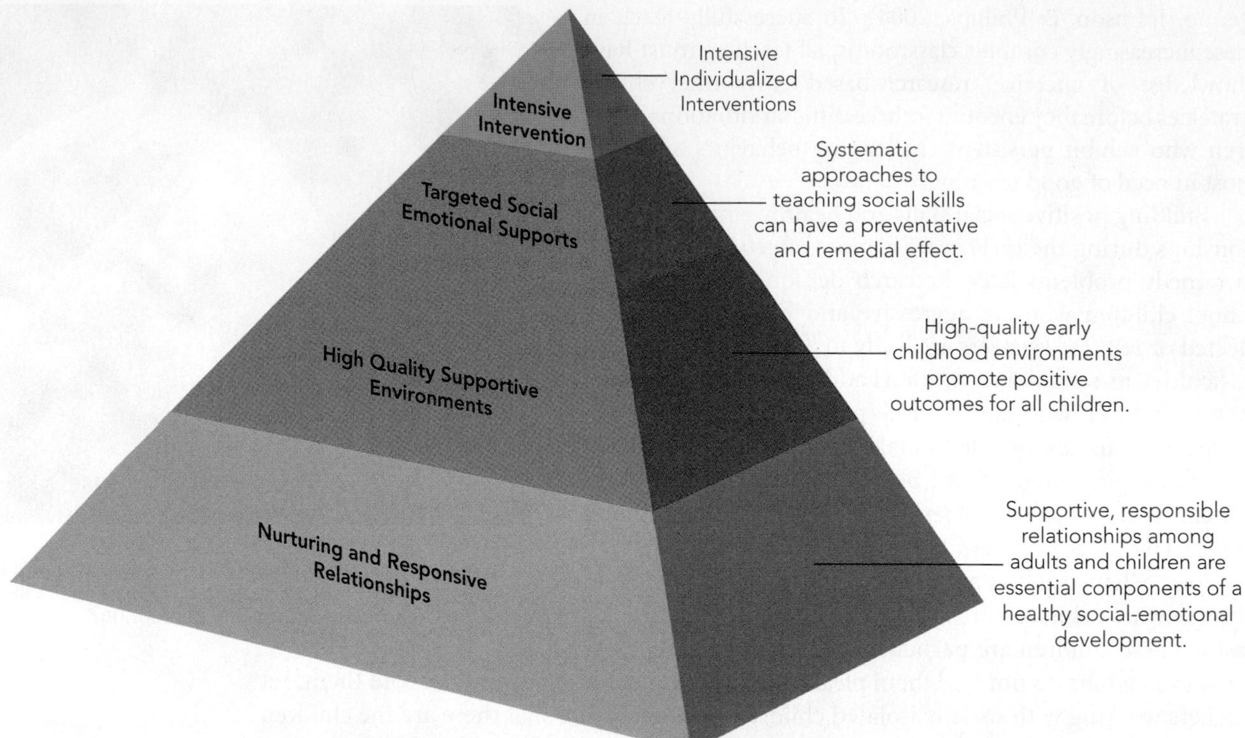
Intensive Intervention
Targeted Social Emotional Supports
High Quality Supportive Environments
Nurturing and Responsive Relationships
Intensive Individualized Interventions
Systematic approaches to teaching social skills can have a preventative and remedial effect.
High-quality early childhood environments promote positive outcomes for all children.
Supportive, responsible relationships among adults and children are essential components of a healthy social-emotional development.

Figure 8.1 Teaching Pyramid Model for Supporting Children's Social and Emotional Development
Source: From *Promoting Social and Emotional Competence in Infants and Young Children.* The Center on Social and Emotional Foundations for Early Learning, www.vanderbilt.edu/csefel. Reprinted by permission.

which is depicted in Figure 8.1. **Challenging behavior** is defined as "any behavior that interferes with children's learning, development, and success at play; is harmful to the child, other children, or adults; and/or puts a child at high risk for later social problems or school failure" (Kaiser & Rasminsky, 2007, p. 9).

Understanding the Pyramid

The Teaching Pyramid is composed of four parts: (1) positive relationships with children, (2) high-quality supportive environments, (3) social and emotional teaching strategies, and (4) intensive individualized interventions. The base of the pyramid is the largest portion because it represents the foundation of positive relationships on which everything else depends. Each subsequent topic on the pyramid builds on the ones below, and represents a proportionately smaller amount of teachers' time and effort. This model indicates that if teachers follow these recommendations, positive behaviors will increase and children's challenging behaviors will diminish.

challenging behavior Any behavior that interferes with children's learning, development, and success at play; is harmful to the child, other children, or adults; or puts a child at high risk for later social problems or school failure.

When teachers encounter children who exhibit negative behaviors such as aggression or hostility, their first inclination is to try to "fix" that child. As teachers, it is natural to assume that if we could just quickly change that child's behavior, everything would be well and our job would be so much easier. The truth is that there are no quick fixes; in fact, the more effective strategy is not to try to fix the child at first. It is always more difficult to change another person's behavior, even if that person is only 3 years old, than to change our own behavior.

The Teaching Pyramid turns our prior assumptions on their head. Rather than trying to change children first, we begin by changing ourselves—that is, we examine our behavior in order to focus on establishing a positive relationship with each child. We recognize that more difficult children will take more effort, but we also acknowledge that the effort will pay off greatly. Next, we evaluate the environment and our teaching to determine whether and what changes need to be made. How can we create an environment that helps children do their best? How can we teach social skills and emotional self-regulation? By asking these questions and seeking solutions, then—and only then—can we attempt to directly address individual children's challenging behaviors.

The Pyramid's Effectiveness

Research demonstrates that when teachers consistently apply the strategies described in the Teaching Pyramid, fewer than 4% children require the more intensive level of interventions (Fox et al., 2003; Sugai et al., 2000). In a group of 20 children, that equates to only one child, or perhaps not even one child. In a center serving 100 children, about 4 children might require this level of intensive assistance. In the following sections, we discuss each level of the Teaching Pyramid and provide examples of effective teaching practices.

Establishing Positive Relationships with Children

A key premise of the Teaching Pyramid is that the most fundamental way to promote healthy development and learning in young children is for teachers to build positive relationships with them. This is the area where teachers need to put most of their energies.

Strategies for Building Relationships with Children

Teachers who have positive relationships with children are significantly more likely to influence their behavior because children pay more attention to responsive, caring adults (Fox et al., 2003). In addition, caring relationships help children develop positive self-concept, confidence, and a sense of safety, which, in turn, reduces the incidence of challenging behavior. In fact, "the time spent building a strong relationship is probably less than the time required to implement more elaborate and time-consuming strategies" to address challenging behaviors (Fox et al., 2003, p. 49).

Teachers need a large repertoire of strategies to use as they build relationships with children, including these with disabilities or special needs and those whose cultural backgrounds may be different from the teacher's own. Human relationships are complex, two-way interactions, and children's behavior influences adults' reactions and behaviors just as much as adults influence children. Therefore, teachers need to spend time reflecting on the basis for their expectations and judgments about children's behavior.

MyEducationLab

Go to the Assignments and Activities section of Topic 9: Guiding Children in the MyEducationLab for your course and complete the activity entitled *Nurturing Relationships*. How does the teacher foster a warm, caring relationship with the toddlers and infant in her care?

Examining Personal, Family, and Cultural Views of Children's Behavior

Each of us has her or his own views about the acceptability of specific behaviors in children based on personal, family, and cultural experiences (Kaiser & Rasminsky, 2003). For example, some adults welcome children's exuberance, whereas others see rambunctious play as misbehavior. Some children are hypersensitive to touch. With 3-year-old Shisuko, pats or hugs would not be welcome, but sitting nearby and talking quietly would. Relationship building, like all other aspects of teaching, requires individualizing.

Because what is considered acceptable behavior in one family, community, or cultural group may be frowned on or prohibited in another (Kaiser & Rasminsky, 2003), teachers should help children learn the kinds of behaviors that predict success in school. In doing so, they can help young children learn that there are different rules of behavior for different

Culture Lens

Helping Children Adapt to School

On the first morning of kindergarten, Miguel Hernandez sets in motion a plan to build a sense of community among the children. His class includes children from many different countries and cultural backgrounds. Miguel greets the children, most of whom arrived by bus, at the door. He hasn't had a chance to meet their families.

He begins the day with a morning meeting and wants the children to introduce themselves. Quickly, however, he changes his plan. In gathering the group and observing them, he realizes how uncomfortable and awkward many of the children would feel if he asked them to speak up in the group. Instead, he introduces himself and reassures them by talking briefly about what will happen today and what they can expect.

Even though Miguel has lived and worked in many different contexts in his life, he remembers vividly his first day of kindergarten. His mother had given him some last minute instructions so that he would be successful in school. She told him to do three things: stand tall, show respect to his teacher, and speak only in English. When he arrived at school the teacher said, "Look at me. Now what's your name?" He was nervous and confused then because he wanted to do what the teacher had told him, but he also wanted to follow his mother's instructions. He knew that looking into the teacher's eyes would be disrespectful, and he was unsure of how to say his name in English. Right at the start of his first day of school, differing cultural expectations clashed and he was caught in the middle.

Fortunately for the children in Miguel's class, he knows not to make assumptions and is sensitive to their needs. He will continue to work toward his goal—to create a caring community of learners—but he also knows that to achieve it, he will have to learn as much as possible about the children's families, their values, and their behavioral repertoires. Although it would have been better for this to happen before the first day, he will find ways to talk with families to discover areas where school and home expectations might differ. Once revealed, he will be able to propose some options to make things easier for a child, and to offer a chance to talk about the differences. For example, "At home you remove your shoes before entering the house. At school we keep shoes on."

Teachers can use the same principle when problems arise over differing expectations about appropriate behavior, which may be more sensitive to discuss with parents, such as the use of profanity. Children may hear and use language at home that is prohibited at school. Helping children adapt to the expectations of school without criticizing their family or community can be a tricky balancing act for teachers, but is likely to be in the child's best interest.

environments. Children make these distinctions all the time. Early on, they learn that what is accepted and safe behavior in their own home is not acceptable behavior in the neighborhood. Read the *Culture Lens: Helping Children Adapt to School* feature for an example of what teachers can do to help children feel comfortable at school.

Examining Adults' Attitudes toward Challenging Behavior

An essential part of your development as a teacher is to examine your own attitudes toward children's challenging behavior. These attitudes are based in your own upbringing, your personal values, your cultural practices, and many other aspects of your prior experiences. Which behaviors do you find most unacceptable? Which behaviors "push your buttons"? Spitting, hitting, name-calling, or bullying? Are they equally unacceptable?

It is also important for you to consider your personal beliefs about the causes of specific types of unacceptable child behavior. Do you attribute motives to certain children but not to others? Do you find yourself thinking that a particularly aggressive child is mean-spirited, or do you think that she wants your attention and is willing to get it any way she can?

mistaken behavior Alternative term for children's misbehavior, recognizing the fact that young children are still learning acceptable behavior and that they are bound to make mistakes.

Mistaken Behavior, Not Misbehavior

Considering the causes for children's behavior is an important part of the reflection process. Dan Gartrell (2004), an expert on guiding children's behavior, prefers the term **mistaken behavior** to *misbehavior*. Young children are still learning acceptable behavior and are bound to make mistakes, just as they make mistakes when learning to tie their shoes or write their names. We not only tolerate, but we expect mistaken behavior as part of the learning process. Why, then, are we so much less tolerant of mistakes in children's social behavior?

Some aspects of children's behavior that disturb adults are actually reflections of children's typical development. For example, toddlers come to love and overuse the word *no* and may accompany their insistent "No!" with temper tantrums. These behaviors demonstrate children's growing independence from adults, their beginning knowledge of the power of language, and frustration over not being able to do everything they would like. Most of the time children grow out of these oppositional behaviors if given appropriate support and nurturance.

Behavior Is Functional

All behavior is a form of communication; it serves a function. Teachers need to understand that even challenging behaviors—those behaviors that are potentially harmful in the short or long term—are conveying some type of message. Experts who study children's behavior have found that most challenging behavior serves one of three functions: It helps children get something, avoid something, or change the level of stimulation (Kaiser & Rasminsky, 2007; Neilsen, Olive, Donovan, & McEvoy, 1999). For example, Brian wants Tonia's truck, so he pushes her down. Tray doesn't want to clean up, so he throws the toys at Emma. Lala is bored waiting in line for the bathroom, so she pinches Mona. As undesirable as these behaviors may be, to effectively handle the children's frustration, the teacher must determine what each behavior is conveying and provide the appropriate support and guidance.

If teachers think about children's challenging behavior as either a mistake on the path to learning or a message they are trying to send, it is likely that their attitudes toward challenging behaviors will change. Instead of blaming children or rejecting them, teachers are more likely to embrace these challenges as problems to solve. Of course, the most effective strategy is to prevent problems in the first place, which is the second step on the Teaching Pyramid.

Organizing High-Quality Supportive Environments

The organization of the learning environment is also very important in creating a caring community of learners and enabling children to do their best. The learning environment includes how the physical space is arranged and furnished as well as how time is organized and used, and how teachers support children's engagement in play and learning. Teachers' work begins before they meet the children in their group. The physical environment, the schedule including use of routines and transitions, and curriculum plan are all important factors in promoting children's positive outcomes and preventing negative behaviors.

Organizing the Learning Environment

Environments send messages, often subtle or even subconscious, about how to behave or which behaviors are acceptable. Libraries convey the message that soft voices and quiet reading are expected. Open spaces and playgrounds invite children to run and chase one another around. With the knowledge that environments send messages, teachers need to consciously think about the messages they want their classroom environments to send to children.

The Physical Space

The classroom needs to be accessible to all children, including children with disabilities, and be organized so that children can interact positively, function as independently

Environments send messages to children about what behavior is acceptable and what is valued. What messages does this classroom environment send to children?

as possible, and learn decision-making skills. For example, teachers should make sure there is enough space for active play that is protected from traffic. They should also make sure to provide enough age-appropriate materials and duplicates of popular toys so children do not always have to share, which can lead to frustration and, ultimately, conflict.

A good early childhood environment is organized into separate **learning centers**, which are defined areas of the classroom that have a particular purpose and that contain relevant furnishings and materials. Learning centers in a preschool typically include a library area, blocks, dramatic play, writing center, art center, manipulative toys near tables, and a group meeting area. Learning centers in a primary grade school are more closely linked to curriculum areas such as reading, math, and science. An environment for babies and toddlers, on the other hand, should be more individualized with large areas for active play and separate spaces for sleeping, feeding, and diapering.

Learning centers enable children to focus their attention, promote small-group interaction, and require children to make choices and experience the consequences of those choices. Figure 8.2 depicts a room arrangement for a preschool classroom that is organized with these guidelines in mind:

- Allow children to independently choose their own activities for part of each day.
- Establish clear boundaries between learning centers by using furniture, floor coverings (carpet, tile), or shelves that help limit the number of children who work or play in each area at one time.
- Locate quiet areas, such as the book, art, writing, and computer centers, next to each other, separated from noisier and more active centers such as blocks, dramatic play, or woodworking.
- Provide easily supervised places for children to be alone or with a friend.
- Locate messy activities such as sand and water play and art projects near a source of water for easy access and cleanup.

learning centers Defined areas of the classroom that have a particular purpose and that contain relevant furnishings and materials.

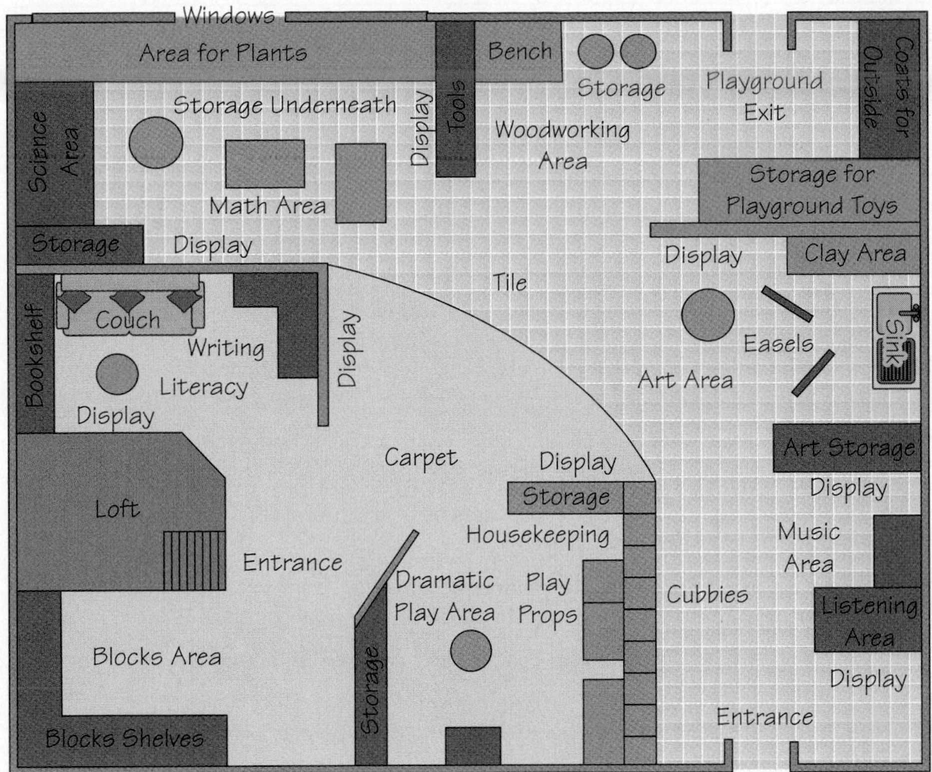

Figure 8.2 Preschool Classroom Room Arrangement

From Wardle, *Introduction to Early Childhood: A Multidimensional Approach to Child-Centered Care and Learning*, p. 141. Published by Allyn and Bacon, Boston, MA. Copyright © 2003 by Pearson Education. Reprinted by permission of the publisher.

- Provide a comfortable meeting space for the whole group to engage in music, movement, book reading, and other large-group activities. Designate seating arrangements so children are not crowded or distracted by toys within reach.
- Eliminate unnecessary clutter, which can distract and agitate some children.
- Avoid large open spaces or corridors that invite children to run.

Organization of the physical environment is one way to positively affect children's behavior. Another way for teachers to support children's development and prevent problems is to carefully plan how time is used.

Organizing the Day

Many of the difficulties that children exhibit in school are related to how the day is organized. These difficulties can be alleviated if teachers provide a consistent, predictable routine that children can rely on. At the same time, teachers need to be flexible so they can easily change plans in response to children's interests or to unanticipated events.

Planning the Schedule

One of the most important aspects of managing the classroom and influencing children's behavior is planning and using time effectively. Young children are often thought to have short attention spans; however, the amount of time they engage in small-group activities that they have chosen is often considerably longer than adults would expect. Children's attention during activities that involve the whole group, such as story reading or morning

Approximate Times (vary by program or school schedule)	Activity
15 to 30 minutes 8:00–8:30	*Arrival:* Teachers greet children and families. Children store belongings, wash hands, find a quiet activity such as looking at books or drawing, or eat breakfast.
15 to 20 minutes 8:30–8:50	*Morning meeting:* Teachers and children gather in whole group to plan for the day and encourage sense of community and belonging in the group. They share music and movement.
60 to 75 minutes 9:00–10:15	*Center time and small groups:* Children play and work in learning centers that the teacher has prepared. Teachers observe and interact one on one with children and also work with small groups on projects, book reading, and playing a math game. Children clean up and wash hands.
15 minutes 10:15–10:30	*Morning snack time:* Teachers sit with children, engage in conversation, and model mealtime behavior. Children serve selves.
15–20 minutes 10:30–10:45	*Group time:* Children share/revisit experiences of the morning. Teachers lead music, movement, and read and discuss book.
30 to 45 minutes 10:45–11:30	*Outdoor play:* Teachers supervise children at play and as they make nature discoveries; they interact with them one on one or in small groups.
10 to 15 minute 11:30–11:45	*Half-day program, group meeting:* Teacher and children reflect on day, plan for tomorrow.
	Full-day program, group meeting: Do a calming activity, prepare for lunch.
30 to 45 minutes 11:45–12:30	*Lunch:* Teachers sit with children, engage in conversation, and model mealtime behavior. Children serve selves.
60 to 90 minutes (varies with age and needs of children) 12:30–2:00	*Full-day program, group meeting, nap, or rest time:* Teachers help children relax. They also supervise and provide quiet activities for those who do not sleep.
15 to 30 minutes 2:00–2:30	*Afternoon snack and activities:* Children have an afternoon snack and engage in quiet activities such as putting puzzles together, book reading, drawing, or writing.
45 to 60 minutes 2:30–3:30	*Full-day program:* Children engage in outdoor play or large muscle experiences indoors. *School-day program, center time, and small groups:* Continue projects from morning and/or make different choices, or outdoor play
10 to 15 minutes 3:15–3:30	*Group time:* Reflect on day and plan for tomorrow.
60 to 90 minutes 3:30–4:30/5:30	*Full-day program center time:* Play, continue projects from morning and/or make different choices.

Figure 8.3 Sample Daily Preschool/Kindergarten Schedule

Source: Based on *Connecting Content, Teaching, and Learning: A Supplement to the Creative Curriculum for Preschool Early Childhood*, 4th ed., by D. T. Dodge, L. J. Colker, and C. Heroman, 2002, Washington, DC: Teaching Strategies.

meetings, is usually more limited and difficult to maintain because there are so many distractions. So time should be planned accordingly. Figure 8.3 provides an example of a daily schedule for a preschool or kindergarten classroom.

Ideally, in an effective classroom, the schedule for the day is posted so that children can predict what is going to happen throughout the day. At times, the schedule will change for planned or spontaneous events, such as a celebration or finding a bird's nest on the playground. But for the most part, a regular schedule allows children to thrive in predictable

environments. If the schedule has to be changed, teachers need to inform the children in advance. The daily schedule should be based on the following guidelines:

- Plan for a balance of learning experiences: large group, small group, and individualized; child initiated and teacher initiated; active and quiet; indoor and outdoor.
- Allow 60 to 75 minutes for learning-center time so children can become deeply engaged in play and projects. In a full-day program, allow at least 1 hour in the morning and another in the afternoon.
- Limit whole-group meeting times to 10 to 20 minutes (allowing more time as children get older) and give opportunities for children to be actively engaged during these experiences.

Ensuring Smooth Transitions

Young children's care and education involves numerous changes in activity and relocation of their physical space. They move from group time to learning centers, eat regularly, wash their hands, use the bathroom, take naps, and go outdoors and return. Each of these situations involves transitions.

Transitions are the changes from one activity or place to another. Although inevitable, transitions can be difficult for very young children who are not particularly good at waiting or who do not adapt well to change. Children who exhibit challenging behaviors tend to display oppositional behavior during transitions. Figure 8.4 lists principles to keep in mind to ease transitions for children.

transitions Changes from one activity or place to another.

Using Routines

The early childhood day is governed by routines of daily living, which, if planned well, can provide children with excellent learning experiences. One study of prekindergarten programs found that on average, children spent 44% of their time in routines and transitions, uninvolved in learning and often waiting idly (Bryant et al., 2005). These regular, informal moments of the day provide valuable opportunities for learning that should not be wasted.

Routines—snacks and mealtimes, cleaning up, washing hands, dressing for outdoors—all provide opportunities for children to practice newly acquired skills and to engage in conversation essential for developing language. In addition, teachers can use routines as times for individual interactions with children such as sitting and talking with children during snacks and meals.

- Prepare ahead of time for the next activity so children do not spend excessive amounts of time waiting. For instance, have several children setting up for snacks while others are cleaning up centers so the transition to snack time is smooth.
- Give children a 5-minute warning before a transition happens, such as, "Five more minutes until cleanup time." Point out the numbers on a digital clock (which becomes a math/addition learning experience) or the hands of the clock to help children grasp the concept of 5 minutes.
- Give children who have particular difficulty with transitions an individual warning and explanation of what is to come, or perhaps a pictorial cue.
- Make transitions learning experiences by singing songs, reciting rhymes or poems, counting steps, following the leader's motions, doing movement exercises, or following specific directions, such as, "If your name starts with a K, get your coat."
- Minimize the number of transitions between activities and the amount of time children spend in transitions.

Figure 8.4 Planning for Smooth Transitions

MyEducationLab

Go to the Building Teaching Skills and Dispositions section of Topic 9: Guiding Children in the MyEducationLab for your course and complete the activity entitled *Guiding Children to Help Ensure Their Success*. As you work through the learning unit, consider how routines can be used to teach and manage the classroom.

Teachers should establish routines that allow children to do as much as possible for themselves. When adults do things for children that they can already do themselves, they rob children of important learning experiences. Routines such as dressing or cleaning up also provide many chances for children to practice fine motor skills, as well as cognitive abilities such as categorization (for example, the long blocks go together and the short blocks go together).

Establishing Clear, Consistent Rules for Behavior

Just as children thrive in predictable physical and temporal environments, they also thrive when the expectations for behavior are clear and predictable. Therefore, it is essential that teachers involve children early on in establishing clear rules, limits, and consequences for behavior. It is equally important that teachers consistently and fairly enforce these rules in order for children to feel safe and secure.

In establishing classroom rules or *guidelines* for behavior, as Gartrell (2004) calls them, teachers need to engage children in discussing and enforcing a manageable number (three to six) of positively stated classroom rules. These discussions should take place during times of calm and quiet reflection. Some teachers may be tempted to focus children's attention on what not to do—don't hit or don't throw toys. However, a more effective approach is to positively state what children should do. Virtually all situations can be covered by these three rules:

1. We take care of ourselves.
2. We take care of other people.
3. We take care of our school.

When we say "Don't run" to young children, their brains may process only the word *run*; they don't process the prohibition. Therefore, it is always more effective to state expectations clearly and positively: "Keep the food on the table" or "Walk inside." It is also important to provide reasons for the expected behavior: "If you run, someone might get knocked over."

Supporting Children to Do Their Best

Earlier, we identified several reasons why children behave as they do: to get something, to avoid something, or to change the level of stimulation. When it comes to "getting something," the object of desire is usually the teacher's attention. Children are willing to do almost anything to attract adults' attention, and they tend not to discriminate between positive and negative attention. To guide children toward using positive strategies to attract attention, teachers must keep in mind that because they have only the power to control their own behavior, they can determine which behaviors of children they give attention to and when. Teachers can ignore mistaken behavior, redirect behavior, and give positive feedback and encouragement.

Ignoring When Appropriate

Behaviors that are not reinforced will be extinguished or eliminated. If the reinforcement that children are seeking is the teacher's attention—and they are behaving inappropriately to receive that attention—then ignoring the inappropriate behavior can be an effective way of extinguishing it. When teachers react to these behaviors, they continue.

Consider, for example, 3½-year-old Curt, who has daily tamper tantrums and lies the floor kicking and screaming. His teacher, Janine, knows that he is too old for this behavior and believes that it is a cry for her attention. She decides to ignore the tantrums by physically removing herself to the other side of the room, but as soon as Curt tires from his explosion and quiets, she returns and invites him to sit by her and read a story. It takes several days during which she has to remind the other children not to pay attention to Curt during these episodes, but gradually Curt's tantrums disappear.

To be effective, teachers must be careful to give more attention to children's positive behaviors than their negative ones. Teachers can identify a select few negative behaviors to ignore and also identify prosocial or positive behaviors to acknowledge that are the opposite of the ones

they are trying to ignore. It may also be necessary to teach the other children to ignore a peer's undesirable behavior since the child may desire the attention of his or her peers as well as the teacher.

Redirecting Behavior

Another strategy for supporting children to do their best is **redirection**, which is the drawing of a child's attention or behavior toward a more desirable alternative. Redirection is especially effective with very young children whose attention is easily distracted. For instance, 18-month-old Jamie appears ready to bite Erika because she has the toy train he covets. His teacher has anticipated this situation and heads it off by offering him an identical engine and turning his attention toward her and away from where Erika is playing.

Redirecting children toward more productive activities is a useful strategy for toddlers who have yet to learn language or other problem-solving strategies and for children who are wandering or withdrawn. As children get older and become more competent problem solvers themselves, adults should rely less on redirection and more on intentionally teaching children to get along with others. Because adults won't always be available to redirect behavior, it is important to use this strategy sparingly.

Giving Positive Attention, Feedback, and Encouragement

One of the most powerful ways teachers have for supporting children's prosocial behavior is to give positive attention when children behave in desirable ways. When teachers use positive feedback and encouragement related to children's appropriate behavior, children feel supported and are more likely to continue to behave acceptably.

If a teacher wants a behavior to continue, it is necessary to provide positive feedback or encouragement. It is important for teachers not to give empty praise such as "Good girl" or "Nice job," but rather to enthusiastically encourage and describe the desired behavior or acknowledge the effort. "Curt, thank you for telling me why you were angry," says his teacher, Jane. "Next time, I'll make sure you get a turn on the balance beam." At times, encouragement will be nonverbal, offering a child a smile, a nod, or a thumbs-up for an achievement.

For positive feedback and encouragement to be effective, teachers need to recognize that there are individual differences in the forms of acknowledgment that children find positive. Communicating with families about what kinds of feedback work for their children may be necessary. One might prefer to sit by the teacher, while another prefers to be given a task to do. When teachers frequently give positive support for appropriate behavior, children will often pick up on their lead, giving positive feedback to each other. Repeating words she has heard her teacher use, 5-year-old Karen says to her friend Darla, "Thanks for helping me clean up this mess. I'll help you next time."

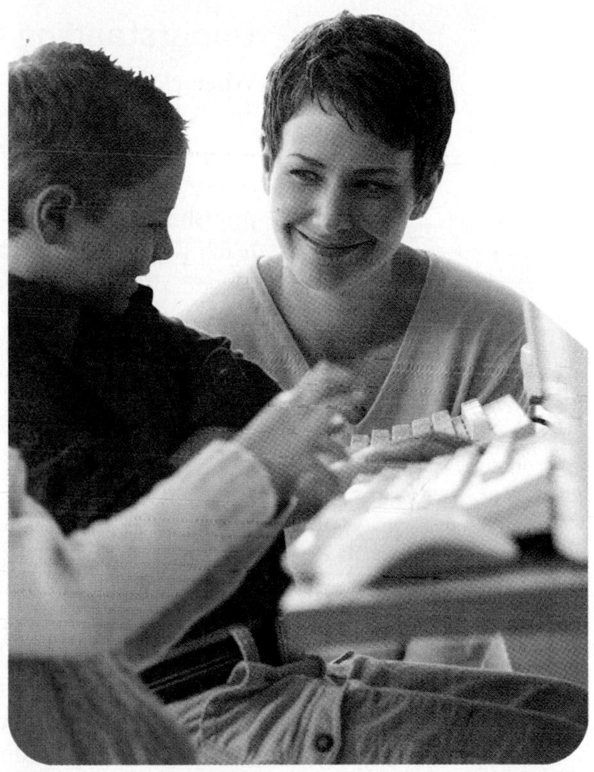

As we see with this first grader, intentional teachers encourage young children's positive behavior. Sometimes just a smile or nod is enough to communicate that you noticed a child's effort or success.

Let's think about how a teacher might use all of these ways of supporting children to do their best when confronted with a challenging situation. Andy picks his nose and it definitely irritates his teacher. She finds this behavior disgusting, but realizes after reflection that she overreacts every time he does it, and the frequency of the behavior is actually increasing, especially during snack times. She decides to encourage more appropriate behavior by giving him his own box of tissues and reminding him in advance how to use them. At first, Andy's nose picking increases, but his teacher decides to ignore it. Instead, when he does anything with the tissue box, even if he simply picks it up, she gives him attention and encouragement. She also gives him positive attention unrelated to the negative behavior:

redirection Drawing a child's attention or behavior toward a more desirable alternative than the one on which the child is currently focusing.

"Andy, you did a good job cutting the bread." Over time, his teacher finds much to enjoy in Andy and the nose picking becomes a rare event.

As we have seen, there are many effective strategies teachers can use to support children to do their best and prevent problem behaviors. In addition to preventing negative behaviors, however, adults have key roles to play in teaching children appropriate behavior, which we examine next.

Promoting Social Competence and Positively Guiding Behavior

Children aren't born with the ability to get along well with other people and regulate their own strong emotions. These social and emotional skills are learned gradually over the first years of life, and they are among the most important accomplishments of children's lives.

Guiding children to function well in a caring community of learners, however, depends on three key aspects of teaching practice: fostering emotional literacy, teaching social skills, and teaching conflict negotiation. Before addressing each of these dimensions of teaching practice, it is important to clarify the distinction between guidance and punishment.

Understanding Guidance and Punishment

When children display unacceptable or inappropriate behavior, which is a natural part of growing up, adults' automatic response is often to discipline them. Consider that the word *disciple* means "to learn." Often when teachers and adults discipline, however, they do so not to teach, but rather to punish. However, children do not learn positive behaviors from punishment. Although punishment may stop a negative behavior temporarily, it does not teach the child what to do instead. Consequently, teachers may find that using the same punishment repeatedly with a child (which they often do) doesn't deter the negative behavior.

> **Effective Teaching**
> Effective teachers develop positive relationships with each child, provide engaging learning environments, intentionally teach social skills, and implement individualized interventions for the children who need them.

One discipline strategy teachers and parents too often use is time-out. **Time-out** is removing a child to a specified chair or area of the room for a period of time following an unacceptable behavior. Many adults think that time-out is a good way to get children to stop their unacceptable behavior. Removing a child from a situation for a period of time, however, can be a form of punishment and, if so, it is unlikely that the child is reflecting on righteousness in this situation. Time-out does not teach the child what to do instead of the negative behavior and, in fact, may achieve the child's purpose by removing him from the situation he sought to avoid, such as helping to clean up. On the other hand, occasionally giving children a brief time away to calm down before negative behavior escalates may be helpful, if the child feels positively supported by the teacher in this situation (Kaiser & Rasminsky, 2007).

Guidance is the process of teaching children the life skills they need to function productively. Instead of punishments, children need adults to actively teach them positive behaviors to replace negative, ineffective behaviors. Children must be taught important life skills, such as appropriate expression of negative emotions, getting along with others, and conflict resolution, using a variety of developmentally appropriate learning experiences and teaching strategies.

time-out Removing a child to a specified chair or area of the room for a period of time following an unacceptable behavior.

guidance The process of teaching children the life skills they need to function productively with other children.

emotional literacy Children's ability to identify their own and others' emotions and to express emotions in a healthy way.

Fostering Emotional Literacy

When children grapple over a toy, hit, or bite, teachers often suggest, "Use your words." This is an effective strategy if, and only if, children have the vocabulary to describe their emotions and the language proficiency to articulate their wants and needs. **Emotional literacy** is "the ability to identify, understand, and respond to emotions in oneself and others in a healthy manner" (Joseph, Strain, & Ostrosky, 2006). Children who have a strong foundation in emotional literacy are more likely to tolerate frustration, fight less, and are less lonely and impulsive. They are also more focused and have greater academic achievement. Developing a vocabulary for ex-

Table 8.1 Strategies for Promoting Emotional Literacy

Strategy	Example
Express your own feelings. Talk out loud and label your own emotions.	"I'm feeling frustrated because this paint jar is stuck. I think I'll take a deep breath and count to five. One . . . two . . . three . . . four . . . five. Now I'll try again."
Label children's feelings.	"You look disappointed that both computers are busy now." "I can tell you're surprised and excited to see your grandmother."
Help children talk about their own and others' emotions and discuss acceptable ways of expressing strong feelings.	"I think you and Rashid are angry with each other. I think you want Rashid to give you a turn at the easel. Can you ask how much longer it will be before you can paint?"
Use songs and rhymes, play games, and read stories that introduce and reinforce feeling words.	Adapt a song to expand feeling vocabulary: "If you're happy and you know it, clap your hands. If you're excited and you know it, jump up high. If you're frustrated and you know it, take a breath."
Narrate and describe ongoing interactions to help children develop vocabulary related to prosocial behaviors.	"Gregory and Keisha, you are working so well together at the computer. You look pleased and proud of the book you've created."
Draw children's attention to the feelings or experiences of others, at times using pictures or photos of people's faces.	"Look at this face. Can you tell how this person feels?" Help them to develop empathy by reminding them of their own similar feelings or experiences. "You know what it feels like when someone says you can't play."
Model caring, positive regard for others.	When a child is absent, remind the others of the friend who is missed. If absences are prolonged, have children make cards or send e-mails or gifts to convey feelings of regard.

Source: Based on *Fostering Emotional Literacy in Young Children: Labeling Emotions* (What Works Brief 21), by G. Joseph, P. Strain, and M. M. Ostrosky, 2006, Urbana-Champaign, IL: Center on the Social and Emotional Foundations for Early Learning. Retrieved July 29, 2009, from http://www.vanderbilt.edu/csefel/briefs/wwb21.html. Reprinted with permission.

pressing feelings is an essential aspect of emotional literacy because the larger a child's emotional vocabulary, the finer distinctions she can make when expressing her feelings to other people.

Think about the number of words you know related to feeling bad: *angry, mad, furious, upset, anxious, unhappy, distraught, disturbed, disappointed, depressed, disgusted, dismayed, frustrated*—we could empty a thesaurus. The same could be said for other emotional states. Being frustrated, however, is not the same as being furious. Children's behavior may be communicating frustration or fury and, without knowing which, we may be more or less effective in helping them. A number of effective strategies can be used to teach emotional literacy, as described in Table 8.1.

An important aspect of emotional literacy is being able to reflect on one's own emotions. Read the *What Works: The Emotion Thermometer* feature for an example of an effective strategy to promote emotional literacy in young children.

Teaching Social Skills

Just as children need adults to teach them how to regulate and express emotions constructively, children need adults to explicitly teach them social skills such as cooperation, social problem solving, and interacting with peers. In addition, children with disabilities may need particular help from adults in forming friendships with typically developing peers (Odom, 2001).

What Works

The Emotion Thermometer

Teaching emotional literacy is a proven strategy for promoting children's social skills and preventing challenging behavior. Teachers can use the emotion thermometer to help children monitor their own feelings. Here is how the strategy works: The children decorate the thermometer with pictures of feeling faces from "happy" and "relaxed" in the blue, cool section of the thermometer all the way up to "angry" or "stressed out" in the red, hot section of the thermometer.

The teacher then asks children to describe a recent conflict and together they retrace the steps that led to the angry outburst. The teacher writes down the child's thoughts, actions, and words that indicated an escalating anger pattern. For example, the child kicks, yells, or thinks, "He always takes my toys." Then the teacher discusses with the child the thoughts, actions, and words that the child can use to reduce her anger.

As the teacher retraces the steps of the angry outburst, he helps the child identify the time or situation that caused her to start getting angry. This is marked as the "Danger Point" on the thermometer. Once children have established their danger points, they name the zone, such as "Chill Out," "Cool Down," "Code Red," or "Hot Engine." Then, in the course of a day, the teacher and child can use this code word as a signal that anger or stress has reached the threshold. This in turn can trigger the use of an agreed-on calming strategy such as taking three deep breaths or visualizing happy and calming places.

Source: From *Fostering Social and Emotional Competence: Implementing Dina Dinosaur's Social Skills and Problem Solving Curriculum in Inclusive Early Childhood Programs,* 2006, by G. E. Joseph, C. Webster-Stratton, and M. Reid. Retrieved August 7, 2009, from http://www.incredibleyears.com/Library/items/fostering-social-emotional-curriculum_06.pdf.

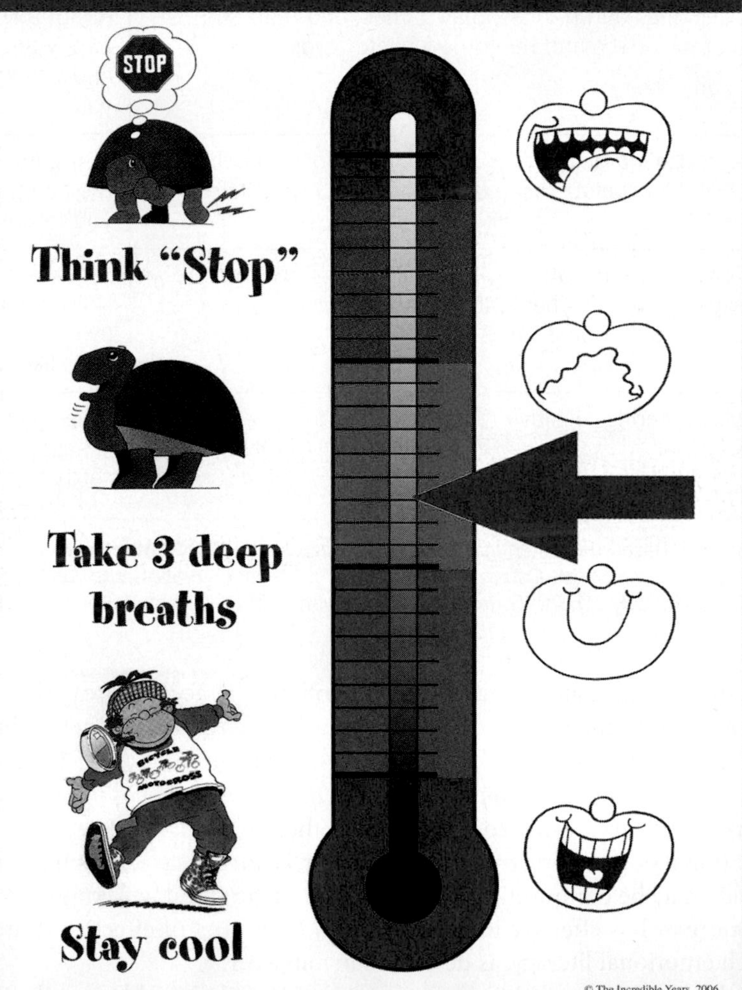

Emotion Thermometer
Source: Copyright © The Incredible Years, 2006.

Including All Children

When to Teach Social and Emotional Skills

The figure below illustrates the cycle of challenging behavior as it typically occurs in early childhood settings. It depicts the point at which teachers are most effective in supporting children's social–emotional development and in preventing challenging behaviors. Consider how the cycle unfolds in the following scenario.

> At choice time, Jessie moves to the block corner, sits down, and begins constructing a boat with the unit blocks. He is serious about his project, but calm and content. His teacher, Sarah, looks around the room and notices that all of the children are happily playing and learning. A few minutes pass and more children are now in the block corner. There are fewer blocks to go around, and it is getting crowded. Still, Jessie is busy concentrating and enjoying his creation.
>
> Fifteen minutes later, Jessie has an idea and searches for the Y-shaped block. He sees a child using it and demands it with angry words, but the other boy continues to claim it.
>
> Sarah hears a scream and rushes to see what happened. Jessie has attacked the boy with the Y-shaped block, who is badly hurt and cries loudly.

At precisely this point—marked by the red arrow—many teachers try to teach Jessie a social skills lesson. For example, teachers might say any of the following: "Use your words!" "Hitting is not okay." "We share our toys." "Say you're sorry!" "You need to calm down. Go to the thinking chair."

It is true that preschoolers need to use words to resolve conflict; to understand that aggression is not okay; to share materials; to know how and when to use an apology; and how to regulate their emotions. However, teaching these skills is ineffective if teachers try to do so at the wrong time. The crisis moment (red arrow) is not a teachable moment for several reasons: (1) The challenging behavior has already occurred. (2) The child who engages in aggression is likely to be upset and agitated and not responsive to a lesson highlighting his or her mistakes. (3) The time and attention the teacher spends trying to teach the child what to do instead (even if it is negative attention) may serve to reinforce the challenging behavior. (4) If the teacher only uses these crisis moments as times to teach social–emotional skills, the child will never receive enough positive learning and practice opportunities to effectively alter his or her behavior.

The most effective teachable moments happen *before* problems occur, when the teacher and children are calm and engaged in appropriate behavior—green arrows. At these times, teachers can build positive relationships and teach key social–emotional skills, such as identifying emotions and resolving conflict.

Source: Based on "The Teaching Pyramid: A Model for Supporting Social Competence and Preventing Challenging Behavior in Young Children," by L. Fox, G. Dunlap, M. L. Hemmeter, G. E. Joseph, and P. S. Strain, 2003, *Young Children, 58*(4), pp. 48–52.

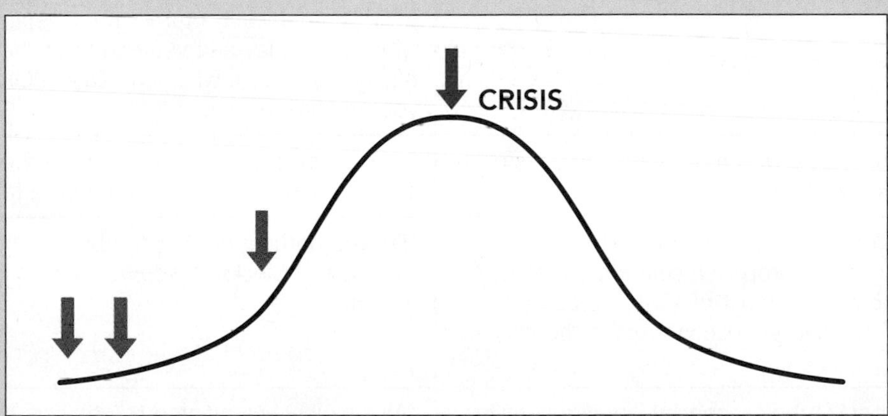

Cycle of Challenging Behavior

One important decision facing teachers is when to teach social skills. Some moments in time are more effective than others to teach social skills. Teachers often try to teach problem solving in the middle of a crisis situation, when intervention is least effective. Read the *Including All Children: When to Teach Social and Emotional Skills* feature to learn timely ways to teach social skills.

Teaching Children to Negotiate Social Conflicts

Conflict is an inevitable part of social interaction, especially with young children who are just developing their ability to get along with other people. Teaching children specific steps in conflict resolution before problems occur and trusting them to solve their own problems are important steps in children's social–emotional development.

During conflicts between students, when teachers remain calm and in control of their own emotions, children feel assured and safe. It is important to acknowledge children's strong feelings and help them learn to describe their feelings and perceptions of the conflict to each other. Rather than asking a question that children will not be able to answer such as "How do you think that made him feel?" ask the child, "What happened? How do you feel?" By giving each child the opportunity to offer solutions to the conflict and by offering their own only if needed, teachers help children become better negotiators and communicators. Table 8.2 describes strategies for teaching conflict resolution.

Table 8.2 Teaching Conflict Resolution

Strategy	Example
Acknowledge, accept, and validate all children's feelings and perceptions of the conflict.	Use "I messages"—sentences that describe your own observations or perceptions about a situation, such as "Katie, I think you are angry because Ally took the blocks you wanted."
Help children verbalize feelings and desires to each other and listen to one another. Use *active listening*, which reflects what you are hearing so the child can agree or disagree.	The teacher says, "Katie, it sounds like you wanted all the big blocks for your bridge." Katie responds, "No, I just want the two biggest and Ally took them."
Clarify and state the problem.	"Katie and Ally, you both want the two biggest blocks."
Give children the opportunity to suggest solutions.	The teacher says, "How could we solve this problem?" Katie says, "I get to have the blocks because I was here first." Ally says, "You have been playing with them the whole time. I want a turn." Katie replies, "I could play with them today and you can have them next week." Ally ponders for a while and says, "Okay, but only if you promise."
Propose solutions when children do not have ideas or if their ideas are too extreme or punitive.	"Next week seems like a long time away," the teacher says. "Maybe tomorrow would be a fairer solution."
Uphold the value of mutual agreement and give children the opportunity to reject proposed solutions. That is, both parties in the conflict must mutually agree on the solution. When both children lose interest in the conflict, do not pursue it.	"Do you both agree that tomorrow Ally can have the two biggest blocks? If so, we'll write it down so we remember."
Help children recognize their responsibility in a conflict situation.	"Ally, I know you wanted the blocks, but Katie got angry when you took them without asking."
Help children repair the relationships, but do not force children to be insincere.	"Ally, you usually like to build with Katie. And I know Katie is your friend."
Encourage children to resolve their conflict by themselves.	"Katie, I know that you and Ally built a hospital together last week so I think you can solve this problem together."

Source: Based on *Moral Classrooms, Moral Children: Creating a Constructivist Atmosphere in Early Education*, by R. DeVries and B. Van, 1994, New York: Teachers College Press.

Helping children learn conflict negotiation skills takes time and practice. Sometimes a conflict does not warrant a full-scale negotiation because one child is not as vested in the issue. But equipping all children with conflict negotiation skills helps ensure that rules are fairly and equitably applied and that the classroom is truly a caring community of learners.

Applying the first three parts of the Teaching Pyramid—establishing positive relationships, organizing high-quality supportive environments, and teaching social and emotional skills—will go a long way toward creating a caring community of learners. Nevertheless, a few children will require more individualized interventions to successfully navigate the classroom and learn optimally, as we discuss next.

MyEducationLab

Go to the Assignments and Activities section of Topic 9: Guiding Children in the MyEducationLab for your course and complete the activity entitled *Peaceful Conflict Resolution*. What are some strategies that this teacher uses to help the children resolve their conflict and avoid future conflicts?

Individualized Interventions for Children with Challenging Behaviors

In most classrooms, it is likely that there will be a few children who demonstrate persistent challenging behaviors. To effectively reach these students it may be necessary to use **individualized intervention**, which is a systematically planned and implemented set of actions designed to alter the course of a child's development or learning.

Research demonstrates that **positive behavior support** (**PBS**) is a highly effective, humane intervention approach for working with children with severe and persistent challenging behaviors (Fox et al., 2003). Positive behavior support is a method of identifying the causes and functions of problem behaviors in order to develop support strategies that prevent such behaviors and teach new, more appropriate skills. In the following sections, we identify and describe challenging behaviors and then explain each of the elements of positive behavior support.

Understanding Challenging Behaviors

A formal definition of *challenging behaviors* is "behaviors that are dangerous, disruptive, or disgusting; cause injury to the child or others; damage the physical environment; interfere with learning; or cause the child to be isolated from peers" (Neilsen et al., 1999). However, each of us defines *challenging behaviors* according to our own values, experiences, and cultural perspectives. Strain and Hemmeter (1999) take a more pragmatic view in their definition: "Challenging behavior is any behavior that is disturbing to you and you wish to see stopped" (p. 17).

Strain and Hemmeter (1999) also offer some practical advice for anyone working with children with challenging behaviors (and that's everyone who works with children!). They advise early childhood professionals to become more "comfortable" with challenging behavior; they emphasize how important it is to recognize that when stressed, embarrassed, disturbed, or feeling hopeless, it is difficult to be effective. To help teachers become more at ease, they suggest that teachers need to acknowledge these feelings and serve as mutual support for each other. Then, if a child loses control and a teacher begins to feel herself losing control as a result, she can turn to a colleague to step in temporarily.

According to Strain and Hemmeter (1999, p.18), becoming more comfortable with disturbing behavior is more likely to be successful when teachers:

- Stop thinking about removing the child as the "real" answer to the problem.
- Stop blaming disturbing behaviors on uncontrollable, extraneous events such as "If only his parents cared more."
- Start celebrating what has been accomplished in comparison to where the situation began. For example, instead of lamenting that Andy still picks his nose, celebrate that he only picked his nose once today instead of 10 times.

individualized intervention A systematically planned and implemented set of actions designed to alter the course of a child's development or learning.

positive behavior support (PBS) A method of identifying the causes and functions of problem behaviors in order to develop support strategies that prevent challenging behaviors and teach new, more appropriate skills.

MyEducationLab

Go to the Assignments and Activities section of Topic 9: Guiding Children in the MyEducationLab for your course and complete the activity entitled *Managing Challenging Behavior: The Teacher's Role*. How do these teachers help manage and resolve conflict? Notice their tone and demeanor.

- Alter expectations about the effectiveness of interventions. Don't expect that an intervention will result in challenging behavior being "fixed for good" or "never ever" occurring.

Positive behavior support involves several steps. The first, and perhaps most important, is determining the function of the child's behavior.

Assessing and Addressing the Function of the Child's Behavior

Functional assessment, also called **functional analysis**, is the process of determining why a child is behaving in a certain way. "Any challenging behavior that persists over time is 'working' for the child" (Strain & Hemmeter 1999, p. 19) and is an attempt to communicate a message such as "You're asking me to do something that is too difficult" (e.g., when a teacher expects preschoolers to sit still for a 30-minute group time) or "I'm bored; pay attention to me."

Acknowledging that children's behavior serves a function and communicates a message helps teachers focus on teaching alternative ways of interacting with other people. Remember Tray, who didn't want to clean up and threw the toys at Emma? If his teacher responds by putting him in time-out, Tray will most likely throw toys again tomorrow because he succeeded in avoiding cleanup time.

Functional assessment is a process of systematic observation and documentation of children's behavior over time involving three steps that are easily remembered using the letters A, B, C (Neilsen et al., 1999):

- A = *Antecedents.* This step is observing what usually occurs before the negative behavior or what conditions trigger the behavior, such as a whole-group time.
- B = *Behavior.* During this step, teachers systematically document what the behavior is and how frequently it occurs.
- C = *Consequences.* During the third step, the teacher or child care provider attempts to determine the function the behavior serves; that is, what does the child get, avoid, and/or change as a result of the behavior?

Identifying Antecedents

Assessing the antecedents (A) of the behavior requires a teacher to carefully observe to determine the conditions or situations that most often trigger the behavior. By identifying key triggers, the teacher can change the conditions to prevent the behavior or redirect the child before the occasion arises. For example, observing that Lala's behavior usually deteriorates during transitions, such as when she pinched Mona while standing in line, her teacher uses a rhyming game to keep her engaged.

Documenting Behavior

The next step is documenting the behavior (B). In using functional assessment, it is important to carefully define and count the frequency (how often) of the behavior to be changed. For example, in the midst of working with a particularly disturbing behavior such as spitting or biting, sometimes teachers lament, "He spits constantly" or "He bites all the time." In fact, a child could not spit or bite "all the time"; even the most avid spitter or biter must come up for air occasionally. Systematic observation and recording of the actual number of unacceptable behaviors is required for successful intervention. In doing so, Andy's teacher finds that he picks his nose 10 times a day and sets out to intervene to decrease this behavior.

functional assessment or functional analysis The process of determining why a child is behaving a certain way, based on the principle that all behavior serves a function or purpose.

Observing Consequences

Objectively observing the consequences (C) of the behavior is essential to form a hypothesis about the function of the child's behavior. What usually happens after the behavior occurs? Does Hans get the Legos after pushing Natasha away from the table? Does Manny avoid reading group because he cries and insists he has a stomachache?

Once antecedents, behavior, and consequences are documented, teachers can assess possible functions that the behavior is serving. What does the child appear to be getting or avoiding? Children most often exhibit challenging behavior to get attention from adults or peers. At times, however, a child wants *power*, the ability to control what is happening to him or others. This may be the case for a child who is experiencing some kind of disruption that is beyond his power to control, such as his parents' divorce or an abusive relationship. Avoiding power struggles with children is always advisable. Adults often lose, and there is nothing scarier to a child than having too much power. If a child is trying to get power, it is best to give him choices and power over manageable things, such as what book to read or who to play with and where.

Objective documentation describes behaviors without adding judgmental comments. Using a form such as the one shown in Table 8.3 facilitates a teacher's objective documentation of an ABC analysis.

With children whose challenging behaviors are severe and persistent, it is especially important to involve a team of people in the process of functional assessment and developing a plan.

Teaming with Families and Professionals to Implement Individualized Plans

Too often teachers, especially new teachers, feel alone and helpless when confronted by children with challenging behaviors. They can find strength and knowledge in a team for

Table 8.3 ABC Analysis for 4-Year-Old Tyler

Date and Time	Antecedent	Behavior	Consequences	Perceived Function/ Comments
	What happened before?	What did the child do?	What happened after?	What was the possible function of the behavior?
1/10 10:30	Three minutes of art activity has passed. Tyler is not participating. The teacher asks Tyler to paint a picture.	Tyler screams, "No!" and throws his paper on the floor.	The teacher walks away. Tyler leaves the art table and goes to the block area to play.	Avoid art activity
1/10 11:30	The teacher announces that it is time to get ready for lunch and takes Tyler's hand to guide him to the sink to wash his hands.	Tyler falls to the floor and starts crying.	The teacher says, "Okay, Tyler, you don't have to wash your hands, but you have to use a handiwipe."	Avoid washing hands. Opportunity to use handiwipe
1/11 8:30	The teacher tells the children it is time to clean up and go to circle. The teacher walks toward Tyler.	Tyler throws a truck and screams, "No! I don't want to clean up!"	The teacher says, "Tyler, no throwing toys. Go to time-out." Tyler sits in a chair while the rest of the children clean up. When cleanup time is over, Tyler goes to the circle with the rest of the children.	Avoid cleanup time

Source: From *Practical Ideas for Addressing Challenging Behaviors* by DEC Staff. Copyright 1999 by Division for Early Childhood. Reproduced with permission of Division for Early Childhood in the format Textbook and Other Book via Copyright Clearance Center.

several reasons. Children are incredibly adept at figuring out how to push adults' buttons. At the same time, children benefit from consistent, clear messages about expectations for their behavior from the significant adults in their lives. Finally, teachers and parents themselves need support to both endure and transform children's challenging behavior.

Although it can be difficult to get some parents involved, intervention is more likely to be successful if family members are involved. Understanding how children behave at home and communicating to parents how their children behave in school is an essential part of the process.

Creating and implementing individualized intervention plans require the expertise of professionals beyond classroom teachers. Early childhood special educators, mental health professionals, social workers, and therapists play key roles in developing the plan. Every state has such resources available to families and child care programs through its public school system and is required by law to provide this assistance to children with disabilities and special needs.

Implementing an Individualized Plan Using Positive Behavior Support

Once a team has been established and a functional assessment completed, the next step is to develop and implement a **behavior intervention plan**, which describes the behavior to be changed and the strategies adults will use to prevent the negative behavior and to teach more acceptable behavior. For example, once a teacher better understands what triggers the behavior, she can prevent or redirect the child before events escalate. In addition, understanding the consequences of a behavior enables the teacher to ensure that the behavior is not effective in achieving its goals.

Although one goal of the behavior plan is to diminish negative behaviors, a more important goal is to teach **replacement behaviors**, which are the prosocial behaviors you want the child to exhibit instead of the problem behaviors. To replace negative, challenging behaviors with prosocial behavior, teachers can use the teaching strategies described previously in this chapter as well as more explicit instruction and reinforcement of acceptable alternatives. Replacement skills should be taught throughout the day, particularly when the problem behavior is not occurring. A functional analysis of Tyler's challenging behavior was presented in Table 8.3 on page 253. Now that we have discussed how to implement an intervention plan, read and discuss the feature titled *How Would You Respond? Implementing a Plan for Tyler's Challenging Behavior.*

The last stage of the behavior plan is to carefully monitor and document the child's progress and make adjustments as needed. Teachers should not become discouraged if results are not immediately positive. The fact is that when interventions are first initiated, children's behavior often gets worse before it improves. As a result, teachers or parents often abandon the intervention too soon. Teachers and team members must continue to observe children's behavior over time and change strategies that are not successful. Working with children with challenging behaviors can be a humbling experience, but the ultimate result can be tremendously rewarding for everyone involved, particularly the child.

In the following sections, we demonstrate how to apply the Teaching Pyramid in specific circumstances that teachers are likely to encounter in practice.

behavior intervention plan Describes the strategies adults will use to prevent a child's negative behavior and to teach more acceptable behavior.

replacement behaviors Desirable prosocial behaviors that replace problem behaviors.

Using the Pyramid Model to Teach Boys More Effectively

Using the Teaching Pyramid to guide teaching practice every day will improve the quality of the educational experience for all children and teachers. In this section we demonstrate how to use the Teaching Pyramid to teach boys more effectively. We realize that addressing the behavior of boys as a group runs the risk of stereotyping. Of course, all

How Would You Respond?

Implementing a Plan for Tyler's Challenging Behavior

Table 8.3 describes a functional assessment of 4-year-old Tyler's challenging behaviors. From these observations, it appears that Tyler is successfully avoiding table activities, hand washing, and cleanup time by crying and engaging in tantrums. How would you respond?

- Teach Tyler to say "Please help" before cleanup time is announced.
- Help Tyler pick up the toys to decrease his challenging behavior.
- Give Tyler a short break before cleanup time.
- Ignore Tyler's crying and tantrums.
- Teach Tyler to say "I'm done" before he starts crying when he's frustrated.
- Teach Tyler to ask for help washing his hands: "Help, please."
- After Tyler picks up a toy or washes his hands, give him positive attention and encouragement.

Which of these actions do you think would be useful and why? What else can you suggest?

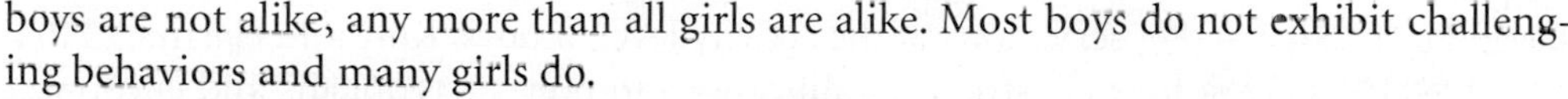

boys are not alike, any more than all girls are alike. Most boys do not exhibit challenging behaviors and many girls do.

However, boys are described as socially immature and developmentally young more often than girls. As a result, boys are more likely to be held back in preschool or kindergarten. In addition, boys are disproportionately labeled as having ADHD, are assigned to special education, and/or are expelled from school (King & Gartrell, 2004), especially boys who are African American and Hispanic (FPG Child Development Institute, 2007a; Gilliam, 2005).

In fact, there are some observable gender differences in the behavior of young children. Boys are more likely than girls to engage in off-task behavior, rough-and-tumble play, and physical aggression, whereas girls are more often verbally aggressive during conflicts (King & Gartrell, 2004).

Teaching Boys

Darlene is the sole kindergarten teacher in a group of 23, 15 of whom are boys. During learning center time, a fight breaks out in the block corner. When Darlene tries to intervene, Jamie screams at her, "You're stupid!" and the other four boys cover their ears and laugh. For 20 minutes at a time, four of the girls happily play in the grocery store Darlene has set up, but Darryl and Jason rush in and knock over the food stands trying to race with the shopping carts. At group time, a group of boys start tickling each other or pushing one another over while Darlene tries to read. Despite years of experience as a teacher, Darlene finds herself struggling to control her emotions, speaking harshly to the boys, and putting them in time-out repeatedly but to no avail.

Perhaps fearing the label of *gender biased*, many educators avoid tackling the topic of boys' behavior. However, many teachers, who are often female themselves, may find active, energetic boys difficult to manage. Denying this fact does not help teachers any more than it helps boys function more successfully in school. Increasing the number of male teachers of young children could alleviate the problem because males might be more understanding and tolerant of boys' typical behavior. However, as of 2008 only about 4% of child care teachers and 2% of prekindergarten and kindergarten teachers were male (MenTeach, 2009).

In the sections that follow, we discuss strategies that can be used within the Teaching Pyramid model to build positive, encouraging relationships with boys; rethink the environment to prevent boys' challenging behaviors; and adapt teaching and intervention strategies for boys.

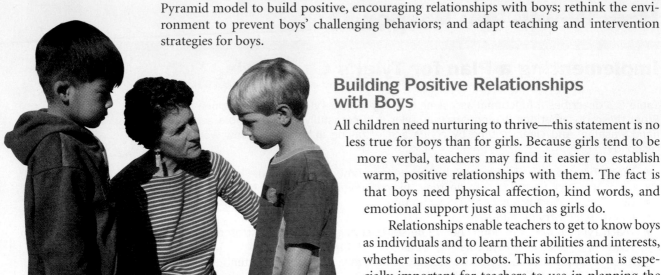

Conflicts are inevitable when children are together in group situations. Effective teachers do not solve problems for children. They teach children the skills they need to resolve their own conflicts.

Building Positive Relationships with Boys

All children need nurturing to thrive—this statement is no less true for boys than for girls. Because girls tend to be more verbal, teachers may find it easier to establish warm, positive relationships with them. The fact is that boys need physical affection, kind words, and emotional support just as much as girls do.

Relationships enable teachers to get to know boys as individuals and to learn their abilities and interests, whether insects or robots. This information is especially important for teachers to use in planning the environment and activities to prevent problem behaviors in boys.

Rethinking the Environment for Boys

Based on research and observations of the activity level of boys, King and Gartrell (2004, pp. 112–115) suggest four classroom modifications to prevent problems and encourage boys to do their best:

1. Increase indoor and outdoor large-motor and whole-body experiences such as "painting" the sidewalk with water, navigating an obstacle course, or allowing rough-and-tumble play.
2. Add sensory exploration and experimentation experiences, such as cutting vegetables for snacks or sand and water play.
3. Adapt building and construction experiences by enlarging and enriching the block area with props such as firefighter hats, and adding a woodworking center with real tools and safety goggles.
4. Increase variety by adding novel dramatic play experiences such as fishing, boating, or camping. Use games and books on topics of interest to boys such as dinosaurs or space travel.

Rethinking the environment with boys in mind will go a long way toward preventing many of the challenging behaviors of boys, especially those that result from their trying to change the level of stimulation. Boys who are engaged in stimulating activities are less likely to be bored and uninvolved and, thus, less disruptive. The next two levels of the Teaching Pyramid—teaching social and emotional skills, and individualized interventions—should also be adapted to ensure successful experiences for boys.

Adapting Teaching and Intervention Strategies for Boys

The Teaching Pyramid strategies described earlier apply to all children; however, King and Gartrell (2004) offer several adaptations to increase the likelihood of success with boys. These suggestions are based on the fact that boys tend to have a strong sense of justice and fair play, and may feel humiliated or unfairly treated by a teacher. Table 8.4 lists effective

Table 8.4 Adapting Teaching and Intervention Strategies for Boys

Strategy	Explanation	Example
Defuse the situation.	Stay observant and downplay conflict before it escalates. Sometimes boys attribute motives where none exist and the teacher can clarify what really happened.	"Josh, Rodney didn't mean to knock over your building. It was an accident. Would you let him help you rebuild it?"
Help children calm down.	Rather than time-out, provide an area of the room for "time away" where a child can select to go before a conflict escalates to calm down and regain composure. Use humor carefully and respectfully to defuse situations.	Use the emotion thermometer (see page 248) and deep breathing to help boys regain composure. "It sounds like a firecracker went off over here. Let's be careful it doesn't fall on our heads."
Talk privately with boys.	Given boys' strong sense of justice, it is important that teachers avoid subjecting them to shame or public embarrassment.	A private talk before a problem or after the child has calmed down should be effective.
Avoid threats.	Threatening a child creates a power struggle that inevitably leads to one person losing, either the teacher or the boy.	Rather than issuing a threat ("Share the blocks or I will take them away"), give boys a meaningful choice: "Josh, you can share all the blocks with Mark and Todd, or you can have ten to play with by yourself."
Follow through.	Boys tend to lose respect if the teacher does not follow through with the consequences of the decision the child made or the negotiated solution to the conflict.	If Josh continues to refuse to share the blocks, the teacher needs to quietly enter the block corner, speak to him at his eye level, and follow through with the choice: "Josh, since you don't want to share all the blocks, I'll help you count ten that you can play with alone."
Teach boys to manage their impulses.	Many boys tend to act impulsively, physically acting out when faced with a conflict.	Coach boys to express their emotions In acceptable ways at times when conflicts are not occurring.

Source: Based on Gartrell, D., *The Power of Guidance,* pp. 112–115. © 2004 Wadsworth, a part of Cengage Learning Inc. Reproduced by permission. www.cengage.com/permissions.

ways of adapting teaching and intervention strategies for boys. These strategies are also likely to be successful with girls.

With these adaptations for boys in mind, kindergarten teacher Darlene rethinks her classroom environment:

> Darlene realizes that with so many boys trying to build, the construction area is too small. By removing some of the puzzles and other table toys that are not used, she creates more space for building. She also obtains additional blocks from one of the other kindergartens where they are not being used. Darlene teaches prosocial behaviors and steps to conflict resolution. "If someone takes the block you're using, Jamie, what could you say to him?" When Jamie and the other boys suggest silly things like "Tell him he's a butthead," Darlene laughs with them. She calmly says, "That's funny now, but I don't think Marco will laugh. What else could you say?"
>
> Darlene also finds the boys are interested in playing ambulance, so she transforms the grocery store into a hospital, which the girls enjoy as well. Instead of reading to the

Effective teachers can apply the Teaching Pyramid to help active boys succeed in school and prevent challenging behaviors. These same strategies will work with girls as well.

whole group, which invites the boys to act out, Darlene reads more books with male characters in smaller groups of eight to actively involve all of the children in talking about the story or acting it out.

Having applied the Teaching Pyramid to working with boys, in the next section we demonstrate its applicability to one of the most common, but challenging behaviors teachers confront that cuts across gender lines—biting.

Using the Pyramid Model to Address Biting

Experienced teachers of toddlers tend to think of dealing with biting as one of the occupational hazards of group care for this age group. Biting is viewed as an aspect of typical development in all children, like separation anxiety or oppositional behavior. Nevertheless, biting is a very emotional experience for the biter, the victim, their parents, and their teachers (Greenman & Stonehouse, 1994). Parents of children who are bitten often become very upset and demand better supervision of their children. Parents of biters may feel they are somehow responsible and fear that if the situation continues the child care center will demand they remove their child.

As we learned from the Teaching Pyramid, teachers in groups where biting occurs need to assume responsibility for the safety and nurturance of all of the children, while also taking steps to prevent biting, teach alternative behaviors, and intervene when it persists. Biting is not a behavior to ignore; once biting starts in a group of toddlers, others may imitate the behavior, leading to an epidemic of biting that is very hard to control.

Why and When Young Children Bite

Biting, like other challenging behaviors, serves a function. There are actually two kinds of biting. The first is a communication strategy, which usually responds to prevention strategies. The second occurs when a child persists in using biting because biting is successful in getting the child what she wants. The persistent form of biting requires systematic intervention.

Biting as Communication

Because most children who bite are under the age of 3 and have not yet developed language, biting is often used as a powerful form of communication. The biter may be saying, "You are too close to me," "I want that toy," or "I'm tired." Biting may occur as a self-defense mechanism by the child who feels threatened.

Biting may occur more frequently when children are feeling stress due to changes in their development or the environment, or lack of attention from caregivers (Greenman & Stonehouse, 1994). When children are undergoing periods of rapid development, such as when they first learn to walk or talk, they can easily become frustrated if their emerging skills do not match their desires for locomotion or communication (Greenman & Stonehouse, 1994). Biting may relieve the stress or enable the child to get what she wants.

Biting and Oral Development

One theory relates biting to children's sensory and oral development (Ramming, Kyger, & Thompson, 2006). During the earliest years of life, "the mouth is the quickest route for

providing sensory information to the brain" and children are literally hungry to experience and make sense of their world (Ramming et al., 2006, p. 21). The hypothesis is that biting may occur because the foods children are offered do not meet their needs for tactile stimulation and do not sufficiently stimulate their senses.

To prevent this type of biting, researchers recommend that caregivers offer toddlers foods with a variety of textures, tastes, and temperatures to suck, gum, munch, or crunch and chew (Ramming et al., 2006). Of course, caregivers must supervise children while eating and make sure foods are the right size to prevent choking. Varying the textures and types of foods, as well as when children are fed, is found to be effective in reducing biting in child care settings (Ramming et al., 2006).

Applying the Teaching Pyramid to Biting

Applying the levels of the Teaching Pyramid to biting begins with making sure that toddlers feel nurtured, loved, and cared for. Having close relationships with very young children and their families enables caregivers to be aware of situations that may contribute to biting, such as the stress of a new baby or divorce, or a developmental transition such as beginning to eat solid food. Children tend to treat others the way they are treated. Therefore, it is important for caregivers to speak softly and be gentle and kind.

Preventing Biting

Most biting is preventable if children are closely supervised. When child care groups are too large (as happens when licensing standards are weak), it is more difficult to prevent biting. In such cases, teachers should separate the large group into smaller groups as much as possible, especially if there is a second adult. In a smaller group, a child is less likely to bite when a peer invades his space. The teacher also has more opportunity to play and talk with children and redirect those who frequently have conflicts.

One of the best ways to prevent biting is to minimize frustration for toddlers. Programs need to provide enough developmentally appropriate toys so children do not fight over them and do not become frustrated if the toy requires skills they do not yet have. For example, large cardboard blocks are lightweight and easily moved by toddlers, whereas smaller toys may be too difficult to manipulate.

Teaching Social–Emotional Skills

An important dimension of responding to biting is to teach children how to express their feelings and desires. In working with very young children who are just learning language, it is important to give them the words. Teachers should model specific language: "Say 'I want it,'" rather than an unhelpful phrase, such as "Use your words." Many of the social and emotional teaching strategies described earlier in this chapter can be used to teach children acceptable behaviors to replace biting.

Intervention for Persistent Biters

If biting persists over time or if children continue to bite beyond the toddler years, then the behavior is working for them in some way. In this situation, caregivers need to apply the fourth level of the pyramid and use functional assessment to determine what conditions tend to trigger the behavior and what function biting is serving for the child. Then a behavior plan can be implemented involving parents and other staff members to eliminate the biting and replace it with more socially acceptable behaviors.

We have seen how the Teaching Pyramid relates to addressing the common phenomenon of biting among young children in groups. In the final section, we apply the framework to one of the most disturbing and potentially destructive of all challenging behaviors—bullying.

Using the Pyramid Model to Alleviate Bullying

Tragic events such as high school shootings and teen suicides have drawn public attention to an age-old societal problem—bullying. **Bullying** occurs when a person repeatedly commits aggressive acts that intend to harm, and an imbalance of power makes it hard for the victim to defend himself or herself (Kaiser & Rasminsky, 2007, p. 232). In the past few decades, school personnel and mental health experts have become much more attuned to the long-term damage that bullying can inflict on bullies and their victims, as well as the bystanders who may assist or incite bullying behavior. For example, one study found that students who killed other students or teachers were twice as likely to have been bullied by their peers, and the most volatile were students who had been both bully and victim (Anderson et al., 2001).

Every teacher needs to be alert to the existence of bullying, take steps to prevent it, and intervene immediately when bullying occurs. Although bullying usually begins to appear during the primary grades of school, there is evidence that the roots of bullying behavior are evident during preschool. Earlier in this chapter, we cautioned teachers to be alert for children who are socially isolated or neglected by peers. These children may become bullies or victims.

What Can Teachers Do about Bullying?

"Bullying is a learned behavior and it can be unlearned and even prevented," (Kaiser & Rasminsky, 2007, p. 241). As with other, less volatile aspects of challenging behavior, solutions to bullying can be found in the framework of the Teaching Pyramid, beginning with the foundation level of relationships.

Olweus (1993) promotes a whole-school approach that involves teachers, administrators, children, counselors, and parents becoming aware of bullying and agreeing on strategies to combat it. The goal is to prevent bullying by restructuring the environment so that there are fewer opportunities for bullying to occur, more reinforcement of positive behavior, and assurance of protection for all children.

Preventing and Intervening in Bullying

Experts on bullying recommend the similar, but more intensive, use of the strategies we discussed earlier. Olweus (1993, as quoted in Kaiser & Rasminsky, 2007, p. 243) concludes that the most important and effective tools adults have are these:

- Their warm and involved relationships with the children
- Firm limits on unacceptable behavior
- Close monitoring and supervision
- Models of the positive use of power and problem solving
- A cooperative classroom climate—what we call a caring community of learners.

bullying Occurs when a person repeatedly commits aggressive acts that intend to harm, and an imbalance of power makes it hard for the victim to defend himself or herself.

Regular class meetings are an effective strategy to involve children in setting limits and establishing clear rules: Don't bully other children, help children who are bullied, and include children who are left out (Kaiser & Rasminsky, 2007, p. 243). Children can discuss and analyze complex topics such as empathy, peer pressure, courage, and the difference between teasing and bullying.

Children who need intensive individualized intervention for persistent challenging behaviors benefit from a team approach. In these situations, it is essential to involve not only teachers and other professionals, but family members as well.

Children also need to learn the difference between *tattling*, the purpose of which is to get someone in trouble, and *telling* to get someone out of trouble, which is necessary when bullying is observed or experienced. Useful strategies include helping children report where they don't feel safe, and in primary grades, providing a box for anonymous reporting of bullying. Meeting times can then be used to discuss prosocial skills such as cooperation and to practice responses.

In this chapter, we discussed the importance of creating a caring community of learners, as well as strategies for positively guiding children's behavior and promoting their social and emotional development. With this information in mind, we return to Sue and Elly's classroom, where we began this chapter.

Revisiting Ms. Brady and Ms. Donahue's Classroom

At the beginning of this chapter, Sue, Elly, and the children in their classroom were having a very bad day. The director of their program worked with them to help them learn about the Teaching Pyramid. Let's revisit their classroom now that these two teachers have begun to implement many of these research-based strategies.

The day begins with Sue and Elly greeting each child individually and talking briefly with their family members. The two teachers have been doing home visits and making phone calls to parents so that they could get to know the children and their interests much better. In addition, they are more aware of the importance of building warm, nurturing relationships with each child in the class (level 1 of the pyramid).

They reorganized their classroom by making signs, labeling bins, organizing shelves, and designating specific areas where materials belong. They also created learning centers where children can comfortably work and play. They've been holding group meetings each morning to talk with children about the class routines and making choices during Center Time, and the children are playing more productively.

Sue and Elly also remember to use quiet voices themselves at all times; when they really want to be heard, they whisper. The noise level is now much more tolerable. When it's time to go outside, they offer Aimee and Edie the choice of what they'd like to carry. The teachers focus a lot of attention on transitions such as preparing for naptime and cleanup because these are times when children have struggled in the past. They now give warnings before transitions, and assign children different responsibilities at cleanup time. At naptime, they play soothing music, turn out the lights, and rub the backs of children who are slow to relax. These changes to the environment and adult–child interactions have made a world of difference for the teachers and children because they are preventing many problems and helping children to do their best (level 2).

Sue and Elly also teach social skills and emotional self-regulation to all the children. For those children who need extra help, however, they use more explicit instruction. For example, Ricky so wants to have friends that he will do anything to get the children's attention. Sue and Elly coach him in acceptable ways to play with others and strategies for joining in a group. Ricky likes Aimee and she has a calming effect on him, so the teachers encourage the two of them to play together. They also suggest to his mother that he bring something interesting from home to gain attention from the other children in a positive way (level 3).

Having attended to the first three levels of the Teaching Pyramid, Sue and Elly have solved almost all of their behavior challenges. However, Booth's physical aggression and unprovoked attacks continue to be a serious problem. The director is aware of the federally funded early intervention services provided by the state. She contacts the school district, which coordinates early intervention consultation to child care centers. The director and Sue initiate a meeting with an intervention specialist and Booth's family to develop an individualized intervention plan (level 4). Sue and Elly now realize that while there are no quick fixes to children's challenging behavior, there are many effective ways to create a caring community of learners.

MyEducationLab

To assess your understanding of how to create a caring community of learners, go to the Book Specific Resources section in the MyEducationLab for your course, select Effective Practices in Early Childhood Education, Chapter 8 of the Study Plan, and then complete the multiple choice questions and activities.

Chapter Summary

- A caring community of learners is a group or classroom in which children and adults engage in warm, positive relationships; treat each other with respect; and learn from and with each other.
- Teachers have a significant role to play in promoting children's social competence, helping them acquire emotional and cognitive self-regulation, and preventing later difficulties.
- The Teaching Pyramid is a research-based framework for promoting social competence and addressing children's challenging behaviors.
- The foundation level of the Teaching Pyramid is teachers' positive relationships with children. Young children learn best when they experience warm, positive, responsive relationships with adults—parents, teachers, and caregivers.
- Level 2 of the pyramid describes high-quality supportive environments that help promote positive outcomes for children and prevent challenging behaviors, such as how the physical space is arranged, how time is organized and used, and how teachers support children's engagement in play and learning.
- Level 3 of the pyramid describes positive ways to guide children's behavior and social and emotional teaching strategies such as emotional literacy, social skills, and conflict negotiation.
- Level 4 describes intensive individualized interventions to address persistent, severe, challenging behaviors. Intervention includes functional assessment, a team approach involving families and specialists, and a behavior plan that includes teaching replacement skills.

key terms

attachment theory
behavior intervention plan
bullying
caring community of learners
challenging behavior
disorganized/disoriented attachment
efficacy
emotional literacy
functional assessment or functional analysis
guidance
individualized intervention
insecure-ambivalent/resistant attachment
insecure-avoidant attachment
learning centers
mistaken behavior
positive behavior support (PBS)
redirection
replacement behaviors
secure attachment relationship
secure base
self-concept
self-esteem
time-out
transitions

readings & websites

Bell, S. H., Carr, V., Denno, D., Johnson, L. J., & Phillips, L. R. (2004). *Challenging behaviors in early childhood settings: Creating a place for all children.* Baltimore: Paul H. Brookes Publishing Co.

Gartrell, D. (2004). *The power of guidance: Teaching social-emotional skills in early childhood classrooms.* Clifton Park, NY: Delmar Learning.

Kaiser, B., & Rasminsky, J. S. (2007). *Challenging behavior in young children: Understanding, preventing, and responding effectively* (2nd ed.). Boston: Allyn & Bacon.

Center on Social Emotional Foundations for Early Learning (CSEFEL)
www.vanderbilt.edu/csefel

Collaborative for Academic, Social, and Emotional Learning
www.casel.org

Technical Assistance Center on Social Emotional Intervention for Young Children (TACSEI)
www.challengingbehaviors.org

1. What is considered acceptable behavior in one family, community, or cultural group may be frowned upon or prohibited in another. The same child may be considered either exuberant or aggressive; either antisocial or quietly respectful. Think of other examples of behaviors that might easily be interpreted differently by different people. What problems might arise for a teacher as a result?
2. Observe the physical environment of a preschool or primary-grade classroom. Is it organized to promote positive outcomes for children and prevent problems? How do you think it could be improved?
3. Observe a classroom to see if and how the teacher intentionally builds positive relationships with children and teaches social and emotional skills. Does she use time-out? If so, what happens? Do you think it is an effective strategy for addressing "mistaken" behavior?
4. Observe a preschool or primary-grade classroom and pay particular attention to boys. Do they "get in trouble" more often than girls? Think about how the environment and schedule could be changed to prevent problems for them. What do you think the teacher could do to help boys (and girls) do their best?
5. Each of us defines the term *challenging behavior* according to our own values and experiences. Reflect on the kinds of behaviors that "push your buttons." What are they? How do you think you would react if children demonstrated these behaviors? Why is it important for teachers to be aware of their own perspectives about challenging behaviors?

9 Teaching to Enhance Learning and Development

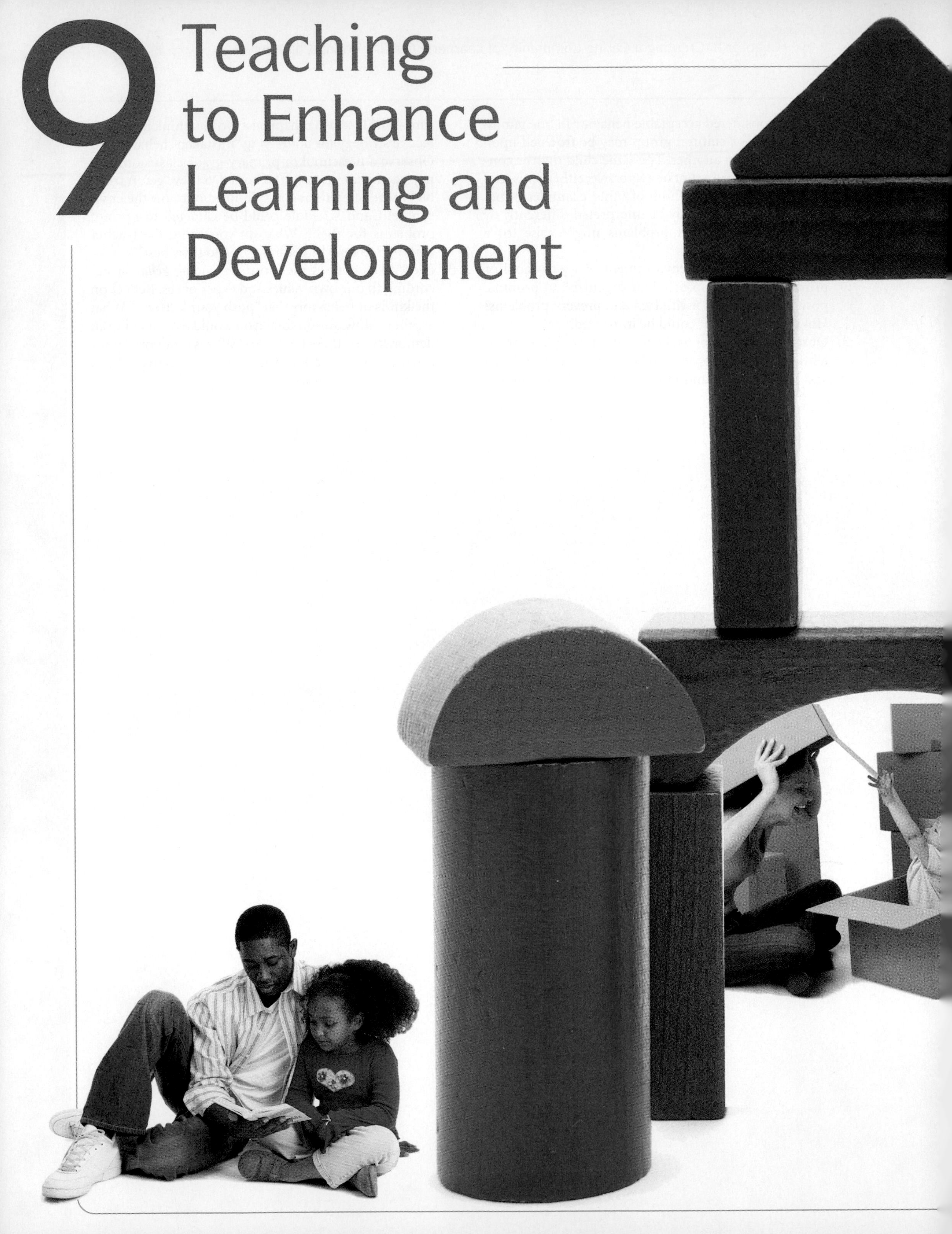

Thinking Ahead

1. How is teaching both a science and an art?
2. What are effective teaching strategies that help children achieve important learning and developmental goals and motivate them to learn?
3. How do teachers create various contexts for learning in an intellectually engaging learning environment?
4. How do teachers use grouping as an instructional strategy?
5. How do teachers use play as a teaching strategy?
6. How can teachers use technology to teach young children?

Sally Hanson is a kindergarten teacher in a large, urban school district. Her class of 23 children includes several children whose home language is not English and two children with IEPs. Some of the children have been in child care since they were infants, but 6 did not attend any early childhood program before entering school. The children's skills and abilities are at different levels. In short, Sally's class is typical; there is a wide range of individual variation in the children's development and learning and in their preparedness to tackle the demands of the kindergarten curriculum.

Among Sally's early literacy goals for the children is having them learn to write their first and last names. When the children arrive each morning, they sign in on an attendance chart that lists their names in alphabetical order. Sally uses this morning ritual as a daily opportunity for children to practice their writing. Jason enters the room, and Sally guides him in finding his name. "Look carefully, Jason. Can you find your *J*? Yes, there it is. Can you make a *J* like that?" Jason is just beginning to learn his letters, so writing a *J* is a wonderful new accomplishment for him.

Elena has only recently arrived from Guatemala and speaks little English. Sally kneels next to her, points to her photo posted by her name on the chart, and gives her a marker. Shyly watching the other children as they write their names, Elena follows suit and makes a straight vertical line next to her name. Smiling, nodding, and making a vertical motion with her finger, Sally says, "Yes, Elena, you made the first part of the *E* in your name." Sally then encourages Lucy, who has Down syndrome, to find her photo. After Lucy makes a straight line followed by a scribble, Sally says, "Lucy, I see you made the beginning of the *L* in your name."

Logan can write his first name in uppercase and lowercase letters with ease, so Sally adds challenge to the task by writing his last name for him to copy. "Logan, now you can try your last name—Jameson. It has some letters you already know how to write. What are they?" Logan looks closely and happily shouts, "It has an *n* like Logan." "Yes, it does," his teacher confirms. "Do you see another letter you already know?"

Marguerite has a long name, struggles to remember the order of the letters, and usually forgets the *E* in the middle. Sally gives her a name card with the middle *E* written in red to draw her attention to the correct order of the letters. With this assistance and reminder, Marguerite spells her name correctly. Some children need little help signing in, so Sally directs them to their journals to begin drawing and writing their plans for today. A few children need more direct instruction in writing their letters. "Tommy, when you write your *T*, make a straight line down. That's right." Pointing to the left side of the paper, Sally says, "Now begin on the left and draw a shorter line across the top." Sally sits with the children, offering guidance and assistance as needed to help them write their names and using strategies adapted to each child's skill level. ▲

As we see in Sally's interactions with each child in her classroom, the early childhood teacher's role is complex. Engaging in developmentally appropriate practice involves knowing the learner, knowing what to teach, and knowing how to teach. Teachers are always teaching *something* to *someone*. In this chapter, we focus on knowing *how to teach* to help children reach challenging and achievable learning goals. Becoming an intentional teacher requires an understanding of the range of effective teaching strategies and how and when they are most useful (NAEYC, 2005h; 2009a). Armed with this knowledge, teachers can intentionally choose the strategies that work best with each learner or group of learners in a given situation.

Because many teaching behaviors in early childhood classrooms are subtle or take place in the context of play or child-initiated learning, the novice may be uncertain of what "effective teaching" actually entails and how to do it. Without knowledge of research-based teaching practices, inexperienced or ill-informed teachers may be too passive and miss important opportunities to promote children's learning. On the other hand, they may err in assuming that the only time they are "teaching" is when they are talking. The fact is that good teaching is a complex interplay of both science and art.

pedagogy What a teacher says or does that engages children and contributes to their learning and development.

effective teaching The use of approaches that are proven to be successful based on scientific evidence and that have a high probability of enhancing children's learning and development.

■ Defining Teaching: Both a Science and an Art

This chapter is about teaching—also known as **pedagogy**—which is what a teacher says or does that engages children and contributes to their learning and development. In this book, we emphasize **effective teaching**, which is the use of an approach that has proven to be successful based on scientific evidence and that has a high probability of enhancing student achievement (Marzano, Pickering, & Pollock, 2001; McCardle & Chhabra, 2004). Using knowledge of research to inform planning and decisions about practice is essential to becoming an intentional teacher.

The Science of Teaching

Since the 1990s and in response to the passage of Public Law 107–220, the No Child Left Behind Act of 2001, the emphasis in education has been on scientifically based practice (McCardle & Chhabra, 2004). Such practice is informed by at least three areas of research: the science of child development, cognitive science or the study of how people learn, and research on effective instructional strategies and contexts.

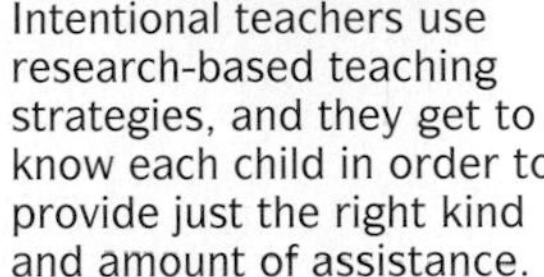
Intentional teachers use research-based teaching strategies, and they get to know each child in order to provide just the right kind and amount of assistance.

Scientific Research

Research is used to answer two sets of questions: (1) What skills and abilities predict children's later outcomes in important areas like reading, writing, and mathematics? and (2) What teaching behaviors, curriculum, and other educational interventions contribute to or inhibit gains in children's skills and abilities in these areas? Systematic reviews of research by experts, such as the National Reading Panel (National Institute of Child Health and Human Development [NICHD], 2000) and the National Early Literacy Panel (2008), have been particularly influential.

Classroom Research

Although debate is ongoing about various aspects of practice, there is strong consensus that the daily interaction among teachers and children is the most important determinant of the quality and effectiveness of programs from infancy through primary grades (Hamre & Pianta, 2005, 2007; NAEYC, 2005f). Regardless of the specific curriculum used or the materials in the environment, everything that happens in the classroom is influenced by the teacher's interactions with children.

This conclusion is supported by two large-scale studies of state-funded prekindergarten and kindergarten classrooms conducted by the National Center for Early Development and Learning (NCEDL) (Early et al., 2005). These studies used a teacher observation tool called the Classroom Assessment Scoring System (CLASS) (Pianta, La Paro, & Hamre, 2008). The CLASS assesses the quality of both the emotional climate and the instructional climate in a classroom.

Emotional Climate. A high score on emotional climate on the CLASS means that teachers are positive, sensitive, and manage the classroom well. In classrooms where teachers score high on emotional climate, children's language improves and they have fewer behavior problems in both preschool and kindergarten (Pianta et al., 2008). On average, the classrooms in the NCEDL studies rated around 5 on a 7-point scale, which indicates that they are generally positive, supportive environments for children.

Instructional Climate. The CLASS instructional climate score indicates how well teachers use a variety of teaching strategies to promote children's concept development and higher order thinking. The classroom's instructional climate has been found to be the strongest and most consistent predictor of children's learning over time (Early et al., 2005). Researchers have found that children gain more from a learning activity when a teacher interacts with them in an intentional way or when the teacher has prepared the environment and supports children's learning during play and other child-initiated activity.

The results of the NCEDL studies, however, found poor-quality instructional climates in the early childhood classrooms studied, with an average score of about 2 on the 7-point scale. Teachers either provided very little instruction at all or tended to rely on worksheets or whole-group repetitive lessons. They also found that children spent more than 40% of their day involved in routines and transitions that did not involve any learning activity. The researchers concluded that most of these classrooms were pleasant places in which there were many missed opportunities for learning (Hamre & Pianta, 2007).

These studies provide a window through which we can assess the quality of teaching practices occurring in early childhood classrooms today. Similar results were found for primary grade classrooms as well (Hamre & Pianta, 2005). In Chapter 8, we described how you as a teacher can provide a positive emotional climate in your classroom. The goal of this chapter is to prepare you to create an effective instructional climate to help all children achieve their learning potential.

The Limits of Research

Early childhood education has a large and growing research base to guide practice. Where research evidence is strong, teachers have a professional responsibility to adhere to its guidance. However, research on effective teaching is an evolving science. Although a great deal of work has been done, we still need answers to questions about which practices work best with which learners.

With classrooms increasingly serving children with diverse language and cultural backgrounds, teachers need to adapt for individual variation of all kinds. Consequently, valid research is not always available to guide practice. In these instances, teachers need to supplement the evidence base with information obtained from families and practical wisdom (Buysse & Wesley, 2006). Even when research is available, applying evidence-based practice in unique classroom situations with diverse groups of children requires considerable skill. Teachers need to respond to situations as they happen, which often requires creativity—more art than science.

The Art of Teaching

Although effective teaching is informed and guided by research, teaching is also an art in that it requires vision, creativity, and decision making. What makes good science is controlling as many variables as possible to be able to determine cause and effect. But in classrooms, there are simply too many variables to control. Effective teaching requires creatively adapting to individual children and to the situations that arise.

Consider the following analogy, comparing the work of a painter to the work of a teacher. Skilled painters are knowledgeable about theories of art, composition, color, and perspective. But each artist, like each teacher, applies her or his knowledge in creative ways. One of the painter's most powerful tools is the use of color, and knowledge of how the myriad of colors in nature can be created by mixing a few basic colors. For example, given the three primary colors—red, yellow, and blue—a skilled painter can create virtually every color of the spectrum. Think of those basic colors as the basic strategies from which teachers create innumerable variations in interactions with individual children and groups. If we add to the color wheel the many gradations of gray—ranging between white and black—and mix these with our primary colors, we have an almost infinite variety of options from which to "color" the world of experiences we provide for children.

We begin our exploration of the science and art of early childhood teaching by examining research-based teaching strategies. This discussion will demonstrate how art and science can coexist to create an enriching classroom filled with color, creativity, and a variety of options for both teachers and children.

Effective teaching is both an art and a science. Intentional teachers ensure that children's experiences in the classroom are as creative and colorful as the world around them.

Building a Repertoire of Effective Teaching Strategies

The most effective teachers have a large repertoire of teaching strategies that they use as situations present themselves. Teachers must first become familiar with the many options. In practice, there is no one teaching strategy that will address all situations.

Children's development and learning are complex processes. Therefore, the more strategies teachers know how to use, the more ways they will be able to meet the needs of diverse learners. Throughout your career as a teacher, you will continue to add to and refine your repertoire of effective teaching tools.

What Are Teaching Strategies?

A **teaching strategy** is a behavior or activity that a teacher deliberately selects and flexibly applies to help students construct meaning (Mehigan, 2005, p. 557). Applying teaching strategies demands conscious thought and flexible decision making, which are the essence of intentional teaching. Earlier, for example, we saw how Sally Hanson encouraged some of the children to practice their writing, while she demonstrated how to write a letter for those who needed more help.

Because the processes of teaching and learning are linked, the most effective teaching strategies parallel learning strategies. A **learning strategy** refers to how children construct meaning in every context or situation. As later examples in this chapter illustrate, some of the most effective teaching strategies are designed to develop students' own learning strategies.

Strategies as Tools

Education is often plagued by *either/or* debates that pit one practice against another, or that dichotomize complex decisions into either/or choices, such as "Which is better, direct instruction or active learning?" As teaching becomes more scientific, we realize that these are the wrong questions. Asking which teaching technique is best is like asking whether a hammer is better than pliers. The answer, of course, depends on what the carpenter needs to do. In teaching as in carpentry, the selection of tools depends on what the teacher is trying to accomplish and with which child; there is no one best teaching practice (National Research Council [NRC], 2000).

The Right Tools

You may have heard the statement—in fact, I've written it myself—that young children are not miniature adults and do not think and learn the way adults or older children do. Although this statement is essentially true, it is equally true that some practices that are inappropriate for young children, such as listening in a whole group for an extended period of time, are not effective for older students either (Marzano et al., 2001; NAEYC, 2009a).

In fact, many of the most effective teaching practices for young children—such as connecting new learning to what students already know and can do—are also effective with college students. The particular strategies teachers use to help children build on prior learning will vary with the age and ability of the learner (that is, if the strategies are developmentally appropriate). All of these strategies can be used in the context of teacher-initiated or child-initiated experiences, which we discuss next.

teaching strategy A behavior or activity that a teacher deliberately selects and flexibly applies to help students construct meaning.

learning strategy How children construct meaning in any context or situation.

teacher-initiated experiences Learning experiences in which teachers take the lead by providing explicit information and modeling or demonstrating a skill, as determined by the teacher's goals and direction.

Teacher-Initiated and Child-Initiated Experiences

Early childhood practices are often described as either teacher-initiated or child-initiated experiences. However, both contexts are important for children's learning. During **teacher-initiated experiences**, teachers take the lead by providing explicit information and modeling or demonstrating skills. Teacher-initiated learning experiences are determined by the teacher's goals and direction, but children should be actively engaged (Epstein, 2007b). Under these conditions, focused, teacher-guided instruction can contribute significantly to children's learning (Hamre & Pianta, 2005, 2007).

By contrast, during **child-initiated experiences**, children acquire knowledge and skills through their own exploration and interactions with objects and other children (Epstein, 2007b, p. 2). Child-initiated experiences grow out of children's interests. However, teachers organize the environment and materials and provide the learning opportunities from which children make choices (Epstein, 2007b). Teachers observe children during child-initiated activities and interact with them to support their continued learning and development. During child-initiated experiences, both teachers and children should be actively involved.

Using an Array of Teaching Strategies

Many different strategies are effective in supporting children's learning and development. Understanding when and how to apply each strategy gives teachers the tools necessary to be a thoughtful, purposeful, intentional teacher (Bowman, Donovan, & Burns, 2001; Copple & Bredekamp, 2009; Epstein, 2007b).

Note, however, that in practice, strategies are used in combination. Observe a skilled teacher at work and you will find it almost impossible to isolate an example of a teaching strategy, even explicit instruction, that doesn't also include some other strategy such as encouragement, modeling, or questioning. For example, a preschool teacher may acknowledge a child's accomplishment by saying, "Luca, you found the two shapes that match." Then she immediately provides specific information, "They have eight sides and they are called octagons," while quickly adding challenge to the task, "Can you find another octagon in our room?"

One particularly effective strategy, which is called *scaffolding*, draws on many different strategies at once; therefore, we discuss it following our description of the individual strategies. In the sections that follow, we define and give examples of a variety of teaching strategies, which are listed in Table 9.1.

Acknowledging and Encouraging

Acknowledging is the positive attention teachers give to children that tells a child the teacher noticed what the child did. Teachers often use this strategy without conscious awareness. Acknowledging is particularly effective in keeping children engaged in desirable behaviors. For example, after observing 3-year-old Keily while she serves as the snack helper, her teacher says, "I see you gave each person a napkin, Keily. Now we're ready for our snack." Noting 2-year-old Bailey's empathic behavior, her teacher says, "Thank you, Bailey, for sitting with Kayla. She was sad that her mommy left." By understanding the power of their acknowledgment of children's competence and performance, teachers are able to influence children to demonstrate desired behaviors.

Encouragement can be conveyed through verbal comments or nonverbal signs such as pats or high fives that promote the child's persistence and effort. While encouragement doesn't directly enhance a child's understanding or skill, it is most valuable in helping children realize that effort is necessary for mastering skills, completing tasks, and solving complex problems. For example, second-grader Jushawn struggles with writing a funny story about his dog. His teacher encourages him to persist by making comments such as "I really laughed when you told me how he spilled his food." When Jushawn finishes, she points out, "You worked hard writing your story and I enjoyed reading it, and I laughed again at your dog's antics."

child-initiated experiences Experiences that allow children to gain knowledge and skills through their own exploration and interactions with objects and other children.

acknowledging Giving positive verbal or nonverbal attention that promotes the child's persistence and effort.

encouragement Verbal comments or nonverbal signs such as pats or high fives that promote the child's persistence and effort.

Giving Quality Feedback

Feedback, in which teachers provide specific information on a child's performance or respond to questions, helps focus the child's attention on the process of learning. Effective

Table 9.1 Effective Teaching Strategies

Teaching Strategy	Definition	Most Effective Uses
Acknowledging and encouraging	Giving positive verbal or nonverbal attention that promotes a child's persistence and effort	Teachers influence children to stay engaged, demonstrate desired behaviors, and help children master skills, complete tasks, and solve complex problems.
Giving quality feedback	Providing specific information on a child's performance or responding to questions and comments	Teachers expand learning and understanding (how children come to solve a problem) rather than focusing only on the correct answer or end product.
Modeling	Showing children a skill or desirable way of behaving or speaking	Teachers promote positive social skills and self-regulation. Teachers model language—repeating and extending children's verbal responses, describing their own and children's actions, and using advanced vocabulary.
Demonstrating	Showing the correct way to perform a skill or procedure while children observe the outcome	Teachers teach skills that require particular steps in a certain order.
Giving cues, hints, and offering assistance	Reminding children of what they already know and can do, and helping them to use that knowledge for new learning	Teachers help children build on prior knowledge to gain new skills and understanding.
Creating and adding challenges	Making learning situations harder by generating a problem, or adding difficulty to a task so that it is a bit beyond what children have already mastered	Teachers add challenge to interest children and motivate them to learn, but not so much that they become frustrated or repeatedly fail. Children continue to make learning and developmental progress.
Questioning	Eliciting different types of responses and promoting different types of thinking	Teachers ask open-ended questions that require children to analyze information or engage in higher-order thinking.
Co-constructing	Thinking with different points of view; working collaboratively to solve a problem or clarify a concept	Teachers and children think and talk together during a joint activity such as a project, and both parties learn from the exchange.
Giving direct or explicit instruction	Explicitly giving directions for completing a task; providing facts, verbal labels, or other specific information; or providing instructions for a child's action or behavior	Teachers transmit knowledge that can only be learned from one person telling another, that is, social–conventional or procedural knowledge.
Scaffolding—using the above strategies in combination	Supporting children's ability to accomplish learning tasks that they could not otherwise accomplish independently; using strategies such as cues, hints, assistance, questions, and so on	Teachers adapt instruction for individual children of different skill levels, cultural backgrounds, personalities, and talents toward new, achievable goals. Teachers help children acquire the skills to eventually achieve the same task independently.

Sources: Based on *Basics of Developmentally Appropriate Practice: An Introduction for Teachers of Children 3 to 6*, by C. Copple and S. Bredekamp, 2006, Washington, DC: NAEYC; and *Developmentally Appropriate Practice in Early Childhood Programs Serving Children from Birth through Age 8*, revised edition, edited by C. Copple and S. Bredekamp, 2009, Washington, DC: NAEYC.

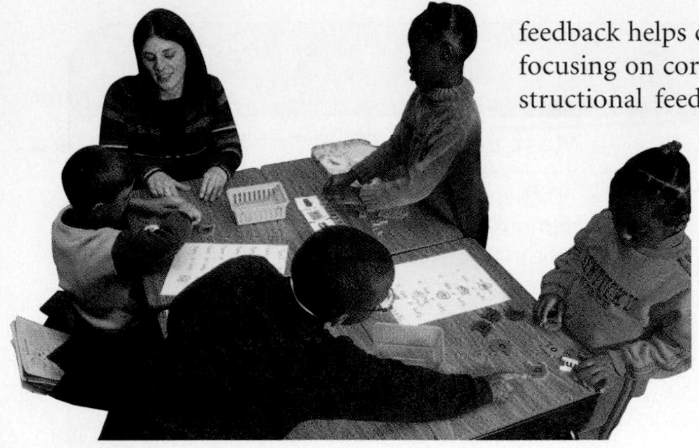

Positive feedback provides children with specific information and helps focus their attention. Back-and-forth exchanges in small groups help everyone learn more.

feedback helps children expand their learning and understanding, rather than focusing on correct answers (Pianta et al., 2008). Research finds that such instructional feedback helps improve literacy and language in preschool and kindergarten children (Howes et al., 2008) and helps close the achievement gap for children in first grade and up (Hamre & Pianta, 2001, 2005).

Effective feedback often involves back-and-forth exchanges between teachers and students. This exchange is called a **feedback loop**, and involves a teacher and a child or small group of children communicating in an effort to reach deeper understanding. Consider the following example of a feedback loop that occurred in a preschool class where the teacher and children were discussing a book about shadows:

Teacher points to a picture in book: What do you think made this shadow?
Various children call out: An animal. A dog. A cat.
Teacher: Kami, why do you think it's a cat?
Kami: The tail.
Teacher: What makes you think that it's a cat's tail?
Kami: Well, it looks like a long tail.
Connor: But dogs have tails, too. It could be a wolf.
Teacher to class: What do you notice about the tail?
Kami: It's a cat's tail. It's skinny, and it has a curl on the end.
Teacher: Oh, so you're sure it's a cat. Let's find out."

Modeling

Teachers are especially powerful models for children with whom they have built positive relationships. **Modeling** is a technique teachers use to show children a skill or desirable way of behaving or speaking.

Language modeling is among the most effective instructional strategies teachers can use. A large body of research demonstrates that teacher's language modeling strongly predicts children's achievement in all areas of learning and development (Early et al., 2005; Hamre & Pianta, 2005, 2007; Pianta et al., 2008).

Effective *language modeling* includes:

- Frequent conversations among teachers and students
- Intentional effort to promote child-initiated conversations
- Use of open-ended questions, which are questions that have more than one answer
- Teachers repeating and extending children's verbal responses
- Teachers verbally describing their own and children's actions
- Teachers using advanced language and vocabulary
- Children engaging in extended conversations with each other (Pianta et al., 2008).

Adult–child language interactions are especially important because the most competent language user in the classroom is the teacher. One of the most effective strategies for developing young children's vocabulary and language use is to engage them in frequent one-on-one conversations, particularly during their play (Dickinson, 2001b; Early et al., 2005; Sylva, Melhuish, Sammons, Siraj-Blatchford, & Taggart, 2004). In the following example, preschool teacher Ms. Lawry models language with children who are pretending to cook in the dramatic play center:

Child: Here's your dinner. It's hot.
Ms. Lawry: Thank you. This soup must be boiling hot. I think I can see steam rising up. I'll just sip it slowly. I don't want it to scald me.
Child: Huh? Scald?
Ms. Lawry: Yes. I don't want it to burn my lips.

feedback loop Back-and-forth communication between a teacher and a child or small group of children in an effort to reach deeper understanding.

modeling Showing children a skill or desirable way of behaving or speaking.

During this pretend scenario, the teacher modeled advanced vocabulary words like *boiling, rising, sip, steam,* and *scald,* and introduced some science concepts at the same time. In some respect, teachers are always engaged in modeling because children pay attention to what teachers do as much as to what they say.

demonstrating Showing the correct way to perform a skill or procedure while children observe the outcome.

apprenticeship The process of children learning by observing adults and more accomplished peers performing tasks and by practicing the skills themselves with adult guidance and support.

facilitating Providing short-term, temporary assistance to help a child achieve the next level of functioning.

supporting Providing assistance that helps the child to accomplish a difficult task by making it easier.

Demonstrating

An effective strategy for teaching skills that require performing particular steps in a certain order is **demonstrating.** When teachers show the correct way to perform a skill or procedure, children are able to observe the outcome. Similar to modeling, demonstrating is more formal and directive, with the adult drawing children's attention to the correct steps necessary to complete a task, as in the following examples:

> Irene demonstrates for her 3-year-olds how to wash their hands thoroughly to prevent the spread of infection. As she washes her own hands, she says, "See? Now I'm drying my hands with the paper towel. Before I throw the towel away, I use it to turn off the faucet. That way, my hands stay really clean. Now you try it."
>
> In the art area, kindergarten teacher Max introduces potter's clay to the group. As he demonstrates, he says, "Watch how I pinch off a little piece of clay and use a small amount of water to make the little piece stick to the bigger piece."

Children often learn by observing not only adults, but also more accomplished peers performing tasks. Such learning has been called **apprenticeship,** and researchers have observed it across cultural groups (Rogoff, 1990, 2003). When young children watch others perform basic skills of living such as dressing, feeding, or tying shoes, they gradually learn how to accomplish these skills themselves. For demonstrating to be effective, children's observations must be followed by opportunities for them to practice the skills themselves with adult guidance and support.

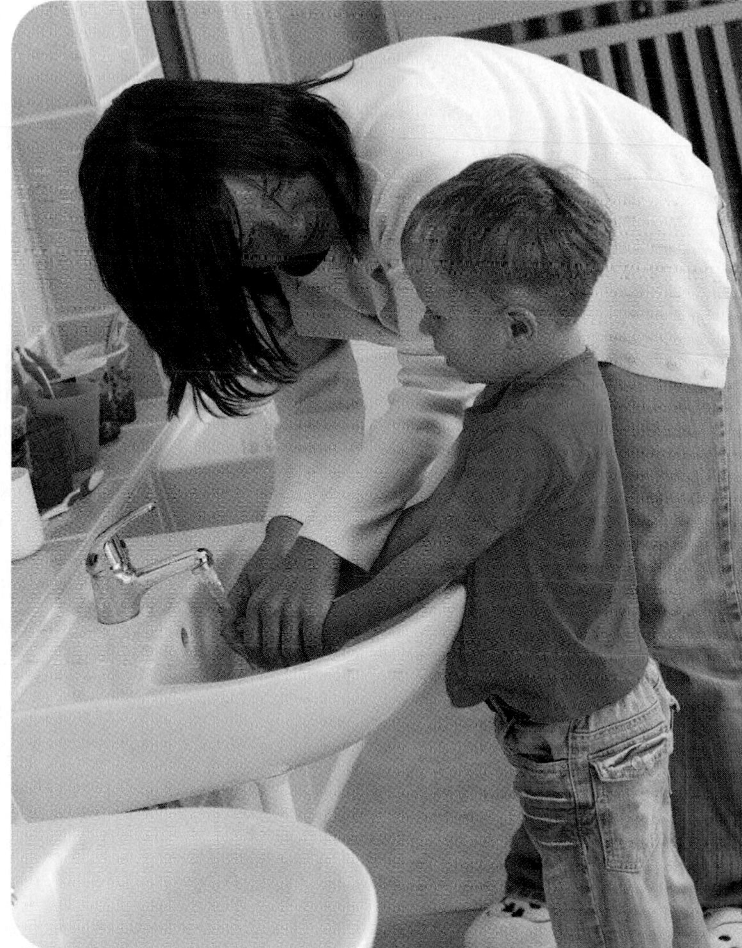

Effective teachers have a large repertoire of strategies to use in different situations. When children need to learn a specific skill, a teacher may intentionally demonstrate it for them.

Giving Cues, Hints, and Offering Assistance

Giving *cues* or *hints* are ways of reminding children what they already know and helping them use that knowledge to build new skills. For example, when a child is reading and is stuck on a word, the teacher may say, "That word has 'ch' at the beginning like another one you know." In this case, the teacher is cueing the beginning reader to compare the new word to one she already knows.

Other common teaching strategies fall in the general category of **facilitating** or **supporting** learning. When teachers *facilitate,* they provide short-term, temporary assistance to help a child achieve the next level of functioning, such as when the teacher gently holds a preschooler's hand as he walks across the balance beam. When teachers *support* learning, they provide a more fixed-form of assistance such as providing word wall (displaying frequently used words) for kindergartners to refer to as they work in their journals. In both facilitating and supporting learning, the teacher provides assistance that helps the child to accomplish a difficult task by making it easier.

Creating and Adding Challenges

Although cues, hints, and other assistance make children's learning tasks easier, effective teachers also intentionally make learning situations harder at times by creating challenge, generating a problem, or adding difficulty to a task so that it is a bit beyond what children have already mastered. For example, Hiroki is especially adept at doing puzzles and quickly completes all that are available in his preschool classroom. His teacher, Keith, brings in an alphabet puzzle with 26 pieces, one for every letter, challenging Hiroki's skill with puzzles to help him learn the alphabet.

In her second-grade classroom, Catarina determines that although most of the children are reading at or below grade level, two of them are much more advanced. She provides fourth- and fifth-grade level reading materials to ensure that they are challenged to continue their reading growth. In addition, she adapts her writing assignments to add challenge. The other children's assignment is to describe their own experiences over the weekend. To add challenge for the more advanced children, Catarina asks them to write a different ending for a story they've read, requiring higher-level comprehension and analysis.

Questioning

One of the most frequently used teaching strategies, **questioning** is used to elicit different types of responses and to promote different types of thinking. Research on questioning finds that higher-level, **open-ended questions**—those that require children to analyze information in some way—are more effective learning tools than lower-level questions (Marzano et al., 2001). Lower-level or **closed questions** have one right answer, usually requiring children to recall information or facts. Closed questions, which are often the type used on tests, may reveal what a child knows, but they do not propel further learning. Open-ended questions, on the other hand, have many possible answers. Indeed, a truly open-ended question is one for which the teacher does not have an answer in mind.

To understand how different types of questions elicit different types of responses, compare the following two questions, asked after a reading of Beatrix Potter's *The Tale of Peter Rabbit*:

Question 1: Where did Peter Rabbit get lost?
Question 2: How would you feel if you were lost like Peter?

Question 1 has one right answer—Mr. McGregor's garden. This question offers little opportunity to generate further conversation. Conversely, question 2 would most likely evoke many different responses from children with various adjectives describing feelings—*scared, afraid, unhappy, sad, tired,* or *hungry*—as well as opportunities for follow-up questions that would extend the conversation. For example, "What would you do?" or "How could you get help?" would elicit a host of responses. Even more beneficial, the open-ended questions would enable children to connect the story to their own experience beyond the classroom, making the reading even more meaningful.

Questions That Promote Problem Solving. Teachers often use questions as ways to cue or prompt children to take the next step in solving a problem or performing a skill. In addition, they may use questions to remind children of what they already know before introducing new information, as well as to focus their attention and thinking in advance.

In the following example, before reading *Caps for Sale* by E. Slobodkina to a group of preschoolers, Carol holds up the book cover and begins a conversation with a question:

Teacher: What do you see in this picture?
Mark: A man with lotsa hats on his head.
Tory: He looks funny. The hats are all different colors.
Teacher: So you think this will be a funny story, Tory?
Tory: I don't know. How can those hats stay on his head? I bet they fall off.
Teacher: Let's read the story and find out.

By asking questions before she reads the book to the children, Carol engages their interest. As soon as Carol begins reading, the children are observing and analyzing the pictures and making predictions about the story. After the story, Carol and the children will discuss whether their predictions were correct.

questioning Eliciting different types of responses and promoting different types of thinking.

open-ended questions Questions that require children to analyze information in some way and that have many possible answers.

closed questions Lower-level questions that have one right answer and usually require children to recall information or facts.

Quality of Questioning. Research on questioning demonstrates its effectiveness as a teaching strategy. However, research also finds that while questions are by far the most frequent verbal interaction among teachers and children, teachers most often ask low-level questions (Marzano et al., 2001). One observational study of preschool classrooms in England (Sylva et al., 2004) found that even in good programs, only about 5% of teachers' questions were open ended. More than 34% of their questions were closed (one-right-answer, low-level questions), and more than 60% were related to controlling behavior and not directly related to pedagogy.

Despite the scarcity of open-ended questions, however, when open-ended questions were asked, they provoked rich conversations and thoughtful speculation and extended children's imaginations. The researchers concluded that given their potential effectiveness, increasing the use of open-ended questions could greatly improve outcomes for children, especially children who are at risk of school failure (Sylva et al., 2004).

Wait Time. An important aspect of questioning is **wait time**, the length of time that a teacher waits for a response after asking a question. Research reveals that when teachers wait briefly—about 5 seconds—for responses from children, it increases the frequency and depth of children's responses (Tharp & Entz, 2003; Tobin, 1987). Wait time is especially valuable for young children who are just beginning to master verbal communication and also for children who are learning a second language (Tabors, 2008).

Wait time also helps extend conversations with children and among groups of children. Sometimes, when children do not immediately respond to adult questions or comments, adults may impatiently talk for them or over them. For teachers who recognize the beauty of wait time, however, it becomes a highly useful strategy to add to their repertoire.

> **Effective Teaching**
> The most effective teachers artfully use a large repertoire of research-based teaching strategies to help each child achieve developmentally appropriate goals.

wait time The length of time that a teacher waits for a response after asking a question or responding to a comment.

Co-Constructing Learning and Understanding

One of the most important ways children learn is by constructing their own understanding of concepts as they actively try to make sense of their experiences. The process of co-construction often happens when children work collaboratively with teachers and/or other children on a joint project or activity (Copple & Bredekamp, 2006). This strategy of working collaboratively to solve a problem or clarify a concept is called **co-construction**, because both parties in the task think and talk together and each learns from it. The value of this strategy was demonstrated in a large-scale observational study in England. The researchers found that in the most effective classrooms, teachers encouraged co-construction during children's play activities, which they called *sustained shared thinking* (Siraj-Blatchford, Muttock, Sylva, Gilden, & Bell, 2003; Sylva et al., 2004), as in this example:

co-construction Teaching strategy that involves thinking and working collaboratively to solve a problem.

> Four-year-old James is watching various objects floating in the water table. "Look at the pine cone. There's bubbles of air coming out," he observes. Modeling curiosity and extending the interaction his teacher says, "It's spinning around." James responds, "That's 'cause it's got air in it." The teacher picks up the cone and shows the children how the scales go round it in a spiral. Then, turning it with a winding action, she says, "When the air comes out in bubbles, it makes the cone spin around." Another child, Kathy, uses a plastic tube to blow into the water. "Look! Bubbles," she says. The teacher asks, "What are you putting into the water to

As you see in this situation, activities such as water play provide rich opportunities for children and teachers to talk and think together—what is called *co-construction*.

make bubbles? What's coming out of the tube?" "Air," Kathy replies. (Adapted from Siraj-Blatchford et al., 2003, p. 51.)

This process of co-construction, or sustained shared thinking, proved to be so predictive of positive outcomes for young children that the researchers concluded that it is a prerequisite of effective preschool education. Co-construction is also one of the most frequently used strategies in the schools in Reggio Emilia, Italy. Although open-ended questioning is one way to initiate co-construction during children's play, teachers need to sustain the back-and-forth conversation and think along with the children to help them construct their understanding of new concepts.

Giving Direct or Explicit Instruction

Direct instruction occurs when a teacher gives explicit directions for completing a task; provides facts, verbal labels, or other specific information; or provides instructions for a child's action or behavior. Direct or explicit instruction is used for transmitting knowledge that can only be learned from one person telling another the culturally agreed-on labels for objects, events, and experiences, which is called *social-conventional knowledge*. For example, the days of the week, letters, or punctuation symbols have conventionally agreed-on names that children learn more easily and efficiently through direct instruction. Writing a question mark on chart paper, first-grade teacher Lydia uses direct instruction when she points out, "This is called a question mark, and we write it at the end of a sentence that is asking a question or making a request."

Teachers also use direct instruction during child-initiated activities and when working with small groups. For example, when working with a group of 4-year-olds' building blocks, their teacher points to a block and says, "This rounded block is called a cylinder. You used four cylinder blocks to hold up your bridge."

Uses and Misuses of Direct Instruction. Direct instruction can be the most efficient and effective way of conveying information and introducing new concepts, procedures, or vocabulary. Like every other strategy, however, it should not be overused. Studies of children's experiences in the primary grades have found that direct instruction in the whole group is the most frequently used teaching strategy (NICHD Early Child Care Research Network, 2002, 2003). In addition, whole-group, direct teaching is used much more often in kindergarten than in preschool (Hamre & Pianta, 2007).

Direct instruction is the easiest and most efficient way to teach some knowledge, such as agreed-on names for tools, and some skills, such as tying shoes. However, this type of instruction is only one part of helping children learn concepts. For example, children can learn aspects of written language through direct instruction, but they need many additional experiences with print to understand the complex concepts that go into learning to read.

Although the list of teaching strategies presented so far is not exhaustive, it provides a basic overview of options teachers can use to become intentional, effective teachers. Next, we turn to a particularly effective teaching strategy, scaffolding, that draws on the strengths of several different strategies at once.

direct instruction Explicitly giving directions for completing a task; providing facts, verbal labels, or other specific information; or providing instructions for a child's action or behavior.

The Power of Scaffolding: An Integrated Approach

We have now discussed a number of effective strategies that will help you create an effective classroom. Yet how do you best guide children of different skill levels, cultural backgrounds, personalities, and talents toward new, achievable goals? Scaffolding is the most effective teaching strategy for such a challenging task.

scaffolding Using a variety of strategies to support children's ability to accomplish learning tasks that they could not otherwise accomplish independently.

Defining Scaffolding

Scaffolding is a metaphor for a series of teacher behaviors that support children's ability to accomplish learning tasks or solve a problem that they could not otherwise accomplish independently (Wood, Bruner, & Ross, 1976). This strategy not only allows children to progress toward challenging goals, but it also gives them the skills to eventually achieve the

same task on their own. Scaffolding may be such an effective teaching practice because it actually draws on the strengths of many of the other teaching strategies all at once.

Literally, scaffolding is a temporary structure, usually an elevated platform, that builders or painters stand on to reach otherwise inaccessible parts of a building. Like the painter's platform, the scaffold used in the classroom is the right amount of teacher support for the learner to achieve a task or accomplish an objective that would be beyond his or her reach without the assistance.

Scaffolding assists a child to work in his or her zone of proximal development—the area just beyond a child's current level of understanding or ability to achieve. What makes scaffolding effective is that it presents learners with just the right amount of challenge—enough so they don't give up or fail, but not so much that they aren't solving the problem themselves (Clark & Graves, 2005).

MyEducationLab

Go to the Assignments and Activities section of Topic 6: Curriculum Planning in the MyEducationLab for your course and complete the activity entitled *Using Guided Learning in a Unit of Study.* How do these intentional teachers artfully scaffold children's learning using many strategies such as co-construction, K-W-L, and questioning?

The Teacher's Role

The process begins with the teacher having responsibility for the learning and gradually releasing more and more of it to the learner until the child is capable of assuming full responsibility for the task. At that point, a new zone of proximal development is created, and a new challenge can be presented, starting the process once again. Alternatively, scaffolding may occur in a situation where a child is close to mastering a task and, therefore, the teacher provides just a little assistance. For example, 7-year-old Barry loves jigsaw puzzles but he is working on a very difficult one. He has completed the outside border but he is struggling with the middle. His family child care provider suggests that he put all the pieces that are the same color together and match the colors first and then try to match the shapes. He finds this suggestion works well and is able to complete the puzzle on his own.

The process of scaffolding comes to life in the example of a kindergarten teacher writing with her class, as depicted in Table 9.2. In this example, we see how the teacher gradually releases responsibility for the learning to the students.

Table 9.2 Scaffolding in Action

At their morning meeting, after discussing a visit to the classroom by a local dentist, Ms. Riley suggests that the kindergarten children write thank-you notes:

High Level of Teacher Support	Scaffolding		Low Level of Teacher Support
I Do . . . You Watch	*I Do . . . You Help*	*You do . . . I Help*	*You Do . . . I Watch*
The teacher leads a class discussion of what they learned from the dentist's visit. Ms. Riley writes their ideas on a chart as they watch. Then she models how to begin a letter: "Dear Dr. Martinez," she writes, pointing out how she used capital letters for the dentist's name and a period after "Dr."	Ms. Riley sits down with a small group. She prompts their memories about the visit. They were impressed by the big brush and set of teeth and the kinds of food, like apples, that help clean teeth. The children take turns copying some of the words on the chart from yesterday with Ms. Riley's help.	During choice time, children visit the writing center and work on writing their thank-you letters to Dr. Martinez. Ms. Riley places the chart the children dictated where they can see it for reference. She is available as they use their own invented spelling to help them sound out the words they want to write. Occasionally she draws attention to the correct spelling of Dr. Martinez's name.	The children create drawings to include in their letters to Dr. Martinez that describe what they learned and what they enjoyed about her visit to the class. Some children decide to make a chart with pictures and words of how to brush teeth and post it in the bathroom.

Source: Adapted from "Teaching in the Kindergarten Year," by C. Heroman and C. Copple, 2006, in *K Today: Teaching and Learning in the Kindergarten Year*, edited by D. F. Gullo, Washington, DC: NAEYC. Reprinted with permission from the National Association for the Education of Young Children.

MyEducationLab

Go to the Assignments and Activities section of Topic 2: Child Development/Theories in the MyEducationLab for your course and complete the activity entitled *Scaffolding Emergent Literacy.* How does the teacher use a variety of teaching strategies to provide just the right amount of assistance for this child?

Intentional teachers use scaffolding and the other teaching strategies described previously to teach all children. However, additional specific adaptations and modifications may be necessary to help children with disabilities make progress toward their individualized learning goals. The *Including All Children: Modifications and Adaptations for Children with Disabilities* feature provides examples of research-based strategies for teaching children with special needs. In addition, these adaptations are helpful for any child who is not making expected progress and for dual language learners as well.

In the previous sections, we described an array of research-based effective strategies. In the following section, we illustrate how intentional teachers apply these strategies in practice to help individual children reach developmentally appropriate goals.

Connecting Teaching and Learning

As you are starting to see, various teaching strategies accommodate different types of knowledge and different ways of learning. Teachers, therefore, must always be open to different ways of teaching. In the volume *Eager to Learn: Educating Our Preschoolers* (Bowman et al., 2001), experts reviewed the research on young children's cognitive development and its implications for teaching. They identified three key principles of early childhood teaching and learning:

1. Effective teachers make learning meaningful by building on what children already know and can do.
2. Effective teachers develop children's conceptual understanding by teaching topics in depth, using many examples, and making connections to children's everyday experiences. For example, learning knowledge and skills (such as identifying letters and numbers) must be framed within the larger, key concepts involved in each domain of learning (such as the written language system in literacy or the concept of quantity in mathematics).
3. Effective teachers promote children's higher-level thinking and problem solving. They encourage children's development of metacognitive skills such as reflecting, predicting, questioning, and hypothesizing.

The above three principles of learning apply to people of all ages (NRC, 2000). Consider what these three principles mean to you as a college student or as a professional who is expanding your knowledge of teaching.

Reflecting on Your Own Learning

During the course of your schooling and from your work experiences, you have probably identified subjects that you are more interested in than others and that you are likely to pursue as a major or minor. Whenever you take an additional course in your major or an area you have studied thoroughly before, it becomes easier for you to understand and learn the material because you already know a great deal about the subject. In short, you begin by activating your prior knowledge, by connecting new learning to what you already know. An additional advantage to you as a learner is that in your preferred subject area, you are gradually building conceptual frameworks, or mental models, to which you can integrate new information, thereby deepening your understanding.

These types of **conceptual frameworks** serve as memory aids when you need to recall something you've learned or apply knowledge to a new situation. In fact, the more you know about a topic, the more necessary these mental models become in helping you organize, retrieve, and use your knowledge. Finally, when you have that level of understanding, you can begin to analyze your thinking, engaging in metacognitive strategies such as reflecting on what you know and don't know, and apply your knowledge to solve new problems.

conceptual frameworks Mental models that connect new learning to prior knowledge, enhance memory, and deepen understanding.

By contrast, consider some of the general electives you were required to take. You might have very little prior knowledge about those subjects—and perhaps even less interest. If you are like many other students, you may resort to memorizing the facts for a test

Including All Children

Modifications and Adaptations for Children with Disabilities

All teachers should be prepared to work in inclusive settings and support the learning and development of children with identified disabilities or special needs. Here we provide descriptions and examples of seven research-based types of modifications and adaptations that teachers can use to help children achieve individual goals.

Type of Modification	Description	Examples
Environmental support and learning	Altering the physical, social, and temporal environment to promote a child's participation and engagement	• If a child has difficulty making transitions, before the transition give the child a picture or symbol representing the area or activity that the child should go to next. The child can take the picture or symbol card to the next area.
Materials modification	Modifying materials so that the child can participate as independently as possible	• If the child has difficulty standing at an art easel, lower the easel and give the child a chair, or cut the legs off an easel and place it on a table. • If a child's feet do not reach the ground in a child-size chair, place a stool under the table so the child can rest her feet on it and stabilize her body. This stability helps children more easily use their fine-motor skills.
Activity simplification	Simplifying a complicated task by breaking it into smaller parts or reducing the number of steps	• If a child is easily distracted when playing with manipulative toys such as puzzles or beads, hand the pieces to the child one by one. Gradually increase the number of pieces the child has at one time. • If a child has to make a long walk from one place to another and dawdles, complains, and sometimes stops and drops to the floor while walking, put photos, posters, or interesting displays at strategic points along the way. Encourage the child to go to the next spot and describe the achievement: "You got to the baby elephant picture. Can you find the baby lion?"
Use of children's preferences	Identifying and integrating the child's preferences for materials or activities so that the child takes advantage of available opportunities	• If a child has difficulty engaging in new activities or learning centers, or perseverates (stays with one activity only), incorporate the child's favorite toy in a different center. For example, if the child loves cars but never goes to the dramatic play area, create a "car wash" in the area. • If a child does not come readily to circle time, begin group time with a favorite activity such as blowing bubbles or singing a favorite song.
Adult support	An adult intervening or joining the activity to support the child's level of participation	• If a child at the sand table dumps and fills repeatedly without paying attention to the effects of his actions, show the child another way to dump and fill with small alterations, such as holding the container up high while you dump it, or dumping it through a funnel or short tube.
Peer support	Utilizing peers to increase a child's participation	• If a child doesn't know how to select an activity or game on the computer, pair the child with a capable peer who can show the child how to select an activity from the menu. • If a child is learning to use words or sign language to request food items at mealtime, have a peer hold the food so that the child will need to request it from the friend instead of always making requests of adults.
Invisible support	A purposeful arrangement of naturally occurring events within an activity	• If a child is a reluctant talker during group activities, give the child a turn to talk after a particularly talkative peer, which can give the reluctant child ideas about what to say. • If a child is just learning to pour out of a pitcher, let other children pour first so that the pitcher is not too full.

Source: Adapted from *Building Blocks for Teaching Preschoolers with Special Needs*, by S. Sandall et al., 2002, Baltimore: Paul H. Brookes Publishing Co., Inc. Adapted with permission.

without developing a deep understanding of the subject. Without a mental framework of concepts to which you can connect and, therefore, retain new information, you soon forget everything you have "learned." In addition, you cannot engage metacognitively in this subject area because you don't know enough about what you know to reflect on it, analyze it, make predictions about it, or evaluate your own thinking in regard to it.

Now that we have introduced teaching strategies and discussed the importance of accommodating each child's needs, we will show how teachers can use these strategies to make learning meaningful for children, to help them develop conceptual understanding, and to build higher-level thinking and problem-solving skills.

Making Connections: Strategies to Make Learning Meaningful

According to the principles identified previously, effective teaching draws out and builds on children's preexisting understandings (Bowman et al., 2001; NRC, 2002). Several strategies are effective in activating and building on children's prior knowledge, including cueing, questioning, and using some form of advance organizer (Ausubel, 1978).

Cueing and Questioning

A straightforward way of activating children's prior knowledge is to provide cues that will spark a connection (Marzano et al., 2001, p. 114). Another strategy is to ask questions. For example, before reading *Caps for Sale,* Carol continues to engage children's prior knowledge to help make the story meaningful:

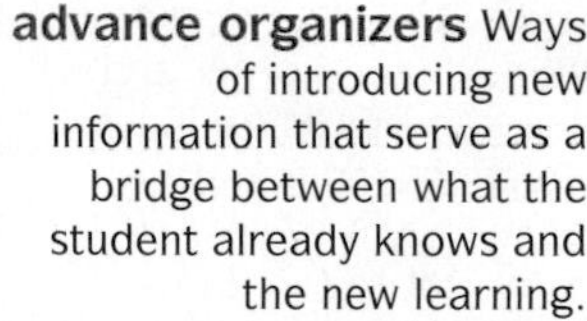

advance organizers Ways of introducing new information that serve as a bridge between what the student already knows and the new learning.

K-W-L An advance organizer strategy in which teachers ask children what they already know (K) about the topic of study, what they want (W) to know, and then what they learned (L).

Teacher: Our story is called *Caps for Sale: A Tale of a Peddler, Some Monkeys, and Their Monkey Business.* You already know what caps are, don't you Jason.

Jason: Yeah. I wore a baseball cap to school today.

Teacher: That's right. It's a kind of hat.

Pressing on with more pointed questions, the teacher continues: "What do you think the author means when he says the story is about 'monkey business'? Have you ever heard that before?"

Marly: When my grandma babysits us, she always tells my mommy that she won't allow any monkey business, but she is smiling when she says it.

Teacher: So what is Marly's grandma talking about, do you think?

Ricardo: I guess she means she won't let anybody act silly.

Prior to reading the story, the teacher used cues and questions to tap into what the children already know and understand. As she reads the story, she connects the antics of the monkeys to children's ideas and effectively builds on their prior knowledge.

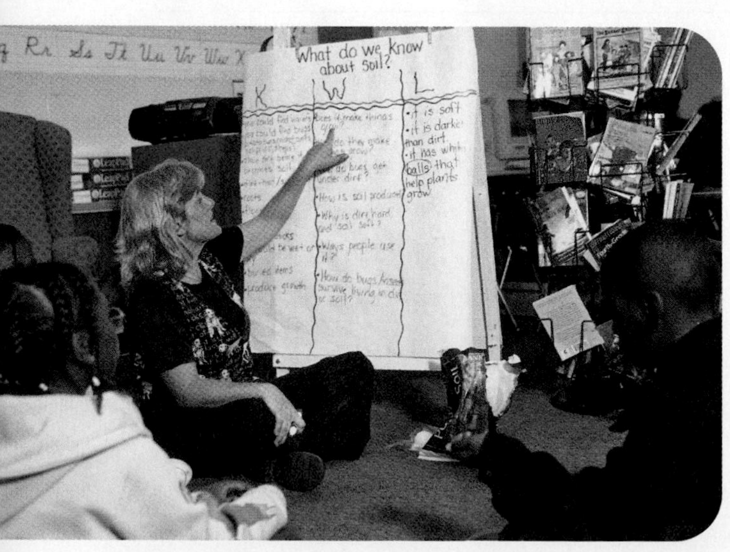

Effective teachers build on what children already know. One way is to use a K-W-L chart, asking children what they know about a topic and what they want to learn. In what other ways could teachers build on children's prior learning?

Using Advance Organizers

Another way teachers help children build on their background knowledge to engage new learning is to use advance organizers. **Advance organizers** are used before introducing new information, and they serve as a bridge between what the student already knows and the new learning (Ausubel, 1978; Marzano et al., 2001). An example of an advance organizer strategy that is widely used in early childhood education is known as **K-W-L** (Ogle, 1986). In using K-W-L, teachers first ask children what they already *know* (K) about the topic of study. Then, they ask children what they *want* (W) to know or what questions they have about the topic. After the study is complete, these responses are compared to the answers children provide to the third question, "What did you *learn* (L)? K-W-L is a useful strategy to build reading comprehension or to organize learning about a science or social studies topic. Consider the following example:

> In his second-grade classroom, Mr. Ivey uses K-W-L to launch a study on wolves with a small group of children:
>
> Mr. Ivey: Today we're going to read a book about wolves. What do you already know (K) about wolves?
>
> Children's responses include these: They live in the forest. They kill other animals. They are scary.
>
> Mr. Ivey: What do you want to find out about wolves? (W)
>
> The children raise many questions: What do they eat? Where do they sleep? Do they sleep all winter like bears? How big do they grow? How do they take care of their babies? Mr. Ivey writes each question on chart paper.
>
> Mr. Ivey: Let's read this book and afterward we'll write down what we've learned.
>
> Following the reading, the children have learned many facts about wolves, but they still don't know if they hibernate.
>
> Mr. Ivey: How could you find out if wolves hibernate?
> Melinda: We could use the Internet or we could e-mail the zookeeper.

MyEducationLab

Go to the Assignments and Activities section of Topic 10: Cultural and Linguistic Diversity in the MyEducationLab for your course and complete the activity entitled *Strategies for Teaching Diverse Learners*. What teaching strategies are demonstrated in the video to make learning meaningful for children and adapt for diverse learners in primary grades?

This process of building on prior knowledge is easier when teachers and children share a common language and similar cultural background. When children's prior knowledge is acquired in a language and/or cultural context that is different from that of the teacher, the task of building on the children's prior knowledge becomes more difficult but no less important. Teachers of dual language learners must become aware of children's abilities and how to build on them. Read the *Language Lens: Teachable Moments with Dual Language Learners* feature for suggested strategies.

Cueing, questioning, and using advance organizers are all effective approaches to activate children's prior knowledge, which, in turn, enhances their understanding and retention of what they learn (Bransford, Brown, & Cocking, 2000). Next, we identify some strategies for building concept development.

Developing Concepts: Strategies to Build Children's Understanding

The second principle of teaching and learning emphasizes the need for children to learn topics in depth rather than amassing a large number of unrelated facts. Such understanding is enhanced when children's factual knowledge is organized into conceptual frameworks with many examples and apparent connections. To help children build conceptual frameworks, teachers can engage them in classification and representation activities.

Classifying and Identifying Similarities and Differences

Teachers can help children build concepts by engaging them in forming **classification systems** that identify similarities and differences or compare and contrast objects and ideas. These cognitive activities begin early for young children.

When interacting with babies, adults continually use comparative language: "Look how big you are! You're bigger than the teddy bear now, but Scruffy is the biggest." Likewise, children learn many mathematical concepts through building classification systems. With her group of 2- and 3-year-olds olds, Thelma helps the children learn the concept of the number *2* by matching pairs of shoes and socks. They soon apply this new concept to their body parts, singing a song while pointing out their two feet, two hands, two legs, two ears, and on and on.

classification systems Systems teachers use to help children build concepts by identifying similarities and differences or by comparing and contrasting objects and ideas.

Language Lens

Teachable Moments with Dual Language Learners

For children who are learning English, every moment in the classroom is a learning experience. They may be wearing winter clothes for the first time, riding a school bus, and meeting people who do not look or sound like them. Learning a new language takes time, effort, and intentional teaching. Teachers need to take advantage of every teachable moment. Here are some points for teachers to keep in mind:

- As a role model of the language, speak slowly but not loudly, simplifying your vocabulary and sentence structure as you might for a younger child. Over time, work toward more challenging vocabulary, sentences, and short conversation.
- Use your body and facial expressions to communicate. For instance, to emphasize words like *under, through*, *around*, or *on top*, play with children around a table to physically demonstrate these words and concepts.
- Use repetition. Be as clear as possible in pronunciation and diction, which may mean opening the mouth wider because children look for facial clues.
- Identify English-speaking children who are willing to be classroom language pals.
- Use large-group time to engage children in the joy of group movement and exercise, singing and choral repetition, and quiet listening time.
- Use small-group time, which is especially effective for dual language learners because it allows for active participation, individual attention, and experiences with objects. For example, if children are learning about vegetables, have real broccoli, carrots, and squash for them to see, touch, and taste.
- Vary the composition of groups, at times bringing together learners who speak the same language and, at other times, children from two or more language groups.
- Outdoor playtime is a great venue for children to learn new English words for physical actions and social interactions. Create games that repeat words like *run, kick, walk, jump, throw over,* or *throw under.* Making friends and playing together motivate children to learn a new language.
- Give special attention to particular sounds that may not exist in the child's home language. For some Spanish-speaking children it may be the */ch/* or */sh/* or */w/* pronunciations; for some Asian children, it may be the */r/* or */th/* sounds.
- Encourage children's efforts at speaking the new language; avoid correcting children by simply rephrasing and repeating.

Creating Graphic Representations

"A picture is worth a thousand words" may seem to be a hackneyed cliché, yet when it comes to developing children's conceptual understanding, the phrase is true. In fact, it is also true for college students. You've probably experienced seemingly endless pages of text or hours of lecture that only become clear to you after you've seen a chart, graph, or Venn diagram. This teaching strategy, called **graphic representation**, is the process of depicting thoughts and ideas through drawing, modeling, or using other media.

Teachers can use representation is many ways. For instance, learning about "quantity," first graders create a graph showing their preference: basketball or soccer. The higher bar, soccer, is the one with "more" votes, providing a visual representation of the concept for the children. They then create a graph comparing the votes of boys and girls.

While teachers' use of graphic representations is an effective way to teach concepts and to engage children, another powerful use of representation is to engage children in creating their own representations. This activity is a defining characteristic of the Reggio Emilia approach and one of their many contributions to the knowledge base of early childhood.

Loris Malaguzzi (1998) described the purpose of representation as clarifying children's understanding. George Forman, one of the earliest disseminators of the Reggio approach in America, described children's use of graphic representation in Reggio as "not learning to draw, but drawing to learn" (Forman, 1994). Reggio educators (Edwards, Gandini, & Forman, 1998) view graphic representation as a communication tool that is simpler and clearer than words and, therefore, an invaluable way to help children clarify and

graphic representation The process of depicting thoughts and ideas through drawing, modeling, or other media.

extend their thinking, that is, deepen their conceptual understanding. Because children are trying to communicate with others through their drawings, clay models, or other representations, they often pause to clarify their ideas before putting them down on paper and making them visible to other people. Important thinking is going on at such moments.

One example of how representation reveals and challenges a child's thinking is related to a study of rain (from the Hundred Languages of Children exhibit, Commune of Reggio Emilia, Italy, cited in Landry & Forman, 1999). After many days of rain, teachers asked children, "Where do you think rain comes from?" Children expressed various theories, such as "the Lord makes the rain." But Simone, age 5½, explained, "The sun heats the rain that has fallen and that's how it goes away afterwards. It goes back into the clouds and then it starts to rain again." From her explanation, it seems that Simone has a good understanding of the rain cycle.

After writing down (representing) children's theories in words, their teacher asked them to draw pictures of where the rain comes from. Simone's detailed drawing included pipes or tubes going up from the ground to the sky to convey the water. Thus, when asked to represent her theory, the child had to further elaborate on it. By engaging children in graphic representation of their theories, the teacher got a much clearer picture of Simone's understanding—somewhat different from her seemingly accurate verbal representation.

Promoting Higher-Level Thinking and Problem Solving

Strategies that are effective in building higher-level thinking and problem solving are those that integrate teaching of metacognitive skills. **Metacognitive activities** engage children in thinking and reflecting about their own learning. Early childhood education has a long tradition of incorporating these strategies in effective ways (Copple, Sigel, & Saunders, 1984; Hohmann & Weikart, 2002). We describe next two strategies that not only engage children's metacognition, but also contribute to their achievement in school and life.

metacognitive activities Activities that engage children in thinking and reflecting about their own learning.

Planning and Reflection

Many early childhood programs offer children choices during center time, but planning is more than making choices. **Planning** requires children to make intentional choices and encourages them to identify their goals, consider the options for achieving them, make predictions, and anticipate consequences (Epstein, 2003).

planning Requires children to make intentional choices and encourages them to identify their goals, consider the options for achieving them, make predictions, and anticipate consequences; helps build children's higher-level thinking and problem solving.

Reflection is remembering with analysis, which is more than just memory and recall of events (Epstein, 2003). Teachers help children go beyond remembering what they did to becoming aware of what they learned, what was interesting, how they felt about the experience, and what they can do to build on and extend the experience. For an example of this effective practice in action, read the feature titled *What Works: Involve Children in Planning.*

reflection Teaching strategy in which teachers help children go beyond remembering what they did to becoming aware of what they learned, what was interesting, how they felt about the experience, and what they can do to build on and extend the experience.

Generating and Testing Hypotheses

Tisha, a second grader, stares up at the sky for a long time and announces, "I think we're going to have a bad storm. It was hot but now it's cold, and see those cumulus clouds." Impressed, her grandma asks her where she learned all that. "We're studying weather all year in my class. We go outside every day."

At least once a week, Tisha's class looks at the weather map on the Internet, discusses what has been happening during the last 24 hours, and then go outside and observe the sky in the morning and again in the afternoon. The children make predictions about what they think will happen before the next school day, explaining the reasoning behind their predictions. The next morning, they discuss their hypotheses and the extent to which they were correct. If their predictions were accurate, they identify the observations that were the most helpful. If their predictions were not accurate, they try to figure out what they missed or misunderstood (adapted from Marzano et al., 2001, p. 103).

In the above scenario, Tisha's teacher uses a teaching strategy that draws on children's metacognitive abilities. **Hypothesis generating and testing** is the strategy of applying

hypothesis generating and testing Applying previously acquired knowledge to a new situation by making a prediction and then observing and reflecting on the outcome.

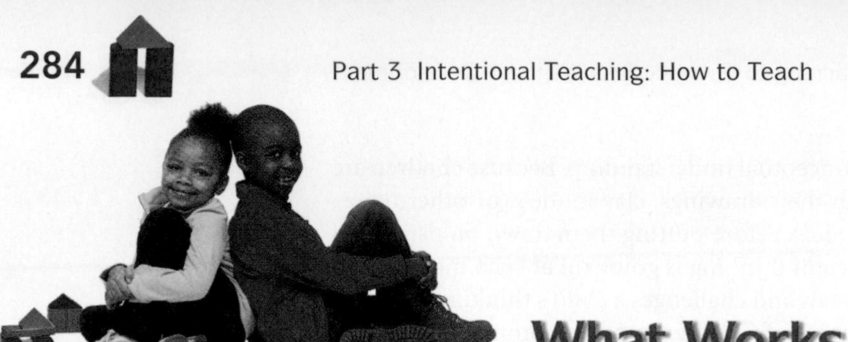

Involve Children in Planning

When children engage in planning, they use their minds actively. As they work out what they will do, children become initiators, problem solvers, and artists who make things happen and create meaning for themselves and others. To help children develop the ability to plan, consider the following strategies.

Make Planning a Regular Part of the Day If tasks that require planning become a routine classroom activity, children are more likely to improve their planning skills. To encourage children to plan tasks and events, it is useful to have a designated planning time, such as just before center time. You can plan with children in small groups, pairs, or individually, making sure each child gets to express his or her intentions. Children benefit from planning in small groups because the thoughts and elaborations of others often spark their own ideas. For example, notice how the teacher is talking with a group of 4- and 5-year-olds about what they will do during center time.

Jason: I'm going to make a race track in the block area.
Teacher: You made a track yesterday that stretched all the way to the bookshelf.
Mike: Me and him made it together. Today we're gonna make a longer one.
Teacher: It sounds like Jason and Mike are planning to work together today.
Darya: I'm going to work together, too.
Teacher: Who are you planning to work with?
Darya: With Mei Lin.
Mei Lin: Let's fill all the jars with water and make them sing.
Darya: First let's make the water orange. I'll mix the watercolors while you get the jars.
Teacher: Let me know when the jars are ready to sing. I want to hear them.

Encourage Children to Elaborate on Their Plans For inexperienced planners, try simple follow-up questions: "What will you need to do that?" Sometimes a comment about what the child is doing elicits more details than a question would. When the teacher observed 4-year-old Mitch's behavior, she said, "You're barking like a dog," to which Mitch replied, "I'm a lost dog and I want you to find me."

In your eagerness to assist younger children, don't overlook opportunities to promote older children's progress as planners as well. Encourage them to give specifics about where they will work, the materials they intend to use, the sequence of their activities, and the outcomes they expect to achieve. When Rachel announces she is going to draw the family dog, her teacher says, "I wonder how you're going to show the puppies growing inside Daisy." This comment encourages Rachel to consider such issues as size and spatial relationships as she plans her drawing.

Write Down Children's Plans Written plans communicate that children's ideas are valuable. Take dictation when children describe what they will do and how they will go about it. Encourage older 4-year-olds and kindergarten children to begin writing their own ideas. Documenting children's work through writing, drawing, and photography—which both children and teachers can be involved in—helps young learners become more conscious of the process and value of planning. Children can also look back to their documented plans as they reflect on their experiences and compare their intentions with the actual outcomes.

Source: Based on "How Planning and Reflections Develop Young Children's Thinking Skills," by A. S. Epstein, 2003, *Young Children, 58*(5), pp. 28–36.

scientific method Method of beginning with a hypothesis, testing it with an experiment, making observations and gathering data, and then confirming or disconfirming the initial hypothesis.

previously acquired knowledge to a new situation by making a prediction and then observing and reflecting on the outcome. Using this strategy, learners activate prior knowledge, gather new information, and expand and deepen their understanding of concepts. The greatest benefit of hypothesis testing comes when learners explain their thinking, which helps deepen understanding (Marzano et al., 2001, p. 105).

Hypothesis testing is used in science curricula because it actively engages children in applying the **scientific method**: Begin with a hypothesis, test it with an experiment, make observations and gather data, and then confirm or disconfirm the initial hypothesis. However, hypothesis testing is not exclusively used for science; in fact, it is used in all kinds of problem-solving situations, such as those encountered in mathematics or social studies or when negotiating social problems among peers. Consider how hypothesis testing is used in the following example:

> A small group of preschoolers wants to construct model cars to use on the race track they have built. Their teacher asks them to hypothesize about what kinds of materials they could use to get the wheels to turn, and the children offer suggestions:
>
> Mary: Straws with buttons glued on the ends.
> Damon: Donuts. (Several children laugh.)
> Teacher: Why do you think donuts wouldn't work?
> Gina: We'd eat them before we finished the car!
> Damon: But maybe something like a donut because a wheel needs to have a hole in the middle.
>
> Damon and his friend Jaleel search for objects among the collage art materials that might work to test their hypothesis, while Mary and her friend pursue gluing the buttons. Later the teacher and children describe what happened with their experiments and whether their hypotheses were accurate. The girls admit that although the buttons are round, the glue makes them stationary and, therefore, not very good wheels.

In the previous sections, we described an array of teaching strategies and how teachers apply them to make learning meaningful for children, to help them learn concepts, and to engage them in higher-level thinking. To be an effective teacher, you will need to have all of these strategies in your repertoire and know when and how to use them.

Using Grouping as an Instructional Strategy

In Chapter 8, we described how the environment influences children's behavior and helps teachers create caring communities. At the same time, the environment provides a powerful context for learning. Environments communicate messages to children about what kind of learning is valued and what their role is in the process. For example, a classroom with rows of individual desks and the teacher's desk in the front sends the message that children work only as individuals and teachers control the dissemination of knowledge.

On the other hand, a classroom with tables that encourage groups of children to work together, an open space for class meetings and discussions, and learning centers for children to choose where they will work and play sends an entirely different message. In the latter environment, the expectation is clear that the teacher and children will work together in various learning contexts.

Organizing the Environment for Learning

Appropriate learning environments for children will vary depending on the age of the children, the time of the year, and the topic of study. Child-centered environments are organized so that many materials are accessible to children. In preschools, children have access to blocks, dramatic play props, puzzles and other manipulative toys, art materials, and books. In primary grade classrooms, children may have books to read, science tools to explore and investigate, math games, computer centers, and other learning materials. Table 9.3 lists the types of centers available in a challenging, engaging kindergarten learning environment and materials that they might include.

An intellectually engaging learning environment provides various contexts for teaching and learning to occur, such as small groups, individual interactions, whole-group meetings, center choice time, and opportunities for play. In the following sections, we describe some of the ways teachers use grouping as an instructional strategy and interact

Table 9.3 Centers and the Materials They Might Include

Learning Center	Examples of Materials
Books	Books of all genres (predictable, informational, poetry, narrative, wordless, decodable), listening center with books on tape or CDs, storytelling and retelling props (flannel boards, puppets, story clothesline)
Writing	Writing paper, envelopes, blank booklets, journals, pencils, pens, markers, word banks, letter stamps, alphabet cards
Mathematics and games	Collections of objects (buttons, stickers, erasers, bottle caps), number cards, interlocking cubes, parquetry blocks, attribute games, graphing mats, sorting trays, decks of cards, board games, dice
Science/discovery	Plants, class pets, nature objects, collections (shells, rocks, leaves, balls, shiny things), tools for investigating (magnifying glasses, magnets, funnels, lenses), science journals, clipboards
Music and movement	Collection of CDs, musical instruments, keyboard with headphones, picture songbooks, song cards (color-coded to correspond with colored instruments), props for movement (scarves, flags, streamers)
Art	Materials to paint and draw on (newsprint, butcher paper, fingerpaint paper, foil), painting and drawing implements (markers, crayons, paints, pens, pencils, charcoal, chalk), materials for molding and sculpting (clay, playdough, tools), cutting and pasting materials (scissors, paste, glue, collage materials), materials for constructing (foam pieces, wood scraps, wire, pipe cleaners, recyclable materials), art books, photographs, posters
Dramatic play	Props and dress-up clothes, homelike materials reflecting children's culture (kitchen furniture, dolls, phone, message board, empty food containers), open-ended materials (large pieces of fabric, plastic tubing, cardboard boxes), literacy materials (magazines, books, pads of paper, cookbooks, junk mail), mathematics and science materials (calculators, kitchen and bathroom scales, calendars, cash registers, measuring cups and spoons, store coupons)
Blocks	Unit blocks, hollow blocks, props (people figures, vehicles, hats, animal figures), open-ended materials (cardboard tubes, cardboard panels, PVC pipes, vinyl rain gutters), literacy materials (writing tools and paper, signs, books about bridges and buildings)
Technology	Computers, printers, optional technology (Web cam, digital camera, scanners, computer microscopes)

Source: Adapted from "Teaching in the Kindergarten Year," by C. Heroman and C. Copple, 2006, in *K Today: Teaching and Learning in the Kindergarten Year*, edited by D. F. Gullo, Washington, DC: NAEYC. Reprinted with permission from the National Association for the Education of Young Children.

with children in different learning contexts. A discussion of play as a learning context follows in a later section of the chapter.

Learning in the Whole Group

Whole group, which is also called *circle time* or *class meeting time*, provides a valuable context for class discussions, music and movement, planning for the day or for special experiences such as visitors or field trips, and for children to share their experiences and ideas. Whole group is a time to build a sense of community and shared purpose. Teachers use this time to introduce a new idea or concept in the whole group using modeling, demonstration, or direct instruction.

Research with preschoolers demonstrates that during large-group times, teachers' explanatory talk and use of challenging vocabulary is related to improving learning outcomes for children (Dickinson, 2001b), as in this example:

> Prior to a visit by a local police officer, Margo gathers her whole class of preschoolers on the rug. She explains, "Officer Gardner is coming tomorrow. She will be wearing her uni-

form, and her badge that identify her to everyone as a police officer. She wants to tell you some ways to stay safe because keeping people safe is the main job of the police. I'll write on our chart some questions you want to ask her." During this brief introduction, Margo provided the children with a concise explanation of what to expect. She also clarified the meanings of the vocabulary she used, such as *uniform*, *badge*, and *identify*.

Teachers may also engage the whole group in discussion, using questions to prompt and sustain the interaction. For example, a teacher might have her third-grade children working in small groups on an investigation of floating and sinking. Each group will share their theories about floating or sinking with the rest of the class.

In general, the younger the child, the shorter the length of time she or he should spend in whole-group experience. Young children are easily distracted, and the context is less effective if overused (Montie, Xiang, & Schweinhart, 2006). Nevertheless, if children are actively engaged in a large group, mentally and/or physically, this setting can be an effective learning context where children have the opportunity to express themselves, to hear the opinions of others, and to feel part of the larger learning community. The important caveat is that teachers need to take their cue from the children. If interest wanes during whole group, it is best to bring the group time to a close and move on to another activity setting or actively engage all the children in singing or movement.

Learning in Small Groups

Small groups, usually composed of four to six children, are especially valuable learning contexts for two reasons. First, they provide the opportunity for more focused attention and individualized instruction from the teacher, and second, they give children the opportunity to interact with peers. Teachers can use small groups for a focused learning experience such as introducing a new skill or concept.

One of the greatest benefits of small-group interaction is the back-and-forth exchanges among children, which can scaffold children's learning just as teacher interactions can. Small groups also provide the opportunity for active engagement in the learning experience. Without such active involvement, the benefit of small groups goes unrealized. Children should have the opportunity to participate in more than one small group each day depending on the instructional goals, working with peers of varying ability levels. For an example of grouping as an instructional strategy, read the feature titled *Becoming an Intentional Teacher: Working in Small Groups*.

MyEducationLab

Go to the Assignments and Activities section of Topic 6: Curriculum Planning in the MyEducationLab for your course and complete the activity entitled *Effective Teaching Strategies in Early Childhood Classrooms*. How do these teachers effectively use grouping as an instructional strategy in both teacher-initiated and child-initiated learning opportunities?

Teaching in Learning Centers

Effective early childhood classrooms provide an extended period of time, from 45 to 90 minutes, for children to engage in child-initiated experiences in learning centers (Epstein, 2007b; Montie et al., 2006; Siraj-Blatchford et al., 2003). These defined areas of the classroom have particular purposes. The library area promotes book reading and listening. A block area provides for building and pretending. Art and writing centers promote creative expression, symbolic representation, and development of fine-motor skills. Manipulative toys, like peg boards, beads, and Legos offer opportunities to practice fine-motor skills and solve problems. The dramatic play area promotes symbolic pretend play, self-regulation, and language interaction among children.

During learning center time, children have opportunities to plan, initiate, and make choices and to practice their developing skills, which is essential for mastery. Learning centers provide natural laboratories for children to work out social problems with other children and practice their language. Center time also promotes decision-making skills because children make choices about how they will spend their time, what they will do, and with whom they will play.

Effective teachers use center time to engage children in one-to-one, extended conversations (Dickinson, 2001). During this period in which children are engaged with various tasks, such as writing, doing a puzzle, or pouring water, teachers are available to scaffold individual

Working in Small Groups

Here's What Happened With my kindergarten class, I decided to play a marble game to engage them in thinking about measurement and also the processes of predicting, observing, and recording results. After explaining the game, I organized children into groups of three or four. Each had a hollow piece of plumbing pipe and a marble. With one end of the pipe on the ground, a child held the other end. Each group dropped a marble down the pipe to see how far it would travel out the other end. After the initial try, the children held the pipe at different angles to see if the angle affected the distance the marble traveled. The children recorded how far the marble went in an initial try and then tried to get it to roll farther based on where they were holding the other end of the pipe. I asked each group questions as the game proceeded to engage them in thinking about and predicting what would happen.

Here's What I Was Thinking I planned the marble game as a small-group activity for several reasons. Small groups of children are better than large groups for focusing their attention on an idea. When each child can participate more actively in investigating, predicting, and recording measurements, they care more about the outcome—in this case, making the marble go farther than it has before. They pay attention to what affects the distance it rolls, and they are motivated to work out a way to measure if they've succeeded in improving their previous results. Small groups not only allow the children to participate, they allow me to observe what each child does and does not understand and engage each child in the learning experience at his or her own level.

I typically put together these small groups during the time that children were in learning centers. I invited a group of children to work with me; if there was something else the children really wanted to do instead, I allowed them to choose. It was rare, however, for them to pass up this opportunity—they loved the extra interaction of small groups and I worked hard to make these experiences engaging.

I formed groups that were mixed with respect to the children's developmental levels, or what I thought their ability would be on this task. I thought that five children were starting to grasp the general idea of standard units in measurement—a big breakthrough that many children don't make until age 7 or 8. I dispersed those children among the five groups I worked with. I encouraged these five children to explain their ideas to the others because it helps them get a firmer understanding of the concepts. And the exposure the less advanced children get gives them a new idea to chew on.

Source: Based on *The Young Child and Mathematics*, pp. 103–104, by J. V. Copley, 2000, Washington, DC: NAEYC.

children's learning as needed. Finally, center time also provides an excellent opportunity for teachers to observe and assess children's developing capabilities in various contexts.

In the previous sections, we described the various contexts commonly found in early childhood classrooms: whole group, small group, and learning centers. Center time is an excellent opportunity for children to engage in their favorite activity—play (Wiltz & Klein, 2001). Play is also a highly effective context for learning and teaching, as described next.

Play as a Teaching Strategy

The word *play* is used to describe different types of activities, including constructive play and games with rules as well as pretend play. In the previous discussion of learning centers, we saw how teachers' behaviors support learning during various forms of play. In this section, we explore teachers' roles during sociodramatic play, a particularly effective form of play for developing children's self-regulation, problem-solving, and language and literacy skills (Berk & Winsler, 1995; Bodrova & Leong, 2001, 2007; Smilansky & Shefatya, 1990).

Rarely is play thought of as a teaching strategy. Researchers define play as child-initiated experience, and, in fact, children themselves see play as something they control (Singer, Golinkoff, & Hirsh-Pasek, 2006; Sutton-Smith, 1980). Nevertheless, decades of research on play demonstrates that teachers have important roles in children's play and they can help play achieve its full potential as an effective learning experience for children (Singer et al., 2006; Zigler, Singer, & Bishop-Josef, 2004).

During sociodramatic play, children pretend, create a theme, use props, develop roles, and follow rules related to the roles. Moreover, sociodramatic play involves language interaction (Berk & Winsler, 1995), as we see in this example:

> In her Head Start classroom, Marita Lewis sets up a grocery store with food boxes, plastic fruit and vegetables, shopping carts, a cash register, and check-out counter. She adds paper and pencils for writing shopping lists, play money, and paper receipts. As 4-year-old Carey pushes her cart up to the counter, the "cashier" Angela, her classmate, asks, "Paper or plastic?" After Carey selects, "Paper," Angela, continues to recite the script of a cashier to the best of her recollection, "Credit card or money?" Meanwhile, sitting nearby, Marita is approached by LaToya who needs help writing her shopping list. She wants to add bananas. Marita says, "BBBBananas" drawing out the */b/* sound at the beginning of the word. "What letter does it start with?" "B!" shouts LaToya, who quickly starts to write a *B* on her list.

Teachers' Involvement during Play

Research reveals that teachers play a variety of roles during children's play that can be placed on a continuum from minimal to maximum teacher involvement (Enz & Christie, 1997; Johnson, Christie, & Wardle, 2005; Roskos & Neuman, 1993). Figure 9.1 depicts the continuum of teacher roles in play (Johnson et al., 2005). As the figure illustrates, the effective, *facilitating* roles are the ones in the middle of the continuum.

The two extremes of teacher behavior, either *uninvolved* or *overly directive*, have a negative effect on play. If teachers are uninvolved and ignore children during play, using playtime to do paperwork or housekeeping tasks, children's pretend play tends to become simplistic, repetitive, and raucous, featuring themes like monsters and superheroes (Enz & Christie, 1997; Johnson et al., 2005). In these situations, the play often turns into a disciplinary situation with the teacher only stepping in to police behavior. Consequently, the learning potential of play is lost.

At the other end of the continuum, teachers are ineffective if they take too much control of children's play, either by trying to direct what children do from the sidelines or by redirecting the play away from what the children are doing toward the teacher's goal. Situations

MyEducationLab

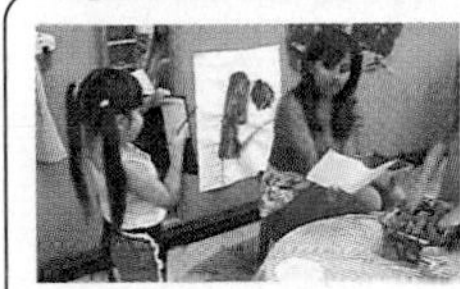

Go to the Assignments and Activities section of Topic 2: Child Development/Theories in the MyEducationLab for your course and complete the activity entitled *The Restaurant.* What roles does the teacher play in the restaurant scenario? How does she support children's engagement in sociodramatic play?

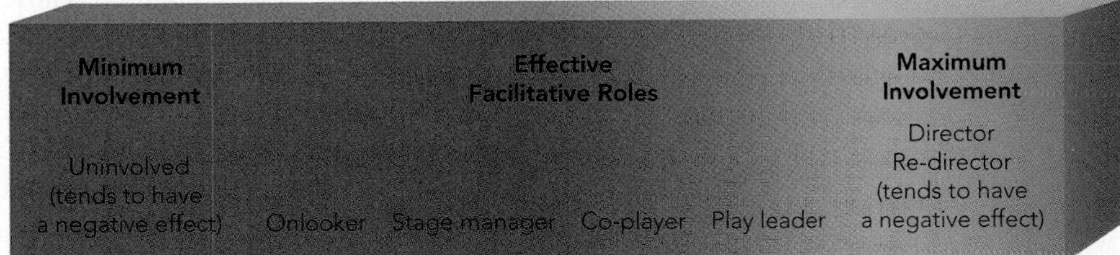

Figure 9.1 Continuum of Teacher Roles in Play

From James E. Johnson et al., *Play, Development and Early Education, 1e*, p. 271. Published by Allyn and Bacon/Merrill Education, Boston, MA. Copyright © 2005 by Pearson Education. Adapted by permission of the publisher.

where teachers are maximally involved cease to be child-initiated play, and most of the time, children will simply withdraw mentally from the pretend scenario or leave the scene entirely.

So we see that using play as a teaching strategy requires teachers to walk a fine line between doing too little and doing too much. Next we discuss several effective roles of teachers during play.

Teacher's Roles during Play

The four roles in the midrange of the continuum are onlooker, stage manager, co-player, and play leader. These roles are all effective in helping children get involved and stay engaged in play situations. In each of these roles, the teacher becomes more involved in the play scene. At the same time, the teacher adapts her role as the children play, depending on their interests and needs.

Onlooker Role

In the **onlooker** role, teachers act as the audience for children's play. They position themselves nearby, acknowledging and encouraging children's play by nodding, smiling, or making positive comments. The onlooker role lets children know that play is valued and important, and encourages them to persist. In the onlooker role, teachers observe and assess children's competencies exhibited during their play interactions. Based on these observations, the teacher intentionally decides whether and how to become more involved in the play (Johnson et al., 2005).

Stage Manager

As the name implies, **stage managers** do not actively enter the play; they instead set the stage by providing the props and theme. They are also available to respond to children's requests for materials or assistance. In the grocery store play described previously, Marita acted as a stage manager, having prepared the setting, which encouraged children's involvement. Stage managers scaffold children's learning such as when Marita helped LaToya with her shopping list. Teachers as stage managers also make suggestions to help extend the play. For example, if LaToya began to lose interest, Marita might ask, "What else do you need for your dinner tonight?"

Co-player

As **co-players**, teachers actually join in and take an active role in the play. Coplayers are equal play partners with children, but it is best if teachers take the subordinate role in the drama, such as the patient in the doctor's office or the passenger on the airplane, leaving the prime roles of doctor or pilot for the children. As a co-player, the teacher is careful to let the children take the lead. This role provides ample opportunity, however, for the teacher to model play skills, including pretending with objects and roles, turn-taking, ways to enter an ongoing scene, and vocabulary (Johnson et al., 2005, p. 272). Consider how the teacher accomplishes all of these goals in the following play situation (cited in Bredekamp, 2004):

> In Evelyn Delgado's preschool, she lies on the floor among several children whose white coats and stethoscopes identify them as medical staff. Evelyn says, "Oh, doctor, I'm so sick and I'm scared." The doctors begin administering shots and discussing what medicine to give her. One of the girls offers Evelyn a phone to call her mommy. Evelyn cries into the phone, "Mommy, I'm so scared. There are doctors all around me." The same little girl shifts roles and returns as Evelyn's mommy, offering to read her a story to make her feel better. Pointing to a page in the book about a visit to the hospital, she comforts Evelyn, "He's not afraid because he's the big brother."

Play Leader

This role involves teachers' direct participation in children's play, but exerts more influence than the co-player's role. As the **play leader**, the teacher deliberately attempts to enrich and

onlooker Teachers act as the audience for children's play.

stage manager Teachers set the stage for children's play by providing the props and theme, and being available to respond to children's requests.

co-player Teachers actually join in and take an active role in children's play.

play leader Teachers participate in children's play; includes making deliberate attempts to enrich and extend the play episode.

extend the play episode, suggesting a theme and introducing new props or plot elements. Teachers become play leaders when children have difficulty beginning sociodramatic play or when play breaks down:

> After several days playing in the grocery store, the children's play becomes repetitive and fewer children choose to play there. To spark some interest, Marita puts herself in the role of store manager.
>
> Marita: This store is losing business. I think it needs some new attractions for shoppers. What if we reduce the prices on everything and have a sale?
> Josh: We'll have to change all the signs.
> Marita: What else could we do to get more customers?
> Toby: We could put in a McDonald's like they have at the mall.
>
> The children quickly embrace Toby's idea. Josh starts to draw a big M for the McDonald's sign, while other children start gathering props for the food. Toby's suggestion leads to many changes in the dramatic play episode with new roles like cook that extend the play over several days.

Sociodramatic play is a valuable context for children's learning. But children don't automatically play productively. How can teachers support play to benefit children without taking over?

Because sociodramatic play is such an effective learning context, teachers need to be aware of and use the full range of roles and strategies available to them in supporting children's make-believe play. While some educators believe that pretend play comes naturally to children and that adults are not needed, this is a misperception. In fact, children who are skilled "players" during preschool most likely had parents or caregivers who played with them beginning as babies and toddlers (Elias & Berk, 2002).

Today's teachers report that many children, often children from low-income backgrounds but also their middle-class peers, are unskilled at pretend play when they come to early childhood programs. Their play tends to be repetitive and immature. In situations such as these, teachers in the role of stage manager can coach children from the sidelines to improve play behaviors, or as co-players or leaders, they can model and scaffold appropriate play behavior. Consider what role or roles you might play as a teacher in the situation described in *How Would You Respond? Helping Children Enter Play*.

Research demonstrates that participation in sociodramatic play has positive effects on children's language, social, and cognitive development (Bodrova & Leong, 2007; Dickinson, 2001). As when using any teaching strategy, to be effective, teachers must be intentional in their role in children's play. Play has a long tradition in early childhood programs as well as a thorough research base. In the next section, we discuss a more recent educational phenomenon, the use of technology.

Teaching with Technology

Young children today are surrounded by technology. Many tools of daily life, such as cell phones, computers, websites, social networking, video games, and digital cameras, are technological. In discussing how to teach, it is important to consider how to use technology most effectively.

Using Computers to Teach

Research on the use of computers with young children demonstrates that they can be highly effective in promoting children's learning (NRC, 2009; Sarama & Clements, 2002). Computers also encourage social interaction among young children. Unlike adults who tend to work at computers in isolation, preschool and primary grade children willingly seek other children's involvement if the software is engaging and interactive. Placing two

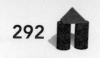

How Would You Respond?

Helping Children Enter Play

The Situation Four-and-a-half-year-old Joseph spends a lot of time watching while the other children play. On the few occasions when he tries to participate in the play, his classmates ignore him. As his teacher, you understand that all young children do some watching—some more than others—and that such onlooking may help him see how children get along with each other. Yet, if a child works and plays alone because he is intimidated and lacks the skills to join in and interact, it is likely he is feeling unhappy about it and is missing out on valuable experiences.

What to Do? While Joseph hardly ever joins the other children to play, you might think that this is a matter of individual style. What might help you determine if this is the case? Let's assume you do decide that Joseph would benefit from being able to work and play more with the other children. Consider whether any of the following strategies might help:

- Each day give Joseph and another child a collaborative task, such as cleaning up with a broom and dustpan, making a sign, or mixing ingredients.
- Join Joseph as he plays alone and ask questions about the activity he is involved in, continuing this one-on-one engagement until he seems comfortable. Next, invite one other child into the activity, gradually adding more children, one at a time, until Joseph seems more at ease with the other children.
- Tell Joseph the words he can use to ask the other children if he can play with them.
- When you see Joseph looking on at children playing, create a role for him that adds to the others' play and gives him a place in it. With time, you can teach him to do this independently, that is, create a role for himself in ongoing play.

Which of these actions do you think would be useful and why? What else might you suggest?

seats in front of a computer encourages this type of interaction, as does locating computers in the classroom as a learning center rather than in a separate computer laboratory.

Teachers should integrate interactive media into the ongoing routine of the classroom. For example, a teacher might introduce a concept like rhyming in whole-group time; during center time, the children can play a rhyming game at the computer center. Children may use a program to create their own story by clicking on the characters and events of their choosing. In addition, the Internet allows communication with other children or adults, such as favorite authors, in other cities, states, or countries. Through technology, a second-grade class can take an electronic field trip and regularly monitor the growth of the baby panda at the National Zoo via the zoo's website.

Technology is a teaching tool that can be used effectively or not. What are some ways in which computers can be used to extend children's learning opportunities?

Computer software programs are available to address the teaching and learning principles described earlier in this chapter: making learning meaningful, promoting concept development, and engaging children in higher-level thinking and problem solving. Other software is primarily designed for children to practice basic skills such as phonics or counting. Choosing appropriate software is like choosing books or any other educational resource. Educators making decisions about purchasing software need to carefully evaluate the philosophy and purpose, as well as the developmental, individ-

ual, and cultural appropriateness of the resource. Providing bilingual software may be an excellent decision, for example, while using a translation program may not.

Just as the Internet has created limitless options for information dissemination, the use of technology in classrooms has endless possibilities. These possibilities are only achieved, however, if intentional teachers make good choices about appropriate interactive media and teach children how to use these resources well.

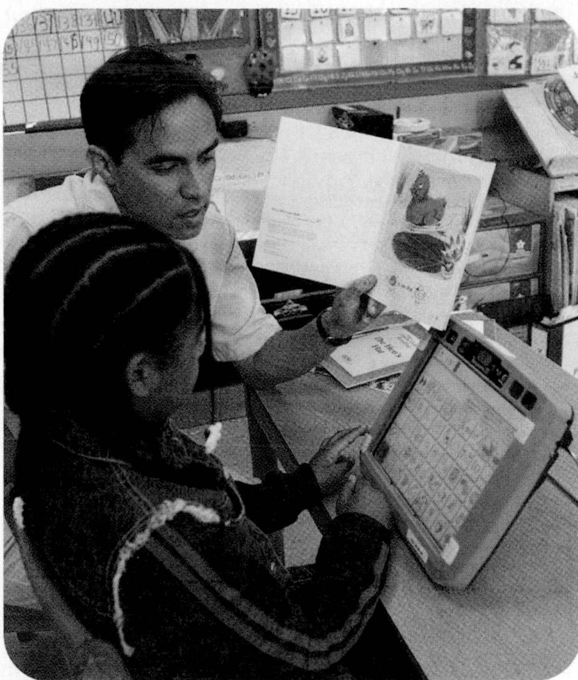

Use of assistive technology may be part of a child's IEP. Well-designed assistive technology can be valuable for children with and without disabilities.

Using Assistive Technology for Children with Disabilities

One of the most valuable uses of technology is that it can empower children with disabilities to participate more fully and successfully in inclusive classrooms.

The Individuals with Disabilities Education Act (IDEA) defines **assistive technology** as "any item, piece of equipment, or product system whether acquired commercially off the shelf, modified, or customized, that is used to increase, maintain, or improve functional capabilities of individuals with disabilities." Assistive technology incorporates a wide range of options designed for many different purposes, offering various benefits to children with special needs. For example, a child with cerebral palsy may use a device that supports him to stand at an easel or another device to help him grip a pencil. A girl with attention deficit disorder may use headphones at a computer to decrease distractions from the classroom. Assistive technologies such as these help children function independently and support their inclusion in classrooms with their peers (Mulligan, 2003). Such technology is valuable for children without disabilities as well.

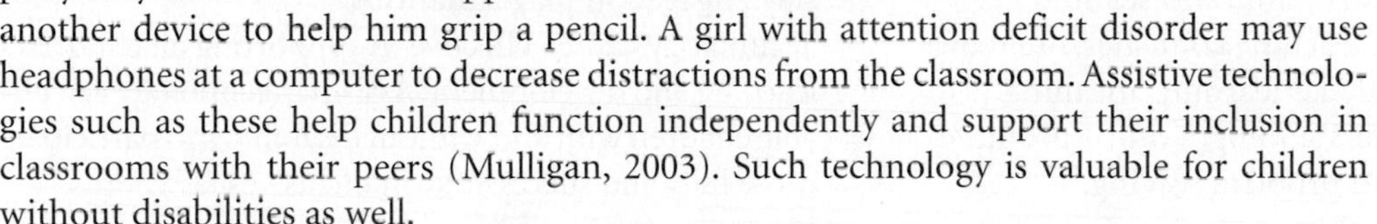

Many assistive technology devices are available, ranging from low-tech toys to complex communication systems (Alliance for Technology Access, 2004). Children who lack the physical ability to write can use voice-activated computer software to express their ideas and feelings. Children who cannot speak can use communication boards that they touch with a hand, foot, or other body part to activate a voice that speaks for them. The options are almost limitless, depending on the creativity of individuals and the resources available.

If appropriate, the use of assistive technology will be part of a child's individual education plan (IEP). Teachers working in inclusive settings need to be prepared to use whatever technology is required to successfully include children with disabilities and special needs and help them achieve individualized learning goals.

■ Revisiting Ms. Hanson's Classroom

In this chapter, we provided a conceptual framework for teachers to build a repertoire of effective teaching strategies. We also cited research demonstrating that current practices in preschool and primary grade classrooms could be improved to reflect what is known about effective teaching. At the outset, we visited Sally Hanson's kindergarten class, where she used various strategies to help the children learn to write their names. Having now explored the array of effective strategies that make up a teacher's repertoire, we can analyze what Sally was doing and why.

Sally's goal was for all of the children to acquire the same necessary skill: writing their name. Because the children came to the task with differing skill levels, however, she adapted her teaching to match their needs. She used *encouragement*, *cueing*, and *questioning* as needed for different children, particularly Jason, Elena, and Lucy. She provided *scaffolding*

assistive technology A piece of equipment or product that is used to increase, maintain, or improve the functional capabilities of individuals with disabilities.

MyEducationLab

To assess your understanding of how to teach to enhance learning and development, go to the Book Specific Resources section in the MyEducationLab for your course, select *Effective Practices in Early Childhood Education,* Chapter 9 of the Study Plan, and then complete the multiple choice questions and activities.

for Elena and Lucy, adapting her instruction to help them do tasks that they could not do independently. By providing preprinted names and photos, she provided the scaffolding needed for many children to function with less of her direct support. Sally provided a more fixed form of *support* for Marguerite to focus her attention on the order of the letters in her name. Sally *activated prior knowledge* for Logan when she helped him find the letters in his last name that he already knows. She used *direct instruction* with Tommy, who was struggling to form the letter *T*. Any one of these strategies would have been less effective if used with every child.

Intentional teachers know the children in their classroom as well as their curriculum goals. They flexibly draw on their professional knowledge of teaching strategies to effectively promote children's learning and development.

Chapter Summary

- Effective teaching is a science, informed and guided by research. Teaching, however, is also an art because it requires vision, creativity, and decision making.
- The most effective teachers have a large repertoire of research-based teaching strategies, including acknowledging and encouraging, giving quality feedback, modeling, demonstrating, giving cues and hints, adding challenge, questioning, co-constructing learning, giving direct instruction, and scaffolding.
- Children learn best when teaching strategies, build on their prior knowledge (make learning meaningful), build conceptual understanding, and promote higher-order thinking and problem solving.
- An intellectually engaging learning environment provides various contexts that offer different opportunities for learning and types of teacher–child interactions: individual interactions, whole-group meetings, small groups, center choice time, and opportunities for play.
- Teachers use play as a teaching strategy by taking on various roles—onlooker, stage manager, co-player, and play leader—to help children get involved and stay engaged in play situations.
- Technology can be effective in supporting all children's learning and development. Assistive technology can enable children with and without disabilities to participate more fully and successfully in inclusive classrooms.

key terms

acknowledging
advance organizers
apprenticeship
assistive technology
child-initiated experiences
classification systems
closed questions
co-construction
conceptual frameworks
co-player
demonstrating
direct instruction
encouragement
effective teaching
facilitating
feedback loop
graphic representation
hypothesis generating and testing
K-W-L
learning strategy
metacognitive activities
modeling
onlooker
open-ended questions
pedagogy
planning
play leader
questioning
reflection
scaffolding
scientific method
stage manager
supporting
teacher-initiated experiences
teaching strategy
wait time

readings & websites

Epstein, A. S. (2007). *The intentional teacher: Choosing the best strategies for young children's learning.* Washington, DC: NAEYC.

HighScope Early Childhood Staff. (2009). *Small-group times to scaffold early learning.* Ypsilanti, MI: HighScope Educational Research Foundation.

Ozretich, R., Burt, L., Doescher, S., & Foster, M. (2010). *Case studies in early childhood education: Implementing developmentally appropriate practices.* Upper Saddle River, NJ: Pearson/Merrill.

Alliance for Technology Access
www.ataccess.org

National Center for Research in Early Childhood Education
www.ncrece.org

National Institute for Early Education Research
www.nieer.org

New Horizons for Learning, Technology in Education
www.newhorizons.org

observe, reflect, decide

1. Observe a preschool classroom for a morning. How much time do children spend in whole group, small group, learning centers, or involved in routines and transitions? Reflect on how children's time is used. Decide if there are missed opportunities for teaching and learning.
2. Reflect on your own childhood. Do you remember playing dress-up and pretending with other children? If so, what are your recollections of these experiences? Think about the children you know today. Do you observe them engaging in mature sociodramatic play? If you did not play this way as a child, do you think it would be difficult for you as a teacher to support this play in children?
3. Observe the teaching strategies a kindergarten teacher uses during a half hour period of time. Reflect on which strategies she uses most often and which she uses less frequently. Does she scaffold individual children's learning? Does she adapt for differences in children's skill levels and interests? In what ways?
4. Observe a first- or second-grade classroom for 1 hour. Try to write down all of the questions the teacher asks. Reflect on the number of open-ended and closed questions, and the children's responses they generated. Decide how more open-ended questions might be infused in the teaching.
5. Consider the numerous types of technology and social networking options available today, such as websites, wikis, Twitter, texting, digital cameras, smart boards, and so on. Reflect on ways these technologies can be effective teaching tools with young children. Think critically about any potential drawbacks to using technology as a teaching tool.

10 Planning Effective Curriculum

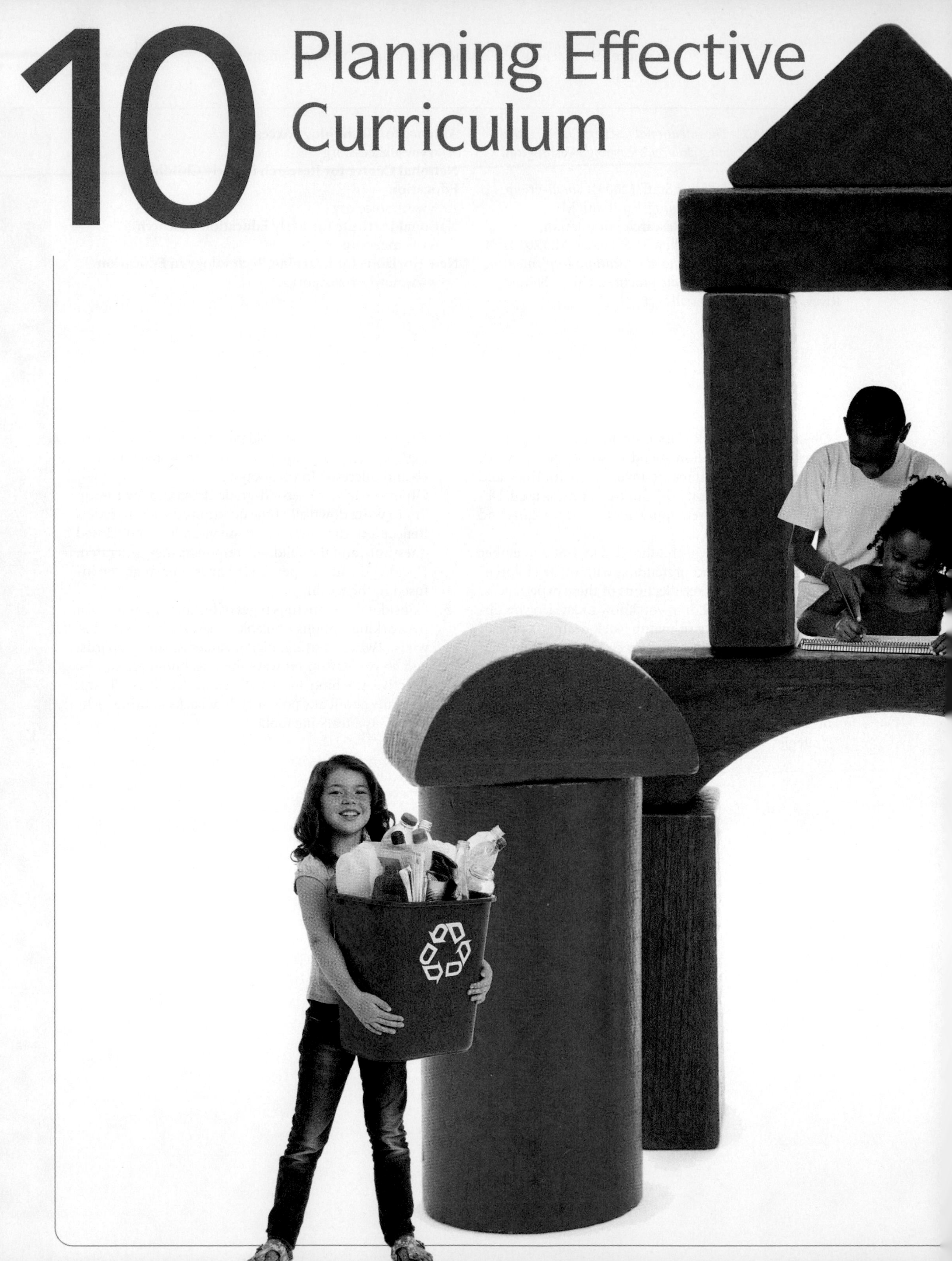

Thinking Ahead

1. What is curriculum? What is scientifically based curriculum?
2. How do various approaches to curriculum planning engage children's interest and promote their learning?
3. What are indicators of effective curriculum?
4. How do standards and outcomes influence curriculum planning?
5. What are the focus and goals of various curriculum models?
6. How can teachers use content standards and child development knowledge in planning effective curriculum?
7. How do teachers adapt curriculum for individual and cultural variation among children?

This is an exciting morning in Mona Amas and Shelley Kadota's class of 3- and 4-year-olds. For several weeks the class has been engaged in a study of animals that hatch from eggs. A focus of the study is the incubator, where each day the children carefully turn the eggs and mark off how many days they must wait until the eggs hatch. When the study began, Mona and Shelley gave the parents and children a homework assignment. Parents (or other family members) were to ask the children what they already know about eggs and what they wanted to learn about eggs. Then Mona and Shelley made large charts of the children's responses to these questions that the group refers to each day. Because most of the children are only 3½-years-old, Mona chose this strategy to launch the unit of study rather than trying to hold the attention of the whole group while answering these questions. Involving the families doubled the children's interest and motivation to engage with the curriculum topic.

Today is special because Shelley has brought in a live hen for the children to see. During center time, several children draw pictures of the incubator and "write" some letters or approximations of words in their journals. Mona sits down in the newly equipped "veterinarian's office," casually tells Liliana and Keanu that someone is calling on the phone, and draws their attention to the appointment book. Two boys gather around the microscope and look at "slides" of the eggs of various animals.

Liliana picks up the stuffed snake and announces, "My snake has an owie."

Mona asks, "What hurts on your snake?"

"His leg," Liliana answers.

Mona replies, "I didn't know snakes had legs."

Liliana takes hold of the end of the snake, wags it, and says, "Here. He's bleeding."

For about 10 minutes, Liliana ministers to the snake, who has a fever and needs bandaging. Grabbing the stethoscope, she says, "He needs to listen to your heart."

Mona calmly responds, "Yes, you can use the stethoscope to listen to his heart."

Meanwhile, Shelley guides small groups of children out to the patio to visit with the hen. She carefully holds the chicken. "I'm holding her tight like this so she won't peck you," she explains. The children gather around and carefully touch parts of the hen, including the comb, beak, and feet, describing what they see and feel, using words like *soft*, *hard*, *rough*, *feathery*, and *pointy*. The children are especially observant of the hen's clawed feet and soon begin comparing them to the webbed duck's foot model that they have seen in the classroom. Shelley leads them in a discussion of why the two feet look so different. She then draws their attention to the fact that the hen's eyes close from the bottom rather than from the top, like people's eyes.

Later, during meeting time, Shelley and Mona share this observation about the hen's eyes with the whole group. Different children offer their hypotheses for why this might be, and they add it to their list of questions about animals that hatch from eggs. During reading and writing time, some children start looking through the science books for information about hen's eyes, while Naia asks her teacher, "Can we look on the computer and find out?" ▲

Integrating curriculum around a science topic engages children's interests and supports their learning in all areas. Here preschoolers' firsthand encounter with a chicken is part of a larger study of animals that hatch from eggs.

Even the most uniformed visitor to Mona and Shelley's class could not fail to observe the content of the curriculum during this brief visit. Clearly, the curriculum is focused on a science topic—the study of animals that hatch from eggs—into which other areas of the curriculum are integrated. The children are reading and writing about this topic and learning new vocabulary words and concepts. Skills such as counting days and hypothesis testing are also addressed. The curriculum theme is literally "played out" in the vet's office, where children use the language they are learning as well as their social skills. Sharing the microscope requires self-regulation as well as turn-taking, and Mona is available to help if the children struggle with this problem. The curriculum is so rich and engaging that there are very few discipline problems; the classroom hums with children's happy voices, smiles, and laughter.

The goal of this chapter is to help you understand the complexity of planning effective curriculum and the intentional teacher's roles in working with curriculum. We begin by defining the term *curriculum* and describe ways of organizing curriculum plans. We discuss the early childhood profession's indicators of effective curriculum and the role of standards. Next, we describe the focus and goals of some frequently used curriculum models. Finally, we present a model for planning curriculum that demonstrates the connection between discipline-based curriculum content and child development knowledge.

Defining Curriculum

Curriculum is usually thought of as the "what"—the content that children are learning—while teaching is the "how." In early childhood education, it is especially difficult to separate curriculum from teaching. There is no one agreed-on understanding of curriculum that is a comfortable fit for this diverse field. In this chapter, however, we present our vision of early childhood curriculum and its contributions to children's learning.

What Is Curriculum?

Curriculum is a written plan that describes the goals for children's learning and development, and the learning experiences, materials, and teaching strategies that are used to help children achieve those goals (Head Start, 1998; National Association for the Education of Young Children [NAEYC], 2005c). The goals include the knowledge, skills, and dispositions (or attitudes and approaches toward learning) that we want children to achieve.

curriculum A written plan that describes the goals for children's learning and development, and the learning experiences, materials, and teaching strategies that are used to help children achieve those goals.

Written Curriculum Plans

Different types of written plans can be used to best meet the needs of specific groups of children. These include teacher-developed and locally developed plans, research-based curricula, and published curriculum resources.

Teacher-Developed Plans

Teachers themselves often prepare their own written plans. For example, Dominique and Tami teach a group of 2-year-olds. Their child care center has goals for the children such as fostering their language and helping them learn about the physical world. Each week Dominique and Tami meet to prepare written plans that help them think in advance about their goals and the kinds of experiences and materials they need to prepare. Such advance planning frees them to focus their attention on the children. This week, the group is exploring water by playing in the water table, splashing in a wading pool outside, and blowing bubbles. Tami suggests putting ice cubes in the water table to encourage new words like *freezing*, *melting*, and *floating*. Dominique thinks of adding food coloring to create more interest and challenge.

Locally Developed Plans

In other cases, an agency such as Head Start, a child care program, or a school district develops a written plan. In these situations, a curriculum specialist or team of teachers develops a plan for children's learning that is designed to achieve the program's goals. For example, Head Start agencies need to help children make progress on the goals outlined in the Head Start Child Outcomes Framework, which addresses all areas of development plus literacy, mathematics, social studies, and science (Head Start Bureau, 2003). Frankie Sanders's job as education leader in her program includes curriculum development. To help ensure consistency across the 10 classrooms in the agency, Frankie prepares a written curriculum plan, with input from the teachers. The teachers will use the plan flexibly, but its existence helps keep them focused on what is important for children and prevents missed opportunities for learning.

Research-Based Curriculum

Despite the early childhood field's long history and comfort with teacher-developed and locally developed curriculum plans, several recent trends have placed more emphasis on formal, research-based curriculum. **Scientifically based curriculum** derives from research evidence about what kinds of learning outcomes relate to later achievement, and what types of teaching and learning experiences help children achieve those outcomes (McCardle & Chhabra, 2004). Scientifically based curriculum has been *validated*, which means that it has been evaluated and has demonstrated its effectiveness in producing desired learning outcomes. A growing number of validated early literacy, mathematics, and social–emotional curricula have been developed for preschool and primary grades (Institute of Education Sciences, 2009; Preschool Curriculum Evaluation Research [PCER] Consortium, 2008).

Published Curriculum

Most elementary schools use some form of commercially published curriculum. These decisions may be made at the state, district, or school level. In such situations, a committee, which usually includes teachers, reviews the available options and makes a decision about which curriculum resource to adopt. For example, every few years, state departments of education review new editions of primary grade curricula in subject areas such as reading, mathematics, and science, and identify a list of approved programs from which schools may choose.

The universal pre-K movement has led to greater involvement of public schools in preschool as well as calls for alignment of pre-K with K–12 curriculum. As a result, all major publishers of K–12 curriculum now publish written curriculum for programs for 3- and 4-year-olds (Goffin & Washington, 2007). The greater availability of published curriculum for preschoolers adds another factor to the curriculum decision-making process at that level (Frede & Ackerman, 2006).

scientifically based curriculum Derives from research evidence about what kinds of learning outcomes relate to later achievement and what types of teaching and learning experiences help children acquire those outcomes.

Written curriculum plans, including those that are commercially published and used in primary grades, are by no means uniform. Some curricula provide an organizing structure and require a lot of initiative on the part of the teacher and children. Others provide goals, suggested activities to help children achieve those goals, and recommended teaching strategies. Usually curriculum packages include teacher's guides with many options for learning experiences, strategies, and resources, from which teachers choose those that fit their goals for children. In other cases, the curriculum is more prescriptive and less choice is available or expected. Regardless of the type of curriculum provided, effective teachers never rely exclusively on prepackaged curriculum; instead, they use it as a springboard from which to adapt plans for groups and individual children.

Why Use a Written Curriculum Plan?

Whereas critics of written plans believe that they limit teachers' creativity, decision making, and responsiveness to individual children, this is not necessarily true. Curriculum plans have several advantages.

Plans Can Be Evaluated

Written plans make it possible for administrators, teachers, families, funders (such as taxpayers, families, or contributors), evaluators, and other interested parties to review, debate, and potentially revise the program's goals, expectations, and learning opportunities for children. Written plans can also be evaluated for their responsiveness to cultural and linguistic diversity and to community values.

In addition, putting expectations for children in writing means that teachers can evaluate whether they are achievable yet challenging. For instance, if the kindergarten curriculum calls for all children to learn to read, teachers who know the children can determine that this expectation is too high for most, but may be appropriate for some.

Curriculum for very young children is often developed by teachers themselves. Even for toddlers, having a curriculum plan helps teachers prepare engaging and interesting learning opportunities.

Plans Assist Teachers

With increasing calls for accountability and rising expectations about children's readiness for school, providing teachers with thoughtfully planned, research-based curriculum resources can free them to focus on adapting their teaching for individual children's abilities, needs, and interests. Instead of using all of their time preparing lessons and locating related resources, teachers can instead spend their valuable time observing and assessing children's learning and adapting their teaching. Written curriculum plans provide support for teachers so they do not have to "make it up" as they go along. In cases such as these, the written plan serves as a scaffold for teachers, providing them with the support they need to go beyond and do more on their own (Kauffman, Johnson, Kardos, Liu, & Peske, 2002). Curriculum plans neither discourage teacher creativity nor take the place of teacher decision making.

Quality Is What Matters

In their position statement on curriculum, NAEYC and the National Association of Early Childhood Specialists in State Departments of Education (NAECS/SDE) (2003) address this question: Should programs use published curricula, or is it better for teachers to develop their own curriculum? A portion of the response follows:

> The *quality* of the curriculum should be the important question. If a published, commercially available curriculum—either a curriculum for one area such as literacy or mathematics or a comprehensive curriculum—is consistent with the position statement's goals and values, appears well suited to the children and families served by the program, and can be implemented effectively, then it may be worth considering, especially as a support for inexperienced teachers. (p. 9)

As for teachers developing the curriculum themselves, the position statement cautions:

> If staff have the interest, expertise, and resources to develop a curriculum that includes clearly defined goals, a system for ensuring that those goals are shared by stakeholders, a system for determining the beneficial effects of the curriculum, and other indicators of effectiveness—then the program may conclude that it should take that route. (p. 9)

Having shared our definition of curriculum, we now turn to a discussion of general approaches to planning curriculum. These approaches share the goal of making curriculum meaningful and interesting to children and, therefore, more effective.

■ Approaches to Planning Curriculum

A plan helps guide teachers in making decisions about what, when, and how to teach. In other words, curriculum is not a set of random activities that children might find enjoyable; instead, the activities must be connected in a coherent way to content goals and teaching strategies (NAEYC & NAECS/SDE, 2003). There are several ways of organizing a coherent curriculum. These include emergent curriculum, integrated curriculum, thematic curriculum, webbing, the project approach, and scope and sequence.

Emergent Curriculum

Some early childhood educators are not comfortable with defining curriculum as a *written* plan or specifying what will be taught in advance. This concern grows out of the strong tradition of emergent curriculum in early childhood education. According to this perspective, the focus should be on children, not on curriculum. **Emergent curriculum** is "what happens in an educational environment, not what is rationally planned to happen but what actually takes place" (E. Jones & Nimmo, 1994, p. 12). Advocates of emergent curriculum believe that children's interests and needs should determine what goes on in a classroom rather than a predetermined plan. They also assume that a written curriculum plan may be too rigid to be responsive to children's individual and cultural variation.

emergent curriculum
Curriculum that develops in an educational environment in response to children's interests and needs rather than according to predeveloped plans.

Although emergent curriculum places considerable emphasis on following children's interests, it does not mean that nothing is planned and that everything emerges solely from the children. Elizabeth Jones, one of the foremost proponents of emergent curriculum, describes it as a *planning process* in which teachers work from children's interests, creating webs of possibilities that become tentative plans for experiences (E. Jones & Nimmo, 1994). What follows depends on children's responses, with the teacher paying attention to what happens and evaluating and adjusting the plans as needed:

> Monday morning in John and Bettina's preschool class begins with a class meeting in which children talk about their weekend experiences.
>
> *Courtney:* "My dad took me and my cousins to a museum and we saw dinosaur bones. They were humongous."
> *Shauntae:* "I went there. My mom only came up to the dinosaur's knee."
>
> The discussion continues with children becoming more animated by the minute. John and Bettina look at each other and smile. Their plan was to introduce a unit on families. They don't think that dinosaurs are the best topic of study because young children can't grasp concepts of historical time and extinction. At the same time, the teachers recognize that young children are drawn to dinosaurs because they are "manageable monsters." They decide that with this much enthusiasm generated, following the children's interest could open up new possibilities.
>
> *Bettina:* "It looks like you want to learn more about dinosaurs. Let's start by thinking about everything we already know and writing down what we want to find out."
>
> Later, Bettina and John meet to map out how a study of dinosaurs can help them meet the goals of their original plan. They decide that it will be a novel way to help children learn math concepts, including classification and measurement, and some of the "big ideas" in science such as change and living/nonliving things.

Effective Teaching
Effective teaching involves goal-directed, written curriculum that is flexible and adapts to children's interests and needs. Emergent curriculum uses children's interests to help them achieve important learning goals.

One of the goals of this chapter is to address the tendency in the field to view emergent curriculum and written curriculum as complete opposites. To be effective, curriculum planning needs to be intentional while at the same time responsive to children's interests and needs. In other words, goal-directed written curriculum must be flexible and adapt to children's interests and needs, and emergent curriculum must use children's interests to help them achieve important learning goals. Whichever approach a program chooses, to be effective, children's learning must benefit. One way to help children achieve important goals while also responding to their interests is to use an integrated curriculum, defined next.

Integrated Curriculum

A curriculum can be focused on one subject area such as mathematics or science, or it can be comprehensive, addressing all learning goals for a specified age or grade level. It may also focus on various developmental domains such as cognitive, physical, language, and social–emotional. **Integrated curriculum** addresses learning goals across multiple areas of curriculum at the same time (Schickedanz, 2008). For example, it might address literacy and social–emotional goals within a single experience or lesson, such as when a preschool teacher reads books about feelings or making friends. A third-grade reading curriculum can include biographies of historical figures such as Harriet Tubman or Abraham Lincoln. In this way, children acquire both knowledge of history and literacy in the same experience.

integrated curriculum Addresses learning goals across multiple areas of curriculum at the same time.

Integrated curriculum is useful for several reasons. First, it helps address the challenge of covering many learning goals in a limited period of instructional time. Recall our visit to Mona and Shelley's class in the opening vignette of this chapter. Rather than devoting separate time periods for literacy instruction and science study, they engaged the children in reading and writing about their science topic, animals that hatch from eggs. At the same time, the children learned concepts such as counting and life cycles. Mona and Shelley integrated curriculum around a topic of study or theme, which we discuss next.

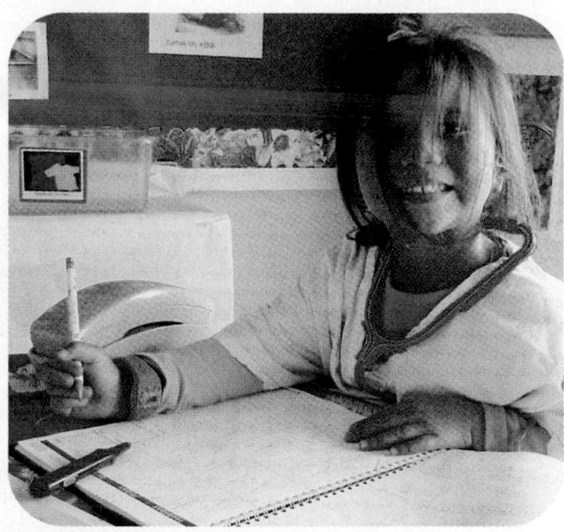

Within a broad topic of study, teachers build children's literacy skills in context. This child writes as she plays the role of veterinarian.

Thematic Curriculum

Another advantage of integrated curriculum is that curriculum can be organized around topics (also called *units*) that children find interesting or engaging. This type of integrated curriculum is called a **thematic curriculum**, in which a broad topic of interest or a "big idea" provides the basis for making connections across learning goals. The life cycle of birds, for example, can be the organizing structure for several weeks or longer.

Thematic curriculum not only motivates children, but also builds deeper conceptual understanding (Bransford, Brown, & Cocking, 2000). For example, a predictable interest of preschool children—building with blocks—provides a basis for integrating curriculum around the theme of construction. Children's interest in building structures becomes a vehicle for teaching concepts of physical science, such as how buildings stand up or how roofs are constructed to make enclosed spaces (Chalufour & Worth, 2004). A construction study helps children understand math concepts like counting, measuring, and classification, which they will need when they decide how to balance a skyscraper. Children also learn vocabulary words related to building. Related books, such as *Alphabet Under Construction* by D. Fleming can bring in literacy skills. A neighborhood walk to see architecture, historical structures, or civic buildings addresses social studies standards.

For thematic curriculum to be effective, however, it is important that teachers select truly "big" ideas—concepts that are rich enough to be studied in depth and lead to new learning. Consider the difference between a unit on teddy bears and one on living bears—there is no comparison in terms of the concepts that can be explored. Yet, young children love teddy bears, so a teacher might be tempted to pursue that interest despite its shallow nature. How then do teachers decide whether a topic is sufficiently rich to pursue? One strategy is to use webbing, discussed next.

Webbing

As we will see, webbing serves many valuable functions in early childhood curriculum. It helps teachers organize their planning and acts as a conceptual organizer for children's thinking and learning.

Teacher Planning

Webbing is a curriculum planning tool that teachers use to organize curriculum content. Figure 10.1 is an example of an initial web Kiara created for her Head Start class of 3-year-olds. The theme of the curriculum is transportation. Her class became interested in this topic because one child's uncle recently started driving a delivery truck. The curriculum web contains ideas for transportation-related teaching and learning experiences in each developmental domain.

One important criterion in planning curriculum is the need to adapt for individual differences in children, including children with special needs. The *Including All Children: Creating Individualized Education Plans* feature illustrates how Kiara also uses her web-based curriculum plan as a framework to plan for children with disabilities.

Kiara uses the topic of transportation, which is of great interest to her children, to plan experiences for all areas of children's development. Over time, she will add new experiences to her web. Kiara's web is a teacher-made planning tool, but webbing is even more useful as a conceptual organizer for children.

thematic curriculum Way of integrating curriculum in which a broad topic of interest or a "big idea" provides the basis for making connections across learning goals.

webbing A planning tool that teachers and children create together to organize curriculum content.

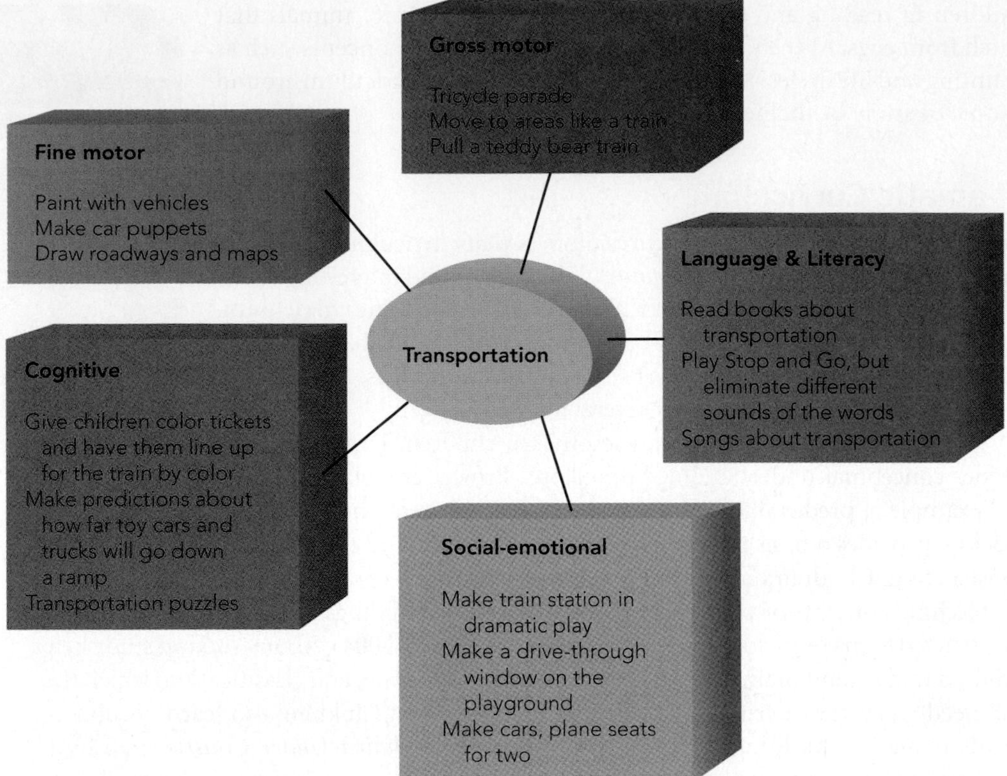

Figure 10.1 Webbing for Curriculum Planning with Class of 3-Year-Olds

Concept Webbing

In Chapter 9, we discussed teaching strategies that build children's understanding. These included using advance organizers such as K-W-L and graphic representations. In K-W-L, children answer the questions, "What do you know?" "What do you want to know?" and then at the end of a study, "What did you learn?" Webbing is a way of graphically representing the answers to these questions, which also illustrates the connections among facts and larger concepts. Figure 10.2 illustrates how Mona and Shelley's class learned about eggs.

Webbing is a useful tool for all of the ways of organizing curriculum discussed thus far: emergent, integrated, and thematic. But it is particularly valuable as a core component of the project approach, a topic to which we turn next.

The Project Approach

project An in-depth investigation of a topic worth learning more about, usually involving a small group, but occasionally the whole class.

project approach Strategy for conceptually organizing curriculum by engaging children an in-depth investigation of a topic, focused on finding answers to questions posed by the children, the teacher, or the teacher working with the children.

Engaging children in projects or investigations, a concept going as far back as John Dewey and an integral part of the Bank Street approach, continues to be one of the most popular activities among early childhood teachers and children (Helm & Beneke, 2003; Helm & Katz, 2001; Katz & Chard, 2000). A **project** is an in-depth investigation of a topic worth learning more about, usually involving a small group, but occasionally the whole class. The key feature of a project is that it is a research effort focused on finding answers to questions posed by the children, the teacher, or the teacher working with the children (Katz, 1994, p. 1).

Benefits of Projects

The **project approach** is not a curriculum; rather it is a way of engaging children's minds with curriculum content and processes (Katz & Chard, 2000). In the project approach, teachers guide children through in-depth studies of real world topics of interest to children. When

Including All Children

Creating Individualized Education Plans

In Kiara's Head Start classroom of fourteen 3-year olds, three of the children, Nikki, Devren, and Theo, have individualized education programs (IEPs). Once a month, Kiara meets with the children's IEP team to brainstorm ideas for addressing their individual goals in the context of the general curriculum and daily routines. First, Kiara and the team consider the current IEP objectives for each child:

- **Nikki.** Improve fine motor skills such as holding writing instruments and cutting; identify colors and shapes; demonstrate one-to-one correspondence.
- **Devren.** Make requests; initiate interactions with his peers; watch, listen, and participate in large-group settings.
- **Theo.** Ask for help when needed; label objects; share toys and materials.

During the meeting, the team considers these individual goals along with the curriculum plan for the entire class, which at the moment is a unit on transportation. With this approach, the children with special needs do not need to be segregated from their peers for one-on-one direct instruction, and they have many opportunities to learn and practice skills. Because the curriculum topic is interesting and motivating for young children, learning occurs more quickly for children with special needs.

To ensure sufficient practice opportunities throughout the day, Kiara prepares an activity matrix (see below) that describes the opportunities to embed the children's learning goals in the daily schedule and lesson plans.

Classroom teachers and early childhood special educators can collaborate to create fun, meaningful curriculum that provides powerful motivation for children, both with and without special needs, to practice important skills throughout their day.

	Nikki	Devren	Theo
Arrival	Have Nikki "sign in" for the day holding an adaptive marker.	Have Devren be the greeter and ask children if they would like to sign in.	Have Theo be in charge of the dry erase markers for sign-in time so that he has opportunities to share.
Breakfast	Nikki will be the helper and set out plates and utensils at each place mat. She will help "take orders" by making a mark on her paper for each child who wants milk.	Serve some of Devren's favorite foods at mealtime to encourage him to verbalize his requests.	Provide Theo's favorite snack (crackers) inside a jar with a lid and wait for a request for help to open and provide the snack. Put the lid back on when done so that Theo will ask for help again.
Group time	Have Nikki hand out colored bus circle time props (she waits for peer to request a specific color). Sing modified version of "Wheels on the Bus," i.e., "The red bus goes. . . ."	Have Devren collect circle time props, initiating to each peer, "___, please hand me your bus."	Have Theo label the color pattern of the bus props the children use: red, green, blue.
Free choice/centers	Provide colored train tickets to correspond with colored train car. Ask Nikki to identify the colors of both.	Devren can be the engineer and request tickets from peers. At art, keep glitter in sight but out of reach and have Devren request to use it.	Have train engineer clothes available for dramatic play. Prompt Theo to ask for help with dressing.
Outdoor play	Take colored sidewalk chalk outside. Have Nikki draw and identify chalk colors.	Put teeter-totter and Sit and Spin (Devren's favorites) outside to increase initiations with peers.	Make a scavenger hunt of transportation objects outside. Have Theo label the items as he finds them.
Small group/tables	Make trains out of shapes. Have Nikki identify different shapes.	Put peer in charge of highly preferred art material. Devren has to initiate with a peer to make a request.	Close lid on glue after each use. Prompt Theo to ask for help.
Story	Ask questions about the colors and shapes in the book.	Let Devren sit close to teacher and hold favorite item during story to increase engagement.	Ask object identification questions after reading the story to Theo.
Departure	Have children identify a shape and color before leaving to get their coats.	Have children identify a shape and color before leaving to get their coats.	Have children identify a shape and color before leaving to get their coats.

What would you like to know about eggs?

1-Why do animals lay eggs?AK
2-What other animals come from eggs?KW, LW
3-Do butterflies lay eggs?LW
4-How long does a chicken have to sit on an egg to make it crack open with a little chick inside?LW
5-How do you cook eggs?KW, KK
6-What shape is the egg?JR
7-Are eggs good for you?GM

Figure 10.2 Concept Webbing

teachers implement the project approach well, children can be highly motivated, feel actively involved in their own learning, and produce high-quality work (Helm & Beneke, 2003).

Well-planned and implemented projects engage children's interests and eagerness to learn, focus their attention, and are lots of fun. More important than simple enjoyment is the fact that projects or investigations are effective ways of integrating curriculum content and promoting children's understanding and thinking. Consider the following example of a project that integrates social studies and other areas of the curriculum, shared by Gail Joseph:

> One morning at the Active Learning Center, the organic milk delivery service mistakenly left chocolate milk. Before she notices, the teacher, Diane, asks Lamont and Sara to bring it to the kitchen because they have the "milk deliverer" job today. Lamont and Sara shriek as they carefully lift a glass bottle filled with chocolate milk out of the box. They head for the classroom to find Diane, but along the way they tell each child in the class about the yummy mistake, "We got chocolate. It's brown!"
>
> By the time they reach Diane, there is a line of children asking if they can have the chocolate milk with their snack. After Diane agrees, a more dedicated line of inquiry ensues. "Who left this for us?" "How do they make it brown?" "Does it cost more money?" "Can we have it again?" Diane sees that the milk mistake has the potential for an interesting project.
>
> At group time, Diane asks the children to list what they know about chocolate milk and what else they want to find out. She records their ideas on chart paper. During the next 2 weeks, the children learn a lot about chocolate milk. They write stories about the "chocolate mistake" in the writing center. They write letters to the milkman, thanking him for the mistake. They examine the price list to compare the cost of chocolate and plain milk. They make chocolate milk and graph how many children like chocolate versus plain milk (a skewed distribution for sure!).
>
> The milk investigation goes into greater depth when the children take a field trip to the dairy and learn about "organic" milk, and why people might prefer it to nonorganic. They observe dairy cows and see milking machines. The children also learn how the milk is transported to the customers, and why they use glass bottles. On the trip they discover that the empty bottles are recycled, which prompts one of the children to propose a "recycler" job in the classroom. The children learn that not all people drink milk and the reasons why. They learned why regular milk is healthier than chocolate.

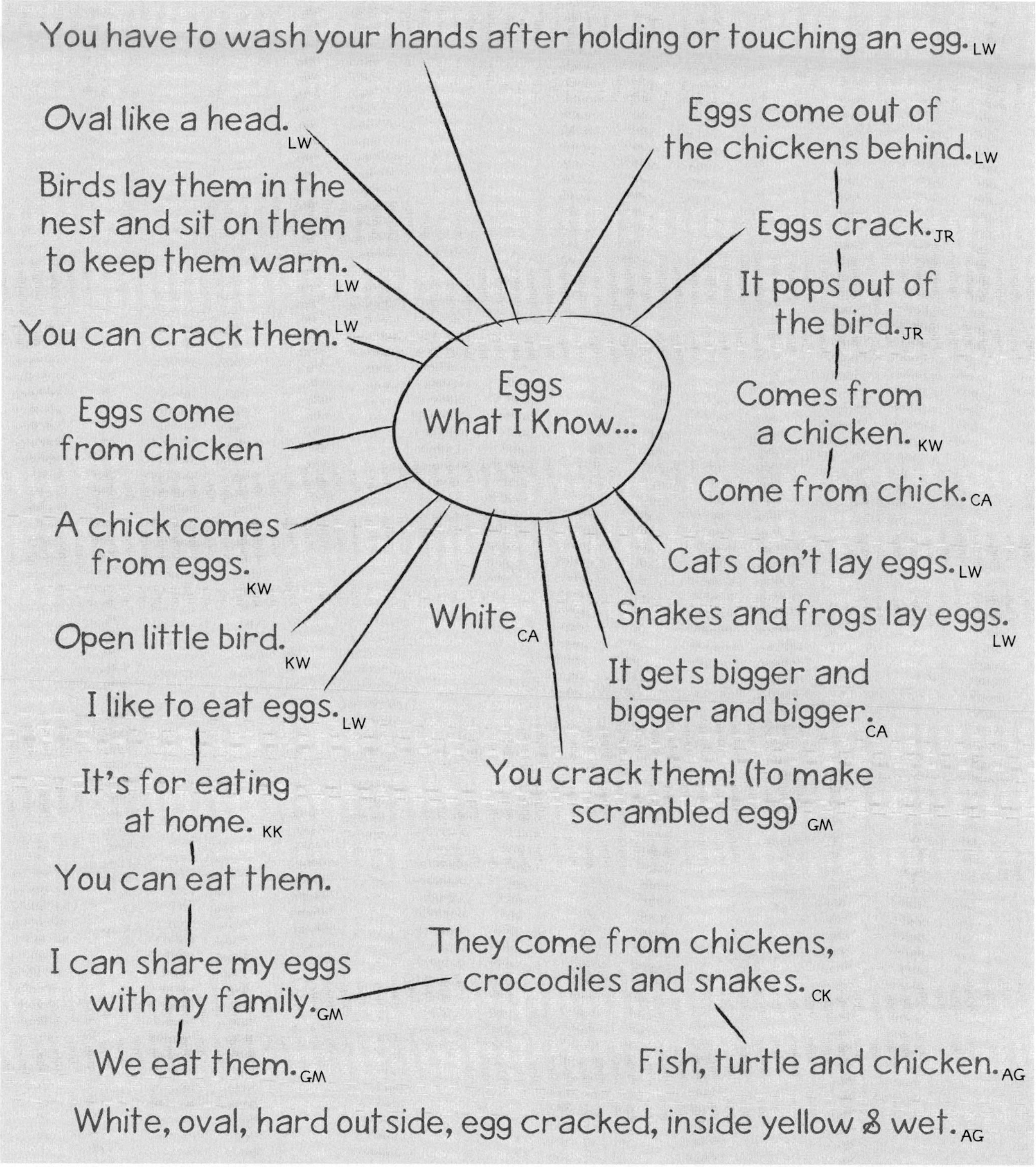

You have to wash your hands after holding or touching an egg. LW

Oval like a head. LW

Birds lay them in the nest and sit on them to keep them warm. LW

You can crack them. LW

Eggs come from chicken

A chick comes from eggs. KW

Open little bird. KW

I like to eat eggs. LW

It's for eating at home. KK

You can eat them.

I can share my eggs with my family. GM

We eat them. GM

Eggs
What I Know...

Eggs come out of the chickens behind. LW

Eggs crack. JR

It pops out of the bird. JR

Comes from a chicken. KW

Come from chick. CA

Cats don't lay eggs. LW

Snakes and frogs lay eggs. LW

White CA

It gets bigger and bigger and bigger. CA

You crack them! (to make scrambled egg) GM

They come from chickens, crocodiles and snakes. CK

Fish, turtle and chicken. AG

White, oval, hard outside, egg cracked, inside yellow & wet. AG

Figure 10.2 Concept Webbing *(continued)*

During the last week, the children decide to have a "chocolate milk celebration" with their families. They make invitations, propose and vote on the menu, and help develop displays documenting their field trip and what they've learned. They also offer a book signing for the class book they title *The Chocolate Mistake*.

At the end of the project, Diane revisits the chart created a few weeks ago and asks the children what they have learned. It is clear that they thoroughly enjoyed the project and learned a lot about chocolate milk. But they learned much more about social studies, including concepts about culture, health, community, the environment, diverse beliefs, production of goods and services, and economics, and they also engaged in reading, writing, mathematics, and science.

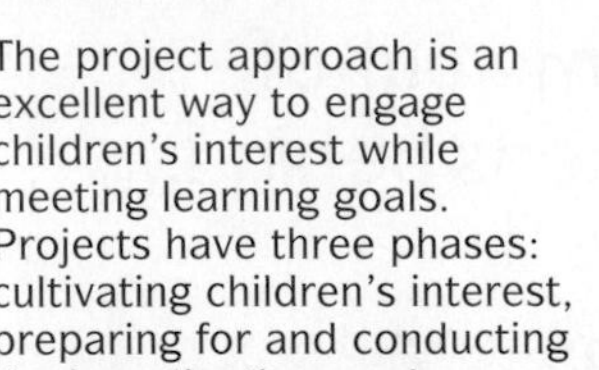
The project approach is an excellent way to engage children's interest while meeting learning goals. Projects have three phases: cultivating children's interest, preparing for and conducting the investigation, and a culminating event.

Phases of a Project

The previous example illustrates the phases of a project:

- *Phase 1: Identify children's interests.* The beginning phase occurs when a possible topic emerges either from the children's interest or from an idea initiated by the teacher. During this phase, the class might create a K-W-L list or web of what they know and what they want to find out. At this stage in a project, the teacher needs to decide if the topic is consistent with the goals of the curriculum, appropriate, and also practical to pursue (Katz & Helm, 2001). In the scenario above, Diane recognizes that the children are very interested in the chocolate milk, although the interest was a fortuitous mistake. Other ways to discover or cultivate children's interest could be through bringing something into the classroom, such as the hen that Shelley brought in, or through a story. The key is to notice what children are interested in and to follow it. The next step is to develop a web of children's thoughts and questions about the topic.
- *Phase 2: Prepare for investigation.* In this phase, children begin to think about and engage in an investigation of the topic. The questions children want answered should be broad enough to allow for substantive research. They might take a field trip as Diane's class did when they went to the organic dairy, hear from visiting experts to learn more about the topic, or conduct experiments.
- *Phase 3: A culminating event.* An event can be arranged that involves communicating, sharing, and presenting the work of the project to others. Diane's class held a chocolate milk celebration to share with their families all they had learned.

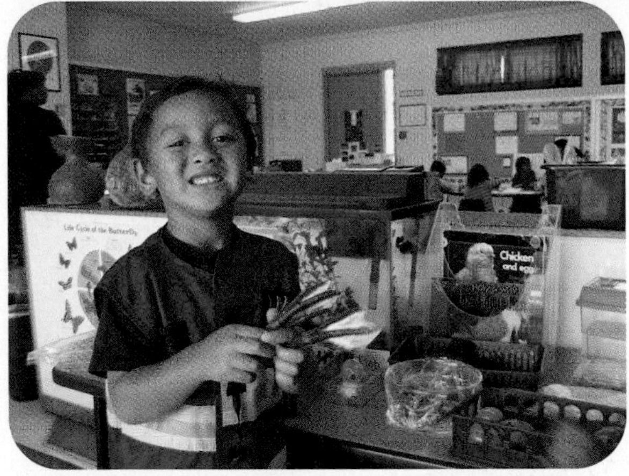

The project approach draws on and cultivates children's interests as it builds their motivation to learn. But more importantly, it engages children in thinking and problem solving, finding answers to their questions, and building content knowledge and skills.

In previous sections, we described several well-known approaches to organizing curriculum content in early childhood settings. Next, we turn to a different approach, organizing curriculum sequentially.

Scope and Sequence

In recent years, research on early learning has provided greater insight about which skills are foundational in content areas such as reading and mathematics (National Council of Teachers of Mathematics, 2000, 2006; National Early Literacy Panel, 2008; National Institute of Child Health and Human Development, 2000; National Research Council, 2009). This knowledge is useful in developing the *scope* and *sequence* of a curriculum, especially in areas where sequential learning is particularly important. In mathematics, for example, children need to have a basic understanding about number before they can tackle number operations like adding and subtracting. **Scope** refers to the particular focus of the curriculum at a given point in time; that is, how much of a larger content area will be addressed. **Sequence**, as the name implies, is the order in which knowledge and skills will be taught.

Scope and sequence, familiar terms to elementary educators but relatively new in the preschool world, provides teachers with guidance about what to teach and when. For example, learning to read involves many different abilities that children acquire over time. A primary grade reading curriculum identifies the expectations for children's reading achievement at each age level (the scope of what is to be learned) and suggests an order in which reading skills should be taught as well. However, because children's acquisition of skills and knowledge does not occur in a predetermined order and because many skills are acquired simultaneously, curriculum sequences should not be applied rigidly. The concept of scope and sequence is familiar in elementary education, where the curriculum is more closely linked to teachers' guides and textbook series used by children.

Now that we have established a common vocabulary with which to discuss curriculum, we turn to a discussion of indicators of effective curriculum.

Indicators of Effective Curriculum

According to the position statement on curriculum, assessment, and program evaluation of NAEYC and the NAECS/SDE (2003), programs should implement curriculum that is "thoughtfully planned; challenging, engaging, and developmentally appropriate; culturally and linguistically responsive; comprehensive and likely to promote positive outcomes for all young children" (p. 1). These guidelines set a high standard for early childhood curriculum.

Before discussing specific indicators of effective curriculum, it is important to consider the challenge of providing culturally and linguistically responsive curriculum. Several different curriculum models have been developed to accommodate dual language learners (Garcia, 2005). Read the *Language Lens: Teaching Dual Language Learners* feature and consider the potential strengths and weaknesses of each approach.

Evaluating Curriculum

To evaluate whether curriculum is effective, NAEYC and NAECS/SDE (2003) identify some key indicators of success. These indicators, listed in Table 10.1, cut across facets of planning, developing, and teaching curriculum.

This brief examination of indicators of effective curriculum demonstrates the influence of standards on current thinking about curriculum. The connections between learning standards and curriculum are becoming increasingly important and powerful in early childhood education.

The Role of Standards in Curriculum

One of the most influential current trends in education is the standards movement. The last decade of the 20th century saw each of the discipline-based content organizations develop standards for what students should know and be able to do at various grade levels.

scope The particular focus of the curriculum at a given point in time; that is, how much of a larger content area will be taught.

sequence The order in which knowledge and skills will be taught.

Language Lens

Teaching Dual Language Learners

Antonia Zapeda, whose family came to the United States from Mexico 1 year ago, is starting kindergarten. Antonia's parents want very much for their children to succeed in school, but they are struggling to learn English themselves. Antonia's language development in Spanish is advanced; however, she tends to be shy in new situations, relying on her brothers to pave the way for her.

The school district's curriculum approach for English language learners like Antonia is likely to have a significant impact on her later success in school and life. Following are brief descriptions of commonly used approaches for educating English language learners. As you read about each approach, put yourself in Antonia's shoes as she encounters school for the first time. What would her experience be like? How would she feel about her home language and family? What will she be learning? How successful will she be in mastering curriculum content?

- **English immersion.** All the instruction is in English throughout the child's school career. Students may receive assistance from specialists in English as a second language, but the classroom teacher uses English only.
- **Bilingual education programs.** These programs use both English and the students' native language instruction, with greater emphasis placed on English.
- **Transitional bilingual programs.** Instruction is provided in the students' home language for up to 3 years during the primary grades, and then the children transition into classes with all of the instruction in English. These programs share the goal of bilingual programs, but recognize that children need more time to learn academic concepts in their native language before focusing on English.
- **Two-way or dual immersion programs.** In these programs, half of the instruction takes place in English and the other half occurs in the second language, usually Spanish but perhaps a Native American language. The goal is for *all* the children to become bilingual and biliterate and achieve standards.

Consider what Antonia's experience might be like in a dual language program. In the morning, Ms. Cafritz does all of the teaching in English, and in the afternoon, Mr. Jimenez teaches in Spanish, or vice versa. All of Antonia's friends at school are learning both English and Spanish. Her new best friend, Joy, speaks English at home and has trouble with some of the sounds in Spanish so Antonia helps her when they are on the playground. They laugh together about how funny each other sounds. During Spanish instruction time, she knows most of the answers to the teacher's questions and often speaks up, while Joy listens more. After several months, Antonia becomes more confident in English, mixing languages on the playground with her friends but trying to answer the teacher's questions in English. Her parents are proud when she begins to read in English as well as Spanish. They are impressed that she is learning so many new Spanish words while also learning English.

Over the course of your career as a teacher, you are likely to work in situations with different policies regarding English language learners. As you do, remember Antonia. Be intentional in your approach, considering children's best interests and respecting the languages and cultures of the families.

Source: Based on *Teaching and Learning in Two Languages: Bilingualism and Schooling in the United States*, by E. E. Garcia, 2005, New York: Teachers College Press.

What Are Standards?

learning standards Expectations for student learning.

content standards Describe what students should know and/or be able to do within a particular discipline such as math or science.

performance standards Describe the knowledge or skill that students should acquire by a particular point in their schooling, usually tied to grade or age level; also known as *benchmarks*.

Every state has standards for K–12 schools and 49 states have developed early learning standards for the preschool level (Scott-Little, Kagan, & Frelow, 2006). To understand the relevance and impact of the standards movement, it is important to understand the language of standards.

- **Learning standards** are expectations for student learning.
- **Content standards** describe what students should know and/or be able to do within a particular discipline such as math or science.
- **Performance standards**, or *benchmarks*, describe the knowledge or skill that students should acquire by a particular point in their schooling, usually tied to grade or age level.

How Do Standards Affect Curriculum?

Standards are not curriculum; nevertheless, they have a powerful influence over curriculum development. Today, curriculum is often designed for the express purpose of helping

Table 10.1 Indicators of Effective Curriculum

Indicators	Key Considerations
Goals are clearly defined and communicated.	Is there a written plan that addresses important goals and can be shared with all who need to know about it?
Curriculum is comprehensive.	Does the curriculum address "the whole child"—all domains of children's development (cognitive, social, emotional, and physical)—as well as all content areas such as literacy, mathematics, science, social studies, health and physical education, and the arts?
Curriculum is evidence based.	Is there research evidence of its effectiveness with a similar group of children, for example, the same age or speaking the same language?
Professional standards validate the curriculum subject matter content.	Does the content of the curriculum reflect the content standards recommended by the subject matter disciplines, such as math educators or reading specialists?
Children are active and engaged.	Do the teaching and learning experiences provide opportunities for children to be active both mentally and physically?
Valued content is learned through investigation and focused teaching.	Is the curriculum delivered through experiences that include both child-initiated exploration and teacher-guided instruction?
Curriculum builds on prior learning and experiences.	Is the curriculum sequenced in logical and reasonable ways? Because children's prior learning experiences will vary, this requires that the teacher individualize the curriculum as much as possible.
The curriculum is developmentally appropriate.	Are the developmental and learning goals challenging and achievable? That is, are the learning outcomes reasonable expectations for most children within the age range for which it is designed?
The curriculum is culturally and linguistically appropriate.	Does the curriculum promote positive images of children's cultural identities and home languages and also recognize and build on their competence?
The curriculum can be adapted for individual differences in children.	Is the curriculum flexible enough for teachers to adapt to individual variation in children? Can the curriculum be adapted for children with disabilities and special needs?
Curriculum is likely to benefit children.	Has the curriculum been found to be effective in producing positive outcomes for children?

Sources: Based on *Developmentally Appropriate Practice in Early Childhood Programs Serving Children from Birth through Age 8. Position Statement,* 2009, Washington, DC: NAEYC. Retrieved August 23, 2009, from http://www.naeyc.org/files/naeyc/file/positions/position%20statement%20Web.pdf; and *Early Childhood Curriculum, Assessment, and Program Evaluation: Building an Effective, Accountable System in Programs for Children Birth through Age 8, Joint Position Statement,* by NAEYC and NAECS/SDE, Washington, DC: NAEYC.

children achieve standards (Seefeldt, 2005; Wien, 2004). Similarly, assessment of learning is linked to achieving standards (Gronlund, 2006). Ideally, the goals of a curriculum include, but are not necessarily limited to, the relevant early learning standards (Bredekamp, 2009). As teachers implement curriculum, they should regularly assess children's learning and adapt the curriculum and their teaching to ensure that children make progress toward the standards. In such a scenario, standards *guide* but do not determine or standardize the curriculum (Bredekamp, 2009).

Because curriculum is influenced by standards, it is essential that standards be comprehensive and developmentally appropriate. Yet, this may not be the case; an evaluation of state early learning standards found uneven attention to all areas of child development

MyEducationLab

Go to the Professional Perspectives section in Topic 4: Observation/ Assessment in the MyEducationLab for your course and select the video entitled *Standards: What Early Childhood Students Need to Know* and watch and listen to Sue Bredekamp discuss this topic.

and learning (Scott-Little et al., 2006). For example, while every state addresses the areas of language and cognition, less consistent attention is paid to social–emotional development, physical health and development, and approaches toward learning, such as curiosity and persistence. In some cases, standards may underestimate children's competence, such as the standard of counting only to 10 in kindergarten (NRC, 2009). In others, they overestimate it, such as expecting 4-year-olds to segment or blend phonemes, a task more appropriate for late kindergarten or first grade (Neuman & Roskos, 2005).

To assist with the task of managing standards, the standards project of the Mid-Continent Regional Education Laboratory in Denver provides a compendium of standards across subject matter areas and grade levels. Figure 10.3 provides an example of how a typical language arts standard is written, followed by benchmarks for two levels, prekindergarten (pre-K) and kindergarten through second grade (K–2).

Language Arts Standard—Uses the general skills and strategies of the writing process

Pre-K Benchmarks

1. Knows that writing, including pictures, letters and words, communicates meaning and information
2. Uses drawings to express thoughts, feelings, and ideas
3. Uses forms of emergent writing (e.g., scribble writing, random symbols, random letter-like marks) to represent ideas
4. Dictates stories, poems, and personal narratives
5. Uses emergent writing skills to write for a variety of purposes (e.g. to make lists, send messages, write stories) and to write in a variety of forms (e.g. journals, sign-in sheets, name cards, cards with words and pictures)
6. Uses knowledge of letters to write or copy familiar words, such as own name
7. Uses writing tools and materials (e.g. pencils, crayons, chalk, markers, rubber stamps, computers, paper, cardboard, chalkboard)

Grade: K-2 Benchmarks

1. Prewriting: Uses prewriting strategies to plan written work (e.g. discusses ideas with peers, draws pictures to generate ideas, writes key thoughts and questions, rehearses ideas, records reactions and observations)
2. Drafting and revising: Uses strategies to draft and revise written word (e.g. rereads; rearranges words, sentences, and paragraphs to improve or clarify meaning; varies sentence type; adds descriptive words and details; deletes extraneous information; incorporates suggestions from peers and teachers; sharpens the focus)
3. Editing and publishing: uses strategies to edit and publish written work (e.g., proofreads using a dictionary and other resources; edits for grammar, punctuation, capitalization, and spelling at a developmentally appropriate level; incorporates illustrations or photos; uses available, appropriate technology to compose and publish work; shares finished product)
4. Evaluates own and other's writing (e.g. asks questions and makes comments about writing, helps classmates apply grammatical and mechanical conventions)
5. Uses writing and other methods (e.g. using letters or phonetically spelled words, telling, dictating, making lists) to describe familiar persons, places, objects, or experiences
6. Writes in a variety of forms or genres (e.g. picture books, friendly letters, stories, poems, information pieces, invitations, personal experience narratives, messages, responses to literature)
7. Writes for different purposes (e.g. to entertain, inform, learn, communicate ideas)

Figure 10.3 Example of Language Arts Content Standard and Benchmarks

Source: Adapted by permission of McREL from *Content Knowledge: A Compendium of Standards and Benchmarks for K–12 Education*. www.mcrel.org/standards-benchmarks.

Consider how the standard described in Figure 10.3 can guide decisions about the kinds of learning experiences incorporated in a curriculum plan. For example, a preschool curriculum designed to help children achieve these learning standards would have to provide materials, time, and opportunities for children to engage in writing. Think back to Mona and Shelley's preschool class described at the opening of this chapter. The science curriculum provided ample opportunities for children to draw and write their observations of the eggs hatching and the hen's visit. In addition, children wrote in journals each morning. These are a few examples of how the curriculum is designed to help children meet learning standards and how standards guide curriculum development.

MyEducationLab

Go to the Assignments and Activities section of Topic 2: Child Development/ Theories in the MyEducationLab for your course and complete the activity entitled *Cognitive and Language Development.* How do the teachers in these videos implement effective curriculum? What learning standards do these classroom experiences address?

Planning Curriculum for Different Age Groups

In each of the broad age periods of early childhood—infants/toddlers, 3- through 5-year-olds, and primary grades—the curriculum takes a different form with different emphases. The NAEYC and NAECS/SDE (2003) position statement on curriculum, assessment, and evaluation describes how the *focus* of curriculum changes at each period of the early childhood age continuum.

Curriculum for Infants and Toddlers

A thoughtfully planned, challenging, and engaging curriculum for infants and toddlers focuses on, but is not limited to (NAEYC, 2005c, p. 30):

- Relationships that promote a sense of security and social interaction
- Language development
- Exploration of the physical world.

High-quality programs for babies and toddlers use an emergent curriculum process (Lally, Mangione, & Greenwald, 2006). Teachers observe the play of very young children, determine what the child is interested in, and respond by enriching and extending the play or by adding novelty and complexity. Effective curriculum for babies and toddlers is highly individualized and responsive to children's needs and interests, while also extending their language and learning (Albrecht & Miller, 2000a, 2000b; Lally et al., 2006; Raikes & Whitmer, 2006).

Curriculum for Preschoolers and Kindergartners

Thoughtfully planned curriculum for 3- through 5-year-olds addresses the development of the whole child including physical well-being and motor development; social and emotional development; approaches to learning, such as curiosity and persistence; language development; and cognition and general knowledge (NAEYC & NAECS/SDE, 2003). At the same time, the curriculum builds knowledge and skill in literacy, mathematics, science, social studies, and the visual and performing arts. During these years, integration across subject matter areas is the primary planning strategy, although at times, the curriculum will focus on one area such as math or print knowledge (NAEYC, 2005c). Play and projects are particularly valuable ways of bringing curriculum content to this age group.

Curriculum in the Primary Grades

In primary school, the curriculum focus shifts to knowledge and skills in the subject matter areas. These include language and literacy, mathematics, science, social studies, health, physical education, and the visual and performing arts (NAEYC, 2005c). Goals should continue to address the importance of social–emotional development and approaches to learning, which includes motivation, curiosity, creativity, and initiative. Other important, non-content goals include: problem solving, memory, and the ability to self-regulate, plan, pay attention, and persist at complex tasks.

A major portion of the day in primary grades is devoted to reading and writing instruction using published curriculum. Intentional teachers know that, regardless of the source of the curriculum, their role is to adapt the plan for individual children.

Challenging and engaging curricula for this age group help children develop and use oral and written language,

How Would You Respond?

Curriculum Decision Making

The Situation You have recently started teaching at an independently owned preschool. The school is taking a look at its curriculum, which was developed by the former director and has evolved over 8 years. Most of the teachers are inclined to stick with the one they are comfortable with, but the parents are asking whether it is up to date and of sufficient quality in light of the state's K–12 standards. The director, remaining noncommittal, has set up a small group of parents and teachers, of which you are one, to review the matter. One of the committee members has identified two commercially published preschool curricula that are being used by other programs in the community.

What to Do? Taking a leadership role, you might recommend that the group do the following:

- Evaluate the program's current curriculum and the two commercial curricula in light of the state standards and the stated goals of the program.
- Poll the parents of the past 4 years to see how satisfied they were with the curriculum, and if they were not satisfied, find out why not.
- Examine the promotional materials as well as sample teacher's guides available from the publishers of the commercial curricula.
- Search for independent research on the effectiveness of the proposed curricula.
- Determine the expense of the new curricula, and the training that would be needed.
- Consider whether the existing curriculum can be integrated with either or both of the commercial curricula and what, if anything, would be gained.

Are there any of these that you would not recommend? Why?

mathematical and scientific thinking, and investigation skills across the disciplines. Curricula in the primary grades should help children develop a sense of their own competence and confidence—Erikson's notion of mastery. The overarching goal of the primary grades, however, is learning to read.

Earlier in this chapter, we described several ways of planning curriculum: emergent, thematic, integrated, webbing, the project approach, and scope and sequence. We also described types of plans, from teacher developed to commercially published. All of these curriculum approaches can be used from preschool through primary grades. For example, although a second-grade teacher is highly likely to use a published reading program of some kind, she may also use an integrated science curriculum and the project approach to teaching social studies. During your career as a teacher, you will be asked to make many decisions about curriculum. To start becoming familiar with the types of issues you could confront, read the *How Would You Respond? Curriculum Decision Making* feature.

Having defined curriculum and explored indicators of effective curriculum, next we go deeper into the concept of curriculum models. In the following section, we describe well-known, though somewhat different, models of early childhood curriculum.

Understanding Curriculum Models

The word *curriculum* is often used in relation to various models, approaches, or frameworks. Because these general terms are sometimes used interchangeably, we provide definitions and examples of each in the next sections. With its strong tradition of emergent and integrated curriculum, early childhood curriculum often means that a program uses a particular model of teaching and learning.

Curriculum Models, Approaches, and Frameworks

A **curriculum model** is a research-based, idealized version of what and how teaching and learning should occur. Widely used early childhood curriculum models include the HighScope curriculum, Creative Curriculum, Montessori method, and Bank Street, which are based on theories of child development and learning. To ensure **fidelity**, that is, faithful implementation of the curriculum model, developers typically provide training of teachers in how to implement the model.

A **curriculum approach** describes the main elements or direction of a program (Roopnarine & Johnson, 2008) and is less detailed than a model. For example, Reggio Emilia educators purposely call their work the Reggio Emilia *approach* and reject the word *model*. They do not see their work as a model to be imitated or adopted, but rather as a set of principles to be applied in various contexts with diverse children, families, and teachers (Edwards, Gandini, & Forman, 1998). Similarly, the project approach is not a curriculum, but a method of engaging children with curriculum content.

Curriculum is sometimes defined as a framework; however, a **curriculum framework** is more precisely defined as a guide for designing or choosing a curriculum. For example, most state departments of education write curriculum frameworks that influence or determine which commercial curriculum packages school districts purchase. For example, in about 100 pages, the California Department of Education's Reading and Language Arts curriculum framework for kindergarten through third grade connects the state standards to effective practices. These include ways of grouping for and differentiating instruction and how much time should be devoted to language arts. A published curriculum that did not address the standards sufficiently or include the recommended practices would be less likely to be used in that state.

Early childhood education has traditionally focused on the process of teaching and learning rather than the content of what children are learning. In the past decade, however, there has been an explosion in early childhood curriculum development. In 2007, the PreK Now website listed 27 "research-based" curricula for preschool children. Despite this trend, there are several curriculum models that are widely used, including HighScope, Creative Curriculum, Core Knowledge, and Tools of the Mind. In this section, we discuss the key components of each of these models.

curriculum model A research-based, idealized version of what and how teaching and learning should occur.

fidelity Faithful implementation of a curriculum model.

curriculum approach Describes the main elements or direction of a program; is less detailed than a curriculum model.

curriculum framework A guide for designing or choosing a curriculum.

validated curriculum Curriculum that has been evaluated and its effectiveness demonstrated.

HighScope Curriculum

The HighScope curriculum model was first developed by David Weikart and his colleagues who launched the Perry Preschool Project in the early 1960s. HighScope is a **validated curriculum** because research has demonstrated that using it has lasting positive effects on children's long-term success in school and in life (Schweinhart, Barnes, & Weikart, 1993; Schweinhart et al., 2005; Schweinhart, Weikart, & Larner, 1986).

The HighScope curriculum is based on a constructivist view of how children learn. The curriculum emphasizes that children need to be engaged in active learning—direct, hands-on experience with people, objects, events, and ideas (Epstein, 2007a; Hohmann & Weikart, 2002). Both teachers and children play an active role in the HighScope curriculum, functioning as partners in learning (Epstein, 2007a).

A key element of the HighScope curriculum is the plan–do–review process. The strategy promotes children's higher order thinking and problem-solving skills.

A key element of HighScope's curriculum is the *plan–do–review process* for organizing the daily routine, an example of which appears on page 284 in Chapter 9's *What Works: Involve Children in Planning* feature. Each day, children engage in 60 to 90 minutes of choice time. Prior to this period, children plan what they want to do, then they engage or "do" what they have planned. Afterward, they review those plans, reflecting on what was learned and what they may wish to do later.

The content of the HighScope preschool curriculum consists of a set of 58 key developmental indicators (previously called *key experiences*) that describe goals

MyEducationLab

Go to the Assignments and Activities section of Topic 5: Program Models in the MyEducationLab for your course and complete the activity entitled *The HighScope Model.* Identify key elements of the HighScope curriculum model and consider why it is effective in promoting long-term positive outcomes for children.

across 10 child development areas. For example, there are two key indicators for the goal area "Approaches to Learning": (1) making and expressing choices, plans, and decisions, and (2) solving problems encountered in play. The key developmental indicators provide a framework for teachers to use as they plan activities and observe children's progress. Recently, HighScope developed a specific literacy component, *Growing Readers*, and a mathematics focused curriculum, *Numbers Plus.* The HighScope curriculum also includes an infant/toddler version.

The HighScope Educational Research Foundation assumes that teachers will need professional development training in addition to their general teacher education to implement the curriculum at a high level. The HighScope curriculum is the most widely used curriculum model in Head Start and public prekindergarten programs (Early et al., 2005; Zill, Sorongon, Kim, Clark, & Woolverton, 2006).

Creative Curriculum

Creative Curriculum, developed by Diane Trister Dodge and her colleagues, strongly emphasizes the learning environment, children's play, and child-initiated activity with teachers serving as facilitators. The learning environment is the organizing framework of the curriculum. Teachers use children's involvement in centers in the classroom including blocks, dramatic play, toys and games, art, library, discovery (science center), sand and water, music and movement, cooking, computers, and outdoors to foster development and learning (Dodge, Colker, & Heroman, 2002).

The Creative Curriculum has evolved over the years, drawing on the work of several learning theorists, including Maslow, Erikson, Piaget, Vygotsky, and Gardner. These influences have contributed to the teacher's role as observing, reflecting, and responding to children in their environment in order to facilitate their development and learning. The Creative Curriculum also has a program for infants and toddlers (Dodge, Rudick, & Berke, 2004), as well as resources for primary grade teachers.

Creative Curriculum's goals are described in a developmental continuum that guides teachers' observations of children's progress and their planning (Dodge, Colker, & Heroman, 2000). Literacy and mathematics supplements are also available that are designed to align the Creative Curriculum with the Head Start Child Outcomes framework and state early learning standards (Copley, 2007; Heroman & Jones, 2004).

Both HighScope and Creative Curriculum are child-centered curriculum models that focus on the process of how children learn and develop, reflecting a constructivist theoretical perspective. HighScope's distinguishing characteristic is the plan–do–review learning process, while Creative Curriculum emanates from the learning environment. Another approach to curriculum development focuses on content: what children should know and be able to do. This is the key component of the Core Knowledge curriculum.

Core Knowledge

In 1986, E. D. Hirsch, Jr., professor at the University of Virginia, founded the Core Knowledge Foundation, a nonprofit organization that promotes greater excellence and fairness in education. The concept is based on the fact that successful education systems in other countries tend to teach a common core of knowledge to all children. The premise of Core Knowledge is that equal educational opportunity can only be guaranteed for every child, including children from low-income families, by explicitly identifying the competencies and knowledge that all children should acquire (Hirsch & Wiggins, 2009). Hirsch believes that the achievement gap in American schools is actually a result of inequity in exposure to curriculum content (Hirsch, 2007). This belief led the Core Knowledge Foundation to develop a curriculum sequence for prekindergarten through eighth grade.

The Core Knowledge preschool sequence (Hirsch & Wiggins, 2009) is designed to be a coherent, content- and language-rich curriculum that offers a progression of skills and

knowledge across all areas of development as well as mathematical reasoning and number sense, orientation in time and space, scientific reasoning and the physical world, and music and visual arts.

These areas of skill and knowledge are similar to those included in the other curriculum models described previously. However, the Core Knowledge preschool sequence differs from those approaches in at least two ways:

- *Specificity regarding content.* The preschool sequence identifies specific experiences, knowledge, and skills for all children including particular stories, fables, legends, nonfiction books, songs, rhymes, and poems. A month-by-month planning guide promotes the concept of a sequence of knowledge and competencies building on one another. Although the program is flexible, it does establish expectations that all the content and language should be incorporated in order to prepare children for the next level of curriculum.
- *Lack of specificity regarding pedagogy.* The Core Knowledge preschool sequence specifies *what* to teach, not *how* to teach. It does not advocate any particular approach, but rather a wide range of strategies that includes both teacher-directed large- and small-group experiences and children's play and discovery learning.

Tools of the Mind

Based on Vygotsky's sociocultural theory of learning, the Tools of the Mind curriculum is designed for preschool through second grade (Bodrova & Leong, 2007). The curriculum provides teachers with ideas and strategies designed to support children's development of early literacy, self-regulation, and cognitive skills. Consistent with Vygotsky's theory of learning, the curriculum emphasizes the teacher's role in guiding and supporting children's learning in a child-centered environment. The curriculum is designed to achieve two main, interrelated goals:

1. Development of foundational cognitive abilities that include self-regulation of behavior, emotions, and cognition; memory; and focused attention
2. Development of specific academic skills such as symbolic thought, literacy, and an understanding of mathematics (Bodrova & Leong, 2007).

Developing Foundational Cognitive Abilities

One of the key aspects of Tools of the Mind is that it is based on the assumption that if children lack underlying cognitive skills such as self-regulation, trying to teach them academic skills is more difficult and inefficient. As a result, activities in Tools of the Mind promote these abilities simultaneously. Teachers also organize the classroom routines to eliminate or minimize situations that tend to interfere with the development of self-regulation, such as long periods of whole-group instruction or lengthy waits for a turn.

Teachers embed self-regulation practice in all classroom activities. For example, in a preschool classroom, a teacher might use props to scaffold children's practice of conversation turn-taking. After her teacher explains what to do with the props, Kesharia holds a cardboard ear to prompt her to listen, while Ashanti holds a cardboard mouth assigning him the role of speaker. Then, they switch roles.

Developing Academic Skills through Play

To accomplish high levels of mature play, teachers engage children in play planning before and even during the play. Children produce their own play plans, which are written or graphic descriptions of what the child intends to do during the play. By writing and/or drawing their plans, the children's writing abilities improve over time, a process called *scaffolded writing*, an example of which is shown in Figure 10.4. Teachers also help children make more complex plans, encouraging two or more children to plan together to build friendships and collaborative learning.

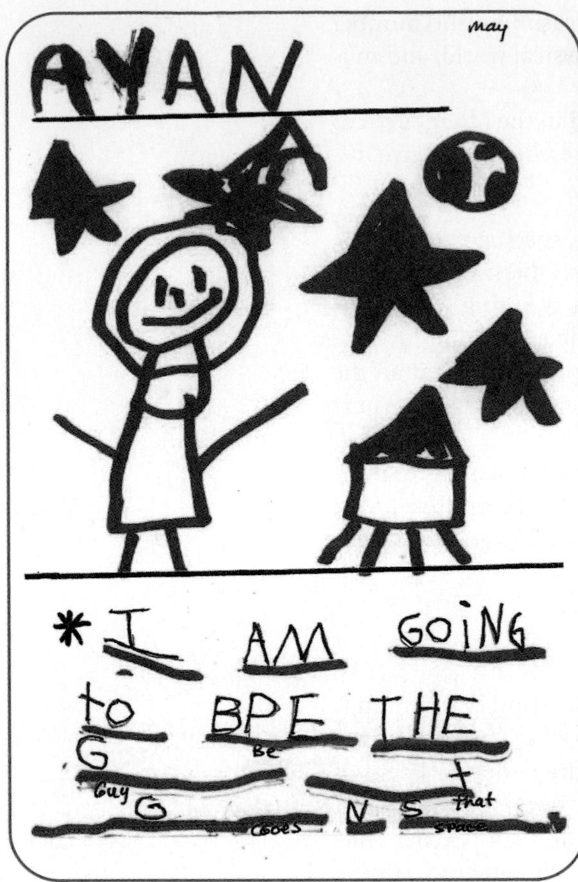

Figure 10.4 Tools of the Mind Sample Play Plan with Scaffolded Writing
Source: Used with permission of Deborah Leong.

To enhance the quality of the play, teachers also provide children with relevant experiences that will inform their play. For example, a trip to the firehouse helps children learn about the roles and scenarios that occur there. But teachers do not leave the learning to chance. They ask the firefighters and other workers to demonstrate for children what they actually say before and after the fire bell goes off. Such experiences expand children's vocabulary and use of complex language, which they then practice during play.

Research on Preschool Curriculum

The irony of mandates for research-based curriculum is that there is a limited body of well-designed research on the comparative effectiveness of preschool curricula (Barnett, Yarosz, Thomas, & Hornbeck, 2006). Most of the existing research compares the effectiveness of teacher-directed instruction and more child-initiated, play-oriented approaches to curriculum. In fact, these studies are more about particular teaching strategies than evaluations of curricula. Conducting research on curriculum can be a challenging process, as described in the *What Works: Examining Curriculum Effectiveness* feature.

Early Curriculum Comparison Studies

The earliest curriculum comparison studies were conducted beginning in the late 1960s. These studies were an attempt to determine which curriculum would most successfully prepare Head Start children for success in school (Datta, McHale, & Mitchell, 1976).

The results of this research reinforced the importance of having clearly defined curriculum goals; however, no one approach was found to be more effective than others. In fact, very different approaches resulted in learning gains for children as long as the curriculum was well planned and implemented. The simplest way to interpret this and other curriculum research is to say that "having a planned curriculum in a preschool program is better than having none" (Bowman, Donovan & Burns, 2001, p. 184).

Recent Preschool Curriculum Research

Since the early 1970s, there has been little rigorous curriculum research in early childhood despite the fact that there has been an explosion in numbers of children attending preschool as well as in newly developed curriculum resources. After an interval of almost 30 years, the federal government again funded a large-scale study to evaluate the effectiveness of various preschool curricula (PCER Consortium, 2008).

After 6 years of work, however, this large-scale study raised more questions than it answered. The results demonstrated that children make learning gains in most well-designed curriculum approaches; however, there are very few significant differences between the curricula. Several lessons can be drawn from the mixed results of curriculum research to date. Ample evidence exists that a well-planned, research-based curriculum is an essential element of an effective early childhood program (Bowman et al., 2001; Landry, 2005a, 2005b; National Center for Children in Poverty, 2007). The bottom line is that to be most effective, teachers need *both* good curriculum knowledge *and* understanding of child development (Cunningham & Davidson, 2007; Siraj-Blatchford, Muttock, Sylva, Gilden, & Bell, 2003). Teachers who have this knowledge possess the fundamental resources for planning an effective curriculum, which is described in the next section.

What Works

Examining Curriculum Effectiveness

The curriculum has important and lasting implications for children's learning. So educators and families naturally would like to know if a particular curriculum gets the results they are seeking. Finding the answer to the effectiveness question, however, is not as straightforward as it might seem.

Curriculum effectiveness can be investigated in one of two basic ways. In the first, researchers can test a single strategy or component to see if it is worthwhile to include in a curriculum. This approach is a bit like a cook investigating what happens when she changes a single ingredient in a recipe. For example, in a literacy curriculum, investigators can assess which is more effective for children: to hear the same book read repeatedly or to hear different books read once. The value of this research approach is finding out just what experiences make a difference. The challenge lies in creating a complete curriculum from such single strands and determining how they fit together for best results. The results can then inform curriculum developers, as well as those choosing a curriculum, about which learning experiences and teaching practices bring results.

Sticking with the cooking analogy, the second method of examining curriculum effectiveness is to see how the complete recipe turns out. In other words, one can test whether the curriculum as a whole yields the desired results. Assuming the research is done competently, the results will show whether or not Curriculum A is more effective than Curriculum B (which may be another curriculum under study, or "business as usual" for the control).

An example is the evaluation of the effectiveness of the Tools of the Mind curriculum, described on page 317 in this chapter. Teachers and preschool children were randomly assigned to either treatment or control classrooms. The treatment classrooms used the Tools of the Mind curriculum, which approaches literacy and other learning through emphasis on self-regulation, development of high-level play skills, and teacher scaffolding. The control group experienced an established district-created model described as a "balanced literacy curriculum with themes." When children were compared on cognitive, linguistic, and social-emotional growth, the Tools of the Mind curriculum was found to yield more progress in language and self-regulation.

This method of testing the curriculum as a whole can be useful, but it has a limitation. It leaves unanswered the question of what aspects from the many activities and strategies are actually making a difference in children's learning. Is everything in the curriculum contributing to the final result? Or are a few features or components helping a lot while others are not? Some parts of the curriculum may be a complete waste of time, or may even be counterproductive. Others may be so effective that doubling or tripling the time spent on them would greatly improve results. Testing the curriculum as a whole indicates that *something* in the "black box" is working but does not reveal what works and what does not. Each of the approaches to evaluating curriculum effectiveness has both value and limitations.

Source: Based on "Educational Effects of the Tools of the Mind Curriculum: A Randomized Trial," by W. S. Barnett et al., 2008, *Early Childhood Research Quarterly, 23*(3), pp. 299–313.

A Model for Planning Effective Curriculum

In this section, we present a general model for planning effective curriculum that applies across the full age range of early childhood as well as in diverse settings. This model for developing and planning curriculum is shown in Figure 10.5 (Bredekamp & Rosegrant, 1995; Rosegrant & Bredekamp, 1992). In the sections that follow, we briefly describe the sources of knowledge that are brought together in a coherent curriculum, and then we provide examples of applying the planning model in action. All good early childhood curriculum needs to focus first on children, as we discuss next.

The Child in the Sociocultural Context

Early childhood curriculum is often called *child centered*; accordingly, this model places the child at the center of curriculum planning. In a child-centered curriculum, learning is

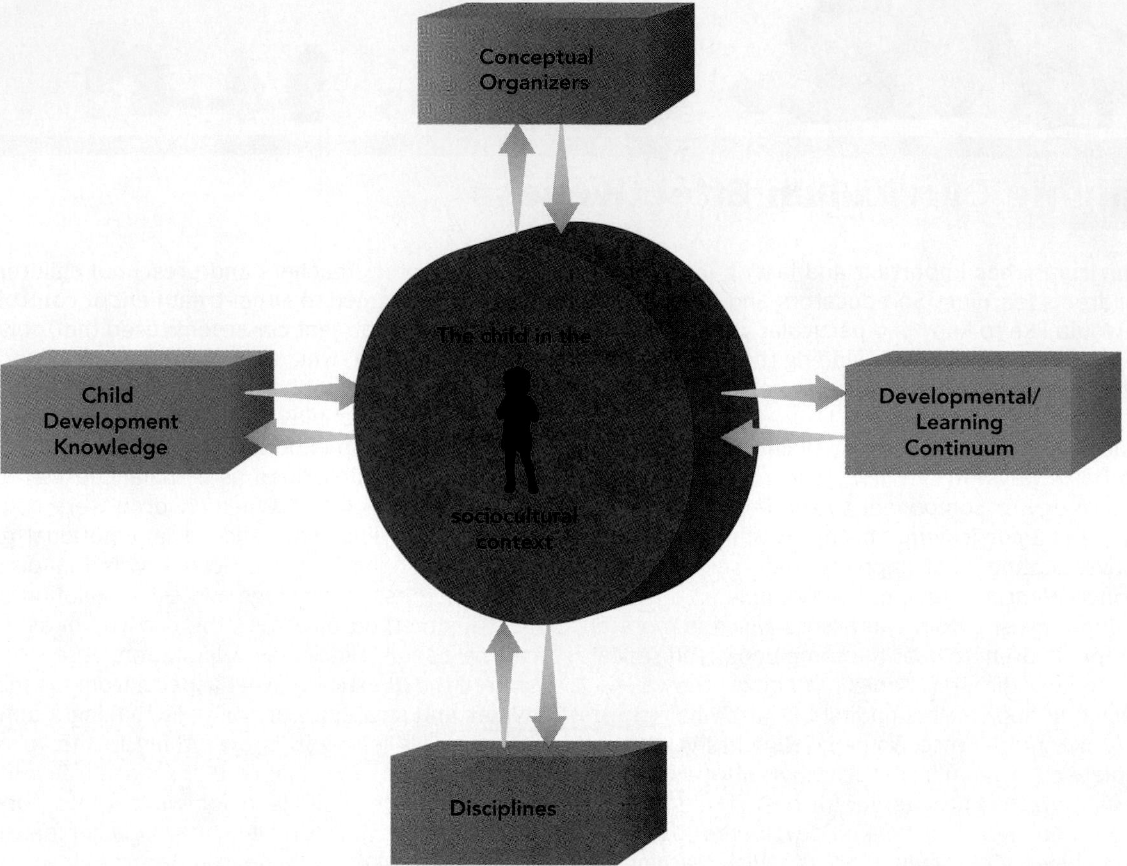

Figure 10.5 Curriculum Planning Model

Source: From "Reaching Individual Potentials through Transformational Curriculum," by T. Rosegrant and S. Bredekamp, 1992, pp. 66–73, in *Reaching Potentials: Appropriate Curriculum and Assessment for Young Children, Vol. 1,* edited by S. Bredekamp and T. Rosegrant, Washington, DC: NAEYC. Reprinted with permission from the National Association for the Education of Young Children.

an interactive process—children change from exposure to the curriculum and the curriculum changes in response to the learner's progress. Teachers involve children in planning by determining what they already know, as well as what they want and need to know. As curriculum is implemented, teachers continually assess children's abilities and interests, and adapt the curriculum and teaching in response.

However, children do not grow and learn in isolation; in early childhood classrooms, children are part of a group. The group, in turn, exists in a larger context of a program or school, a community, state, and nation. Therefore, the model situates the child in a sociocultural context that influences what is included in the curriculum (Bronfenbrenner, 1979).

The cultural values of families and the larger community always influence curriculum decisions. For example, a faith-based private school may include religious study in its curriculum, whereas a public school may avoid reference to religious activity of any kind. In this model of curriculum planning, culture is not viewed as a separate source of curriculum, but rather as the context within which all curriculum decisions are made. Therefore, culture influences all of the aspects of curriculum planning, as we describe in the sections that follow on each dimension of the model.

Sources of Curriculum

As illustrated in Figure 10.5, curriculum planning draws on four sources:

1. *The content of the disciplines.* Much of the curriculum comes directly from the subject matter disciplines: what children need to know and be able to do in science, mathe-

matics, language arts, health, social studies, and the arts. Such content gives curriculum intellectual integrity; that is, it teaches accurate information about how the world works and how to obtain new knowledge. However, the content of the disciplines can be abstract and removed from children's direct experiences. Therefore, early childhood curriculum needs to be conceptually organized.

2. *Conceptual organizers.* We have already discussed several approaches to conceptually organizing curriculum. **Conceptual organizers** make content knowledge more meaningful, interesting, and understandable for young children. For example, children can learn key scientific concepts by planting a garden or studying the effects of light on shadows.
3. *Child development knowledge.* Knowledge of how young children develop and learn is critical in planning curriculum that will reach all children. Research on children's cognitive, language, social, emotional, and physical development allows teachers to anticipate whether curriculum goals will be achievable and challenging (that is, developmentally appropriate).
4. *Developmental/learning continuum.* A **developmental continuum** is a predictable, but not rigid, sequence of typical developmental accomplishments within age ranges (McAfee & Leong, 2007). A **learning continuum** (also called a **learning trajectory** or **learning path**) is similar to a developmental continuum, but focuses on sequences of knowledge or skill in a content area such as mathematics or physical education, with each level more sophisticated than the last (Sarama & Clements, 2009a, 2009b). (The terms *developmental continuum* and *learning trajectory* or *learning path* are often used interchangeably.) Research-based developmental and learning continua are the basis for planning the scope and sequence of a curriculum. Teachers use a continuum of development and learning in a curriculum area to determine when, where, and how to provide individual instruction and scaffolding.

conceptual organizers Ways of organizing curriculum, such as the project approach, that make content knowledge more meaningful, interesting, and understandable for children.

developmental continuum A predictable, but not rigid, sequence of typical developmental accomplishments within age ranges.

learning continuum, learning trajectory, or learning path Similar to a developmental continuum, but focuses on sequences of knowledge or skill in a content area.

This model illustrates how both content knowledge and child development knowledge must be considered in planning effective early childhood curriculum. The goal of this curriculum planning model is for early childhood programs from birth through age 8 to teach the *whole child*—the thinking, feeling, moving, expressing, creating, problem-solving, interacting human being.

Applying the Curriculum Model in Practice

In the following example, we see teachers putting the planning model into practice (based on Bredekamp & Rosegrant, 1995):

> One of the favorite spots in Helen and Callie's classroom of 3- and 4-year-olds this week is the play shoe store. Shelves are piled high with shoe boxes of every kind, and children enjoy being customers or sales clerks.
>
> *Angelique:* I'm going to a wedding, so I need a pair of beautiful high heels.
> *Mitchell, as he pulls out a shoe measure:* What size?
> *Angelique, pointing to her toes:* I want pink ones.
> *Mitchell sorts through his boxes and replies:* We got red, green, and blue. No pink. Here's a catalog.
> *Angelique:* I guess I'll get 'em on eBay.
>
> Meanwhile, Helen is reading *The Elves and the Shoemaker* to four children. Callie is playing a math game with several others, challenging them to find everything in the classroom that comes in pairs. After looking everywhere and feeling stumped, Ross shouts with glee, "Ears!"

Intentional teachers can use children's interests to plan curriculum that meets many learning goals. This child looks like she is just playing, but what can her teacher help her learn as she plays shoe store?

This glimpse into Helen and Callie's classroom finds happy children, laughing and playing together. What is not immediately apparent, however, is the planning that has gone

MyEducationLab

Go to the Building Teaching Skills and Dispositions section of Topic 6: Curriculum Planning in the MyEducationLab for your course and complete the activity entitled *Planning the Curriculum: Methods, Effective Teaching Strategies, and Standards.* As you watch the videos, consider how the curriculum in each of these classrooms builds content knowledge in meaningful ways and supports individual children's development and learning.

into this day. To begin, the teachers identified the topic of shoes as a conceptual organizer for several reasons. They had observed how much time the children spend talking about and focusing on shoes (put your shoes on, take your shoes off, put on your boots, see my new shoes, my basketball shoes help me jump). Children take great interest in their own and each other's shoes.

Next, the teachers considered how well the topic promotes child development. They agreed that it would provide opportunities to build cognitive processes such as matching, describing, organizing, and categorizing by size, color, and function (dress-up, athletics, inclement weather). The topic promotes physical development such as walking, running, and balancing, and also independent practice of fine motor skills getting in and out of shoes several times a day. The shoe store and other activities encourage social interaction and turn-taking as well as language development.

As for content knowledge, the shoe unit supported children's learning in every discipline area listed below.

Mathematics: counting by ones and twos; measuring; ordering by size; learning about patterns and relationships (shoe designs are in patterns; shoes have similarities and differences)

Science: learning technology about the tools and materials to make shoes; physical properties (some shoes are water repellant, others are not)

Language and literacy: vocabulary (*heel, instep, rubber, canvas*); books and songs

Social studies: economics of buying and selling shoes; cultural differences related to when and what kind of shoes to wear

Health: shoes for protecting feet from injury and weather.

The final element of the curriculum model is that teachers need to know the continuum of development and learning in each area so they can adapt the curriculum to accommodate individual differences in children. Although we raise this issue at the end of the chapter, it is the most important aspect of implementing an effective curriculum.

Adapting for Individual Differences

Teachers must take into account that children vary enormously on practically every dimension of development and learning. These differences are manifest in rates of development; prior experiences, which greatly influence learning; diverse cultural and linguistic backgrounds; and the existence of specific abilities and disabilities.

Understanding students' diverse needs is critical in implementing curriculum and adapting for individual variation. Regardless of the type of curriculum used, teachers need to apply their professional expertise. Adaptation may take many forms, such as adjusting the groupings, the time schedule, the nature of teacher–child interactions, or the amount and kind of scaffolding provided. The feature *Becoming an Intentional Teacher: Shape Curriculum to Connect with Children* describes one teacher's thinking as she works to meet the individual needs of her students.

Effective curriculum planning involves several key steps, whether curriculum is locally developed or purchased. Curriculum should be selected or developed using the NAEYC key indicators. If teachers use a published program, they need to use it flexibly, and adapt it in response to children's cues and information obtained from ongoing assessment. Similarly, if teachers develop their own curriculum plans, they need to ensure that those plans reflect the most current knowledge from the disciplines as well as research on child development and learning.

Becoming an Intentional Teacher

Shape Curriculum to Connect with Children

Here's What Happened I've been teaching first grade for 4 years now, and this year the district adopted a K–2 curriculum. It isn't bad, but I believe it's far more effective when used with flexibility and a close eye on what the children need and are ready for. Consequently, I make quite a few changes. My principal so far has agreed to my modifications as long as I can make a good case for them.

Last month we were working on measurement, and the kids wanted to measure their bean plants. Some of the plants were growing like gangbusters and others were not. We made a chart of the plants' heights, and the kids wanted to know why some plants grew a lot and some didn't. This seemed like the perfect time to get into the unit on plant growth, so I moved this lesson up in the curriculum sequence. We did several experiments on effects of water and light, giving the children more experiences in measurement and recording results.

Here's What I Was Thinking When I switch the order of the curriculum plan, there's always a good reason. As in this case, I like to capitalize on what the children are engaged in right then and make the learning more meaningful, as I hoped to do with the bean plants. Some areas of the curriculum, such as phonological awareness or number, have a learning path that is sequenced, with one concept or skill building on another. For other things in the curriculum, the order doesn't matter so much. Before changing the order of topics substantially, I have to think about this. I have to consider whether the change would affect the way the children's learning proceeds and whether there are any related skills where the learning path would be negatively affected.

Besides changing the order of lessons in the packaged curriculum, I sometimes adjust the pace. I may see that we need a detour or to slow down to work on a skill the children must master before going on. In other cases, some children may be ready for more challenge and I want to keep them engaged. Sometimes it's just a few children who need these kinds of adaptations; sometimes it's the class as a whole.

Revisiting Ms. Amas and Ms. Kadota's Classroom

In this chapter, we described indicators of effective curriculum and provided a model for planning curriculum that draws on both content knowledge and knowledge of child development, while also placing children at the center of the planning process. At the outset, we saw the children in Mona and Shelley's classroom involved in their study of animals that hatch from eggs. Now we can revisit their classroom and think about it in relation to what we have learned about curriculum.

To implement the principles of effective curriculum, we saw that Mona and Shelley had thoughtfully planned what they wanted children to think about and learn during this study. Children were active and engaged as they interacted with the visiting hen, drew pictures of her, and wrote in their journals. This preschool activity illustrates integrated curriculum in action, with children's experiences contributing to different areas of their development and learning at the same time.

With regard to the planning model used in this classroom, the curriculum is based in the discipline of science but made accessible to children through a topic with which they are fascinated: the hatching eggs. At the same time, children are learning the key concepts and tools of inquiry used by scientists. For example, they employ the scientific method as they predict when the eggs will hatch, and observe what happens with the incubator. They enhance their language and literacy as they learn new words and concepts related to the hen.

Child development knowledge is reflected in providing developmentally appropriate experiences, including sociodramatic play and book reading, throughout the day. At the same time, Mona and Shelley assess each child's progress in relation to learning goals, and support their developing abilities, as when Mona assisted the children in the "vet's office," with language and sharing. As this classroom demonstrates, effective early childhood curriculum is not only motivating and engaging, but also intellectually challenging for children and teachers.

MyEducationLab

To assess your understanding of how to plan effective curriculum, go to the Book Specific Resources section in MyEducationLab for your course, select *Effective Practices in Early Childhood Education,* Chapter 10 of the Study Plan, and then complete the multiple choice questions and activities.

Chapter Summary

- Curriculum is a written plan that describes the goals for children's learning and development, and the learning experiences, materials, and teaching strategies that are used to help children achieve those goals.
- Effective approaches to planning early childhood curriculum include emergent curriculum, integrated curriculum, thematic curriculum, webbing, the project approach, and scope and sequence.
- Effective curriculum is thoughtfully planned; challenging, engaging, and developmentally appropriate; culturally and linguistically responsive; comprehensive; and likely to promote positive outcomes for all young children.
- Learning standards define what is to be taught and what kind of performance is expected. Standards can provide useful guidance to curriculum developers and teachers about what and when to teach particular content.
- Curriculum models are idealized versions of what and how teaching and learning should occur. Frequently used early childhood curriculum models include HighScope, Creative Curriculum, Core Knowledge, and Tools of the Mind.
- Scientifically based curriculum derives from research evidence about what kinds of learning outcomes relate to later achievement, and what types of teaching and learning experiences help children acquire those outcomes. Scientifically based curriculum has been evaluated and demonstrated its effectiveness.
- A child-centered model of curriculum planning draws on content knowledge, conceptual organizers, knowledge of child development, and learning developmental and learning continua. All four dimensions of the model are influenced by sociocultural contexts.

key terms

conceptual organizers
content standards
curriculum
curriculum approach
curriculum framework
curriculum model
developmental continuum
emergent curriculum
fidelity
integrated curriculum
learning continuum, learning trajectory, or learning path
learning standards
performance standards
project
project approach
scientifically based curriculum
scope
sequence
thematic curriculum
validated curriculum
webbing

Frede, E., & Ackerman, D. J. (2007). *Curriculum decision-making: Dimensions to consider*. New Brunswick, NJ: National Institute for Early Education Research.

Gronlund, G. (2006). *Make early learning standards come alive: Connecting your practice and curriculum to state guidelines*. St. Paul, MN: Redleaf Press.

Helm, J. H., & Beneke, S. (2003). *The power of projects: Meeting contemporary challenges in early childhood classrooms—Strategies and solutions*. New York: Teachers College Press.

Association for Supervision and Curriculum Development (ASCD)
www.ascd.org

Mid-continent Regional Educational Laboratory
www.mcrel.org

Project Approach
Website directed by Sylvia Chard with resources for teachers using the project approach.
www.projectapproach.org

1. Observe two preschool programs that use the same curriculum model. Reflect on how the implementation of the curriculum looks similar or different in the two settings. How much influence do you think specific curriculum models have on actual practice in preschool programs?
2. Observe at an infant/toddler child care facility. Ask the teachers how they decide what they will do with the children. Reflect on whether there is a "curriculum" in the program and whether it is appropriate for infants/toddlers.
3. Observe a first-grade reading/language arts period. Does the teacher use a published curriculum? If so, to what degree does the teacher follow the prescribed plan or adapt the instruction to individual children's needs? Decide how you would feel as a teacher using this particular reading program.
4. Visit the websites of two publishers of K–3 curriculum. Find out as much as you can about the different products available. How would you feel about using any of these products? Which do you feel would be most effective in teaching diverse learners? Why? How would you adapt it for individuals?
5. Interview an experienced kindergarten, first-, second-, or third-grade teacher. Ask how he or she thinks the standards movement has affected the curriculum for the age group he or she teaches. Try to determine both the positive and negative impact on standards on schools.

11 Assessing Children's Learning and Development

Thinking Ahead

1. What is assessment literacy? What terms do teachers need to know and use to become assessment literate?
2. What are the most important indicators of effective assessment?
3. What are the primary purposes for assessing young children?
4. What are effective strategies for observing, gathering, and recording evidence to support children's learning and development?
5. How do teachers use assessment strategies to improve child outcomes and individualize teaching?
6. What is standardized testing, and what are appropriate and inappropriate uses of standardized tests?

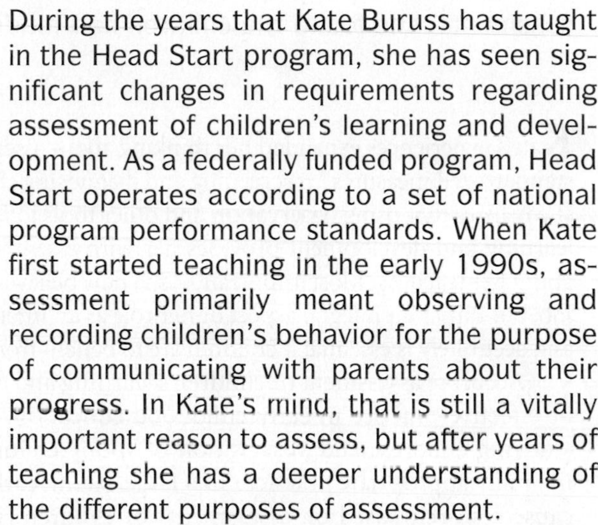

During the years that Kate Buruss has taught in the Head Start program, she has seen significant changes in requirements regarding assessment of children's learning and development. As a federally funded program, Head Start operates according to a set of national program performance standards. When Kate first started teaching in the early 1990s, assessment primarily meant observing and recording children's behavior for the purpose of communicating with parents about their progress. In Kate's mind, that is still a vitally important reason to assess, but after years of teaching she has a deeper understanding of the different purposes of assessment.

Early in the school year, Kate uses a developmental screening instrument to determine whether any of the children might be at risk for serious developmental or learning problems. She takes this responsibility very seriously. Most years, the screening process identifies a few children who require further diagnosis and intervention services. This year, Kate is grateful that Jared and Bethany are getting speech therapy for their language delays. She feels confident that Julio does not have a speech delay because further evaluation, after screening, found that his language is developing just fine. Health screenings also benefit the children. Kate will always remember 4-year-old Eileen's joy when she got her new glasses following the vision screening at Head Start. Eileen came to school that day and announced to Kate with wonder in her voice, "I see little leaves on the trees."

In the late 1990s, when Head Start began requiring systematic assessments of children's learning progress three times each year, Kate was wary. She thought that too much time would be devoted to assessing children and that it would take away from their learning experiences. During the first year of implementing this requirement, however, Kate was stunned to learn that many of the children scored no better on measures of vocabulary and alphabet knowledge at the middle of the year than they had at the beginning. These data propelled Kate to adapt her teaching and curriculum to focus more on language and literacy. She also began to pay more attention to assessing individual children's literacy skills on a regular basis. She focused more energy on involving parents in the assessment process in order to find out how the children perform away from school. Sharing children's writing and drawing samples in conferences with their families left parents amazed at what these small people can do. When Kate conducted the year-end assessments, she found the children had made considerable progress. ▲

Kate's experiences expanded her thinking about assessment. She knows the benefits of using standardized measures for screening and diagnosing children's special needs. At the same time, she realizes that using observation and other tools to formally and informally assess children's learning and development provides her with essential information to make good decisions about her teaching. Most importantly, she now believes that assessment is not an add-on to her job, but rather an integral aspect of her role as an intentional teacher. Using assessment wisely and accurately is essential if children are to benefit from their school experiences.

Accurate assessment of children's learning and development is an integral component of effective practice in early childhood education. The profession has a long history of studying children, and observation of young children is essential to providing developmentally appropriate practice. To a large extent, early childhood education has grown because research based on assessments of children's learning has found that high-quality programs have positive, lasting effects on children's development. The closely related field of early intervention is steeped in the necessity for and value of assessment for educating children with special needs. Recently, the school accountability movement has placed considerable emphasis on testing in the early years of school to ensure that all children achieve basic reading and mathematics skills.

The goal of this chapter is to prepare you to achieve the most important purpose of assessment: to improve children's learning and development. If children are to benefit fully from early childhood programs, intentional teachers must know why, what, and how to assess. Like many other areas of education, assessment has its own—sometimes bewildering—vocabulary and jargon. We begin by helping you learn the language of assessment. Then we present indicators of effective assessment. We discuss four fundamental purposes of assessment and connect these to various tools and procedures. The chapter concludes with a discussion of appropriate and inappropriate uses of standardized tests and of program evaluation and accountability.

assessment The ongoing process of gathering evidence of children's learning and development for informed decisions about instructional practice.

evidence An outward sign or indication of children's learning, such as their response to a question or their solution to a problem.

■ Learning the Language of Assessment

The first step in understanding and using assessment appropriately and accurately is for teachers to acquire the vocabulary of assessment. As teachers become more experienced in using various assessment methods and tools, their knowledge of assessment—their *assessment literacy*—grows and deepens. Broadly defined, **assessment** is the ongoing process of gathering evidence of children's learning and development, then organizing and interpreting the information in order to make informed decisions about instructional practice (J. Jones, 2004; McAfee, Leong, & Bodrova, 2004). **Evidence** is an outward sign or indication of children's learning, such as their response to a question or their solution to a problem (McAfee et al., 2004). Therefore, assessment involves using multiple sources of evidence systematically collected over time from which professionals make judgments about specific actions to take on behalf of children.

formative assessment The process of gathering information about children's learning and using it to provide the right kind and amount of support.

curriculum-embedded assessment Formative assessment that is integrated into the curriculum; this assessment does not occur as a separate procedure.

play-based assessment Similar to curriculum-embedded assessment, but the context for observing and interacting with children is the children's play.

summative assessment Assessing student learning at the end of an educational experience to evaluate the effectiveness of the experience.

evaluation The process of making a judgment about assessment results; frequently considered the last step in assessment.

informal assessment Information is gathered for teacher's use to make everyday classroom decisions or adjustments to teaching.

Understanding Assessment

Each of the many different types of assessment has various implications for how and when it is conducted. We begin by describing assessment in its broadest terms—formative and summative—and then describe more specific types of assessments.

Formative Assessment

Formative assessment is the process of gathering information about children and using it to provide the right kind and amount of support to help them progress. The information obtained from formative assessment helps *form* the next steps in the teaching and learning process. In practice, formative assessment is so closely linked to teaching and curriculum that teachers may not even recognize it as assessment.

One type of formative assessment, for example, is **curriculum-embedded assessment**, which is integrated into the curriculum and not conducted as a separate procedure. The teacher assesses the children while teaching, using the classroom activity itself, such as when a teacher listens to children describe their reasoning or watches them write. **Play-based assessment** is similar to curriculum-embedded assessment, but the context for observing and interacting with children is the children's play.

Summative Assessment

At the end of an educational experience, student progress is assessed using a **summative assessment**, which *sums up* or evaluates the effectiveness of an experience after it concludes. **Evaluation** is the process of making a judgment about assessment results and is frequently considered the last step in assessment (McAfee et al., 2004). In a college English course, for example, the instructor's feedback on student essays is formative assessment, whereas the final exam is summative. Similarly, in a preschool or primary classroom, summative assessment may occur at the end of the year, when teachers compare their observations of children's progress to those they conducted when the school year began.

Accurate assessment is essential for effective practice. Intentional teachers observe children and gather information about their learning and development to plan curriculum and adapt their teaching.

Informal and Formal Assessments

Assessments are often identified as informal or formal. **Informal assessment** refers to information that is gathered for teachers' use to make everyday classroom decisions or adjustments to teaching (McAfee et al., 2004). For instance, while reading a storybook to her preschool class, Abby Cosgrove observes that some children are listening intently while others are clearly uninterested and not following the story. She uses this informal observation of children's cues to quickly adapt her behavior. "This is a very long story," she says. "I will finish reading it during choice time if you want to hear the rest. Right now, let's all reach for the sky . . . turn around . . . touch the ground . . . and sit down." As Abby slowly gives each direction, all of the children become engaged in the physical movement and return their attention to her. "Now who has a song for us to sing?" In this example, Abby used her informal assessment of the children to adapt her teaching and engage them in the learning process.

A **formal assessment** is an assessment that follows a specific procedure and uses a specially designed instrument or tool. Teachers often use such assessments to report results to others. Formal assessments include structured child observations or assessments that produce specific scores. Formal assessment, in contrast to informal assessment, is also used to describe any method of gathering information that is standardized, a topic discussed later in this chapter.

formal assessment Assessment that follows a specific procedure and uses a specially designed instrument or tool.

performance assessment Determines what children know and can do from their demonstration of a skill or their creation of a product; also known as *authentic assessment*.

alternative assessments Assessments that call for a child to produce a response rather than select from a list of possible responses.

dynamic assessment Analyzes a child's performance not just in terms of what the child can do independently, but what the child can do with the assistance of a teacher or peer.

standardized assessment Assessment of all children using the same procedures and performing the same task under the same conditions.

Performance Assessment

Performance assessment, also known as **authentic assessment**, is used to determine what children know and can do from their demonstration of a skill or their creation of a product. Consider, for instance, how figure skaters are judged on the basis of their skating *performance*, not on whether they can draw a skating maneuver or write a description of how to do a triple axel.

For children, authentic assessment engages them in tasks that occur in real-life contexts whether in the classroom or on the playground, or in situations as close as possible to that context. For example, to assess children's reading ability, a teacher listens to them read aloud rather than giving them a multiple-choice test. Assessments such as this, which call for a child to produce a response rather than select from a list of possible responses, are also called **alternative assessments** (Gullo, 2006).

Dynamic Assessment

Based on Vygotsky's concept of the zone of proximal development, **dynamic assessment** analyzes a child's performance not just in terms of what the child can do independently, as most assessment procedures require, but what the child can do with the assistance of a teacher or peer (McAfee & Leong, 2007). A teacher may provide prompts, cues, hints, or questions that elicit a child's response. Analyzing the amount and kind of assistance the child needs to perform a task provides information about the child's current level of understanding and skill and also guides the next steps in teaching (McAfee & Leong, 2007).

Understanding Standardized Testing

Many people hear the word *assessment* and automatically think of testing. **Standardized assessment** refers to the assessment of all children using the same procedures and performing the same task under the same conditions. The thought behind standardizing procedures is that it leads to less biased and more objective results.

Although assessment is sometimes used as a synonym for testing, testing is only one part of the larger concept of assessment. **Testing** is a systematic procedure for evaluating a child's behavior and knowledge that results in the assignment of a score (McAfee et al., 2004). Therefore, a test is a snapshot of a child's performance or knowledge that is administered to an individual or group under controlled conditions. Some tests are teacher developed, whereas others are developed by test publishing companies. Some, but not all, commercially published tests are standardized.

Dynamic assessment involves finding out what children are capable of doing with the assistance of other children or the teacher. Why would this information be valuable?

Reliability and Validity in Testing

Standardized testing uses prescribed methods for administering and scoring and needs to meet technical standards for educational and psychological testing (American Educational Research Association, American Psychological Association, & National Council on Measurement in Education, 1999). These standards are designed to ensure that tests have high levels of reliability and validity.

Reliability.

Reliability is the extent to which the results obtained from a test are accurate and consistent over time. A test is said to be reliable if the tool is likely to get the same or similar results when used by different people or on different days. To understand the concept of reliability, consider an example unrelated to education: measuring cooking ingredients. If a recipe calls for 1 cup of flour, even a beginning cook would reach for a standard, 8-ounce measuring cup. If one cook used a demitasse cup, another chose a giant-size coffee mug, and another filled a tea cup half full, the final results would vary considerably. The standard measuring cup, therefore, is reliable, whereas the other cup selections are not.

Validity.

Validity means that the instrument measures what it purports to measure. For example, a test designed to measure children's physical skills should not depend heavily on children's ability to understand verbal directions; in such a case, the test is really a measure of the children's language.

In revisiting our cooking example, suppose we are trying to measure volume. There are a number of ways to measure volume, such as using a liquid measuring cup or an 8-ounce standard cup, which would yield an equally accurate amount of flour for a recipe. However, if we tried to measure flour with a yardstick which is for measuring length, the results would be not only messy but also inaccurate and, therefore, lacking validity. If a standardized test lacks reliability or validity, the results it yields are meaningless.

Scoring Standardized Tests

In addition to reliability and validity, standardized tests involve one of two ways of scoring. They may be either norm referenced or criterion referenced.

Criterion-Referenced Tests.

Criterion-referenced tests compare a person's score to a predetermined level of performance. They are designed to measure how well an individual has learned a specific body of knowledge and skills (FairTest, 2007). Third-grade standardized achievement tests administered by state departments of education are criterion-referenced tests. The criterion for passing is a preset number of correct answers, which presumably represents how much a child has learned. Similarly, the SAT test is a criterion-referenced test, with different colleges setting the cut-off score, or criterion, needed for admission.

Norm-Referenced Tests.

By contrast, **norm-referenced tests** compare an individual's score to that of other test takers—who knows the most and who the least? Scores are reported by percentage rank with half scoring above and half scoring below the midpoint or average (FairTest, 2007). Many school-administered tests are norm referenced. For example, screening or diagnostic tests used in the process of identifying children's special needs compare children's scores to that of other children to determine if their development is within the typical, or "normal," range.

Norm-referenced tests are developed by giving the tests to large numbers of children and comparing their scores. These tests result in a distribution of scores that look like a bell or **normal curve**, with most people scoring at the midrange and fewer scoring at the higher and lower ends. For example, on a hypothetical vocabulary test of 4-year-olds, most children's vocabulary might average about 1,200 words, while some know as many as 2,500 and others know as few 400.

testing A systematic procedure for evaluating a child's behavior and knowledge that is then assigned a score.

standardized testing Uses prescribed methods for administering and scoring.

reliability The extent to which the results obtained from a test are accurate and consistent over time.

validity The degree to which an instrument measures what it purports to measure.

criterion-referenced tests Tests that compare a person's score to a predetermined level of performance.

norm-referenced tests Tests that compare an individual's score to that of other test takers.

normal curve A distribution of scores that looks like a bell shape, with most people scoring at the midrange and fewer scoring at the higher and lower ends.

Accurate assessment of children whose home language is not English is difficult. Standardized tests are often not reliable. How can teachers get accurate information about the abilities of English language learners?

In administering a norm-referenced test, it is essential to know the characteristics of the group used to develop the norms, that is, the *norming group*. In the vocabulary test example, the norming group is the thousands of 4-year-olds whose vocabularies were measured. If a norm-referenced test is used, the administrator needs to consider the composition of the norming group in terms of gender, ethnicity, age, socioeconomic background, culture, language, and inclusion of children with disabilities. If the norming group differs a great deal from the group of children with whom the test will be used, the results may not be accurate or reliable. For example, if a vocabulary test designed to identify language delays were given to a child who is learning English, the result might indicate a learning problem when none actually exists.

Types of Standardized Tests

There are many types of standardized tests. Most standardized tests can be categorized as achievement tests, aptitude or ability tests, readiness tests, or screening and diagnostic tests (McAfee & Leong, 2007).

Achievement Tests

Anyone who has attended school in America is familiar with standardized **achievement tests** such as the SAT, the Iowa Test of Basic Skills, or the California Achievement Test. Achievement tests are designed to measure what children have learned in general or in a content area such as reading or mathematics. The test items are a sample of the curriculum content, and children's responses are an indication of what they have learned. Most recent examples of achievement tests are those administered to meet No Child Left Behind requirements or state learning standards.

Aptitude or Ability Tests

Aptitude tests are presumably designed to measure not what children have already learned, but their potential for learning in the future (McAfee & Leong, 2007). Consequently, scores on aptitude tests are intended to predict future performance. One example is a career aptitude test used to determine if an individual's abilities are a good match to learn the skills required of a job, such as piloting an airplane.

In education, intelligence or IQ tests such as the Stanford-Binet or the McCarthy Scales of Children's Abilities are aptitude tests. Such tests are controversial because children's scores will naturally be influenced by their previous opportunities to learn. If children do not perform well on such tests, it may be because they have not had the opportunity to learn rather than because they are incapable of learning.

Readiness Tests

School **readiness tests** are typically administered before entrance to kindergarten (Maxwell & Clifford, 2004; Meisels, 1999). Some norm-referenced readiness tests are considered aptitude tests because they purport to predict whether children are sufficiently developed to benefit from kindergarten instruction. These tests are especially problematic because the younger the child, the more difficult it is to obtain an accurate assessment of what she or he has learned, much less what the child is capable of learning in the future (National Association for the Education of Young Children [NAEYC] & National Association of Early Childhood Specialists in State Departments of Education [NAECS/SDE], 2003).

The fact is that children's scores on readiness tests actually reflect their past experiences and opportunities to learn and, hence, are more accurately categorized as achievement tests (K. L. Snow, 2006). The use of readiness tests to keep children out of kindergarten is considered inappropriate by NAEYC because it denies children what they need most: the opportunity to attend school (NAECS/SDE, 2000; NAEYC, 1995).

achievement tests Tests designed to measure what children have learned in general or in a content area like reading or mathematics.

aptitude tests Tests designed to measure children's potential for learning in the future.

readiness tests Achievement tests administered to children at entry to kindergarten.

Screening and Diagnostic Tests

Screening and diagnostic tests are used as part of a two-step process of identifying children who may have disabilities or special learning or developmental needs. **Screening tests**, also called *developmental screening*, are administered to all children, usually in preschool or kindergarten, as the first step in a process to determine which children are at risk of a possible disability or learning problem. Administered by specially trained professionals, **diagnostic tests** are designed to identify the specific learning or developmental problems a child has and to plan interventions.

High-Stakes Testing

High-stakes testing refers to the use of standardized test scores to make decisions about individual children, teachers, or schools that have potential long-term consequences. For example, accurate tests are essential when children are identified for special services. Misidentification may mean that one child who needs services is denied them, or another child is assigned to special education needlessly.

Today's school accountability movement has increased the amount of high-stakes testing. Test results can lead to children being retained in grades, a decision with lifelong consequences. School districts use children's test scores in teacher performance evaluations and even for decisions about teacher pay. Schools are ranked in the newspapers and on websites according to test scores. When the stakes surrounding testing become so high, unintended consequences may result, such as narrowing the curriculum to teach only what is tested, or even cheating by giving children assistance or changing the conditions under which a test is administered (Asp, 1998; Au, 2007; Meisels, 2007).

The language of assessment is complex. In practice, terminology is often misused or used inconsistently. Teachers need to be clear about the concepts underlying the words; they need to become assessment literate. Now that we have established a common vocabulary with which to discuss assessment, in the next section we describe indicators of effective assessment.

Indicators of Effective Assessment

According to the NAEYC and NAECS/SDE (2003), ethical, appropriate, valid, and reliable assessment is a central part of early childhood education. These professional associations call for assessment methods that are "developmentally appropriate, culturally and linguistically responsive, tied to children's daily activities, supported by professional development for teachers, inclusive of families, and connected to beneficial purposes" (NAEYC & NAECS/SDE, 2003, p. 2). The ultimate goal of all early childhood assessment should be to benefit children by making sound decisions about teaching and learning, providing access to intervention services, or improving the quality of the program.

Effective Assessment Practices

Early childhood professional organizations have established guidelines for effective assessment and evaluation (Division for Early Childhood [DEC], 2007; NAEYC & NAECS/SDE, 2003). Key indicators of effective assessment practices are listed and described in Table 11.1.

To implement the assessment practices advocated by NAEYC and NAECS/SDE (2003), teachers need to understand the implications of terms like *developmentally appropriate* and *culturally and linguistically responsive*. Considerations for assessing very young children, English language learners, and children with special needs are discussed in the sections that follow.

Developmentally Appropriate Assessment

Most parents, grandparents, and teachers would agree with the statement "Young children are not good test takers." But why is this statement a truism? Sound assessment of young children

screening tests Tests administered to all children, usually in preschool or kindergarten, as the first step in a process to determine which children are at risk of a possible disability or learning problem; also called *developmental screening*.

diagnostic tests Tests designed to identify the specific learning or developmental problems a child has and to plan interventions; must be administered by specially trained professionals.

high-stakes testing Using standardized test scores to make decisions about individual children, teachers, or schools that have potential long-term consequences.

Table 11.1 Achieving Effective Assessment Practices

Indicators	Key Considerations
Ethical principles guide assessment practices.	Children should never be denied opportunities or services on the basis of assessment findings. Decisions should never be made on the basis of a single assessment or test score. Assessment findings should remain confidential.
Assessment instruments are used for their intended purposes.	Using a measure for a different purpose inevitably invalidates the results. For example, a developmental screening test should be used as the first step in an identification process, not as a measure of kindergarten readiness.
Assessments are appropriate for the ages and other characteristics of children being assessed.	Assessments should be used with groups of children who are similar to the group with which the measure was validated in terms of age, culture, home language, socioeconomic status, and abilities and disabilities.
Assessment instruments comply with professional criteria for quality.	Test development must meet technical guidelines for reliability and validity.
What is assessed is developmentally and educationally significant.	Because assessment takes up considerable time and resources, it should address the important learning goals and standards that are emphasized in the curriculum.
Assessment evidence is used to understand and improve learning.	Good assessment teaches teachers about children. That knowledge needs to be put to use in individualizing instruction or adapting curriculum or else both teachers' and children's time and effort are wasted.
Assessment evidence is gathered in realistic settings and situations that reflect children's actual performance.	This indicator calls for authentic performance assessment based on the results of teachers' observations of children in context, interviews, and on collections of children's work.
Assessments use multiple sources of evidence gathered over time.	Repeated, systematic observation, documentation, and other forms of criterion- or performance-based assessment are needed to accurately assess young children.
Screening is always linked to follow-up.	When screening or informal assessment indicates a possible problem, referral to specialists for diagnostic assessment follows. Labeling a child as having a disability is never made on the basis of a brief screening or one-time assessment.
Use of individually administered, norm-referenced tests is limited.	Formal, standardized, and norm-referenced tests are potentially beneficial as part of the process of identification and diagnosis of special needs.
Professionals and families are knowledgeable about assessment.	Both teachers and families need to see assessment as a tool to improve outcomes for children. Parents are not simply audiences for assessment information; they are also important sources of information about children's capabilities at home and in the community that must be considered in the assessment process.

Sources: Based on "Assessing Young Children's Learning and Development," by S. Bredekamp and L. Shepard, 1998, pp. 93–108, in *Assessing Student Learning: New Rules, New Realities*, edited by R. Brandt, Arlington, VA: Educational Research Service and Alliance for Curriculum Reform; and *Early Childhood Curriculum, Assessment, and Program Evaluation: Building an Effective, Accountable System in Programs for Children Birth through Age 8. Joint Position Statement*, by National Association for the Education of Young Children and National Association of Early Childhood Specialists in State Departments of Education, 2003, Washington, DC: NAEYC.

is difficult for several reasons: the nature of typical child development, children's sensitivity to context, and their lack of motivation for the assessment process, as well as their inability to perform many of the tasks required by traditional assessments (McAfee et al., 2004). For assessment to be developmentally appropriate, each of these factors must be taken into consideration.

Characteristics of Development

Many of the characteristics of young children make it difficult to obtain trustworthy assessment information. Children's development is rapid, uneven, and embedded in specific cultural and linguistic contexts (Shepard, Kagan, & Wurtz, 1998). For example, 2½-year-old Brian barely said a word at child care, and then one day he got so excited about the new set of trucks that he couldn't stop talking. Four-year-old Wyatt spent all day showing off how he could balance on one foot, but when his aunt arrived to pick him up, he refused to demonstrate this newly acquired skill.

Young children's development and learning is marked by spurts and plateaus (McAfee et al., 2004). For months, 6-year-old Aura struggled during language arts period. Then in March, she seemed to have an "ah-ha" moment. She stopped guessing at words she didn't know and began really reading for the first time. At times, children's development may even go backward. Three-year-old Jacob seemed to have thoroughly mastered the potty until his baby sister was born, and then he started having accidents every day.

Children's progress is also uneven across different developmental areas. Five-year-old Claudio has the vocabulary of an 8-year-old and can read at the second-grade level, but he struggles to regulate his emotions and is aggressive when frustrated. If only Claudio's reading skills were assessed, we would have a skewed picture of his school performance.

Language development is also a work in progress during the first 8 years of life. Most types of assessment require that children understand directions, know particular vocabulary words, or be understood by an adult, perhaps even a relative stranger. Limited language skills can easily interfere with obtaining an accurate picture of children's competence. Accurate assessment of children who are learning two languages raises an additional set of concerns that are addressed later in this chapter.

Importance of Context

The context where an assessment takes place, either informal or formal, can affect children's performance. Context includes the physical setting, whether in the classroom, home, or on the playground, and the social setting: one on one, small group, or whole group. A familiar context can serve to make children comfortable and relaxed and more likely to perform naturally and do their best.

A strange or unfamiliar context, either in terms of the place or the people, can be distracting or even stressful. Consider Hugo, who is a relatively fearless 5-year-old. Because Hugo usually charges into new situations head first, his mother wasn't concerned about taking him to the community center for kindergarten readiness testing. But Hugo became so interested in seeing the other children and examining the lines on the floor of the basketball court that he didn't attend at all to the tasks the kindergarten teacher asked of him.

Performance assessment is one of the best ways for teachers to assess children's capabilities. Teachers can find out more by listening to a child read than by looking at a score on a standardized test.

Context influences not only children's attention to the assessment task, but also their actual performance. Young children behave differently at home than at family child care, the child care center, or school. Five-year-old Dolly goes to gymnastics with her dancer mom and can do backflips and cartwheels, but when her teacher at school asks her to skip, Dolly says, "I don't know how." Perhaps Dolly didn't demonstrate her advanced physical skills at school because she didn't want to be different from the other children, but maybe she just wasn't interested in skipping. Motivation, as well as context, is a big factor in obtaining accurate assessment of young children.

Influence of Motivation

Assessment is "an adult's agenda" in which young children have little interest (Hills, 1992). Children are most likely to be motivated in situations that appeal to their interests and cultivate their curiosity, that offer choices of activities and materials, and that provide active involvement with other people. Many formal assessment procedures do not allow for any of these conditions. Young children are not interested in being assessed. They may be removed from the usual activity setting, and their movement, talk, and expression of feelings may be restricted (Hills, 1992).

As children get older, they can reflect more on their performance and competence and can be encouraged to do their best in an assessment situation (Hills, 1992). For some children, demonstrating their competence will become intrinsically motivating. In general, however, assessment results will be more accurate if children's interests are taken into consideration. For example, second-grader Laticia loves stories about animals and reads these stories with more expression than other books.

A final developmental constraint on assessment is children's ability to perform the tasks required. Group-administered, paper-and-pencil tests are especially challenging for children before third grade (NAEYC & NAECS/SDE, 2003). They may not be able to follow the directions and may not understand why the teacher can't help today. Some children may not have the fine-motor skill to fill in the bubble carefully or may generally operate at a slower pace than the others or the test administrator.

Considerations for Developmentally Appropriate Assessment

Even a cursory discussion of typical child development characteristics leads to the conclusion that the younger the child, the more difficult it is to obtain accurate assessment data (Bredekamp & Shepard, 1998; Shepard et al., 1998). Therefore, assessment can be considered developmentally appropriate if, and only if:

- Assessment draws on multiple sources of evidence, especially observations by teachers and parents who can observe children's performance in various contexts over time.
- Assessment occurs in a variety of situations representing children's typical range of activities, in the regular classroom or at home.
- Children are made to feel comfortable, which means that they are assessed by familiar adults, or that parents or other known adults can stay with them.
- Assessment information is gathered frequently to accommodate children's rapid developmental changes. This doesn't mean that assessment consumes other important teaching and learning experiences, but rather that it is embedded in children's ongoing experiences.
- Assessment tasks are of interest to children and within their range of ability. For example, instead of requiring a child to circle the picture of four kittens, the item requires the child to count four toy plastic kittens, one for each of her friends.

Culturally and Linguistically Responsive Assessment

Developmentally appropriate assessment must be culturally and linguistically responsive (NAEYC, 2005g). One of the biggest challenges is serving the needs of dual language learners because, to some extent, all assessments of young children are fundamentally measures of language ability (Garcia, 2005). Children's ability to demonstrate their learning depends a great deal on their language capacity, both to understand the demands of the task and to respond either to a teacher's informal question or a written test. While the role of language in assessment is relevant for all children, it is of special concern for children whose home language is not English.

In many instances, the only way to get a fully accurate picture of children's learning is to assess them in their home language. But even if valid and reliable assessment tools were available in multiple languages, which they are not, such assessments are not a foolproof solution. All languages, including English, have dialects, so translations do not always solve the problem. A child from Mexico and one from Peru may not understand the same Spanish translation of a test.

Determining whether a child is sufficiently proficient in English for accurate testing is also difficult. Academic language used in schools is quite different from the conversational language children use on a daily basis. Linguists estimate that it takes 4 to 7 years to acquire proficiency in academic English (Garcia, 2005). A child may speak English well on the playground or in casual conversation, yet struggle with the language of an assessment. The importance of linguistically appropriate assessment is illustrated in the *Language Lens: Testing Dual Language Learners* feature.

Children's language and prior knowledge are closely tied to their culture, yet assessment materials do not take into account culturally influenced variations in knowledge and skills. For example, a language assessment may ask children to identify items that are unique to U.S. culture, such as a hamburger. Inclusion of many such culturally biased items in a measure biases the outcome for individual children and misrepresents their abilities.

Language Lens

Testing Dual Language Learners

Accurate assessment of English language learners poses difficult challenges for teachers and educational leaders. High-stakes standardized testing is particularly problematic, as the following example demonstrates.

In 2007, as part of No Child Left Behind accountability testing, the U.S. Department of Education required that immigrant children who had been in the country at least 1 year had to be tested in reading and mathematics in third grade using tests written in English. The government threatened to withhold federal funding from Fairfax County, Virginia, because the county was giving children with limited English proficiency tests of their knowledge of English rather than the more difficult subject matter tests.

Fairfax County educators argued strongly against subjecting young children, who are adjusting to a new country, language, and culture, to tests that they would inevitably fail. Fairfax County second-grade teacher Carole Puckett provided the following examples of items on Virginia's third-grade test to demonstrate the challenge of accurately assessing the competence of English language learners.

- You can't ______ that heavy turnip on the ______ scale because it would break it! Which pair of words makes the sentence correct?
  a. way, knew
  b. weigh, knew
  c. way, new
  d. weigh, new
- Wouldn't it be wonderful to live in a caboose? Which of these is another way to write "wouldn't"?
  a. Will not
  b. Would not
  c. Will never
  d. Would never

Puckett asks:

> Does anyone actually believe these are appropriate questions to gauge whether an 8-year-old has mastered the English language in 13 months? Why is it important for an 8-year-old to understand the words "turnip" and "caboose"? And who would ever say, "Would not it be wonderful to live in a caboose?" As a teacher, we are the ones teaching English. We are the ones teaching math and science and social studies to non-English speakers. And the students are learning it. Don't diminish our efforts with inappropriate, poorly designed tests.

Advocates for dual language learners, like those in Fairfax, were successful in convincing the U.S. Department of Education to reexamine its requirements for testing dual language learners, although challenges continue. Nevertheless, this example is a powerful reminder of the importance of using linguistically appropriate assessment tools, and the risks of high-stakes testing.

Source: Excerpts from Carole Puckett, "Counties Know Best How to Test" March 11, 2007, *The Washington Post*. Reprinted with permission of Carole Puckett.

Children's learning is a product of their experiences, which occur in cultural contexts. For example, a standardized test asks where to find a lion, and 4-year-old Omari replies, "In the park." His answer, accurate in his native Kenya, is marked incorrect because the correct answer in the test manual is "in the zoo." Such cultural influences exist within the United States as well. Consider a test item that asks children to point to a picture of a *swamp*. Imagine the blank stares of children living in New York City or rural Nebraska when presented with such a request compared to the nodding heads of those from parts of Florida or Louisiana.

Individually Appropriate Assessment for Children with Special Needs

Young children with disabilities or special needs face a lifetime of being assessed. Federal laws govern how, when, and under what conditions children with disabilities are to be assessed and how assessment information should be used by teachers in implementing individualized education plans and individualized family service plans. Ensuring that assessments are *individually appropriate* for all children may require accommodations or modifications to the tools or procedures used.

Accommodations are changes in assessment procedures, materials, or setting to eliminate barriers related to the child's disability that might keep children from demonstrating their full capabilities (Neisworth & Bagnato, 2005). A child with a physical disability might be allowed to answer questions verbally rather than in writing. A child with attention deficit/hyperactivity disorder (ADHD) might be given more time or allowed to take a test in a separate place away from distractions.

Modifications are changes in the assessment that alter what the assessment measures or what the results mean (McAfee et al., 2004). For example, rather than asking Jade, a child with special needs, to point to pictures of objects to measure her receptive vocabulary, her teacher talks with Jade as she plays with real toys and makes notes of which ones Jade names correctly.

The process of identifying children for special education services is an example of a high-stakes decision that requires the use of many different sources of information, including standardized, norm-referenced tests. Even with these various sources, however, the wide use of standardized tests with children who have special needs is fraught with problems (Neisworth & Bagnato, 2005). Because standardized tests are based on norms of typically developing children, the results are often not relevant or useful to the goals for a child who has a disability. Moreover, considerations needed to make assessment developmentally appropriate are even more important for children with special needs, such as ensuring their comfort and engaging their interest.

Early childhood special educators strongly advocate a play-based approach to assessment that focuses on children's **functional skills**, the essential abilities needed to fulfill goals parents have for their children such as communicating, making friends, and learning self-help skills (Bagnato & Neisworth, 2005). As described earlier in this chapter, play-based assessment involves systematic observation of children's behavior and skills in the context of their play. The feature titled *Including All Children: Individually Appropriate Assessment Practices* discusses assessment practices for children with special needs.

In this section, we described indicators of effective assessment. Next, we turn to a discussion of the various purposes of assessment.

accommodations Changes in assessment procedures, materials, or setting to eliminate barriers related to the child's disability that might keep children from demonstrating their full capabilities.

modifications Changes in an assessment that alter what the assessment measures or what the results mean.

functional skills The essential abilities needed to fulfill goals parents have for their children such as communicating, making friends, and learning self-help skills.

Purposes of Assessment: Why Assess?

Before engaging in any form of assessment, teachers need to ask, "What is the purpose of the assessment?" The answer to this question determines all aspects of how the assessment will be conducted including:

- Who is to be assessed
- What is to be measured and with what tool

Including All Children

Individually Appropriate Assessment Practices

Individually appropriate assessment of young children with special needs requires that professionals and family members work together and respectfully share useful information. In the following contrasting scenarios, we see how important individually appropriate assessment practices are for both children and their families:

> The O'Briens' 4-year-old son, Dan, has been diagnosed as developmentally delayed. During a conference with his teacher, Ms. Blako, about Dan's progress, Mrs. O'Brien becomes increasingly discouraged as she is told, once more, what her child cannot do and that he is functioning at the 24-month level on a norm-referenced test. Ms. Blako explains that they will continue to work with Dan on colors, writing his first name, and counting to 20. Mr. O'Brien is frustrated because these are the same skills Dan has been working on all year. Mrs. O'Brien is concerned that Dan still isn't potty trained and doesn't seem to have friends. Ms. Blako smiles and suggests some good books on toilet training. The O'Briens' leave feeling belittled, apprehensive, and concerned about Dan's remaining preschool year and pending transition to kindergarten.
>
> In contrast, consider the conference between Larisha's mother, Tina, and the preschool teacher, Stephanie. Larisha, who has cerebral palsy, attends an inclusive preschool. The meeting is attended not only by Tina and Stephanie, but also the physical therapist, speech-language pathologist, and psychologist, who all know Larisha and her family well. The purpose of the conference is to discuss what Larisha does well at home and at school and to set new goals for her. Stephanie shares the results of her observations of physical, language, social, and emotional skills that Larisha displayed during the last several months. Tina shares what she has observed Larisha doing at home. The team agrees that Larisha is showing impressive growth and they identify target skills to work on with her over the next few months:
>
> 1. Initiate play with peers, not just her cousins at home.
> 2. Watch, listen, and participate in small- and large-group times. Larisha can sit in a supportive chair to stabilize her trunk (rather than on the carpet).
> 3. Pedal and steer a tricycle. The physical therapist agrees to modify the trike so Larisha can reach the pedals and grasp the handles better.
> 4. Recognize when she needs to use the restroom, notify the teacher, and complete toileting activities independently. Stephanie will provide information for how to work on this at home as well.
>
> Tina says that her number one priority is for Larisha to have friends and the team agrees to make this their focus. Tina leaves the conference feeling heard, valued, and inspired about Larisha's progress and her future skill development.

The difference between these two assessment scenarios is profound. Dan's parents were passive recipients of information. Dan's assessment focused on traditional academics rather than his overall development. This led to underestimating his skills, as well as to setting goals that are of questionable value to his family.

In sharp contrast, Larisha's family is part of the team, providing valuable information about her development. Her teacher uses observational assessment, focusing on skills in all developmental domains—the skills that Larisha needs to function well in the classroom, on the playground, or at home. Both her teacher and mother can use the assessment information to identify goals for Larisha's further development.

- Who will conduct the assessment and when
- What technical requirements are needed for the assessment
- How the results will be interpreted and used.

In early childhood programs, the four basic purposes of assessment are (1) to inform teaching and promote learning, (2) to identify children with special learning or developmental needs, (3) to evaluate programs, and (4) to demonstrate accountability (National Research Council, 2008; Shepard et al., 1998). First, we discuss these purposes and then we give examples of informal and formal assessments related to them.

Assessing to Inform Teaching and Promote Learning

Effective teaching cannot occur without ongoing assessment. The first step in developmentally appropriate practice—*meeting the learner* or monitoring children's progress—

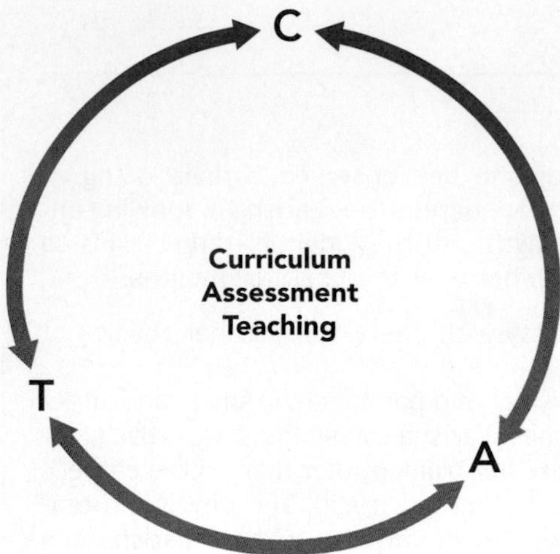

Figure 11.1 Relationship of Curriculum, Assessment, and Teaching

Source: Based on "The Relationship between Large-Scale and Classroom Assessment: Compatibility or Conflict?" by E. Asp, 1998, pp. 17–46, in *Assessing Student Learning: New Rules, New Realities*, edited by R. Brandt, Arlington, VA: Educational Research Service and Alliance for Curriculum Reform.

requires assessment. Consider the following examples of how teachers use the information they gather to make decisions about curriculum planning and teaching:

> In David Billings's preschool, a curriculum goal is for children to distinguish beginning and ending sounds in words. David first introduced these skills using poems and songs during whole-group time. But when he finds that a few children can't pick out the rhyming sounds, he plans to work with them in a small group, playing rhyming games and reading rhyming books.
>
> Margie Wasky regularly monitors whether her second graders comprehend what they read. She discovers a few children who read very fast but can't accurately answer questions about the passages they read. She has these children read aloud to each other in pairs, and finds that reading more slowly with expression to a partner improves their understanding of what they've read.

In these examples, we see that planning and adapting curriculum and teaching practices requires ongoing assessment. Although we address teaching, curriculum, and assessment in separate chapters in this book, in reality they are integrally connected. What happens in one area influences and is influenced by what happens in the others, as depicted in Figure 11.1.

Teachers are the primary assessors as well as the primary audiences for classroom assessment. In early childhood, much classroom assessment is informal and performance based, relying heavily on teacher observations. Because everyday decisions are not high stakes, and easily corrected if inaccurate, classroom assessment does not need to meet technical standards for reliability and validity (Bredekamp & Shepard, 1998). For instance, if participation in the small group doesn't help Jamal's rhyming, David begins working with him one-on-one and also gives his mother some ideas to try at home.

Nevertheless, teacher observations and judgments can be unreliable, invalid, or biased. This is why teachers need to draw on many sources of information. They should observe children in different situations over time, rather than base their conclusions about children's ability on one encounter. Intentional teaching depends on accurate classroom assessment tools, which we discuss later in this chapter.

Identifying Children with Special Learning or Developmental Needs

This purpose of assessment encompasses both routine checks for vision, hearing, and immunization to ensure healthy development, and identification of physical, cognitive, or emotional disabilities. Regular health checks by physicians beginning at birth may also uncover possible disabilities or special needs. Vision and hearing problems, if undetected, can have long-term consequences for children's learning, so early health screenings are essential for every child.

Because the benefits of early intervention are well established, professionals have an ethical as well as legal responsibility to accurately identify young children with special needs and help them access appropriate services (DEC, 2007; Sandall, Hemmeter, Smith, & McLean, 2005). These decisions have lasting consequences for individual children; therefore, the instruments used need to meet high standards of reliability and validity (J. Jones, 2004). Assessment for identification of special needs is conducted in two stages: screening and diagnosis.

MyEducationLab

Go to the Assignments and Activities section of Topic 4: Observation/Assessment in the MyEducationLab for your course and complete the activity entitled *Hearing and Vision Screening*. How do the screeing procedures used in the program demonstrate effective, developmentally appropriate assessment practices for young children?

Screening

The first stage is screening (Meisels & Atkins-Burnett, 2005). Teachers or other professionals administer these brief tests, which include general items on motor development, perception, language, and cognitive development. A screening test is like the toy screen used in a sandbox; most of the grains of sand will pass through readily, but a few will be left for closer inspection.

In many preschools and child care programs, screening is a well-established rite of fall.

The process is not foolproof, and some children may have problems that go undetected. Therefore, teachers play a critical role in contributing information to the screening and identification process. As teachers assess children's progress on a daily basis, they may obtain information that raises concerns that formal screening may confirm or deny. Those few children who do not pass the initial screening may or may not have a more serious condition; to make this determination, diagnostic testing is required (McAfee & Leong, 2007).

One of the most important purposes of assessment is screening and identification of children with special needs. To ensure accurate identification, valid and reliable measures must be used along with information from parents and teachers.

Diagnostic Testing

The second stage is a complete diagnostic evaluation that is designed to not only identify the child's areas of need and strength, but also to prepare an individualized intervention plan. Multiple sources of information such as teacher and parent observations, medical evaluations, and standardized tests are used. Diagnostic tests require specialized training to administer and interpret and, therefore, are given by special educators, school psychologists, speech pathologists, or therapists.

For the first two purposes of assessment—to support learning and to identify children with special needs—the target of assessment is the individual child. Next we turn to assessment purposes for which information is gathered on groups of children.

Evaluating Program Quality

Program evaluation is the process of gathering information about the quality of the classroom and its effects to determine if the program is achieving its goals and objectives. Some types of program evaluation, like licensing or accreditation, may not require information about children's performance. Increasingly, however, program evaluation includes data on child outcomes—how well the group of children as a whole is achieving the goals of the program. The results of assessment for program evaluation are usually *aggregated*, that is, they are combined and reported as total scores for the group rather than scores attached to individual children.

The audience for program evaluation data is usually policy makers or funders who want to know if a program represents a cost-effective use of public or private dollars. Although stakeholders need accurate program evaluation data for future decision making, the stakes for such assessment are not as high as for accountability assessment.

Assessing for Accountability

Closely related to program evaluation, assessment for accountability is, by definition, high-stakes testing. **Accountability** is "holding teachers, schools, or programs responsible for meeting a required level of performance" (McAfee et al., 2004, p. 8). Accountability requirements often specify what children should know and be able to do, based on state learning standards. The audiences for accountability data include federal, state, and local policy makers, parents, and the general tax-paying public.

As we discussed earlier in this chapter, the stakes attached to accountability testing are high. By the same token, holding schools accountable can lead to more attention being focused on the children who need it and improvements in teaching and learning (Au, 2007). The standards for accuracy of accountability testing must be extremely rigorous because scores are attached to individuals—children and teachers—rather than an aggregate group or program (Bredekamp & Shepard, 1998).

program evaluation The process of gathering information about a program's quality and effectiveness.

accountability The process of holding teachers, schools, or programs responsible for meeting a required level of performance.

Table 11.2 Matching Purpose and Types of Assessment

Purpose	Types of Assessment	
	Formal	*Informal*
To monitor children's progress and make decisions about teaching and learning	Published, validated observation tools and rating scales; criterion-referenced achievement tests	Observation; interviews, analysis of work samples; teacher-made tests and procedures
To identify children who may have special needs	Developmental screening tests to be followed by diagnostic evaluation for those identified; norm-referenced standardized tests with high reliability and validity	Structured observation of behavior and performance by teachers; information from parents
Program evaluation	Validated observational measures of classroom quality and teacher–child interactions; criterion-referenced tests for samples of children keyed to program goals	Surveys of children, teachers, and parents; data collected by teachers from informal classroom assessments including observations, performance assessments, and portfolios
Accountability	Criterion-referenced standardized achievement tests	Data collected by teachers from informal classroom assessments including observations, performance assessments, and portfolios

Source: Adapted from "Reaching Potentials through Appropriate Assessment," by T. W. Hills, 1992, pp. 43–63, in *Reaching Potentials: Appropriate Curriculum and Assessment for Young Children, Vol. 1*, edited by S. Bredekamp and T. Rosegrant, Washington, DC: NAEYC. Reprinted with permission from the National Association for the Education of Young Children.

Connecting Purposes and Types of Assessment

As we have seen, each of the four purposes of assessment demands various types of tools and procedures. Given that all effective assessment decisions require multiple sources of information, teachers need to know which kinds of assessment are most effective for which purposes. Table 11.2 provides examples of formal and informal assessment tools appropriate for each of the four purposes.

With increased demands for demonstrating program effectiveness and accountability, teachers must be knowledgeable consumers of assessment information. It is usually the classroom teacher who must explain the results of testing to parents or children, and teachers themselves most often feel the pressure of testing and assessment. Nevertheless, teachers' most important use of assessment is to improve learning outcomes for children, as discussed next.

Assessment to Improve Teaching and Learning

Like every other aspect of intentional teaching, assessment engages teachers in professional decision making. They must decide what evidence is important to collect, as well as how and when to gather information. The process of gathering evidence of children's learning is also called *documenting*, and involves two kinds of decisions: (1) how to gather information about children and (2) how to record the findings (McAfee et al., 2004). Thinking of these processes separately opens up more options for assessment, or more "windows" into children's learning (McAfee & Leong, 2007). Observation, for instance, is the most frequently used method of gathering information. However, there are many ways of recording findings from observation—among them, *anecdotal records*, *checklists*, or *rating scales*—that increase teachers' options for learning about children.

In the sections that follow, we describe ways teachers can collect information about children and then we describe various ways to record or document the information for later analysis. In addition, we present advantages and limitations of each method.

Observing and Gathering Evidence

The most effective classroom assessment procedures need to be part of every teacher's repertoire. These include systematic observation, eliciting responses from children, collecting work products, and gathering information from family members and other adults (McAfee & Leong, 2007). We begin with observation, which is the foundation of effective, developmentally appropriate practice.

Observing Children's Behavior and Performance

Keen observation skills are the most important assessment tool a teacher can develop and use. This is especially true when working with infants, toddlers, and young preschoolers who have limited ability to create products and communicate verbally. During preschool, kindergarten, and the primary grades, teachers continue to regularly observe children's interests, interactions, and performance of tasks to assess their skills and understanding as part of an overall assessment plan (NAEYC, 2005a).

Accurate, objective observation can be quite difficult. Consider the fact that eyewitness accounts of events tend to vary considerably. Likewise, even everyday experiences may be described differently by different participants. For instance, a teenager's view of a holiday gathering she didn't want to attend would be quite different from her grandmother's, who savored seeing the whole family together. Similarly, if two teachers observe the same preschooler's boisterous behavior, one might see happiness, whereas the other sees rowdiness.

> **Effective Teaching**
> Intentional, effective teaching begins with observing and getting to know each child.

Systematic Observation. Systematic observation means that teachers focus their attention on individual children or groups, watch what children do as they work and play together, and listen carefully as they speak. At times, teachers stand back and observe children as they engage in the ongoing life of the classroom or on the playground. Who does Marcus play with and for how long? Does he play alone or with a friend? At other times, teachers arrange specific tasks or activities and observe children's performance. First grade teacher Ms. Victor adds frequently used words to the "word wall" each week and observes which children refer to them as they are writing.

Observation is most effective if teachers think in advance about what they want to observe while remaining flexible to observe events as they proceed. Janice planned to observe the babies in her care during feeding time to see how their fine-motor skills were developing. She observed that two of the 13-month-olds, Josie and Ana, could pick up the cereal on the highchair tray. However, 15-month-old Tania became frustrated and started to cry. Janice watched to see whether and how soon Tania would calm herself before she had to intervene. In this case, an observation of fine-motor skill turned into an observation of emotional self-regulation, an example of the kind of shift that occurs constantly in early childhood programs.

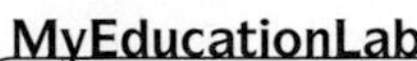

Go to the Assignments and Activities section of Topic 4: Observation/ Assessment in the MyEducationLab for your course and complete the activity entitled *Observing Children in Authentic Contests.* How does this teacher effectively use systematic observation to assess children's development and learning, and adapt her teaching?

Advantages and Disadvantages of Observation. Observation has the distinct advantage of being a truly authentic assessment. Teachers can observe without interfering with the ongoing activities in the classroom. They can see children's performance in a relevant context, whether during play, routines, collaborative projects, or outdoors.

Observation is not effective for all assessment purposes, however. Although it is the best way to obtain information about children's behavior, their thinking or problem solving cannot be directly observed. In addition, systematically observing an individual or small group of children is time consuming and can distract teachers from interacting with children.

The biggest risk of observation is that personal bias cannot be eliminated. The eye of the beholder will always influence not only what is seen, but how it is interpreted. As you think about becoming an intentional, effective observer, remember that individual and cultural differences can influence teachers' perceptions.

Eliciting Responses from Children

Aspects of children's learning and development that cannot be directly observed, such as their conceptual understanding or reasoning, can be elicited from children through questioning, conversation, or other informal teacher–child interactions. Eliciting children's responses—drawing out their ideas or reflections—is an efficient way of gathering information; this way, teachers do not have to wait for behaviors or responses to occur spontaneously (McAfee et al., 2004).

Interviews, Conferences, and Discussions. Teachers can have interviews and conferences to elicit children's ideas, problem-solving strategies, and feelings (McAfee & Leong, 2007). **Interviews** usually involve the teacher asking predetermined questions that are designed to reveal what children understand. For example, rather than asking a closed question such as "How many is 9 + 5?" the teacher might ask, "How would you figure out what 9 + 5 is?" Such an open-ended question is valuable because it requires an extended response that reveals more about children's thinking and understanding. (For another example, read Chapter 4's *Becoming an Intentional Teacher* feature on page 112.)

Conferences engage children in reflecting on their own work. Second-grade teacher Ernestine Cunningham holds regular writing conferences with her students to discuss the child's writing samples and identify ways to edit or improve them.

Small-group discussions provide opportunities to elicit children's thinking in collaboration with other children. At the end of each science unit, rather than giving a multiple-choice test to see what facts children remember, third-grade teacher Devon Kerns meets with small groups of children and asks them to discuss the phenomenon they have been studying. During one such discussion, Devon begins this way: "We've been learning about sinking and floating. So why don't giant ships weighing several tons sink?" The children's responses reveal varying degrees of understanding of the concept of displacement. Barry stays silent until the end when he admits, "I think there's something magic going on."

interviews Teacher–created, predetermined questions that are designed to reveal what children understand.

Advantages and Disadvantages of Eliciting Responses. The various ways of eliciting responses from children offer several advantages for teachers. They save time while providing insight into complex learning that cannot be directly observed. Interviewing or conferencing also engages children in thinking and reflecting about their own learning, which are important metacognitive processes that contribute to further development.

Like other assessment procedures, eliciting responses has limitations. When children do not respond, teachers should not automatically assume that they don't know the answer. The wording of the question may influence the child's response, or the child may be inhibited because of certain cultural factors or emotional factors such as lack of self-confidence (McAfee & Leong, 2007).

Observing children's behavior is important, but it doesn't reveal what children are thinking. To find out more, intentional teachers interview individuals or conference with small groups of children.

Collecting Work Products

Much of children's work and play produces a product such as a drawing, a painting, a construction in a particular medium, a piece of writing, a dramatic performance, and speaking in a group. These products, if systematically collected over time, provide evidence of changes in children's development and learning. Examples of in-

dividual work might be one child's journal or an art project. Teachers may also collect or evaluate the work of a group, such as a mural, or a compilation of children's observations from a field trip, such as a PowerPoint presentation with digital photos.

Collecting samples of children's work has several advantages. Teachers can use the evidence gathered over time to evaluate children's progress. By collecting writing samples at regular intervals, for instance, a teacher can not only document a child's progress, but also analyze where help is needed.

Tangible products are also excellent ways to demonstrate children's learning progress to parents and to children themselves. Although products are relatively easy to collect, such collection creates additional challenges for teachers. They may not be sure which products to keep, how many to save, and how to evaluate them. Portfolio assessment, which is discussed later in the chapter, is one strategy for systematically collecting and analyzing children's work samples.

Gathering Information from Family Members

Parents are often thought of as the audience for assessment information, passively receiving report cards or listening attentively during parent–teacher conferences. However, teachers must not only *give* information *to* parents, they must *get* information *from* parents as well. Parents can provide insights about children's behavior and capabilities outside the school or child care center. They can also serve as key informants about children's culture and language. Family involvement is so necessary to valid assessment of children with disabilities and special needs that it is legally required (Sandall et al., 2005).

Effective assessment systems—those that provide valid, reliable, and useful information for decision making—use all the ways of gathering evidence discussed in previous sections. Intentional teachers regularly gather evidence and then use it to inform their teaching decisions about individual children. In the feature box titled *Becoming an Intentional Teacher: Using Assessment to Inform Teaching*, we see this process in action for one teacher.

Recording What Children Know and Can Do

Observation, eliciting children's responses, collecting work samples, and other authentic assessment procedures are generally informal and, therefore, not subject to the technical requirements of standardized testing. Nevertheless, for informal assessment results to be accurate and useful, they need to be as objective and nonbiased as possible. Various methods of documenting assessment are designed to increase the likelihood of gathering reliable and valid information. We turn now to a description of the most commonly used methods of documentation. These methods include descriptive records, frequency counts, checklists, rating scales and rubrics, and portfolios. Technology, such as hand-held devices and laptops, is now available to facilitate data collection for these methods.

Using Descriptive Records

Narratives are stories in which the narrator stands outside the experience and describes the people, situation, and events that occur. The same is true of narrative approaches to observation. **Narrative records** are teachers' attempts to record detailed descriptions of children in a situation or event that is the focus of the observation (Hills, 1992; McAfee et al., 2004). It is important for narrative records to focus on the observed behavior rather than implying judgment. "Kery kicked over Stan's building, threw the sand toys on the floor, and pushed Mimi down" is much more informative and useful later than "Kery was disruptive at school today."

Narrative records should include (Day, 2004):

1. Date and time of observation
2. The names of children involved
3. The location of the incident, such as lunch table, hallway, or library area
4. What the children said and exactly what they did.

narrative records
Teachers' attempts to record detailed descriptions of children in a situation or event that is the focus of the observation.

Becoming an Intentional Teacher

Using Assessment to Inform Teaching

Here's What Happened Marcus, 3½ years old, is a gentle, cooperative boy, but he is very quiet. Thinking about him recently, I realized I wasn't sure what accounted for his speech delay. Because hearing tests are done when children enter the program, I was able to rule out hearing loss. I made a point of watching Marcus with other children, with his mother or grandmother when they picked him up, and when we were doing things that really interested him. I also talked with Marcus's family about how he is at home—does he talk much there? They told me he didn't have a whole lot to say, but that he seemed to understand them. In my discussion, I also learned that his older sister Tessa is a big talker. I wondered if she might be doing the talking for him.

I decided to read a book with Marcus every day so I could build a closer relationship that might allow me to get a better sense of his language abilities. As we enjoyed a story together, I prompted him to show me where things were on the page, "It says, 'The worm has a long skinny car.' Can you find that one?" He did pretty well with such questions, although there were some words that drew a blank, especially when he didn't hear them in context.

Here's What I Was Thinking Before I can take action to help a child, I need to know as much as possible about the child's skills, abilities, and needs. That's where assessment comes in. Maybe Marcus was just quiet but understood most of what he was hearing, in which case I should focus not so much on his language development as on helping him become more comfortable expressing himself. Or maybe he was behind in language and vocabulary development, so I should work on that. Observing him in different situations was the key. In reading with him, I could find out more about his receptive vocabulary—the words he understands even though I don't hear him using them.

From my observations and conversations with Marcus's family, I now have a working hypothesis. It seems likely that not participating in conversation very much (maybe because of his chatty sister) has somewhat limited Marcus's vocabulary growth and linguistic competence. To help Marcus with both of these issues, I will set up situations to encourage his ease when talking with others. I will also plan some activities that work directly on his vocabulary.

Here are some types of narrative records:

- A *diary description* is a chronological record of an individual child's behavior that helps teachers better understand that behavior. (Hills, 1992). The diary format allows the teacher to compare and analyze a child's behavior and development over time. Ms. Dollan worries about Jennifer's shyness and is concerned that it is interfering with her ability to become involved and learn in kindergarten. She keeps a diary for 1 week, noting as many of Jennifer's social interactions as she can observe. At the end of the week, Ms. Dollan is surprised to find that Jennifer engages much more than she thought; Jennifer just tends to wait and observe before she gets involved.
- **Anecdotal records** are short descriptions of incidents, or anecdotes, involving one or more children (McAfee et al., 2004). "Monday 5/8—When I read *Hansel and Gretel* to 5 children, Sam (a child with special needs) sat up front and counted the pebbles on the page. He kept his eyes glued to the story the entire 15 minutes. He frowned when the children were lost and smiled at the ending. He picked up the book on his own afterward." When his teacher, Joanne, reflects on her anecdotal record about Sam, she

anecdotal records Short descriptions of incidents, or anecdotes, involving one or more children written by teachers and based on observations.

realizes that previously she underestimated Sam's attention span. Sam's attention during whole group wanders, but she had never assessed it in the small-group context before. Joanne is looking forward to sharing this newly found strength with Sam's dad.

- *Videotapes, audiotapes*, and *digital photography* are tools for capturing ongoing streams of behavior or performances that are difficult to document in writing. Doreen videotaped a small group of 5-year-olds as they discussed how they would build a replica of the zoo's panda house in their classroom. When she played back the tape with the children, she discovered that the group really listened to each other's ideas, abandoned some, and agreed on others, which she later helped them implement.

Narrative records, like all methods, have advantages and disadvantages. The benefits of such detailed observations are that they are open-ended and flexible and can provide a wealth of information about children. Children can be assessed in the context of regular classroom routines and activities so their behavior is most natural and authentic. The primary disadvantage of narrative records, on the other hand, is that they are time consuming to both record and interpret. Technology, such as video and digital cameras, can help teachers collect evidence, but it doesn't completely circumvent the difficulties. Given the disadvantages, however, several other tools and methods are available that essentially count or tally what is observed.

Using Frequency Counts

In some cases, teachers need to know how often a behavior occurs, the *frequency*, and/or how long it lasts, the *duration*. For example, to intervene with a child who hits, teachers begin by keeping track of how often the negative behavior occurs. Then, once an intervention plan is in place, they can use a frequency count to evaluate its effectiveness.

Teachers can also use **frequency counts** to keep track of children's activities, as shown in Figure 11.2. The teacher simply makes a mark whenever a child participates in an activity. At the end of the week, she can see which children were involved in each kind of activity and plan ways to engage them in diverse experiences. For example, Chaka didn't choose

frequency counts Method used by teachers to keep track of how often a behavior occurs.

Week: October 25

Children:	Kiru	Chaka	Vicki	Seth
Learning Experience:				
Read books	I	~~IIII~~ I	II	0
Blocks	III	0	I	~~IIII~~
Dramatic play	0	~~IIII~~	IIII	0
Board games	~~IIII~~	0	I	III
Art center	I	III	~~IIII~~	I
Water play	III	I	II	IIII

Figure 11.2 Sample Frequency Count Chart

Source: From *Essentials for Child Development Associates Working with Young Children*, by C. B. Day, 2004, Washington, DC: Council for Professional Recognition. Reprinted with permission.

blocks or board games, which are useful for learning math, so the teacher might find ways to entice her to those areas or plan other mathematics activities for her.

Frequency counts serve a valuable but limited function. They are easy to use and help teachers quickly gather general information about children's participation and experience. However, they do not provide contextual information about what occurs before and after a specific behavior. For that evidence, teachers need to supplement frequency tallies with narrative records or checklists, addressed next.

Using Checklists

One of the most commonly used recording methods, **checklists** are practical and versatile tools for gathering assessment information about almost any aspect of children's behavior, skills, or attitudes (McAfee & Leong, 2007). They can be based on learning standards in literacy or mathematics, or on sequences of development such as physical development or social skills. Some checklists are designed by teachers while others are commercially published.

Some checklists only require marking "yes" or "no" as to whether a child engages in a behavior (such as "Follows two directions"). Other, more open-ended checklists require the teacher to make a judgment of the degree to which a child has mastered a skill. Teachers may make notes while observing children and then use those notes to complete the checklist at a later time. One of the strengths of checklists is that they focus teachers' observations; in effect, checklists tell teachers what to look for and which skills or standards are important. Checklists can provide data that can be analyzed and compared over time and also aggregated for a group of children. Their limitation is that no checklist can adequately capture the complexity of an individual child's competence.

Using Rating Scales and Rubrics

Rating scales and *rubrics* record teachers' judgments about how a child's performance compares to that of peers or to a predetermined standard (McAfee & Leong, 2007). Ratings should be based on sound assessment evidence collected over time. **Rating scales** require the assessor to evaluate an individual on a characteristic and then rank the individual's ability on a continuum from low to high frequency or quality (McAfee & Leong, 2007). For example, a frequency scale might rate whether a child performs a skill "usually," "sometimes," "seldom," or "never." A scale designed to rate quality might be "exceeds standard," "meets standard," or "making progress toward standard."

Rubrics are descriptive rating scales that include clear descriptions of each point on the scale or guidelines for making judgments about a rating (McAfee & Leong, 2007). Figure 11.3 shows a sample rubric for assessing a child's ability to make choices and plan, taken from the HighScope Child Observation Record.

Rating scales and rubrics are relatively quick and systematic ways of keeping track of children's progress, and they assist teachers by focusing their observations and evidence collections. Rubrics are more reliable than rating scales because the guidelines for rating are explicit, which helps teachers make more accurate judgments. Rating scales and rubrics also help teachers identify where children are in relation to program objectives, and help guide curriculum planning and teaching. Some commercially published authentic assessment tools that use rating scales and/or rubrics have been validated (i.e., they meet standards for reliability and validity).

Using Portfolios

Portfolios are systematic and organized collections of children's work and demonstrations of their progress relevant to the goals of the curriculum (Gullo, 2006). Portfolios have several benefits. They focus on how individual children change over time, rather than comparing children to each other. Teachers create portfolios to document how well children are learning the content of the curriculum. In addition, portfolios provide concrete and meaningful information about children's progress to share with parents, other teachers, administrators, specialists, and even the general public (Gullo, 2006).

checklists Practical and versatile tools for gathering assessment information about children's behavior, skills, or attitudes.

rating scales Method of recording teacher's judgments about how a child's performance compares to that of peers or to a predetermined standard.

rubrics Descriptive rating scales that detail the qualities related to each rank on the scale; includes clear descriptions of each point on the scale or guidelines for making judgments about a rating.

portfolios Systematic and organized collections of children's work and demonstrations of their progress relevant to the goals of the curriculum.

ITEM: INITIATIVE—MAKING CHOICES AND PLANS

LEVEL 1 • Child indicates a choice by pointing or some other action.
The child expresses choices, decisions, and plans through simple actions, such as pointing, going and getting an object, or just starting an activity with no prompt.

LEVEL 2 • Child expresses a choice in one or two words.
The child states a choice or plan by using a word or a short phrase. The child may state this plan in response to adult prompting, as long as the adult has asked an open-ended question ("What will you do in the art area?") rather than a yes–no question ("Do you want to color?").

LEVEL 3 • Child expresses a choice with a short sentence.
The child expresses a choice or plan in a short sentence, adding no details about how the plan will be carried out. If the child just identifies the play activity ("I'm going to play with the truck") without adding any more elements (such as the location or additional materials to be used), this is considered a level 3 plan. A plan that flits from place to place, such as "I'm going to the house area, and then to the art area, and then to the book area, and then...," should be scored at this level, because it includes no details about what the child will actually do.

LEVEL 4 • Child makes a plan with one or two details.
At this level, the child is able to add a bit more detail to a plan. This might include specifying a play location, a playmate, or the toys or materials to be used. If the child just says where he or she will play, this is not sufficient and should be scored as a 3 rather than a 4.

LEVEL 5 • Child makes a plan with three or more details.
The child makes complex plans and describes in some detail what will be used and how the plans will be accomplished. For a level 5 score, the child's plan must include a least three elements: for example, identifying the play activity and two materials to be used or naming the activity, the location, and two playmates.

Figure 11.3 Rubric of Child's Planning Skills
Source: From *Preschool Child Observation Record*, 2nd edition, 2003, Ypsilanti, MI: HighScope Educational Research Foundation. Reprinted with permission.

MyEducationLab

Go to the Assignments and Activities section of Topic 4: Observation/ Assessment in the MyEducationLab for your course and complete the activity entitled *Portfolio Exhibitions*. How do portfolios help teachers effectively assess children's learning and also involve children and their families in the assessment process?

The materials contained in a portfolio provide teachers and children with the opportunity to reflect together on children's progress. Most teachers involve children in selecting work to be included in a portfolio. This requires children to think about which of their products are worth keeping and evaluate the quality of their own performances.

Portfolio Contents. The contents of portfolios can vary, but they need to be consistent among children in a group. Generally, portfolios include dated samples of children's work representing at least the beginning, middle, and end of a school year. These samples should include teacher notes about context or children's verbal comments made about the work. A portfolio may also include anecdotal or other narrative records plus observational checklists related to curriculum goals. One widely used, validated portfolio assessment system that includes all these elements is the Work Sampling System, designed for children from preschool to grade 6 (Meisels, Jablon, Dichtelmiller, Dorfman, & Marsden, 2001).

Portfolios are a valuable alternative to standardized testing for evaluating children's learning. Parents can see authentic evidence of children's progress, and children themselves can feel proud of their accomplishments.

Advantages and Disadvantages of Portfolios. Despite the potential benefits of portfolios, portfolio assessment can be both time consuming, expensive, and ineffective if teachers are not adequately trained (Horton & Bowman, 2002). One solution to these challenges is the use of technology. Educational software companies have stepped in to provide electronic portfolios that can be used to create, preserve, and store children's work using digital technology (McAfee & Leong, 2007). With digital cameras and scanners as well as video and audio features, the possibilities for storing work samples and performances are almost endless. The long-term storage capabilities make it possible to continue to track children's progress across grades and to produce a permanent record of children's progress for their families.

MyEducationLab

Go to the Assignments and Activities section of Topic 4: Observation/ Assessment in the MyEducationLab for your course and complete the activity entitled *Assessment in Reggio Emilia.* As you watch the video, consider how documentation differs from other forms of assessment and how it is used to both promote and assess children's learning.

Using Documentation as Part of Dynamic Assessment

Earlier in this chapter, we defined documenting as the process of collecting and recording evidence about children's learning and development. The word *documentation* is often used to refer to the recorded evidence that is then analyzed and interpreted. However, the influence of the Reggio Emilia approach on early childhood practice (Edwards, Gandini, & Forman, 1998) created a new, expanded definition of documentation.

Characteristics that make documentation a unique assessment tool include the following (Helm & Beneke, 2003; Helm & Katz, 2001):

- It involves teachers intensely observing and recording, using all of the tools of technology and displaying children's processes of thinking and problem solving as they work together on projects.
- It captures the collaborative interaction that occurs among teachers and children. It depicts the process of learning, rather than any one product.
- It encourages children to revisit and remember their experiences as they examine the documentation, which extends and deepens their learning.
- Its displays draw parents into the life of the school through compelling, visual evidence of their children's competence.
- For teachers, it serves as research on children's thinking and learning processes that contributes to their professional development.
- It provides evidence of children's competencies, such as their ability to collaborate with other children, that cannot be measured on more formal tests.

To learn more about this powerful assessment process, read the *What Works: Assessing Children's Learning through Documentation* feature.

Interpreting and Using Evidence to Improve Teaching and Learning

So far we have described two major steps in classroom assessment: gathering evidence of children's development and learning and recording the findings. The next step is interpreting and using the evidence to plan curriculum or adapt teaching strategies.

Accurate interpretation and effective use of assessment evidence depend on how well teachers know what children should accomplish at developmental junctures and when those junctures occur. This means that every teacher needs to be familiar with the continuum of development and expected learning sequences relevant to the age range he or she teaches. Given the wide range of individual variation, in fact, early childhood teachers should be familiar with the full range of development from birth through age 8.

developmental continuum A predictable, but not rigid, sequence of typical accomplishments within age ranges that is used to plan curriculum; also an effective assessment tool used to focus teacher attention on what is important to assess—what children can do—and to identify goals for continued progress.

A **developmental continuum** is a predictable, but not rigid, sequence of typical accomplishments within age ranges that is used to plan curriculum. A developmental continuum is an effective assessment tool because it helps teachers to focus attention on what is important to assess—what children can do—and to identify goals for continued progress (Dodge, Colker, & Heroman, 2000; McAfee & Leong, 2007). When teachers are familiar with predictable sequences of learning and development, they can use these to assess where children are in the sequence and adjust their teaching to help them progress.

Learning standards set curriculum goals for what a child should know and be able to do. They also guide the development of assessments. Effective teachers interpret and use

What Works

Assessing Children's Learning through Documentation

One way teachers can assess children's learning is by documenting a project or activity through note-taking, photography, audiotaping, videotaping, and collecting samples of student work. Through the children's verbal expression, writing, drawing, and construction, researchers and teachers are able to see what the children understand and how they convey their ideas and knowledge. Here is an example from one Illinois school:

> In the course of a first-grade class's project on water, Ms. Fisher asked Mr. Vaughn from the city's Maintenance Department to give the children a tour of the town water tower and reservoir. Before their visit, Ms. Fisher involved the children in discussing what they wanted to know about how water is collected and how it moves from the reservoir to their faucets. Each child took responsibility for asking Mr. Vaughn certain questions. On their return, the children recorded what they had learned in their drawings, descriptions, and written language.

Kyle's drawing of the water tower is below along with his account of what he learned when he asked Mr. Vaughn why the tower is so tall. He wrote: "to hold the water and keep the pressure. The higher it is off the ground, the water comes out of your faucet faster."

Kyle–Ask Mr. Vaughn why the water tower is so tall.
Draw the water tower.

to hold the water
and keep the pressure.
The higher it is off the
ground, the water comes
out of your faucet faster.

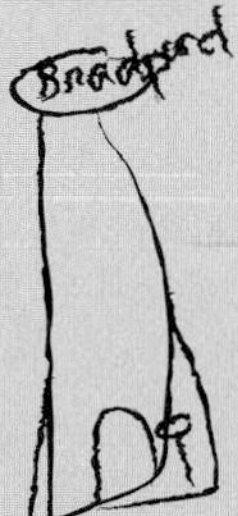

Kyle's Drawing

Source: Reprinted with permission of the Publisher. From Judy Harris Helm, Sallee Beneke, and Kathy Steinheimer, *Windows on Learning: Documenting Young Children's Work, 2e*, New York: Teachers College Press. Copyright © 2007 by Teachers College, Columbia University. All rights reserved.

Ashley–
Ask how water gets to school. Draw it.
57 Feet
B

Ashley's Drawing

Source: Reprinted with permission of the Publisher. From Judy Harris Helm, Sallee Beneke, and Kathy Steinheimer, *Windows on Learning: Documenting Young Children's Work, 2e*, New York: Teachers College Press. Copyright © 2007 by Teachers College, Columbia University. All rights reserved.

Ashley's drawing of how the water gets to the school shows the underground pipes connecting the water tower and the school.

Ms. Fisher asked the children questions and encouraged them to share through words and drawings their new knowledge and ideas about the water system and how it works. Kyle, Ashley, and the other first graders thought back to what they had seen and heard at the water facility, consulted their notes, and worked to represent their experiences and ideas accurately.

From carefully studying the children's work and tapes of their discussions, Ms. Fisher is able to see what misconceptions and areas of incomplete knowledge the children have regarding the dynamics of the water system, as well as in their writing, communication skills, and pictorial representation. This information guides her planning of what additional experiences and instruction to provide.

Yet another benefit of the documentation is that it can be publicly displayed. Seeing the visible evidence of the thought, intelligence, and passion the children bring to their work, families and communities gain appreciation for the children's capabilities and for the school's excellence.

Source: Adapted from *Windows on Learning: Documenting Young Children's Work*, 2nd edition, by Judy Harris Helm, Sallee Beneke, and Kathy Steinheimer, 2007, New York: Teachers College Press.

the assessment information they have gathered and recorded in relation to learning standards. For instance, Micah observes that at the midpoint of the year, most of the children in his Head Start class can recognize the first letter in their names and maybe one other letter. Is this good or bad? Unless Micah is familiar with early learning standards in the area of literacy, he can't make a judgment about whether his children are achieving at an acceptable rate. Similarly, four of the children in Micah's class do not speak in complete sentences. Because Micah is familiar with the developmental continuum of language, he realizes these children are significantly behind their peers in language. He adds book reading and additional one-on-one conversation time to his teaching plan, continues to observe and record their language, and seeks out the speech pathologist to consider systematic evaluations.

Effective assessment systems—those that provide valid, reliable, and useful information for decision making—gather evidence from many sources. An example of such a system designed for children from birth to 3½ years of age, a notoriously difficult age group to accurately access, is the Ounce Scale (Meisels, Marsden, Dombro, Weston, & Jewkes, 2003). The tool includes an Observation Record, an album for gathering the family's responses, and Developmental Profiles and Standards to use in completing the observation and analyzing the evidence.

The role of assessment in effective practice for children from birth to age 8 is now widely accepted (Dichtelmiller, 2004; Horton & Bowman, 2002). At the same time, educational policy and practice in elementary schools has become increasingly dominated by standardized testing, a controversial topic that is discussed next.

Standardized Testing of Young Children

Anyone who has attended school in the United States in the past half century is intimately familiar with the regular rituals of standardized testing. We have all taken some form of state-mandated achievement test at some time in our educational careers. Most of us took the SAT or ACT to get into college. In many states, passing standardized tests is required to become a certified teacher. Despite educators' concerns and increasing doubts expressed by the general public (Whoriskey, 2006), standardized testing is inescapable in today's political climate. Therefore, teachers must be more knowledgeable than ever about the content that will be tested, as well as the appropriate and inappropriate uses of standardized tests. Before addressing the controversies and concerns about standardized testing, it is important to recognize the benefits and well-intended purposes for using standardized tests.

Appropriate Uses of Standardized Testing

Standardized tests are not inherently good or evil. Although some published tests do not meet technical requirements for reliability and validity, many others are technically sound. As described earlier in this chapter, standardized tests have particular characteristics and specific purposes for which they have been developed. When used for these purposes, they can have **utility**, that is, they can be used to benefit children. The most positive uses of standardized tests are these: (1) to help identify and diagnose children with special needs, (2) to serve as a source of information for assessing children for instruction, and (3) to provide information for program evaluation and accountability. Tests are also used for research purposes.

Standardized testing has appropriate uses as long as the instruments are technically sound, used for the purposes for which they were designed, used to benefit children, and used in conjuction with other sources for decision making. Throughout your career as a teacher, you will face decisions about using standardized tests. Think about and discuss with your colleagues what you would do in the situation faced by the teacher in the *How Would*

utility Used to benefit children.

How Would You Respond?

Testing Early Literacy Skills

The Situation You have been told that your preschool program and others will be required to give children a certain test of early literacy skills. You know little about the test, except that it takes about 20 minutes to administer to each child and will be given in a quiet area outside of the classroom by program staff who will receive training. You have concerns about the value of the test and what the results will be used for.

What to Do? Various attitudes and actions are possible in this situation. Which do you think would be most useful and why?

- Accept that there is nothing you can do about the test requirement. Just teach the children the best you can and don't worry about how they perform on the test.
- Find out how the test results will be used. Is the test being given for evaluating the program, the teacher, or the child?
- Find out whether "high-stakes" decisions will be made about any of these—the child, teacher, or program—on the basis of the test.
- Consider other assessment information about children's literacy learning that you are gathering or could gather that could be used along with the results of this test, for example, work samples, observations, and questions you can ask when reading with a child.
- Oppose use of any standardized test with preschool children as developmentally inappropriate.

Can you suggest other strategies that might be useful in this situation?

You Respond? Testing Early Literacy Skills feature. Although there are appropriate uses for standardized testing, there are controversies and concerns that surround their use, which we discuss next.

Concerns about Standardized Testing

High-stakes accountability testing can have adverse consequences for teaching practices in primary grades that trickle down into kindergarten and preschool. Among the major concerns about standardized testing are potential for bias and negative effects on curriculum and teaching.

Bias in Standardized Testing

One of the biggest fallacies of standardized tests is that they are completely fair and objective (Horton & Bowman, 2002; Santos, 2004). Although objectivity is the intent behind standardization, that goal has not been reached. The only truly objective part of standardized tests is the scoring, often done by machine (FairTest, 2006b). The choice of test content, wording of items, and determination of the correct answer is decided by human beings who have their own subjective perspectives (FairTest, 2006). As a result, it is virtually impossible to develop a truly objective test, free of all cultural and other forms of bias.

Negative Effects on Curriculum and Teaching

The power of paper-and-pencil, multiple-choice tests to drive what happens in schools is well documented (Asp, 1998; Au, 2007). Although testing was a controversial issue before No Child Left Behind, since it went into effect, schools report narrowing of the curriculum to put more focus on the subject matter that is being tested, especially reading and math. This means that other areas of the curriculum such as physical education, the arts, and even academic subjects such as social studies are sacrificed. Some schools have even taken away recess to allow more time for reading practice.

Another negative effect of standardized testing is on instruction itself. Because multiple-choice tests tend to measure basic skills and factual knowledge, instructional practices are adversely affected. Instead of using effective teaching practices that emphasize learning as a socially constructed process, direct instruction on the basic skills that will be tested takes precedence in many classrooms (Gullo, 2006).

Perhaps the biggest problem with large-scale standardized testing for accountability is that it often fails to achieve its well-intended purpose, which is to improve learning outcomes for individual children (Asp, 1998). Test scores become available after children have moved on from the classroom that is being evaluated. More importantly, the results of such tests are not useful for informing curriculum and teaching. A single score in no way describes the complexity of children's achievement, as the following example demonstrates.

A study that analyzed the results of children who failed the state fourth-grade reading test shows the ineffectiveness of large-scale testing in improving teaching (Valencia & Buly, 2004). The researchers wanted to understand why these children were experiencing reading difficulty. Among the students in their study, they identified six very different clusters of reading problems. For example, one group of children could read fast, but didn't understand what they read. Another group of children had good comprehension skills but slow decoding ability, which interfered with their comprehending what they read. In addition, the researchers found considerable variance among individual children that would call for different kinds of reading support. Some of the children failed the test by only one or two points. Fewer than 10% of the children were identified as "disabled" readers. These few children are what we picture when we hear that large numbers of children failed the state reading test.

As the researchers concluded, the standardized test score alone does not begin to describe the complexity and diversity of the reading difficulties children face. Neither is it useful in helping teachers address children's individual problems. While their conclusion could extend to other areas of the curriculum as well, it is particularly ironic, since improving reading achievement is the primary goal of so many accountability efforts.

Despite the challenges and controversies surrounding testing of young children, accurate assessment of young children's development and learning is an essential component of developmentally appropriate practice. Intentional teachers use the effective assessment strategies described in this chapter to meet children where they are in order to plan curriculum and adapt their teaching to help children achieve challenging goals.

Revisiting Ms. Buruss's Classroom

At the outset of this chapter, we met a Head Start teacher, Kate Buruss, whose years of teaching experience were marked by many changes in assessment requirements in the federally funded program. Kate's work demonstrates the positive power of formal as well as informal, performance-based assessment to improve teaching and learning outcomes for young children. The children in her classroom clearly benefit from Head Start's emphasis on screening and diagnosis of special needs—and vision, hearing, and health screening in general enable children to access essential services.

Kate uses assessment information to improve her teaching as well as the program as a whole. The families she works with are integrally involved and marvel at their own children's competence. In Kate's program, assessment meets the ultimate test—it benefits children and their families.

MyEducationLab

To assess your understanding of how to assess children's learning and development, go to the Book Specific Resources section in the MyEducationLab for your course, select *Effective Practices in Early Childhood Education,* Chapter 11 of the Study Plan, and then complete the multiple choice questions and activities.

Chapter Summary

- Assessment literacy is teachers' understanding and using the vocabulary of assessment and testing.
- Assessment is the ongoing process of gathering evidence of children's learning and development, and then organizing and interpreting that information in order to make informed decisions about instructional practice.
- Indicators of effective assessment include (1) using multiple sources of evidence; (2) using assessments only for the purpose for which they are reliable and valid; and (3) considering what is developmentally appropriate, culturally and linguistically responsive; and individually appropriate for all children, including children with special needs.
- Early childhood programs have four basic purposes for assessment: (1) to inform teaching and promote learning, (2) to identify children with special learning or developmental needs, (3) to evaluate programs, and (4) to demonstrate accountability.
- The most effective methods for collecting evidence to improve learning and development are observing children's behavior and performance, eliciting responses from children, collecting work products, and gathering information from family members.
- Accurate interpretation and effective use of assessment evidence depend on teachers' knowing what and when children should be accomplishing certain developmental tasks and learning skills.
- Benefits of standardized tests include these: (1) they help to identify and diagnose children with special needs, (2) they serve as a source of information for assessing children for instruction, and (3) they are one source of information for program evaluation and accountability.
- High-stakes accountability testing can have adverse consequences for teaching practices in primary grades that trickle down into kindergarten and preschool, including biased results and negative effects on curriculum and teaching.

key terms

accommodations
accountability
achievement tests
alternative assessments
anecdotal records
aptitude tests
assessment
authentic assessment
checklists
criterion-referenced tests
curriculum-embedded assessment
developmental continuum
diagnostic tests
dynamic assessment
evaluation
evidence
formal assessment
formative assessment
frequency counts
functional skills
high-stakes testing
informal assessment
interviews
modifications
narrative records
normal curve
norm-referenced tests
performance assessment
play-based assessment
portfolios
program evaluation
rating scales
readiness tests
reliability
rubrics
screening tests
standardized assessment
standardized testing
summative assessment
testing
utility
validity

readings & websites

Gullo, D. F. (2005). *Understanding assessment and evaluation in early childhood education* (2nd ed.). New York: Teachers College Press.

Jablon, J. R., Dombro, A. L., & Dichtelmiller, M. L. (2007). *The power of observation for birth through eight* (2nd ed.). Washington, DC: Teaching Strategies and NAEYC.

McAfee, O., & Leong, D. (2007). *Assessing and guiding young children's development and learning* (4th ed.). Boston: Pearson Allyn & Bacon.

National Association for the Education of Young Children (NAEYC)
Position statement on curriculum, assessment, and program evaluation.
www.naeyc.org/positionstatements/cape

National Center for Fair and Open Testing
www.fairtest.org/K-12

National Institute for Early Education Research (NIEER)
Information on most frequently used assessment tools for young children.
www.nieer.org/assessment

SERVE Center at the University of North Carolina Greensboro, Southeast Regional Educational Laboratory
http://serve.org/assessment

observe, reflect, decide

1. Interview a preschool teacher to get her or his views on assessment. Reflect on how what you learn compares to what we know about effective assessment practices in early childhood education. Decide how you think the center or school's assessment practices could be improved to more effectively serve children.
2. Observe in an infant/toddler classroom. Ask the teacher how he or she assesses and documents children's development. Reflect on the challenges of accurately assessing this age group.
3. Observe in a preschool or kindergarten classroom. Examine the displays of children's work. Do you see evidence of children's learning progress in the work displayed?
4. Interview a primary grade teacher about her or his experience with standardized testing. Ask if high-stakes testing has had an impact on her or his teaching and, if so, how. Consider both the advantages and disadvantages of testing for accountability.
5. Reflect on your own testing experiences as a student. What role do you think testing and assessment has played in your educational experience? What do you think about the accuracy of standardized tests and other forms of assessment in evaluating the competencies of learners? How might your experiences and opinions influence you as a teacher?

part four

Implementing an Effective Curriculum

12 Teaching Children to Communicate: Language, Literacy, and the Arts

Thinking Ahead

1. How do young children develop language from birth to age 8?
2. What are effective strategies teachers can use to promote children's language learning?
3. How do children acquire a second language?
4. What key early literacy skills predict later success in learning to read and write?
5. What curriculum and teaching strategies are effective in promoting children's early literacy skills?
6. What are the components of effective literacy instruction in the primary grades?
7. How do children learn to communicate through the visual arts, music, movement, and dance, and drama? What are effective strategies for engaging children in arts education?

Thurgood Marshall Early Learning Center is a public school, serving prekindergarten through second grade. In April, the whole school faculty plans to focus on art appreciation and communication. Each class takes a field trip to the local art museum. In preparation, the kindergarten teacher, Ms. Barker, displays posters of several paintings in the gallery. Each group of four children focuses on one painting, such as one depicting bright sunflowers by Vincent Van Gogh. Meeting with children in small groups, Ms. Barker stimulates their conversations with open-ended questions such as "What do you see in this painting? What do you think the artist was feeling/thinking?"

After their discussions, each group tries their hand at producing paintings on the same theme as the artist. Using their own attempts at spelling, children write about or dictate to the teacher descriptions of their paintings and how they compare to the original: "I painted yellow flowers, too, but mine are little," explains Elijah.

Before the visit, the teacher gives each child a postcard of the painting to focus their attention. At the gallery, the groups look carefully for their "own" painting and the teacher asks if they are surprised by anything about the paintings.

Bruce (upon encountering the Van Gogh): It looks rough!

Ms. Barker: How a painting feels is called texture. The painter used thick layers of paint.

Marion (pointing to his postcard): But here it looks smooth.

Ms. Barker reinforces the new word: That's true. The texture of the postcard isn't rough. It's smooth.

Tallulah: The sunflowers are so yellow. They almost hurt my eyes.

Ms. Barker: The color in the painting is brighter and more intense than on the postcard.

After the trip, children discuss and write about what they observed, and do more painting. Their paintings and the words they use to describe them are far more detailed than before their visit. Similar experiences occur in other classes, and the teachers set up an art gallery in the hallway. Children display their paintings next to the posters of the great artists' works that inspired them. In the first and second grades, the teachers read short biographies of some of the famous artists with the children and write summaries to display on the walls of their gallery. The first graders are surprised to learn that many famous artists painted outside. The teachers set up easels outside so children can paint the views from their school. Their vocabulary for colors expands as they try to mix new variations to match what they see, such as *lavender, chartreuse,* or *magenta*.

The art study lasts several weeks during which children increase their language and literacy skills. They sharpen their observation skills, learn descriptive vocabulary, and broaden their understanding of how art is used for communication and expression. ▲

MyEducationLab

Go to the Book Specific Resources in the MyEducationLab for your course and select Author Interviews in Chapter 12 to watch and listen to the video *Early Childhood Curriculum*. What does Sue Bredekamp say about importance of early childhood curriculum?

In this chapter, we address fundamental areas of the early childhood curriculum: language and literacy development. Speaking and understanding, reading and writing are the foundation of all other learning in school and essential for success in life.

Also in this chapter, we address the arts, a content area that, in contrast to literacy, is often seen as expendable. Today's emphasis on reading and test scores now drives the curriculum to a large extent. Some schools have eliminated the arts altogether, while others use them only as a reward for good behavior. This chapter views the arts as an essential means of communication for young children and demonstrates their connection to other areas of communication: language and reading. Although we focus on the integration of the arts, we also believe in art for art's sake, especially for young children for whom art experiences contribute to development in so many ways.

First, we address the all-important area of language development—how both first and second language develops and ways teachers can enhance children's language learning. Next, we discuss the foundations of literacy from birth through age 5, as well as the key components of reading instruction in the primary grades. We then turn to the creative arts, describing goals for early childhood art education and teaching strategies to enhance children's enjoyment and engagement in the arts.

Understanding Children's Language Development

After 3 months of separation, 4-year-old Liam is excited to see his Nana. He talks and talks as she tries to quiet him for bedtime. Finally, in exasperation, he says to her, "But I have so many words for you, and they never get tired."

Seeing their language skills blossom is one of the most delightful aspects of teaching young children. Perhaps the most important task of the first 5 years of life is development of language because it supports learning in so many other areas. Language is a very strong predictor of later success in learning to read and write (National Institute of Child Health and Human Development [NICHD], 2000; Snow, Burns, & Griffin, 1998). Likewise, children who are skilled communicators demonstrate better social competence and emotional self-regulation.

The Critical Importance of Language Development

Because children seem to learn language naturally, adults often assume that it is simply the product of maturation, like learning to walk. But it is not. Biology primes humans for language, but the language children speak is learned over many years through verbal interaction with adults and other children (Weitzman & Greenberg, 2002). By the time they reach preschool, children are experienced users of language. However, the language they use may differ from the language used in the school because children's speech is acquired in the context of their home and cultural and linguistic community.

Language learning is far from complete when children enter kindergarten or even finish elementary school. Human beings learn language throughout school and life. Undoubtedly, as a college student, you continually add new words to your vocabulary. As a teacher working with a diverse population of children and their families, your vocabulary will continue to expand.

receptive language The ability to understand what is being said.

expressive language The ability to communicate; use and knowledge of spoken language.

vocabulary A combination of receptive and expressive language; the number of words a person knows and uses when listening or speaking.

syntax Grammar and sentence structure.

Understanding Types of Language

There are basically two types of language: receptive and expressive. **Receptive language** is the ability to understand what is being said. **Expressive language** is the ability to communicate, their use and knowledge of spoken language. Receptive language skills—listening and understanding—develop earlier than the expressive abilities of speaking and communicating. At any point in time, children understand more words and more advanced sentence structures than they use.

Vocabulary

Vocabulary is a combination of receptive and expressive language, that is, the number of words a person knows and uses when listening or speaking (Snow et al., 1998). An important goal of all teaching is to increase both the quantity and quality of children's receptive and expressive vocabulary. It is not enough that children speak a lot. We must pay attention to the range of words they understand and use—the use of pronouns, prepositions, adverbs and adjectives, and other parts of speech (Snow et al., 1998).

Vocabulary words are the labels children use for concepts that they are learning, as well as for those they already know and understand. Consequently, the more limited the vocabulary, the more limited the child's understanding of the world is. A child who knows the words *mail*, *stamp*, *envelope*, *address*, *package*, and *delivery* has a more refined concept of the postal system than a child who refers to all of those concepts as *mail*.

Children's language development affects all areas of their learning as well as their social–emotional development. Intentional teachers use every opportunity to help children learn language.

Grammar

Another important element of language development is the complexity of sentence structure children use, referred to as **syntax** or grammar. As children become more skilled users of language, their syntax becomes more complex. For example, a toddler may say, "Me go" to indicate he wants to play outside. But a preschooler will use a more conventional sentence structure such as "I wanna go to the playground and climb the ladder swing."

A related learning goal is for children to begin to acquire **script language**—the typical ways that people communicate in different contexts or settings. For example, what the doctor says is different from what the grocery clerk says. Similarly, the way one talks at school is different from the way one talks at home or on the playground. Learning the language of school, what is called **academic discourse**, is important for school success, and it is not an automatic process. For example, if you have ever seen children "play school," you have seen how they rehearse the script that teachers use (and it is not always comfortable for adults to watch their behavior played back for them).

Working with Language Differences in Children

During the preschool years, language develops far more rapidly than at any other time, but there are enormous individual differences (Hart & Risley, 1999). Of particular concern is that differences in children's language abilities exist between socioeconomic groups at entrance to school (Bardige, 2005; West, Denton, & Germino-Hausken, 2000). These differences become greater over time and contribute to the persistent achievement gap in our country (Hirsch, 2003, 2007b; Neuman, 2006). Therefore, programs serving children from low-income families and children from diverse linguistic and cultural backgrounds must take on the challenge of accelerating children's language progress.

Effects of Early Language Experience

A classic study of early language acquisition found that socioeconomic background was a major factor affecting young children's language development (Hart & Risley, 1995). The researchers videotaped language interactions between parents of different income levels and their children from infancy to age 3. The study found that, over the course of a year, children of parents who were professionals were exposed to more than 11 million words. In contrast, children whose families were receiving public assistance were exposed to only 3 million words.

Researchers estimated that during the first 4 years of a child's life, an average child in a professional family would have accumulated experience with almost 50 million words, whereas an average child living in poverty would have been exposed to 13 million words (Hart & Risley, 1995). Consequently, children's vocabulary growth reflected their experience. By age 4, children from more affluent homes had vocabularies approximately three times as large as those of children living in poverty. It is important to note that in this study, economic advantage was the *only* factor related to language differences (Hart & Risley, 1995). Race/ethnicity, gender, or birth order of the child made no difference. The researchers also cautioned about negatively judging these parents who are coping with the many stresses of poverty:

> Particularly striking among the welfare parents was their resilience and persistence in the face of repeated defeats and humiliations, their joy in playing with their children, and their desire that their children do well in school. They could spend an hour on a bus holding a feverish child and wait longer than that in a public health clinic. But these parents did not talk to their children very much. (Hart & Risley, 1995, pp. 69–70)

To address this gap in children's language development, teachers must first understand how language typically develops. Teachers must also be aware that many types of disability affect communication; some individual children will need access to assistive technology—called *augmented communication devices* and/or sign language.

script language The typical ways that people communicate in different contexts or settings.

academic discourse The language of school, which is important for school success.

The Developmental Continuum of Language Acquisition

Language development follows a relatively predictable sequence, but there are individual differences that are well within the range of normal (Hart & Risley, 1999). In addition, as we saw in research cited earlier, if children have many opportunities to speak and be spoken to, they

are likely to develop richer, more complex language. Table 12.1 provides an overview of the typical progression of language development and how children of different ages communicate.

In the previous sections, we described the critically important role of early experience to language development and developmental expectations across the period from birth to age 8. Next, we describe what adults can do to help develop children's communication skills.

cooing Vocalizing vowel sounds.

babble Produce consonant/vowel sounds such as "ba ba."

telegraphic speech Combining words into two-word utterances.

Table 12.1 Developmental Continuum of Oral Language

Age of Child	Developmental Expectations
Birth to about 8 months	• Communicate through behaviors rather than words; signal distress by crying. Caregivers need to interpret babies' sounds and gestures. • Smile or vocalize if they want someone to pay attention or play. • Begin vocalizing vowel sounds called **cooing**. Soon after, begin to **babble**, producing consonant/vowel sounds such as "ba ba." • Continue to babble using all kinds of sounds and will play with sounds when alone. • Begin to understand familiar names like those of siblings or pets. • Laugh and appear to listen to conversations.
Between 8 and 18 months	• Become more purposeful in their communications. • Use facial expressions, gestures, and sounds to get their needs met. (If a bottle falls from a highchair tray, instead of just crying the 14-month-old may grunt and wave at the floor.) • Understand many more words than they can say. • Speak in long, babbled sentences that mirror the cadence of conventional speech. • Soon start to shake their head "no" and begin to use the word *me*. • Usually crack the language code and begin to use their first words between 12 and 18 months.
From 18 to 24 months	• Experience a burst in vocabulary and begin to combine words into two-word utterances called **telegraphic speech**. Like old-fashioned telegrams, they waste no words in communicating their message: "No bed."
Ages 2 to 3	• Progress from using two-word combinations (my truck) to three- and four-word sentences with words in the correct order more often (Where's my truck?). • Speaking vocabulary may reach 200 words. • Use adjectives and adverbs. (Give me my blue truck now.) • Most children's speech becomes more understandable. Constantly ask, "Wassat?" as they seem to want to name everything.
Ages 3 to 6	• Have a vocabulary of about 1,000 words. • Although some may still have difficulty, most are better able to articulate some of the more difficult sounds, like *s, th, z, r*, and *l*. • Can initiate and engage in more complex conversations. • Use 1,500 to 2,000 words as vocabulary expands rapidly during kindergarten. • Usually speak clearly and are lively conversation partners with adults and other children.
The primary grades	• Language development continues at a rapid pace. • During these years, children need a large vocabulary to learn to read and to comprehend what they read. Explicit teaching of vocabulary needs to be an instructional goal. • At the same time, the more children read, the more words they learn because the language of books is more elaborate than everyday conversation. Some researchers estimate that children need to learn 3,000 words a year throughout the elementary school years.

Sources: Based on *Bringing Words to Life: Robust Vocabulary Instruction*, by I. L. Beck, M. G. McKeown, and L. Kucan, 2002, New York: The Guilford Press; *Young Children and Picture Books*, 2nd edition, by M. R. Jalongo, 2004, Washington, DC: NAEYC; *Assessing and Guiding Young Children's Development and Learning,* 4th edition, by O. McAfee and D. Leong, 2007, Boston: Pearson, Allyn & Bacon; and *Learning Language and Loving It: A Guide to Promoting Children's Social, Language, and Literacy Development in Early Childhood Settings*, 2nd edition, by E. Weitzman and J. Greenberg, 2002, Toronto: The Hanen Centre.

Supporting Children's Language Development

Children learn language and expand their vocabulary from their interactions with more competent speakers. However, effective teaching strategies differ based on the age of the children. Next we discuss developmentally appropriate ways of promoting language in each age group.

Fostering Language Development with Babies and Toddlers

Depicting language development as a progression may imply that it happens automatically. Although children do learn to talk without formal instruction, adults play a critical role in supporting that process.

Talking to Babies and Toddlers

The role of conversational partner is especially important for teachers working with babies and toddlers because the first 3 years of life are prime time for developing language. Nevertheless, some teachers and parents of very young children persist in the view that there is no reason to talk to children who can't talk back. The opposite is true. From the earliest moments of life, babies are trying to communicate. Teachers need to talk as if the child can talk back and respond to almost any attempt to communicate.

Effective communication begins as babies pay attention and respond to the sound of **parentese** or *motherese*, the high-pitched tone of voice that adults and older children tend to use naturally with babies (Weitzman & Greenberg, 2002). When the child initiates, teachers need to respond enthusiastically and then wait for a response. They interpret what babies are trying to communicate and expand on the message with words.

parentese The high-pitched tone of voice adults and even children tend to use naturally with babies; also called *motherese*.

play-by-play language Language that describes what is happening during routines and social interactions with babies and toddlers; also called *running commentary*.

Teachers shouldn't pressure young children to talk. Communication needs to be meaningful; it should not test children with obvious questions such as "What are you doing?" or direct them with comments like "Put the car on the road" (Weitzman & Greenberg, 2002). Instead, the teacher might say, "Your car is going fast." If the comment sparks the child's interest, the child might respond, "Fast." Then it's the teacher's turn: "You're making the car go very fast."

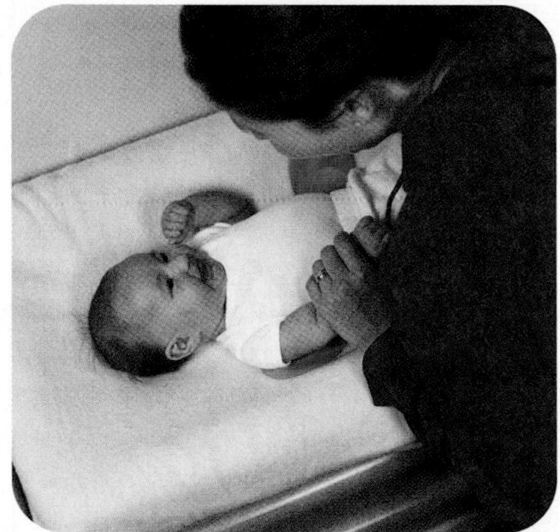

Infant/toddler teachers intentionally describe their actions for babies. This type of talk, called "play-by-play," is similar to what sportscasters do on television and helps babies learn the words for objects and experiences.

Describing Their Experiences

One of the most effective ways of building language in babies and toddlers is to use **play-by-play language** or *running commentary* during routines and social interactions with babies and toddlers. Think of watching a sporting event on TV. A play-by-play announcer describes the action even though you're seeing it before you. This sort of commentary connects actions and objects with words and familiarizes babies with the cadences of speech. Here's an example of play-by-play during a typical routine with the words tied to each action: "Let's change your diaper now. I need to pick you up. You're such a big boy. Let's lie down on the changing table. You can hold your horsie. We need to take off these wet pants" and on and on.

Finally, to promote language in babies and toddlers, two very important points must be kept in mind. First, children need a lot of opportunities to play with different kinds of toys, to touch real objects, and to move around. Think of the many different words a child could learn from playing in water, eating applesauce, climbing on a low ramp, rolling a ball, or looking at a cardboard book. Secondly, in each of these situations, teachers need to supply the words. While children play on a ramp, the teacher can introduce the words *slide, roll, climb, fast, shiny, push*, and many more.

As children's understanding and language use improves, teachers need to adapt their language by using longer, more complex comments and more sophisticated vocabulary. Many of these same strategies apply to promoting language with preschoolers, discussed next.

Promoting Preschoolers' Language and Vocabulary

Research demonstrates that several strategies are particularly effective in promoting preschooler's language acquisition (Dickinson, 2001b; Whitehurst et al., 1988). These strategies include modeling language, conversation, listening, decontextualized speech, and intentional teaching of new words.

Modeling Language and Complex Vocabulary

Teachers do a lot of talking and are important role models for children. Therefore, they need to use standard grammatical speech. They also need to recognize that many of the grammatical errors children make, such as *I goed to the store* or *three sheeps,* show their efforts to learn a language rule. As they learn the rule, like using *s* to indicate plural, they overgeneralize it. Instead of pointing out the mistake, a more effective approach is to pick up on what the child says and say it correctly. A child might say, "I gots two foots," to which the teacher replies, "Yes, you have two feet so you need two socks."

Similarly, if children speak a dialect or vernacular version of English, teachers should not correct or prohibit their speech. Doing so tells children that the speech of their family and their cultural group is inferior. This negative message may inhibit children's attempts to communicate. A more effective alternative is to help children see that there are different ways to say the same thing. For example, a child might say, "He ain't got no shoes." Rather than correcting the double negative, the teacher could say, "Yes. He doesn't have any shoes. He's barefoot."

Especially as children get older, the teacher should intentionally draw their attention to the fact that there are different ways to say the same thing. When children understand and use both the mainstream version of English and their home language or dialect, they are said to be able to **code switch**. Code switching is a well-developed skill in many bilingual individuals, and it contributes to their ability to think and analyze complex problems (Garcia, 2005). To learn more about this skill, read the *Culture Lens: Code Switching* feature.

MyEducationLab

Go to the Assignments and Activities section of Topic 2: Child Development/Theories in the MyEducationLab for your course and complete the activity entitled *Accommodating for Development Differences.* How does the teacher in this video model, encourage, and extend conversation to promote language development in a child whose language is delayed?

Using One-to-One Conversation

One of the most effective strategies for promoting children's language development is engaging them in one-to-one conversations (Dickinson & Tabors, 2001; Sylva, Melhuish, Sammons, Siraj-Blatchford, & Taggart, 2004). When children are served in groups, the task of supporting each child's language acquisition and understanding what they are trying to say can be daunting. Too often, the children whose language is most advanced are spoken to more often. This leads to a vicious cycle where those children who are lagging behind get less language interaction than they need, while those who need less actually get more (Bredekamp, 2002).

Extending Conversation

One of the best ways to build children's vocabulary is to increase the amount of talk in the classroom and to intentionally extend conversations. **Extended discourse** occurs when adults talk with children in ways that build on and expand what the children say. (Dickinson & Tabors, 2001). Researcher David Dickinson encourages teachers to "strive for five," that is, five back-and-forth exchanges during a conversation with a child. In

code switch The ability to understand and use both the mainstream version of English and the home dialect or language.

extended discourse Talking with children in ways that build on and expand what they say.

Culture Lens

Code Switching

Growing up in 1950s Harlem, young Dana finds herself as one of the few African American children selected to integrate a white school. Soon her teacher singles her out for her "improper speech." Trying to fit in and learn the language of the school, Dana struggles to convince her neighborhood friends that she is still the same person. This true story is related in *Don't Say Ain't* (Smalls & Bootman, 2003), a children's book about how one young girl learns to survive and succeed in two different worlds.

Dana's story and similar books can help children learn the concept of *code switching*, the ability to understand and use both the mainstream version of English and the home dialect or language. The goal is for children to develop the capacity to use both languages, switching between the two as the situation requires.

When it comes to children who are from ethnically distinct language communities, such as Spanish-, Amharic-, or Farsi-speaking communities, the discussions can be heated, but are fairly straightforward. However, the debate becomes emotionally charged with regard to African American children because of controversy about the language of the black community, whether it is called *ebonics* or *black English*. Some believe it is a dialect or broken form of English; others argue that because the verb forms (such as past tense or the verb *to be*) are West African in origin, the language is really more like a second language when compared to English. Putting aside value judgments about the language, in either case, principles from second language learning can be applied to promote the development of language and literacy among African American children.

Using literature is one innovative approach to help speakers of black English become proficient in mainstream English and be able to switch back and forth between the two languages when necessary. For example, many years ago the Chicago school system developed a reading series where two sets of books were used. One primer related a story in "everyday talk," while the other told the same story in "school talk." Consider the following examples from the book entitled *I Am Scared When . . .*

Written in everyday talk: I be scared when I get shots. I be scared of the doctor. He give you shots. I don't like no shot. Shots hurt. I be crying. My baby be yelling.

Written in school talk: I am scared when I get shots. I am scared of the doctor. He gives you shots. I don't like shots. Shots hurt. I cry. My baby yells.

Another example of code switching can be found in *Flossie and the Fox* (McKissick & Isadora, 1986), a folktale told in the rich black language of the rural South. The story raises the issue of people's perceptions about speech. Flossie is told that she "sounds dumb" because of the way she talks, but in the end, she outsmarts the wily fox. A story such as this demonstrates respect for children's language while also introducing the concept of negative perceptions about language and helping children understand the value of code switching.

Teaching and encouraging children to code switch honors the language system that they already possess and helps them adapt to different communication requirements in different situations. Teachers don't need to rely on preset curriculum to accomplish this, but can create and use their own tools and techniques. For example, teachers can give children a microphone to practice talking as if they were on TV. Or children can make dictionaries or thesauruses of different words or phrases that say the same thing in different ways. Teachers can also create a classroom climate in which children feel safe to self-correct or correct each other's speech. Capable code switchers acquire the ability to think about their own use of language, which serves them well in other learning situations.

References: Chicago Board of Education. (1968). *I am scared when*... (Psycholinguistic Reading Series). Chicago: Author; McKissick, P., & Isadora, R. (1986). *Flossie and the fox*. New York: Dial Books/Penguin Books; Smalls, I., & Bootman, C. (2003). *Don't say ain't*. Waterton, MA: Charlesbridge.

short, teachers need to use fewer conversation closers and more conversation stretchers, as described in Table 12.2.

Building Listening Comprehension

Conversation involves turn-taking. One person speaks and the other person listens. Listening is critical to understanding what is said. In addition, listening comprehension prepares young children for later reading comprehension (Jalongo, 2008). As important as listening is, most teachers do not treat it as a skill to be taught. When adults tell children to "Listen," they often mean "Behave" or "Do as I say." No wonder children often tune out the word.

Table 12.2 Improving Teacher–Child Conversations

AVOID Conversation Closers—Types of Teacher Talk That Cut Off Conversation with Individual Children

Conversation Closers	Examples
Answering own questions—talking for children or over children	Teacher speaking without waiting for a reply: "How did you like our trip to the firehouse, Jack? I bet you liked hearing the fire bell. I saw you looking at the pole. That was neat."
Moralizing	Jack: "I wanna ring that bell." Teacher: "You can't ring the bell. It's not allowed."
Using empty praise or phrases	Teacher: "That's nice, Jack." "Good boy."
Time-passing remarks	Jack: "Can we drive the truck?" Teacher: "We'll be going pretty soon."
Focusing on safety and rules	Jack: "Look, I found a caterpillar." Teacher: "You'll have to wash your hands now."

INCREASE Conversation Stretchers—Types of Teacher Talk That Extend One-to-One Conversation and Contribute to More Turn-Taking

Conversation Stretchers	Examples
Focusing on and adding details	"The firefighter's boots are tall. Let's see how big they are compared to your shoes, Jack. They're gigantic. Why do you think they have these handles?"
Expanding and asking questions	"It sounds like you want to build a firehouse out of your blocks with a pole. What materials will you need?"
Repeating important words	"Here's the fire extinguisher. We have a fire extinguisher like this at school. Who remembers where we keep the extinguisher?"
Sharing own experiences	"When I was on my way to school, I heard an ambulance siren. It startled me."
Explaining terms	"A false alarm. *False* means it is not real. So a false alarm means there isn't a real fire."
Wondering aloud	"I wonder what it would be like to work in a fire station. . . ."
Using wait time	Give plenty of time (5 to 10 seconds) for children to respond, especially less verbal children. The other children and you will learn that waiting for a less verbal child can sometimes yield keen insights.

Sources: Based on *Oral Language and Early Literacy in Preschool: Talking, Reading, and Writing*, by K. A. Roskos, P. O. Tabors, and L. A. Lenhart, 2004, Newark, DE: International Reading Association; and *Learning Language and Loving It: A Guide to Promoting Children's Social, Language, and Literacy Development in Early Childhood Settings*, 2nd edition, by E. Weitzman and J. Greenberg, 2002, Toronto: The Hanen Centre.

Young children need to listen in order to learn; therefore, they need to learn to listen (Jalongo, 2008). Because teachers or parents tell children, "Be quiet, sit still, and listen," listening may seem to be a passive activity. However, effective listening is an active process. **Listening** is "the process of taking in information through the sense of hearing and making meaning from what was heard" (Jalongo, 2008, p. 12).

listening The process of taking in information through the sense of hearing and making meaning from what is heard.

Kindergarten children enjoy playing word games, which have the added benefits of expanding vocabulary and enhancing reasoning and problem solving.

To promote listening and understanding, teachers should model good listening for children. They can use the conversation stretchers and avoid the conversation closers, listed in Table 12.2 and depicted in the following example:

> Ms. Abell's kindergarten class gathers around her for meeting time. The children become excited when they spy the "mystery box," which signals that they are going to play one of their favorite games.
>
> *Ms. Abell, putting her hand inside the box:* I'm touching something that is hard and has points on one end.
> *The children take turns guessing:* A pencil.... A knife.... A carrot.
> *Ms. Abell:* Listen to my clue. I said *points*.
> *Ashley:* I know. It's scissors. (The other children nod and agree.)
> *Ms. Abell, feeling in the box:* "That's close, but it has four points, called prongs."
>
> Because *prongs* is a new word for them, the children need other clues. Ms. Abell says, "Who can remember all the clues?" After Dorsey lists the clues so far, Ms. Abell adds another one: "You use it at lunchtime." Soon, Robin figures out that the mystery item is a fork.

This game is only one of the ways in which Ms. Abell promotes listening skills. During center time, a group plays a matching sounds Lotto game. Two children from Cambodia listen to a story on tape in their home language. Ms. Abell sets up a treasure hunt where children must listen and follow a series of directions to find the surprise.

Using Decontextualized Speech

One of the most effective ways to expand children's language is to use **decontextualized speech**. This is talk about events, experiences, or people that are beyond the here and now or that inhabit children's imaginations. Such interaction requires children and adults to use more complex and varied vocabulary in explanations, descriptions, dialogue, and pretend talk.

Decontextualized speech can be complicated because the speaker and the listener can't rely on cues from the context to understand the communication. When children talk about the here and now, the context permits using words like *this*, *that*, *there*, *here*, and *it*. These are words that children already know. Such conversation doesn't require or challenge them to use more descriptive language to be understood.

Furthermore, decontextualized speech is valuable preparation for reading (Snow et al., 1998). In spoken communication, lots of cues such as gestures, facial expressions, physical space, and objects are available. If someone says, "Take your seat," the listener quickly understands if he is being told to sit down. But if the same sentence appears in writing, the reader would have to figure out whether it means *sit in a chair* or *pick up a cushion*. This is just one example of the important connection between speaking and reading.

Teaching New and Rare Words

Four-year-old Liam has a new baby brother named Ryan. Liam decides that the baby should be named Nathan, after his best friend at preschool. The first few days after Ryan comes home from the hospital, Liam persists in calling him Nathan. His parents don't correct him, but they keep calling the baby *Ryan*. Sitting next to his mom and Ryan on the couch one day, Liam thoughtfully says, "We can call him Rynathan. That will be a compromise."

Liam's advanced vocabulary, which also includes words such as *actually*, *amazing*, *entertaining*, and *decision*, did not develop by chance. His parents and preschool teachers talk with him, use these words regularly, and explain and show what they mean.

decontextualized speech Talk about events, experiences, or people that are beyond the here and now or that inhibit children's imaginations.

Learning new words occurs through repeated exposure to the words in a context where the meaning becomes clear. Liam's parents undoubtedly negotiate with him rather

than get into power struggles. For example, if he wants to watch TV and his mother wants him to go outside, she might say, "Let's compromise. You can go outside while it's still light, and we'll tape the program so you can watch it later." After hearing and using this word several times, Liam begins to use it himself.

Teachers need to use explicit instruction to expand children's vocabulary, and should intentionally introduce new and **rare words**—multisyllable words that are not typically part of a preschooler's vocabulary (Dickinson, 2001b; Schickedanz, 1999). For example, a teacher might say, "Today I want to show you our new *magnifying* glass. When we hold it up, *objects* look bigger. They are *magnified*. Even tiny seashells may look *enormous*." To reinforce the learning, the teacher can use the new words repeatedly and encourage children to use them correctly when they play with the magnifying glass.

Using Play to Promote Language and Early Literacy

After a visit to the local airport, Ms. Keegan's preschool class wants to take an airplane ride. They organize all of the chairs into the two aisles of the plane and choose roles. Two children are the pilots, three are the flight attendants, one is the ticket agent, another is the baggage handler, and the rest are passengers. In preparation, one group makes tickets while another sets up a beverage cart. As the plane loads, Grayson, the flight attendant, greets each passenger with a, "Welcome aboard" and tells the assembled group to fasten their seat belts. The pilots announce that the plane is going to Disneyland. Most children get deep into the scenario and stay with it for 20 minutes or more. The play is repeated for several days with children exchanging roles and practicing the language of air travel.

Value of Pretend Play

One of the defining characteristics of sophisticated sociodramatic play is the use of language. During such play, children try to imitate adults and their language becomes more complex and sophisticated (Christie & Roskos, 2006). Similarly, when children play out specific roles in pretend contexts, they adapt their speech style and employ the familiar scripts common to those settings. The airport, space shuttle launch, and restaurant are different contexts, each with its own vocabulary and script.

To stimulate language, teachers may need to take a role in play to get it going or to extend it to include more language. For instance, the teacher might arrive at the airport and say, "I almost missed the plane. Can you tell me what to do in case of emergency? How does the oxygen mask work?" Play provides many opportunities to practice such verbal interaction with other children and occasionally with adults.

rare words Multisyllable words that are not typically part of a young child's vocabulary.

Using Interactive Book Reading

One of the most effective ways to promote children's language and increase their vocabulary is to engage in interactive book reading (Dickinson & Smith, 1993; Karweit & Wasik, 1996; Whitehurst & Lonigan, 1998). In many classrooms, storybook reading is the favorite activity of both teachers and children. However, teachers usually read books only to the whole group (Dickinson, 2001a). At times, reading is seen as entertainment only; at other times, teachers use it as a transition activity with children taking turns to go wash their hands while the teacher reads (Dickinson, 2001a; Schwanenflugel et al., 2005). These practices are missed opportunities for learning.

Effective teachers read to children in small groups. In a group of four to six, children can see the pictures, ask questions, and talk about the story before and after the reading.

Reading in Small Groups

Research shows that book reading is most effective when it occurs in groups of four to six children (Karweit & Wasik,

What Works

Dialogic Reading

Dialogic reading is interactive, shared picture book reading that enhances children's language and literacy skills, according to the What Works Clearinghouse at the U.S. Department of Education. During the shared reading practice, the adult and child gradually switch roles so that the child learns to become the storyteller with the assistance of the adult, who plays the role of active listener and questioner.

Teachers can use dialogic reading with children individually or in small groups. While reading books with the children, the teacher uses five types of prompts or questioning strategies to stimulate children's language interaction. A handy mnemonic device to remember the prompts is the word *CROWD*. The table below lists the prompts with examples of questions from a reading of *The Tale of Peter Rabbit* by Beatrix Potter.

The CROWD prompts are used by the adult in a reading technique called PEER:

P: Adult prompts the child to say something about the book.
E: Adult evaluates (listens to) the child's response to decide how to respond.
E: Adult expands the child's response.
R: Adult repeats the prompt.

As the child becomes increasingly familiar with a book, the adult reads less, listens more, and gradually uses more higher-level prompts to encourage the child to go beyond naming objects in the pictures to thinking about what is happening in the pictures and how this relates to the child's own experiences.

Research on dialogic reading demonstrates that it enhances the language skills of children from middle- and upper-income families more than typical picture book reading alone. More importantly, studies conducted with children from low-income families found substantial positive changes in the development of children's language.

Prompt	Description	Example
Completion prompt	Child completes an incomplete sentence.	Teacher: "Peter Rabbit got stuck in ____."
Recall questions	Teacher asks questions about the book the child has read.	Teacher: "What did Peter lose in the garden?"
Open-ended questions	Teacher encourages child to tell what is happening in a picture.	Showing the picture of Peter caught and the birds flapping their wings, the teacher asks: "How do you think Peter is feeling now?"
***W**h*- questions	Teacher asks *Wh*- questions about the pictures in books. These questions help children think about a character's motives or feelings.	Teacher: "Why do you think Peter went in the garden even though his mother told him not to?"
Distancing questions	Teacher relates pictures and words in the book to children's own experiences outside of the book.	Teacher: "Have you ever been scared like Peter? What happened? What did you do?"

Source: Based on *Dialogic Reading* (What Works Clearinghouse Intervention Report), by Institute of Education Sciences, February 2007, Washington, DC: U.S. Department of Education. Retrieved September 2, 2009, from http://www.eric.ed.gov/ERICDocs/data/ericdocs2sql/content_storage_01/0000019b/80/29/e1/30.pdf.

1996; Morrow, 1988). The power of reading is not in the book alone, but in the conversation about the book among teachers and children (Whitehurst et al., 1988). This type of interaction is more likely to occur in a small group than in the whole group or even in a one-on-one reading situation (Morrow, 1988; Wasik & Bond, 2001).

Reading in small groups and rereading the same book are especially effective ways of promoting language and literacy skills in children from low-income families (Karweit & Wasik, 1996; McGee & Schickedanz, 2007). By contrast, those from middle-class families who have been read to often do not benefit as much from rereading and may get bored with the same book.

Small groups make it possible for each child to see the pictures, follow the print, participate in a discussion, and comprehend the story better. Small-group reading makes it more feasible for teachers to interact with children before, during, and after reading. This is particularly valuable when the book has a complex narrative and rare words. A **narrative** is a story with a beginning, middle, and end; characters; dialogue; and a plot with a problem to solve or a dilemma to be resolved. Interactive, shared book reading is a highly effective strategy for expanding children's language and listening comprehension. To learn more about this research-based practice, read the *What Works: Dialogic Reading* feature.

Reading to the Whole Group

The effectiveness of small-group reading does not mean that teachers should never read to the whole group. If the book is relatively short and involves children's active participation and *predictable* text, whole-group reading may be the best choice. **Predictable books** use parallel text structures that become familiar to children, such as those in Bill Martin's *Brown Bear, Brown Bear* or Dr. Seuss's *Hop on Pop*. The whole group can chime in during Eric Carle's *The Very Hungry Caterpillar* with predictable text such as "But he was still hungry."

Throughout the first 5 years of life, children develop language and early literacy skills simultaneously, and the two are interrelated (Dickinson & Tabors, 2001; National Early Literacy Panel [NELP], 2008). Reading to children enhances their language because the structures and words used in books are more complex than those used in everyday speech. Knowing more words, in turn, helps children make sense of print and find what they read more meaningful and interesting. Talking with children about what is read further boosts vocabulary and comprehension. But what about children who don't speak the language of the classroom? Next, we discuss the timely topic of learning in two languages.

Learning a Second Language

Consider these two phrases: *English language learners* and *dual language learners*. The first communicates that the focus is on children learning English. In contrast, **dual language learning** conveys that children are simultaneously learning two languages—their home or first language as well as English or another second language.

Effective teachers understand the process by which children acquire a second language and how best to support children as they learn two languages (Espinosa, 2010; Head Start, 2008a).

Developmental Sequence of Second Language Acquisition

Just as with primary language development, there is a developmental sequence of second language acquisition, which is depicted in Table 12.3. The length of time individual children spend at each level varies, and unlike learning their home language, learning a second language is a conscious process that requires effort.

dialogic reading Interactive, shared picture book reading during which the adult and the child gradually switch roles so that the child learns to become the storyteller with the assistance of the adult, who plays the role of active listener and questioner.

completion prompt A prompt that requires the child to verbally complete the end of a sentence.

recall questions Questions asked by the teacher about a book to see what children remember.

open-ended questions Questions asked by the teacher that encourage a child to tell what is happening in a picture.

***Wh-* questions** Questions that begin with "Why" or "What" to get children thinking about characters' motives or feelings.

distancing questions Questions that relate pictures and words in the book to children's own experiences beyond the book.

narrative A story with a beginning, middle, and end; characters; dialogue; and a plot with a problem to solve or a dilemma to be resolved.

predictable books Books with controlled vocabulary using parallel text structures that become familiar to children.

dual language learning Simultaneously learning two languages: the home or first language as well as English or another second language.

Table 12.3 Stages of Second Language Learning

Stage	Description	What Teachers Can Do
Stage 1: Home language use The child speaks the home language only.	Even though other people are speaking English, children may not realize or understand that the two languages differ. At first, they try to use their home language, but soon learn that this isn't working. At some point, this becomes frustrating and they stop trying, leading to the second stage.	Teachers provide cues to help children make sense of words by pointing to and labeling objects. At lunchtime, Rachel sits with a group of Spanish-speaking 4-year-olds. As they eat, she labels the utensils and food, speaking slowly and distinctly. "Spoon," she says as she picks up her own. "Here's your spoon for your soup," as she guides Carlos to follow her directions.
Stage 2: Nonverbal or silent period After children stop trying to speak in their first language, they enter a period where they do not talk at all, but rather listen and observe.	This period can last for a long time or can be relatively brief, depending on the individual. This stage is sometimes called the silent period, but a better name is the nonverbal period. *Silent* implies that no communication occurs. Actually, during this period, children are learning a lot about the new language by listening and observing, but they are not verbal themselves. Children may not be talking, but that does not mean they are not communicating.	Teachers should not force nonverbal children to speak. Instead of talking, children may try to communicate nonverbally to get help from adults or other children. They may point to the object they want or smile when their request is granted. Gradually, they begin to rehearse the new language by speaking some words quietly to themselves or playing with the sounds. A child says, "Paint paper" and the teacher interprets whether the child wants to paint or to take her picture home.
Stage 3: Early language production Children have a small, working vocabulary in the second language and begin to use it out loud.	Children speak in one- or two-word utterances and repeat routine phrases without understanding what they mean. At story time, Carlos automatically says, "It's circle time" because he has heard these words in this context many times.	Teachers give simple choices that require "yes" or "no" responses, such as "Do you want to play with blocks or paint?" Children can also answer simple *who*, *what*, or *where* questions.
Stage 4: Speech emergence Children begin producing the new language. This stage can take 1 to 2 years during which children gradually produce longer sentences.	Listening comprehension improves as receptive language increases. Children use the social language of the classroom or playground, such as "My turn now" or "Be my friend." They begin to apply the grammar rules of the new language, but not consistently. Children are better able to participate in academic learning.	Rather than correcting "errors," teachers strive for communication. Carlos might say, "I like my school big" rather than "I like my big school." His teacher responds, "I'm glad you like our big school." Teachers ask *how* and *why* questions that require short responses: "How did your shoes get wet?"
Stage 5: Fluent second-language production Moving from emergent to fluent language production can take 1 to 2 years.	Children can understand what is said in the classroom and begin to understand written communications.	Teachers use open-ended questions that engage children in producing more complex sentences. Second language learners will probably need extra help in the early grades, where the curriculum focuses on learning to read. Teaching reading in the home language is most effective.
Stage 6: Advanced language proficiency	Children have developed understanding of specialized, content-related vocabulary. It can take from 5 to 7 years for children to master this level of cognitively demanding language.	Teachers intentionally teach the vocabulary and language skills required for academic achievement in school. For example, mathematics requires knowing words like *addend* or *double-digit multiplication* that are not used in everyday speech.

Sources: Based on *Assessing Language Development in Bilingual Preschool Children*, by B. McLaughlin, A. G. Blanchard, and Y. Osanai, 1995, Washington, DC: National Clearinghouse for Bilingual Education; and *Oral Language and Early Literacy in Preschool: Talking, Reading, and Writing*, by K. A. Roskos, P. O. Tabors, and L. A. Lenhart, 2004, Newark, DE: International Reading Association.

Supporting Dual Language Learners

The reality of so many dual language learners means that teachers have a special responsibility to help children make progress in understanding and speaking *both* English and their home language. Research finds that supporting home language has distinct benefits for children, as discussed in the *Language Lens: Speaking Two Languages* feature.

Teachers can help parents understand that it is important for children to have a strong foundation in their home language (Espinosa, 2007, 2008). The more words and concepts children know in their first language, the more likely that knowledge will transfer as children become proficient in English. Moreover learning to read is more effective when instruction occurs in the home language (Slavin & Cheung, 2005).

In the previous sections, we described how children learn both their first and second languages and ways to promote language development from birth through primary grades. Next we turn to the related topic of how children become literate.

Language Lens

Speaking Two Languages

Of 16 children in Pedro Cordero's Head Start classroom, 12 speak Spanish as their home language. Pedro uses both English and Spanish in his interactions with the children. During conversations with individual children, he often speaks Spanish, finding that it helps him get to know the children and build positive relationships with them. During more formal gatherings such as story time or small-group activities, he often speaks English. But he connects new words to real objects or pictures, and he checks children's understanding regularly. Pedro's assistant teacher only speaks English; she and the English-speaking children provide language models for the dual language learners.

In many states in the United States today, the type of teaching Pedro does would be prohibited by law. In the belief that bilingual education harms children, prevents learning English, and hurts academic success, some states have adopted "English-only" laws.

But what does research say about English-only teaching and children's success in school? Researchers in a large-scale study observed 345 Spanish-speaking children in 161 prekindergarten programs, and asked teachers to rate children's social and behavior skills and the quality of their relationships with them. In the classrooms observed, about two-thirds of the parents said their child did not speak English at home. The study found that when teachers spoke some Spanish, Spanish-speaking children were found to have better social skills than children whose teachers spoke only English.

In addition, children whose teachers spoke some Spanish were less likely to be victims of aggression, bullying, or teasing, and their teachers were more likely to have a positive relationship with them. The amount of Spanish that teachers spoke was significantly related to teachers' ratings of children's assertiveness, attention and task persistence, and ability to get along with other children. On the other hand, the more English interactions children had, the more likely they were to have behavior and learning problems and become easily frustrated.

An important—and seemingly contradictory—finding was that the amount of Spanish spoken in the classroom was not related to a child's English proficiency. In the study, teachers spoke Spanish with Spanish-speaking children only 20% of the time. When speaking directly to Spanish-speaking children, teachers who spoke some Spanish still used English two-thirds of the time. When speaking to a group, teachers tended to use English. When teachers spoke Spanish, however, they had more elaborate conversations with children, a key finding considering the research on the value of extended conversations for vocabulary development.

The researchers concluded that contrary to popular belief, English-only teaching of young children may contribute to the achievement gap rather than help close it. From the perspective of research, both the Spanish-speaking and English-speaking children in Pedro Cordero's Head Start class should benefit from his approach to teaching.

Sources: Based on "Spanish Speaking Children's Social and Language Development in Pre-Kindergarten Classrooms," by F. Chang, G. Crawford, D. Early, and D. Bryant, 2007, *Journal of Early Education and Development, 18*(2), pp. 243–269; and *Is Public Pre-K Preparing Hispanic Children to Succeed in School?* (Preschool Policy Brief 13), by L. M. Laosa, and P. Ainsworth, 2007, New Brunswick, NJ: National Institute for Early Education Research.

Promoting Early Literacy in Children: Birth through Age Five

Young children begin the process of learning to read and write long before they enter formal school. Decades of research shows that children who enter kindergarten with specific kinds of knowledge and skill are more likely to become successful readers and writers. (NELP, 2008; NICHD, 2000; Snow et al., 1998).

The Continuum of Early Literacy Learning

Table 12.4 presents some of the widely held expectations for children's literacy development from birth through age 5, assuming that they have good learning opportunities. Individual children's progress will vary depending on their prior experiences with written language and other factors.

Teachers need to be intentional in promoting children's language and literacy learning. This means that they thoughtfully plan and prepare in advance but are also playful (Roskos et al., 2004). Children need to playfully explore and engage in activities involving reading, writing, and learning letters and sounds. These opportunities are more likely to occur in a literacy-rich environment.

Table 12.4 Continuum of Early Literacy Learning

Age Range	Widely Held Expectations
Birth to Age 3—Beginning Awareness and Exploration Babies and toddlers become aware of and begin to enjoy books and sounds of language.	**By age 3, most children:** • Recognize favorite books by their cover. • Listen to short stories and enjoy book reading routines with caregivers, such as lap book reading. • Label objects pictured in books. • Scribble and gradually produce increasingly controlled scribbles with some letter-like forms (circles and lines). • Begin to pay attention to print, especially the first letter of their name. • Play with sounds and enjoy rhymes and songs.
Preschool (3- to 5-Year-Olds)—Exploration and Investigation During the preschool years, children explore their environment and build the foundations for learning to read and write.	**Most 3- to 5-year-olds:** • Enjoy listening to and talking about age-appropriate story books and information books. • Understand that print carries a message. • Can follow the sequence of events in a story and answer questions that demonstrate listening comprehension. • Pretend to read and attempt to write. • Recognize familiar labels and environmental print (signs for stores, street signs). • Attend to chunks of sound in spoken language, identify rhymes and alliteration (silly Susie), clap syllables. • Recognize many letters, especially those in meaningful words. • Make some letter–sound matches (as when attempting to write words). • Use known letters and letter-like symbols to represent written language.

Sources: Based on *Learning to Read and Write: Developmentally Appropriate Practices for Young Children: A Joint Position Statement*, 1998, International Reading Association and National Association for the Education of Young Children, 1998, Washington, DC: NAEYC; and *Preventing Reading Difficulties in Young Children*, edited by C. E. Snow, M. S. Burns, and P. Griffin, 1998, Washington, DC: National Academies Press.

Creating a Literacy-Rich Environment

Some children grow up in homes where they observe family members reading books and magazines, writing lists, browsing the Internet, or answering e-mail. But access to literacy is unequal in our society. Affluent American children may have as many books in their bedrooms as poor children have in their entire neighborhoods (Krashen, 1998; Neuman & Celano, 2002).

From their environment, children learn whether literacy is valued and important. Therefore, every classroom needs to be rich in literacy-enhancing materials and experiences (Neuman & Roskos, 1992, 1993; Roskos & Neuman, 2001). To picture a literacy-rich environment, consider the following example:

> A look into Ms. DeSoto's preschool classroom reveals the many ways she creates an environment that communicates the value of literacy to children and teaches them important skills. In strategic places, she posts signs, labels, and other print materials that have real purposes such as the names of today's helpers, classroom attendance, message boxes, menus, and directions. But she is careful not to clutter the classroom because too much print on the walls becomes as meaningless to children as wallpaper. Instead, she engages children in creating and using the print, and calls children's attention to it as when she points to the written schedule on the wall and says, "Let's look at the schedule and see what we will do after lunch."
>
> One of the children's favorite spots is the cozy, well-lit library area with its comfortable, child-size furniture and pictures of favorite story characters. Books are attractively displayed on open shelves, accessible to children and inviting their interest, much as bookstores do when they attractively display covers of new titles. The classroom library is well stocked with at least five books per child, with two to three per child on display at one time. The collection includes culturally and developmentally appropriate storybooks, information books, wordless picture books, and poetry.
>
> Ms. DeSoto places books and writing tools in centers where they are relevant, such as a book on construction in the block area and paper and markers to make signs. Even a casual observer notices that books are in children's hands throughout the day, not just in the teacher's hands during story time. Shelves are stocked with games, toys, and equipment that promote knowledge of letters and sounds such as alphabet blocks, magnetic letters, an alphabet puzzle, and a CD player.

MyEducationLab

Go to the Assignments and Activities section of Topic 7: Curriculum/Content Areas in the MyEducationLab for your course and complete the activity entitled *Planning and Teaching the Communication Curriculum.* Observe how these teachers implement effective practices for promoting both first and second language and early literacy learning?

early literacy Skills and knowledge that come before and lead up to (forerunners) conventional reading and writing.

predictors Set of early literacy skills and knowledge that increases the likelihood of later success in learning to read and write.

Early Literacy Skills and Abilities from Birth to Kindergarten

Early literacy is the knowledge and skills that are the forerunners of conventional reading and writing. Research demonstrates that specific early literacy skills predict later success in learning to read and write (NELP, 2008; NICHD, 2000; Snow et al., 1998). These **predictors** do not guarantee success, but they do increase the likelihood of success. More importantly, without these abilities upon entrance to kindergarten, children are more likely to encounter difficulties in learning to read (NELP, 2008; Snow et al., 1998).

Research-based early literacy skills include phonological awareness, alphabet knowledge, print awareness, and vocabulary. Other important skills that contribute to later reading include early writing, listening comprehension, and motivation to read. In the following sections, we define and describe each of these skills and effective ways teachers promote children's literacy learning. (In the previous sections, we described numerous strategies for building vocabulary.)

Literacy-rich environments help children experience the pleasure and power of reading and writing. In classrooms such as this one, children use print for real purposes. What would children learn about literacy in this environment?

Phonological Awareness and Letter Knowledge

Written language is a symbol system—a code that children need to learn. This code may seem abstract and beyond young children's capacity to learn. However, children are constantly exposed to abstract symbols, including *walk/don't walk* symbols, computer icons, pictures to signify male and female restrooms—the list is endless.

Precisely because written language is a complex symbol system, children need practice playing with it over many years to become proficient users (Yopp & Yopp, 2009). At preschool, the two important skills for learning the code are phonological awareness and learning the alphabet (Ehri & Roberts, 2006; NELP, 2008).

Understanding Phonological Awareness

Phonological awareness is the consciousness that the stream of spoken language is made up of smaller units or chunks of sound (Goswami, 2001; Stahl, 2001). Phonological awareness develops along a continuum, from recognizing the larger units of sound, such as **rhymes** (two words ending with the same sound) and **alliteration** (two words beginning with the same sound), to the smaller units such as syllables. A more complex level of phonological awareness involves awareness of parts of syllables.

The most difficult level is **phonemic awareness**, or recognizing that spoken words are made up of individual sounds called **phonemes**. English has approximately 44 phonemes that are represented by the 26 letters of the alphabet either alone or in combination. The letter *m* stands for a sound, while the letters *th* stand for another sound. The word *bat* is made up of three phonemes: /b/, /a/, and /t/. If one phoneme is changed—using /m/ instead of /b/—the meaning of the word is changed. Phonemes are important to later reading because written language represents these sounds.

Teaching Phonological Awareness

Like virtually every other early literacy skill, children do not automatically acquire phonological awareness. Teachers need to intentionally plan experiences that focus children's attention on the sounds in words and speech, beginning with the bigger chunks of speech (words) and eventually moving to the smallest ones (individual phonemes). But these activities need to be fun and playful to ensure children's participation, motivation, and interest (Yopp & Yopp, 2009). For an example of how to accomplish this task, read the *Becoming an Intentional Teacher* feature.

phonological awareness Consciousness that the stream of spoken language is made up of smaller units or chunks of sound.

rhyme Two words ending with the same sound.

alliteration Two words beginning with the same sound.

phonemic awareness Recognizing that spoken words are made up of individual sounds that can be manipulated.

phonemes The individual sounds of spoken language; changing one in a word changes the meaning of the word.

alphabetic principle The understanding that there is a systematic relationship between letters and sounds, and that all spoken sounds and words can be represented by a limited set of agreed-on symbols called *letters*.

Learning the Alphabet

The ability to read and write depends on mastering the **alphabetic principle**, the understanding that there is a systematic relationship between letters and sounds, and that all spoken language can be represented by a set of agreed-on symbols called *letters* (Adams, 1990). Children will not master the alphabetic principle in preschool, but knowing the alphabet at kindergarten entry is one of the strongest predictors of success in reading during first grade (NELP, 2008; Snow et al., 1998). *Knowing letters* means remembering their shapes, names, and sounds.

Teaching the Alphabet

Katya, age 2½, and her dad drive to Kmart to buy some clothes. Her dad points to the large sign and says, "Look, Katya, there's your K." Katya wonders, "This is my store. Why are these people here?"

Like many children her age, Katya has discovered her letter and she feels personal ownership. But how did this important discovery occur? As her father demonstrated, Katya's parents helped her learn the first letter in her name. As with phonological awareness, children need adult support to learn the alphabet.

The alphabet is a set of arbitrary symbols with preset names that require instruction. Teaching the alphabet is necessary, but how it is taught is also important. Because adults clearly value this skill, most children are motivated to learn the letters. However, teachers

Becoming an Intentional Teacher

The Rhyming Song

Here's What Happened I introduced a large group of my 4-year-olds to an illustrated poetry book. One of the children's favorites was "Hickory Dickory Dock," and soon, aided by the illustrations, they were chanting along. They laughed at the picture of the mouse on top of the clock being startled by the chime. During the next 2 days in groups of three or four children at a time, I took the rhyming one step further, involving them in supplying rhyming phrases for new variations, such as "Hickory Dickory Dare." Most of the children were able to make rhymes right away or after listening to the others. They suggested phrases such as "The mouse ran up the chair," "The mouse ran into my hair," "The mouse ran away from the bear." Five children didn't seem to get the rhyming idea, although three of them caught on when I grouped them with proficient rhymers.

With the two others, Marina and Seth, I played a game where there were two choices pictured on cards, one of which was a rhyme. For example, if the object was a fish, they would see a dish and a cup. If it was a rhyme, there was a star on the back of the card. While we played, I would sometimes model thinking-aloud things like "Fish–cup? No, they don't rhyme. How about fish–dish? Fish–dish. Yes, that's a rhyme." After awhile, Marina and Seth were able to choose from two options and then create their own rhymes.

Here's What I Was Thinking I saw whole group as the best time to introduce the poem and give the children the idea of rhyming, which is an early step in phonological awareness. I followed up with small groups and had the children generate their own rhymes because I wanted to find out what each child was able to do with rhyming and hearing the separate sounds that make up words. We also began varying the poem to play with alliteration. I changed "Dickory Dare" to "Hickory Bickery Bow," and the children came up with their own variations: "Hickory, Slickery, Slow."

For the children who have mastered rhyming and alliteration easily, I next plan to introduce the more difficult task of blending sounds in syllables. We will play a game where I say "/b/" and then "it" and see if they say "bit." For the children who didn't seem to get rhyming, I needed more information as to why not. Marina and Seth might be recognizing rhymes, I thought, even though they couldn't yet generate rhyming words themselves. That was a possibility I wanted to check out. So I decided to make a simple two-choice game we could play. Then I made sure to emphasize the sound of the words, saying them side by side to make it easier to hear the rhyme, as in "Fish–dish."

need to make learning the alphabet meaningful. Teaching letters in isolation without any connection to words and sounds that children know can lead to frustration or memorization, which doesn't predict later reading success (Adams, 1990).

As Katya did, children approach letter learning by first focusing on the letters in their own names. If they frequently see their name in writing, at some point between about 18 months and age 3, they will identify the first letter as their own. A child may even be affronted if someone else claims the letter, too. Toddlers love to sing the alphabet song, play with alphabet blocks, and look at alphabet books.

In the classroom, letters should be the type children can see, touch, and manipulate, such as magnetic or sandpaper letters (Neuman, Copple & Bredekamp, 2000). Children need to see both uppercase and lowercase letters and different fonts of the same letter. This way, children learn the "essence" of the letter symbol rather than only one representation of it.

Knowing the alphabet at kindergarten entry is one of the best predictors of later success in learning to read. What are some developmentally appropriate ways to teach letters to young children?

Developing Print Awareness

Print awareness is beginning knowledge about written language. Various purposes of print include communication, expression, explanation, direction, and information. Concepts and abilities related to print awareness include (Head Start, 2003; Schickedanz & Casbergue, 2004):

- Understanding that print performs a variety of functions and purposes
- Recognizing print in the environment (such as in signs or labels)
- Knowing that print, not pictures, carries the message in the story
- Understanding the concept of *word*, that is, that specific clusters of letters on the page with spaces between them represent the words said by the reader
- Realizing that print represents speech or thought that is written down
- Realizing that print in English is read left to right, top to bottom.

The skills listed above—also called **concepts of print**—are important elements of literacy learning (Clay, 1985). These developmentally appropriate outcomes are challenging but achievable for preschool children if they have good teaching and planned learning experiences.

Developing Early Writing Skills

Encouraging young children to write is an effective way to help them learn to read (Dyson, 2001; Schickedanz & Casbergue, 2004). Research demonstrates that talking, reading, and writing are developing simultaneously and that progress in one area supports learning in the others (NELP, 2008; Snow et al., 1998).

Continuum of Early Writing

As children try to write on their own, the writing process promotes print awareness as well as many other early literacy skills (Vukelich & Christie, 2004). Children's writing is another area that tends to follow a developmental sequence, as described in Table 12.5. At first, they do not distinguish drawing and writing. But over time they learn the difference and will label scribbles that are indistinguishable to adults as one or the other. Pointing to one circular scribble, 2-year-old Mackenzie says, "This is my house." She points to an elongated scribble and identifies it as her name.

Gradually children's scribbles become more deliberate and controlled. Between the ages of 3 and 4, children incorporate letter-like shapes or symbols (circles and straight lines) in their drawings and random strings of letters. Some children begin to identify sounds within words, and some 4-year-olds begin to use *invented spelling*, at least with initial consonants in English. Spanish-speaking children tend to use vowels first (Snow et al., 1998).

Temporary **invented spelling**, also called *developmental* or *phonetic spelling*, represents children's initial attempts to associate sounds with letters, as when a 4-year-old writes "Mk" for "Mike." This process of trying to figure out how to write words is an important step on the way to learning conventional spelling. Observing and talking with children as they produce these spellings enables teachers to monitor children's understanding of letter–sound relationships. For example, 6-year-old Katie writes: "Good moraning. We are going to be bise [busy]. We are genu go to the postofs [post office]."

Using invented spelling does not interfere with learning conventional spelling. In fact, the opposite is true. Invented spelling actually accelerates children's development of phonemic awareness and conventional spelling when it is taught in the primary grades (Clarke, 1988; Snow et al., 1998). The progression of children's writing and drawing is depicted in the examples in Figure 12.1.

print awareness Beginning knowledge about written language.

concepts of print Beginning understandings about the forms and functions of written language, such as that words carry messages.

invented spelling Developmental or phonetic spelling that represents children's initial attempts to associate sounds with letters.

Teaching Early Writing Skills

When children see adults writing, they want to write themselves. To encourage writing, teachers need to reinforce children's sense of competence. Curriculum should expose children to various types of writing. A cooking project requires them to attend to a recipe. Sci-

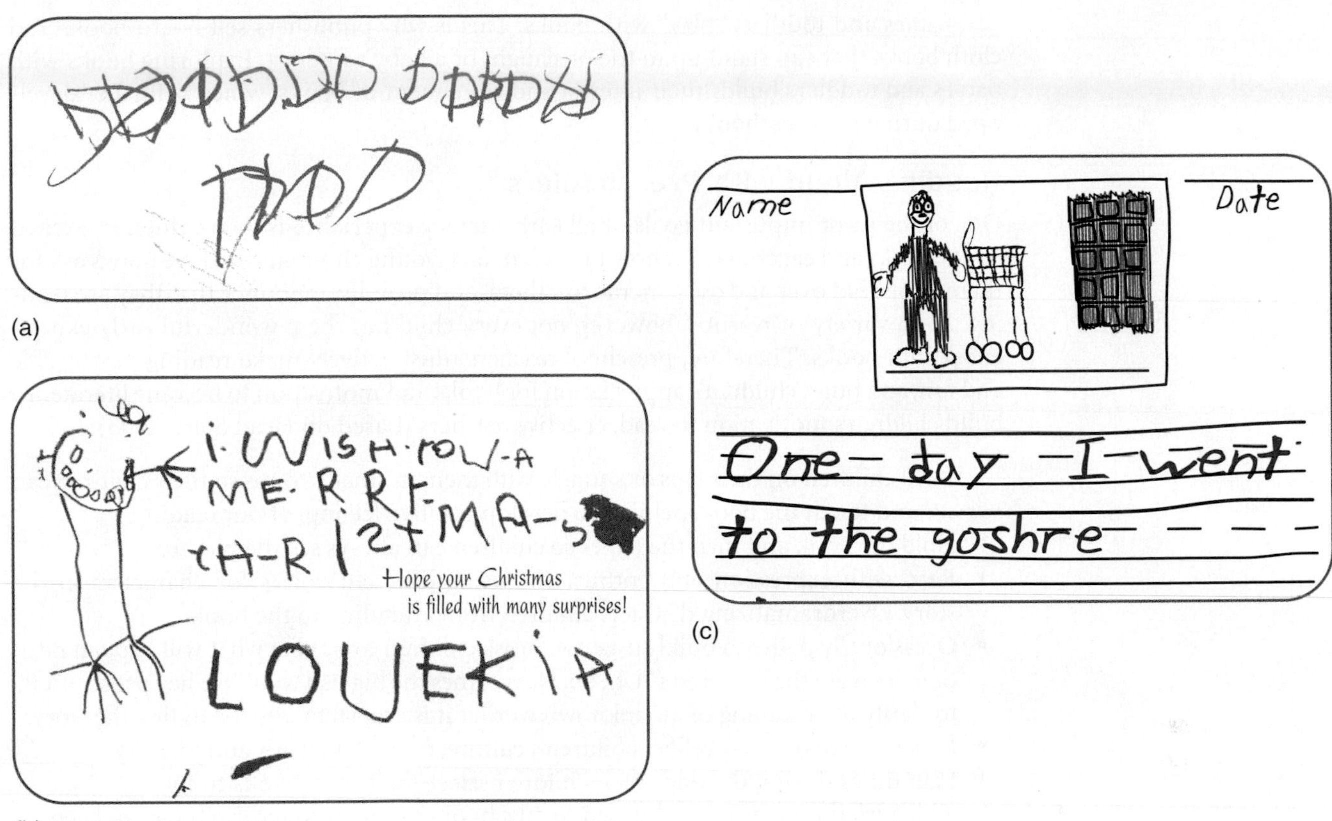

Figure 12.1 Progression of Child's Writing
(a) Age 2 years, 10 months; (b) age 3 years, 4 months; (c) age 5 years.

ence experiments require data collection. Children's desire to protect a block structure motivates them to write a sign.

It is important that teachers not focus on children's forming letters properly because that approach is likely to be less meaningful and potentially frustrating for children. Teachers and parents should not be alarmed when children reverse letters or even write words as if in mirror-image. These "errors" are normal at this age (Schickedanz & Casbergue, 2004). If children persist in writing letters backwards, however, teachers may want to scaffold more correct production. For example, 4½-year-old Franklin tends to write his name backwards. Mr. Gandini notices that he starts writing on the right-hand side of the page and usually runs out of room, so he continues toward the left. He simply says, "Franklin, why don't you start your name up here in the left-hand corner of your paper, the way I write people's names on their paintings. Then you have plenty of space."

Promoting Book Appreciation and Motivation to Read

Children who are motivated to read show interest in books and reading, connect reading events to real life, and experience the pleasure and power of reading (Neuman et al., 2000). All children can come to appreciate books and find that reading is enjoyable.

Reading with Babies and Toddlers

Earlier in this chapter, we described how interactive book reading facilitates language development. But reading aloud is also valuable for promoting children's literacy skills and motivation to read. Like so many other aspects of teaching, appropriate use of books varies with the age of the child.

Babies and toddlers "play" with books. This is why publishers sell board books and cloth books that can stand up to the onslaught of a baby's interest. Exploring books with babies and toddlers builds their interest and enjoyment of books, which is further developed during the preschool years.

Reading Aloud with Preschoolers

One of the most important goals of all early literacy experience is to get children excited about books and eager to learn how to read. In fact, young children who love books ask for them to be read over and over, memorize them, and proudly announce that they are reading. For a variety of reasons, however, not every child has these wonderful early experiences with books. Therefore, preschool teachers must actively make reading pleasurable and fun, and build children's appreciation for books and motivation to become literate. To build children's motivation to read, effective teachers (based on Head Start, 2003):

- Hold children on their laps or snuggle with them in small groups so their children can see and touch the book, helping to develop positive feelings about reading.
- Hold the book and turn the pages so children can always see the pictures.
- Read with expression and enthusiasm, using different voices for characters in the story. Overdramatizing distracts children from attending to the book.
- Occasionally pause to build suspense, to ask children to predict what will happen next, or to increase their interest ("Uh, oh. Here comes the big bad wolf!"). They pause briefly to clarify the meaning of an unknown word if it is crucial to understanding the story.
- Make sure that books reflect children's culture, home language, and identity.
- Plan times during the day when children select their own books to look at alone or with a friend. They allow children to take books home or to receive books to keep.
- Read to children several times a day, every day, expressively and enthusiastically.
- Read favorite books repeatedly when requested. They talk with children about their favorite books and authors, and encourage children to write or e-mail them. They also use the Internet to get more information about authors' lives and work.

> **Effective Teaching**
> Effective teachers thoughtfully plan for children's language and literacy learning, but they are also playful and make learning meaningful and enjoyable.

For nearly every child, the process of learning to read becomes difficult at some point, whether in first grade, when decoding becomes the focus of instruction or in third grade, when comprehension takes center stage (Snow et al., 1998). Children who are motivated to read are more likely to persist when they encounter these challenges. Motivation is also important because the more a child reads, the better reader he or she becomes (Snow et al., 1998; Stanovich, 1986). Children who like reading and, therefore, choose to read are almost always very good readers.

Integrating Literacy and Building Background Knowledge

Early literacy experiences are now a key part of every good early childhood program, but they should not become the whole curriculum. Because the curriculum lends itself to integration, many teaching strategies are effective for multiple goals. For example, storybook reading promotes listening and understanding, vocabulary, development, phonological awareness, alphabet knowledge, print awareness, knowledge in a subject area such as science, and even social problem-solving skills. Learning curriculum content builds all-important **background knowledge**, concepts, and basic information about how the world works. Background knowledge is essential for reading comprehension.

Covering the curriculum is always a challenge for teachers, especially now that so much emphasis is placed on literacy even in preschool. Therefore, integrated curriculum becomes all the more important. Read the *How Would You Respond? Integrating Language and Literacy* feature and consider ways in which you might connect language and literacy goals to other areas of the curriculum.

background knowledge Concepts and basic information about how the world works that is essential for reading comprehension.

The predictors described in the previous sections are the forerunners of successful reading and writing. We now turn to the topic of the formal teaching of reading in the primary grades.

How Would You Respond?

Integrating Language and Literacy

The Situation Like most primary teachers today, you struggle with fitting everything in the standards into the day in your second-grade classroom. You have heard from a fellow teacher that science is full of opportunities for developing children's language and literacy. Thinking about it, you realize that when children use reading or writing in science investigations, they may be more likely to see a purpose, such as when they need to chart their observations or figure out what the word *thermometer* means in an information book on weather. As part of a larger science study on earth science, you decide to have the children learn about seasonal change.

What to Do? What potential benefits and drawbacks do you see in each of the following possible teacher actions?

- Before starting anything else in the unit, have the children read a book about seasons and write book reports.
- Have the children measure and record the temperature each day in the classroom and outdoors.
- Have the children write in their field notebooks their predictions about the weather, what they observe, and what they think will happen next.
- Use a digital camera to take photos around the school at various points in time, get the children to describe what they see, and record what they say.
- Have the children compare the photos and descriptions of the changing weather conditions with what they previously wrote as predictions for what they would see.

What other ideas can you think of to integrate reading and writing throughout the curriculum?

Learning to Read and Write in the Primary Grades

In this section, we introduce some of the key terms and issues in teaching reading. We revisit the reading and writing developmental continuum. Then, we describe the components of an evidence-based reading program and conclude with a brief description of effective practices for teaching beginning reading.

Learning to Read

Conventional reading is reading in which the reader gains meaning from unfamiliar text. This is what we think of when we talk about being literate—the ability to read without conscious effort, the way adults and older children read. English is an alphabetic language, as are Spanish and many other languages. In these languages, we translate or **encode** speech sounds into symbols—the letters of the alphabet—to create writing. Reading requires the ability to **decode**, that is, to figure out what those symbols represent.

Basically, reading involves two processes:

1. **Word identification**: the process of decoding unfamiliar words and recognizing high-frequency (both regularly and irregularly spelled) words by sight, such as *the, with, that, house, dog*
2. **Comprehension**: the ability to understand what is read and to interpret and analyze the author's meaning.

conventional reading Reading in which the reader gains meaning from unfamiliar text.

encode Translating speech sounds into symbols—the letters of the alphabet—to create writing.

decode The ability to figure out what written symbols—letters of the alphabet—represent.

word identification The process of decoding unfamiliar words and recognizing high-frequency (both regularly and irregularly spelled) words by sight.

comprehension The ability to understand what is read and to interpret and analyze the author's meaning; the ability to make sense of what is read.

MyEducationLab

Go to the Assignments and Activities section of Topic 2: Child Development/Theories in the MyEducationLab for your course and complete the activity entitled *Literacy Development in the Primary Grades*. What do these artifacts of children's writing reveal about their literacy development?

For many decades, there have been heated debates about which of these processes is more important and needs more attention when teaching beginning reading. Today, most researchers agree that effective reading instruction helps children master the alphabetic principle *and* acquire meaning from text—what is called a **balanced approach** (International Reading Association [IRA] & National Association for the Education of Young Children [NAEYC], 1998; Kim, 2008; Snow et al., 1998). Such an approach is more likely to be meaningful and motivating for children and, therefore, more likely to help them become successful readers.

Learning to read is an example of a *both/and*, not an *either/or* choice—both decoding and comprehension are required. Teachers need to realize that it is impossible to understand what you cannot decode, but it is possible to decode what you cannot understand. Those of us who have never studied physics, for example, would probably be able to "read" (that is, decode) the words in a physics textbook, but would have no idea what we've read.

Continuum of Literacy Learning in the Primary Grades

Literacy goals for the primary grades are listed in Table 12.5. Being familiar with such a continuum is useful for teachers because it identifies the goals for literacy instruction at each age level and helps them assess children's progress toward those goals (IRA & NAEYC, 1998; McAfee & Leong, 2007).

Children's progress along the continuum depends to a large extent on their earlier experience. Children will arrive at kindergarten and first grade with very different abilities. Some will already be reading, while others may know only a few letters. Therefore, teachers must adapt their instruction to start where children are and help them make continuing progress.

balanced approach Effective reading instruction that helps children master the alphabetic principle *and* acquire meaning from text.

phonics A system of teaching the correspondences between letters or groups of letters and the sounds they represent.

Evidence-Based Reading Instruction

Given the current understanding of research, the National Reading Panel identified five components of an evidence-based reading program that are now widely used in planning and evaluating curriculum (NICHD, 2000). Each of these components—phonemic awareness, phonics, fluency, vocabulary, and comprehension—is described in the sections that follow.

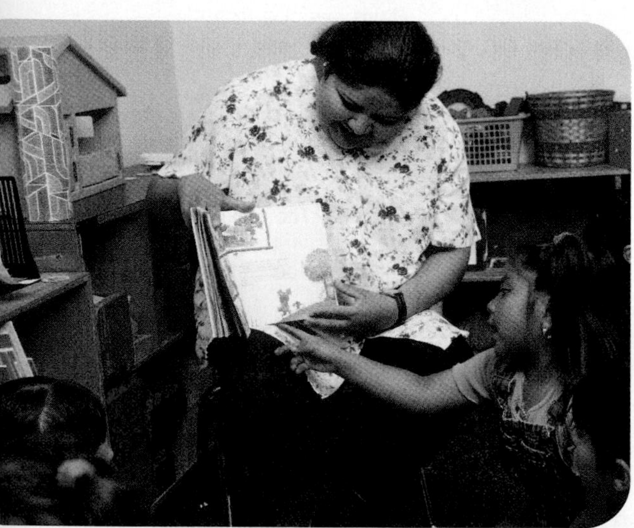

Schools today have increasing numbers of children who speak a language other than English at home. Every early childhood teacher needs to understand the process of second language acquisition and effective ways to teach English language learners.

Developing Phonemic Awareness

Phonemic awareness is one of the strongest predictors of success in reading (Richgels, 2001; Stahl, 2001). Without it, later instruction in phonics doesn't make sense. However, although research has found that phonemic awareness is absolutely necessary for success in reading, it is not by itself sufficient; there is much more to beginning reading than the spoken sounds of words (NICHD, 2000).

Teaching Phonics

Phonics is a system of teaching the correspondences between letters or groups of letters and the sounds they represent. Although the use of phonics to teach reading has been hotly debated, the value of phonics has long been established as a necessary component in an effective, research-based program (R. C. Anderson, Heibert, Scott, & Wilderson, 1985; Chall, 1967). The major issue concerning phonics instruction is not whether to teach phonics and other skills like spelling, but how to teach them in engaging ways that support children's continued reading development as well as their motivation to read. While some children need extensive help with phonics, other children do not (Strickland, 1998).

Table 12.5 Continuum of Literacy Learning in the Primary Grades

Age/Grade Level	Widely Held Expectations
First Grade—Early Reading and Writing Children begin to read simple stories and can write about a meaningful topic, such as a pet.	**Most first graders:** • Make the transition from experimental to "real" or conventional reading. • Read aloud accurately and with reasonable fluency texts appropriate for beginning grade 1. • Use letter–sound associations, word parts, and context to identify new words. • Use strategies when comprehension breaks down (rereading, predicting, questioning, or using context clues). • Use reading and writing for various purposes on their own initiative. ("I want to write a Valentine for my mom.") • Sound out and represent all substantial sounds when spelling a word. • Identify an increasing number of words by sight, including common irregularly spelled words, such as *said*, *where*, *two*. • Write various kinds of texts about meaningful topics (journals, stories). • Begin to use some punctuation and capitalization correctly.
Second Grade—Transitional Reading and Writing Children read more fluently and write various text forms using simple and more complex sentences.	**Most second graders:** • Read with greater fluency. • Use strategies to aid comprehension, such as rereading, questioning, using context, more efficiently. • Use word identification strategies to figure out unknown words. • Identify an increasing number of words by sight. • Write about a range of topics for different audiences. • Use common letter patterns to spell words. • Punctuate basic sentences correctly and proofread their writing. • Read daily and use reading to get information on topics of study.
Third Grade—Independent and Productive Reading and Writing Children continue to extend and refine their reading and writing for various purposes and audiences.	**Most third graders:** • Read fluently and enjoy reading. • Use a range of strategies to make meaning from unfamiliar text. • Use word identification strategies appropriately and automatically when encountering unknown words. • Recognize and discuss elements of different text structures. • Write expressively in various forms such as stories, reports, letters. • Use a rich vocabulary and complex sentence structure. • Revise and edit their own writing during and after composing. • Spell words correctly in final drafts.

Sources: Based on *Learning to Read and Write: Developmentally Appropriate Practices for Young Children: A Joint Position Statement*, 1998, International Reading Association and National Association for the Education of Young Children, 1998, Washington, DC: NAEYC; and *Preventing Reading Difficulties in Young Children*, edited by C. E. Snow, M. S. Burns, and P. Griffin, 1998, Washington, DC: National Academies Press.

Building Fluency

Fluency refers to rapid, efficient, and accurate word recognition skills that permit the reader to comprehend the meaning of text (Pikulski & Chard, 2005). Fluency is first apparent when children are able to read out loud quickly, accurately, and with appropriate expression. This ability then leads to their ability to comprehend what they read silently.

Fluency is like the bridge between phonics and comprehension (Pikulski & Chard, 2005). If children's decoding skills are inadequate, they must slowly sound out and stumble over each word. By the time they've reached the end of the sentence, they've forgotten the words they've read and, as a result, the sentence doesn't make sense.

fluency Rapid, efficient, and accurate word recognition skills that permit the reader to comprehend the meaning of text.

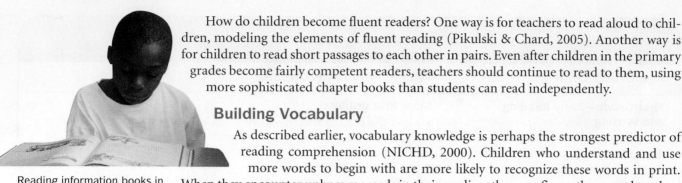

Reading information books in primary grades serves the dual purpose of building word identification skills and background knowledge. Both are needed for reading comprehension.

How do children become fluent readers? One way is for teachers to read aloud to children, modeling the elements of fluent reading (Pikulski & Chard, 2005). Another way is for children to read short passages to each other in pairs. Even after children in the primary grades become fairly competent readers, teachers should continue to read to them, using more sophisticated chapter books than students can read independently.

Building Vocabulary

As described earlier, vocabulary knowledge is perhaps the strongest predictor of reading comprehension (NICHD, 2000). Children who understand and use more words to begin with are more likely to recognize these words in print. When they encounter unknown words in their reading, they can figure them out based on what they already know (Snow et al., 1998).

Because children in the primary grades need to grow their vocabularies by about 3,000 words per year, they need to learn about 15 words per day (Beck et al., 2002). Consequently, vocabulary instruction needs to be intentional and focused during these years, especially for children who are behind in vocabulary development at school entry (Beck et al., 2002; Juel, Biancarosa, Coker, & Deffes, 2003).

Improving Reading Comprehension

Reading comprehension is the construction of meaning from unfamiliar text, the ability to make sense of what is read. A prerequisite for high levels of reading achievement is a rich amount of background and content knowledge. The content that children learn in social studies, science, and other areas provides essential background knowledge to comprehend what they read.

MyEducationLab

To observe a first grade teacher using a balanced approach to reading instruction, go to the Video Examples section of Topic 7: Curriculum/ Content Areas in the MyEducationLab for your course and watch the video entitled *Teaching Reading.* What elements of evidence-based reading instruction does she use?

A solid base of knowledge is essential for becoming a skilled reader and succeeding in school (NICHD, 2000). By third grade, the curriculum shifts from a focus on learning to read to an expectation that children read to learn, as they encounter increasingly more complex textbooks. In fact, the fourth-grade reading slump that typically occurs in American schools may be caused in part by children's lack of content knowledge from which to make sense of more challenging texts (Hirsch, 2003, 2007b).

In previous sections, we discussed the development and learning of verbal and written communication skills. In the final sections, we address another dimension of human communication—the creative arts.

Communicating through the Arts

We began this chapter with a visit to a primary school where teachers used children's art production and appreciation to teach language, reading, and writing. In previous sections, we focused on two dimensions of communication: language and literacy. While it is true that speaking, listening, reading, and writing skills are essential for school success, they are not the only ways of communicating and learning, as is clear from Gardner's theory of multiple intelligences.

Young children, who tend to be less inhibited than older children and adults, use their entire bodies to express their ideas and emotions. If encouraged and provided a range of interesting materials, they can be incredibly creative in representing their world through various art media. Children's enjoyment and accomplishment in the creative arts depends, in part, on teachers providing adequate materials, time, and instruction in specific art techniques.

The Value of Creative Arts

When we discuss the creative arts, we are referring to visual arts, music, movement, dance, and drama. Each type of creative art supports children's imaginative thinking and expression of their ideas and emotions (Isenberg & Jalongo, 2006). Participation in the arts achieves several goals for children: enhanced cognitive development, promotion of symbolic representation, support for creativity, and engagement of children from all cultural and linguistic backgrounds.

Creative Arts and Cognitive Development

The creative arts contribute to children's development in many ways. Engaging in the arts helps children reflect on their own thinking, which becomes more complex as a result. The following example illustrates this relationship between the arts and cognition:

> Karen Spitzer's kindergarten class is involved in a yearlong study of plants and growing things. In the early days of spring, the children become very excited by the flowers bursting forth on the grounds surrounding their rural school. Karen guides the children to observe several types of roses closely. The children take sketch pads outside and draw the roses. When they return to the classroom, Karen reads an information book about flowers. The children write short poems or sentences about how the flowers make them feel. Next, they create pictures using various media such as tempera paint, watercolors, colored pencils, and chalk. Then, the children examine and discuss each other's pictures:
>
> *Kehembe:* I wanted my roses to be pink, but they look too red.
> *Chrystal:* Yeah. Maybe you could add more white next time.
> *Tyree:* Why don't you try the chalks? They come in more shades than the watercolors. Or try the paints because they're easier to mix colors.
>
> The next day, Karen brings in a dozen roses. She places them in water near the art area and gives each child one to hold.
>
> *Karen:* Now look very carefully at your flower and compare it to your picture. What do you see?
> *Chrystal:* Ouch! I forgot about the thorns. I'm going to put some in my painting.
> *Kehembe:* My rose isn't just one color. Even though it's mostly light pink, there's white and some darker pink, too. And the stem is way longer than I thought.
> *Tyree:* I'm going to try making a rose from wire and colored tissue paper so it will look more like a real one, not flat on the paper.

symbolic representation The process of mentally using one thing to stand for something else.

In the above example, many important things are going on. Children are having fun creating art. But even more important, they are developing two key abilities: *symbolic representation* and *visual literacy* (discussed later in this chapter)—that support language and literacy as well as thinking in all areas (see Figure 12.2).

Figure 12.2 A Kindergarten Child's Creativity and Symbolic Representation Abilities

Using Art to Promote Symbolic Representation

Symbolic representation is the process of mentally using one thing to stand for something else. When children engage in the visual arts, they are using various media to represent their concepts of the real world (C. M. Thompson, 2006). Language is a representation of objects, experiences, feelings, and concepts. For example, in English we use the word *chair* to represent an object with four legs that we sit on. Other languages use a different word to stand for the same object. Written language is also an example of symbolic representation. The letters of the alphabet are symbols to represent the sounds of the spoken language. Developing symbolic representation is essential to speaking and reading.

Consider how Karen Spitzer, in the previous example, uses the arts to build symbolic representation in her kindergartners. The children represented the flowers in their initial drawings, in verbal descriptions, and in writing, and they read about them in books. Using different media, such as paint and sculpture tools, they again represented the roses. Then they observed real roses closely and discussed their pictures, reflecting on each other's representations. Finally, they were able to add more realistic detail, representing their more accurate concepts of a rose. The processes that Karen used with her class promoted their creativity, artistic ability, and symbolic representation skills. The activities were part of a science unit that also integrated language and literacy skills.

Supporting Creativity

Individuals are *creative* when they take existing objects or ideas and combine them in different ways for new purposes. Creative individuals use their ever-growing body of knowledge to generate new and useful solutions to everyday challenges (Isenberg & Jalongo, 2006). Therefore, creativity applies not only to the arts, but to all aspects of children's experience.

To support children's involvement in the creative arts, effective teachers need to understand their role. Teachers can err in doing either too little or too much (Isenberg & Jalongo, 2006). Some teachers are too passive, providing no help with art techniques. They merely provide materials and stand back. The commonly heard phrase "It's not the product, it's the process" relates to this view of creativity. The assumption is that whatever children produce is unimportant compared to their creative use of materials.

By contrast, some teachers are too controlling, overemphasizing the finished product. These teachers may assume that parents want children to color within predrawn lines or produce art that conforms to adult-made models. Envision a classroom wall decorated with a series of rabbits that look like they came off an assembly line. The rabbit ears and other parts were obviously cut out by the teacher.

The best approach is for teachers and children to value *both* the process *and* the product. Teachers need to understand that the process of producing art is more satisfying and valuable if children have been taught some techniques (Epstein, 2007b). Children will enjoy the process more and become less frustrated. At the same time, they will feel prouder about the products they themselves produce.

Teachers can also encourage creativity and learning through the arts by introducing children to excellent examples of art. As the teachers from the Thurgood Marshall School did at the beginning of the chapter, they can involve children in noticing, thinking about, and discussing the work of other artists. Then, to promote discussion, effective teachers use open-ended questions, which invite children to observe, critique, evaluate, and develop their own aesthetic preferences.

Engaging Every Child

All areas of the arts can involve and engage diverse groups of children. It is always important to adapt materials and experiences to ensure that children with disabilities can fully engage in the creative arts.

Art, music, and movement are areas where dual language learners can be included without needing to rely on their English language skills. All children can enjoy learning a song in either English or another language. In addition, when singing a song, there is a clearer distinction between each word than in speaking. With her 3-year-olds, Derry sings, "Head, shoulders, knees, and toes . . . and eyes, and ears, and a mouth and nose," touching each body part as she sings. Such a rhyme or song helps dual language learners by connecting physical movements with words.

Every cultural group has its tradition of artistic expression. Consider origami in Asian cultures or African masks. Teachers can involve families by inviting them to share creative art from their own culture. Exploring children's cultural diversity should not be limited to examining such artifacts, but including them is important.

In the following discussion, we describe and give examples of effective teaching strategies in each area—visual arts, music, movement, and dance, and drama.

MyEducationLab

Go to the Assignments and Activities section of Topic 2: Child Development/Theories in the MyEducationLab for your course and complete the activity entitled *Art Development in Preschool.* Consider these artifacts as well as the ones in the chapter to learn how children's drawing develops over time and with experience.

Visual Arts

The **visual arts** are creative processes and products that involve drawing, painting, sculpting with clay, or making models of objects using a variety of materials. Art experiences allow children to convey their ideas, feelings, and knowledge in visual forms. Individually and in groups, children use materials such as crayons, markers, paint, playdough, clay, wire, found objects, glue, tape, and paper, along with tools such as scissors, brushes, rolling pins, and cookie cutters. Developing an appreciation for and an aesthetic awareness of art is another important element. Including art forms, materials, and techniques from children's home cultures can increase their motivation and interest in art.

Understanding Children's Artistic Development

The arts are part of the curriculum and, therefore, are influenced by children's development just like literacy or mathematics. To plan and implement a challenging and achievable arts curriculum, teachers need to understand the typical course of children's artistic development. As with other developmental areas, children pass through several stages as they progress in drawing and painting (C. M. Thompson, 1995). These stages are similar to those in early writing development, described earlier in Table 12.5.

When 2-year-olds begin to draw, they first make random scribbles, lines, zigzags, and circles that may cover the whole paper (see Figure 12.3a). As they gain experience, 3- and 4-year-olds begin to produce shapes such as crosses, squares, and rectangles. Then they combine shapes, making sun-like objects using circles and lines (see Figure 12.3b). Soon children make figures that look like humans (stick figures that gradually get more features), animals, houses, and trees.

With experience and adult scaffolding, children's artwork becomes more and more representational over time. They talk about the process they used and what the product represents. Increasingly, they plan what to create and decide which materials and techniques they will need (Epstein, 2007b).

visual arts Creative processes and products that involve drawing, painting, sculpting with clay, or making models of objects using a variety of materials.

Understanding the typical sequence of children's artistic development helps teachers know what kinds of materials and experiences will be safe, interesting, achievable, and challenging for each age group; that is, what art is developmentally appropriate. For example, with

(a)

(b)

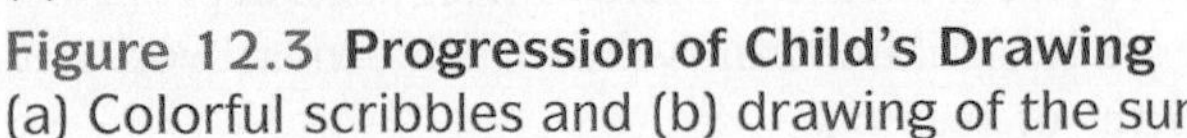

Figure 12.3 Progression of Child's Drawing
(a) Colorful scribbles and (b) drawing of the sun.

MyEducationLab

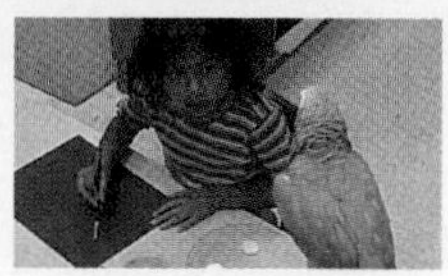

To observe an effective teacher using the visual arts to scaffold children's symbolic representation abilities, creativity, language, and literacy skills, go to the Video Examples section of Topic 7: Curriculum/ Content Areas in the MyEducationLab for your course and watch the video entitled *Birds, Part 2*.

a group of toddlers, representational drawing is an unrealistic expectation; but teachers can expect that recognizable objects will be increasingly present in preschoolers' work, especially if they provide scaffolding as Karen Spitzer did in the earlier example of drawing flowers.

Artistic skills are related to physical development. When finger painting or sculpting with wire, playdough, or clay, children use their senses, explore the properties of the materials, build fine-motor skills, and practice eye–hand coordination (Head Start, 2003). Children build the same muscles and skills they need for writing.

Scaffolding Artistic Development and Learning

Many people think that creativity is inborn. Actually, children's ability to be creative depends in large part on their skills in producing art. Children who lack the skills to model with clay, for instance, may continue to roll clay into balls or make "snakes," but they won't advance to sculpting objects. Soon they may lose interest in working with clay altogether.

When teachers provide adequate materials, time, instruction in specific techniques, and assistance when needed, children's skills continue to develop (Epstein, 2007b; Epstein & Trimis, 2002). For example, after observing the art center in her kindergarten, Lara Mann sees that Duane has a tendency to use too much water, sopping the paper, that he inevitably wads up and tosses away. With a little instruction in how to use watercolors effectively, Duane produces a painting he wants to take home.

Specific art skills that can be taught can be as simple as tapping the paint on the side of the can to get a more controlled stroke, as complex as using potter's clay to make elaborate and durable sculptures. Effective teachers encourage children by making positive, specific comments rather than by giving compliments. Instead of saying, "What a beautiful picture," they say, "I see you've made a pattern—two red stripes, two blue stripes, two red stripes, two blue stripes." The following example illustrates how important teacher scaffolding can be to maintaining children's enjoyment of art:

> Three-year-old Emily, budding artist, loves to paint. She often spends long periods of time at the easel, layering colors of thick paint until her paper is wet through. After weeks of this activity, she tells her teacher, Lelia, that she doesn't want to paint anymore. When Lelia asks why, Emily says, "It always comes out brown." At this point, Emily's teacher has a choice. She can smile and ignore Emily's problem, or she can see the situation as a teachable moment.
>
> *Lelia begins by asking:* Emily, let's think about why your pictures turn brown. What color do you put on first?
>
> *Emily:* I like red best. And I like blue and yellow, too.
> *Lelia:* Those are all pretty colors. Let's mix them together and see what color we get.
>
> As Lelia and Emily mix the colors, Emily's eyes get very wide.
>
> *Emily:* It makes brown! Let's try it again.
>
> After they mix the color brown over and over, Lelia asks, "What could you do next time you paint a picture so it won't come out brown?" With such minimal assistance, Lelia supports Emily to find the solution of separating colors on her paper instead of continually painting over the same spot and renews Emily's enthusiasm for painting.

To effectively support children's artistic development and creativity, teachers need to organize the environment to provide sufficient space and materials for messy activity, clean up, and storage of children's work and work-in-progress. Also critically important is for teachers to treat children's work with respect. To do so, teachers display children's work with their permission. They can also mat or frame selected works for each child to display and keep. Teachers encourage children to take art home to share with families. In preschool and in kindergarten and the primary grades, children can evaluate their own artwork and decide which products they judge worthy of keeping.

Promoting Visual Literacy

All of the experiences described previously contribute to the development of children's visual literacy. **Visual literacy** is the "ability to create visual messages and to 'read' messages contained in visual communications; to perceive, understand, interpret, and evaluate the visual environment" (Johnson, 2008, p. 74). To build children's visual literacy experiences, teachers engage them in: talking about art; extending their thinking about art; and reflecting on art (Johnson, 2008). These processes are similar to the connections that exist among speaking, reading, and writing.

Intentional teachers use the visual arts to promote creativity, symbolic representation, visual literacy, and much more. Creative arts should be an integral part of the early childhood curriculum.

Teachers engage children in talking about their art by commenting on colors, textures, techniques, and patterns. They also lead children through thinking and problem solving by asking open-ended questions such as "What materials did you use to make this flower sculpture?" and "How can you make a door in your house structure? What will you need? What could you do first?"

As in the vignette that opened this chapter, teachers can help children observe, compare, and respond to the properties of artistic works. With a teacher's guidance, children can discuss the artist's use of color, shape, line, pattern, texture, and more. Typical comments might include "Look at the big blocks of color in the Mondrian painting." "Look very closely. Can you see how the people in this picture by Seurat are painted with tiny dots of color?" To bring art closer to children's firsthand experience, local artists can share and discuss a work-in-progress or display their work in the classroom.

Music, Movement, and Dance

On the first day of school for her preschool class, Yasmine gathers the children on the rug and begins to sing a simple song with corresponding hand gestures: "Open, shut them. Open, shut them. Give a little clap. Open, shut them. Open, shut them. Put them in your lap. Creep them, creep them. Creep them, creep them, right up to your chin. Open wide your little mouth . . . but do not let them in!" The children are enchanted and their attention is fully engaged. They beg for her to do it again. Many of them begin following her movements and mimicking the words immediately. Right from the start, the children learn that music will be a fun and active part of every day in Yasmine's room.

Developmentally appropriate music and movement experiences for young children involve singing, creating, listening to, learning about, and making and moving to music (National Association for Music Education, 1995). Music and movement should be a primary focus of the early childhood curriculum and should also be used to accomplish other curriculum goals. Every day teachers can provide opportunities for children to sing favorite songs, learn new ones, and make up their own. Children should also use simple rhythm instruments to create music or to accompany live or recorded music.

Music in the Lives of Young Children

Children's experiences and connections with music begin at birth, when they are comforted by lullabies or the soft humming of their mothers' voices. Some families make music an integral part of their lives. By the time they reach the toddler years, many children have favorite songs and musical pieces. They listen attentively, sing along with a familiar chorus, move to the music, and begin making their own music by shaking a tambourine or banging on a pot or drum. As language skills develop, toddlers begin making up their own songs. If they have had many opportunities to listen to and talk about music, they can identify the sounds made by specific instruments such as a trumpet, drum, or violin.

Music experiences play an important role in children's lives. Music and dance influence children's identities, connect them to their cultural group and the larger society, help them experience and express emotions and ideas, and support their learning across the curriculum. Moreover, music and dance can be lots of fun.

visual literacy Ability to create visual messages and to interpret messages contained in visual communications.

Every cultural group has a musical tradition, such as gospel music in the African American community or salsa among Latinos. As communities connect within a broader culture, these musical traditions are shared and influence each other. Rock and roll began as a blending of several musical forms, including the blues and gospel. This is what makes music a part of children's identities and why it is important to incorporate the music of children's cultures and home languages into the curriculum. If children don't know the songs, they can sing along with a recorded version of a song, such as "Abiyoyo," until everyone learns the words. Teachers can also introduce real or homemade versions of instruments that are typical of children's cultures.

Because popular music is such a part of the larger culture, children will embrace musical styles and lyrics meant for older audiences. Preschoolers will imitate their favorite TV or recording stars, singing into a microphone and dancing to the music. Teachers may need to talk with families about the role of popular music in the classroom.

Memory and sequencing are required to coordinate music and movement, and both require children to follow directions. The skills and knowledge that children gain from participating in music and dance include these (Head Start, 2003; Isenberg & Jalongo, 2006):

- Listening, as when children try to identify the words in a lyric or sounds made by different instruments
- Responding by clapping to the beat or marching around the room
- Creating music, by exploring the sounds made by different instruments and making up a new song or a verse for a familiar song
- Understanding, such as whether a piece of music has a slow or fast beat
- Playing music, such as when they use bells or rhythm sticks to accompany a song
- Moving and dancing with or without music—swinging, rotating, twirling, twisting, or shaking their bodies.

Incorporating Music and Movement in the Classroom

Exposing children to all kinds of music provides many different opportunities for learning. First-grade teacher Malique is an amateur guitarist and music lover. Even though he doesn't sing very well, he never lets that stop him from singing with the children. He knows that children don't mind if the song is off-key as long as they can sing along, too. Malique introduces a different kind of music each week and provides follow-up activities. To launch this music appreciation curriculum, Malique invites sixth-grade band members to bring their instruments and demonstrate the sounds. The children love seeing the instruments up close and learning how to care for them. Then he plays a recording of portions of *Peter and the Wolf* and asks children to listen to how the instruments sound like animals.

Whatever music Malique uses in his classroom, he involves children in thinking and talking about their experiences. He asks questions such as "How does it make you feel?" "What do like or dislike about it?" "How is it similar to and different from other music you have heard?" "What instruments do you hear in different pieces of music?" In this way, children can become critical thinkers about music as well as music appreciators.

Every cultural group has its own musical tradition. Music is one way for children and their families to share a similar experience.

Drama

Pretend play and dramatization involve creative production and demonstration (Head Start, 2003). We have already discussed the benefits of sociodramatic play for language and early literacy skills. Dramatization, however, is more closely tied to a specific story or script. Children in primary grades are more likely to

engage in dramatization than younger children, although preschoolers do act out favorite stories. Children can also dramatize traditional stories from their own cultures.

Teachers can structure a drama session to promote literacy skills in story sequence, character development, and plot. Many dramatizations, both child initiated and teacher guided, involve retelling familiar stories. After reading *Three Billy Goats Gruff* to her class of 4- and 5-year-olds, Marissa Reese helps them act it out. First, she encourages their recall and story sequencing skills by asking them to tell what happened: "How did the story start?" "What happened next?" She helps them identify emotions or problems that surface in the dialogue: "How did the little billy goat feel?" As the children practice acting out the different roles, they get an opportunity to play with dialogue, changing their tone of voice and expression to fit the character of each goat or the troll.

Scaffolding Drama

Scaffolding dramatization requires providing different kinds and the right amount of support for different children (Davidson, 1996). Providing props of varying realism can meet the needs of both inexperienced and capable players. Some will need realistic props to get into character, such as a variety of dress-up clothes or the actual props used by characters in a story. For example, after reading *The Little Old Lady Who Was Not Afraid of Anything* (Williams, 1988), a kindergarten teacher gives children props to act out the story—shoes, pants, shirts, and a hat—and create a scarecrow at the end. Other children can take on a creative role with more open-ended objects such as cardboard tubes, unit blocks, or pieces of cloth.

Seeing the Arts with New Eyes

Pablo Picasso once said every child is an artist (cited in Arts Education Partnership, 1998). But given the current emphasis on the basics of reading, writing, and mathematics in early schooling, time and resources for arts education are diminishing. Many children today have less opportunity to experience the arts. However, all forms of art offer new ways in which children can build language and literacy skills, learn about their own and other cultures, and develop cognitive and social skills. Each of the creative arts can enhance development and learning in other areas. For example, children might count musical beats, draw or construct a model of the earth, analyze the message in a painting, or write dialogue for a drama.

A growing body of research on the effects of early arts experiences finds a positive relationship with improved academic performance (Arts Education Partnership, 1998). Research in the arts also demonstrates that when creativity is developed at an early age, its results transfer to many intellectual tasks (Arts Education Partnership, 1998; Isenberg & Jalongo, 2006; C. M. Thompson, 2006). Given the power of the creative arts to promote children's learning and enrich their lives, teachers can use all forms of art in their teaching to keep students engaged and excited about learning.

Today, state standards and program goals for early childhood education always include language and literacy. Reading proficiency has become the overarching purpose of primary grades. Teachers who know and love young children, however, never lose sight of the long-term goal: learning to communicate creatively in all of its forms.

■ Revisiting Thurgood Marshall School

At the beginning of this chapter, we visited a primary school where a schoolwide art project was occurring. The curriculum at Thurgood Marshall, like every other school in the United States, is full to the brim. Teachers need to be creative to cover the breadth of the curriculum while helping children gain depth in important subject areas. The art study was an excellent example of how teachers can integrate curriculum in meaningful ways. Teachers didn't miss an opportunity to infuse language and literacy throughout the day in all areas of study.

MyEducationLab

To assess your understanding of how to teach children through language, literacy, and the arts, go to the Book Specific Resources section in the MyEducationLab for your course, select *Effective Practices in Early Childhood Education.* Chapter 12 of the Study Plan, and then complete the multiple choice questions and activities.

Having examined how children acquire language and become literate, we can now see how the art project promoted these skills. Children learned new vocabulary words and used language in conversation and analysis. They also read books at appropriate levels on topics of interest, thus promoting their motivation to read. They produced their own art and learned to appreciate and evaluate the work of other artists. These experiences developed symbolic representation ability and visual literacy. Firsthand experience with art sharpened children's observations and critical-thinking skills. All of these experiences motivated the children to become more competent and confident readers, writers, speakers, and artists.

Chapter Summary

- Children gradually learn language over many years from verbal interaction with adults and other children. Language development follows a relatively predictable sequence, but there is a wide range of individual variation that is well within the range of normal.
- Research-based vocabulary-building strategies include one-to-one and extended conversations, listening, decontextualized speech, intentional teaching of new and rare words, play, and interactive book reading.
- The developmental sequence of second language acquisition is similar but not identical to first language learning. To help children acquire English while also maintaining their home language, teachers must work effectively with parents and use proven classroom strategies including play.
- Literacy is the result of many cumulative, interrelated experiences beginning at birth. Research demonstrates that there is a specific set of early literacy skills and knowledge that predict later success in learning to read and write: phonological awareness, alphabet knowledge, print awareness, and vocabulary. Other important skills that contribute to later reading ability include early writing, listening comprehension, motivation to read, and background knowledge.
- Conventional reading is the ability to gain meaning from unfamiliar text. The most effective reading instruction helps children master the alphabetic principle *and* acquire meaning from text in what is called a balanced approach. Components of an evidence-based reading program include phonemic awareness, phonics, fluency, vocabulary, and comprehension. Motivation is key to reading achievement.
- Children learn to communicate through the creative arts: visual art, music, movement, dance, and drama. The arts promote the development of symbolic representation, creativity, and visual literacy. Children's enjoyment and accomplishment in the creative arts depends in part on teachers providing adequate materials, time, and instruction in specific artistic skills.

key terms

academic discourse
alliteration
alphabetic principle
babble
background knowledge
balanced approach
code switch
completion prompt
comprehension
concepts of print
conventional reading
cooing
decode
decontextualized speech
dialogic reading
distancing questions
dual language learning
early literacy
encode
expressive language
extended discourse
fluency
invented spelling
listening
narrative
open-ended questions
parentese
phonemes
phonemic awareness
phonics
phonological awareness
play-by-play language
predictable books
predictors
print awareness
rare words
recall questions
receptive language
rhyme
script language
symbolic representation
syntax
telegraphic speech
visual arts
visual literacy
vocabulary
Wh- questions
word identification

readings & websites

Althouse, R., Johnson, M. H., & Mitchell, S. T. (2003). *The colors of learning: Integrating the visual arts into the early childhood curriculum.* New York: Teachers College Press. Washington, DC: NAEYC.

California Department of Education Child Development Division. (2007). *Preschool English learners: Principles and practices to promote language, literacy, and learning—A resource guide.* Sacramento, CA: CDE Press.

Roskos, K. A., Tabors, P. O., & Lenhart, L. A. (2009). *Oral language and early literacy in preschool: Talking, reading, and writing* (2nd ed.). Newark, DE: International Reading Association.

Weitzman, E., & Greenberg, J. (2002). *Learning language and loving it: A guide to promoting children's social, language, and literacy development in early childhood settings* (2nd ed.). Toronto: The Hanen Centre.

Association for Library Services to Children
www.ala.org

International Reading Association
www.reading.org

National Art Education Association
www.arteducators.org

National Association for Music Education
www.menc.org

National Center for Family Literacy
www.famlit.org

observe, reflect, decide

1. Listen to parent–child interactions wherever you go—in the grocery store, on the subway or bus, on a playground. How do parents talk to their children? Do they initiate conversations? Do they respond when children initiate? Or do they tell the child to be quiet? How does the child react? What effect do you think parental interactions are having on the child's language development?
2. Visit a preschool classroom. Observe and record the language interaction. Does teacher-talk dominate the classroom? When teachers talk, are they mostly issuing directives like "Do this" or "Don't do that"? Or are children and teachers engaged in extended conversations? Do teachers use more conversation closers or conversation stretchers?
3. Observe in a preschool or kindergarten classroom. Look for evidence of literacy. Is the classroom a literacy-rich environment? Where and how are books used? Do teachers ever read books to small groups? Are children encouraged to write? Does the teacher support alphabet learning? Can you find any missed opportunities for supporting literacy learning?
4. Observe in a classroom that includes dual language learners. Do you observe different levels of second language acquisition among the children? What does the teacher do to help make learning comprehensible for those children who are learning English? Are there more effective strategies the teacher could employ?
5. Observe reading instruction in a first- or second-grade classroom. Are teachers helping children learn phonics *and* comprehension strategies? Do children seem interested and motivated to learn to read? Can you think of ways the teacher could be more responsive to children's individual differences in reading ability?
6. Reflect on your own experiences in primary school. How much opportunity did you have to engage with the visual arts, music, movement, dance, and drama? What effect did those experiences have on your creativity, enjoyment of school, and critical thinking? Can you think of ways the arts could be better incorporated in early childhood instruction?

13 Teaching Children to Investigate and Solve Problems: Mathematics, Science, and Technology

Thinking Ahead

1. How can early education address issues of equity and narrow the achievement gap in math and science?
2. How does cognitive development relate to learning mathematics and science?
3. What teaching strategies and curricula are effective in helping children learn mathematics?
4. What teaching strategies and curricula are effective in helping children learn science?
5. How can technology be used effectively to teach mathematics and science?

Darrell Burns and Sofia Moreno co-teach in a state-funded prekindergarten program that is operated in a local child care center. The school district has just introduced a new preschool curriculum to align with the K–3 math curriculum. At first, Darrell and Sofia are skeptical about their children's ability to learn the content, and they feel somewhat anxious about tackling mathematics education themselves. "Math was always my worst subject," Darrell admits. "I majored in early childhood education rather than elementary because I didn't want to teach math." Sofia nods. "I know how you feel. I kind of memorized stuff for the test and never really understood it."

After several weeks, however, the teachers' attitudes change. The curriculum plan helps them understand the number and geometry concepts that they are teaching as well as the important sequences of mathematics learning. Much to their surprise, the children are capable of learning sophisticated math concepts, and truly enjoy the activities in which they participate.

Darrell and Sofia find that opportunities for learning math abound in their classroom. During center time, Sofia works with a small group of children on basic counting principles, using 1-inch cubes. Four-year-old Tori points at the blocks as she says, "One, two, three, five, seven, eight." "No, no," says her friend Parker, "You skipped four! I'll show you." Parker proceeds to say all the numbers in the correct order, but touches some blocks twice. Instead of counting six blocks, he comes up with eight. Sofia notes that Tori has yet to master the number word list, so she'll engage Tori in verbal counting more often. As for Parker, Sofia simply says, "Slow down a little, and touch each block as you say the word." After two more tries, Parker successfully counts six blocks.

Darrell oversees four children playing a board game with a number on each square. Two girls are working at the computer, moving shapes to complete puzzles. Several children are building with unit blocks on the floor. Darrell observes them and adds math words to their play: "Dante, you've made a rectangle space with these cylinder blocks. Can someone else figure out how to make a rectangle?"

As the children become more interested in math, they start counting everything in sight and looking for shapes, in the classroom and on the playground. They figure out ways to create new shapes, such as putting two triangle blocks together to form a square. The children especially like taking digital photos of three-dimensional shapes like spheres and cones, which they use to make a book on shapes. Sofia and Darrell help them make connections between what they are learning about math and their physical science study of the characteristics of light. The children look forward every day to measuring and comparing their shadows on the playground. ▲

The teachers in this classroom, like many early childhood teachers, were initially intimidated by the thought of teaching mathematics. But with knowledge and a well-designed curriculum plan, they realized what capable learners young children can be.

This chapter addresses three separate but interrelated aspects of the curriculum: mathematics, science, and technology. First, we present the content and processes of the early childhood mathematics curriculum and effective teaching strategies that lay the foundation for later school mathematics. Next, we describe the science curriculum and how teachers can engage children in the scientific process. Throughout the chapter, we describe ways to use technology in teaching and learning math and science. A key goal is to raise awareness of the importance of math and science for *all* children. We particularly focus on the need to narrow the persistent achievement gap in mathematics between children from low-income families and their more affluent peers.

■ The Importance of Mathematics and Science

In recent years, mathematics and science education have generated considerable interest for several reasons. The first is widespread concern about the nation's ability to produce a workforce qualified to compete in the global economy. Second is the issue of equal educational and economic opportunity for all citizens.

With so many competing goals in early childhood programs, why is mathematics important? Preschool math matters because it is highly related to later math achievement and because effective curriculum and teaching can narrow the knowledge gap early on (Duncan et al., 2007; Sammons et al., 2008). Research demonstrates that young children are capable of learning important mathematics and science concepts, but they are usually not given the opportunity to do so (National Research Council [NRC], 2009).

The Need for an Educated Workforce

In today's global economy, a large number of jobs require mastery of what is called STEM—science, technology, engineering, and mathematics (NRC, 2001). However, in international comparisons of mathematics and science achievement, children in other nations regularly outperform American children (Mullis, Martin, & Foy, 2008). Moreover, these differences in mathematics knowledge are apparent as early as age 4 or 5 (Starkey & Klein, 2008; Starkey et al., 1999).

Although achievement in science and technology is important, understanding mathematics is strongly connected to both of these areas. As a result, considerable emphasis is now being placed on children developing a firm foundation in mathematics during the early years of school. As early as 2002, the National Association for the Education of Young Children (NAEYC) and the National Council of Teachers of Mathematics (NCTM) issued a joint position statement on math education for 3- through 8-year-olds. In 2009, the NRC issued a major report on early childhood mathematics that outlined recommendations for improving mathematics teaching and learning for all children ages 3 to 6.

Young children are more capable of learning sophisticated math concepts than previously thought. As you can see in this preschool classroom, children are interested in and enjoy learning about mathematics.

Addressing the Mathematics Achievement Gap

Significant gaps exist not just between our country and others, but within our country. As in reading, a mathematics achievement gap exists between children growing up in more affluent communities and those living in poverty (Denton & West, 2002; National Center for Children in Poverty, 2007; NRC, 2009).

Mathematics Predicts School Success

Although reading has received much more attention, research now demonstrates that math skills at kindergarten entry are the *strongest* predictor of later school achievement (Duncan et al., 2007). In an analysis of six large-scale longitudinal studies in the United States, Great Britain, and Canada, researchers found that early math skills predicted not only later math ability, but also success in reading (Duncan et al., 2007). By contrast, early literacy skills were related only to later reading. Apparently, the cognitive abilities employed in mastering mathematics apply broadly to other curriculum content areas.

Mathematics is a cumulative topic of study. Later understanding not only builds on earlier concepts but *depends* on them. Many adults who struggled with and disliked math in school did not have a firm foundation on which to build. As a result, in later grades, more complex math didn't make sense and they began to feel less competent. Early education can narrow the gap. Research in the United States and other countries demonstrates that using a math-focused curriculum can significantly improve the math achievement of children living in poverty (Clements & Sarama, 2007a, 2008; Griffin, 2004; Preschool Curriculum Evaluation Research Consortium [PCERC], 2008; Starkey, Klein, & Wakeley, 2004).

MyEducationLab

Go to the Professional Perspectives section in Topic 6: Curriculum Planning in the MyEducationLab for your course and select the video entitled *Conclusions and Recommendations for Early Childhood Mathematics* and watch and listen to Sue Bredekamp discuss this topic.

International Research Can Inform U.S. Instruction

One international study compared mathematics learning among preschoolers of high and low socioeconomic status (SES) in China and the United States (Starkey, 2007). Two findings were noteworthy. First, Chinese 3-year-olds started out knowing more about math than their American counterparts regardless of their SES status. In fact, the low SES Chinese group knew more math than the high SES Americans. Nevertheless, a knowledge gap between socioeconomic groups existed in both countries at age 3. But by the end of preschool, the gap between the two groups had narrowed considerably for the Chinese youngsters, but had actually widened for the Americans. What accounts for these differences? There are two feasible explanations:

1. Teaching mathematics in preschool and promoting mathematics at home is a higher priority in countries like China and Japan than in the United States (Starkey &

Mathematics knowledge in preschool is a strong predictor of later success in learning both math and reading. Although an achievement gap exists as early as preschool, research shows that good teaching and math experiences can narrow the gap early on.

Klein, 2008). The studies demonstrate that when young children, even those growing up in poverty, are taught more focused math, they learn it and carry it into later schooling.

2. There seems to be a fundamental cultural difference in the value these countries place on learning mathematics and their beliefs about what it takes to succeed. In the United States, we tend to assume that mathematics achievement results from having talent or innate ability; by contrast, in Eastern countries, the assumption is that students can achieve in mathematics if they work hard enough (NRC, 2001).

In the previous sections, we present the case for teaching and learning mathematics in the early years. To truly understand the learning process, it is important to be aware of the cognitive foundations that underlie early mathematics learning.

The Role of Cognitive Development

Several aspects of general cognitive development are strongly related to how children learn mathematics and science. These include informal, everyday math and science applications, concrete and abstract thinking, and the role of language and cognitive development (Ginsburg, Lee, & Boyd, 2008).

Informal, Basic Mathematics

One of the first words babies utter is *more*—evidence of their intuitive understanding of quantity. As they grow, they pay considerable attention to who is bigger and when something is "All gone." Well before school entry, children of all socioeconomic groups demonstrate considerable informal math knowledge.

Informal knowledge about math, including basic ideas about quantity (more and less), size, shape, and pattern, is also called **everyday mathematics** (Ginsburg et al., 2008). Research demonstrates that by age 5, everyday mathematical knowledge is essentially a universal aspect of cognitive development (NRC, 2009). Even babies and toddlers demonstrate basic understandings about some math and science concepts. When they reach out to make a toy move or repeat a sound, they begin to understand the idea of cause and effect (Gelman & Brenneman, 2004). These intuitive ideas about mathematics and science are prior knowledge on which teachers can build.

Children's Interests

Four-year-old William was thrilled when his teacher showed the class a new set of multicolored magnetic blocks. The teacher explained, "There are a hundred pieces in this box." William's eyes lit up and he exclaimed, "One hundred! That's my favorite number!"

Like William, most young children have a natural interest in mathematical and scientific ideas, spontaneously count, and love big numbers (Gelman & Gallistel, 1978; Ginsburg et al., 2008; Greenes, Ginsburg, & Balfanz, 2004). Children's play is full of mathematical and scientific ideas. They order blocks by size, create and extend interesting patterns, and conduct their own experiments, such as seeing if a ball rolls faster down a steeper incline (Seo & Ginsburg, 2004; Worth & Grossman, 2003).

everyday mathematics
Informal, intuitive knowledge about math, including basic ideas about quantity (more and less), size, shape, and pattern.

Children's Thinking

In the past, educators assumed that young children had little capacity to learn mathematics; therefore, teachers often considered it developmentally inappropriate to teach math

(Ginsburg et al., 2008). Researchers today believe children are more competent than previously thought and capable of learning sophisticated math ideas (Clements, Sarama, & DiBiase, 2004; Gelman & Gallistel, 1978).

Both Competent and Incompetent

Children's minds are not simple, however. Compared to adults, children are *both* competent *and* incompetent; they are *both* concrete *and* abstract thinkers (Ginsburg et al., 2008). On the one hand, from an early age, they spontaneously demonstrate math interest and ability well before entering school. At the same time, children display certain kinds of mathematical incompetence, as when they struggle with *conservation* problems (Piaget, 1952). Recall from Chapter 4 that conservation is the understanding that the quantity of objects stays the same regardless of changes in appearance. For example, Noah and Martina each have four graham crackers. Martina lines her crackers up with spaces in between, looks over at Noah and declares, "I gots more than you." Typically, children of this age cannot reverse the operation in their minds to realize that no more crackers were added. In certain situations, however, children can perform conservation tasks depending on how an adult asks the question or alerts children to events they might not have focused on.

Both Concrete and Abstract

Even 3-year-olds can look at a small set of objects (four or fewer) and know how many there are without counting, a skill called **subitizing**, a necessary precursor to later math competence (Clements & Sarama, 2007a). They can see that a set of three toy bears is smaller than a set of five.

MyEducationLab

Go to the Assignments and Activities section of Topic 2: Child Development/ Theories in the MyEducationLab for your course and complete the activity entitled *Development of Preschoolers*. What do you observe about the intellectual competence of this child? How is her thinking both concrete and abstract?

In other ways, however, young children's thinking is abstract. Consider 4-year-old Francine counting her stuffed animals. She touches each one as she says, "One, two, three, four, five." Her teacher asks, "How many animals do you have?" Francine answers "Five," which seems like a very simple thing to do. However, this little girl had to know and say the counting words in the right order; connect each word to one and only one bear; and know that the last word said in the sequence not only stood for the last bear but also represented the total number of bears. That is, she had to remember that she had counted five bears in order to answer that she had five altogether—she had to hold two thoughts in her head at once. And she had to think about a very abstract concept—what *five* is. Five is still five whether it refers to five bears, five chairs, five children, or five fingers. She also sees, reads, and has to interpret an abstract symbol—the numeral 5—in different places. The numeral 5 is posted by the climbing loft because only five children are allowed at a time.

Conceptions and Misconceptions

Children are actively thinking all the time as they try to make sense of their world. Some of these conceptions are accurate, such as Francine's computation of the five bears, while others are not. For example, a common "mistake" young children make is to assume that a "skinny," elongated triangle cannot be a triangle; they think that true triangles can only be equilateral triangles—ones with three equal sides (Clements & Sarama, 2007a). Children also form their own hypotheses about events, some of which seem like magical thinking. They may assume that the sun goes to bed because they do, not the other way around.

Most misconceptions are actually partial hypotheses, or early theories, about how the world works. For example, 5- to 7-year-olds can readily state that the earth is round because they have been taught this fact. However, when asked to draw a picture of the earth and where the people live, their representations reveal their understanding (Hannust & Kikas, 2007). They may actually think the earth is a flattened sphere with the people living on top or that the earth is hollow and the people live inside. These partial hypotheses are gradually replaced by more accurate ones because, as children get older, their thinking becomes more abstract, and experience challenges their earlier ideas.

subitizing The ability to look at a small set of objects (four or fewer) and know how many there are without counting.

Some misconceptions can be prevented by broadening children's experiences. For example, unless children are helped to understand the common properties that make a shape a

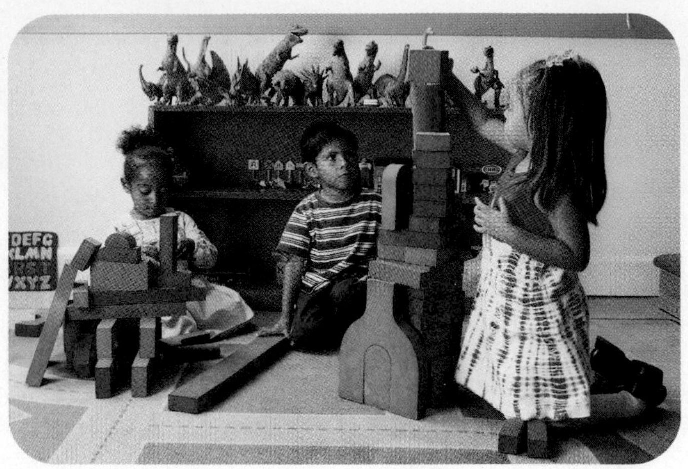

Young children's play is rich in "everyday mathematics." This informal knowledge provides a foundation for later mathematics learning, when intentional teachers introduce the language of math—words that describe quantity and relationships.

triangle, they will persist in thinking that "skinny" versions are not really triangles. It is normal for preschool children to make "errors" as they learn counting and other math and science concepts. Therefore, teachers should be cautious about correcting "errors"; they should encourage children's enthusiasm instead of making them hesitant to voice their own ideas (NRC, 2009).

The Role of Language and Cognition

Language plays a key role in learning mathematics and science. From about age 2, children begin learning the language of counting. The first 10 or so number words are essentially meaningless—children memorize these words by rote (NRC, 2009). Even though this skill is learned before it has true meaning, knowing the number sequence is not the same thing as being drilled on it. Children memorize the sequence by playfully repeating it over and over, the same way they learn the alphabet sequence by singing the alphabet song long before the letters are fully meaningful. Knowing the alphabet sequence, however, is only useful for *alphabetizing*, a skill that preschoolers do not yet need; by contrast, learning the number sequence is absolutely essential.

The Language of Mathematics

Beyond the first 10 numbers, language reflects the underlying structure of the number system. For example, in English, after the child learns "twenty," all he has to do is repeat "twenty" and add the numbers one to nine up to "twenty-nine." Thus, saying the number words goes beyond simple memory to reflect the organization of the **base ten place value system**. The base ten system is a highly efficient way of using just 10 symbols—0, 1, 2, 3, 4, 5, 6, 7, 8, 9—to write any counting number, no matter how large (NRC, 2009). To do so, we use place value in which the meaning of a numeral depends on where it is placed within the number—that is, the numeral 1 can stand for 1 or 1 trillion.

Children also learn other kinds of mathematical language, such as the names of shapes and words for quantity (*more, less*), position (*under, inside*), and relationship (*bigger, smaller, first*) (Ginsburg et al., 2008). These words are so commonly used that we don't even think of them as mathematical or scientific terms. Most importantly, language is necessary to express and explain mathematical thinking. Consider this example:

> Mr. Blaine's kindergarten class needs to divide into four groups. He explains that there will be four chaperones to accompany children to different sections of the zoo and he asks for suggestions:
>
> *Naomi suggests:* Let's just pick the group we want.
> *Darius notes:* But what if we all pick the same one? It will be too crowded and we won't learn different things to tell the other kids about.
> *Flair:* There are twenty kids. How can we divide up? We could line up in four lines.
> *Mr. Blaine asks:* How would that help?
> *Flair:* We need four groups and four lines are four groups.
> *Doug jumps in:* That would work. But it would be easier if we just drew four lines on the chart paper and wrote our names where we want to go.
> *Darius is still skeptical:* But what if we all put our name in the same box?

After each suggestion, Mr. Blaine asks each child to explain why her or his idea would work. The explanations reveal and extend their ideas about how to compose equal-size groups.

base ten place value system Highly efficient system of using just 10 numerals to write any counting number no matter how large, in which the meaning of a numeral depends on where it is placed within the number.

The Language of Science

Science, too, has its own vocabulary and exposes children to a vast array of words—both nouns and verbs—that they might not otherwise encounter. Children are eager to and capable of learning "big" words, such as *hypothesis*, *prediction*, *observe*, *reflect*, and *decide*. They also learn the vocabulary attached to scientific information, words like *incline*, *magnifier*, or *telescope*.

Science information books are rich sources of language along with hands-on experiences. Language is such an important part of children's cognitive development, as well as science and mathematics learning, that teachers should take every opportunity to introduce and reinforce this rich vocabulary (Gelman & Brenneman, 2004).

Mathematical Language and the Achievement Gap

Evidence suggests that the mathematics achievement gap exists because low-income children do not have sufficient opportunity to learn the language of mathematics (Ginsburg, 2006; Ginsburg & Pappas, 2004). How do we know this? Observations of lower- and middle-income preschoolers find little difference in the everyday mathematics they spontaneously demonstrate during free play (Ginsburg, 2006). Both groups exhibit a good deal of mathematical competence on which to build. The main difference is that children living in poverty are generally provided less support and opportunity to learn the language that connects their informal, basic math knowledge to later, more abstract school mathematics. To do so, teachers must help children *mathematize* their everyday experiences, a critically important process described next.

Learning to Mathematize Experience

To **mathematize** means to understand and think about everyday problems and experiences in explicitly mathematical terms (NRC, 2009). When children mathematize, they focus on the mathematics aspect of a situation; they learn to represent and think about its quantitative or spatial aspects; and they create a mathematical model of the situation to solve problems (NAEYC & NCTM, 2002; NRC, 2009).

mathematize To understand and think about everyday problems and experiences in explicitly mathematical terms.

Mathematical models can be created with objects (such as beads or paper), actions (such as counting), or through solving real-life problems mathematically. For example, children building a house create a model of mathematics learning when they figure out how many more blocks they need to make the house twice as tall.

To link the concrete world to the abstract world of math, teachers need to help children learn to mathematize, to connect the informal experiences they have to mathematical ideas and symbols (Ginsburg et al., 2008). Consider the following situation. Children are often asked to share toys. Teachers tend to think of sharing as a social skill, but it can also be considered mathematically—as addition, subtraction, and division. When 4½-year-old Corky wants more toy cars than Eugene, the situation is actually a math problem. If he takes two cars from Eugene, he is adding, while Eugene experiences subtraction (take away). If Corky gets two more cars from the shelf, Eugene's pile stays the same. Corky then has to figure out whether either solution gives him more than Eugene. Unless he knows how many they both started with, he can't be sure if either of his solutions worked. His teacher could step in and simply prevent a squabble by dividing the cars herself or telling Corky he has to share. Or she could engage them in a conversation about how to create two equal sets of cars or one set that is two cars larger.

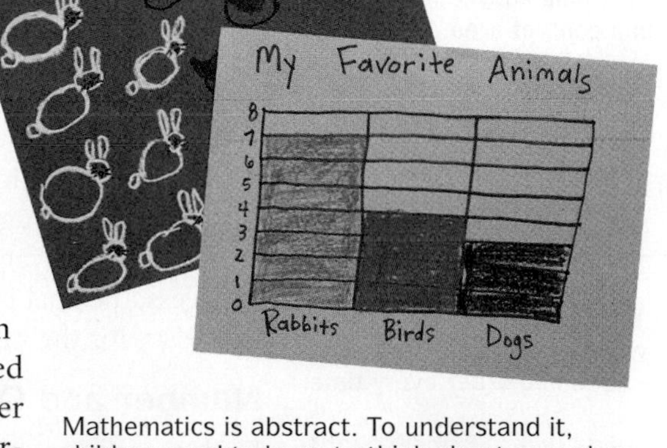

Mathematics is abstract. To understand it, children need to learn to think about everyday experiences and problems in mathematical terms. Children can create concrete mathematical models such as these that make complex concepts more meaningful.

Helping Children Learn Mathematics

Teaching mathematics involves several key elements. First, teachers must know the math concepts and skills or operations themselves. This should go without saying, but many early childhood teachers like Darrell and Sofia, whom we met at the beginning of this chapter, do not fully understand the mathematics concepts they are expected to teach (Ginsburg et al., 2008). In fact, college-level math courses are often not helpful or relevant to early childhood mathematics. For this reason, the 2009 NRC report includes a chapter, "Foundational Mathematics Content," that explains the fundamentals of beginning mathematics for teachers.

The other elements of teaching mathematics to young children are interrelated. Teachers need to know (1) the math content and processes that children need to learn and when they are most effectively taught, and (2) how to plan and implement effective curriculum and teaching strategies.

The Content of Early Childhood Mathematics Curriculum

A broad consensus exists about the early childhood mathematics curriculum based on standards developed by the National Council of Teachers of Mathematics (2000). In 2006, NCTM published *Curriculum Focal Points*, which identifies the math content to focus on at each grade level to ensure that children gain deep understanding of the key concepts and skills needed for later learning.

These documents identify the *big ideas of mathematics*—the overarching concepts and skills of the early childhood curriculum. From age 3 to grade 3, the content goals focus on number and operations, and geometry, spatial relations, and measurement.

Mathematics Teaching–Learning Paths

The NRC (2009) report on early childhood mathematics goes further than NCTM by specifying the **teaching–learning paths** for children age 2 to first grade. These describe the goals or significant steps, with each new step building on the earlier step. Teaching–learning paths are also called *learning trajectories* (Sarama & Clements, 2009) and *developmental* or *learning continua*, and they are a key part of curriculum planning.

Teaching–learning paths have two sources (NRC, 2009):

1. The content of the discipline, that is, the mathematics skills and knowledge that provide the foundation for later learning
2. What is achievable and understandable for children at a certain age.

Teaching–learning paths are linked to age/grade levels and are valuable because they can guide curriculum planning and help teachers use formative assessments to scaffold children's learning along the path (Clements & Sarama, 2007a; NRC, 2009). Table 13.1 provides an example of a teaching–learning path for learning to count from age 1 to 7.

teaching–learning paths Sequence of teaching and learning knowledge or skills in a content area. Also called *learning trajectories* and *developmental* or *learning continua.*

enumeration The act of counting.

stable order principle Principle that states number words need to be said in the same order every time.

one-to-one correspondence Attaching one and only one number word to each object being counted.

One important NRC (2009) recommendation in planning math curriculum is that equal attention should not be given to all topics. There is always limited time in the school day, and decisions need to be made about priorities. In preschool and kindergarten, more focused time should be devoted to number competence (NRC, 2009). This does not mean that number is taught in isolation, nor does it mean that geometry and measurement are unimportant. In fact, learning in these areas can promote learning number concepts. Nevertheless, the goal is that children achieve the foundational number and operations goals necessary for their continued progress in primary grades.

Number and Operations

Understanding number, even the seemingly simple act of counting—called **enumeration**—involves several key concepts (Gelman & Gallistel, 1978). Children need to know that number words should be said in the same order every time—the **stable order principle**. They need to know **one-to-one correspondence**—that one and only one number word should be

Table 13.1 Learning Trajectory for Counting

Age	Developmental Progression
1 year	**Pre-counter** *Verbal* No verbal counting. Names some number words with no sequence. **Chanter** *Verbal* Chants "sing-song" or sometimes indistinguishable number words.
2 years	**Reciter** *Verbal* Verbally counts with separate words, not necessarily in the correct order above five ("one, two, three, four, five, seven"). Puts objects, actions, and words in many-to-one correspondence or overly rigid one-to-one correspondence (e.g., counts two objects "two, two, two"; if knows more number words than number of objects, rattles them off quickly at the end; if more objects, "recycles" number words).
3 years	**Reciter (10)** *Verbal* Verbally counts to 10, with some correspondence with objects, but may either continue an overly rigid correspondence or exhibit performance errors (e.g., skipping, double-counting). Producing, may give desired number. **Corresponder** Keeps one-to-one correspondence between counting words and objects (one word for each object), at least for small groups of objects laid in a line. May answer a "How many?" question by recounting the objects or may violate the one-to-one correspondence or word order to make the last number word be the desired or predicted word.
4-5 years	**Counter (Small Numbers)** Accurately counts objects in a line up to five and answers the "How many?" question with the last number counted. When objects are visible, and especially with small numbers, begins to understand cardinality: _ _ _ _ "1, 2, 3, 4 ... *four!*" **Counter (10)** Counts arrangements of objects to 10. May be able to write numerals to represent 1 to 10. Accurately counts a line of 9 blocks and says there are 9. May be able to tell the number just after or just before another number, but only by counting up from 1. What comes after 4? "1, 2, 3, 4, 5. *Five!*" Verbal counting to 20 is developing. **Producer (Small Numbers)** Counts out objects to five. Recognizes that counting is relevant to situations in which a certain number must be placed. Produces a group of four objects. **Counter and Producer (10+)** Counts out objects accurately to 10, then beyond (to about 30). Has explicit understanding of cardinality (how numbers tell how many). Keeps track of objects that have and have not been counted, even in different arrangements. Writes or draws to represent 1 to 10 (then 20, then 30). Gives next number (usually to 20s or 30s). Separates the decade and the ones part of a number word, and begins to relate each part of a number word/numeral to the quantity to which it refers. Recognizes errors in others' counting *and* can eliminate most errors in own counting (point-object) if asked to try hard. **Counter Backward from 10** *Verbal and Object* Counts backward from 10 to 1, verbally, or when removing objects from a group: "10, 9, 8, 7, 6, 5, 4, 3, 2, 1!"
6 years	**Counter from N (N + 1, N − 1)** *Verbal and Object* Counts verbally and with objects from numbers other than 1 (but does not yet keep track of the number of counts). Asked to "Count from five to eight," counts "5, 6, 7, 8!" Determines numbers just after or just before immediately. Asked, "What comes just before seven?" says, "Six!" **Skip Counter by 10s to 100** *Verbal and Object* Skip counts by tens up to 100 or beyond with understanding; e.g., "sees" groups of 10 within a quantity and counts those groups by 10 (this relates to multiplication and algebraic thinking): "10, 20, 30 . . . 100." **Counter to 100** *Verbal* Counts to 100. Makes decade transitions (e.g., from 29 to 30) starting at any number. " . . . 78, 79 . . . 80, 81. . . . " **Counter on Using Patterns** *Strategy* Keeps track of a few counting acts, but only by using numerical pattern (spatial, auditory, or rhythmic). "How much is three more than five?" Child feels three "beats" as counts, "5 . . . *6, 7, 8!*" **Skip Counter** *Verbal and Object* Counts by fives and twos with understanding. Child counts objects: "2, 4, 6, 8 . . . 30." **Counter of Imagined Items** *Strategy* Counts mental images of hidden objects (as when asked, "There are five chips here and five under the napkin. How many are there in all?"). **Counter on Keeping Track** *Strategy* Keeps track of counting acts numerically, first with objects, then by "counting counts." Counts up 1 to 4 more from a given number. "How many is three more than six?" "Six . . . 7 [puts up a finger], 8 [puts up another finger], 9 [puts up third finger]. *9*." "What is eight take away two?" "Eight . . . 7 is one, and 6 is two. *6*." **Counter of Quantitative Units/Place Value** Begins to understand initial ideas about the base ten numeration system and place-value concepts, including ideas of counting in units and multiples of hundreds, tens, and ones. When counting groups of 10, can decompose into 10 ones if that is useful. Understands value of a digit according to the place of the digit within a number. **Counter to 200** *Verbal and Object* Begins to understand counts accurately to 200 and beyond, recognizing the patterns of ones, tens, and hundreds.

(continued)

Table 13.1 Learning Trajectory for Counting *(continued)*

Age	Developmental Progression
7 years	**Number Conserver** Consistently conserves number (i.e., believes number has been unchanged) even in face of perceptual distractions such as spreading out objects of a collection. **Counter Forward and Back** *Strategy* Counts "counting words" (single sequence or skip counts) in either direction. Recognizes that decades sequence mirrors single-digit sequence. Switches between sequence and composition views of multidigit numbers easily. Counts backward from 20 and higher with meaning.

Source: From *Learning and Teaching Early Math* by Douglas Clements and Julie Sarama, Table 3.1, pp. 30–41. Copyright 2009 by Taylor & Francis Group LLC–Books. Reproduced with permission of Taylor & Francis Group LLC–Books in the formats Textbook and Other Book via Copyright Clearance Center.

attached to each object. They also need to learn **cardinality**, the concept that the last number said stands for the total number in the set. Another key idea, called **abstraction**, is that anything can be counted, whether bears, toes, or people. Finally, counting involves the **order irrelevance principle**, the idea that counting can begin with any object in the set as long as each is counted only once.

The term **operations** refers to working with and solving problems about relationships, such as *more than* or *less than*, and addition and subtraction. Operations should use real objects and word problems. For example, in meeting with her kindergartners, Ms. Guiffre raises a real-world math problem:

> *Ms. Guiffre:* There are four people absent today, and we usually have twenty-two people in our class. We need to send our lunch count to the cafeteria staff. How can we figure out the number of lunches we need?

The children offer several suggestions and then try out some of them.

> *Melissa:* We can count out twenty-two little blocks and take away four, and then count out how many we have left.
>
> *Tyrone:* I know. Let's count our coat hooks on the wall. But not the ones for the kids who aren't here.

Teaching–learning paths are useful for helping teachers guide children along the path (NRC, 2009; Sarama & Clements, 2009b). For example, teachers use strategies to help children learn to count accurately and efficiently, such as slowly touching each object as each number name is said. Teachers should also encourage children to use their fingers to count and explore part/whole relationships (a concept that underlies addition and subtraction). The teacher might say, "Brianna is showing us how old her brother is by holding up five [fingers] and two. What's another way to show seven with your fingers?"

Counting on your fingers is an important part of learning about number. Teachers may not realize, however, that there are cultural differences in how children count on their fingers. To broaden your view of finger counting, read the *Culture Lens: Finger Counting in a Cultural Context* feature.

cardinality The concept that the last number said stands for the total number in the set.

abstraction The concept that anything can be counted.

order irrelevance principle The concept that counting can begin with any object in the set as long as each is counted only once.

operations Working with and solving problems about relationships such as *more than* or *less than*.

geometry The study of shapes and space, including flat, two-dimensional space and three-dimensional space.

Geometry, Spatial Relations, and Measurement

In addition to number and operations, a second area of focus for the early childhood math curriculum is geometry, spatial relations, and measurement (NRC, 2009).

Geometry. Children are naturally motivated to engage with **geometry**, the study of shapes and space, including flat, two-dimensional space and three-dimensional space (Clements & Sarama, 2007b). Geometry involves size, position, direction, and movement, and describes and organizes the physical world in which we live. Children can learn about

Culture Lens

Finger Counting in a Cultural Context

Located in a downtown office building in a large city, West Street Early Learning Center is an employer-sponsored child care center that serves a diverse group of children and families from all over the world. Today is the first day of class for the 3-year-olds. Ella, a new teacher, is just getting to know the children. To draw out one of the shy little boys, she stoops down in front of him and asks, "How old are you, Kenny?" "Free," he replies, and counts off his middle three fingers. Turning to Mizuki, whose family is Japanese, Ella asks the same question. Mizuki doesn't say anything and appears to wave her fingers. Ella is confused. Certainly, she thinks, Mizuki knows how old she is.

Just like most 3-year-olds, Mizuki does know her age. However, her way of communicating this knowledge to Ella reflects her cultural background. Most countries around the world actually use one of three ways of raising fingers to show numbers. In early childhood programs that serve children from different parts of world, teachers are likely to see these different methods.

The most common way—used frequently in Latin American countries—is to raise the thumb first and then the fingers across to the smallest one. In the United States, the most common method is to raise the index finger first, then the other fingers in order (holding down unused fingers with the thumb), and then lastly the thumb—as Kenny did. Another way, also used in some Latin American countries is to begin with the little finger and move across to the thumb.

Other methods are less frequently used such as Mizuki's, where fingers are raised and then lowered. Mizuki wasn't just waving her fingers, she was raising and lowering three fingers to show her age. In India, children may count by touching the lines of the fingers with the thumb.

Given that many programs in the United States serve children from throughout the world, teachers may encounter some of these different finger counting methods. Fingers are a very important tool for young children to solve numerical problems, not just to show their age. Therefore, teachers should recognize that there are different ways of counting on fingers and not try to change what's working for a child.

Source: Based on *Mathematics Learning in Early Childhood: Paths Toward Excellence and Equity*, National Research Council Committee on Early Childhood Mathematics, 2009, Washington, DC: National Academies Press.

angles, shapes, and solids by observing and manipulating objects in the physical world and in the virtual one via technology (Clements & Sarama, 2007b).

Research finds that most early childhood curricula severely underestimate children's ability to learn geometry (Clements & Sarama, 2007a). Teachers continue to focus only on naming basic shapes (circle, triangle, square) long after children have mastered these concepts. Geometry is far more complex, and involves the ability to put together and take apart shapes (composing and decomposing), as well as talk about the properties of shapes (number of angles, sides, orientation).

Spatial Relations. Learning about **spatial relations** gives children an awareness of themselves in relation to the people and objects around them. Spatial sense and familiarity with shape, structure, and location help children understand both their spatial world and also other mathematics topics (Clements et al., 2004). For instance, as Carmel examines a three-dimensional pyramid, her teacher encourages her to explore number concepts as well. For example, the teacher asks: "How many sides does a pyramid have? Why is it hard to figure out?"

Measurement. **Measurement** is the process of determining size, length, area, or volume using a standard unit (inch, gallon). Young children look for and analyze relationships in the real world using measurement. Measurement is a learning goal in itself, but it also plays a useful role in building children's understanding of number and spatial relations. When children measure and compare the length, height, and weight of objects, they use *units* such as inches, feet, or pounds. In working with measurement, children focus on how big, little, long, or short things are and how to figure that out.

Children will sometimes explore measurement by using parts of their body or toys in the classroom—what are called *nonstandard units*. For example, Damien and Issata use their own

spatial relations Spatial sense and familiarity with shape, structure, and location.

measurement The process of determining size, length, area, or volume using a standard unit.

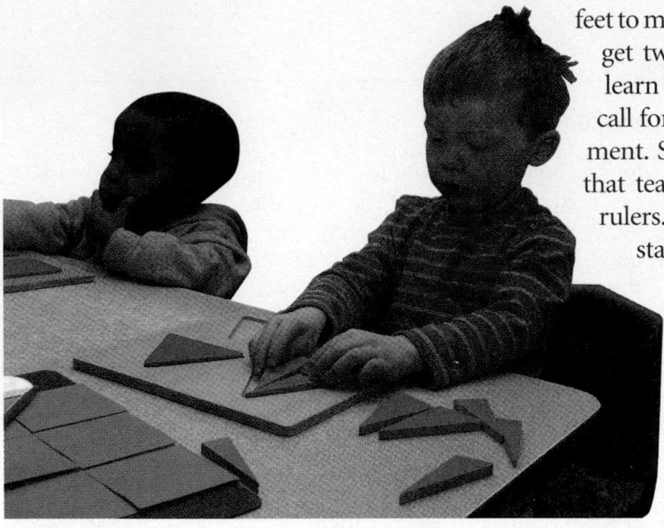

A favorite activity for young children, puzzles help them learn spatial relationships and basic geometry concepts.

feet to measure the length of the boat they've built and discover that they get two different answers. Because children naturally use and can learn from nonstandard measurement, many state math standards call for children to use nonstandard and standard units of measurement. Such a standard has sometimes been misinterpreted to mean that teachers should withhold standard measurement tools such as rulers. But this is not the case. Children enjoy and can learn about standard units using rulers and scales, and doing so can prevent the development of misconceptions about measurement (Clements & Sarama, 2007a).

For example, Mina puts out rulers for her kindergartners to explore during center time. At first, they play with the rulers, pretending that they are objects such as magic wands or pirate swords. But when the children become interested in earthworms on the playground, Mina brings out the rulers and the children begin to pay attention to the numbers on the rulers and what they mean. They get excited about measuring and comparing the length of the worms, and begin to use the rulers for other purposes as well.

Measuring Time: A Word of Caution. Many teachers spend time every morning "doing" the calendar because they think it is a good way to teach math. In fact, more than 90% of kindergarten teachers teach the calendar every day (NRC, 2009). Although the calendar can be used to plan and anticipate future events, it has limited value as a math teaching tool (Beneke, Ostrosky, & Katz, 2008; NRC, 2009).

The calendar's organization—7-day weeks—bears no resemblance to the base-10 number system that children need to master (NRC, 2009). Most of the time children simply recite the numbers in order while someone points to blocks on the calendar. This task is repeated long after the children have mastered the number list and long before they can fully understand the concept of time (Beneke et al., 2008). In addition, pointing to the spaces on the calendar is not as effective for teaching number as counting real objects. The amount of time spent on the calendar each day could be better spent helping children make progress on the mathematics learning paths. More valuable experiences that help children begin to develop understanding of time concepts include the following:

MyEducationLab

To observe a teacher introducing the language of math in children's block play, go to the Video Examples section of Topic 6: Curriculum Planning in the MyEducationLab for your course and watch the video entitled *Building Blocks: Small Group Activity.*

- Children compare one activity with another in terms of which takes more time, "Who can stand on one foot longer?"
- Teachers point out the time schedule and the passing of time, with ideas like *after lunch* or *before story time,* or using more abstract notions like *yesterday*, *today*, and *tomorrow*, although they don't expect children to fully comprehend.
- Teachers use a calendar in much the same way people use one in their homes—to note, plan for, anticipate, and remember significant events such as birthdays, trips, and visitors. They place calendars in the house or office center, where it is used in the real world. They introduce names of days of the week and months of the year, but don't drill children on these ideas.

Mathematics Process Skills

Math experts consistently identify five general process goals that cut across content areas and that should be interwoven throughout the teaching and learning of mathematics for all age groups (NCTM, 2006; NRC, 2009). These processes are problem solving, reasoning, communicating, making connections, and designing and analyzing representations. Any mathematics learning experience might involve all of these processes. These processes are also relevant for other areas of the curriculum, especially for science. All of these processes are part of the larger process of mathematizing. Perhaps most important, these learning processes build

children's curiosity, creativity, and willingness to take risks, all of which may be the most long-lasting and important goals of mathematics education (Clements & Sarama, 2007a).

Problem Solving and Reasoning

Mathematics is about thinking. It is not simply manipulating objects, but constructing mathematical meaning from the experience (Seo, 2003). To become mathematical thinkers, children need to solve problems and reason about number and operations, geometry, spatial relations, and measurement. They need to understand that there are different ways to solve a problem and that more than one answer is often possible. Even in situations where one correct answer exists ("We need fifteen chairs for fifteen children"), there are usually a number of ways to arrive at that solution ("We can give each person his or her own chair" or "We can count fifteen chairs").

Reasoning is thinking logically to come to a conclusion or find a result. As children tackle problems, teachers should encourage them to talk about—mathematize—their thinking. This brings their reasoning to a conscious level, where other children or the teacher can expand on it. Teachers need to create a learning environment in which children feel free to take risks and search for solutions to problems.

> **Effective Teaching**
> Intentional teaching of mathematics leads to better math outcomes for children, especially children from low-income families.

Communicating

To promote children's mathematical thinking, one of the most important things teachers can do is to talk with them about problems, relationships, and mathematical connections. It is equally, if not more, important to listen to what they say. When children discuss their thinking and describe what they are doing, their own thoughts become clearer (NCTM, 2000).

In addition, when children and teachers describe and debate their reasoning, they use the language of math. Teachers can use these occasions to introduce and reinforce math vocabulary. Open-ended questions such as "How do these blocks compare to each other?" and "How do you know that a square is a rectangle?" increase the amount of math talk. Gradually children internalize these questions (ask them of themselves) and are more likely to understand the world from a mathematical perspective.

Making Connections

In mathematical terms, making **connections** refers to understanding links between different areas of math as well as connecting math concepts to real-world problems. For example, measurement can be connected to number because it involves counting units of measurement (i.e., inches), or it could be used to figure out if a shoe fits.

Designing and Analyzing Representations

Exploring ways of expressing mathematical ideas with words, diagrams, pictures, and/or symbols, called **representing**, is an essential part of mathematizing. Imagine a group of kindergartners singing the song "Five Little Monkeys Jumping on the Bed." The teacher first uses her fingers to represent the monkeys as the children sing "One fell off and bumped his head." Soon the children follow her lead with their own fingers. From these concrete representations, the children begin to picture the monkeys in their heads—they form a mental image. Other ways they can represent the monkeys include scribbling circles or drawing pictures of them. Their representations gradually become more abstract. They may make marks on the page to represent the monkeys as the number goes from 11111 to 1111 down to 1. Eventually, children will represent these subtraction problems in symbols: $5 - 1 = 4$.

There are many ways to involve children in designing and analyzing representations of math concepts and problems as well as talking about them. Figure 13.1 is a preschool class's representation of seven eggs and how the class kept track of the 21 days required for them to hatch. Note how the days are in units of 10 rather than 7-day weeks.

reasoning Thinking logically to come to a conclusion or find a result.

connections Refers to understanding links between different areas of math and connecting math concepts to real-world problems.

representing Expressing mathematical ideas with words, diagrams, pictures, and/or symbols.

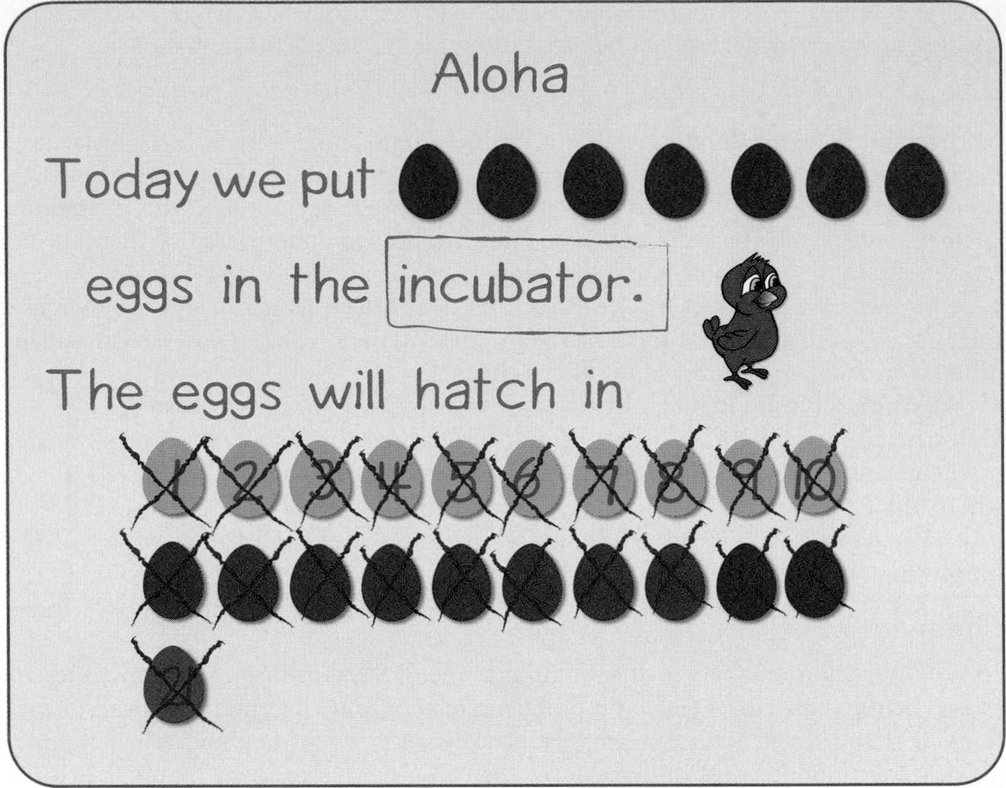

Figure 13.1 Artifact Representing and Analyzing Mathematical Ideas

In addition to these general processes, some specific mathematical processes are used across content areas, such as identifying patterns and solving problems that involve putting together/taking apart, which we discuss next.

Identifying Patterns

In recent years, math standards have included learning about patterns as a specific area of curriculum content that is particularly related to later algebra learning (NCTM, 2000). The ability to identify patterns, however, is a process skill that cuts across all math content areas (NRC, 2009). For instance, geometry and spatial relations involve composing and analyzing patterns. The number list is a pattern in which each new number is one more than the last; counting can be done in patterns (by twos, fives, or tens). Classifying objects by some attribute such as size or shape also involves seeing patterns. Following are strategies for building children's awareness of patterns (Head Start, 2003):

- Help children find patterns (*ab*, *ab* or *abc*, *abc*) in designs and pictures, as well as in movement and in recurring events such as the daily schedule.
- Sing songs with patterns—"If You're Happy and You Know It"; march or move to a rhythm; and clap patterns.
- Play detective and spy patterns in the classroom, on the playground, or in children's clothes.
- Engage children in creating and noticing patterns as they string beads, place shapes or blocks into arrays, and arrange other materials. Over time children can reproduce and create more complex patterns.

Putting Together and Taking Apart

Mathematics at all levels involves putting groups together and taking them apart—the processes of **composing** and **decomposing** (NRC, 2009). These processes are the basic components of addition, subtraction, multiplication, and division. Measurements are composed of larger units (feet) that can be decomposed to smaller units (inches).

Understanding these concepts begins with experiences during early childhood. From age 2 through primary grades, children create collections of objects. Toddlers love stacking toys and filling and dumping containers. Preschoolers will repeatedly compose and decompose puzzles, challenging themselves to do it faster each time. Children can sing a song like "B-I-N-G-O" in which the word starts out composed (with all the letters), and then is decomposed as each letter of the word is no longer articulated. Primary grade children learn about fractions by dividing a pizza.

In the previous sections, we described the important mathematics content and processes that children are learning in progressively more complex and sophisticated form from infancy through the primary grades. Next we describe mathematics curriculum and teaching strategies.

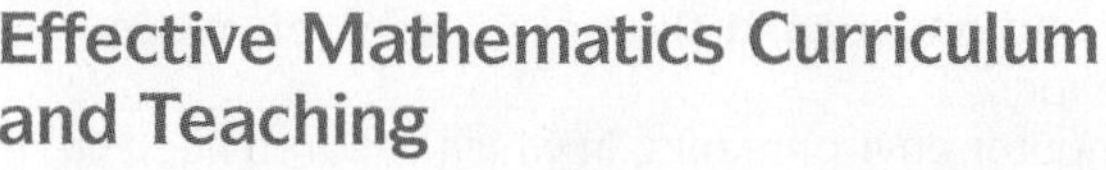

As you can see, even toddlers experiment with basic mathematics concepts, such as putting together and taking apart.

Effective Mathematics Curriculum and Teaching

Responding to children's natural interest in math and problem solving and taking advantage of the teachable moments during children's play and routines are valuable ways to promote math learning, but they are not enough (Ginsburg et al., 2008). An effective curriculum is more than a collection of activities; it must be coherent, focused on important mathematics, and well articulated across the grades (NAEYC & NCTM, 2002; NRC, 2009).

One of the key findings of the NRC (2009) report on early childhood mathematics is that very little time is devoted to mathematics. Most programs do not include experiences in which mathematics is the primary goal. Instead, they address math as part of an integrated curriculum in which mathematics is a secondary goal; as a result, math teaching occurs only occasionally and rarely in depth (PCERC, 2008). However, studies have found that integrated math instruction is less effective than learning activities in which mathematics is the primary goal (NRC, 2009; PCERC, 2008).

A focused mathematics curriculum not only improves children's math skills but also increases their interest in math (Arnold, Fischer, Doctoroff, & Dobbs, 2002). Teachers, too, report that they increase their knowledge and enjoyment in implementing math activities. At the very least, studies on the effects of mathematics curricula indicate that more intentional teaching of math leads to better math outcomes for children, especially children from low-income families and English language learners (Arnold et al., 2002). Read the *What Works: Using a Coherent, Focused Math Curriculum* feature to learn more about curriculum in which mathematics is the primary goal.

Intentional Teaching of Early Childhood Mathematics

In this section, we present research-based ways of intentionally teaching mathematics. They include specific teacher behaviors that relate to positive outcomes, math talk, and grouping. We then discuss the role of play when teaching math.

Teacher Behaviors

Recent research demonstrates the effectiveness of specific teaching behaviors that are related to positive learning outcomes for children (Clements & Sarama, 2008). Doug Clements and Julie Sarama (2007) developed the *Classroom Observation of Early Mathematics—Environment and Teaching* (COEMET), a useful observation instrument to evaluate the quality of mathematics instruction. Some specific teacher behaviors on the COEMET are

composing/decomposing Mathematical processes of putting together and taking apart (for example, addition and subtraction).

What Works

Using a Coherent, Focused Math Curriculum

Valuable math experiences for young children engage their thinking and reasoning and lay a solid foundation for later mathematics learning. An effective math curriculum builds on children's experiences with mathematics and involves them actively in "doing mathematics." Also important are making good use of technology and incorporating assessment as an integral part of learning experiences. Finally, research evidence documenting the effectiveness of the curriculum is essential.

A curriculum that meets all of these criteria is *Building Blocks—Foundations for Mathematical Thinking*, developed by Douglas Clements and Julie Sarama at the State University of New York at Buffalo. Because this model has been used in a great many classrooms and shown to produce robust learning outcomes in well-designed research studies, *Building Blocks* exemplifies what works, according to the Institute for Education Sciences' What Works Clearinghouse.

In programs that use a coherent math curriculum, such as *Building Blocks*, children encounter math experiences in small and large groups, and in their everyday experiences with blocks, art, puzzles, dramatic play, and music. They also learn math by using computers and specially designed software that makes the most of computers' capacities for supporting learning.

For example, young children are limited in their ability to mentally manipulate shapes—to imagine the shapes turned or flipped, for example. Once children accumulate experiences in sliding, rotating, and flipping objects—whether with physical objects or a computer tool—they will be able to develop skills of mental imagery and understand the possibilities for manipulating shapes.

Computer environments, in which children need to think abstractly and give concrete and precise commands, can be particularly helpful in getting a feel for such transformations and for other aspects of mathematical thinking.

A number of other primary mathematics curricula include some of the elements listed here and, to varying degrees, have supportive research. Such programs include *Number Worlds* (Griffin, 2004), *Big Math for Little Kids* (Greenes et al., 2004), and *Pre-K Mathematics* (Starkey et al., 2004).

listed next that relate to children's improved math knowledge (Clements & Sarama, 2007b, 2008; Sarama & Clements, 2007):

1. How much time the teacher is actively engaged in math activities
2. Whether the teacher builds on and elaborates children's mathematical ideas and strategies
3. How much the teacher facilitates children's responding to math questions and situations.

The COEMET describes both high-quality and poor-quality teaching, some examples of which appear in Figure 13.2. Other teacher behaviors that strongly relate to children's math learning include (Clements & Sarama, 2007b, 2008; Sarama & Clements, 2007):

- Teachers' curiosity about and enthusiasm for mathematics
- Teachers' ability to set high but realistic expectations
- Teachers observations of children, note taking to record their observations, and use of learning trajectories to individualize instruction.

Math Talk

Tamara's kindergarten is well stocked with board games that the children enjoy playing. But Tamara observes that some children rarely use them. One day, she invites four of the reluctant players to join her. Tamara introduces the activity: "For this game, we need to roll the dice. Look carefully at this cube. What do you observe about the dots?" As the children examine the dice and count the dots on each side, Tamara extends the math

EXAMPLE 1: The teacher showed curiosity about and enthusiasm for math ideas and connections to other ideas or real-world situations.

- commented on or discussed mathematical ideas in reading a story
- showed interest in the mathematics that emerged in children's play, construction, or discussions

Situation

The children are building with blocks. The teacher says, "What are you making?" Children respond that it's a skyscraper.

Low-Quality Instruction	***High-Quality Instruction***
• The teacher says, "Nice. Be careful it doesn't fall on you."	• The teacher says, "It looks the same on this side [gesturing] as it does on this side [gesturing]. It's symmetrical! Are you going to keep building a symmetric building?" • The teacher asks, "I wonder how tall it is?" • The teacher says, "I see you put the long blocks at the bottom and the smaller ones on top. Could you tell me how that helped you make your building?" "What might happen if you put the long ones on the top?" • The teacher asks, "If you put these curved ones here, can you build more on top of them or not? What would happen if you did?"

EXAMPLE 2: The teacher *facilitated* children's responding.

- elicited many solution methods for one problem
- encouraged elaboration of children's responses
- waited for and listened attentively to individual children
- responded to errors as learning opportunities

Situation

The teacher asks one child to figure out how many 1 more than 3 is.

Low-Quality Instruction	***High-Quality Instruction***
• When a child has difficulty, the teacher says, "Someone else can answer." • When another child gives the correct answer, the teacher moves to the next task.	• When a child has difficulty, the teacher says, "Can you show me 3 to get started?" • The child says, "Four." The teacher asks, "Can you teach us how you did that?" • The teacher asks, "Did anybody do it a different way?"

Figure 13.2 Examples of High- and Low-Quality Mathematics Teaching

Source: From *Manual for Classroom Observation of Early Mathematics—Environment and Teaching (COEMET), Version 3*, by J. Sarama and D. H. Clements. Copyright © Sarama and Clements, 2007. Reprinted with permission.

talk: "What's the largest number you can get when you roll one die?" After turning the dice around, the children finally agree on "six." As the conversation continues, Tamara introduces math talk such as "What do you observe about the number of dots on each side of the cube? How are they different? Do you see a pattern? The dice is shaped like a cube. What do the dots tell you about cubes?" After the children have mastered the game using one die, Tamara brings out a second one and further extends the math learning, "You rolled a four and a five, so how many spaces can you move?"

MyEducationLab

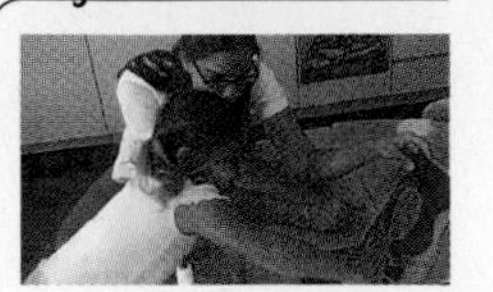

To observe an effective teacher using a variety of high quality teaching strategies to help two young girls learn number and geometry concepts, go to the Video Examples section of Topic 2: Child Development/Theories in the MyEducationLab for your course and watch the video entitled *Samantha Makes an Octopus Puppet.*

This scene from Tamara's classroom demonstrates how even a simple board game provides a great opportunity for **math talk**. Given the critical role of language in learning math, it is not surprising that one of the most effective teaching strategies is what is simply called *math talk*. Teachers should also point out that in these situations children are "doing" math.

The amount of math-related talk children experience is positively related to their mathematical knowledge (Klibanoff, Levine, Huttenlocher, Vasilyeva, & Hedges, 2006). However, there is an enormous amount of variation in the amount of math talk that children experience. One study found that in a 1-hour observation of 26 preschool classrooms, teachers' math talk ranged from 1 to 104 math-related words (Klibanoff et al., 2006).

Grouping as a Teaching Strategy

Alice's preschool children love it when she brings out the plastic attribute blocks which vary by color, shape, size, and thickness. She introduces the activity by saying, "There are so many ways these blocks are the same, but they are also different. Yesterday, we sorted them into groups by two attributes: color and shape. Today, let's see if we can sort them another way. Does anybody have an idea?"

Alfredo says, "Some are big and some are little."

"That's boring," counters Bernadette.

"Okay, you want a challenge," Alice responds. "We'll play a game. I'll give clues and you try to find the shape. Alfredo, can you find the big, fat, blue pentagon?"

Small-group activities for four to six children are especially useful for teaching mathematics, and the skills children acquire during small-group instruction can transfer to knowledge and abilities that have not been taught (Clements & Sarama, 2007a).

Although whole-group time can also be used to teach mathematics, to be effective, it should only be one component of instruction, along with small groups, individual activity, and computer-based programs (Clements & Sarama, 2007b, 2008). The most effective whole-group interactions include a combination of teacher-led brief discussions, problem solving with a partner (another child or an adult), and physical activities, such as marching while counting or doing a shape hunt (Clements & Sarama, 2007a, 2008).

The Role of Play in Teaching and Learning Mathematics

Opportunities for mathematics learning abound in different types of play: block building, sociodramatic play, exploration and practice during play, playing games, using table toys (manipulatives, puzzles, etc.), and book reading.

Block Building

As we have seen, block play provides valuable opportunities for children to explore and engage in mathematical activity on their own (Ginsburg, 2006; Hirsch, 1996). Young children enjoy building with blocks and they naturally engage in mathematical play with them (Seo & Ginsburg, 2004).

However, block building during free play alone doesn't automatically result in math learning. When teachers discuss mathematical ideas with children during block play, their learning is enhanced (Clements & Sarama, 2007b). Teachers can introduce new words such as *unit* or *equal*, and raise problems, such as "How can you make your bridge high enough for the biggest boat to go under?" When teachers provide this kind of support, it

math talk Using the language and vocabulary of mathematics.

enhances children's learning at the time, but is also valuable because children incorporate these new ideas when they play on their own (Clements & Sarama, 2007a). Block building contributes to children's knowledge of geometry and spatial relations, especially three-dimensional shapes.

Small-group experiences like playing board or card games are very effective for teaching mathematics. What other kinds of games might be fun ways of learning mathematics?

Sociodramatic Play

Sociodramatic play contributes to the development of self-regulation and executive function in children (Bodrova & Leong, 2007). Because these two basic cognitive abilities are essential for mathematics understanding, sociodramatic play is an important opportunity to promote math and science learning.

Sociodramatic play provides a context for children to use their developing math skills. For example, while playing restaurant, children write and read the prices on a menu, count their "money," and use one-to-one correspondence as they set the table. Pretend play also provides many opportunities for children to practice their developing math skills, as we describe next.

Exploration and Practice during Play

Many mathematics competencies such as counting require a lot of practice, as well as demonstration, modeling, or scaffolding from adults (Fuson, 1988). Children need practice to master these skills, but such practice should be meaningful and motivating for children and play is an excellent context for it.

During play, children will often initiate their own practice. For example, 2-year-olds will repeat a drumbeat until adults get tired (Geist, 2003). Three- and four-year-old children will repeatedly string a set of beads in a pattern until they have mastered the skill to their personal satisfaction. During recess, several girls take turns pushing each other and count the pushes as they go along. When they get to 20, they switch places. Seven-year-old Garrett repeatedly asks his mom to try to stump him with two-digit addition and subtraction problems as she puts him to bed each night.

Games

Board games in which children count spaces along a number list (squares with numbers on them) are an effective way to develop young children's numerical knowledge. The power of such games is demonstrated in an experiment conducted in a Head Start program (Siegler & Ramani, 2008). Children who played a board game similar to Chutes and Ladders became more skilled at counting, comparing, naming, and estimating numbers. This study showed how something as basic as playing a board game with numbered squares can significantly improve the number knowledge of children from low-income families, many of whom don't have the opportunity to play such games at home. Various games such as cards and dominoes are also fun as long as they don't become too competitive.

Using Table Toys

One of the most effective ways for children to learn math is to use concrete materials, such as puzzles, matching games, and manipulatives. **Manipulatives** are small-sized blocks, cubes, pattern blocks, beads, pegs, and the like that are designed for children's play and learning.

Puzzles and manipulatives can enhance math knowledge, especially geometric and spatial thinking, in both preschool and elementary-age children (Clements & Sarama, 2007a, 2007b). Up to about age 5½, children need concrete objects to learn counting and to solve larger number problems using addition and subtraction (Levine, Jordan, & Huttenlocher, 1992). Manipulatives make abstract tasks meaningful.

manipulatives Small-sized blocks, cubes, pattern blocks, beads, pegs, and the like that are designed for children's play and learning.

However, simply providing manipulatives and other concrete materials does not ensure learning. Rather, teachers need to help children use manipulatives and scaffold their learning if they get stuck using the materials in the same way over and over. Six-year-old Martha loves to play with Unifix cubes, and for several days she creates one row of 10 cubes. Her teacher says, "Martha, you seem to like counting to ten. What if we make two rows of ten? How many cubes do you think we'll need altogether?"

Book Reading

Books have great potential for teaching mathematics and are often used to integrate math into other areas of the curriculum, especially literacy (Casey, 2004; Casey, Erkut, Ceder, & Young, 2008; Schickedanz, 2008). Math concepts can be found in an enormous number of storybooks. In some stories, such as *The Three Bears*, math concepts are readily apparent. In other stories, the math is more implicit, such as in *Rosie's Walk* (Hutchins, 1968), which uses spatial vocabulary to describe a fox following a hen on her winding way (Schickedanz, 2008). In such books, math learning is secondary to another goal, usually language and literacy. Numerous children's books are also published each year for the explicit purpose of teaching math and science.

The use of books is especially powerful, however, when the primary goal is teaching math. The work of Beth Casey and her colleagues (2008) provides strong evidence that presenting math content (such as spatial and number skills) as part of a meaningful story is more effective than teaching the content alone. They developed *Storytelling Sagas*, a series of specially written math storybooks for children in preschool through grade 2 that have proven to be very effective—especially with girls—in teaching math.

In previous sections, we described the importance of building a firm foundation in mathematics understanding for all young children. Next we turn to the topic of science, which is often integrated with mathematics curriculum in the early years.

Helping Children Learn about Science

Young children tend to be curious and inquisitive. They constantly ask questions such as "What's that?" "Why?" "How come?" They also are inclined to actively explore and observe their environment. They want to know "What would happen if . . . ?" To find answers, they readily dig in the mud, dump and splash water, or move their bodies in every way imaginable. At the same time, they try to make sense of these experiences, so they develop and test their own theories about how the world works. As a result, children are often called "natural scientists" (Worth & Grollman, 2003).

In the following sections, we describe the early childhood science curriculum—the content and processes that children from infancy through third grade can and should be learning. Then, we describe effective teaching strategies to promote children's scientific knowledge and understanding. We begin with the role of science in an integrated curriculum.

Science and Technology in the Early Childhood Curriculum

The purpose of **science** is to study and understand the physical and natural world, especially by observing and experimenting. Science plays two important roles in the early childhood curriculum. The primary role is to lay a foundation of conceptual understanding and knowledge that will deepen and broaden as children move through school. Second, science exploration is an excellent way of integrating learning across the curriculum, as the following example illustrates:

> Rose Grindel's first graders are studying life science and exploring concepts such as living and nonliving things and growth and change. As part of their study, they visit a nearby apple orchard. Before their visit, Rose brings in types of apples for tasting (Mackintosh, Granny Smith) and the children graph their preferences. A lively debate ensues about why apples look and taste different. Theo comes to the wise conclusion that apples must be kind of like people: They are the same in most ways, but they look different.

science Study of the physical and natural world, especially by observing and experimenting.

Rose continues, "I guess we need to find out the kind of apples that grow at the orchard. Are there other things you want to find out? Do you think apples are alive?" This last question draws laughs, but then some other queries. Grason says, "Well, trees are alive and apples grow on trees. So they could be alive, too." Grason's comment sparks a debate about what the word *living* means. This topic will be further explored throughout the month as children explore the characteristics of living and nonliving things.

At the orchard, children write down the farmer's answers to their questions and take photos to document their visit. Hunter wants his picture taken next to a tree as a way to measure it. Later in the year, the class will return and compare their photos of the fruit-bearing trees to the flowering trees in spring. Their documentation will pique memories. Hunter thinks his photo will show how much the tree grows.

At the farm, each child picks 10 apples (counting by ones), and back at school they group the apples by tens. The children come up with several ways to figure out that the total number they picked is 210! They also organize the apples by size, and choose the smallest to cook and the larger ones to eat. Because they picked so many apples, Ebony suggests that they donate some to the food bank. When the children cut the apples, they work with halves and quarters. They also bake apples and make applesauce, all the while predicting and observing the changes that take place.

In the previous example, life science is the main curriculum focus. Children learn science facts and concepts while *doing* science—asking questions, predicting, observing, and drawing conclusions. But other curriculum areas are well integrated. Children represent their learning in many ways—drawing pictures, taking photos, and writing about the apple orchard. Mathematics learning includes number and operations (counting, adding, and dividing); creating and analyzing data (graphing), and measurement. Language and literacy are also involved, with children reading information books and discussing and learning new vocabulary.

The Early Childhood Science Curriculum

Scientists and science educators agree on the goals of the science curriculum from preschool through third grade (American Association for the Advancement of Science [AAAS], 2009; NRC, 1996). The content of early childhood science is directly related to young children's natural interest and curiosity about how the world works, living things, their bodies, the environment, animals, and other topics they find fascinating (Head Start, 2003).

As in mathematics, both content and process are not only essential, but also integrally connected. Children can't do a science experiment that isn't connected to science knowledge and concepts, nor can they make sense of discrete facts and concepts presented apart from meaningful context. In short, children can't learn science from a book alone; they have to *do* science.

MyEducationLab

To observe an effective science curriculum and teaching in action, go to the Video Examples section of Topic 7: Curriculum/Content Areas in the MyEducationLab for your course and watch the video entitled *Science*. What science content are these children learning? In what ways are they "doing" science like real scientists?

Scientific Knowledge Goals

As important as it is to foster children's interest and active engagement in doing science, equally important is to expand their content knowledge. The curriculum includes physical, life, and earth and space science. Following are definitions of these science topics and some related goals (AAAS, 2009).

Physical Science. In the area of **physical science**, children learn basic ideas about the properties of liquids and solid materials and objects (size and shape). They learn how things move and change position. They show increasing understanding of cause-and-effect relationships, for instance, how force affects the distance a ball rolls. They also explore characteristics of sound and light—how shadows are produced and change, or how sound results from vibrations.

physical science Basic ideas about the properties of liquids and solid materials, how things move and change position, and cause-and-effect relationships.

From infancy, children gain knowledge of the physical world by acting on objects to see what happens; babies love to throw their bottle out of a high chair over and over to see what happens. At times they act to get a desired effect—rolling, pushing, and dropping objects. To extend learning, teachers can ask children what will happen if they squeeze an object or

Young children are naturally interested in investigating the world around them. As you can see, these preschoolers are fascinated by observing flowers.

challenge them to blow on a spool to make it move. Often children explore and manipulate effects without knowing how they achieved the results; when teachers ask children how or why they think something happened, an everyday experience is turned into a scientific event (Head Start, 2003).

Life Science. **Life science** is the study of the characteristics, life cycles, and environments of organisms. Children identify features of plants and animals, their habitats, and needs (food and water). They learn about living and nonliving things, and how living things grow and change. They also learn parts of the human body, how they function, what people need to stay healthy, and how human beings are alike and different.

Earth and Space Science. This topic involves studying properties of earth materials, changes on the earth, and patterns of movement and changes of the sun and moon. The learning goals of **earth and space science** include:

- Recognizing repeating patterns in nature (day and night; seasons)
- Observing weather changes
- Understanding the effect of people on the environment
- Learning about geographic features of the earth (mountains, oceans) and the movement of objects in the sky.

Key Scientific Concepts

Across the three content areas of science are several key concepts or big ideas that create a strong foundation for later science learning. These concepts include *understanding change* and *cause-and-effect relationships*. Another concept that is revisited through school is the *idea of a system*—that a whole is composed of related parts that affect each other. For example, the human body is a system; there are weather systems and, of course, the vast solar system.

These complex concepts are vital to the work of all scientists. Preschoolers can grasp such concepts at a basic level when teachers draw attention to them in planned and spontaneous learning experiences. For example, when Jonah asks why insects fly and birds fly, but fish that also have wings don't fly, his teacher poses the question to the class. A lively discussion ensues about the differences between wings and fins and how some birds, like ducks, both swim and fly.

Children's conceptual understanding deepens when they have a variety of experiences related to the same concept (Gelman & Brenneman, 2004). For example, children deepen their understanding of the concept of life cycles by planting and tending a garden, observing a class pet, and studying how humans grow.

Change can be continually observed in the natural world. Some changes occur too rapidly to be observed without special tools such as microscopes, whereas others occur too slowly for children to fully comprehend, such as the changing seasons (Head Start, 2003). On the other hand, some changes can be readily observed and investigated by any age child. Teachers can encourage children to look for all sorts of changes:

- What happens to the plant when it is left in the dark?
- What happens to your shadow at different times of the day? Is your shadow there every day?
- What changes can be reversed? Can water be turned into ice and back into water?

Scientific Inquiry

An overarching aspect of the curriculum is the process of doing science, or **scientific inquiry.** Scientific inquiry involves children in several processes such as observing, predicting, and investigating (Worth & Grollman, 2003). In Table 13.2, we list these processes and illustrate them with a physical science example—children studying shadows to learn the properties and characteristics of light.

life science The study of the characteristics, life cycles, and environments of organisms.

earth and space science Studying properties of earth materials, changes on the earth, patterns of movement, and changes of the sun and moon.

scientific inquiry Involving children in observing, predicting, and investigating.

Table 13.2 Scientific Inquiry Processes in Children

Process of Scientific Inquiry	Example: Properties of Light
Noticing, wondering, exploring, and asking questions out of curiosity or to further existing knowledge	On a bright, sunny day outdoors, preschoolers notice and play with their shadows, exploring how to make the shadows longer or shorter and wondering whether they can "get away" from them. The teacher asks, "Where do you think a shadow comes from?"
Formulating preliminary predictions, explanations, or hypotheses to answer questions	Children offer their theories about shadows: People make shadows; shadows follow you; shadows are skinny; only the sun makes shadows. Some think shadows go away at night and some disagree.
Gathering evidence by actively observing, investigating, and/or experimenting	The children observe and gather evidence about shadows: They trace their shadows at different times of the day outdoors; they play with a shadow theater indoors (a sheet in front of a large window), guessing the objects creating the shadows.
Recording, reporting, explaining, discussing, and reflecting on evidence	The children refine their ideas about shadows: Other sources of light make shadows, not just the sun; people need light to make shadows; shadows change shape.
Refining questions, refocusing observations, and engaging in more focused explorations	The teacher sets up an overhead projector for children to focus on what more can be learned about shadows. The teacher sends home a letter to families encouraging them to help children observe shadows at night.
Sharing and discussing ideas, listening to other perspectives, and asking new questions	Children share their observations from home, such as street lights can make shadows, and they ask new questions: "Can the moon make shadows?" The study continues with new questions and interests.

Source: Based on *Worms, Shadows and Whirlpools: Science in the Early Childhood Classroom*, by K. Worth and S. Grollman, 2003, Portsmouth, NH: Heinemann.

Effective Science Teaching

The fact that most young children are naturally curious and inclined to explore and investigate does not mean that they "naturally" or automatically learn science concepts and processes. To understand concepts and acquire skills, children need intentional teachers who plan and implement a coherent science curriculum. Science learning is too important to be left to chance. Intentional teachers promote science learning by carefully organizing the environment, providing focused learning experiences, and integrating science into children's play and everyday routines (Head Start, 2003).

Organizing the Environment

Science requires a planned environment, materials, and tools, such as cups, containers, trays, and jars, to help children observe, collect, organize, and display evidence. Children need tools for investigation including a variety of magnifying glasses, binoculars, mirrors, flashlights, magnets, levers, pulleys, and scales. Information books and access to the Internet are also essential resources for studying science.

Recording and representing evidence and conclusions requires tools as simple as notebooks, writing implements, and chart and graph paper, and as technologically sophisticated as digital and video cameras, computers, and whiteboards. For example, an Eyeclops™ is a computerized magnifier that can project onto a wall or screen. Children can aim it at all kinds of objects—their skin, the inside of a seed, or a butterfly in a jar.

Children learn by *doing* science. They need to use the methods of scientists—questioning, predicting, investigating, experimenting, and drawing conclusions.

Providing Focused Experiences

An effective science curriculum should reflect a scope and sequence that provides a coherent progression of science skills and content (Albert Shanker Institute, 2009). Learning goals and topics should build on one another so that children develop progressively more complex understandings. Content should align with state or national science benchmarks and standards.

Teachers can plan in-depth projects or topics of study related to science knowledge that build on and expand children's interests. Sufficient time should be devoted to topics for children to go into some depth. For instance, in a class study of animals, small groups of children or individuals might study one animal and report their findings to the others in the group.

Curriculum should focus on knowledge that is familiar and meaningful to children, such as concepts of temperature based on their experiences with weather. Although children are more capable of abstract learning than previously thought, it is usually easier to begin with more concrete, accessible experiences such as scientific phenomena that can be directly seen, touched, tasted, or heard. In addition, teachers shouldn't impose scientifically accurate explanations for phenomena before children are able to grasp their meaning (Worth & Grollman, 2003).

Integrating Science in Play and Routines

Science is everywhere. Children learn science when they play in the water table, ride down a slope on a tricycle, or observe ants on a sidewalk. Rich science opportunities occur in blocks, sand, clay, and other materials; cooking, art, music, and movement; stories; and outdoor experiences.

Adapting for Individual and Cultural Diversity

Science is engaging, interesting, and fun for many children. But every child is different. Teachers need to pay particular attention to adapting learning experiences for children with special needs and dual language learners. They also need to be mindful of providing girls with equal opportunities to learn science.

Children with Special Needs. Providing access to science experiences for children with disabilities is an especially important task for teachers. To widen your view of effective science teaching, read the *Including All Children: Science Exploration* feature.

Dual Language Learners. Science presents an opportunity as well as a challenge for children who are learning English. Because science involves real things and events, it can help children learn vocabulary words, especially names of objects, living things, and tools. On the other hand, specific scientific terms such as *inquiry* or *evidence* can be especially difficult for dual language learners (Albert Shanker Institute, 2009). These children will need lots of cues, gestures, and repetition to learn these words in meaningful context.

Gender Differences. During a visit to the nature center, first-grade teacher Trula Mann is startled when the naturalist brings out a snake for the children's inspection. She hates snakes and cringes at the thought of touching it. She sees that the boys eagerly gather around the snake while most of the girls look frightened and withdraw. Trula swallows her anxiety and reaches out to touch the snake. She is surprised to find that it is not at all slimy. The naturalist asks, "How can a snake find food or defend itself since it doesn't have arms or legs?" At the end of the discussion, the children conclude that they would bite, too, if they were a snake who was threatened. In overcoming her trepidation, Trula served as a valuable model for the children, especially some of the girls.

Including All Children

Science Exploration

Science is an excellent vehicle for integrating curriculum content in early childhood. Most children are naturally interested in science topics and motivated to engage in investigations using all of their senses. However, children with sensory disabilities may lose out on such learning unless teachers make appropriate accommodations.

Sheila Kohn loves science, and so do the children in her first grade class. Currently, the curriculum topic is earth science. The children have formulated questions and are exploring a wooded area near the school. They want to know what lives under the ground and how it survives. They have brought little shovels, collection containers, and magnifying glasses for observation. Their questions include these: How does the earth smell? How does it feel? What lives in a small amount of earth? How do they breathe? What do they eat? What happens if it rains?

Most of the children are very excited and eagerly approach the investigation. Delores, however, has a vision impairment. The trek outside intimidates her, and all the talk of observing and using the magnifying glass makes her feel left out. Sheila discusses the situation with Delores and they agree on a plan. Together they will visit the outdoors in a small group, and Delores will use her other senses to investigate the earth. Delores will be in charge of the questions that she is most able to address: What does the earth feel like and how does it smell? Delores is an especially astute listener as well, so she will also report on what she hears outside. Because the other children focus on what they see, they usually miss a great deal of information that can be obtained through their other senses.

Ira has a different special need—sensory integration disorder—which requires an altogether different accommodation. Children who have sensory integration disorders have difficulty processing and connecting sensory information. Each of the five senses obtains information from the environment in different ways. In the course of typical development, the senses work together to sort out and make sense of the input. Children with sensory integration disorders, however, may be overly sensitive to one or more of the senses—touch or sound, for example. Or they may fixate on one sense such as sight or smell.

In Ira's case, the busyness of the classroom overwhelms him at times. He is especially disturbed by confusing experiences like science study that seem to come at him from all directions. To ensure Ira's successful participation, Sheila includes him in the small group with Delores on the walk. Unlike Delores, however, who is encouraged to use as many senses as possible, Sheila helps Ira limit his sensory input. She gives him earplugs to lessen the noise and sunglasses to minimize the light. Under such conditions, Ira is an astute observer and spends a long time carefully watching a worm wiggling through his pile of earth.

As we see from Delores's and Ira's situations, successful inclusion of all children requires knowledge of each child's needs and strengths and individually planned accommodations and modifications.

Because the science and engineering professions have been traditionally dominated by white males, particular efforts need to be made to address stereotypes and open the fields early on to girls and to children from diverse linguistic and cultural groups. Such gender differences are apparent as early as preschool. For example, one study found that boys demonstrated more curiosity, spontaneity, and extensive knowledge about nature and vertebrate and invertebrate (worms, snakes) animals than did girls (Desouza & Czerniak, 2002). On the other hand, girls, although more fearful, were also more concerned about the welfare of animals. Boys and girls also differed in their play preferences, with boys more active and more likely than girls to bring into their play the science concepts that were introduced at group time the day before. Given that gender differences in both science and mathematics begin early and persist, it is never too early to introduce powerful role models such as female astronauts, inventors, or architects.

The Teacher's Role in Supporting Science Learning

Providing a scientifically engaging learning environment and opportunities to explore are essential, but children do not learn science from manipulating materials alone. They need intentional teachers to connect the experience to scientific concepts and vocabulary, as described in the feature titled *Becoming an Intentional Teacher: Science in Block Building.*

Becoming an Intentional Teacher

Science in Block Building

Here's What Happened The block area was running smoothly, but I wanted to take my preschoolers' block building experiences to a new level and extend their awareness of the physical science in construction. I took the following actions:

1. Took photos of various details of our building's interior and exterior and gathered pictures of different kinds of constructions (e.g., fort, barn, tower) to post in the block area.
2. Put away the blocks that stick together, such as Legos and Duplos.
3. Began observing in the block area and talking with children about construction.

Here's What I Was Thinking Physics principles are at the heart of block construction, but I felt that in my classroom we weren't using the full potential of blocks for exploring these ideas. Here is the thinking behind my actions:

1. I posted photos and other images of buildings in the block area and talked with the children about them in order to increase their awareness of various types of buildings and encourage them to branch out in their construction. Such pictures were handy, too, for children to refer to as they grappled with creating various kinds of buildings.
2. Because I wanted the children to get into exploring balance and stability, I decided to remove for the time being all of the blocks that stick together.
3. I observed in the block area to get a feel for the kinds of things the children were doing there. I noted that they usually were not interested in creating complex structures. If I asked questions related to the building ("What could you do to make the walls of your fort stronger?"), as often as not they ignored me. I wanted to extend their thinking without interfering with their play.

Instead of intervening during center time, I eventually found that using another time, such as large or small group, worked better for introducing new building materials or a new challenge. I found that the children often incorporated such elements in their block play and discussed them—with me and with one another—yet the construction and play were under their control.

Source: Based on a teacher's experiences as described in *Worms, Shadows, and Whirlpools: Science in the Early Childhood Classroom*, by K. Worth and S. Grollman, 2003, Portsmouth, NH: Heinemann.

Table 13.3 lists key strategies that teachers can use to promote children's enthusiasm and understanding of science knowledge, concepts, and methods. These strategies are also effective for teaching mathematics.

Teaching and Learning with Technology

While science is the study of the natural world, the goal of **technology** is to change or modify the natural world to meet human needs (NRC, 1996). Technology, in its many forms, is a tool for all kinds of learning throughout life. It can be as simple as a handheld magnifying glass or as complex as the Hubble space telescope exploring the origins of the universe. Both of these tools make it possible for people to see things beyond the capability of the human eye. Technology in itself is neither good nor bad; the same tool—such as a computer—can be used productively or destructively.

technology Tools used to change or modify the natural world to meet human needs.

Table 13.3 Science Teaching Strategies

Science Teaching Strategy	Explanation
Model and welcome curiosity, openness, and flexibility to questioning without needing to know all the answers. Teachers are sometimes intimidated by science because they don't have enough knowledge themselves.	While teachers don't need vast knowledge before tackling a topic, they do need to prepare and learn as much as possible. When they don't know an answer to a child's question, the best response is, "I don't know. What do you think?" or "How could we find out?"
Be open to and appreciate creativity and beauty in science. Sometimes science is erroneously thought to be only about cold, hard facts.	Examine NASA-produced photos of sunrise on Mars or the rings around Jupiter. Watch a butterfly emerge from its cocoon. Such experiences can inspire children to produce their own creative representations of the natural and physical world.
Encourage children to reflect on their experiences and share their ideas with others. Direct experience with materials is important to their science learning, but it is not enough.	Engage children in thinking about, representing, and discussing their experiences and observations. Discussion among teachers and children, informally and in planned groups, gives children the chance to hear others' thinking and perspectives and to develop skills communicating about science.
Teach children observation skills.	Encourage children to go beyond just looking. Have children describe, draw, discuss, redraw, and describe again to refine observation skills and build vocabulary.
Provide a variety of ways for children to document and represent their work.	Give children journals, writing tools, and digital cameras to record their observations, gather data, and communicate their findings to others.
Listen to children and ask about what they are seeing and doing.	When children talk with interested adults about what they see, hear, and think, they do more noticing, wondering, and reflecting. They make connections, think about causes, and learn new, often rare words.
Build on and extend children's interests in the natural world and living things.	Use information books, field trips, technology, and visitors, to open up the classroom.
Engage children in formulating their own questions (*What do you want to know?*), designing experiments (*How can we find out?*), and making predictions (*What do you think will happen if…?*).	Children attend more closely to what they see, hear, smell, and feel when they have put forth their own prediction or question or have considered how to go about investigating something. They are also more likely to think about what their observations mean.
Don't bombard children with talk as they explore and investigate. Instead, watch closely and use a well-timed question or comment.	Prompt children to: • Make a prediction (*What will it look like if…?*). • Think aloud (*What are you doing now? What next?*). • Reflect on their actions (*What did you do before that happened? How do you know? How did you figure that out?*).

Sources: Based on *Benchmarks for Science Literacy*, American Association for the Advancement of Science, 2009, Washington, DC: Author, retrieved September 15, 2009, from http://www.project2061.org/publications/bsl/default.htm; and *The Head Start Leaders Guide to Positive Child Outcomes: Strategies to Support Positive Child Outcomes*, Head Start, 2003, Washington, DC: Department of Health and Human Services.

Children today need to learn with and about technology. How can teachers use technology to promote mathematics and science learning?

A Developmentally and Technologically Appropriate Classroom

A preschool teacher creates a class website that is updated regularly. The children create a slide show about their class pet using Kid Pix software to share with families. For an integrated science study on the properties of water, kindergartners produce information books on the computer using digital photos of their water experiments.

First graders work together using an interactive whiteboard, a large digital touch screen with a computer, and the Internet. They explore pictures and information about birds in different parts of the world. They e-mail their questions to a first-grade class in Australia.

These are some examples of how creative teachers use technology to expand children's worlds beyond the classroom. In some cases, a relatively inexpensive form of media is used such as a digital camera, while an interactive whiteboard constitutes a much larger investment. Given the costs, educators must make informed decisions and be taught to use the tools effectively.

Choosing Appropriate Interactive Media

As with books and toys, every year hundreds of children's media products flood the marketplace, for both home and school use. Given limited budgets and the vital importance of choosing developmentally and culturally appropriate tools, early educators need help making decisions. Warren Buckleitner, an authority on interactive media for children, provides an online service for this purpose, *Children's Technology Review*. In addition, the NAEYC Technology and Young Children Interest Forum (2008) provides an interactive support group for teachers through its website.

Decisions about technology should be based on how well the particular tool serves the purposes of the classroom and the teaching and learning goals for children. "Technology does not drive purposeful learning; teachers' intentional instructional planning does" (NAEYC Technology and Young Children Interest Forum, 2008, p. 50).

Promoting Learning with Technology

Technology has many uses, from complex problem solving to practice on individual skills, managed at the children's level of thinking (Clements & Sarama, 2003). Working with appropriate software builds collaboration, creativity, and language. In fact, preschoolers actually talk almost twice as much at the computer than during any other activity, including blocks and art (Clements & Sarama, 2003).

Computers allow children to break free of the physical world and manipulate objects and space in ways that are otherwise impossible (Clements & Sarama, 2003; Sarama, 2004). For example, when children put together a wooden puzzle, there are strict limits on how pieces can be placed. Similarly, trying to correct or change marks formed on paper can be difficult and frustrating. By contrast, with Kid Pix drawing software and many other programs like it, a child can take actions that are impossible in the real world—change the shape of a design or instantly change colors—and easily alter their creations. In this way, the computer helps children become explicitly aware of and intentional about what they are doing (Clements & Sarama, 2007a).

Ensuring Access for All Children

Technology is expensive, and some question whether and how limited resources should be devoted to it (Blagojevic, 2003). Others raise the issue of equity because some children have

How Would You Respond?

Computer Access

The Situation Suppose you have children in your first-grade class who are computer savvy and others who have very little familiarity with computers. There are two computers in your classroom, and the daily schedule includes several periods when children work independently on various activities and projects (in writing, math, social studies, science, etc.), some of which can involve the computer. You want the children who have had very little computer experience to gain skills and confidence with the technology and begin to use it in productive learning experiences.

What to Do? Various courses of action are possible in this situation. Which of the following do you think would be most useful and why?

- Ensure that all the children who want time with the classroom computers have access.
- For certain activities, pair children who are less experienced with those who are more computer competent to help the novices catch up.
- Set up the computers so each child can work on his or her own and have privacy so less experienced children won't be embarrassed by their lack of computer skills.
- Invite parents who don't have computers at home to use the classroom computers after the school day (with the assistance of a tech-savvy parent or teen volunteer) and encourage the parents to involve their child in what they are doing.

Can you suggest other strategies that might be useful?

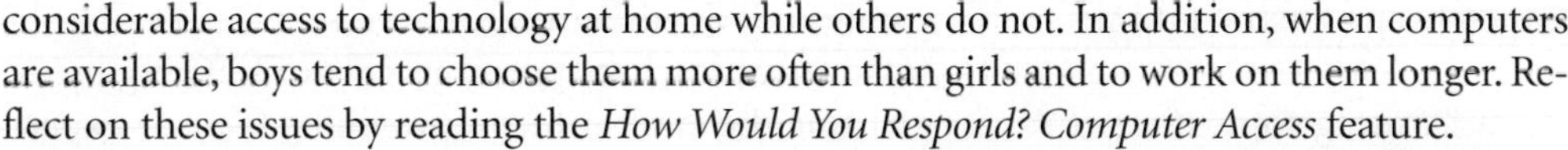

considerable access to technology at home while others do not. In addition, when computers are available, boys tend to choose them more often than girls and to work on them longer. Reflect on these issues by reading the *How Would You Respond? Computer Access* feature.

For interactive media to be effective, teachers need to teach children the basics of how to use it along with the vocabulary (i.e., *mouse, cursor*); then they can encourage experimentation with open-ended problems. They also need to use a wide range of teaching strategies to encourage, question, prompt, model, demonstrate, and give children choices without taking over or limiting children's opportunities to explore. Developmentally appropriate software allows children to be in control, to function independently, and to create and invent their own activities; it also needs to be flexible and allow for more than one correct response (NRC, 2009).

In this chapter, we explored the importance of providing developmentally appropriate, effective curriculum and intentional teaching in the related areas of mathematics, science, and technology. We described how teachers can help children become effective problem solvers and investigators. With this knowledge in mind, we return to Darrell and Sofia's classroom.

Revisiting Mr. Burns and Ms. Moreno's Classroom

At the beginning of this chapter, we met Darrell and Sofia who, like many Americans, feel math anxiety. Using a well-planned, focused curriculum, they found that young children are not only capable of learning significant mathematics, but also enjoy and are interested

MyEducationLab

To assess your understanding of effective curriculum and teaching strategies in mathematics, science, and technology, go to the Book Specific Resources section in the MyEducationLab for your course, select *Effective Practices in Early Childhood Education,* Chapter 13 of the Study Plan, and then complete the multiple choice questions and activities.

in learning it. They incorporated mathematics learning goals and introduced mathematics language into children's play. The teachers worked with children in small groups using math manipulatives and games. They also individualized their teaching to help each child make progress along the learning paths that lay the essential foundation for later math understanding.

These teachers also integrated part of the curriculum around a science topic that was motivating for children and created a meaningful way for them to apply math concepts in context—a shadow study that included measurement. They used technology—digital cameras, computers—as a tool to build on and expand children's interest and extend their experiences beyond the classroom.

Chapter Summary

- A math achievement gap among lower SES and higher SES groups of children is present at the time of kindergarten entry and tends to widen as children progress through school. This knowledge gap exists to some extent because children living in poverty do not have sufficient opportunity to learn the language of mathematics that connects their informal, basic math knowledge to later more abstract school mathematics.
- Several aspects of general cognitive development are strongly related to how children learn mathematics and science. These include informal, everyday math and science applications, concrete and abstract thinking, and language.
- Young children are capable of learning sophisticated mathematics, and they are interested in learning it. Teachers can contribute to narrowing the achievement gap and improving the math learning of all children by helping children mathematize their play and everyday experiences as well as by planning specific, math-focused curriculum.
- Broad consensus exists among mathematics experts that from age 3 to grade 3 content goals should focus on these topics: number and operations and geometry, spatial relations, and measurement. Mathematics process goals include problem solving, reasoning, communicating, connecting, and designing and analyzing representations.
- Early childhood science curriculum includes knowledge and concepts of life science, physical science, earth and space science, and the process of scientific inquiry: questioning, predicting, observing, investigating, and documenting.
- Intentional teachers promote science learning by organizing the environment, providing focused experiences, and integrating science in play and routines.
- Interactive media are effective tools for teaching young children curriculum content and for expanding their thinking and communication skills.

key terms

abstraction
base ten place value system
cardinality
composing/decomposing
connections
earth and space science
enumeration
everyday mathematics
geometry
life science
manipulatives
math talk
mathematize
measurement
one-to-one correspondence
operations
order irrelevance principle
physical science
reasoning
representing
science
scientific inquiry
spatial relations
stable order principle
subitizing
teaching–learning paths
technology

Clements, D. H., & Sarama, J. (2009). *Learning and teaching early math: The learning trajectories approach.* New York: Routledge.

National Research Council, Committee on Early Childhood Mathematics. (2009). *Mathematics learning in early childhood: Paths toward excellence and equity.* Washington, DC: National Academies Press.

Seefeldt, C., & Galper, A. (2007). *Active experiences for active children: Science.* Upper Saddle River, NJ: Pearson.

Worth, K., & Grollman, S. (2003). *Worms, shadows and whirlpools: Science in the early childhood classroom.* Portsmouth, NH: Heinemann.

Children's Technology Review
www.childrenssoftware.com/aboutcsr.html

NAEYC Technology and Young Children Interest Forum
www.techandyoungchildren.org

National Council of Teachers of Mathematics
Search this site to find *NCTM Curriculum Focal Points, PreK to Grade 3.*
www.nctm.org

ScienceStart!
www.sciencestart.com

readings & websites | observe, reflect, decide

1. Listen to conversations among your peers about mathematics. Reflect on whether they convey positive or negative attitudes about math and their own abilities. Reflect on your own experiences with mathematics in school. Are you math-phobic? If yes, why? How will you confront these phobias?
2. Observe in a preschool, child care classroom, or family child care home. Watch carefully for examples of mathematics learning. Reflect on whether there are missed opportunities for teaching mathematics. How could teachers be more intentional in teaching mathematics with this age group? How could they incorporate mathematics into the day?
3. Visit http://ecetechshowcase.wikispaces.com. Explore the many ways technology is being used with young children. Read at least one of the teacher blogs and reflect on what you learn about teaching with technology.
4. Observe in a preschool or kindergarten classroom. How much, if any, time is spent on the calendar? If math is only taught in a whole-group session, reflect on how effective it is. Decide if the environment helps or hinders children's active involvement in learning mathematics or science.
5. In a primary grade classroom, look for evidence of science curriculum and teaching. Are science books and tools of inquiry available? Are boys and girls equally involved in science experiences? Reflect on whether science is valued in the school. Decide if more time and resources should be devoted to science.
6. Observe how technology is used in two elementary schools—one serving a low-income population and another serving a more affluent community. Reflect on the similarities and differences you see. Decide whether inequities exist and explain how they might be addressed.

14 Teaching Children to Live in a Democratic Society: Social–Emotional Learning and Social Studies

Thinking Ahead

1. How do young children develop socially and emotionally?

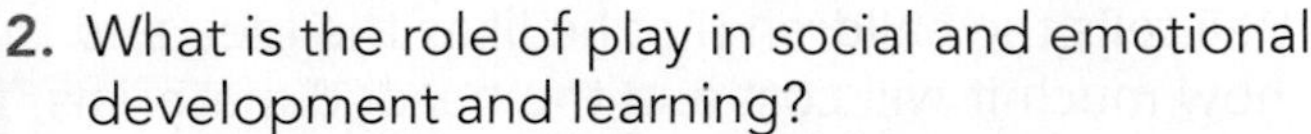

2. What is the role of play in social and emotional development and learning?
3. How can understanding the continuum of social and emotional development help teachers to foster children's social–emotional learning?
4. What are effective strategies for teaching children social problem-solving skills?
5. What is the content of the early childhood social studies curriculum?
6. What are some effective, developmentally appropriate strategies for teaching social studies?

It is Waylon's birthday and he gets to be the "Big Cheese" in his kindergarten class at Jefferson Elementary School. He bounds in the door with his "About Me, My Family, and My Community" poster, featuring a collage of photos including his grandparents' wedding, his first birthday, his first haircut, and his pet dog. His mom will visit at circle time to share the story of how they picked his name and what it means. Waylon gets to deliver the attendance sheet to the office and select a friend to accompany him. Later Waylon's teacher, Ms. Hans, asks the class to vote for which of Waylon's two favorite books to read. A few more votes are cast for *Leonardo the Terrible Monster* and the children know that the majority rules. Ms. Hans begins reading and the children visibly relax while listening to the story about friendship.

Down the hall, Mr. Bell is working with a small group of third graders on their relief maps of Iraq. Four children are working on a report about oil: what it is used for, how much we use in America, and how much we get from foreign sources. The group is huddled around a computer, searching the Internet for some of these answers. Another group is brainstorming ways to support the children on the nearby army base who have parents deployed to Afghanistan and Iraq. They decide on a stuffed toy drive for the younger children, a "letter buddy" system, and a care package drive. The group excitedly tells

Mr. Bell about the buddy project. Eight-year-old Tasha explains, "Well, you see, third graders—like us—will be paired with kindergarten and first graders from the base school to help write letters to their parents."

Mr. Bell tells the children that he likes the idea and that they need to figure out how much it will cost and the needed materials. Mr. Bell's class has been studying Iraq for weeks. He incorporates reading, writing, and mathematics into the social studies unit. ▲

In this chapter, we discuss how social–emotional learning and the social studies curriculum prepare children for life in a democracy and in a global society. **Social–emotional learning** (also called *social competence*) is children's ability to recognize and regulate their emotions, establish and maintain positive relationships, make responsible decisions, and solve social problems constructively (Epstein, 2009). **Social studies**, the integrated study of history, geography, economics, political science, and other related subjects, contributes to the development of competent citizens (National Council for the Social Studies [NCSS], 1994). During early childhood, social studies and social–emotional learning are inextricably connected. Learning to live in a democratic society—the overarching goal of social studies—is predicated on social–emotional competence.

In this chapter, we focus on how the social studies prepare children to be **engaged citizens**—change agents in their schools, communities, and eventually in the world. As we saw in Mr. Bell's class, he extends his class's learning beyond the community to the Middle East and helps children learn history and geography while working to make the world a better place. In Ms. Hans' kindergarten, she lays the foundation for engaged citizenry with her focus on social–emotional learning. The children learn about themselves and others and engage in beginning democracy by voting on activities such as which book to read.

We begin with an overview of children's social and emotional development from birth through age 8 and ways teachers can foster children's social–emotional learning. Then we discuss social studies content and effective teaching and curriculum approaches.

Social–Emotional Development and Learning

Research demonstrates the critical importance of social–emotional learning for school success (Boyd, Barnett, Bodrova, Leong, & Gomby, 2005; Payton et al., 2008). The foundation of active citizenship is the ability to establish positive relationships with other people and solve social problems.

Development in the social and emotional domains is inextricably linked; consequently, they are often referred to as one concept, *social–emotional development*. When children establish warm and responsive relationships with adults—the foundation of social development—they are more likely to develop important emotional skills such as identifying feelings and learning to regulate their emotions and express them appropriately. In turn, these emotional skills pave the way for the development of interpersonal problem solving, an essential social skill. The following example illustrates the interaction of social and emotional development.

> Louise was overjoyed the day her daughter Kate was born. Louise's friends tease her that she never puts Kate down for a moment. Indeed, Louise often holds and gazes at her baby. She imitates her expressions and, at first, picks her up whenever she cries. As a newborn baby, Kate is beginning to trust Louise to meet her needs. Kate generalizes this trust to other adults in her life. In the context of these relationships, Kate is also learning key emotion words that eventually will help her to regulate her emotions and, in turn, to solve interpersonal problems. Ever since Kate was a tiny baby, her parents have labeled her various states with feeling words, "You are sad. . . . Katie is frustrated. . . . Katie loves her

social–emotional learning Children's ability to recognize and regulate their emotions, establish and maintain positive relationships, make responsible decisions, and solve social problems constructively. Also called *social competence*.

social studies The integrated study of the history, geography, economics, political science, and other related aspects of societies of the past, present, and future.

engaged citizens Children as change agents in schools, communities, and eventually in the world.

mommy. . . . Katie is happy to see her grandma. . . ." When Kate begins to talk, her sentences are often peppered with feeling words that help her parents, teachers, and peers understand what she needs and how to help.

Social–emotional learning is to a large extent the product of development—relatively predictable, age-related changes in children. At the same time, social and emotional skills are learned and, therefore, can be taught. We begin by addressing the topics separately, but because they are so closely connected, the remainder of the chapter addresses these topics in a more integrated way.

Social–emotional learning and social studies during early childhood lay the foundation for children to become engaged citizens in their community and the world.

Understanding Social Development and Learning

Social development refers to young children's ability to form and sustain positive relationships with adults and other children. Like other domains, social learning occurs along a developmental continuum. Skills become more complex as children are placed in more demanding social situations, such as early childhood programs, schools, after-school programs, and special interest clubs and classes.

As children grow, their ability to establish friendships with peers becomes more important and influences how children view themselves and the world (Ladd, Herald, & Andrews, 2006). Within the context of these relationships, children learn and practice cooperation, the ability to form and sustain relationships, and the ability to solve interpersonal problems in positive ways. Cooperation with peers requires that children understand other people's rights and perspectives, empathize, and balance their own needs and desires with those of others. For example, when Mimmo, Bart, and Chelsea want to play restaurant, they can't all be the waiters; they have to work together and figure out who will do what. Similarly, when Sasha tries to join the group, further cooperation is required to see how she will fit in.

Understanding Emotional Development and Learning

Emotional development is children's increasing ability to identify their own and others' emotions, to express emotions in a healthy way, and to regulate their feelings (Epstein, 2009). **Emotional literacy** helps children self-regulate, both in personal situations, such as when they become frustrated or discouraged, and in social contexts, such as when their feelings are hurt. Teachers must also understand that individual and cultural differences affect social–emotional development.

social development Young children's ability to form and sustain positive relationships with adults and other children.

emotional development Acquisition of important emotional skills such as identifying feelings and learning to regulate emotions and express them appropriately.

emotional literacy Children's ability to identify their own and others' emotions, to express emotions in a healthy way, and to self-regulate their feelings.

Valuing Individual and Cultural Diversity

The values and practices of each child's family and community shape the feelings, knowledge, and expectations that influence social and emotional development (Hanson & SooHoo, 2007). For example, Waylon's enthusiasm for being the "Big Cheese" might not be shared by a child from another cultural group.

Children need to develop respect for people with ideas and experiences that are both similar to and different from their own. Lulu's best friend in preschool is Bethel. When Lulu invites Bethel to her birthday party and Bethel doesn't come, Lulu's feelings are hurt. Angela, the girls' teacher, notices that Lulu doesn't want to play with Bethel anymore. Angela explains to Lulu that Bethel's family does not celebrate birthdays or holidays. Her not attending Lulu's party doesn't mean that Bethel doesn't like Lulu. Angela draws a parallel to Lulu's family being vegetarian. When this is explained to Lulu, she understands and readily seeks out Bethel as a playmate again.

Healthy social–emotional development is influenced by the match between children's feelings and expressive behaviors and the expectations of the social situation in which they find themselves. Teachers need to provide a respectful atmosphere in which cultural, religious, racial, linguistic, age, gender, and ability differences are valued.

Supporting Children with Disabilities

Children who have disabilities, developmental delays, or who are at risk for developmental delays may require special attention and support to promote their social–emotional development. Some children with special needs may face particular challenges in developing successful peer relationships. To consider social–emotional development through the wider lens of special education, read the *Including All Children: Social Development in Children with Disabilities* feature.

Children with even mild delays tend to participate less in sustained play, spend more time alone when other children are playing, express more sadness when playing with other children,

Including All Children

Social Development in Children with Disabilities

Children with disabilities may have difficulty making friends and being accepted by other children in the group. Peer rejection is harmful for every child, but especially painful for children with disabilities who face multiple developmental challenges. And many parents of children with disabilities want most of all for their children to have friends and be treated like their typically developing peers. To achieve these goals, children with special needs often need adults—teachers and parents—to intervene, as the following example illustrates.

> Tommy is a 5-year-old child with Down syndrome. He has attended preschool for the past 2 years and is now in kindergarten. Tommy's social relationships with the other children have been generally positive, especially with several children from his preschool class. Recently, however, both Tommy's parents and teachers have noticed that other classmates have begun to tease Tommy, and former playmates are less interested in including him in their play unless he takes on the role of the baby. In fact, as one playmate points out, "Tommy still wets his pants, so he has to be the baby."
>
> Tommy's teacher, Ms. Wasky, was trained in early childhood education and has little experience in or knowledge about special education. She strives to provide interesting learning experiences that keep children engaged. She believes strongly in activating children's intrinsic motivation to learn rather than using external reinforcements like stickers or happy faces. She talks with the children and encourages them to include Tommy. Under Ms. Wasky's supervision, a few children grudgingly let Tommy join them, but then they ignore him. She is concerned that Tommy's social development is regressing.
>
> Ms. Wasky meets with Tommy's parents and members of his IEP team to discuss ways to help him become more accepted by his peers. Both the parents and teacher believe that Tommy is physically capable of self-toileting and, in fact, the pediatrician agrees. All adults involved want to allow Tommy to achieve this important developmental task on his own terms rather than rely too heavily on external reinforcement.
>
> The dilemma they confront is weighing the risk of waiting longer while Tommy continues to be rejected by his peers, against the risk of Tommy possibly becoming dependent on extrinsic reinforcement. Their growing concern about the social costs of peer rejection or infantilization of Tommy leads them to decide on a behavioral intervention. Tommy's teacher and parents, in consultation with the special education team members, decide to initiate a behavioral intervention that uses operant conditioning. They begin with concrete reinforcers for appropriate toileting behavior (in this case, stickers that Tommy selected). Eventually the reinforcement shifts to tokens that Tommy can trade for extra time on the computer or other experiences he especially likes.

As a result of this intervention, Tommy becomes more aware of and gradually learns to anticipate and respond appropriately to his toileting needs. As a result of this explicit teaching strategy, Tommy not only experiences the intrinsic satisfaction of controlling his own toileting practices, but this functional achievement also significantly contributes to an improvement in his social status in the classroom. No longer is he relegated to the role of the baby on every occasion.

Source: Adapted from "Developmentally Appropriate Practice: The Early Childhood Teacher as Decision-Maker," by S. Bredekamp, 1997, p. 48, in *Developmentally Appropriate Practice in Early Childhood Programs*, revised edition, edited by S. Bredekamp and C. Copple, Washington, DC: NAEYC. Reprinted with permission from the National Association for the Education of Young Children.

get angry more, and use less effective conflict resolution strategies (McConnell & Odom, 1999). Some children will need extra assistance from teachers when building these skills.

The Role of Play in Social–Emotional Learning

Because peer relationships are such a critical component of social–emotional development, play is an especially important context for children to acquire and practice social skills and emotional self-regulation.

Social Development and Play

Children's play has been a topic of study for centuries. Early in the 20th century, researchers began to systematically observe and record how young children's social interactions during play changed over time.

Development of Social Play

Now-classic studies conducted by Parten (1933) identified four developmental levels of social play and approximate ages when each type of play dominates, as presented in Table 14.1. Parten also identified unoccupied and onlooker behavior as two situations in which children do not engage in play.

Current Views of Social Play

Although most play researchers still agree that children engage in these different types of social play, they do not agree about the order or the ages at which children progress

solitary play Children play alone, usually with toys or objects.

parallel play Children play next to each other, but not with each other; they may speak, but don't really converse.

associative play Children play and share with each other, usually one other child.

cooperative play Children assume different roles and share a purpose for the play.

Table 14.1 Levels of Social Play

Type of Social Play	Approximate Age	Example
Solitary play—children play alone, usually with toys or objects.	2 to 2½ years old (according to Parten) All ages (as understood today)	Two-year-old Jeannette pounds her plastic hammer on her workbench or tucks her baby doll into bed. Five-year-old Imelda pretends to be a doctor, dresses up in a lab coat with a stethoscope, and starts treating the dolls and stuffed animals.
Parallel play—children play next to but not with each other. They may speak but don't really converse.	2½ to 3½ years old	Three-year-olds Nina and Dora sit next to each other with their dolls. Nina says, "My baby is sick." Dora says, "I'm going to grandma's house."
Associative play—children play and share with each other, usually one other child.	3½ to 4½ years old	Four-year-olds Chris and Cory are each building a tower with blocks. Cory says, "You need a pointy one on top. Here's one."
Cooperative play—children assume different roles and share a purpose for the play.	4½ years and older	Four preschoolers build a bus with the hollow blocks. Sasha says, "I'm the driver, but I need a ticket taker. You take the tickets, Rinaldo." Toya states, "Me and Isaac will be passengers. Take us to the circus. Then I get to drive."

Source: Based on "Social Participation among Preschool Children," by M. Parten, 1933, *Journal of Abnormal and Social Psychology, 27,* pp. 243–269.

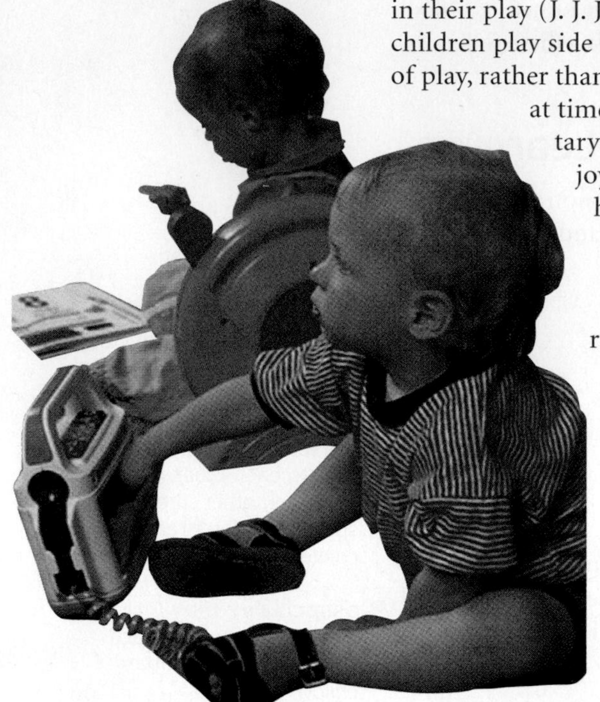

Social development begins in play. As you can see, these toddlers are parallel playing, a first step in learning to play with other children.

in their play (J. J. Johnson, Christie, & Wardle, 2005). For example, parallel play, where children play side by side but do not interact, is now considered the least mature form of play, rather than solitary play. Older children continue to engage in solitary play and, at times, switch back and forth between cooperative and solitary play. Solitary play can involve toys/objects or make-believe. For example, Toya enjoys the cooperative scenario of taking the trip, but afterward she sits by herself and pretends to drive the bus. Even after children develop more socially complex play abilities, they will use all types of play at times. Imelda may share her stethoscope with Lora who also wants a turn—associative play—without cooperating in the shared goal of running a hospital.

In fact, solitary play may be evidence of a personality trait; some people are just more social than others. But if children never play with others, they miss the valuable learning opportunities that play affords. Additionally, if children do not move beyond solitary play, this may signal a difficulty in children's social development (J. J. Johnson et al., 2005). Teachers need to be aware of children's play patterns and intervene if necessary; for example, if children watch others play and appear to want to join in but don't know how or are rejected by their peers, teachers need to model the words to say or suggest other strategies to use.

Emotional Development and Play

Play has long been linked with emotional development and helps children in several ways (Hyson, 2004; Sutton-Smith, 1980). Play provides a context for children to address their fears, develop coping skills and resilience, and feel in control of their environment.

Play and Fears

During the preschool years and as children's cognitive development progresses, they acquire a well-developed imagination. Along with this new flexibility in thinking comes an increase in their fears. Three-, four-, and five-year-olds may be afraid of animals, the dark, monsters, or whatever they can conjure up. Given the dangers in today's world—strangers, violence, and abuse—their fears may be real as well as imaginary. Consider this example:

> Four-year-old Taylor is afraid of dogs, especially the big boxer that just moved in next door. He cries every time he leaves home and doesn't want to go to school anymore. After talking to Taylor's mother, Ms. Jerome purchases a set of plastic dogs for the classroom and sets up a pretend dog training school. Taylor gradually begins to play with the plastic dogs and Ms. Jerome overhears him saying to the boxer, "Bad dog. Don't jump. Stay in your yard. No barking." After a few days, Taylor takes over the dog training school, and tells the stuffed dogs that they better be good or he will tell their mommies. Taylor's mother also talks to the neighbor about controlling the dog, but his play experiences at school help Taylor work through his fear.

In play, children like Taylor can pretend to be mighty and strong and conquer their fears. They fantasize that they are the giant animal or the monster, thus giving themselves power over the feared creature.

Building Coping Skills and Resilience

Young children experience all kinds of stresses in their everyday lives: going to child care when they want to stay home, moving to a new house, going to the doctor, and so forth. At times, extraordinary stressors occur—a death in the family, illness or injury, observing or being a victim of violence. Play helps children develop the ability to cope with life's traumas and acquire resilience.

Play can serve as a cathartic activity for children to express the negative emotions that life events precipitate. Three-year-old Grace has a new baby brother, Miles. Her mother assures her teacher that Grace just loves the baby and isn't jealous at all. But during playtime, her teacher observes Grace shaking a baby doll and saying in a harsh voice, "Get in your bed and stop crying." Obviously, Grace knows she can't treat baby Miles this way. By playing out her resentment and jealousy at school, however, she can cope more effectively with this major change in her life.

Gaining Control through Play

In general, young children's lives are not in their control. Grown-ups and older children make them do things that they don't want to do: eat what is served, pick up their toys, get dressed, go outside, take a nap. Sometimes they resist even when they want to do something simply because it wasn't their idea.

Children love to play (and it is so emotionally supportive) because it is *child initiated* and controlled (J. J. Johnson et al., 2005; Wiltz & Klein, 2001). They decide when to start and stop, what to do, and whom to do it with. If teachers intrude on children's play—try to take over or direct the play to their own ends—children will usually stop playing. It's no longer fun. Child-initiated play affords children power in a safe environment and also helps them learn to make choices and live with the consequences of their choices. If Chloe chooses to build with blocks, she may not have time to do puzzles or paint at the easel.

The Continuum of Social and Emotional Development

In this section, we describe some of the typical social and emotional accomplishments that occur for children from birth through age 8. These descriptions, in which the role of play is apparent, are followed by examples of how teachers can support children's progress.

It is important to note that individual differences are present even at birth and that children's experiences at home, in child care, and at school make a big difference in how and when they develop these abilities. Because children's social and emotional development are linked to the contexts, cultures, and relationships in which they grow and learn, adults play a critical role in shaping children's positive social and emotional development.

> **Effective Teaching**
> Intentional teaching, support, and encouragement are necessary to foster crucial social–emotional skills in young children.

Infants and Toddlers

The major social–emotional task for babies is the development of a warm and responsive relationship with primary caregivers (Shonkoff & Phillips, 2000). Between birth and 12 months, an indicator of emotional development is the ability to quiet when comforted. Babies also begin to show preferences for primary caregivers and work to maintain interactions with caregivers. For example, babies imitate caregivers' gestures and sounds and also initiate interaction by patting the caregiver or through eye gaze and smiles.

Toward the first birthday, babies show a preference for familiar people. This time period may also be marked by **separation anxiety**, in which a child cries when the caregiver is not in sight or clings to a caregiver in the presence of strangers; such anxiety diminishes over time. In the second year, toddlers continue to demonstrate a strong attachment to caregivers and initiate interactions with familiar adults.

separation anxiety
Feeling a baby experiences when the caregiver is not in sight; the baby may cry or cling to a caregiver in the presence of strangers; usually occurs around 8 months of age.

Fostering Social Development in Infants and Toddlers

During the first year, babies show interest in other children, particularly siblings, by watching them and tracking their behavior. They smile spontaneously at other children and show enjoyment in interactions with peers, as expressed in gestures, facial expressions, and

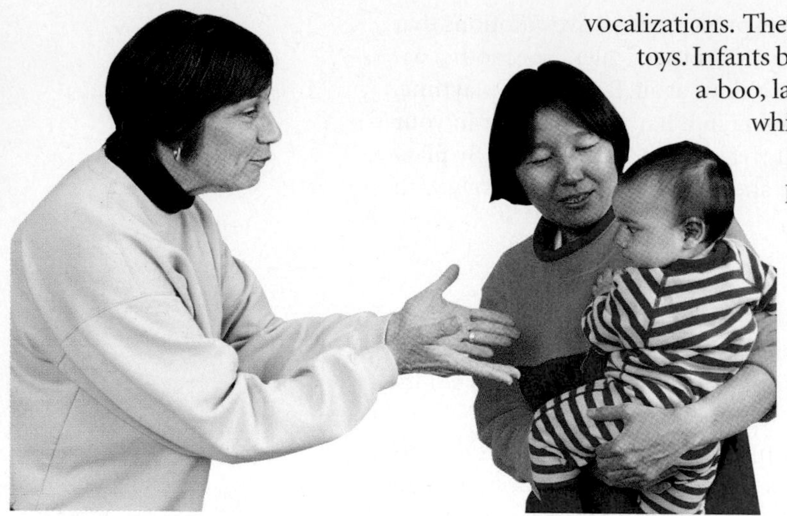

Separation anxiety is a natural part of social-emotional development at about 8 to 10 months of age, but it can make parents anxious as well. What can teachers do to help ease this experience for babies and families?

vocalizations. They may reach out to touch other children or grab their toys. Infants begin to take turns with teachers during play, as in peek-a-boo, laying a foundation for turn taking with other children, which develops during the second and third years of life.

Toddlers and 2 year olds often engage in parallel play. They observe and imitate another child's behavior or activity and by age 3, they initiate social interactions with peers. They may approach another child and ask to play, but will also be quick to assert ownership of toys by saying "Mine." Between 2 and 3 years of age, children start to show preferences for familiar playmates.

Fostering Emotional Development in Infants and Toddlers

In the second and third year of life, toddlers begin to name their own and other's emotions, and they demonstrate empathy by noticing how adults or peers feel and trying to comfort them. For example, Levi brings a stuffed animal to Francie who is sad because her mommy just left. His teacher quickly reinforces Levi's behavior, "What a caring friend you are, Levi."

These first years are also marked by tremendous growth in self-awareness and awareness of others. Infants will observe themselves in mirrors and notice other's physical characteristics and when a member of the group is missing. For example, a toddler may pat a child's head to feel her curly hair. They explore their own body, observing their hands or reaching for their toes; they may explore the face and body parts of others.

Toddlers begin to identify gender and other basic similarities and differences, although they may think that changing clothes changes their gender. They also begin to test limits and strive for independence. They notice when others are looking at them, and they often exaggerate movements or act silly when they are being watched. Table 14.2 lists some of the key indicators of social–emotional development in infants and toddlers and ways that teachers can help promote the development of these competencies.

Preschool and Kindergarten

During preschool and kindergarten, children become increasingly adept at building relationships. Preschoolers begin to try to please adults and use adults for assistance in solving problems, for getting their needs met, and for emotional support.

One of the greatest joys of the preschool years is making friends. Having friends contributes to social–emotional development and later success in school and life.

Social Development in Preschool and Kindergarten

The preschool and kindergarten years are marked by tremendous growth in interactions with peers. Children initiate interactions with other children and will make and maintain a friendship with at least one other child. These relationships contribute to cognitive and language development and to overall well-being (Buysse, Goldman, West, & Hollingsworth, 2007). With occasional assistance from teachers, children can share toys and materials during play and use simple strategies to solve social problems appropriately, as discussed later in this chapter.

Preschoolers can give reasons for a position, such as "I don't want to play right now because I am tired." By the end of preschool, children can understand the effects of their actions on others as in "I took the marker away from her and now she is crying." This accomplishment is essential to interpersonal problem solving.

Table 14.2 Fostering Social–Emotional Development in Infants and Toddlers

Some Indicators for Children	How Teachers Can Help
Quiets when comforted.	Hold, cuddle, hug, smile, and laugh with the child.
Establishes and maintains interactions with parents and teachers.	Consistently and promptly respond to child's needs for comfort and reassurance.
Shows affection for adults through facial expressions and gestures.	Talk and sing to child frequently, especially during feeding and diaper changes.
Exhibits separation anxiety by crying when caregiver is not in sight or clinging to caregiver in the presence of strangers.	Provide environment with consistent, small number of trustworthy adults and give child sense of security when around unfamiliar adults.
Establishes an attachment with a consistent adult other than the primary caregiver.	Respond to child's emotional and physical needs, verbal and nonverbal communications.
Smiles spontaneously at other children and shows interest in other children by watching them and tracking their behavior.	Provide opportunities for children to play and interact with other children; carefully supervise so that children don't hurt each other.
Seeks adult assistance with challenges.	Respond positively to child's questions and calls for assistance.
Plays side by side with other children at times.	Provide enough toys of the same kind so children can play side by side but don't have to share.
Takes turns at times during play, with considerable assistance (2-year-olds).	Play turn-taking games like pat-a-cake with babies. Help children learning turn-taking skills: "It's Curtis' turn to sit on my lap. You're next, Cassie."
Learns consequences of a specific behavior, but may not understand why the behavior warrants the consequence.	Describe for children how their behavior might make others feel: "You got in Peter's space, Mahvdi. That's why he screamed."

Source: Based on *Washington State Early Learning and Development Benchmarks*, State of Washington, 2005. Retrieved September 16, 2009, from http://www.k12.wa.us/EarlyLearning/Benchmarks.aspx.

Emotional Development in Preschool and Kindergarten

During these years, most children become increasingly capable of regulating their own emotions. Most preschoolers can wait for a turn and sometimes, though not always, show patience during group activities, a skill that improves in kindergarten. With guidance from teachers, most preschoolers can calm themselves after feeling strong emotions, going to a quiet corner or requesting a favorite book to be read when upset. At this age, children can associate emotions with words and facial expressions and use pretend play to understand and respond to emotions, such as when pretending to be a fierce animal to express negative emotions.

Preschool and kindergarten children also demonstrate growth in self-concept and self-esteem. They describe themselves as a person with a mind, body, and feelings, and they often exert their will and have strong preferences for certain foods, toys, or activities. They also tend to overestimate their own competence, and experiment with their own abilities, try new activities, and test limits such as "skipping bars" on the monkey bars at the playground.

All of the social–emotional skills described here require teachers to provide more or less assistance, depending on individual children's needs and abilities. Table 14.3 lists indicators of children's social–emotional learning and effective teaching strategies to promote it.

MyEducationLab

To observe children's social-emotional development in the context of play, go the Video Examples section of Topic 2: Child Development/Theories in the MyEducationLab for your course and watch the video entitled *Building with Blocks*. What do you observe about the social skills of these boys? What could an effective teacher do to help the boys who don't actively participate?

Table 14.3 Fostering Social–Emotional Development in Preschool and Kindergarten

Some Indicators for Children	How Teachers Can Help
Expresses affection for significant adult.	Be an appreciative audience and model appropriate affection.
Approaches adults for assistance and offers to assist adult.	Support and validate child's feelings and reinforce the child's positive problem-solving skills.
Brings simple problem situations to adults' attention.	Show respect for child's choices and attempts at solving problems.
Shows enjoyment in playing with other children.	Provide opportunities for child to engage in a variety of play activities with other children (e.g., dramatic play, art projects, free play outside, and dance and movement).
Makes and maintains a friendship with at least one other child.	Provide opportunities for children to choose activities that interest them, the time to pursue these activities, and the freedom to interact with preferred playmates who share similar interests. Give ample time for children to be silly and enjoy each other's company. Read stories about friendship and discuss the behaviors that made the character in the story a good friend.
Cooperates with other children and shares materials and toys during play.	Acknowledge cooperation when child plays with other children and provide opportunities for children to share materials.
Demonstrates understanding of the consequences of own actions on others.	Provide opportunities for dramatic play so that child can practice taking another's role or perspective ("Pretend you're Gera and can't have a turn. How do you think she is feeling?").
Identifies self as member of a group.	Promote a sense of community and membership within groups (e.g., acknowledging everyone at group time and noticing who is absent).
Notices and shows concern for peer's feelings.	Name and discuss feelings throughout the day (e.g., "You're sad because . . .").
Comforts peers when they are hurt or upset.	When there is a conflict between two children, demonstrate empathy for both children.
Develops awareness and appreciation of own gender and cultural identity.	Provide opportunities for children to describe and see positive images of their own cultural and physical characteristics.

Source: Based on *Washington State Early Learning and Development Benchmarks*, State of Washington, 2005. Retrieved September 16, 2009, from http://www.k12.wa.us/EarlyLearning/Benchmarks.aspx.

Primary Grades: Fostering Social–Emotional Development

During the primary grades, peer relationships become increasingly important. Most primary grade children show loyalty to friends. They sustain friendships by cooperating, helping, sharing, and suggesting new ideas for play. At this age, most children prefer friends of the same gender.

Interpersonal problem solving becomes more complex during the primary grades. Children attempt to settle disputes or solve problems with another child through negotiation, addressing their own rights as well as the other child's needs, sometimes still with assistance from teachers. Children in primary grades can participate in cooperative groups and take different roles at times—sometimes leader, sometimes follower. Primary grade children become excessively concerned about fairness within peer groups and can recognize stereotypes and culturally or linguistically unfair or biased behavior.

In terms of self-esteem, a major development during the primary years is that children gain the ability to realistically judge and compare their own academic, physical, and social abilities to those of other children. Unlike preschoolers, who overestimate their competence, primary grade children may judge themselves too harshly; for example, "I'm not smart like Natalie" or "I can't play baseball." Table 14.4 describes indicators of social–emotional learning during the primary grades and effective ways teachers can support this learning.

Table 14.4 Fostering Social-Emotional Development in the Primary Grades

Some Indicators for Children	How Teachers Can Help
Describes their emotions and the situations that cause them and demonstrates constructive ways to deal with emotions.	Have children discuss situations that trigger strong emotions and role-play strategies to cope with them.
Identifies own likes and dislikes. Describes things they do well and not well.	Help children to make accurate, realistic assessments of their own competence ("It's true that this math lesson is hard, but I can see how hard you're working and how much you've learned since last week").
Understands expectations and responsibility to promote a safe and productive environment. Demonstrates understanding of when to bring issues to adult attention.	Help children feel comfortable in coming to you with questions and assistance, but also encourage them to try to solve problems independently. Model cross-cultural communication and provide strategies for child to address bias. Actively address bullying or children's attempts to exclude others.
Shows loyalty to friends; prefers same-sex peers.	Provide opportunities for children to play and work with friends in self-selected groups. At times, organize mixed-gender or other diverse groups to ensure that children do not limit their interactions or consistently exclude others.
Follows suggestions given by a friend about how to proceed in their play.	Provide opportunities for children to be part of group activities (e.g., games, cultural events).
Works with other children to overcome challenges.	Discuss and demonstrate how different things can be achieved when children work together (dramatizing a story or building a model). Children can read (or be read to) and write stories about actual people who have overcome challenges, such as Jackie Robinson. Model and promote respect for diversity in all its forms.
Uses multiple strategies to resolve social conflicts.	Guide children through conflict resolution. Support children's attempts to solve social problems.
Feels empathy for other people and describes how own actions make others feel and behave. Recognizes that others may have different perspectives or feelings than own. Recognize words and actions that hurt others.	Read or help children read chapter books, such as *Charlotte's Web*, that depict emotionally challenging events or social situations. Demonstrate and provide opportunities for children to take another's perspective before making decisions (e.g., "What would Ella think if you gave her your book?").
Participates cooperatively in large- and small-group activities, play, and games.	Provide opportunities for small-group projects (creating a map, planning and carrying out an experiment). Encourage participation in group games, allowing children to make or modify rules.
Communicates about others' feelings.	Provide opportunities for child to share and discuss feelings. Discuss why a character reacts as he/she did in a story, taking cultural differences into consideration.

Source: Based on *Assessing and Guiding Young Children's Development and Learning*, 4th ed., by O. McAfee and D. Leong, 2007, Boston: Pearson Allyn & Bacon.

How Would You Respond?

Individual Differences

The Situation Kareem is 6 years old and a recent immigrant from Cameroon. Unlike all of the other first graders, he has not been in school before. He speaks English as well as French, his native language. However, he speaks English with a British accent and the other children don't always understand him; in fact, they sometimes make fun of and imitate him. Several times during each day—for morning meeting and sometimes for math or reading—the teacher gathers the whole group together. Kareem refuses to join the group, although he is not disruptive.

What to Do? In situations like this, teachers have various options to pursue. Which do you think would be most useful and why?

- Insist that Kareem sit with the group even if he becomes uncomfortable, upset, or fearful. Other children don't have an option and they might start refusing to join the group, too.
- Give Kareem another quiet activity to do during group time, such as looking at a book on his own.
- Permit Kareem to sit outside the group a little distance. Don't draw attention to him, but give him frequent eye contact, smiles, and encouragement, especially when he appears to be listening or observing.
- Meet with Kareem's mother to talk about ways you and she could work together to help him adjust to the expectations of the classroom.
- Talk privately to Kareem to uncover his feelings about group time and to generate solutions. Perhaps he is afraid he will have to speak and the children will laugh at him. Or maybe he doesn't like to be touched and there isn't enough space for him to feel physically comfortable.

Can you suggest other strategies that might be useful?

Teachers need to understand the continuum of social–emotional development to have realistic expectations for children's behavior and to provide effective amounts and kinds of assistance. For example, willful behavior on the part of 2-year-olds is typical, as is strong insistence on fairness among second graders.

Although we offer these descriptions of "typical" social and emotional learning, teachers need to remember that there is no such thing as a typical child. Individual and cultural differences play a significant role in how children express their emotions and how they behave in groups. Read the *How Would You Respond? Individual Differences* feature and consider how you might help a child who is struggling to fit in emotionally and socially.

Teaching and Learning Social Problem Solving

Children's problem-solving skills are a key feature in the development of social competence (Webster-Stratton, 1999). The power of problem solving lies in three areas. First, these skills travel well with children; they can be used in any social situation to resolve any number of social dilemmas. Second, these skills prevent challenging behavior. Finally, problem-solving skills allow children to quickly repair breaches in their relationships with peers, such as typical squabbles over toys, taking turns, or competition among friends.

Teaching Problem-Solving Skills

Problem solving is a highly effective deterrent to aggression and antisocial behavior. Consequently, every validated curriculum designed to teach social competence includes in-

struction in these skills (Joseph & Strain, 2004). Teachers can help children learn the following problem-solving steps that are common to most evidence-based curricula, such as ICPS: I Can Problem Solve and The Incredible Years (see the Readings and Websites section at the end of this chapter):

MyEducationLab

Go to the Assignments and Activities section of Topic 9: Guiding Children in the MyEducationLab for your course and complete the activity entitled *Managing Challenging Behavior: The Teacher's Role.* As you watch the videos, consider what effective strategies these teachers are using to promote children's social problem solving skills and positive social-emotional development.

1. What is my problem?
2. What are some solutions?
3. What would happen next?
4. Give the solution a try!

Step 1: What Is My Problem?

As a first step in problem solving, children should be taught to pay attention to their feelings. When they are experiencing a negative emotion such as anger or frustration, that is their cue that they have a problem. This is why teaching young children an emotional vocabulary is essential for effective problem solving (Joseph & Strain, 2003a; Webster-Stratton, 1999).

After children recognize they have a problem, they need to describe it. Adults and/or puppets can model the process of describing a problem for children. Initially, children will need guidance to reframe the situation from the other person's problem to their own. For example, instead of "They won't let me play," the problem becomes "I want to play with them." This reframing, although subtle, helps children generate more appropriate solutions.

Step 2: What Are Some Solutions?

Young children need help generating several alternative solutions to interpersonal problems. Children who engage in aggression and antisocial behavior have fewer solutions than their typically developing peers (Joseph, 2002). These children may in fact have a positive solution in their repertoire, but tend to have only one, such as saying "please." Their other solution is aggression, which in the short run is often more effective and efficient at getting their needs met.

Children who have more solutions to choose from usually solve the problem before resorting to aggression. For these reasons, teachers need to teach children alternative solutions to common problems and have children generate their own solutions. Because no one solution is always effective, the key is to teach children to generate as many different solutions as possible, as illustrated in the following example:

> Preschool teacher Ms. Trina brings both hypothetical and real problems to the group and challenges the class to come up with multiple solutions to the problem. Yesterday, Ms. Trina asked the class what they would do if they were feeling lonely and wanted to join a group of children playing on the Big Toy structure.
>
> *Tobias:* You could ask them.
> *Ms. Trina:* Yes, you could ask them. That is a solution. What else could you try?
> *Savannah:* If they said no, you could find another friend to play.
> *Ms. Trina:* Yes, that is another solution. So far we have two solutions. Let's try to think of five more.

Step 3: What Would Happen Next?

After children generate many alternative solutions to problems, they can begin to evaluate consequences. Teachers ask, "What would happen next?" Three questions can guide a child's decision to determine if the consequences would be good or bad (Webster-Stratton, 1999):

- Will this solution keep our bodies, feelings, and things safe?
- Is the solution fair?
- How will everyone feel?

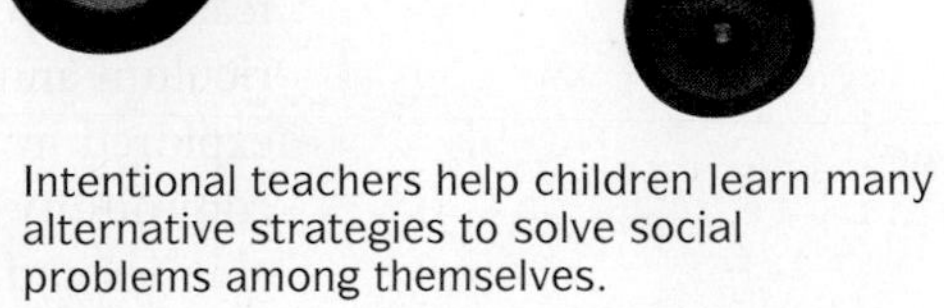

Intentional teachers help children learn many alternative strategies to solve social problems among themselves.

Once again, teachers can use role-play to help children learn these strategies. Feeling satisfied with the number of diverse solutions the children generated, Miss Trina helps them evaluate the consequences of solutions, using a puppet to introduce the three criteria for evaluating solutions. For example, the puppet demonstrates their solution of taking turns, and then asks the children, "Is it safe?" Aaron and Javier shout, "Yes!" The puppet congratulates them on good thinking and then demonstrates another solution, grabbing toys. The puppet asks, "Is it safe?" When the children respond, "No," the puppet asks, "Why not?"

Step 4: Give the Solution a Try!

At this step, children are taught to act on the best solution that they generated and what to do if a solution does not work. When a prosocial solution does not work, children can draw on the other solutions they generated in step 2 that might have positive consequences. When teachers focus on building problem-solving skills, children are likely to begin supporting and encouraging each other's efforts.

Supporting Children to Solve Problems in the Moment

Many unanticipated social–emotional problems occur throughout each day. Teachers need to assist children with problem solving on a moment-to-moment basis. At times, it's enough for teachers to anticipate a problem and be nearby to prompt a child through the problem-solving steps. For example, 6-year-old Oralie got off the bus this morning with a scowl on her face. Her teacher keeps an eye on her, and when Oralie squabbles with Clancy over using the computer, her teacher is there to encourage them to think of and try various solutions.

Children need support from teachers to remember the problem-solving steps and to stay in the situation. Those who are not skilled problem solvers may be prone to flee. Others may lose control of their temper and have an emotional meltdown. Teachers need to be equipped with strategies to support children through these difficult moments. One research-based strategy, the Turtle Technique, is described in the *What Works* feature.

We now turn to the related area of the curriculum in which children see these skills in action in themselves and other people—social studies.

The Social Studies Curriculum

Positive social–emotional development is integrally connected to other areas of development such as language and to learning curriculum content, particularly in social studies. In Chapter 10, we described a model for curriculum planning that draws on content knowledge from the disciplines as well as knowledge of child development. Social studies content comes from the subject matter disciplines of history, geography, political science, and economics. These provide the key concepts—the "big ideas"—and processes that children need to learn. Understanding typical patterns and sequences of child development determines which of these concepts to include in the curriculum for different ages. In addition, knowing children's predictable interests and capabilities makes it possible to teach relatively complex concepts in ways that are meaningful and accessible for children.

For example, one big idea in social studies is that institutions such as the family, community, and government play key roles in individuals' lives. At the college level, these concepts are part of courses in sociology and political science. By contrast, in preschool, teachers tap into children's natural interest in their families as a theme for organizing curriculum and teaching how people depend on and help each other. This same topic can be explored in greater complexity as children get older. First graders might study how their community supports families by investigating if the park is accessible for persons with disabilities and, if not, sending e-mails to town council members to call for change.

What Works

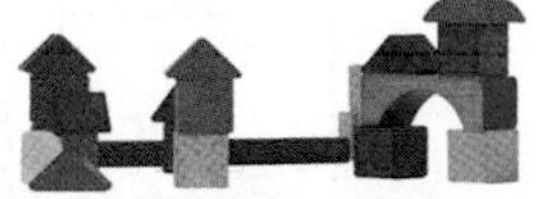

The Turtle Technique

Four-year-old Maxim has only been in preschool a few weeks. It is his first group experience and, as an only child, he has not been around other children very often and has never had to share his toys. Maxim tends to play alone and will spend 20 minutes or more with playdough, which is his favorite activity. One day, Nate sits down beside Maxim and reaches for some playdough and plastic molds. Maxim immediately pulls the toys out of Nate's hands and pushes him away. When Nate resists, Maxim loses control entirely; he falls on the floor and wails that he wants to go home. He is inconsolable until snack time distracts him from his anger.

When Maxim's mother comes to pick him up at the end of the day, the teacher, Ms. Gallo, tells her about the incident and his mother worries that Maxim is too immature for preschool. Ms. Gallo, who has taught preschool for many years, reassures her that preschool is where Maxim needs to be to learn to regulate his emotions and express them more constructively. She explains that in the future she will use a research-based strategy, the Turtle Technique.

When a teacher notices a child getting agitated and upset she can cue the child to "calm down" by remembering the Turtle Technique. The Turtle Technique was originally developed to teach adults anger management skills, and then was successfully adapted and integrated into social skills curricula for school-age and preschool children. The basic steps of the Turtle Technique are as follows:

1. Recognize that you feel angry.
2. Think "STOP."
3. Go into your "shell" and take three deep breaths and think calming, coping thoughts: "It was an accident. I can calm down and think of good solutions. I am a good problem solver."
4. Come out of your "shell" when calm and think of some solutions to the problem.

Teaching the Turtle Technique to young children can occur during large- and small-group times. A turtle puppet is helpful and keeps children engaged during the lesson. The teacher can begin by introducing the turtle to the class. After the children get a chance to say hello and perhaps give a gentle pat, the teacher shares the turtle's special trick for calming down. The turtle explains a time when he got upset (selecting an incident familiar to the children is best). He demonstrates how he thinks to himself "STOP," then goes in his shell and takes three deep breaths. Then he thinks to himself, "I can be calm and think of some solutions to solve my problem." When he is calm, he comes out of his shell and is ready to solve the problem peacefully with the teacher nearby for support.

Rather than singling out Maxim for instruction, the next day, Ms. Gallo uses the turtle puppet to teach the technique to all of the children. During center time, she reminds children to practice the technique when they feel frustrated or angry. It takes several weeks for Maxim to successfully use the technique to calm himself. But in the meantime, Nate is more successful in playing near him, and soon they are best friends.

Source: Based on "The Turtle Technique: An Extended Case Study of Self-Control in the Classroom," by A. Robin, M. Schneider, and M. Dolnick, 1976, *Psychology in the Schools, 13*, pp. 449–453.

What Is Social Studies?

Social studies is not a single topic or field of study. According to the National Council for the Social Studies (1994):

> The social studies are the study of the political, economic, cultural, and environmental aspects of societies of the past, present, and future. The social studies equip children with knowledge and understanding of the past necessary for coping with the present and planning for the future, enable them to understand and participate effectively in their world, and explain their relationship to other people and to social, economic, and political institutions. Social studies can provide students with the skills for productive problem solving and decision making, as well as for assessing issues and making thoughtful value judgments. Above all, the social studies help

students to integrate these skills and understanding into a framework for responsible citizen participation, whether in their play group, the school, the community or the world.

As we see from this definition, there is considerable overlap between the goals inherent in teaching social–emotional learning and in social studies.

Social Studies Content Goals

Although social studies are comprised of a vast amount of content, a relatively small share of curriculum time is allotted to it, especially in primary grades (McGuire, 2007). So what can and should children learn about social studies in the early years? The NCSS (1994) suggests thematic strands that serve as the basis for social studies standards in many states. Each theme includes concepts that are most easily understood as well as relevant and engaging for young learners. Table 14.5 lists nine social studies themes and key concepts for young learners.

Table 14.5 Social Studies Themes and Concepts

Theme and Traditional Discipline(s)	Big Ideas from the Discipline	Key Concepts for Young Learners
Individual Development and Identity (Psychology)	Personal identity is shaped by one's culture, by groups, and by institutional influences.	Developing a positive self-concept and feelings of self-efficacy; making and keeping friends.
Individuals, Groups, and Institutions (Sociology, Political Science)	Institutions such as families, schools, government agencies, and the courts play a role in people's lives.	Different kinds of families, making group decisions, living in a democracy.
Culture (Anthropology)	Aspects of human cultures—art, language, history, and geography—exhibit both similarities and differences.	Concepts such as alike and different, appreciation and respect for diversity in all of its forms.
Time, Continuity, and Change (History)	Children come to understand themselves in terms of the passage of time and develop the skills of the historian.	Routines that teach time sequencing; projects that teach how things change over time.
People, Places, and Environment (Geography, Archeology, Ecology)	Children learn to locate themselves in space, become familiar with landforms in their environment, and develop an understanding of the human–environment interaction.	Mapping for young children, beginning with picture maps of their classroom and extending to their community; caring for and protecting the environment.
Production, Distribution, and Consumption (Economics)	Projects address questions such as "What is to be produced?" and "How is production to be organized?"	Understanding that everyone has wants and needs and how these can be fulfilled.
Science, Technology, and Society (Mathematics, Science, and Technology)	Modernity is characterized by technology and the sciences that support it.	Becoming familiar with and using various technologies.
Global Connections (Political Science, Ecology, Economics)	We have connections and tensions with the rest of the world.	Being stewards of the environment; human rights; economic competition.
Civic Ideals and Practices (Political Science, Civics)	Children need an understanding of civic ideals and the practices of citizenship.	Involving children in developing the rules and holding class meetings to resolve conflicts.

Source: Based on *Social Studies for Early Childhood and Elementary School Children Preparing for the 21st Century: A Report from the NCSS Task Force on Early Childhood/Elementary Social Studies*, National Council for the Social Studies, 1998, Silver Spring, MD: Author.

In the sections that follow, we briefly describe many of the themes and ways teachers can help children learn key social studies concepts.

MyEducationLab

Go to the Assignments and Activities section of Topic 7: Curriculum/Content Areas in the MyEducationLab for your course and complete the activity entitled *Social Studies*. How are these teachers implementing effective curriculum to promote social-emotional competence and understanding of the social studies?

Fostering Children's Sense of Identity

A major goal of the social studies for young children is to help them develop a positive **identity**. Children need to understand that they are unique, but that they also have some commonalities with other children. General principles for helping young children develop a sense of identity include:

- Have children share information about their interests and families.
- Provide opportunities for children to make appropriate and varied decisions.
- Delight in children's accomplishments and explorations.
- Ensure that children can see themselves in books, pictures, and play materials.
- Help children distinguish people and relationships.

Valuing Diversity

An overarching goal of social studies is to create an engaged citizenry in which democratic values are an essential element of early education. James Banks (2008), director of the Center for Multicultural Education at the University of Washington, coined the term **equity pedagogy**, the idea that teaching about differences needs to include teaching about oppression, equity, and the rights of diverse people, as this example illustrates:

> Gail and Jim co-teach in a preschool classroom and decide to read some classic fairy tales. Fully aware that fairy tales often convey racism, sexism, and ageism, the two decide to incorporate the goal of teaching about equity. After reading versions of *Sleeping Beauty* and *Cinderella*, Jim asks the children why they think the princesses always have blonde hair and light skin. The children decide that this was because the author chose to draw only white people. The class collectively decides to "rewrite" the fairytales, featuring characters of color. The children also reenact the stories with princesses saving princes. In this example, Jim and Gail are teaching children to value diversity and also to think critically about books, movies, television, and other media.

Learning about diversity often focuses on differences; however, children need to understand that people are similar as well as different. The Milestones Project, described in the *Culture Lens* feature, is designed to accomplish this important goal.

Understanding Families and Communities

Helping young children develop a sense of self and a positive identity begins with learning about the important people in their environment. A wide variety of activities help children think about who is in their family—immediate and extended—and community. These themes date back to the **widening horizons approach** to social studies curriculum developed by Lucy Sprague Mitchell and incorporated in the Bank Street approach. This approach to curriculum planning is designed to begin where "children are" and then expand outward. Although the basic concept of widening horizons is still relevant today, social studies should not be limited to immediate, firsthand experiences. Children's horizons are and can be much wider today. Consider how the widening horizons approach is used in the following example:

> Lily Nguyen teaches in an inclusive preschool classroom. For a study about families, she plans a project that families can work on together. Lily sends home colorful construction paper, child-sized scissors, glue sticks, crayons, stickers, and directions to trace one hand from each person in the family, decorate it, and then glue it to the large piece of construction paper. When the hand pages come back, Lily is delighted. The families are very creative and many note that they had great fun with the activity. After laminating the pages and compiling them into a book,

identity Characteristics that individuals recognize as constituting their sense of self and belonging to a group.

equity pedagogy The idea that teaching about differences needs to include teaching about oppression and equity.

widening horizons approach Approach to social studies curriculum planning designed to begin where "children are" and then expand outward.

Culture Lens

Milestones Project

When teachers think about culture, the focus is almost always on differences. However, human beings from diverse cultural backgrounds are not only different, they also share many similarities. The Milestones Project is designed to focus more attention on the ways people across cultures are alike.

Deeply concerned over divisive world events such as ethnic cleansing, religious hatred, and racism, Richard and Michele Stickel launched the Milestones Project in 1998 (www.milestonesproject.com). They believe that if more people could see how all humans are alike, people would be more accepting, understanding, and respectful of each other. To achieve this goal, the Stickels travel the world, photographing children of various nationalities, races', religions, and cultures. They document the same milestones in children's development at about the same points in time. Milestones include such significant achievements and events as first step, first tooth, first day of school, and best friend. Subjects also write or dictate stories about these life experiences. The Milestones website makes the photos and narrative accounts available for anyone in the world to see. They have also published books, including an interactive workbook in English and Spanish co-authored with the Great Kids Head Start program in Denver, Colorado.

Inspired by the Milestones Project, first-grade teacher Kay Isaacs decided to do a similar project in her classroom. Her school is located near a large city in a neighborhood that is sometimes called a mini-United Nations. A local store contributed digital cameras to the school and the project was launched.

Kay began by having the children visit the Milestones website in pairs. She asked them to record their responses to what they saw. The children's notes included statements like "Kids everywhere like to have friends." "Boys always like boys best." "Most kids lose a tooth when they are in first grade." "Everybody smiles the same."

The children became so excited looking at the photos and reading other children's stories that they wanted to produce their own Milestones Project. Kay organized them into small groups to decide which milestones each group wanted to study. Some groups simply picked the same ones they saw on the web. Others were more creative. One group picked older people (their grandparents or great-grandparents), choosing to document what they look like when their grandchildren visit or when they get a present. Each group identified people—either their own families or neighbors—representing various races, ethnicities, religions, and cultures. Then they used digital cameras to capture faces and tape-recorded stories or reactions from the participants.

As a culminating event, Kay's class prepared a PowerPoint presentation featuring quotes from the participants and beautiful color photos, which they shared with their families at a parent meeting. The other first-grade classrooms in the school also viewed the show and decided to do their own Milestones Projects.

The Milestones Project is one example of how early childhood teachers can support children's identity and build respect for cultural diversity at the same time.

For a complete description of the project and to view the wonderful photographs, visit www.milestonesproject.com.

Lily shares the completed project with the children, stopping after each page to count and discuss the members of each family. The children then help graph the number of family members each child has.

In this project, Lily has many opportunities to talk about and demonstrate respect for diverse families. The children come from a variety of family structures, such as single parents, gay and lesbian families, extended families, and foster families. An additional subject emerges as Lily's class discusses families. Some children talk about relatives who are no longer living. This topic leads into another social studies theme and related concepts—history and how people change over time.

Learning about the Past and the Concept of Time

Social studies can equip young children with knowledge and understanding of the past and how things, people, and places change over time. Preschoolers begin learning concepts of time by experiencing a predictable schedule. As children get older, they are increasingly able to mark the passage of time and how things change over days, weeks, months, and seasons.

Children can also learn to use the methods used by historians, such as identifying problems and questions, collecting information and artifacts, and observing and reaching conclusions about the past. Elementary-age children learn about the past by engaging in "living history" projects in which they interview older members of their family or community. The *Becoming an Intentional Teacher* feature illustrates how one teacher engaged children in a living history project to integrate social studies and other curriculum areas.

Becoming an Intentional Teacher

Integrating Social Studies Content and Meeting Standards

Here's What Happened I teach second grade in a rural public school. Seven-year-old Amy's great-grandmother, whom she calls Gigi, recently came to live with the family. Prior to this move, Gigi lived in the same farmhouse where she grew up. Amy tells me that Gigi isn't happy. Amy tries to cheer Gigi up by asking her to tell stories, which sometimes works.

With Amy's agreement, I invite Gigi to visit our class to talk about what life was like in our community when she was a little girl. At first Gigi is hesitant, but with much encouragement, Gigi agrees to come. To prepare for her visit, the children generate a list of questions to ask her: "What was your school like?" "How did you get there?" "How did you talk to people far away?" "How did you get food?" The list goes on and on. Carl suggests that it would be neat if we could videotape Gigi's interview, and she grants permission.

On the day of Gigi's visit, Amy proudly introduces her great-grandmother, who says that she is 89 years old. The children do the math to figure out what year she was born and how much older she is than they are. The interview lasts 30 minutes. The children can hardly imagine what it must have been like not to have e-mail or cell phones, much less not to have phones at all! They also can't believe that Gigi's father was a blacksmith and that, in earler days, people used horses to travel. A few people had cars, but they were very expensive and there weren't many paved roads. Gigi has brought some black-and-white photos that show her family and farm and the buildings in the small town back then.

Gigi's visit generates a great deal of interest among the children. She returns for several more interviews, and the children produce a documentary video as the culmination of their living history project. The children seek out other elders in the community to learn about their lives when they were young, their jobs, and how the area looked at the time.

Here's What I Was Thinking Our school curriculum reflects the state learning standards. For second grade, the history, geography, and economics standards require children to learn key concepts and processes for studying the discipline. One such history concept—continuity and change—is related to the standard "Children understand that basic human needs remain the same but how they are met changes with technology."

I find it difficult to teach abstract concepts such as this. And there isn't time in the day to address all of these standards, especially because in second grade we need to focus so much on reading and math. In my experience, however, children learn best when their interests are piqued and they actively inquire about a meaningful problem or question.

I saw an opportunity for integrating many key social studies concepts into the living history project. After the children generated their list of questions and decided how they would get answers, I went through the state standards and noted which ones related to this study. I also planned for children to use the actual processes and tools of historians. For example, they interviewed subjects, recorded data, examined old photos and documents, read books about the period, and came to conclusions based on the evidence. Thus, children practiced their reading and writing skills during the living history project as well.

A serendipitous outcome of the project was that Gigi became an honorary member of our second-grade class. Children frequently consult her when they have questions about past and even current events. And since Amy taught her to use e-mail, communication with her became even easier.

Learning about Where We Live: Geography and Mapping

Geography is an important part of our daily lives and of the early childhood curriculum. Children learn geographic concepts through active experiences and engaging in geographic thinking. For example, preschoolers can take a walk around the school and collect objects or take pictures along the way, and then place the items or photos on a map of the school grounds. Kindergartners and primary grade children can construct maps of their classrooms, school, or neighborhood by placing objects, pictures, or symbols in relation to each other.

The national geography standards, *Geography for Life* (National Council for Geographic Education [NCGE], 1994), identify five skills that children begin developing during their preschool and primary years. These are listed in Table 14.6 with suggestions for how teachers can help children learn these skills.

The *Geography for Life* national standards (NCGE, 1994) identity five central themes to be used in geographic inquiry:

1. *Location: position on the earth's surface.* The theme of location tells us exactly where in the world something is, as well as why things are located in certain places. For young children, this begins when they notice features of their immediate surroundings (Fromboluti & Seefeldt, 2000).
2. *Place: physical and human characteristics.* The characteristics of any given place tell a lot about where people live, why they settle there, and how they use natural resources. A complete understanding of the earth and its features is not achievable for young children. But by asking questions with this geography theme in mind, teachers can help children develop an understanding of places and their distinctive characteristics (Seefeldt, Castle & Falconer, 2010).
3. *Relationships within places.* This theme, which has been getting more attention because of issues such as global warming, explores how humans impact the environment as well as how the environment influences human behavior (Seefeldt, Castle, & Falconer, 2010).
4. *Movement: travel from place to place.* The fourth theme focuses on how people, things, ideas, products, and information move from one place to another. The most common movement children see and think about is people traveling every day to school or work. Some children will have traveled much farther afield.

Table 14.6 Geography Education Standards

Geographic Skill	How Teachers Can Help
Asking geographic questions	Acknowledge and encourage geographic questions. Join children in their sense of wonder about the natural world and how it formed (e.g., "Where does rain come from?" "How do mountains grow?"). Model asking geographic questions ("Which way do you come to school?").
Acquiring geographic information	Provide children with resources such as maps, globes, map puzzles, relief maps, and books depicting other lands and people.
Organizing geographic information	Provide children with materials and inspiration to draw maps, construct graphs, and tell and write stories about places they have been or want to go.
Analyzing geographic information	Show children how to locate themselves on maps and globes. Locate the places of origin of children's families, especially immigrant families.
Answering geographic questions	Have children present their maps, stories, buildings, drawings, and findings of other places to their peers. Teachers and peers can ask questions about the child's work.

Source: Based on *Geography for Life: The National Geography Standards,* 1994, Washington, DC: National Geography Society Committee on Research and Exploration. Retrieved October 1, 2009, from http://www.ncge.org/i4a/pages/index.cfm?pageid=3314.

Table 14.7 Children's Books to Address Five Themes of Geography

Theme	Children's Book	Ideas for Teaching
Location	*Arthur Lost and Found* (M. Brown, 1998)	Questions to consider: • Where were Arthur and Buster supposed to get off the bus? • Where are Arthur and Buster now? • How can they find their way home?
Place	*Masai and I* (Kroll, 1997)	Read in pairs with one person reading the section from the United States and the other reading the Masai section. Contrast a typical day of an American student with Ahmed's day and share how much they have learned about life in Cairo.
Human/ environment	*The Little House* (Burton, 1969)	Compare the little house's life before and after urbanization: • Where was the little house located? • What was her life before the encroaching of the city? • How did she feel after she found herself cut off from nature and the countryside?
Movement	*Grandfather's Journey* (Say, 1993)	Notice how Allen's grandfather • Traveled through America by riverboat, train, and on foot. • Met various people. • Saw deserts and oceans. • Visited rural towns and industrial cities. Have children discuss the ways they get to school each morning and then graph this information.
Region	*Bread, Bread, Bread* (Morris, 1993)	Ask children to note the many shapes bread takes and the many different ways bread is transported and eaten. See how many breads can be named and guess the location of the breads. Note how other cultures have adopted "American" bread—evidence of our global village.

Source: From "Teaching Young Children Basic Concepts of Geography: A Literature-Based Approach," by M. A. Z. Hannibal, R. Vasiliev, and Q. Lin, 2002, *Early Childhood Education Journal*, *30*(2), pp. 81–86. Reprinted with kind permission from Springer Science + Business Media.

5. *Regions: united by similar physical conditions and common cultural traits.* This theme includes questions about how human actions modify the physical environment, how physical systems affect human systems, and about the changes that occur in the meaning, use, distribution, and importance of resources.

One effective way to teach young children geographical concepts is through literature. Some examples are presented in Table 14.7.

Learning about Wants and Needs: Early Economics

Economic concepts are basic to children's lives. All young children have wants and needs that act as powerful motivation to begin understanding economic systems. Table 14.8 presents six key early economics concepts young children can learn along with examples of teaching strategies.

Learning about Living in a Democracy: Making Choices and Voting

John Dewey strongly believed that an essential purpose of education is to empower an engaged citizenry. In a democracy, people have the power to make a variety of meaningful choices pertaining to their daily lives—to become agents of change. In early childhood

Table 14.8 Teaching Early Economics

Economics Concept	Teaching Strategies
Scarcity means that there is always a conflict between never-ending wants and limited resources.	Comment on the scarcity of materials when children engage in conflict over toys. Explain that there are limited numbers of toys, and more children want them than there are toys to go around.
Because resources are limited, people must choose some things and give up others.	Building on the example above, this is a time to talk about other solutions to problems involving scarce materials. Ideas include sharing, getting another toy to play with, or waiting for a turn.
People produce and consume. When they produce, they make goods. When they consume, they use goods and services.	Ask family members to share their work with the class, and (if possible) to share active experiences with the children (cooking, making art, writing). Create a "market day" where children produce and sell things. The class can vote on how the profits will be spent.
Money and trade or barter are used to obtain goods and services.	Create a store in the classroom. Include merchandise, a cash register, play money and food stamps, pads for receipts, and props for workers and consumers.
People work in a variety of jobs.	Take field trips to local businesses and organizations or invite parents to visit the class and discuss what they do.
Helping others who do not have their basic needs met is socially desirable.	Host a class clothing drive. Children can make signs about the drive, collect and organize clothing, and count and graph the types and sizes of clothing collected.

Source: Based on *Active Experiences for Active Children: Social Studies,* 2nd edition, by C. Seefeldt and A. Galper, 2007, Upper Saddle River, NJ: Pearson Prentice Hall.

programs, children are not just preparing to become members of a democratic society; they actually are citizens of a democracy (Dewey, 1916). Therefore, teachers need to engage them in group decision-making and discussion of differing opinions during class meetings and help them understand the concepts of voting and majority.

In previous sections, we presented some of the social studies curriculum themes recommended by the National Council for the Social Studies, the key concepts for children to learn, and examples of teaching strategies. Next we discuss effective approaches for planning and implementing social studies curriculum.

Developmentally Appropriate Social Studies Teaching

One of the biggest challenges in teaching social studies is deciding what content and topics are developmentally appropriate for young children; that is, which learning goals are achievable for children and when? These decisions are particularly difficult in social studies because subjects such as history and geography involve highly abstract ideas. For example, comprehending history requires understanding chronological time—an ability that is not fully developed until age 11 or later (Seefeldt et al., 2010). Similarly, geography requires an understanding of complex concepts such as location and direction and that maps and globes are abstract representations of reality (Seefeldt et al., 2010).

Using the NCSS themes to plan early childhood social studies curriculum is a good way to make such abstract concepts more understandable for young children and, therefore, more developmentally appropriate. It is also important to use teaching strategies that build on what children already know, help them make sense of new experiences, and connect facts to larger concepts and ideas. Three commonly used, developmentally appropriate approaches to social studies curriculum meet those criteria: (1) engaging children in play and active learning, (2) using a project approach to integrate social studies, and (3) using technology to expand children's firsthand experiences and worldview.

Engaging Children in Play and Active Learning Experiences

"Children are born into social studies. From birth, they begin exploring their world" (Mindes, 2006, p. 4). In good schools for young children, social studies take place naturally (Seefeldt et al., 2010). Such schools allow children to experience the curriculum firsthand through child-guided exploration and play within a carefully planned environment. Children learn social studies when they interact to solve problems such as how to make mud on the playground or how to produce a guidebook for school visitors.

Teachers can extend this learning by inviting guest speakers for children to meet and interview. However, teachers should prepare guests in advance; people who have not had experience with young children may have developmentally inappropriate expectations for their behavior, such as expecting them to remain quiet for a lecture. A more successful approach is for guests to bring hands-on materials such as antique tools from the history museum for the children to see, touch, and talk about.

Field work is another active way to extend social studies learning, whether in the form of an exploration of the school building, a visit to the florist, or a trip to the planetarium. However, like all early childhood experiences, successful field trips are not automatic. Field trips should be structured to achieve maximum success, safety, and active learning. Below are a few suggestions for getting the most out of a field trip (Seefeldt et al., 2010):

- Have a clear purpose for the trip. Identify how the trip will help achieve specific learning goals for children.
- Visit in advance. Note where the bus or cars should park, tricky crosswalks, access for children with disabilities, and any potential hazards.
- Prepare adults who will speak with children at the site. Remind them to talk for a short time and encourage children's participation.
- Notify the parents any time children leave the building. Follow the school's procedures for obtaining written permissions for outings beyond the school grounds.
- Discuss the field trip with the children beforehand, show them pictures of where they are going, and respond to any questions or concerns from children who are anxious.
- Develop questions to answer or identify things to look for to focus children's attention during the field trip and enhance their learning experience.

Field trips are effective ways to extend children's social studies learning beyond the classroom. Effective teachers carefully plan field trips in advance and follow up to ensure maximum benefit for children.

- During the trip, ask children to document their experiences, take photos, and record answers to questions and/or observations. Older children can take written notes.
- Provide follow-up experiences that connect the trip to ongoing study in the classroom. Children can discuss and record their memories in writing, drawing, painting, or through other forms of creative expression. They can work their experiences into their play with appropriate props; for example, they might create a pretend flower shop after a visit to the florist. They also can extend learning by reading books and through technology such as looking on the NASA website following a planetarium trip.

Field trips have the potential to expand children's horizons in many ways. However, trips can also be missed opportunities for learning if the experience is just a whirlwind of unfocused activity. When asked what they remember from a trip to the nature center, children might say "Tasha got sick" or "I jumped in the puddle of water." While these reports are undoubtedly factual, they should not be all the children bring back from the experience.

An Integrated Approach to Teaching Social Studies

There is a limited amount of time in the school day and year to address all of the content that comprises the social studies. Fortunately, the various strands of social studies lend themselves to planning an integrated curriculum, as the following example illustrates:

> One winter day, Gabriella Johnson notices that someone put several unkempt duffle bags and a sleeping bag on the back porch of the child care center. Gabriella sees a note that reads: "I am homeless right now. Please do not remove my things. If I need to move them, let me know."
>
> At circle time, Gabriella reads the note to the children and describes the possessions. The children have many questions. Lani asks why the person is homeless. Leo asks if it is a man or a woman. Jeremiah wants to know where the person is right now. Helen wonders if he is going to sleep there. A rich discussion ensues, and Gabriella explains that she doesn't have the answers to the questions.
>
> The children take a vote and decide the things can stay. Alexa wants to write the person a note. Gabriella helps the children write notes explaining that the stuff can stay and asking some of their questions. The next day, the notes are gone, but the person leaves one for the children that says "Thanks." The children are disappointed that the person didn't answer their questions and think of reasons why, but also are glad the belongings are still there. Leo worries that the person might not have enough to eat, so he asks if they could put the leftovers from lunch on the back porch.
>
> The discussions, note writing, and caretaking continue for several weeks, until the person removes the bags. The children make up stories about where he went. Jackson wonders aloud if the person moved into the shelter he and his mom stayed in at the beginning of the year. Gabriella decides to invite one of the soup kitchen volunteers to visit and talk about her work. This inspires the children, and Gabriella arranges for a service learning opportunity for them to organize a food drive. Tanya suggests that the food drive include pet food, too. The children make signs, set goals, write letters, and graph the amount and types of food they collect.

Gabriella takes an opportunity to build a powerful social studies project from this event. Throughout the project, the children learn concepts of culture, wants and needs, power and privilege, fairness, similarities and differences, and the importance and value of service learning—all while building language, literacy, and math skills.

Using Technology to Teach the Social Studies

Two of the NCSS standards that we have not yet discussed specifically relate to technology and global connections. Technology can be used for children to expand their worldviews, to learn about social studies, and to document their learning. For example, when children are learning about mapping, they can use websites that feature aerial maps of their neighborhoods, such as the Google Earth website. Through this technology, children can try to find their house or school; they can focus in on anywhere in the world and learn about the "bird's-eye view" offered by overhead maps.

The Internet makes it possible for children to take virtual field trips to anywhere in the world. What other ways can technology support social studies learning?

Children can also use global positioning system (GPS) devices during field trips to learn about newer technologies related to geography. To learn more about the world at large, children can explore other cultures and places with Internet searches and electronic pen pals. Many schools, for example, send e-mails and photos of their drawings to children in other schools, particularly ones in the hometowns or countries of children in the class.

Children can also produce and disseminate projects on the web. For example, young elementary-age children might put together a web page about the topics they are studying. Children could also prioritize a "wish list" that includes items to be used in the class; this allows the class to explore economics learning.

Travel costs and supervision concerns often limit opportunities to take field trips. However, **virtual field trips** allow children to use the Internet to go anywhere in the world. In this way, children can explore another community, state, or even country. They also can interview experts online via e-mail or participate in live chats with other children or workers in various jobs. The possibilities of using technology to teach social studies are limited only by the technology available to children.

Revisiting Jefferson Elementary School

virtual field trip Trip taken via the Internet in which children can go anywhere in the world.

At the beginning of this chapter, we visited the kindergarten and third-grade classrooms at Jefferson Elementary School. Having discussed social–emotional development and learning, as well as social studies curriculum and teaching, we can now revisit the school and see more clearly what and how children are learning about social studies.

It is evident from Waylon's experiences in kindergarten that his teacher focuses on both social–emotional development and social studies in her curriculum. Each child has an opportunity to develop a strong sense of identity, while all the children learn about each other, their family history, and the community in which they live. Ms. Hans, his teacher, operates her classroom as a mini-democracy in which children make choices, accept responsibility, and learn how voting functions to make group decisions.

MyEducationLab

To assess your understanding of social-emotional learning and development and how to effectively teach social studies, go to the Book Specific Resources section in the MyEducationLab for your course, select *Effective Practices in Early Childhood Education,* Chapter 14 of the Study Plan, and then complete the multiple choice questions and activities.

The in-depth study of Iraq in Mr. Bell's third grade is an example of integrated social studies curriculum. Current events in the news and in the lives of people in their community motivate the children to learn more and get actively involved as citizens in helping others. They also learn about global connections between products developed and used in different places. The topic is rich with opportunities to learn geography, economics, and history while also developing skills in reading, writing, and researching.

Chapter Summary

- Social–emotional learning (also called social competence) is children's ability to recognize and regulate emotions, establish and maintain positive relationships, make responsible decisions, and solve social problems constructively.
- Play is a vital context for children to develop positive peer relationships and practice social skills. Play is equally important for emotional development, providing a context for children to address their fears, develop coping skills and resilience, and feel in control of their environment.
- Teachers need to understand the developmental continuum of significant social–emotional accomplishments across the period from birth to third grade to have appropriate and realistic expectations for children's behavior, and to know how and when to effectively promote social–emotional learning.
- Children's problem-solving skills are a key feature in the development of social competence. Effective social–emotional curricula include specific strategies for teaching social problem-solving skills.
- Social studies—the integrated study of history, geography, economics, political science, and other related subjects—contributes to the development of competent citizens. During early childhood, social studies topics and social–emotional learning are inextricably connected. Learning to live in a democratic society—the overarching goal of social studies—is predicated on social–emotional learning.
- Developmentally appropriate, effective approaches to teaching the social studies in early childhood programs include engaging children in play and active learning experiences, using an integrated approach to link social studies learning and other curriculum areas, and using technology to expand children's worldviews.

key terms

associative play
cooperative play
emotional development
emotional literacy
engaged citizens
equity pedagogy
identity
parallel play
separation anxiety
social development
social–emotional learning
social studies
solitary play
virtual field trip
widening horizons approach

readings & websites

Epstein, A. S. (2009). *Me, you, us: Social–emotional learning in preschool.* Ypsilanti, MI: HighScope Educational Research Foundation.

Hyson, M. (2004). *Emotional development of young children: Building an emotion-centered curriculum* (2nd ed.). New York: Teacher's College Press.

Seefeldt, C., Castle, S., & Falconer, R. C. (2010). *Social studies for the preschool/primary child* (8th ed.). Upper Saddle River, NJ: Pearson.

Seefeldt, C., & Galper, A. (2006). *Active experiences for active children: Social studies* (2nd ed.). Upper Saddle River, NJ: Pearson Merrill/Prentice Hall.

Collaborative for Academic, Social, and Emotional Learning
www.casel.org

Educators for Social Responsibility
www.educatorssocialresponsibility.org

The Incredible Years (C. Webster-Stratton)
www.incredibleyears.com

ICPS: I Can Problem Solve (M. B. Shure)
www.researchpress.com/product/item/4628

National Council for the Social Studies
www.ncss.org

National Geographic Society
www.nationalgeographic.com

National Multicultural Education Association
www.name.org

1. Observe a kindergarten or early primary grade and decide if you see evidence of the classroom being organized and led as a democracy. Do children have a say in what they will do during the day? Are children provided with responsibilities and tasks that support the whole class? Are children given opportunities to voice their concern and to resolve conflicts?
2. Observe a preschool classroom. What evidence of social–emotional learning do you see? How does the teacher use "feeling" words? What happens when children have difficulty sharing or playing together? Did you notice any missed opportunities to teach problem-solving skills?
3. Take a drive or walk around the community where you live. What places of interest are available that might extend children's social studies learning? For example, what landforms do you observe? What are the physical characteristics of the area that make it unique? How could a walk around the community deepen children's understanding of socials studies and geography in particular?
4. Observe in a first- or second-grade classroom. Do you see evidence of social studies learning? Are the children studying a social studies topic? If so, what strategies does the teacher use to teach social studies?
5. View online the learning standards of one of the professional organizations: *Curriculum Standards for Social Studies: Expectations of Excellence* (National Council for the Social Studies), *National Standards for Civics and Government* (Center for Civic Education), *National Standards for United States History: Exploring the American Experience, K–4* (National Center for History in the Schools), or *Geography for Life: National Geography Standards* (National Council for Geographic Education). Discuss with other students whether you think these standards are achievable for the intended age groups. What do you think are the benefits of having discipline standards such as these? What are the drawbacks?

15 Teaching Children to Be Healthy and Fit: Physical Development and Health

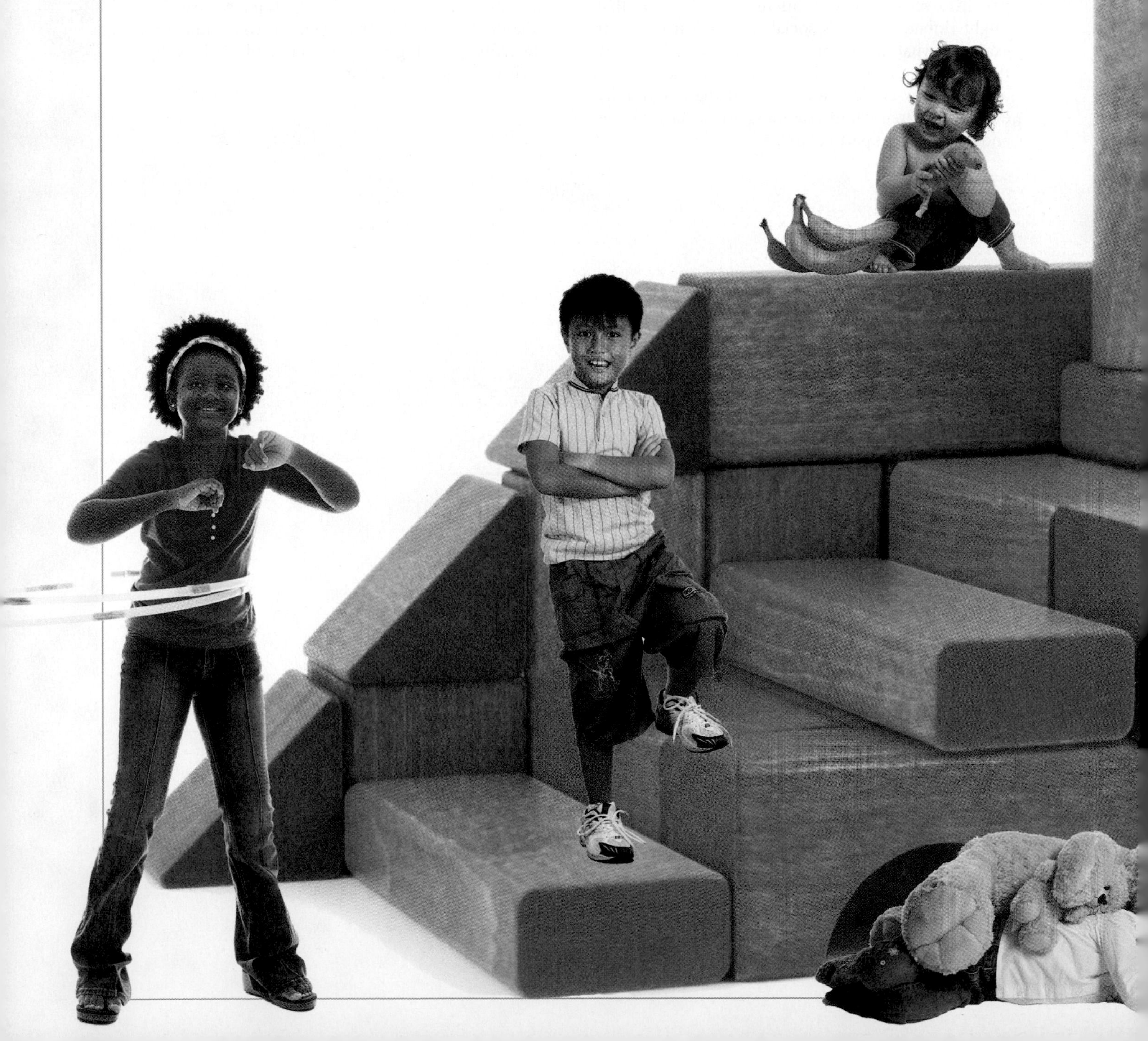

Thinking Ahead

1. Why are physical fitness and health so important? Why are they a concern for young children today?
2. What are the predictable sequences of gross-motor, fine-motor, and perceptual-motor development in young children?
3. How can teachers foster children's development of motor skills?
4. What is the role of indoor and outdoor play in promoting children's physical development, fitness, and health?
5. What are effective strategies for promoting wellness and preventing illness and injury?
6. How can curriculum promote physical development, fitness, and health?

Ms. Perez's class of 3- to 5-year-olds joyfully bounds out the door for their favorite part of the day—outdoor play. A well-planned environment greets the children on the playground. In addition to choosing from the permanent options of a climbing structure and tricycle path, today they can paint on a long piece of paper attached to the fence, water the class garden, or play with the ball collection in the large grassy area.

In less than a minute, all of the children except Allison choose an activity and are busy playing. She is standing by the balls, but hasn't picked one up. Ms. Perez asks, "Allison, do you want to play catch?"

Allison replies, "No, I want to kick the ball but I can't do it."

Ms. Perez smiles and says, "I can help you learn." The teacher sets the balls up in a straight line, positions Allison in front of one ball, stands next to her, and demonstrates how to kick the ball. Allison tries and the ball rolls slowly away to the side without much motion. Ms. Perez says, "You kicked it! Let's see what happens to the next kick. I bet it goes further." Allison is excited about this possibility. Ms. Perez demonstrates again, commenting on the position of her foot in relation to the ball. Allison kicks the ball again—a longer way this time. Ms. Perez steps back and says, "That was a big kick."

Allison continues to kick the balls until they are all over the playground. Drew arrives and says, "I want a turn." Ms. Perez suggests that Drew ask Allison if he can play. He does, and Allison says, "Yes, but I go first." Drew agrees and together Allison and Drew collect the balls, line them up, and kick each one. They run off to collect the balls to repeat the game and play together until it is time to go inside.

After 45 minutes outside, Ms. Perez calls the children inside. They wind down by doing quieter activities. JaNaye and her two friends continue working on the collages they began this morning using objects such as buttons, foam cutouts, scraps of ribbon, rickrack, and lace. Mitchell and Carletta write notes to friends. Another teacher, Ms. Aliote, assists four children as they string beads and use small pegboards to create patterns. Seth and Asia use a computer program to draw pictures, changing colors and line width by clicking the mouse. As lunch arrives, Regina and Alexei help set the table, and the children take turns at the sink next to a child-sized poster reminding them how to properly wash their hands. Their meal is served family style, with children maneuvering serving spoons and passing dishes to each other. Brooks exclaims, "Look, Ms. Perez, I poured my milk and no spills." ▲

As in any high-quality early childhood program, movement is an essential part of living and learning in Ms. Perez's classroom. From tiny babies to active second graders, young children take on and embrace the world with their whole bodies. Healthy children of all ages love physical activity and play, but more than fun is involved. With the help of parents and teachers, children master critically important physical skills and also establish habits related to fitness and health that can last a lifetime.

In this chapter, we address the critical health and fitness issues facing our nation's children today. We discuss the continuum of children's motor development from birth through age 8, and how intentional teachers promote optimal development through play and focused teaching of physical skills. We also discuss curriculum and teaching practices that promote children's fitness, health, and nutrition, and those that prevent illness and injury.

The Importance of Physical Fitness and Health

Physical fitness refers to children's overall physical condition: growth, strength, stamina, and flexibility. Children's physical fitness depends on a number of factors, including heredity, access to good nutrition and health care, and participation in fitness-enhancing activities. Most physically active children grow up to be physically active adults. On the other hand, only 2% of adults who were inactive as children become active in adulthood (National Association for Sports and Physical Education [NASPE], 2004).

The Benefits of Physical Fitness

When they feel strong and fit, children are more confident; they are likely to gain self-esteem, enjoy playing and learning with others, and eagerly take on new challenges (Sanders, 2002). Healthy physical development is closely and consistently linked to children's subsequent academic success (Grissom, 2005). In addition, ample evidence (American Heart Association, 2009; Centers for Disease Control and Prevention [CDC], 2009; Sanders, 2002) confirms that regular physical activity helps children by:

physical fitness Children's overall physical condition: growth, strength, stamina, and flexibility.

- Building and maintaining healthy bones, muscles, and joints
- Controlling weight
- Building lean muscle and reducing fat

- Preventing or delaying high blood pressure and cholesterol and type 2 diabetes
- Reducing feelings of depression, stress, and anxiety
- Improving physical fitness
- Increasing capacity for learning.

Physical development is largely controlled by biological growth, but children do not acquire physical skills automatically. Intentional teachers help children as they gain more control over their bodies and teach motor skills.

Health-related fitness is the aspect of health that can be improved by exercise and activity. It consists of the following four components (Gallahue & Ozmum, 2002, 2006):

1. The **cardiorespiratory**, or **aerobic**, **system** includes the heart, lungs, and blood. When working well, this system provides the stamina needed to actively participate for a long period of time.
2. **Muscular strength and endurance** allow for effective use of muscles. *Strength* allows children to use force to perform a task such as kicking a ball or hammering a nail. *Endurance* is the ability to keep moving without stopping because of fatigue.
3. **Flexibility** is the ability to bend and stretch easily, which helps prevent muscle and tendon injuries.
4. **Body composition** refers to weight and body fat. Excess fat puts stress on ligaments, tendons, bones, and tissues that support the body's weight.

All of these components are important parts of children's fitness and health. Each should be considered in planning effective early childhood programs. In recent years, however, children's health-related fitness has become an urgent concern as the rate of childhood obesity in America has increased significantly (Land, 2008).

Addressing the Childhood Obesity Crisis

The CDC reports huge increases in childhood obesity during the past 30 years. Between 1976 and 2006, the percentage of obese 2- to 5-year-olds increased from 5% to 12.4% (CDC, 2009; Land, 2008). In 6- to 11-year-olds, the percentage went from 6.5% to 17%. These problems often continue into adulthood: 70% of severely overweight children become obese adults (Sacther, 2005).

The causes of obesity are complex and involve genetics, lifestyle, and poor nutrition. But the consequences are profound. Overweight children are at greater risk of cardiovascular disease and other serious illnesses, miss four times as much school as normal-weight children, and can suffer from other health consequences such as depression and anxiety disorders (Schwimmer, Burwinkle, & Varni, 2003). Obese children are also more likely to be socially isolated from their peers and have low self-esteem, which negatively affects their academic performance (CDC, 2009; Grissom, 2005). A higher percentage of children from low-income families have poor nutrition and are also more likely to be overweight or obese (Case, Lubotsky, & Paxson, 2005), which becomes another risk factor associated with poverty.

The following recommendations are designed to counter the obesity crisis and improve physical fitness in all young children (CDC, 2009; NASPE, 2002; U.S. Department of Agriculture [USDA], 2009):

- Children should engage in 60 minutes or more of moderate to vigorous physical activity every day. When children engage in moderate aerobic activity, their heart beats faster and they breathe faster than normal; during vigorous exercise, heart and respiration rates are much faster.
- Physical activity for preschoolers should include at least 60 minutes of **structured physical activity** (in short, 15-minute segments), which is adult-guided play designed for a purpose such as increasing endurance or flexibility, such as when a teacher leads a game

health-related fitness Any aspect of health that can be improved by physical exercise and activity.

cardiorespiratory (aerobic) system Body system made up of the heart, lungs, and blood; provides the stamina needed to be active for a long period of time.

muscular strength and endurance The ability to keep moving without stopping because of fatigue.

flexibility The ability to bend and stretch easily.

body composition Weight and body fat.

structured physical activity Adult-guided play that is designed for a purpose such as increasing endurance or flexibility.

When children's motor skills develop optimally, they are more likely to enjoy and engage in physical activity. Fun outdoor play and physical activity can build children's health and fitness and fight today's childhood obesity crisis.

of Simon Says). In addition, preschoolers need between 60 minutes and several hours of daily, unstructured free play. **Unstructured free play** is chosen and initiated by children, such as that which occurs on a playground.

- Television viewing and other screen time should be limited to less than 2 hours per day. Children should not sit for more than 60 minutes in any activity.
- Children's diets need to be improved with decreased intake of fast food and increased intake of fruits, vegetables, and whole grains.

These recommendations have direct implications for early childhood programs and schools, especially considering a program's hours of operation. For example, in a full-day child care center where children might spend 8 to 10 hours a day, it is essential to provide significant amounts of time for structured and unstructured physical activity. The children may have limited time for active play once they leave the center. If children spend 3 or 4 hours in a program, teachers should plan at least 30, and preferably 45 minutes, of gross-motor play, in one or two time periods. Family child care may provide greater flexibility.

Given the benefits of physical activity for young children as well as the risks of poor levels of fitness, teachers need to ensure that promoting physical development and health are core curriculum goals and not simply add-ons. Movement is fun and most children love it, but the many benefits of physical activity for children's health and well-being are a serious justification for including it in the early childhood curriculum.

Understanding Physical Development

Physical development during early childhood may seem a little magical; it begins at the moment of conception and continues throughout the life span. Yet physical development is anything but effortless. Individual children's physical growth and development varies considerably depending on heredity, environmental factors, nutrition, gender, and access to health care. Over time, the interplay brings on dramatic, noticeable changes in children.

The Nature of Physical Development

Changes in physical development are rapid, with later abilities, skills, and knowledge building on already acquired skills. Although children's development follows a relatively predictable sequence, variation exists, most notably in the pace of development. For example, while most children jump first with both feet and then learn to balance on one foot, Kinisha begins to balance at age 3, while Jarrod acquires this skill at 4.

Children's ways of perfecting physical skills are also different. Brent tries hopping, but falls when he loses his balance. Amalie hops while holding hands with a friend or while holding onto a railing. Li watches others hop, learning from their successes and failures before trying the skill. Another aspect of individuality is the sporadic and uneven nature of development. Physical growth in children sometimes occurs in spurts, while at other times development is steady and incremental.

unstructured free play Play that is chosen and initiated by children, such as that which occurs on a playground.

Types of Physical Development

There are three types of physical development:

1. **Gross-motor development** refers to physical skills related to moving the whole body or major parts of the body. For babies, one of these skills is gaining control of the head, neck, and torso to enable sitting, and later, standing. In preschoolers, gross-motor skills are walking, running, and jumping.
2. **Fine-motor development** involves changes in skills related to the small muscles found in individual body parts, especially those in the hands and feet. As children increasingly direct the movements of their fingers, hands, and wrists, they learn to perform more complex fine-motor tasks such as tying shoes and drawing or writing.
3. **Perceptual-motor development** involves children using their senses to take in information about objects in the environment and then using this information to coordinate their movements. Information collected by the senses helps determine how the muscles of the body respond.

MyEducationLab

Go to the Assignments and Activities section of Topic 2: Child Development/ Theories in the MyEducationLab for your course and complete the activity entitled *Physical Development.* As you observe the enormous physical changes that occur in children from birth through age 8, consider effective ways teachers can support children's physical development, fitness, and health.

Characteristics of Physical Development

Although individual differences exist, three general principles of muscle development apply:

1. In general, the *direction* of muscle development is from top of the head to the tips of the toes. Babies learn to lift their heads before they can raise their torsos and use their arms before they can stand with, and then without, support.
2. The *sequence* of muscle development begins with those closest to the center of the body and progresses to those in the extremities—the hands and feet. Most children learn to crawl before they can pick up objects using the thumb and forefinger, called the **pincer grasp.** Thus, children refine their gross-motor movements, such as those used to walk or throw a ball, before they can control the fine-motor skills used to zip a jacket or turn the pages of a book.
3. The *process* of physical development is a result of experience—the opportunities children have to explore, practice, refine, and increasingly coordinate those motor movements that drive physical development.

As children learn to roll over, sit, stand, walk, and run, the impact of exploration and practice is clear in gross-motor skill acquisition. In addition, adult guidance and, sometimes, direct teaching stimulate physical development, as when children learn to swim, balance on a beam, or throw a basketball through the hoop. The direction, sequence, and process of physical development are not the same for all children, especially for those with physical disabilities. However, relatively predictable, though not rigid, sequences exist in each of these areas of motor development, as we see in the next section.

gross-motor development Physical skills related to moving the whole body or major parts of the body.

fine-motor development Physical skills related to the small muscles found in individual body parts, especially those in the hands and feet.

perceptual-motor development Occurs when children use their senses to take in information about objects in the environment and use this information to coordinate their movements.

pincer grasp Grasp used to pick up objects with the thumb and forefinger.

The Continuum of Motor Skill Development

During the first 3 years of life, the pace of physical development is staggering as children go from newborn helplessness to competence in controlling their own bodies in space and coordinating their arm, hand, and finger movements. The pace slows down somewhat during the preschool years as children gain greater control over these skills. During the primary years, children develop increasing coordination of their arms and legs as well as better control and refinement of skills.

Phases of Motor Development

The four broad phases of motor development from infancy to age 8 (Gabbard, 2007; Gallahue & Ozmun, 2006) are presented in Table 15.1. Although the sequence of motor skill

Table 15.1 Phases of Motor Development

Typical Age	Movement Phase	Movement Characteristics
Infants—birth to age 1	Reflexive movement phase	Babies gradually replace inborn reflexive movements, such as sucking, with more voluntary movements.
Toddlers—to age 2	Rudimentary movement phase	As infants become toddlers, they gain more control over their bodies as characterized by grasping, sitting, standing, and walking.
From ages 2 to 7	Fundamental movement phase	During this phase, children master most of the locomotor skills of walking, running, jumping, hopping, galloping, and skipping.
Begins about age 7 and continues to adolescence	Specialized movement phase	Children combine fundamental movements with other skills to develop coordinated, specialized skills such as running and kicking a soccer ball.

Source: Based on "Motor Development in Young Children," by D. L. Gallahue and J. C. Ozmun, 2006, pp. 105–120, in *Handbook of Research on the Education of Young Children*, edited by B. Spodek and O. N. Saracho, Mahweh, NJ: Lawrence Erlbaum Associates.

acquisition is similar in typically developing children, the age range varies considerably. For example, children learn to skip between 5 and 7 years of age (Gallahue & Ozmun, 2006). As children get older, individual differences only increase because children have such widely varying opportunities to participate in physical activities; for instance, while one child constantly watches television, another child may ski and swim regularly.

These phases and related skills constitute the goals of the physical education curriculum. From ages 2 to 7, the goal is for children to develop and refine the following fundamental movement skills (Gallahue & Ozmun, 2006):

- **Locomotor movements**, through which the body proceeds in a horizontal or vertical direction from one place to another, such as walking, running, leaping, or jumping
- **Gross motor manipulative movements**, through which the body gives or receives force from objects such as throwing, catching, or kicking
- **Stability movements**, in which the body remains in place but moves around its horizontal or vertical axis, such as balancing, dodging, starting, and stopping.

In the sections that follow, we present the typical expectations for gross-, fine-, and perceptual-motor development and explain how teachers can foster development in each area.

locomotor movements Movements that allow the body to proceed in a horizontal or vertical direction from one place to another, such as walking, running, leaping, or jumping.

gross-motor manipulative movements Large muscle movements involving giving or receiving force from objects such as throwing, catching, or kicking.

stability movements Movements in which the body remains in place, but moves around its horizontal or vertical axis; examples include balancing, dodging, starting, and stopping.

Fostering Gross-Motor Development

Even though physical development is strongly influenced by biological growth, teachers need to be intentional in promoting children's physical development.

Gross-Motor Development in Babies, Toddlers, and Twos

Remarkable physical change happens to babies during the first year or so of life. During infancy, babies learn to control and lift their heads and turn from side to side. Next, they roll from back to side, then front to side, and then completely over. This ability to change position is followed fairly rapidly by scooting, sitting, crawling, pulling to a stand, and walking with support.

Between 14 months and the second birthday, toddlers typically perfect walking without support and learn to squat down and stand back up, carry large objects, and sweep things off of tables and shelves. Twos are quite good at dumping out containers of toys and materials, propelling riding toys with their feet, walking tentatively up stairs one foot at a

Table 15.2 Fostering Gross-Motor Development in Infants and Toddlers

Some Indicators for Children	How Teachers Can Help	Considerations
Infants demonstrate slow but steady growth in being able to control reflexive movements and direct motor movements more purposefully.	Respond to babies and take delight in their motor skills; smile and laugh as they kick their legs over and over.	Provide constant supervision and a safe environment for babies, (e.g., keep their environment free of objects that might be swallowed).
Infants show intense fascination with motor practice and repeat gross motor movements until they become more coordinated.	Give babies opportunities to control their own bodies without restraint or external support.	Avoid the use of infant seats, swings, play pens, and other equipment that restricts movements or limits exploration and repetition.
Infants move around independently by rolling, scooting, and crawling.	Give babies places and spaces to explore in a safe environment.	Provide floor time; a clean carpet or blanket on the floor is a good choice.
Toddlers begin climbing and exploring the world around them.	Provide sufficient space and indoor climbing equipment for children to engage in gross-motor activities.	Pay particular attention to children's safety as they explore and take risks.

Sources: Based on *Innovations: The Comprehensive Infant Curriculum*, by K. Albrecht and L. G. Miller, 2000, Beltsville, MD: Gryphon House; *Innovations: The Comprehensive Toddler Curriculum*, by K. Albrecht and L. G. Miller, 2000, Beltsville, MD: Gryphon House; *Innovations: Infant and Toddler Development,* by K. Albrecht and L. G. Miller, 2001, Beltsville, MD: Gryphon House; and *Developmentally Appropriate Practice in Early Childhood Programs Serving Children from Birth through Age 8*, revised edition, edited by C. Copple and S. Bredekamp, 2009, Washington, DC: NAEYC.

time, and carrying large objects from one place to another. Table 15.2 describes some indicators of gross motor development in babies and toddlers and ways teachers can help with that development.

As toddlers continue to explore the world and begin to mimic the gross-motor behaviors of older children and adults, their actions become more purposeful. Two-year-old Chad is helped out of his car seat by his mother and stands by the car as she hands him his diaper bag. He puts it on his shoulder, bending his body sideways and raising his arm high in the air to keep it on his shoulder. This awkward position barely keeps the bag from dragging on the ground as he takes his mother's hand and walks toward his child care center. When his mother offers to carry it, he says emphatically, "No, my bag!" and toddles off.

Fostering gross-motor development during this stage is often about getting out of the way! During this period, most children have a built-in drive to master and move on. Creating safe and well-supervised opportunities to continue gross-motor practice is the primary task for teachers of babies and toddlers.

It is also important to remember that cultural groups differ in their views of appropriate child-rearing practices; therefore, infants' and toddlers' gross-motor experiences will vary among diverse cultures. For examples of diverse cultural practices that impact gross-motor development, read the *Culture Lens: Infants' Freedom of Movement across Cultures* feature.

As these children demonstrate, there are many ways that teachers can provide equipment, materials, and opportunities to promote gross-motor development indoors. Can you think of other strategies for teachers to use?

Gross-Motor Development in Preschoolers and Kindergartners

Gross-motor play continues to be important during the preschool and kindergarten years. Children during this period need physical activity throughout the day to maintain their focus and on-task behavior during the more structured parts of the school day. By age 3, children learn to climb stairs, walking up and down, as well as how to alternate feet as they

Culture Lens

Infants' Freedom of Movement across Cultures

Children's physical development is strongly influenced by biology, and yet cultural experience plays a key role. Consider two very different approaches to infant caregiving and their effects on babies' motor development.

The Pikler Institute is a residential nursery (previously called an orphanage) located in Budapest, Hungary, that was founded after World War II to serve children left without families. Dr. Emmi Pikler created a program for children, birth through age 3, that focuses on freedom of movement, which means that babies are never put in positions that they cannot get into on their own. For example, they aren't placed in restrictive devices such as infant seats, high chairs, jumpers, or walkers. They lie on their backs, awake or asleep, until they are able to roll over by themselves and move into different positions. The rule is "No adult interference with children's movement."

Allowing infants to move freely results in remarkable competence, balance, coordination, and calculated risk-taking. Visitors to the Pikler Institute are impressed with the ease and confidence with which very young children move their bodies. The children know how to handle their bodies, have impressive equilibrium, and their body awareness is far above average. In addition, there is a very low accident rate at the Institute.

Sixty years ago, no one was talking about "Back to Sleep," placing babies on their backs to prevent sudden infant death syndrome (SIDS). However, Pikler was doing it—back to sleep and back to play as well, without one SIDS incident ever. American advocates for "tummy time" fear that too much time on their backs will compromise infant development and misshape heads. Neither of these problems is evident at the Pikler Institute even though babies are never on their tummies until they can turn over by themselves. Freedom of movement promotes gross-motor development as well as a strong sense of competence within babies who find out that they can move and learn on their own without the assistance of an adult.

Contrast the Pikler approach to the child-rearing practice of the Au people of Papua, New Guinea. Anthropologist David Tracer has documented that during the first 12 months of life, Au babies are carried by their mothers or siblings 86% of the time. When they are put down, they are usually placed in a sitting position, not on their stomachs. Instead of crawling, Au babies go through a "scooting" phase—pushing themselves along with their hands and scooting on their backsides. Au parents discourage crawling to reduce the risk of their babies contracting disease. Their babies do not crawl; they learn to walk, although a few months later than children in the United States and Europe.

These examples and countless others demonstrate how cultural practices influence children's development—even their physical development—which is so dependent on biology and maturation. Consider how these approaches compare to the expectations for babies' freedom of movement in your own cultural group.

Note: For more information on the other components of the Pikler program and the institute, go to www.pikler.org.

Sources: "The Pikler Institute: A Unique Approach to Caring for Children," by J. Gonzalez-Mena, E. Chahin, and L. Briley, 2005, *Exchange, 166*(November–December), pp. 49–51; and *Will Baby Crawl?*, National Science Foundation Discoveries, 2005, retrieved September 18, 2009, from http://www.nsf.gov/discoveries/disc_summ.jsp?cntn_id=103153&org=NSF.

climb. Preschoolers get better at running, pedaling a tricycle, and jumping up and down on both feet. Endurance increases, although younger children still fatigue easily. Coordination and balance improve as kindergartners learn to jump rope, hop on one foot, and skip. An increasing awareness of their own skills and abilities leads to better understanding of unsafe behaviors; however, children can still lose control, and become overexcited or unable to manage during large-group activities.

The ability of the brain to conceive, organize, and carry out a series of unfamiliar actions is called **motor planning** and takes center stage as children work to gain control over their growing bodies. For example, 2½-year-old Lena tries to catch a ball by extending her arms. She knows what should happen, yet ends up with the ball bouncing off. By contrast, 4-year-old Derek moves his body so he can enclose the ball in his arms. Finally, kindergartner Julianne moves her body around so she can catch the ball between her hands with no assistance from her forearms.

motor planning The ability of the brain to conceive, organize, and carry out a series of unfamiliar actions.

The primary goal of the curriculum for preschoolers and kindergartners is to help them make progress on fundamental motor skills. In acquiring physical skills, competence leads to confidence and further persistence, so success matters. Therefore, it is important for teachers to intentionally teach fundamental motor skills, just as Ms. Perez did with Allison at the beginning of this chapter. Intentional teachers provide encouragement, coaching, and modification of the toys and materials to increase the chances of successful skill learning. They offer cues about how to perform specific skills, such as suggesting that children widen their stance to increase stability while bending forward. They also challenge children to extend, hold, or repeat skills as they practice, or they may add a challenge such as "Recite a poem while balancing on one foot." Table 15.3 describes effective strategies and examples of how teachers can promote gross-motor development in 3- to 6-year-olds.

Table 15.3 Promoting Gross-Motor Development in Preschool and Kindergarten

Teaching Behavior/Strategy	Examples
Provide periods of time for uninterrupted gross-motor play.	Organize the classroom to provide sufficient indoor space so that children can move without getting in each other's way.
Provide active outdoor play.	Provide space and time for children to freely engage in unstructured play and physical activity such as running, climbing, digging, and tricycle riding.
Provide opportunities to build and practice gross-motor skills indoors.	Act out the movements to songs, rhymes, chants, and finger plays.
Provide gross-motor opportunities that use a range of different skills and combine skills in novel and interesting ways.	Set up an obstacle course or play a game such as having children move to music and freeze their bodies in place when the music stops.
Provide appropriate toys and materials.	Supply balance beams, ladders, large wooden and plastic blocks, jump ropes, balls, floor puzzles, push carts, tumbling mats, scooter boards, and so forth.
Provide structured play experiences that help children build and practice fundamental motor skills.	Engage children in activities such as rolling balls, bowling, tossing bean bags into baskets, climbing stairs, or tumbling on mats. Have children play games using hula hoops, streamers, parachutes, or beach balls. Have them participate in music activities such as marching to the beat of a muscial selection.
Use motor movements during routines and transitions.	Have children waddle like a duck or jump like a frog to get from the classroom to the cafeteria.
Integrate movement with other curriculum topics such as literacy or music.	Select action-oriented books to read to children and then add movements to the stories (e.g., *Dinosaur Roar!*).
Consciously choose, adapt, and use materials to ensure maximum participation by all children, including children with disabilities.	Provide equal encouragement to boys and girls. If children have difficulty with materials, adapt them by adding handles, buttons, or knobs; prevent slipping with Velcro or mats. Simplify the task by limiting the range of difficulty; by adding sensory cues such as color, sound, textures, or scents; or by encouraging cooperation among children who can do the gross-motor activities and those who cannot.

Sources: Based on *Innovations: The Comprehensive Preschool Curriculum*, by K. Albrecht and L. G. Miller, 2004, Beltsville, MD: Gryphon House; and "Developmentally Appropriate Practice in the Kindergarten Year—Ages 5–6: An Overview," by H. B. Tomlinson, pp. 187–216, and "Developmentally Appropriate Practice in the Preschool Years-Ages 3–5: An Overview," by H. B. Tomlinson and M. Hyson, pp. 111–148, both in *Developmentally Appropriate Practice in Early Childhood Programs Serving Children from Birth through Age 8*, revised edition, edited by C. Copple and S. Bredekamp, 2009, Washington, DC: NAEYC.

Inclusion of children with disabilities requires that they participate as fully as possible in all activities. **Universal design** is the concept that materials and environments need to be usable by everyone, including those with disabilities, to the greatest extent possible. Read the *Including All Children* feature about universal design to learn principles for successfully including children with disabilities in physical education experiences.

Gross-Motor Development in the Primary Grades

During the primary grades, children practice and perfect a wide range of gross-motor skills, often connected to their interests. They have high energy levels and rarely show physical fatigue. Interest in group games increases as children are able to coordinate more than one gross-motor activity at a time, such as hitting a pitched ball. They can coordinate the movements required for dancing, skating, bike riding, swimming, and playing games such as soccer, basketball, and volleyball. As they practice using motor, balancing, and manipulative skills, they become increasingly competent and coordinated, often perfecting the skills needed to participate successfully in a wide range of games and sports. Table 15.4 lists strategies and examples of how teachers can promote gross motor development in the primary grades.

universal design The concept that materials and environments need to be usable by everyone, including those with disabilities, to the greatest extent possible.

Including All Children

Begin with Universal Design

Universal design refers to the creation of preplanned products and environments that can be used by all people to the greatest extent possible. For example, curbside ramps are essential for people in wheelchairs, but they also benefit skateboarders and cyclists. Universal design prevents the need to modify later. Other examples in the wider world include automatic doors, public signs with internationally recognized symbols, and closed captioning.

Consider how universal design applies in preschool, as three children play with brightly colored wooden puzzles. Paola traces her fingers over and around a bumpy tree-shaped piece as she searches for its place in the puzzle. Mackenzie grabs the knob on the final piece of a truck puzzle, twists it into place, and says, "Let's do it again, Mason!" Grinning broadly, Mason spills all of the pieces out for the tenth time!

Nothing is unusual about this joyful activity except that Paola is legally blind and Mason has cerebral palsy and struggles to control his hands and arms. Although the puzzles are typical enough, they were deliberately chosen and creatively used to foster play and learning for all children. For example, the puzzles' bright colors and interesting textures draw all the children in, but are essential supports for Paola's success. The large knobs on the truck puzzle help Mason as he develops coordination skills. He loves tipping out the pieces for Mackenzie, learning turn-taking in the process. The space is wide enough for Mason to maneuver his wheelchair around the table. A puzzle piece has been glued to the shelf for Paola to feel to help her during cleanup. Nonskid mats on the table keep puzzle pieces from sliding around and help children organize their materials as they work.

Teachers in this program have chosen other materials with universal design principles in mind.

- A basket full of balls can include rubbery, knobby, squishy Gertie balls, which bump along more slowly, making them easier to track and catch. Tennis ball–sized Fling Socks with long colorful tails are also easy to track and catch, and balls like the Wiggly, Giggly balls make noise or light up as they roll or bounce providing extra cues for children with sensory impairments.
- Blocks are an excellent example of universal design. They don't need instructions and can be used by all. Blocks with magnets aid stacking; those with textured sides and noisemakers add sensory experiences.
- Books with a variety of illustration sizes, text sizes, and color variations and those with textures, flaps, cutouts, and pop-ups invite children to explore. Board books make page-turning easier; books that make sounds or read the text when a button is pushed help children with hearing disabilities participate and explore the world of literacy.

Sources: Adapted from "Learning Materials for Children of All Abilities: Begin with Universal Design," by K. Haugen, 2005, *Exchange, 161* (January/February), pp. 45–47; and *Steps for Adapting Materials for Use by All Children*, by K. Haugen, retrieved September 18, 2009, from http://www.childcareexchange.com/library/5016101.pdf. Reprinted by permission.

Table 15.4 Teaching Motor Skills in the Primary Grades

Teacher Behavior/Strategy	Examples
Arrange the classroom to allow for movement activities.	Arrange desks or tables to allow room for calisthenics and movement accompanied by music.
Plan breaks throughout the day for physical exercise and stress relief.	Have children stand, stretch, do motor mirroring (pairs of children mirror each other's movements), or move from place to place.
Integrate motor skill learning and practice into other areas of the curriculum.	Have children act out rhymes and stories, dance, repeat rhythms, express emotions with the entire body, play charades, and pantomime stories.
Offer opportunities for children to create, modify, and play group games and child-initiated team sports.	Encourage children to choose and participate in noncompetitive games, such as hopscotch, jump rope, parachute games, hula hooping, and playing tag and games such as Red Light/Green Light.
Plan activities in which everyone has a chance to participate as opposed to organized sports where only the best players make the team and get to play.	Because of primary grade children's growing inclination to compare themselves with others, avoid pushing competitive activities. Instead, help children compete with their own prior performances rather than those of other children ("Last time you only hit the target once. Today you hit it three times").
Collaborate with physical education, music, and fine arts specialists to make sure that children have opportunities for motor skill learning every day.	At the elementary level, teachers are not likely to be in control of physical education activities, but they can work with other professionals to ensure that children have many rich opportunities to learn and practice motor skills throughout the school day.

Sources: Based on "Developmentally Appropriate Practice in the Primary Grades—Ages 6–8: An Overview," by H. B. Tomlinson, pp. 257–288, in *Developmentally Appropriate Practice in Early Childhood Programs Serving Children from Birth through Age 8*, revised edition, edited by C. Copple and S. Bredekamp, 2009, Washington, DC: NAEYC.

Because motor skill development is closely tied to opportunity, recess is not a luxury for children in the primary grades (Pellegrini & Holmes, 2006). As the pressure to improve scores on standardized tests has increased, as many as 40% of elementary schools have severely limited or eliminated recess (Pellegrini, 2005; Pellegrini & Holmes, 2006). Many consider this trend troubling and potentially damaging to children's academic achievement—opposite of the desired effect (Grissom, 2005; National Association of Early Childhood Specialists in State Departments of Education, 2002).

A large body of research demonstrates the educational, social, and physical benefits of recess (Pellegrini & Bohn, 2005; Pelligrini & Holmes, 2006). Playful breaks maximize children's ability to perform higher-level cognitive tasks and improve social competence, adjustment to school, and physical health. Some think that recess interferes with children's attention spans, but the opposite is true; research finds that in kindergarten and primary grades, children are more inattentive before than after recess (Pellegrini & Holmes, 2006). Recess increases the amount of time children stay on task and reduces fidgeting (Jarrett et al., 1998). Read the *How Would You Respond?* feature and consider how you might defend recess against those who would eliminate it.

Fostering Fine-Motor Development

The term **fine-motor manipulative movement** refers to control, precision, and accuracy of small muscle movement, such as those inherent in picking up objects with the thumb and forefinger, tying shoes, cutting with scissors, or using a keyboard. Fine-motor skills allow children

fine-motor manipulative movements Control, precision, and accuracy of small muscle movement.

How Would You Respond?

Threats to Recess

The Situation To make more time for instruction and try to raise test scores, your elementary school has eliminated recess, and physical education is now only once a week. Your first graders are stressed and restless. The children are too fidgety to concentrate, and you are concerned about their lack of exercise and learning opportunities in physical skills.

What to Do? Various courses of action are possible in this situation. Which do you think would be most useful and why?

- Educate yourself, your colleagues, and families on how children benefit from these activities to become a more effective advocate for recess and physical education.
- Provide more breaks during the day for children to stretch or move around the classroom to reduce fidgeting.
- Incorporate movement into some of your classroom instruction, to meet children's needs that previously were met by recess and a daily physical education period.
- Look for opportunities both in your classroom and in cooperation with teaching specialists to integrate movement into the school day. For example, work with the music teacher to combine movement with music or plan outdoor science experiences.
- Plan outdoor activities, such as neighborhood walks, that relate to what the children are studying in science or other curriculum areas.
- Encourage families to enroll their children in organized sports after school and/or to send them outdoors to play after school.

Can you suggest other strategies that might be useful?

to explore how things work, get dressed, use writing tools, put puzzles together, prepare snacks and meals, and engage in many more activities that require hand, finger, and wrist movements. Strength, control, and coordination of hand, finger, and wrist movements are part of fine-motor development. Strength is needed to cut with scissors; control allows for buttoning and zipping; coordination is used to put together puzzles and thread beads on laces.

Fine-motor play is important to healthy brain development. When the small muscles of the body move, brain circuitry is stimulated and strengthened, and the coordination between neurons and between the parts of the brain improves (Levitt, 2008). As children repeat fine-motor skills, such as stringing beads, working with clay, and putting pegs in pegboards, they not only refine these skills but also improve brain connections.

Fine-motor development progresses slowly as individual children experience different degrees of difficulty in performing fine-motor tasks. Children often encounter failure and become frustrated as they try to master these difficult skills; consequently, they need adequate time and adult support to keep them interested enough to practice.

Fine-Motor Development in Babies, Toddlers, and Twos

Babies spend the first year of life working on grasping objects and tracking movements with their eyes and heads. They perfect picking up objects with their whole hand, pointing, putting objects into containers, and drinking from a cup.

Toddlers begin to use a spoon to eat, turn pages, stack blocks, scribble with crayons or markers, hold drinking cups, and remove clothing. By age 2, they are able to remove shoes and some clothing, hold a cup or glass in one hand, unbutton large buttons, turn doorknobs, stack small blocks, fit large pegs in pegboards, pour and fill containers at a sensory table, unzip large zippers, and begin to show a preference for one hand. Toward the end of

Table 15.5 Fostering Fine-Motor Skills in Infants and Toddlers

Teacher Behavior/Strategy	Examples
Give babies and toddlers many opportunities to explore objects, people, and things using the muscles necessary for reaching, grasping, pulling, picking up, chewing, holding, and letting go.	Play interactive games like peek-a-boo; look at picture books, particularly books with textures, sounds, and actions to imitate; display images that are interesting from a baby's or toddler's perspective, taking into account that very young infants are usually looking up from their backs at the world.
Provide developmentally appropriate toys such as action/reaction toys that help children connect cause and effect as well as stimulate fine-motor skills.	Provide appropriate toys that make noise and respond to the child's manipulation in interesting ways such as rattles, teethers, toys to stack and sort, pull toys, soft blocks, and toys that pop up or roll away. Children who aren't mobile like play mats with objects to kick or reach for, while toddlers can do puzzles with a few separate pieces, stack blocks, and roll wheeled toys.
Provide developmentally appropriate materials and equipment.	Provide eating utensils for children in graduated sizes and complexity to provide incremental motor practice using the small muscles of the fingers and the hand, e.g., spoons, then forks; bowls, then plates.
Provide age appropriate materials. Ensure that most fine-motor toys and materials are easy to clean and sanitize and large enough that they do not present a choking hazard.	Babies put almost everything into their mouths—as they use the sense of touch, taste, and smell to gather information about the object with which they are playing. Toddlers like to tear paper, pull things off of shelves, dump toys out of containers, and play with miniatures such as interconnecting blocks. Banging and clapping are great fun, as is playing with sand, water, and playdough.
Provide art materials such as large crayons, watercolor markers, and a variety of sizes and types of paper.	Let children explore materials. Be realistic about the amount of mess.

Sources: Based on *Innovations: The Comprehensive Infant Curriculum*, by K. Albrecht and L. G. Miller, 2000, Beltsville, MD: Gryphon House; *Innovations: The Comprehensive Toddler Curriculum*, by K. Albrecht and L. G. Miller, 2000, Beltsville, MD: Gryphon House; *Innovations: Infant and Toddler Development*, by K. Albrecht and L. G. Miller, 2001, Beltsville, MD: Gryphon House; and *Developmentally Appropriate Practice in Early Childhood Programs Serving Children from Birth through Age 8*, revised edition, edited by C. Copple and S. Bredekamp, 2009, Washington, DC: NAEYC.

toddlerhood, children tackle toileting, which involves many motor skills such as pulling underwear down and up and controlling the small muscles that hold and release bodily functions. Table 15.5 provides examples of ways teachers can promote fine-motor skills in very young children.

Fine-Motor Development in Preschoolers and Kindergartners

By age 3, children usually exhibit a preference for one hand (although they don't know left from right) and can complete puzzles, string beads, put pegs in pegboards, easily turn the pages of a book, grasp a pencil or marker (though not always with an adult-like grip), and draw and write with crayons and markers. Four- and five-year-olds complete board and floor puzzles; draw recognizable images; copy shapes, letters, and numbers; cut with scissors; button their clothes; and pour from a pitcher into a glass.

Many preschoolers and most kindergartners print letters recognizably, disassemble and reassemble manipulative constructions, use scissors to accomplish desired tasks, hit nails with a hammer head, and use a keyboard and mouse with age-appropriate computer programs. By age 5, children's drawings are more detailed and they may be able to tie their own shoes.

Table 15.6 Fostering Fine-Motor Skills in Preschool and Kindergarten

Teacher Behavior/Strategy	Examples
Provide a range of materials and activities for children.	Use materials and activities in which children with different levels of fine-motor skills can participate with success, such as puzzles with different numbers of pieces and more or less complexity.
Provide appropriate toys and materials.	Supply objects to sort, count, and put into patterns; pegboards and beads to string; clothing and other items that zip and button for dress-up play; drawing and writing materials; scissors, paint, and clay.
Offer opportunities to practice functional skills.	Allow children to pour milk, hammer nails, and use other tools. These activities may require accommodation or modification for all children to use them successfully or when materials cause frustration or fatigue.
Provide open-ended activities that allow children to practice fine-motor skills. Choose activities that fit their current level of competence as well as those that are more challenging yet within reach.	Arrange for open-ended experiences such as drawing and painting, working with playdough or clay, building with blocks, and constructing with Duplos and Legos and other interconnecting blocks.

Sources: Based on *Innovations: The Comprehensive Preschool Curriculum*, by K. Albrecht and L. G. Miller, 2004, Beltsville, MD: Gryphon House; and "Developmentally Appropriate Practice in the Kindergarten Year—Ages 5–6: An Overview," by H. B. Tomlinson, pp. 187–216, and "Developmentally Appropriate Practice in the Preschool Years–Ages 3–5: An Overview," by H. B. Tomlinson and M. Hyson, pp. 111–148, both in *Developmentally Appropriate Practice in Early Childhood Programs Serving Children from Birth through Age 8*, revised edition, edited by C. Copple and S. Bredekamp, 2009, Washington, DC: NAEYC.

Gender differences in motor skills are evident in this period. In general, girls tend to be more advanced than boys in fine-motor skills and in gross-motor skills that require precision, whereas boys tend to do better with skills that require force and power (Berk, 2008). Table 15.6 presents ways to help preschoolers and kindergartners master fine-motor skills.

When fine-motor experiences lead to frustration and fatigue or when children prefer gross-motor activities, they need encouragement and support and sometimes instruction in skills or models of what to try next. Teachers need to carefully observe children to be sure they are ready to tackle the next challenge. Here again, intentional teaching is important, as described in the feature *Becoming an Intentional Teacher.*

Fine-Motor Development in the Primary Grades

Fine motor development in primary grade children is all about refinement. Writing, drawing, and computer skills are more precise. By second grade, wrist, hand, and finger muscles are more coordinated, writing becomes more uniform, and drawing skills include detail and display early attempts at perspective. Primary-age children master the ability to coordinate movements they can cut with scissors while turning the paper to make arches, angles, borders, and other cutouts. They enjoy working on projects or crafts over time, and rather than finish an activity in one session, they will return repeatedly to it if it interests them.

In general, during this time, girls are ahead of boys in fine motor development (Haywood & Gretchell, 2005). However, gender differences are at least partially the result of differences in practice opportunities, with boys and girls developing at a similar pace given similar opportunities (Craig & Baucum, 2002). This research highlights the importance of providing equal opportunities to all children to develop physical skills.

Children in the primary grades like to use real things, such as hammers and nails and scrap lumber, rather than toys. They need instruction about how to use the tools, but will often resist the offer of support until they have tried their own ideas. Teachers can draw

Becoming an Intentional Teacher

Teaching Fine-Motor Skills

Here's What Happened In my kindergarten class I have three boys whose lack of fine-motor skills is holding them back in writing. They're all very physical and love to run, jump, and climb. They aren't attracted to puzzles, working with playdough, or stringing beads, although they do build with blocks at times. I brought in some mini-Legos and small cars, and they began building garages and race tracks for the cars. I've given them writing tools and various kinds of paper and encouraged them to make signs for their race track. Also, I have begun pairing the three boys with other kids at the computer using software I think will get their interest.

Here's What I Was Thinking Boys are sometimes behind girls in their fine motor development, and this seems especially likely when they don't spend much time in activities that involve the small hand muscles. Some of my fellow teachers told me that I should just make the boys practice writing more. But I observed that they fatigued while trying to write and became easily frustrated. Instead, I thought about what these three boys are interested in. A lot of it is large-motor play, but they sometimes build with blocks, and outside they ride their trikes and pretend they're race car drivers. These interests hadn't gotten them involved with much fine-motor activity when they worked with the usual materials. But I thought if I brought in small-scale materials for them to build and pretend with, there might be a change. And I thought that getting them to write for a real purpose would also help. As for the computer, I had two thoughts in mind. One idea was that the computer will allow the boys to do some writing without the difficulty of forming the letters slowing them down so much. And at the same time they'll be working with the mouse and keyboard, which are good tasks for promoting fine-motor skills.

on their interests, arranging for them to create friendship bracelets or bird houses. Six- to eight-year-olds will work for extended periods of time on projects, particularly if they result in "real" products.

Control over fine-motor skills develops later than gross-motor skills, and children need a lot of practice to master them. Otherwise, they can easily become frustrated.

Fostering Perceptual-Motor Development from Birth through the Primary Grades

Perceptual-motor development plays an important role in learning fundamental movement skills. Perceptual-motor skills include auditory, visual, and tactile-kinesthetic skills as well as body awareness. Children develop these skills while using their senses to collect, monitor, interpret, and respond to information from the environment. As their ability to collect and use information improves, motor skills grow and develop, as we see in the following example.

> Fourteen-month-old Tara sits on her teacher's lap with her finger in the air. Her teacher, Miss Laura, begins the finger play she knows Tara is asking her to say. She points to Tara's facial features gently as she repeats the rhyme: "Eye winker (touches one eyelid), tom tinker (then the other eyelid), nose smeller (touches the tip of her nose), mouth eater (points to her mouth), chin chopper (touches her chin), gully, gully, gully (gently tickles her neck)." Tara is already showing her teacher how she perceives input from her senses (the words she hears, the touch she feels) and combines them with her memory of previous times when the teacher played this game to anticipate what will happen next. Tara closes her eyes before they are touched, sticks her nose in the air as Laura says "nose smeller," and lowers her chin and laughs heartily in anticipation of the gentle tickle on her neck.

Perceptual-motor development is maturational—as attention to and perception of sensory information improves, subsequent motor coordination improves. This growth is largely dependent on the development of the brain and central nervous system, although the timing of such maturity varies. Perceptions of where the body is (**spatial awareness**), speeding up or slowing down a movement (**temporal awareness**), anticipating which way to go (**directional awareness**), and listening to verbal input or distinguishing between different sounds (**auditory awareness**) are all part of perceptual-motor development.

Perceptual-Motor Development in Babies and Toddlers

Babies and toddlers learn through movement. As they move their arms, legs, and bodies, they encounter the world by touching it and being touched by it. They explore using all of the senses, particularly touch and taste. Babies begin processing sensory information and trying to make sense of it, anticipating, for example, that pushing a button on a toy will produce a sound. They manipulate tools, such as spoons or a cup, and demonstrate a basic understanding of quantities of more or less.

Toddlers continue the exploration, now from an upright vantage point. They increasingly manipulate objects with a purpose, such as stacking blocks or lining up cars. They gather sensory data from watching others and imitate other children and adults.

Perceptual-Motor Development in Preschoolers and Kindergartners

During the preschool and kindergarten years, the senses of sight, smell, touch, taste, and hearing are all well developed. However, in spite of their physical capacities for excellent sensation and perception, this age group's processing of the incoming information is not complete; children have yet to develop some of the cognitive strategies and language needed to make sense of all the information coming in through their senses.

Children's ability to perceive patterns and discriminate various forms improves during the preschool years. Visually, preschool children are farsighted; they have trouble switching focus between close and distant targets and are still developing binocular vision (the ability of the eyes to work together), which necessitates larger print. Their depth perception is still developing and they tend to run into things and each other (Pica, 2006).

Preschoolers and kindergartners may make letter reversals (confusing the letters *q* and *p* or *d* and *b*), but this is not a perceptual problem. It is a natural confusion based on experience with objects in the physical world that have the same function regardless of their directional orientation—a chair is still a chair whether it is facing left or right.

Hearing is also well developed; this age group loves listening to music, stories, and conversations. They begin to recognize rhyming words and play with the sounds of language. They perceive when two words sound the same or begin with the same sound (Wasik, 2001). When children do not participate or respond during these types of activities, it may be a sign of hearing problems due to chronic middle ear infections or other causes that should be evaluated by a physician.

Perceptual-Motor Development in the Primary Grades

Children in the primary grades have learned to use all of the senses to influence their motor movements. As their ability to simultaneously take in sensory input and make modifications to their motor movements improves, so does motor coordination, balance, and timing. Increasingly, children are able to integrate previously acquired skills into more complex actions, particularly if they have had considerable practice.

Environments filled with interesting things to touch, smell, see, listen to, and manipulate provide sensory input for children to perceive and interpret. From birth to age 8, similar types of experiences promote perceptual-motor development, as listed in Table 15.7.

As children gain perceptual-motor skills and their body awareness increases, teachers can increase the level of difficulty and challenge of the tasks to help them refine these skills further. In the next section, we turn to the all-important contribution of play to children's physical fitness and health.

spatial awareness Perceptions of where the body is.

temporal awareness Speeding up or slowing down a movement.

directional awareness Anticipating which way to go.

auditory awareness Listening to verbal input or distinguishing between different sounds.

Table 15.7 Fostering Perceptual-Motor Development from Birth to Age 8

Teacher Behavior/Strategy	Examples
Provide a variety of interesting sounds and rhythms to hear.	Use songs, rhymes, finger plays, and chants to provide interesting sounds and rhythms. Finger plays (such as "The Itsy, Bitsy Spider"), which require the coordination of the spoken word with hand or body movements, are good perceptual motor experiences for children ages 5 and under. Primary-age children often add hand and body movements to familiar songs, rhymes, and chants. Build auditory awareness by adding novel input, such as the sounds of orchestra instruments or nature.
Stimulate visual acuity for all ages by providing interesting pictures and displays at children's eye level in the environment.	Provide visual stimulation for young children. Babies spend long periods of time gazing at things that interest them while toddlers and twos will explore photographs and pictures. Have preschoolers, kindergartners, and primary grade children examine pictures from a variety of sources, including the Internet and magazines, and use digital and video cameras to enhance visual awareness.
Offer a variety of textures and objects to feel, see, smell, and manipulate to provide sensory input for children to perceive and interpret.	Provide experiences that require children to use the senses independently, such as having them identify hidden objects by touch or various odors by smell. Also have them use the senses together to figure things out: they might smell the results of a cooking project and see food change form as it is cooked.
Help children explore space to build awareness of their body to learn about the parts of their bodies, to become aware of how much space their bodies take up, and to learn how to control their body as they move from one place to another.	Support perceptual motor skills by giving children freedom to explore under tables and chairs and inside of cozy spaces. Balance the familiar perspective of not being as tall as adults with the unfamiliar perspective of being taller by encouraging children to visit the loft or use the climber.
Give children a variety of points of view within and beyond the classroom.	Provide multiple levels with raised platforms or use foam structures or pits. Peek-a-boo hideouts and windows into the next classroom are sources of visual and auditory stimuli, as are low windows that provide a view of the world beyond the classroom.
Provide experiences that promote visual, body, and directional awareness.	Use obstacle courses to build understanding of directions in space such as *under*, *over*, *around*, and *through*. Ask children to imitate body movements: move like an animal, insect, or amphibian. Have children use their body to make letters or numbers.

Sources: Based on *Innovations: The Comprehensive Preschool Curriculum*, by K. Albrecht and L. G. Miller, 2004, Beltsville, MD: Gryphon House; and "Developmentally Appropriate Practice in the Kindergarten Year—Ages 5–6: An Overview," by H. B. Tomlinson, pp. 187–216, and "Developmentally Appropriate Practice in the Preschool Years–Ages 3–5: An Overview," by H. B. Tomlinson and M. Hyson, pp. 111–148, both in *Developmentally Appropriate Practice in Early Childhood Programs Serving Children from Birth through Age 8*, revised edition, edited by C. Copple and S. Bredekamp, 2009, Washington, DC: NAEYC.

The Important Role of Play

From our previous discussion of types of motor skill learning, we have seen that play is an essential context in which children acquire and practice physical abilities. Different types of play have different benefits, and are developmentally appropriate for children at different age levels (Ginsberg, 2007). Here, we focus on the critical role of outdoor play. The outdoors is one of the most stimulating, engaging contexts for children's development and learning. However, current changes in children's lives threaten their exposure to nature, as described next.

Childhood Experiences with the Natural Environment

Richard Louv, in his book *Last Child in the Woods* (2006), chronicles changes in children's exposure, contact, and experience with the natural world and concludes that something

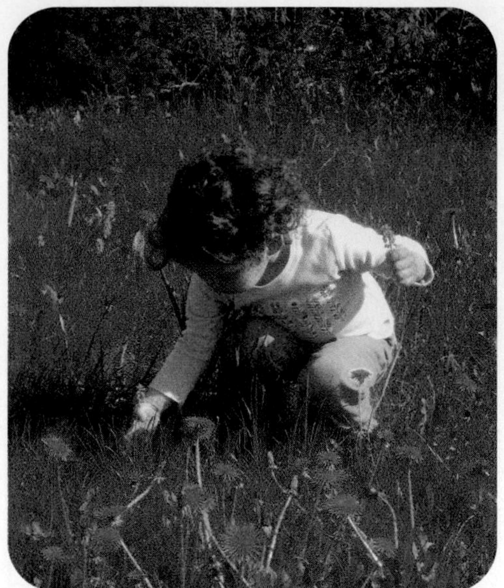

Children today are more likely to spend time watching television or playing video games than experiencing nature firsthand, leading to "nature deficit disorder." Natural play environments address this problem and also provide laboratories for scientific investigation.

important has been lost as children's time in natural environments has diminished. This concern is shared by many early childhood educators (Cuppens, Rosenow, & Wike, 2007; Rivkin, 1995). As the late Jim Greenman, author of *Caring Spaces, Learning Places* (2005a), states: "Children are losing habitat—the real world of people and nature and machines and an opportunity to explore that world (directly, not just electronically) and be a part of it" (Greenman, 2005b, p. 2).

Addressing Nature Deficit

Louv (2006) proposes that children, families, and communities are experiencing "**nature deficit disorder**." The hypothetical disorder describes the human costs of alienation from nature that include "diminished use of the senses, attention difficulties, and higher rates of physical and emotional illnesses" (Louv, 2006, p. 34). These concerns led to an examination of how outdoor environments are designed and constructed and to a movement toward more natural outdoor playgrounds (Keeler, 2008).

A growing trend among playground planners rejects the idea of playgrounds full of commercially purchased plastic, metal, or wood structures surrounded by safety zones filled with wood chips. Instead these planners favor environments that make creative use of natural features and objects while still meeting the health and safety standards required for children's outdoor playgrounds (see American Academy of Pediatrics, American Public Health Association, & National Resource Center for Health and Safety in Child Care and Early Education, 2002). They believe that playgrounds should have areas with trees, grass, shrubs, planters, pots, and paths to show children what the world is made of—the real stuff, not a plastic or simulated version (Keeler, 2008).

Benefits of Natural Environments

Contact with nature has restorative powers for children. Nature buffers the impact of life stresses and lowers the incidence of behavior disorders, anxiety, and depression; children who play outside are sick less often and have a higher measure of self-worth (Wells & Evans, 2003).

The quality of children's experience is different when they play in natural environments; it is more diverse, imaginative, and creative. Such play fosters language and collaborative skills and stimulates social interaction between children (Bixler, Floyd, & Hammutt, 2002; Fjortoft, 2001). Children who play regularly in natural environments show more advanced motor fitness, including coordination, balance, and agility, and are better able to concentrate after contact with nature (Fjortoft & Sageie, 2000).

Natural environments also build an understanding of science and keep children engaged in their learning (J. Thomas, 2007). For those children experiencing developmental, psychological, or relational disorders, research suggests that their symptoms are relieved after contact with nature (Taylor, Kuo, & Sullivan, 2001) and that bullying behavior is reduced by frequent play in natural environments (Malone & Tranter, 2003).

Characteristics of Outdoor Environments

Good outdoor environments have similar characteristics (Cuppens et al., 2007; Greenman, 2005a, 2005b). Space is typically divided into defined areas for different kinds of activities. Areas are dedicated to motor activities such as:

- Climbing, sliding, and crawling
- Riding wheeled toys and transporting things
- Building and construction
- Gross motor activities such as running, jumping, throwing, kicking, bouncing, and balancing
- A messy play area for sand and water play

nature deficit disorder
Hypothetical disorder related to lack of exposure and experience outdoors and in the natural world.

- Places to pretend and for creative expression
- A gardening or digging area
- A place for swings and other dynamic equipment
- An area for art activities
- Places to watch, get away from it all, or slow down.

Outdoor play is essential for children's physical fitness and health. How would a playground such as this benefit children's development?

On playgrounds, climbing structures for children need to be sturdy and well anchored. But children also need equipment and materials that they can arrange in a variety of ways—providing experience with controlling the environment. Children like to rearrange crates, planks, boxes, blocks, and toys. They like tents, fabric scraps, and beach umbrellas to create places to climb into, under, or around.

Spacious settings equipped with age-appropriate toys, materials, and apparatus are also important for primary grade children. Outdoor settings with hills, obstacle courses, softball diamonds, mazes, basketball hoops, tunnels, four-square and hopscotch grids, and volleyball nets are likely to interest children. Walking and running tracks, tether ball poles, and plenty of movable parts such as planks, large blocks, and tree trunks and branches help children sustain gross-motor play. Additional materials, such as balls of all types (large and small playground balls, softballs, basketballs, soccer balls, sensory balls), parachutes, jump ropes, hoops, cones, and beanbags add variety and give children opportunities to practice a variety of physical skills.

Schools should have outdoor equipment such as balance beams that are low to the ground to encourage children to practice skills at their own level. Such equipment limits spills to tumbles instead of serious falls. Digging in the sand or soil is another great outdoor motor activity for children. Water added to dry sand and soil or placed in a water table adds interest as children explore these components of the natural world.

When children are given ample time to play outdoors, they can practice and perfect many physical skills; they feel powerful and successful. For this reason, most children love the outdoors—it is a "can do" place. Yet the fast-paced activity of the outdoors can also be overstimulating and overwhelming for some. Children need quiet places to cool off, calm down, or rest; they also need water available to quench their thirst. A blanket in the shade can provide a place for children to spend some time with the teacher, refueling and recharging before heading back out to explore the world again. Time outdoors provides a change of pace, freedom from being close to other children, and a constant source of interesting stimuli.

Promoting Health and Preventing Illness and Injury

Children's success in school and life is integrally connected to their health. Teachers have a responsibility to keep children safe and prevent disease. In the sections that follow, we discuss ways of supporting children's health and wellness and teaching practices that prevent illness and injury.

> **Effective Teaching**
> Intentional teachers find creative ways to build physical fitness, health and safety, and nutrition education into curriculum every day.

Keeping Children Healthy and Safe

Adults must be vigilant to protect young children's health and safety. NAEYC (2005e) accreditation standards for health and safety are an excellent resource to guide teachers. Keeping children safe requires adequate and attentive supervision during all activities and

MyEducationLab

To observe effective teaching practices for promoting children's health, go the Video Examples section of Topic 12: Professionalism/Ethics in the MyEducationLab for your course and watch the video entitled *Health Lesson: Brushing Habits*. What is the teacher's role in keeping children healthy and preventing illness?

experiences, and providing safe, appropriate furniture, toys, and materials and systematic monitoring to keep them that way.

By nature, children are messy beings. In the early childhood setting, this translates into the need to keep everything clean and sanitized so as to prevent the spread of germs. Adults who model keeping the environment clean teach children how to clean up after themselves. Disease prevention starts with preenrollment requirements such as immunization and physical checkups, and continues with instilling habits that will lead children to eat well, get adequate rest, and participate in plenty of vigorous exercise.

Emergency preparedness is another dimension of health and wellness. In schools, sheltering-in-place strategies and evacuation procedures and drills need to be understood by all and practiced until they become routine for both adults and children. Natural disasters such as hurricanes, tornadoes, or earthquakes are prevalent in certain geographic areas and require specific disaster preparedness plans. In addition to natural disasters, our world today is threatened by terrorism and criminal behavior, and emergency preparedness must address these possibilities as well (Greenman, 2001).

The Teacher's Role in Preventing Illness

Preventing the spread of germs is an essential disease prevention strategy for young children to learn. Most experts agree that the single most effective practice that prevents the spread of germs is proper hand washing by adults and children. Teachers can stop the spread of germs by washing their hands and teaching children correct hand-washing practices. NAEYC accreditation standards as well as state licensing standards require regular, systematic hand washing at specific times for adults and children, such as before and after eating, using the toilet, or diapering. Despite the critical importance of these procedures, these standards are among the least frequently met in early childhood programs. Hand washing that actually prevents the transfer of germs is a process with specific steps, as described in Figure 15.1.

- Always use warm, running water and a mild, preferably liquid, soap. Antibacterial soaps may be used, but are not required.
- Wet the hands and apply a small amount (dime to quarter size) of liquid soap.
- Rub hands together vigorously until a soapy lather appears and continue for at least 15 seconds. Be sure to scrub between fingers, under fingernails, and around the tops and palms of the hands.
- Rinse hands under warm running water. Leave the water running while drying hands.
- Dry hands with a clean, disposable (or single use) towel, being careful to avoid touching the faucet handles or towel holder with clean hands.
- Turn the faucet off using the towel as a barrier between your hands and the faucet handle.
- Discard the used towel in a trash can, lined with a fluid-resistant (plastic) bag. Trash cans with foot-pedal operated lids are preferable.
- Consider using hand lotion to prevent chapping of hands. If using lotions, use liquids or tubes that can be squirted so that the hands do not have direct contact with container spout to avoid contaminating the lotion inside the container.
- When assisting a child in handwashing, either hold the child (if an infant) or have the child stand on a safety step at a height at which the child's hands can hang freely under the running water. Assist the child in performing all of the above steps and then wash your own hands.

Figure 15.1 Proper Hand-Washing Procedures

Source: Reprinted from *Handwashing Procedure,* Centers for Disease Control and Prevention. Retrieved September 18, 2009, from http://www.cdc.gov.ncidod/hip/abc/practic6.htm.

The Teacher's Role in Injury Prevention

When children are involved in active play, the role of the teacher is to provide constant attention and supervision. Teachers need to observe zones of the outdoor area and pay close attention to what children are doing so that they can intervene quickly, remind children of safety considerations, and be close enough to step in and stop risky behavior when it occurs.

Teachers also need to teach children about accident prevention, tricycle and bicycle safety, and preparedness for emergencies. The majority of injuries that occur at school happen on the playground (Phelan, Khoury, Kalkwarf, & Lanphear, 2001; Wallis, Cody, & Mickalide, 2003). Nonfatal playground injuries are most often caused by falls. Children under age 4 are more likely to suffer head and face injuries, whereas children ages 5 to 14 are more likely to suffer injuries to the arms and hands (Mack, Hudson, & Thompson, 1997).

Balancing Risk and Challenge

In striving to protect children's safety and health, however, early childhood educators need to understand the impact of the amount of risk and challenge in the environment, what is called the **risk vs. challenge continuum** (Greenman, 2005a). The concept is that extremes of either risk or challenge—too much or too little—are not in the best interest of children. Too little risk and children may withdraw or try harder to make something happen by using inappropriate or dangerous behaviors (Greenman, 2005a). Too much risk will certainly result in accidents and injuries.

risk vs. challenge continuum Concept that children not only need to be safe but they also need to be challenged if they are to advance their skills and learn how to keep themselves safe.

Concern for children's safety is absolutely necessary and environments should be designed to minimize risks, hazards, and potential dangers. At the same time, an attempt to eliminate all risk can lead to eliminating all challenge. Children not only need to be safe, they also need to be challenged if they are to advance their skills and learn how to keep themselves safe.

From infancy on, children try out challenging activities that might put them at risk for injury, most of them as a part of normal exploration. Consider the concept of risk vs. challenge in deciding whether children should be allowed to climb trees. From a pediatrician's perspective, the risk of injury is too high, so tree limbs on children's playgrounds should be trimmed to prevent tree climbing (Aronson, 1993). However, from the perspective of a veteran child care center director, tree climbing is a learnable skill that can be safely taught to children and practiced with careful supervision (Stephens, 1993).

Curriculum to Promote Physical Fitness and Health

The purpose of developmentally appropriate physical education is to help children learn to move and learn through movement (Gallahue, 1995). In the sections that follow, we first describe curriculum and teaching strategies to promote physical development. We then address how to plan a health education curriculum.

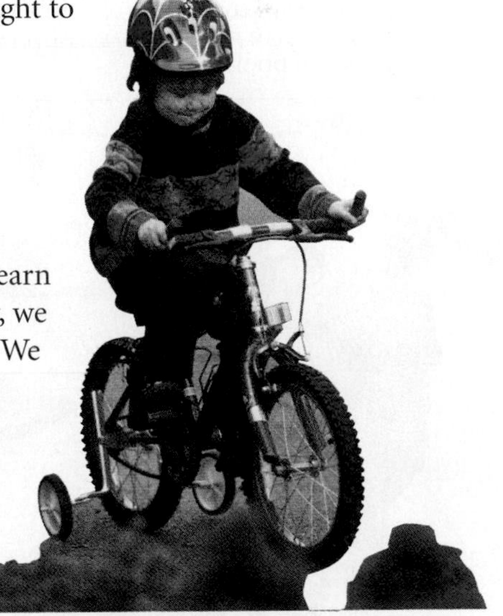

Young children are vulnerable to illness and injury and need adult protection. But they also need challenges to help them learn how to keep themselves safe. How can early childhood teachers find a balance of risk and challenge for children's physical activity?

Planning Meaningful Curriculum

You will recall from Chapter 10 that curriculum planning draws on both the content of the disciplines and knowledge of child development. In planning curriculum for physical development, the disciplines of physical education, nutrition, and health provide the learning goals for children. To make these goals meaningful and accessible to young children, teachers need to translate them into topics of interest. The teachers then plan the learning experiences keeping in mind what they know about the continuum of physical development so they can set achievable goals for children's gross-motor and fine-motor skills.

MyEducationLab

Go to the Assignments and Activities section of Topic 7: Curriculum/Content Areas in the MyEducationLab for your course and complete the activity entitled *Get Up and MOVE!* What are some playful, developmentally appropriate learning experiences and teaching strategies that promote physical activity, fitness, and enjoyment for young children?

Then, based on their observation and assessment, teachers set goals for individual children, as the following example illustrates:

> The 4-year-olds in Betty Bartock and Jake Springer's child care class eagerly anticipate the arrival of the circus in their small town. Betty and Jake decide to make the circus the theme for planning curriculum to address their goals for children's physical development and health. The group has read books about the circus and learned circus songs and games. When they discuss the topic with the children in a group meeting, many ideas are generated. "I'll be the tightrope walker," says Barton, who is proud of his skill on the high balance beam. "We can have a parade. We can pretend we're different animals and walk like them," suggests Deretha. "Let's dress-up like clowns." "I'm going to be the animal tamer. I'll use the stuffed animals," states Maggie.
>
> The circus project becomes one of the highlights of the year. Betty and Jake use it to motivate several of the reluctant children to try out new physical skills like balancing on one foot. They observe that Durrell's eye–hand coordination is exceptional for his age. Although Durrell is often disruptive in class, the circus tasks focus his attention, and he becomes the "juggler"—perfecting his ability to toss a small ball hand to hand.
>
> After a few weeks of circus-inspired physical activity, Betty and Jake decide to share the fun with families. The children write invitations to their circus, plan costumes, and paint advertising signs. For the big day, they need refreshments. This generates a lengthy discussion of what kinds of "circus" foods are healthy. The children settle on unbuttered popcorn and Rice Krispies treats, which they prepare. Many family members attend the circus, watching the parade and enjoying the children's performances of songs and skills. Then they visit the various "acts" arranged in sections of the room or stop to pay a penny for a treat at the food booth.

The circus theme was a big hit with children, families, and teachers. But it also provided a framework for Betty and Jake to help children make progress in the areas of physical development, motor skill acquisition, and health. They were able to use children's interests to help them achieve goals, such as building Durrell's fine-motor skill or getting a less-skilled child to try out the balance beam.

Teaching Motor Skills

The context of a meaningful curriculum topic, such as the circus theme, provides numerous opportunities for teaching children physical skills. Just growing up is not enough to ensure that all children develop the fundamental motor skills they need. They require more than an appropriate environment and supportive adults; children also need instruction (Manross, 1994, 2000; Pica, 2006). Effective teaching strategies to build physical skills include movement exploration, explicit teaching, and teacher-supported practice (Patterson & Van der Mars, 2008; Pica, 2006).

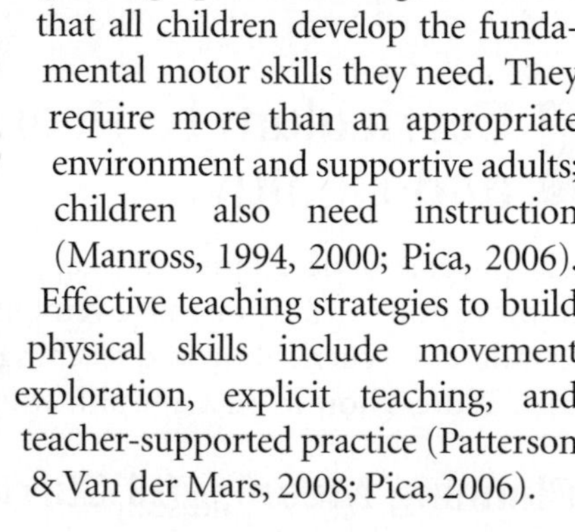

Playing outside is one of the greatest joys of childhood. What other ways could teachers promote movement, particularly in primary grades?

Movement Exploration

Movement exploration gives children a role in learning the skills being taught and allows for wider experimentation as the learning unfolds (Pica, 2006). Tina Sabuco, the founder of Arts Alive! in Houston, Texas, asks preschool and kindergarten children during her movement classes to find a way to connect with each other without touching. As children explore this idea, they discover ways to encircle each other's legs or arms, straddle another person's reclined body, crawl through spread legs, or mirror another child's hand or foot movements—all appropriate though different solutions to the challenge. As children discover their own motor solutions, they develop self-confidence and independence, and their fear of failure lessens. In the current educational milieu of high-stakes testing, where there is often only one right answer to any question, movement exploration is invaluable for solidifying children's view of themselves as able to make things happen and to figure out solutions.

Explicit Teaching and Opportunity to Practice

Some children benefit from a more direct approach. Teachers using a direct approach describe, model, and demonstrate the necessary components of the physical skill being taught. A benefit of the direct approach is that it is immediately clear if children can or cannot perform the skills.

An additional benefit of explicit teaching is that it is efficient. It takes less time to show children how to do movements than to let them figure them out on their own. It also can help children learn to do the skills correctly, which can prevent injuries. On the other hand, the direct approach leaves little room for creativity and individuality. During the early childhood years, the direct approach should be used infrequently and in an individualized way rather than as a primary teaching strategy (Pica, 2006).

Even when teachers use appropriate teaching strategies, children still need plenty of practice to master physical skills. Without opportunities to practice and perfect what they are learning to do, they may never achieve proficient levels of skill. While they are practicing and particularly when they are learning to control new skills, children also need verbal prompts and reminders, feedback on performance, and encouragement to keep trying (Patterson & Van der Mars, 2008). Read the *What Works* feature for examples of effective ways to teach physical skills.

Teachers' attitudes are extremely important. When adults are not enthusiastic about motor play and do not engage with children, children are unlikely to be enthusiastic and persist. The first step to effective teaching is for teachers themselves to be physically active and interested in meaningful physical activity.

Planning Curriculum to Support Health and Wellness

Teaching children healthy and safe practices is the best way to support health and wellness. Nutrition education is also an essential part of the curriculum.

Preventing Injury

An important curriculum goal is educating children about accident prevention, particularly on the playground. Accidents are actually preventable injuries. Teachers need to teach children safe ways to play and interact in both the indoor and outdoor environments to prevent injuries, particularly falls. Safety should be considered from the perspectives of both adults and children.

Learning how to use wheeled toys safely is an important curriculum goal. Universal use of helmets by children ages 4 to 15 when riding tricycles or bicycles could prevent deaths, head injuries, and scalp and face injuries annually (T. R. Miller et al., 1994). Children need to understand how to operate wheeled toys without injuring themselves or others—in other words, they need to learn the rules of the road.

Preventing Illness and Promoting Health

The curriculum goal of disease prevention is a natural extension of children's interest in their own bodies (Hendricks & Smith, 1995). Children's shared experiences of visiting the doctor and dentist and getting regular immunizations are conceptual organizers for this topic. They can also learn about germs and how germs are spread from one person to

What Works

Teaching Physical Skills

Children don't automatically develop the skills of throwing, catching, kicking, skipping, climbing, balancing, and the like; they require instruction and practice. To acquire foundational skills, children need the guidance of involved adults within an environment that has developmentally appropriate equipment. They learn both through free play and exploration and through adult-guided instruction. Young children are most likely to learn physical skills and develop enjoyment and confidence in physical activity when teachers use these strategies:

- *Design tasks for gradual and sequential learning.* Keep in mind that tasks should be more general than specific. You could say, "Show me that you can throw the ball at the wall," rather than "See if you can hit the bull's-eye."
- *Break down motor skills into small, "do-able" actions.* The goal is for everyone to participate, even if this means partial participation for some. For instance, if a child cannot grip a racket to strike a balloon, encourage her to strike the balloon with her hand.
- *Provide cues that help children refine specific skills.* Observe their movements and make helpful, concrete suggestions. The best cues provide children with little steps that help them learn a skill more quickly and correctly and, at the same time, keep them from forming bad habits. When children are learning to catch, for example, some will benefit from the tip "Keep your eye on the ball."
- *Embed skills in playful experiences.* Suggest that children who are learning to hop can pretend to be rabbits. When they're practicing long jumps, place mats in a row to be the river they are trying to jump across. Give them fun challenges, such as "Let's see how many ways we can think of to get across the room besides walking."
- *Individualize.* Simplify or add complexity to fit the child's skill level. For example, if a child is having trouble throwing a ball into the air and catching it, try giving him a larger rubber ball and asking him to bounce and catch it.
- *Show skills in action.* Many children have difficulty learning physical actions from verbal instruction alone; they may do better when they can watch someone modeling the skill.
- *Offer a variety of tasks, materials, and learning centers.* Help children practice specific skills and learn to use different types and sizes of equipment by offering them variety. For example, provide balls of all sizes, shapes, and weights in the form of beanbags, yarn balls, sock balls, and rubber and plastic balls. Then set up centers to allow children to practice throwing, bouncing, and rolling the balls in different ways.

Source: Excerpted and adapted from "Physical Education in Kindergarten," by S. W. Sanders, pp. 135–137, in *K Today: Teaching and Learning in the Kindergarten Year,* edited by D. F. Gullo, 2006, Washington, DC: NAEYC. Used with permission

another. Many children's books treat the topic of visiting the physician and other health and wellness topics. Examples include *Corduroy Goes to the Doctor* (Freeman, 2001), *Wash Your Hands!* (Ross, 2000), and *Germs Are Not for Sharing* (Verdick, 2006).

Nutrition Education

Good nutrition in early childhood is related to children's readiness for school and academic success (Sacther, 2005). Children who eat a nutritionally poor diet during the brain's formative years score lower on tests of vocabulary, reading comprehension, mathematics, and general knowledge (Brown & Pollit, 1996). Even skipping breakfast decreases children's ability to perform well on problem-solving tests (Pollitt, Leibel, & Greenfield, 1991).

The goals of nutrition education are teaching children about healthy eating, introducing children to different types of foods, and promoting exploration of and interest in a well-balanced diet (Bernath & Masi, 2006; USDA, 2009). Nutrition education has the potential to impact children's health behaviors for a lifetime, particularly when the family is included in the education process. Educating children begins by offering them a variety of foods as part of a balanced diet and continues by interesting children in where food comes from, how it is prepared, and the wide variety of food that is available for inclusion in a balanced diet to help children grow up healthy.

MyEducationLab

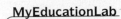

To observe how a routine like feeding babies can promote healthy development in all areas, go the Video Examples section of Topic 12: Professionalism/Ethics in the MyEducationLab for your course and watch the video entitled *Infant Feeding*. How does this teacher's responsive relationship with the baby demonstrate beginning nutrition education?

For babies and toddlers, teachers can start by offering food on demand and at regular intervals. Then, as toddlers begin to eat table food, teachers give them repeated opportunities to try new foods. Dimensions such as color, texture, and temperature may be as important as taste during initial offerings.

Preschool and kindergarten children often have a reputation as picky eaters. This suggests a go-slow approach to introducing new food choices and refraining from too much external pressure to try new things. Children need repeated opportunities to try new foods; they may need to see a new food many times before they are willing to taste it. One strategy is to set up a self-serve snack center, similar to the other learning centers in the classroom (Bernath & Masi, 2006). Food is presented in small store-bought packages or preproportioned in cups with napkins, plates, and utensils for children to serve themselves.

Cooking with Children

Cooking is an excellent way to introduce and encourage children to try new foods. Classroom cooking offers many learning opportunities including seeing foods change state as they cook (science), measuring and mixing ingredients (mathematics), introducing new vocabulary and reading recipes (language and literacy), and predicting outcomes (science) and preferences. Many resources such as children's books and simple recipes are available to help early childhood teachers cook with children in the classroom (Colker, 2005; Johnson, 2001).

Routines That Promote Health and Wellness

Young children need adult support to remember and practice what they have learned about health and wellness. Without including healthy practices in the daily, weekly, and monthly routines, children aren't likely to integrate them into their lives and apply them at home and in other spheres.

Children's health is also affected by their growing independence in carrying out personal routines, their awareness of health and safety concerns, and their ability to follow rules and take steps to keep themselves safe and healthy. Teachers can use different strategies with different children to teach health and wellness practices, such as hand washing or sanitizing table tops before lunchtime, offering specific feedback (such as washing the front, back, and in between the fingers), creating or adding a challenge such as washing for as long as the child sings "Happy Birthday," or modeling appropriate hand washing for a child who skips steps.

We began this chapter with alarming statistics about the health and fitness of our nation's children and the disturbing childhood obesity crisis. Having explored the continuum of motor development and effective curriculum and teaching strategies for promoting health and fitness, we return to Ms. Perez and Ms. Aliote's classroom to see how they implement these practices.

Children love to cook and are often more likely to eat new foods if they have helped prepare them. Cooking with children is an excellent way to bring nutrition education into the curriculum.

Revisiting Ms. Perez and Ms. Aliote's Classroom

At the beginning of this chapter, we visited the classroom of Ms. Perez and Ms. Aliote. These teachers plan indoor and outdoor environments that foster children's physical development and learning. They encourage gross-motor and fine-motor skills with a wide variety of materials and activities in the classroom and on the playground.

Outdoors, children engage in unstructured play such as tricycle riding, climbing, and running, as well as structured physical activities—learning how to kick a ball at a higher level of proficiency and playing kickball with a friend. These teachers use a variety of effective teaching strategies and adapt for individual children's needs. Ms. Perez intentionally taught Allison the skills she needed for kicking the ball. At the same time, she helped Drew build his social–emotional and language skills as she encouraged him to ask Allison if he could play, and they began to play cooperatively.

The teachers incorporate health education in their day by offering healthy food choices and prompting children to wash their hands before eating. Children's physical fitness and health are priorities in this classroom. Their teachers integrate these topics in fun and meaningful ways throughout the day. The end result is that these children are more likely to remain active and healthy throughout their lives.

MyEducationLab

To assess your understanding of how to teach children to be healthy and fit, go to the Book Specific Resources section in the MyEducationLab for your course, select *Effective Practices in Early Childhood Education*, Chapter 15 of the Study Plan, and then complete the multiple choice questions and activities.

Chapter Summary

- Given the benefits of physical activity for young children as well as the risks of poor levels of fitness, teachers need to ensure that promoting physical development and health are core curriculum goals and not simply add-ons. Children's physical fitness and health have become urgent concerns as the rate of childhood obesity in America has increased significantly.
- Physical development—gross-motor, fine-motor, and perceptual-motor development—follows a relatively predictable sequence that is influenced by both maturation and experience.
- Teachers foster children's physical development by providing age-appropriate materials and learning environments, supporting play and movement exploration, and explicitly teaching motor skills.
- Children need opportunities for unstructured and structured play throughout the day to promote physical activity and develop skills. Outdoor play is a particularly valuable context for promoting physical activity. Some children today do not get enough exposure to nature and its many benefits.
- Physical fitness and health and wellness habits are formed early in life. Children benefit from teachers who intentionally plan engaging curriculum to promote physical development and fitness.
- Health education curriculum goals include teaching children health and safety procedures such as emergency preparedness, practices for preventing illness and injury, and good nutrition.

key terms

auditory awareness
body composition
cardiorespiratory (aerobic) system
directional awareness
fine motor development
fine motor manipulative movements
flexibility
gross motor development
gross motor manipulative movements
health-related fitness
locomotor movements
motor planning
muscular strength and endurance
nature deficit disorder
perceptual motor development
physical fitness
pincer grasp
risk vs. challenge continuum
spatial awareness
stability movements
structured physical activity
temporal awareness
universal design
unstructured free play

readings & websites

Aronson, S., & Shope, T. R. (2008). *Managing infectious diseases in child care and schools: A quick reference guide* (2nd ed.). Chicago: American Academy of Pediatrics.

Greenman, J. (2005). *Caring spaces, learning places.* Redmond, WA: Exchange Press.

National Association for the Education of Young Children. (2005). *Health: A guide to the early childhood program standard and related accreditation criteria.* Washington, DC: Author.

Rae, P. (2008). *Physical education for young children: Movement ABCs for little ones.* Champaign, IL: Human Kinetics.

Sorte, J., Daeschel, I., & Amador, C. (2011). *Nutrition, health, and safety for young children: Promoting wellness.* Upper Saddle River, NJ: Pearson.

American Alliance for Health, Physical Education, Recreation and Dance
www.aahperd.org

International Association for the Child's Right to Play
www.ipausa.org

National Association for Sport and Physical Education
www.aahperd.org/NASPE

U.S. Department of Agriculture Nutrition Programs for Preschoolers and Elementary Children
www.mypyramid.gov

observe, reflect, decide

1. Observe in a full-day child care center or family child care home. How much time do children spend in physical activity during the entire day? Do they have 60 minutes or more of unstructured play? Do teachers provide structured physical activity to promote physical skills? Did you observe missed opportunities for encouraging physical health and skill development? What else might teachers do to enhance children's physical development and learning?
2. Observe a community-based early childhood program, public pre-K program, kindergarten classroom, or primary grade classroom. What examples did you see of curriculum and teaching focused on physical development? Did you see examples of integrating physical development and learning into other content areas such as literacy, mathematics, music and the arts, science, or social studies?
3. Consider the concept of the risk vs. challenge, continuum in light of your own experiences as a child and the experiences of children you know today. Did you have freedom to take risks or were concerns about your safety paramount? Do you think the children you know experience enough challenge, or are they overly protected? What do you think is the right balance of risk vs. challenge in children's lives?
4. Review NAEYC program accreditation standards on health (www.naeyc.org/accreditation). Reflect on your role as a teacher in meeting these standards and how important they are to keeping children safe and healthy in early childhood centers and schools.
5. Consider the obesity crisis in children today and the resulting threats to children's health and well-being. In your opinion, what factors account for this trend? Given the sensitive nature of the topic and the many contributing factors, what should be the role of teachers in addressing and counteracting childhood obesity?

16 Putting It All Together in Practice: Making a Difference for Children

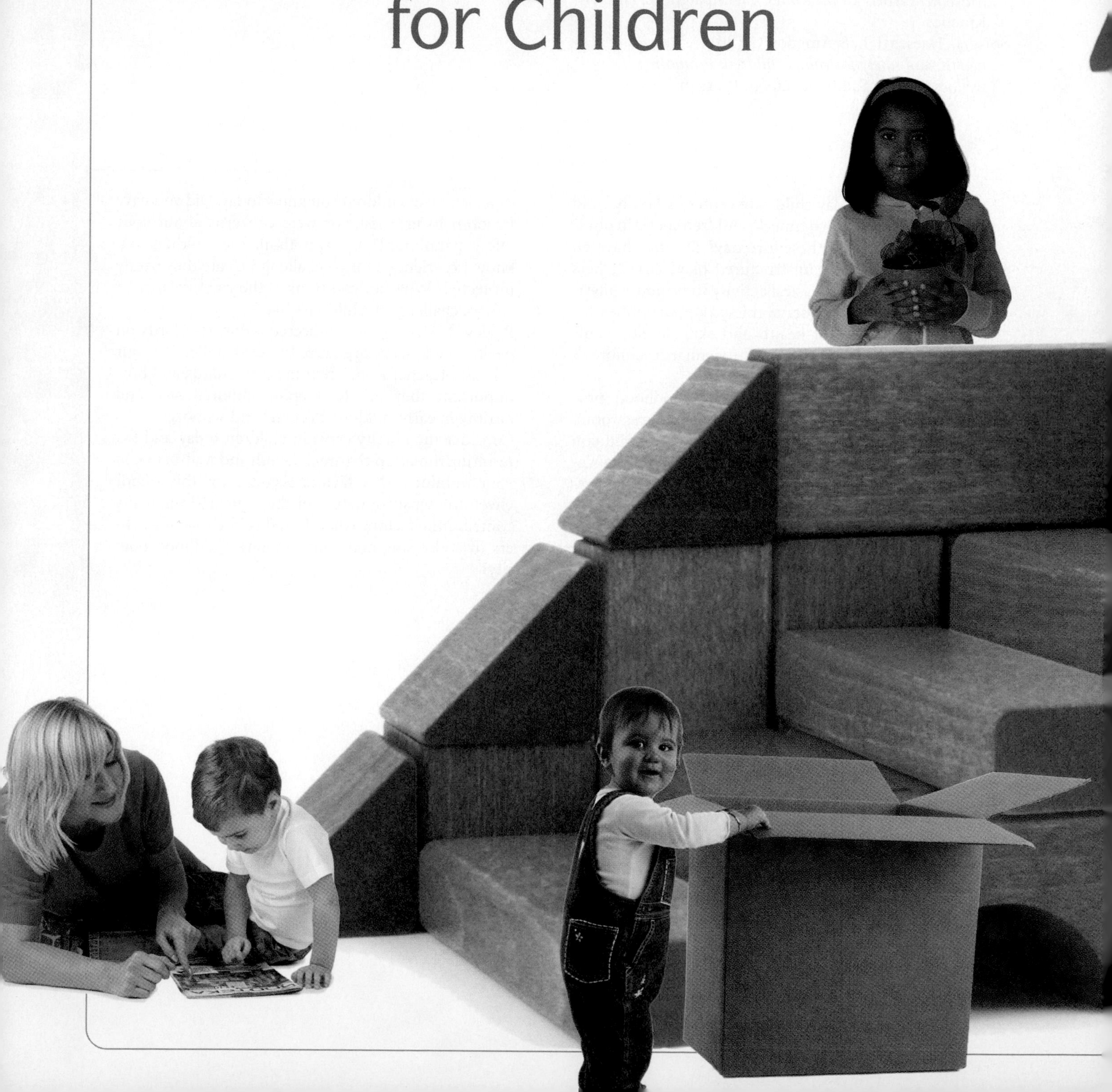

Thinking Ahead

1. What is it like to be a teacher of infants and toddlers? A preschool or kindergarten teacher? A teacher in primary grades? What are some factors to consider in deciding which age group you want to teach?
2. What is the NAEYC Code of Ethical Conduct and how should it be used?
3. What is informed advocacy? What are the important advocacy roles of early childhood professionals?
4. What does it mean to become a professional early childhood educator? What are the obligations and commitments to children that early childhood professionals must understand and embrace? ▲

Every morning in communities across the country, young children arrive at child care centers and family child care homes, preschools, Head Start programs, and K–3 primary schools. Their teachers are there to greet them and to help them take another step on the lifelong journey of development and learning. At the same time, the teachers themselves are on a journey—to be and become the most caring, informed, and effective early childhood professionals possible.

In this chapter, we visit some of those teachers to see what life is like for them in their chosen careers. Then we discuss some of the broader aspects of an early childhood professional's journey.

Throughout this book we describe ways that effective teachers help build strong foundations of development and learning for young children. This work has three interconnected dimensions. Effective teachers must:

- Know children—*who* they teach.
- Understand *how* to teach—the complex roles of the teacher, which include working with families, planning and implementing curriculum, assessing children, and adapting teaching strategies.
- Know *what* to teach—the goals for children's learning and development.

Experienced teachers know that these dimensions of their work cannot be separated. They teach the whole child. And they do not work in isolation; they are connected to colleagues, families, and communities. One of the biggest challenges for teachers is putting it all together.

MyEducationLab

Go to the Professional Perspectives section in Topic 12: Professionalism/ Ethics in the MyEducationLab for your course and select the video entitled *Advice for Those Entering Early Childhood Education: Part 1* and watch and listen to Sue Bredekamp discuss this topic.

Experiencing Life as an Early Childhood Educator

Among the major questions early childhood educators face is which age group they would most like to work with and why. Many teachers change jobs, settings, and/or age levels over the course of a career; however, most early childhood teachers gravitate toward one age group and stay there.

The following sections describe things to consider as you weigh your career options. After reading about a "day in the life" of teachers in diverse settings, you will see some ways in which teachers engage in effective practices. In reality, there is no such thing as a typical day in any program for children. There should be a predictable schedule and routine, a prepared age-appropriate environment, and a planned curriculum. But children themselves are unpredictable. They change from day to day, in wonderful and challenging ways, and they come up with great ideas that lead in new directions. In addition, conditions impinge that are beyond a teacher's control, for example, an emergency or a serendipitous event. Teachers need to be prepared to handle any and all situations.

In many ways, it is the unpredictable nature of teaching young children that makes it such fascinating work. A career in early childhood education is filled with never-ending rewards and challenges. It is a field like no other, as we see from brief visits to classrooms in the following sections.

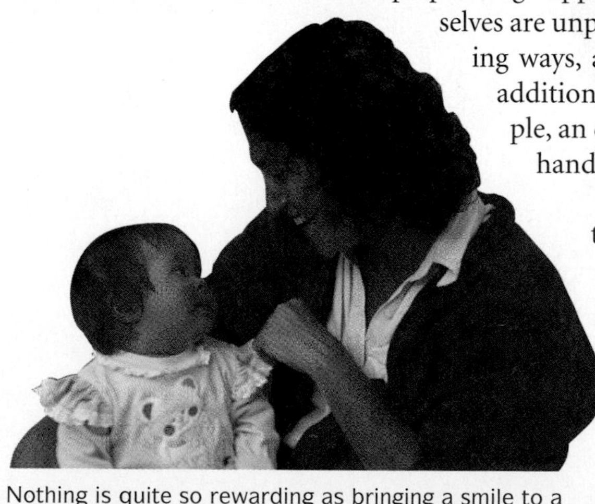

Nothing is quite so rewarding as bringing a smile to a baby's face. These warm, positive relationships between infants and their teachers build a foundation for all later learning.

Caring for and Educating Infants and Young Toddlers

Some people do not consider those who work with babies and toddlers to be teachers. Because much physical care is required for this age group, the term *caregiver* is often used for this role. Neverthe-

less, babies are always learning in the context of loving care. We choose to call all professional caregivers *teachers*.

MyEducationLab

Go to the Assignment and Activities section of Topic 5: Program Models in the MyEducationLab for your course and complete the activity entitled *Infant and Toddler Settings*. Would you enjoy teaching very young children whose rapid brain development necessitates warm, caring relationships, play, and interesting things to do and learn?

A Day in the Life of an Infant/Toddler Teacher

Victoria Thomas and Luisa Franco co-teach a group of eight babies and young toddlers. Their children stay with them for about 2½ years to provide continuity of care and secure relationships for the children and their families. Each morning as the children arrive, Victoria and Luisa greet them warmly and casually chat with the family member who drops them off. They learn vital information about the baby's sleeping and eating patterns, as well as who is feeling fussy or especially happy. Luisa positions the three nonmobile babies where they can watch the action and hear her talking as she picks up little Ella, who is clearly in need of a diaper change. Throughout the day, the teachers will engage in feeding, diapering, and hand-washing routines as the children eat and rest on their own schedules.

After meeting Ella's immediate needs, Luisa puts Sam down for his midmorning nap and then positions Foster and Lydia on the rug for some tummy time. She gets down and plays with them at their eye level with a ball that makes music as it rolls. The babies love swatting the ball to produce the sounds.

Meanwhile, across the room, Victoria calmly plays on the rug with the mobile toddlers, who are just beginning to talk. They are enchanted by a set of large, plastic, colored blocks that they can pick up and place together, forming a big pattern on the floor. Victoria describes what they are doing as it happens: "Alan has a red peg. He put it next to the green one." Alan starts to fuss when Wanda pushes against him. "Wanda, you are in Alan's space. Can you move just a little?" asks Victoria in a soft voice. Alan calms and Wanda smacks a kiss on his cheek. Victoria smiles, "You're a good friend, Wanda."

As the play time comes to an end, Victoria says, "Let's see who is big and strong and can help me pick up the pegs." As Victoria places the full bin onto the shelf, Gary holds on, too. Victoria says, "It's heavy. We have to lift it up high." Gary responds, "Up," and Victoria says, "Yes, let's put it *up* on the shelf. Now, let's go outside. It's warm and we can play on the ride-on toys or go for a walk in the stroller."

In this brief scene, we see effective practices in action. Victoria and Luisa create a calm and warm climate for these young children, focusing on building a relationship with each child. They model kindness and social skills, which even these very young children are starting to emulate. They weave into play ways to support all areas of development and learning. The teachers help the children develop physical skills (rolling the ball, placing the pegs) and knowledge about the world while building language skills. They model rich vocabulary such as spatial relation words like *next to* and *up* and explain the phrase "You're in his space." And they are keen to create new experiences to stimulate children's senses and interests such as being outside in nature, the beginning of science learning.

Throughout the day, Victoria and Luisa keep careful records about each baby—what they eat and drink, bowel movements, their moods, and any special accomplishments—to share with parents at the end of the day. Observing and recording is an effective way of assessing children and communicating what families want and need to know. These exchanges help build close relationships with the families, which then feel more secure about leaving their precious infants in the care of others.

Considerations for Working with Infants and Toddlers

Some parents of babies and toddlers would never consider working while others can think of nothing more rewarding. Teachers of infants and toddlers usually work in child care centers, Early Head Start programs, or family child care homes. Table 16.1 lists some considerations in deciding whether to work with these very young children.

Table 16.1 Considerations for Infant/Toddler Teachers

If you are thinking of teaching infants and toddlers, you might consider that:

On the One Hand	On the Other Hand
A great deal of physical care is required—diapering, feeding, dressing, frequent hand washing, and constant supervision.	Caregiving routines provide time to connect and talk one-on-one with babies and to build loving relationships.
Babies' actions are repetitive and can be frustrating—they drop the cup off the high chair again and again to see what happens.	Babies' actions are obvious evidence of their development and opportunities to share in their joy of discovery.
Babies and toddlers grow and develop so rapidly that just when you think you know what to expect, they change.	From the earliest moments of life, young children demonstrate that they are unique, so life with them is always challenging and never boring.
Caring for babies requires close, constant communication with families. Relationships can be difficult due to competition, differences of opinion, or diverse cultural values.	Relationships with families can be close and rewarding, marked by shared power and responsibility as teachers and parents learn from each other and work toward common goals.
Babies and toddlers are so vulnerable and dependent on adults to protect their health, safety, and emotional security that the responsibility can feel overwhelming.	Protecting very young children from harm as they discover and rediscover the world every day is immensely rewarding.
Babies and toddlers can't tell you what they want and need. They cry and fuss and can make adults feel helpless or inadequate.	Babies and toddlers communicate their needs and wants through cries, expressions, and gestures. Nothing compares with baby's or toddler's smile and belly laugh.

Teaching the Whole Child in the Preschool

Three- to five-year-olds are some of the most interesting people in the world. They are miniature navigators, explorers, writers, artists, acrobats, linguists, and comedians (although much of their humor can be silly or of the bathroom variety). At this age, their potential seems boundless.

Teachers who are drawn to preschoolers have many choices of work site or employer. They may choose Head Start, a child care center, family child care, or a public or private preschool. The length of time the children spend in the program will make some difference in what a teacher's day is like. Although preschoolers are more capable of taking care of their own needs, they continue to need vigilant supervision and a lot of physical care and attention. They also need experiences that engage their minds and actively involve them in the world around them (Katz & Chard, 2000). Most of all, they need intentional teachers to help them achieve their full potential (Epstein, 2007b).

A Day in the Life of a Preschool Teacher

As a white van pulls up at Small Steps Learning Center, Masami and his assistant teacher, Ana, greet the children—some in English and some in Spanish. The children head off to wash their hands and settle in for breakfast. Ana helps them serve oatmeal and orange slices and pour their own milk, while Masami sits and begins a conversation about the bus ride.

The sixteen 3- and 4-year-olds live in an economically disadvantaged community. Some have been exposed to violence and a few have serious emotional problems. Masami and Ana's program places a strong emphasis on building social skills and emotional self-regulation. They use a comprehensive curriculum that promotes language and thinking through interesting projects that build science, math, and literacy skills. It also includes lots of art and music. To achieve the curriculum goals and build secure, continuous relationships, Masami and Ana each work with a group of eight children at times during the school day, which lasts from 8:30 to 3:30. For instance, half the group will go outside with Ana while the rest stay in with Masami, and then they switch.

After breakfast, Masami leads the children in singing songs and then reads a book about a new baby. The group is involved in a long-term life science project about how people grow and change. Then they discuss the choices for center time. Learning centers include dramatic play (set up as a hospital with props and dress-up materials), creative art, math/manipulatives, writing center, library area, and blocks. Masami talks with the children about where they plan to play and what they'd like to do, which helps them regulate their behavior and thinking. The children are becoming better listeners. As they describe their plans, Ana helps them leave the group and transition to the next activity. Sharde calls out, "I got room at my table for Keyona's wheelchair."

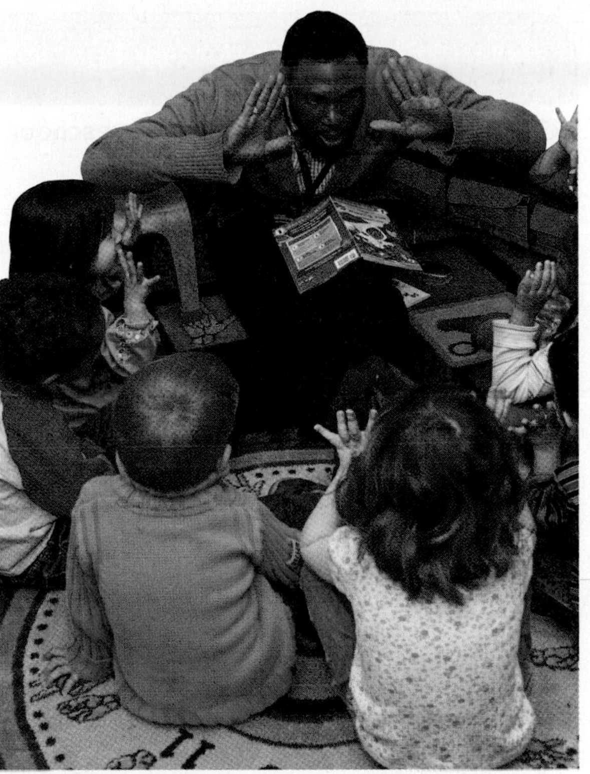

Intentional preschool teachers work with small groups of children at times during the day to assess their current levels of ability and scaffold their learning.

During center time, Masami works with a small group in the art center. They examine their own baby pictures, look in the mirror, and use different media to represent how they look. The discussion centers on how big they can make their drawings. Some children write recognizable letters on their pictures, while others dictate their thoughts for Masami to write. In the dramatic play area, Assata dresses as the doctor while Ben and Rhonda bring their new baby for a check-up. Ayah goes to the writing center, makes marks on a piece of paper, and hands it to Assata, "Here's a letter."

Mia, who has just turned three, heads toward the restroom. Ana congratulates her on listening to her body and getting to the toilet in time. Mia beams in response. Ana helps her get her pants buttoned (she pulls them up all by herself) and then they wash their hands. In the library area, Arturo studies an information book about baby animals. Ana talks with him about how some look like their mothers, and some do not. Their conversation continues as Arturo, who was adopted from Costa Rica, explains that he doesn't look like his mom either.

After cleanup, the children join Masami on the carpet and tell him about what they did during activity time. Mia proudly says she went to the toilet (although that is not exactly what she said!). Arturo says he read a book; others talk about how they observed each other's drawings of themselves, "Marco has brown eyes and he made them blue."

On the playground, Arturo and Kiesha ride on the wheeled toys. Mia starts climbing to the loft of the playhouse. Jorge calls to her to join him in the sandbox. Masami asks Mia if she heard Jorge's invitation. She nods. He coaches her to tell Jorge she wants to climb, so he will know what her answer is.

After lunch, the children settle in for naps. Ana and Masami play soft music, pat a few backs and soon the children sleep. After naptime, the children find several activity areas, including a self-service snack area. Children write their names or make a mark by their photo when they wash their hands and serve themselves a snack.

At the end of the day, Masami and Ana meet to review the day, and record their observations of the children's progress. Masami plans to inform Mia's mother about her toileting success, and Arturo's mother about his reflections on adoption. They also plan ways to build vocabulary through children's interests in babies and their growing bodies.

Considerations for Working with Preschoolers

Ana and Masami's day is far busier than this general portrait can communicate. As we saw in the brief interactions with Mia, they must know each child and how to support her or his progress. They plan ahead, but are constantly thinking on their feet as they interact with individuals and groups. Table 16.2 lists some things to consider in contemplating becoming a preschool teacher.

Table 16.2 Considerations for Preschool Teachers

If you are thinking of teaching preschool, you might consider that:

On the One Hand	On the Other Hand
Preschoolers become increasingly capable of taking care of their own physical needs, but still need help with skills like toileting, feeding, and dressing (zipping, tying). Messiness and spills are normal.	Routine caregiving and meals provide times to interact one-on-one or in small groups and enjoy children as individuals. They also provide learning opportunities.
Many preschoolers have difficulty regulating their emotions and behavior and can be aggressive. Teachers can feel like they spend all their time guiding behavior.	Effective teachers see children make great strides in social–emotional learning and development. Behavior is less of a problem when children have interesting things to do and learn.
Preschool children are active and curious and can be loud and boisterous. Teaching them requires patience and can be exhausting.	Preschoolers are competent, active learners both physically and mentally. They try to make sense of the world and take on new challenges. Preschool teachers are constantly learning with and about them, and taking on new challenges, too.
Preschool children are all different in so many ways, making it hard to teach a large group. Working with diverse cultural groups and languages can be daunting. Successful inclusion of children with special needs can be difficult.	Individual differences in children are what make preschoolers so interesting and enjoyable. Cultural backgrounds and language are fascinating aspects of everyone's identity. Inclusion, with appropriate support, benefits all children.
Preschool programs must meet standards for operation that can seem onerous. Some preschools measure child outcomes and stress teachers' accountability for children's learning.	Standards are designed to protect children and support their healthy development. Meeting them also protects teachers. Professional educators care about children achieving developmentally appropriate goals and are willing to be accountable for children's progress and learning.
Preschools are usually staffed with a teacher and an assistant, requiring skills for working with and perhaps supervising another adult, as well as working with children.	Having two teachers provides better teacher–child ratios, creating more opportunity for individual attention and small-group interaction. Different teachers have different interests and abilities to bring to the class. Collaborating, they can be more creative and effective than alone.
Working with preschoolers requires frequent, almost daily communication with families. Some families are demanding, while others are uninvolved.	Partnering with families makes teachers more effective. Children sense when their parents are respected and feel more comfortable and connected to teachers.

Teaching the Whole Child in the Kindergarten

Kindergarten holds a special place in children's lives. Even if a child has been in child care for the previous 5 years, entering kindergarten marks the major transition to formal school. Given the momentous event, kindergarten teachers are very important to children. They help children negotiate a significant life change and build the foundation for their future educational career.

A Day in the Life of a Kindergarten Teacher

The morning bell rings as Hope Millner greets her 21 kindergartners at the classroom door. Toting backpacks and displaying mostly grins, these 5- and 6-year-olds feel very grown-up as they navigate the corridors and expectations of "real" school. After a brief settling-in period, the group gathers on the rug for a morning meeting.

"Let's review what happened yesterday, and think ahead to today's plans," Hope suggests. The children wave their hands in the air for a turn to talk about the visit to the aquarium. While the sharks made the biggest impression, some children were enthralled by the stingrays. "I hear from your descriptions that you were observing very carefully," Hope says. "I know that most of you used your clipboards and made some drawings. During choice time this morning, I'd like you to refer to those and write in your journals about what you saw and learned. We also have digital photos that we'll put on the computer and project on the wall to help you remember details. Now, I'm going to read parts of an information book about sea life that you can look at later in the library area."

Most public school kindergartens today set high expectations for children's reading progress. How can kindergarten teachers use developmentally appropriate practices to help children build early literacy skills?

During the morning activity period, two children feed the fish in the classroom aquarium, and write a brief note: "Fsh et." Hope assists the children in their journal writing, helping them with letters and words, but emphasizes communicating their ideas rather than correct spelling. She also works with a small group who are still struggling with recognizing letters. An inviting library area is stocked with a variety of diverse, high-quality books at varying reading levels, including multiple copies of kindergarten-level texts. Storybooks and information books reflect the cultural and linguistic diversity of the group. Some children listen to audio books and follow along in the printed book.

Following the midmorning snack, children independently browse or read self-selected familiar books, especially ones that Hope has previously read aloud, such as the fish book. The field trip, books, and ongoing science study of sea life broaden the children's background knowledge and vocabulary. To build reading comprehension, Hope guides discussions about what is being read or listened to. She asks the children to predict events, retell or act out stories, and notice when a text does not make sense.

The kindergartners also have physical education classes three times a week. Working with Hope, the PE teacher plans related movement activities—How would you move like you're swimming? What if you were a fish and there was no water? In the classroom, Hope has a creative art center where some children make representations of their favorite fish and underwater environments while others create simply from their imaginations. After lunch and outdoor play, the children have another 60-minute choice period before dismissal. This is a favorite time for many because they especially like dramatic play, block building, and board games. During this time, Hope works with small groups on the mathematics curriculum goals. Today, a group spontaneously decides to replicate the aquarium with unit blocks. This leads to lengthy debates about how to re-create the water because a flat piece of blue paper wouldn't really hold up the fish. At the end of the day, the group meets to reflect on their day and look forward to tomorrow.

Considerations for Teaching Kindergarten

Hope Millner has taught kindergarten in a suburban school district for 15 years. In that time, she has seen changes in the curriculum with much more emphasis on literacy, and secondarily mathematics, and less administrative support for play. She has also observed that a higher proportion of her students now attend preschool and enter school with more basic knowledge about how the written language system works. At the same time, Hope knows that, developmentally, 5- and 6-year-olds haven't fundamentally changed and that they benefit from both "learningful play and playful learning" (Graue, 2006). Her task is to make the curriculum meaningful and engaging, and to use play and other effective teaching strategies to intentionally promote each child's continuing progress. Teaching kindergarten today involves balancing some potentially conflicting needs and goals, as demonstrated in Table 16.3.

Table 16.3 Considerations for Kindergarten Teachers

If you are thinking of teaching kindergarten, you might consider that:

On the One Hand	On the Other Hand
Kindergarten is part of the formal school system, often more structured and with more challenging curriculum expectations than in the past.	Teachers are still the most important influence on the quality and appropriateness of children's experiences in school. The school system tends to offer higher salaries, better benefits, and more job security than child care or preschool programs.
Kindergartners vary widely in their prior learning opportunities both at home or in preschool. Teachers face the challenge of teaching a general curriculum to diverse learners.	Effective teachers don't expect all the children to achieve the same thing, at the same time, in the same way. By individualizing teaching and working with small groups, teachers experience the rewards of seeing children who are initially behind their peers make great strides.
Kindergartners don't think and learn exactly like adults and older children—there are limits to their understanding of complex concepts.	Kindergartners are more competent learners and thinkers than many people assume. They strive to make sense of the world, solve problems, and are fascinated by learning about topics that interest them.
Kindergarten classes are usually larger than those in preschool and teachers do not always have the benefit of an assistant, making it more difficult for teachers to individualize their teaching.	Most schools have multiple kindergarten classrooms, and teachers can collaborate with colleagues within grade level and across grades. Specialists in music, art, physical education, and special education may also be available to offer support.
Kindergartners can function independently in self-help skills and need less adult support than preschoolers.	Kindergartners are still young children who rely on teachers for emotional as well as physical support and usually want to please their teachers.
The kindergarten curriculum tends to focus on literacy and math, raising concerns that there is insufficient attention to social–emotional development.	Good kindergarten teachers know that both children's cognition and social development are essential. Their teaching integrates academic skills and concepts with positive social–emotional development.
Kindergarten may be included in school district accountability requirements. Children are sometimes tested inappropriately.	Effective teachers use ongoing assessment of children's learning to adapt curriculum and teaching. They don't place undue emphasis on formal tests, but do hold themselves accountable to children and families.

Teaching the Whole Child in the Primary Grades

A great deal of growth and change takes place from ages 6 through 8. Similarly, the curriculum and, therefore, teachers' experiences will vary if they are teaching in the first, second, or third grade. Here we visit a first-grade classroom, but the considerations for teaching in the primary grades generally apply across the age span.

A Day in the Life of a First-Grade Teacher

Lina Truesdale's 22 first graders have very different backgrounds and abilities. Early in the school year, Lina spent time getting to know the children and assessing their abilities. She found that 5 of them were reading at the second-grade level or above, and 4 did not know all the letters and sounds. The district curriculum is designed for children somewhere in the middle. But like every good first-grade teacher, Lina knows that she teaches children first and curriculum second.

The school district requires that there be a 90-minute language arts block each morning in first grade. Lina knows that the children are more likely to stay energetic and focused if she varies the activities during this time, and makes sure that the children are as active as possible, both mentally and physically. She begins the morning with whole-group instruction and discussion of new concepts, introducing and explaining new vocabulary words in everyday language. Then the class divides into smaller groups. Each day, Lina works with small groups on guided reading, during which she assesses their reading comprehension and ability to monitor themselves for understanding. She coaches them to ask questions such as "Does that make sense?" and "What does that mean?"

A major portion of the day in primary grades is devoted to reading and writing instruction. What are some ways that intentional teachers can integrate other areas of the curriculum such as science and social studies with reading and writing?

At the same time, others read independently or in pairs. Then, children continue with individual work, such as writing in journals, while Lina observes and offers individual help as needed. She ends the language arts period with a whole-group read-aloud, which the children love. At this point in their reading journey, the books the children can decode on their own have limited vocabulary and are not as interesting as the stories that Lina reads to them. Lina keeps careful records of children's reading progress. She takes great pride in their achievements, while also focusing on ways to adapt her teaching for those who are behind.

Some days the class has physical education before lunch, and other days they have music. After lunch, they play outside for 25 minutes and then return for focused math time. Again, Lina varies the teaching context. She may introduce a new math concept, such as a put-together/take-apart problem, to the whole group. Then she gives them a problem to discuss with their neighbors: "Six plus what number equals nine?" The children report their solutions and reasoning to the whole group. Seven-year-old Nancy explains, "We got three. We started with six and counted seven, eight, nine, and that's three numbers." Lina says, "That's one way to solve the problem. Is there another way?"

Lina observes children's grasp of the problem. Then, she follows the whole-group time with small-group work during which she focuses on those who haven't grasped the new concept or gives more difficult problems to those who need challenge. Science or social studies projects follow that integrate literacy, language, and mathematics goals.

At the end of her day, Lina meets with the other first-grade teachers to talk about effective ways of helping struggling readers and children who are having trouble grasping basic math concepts. She also seeks their advice on ways to assist Irina and Carlos, who are learning English. She plans to communicate with their families as well.

MyEducationLab

To hear a primary grade teacher talk about the rewards of her work, go to the Video Examples section of Topic 12: Professionalism/Ethics in the MyEducationLab for your course and watch the video entitled *Teaching First Grade.* What influenced her to become a teacher?

Considerations for Teaching in the Primary Grades

Do you remember your first-grade teacher? What experiences come to mind? Of all your teachers between kindergarten and third grade, which ones do you remember best, and for what reasons?

The primary grades—first through third—are prime time for learning. They set the stage for much that comes after. Primary grade teachers have a significant, measurable impact on children's educational careers and, hence, their lives. They have the opportunity to make lasting contributions to the world; their work is both demanding and stimulating, as described in Table 16.4.

In this section, we used broad strokes to paint images of life in classrooms for teachers of children from birth through age 8. However, teachers lead important professional lives beyond the classroom, as discussed in the next section.

Table 16.4 Considerations for Primary Grade Teachers

If you are thinking of teaching in the primary grades, you might consider that:

On the One Hand	On the Other Hand
Primary grade children have longer attention spans and are increasingly capable of independent work.	Primary grade children are still in their early childhood. They become more inattentive and exhausted from sitting and listening for long periods than from movement. Good teachers respect their need to be physically and mentally active.
By third grade, children's academic ability and social skills are well established and become more difficult to change.	Teachers have the power to really make a difference to children's academic and social success through positive relationships and intentional teaching.
The primary grade curriculum tends to be so focused on reading that little time is left over for other subject areas.	Teaching a child to read, which for some children is a relatively easy task while for others a seemingly overwhelming hurdle, is one of the most satisfying experiences of a teacher's life.
The primary school curriculum is usually dictated by the district or state and can be overly prescriptive with little room for flexibility on the part of teachers.	Teachers know that children cannot be scripted. They take their cues from children and follow their lead more than they follow the prescribed lesson plan.
Primary grade children tend to develop focused interests such as collecting, sports, music, or art.	Children's interests can be the vehicles for teaching them important skills and content. They can read and write about sports or practice number problems with a collection of their favorite objects.
Schoolwork gets harder during the primary grades, requiring greater attention and sustained effort. This discourages some learners.	Throughout the primary grades, if they have engaged and talented teachers, most children are motivated to learn and, therefore, like school.
Standardized achievement testing in third grade (and sometimes earlier) can place considerable stress on children and teachers. Test scores may be used as the sole measure of accountability.	Teachers can work across grade levels and with families to focus on helping every child learn and succeed, resisting the pressure to narrow the curriculum to what is tested. Good teachers have high expectations for every child and do not assign blame when children are behind or need extra help.

MyEducationLab

Go to the Professional Perspectives section in Topic 12: Professionalism/ Ethics in the MyEducationLab for your course and select the video entitled *Advice for Those Entering Early Childhood Education: Part 2* and watch and listen to Sue Bredekamp discuss this topic.

Beginning Your Journey as an Early Childhood Professional

Becoming a professional early childhood educator involves commitments in addition to working with children and families. In its *Standards for Early Childhood Professional Preparation*, NAEYC (2009b) describes the following aspects of becoming a professional:

- Identifying and involving oneself with the early childhood field
- Knowing about and upholding ethical standards and other professional guidelines
- Engaging in continuous, collaborative learning to inform practice
- Integrating knowledgeable, reflective, and critical perspectives on early education
- Engaging in informed advocacy for children and the profession.

Becoming a Professional

profession An occupation that requires extensive education and/or specialized training.

A **profession** is an occupation that requires extensive education and/or specialized training, such as the legal or medical professions. Professionals draw on this specialized body of knowledge and expertise to guide their decisions and behavior, but not prescribe it (Feeney & Freeman, 2004). Professions also mandate requirements for entry and standards for practice by their members. They tend to be exclusive in that only those individuals who meet the requirements can call themselves members of the profession (Goffin & Washington, 2007).

Although some positions in the early childhood field abide by this strict definition of a professional, others do not. In general, teachers at the elementary level are considered professionals because they are required to have baccalaureate degrees and licenses and to participate in continuing professional development to stay current in the field. By contrast, there are no uniform educational requirements for teachers of children from birth to age 5. Nevertheless, early childhood education is evolving and can boast several key characteristics of a profession, such as a commitment to a greater good—the welfare of children, a body of knowledge to guide practice, professional associations, and a code of ethics (Feeney & Freeman, 2004).

Effective Teaching
Effective early childhood educators work collaboratively as team members and continue to learn and grow as professionals throughout their careers.

Being a Member of the Early Childhood Field

One of the most valuable steps in becoming a professional is joining an organization that offers resources and services to its members such as conferences and publications. These affiliations provide a sense of identity, the opportunity to establish relationships with like-minded people, and access to the most current research and information about the field. Professional associations, such as the American Medical Association, restrict membership to qualified individuals. Early childhood education, on the other hand, has several professional associations, but membership in them is open to all.

The National Association for the Education of Young Children (NAEYC) is the largest association of individuals who work with and for children from birth through age 8. Other organizations also strengthen individuals' ties to their chosen field and advocate on behalf of children, including the National Black Child Development Institute, National Council of La Raza, National Head Start Association, and the National Association for Family Child Care. Most national associations such as these also have state and/or local affiliate groups through which new and experienced teachers can find support from colleagues and mentors.

Most elementary school teachers belong to one of the two teacher unions: the National Education Association or the American Federation of Teachers. Increasingly, child care professionals are joining unions as well in order to band together for improved wages and working conditions.

Upholding Professional Standards

Because young children are at such a critical point in their development and learning, and because they are vulnerable and cannot articulate their own rights and needs, early childhood professionals must know about and uphold professional and ethical standards (NAEYC, 2009b).

Standards and guidelines vary depending on the type of program or school, but they may include those for program accreditation (NAEYC, 2005d) and for developmentally appropriate practice (NAEYC, 2009a). Other relevant professional standards may include:

- Child care licensing requirements
- Requirements for reporting and preventing child abuse
- National, state, or local standards for curriculum content and child outcomes.

Upholding the NAEYC Code of Ethical Conduct

One of the hallmarks of a profession is the existence of a **code of ethics**, which defines the core values of the field and provides guidance for what professionals should do when they encounter difficult or conflicting obligations or responsibilities in their work. The *NAEYC Code of Ethical Conduct* (2005b) guides early childhood educators in their relationships with children, families, colleagues, and the broader society. Supplements to the code also exist for program administrators, principals, teacher educators, and others involved in professional development.

code of ethics Defines the core values of a profession and provides guidance for what professionals should do when they encounter difficult or conflicting obligations or responsibilities in their work.

Individual people have their own personal views about **morality**—what they think is right and wrong, and how they should behave. **Ethics** involves critical thinking about morality and the ability to make choices about their own values. In contrast to individual morality, **professional ethics** are "the kinds of actions that are right or wrong in the workplace and are a public matter" (Feeney & Freeman, 2004, p. 6). They help individuals resolve moral dilemmas they encounter in their work.

Understanding Ethical Responsibilities. **Ethical responsibilities** refer to the obligations that every teacher agrees to uphold with honesty, integrity, and respect. In fulfilling these responsibilities, early childhood educators should adhere to principles articulated in NAEYC's Code of Ethical Conduct. For example, the first principle is the most important and takes precedence over all others:

> Above all, we shall not harm children. We shall not participate in practices that are emotionally damaging, physically harmful, disrespectful, degrading, dangerous, exploitative, or intimidating to children. (NAEYC, 2005b, p. 3)

Other examples of teachers' ethical responsibilities include never sharing confidential information about a child or family with a person who has no legitimate need for knowing, obeying relevant laws (especially those regarding child abuse), and respecting the rights of children with disabilities. In difficult situations, teachers should consult the code for guidance about their ethical responsibilities, as illustrated in the following situation:

morality Personal views about what is right and wrong and how to behave.

ethics Critical thinking about morality and people's ability to make choices about their own values.

professional ethics The kinds of actions that are right or wrong in the workplace and are a public matter.

ethical responsibilities The obligations that every teacher agrees to uphold with honesty, integrity, and respect.

ethical dilemma Deciding the right thing to do when two or more values conflict.

> Daniel is a child in Kiera Blaine's kindergarten class. His parents are divorcing and involved in a nasty custody battle. Kiera has had several conferences with Daniel's father because he is concerned about the effect of the divorce on his son. Daniel's mother hasn't said anything to Kiera. After several months, Daniel's father asks Kiera to testify on his behalf in the custody case. Kiera feels bad for Daniel's father and wants to help him, but isn't sure if she should.

Here is a case in which consulting the code can ease Kiera's mind and help her do the right thing. The code clearly states: "In cases where family members are in conflict with one another, we shall work openly, sharing our observations of the child, to help all parties involved make informed decisions. We shall refrain from becoming an advocate for one party" (NAEYC, 2005b, p. 4).

Resolving Ethical Dilemmas. Sometimes the right answer in a difficult situation is not clear. An **ethical dilemma** involves deciding the right thing to do when two or more values conflict, as in the following case:

> Little Achievers is a well-respected child care center in a relatively affluent community with a long waiting list for admission. Beverly Stanos is excited to get a job there as an infant/toddler teacher that pays more than any other position she has had. Soon she begins to feel bewildered and conflicted. The center moves the babies and toddlers to a new group every 6 months; the director explains that they do this so that the babies don't get attached to the teachers.
>
> Beverly is upset; this practice goes against everything she has learned in her teacher education program about the importance of early attachments for babies' development. She checks the licensing standards and finds nothing to prohibit the practice. Finally, she meets with the director to try to get her to change the policy based

Teachers inevitably find out about private information and issues concerning children and their families. Maintaining confidentiality is one of the most important ethical responsibilities of every early childhood teacher.

on research about child development. The director dismisses Beverly's ideas because she says the policy is a good selling point with parents who don't want their babies to become attached to anyone but them. On the one hand, Beverly thinks she should quit this job, but she knows that if she just quits nothing will change. On the other hand, she feels an obligation to tell the parents that the policy is wrong.

Over the course of your teaching career, you are likely to encounter difficult situations in which you aren't sure about the right decision. In these cases, NAEYC's Code of Ethical Conduct will help you resolve ethical dilemmas.

Although many early childhood professionals choose their jobs based on the philosophy of the school or program, many find that at some point in their career, they may encounter an ethical dilemma, as Beverly does, in which values conflict. In Beverly's case, several principles in the code apply and she should weigh them as she attempts to resolve the dilemma:

- The code states that early childhood professionals should be familiar with the knowledge base of the profession and appreciate the vulnerability of children and their dependence on adults, which Beverly clearly does in this case.
- The code also guides her to acknowledge families' child-rearing values and their right to make decisions for their children.
- The code directs early childhood educators "to do nothing that diminishes the reputation of the program in which we work unless it is violating laws and regulations designed to protect children or is violating the provisions of this Code" (NAEYC, 2005b, p. 5).

Beverly's dilemma causes her to feel stress and discomfort and forces her to consider:

- Who she is most obligated to in this situation
- What she should do to address her dilemma
- Examining the code for additional guidance.

As an early childhood professional, you will most likely encounter ethical dilemmas of your own. Knowing the resources and tools to refer to is a first step in resolving the conflict. It is also important to understand the philosophy of any place where you are considering taking a position. If Beverly had known from the start what the program's practice was for moving children from one group to the next, she very well might have continued her job search.

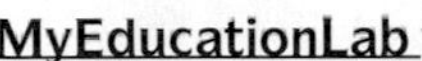

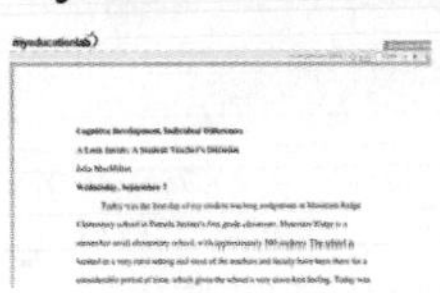

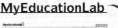

Go to the Assignments and Activities section of Topic 12: Professionalism/Ethics in the MyEducationLab for your course and complete the activity entitled *Ethics and the Early Childhood Professional*. Why is it so important for early childhood teachers to know about and use the NAEYC Code of Ethical Conduct?

Engaging in Continuous, Collaborative Learning to Inform Practice

Knowledge about child development and learning and about effective curriculum and teaching is always changing and expanding. Early childhood educators have an obligation to keep up to date with the latest research developments in the field. Professional education doesn't end with completion of a degree or initial licensure. Rather, teachers commit themselves to ongoing professional development and lifelong learning.

Teachers can learn much directly from children and from other teachers. For this reason, NAEYC (2009b) calls for teachers to collaborate with colleagues on their own classroom-based research, investigate ways to improve their own practices, participate in conferences, and stay current by reading and discussing publications and Internet sites. For example, a group of kindergarten teachers might figure out how to share a limited set of materials across classrooms to enhance the complexity of children's play. A team of preschool teachers might meet regularly to compare observations of children's interests and thinking. The staff of a child care center might read an article on biting and agree on ways to handle the problem with toddlers and families.

Professionals reflect on their decisions and discuss, debate, and analyze their practices with their colleagues. Becoming a professional teacher means committing to becoming a lifelong learner.

Integrating Knowledgeable, Reflective, and Critical Perspectives on Early Education

Even relatively routine decisions about which book to read, how to help children settle a dispute, or how to organize a safe, educational field trip require teachers to draw on professional knowledge and values. Developmentally appropriate practice is a decision-making process that requires teachers to be knowledgeable about the latest research findings in the field.

However, none of the professional guidelines or standards, including the Code of Ethical Conduct, contains one simple, true answer to any of the myriad questions teachers confront. In fact, early childhood professionals who share the same core values do not agree on the answers to some of the most central questions such as name of the field, the proper balance of teacher-guided and child-guided experience, or what *developmentally appropriate* really means (Goffin & Washington, 2007; NAEYC, 2009a). Therefore, professionals need to be reflective and critical, analyzing and evaluating the effectiveness of their own practices to improve their work with young children. They also must be open to views that differ from their own.

MyEducationLab

To observe an example of advocacy in action, go to the Video Examples section of Topic 12: Professionalism/Ethics in the MyEducationLab for your course and watch the video entitled *Walk and Bike to School Day.* How are early childhood professionals more effective advocates for children and families when they involve the community?

Becoming an Informed Advocate for Children and the Profession

Early childhood education is an imperfect field. The quality of services for children is uneven and, in many cases, inadequate. High-quality programs are expensive and many families cannot afford them. Early childhood teachers, whose jobs require a high level of professional knowledge and responsibility, are grossly undercompensated.

To make a real difference in children's lives, early childhood professionals have the additional obligation of becoming informed advocates for children and the profession (NAEYC, 2009b). **Advocacy** is aiding a cause that you believe in. It can be as personal as referring a family for counseling or as political as lobbying your representative for an increase in Head Start funding.

The key word is *informed*. Effective advocates present valid information and draw on their knowledge of research and real-world experience. Representatives are more likely to vote for increased funding if they are convinced that such programs work. Successful advocates present research on program effectiveness, but they also share the stories of children and families whose life experience is represented by the data.

Informed advocacy requires that early childhood professionals be familiar with the central policy issues affecting the field, including compensation for teachers, financing of the early education system, standards for curriculum, and appropriate methods of assessment. They also need to understand how public policies are developed and demonstrate essential advocacy skills, such as clear verbal and written communication skills and the ability to work effectively with others toward a common goal (Robinson & Stark, 2005). Figure 16.1 lists ways in which informed advocates act on behalf of children and the profession.

Joining a Profession That Makes a Difference

advocacy Aiding a cause that you believe in.

Teaching young children is a career that brings great personal fulfillment. Every hour, your small charges burst into laughter, need comforting, figure something out, and learn new words. Each day has its small rewards—a wilting buttercup, a shared joke, an "Ah-ha!" ex-

- Write letters or e-mails to support better child care licensing standards or legislation to support funding for child care assistance.
- Join a child advocacy group such as NAEYC, NBCDI, or NHSA, and stay informed about policy issues through their websites and e-mail alerts.
- Provide information for parents to help them advocate for their children.
- Get to know and collaborate with colleagues across the full age spectrum of birth through 8. Avoid pitting the needs of one age group or sector against those of another.
- Participate in efforts to improve compensation and benefits for early childhood professionals.
- Advocate for sufficient funding and effective services for all children, including children with disabilities.
- Build your knowledge and understanding of cultural and linguistic diversity by reading and joining diverse civic, community, volunteer and/or faith-based groups.
- Attend school board meetings and voice your opinion on educational issues such as developmentally appropriate practice, or appropriate curriculum and assessment.
- Share your critical views with manufacturers of children's products such as violent video games or advertisers of junk food aimed at children.
- Vote in every election, help register parents to vote, and/or run for public office.

Figure 16.1 Becoming an Informed Advocate

Sources: Based on *Advocates in Action: Making a Difference for Young Children*, revised edition, by A. Robinson and D. R. Stark, 2005, Washington, DC: NAEYC; and *Essentials for Child Development Associates Working with Young Children*, revised edition, by C. B. Day, 2004. Washington, DC: Council for Professional Recognition.

pression of understanding, or a whispered "I love you, Teacher." Looking back at the end of every year, teachers can't believe how far most of their children have come and they regret that some have not come farther. Over time, teachers learn more *about* children but mostly *from* children, and they are humbled by the job. They realize how much they don't know and that there are no simple answers to complex questions. They are awed by the trust that children and parents place in them and they use their power wisely. Most of all, they know that the lives they touch will be changed as will their own. They are committed to making a positive difference in children's lives.

We end with a succinct statement of the early childhood professional's commitment to children. The *Statement of Commitment* (NAEYC, 2005b) in Figure 16.2 is not an official part of the NAEYC's Code of Ethical Conduct, but rather a personal acknowledgment of the individual's willingness to embrace the values and moral obligations that lead to becoming part of the early childhood profession.

We began this journey by looking back at the beginnings of early childhood education and the contributions of dauntless women and men who provided the foundations on which it stands today. While those foundations are firm, they are not limiting. The future of children and of early childhood education continues to be built as we learn more about effective practices and our country commits more resources to improving schools for young children. Early childhood education is indeed a field on the rise. If you join this profession, you will discover that you have the power to shape that future for the better.

MyEducationLab

To assess your understanding of the professional opportunities and choices available to you in early childhood education, go to the Book Specific Resources section in the MyEducationLab for your course, select *Effective Practices in Early Childhood Education*, Chapter 16 of the Study Plan, and then complete the multiple choice questions and activities.

As an individual who works with young children, I commit myself to furthering the values of early childhood education as they are reflected in the ideals and principles of the NAEYC Code of Ethical Conduct. To the best of my ability I will:

- Never harm children.
- Ensure that programs for young children are based on current knowledge and research of child development and early childhood education.
- Respect and support families in their task of nurturing children.
- Respect colleagues in early childhood care and education and support them in maintaining the NAEYC Code of Ethical Conduct.
- Serve as an advocate for children, their families, and their teachers in community and society.
- Stay informed of and maintain high standards of professional conduct.
- Engage in an ongoing process of self-reflection, realizing that personal characteristics, biases, and beliefs have an impact on children and families.
- Be open to new ideas and be willing to learn from the suggestions of others.
- Continue to learn, grow, and contribute as a professional.
- Honor the ideals and principles of the NAEYC Code of Ethical Conduct.

Figure 16.2 NAEYC Statement of Commitment

Source: From *Code of Ethical Conduct and Statement of Commitment*, revised edition, April 2005, Washington, DC: NAEYC. Retrieved September 21, 2009, from http://www.naeyc.org/about/positions/pdf/PSETH05.pdf. Reprinted with permission from the National Association for the Education of Young Children.

Chapter Summary

- A career in early childhood education is filled with never-ending rewards and challenges. Among the major questions early childhood educators face is which age group(s) they would most like to work with and why. For each age group/position, there are interesting points to consider.
- The NAEYC Code of Ethical Conduct guides early childhood educators in making decisions about their professional responsibilities and resolving ethical dilemmas that arise in their relationships with children, families, colleagues, and society.
- Early childhood educators are also effective advocates for children and the profession. They know about the central policy issues in the field, including professional compensation, financing of the early education system, and standards for curriculum and assessment.
- Early childhood teachers have the opportunity to make lasting, positive contributions to the lives of children and to make a significant difference in the world.

key terms

advocacy
code of ethics
ethical dilemma
ethical responsibilities
ethics
morality
profession
professional ethics

Kieff, J. (2009). *Informed advocacy in early childhood care and education: Making a difference for young children and families.* Upper Saddle River, NJ: Pearson Education.

Moravcik, E., Freeman, N. M., & Feeney, S. (2000). *Teaching the NAEYC Code of Ethical Conduct: Activity sourcebook.* Washington, DC: NAEYC.

Ozretich, R., Burt, L., Doescher, S., & Foster, M. (2010). *Case studies in early childhood education: Implementing developmentally appropriate practices.* Upper Saddle River, NJ: Pearson Education.

Men Teach
Provides information on careers and resources for men in early childhood education.
www.menteach.org

National Association for Family Child Care
www.nafcc.org

National Black Child Development Institute
www.nbcdi.org

National Council of La Raza
www.nclr.org

National Head Start Association
www.nhsa.org

Southern Early Childhood Association
www.seca.org

readings & websites

1. Observe a "day in the life" of a teacher in an infant/toddler, preschool, kindergarten, primary grade classroom, or in a family child care home. Reflect on the rewards and challenges of working with the age group you observed. Weigh the pros and cons of the age group and setting you observe to determine if it might be a good fit for you.
2. Visit several websites of national early childhood organizations or attend a meeting of a child advocacy group. Which site or meeting provided you with information that you will be able to use as a new teacher? Do you think joining one of these organizations and/or the advocacy group would be a worthwhile investment? If so, which you would choose to join and why?
3. Interview an experienced early childhood teacher. Ask if he or she has encountered an ethical dilemma and how he or she handled it. (Make sure the person is willing to describe the issue without revealing confidential information.) Reflect on what you might do in a similar situation. Decide how the NAEYC Code of Ethical Conduct could be useful in resolving such an ethical dilemma.
4. With your fellow students or colleagues, discuss the ethical dilemma that Beverly faced with her employer at Little Achievers center that is described on pages 494–495. Consider the various alternatives and decide what you would do in this situation.
5. Observe trends in the news related to policies or services that impact young children. Become informed and reflect on your own position on the issue. Decide on an action to take to influence policy or advocate for your cause.

observe, reflect, decide

Glossary

absorbent mind—Maria Montessori's image of the child as actively learning from sensory experiences.

abstraction—The concept that anything can be counted.

academic discourse—The language of school, which is important for school success.

accommodation—When new information or experience doesn't fit within an existing concept (scheme), the child must modify it or construct a new scheme.

accommodations—Changes in assessment procedures, materials, or setting to eliminate barriers related to the child's disability that might keep children from demonstrating their full capabilities.

accountability—The process of holding teachers, schools, or programs responsible for meeting a required level of performance.

accreditation system—NAEYC's voluntary system for identifying high-quality early childhood centers and schools serving children from birth through kindergarten.

acculturation—The process whereby children learn expected rules of behavior.

achievement tests—Tests designed to measure what children have learned in general or in a content area like reading or mathematics.

acknowledging—Giving positive verbal or nonverbal attention that promotes a child's persistence and effort.

adaptation—The mental process of altering concepts (schemes) in response to experience, which occurs in two ways: through assimilation and accommodation.

advance organizers—Ways of introducing new information that serve as a bridge between what the student already knows and the new learning.

advocacy—Aiding a cause that you believe in.

age appropriate—Age-related human characteristics that allow teachers to make general predictions within an age range about what materials, interactions, and experiences will be safe, interesting, challenging, and within reach for children and, thus, likely to best promote their learning and development.

aggressive communication—Speaking the truth in a hurtful way.

alignment—Coordination of the curriculum from one level of education to the next in order to build on what children have already learned and to ease transitions for students between schools and school levels.

alliteration—Two words beginning with the same sound.

alphabetic principle—The understanding that there is a systematic relationship between letters and sounds, and that all spoken sounds and words can be represented by a limited set of agreed-on symbols called *letters*.

alternative assessments—Assessments that call for a child to produce a response rather than select from a list of possible responses.

anecdotal records—Short descriptions of incidents, or anecdotes, involving one or more children written by teachers and based on observations.

anti-bias curriculum—Curriculum that involves learning experiences and teaching strategies that are specifically designed to counter stereotyping and guard against expressions of bias.

apprenticeship—The process of children learning by observing adults and more accomplished peers performing tasks and by practicing the skills themselves with adult guidance and support.

approaches to learning—Behaviors, tendencies, or typical patterns that children use in learning situations that include both how they feel about learning—their level of enthusiasm, interest, and motivation—and how they engage with learning.

aptitude tests—Tests designed to measure children's potential for learning in the future.

assertive communication—Telling the truth in a thoughtful and considerate way; considered the most effective form of communication.

assessment—The ongoing process of gathering evidence of children's learning and development, and then organizing and interpreting the information to make informed decisions about instructional practices.

assimilation—When new information or experience is understood in connection with existing knowledge (schemes).

assistive technology—A piece of equipment or product that is used to increase, maintain, or improve the functional capabilities of individuals with disabilities.

associative play—Children play and share with each other, usually one other child.

attachment theory—The theory that children's ability to learn depends on their developing trusting relationships with caregivers.

auditory awareness—Listening to verbal input or distinguishing between different sounds.

authentic assessment—Used to determine what children know and can do from their demonstration of a skill or their creation of a product; also known as *performance assessment*.

babble—Produce consonant/vowel sounds such as "ba ba."

background knowledge—Concepts and basic information about how the world works that is essential for reading comprehension.

balanced approach—Effective reading instruction that helps children master the alphabetic principle *and* acquire meaning from text.

Bank Street approach—Originating with Lucy Sprague Mitchell at Bank Street College, a curriculum framework based on individual children's development, emphasizing that learning begins in children's experiences in the immediate environment (here and now).

base ten place value system—Highly efficient system of using just 10 numerals to write any counting number no matter how large, in which the meaning of a numeral depends on where it is placed within the number.

behavior intervention plan—Describes the strategies adults will use to prevent a child's negative behavior and to teach more acceptable behavior.

behaviorism or behavioral learning—Theory that learning is a change in behavior that is controlled by the consequences, either positive or negative, that follow the behavior.

bias—Negative feelings and expressions toward groups or individuals.

bicultural—Capable of operating successfully in both the home environment and the dominant culture of the larger world.

body composition—Weight and body fat.

Bronfenbrenner's ecological model—Describes the diverse, interactive contexts that influence the development of individuals and families over time.

bullying—Occurs when a person repeatedly commits aggressive acts that intend to harm, and an imbalance of power makes it hard for the victim to defend himself or herself.

cardinality—The concept that the last number said stands for the total number in the set.

cardiorespiratory (aerobic) system—Body system made up of the heart, lungs, and blood; provides the stamina needed to be active for a long period of time.

caring community of learners—A group or classroom in which children and adults engage in warm, positive relationships, treat each other with respect, and learn from and with each other.

challenging behavior—Any behavior that interferes with children's learning, development, and success at play; is harmful to the child, other children, or adults; or puts a child at high risk for later social problems or school failure.

charter schools—Independently operated, publicly funded schools that have greater flexibility than regular schools in meeting regulations and achieving goals.

checklists—Practical and versatile tools for gathering assessment information about children's behavior, skills, or attitudes.

Child Care and Development Block Grants (CCDBG)—Federal funds allocated to states for low-income working families to purchase child care.

child care center—Group program that provides care and education for young children during the hours that their parents are employed.

child care licensing standards—Minimum requirements, legally established by each state, for a child care program to operate.

child-centered curriculum—John Dewey's idea that curriculum should reflect the concepts and topics that the child is interested in and capable of learning.

Child Development Associate (CDA) credential—National competency-based credential for entry-level early childhood educators.

child-initiated experiences—Experiences that allow children to gain knowledge and skills through their own exploration and interactions with objects and other children.

children with disabilities—Children who have been identified as having a specific category of disability, such as autism or cerebral palsy.

children with special needs—A broad term used to describe children who may have multiple risk factors, specialized health care needs, mental or emotional health concerns, severe allergies, or physical and/or cognitive disabilities.

child study movement—Early 20th century effort to scientifically observe and systematically document children's individual development under the leadership of G. Stanley Hall and Arnold Gesell.

classification systems—Systems teachers use to help children build concepts by identifying similarities and differences or by comparing and contrasting objects and ideas.

Classroom Assessment Scoring System (CLASS)—Preschool and elementary classroom observational instrument that focuses on the instructional strategies teachers use to support children's learning and the quality of their relationships with children.

closed questions—Lower-level questions that have one right answer and usually require children to recall information or facts.

co-construction—Children learning by solving problems collaboratively with the teacher's support or by working with peers; also called *social construction of knowledge.*

code of ethics—Defines the core values of a profession and provides guidance for what professionals should do when they encounter difficult or conflicting obligations or responsibilities in their work.

code switch—The ability to understand and use both the mainstream version of English and the home dialect or language.

collectivist cultural groups—Cultural groups that focus on the needs of the group rather than those of the individual.

competent child—The image of children as active players in their own development and learning.

completion prompts—A prompt that requires the child to verbally complete the end of a sentence.

composing/decomposing—Mathematical processes of putting together and taking apart (for example, addition and subtraction).

comprehension—The ability to understand what is read and to interpret and analyze the author's meaning; the ability to make sense of what is read.

concepts of print—Beginning understandings about the forms and functions of written language, such as that words carry messages.

conceptual frameworks—Mental models that connect new learning to prior knowledge, enhance memory, and deepen understanding.

conceptual organizers—Ways of organizing curriculum, such as the project approach, that make content knowledge more meaningful, interesting, and understandable for young children.

connections—Refers to understanding links between different areas of math and connecting math concepts to real-world problems.

consequences—Principle of operant conditioning that behavior changes as a result of what occurs immediately afterward.

conservation—The understanding that the quantity of objects stays the same regardless of changes in appearance.

constructivism—Learning theory derived from the work of Jean Piaget which assumes that children actively build their knowledge from firsthand experiences in stimulating environments.

content standards—Describe what students should know and/or be able to do within a particular discipline such as math or science.

conventional reading—Reading in which the reader gains meaning from unfamiliar text.

cooing—Vocalizing vowel sounds.

cooperative play—Children assume different roles and share a purpose for the play.

co-player—Teacher's actually join in and take an active role in children's play.

Council for Exceptional Children (CEC)—The national professional association for special educators.

criterion-referenced tests—Tests that compare a person's score to a predetermined level of performance.

cultural competence—The ability to work effectively across cultural groups.

culturally appropriate—Applying knowledge of the social and cultural contexts in which children live, which helps teachers build on children's prior knowledge and make experiences meaningful and responsive.

culture—The explicit and implicit values, beliefs, rules, and expectations for behavior of members of a group that are passed on from one generation to the next. These rules determine to a large extent what group members regard as important, and what values shape their actions and judgments.

curriculum—A written plan that describes the goals for children's learning and development, and the learning experiences, materials, and teaching strategies that are used to help children achieve those goals.

curriculum approach—Describes the main elements or direction of a program; is less detailed than a curriculum model.

curriculum-embedded assessment—Formative assessment that is integrated into the curriculum; this assessment does not occur as a separate procedure.

curriculum framework—A guide for designing or choosing a curriculum.

curriculum model—A research-based, idealized version of what and how teaching and learning should occur.

day nurseries—Programs designed to serve working families in the late 19th and early 20th centuries; the forerunner of present-day child care centers.

decode—The ability to figure out what written symbols—letters of the alphabet—represent.

decontextualized speech—Talk about events, that are beyond the here and now or that inhibit children's imaginations.

demonstrating—Showing the correct way to perform a skill or procedure while children observe the outcome.

development—Age-related change that results from an interaction between biological maturation and a physical and/or social experience; development occurs as children grow, adapt, and change in response to various experiences.

developmental continuum—A predictable, but not rigid, sequence of typical developmental accomplishments within age ranges.

developmental domain—An area of development such as fine and gross motor skills, cognitive abilities, self-help capabilities, and social and communication skills.

developmentally appropriate practice (D.A.P)—Ways of teaching that engage children's interests and adapt for their age, experience, and ability, to help them meet challenging and achievable learning goals.

diagnostic tests—Tests designed to identify the specific learning or developmental problems a child has and to plan interventions; must be administered by specially trained professionals.

dialogic reading—Interactive, shared picture book reading during which the adult and the child gradually switch roles so that the child learns to become the storyteller with the assistance of the adult, who plays the role of active listener and questioner.

differentiated instruction—The creation of multiple paths so that children of different abilities, interests, and learning needs experience equally appropriate ways to achieve important learning goals.

direct instruction—Explicitly giving directions for completing a task; providing facts, verbal labels, or other specific information; or providing instructions for a child's action or behavior.

directional awareness—Anticipating which way to go.

disequilibrium—An imbalance in thinking that occurs when new information or physical experience cannot be understood in terms of what is already known (cannot be assimilated).

disorganized/disoriented attachment—Seen in children who lack secure attachments with adults due to having experienced neglect, abuse, or violence in the home, who have not developed useful strategies for seeking comfort or attention or handling difficulties.

distancing questions—Questions that relate pictures and words in the book to children's own experiences beyond the book.

Division for Early Childhood (DEC)—Subdivision of the Council for Exceptional Children that is the national professional organization for early childhood special educators and early intervention specialists.

dual language learner—Someone who is learning more than one language at a time.

dynamic assessment—Analyzes a child's performance not just in terms of what the child can do independently, but what the child can do with the assistance of a teacher or peer.

early childhood education—Education and child care services provided for children from birth through age 8.

Early Childhood Environment Rating Scale (ECERS-R)—Observational instrument used to rate program quality on a 7-point scale from indadequate to excellent.

early childhood special education—Services for children with disabilities or special needs who meet eligibility guidelines that are determined on a state-by-state basis according to the Individuals with Disabilities Education Act.

Early Head Start—Federally funded program serving low-income pregnant mothers, infants, and toddlers that promotes healthy family functioning.

early intervention—Services for infants and toddlers who are at risk of developmental delay and their families.

early literacy—Skills and knowledge that come before and lead up to (forerunners) conventional reading and writing.

earth and space science—Studying properties of earth materials, changes on the earth, patterns of movement, and changes of the sun and moon.

effective teaching—The use of approaches that are proven to be successful based on scientific evidence and that have a high probability of enhancing children's learning and development.

efficacy—Children's belief in their own ability to accomplish what they set out to do.

egocentrism—The process whereby very young children tend to see everything from their own intellectual and emotional point of view.

eligibility guidelines—Guidelines established on a state-by-state basis according to the IDEA that determine whether children may receive special education services.

emergent curriculum—Curriculum that develops in an educational environment in response to children's interests and needs rather than according to predeveloped plans.

emotional development—Acquisition of important emotional skills such as identifying feelings and learning to regulate emotions and express them appropriately.

emotional literacy—Children's ability to identify their own and others' emotions and to express emotions in a healthy way.

encode—Translating speech sounds into symbols—the letters of the alphabet—to create writing.

encouragement—Verbal comments or nonverbal signs such as pats or high fives that promote the child's persistence and effort.

engaged citizens—Children as change agents in schools, communities, and eventually in the world.

enumeration—The act of counting.

equilibration—The process whereby humans try to make sense of new experiences by creating new concepts (schemes) or adapting existing ones.

equity pedagogy—The idea that teaching about differences needs to include teaching about oppression and equity.

ethical dilemma—Deciding the right thing to do when two or more values conflict.

ethical responsibilities—The obligations that every teacher agrees to uphold with honesty, integrity, and respect.

ethics—Critical thinking about morality and people's ability to make choices about their own values.

ethnicity—The shared characteristics and experiences of a group of people, such as nationality, race, history, religion, and language.

evaluation—The process of making a judgment about assessment results; frequently considered the last step in assessment.

everyday mathematics—Informal, intuitive knowledge about math, including basic ideas about quantity (more and less), size, shape, and pattern.

evidence—An outward sign or indication of children's learning, such as their response to a question or their solution to a problem.

exceptional children—An all-encompassing term used to communicate inclusion of gifted and talented children as well as children whose development is below the expected range.

executive function—The ability to control emotions, focus attention, plan and think ahead, and monitor cognitive processes.

exosystem—Society's larger systems and policies that affect the development of human beings over the course of a lifetime, including economics, education, the media, politics, communication, health, and the law.

expressive language—The ability to communicate; use and knowledge of spoken language.

extended discourse—Talking with children in ways that build on and expand what they say.

extinction—The process whereby a conditioned behavior diminishes and eventually disappears when reinforcers are removed.

facilitating—Providing short-term, temporary assistance to help a child achieve the next level of functioning.

family-centered practice—Providing resources and supports to families that promote children's development and learning and at the same time, strengthen the competency of families in their role.

family child care home—Child care in which caregivers provide care in their own homes for a small group of children, often multi-age groups.

family systems theory—Views family members as interconnected parts with each member influencing the others in predictable and recurring ways.

feedback loop—Back-and-forth communication between a teacher and a child or small group of children in an effort to reach deeper understanding.

fidelity—Faithful implementation of a curriculum model.

fine motor development—Physical skills related to the small muscles found in individual body parts, especially those in the hands and feet.

fine motor manipulative movements—Control, precision, and accuracy of small muscle movement.

5- to 7-year shift—Major transition in cognitive abilities that gradually occurs between 5 and 7 years of age, resulting in increased ability to think logically, self-regulate, and solve problems.

flexibility—The ability to bend and stretch easily.

fluency—Rapid, efficient, and accurate word recognition skills that permit the reader to comprehend the meaning of text.

formal assessment—Assessment that follows a specific procedure and uses a specially designed instrument or tool.

formative assessment—The process of gathering information about children's learning and using it to provide the right kind and amount of support.

free appropriate public education (FAPE)—Education for children with disabilities that is required by IDEA, so that children with disabilities are not denied the same opportunities offered to everyone else.

frequency counts—Method used by teachers to keep track of how often a behavior occurs.

Froebel's occupations and gifts—Invented by Froebel for kindergartners, occupations were planned experiences designed to train children's eye–hand coordination and mental activity, and gifts were concrete materials, many of which influenced later toy development.

functional assessment or analysis—The process of determining why a child is behaving a certain way, based on the principle that all behavior serves a function or purpose.

functional skills—Skills that are useful to children in their everyday lives.

generative skills—Skills that can be used across settings, people, events, and objects.

geometry—The study of shapes and space, including flat, two-dimensional space and three-dimensional space.

graphic representation—The process of depicting thoughts and ideas through drawing, modeling, or other media.

gross motor development—Physical skills related to moving the whole body or major parts of the body.

gross motor manipulative movements—Large muscle movements involving giving or receiving force from objects such as throwing, catching, or kicking.

guidance—The process of teaching children the life skills they need to function productively with other children.

Head Start—Federally funded, national program that promotes school readiness by enhancing the social and cognitive development of children ages 3, 4, and 5 through providing educational, health, nutritional, social, and other services to the nation's poorest children and families.

Head Start Program Performance Standards—National standards that establish the level of quality of services provided by every Head Start program.

health-related fitness—Any aspect of health that can be improved by physical exercise and activity.

high-context culture—Culture in which communication relies less on words and more on contextual cues, such as facial expressions, gestures, or other physical clues, to convey meaning.

high-stakes testing—Using standardized test scores to make decisions about individual children, teachers, or schools that have potential long-term consequences.

home visiting—Visits made by a teacher to the child's home on a regular basis to exchange information with parents.

hypothesis—An assumption about or tentative explanation of a phenomenon.

hypothesis generating and testing—Applying previously acquired knowledge to a new situation by making a prediction and then observing and reflecting on the outcome.

identity—The collection of characteristics that individuals recognize as constituting their sense of self and belonging to a group.

inclusion—Participation and services for children with disabilities and special needs in programs and settings where their typically developing peers are served.

individualistic cultural groups—Cultural groups that focus on the needs of the individual, independence, self-expression, and personal property and choice.

individualized education program (IEP)—A written plan designed to meet the unique needs of a child with a disability or special need; it is developed, reviewed, and revised by an IEP team during meetings for each child who is eligible for special education services.

individualized family service plan (IFSP)—Documents and guides the early intervention process for children with disabilities from birth to age 3 and their families; contains information about the services necessary to facilitate a child's development and enhance the family's capacity to facilitate the child's development.

individualized intervention—A systematically planned and implemented set of actions designed to alter the course of a child's development or learning.

individually appropriate—Information about the strengths, interests, abilities, and needs of each individual child in the group that enables teachers to adapt to and be responsive to individual variation.

Individuals with Disabilities Education Act (IDEA)—Federal law governing provision of services for children with disabilities and special needs.

informal assessment—Information is gathered for teacher's use to make everyday classroom decisions or adjustments to teaching.

insecure-ambivalent/resistant attachment—Children's inability to trust adults to keep them safe due to neglect, abuse, or other difficult circumstances that results in a lack of social competence.

insecure-avoidant attachment—Rejection and insensitivity from adult caregivers that causes children to turn away from or avoid adults and not seek their comfort.

integrated curriculum—Learning plan that addresses goals across multiple areas of the curriculum at the same time.

intentional teachers—Professionals who have a purpose for the decisions they make and can explain that purpose to others.

interviews—Teacher-created, predetermined questions that are designed to reveal what children understand.

invented spelling—Developmental or phonetic spelling that represents children's initial attempts to associate sounds with letters.

kindergarten—Typically considered the first year of formal schooling; serves 5-and 6-year-olds.

K-W-L—An advance organizer strategy in which teachers ask children what they already know (K) about the topic of study, what they want (W) to know, and then what they learned (L).

laboratory school—School operated by colleges and universities that usually serves children of students and faculty and also act as models of excellent education for student teachers.

Lanham Act—Federal legislation to provide emergency child care and other services for families employed in the war effort during World War II.

learning—A change in knowledge or skill that results from experience or instruction.

learning centers—Defined areas of the classroom that have a particular purpose and that contain relevant furnishings and materials.

learning continuum, trajectory, or path—Similar to a developmental continuum, but focuses on sequences of knowledge or skill in a content area.

learning standards—Expectations for student learning.

learning strategy—How children construct meaning in any context or situation.

life science—The study of the characteristics, life cycles, and environments of organisms.

listening—The process of taking in information through the sense of hearing and making meaning from what is heard.

locomotor movements—Movements that allow the body to proceed in a horizontal or vertical direction from one place to another, such as walking, running, leaping, or jumping.

logico-mathematical knowledge—The relationships that are constructed in our minds between objects or concepts.

low-context culture—Culture that focuses on direct, logical, precise verbal communication.

macrosystem—The overarching cultural context of the values and beliefs that influence society at large as well as individuals within that society.

manipulatives—Small-sized blocks, cubes, pattern blocks, beads, pegs, and the like that are designed for children's play and learning.

mathematize—To understand and think about everyday problems and experiences in explicitly mathematical terms.

math talk—Using the language and vocabulary of mathematics.

maturationist—Theory of development that assumes that the sequence of changes in abilities and behavior is largely predetermined by children's biological growth processes rather than by their experiences or learning.

measurement—The process of determining size, length, area, or volume using a standard unit.

mesosystem—How events that occur within the microsystem interact and affect each other.

metacognitive activities—Activities that engage children in thinking and reflecting about their own learning.

microsystem—The interactions in which people are most directly involved, including the family, school and child care programs, religious institutions, and the community.

mistaken behavior—Alternative term for children's misbehavior, recognizing the fact that young children are still learning acceptable behavior and that they are bound to make mistakes.

modeling—Teacher showing children a skill or desirable way of behaving or speaking; also children imitating the behavior of others.

modifications—Changes in an assessment that alter what the assessment measures or what the results mean.

morality—Personal views about what is right and wrong and how to behave.

motor planning—The ability of the brain to conceive, organize, and carry out a series of unfamiliar actions.

muscular strength and endurance—The ability to keep moving without stopping due to fatigue.

narrative—A story with a beginning, middle, and end; characters; dialogue; and a plot with a problem to solve or a dilemma to be resolved.

narrative records—Teachers' attempts to record detailed descriptions of children in a situation or event that is the focus of the observation.

National Association for the Education of Young Children (NAEYC)—The world's largest organization of early childhood educators, whose mission is to act on behalf of the needs and interests of children from birth through age 8. NAEYC establishes standards for teacher preparation and accreditation of early childhood programs.

natural learning environments—Settings that are natural or normal for the child's same-age peers without disabilities such as child care centers, parks, a neighbor's house, or the zoo, as opposed to hospitals, clinics, and therapy offices.

naturally occurring reinforcers—Consequences that are likely to occur *whenever* the child performs the skill and are, therefore, highly effective.

nature—The hereditary or genetic contributions to human development.

nature deficit disorder—Hypothetical disorder related to lack of exposure and experience outdoors and in the natural world.

negative reinforcement—An unpleasant consequence that is avoided if the person performs a desired behavior more frequently.

neurons—Nerve cells in the brain that receive information through the senses or from other neurons, and then communicate information back to other parts of the body.

No Child Left Behind Act (NCLB)—Federal law passed in 2001 to increase school accountability, improve reading and mathematics achievement, and narrow the achievement gap. It emphasizes improved scores on standardized tests beginning in the third grade.

normal curve—A distribution of scores that looks like a bell shape, with most people scoring at the midrange and fewer scoring at the higher and lower ends.

norm-referenced tests—Tests that compare an individual's score to that of other test takers.

nursery schools—Schools serving children younger than kindergarten age; out-of-date term for preschool or prekindergarten.

nurture—Environmental factors and experiences that influence human development and behavior.

object permanence—A concept that babies lack early in the period of sensorimotor development, so that when an object is no longer in their sight, it ceases to exist for them.

one-to-one correspondence—Attaching one and only one number word to each object being counted.

onlooker—Teachers when they act as the audience for children's play.

open-ended questions—Questions that require children to analyze information in some way and that have many possible answers.

operant conditioning—The process of using pleasant or unpleasant consequences to control behavior.

operations—Working with and solving problems about relationships such as *more than* or *less than.*

order irrelevance principle—The concept that counting can begin with any object in the set as long as each is counted only once.

parallel play—Children play next to each other, but not with each other; they may speak, but don't really converse.

parent cooperative—Preschool program owned, operated, and partially staffed by parents.

parentese—The high-pitched tone of voice adults and even children tend to use naturally with babies; also called *motherese.*

passive communication—Speaking in a way that is sensitive to the listener's feelings, but so vague that the message is easily misunderstood.

pedagogy—What a teacher says or does that engages children and contributes to their learning and development.

perceptual motor development—Occurs when children use their senses to take in information about objects in the environment and use this information to coordinate their movements.

performance assessment—Determines what children know and can do from their demonstration of a skill or their creation of a product; also known as *authentic assessment.*

performance standards—Describe the knowledge or skill that students should acquire by a particular point in their schooling, usually tied to grade or age level; also known as *benchmarks.*

person-first language—Language that recognizes that a child is a child first, whether or not he or she has a disability (e.g., saying "child with special needs" as opposed to "special needs child").

phonemes—The individual sounds of spoken language; changing one in a word changes the meaning of the word.

phonemic awareness—Recognizing that spoken words are made up of individual sounds that can be manipulated.

phonics—A system of teaching the correspondences between letters or groups of letters and the sounds they represent.

phonological awareness—Consciousness that the stream of spoken language is made up of smaller units or chunks of sound.

physical fitness—Children's overall physical condition: growth, strength, stamina, and flexibility.

physical knowledge—Understanding how objects move and function in space and how the physical world works.

physical science—Basic ideas about the properties of liquids and solid materials, how things move and change position, and cause-and-effect relationships.

pincer grasp—Grasp used to pick up objects with the thumb and forefinger.

planning—Requires children to make intentional choices and encourages them to identify their goals, consider the options for achieving them, make predictions, and anticipate consequences; helps build children's higher-level thinking and problem solving.

plasticity—The brain's ability to develop and change in response to experiences.

play-based assessment—Similar to curriculum-embedded assessment, but the context for observing and interacting with children is the children's play.

play-by-play language—Language that describes what is happening during routines and social interactions with babies and toddlers; also called *running commentary*.

play leader—Teachers participate in children's play; includes making deliberate attempts to enrich and extend the play episode.

portfolios—Systematic and organized collections of children's work and demonstrations of their progress relevant to the goals of the curriculum.

position statement—A document that articulates a stance, usually research based, that an organization is taking in response to an issue or a problem.

positive behavior support (PBS)—A method of identifying the causes and functions of problem behaviors in order to develop support strategies that prevent challenging behaviors and teach new, more appropriate skills.

positive reinforcement—A reward or pleasant consequence that follows a behavior, causing that behavior to be repeated.

predictable books—Books with controlled vocabulary using parallel text structures that become familiar to children.

predictors—Set of early literacy skills and knowledge that increases the likelihood of later success in learning to read and write.

prekindergarten (pre-K)—Educational programs serving 3- and 4-year-olds, usually in public schools.

preschool—Educational programs serving 3- and 4-year-olds delivered under various sponsorships.

primary grades—First, second, and third grade; sometimes includes kindergarten.

print awareness—Beginning knowledge about written language.

private speech—The process whereby interpersonal understanding or socially constructed knowledge is turned into intrapersonal knowledge (thinking aloud becomes thinking to oneself).

process quality—The quality of the relationships and interactions among teachers and children, and the appropriateness of the materials, learning experiences, and teaching strategies occurring in an early childhood program.

profession—An occupation that requires extensive education and/or specialized training.

professional ethics—The kinds of actions that are right or wrong in the workplace and are a public matter.

professionals—Members of an occupational group that make decisions based on a specialized body of knowledge, continue to learn thoughout their careers, and are committed to meeting the needs of others.

program evaluation—The process of gathering information about a program's quality and effectiveness.

progressive education movement—Major effort to reform schooling in the early 20th century to make it more democratic and responsive to children's needs. This movement was highly influential on early childhood education and later ideas about developmentally appropriate practice.

project—An in-depth investigation of a topic worth learning more about, usually involving a small group, but occasionally the whole class.

project approach—Strategy for conceptually organizing curriculum by engaging children an in-depth investigation of a topic, focused on finding answers to questions posed by the children, the teacher, or the teacher working with the children.

prompts—Gestural, model, physical, pictorial, or verbal clues that elicit responses from children to assist them in using a specific skill.

protective factors—Mechanisms, both inherited and experiential, that may minimize the potentially negative effects for children living in identified high-risk situations.

pruning—The process whereby the brain eliminates unnecessary or unused synapses, which contributes to efficient brain operation, aids learning and memory, and increases the brain's flexibility.

punishment—An unpleasant consequence that stops or decreases the frequency of a behavior.

quality rating systems (QRS)—State-operated systems that evaluate and rate the quality of child care programs according to achievement of benchmarks beyond those required for minimal licensing, such as having more highly qualified teachers or better ratios.

questioning—Eliciting different types of responses and promoting different types of thinking.

rare words—Multisyllable words that are not typically part of a young child's vocabulary.

rating scales—Method of recording teacher's judgments about how a child's performance compares to that of peers or to a predetermined standard.

readiness tests—Achievement tests administered to children at entry to kindergarten.

reasoning—Thinking logically to come to a conclusion or find a result.

recall questions—Questions asked by the teacher about a book to see what children remember.

receptive language—The ability to understand what is being said.

reciprocal relationship—A two-way relationship in which information and power are shared evenly.

Recognition & Response (R&R)—A three-tiered model, also called *RTI Pre-K*, for providing high-quality early childhood education and targeted interventions matched to the learning needs of 3- to 5-year-old children.

redirection—Drawing a child's attention or behavior toward a more desirable alternative than the one on which the child is currently focusing.

reflection—Teaching strategy in which teachers help children go beyond remembering what they did to becoming aware of what they learned, what was interesting, how they felt about the experience, and what they can do to build on and extend the experience.

Reggio Emilia approach—Principles of early childhood education practice developed in schools in Reggio Emilia,

Italy; emanates from the image of the child rich in potential and as a citizen with rights.

reinforcer—Consequence—either positive or negative—that increases or strengthens a behavior.

reliability—The extent to which the results obtained from a test are accurate and consistent over time.

replacement behaviors—Desirable prosocial behaviors that replace problem behaviors.

representing—Expressing mathematical ideas with words, diagrams, pictures, and/or symbols.

resilience—A child's ability to overcome, adapt to, or minimize the damaging effects of adversity.

Response to Intervention (RTI)—A three-tiered framework intended to prevent learning delays in primary grades from becoming learning disabilities.

rhyme—Two words ending with the same sound.

risk factors—Inherited or experiential conditions that potentially contribute to poor developmental outcomes for children, such as peer rejection, academic failure, juvenile delinquency, and school expulsion.

risk vs. challenge continuum—Concept that children not only need to be safe but they also need to be challenged if they are to advance their skills and learn how to keep themselves safe.

rubrics—Descriptive rating scales that detail the qualities related to each rank on the scale; includes clear descriptions of each point on the scale or guidelines for making judgments about a rating.

scaffolding—The assistance, guidance, and direction teachers provide children to help them accomplish a task or learn a skill (within their ZPD) that they could not achieve on their own.

scheme or schema—The organization of mental structures people use to think or guide behavior; the structures develop and change with age and experience.

school readiness—Children's competencies related to success in kindergarten, including physical development, health, and well-being; social-emotional development and learning; cognitive development and general knowledge, such as mathematics and science; positive approaches to learning such as curiosity and motivation; and language development and early literacy skills.

science—Study of the physical and natural world, especially by observing and experimenting.

scientifically based curriculum—Derives from research evidence about what kinds of learning outcomes relate to later achievement, and what types of teaching and learning experiences help children acquire those outcomes. Such a curriculum has been evaluated and its effectiveness demonstrated.

scientifically based instructional practices—Curriculum and instructional practices that research has demonstrated improve learning outcomes.

scientific inquiry—Involving children in observing, predicting, and investigating.

scientific method—Method of beginning with a hypothesis, testing it with an experiment, making observations and gathering data, and then confirming or disconfirming the initial hypothesis.

scope—The particular focus of the curriculum at a given point in time; that is, how much of a larger content area will be taught.

screening tests—Tests administered to all children, usually in preschool or kindergarten, as the first step in a process to determine which children are at risk of a possible disability or learning problem; also called *developmental screening.*

script language—The typical ways that people communicate in different contexts or settings.

secure attachment relationship—A responsive and sensitive relationship with caregivers that allows children to venture forth and comfortably explore and learn about the world.

secure base—An attachment figure (mother or caregiver) who serves as an anchor for children to rely on and from which children can safely venture out and explore.

self-actualization theory—Maslow's view that behavior and learning are motivated by a hierarchy of needs.

self-concept—Children's stable perceptions about themselves despite variations in their behavior.

self-esteem—Children's perception of their own worth.

self-regulated learning—Bandura's theory that people not only learn by modeling the behavior of others, but by observing and evaluating their own.

self-regulation—The ability to adapt or control behavior, emotions, and thinking.

separation anxiety—Feeling a baby experiences when the caregiver is not in sight; the baby may cry or cling to a caregiver in the presence of strangers; usually occurs around 8 months of age.

sequence—The order in which knowledge and skills will be taught.

shaping—Teaching a new skill or behavior by rewarding each step or successive approximation toward the goal.

slippery egg messages—Communications that are difficult to toss (send) and catch (receive), and must be expressed gently to be sure that the catcher receives the communication as intended.

social acceptance—Occurs when a child is treated as a member of the group; other children play, smile, and sit beside the child throughout the day.

social cognitive theory—Bandura's theory that people can learn efficiently from observing the consequences of another person's behavior.

social-conventional knowledge—The culturally agreed-on names and symbols that need to be transmitted to the learner directly.

social development—Young children's ability to form and sustain positive relationships with adults and other children.

social-emotional learning—Children's ability to recognize and regulate their emotions, establish and maintain positive relationships, make responsible decisions, and solve social problems constructively. Also called *social competence.*

social rejection—Occurs when peers choose not to play with a child or outwardly refuse the child's requests to join in their play.

social studies—The integrated study of the history, geography, economics, political science, and other related aspects of societies of the past, present, and future.

sociocultural theory—Vygotsky's theory that children learn from social interaction within a cultural context.

socioeconomic status (SES)—Family income level.

solitary play—Children play alone, usually with toys or objects.

spatial awareness—Perceptions of where the body is.

spatial relations—Spatial sense and familiarity with shape, structure, and location.

specialized instruction—Involves teachers matching an individual child's goals and objectives with appropriate teaching methods and materials, deciding what amount of assistance each child with special needs requires, providing the assistance, and then determining whether the instruction was effective.

stability movements—Movements in which the body remains in place, but moves around its horizontal or vertical axis; examples include balancing, dodging, starting, and stopping.

stable order principle—Principle that states number words need to be said in the same order every time.

stage manager—Teachers set the stage for children's play by providing the props and theme, and being available to respond the children's requests.

standardized assessment—Assessment of all children using the same procedures and performing the same task under the same conditions.

standardized testing—Uses prescribed methods for administering and scoring.

structural quality—Features of an early childhood program, such as maximum group sizes, teacher/child ratios, and teacher qualifications, that are relatively easy to quantify and measure.

structured physical activity—Adult-guided play that is designed for a purpose such as increasing endurance or flexibility.

subitizing—The ability to look at a small set of objects (four or fewer) and know how many there are without counting.

successive approximations—Behaviors that are reinforced (shaped) that are not the actual desired behaviors, but each approximate behavior that is closer to the goal.

summative assessment—Assessing student learning at the end of an educational experience to evaluate the effectiveness of the experience.

supporting—Providing assistance that helps the child to accomplish a difficult task by making it easier.

symbolic representation—The process of mentally using one thing to stand for something else.

synapses—Connections in the brain that carry information between neurons.

syntax—Grammar and sentence structure.

teacher-initiated experiences—Learning experiences in which teachers take the lead by providing explicit information and modeling or demonstrating a skill, as determined by the teacher's goals and direction.

teaching–learning paths—Sequence of teaching and learning knowledge or skills in a content area. Also called *learning trajectories* and *developmental* or *learning continua*.

teaching strategy—A behavior or activity that a teacher deliberately selects and flexibly applies to help students construct meaning.

technology—Tools used to change or modify the natural world to meet human needs.

telegraphic speech—Combining words into two-word utterances.

temperament—The pattern of arousal and emotionality that is characteristic of an individual.

temporal awareness—Speeding up or slowing down a movement.

Temporary Assistance for Needy Families (TANF)—Federally funded program, more commonly known as Welfare to Work, that provides temporary financial aid, but requires recipients to move into the labor force or schooling.

tennis ball messages—Communications that are easily "tossed" and easily received and that help form the foundation of a relationship; they constitute the everyday chitchat between teachers and parents.

testing—A systematic procedure for evaluating a child's behavior and knowledge that is then assigned a score.

thematic curriculum—Way of integrating curriculum in which a broad topic of interest or a "big idea" provides the basis for making connections across learning goals.

theory—An explanation of how information and observations are organized and relate to one another.

theory of multiple intelligences—Theory developed by Howard Gardner that identifies eight different intelligences as opposed to a single score on an intelligence test; this theory is useful for thinking about variation among children and teaching to their strengths.

time-out—Removing a child to a specified chair or area of the room for a period of time following an unacceptable behavior.

tourist curriculum—An approach in which a culture is visited as though it were an exotic destination where people dress, talk, dance, and eat differently before returning to the "normal" place where we all live.

transactional theory of development—Theory that development is the result of both biology and experience and how they influence each other.

transitions—Changes from one activity or place to another.

universal design—The concept that materials and environments need to be usable by everyone, including those with disabilities, to the greatest extent possible.

universal voluntary prekindergarten—Publicly funded preschool usually for 4-year-olds, but sometimes 3-year-olds; available to any family that chooses to use it.

unstructured free play—Play that is chosen and initiated by children, such as that which occurs on a playground.

utility—Used to benefit children.

validated curriculum—Curriculum that has been evaluated and its effectiveness demonstrated.

validity—The degree to which an instrument measures what it purports to measure.

vicarious learning—Learning by observing the effects of other people's behavior, rather than experiencing rewards or punishments directly.

virtual field trip—Trip taken via the Internet in which children can go anywhere in the world.

visual arts—Creative processes and products that involve drawing, painting, sculpting with clay, or making models of objects using a variety of materials.

visual literacy—Ability to create visual messages and to interpret messages contained in visual communications.

vocabulary—A combination of receptive and expressive language; the number of words a person knows and uses when listening or speaking.

wait time—The length of time that a teacher waits for a response after asking a question or responding to a comment.

webbing—A planning tool that teachers and children create together to organize curriculum content.

***Wh-* questions**—Questions that begin with "Why" or "What" to get children thinking about characters' motives or feelings.

widening horizons approach—Approach to social studies curriculum planning designed to begin where "children are" and then expand outward.

windows of opportunity—Periods of time during which human brains are particularly susceptible and responsive to certain types of experience.

word identification—The process of decoding unfamiliar words and recognizing high-frequency (both regularly and irregularly spelled) words by sight.

WPA nurseries—Federal emergency relief nursery schools, funded by the Works Progress Administration (WPA) during the Great Depression, designed to support the economy by providing jobs for those who worked on the site and child care services to families seeking work.

zone of proximal development (ZPD)—The distance between the actual developmental level an individual has achieved (her independent level of problem solving) and the level of potential development she could achieve with adult guidance or through collaboration with other children.

References

Adams, M. (1990). *Beginning to read: Thinking and learning about print*. Cambridge, MA: MIT Press.

Ainsworth, M. D. S., Blehar, M. C., Waters, E., & Wall, S. (1978). *Patterns of attachment*. Hillsdale, NJ: Lawrence Erlbaum Associates.

Albert Shanker Institute. (2009). *Preschool curriculum: What's in it for children and teachers*. Washington, DC: Author.

Albrecht, K., & Miller, L. G. (2000a). *Innovations: The comprehensive infant curriculum*. Beltsville, MD: Gryphon House.

Albrecht, K., & Miller, L. G. (2000b). *Innovations: The comprehensive toddler curriculum*. Beltsville, MD: Gryphon House.

Albrecht, K., & Miller, L. G. (2001). *Innovations: Infant and toddler development*. Beltsville, MD: Gryphon House.

Albrecht, K., & Miller, L. G. (2004). *Innovations: The comprehensive preschool curriculum*. Beltsville, MD: Gryphon House.

Alliance for Technology Access. (2004). *Computer resources for people with disabilities: A guide to assistive technologies, tools and resources for people of all ages* (4th ed.). Alameda, CA: Hunter House.

Althouse, R., Johnson, M. H., & Mitchell, S. T. (2003). *The colors of learning: Integrating the visual arts into the early childhood curriculum*. New York: Teachers College Press; Washington, DC: National Association for the Education of Young Children.

American Academy of Pediatrics, American Public Health Association, & National Resource Center for Health and Safety in Child Care and Early Education. (2002). *Caring for our children: National health and safety performance standards: Guidelines for out-of-home child care programs* (2nd ed.). Elk Grove Village, IL: American Academy of Pediatrics; Washington, DC: American Public Health Association. Retrieved August 31, 2009, from http://www.eric.ed.gov/ERICDocs/data/ericdocs2sql/content_storage_01/0000019b/80/14/0d/14.pdf

American Association for the Advancement of Science. (2009). *Benchmarks for science literacy*. Washington, DC: Author. Retrieved September 15, 2009, from http://www.project2061.org/publications/bsl/default.htm

American Educational Research Association, American Psychology Association, & National Council on Measurement in Education. (1999). *Standards for educational and psychological testing*. Washington, DC: AERA.

American Heart Association. (2009). *Ten ways to help children develop healthy habits*. Retrieved January 16, 2009, from http://www.americanheart.org/presenter.jhtml?identifier=3030485

Ames, L. B., & Ilg, F. (1979). *The Gesell Institute's child from one to six*. New York: Harper & Row.

Anderson, M., Kaufman, J., Simon, T., Barrios, L., Paulozzi, L., Ryan, G., et al. (2001). School-associated violent deaths in the United States, 1994–1999. *Journal of the American Medical Association, 286*, 2695–2702.

Anderson, R. C., Heibert, E. H., Scott, J. A., & Wilderson, I. A. (1985). *Becoming a nation of readers: The report of the commission on reading*. Washington, DC: National Institute on Education.

Arend, R., Grove, F., & Sroufe, L. A. (1979). Continuity of individual adaptation from infancy to kindergarten: A predictive study of ego-resiliency and curiosity in preschoolers. *Child Development, 50*, 950–959.

Aries, P. (1962). *Centuries of childhood: A social history of family life*. New York: Vintage Books.

Arnold, D. H., Fischer, P. H., Doctoroff, G. L., & Dobbs, J. (2002). Accelerating math development in Head Start classrooms. *Journal of Educational Psychology, 94*(4), 762–770.

Aronson, S. (1993, May/June). Tree climbing and care of sand areas. *Exchange, 90*, 79–80.

Arts Education Partnership. (1998). *Position paper for task force on children's learning and the arts: Birth to age 8*. Washington, DC: Council of Chief State School Officers.

Asher, S., Hymel, S., & Renshaw, P. (1984). Loneliness in children. *Child Development, 55*, 1456–64.

Asp, E. (1998). The relationship between large-scale and classroom assessment: Compatibility or conflict? In R. Brandt (Ed.), *Assessing student learning: New rules, new realities* (pp. 17–46). Arlington, VA: Educational Research Service and Alliance for Curriculum Reform.

Au, W. (2007). High-stakes testing and curricular control: A qualitative metasynthesis. *Educational Researcher, 36*(5), 258–267.

Ausubel, D. P. (1978). *Educational psychology: A cognitive view* (2nd ed.). Boston: Holt McDougal.

Baker, A. C., & Manfredi/Petitt, L. A. (2004). *Relationships, the heart of quality care: Creating community among adults in early care settings*. Washington, DC: National Association for the Education of Young Children.

Bandura, A. (1973). *Aggression: A social learning analysis*. Englewood Cliffs, NJ: Prentice Hall.

Bandura, A. (1986). *Social foundations of thought and action: A social-cognitive theory*. Englewood Cliffs, NJ: Prentice Hall.

Bandura, A. (1997). *Self-efficacy: The exercise of control*. New York: Freeman.

Banks, J. A. (2008). *An introduction to multicultural education* (4th ed.). Needham Heights, MA: Allyn & Bacon.

Barbarin, O., & Crawford, G. (2006). Acknowledging and reducing stigmatization of African American boys. *Young Children, 61*(6), 79–86.

Barbour, C., Barbour, N. H., & Scully, P. A. (2005). *Families, schools, and communities: Building partnerships for educating children* (3rd ed.). Upper Saddle River, NJ: Pearson Merrill Prentice Hall.

Bardige, B. (2005). *At a loss for words: How America is failing our children and what we can do about it*. Philadelphia: Temple University Press.

Barker, K. (2005, November 30). Paparazzi get an audience with the panda. *Washington Post*, p. B5.

Barnett, W. S. (2003). Better teachers, better preschools: Student achievement linked to teacher qualifications. *Preschool Policy Matters, 2*. New Brunswick, NJ: National Institute for Early Education Research.

Barnett, W. S. (2008). *Preschool education and its lasting effects: Research and policy implications*. Boulder, CO, and Tempe, CO: Education and the Public Interest Center & Education Policy Research Unit. Retrieved February 23, 2009, from http://epicpolicy.org/publication/preschooleducation

Barnett, W. S., Epstein, D. J., Friedman, A. H., Boyd, J. S., & Hustadt, J. T. (2008b). *The state of preschool 2008: State preschool yearbook*. New Brunswick, NJ: National Institute for Early Education Research.

Barnett, W. S., Jung, K., Yarosz, D. J., Thomas, J., Hornbeck, A., Stechuk, R., & Burns, S. (2008a). Educational effects of the Tools of the Mind Curriculum: A randomized trial. *Early Childhood Research Quarterly, 23*(3), 299–313.

Barnett, W. S., Lamy, C., & Jung, K. (2005). *The effects of state prekindergarten programs on young children's school readiness in five states* (National Institute for Early Education Research Policy Report). New Brunswick, NJ: National Institute for Early Education Research. Retrieved October 9, 2009, from http://nieer.org/docs/index.php?DocID=129

Barnett, W. S., & Yarosz, D. J. (2007, November). *Who goes to preschool and why does it matter?*

(Preschool Policy Brief, Issue 15). New Brunswick, NJ: National Institute for Early Education Research. Retrieved October 9, 2009, from http://nieer.org/resources/policybriefs/15.pdf

Barnett, W. S., Yarosz, D. J., Thomas, J., & Hornbeck, A. (2006). *Educational effectiveness of a Vygotskian approach to preschool education: A randomized trial.* Rutgers, NJ: National Institute for Early Education Research.

Barrera, I., & Corso, R. M., with Macpherson, D. (2003). *Skilled dialogue: Strategies for responding to cultural diversity in early childhood.* Baltimore: Paul H. Brookes.

Beck, I. L., McKeown, M. G., & Kucan, L. (2002). *Bringing words to life: Robust vocabulary instruction.* New York: Guilford Press.

Bell, S. H., Carr, V., Denno, D., Johnson, L. J., & Phillips, L. R. (2004). *Challenging behaviors in early childhood settings: Creating a place for all children.* Baltimore: Paul H. Brookes.

Beneke, S. J., Ostrosky, M. M., & Katz, L. G. (2008). Calendar time for young children: Good intentions gone awry. *Young Children, 63*(3), 12–16.

Bennett, T., Eatman, J., Garcia, G. E., Halle, J., McCollum, J., Ostrosky, M., et al. (2001). *Cross-cultural considerations in early childhood special education* (Technical Report #14). Urbana-Champaign, IL: University of Illinois, Culturally and Linguistically Appropriate Services (CLAS).

Berk, L. E. (2006). Looking at the kindergarten child. In D. F. Gullo (Ed.), *K today: Teaching and learning in the kindergarten year* (pp. 11–25). Washington, DC: National Association for the Education of Young Children.

Berk, L. E. (2008). *Infants and children: Prenatal through middle childhood* (6th ed.). Boston: Pearson/Allyn & Bacon.

Berk, L. E., Mann, T. D., & Ogan, A. T. (2006). Make-believe play: Wellspring for development of self-regulation. In D. G. Singer, R. M. Golinkoff, & K. Hirsh-Pasek (Eds.), *Play = learning: How play motivates and enhances children's cognitive and social-emotional growth* (pp. 74–100). New York: Oxford University Press.

Berk, L. E., & Winsler, A. (1995). *Scaffolding children's learning: Vygotsky and early childhood education.* Washington, DC: National Association for the Education of Young Children.

Bernath, P., & Masi, W. (2006). Smart school snacks: A comprehensive preschool nutrition education program. *Young Children, 61*(3), 20–24.

Berrueta-Clement, J. R., Schweinhart, L. J., Barnett, W. S., Epstein, A. S., & Weikart, D. P. (1984). *Changed lives: The effects of the Perry preschool program on youths through age 19.* Ypsilanti, MI: High/Scope Press.

Bierman, K. L., Domitrovich, C. E., Nix, R. L., Gest, S. D., Welsh, J. A., Greenberg, M. T., et al. (2008). Promoting academic and social–emotional school readiness: The Head Start REDI program. *Child Development, 79*(6), 1802–1817.

Bixler, R. D., Floyd, M. E., & Hammutt, W. E. (2002). Environmental socialization: Qualitative tests of the childhood play hypothesis. *Environment and Behavior, 34*(6), 795–818.

Bjorkqvist, K. (1994). Sex differences in physical, verbal, and indirect aggression: A review of recent research. *Sex Roles, 30,* 177–188.

Blagojevic, B. (2003). Funding technology: Does it make cents? *Young Children, 58*(6), 28–33.

Blair, C., & Razza, R. C. (2007). Relating effortful control, executive functional and false belief understanding to emerging math and literacy ability in kindergarten. *Child Development, 78*(2), 647–663.

Block, J. H. (1983). Differential premises arising from differential socialization of the sexes: Some conjectures. *Child Development, 54*(6), 1335–1354.

Bodrova, E., & Leong, D. J. (2001). *The Tools of the Mind project: A case study of implementing the Vygotskian approach in American early childhood and primary classrooms.* Geneva: International Bureau of Education, UNESCO.

Bodrova, E., & Leong, D. J. (2003). The importance of being playful. *Educational Leadership, 60*(7), 50–53.

Bodrova, E., & Leong, D. J. (2005). Uniquely preschool. *Educational Leadership, 63*(1), 44–47.

Bodrova, E., & Leong, D. J. (2006). Self-regulation as a key to school readiness: How early childhood teachers can promote this critical competency. In M. Zaslow & I. Martinez-Beck (Eds.), *Critical issues in early childhood professional development* (pp. 203–224). Baltimore: Paul H. Brookes.

Bodrova, E., & Leong, D. J. (2007). *Tools of the Mind: The Vygotskian approach to early childhood education.* New York: Merrill/Prentice Hall.

Bogard, K., & Takanishi, R. (2005). PK–3: An aligned and coordinated approach to education for children 3 to 8 years old. *Social Policy Report, 19*(3).

Bowlby, J. (1969/2000). *Attachment. Vol. 1 Attachment and loss.* New York: Basic.

Bowman, B. T. (1992). Reaching potentials of minority children through developmentally and culturally appropriate programs. In S. Bredekamp & T. Rosegrant (Eds.), *Reaching potentials: Appropriate curriculum and assessment* (Vol. 1, pp. 128–136). Washington, DC: National Association for the Education of Young Children.

Bowman, B. T. (2006). Standards: At the heart of educational equity. *Young Children, 61*(5), 42–48.

Bowman, B., Donovan, M. S., & Burns, S. (Eds.). (2001). *Eager to learn: Educating our preschoolers* (National Research Council, Committee on Early Childhood Pedagogy Report). Washington, DC: National Academies Press.

Bowman, B. T., & Stott, F. M. (1994). Understanding development in a cultural context: The challenge for teachers. In B. L. Mallory & R. S. New (Eds.), *Diversity and developmentally appropriate practices: Challenges for early childhood education* (pp. 119–133). New York: Teachers College Press.

Boyd, J., Barnett, W. S., Bodrova, E., Leong, D. J., & Gomby, D. (2005, March). *Promoting children's social emotional development through preschool* (Preschool Policy Report). New Brunswick, NJ: National Institute for Early Education Research.

Bransford, J. D., Brown, A. L., & Cocking, R. R. (Eds.). (2000). *How people learn: Brain, mind, experience and school* (expanded ed.). Washington, DC: National Academies Press.

Brazelton, T. B., & Greenspan, S. I. (2000). *The irreducible needs of children: What every child must have to grow, learn, and flourish.* New York: Perseus.

Bredekamp, S. (Ed.). (1987). *Developmentally appropriate practice in early childhood programs serving children from birth through age 8* (expanded ed.). Washington, DC: National Association for the Education of Young Children.

Bredekamp, S. (1997a). Developmentally appropriate practice: The early childhood teacher as decision maker. In S. Bredekamp & C. Copple (Eds.), *Developmentally appropriate practice in early childhood programs* (rev. ed., pp. 33–52). Washington, DC: National Association for the Education of Young Children.

Bredekamp, S. (1997b). NAEYC issues revised position statement on developmentally appropriate practice in early childhood programs. *Young Children, 52*(2), 34–40.

Bredekamp, S. (2001). Improving professional practice: A letter to Patty Smith Hill. In *NAEYC at 75: Reflections on the Past, Challenges for the Future* (pp. 89–124). Washington, DC: National Association for the Education of Young Children.

Bredekamp, S. (2002). Language and early childhood programs. In C. T. Adger, C. E. Snow, & D. Christian (Eds.), *What teachers need to know about language.* Washington, DC: Center for Applied Linguistics.

Bredekamp, S. (2004). Play and school readiness. In E. F. Zigler, D. G. Singer & S. J. Bishop-Josef (Eds.), *Children's play: The roots of reading* (pp. 159–174). Washington, DC: Zero to Three Press.

Bredekamp, S. (2008a). Beyond developmentally appropriate practice. Keynote address at the annual meeting of the Southern Early Childhood Association, Covington, KY.

Bredekamp, S. (2008b). Malaguzzi's metaphors: The power of imagery to transform educational practice and policy. In L. Gandini, S. Etheredge, & L. Hill (Eds.),

Insights and inspirations from Reggio Emilia: Stories of teachers and children from North America (pp. 48–49). Worcester, MA: Davis Publications.

Bredekamp, S. (2009). Early learning standards and developmentally appropriate practice: Contradictory or compatible? In S. Feeney, A. Galper, & C. Seefeldt (Eds.), *Continuing issues in early childhood education* (pp. 258–271). Upper Saddle River, NJ: Pearson Merrill.

Bredekamp, S., & Copple, C. (Eds.). (1997). *Developmentally appropriate practice in early childhood programs* (rev. ed.). Washington, DC: National Association for the Education of Young Children.

Bredekamp, S., & Glowacki, S. (1996). The first decade of NAEYC Accreditation: Growth and impact on the field. In S. Bredekamp & B. A. Willer (Eds.), *NAEYC accreditation: A decade of learning and the years ahead* (pp. 1–10). Washington, DC: National Association for the Education of Young Children.

Bredekamp, S., & Rosegrant, T. (Eds.). (1992). *Reaching potentials: Appropriate curriculum and assessment for young children* (Vol. 1). Washington, DC: National Association for the Education of Young Children.

Bredekamp, S., & Rosegrant, T. (Eds.). (1995). Reaching potentials through transforming curriculum, assessment, and teaching. In S. Bredekamp & T. Rosegrant (Eds.), *Reaching potentials: Transforming early childhood curriculum and assessment* (pp. 15–22). Washington, DC: National Association for the Education of Young Children.

Bredekamp, S., & Shepard, L. (1998). Assessing young children's learning and development. In R. Brandt (Ed.), *Assessing student learning: New rules, new realities* (pp. 93–108). Arlington, VA: Educational Research Service and Alliance for Curriculum Reform.

Bretherton, I., & Munholland, K. A. (2008). Internal working models in attachment relationships: Elaborating a central construct in attachment theory. In J. Cassidy and P. Shaver (Eds.), *Handbook of attachment: Theory, research and clinical application* (2nd ed.). New York: Guilford Press.

Bricker, D. (Ed.). (2002). *Assessment, evaluation, and programming system (AEPS) for infants and children.* Baltimore: Paul H. Brookes.

Bricker, D., Pretti-Frontczak, K., & McComas, N. R. (1998). *An activity-based approach to early intervention* (2nd ed.). Baltimore: Paul H. Brookes.

Bronfenbrenner, U. (1979). *The ecology of human development: Experiments by nature and design.* Cambridge, MA: Harvard University Press.

Bronfenbrenner, U. (Ed.). (2004). *Making human beings human: Bioecological perspectives on human development.* Thousand Oaks, CA: Sage.

Brown, L., & Pollitt, E. (1996). Malnutrition, poverty, and intellectual development, *Scientific American, 274,* 38–43.

Brown, M. (1998). *Arthur lost and found: An Arthur adventure.* New York: Little, Brown & Co.

Bruder, M. B. (2001). *The individual family service plan (IFSP)* (ERIC Digest). Retrieved November 27, 2007, from http://www.ericdigests.org/2001-4/ifsp.html

Bryant, D., Barbarin, O., Bryant, D., Burchinal, M., Chang, F., Clifford, R., et al. (2005). *Six-state prekindergarten study.* Chapel Hill, ND: Frank Porter Graham Child Development Institute, National Center for Early Development and Learning.

Bryant, D. M., Burchinal, M., Lau, L. B., & Sparling, J. J. (1994). Family and classroom correlates of Head Start's developmental outcomes. *Early Childhood Research Quarterly, 9,* 289–309.

Bukatko, D., & Daehler, M. W. (2003). *Child development: A thematic approach* (4th ed.). Boston: Houghton Mifflin.

Bukowski, W. M., & Sandberg, D. (1999). Peer relationships and quality of life. *Acta Pediatrica Supplements, 428,* 108–109.

Burchinal, M., Howes, C., Pianta, R., Bryant, D., Early, D., Clifford, R., et al. (2008). Predicting child outcomes at the end of kindergarten from the quality of pre-kindergarten teacher–child interactions and instruction. *Applied Developmental Science, 12*(3), 140–153.

Burchinal, M. R., Peisner-Feinberg, E., Pianta, R., & Howes, C. (2002). Development of academic skills from preschool through second grade: Family and classroom predictors of developmental trajectories. *Journal of School Psychology, 40,* pp. 415–436.

Burton, V. L. (1969). *The little house.* New York: Houghton Mifflin.

Burts, D. C., Hart, C. H., Charlesworth, R., DeWolf, D. M., Ray, J., Manual, K., et al. (1993). Developmental appropriateness of kindergarten programs and academic outcomes in first grade. *Journal of Research in Childhood Education, 8,* 23–31.

Burts, D. C., Hart, C. H., Charlesworth, R., Fleege, P. O., Mosely, J., & Thomasson, R. H. (1992). Observed activities and stress behaviors of children in developmentally appropriate and inappropriate kindergarten classrooms. *Early Childhood Research Quarterly, 7,* 297–318.

Buysse, V., Goldman, B. D., West, T., & Hollingsworth, H. (2007). Friendships in early childhood: Implications for early education and intervention. In W. H. Brown, S. L. Odom, & S. R. McConnell (Eds.), *Social competence of young children: Risk, disability, and evidence-based practices* (2nd ed.). Baltimore: Paul H. Brookes.

Buysse, V., Peisner-Feinberg, E., & Berger, L. (2008). Recognition & Response: RTI goes to pre-K. Paper presented at the Global Summit 2008, U.S. Department of Education.

Buysse, V., & Wesley, P. (Eds.). (2006). *Evidence-based practice in the early childhood field.* Washington, DC: Zero to Three Press.

California Tomorrow. (2007, Summer). *Changing times* (newsletter). Oakland, CA: Author.

Calkins, S. D., & Williford, A. P. (2009). Taming the terrible twos: Self-regulation and school readiness. In O. A. Barbarin & B. H. Wasik (Eds.), *Handbook of child development and early education: Research to practice* (pp. 172–198). New York: Guilford Press.

Campbell, F. A., Ramey, C. T., Pungello, E. P., Sparling, J. J., & Miller-Johnson, S. (2002). Early childhood education: Young adult outcomes from the Abecedarian Project. *Applied Developmental Science, 6,* 42–57.

Campbell, F. A., Wasik, B. H., Pungello, E. P., Burchinal, M., Barbarin, O., Kainz, K., et al. (2008). Young adult outcomes from the Abecedarian and CARE early childhood educational interventions. *Early Childhood Research Quarterly, 23*(4), 452–466.

Campbell, N. D., Appelbaum, J. C., Martinson, K., & Martin, E. (2000). *Be all that you can be: Lessons from the military for improving our nation's child care system.* Washington, DC: National Women's Law Center.

Carle, E. (1969). *The very hungry caterpillar.* New York: Philomel, Penguin Group.

Carter, M., & Curtis, D. (1994). *Training teachers: A harvest of theory and practice.* St. Paul, MN: Redleaf Press.

Case, A., Lubotsky, D., & Paxson, C. (2005). Economic status and health in childhood: The origins of the gradient. *American Economic Review, 12,* 1308–1334.

Case, R., & Okamoto, Y. (1996). *The role of central conceptual structures in the development of children's thought* (Monographs of the Society of Research in Child Development, Vol. 61, No. 2, Serial no. 246). Chicago: University of Chicago Press.

Casey, B. (2004). Mathematics problem-solving adventures: A language-arts-based supplementary series for early childhood that focuses on spatial sense. In D. H. Clements, J. Sarama, & A.-M. DiBiase (Eds.), *Engaging young children in mathematics: Standards for early childhood mathematics education* (pp. 377–389). Mahwah, NJ: Lawrence Erlbaum Associates.

Casey, B., Kersh, J. E., & Young, J. M. (2004). Storytelling sagas: An effective medium for teaching early childhood mathematics. *Early Childhood Research Quarterly, 19*(1), 167–172.

Casey, M. B., Erkut, S., Ceder, I., & Young, J. M. (2008). Use of a storytelling context to improve girls' and boys' geometry skills in kindergarten. *Journal of Applied Developmental Psychology, 29,* 29–48.

Center on the Developing Child. (2007). *A science-based framework for early childhood policy: Using evidence to improve outcomes in learning, behavior, and health for vulnerable children*. Cambridge, MA: Harvard.

Centers for Disease Control and Prevention. (2009). Childhood overweight and obesity. Retrieved October 21, 2009, from http://www.cdc.gov/obesity/childhood/index.html

Cervantes, A., & Callanan, M. (1998). Labels and explanations in mother–child emotion talk: Age and gender differentiation. *Developmental Psychology, 34*(1), 88–98.

Chall, J. (1967). *Learning to read: The great debate*. New York: McGraw Hill.

Chalufour, I., & Worth, K. (2004). *Building structures with young children* (Young Scientist Series). St. Paul, MN: Redleaf Press.

Chalufour, I., & Worth, K. (2005). *Exploring water with young children* (Young Scientist Series). St. Paul, MN: Redleaf Press.

Chang, F., Crawford, G., Early, D., & Bryant, D. (2007). Spanish-speaking children's social and language development in pre-kindergarten classrooms. *Journal of Early Education and Development, 18*(2), 243–269.

Child Trends Data Bank. (2005). *Racial and ethnic composition of the child population*. Washington, DC: Author.

Child Trends. 2007. Child Trends data bank. http://www.childtrends.org.

Child Welfare Information Gateway. (2008). *Parent education*. Washington, DC: U.S. Children's Bureau. Retrieved October 9, 2009, from http://www.childwelfare.gov/pubs/issue_briefs/parented

Children's Defense Fund. (2007). Cradle to grave pipeline: Poverty. Retrieved from http://www.childrensdefense.org/site/PageServer/pagename=Programs_Cradle_Poverty

Christian, L. G. (2006). Understanding families: Applying family systems theory to early childhood practice. *Young Children, 61*(1), 12–20.

Christie, J. F., & Roskos, K. A. (2006). Standards, science, and the role of play in early literacy education. In D. G. Singer, R. M. Golinkoff, & K. Hirsh-Pasek (Eds.), *Play = learning: How play motivates and enhances children's cognitive and social-emotional growth* (pp. 57–73). New York: Oxford University Press.

Cipani, E. C., & Spooner, F. (1994). *Curricular & instructional approaches for persons with severe disabilities*. Boston: Allyn & Bacon.

Clark, K. F., & Graves, M. F. (2005). Scaffolding students' comprehension of text. *The Reading Teacher, 58*(6), 570–580.

Clarke, L. K. (1988). Invented versus traditional spelling in first graders' writings: Effects on learning to spell and read. *Research in the Teaching of English, 22*, 281–309.

Clay, M. (1985). *The early detection of reading difficulties* (3rd ed.). Portsmouth, NH: Heinemann.

Clements, D. H., & Sarama, J. (2003). Young children and technology: What does the research say? *Young Children, 58*(6), 34–40.

Clements, D. H., & Sarama, J. (2007a). Early childhood mathematics learning. In F. K. Lester, Jr. (Ed.), *Second handbook of research on mathematics teaching and learning* (pp. 461–555). New York: Information Age Publishing.

Clements, D. H., & Sarama, J. (2007b). Effects of a preschool mathematics curriculum: Summative research on the Building Blocks project. *Journal for Research in Mathematics Education, 38*(2), 136–163.

Clements, D. H., & Sarama, J. (2008). Experimental evaluation of the effects of a research-based preschool mathematics curriculum. *American Educational Research Journal, 45*, 443–494.

Clements, D. H., & Sarama, J. (2009). *Learning and teaching early math: The learning trajectories approach*. New York: Routledge.

Clements, D. H., Sarama, J., & DiBiase, A. M. (Eds.). (2004). *Engaging young children in mathematics: Standards for early childhood mathematics education*. Mahwah, NJ: Lawrence Erlbaum Associates.

Coleman, M. R., Buysse, V., & Neitzel, J. (2006). Establishing the evidence base for an emerging early childhood practice: Recognition & Response. In V. Buysse & P. W. Wesley (Eds.), *Evidence-based practice in the early childhood field* (pp. 196–225). Washington, DC: Zero to Three Press.

Coleman, M. R., Roth, F. P., & West, T. (2009). *Roadmap to Pre-K RTI: Applying Response to Intervention in preschool settings*. New York: National Center for Learning Disabilities. Retrieved October 9, 2009, from http://www.rtinetwork.org/PreKRTIroadmap

Colker, L. (2005). *The cooking book: Fostering young children's learning and delight*. Washington, DC: National Association for the Education of Young Children.

Colker, L. (2008). Twelve characteristics of effective early childhood teachers. *Young Children, 63*(2), 68–73. Retrieved from http://www.journal.naeyc.org/btj/200803

Comune di Reggio Emilia. (1987). *The hundred languages of children: Narrative of the Possible* (Exhibition Catalog).

Congressional Research Service. (2005). *Homelessness: Recent statistics, targeted federal programs, and recent legislation*. Washington, DC: Library of Congress.

Copley, J. V. (2007). *Mathematics: The creative curriculum approach*. Washington, DC: Teaching Strategies.

Copple, C., & Bredekamp, S. (2006). *Basics of developmentally appropriate practice: An introduction for teachers of children 3 to 6*. Washington, DC: National Association for the Education of Young Children.

Copple, C., & Bredekamp, S. (Eds.). (2009). *Developmentally appropriate practice in early childhood programs serving children from birth through age 8* (rev. ed.). Washington, DC: National Association for the Education of Young Children.

Copple, C. E., Cocking, R. R., & Matthews, W. S. (1984). Objects, symbols, and substitutes: The nature of the cognitive activity during symbolic play. In T. D. Yawkey & A. D. Pellegrini (Eds.), *Child's play: Developmental and applied* (pp. 105–124). Hillsdale, NJ: Lawrence Erlbaum Associates.

Copple, C., Sigel, I. E., & Saunders, R. (1984). *Educating the young thinker: Classroom strategies for cognitive growth*. Hillsdale, NJ: Lawrence Erlbaum Associates.

Cost, Quality and Child Care Outcomes Study Team. (1995). *Cost, quality, and child care outcomes in child care centers* (2nd ed.). Denver: University of Colorado at Denver, Economics Department.

Costin, S. E., & Jones, D. C. (1992). Friendship as a factor of emotional responsiveness and prosocial interventions among young children. *Developmental Psychology, 28*, 941–947.

Council of Chief State School Officers & Early Childhood Education Assessment Consortium. (2007). *The words we use: A glossary of terms for early childhood education standards and assessment*. Retrieved March 2009, from http://www.ccsso.org/Projects/scass/projects/early-child-education-asessment-consosrtium/puiblications-and-products/2892.cfm

Craig, G. J., & Baucum, D. (2002). *Human development* (9th ed.). Upper Saddle River, NJ: Prentice Hall.

Crick, N., Casas, J. F., & Mosher, M. (1997). Relational and overt aggression in preschool. *Developmental Psychology, 33*(4), 579–588.

Crick, N. R., & Grotpeter, J. (1995). Relational aggression, gender, and social-psychological adjustment. *Child Development, 66*, 710–722.

Cripe, J. W., Hanline, M. F., & Daley, S. E. (1997). Preparing practitioners for planning intervention for natural environments. In P. J. Winton, J. A. McCollum, & C. Catlett (Eds.), *Reforming personnel preparation in early intervention: Issues, models, and practical strategies* (pp. 337– 362). Baltimore: Paul H. Brookes.

Cummins, J. (1979). Linguistic interdependence and the educational development of bilingual children. *Review of Educational Research, 49*, 222–251.

Cunningham, A. E., & Davidson, M. (2007). Professional development in preschool literacy curricula: Developing a framework for increasing teacher knowledge and skills. Paper presented at the biennial meeting of the Society for Research in Child Development, Boston, MA.

Cunningham, C. E., & Osborn, D. K. (1979). A historical examination of blacks in early childhood education. *Young Children, 34*(3), 20–29.

Cuppens, V., Rosenow, N., & Wike, J. R. (2007). *Learning with nature idea book*. Lincoln, NE: National Arbor Day Foundation.

Datar, A. (2003). The impact of changes in kindergarten entrance age policies on children's academic achievement and the child care needs of families (RAND Dissertation Series). Retrieved from http://www.rand.org

Datta, L., McHale, C., & Mitchell, S. (1976). *The effects of Head Start classroom experience on some aspects of child development: A summary report of national evaluations, 1966–1969* (DHEW Publication No. OHD-76-30088). Washington, DC: U.S. Government Printing Office.

Davidson, J. (1996). *Emergent literacy and dramatic play in early education.* Albany, NY: Delmar.

Day, C. B. (2004). *Essentials for child development associates working with young children* (rev. ed.). Washington, DC: Council for Professional Recognition.

Day, C. B. (Ed.). (2005). *Essentials for child development associates working with young children: Seminar instructor's guide* (rev. ed.). Washington, DC: Council for Professional Recognition.

Day, C. B. (2006a). Every child is a cultural being. In J. R. Lally, P. L. Mangione, & D. Greenwald (Eds.), *Concepts for care: Essays on infant/toddler development and learning* (pp. 97–99). San Francisco: WestEd.

Day, C. B. (2006b). Leveraging diversity to benefit children's social–emotional development and school readiness. In B. Bowman & E. K. Moore (Eds.), *School readiness and social–emotional development: Perspectives on cultural diversity* (pp. 23–32). Washington, DC: National Black Child Development Institute.

De Bellis, M. D., Keshaven, M. S., Clark, D. B., Caseey, B. J., Giedd, J. B., Boring, A. M., et al. (1999). Developmental traumatology. Part 2: Brain development. *Biological Psychiatry, 45,* 1271–1284.

Delpit, L. (2006). *Other people's children: Cultural conflict in the classroom* (updated ed.). New York: New Press.

Denham, S. A. (2006). The emotional basis of learning and development in early childhood education. In B. Spodek & O. N. Saracho (Eds.), *The handbook of research on early childhood education* (2nd ed., pp. 85–103). Mahwah, NJ: Lawrence Erlbaum Associates.

Denham, S., & Weissberg, R. P. (2004). Social–emotional learning in early childhood: What we know and where to go from here. In E. Chesebrough, P. King, T. Gullato, & M. Bloom (Eds.), *A blueprint for the promotion of prosocial behavior in early childhood.* New York: Kluwer Academic/Plenum Publishers.

Denton, K., & West, J. (2002). *Children's reading and mathematics achievement in kindergarten and first grade.* Washington, DC: National Center for Education Statistics.

Derman-Sparks, L. (1992). Reaching potentials through antibias, multicultural curriculum. In S. Bredekamp & T. Rosegrant (Eds.), *Reaching potentials: Appropriate curriculum and assessment for young children* (Vol. 1). Washington, DC: National Association for the Education of Young Children.

Derman-Sparks, L., & ABC Task Force. (1989). *Anti-bias curriculum: Tools for empowering young children.* Washington, DC: National Association for the Education of Young Children.

Derman-Sparks, L., & Edwards, J. O. (2010). *Anti-bias education: Empowering our children and ourselves.* Washington, DC: National Association for the Education of Young Children.

Derman-Sparks, L., & Phillips, C. B. (1997). *Teaching/learning anti-racism: A developmental approach.* New York: Teachers College Press.

Derman-Sparks, L., & Ramsey, P. G. (2006). *What if all the kids are white? Anti-bias, multicultural education with young children and families.* New York: Teachers College Press.

Desouza, J. M. S., & Czerniak, C. M. (2002, Summer/Spring). Social behaviors and gender differences among preschoolers: Implications for science activities. *Journal of Research in Childhood Education, 16*(2), 175–188.

DeVries, R., & Van, B. (1994). *Moral classrooms, moral children: Creating a constructivist atmosphere in early education.* New York: Teachers College Press.

Dewey, J. (1900). *The school and society.* Chicago: University of Chicago Press.

Dewey, J. (1916). *Democracy and education.* New York: Free Press.

Dewey, J. (1929). *My pedagogic creed.* Washington, DC: Progressive Education Association.

Dichtelmiller, M. L. (2004). New insights into infant/toddler assessment. *Young Children, 59*(1), 30–33.

Dickinson, D. K. (2001a). Book reading in preschool classrooms: Is recommended practice common? In D. Dickinson & P. Tabors (Eds.), *Beginning literacy with language: Young children learning at home and school* (pp. 175–203). Baltimore: Paul H. Brookes.

Dickinson, D. (2001b). Large-group and free-play times: Conversational settings supporting language and literacy development. In D. Dickinson & P. Tabors (Eds.), *Beginning literacy with language: Young children learning at home and school* (pp. 223–256). Baltimore: Paul H. Brookes.

Dickinson, D. K., & Neuman, S. B. (Eds.). (2006). *Handbook of early literacy research* (Vol. 2). New York: Guilford Press.

Dickinson, D., & Smith, M. W. (1993). Long-term effects of preschool teachers' book readings on low-income children's vocabulary and story comprehension. *Reading Research Quarterly, 29*(2), 104–122.

Dickinson, D., & Tabors, P. (Eds.). (2001). *Beginning literacy with language: Young children learning at home and school.* Baltimore: Paul H. Brookes.

Division for Early Childhood. (2007). *Promoting positive outcomes for children with disabilities: Recommendations for curriculum, assessment, and program evaluation.* Missoula, MT: Author.

Division for Early Childhood & National Association for the Education of Young Children. (2009). *Early childhood inclusion: A joint position statement of the Division for Early Childhood (DEC) and the National Association for the Education of Young Children (NAEYC).* Chapel Hill: The University of North Carolina, FPG Child Development Institute. Retrieved October 9, 2009, from http://community.fpg.unc.edu/resources/articles/Early_Childhood_Inclusion

Dodge, D. T., Colker, L. J., & Heroman, C. (2000). *Connecting content, teaching, and learning: A supplement to the creative curriculum for early childhood.* Washington, DC: Teaching Strategies.

Dodge, D. T., Colker, L. J., & Heroman, C. (2002). *The creative curriculum for preschool* (4th ed.). Washington DC: Teaching Strategies.

Dodge, D. T., Rudick, S., & Berke, K. (2004). *The creative curriculum for infants, toddlers, and twos* (2nd ed.). Washington, DC: Teaching Strategies.

Dolgin, K., & Kim, S. (1994). Adolescents' disclosure to best and good friends: The effects of gender and topic intimacy. *Social Development, 32,* pp. 146–157.

Duncan, G. J., Dowsett, C. J., Claessens, A., Magnuson, K., Huston, A. C., Klebanov, P., et al. (2007). School readiness and later achievement. *Developmental Psychology, 43,* 1428–1446.

Dunst, C. (2001). Participation of young children with disabilities in community learning activities. In M. J. Guralnick (Ed.), *Early childhood inclusion: Focus on change.* Baltimore: Paul H. Brookes.

Dunst, C. J., Hamby, D., Trivette, C. M., Raab, M., & Bruder, M. B. (2000). Everyday family and community life and children's naturally occurring learning opportunities. *Journal of Early Intervention, 23,* 151–164.

Dyson, A. H. (2001). Writing and children's symbolic repertoires: Development unhinged. In S. B. Neuman & D. K. Dickinson (Eds.), *Handbook of early literacy research.* New York: Guilford Press.

Early, D. M., Barbarin, O., Bryant, D., Burchinal, M., Chang, F., Clifford, R., et al. (2005). *Prekindergarten in eleven states: NCEDL's multi-state study of pre-kindergarten and study of state-wide early education programs (SWEEP).* Chapel Hill, NC. Retrieved August 8, 2008, from http://www.fpg.unc.edu/NCEDL/pdfs/SWEEP_MS_summary_final.pdf

Early, D. M., Bryant, D. M., Pianta, R. C., Clifford, R. M., Burchinal, M. R., Ritchie, S., et al. (2006). Are teachers' education, major, and credentials related to classroom quality and children's academic gains in pre-kindergarten? *Early Childhood Research Quarterly, 21*(2), 174–195.

Early, D. M., & Winton, P. (2001). Preparing the workforce: Early childhood teacher preparation at 2- and 4-year institutions of higher education. *Early Childhood Research Quarterly, 16*(3), 285–306.

Edwards, C., Gandini, L., & Forman, G. (1998). *The hundred languages of children: The Reggio Emilia approach—Advanced reflections* (2nd ed.). Greenwich, CT: Ablex.

Ehri, L. C., & Roberts, T. (2006). The roots of learning to read and write: Acquisition of letters and phonemic awareness. In D. K. Dickinson & S. B. Neuman (Eds.), *Handbook of early literacy research* (Vol. 2, pp. 113–131). New York: Guilford Press.

Elias, C. L., & Berk, L. E. (2002). Self-regulation in young children: Is there a role for sociodramatic play? *Early Childhood Research Quarterly, 17*(2), 216–238.

Elkind, D. (2001). *The hurried child: Growing up too fast, too soon* (2nd ed.). Cambridge, MA: DaCapo Press.

Elkind, D. (2008). *The power of play: Learning what comes naturally*. Cambridge, MA: DaCapo Press.

Enz, B., & Christie, J. (1997). Teacher play interaction styles: Effects on play behavior and relationships with teacher training and experience. *International Journal of Early Childhood Education, 2,* 55–69.

Epstein, A. S. (2003). How planning and reflections develop young children's thinking skills. *Young Children, 58*(5), 28–36.

Epstein, A. S. (2007a). *Essentials of active learning in preschool: Getting to know the High/Scope curriculum*. Ypsilanti, MI: High/Scope Press.

Epstein, A. S. (2007b). *The intentional teacher: Choosing the best strategies for young children's learning*. Washington, DC: National Association for the Education of Young Children.

Epstein, A. S. (2009). *Me, you, us: Social–emotional learning in preschool.* Ypsilanti, MI: High/Scope Educational Research Foundation.

Epstein, A. S., Schweinhart, L. J., & McAdoo, L. (1996). *Models of early childhood education*. Ypsilanti, MI: High/Scope Educational Research Foundation.

Epstein, A. S., & Trimis, E. (2002.) *Supporting young artists: The development of the visual arts in young children*. Ypsilanti, MI: High/Scope Educational Research Foundation.

Epstein, J. L., Sanders, M. G., Simon, B., Salina, K., Jansorn, N., & Van Voorhis, F. (2002). *School, family, and community partnerships: Your handbook for action* (2nd ed.). Thousand Oaks, CA: Corwin Press.

Erikson, E. (1950/1963).*Childhood and society* (2nd ed.). New York: Norton.

Erwin, P. (1998). *Friendship in childhood and adolescence*. New York: Routledge.

Espinosa, L. (2007). English language learners as they enter school. In R. Pianta & K. Snow (Eds.), *School readiness, early learning, and the transition to school.* Baltimore: Paul H. Brookes.

Espinosa, L. (2008). *Challenging common myths about young English language learners*. New York: Foundation for Child Development.

Espinosa, L. M. (2010). *Getting it right for young children from diverse backgrounds: Applying research to improve practice.* Upper Saddle River, NJ: Pearson.

FairTest. (2006). *What's wrong with standardized tests?* Boston: National Center for Fair and Open Testing. Retrieved October 9, 2009, from http://www.fairtest.org/facts/whatwron.htm

FairTest. (2007). *Criterion- and standards-referenced tests*. Boston: National Center for Fair and Open Testing. Retrieved August 31, 2009, from http://fairtest.org/facts/csrtests.html

Fantuzzo, J., Perry, M. A., & McDermott, P. (2004). Preschool approaches to learning and their relationship to other relevant classroom competencies for low-income children. *School Psychology Quarterly, 19*(3), 212–230.

Fass, S., & Cauthen, N. K. (2008). *Who are America's poor children? The official story*. New York: National Center for Children in Poverty.

Feeney, S., & Freeman, N. K. (2004). *Ethics and the early childhood educator: Using the NAEYC code*. Washington, DC: National Association for the Education of Young Children.

Feeney, S., Freeman, N. K., & Moravcik, E. (2000). *Teaching the NAEYC code of ethical conduct.* Washington, DC: National Association for the Education of Young Children.

Feingold, A. (1994). Gender differences in variability in intellectual abilities: A cross-cultural perspective. *Sex Roles, 30,* 81–91.

Fernald, A., & Kuhl, P. (1987). Acoustic determinants of infant preference for motherese speech. *Infant Behavior and Development, 10,* 279–293.

Fisher, R., Ury, W., & Patton, B. (1992). *Getting to yes: Negotiating agreement without giving in* (2nd ed.). Boston: Houghton Mifflin Harcourt.

Fjortoft, I. (2001). The natural environment as a playground for children: The impact of outdoor play activities in pre-primary school children. *Early Childhood Education Journal, 29*(2), 111–117.

Fjortoft, I., & Sageie, J. (2000). The natural environment as a playground for children: Landscape description and analysis of a natural landscape. *Landscape and Urban Planning, 48*(1/2), 83–97.

Forman, G. (1994). Different media, different languages. In L. G. Katz & B. Cesarone (Eds.), *Reflections on the Reggio Emilia approach*. Urbana, IL: ERIC Clearinghouse on Elementary and Early Childhood Education.

Foundation for Child Development. (2008). *America's vanishing potential: The case for pre-K–3rd education.* New York: Author.

Fox, L., Dunlap, G., Hemmeter, M. L., Joseph, G. E., & Strain, P. S. (2003). The teaching pyramid: A model for supporting social competence and preventing challenging behavior in young children. *Young Children, 58*(4), 48–52.

FPG Child Development Institute. (2007a). Helping boys of color succeed. *Early Developments, 11*(2), 7–12.

FPG Child Development Institute. (2007b). RTI goes to pre-K: An early intervening system called Recognition and Response. *Early Developments, 11*(1), 7–10.

FPG Child Development Institute. (2008). How is pre-K quality measured? Findings from NCEDL suggest new directions. *Early Developments, 12*(1), 5–9.

Frede, E., & Ackerman, D. J. (2006). *Curriculum decision-making: Dimensions to consider*. New Brunswick, NJ: National Institute for Early Education Research.

Frede, E., & Barnett, S. (1992). Developmentally appropriate public school preschool: A study of implementation of the High/Scope curriculum and its effects on disadvantaged children's skills at first grade. *Early Childhood Research Quarterly, 7*(4), 483–499.

Freeman, D. (2001). *Corduroy goes to the doctor*. New York: Penguin Putnam.

French, L. (2004). Science as the center of a coherent, integrated early childhood curriculum. *Early Childhood Research Quarterly, 19*(1), 138–149.

Fromboluti, C. S., and Seefeldt, C. (2000). *Early childhood: Where learning begins. Geography, with activities for children ages 2 to 5 years of age* (2nd ed.). Washington, DC: National Institute on Early Childhood Development and Education.

Fuller, B. F. (2007). *Standardized childhood: The political and cultural struggle over early education.* Palo Alto, CA: Stanford University Press.

Fuson, K. C. (1998). *Children's counting and concept of number.* New York: Springer-Verlag.

Gabbard, C. P. (2007). *Lifelong motor development* (5th ed.). Boston: Allyn & Bacon.

Galinsky, E. (2006). *The economic benefits of high-quality early childhood programs: What makes the difference?* Washington, DC: Committee for Economic Development.

Gallahue, D. L. (1995). Transforming physical education curriculum. In S. Bredekamp & T. Rosegrant (Eds.), *Reaching potentials: Transforming early childhood curriculum* (Vol. 2, pp. 125–144). Washington, DC:

National Association for the Education of Young Children.

Gallahue, D. L., & Ozmun, J. C. (2002). *Understanding motor development: Infants, children, adolescents, and adults.* Dubuque, IA: McGraw-Hill.

Gallahue, D. L., & Ozmun, J. C. (2006). Motor development in young children. In B. Spodek & O. N. Saracho (Eds.), *Handbook of research on the education of young children* (pp. 105–120). Mahwah, NJ: Lawrence Erlbaum Associates.

Gallimore, R., Weisner, T. S., Bernheimer, L. P., Guthrie, D., & Nihira, K. (1993). Family responses to young children with developmental delays: Accommodation activity in ecological and cultural context. *American Journal on Mental Retardation, 98,* 185–206.

Gandini, L. (1993). Fundamentals of the Reggio Emilia approach to early childhood education. *Young Children, 49*(1), 4–8.

Gandini, L. (2008). Introduction to the schools of Reggio Emilia. In L. Gandini, S. Etheredge, & L. Hill (Eds.), *Insights and inspirations from Reggio Emilia: Stories of teachers and children from North America* (pp. 24–27). Worcester, MA: Davis Publications.

Garbarino, J. (1995). *Raising children in a socially toxic environment.* San Francisco: Jossey Bass.

Garcia, E. E. (2005). *Teaching and learning in two languages: Bilingualism and schooling in the United States.* New York: Teachers College Press.

Gardner, H. (2004). *Frames of mind: The theory of multiple intelligences* (20th anniversary ed.). New York: Basic Books.

Gardner, H. (2006). *Multiple intelligences: New horizons in theory and practice.* New York: Basic Books.

Gartrell, D. (2004). *The power of guidance: Teaching social–emotional skills in early childhood classrooms.* Clifton Park, NY: Delmar Learning.

Geist, E. (2003). Infants and toddlers: Exploring mathematics. In D. Koralek (Ed.), *Spotlight on young children and math* (pp. 4–7). Washington, DC: National Association for the Education of Young Children.

Gelman, R. (2000). Domain specificity and variability in cognitive development. *Child Development, 71,* 854–856.

Gelman, R., & Baillargeon, R. (1983). A review of some Piagetian concepts. In Ph. M. Mussen (Ed.), *Handbook of child psychology* (Vol. 3, pp. 167–230). New York: Wiley.

Gelman, R., & Brenneman, K. (2004). Science learning pathways for young children. *Early Childhood Research Quarterly, 19*(1), 150–158.

Gelman, R., & Gallistel, C. R. (1978). *The child's understanding of number.* Cambridge, MA: Harvard University Press.

Genesee, F., Paradis, J., & Crago, M. G. (2004). *Dual language development and disorders: A handbook on bilingualism and second language learning.* Baltimore: Paul H. Brookes.

Gersten, R., Compton, D., Connor, C. M., Dimino, J., Santoro, L., Linan-Thompson, S., et al. (2008). *Assisting students struggling with reading: Response to Intervention and multi-tier intervention for reading in the primary grades. A practice guide* (NCEE 2009-4045). Washington, DC: National Center for Education Evaluation and Regional Assistance, Institute of Education Sciences, U.S. Department of Education. Retrieved from http://ies.ed.gov/ncee/wwc/publications/practiceguides

Gesell, A. (1940). *The first five years of life.* New York: Harper & Row.

Gestwicki, C. (2006). *Developmentally appropriate practice, curriculum, and development in early education.* Clifton Park, NY: Thomson Delmar Learning.

Gilliam, W. S. (2005, May). *Prekindergarteners left behind: Expulsion rates in state prekindergarten programs* (FCD Policy Brief Series No. 3). Retrieved October 14, 2009, from http://www.fcd-us.org/usr_doc/ExpulsionPolicyBrief.pdf

Ginsberg, K. R. (2007). The importance of play in promoting healthy child development and maintaining strong parent–child bonds. *Pediatrics, 119*(1), 182–191.

Ginsburg, H. P. (2006). Mathematical play and playful mathematics: A guide for early education. In D. Singer, R. M. Golinkoff, & K. Hirsh-Pasek (Eds.), *Play = learning: How play motivates and enhances children's cognitive and social-emotional growth* (pp. 145–165). New York: Oxford University Press.

Ginsburg, H. P., Lee, J. S., & Boyd, J. S. (2008). Mathematics education for young children: What it is and how to promote it. *Social Policy Report, XXII*(I), 3–23.

Ginsburg, H. P., & Pappas, S. (2004). SES, ethnic, and gender differences in young children's informal addition and subtraction: A clinical interview investigation. *Journal of Applied Developmental Psychology, 25,* 171–192.

Goffin, S. G., & Washington, V. (2007). *Ready or not? Leadership choices in early care and education.* New York: Teachers College Press.

Goldstein, L. S. (2007a). Beyond the DAP versus standards dilemma: Examining the unforgiving complexity of kindergarten teaching in the United States. *Early Childhood Research Quarterly, 22*(1), 39–54.

Goldstein, L. S. (2007b). Embracing multiplicity: Learning from two practitioners' pedagogical responses to the changing demands of kindergarten teaching in the United States. *Journal of Research in Childhood Education, 21*(4), 378–399.

Gonzalez-Mena, J. (2006). *The young child in the family and the community* (4th ed.). Upper Saddle River, NJ: Pearson Merrill Prentice Hall.

Gonzalez-Mena, J. (2008). *Diversity in early care and education: Honoring differences* (5th ed.). Boston: McGraw-Hill.

Gopnik, A., Meltzoff, A. N., & Kuhl, P. K. (1999). *The scientist in the crib: Minds, brains, and how children learn.* New York: William Morrow.

Gormley, W. T., Gayer, T., Phillips, D., & Dawson, B. (2005). The effects of universal pre-K on cognitive development. *Developmental Psychology, 41*(6), 872–884.

Gormley, W. T., Phillips, D., & Gayer, T. (2008). Preschool programs can boost school readiness. *Science, 320,* 1723–1724.

Goswami, U. (2001). Early phonological development and the acquisition of literacy. In S. B. Neuman & D. K. Dickinson (Eds.), *Handbook of early literacy research* (Vol. 1, pp. 111–125). New York: Guilford Press.

Graham, T. A., Nash, C., & Paul, K. (1997). Young children's exposure to mathematics: The child care context. *Early Childhood Education Journal, 25*(1), 31–38.

Graue, M. E. (2006). This thing called kindergarten. In D. F. Gullo (Ed.), *K today: Teaching and learning in the kindergarten year* (pp. 3–10). Washington, DC: National Association for the Education of Young Children.

Graue, M. E., Kroeger, J., & Brown, C. (2003, Spring). The gift of time: Enactments of developmental thought in early childhood practice (online). *Early Childhood Research & Practice.* Retrieved October 14, 2009, from http://ecrp.uiuc.edu/v5n1/graue.html

Greenberg, M., & Snell, J. (1997). Brain development and emotional development. The role of teaching in organizing the frontal lobe. In P. Salovey and D. Sluyter (Eds.). *Emotional development and emotional intelligence: Educational implications* (pp. 93–119). New York: Basic Books.

Greenberg, P. (1987). Lucy Sprague Mitchell: A major missing link between early childhood education in the 1980s and progressive education in the 1890s–1930s. *Young Children, 42*(5), 70–83.

Greenes, C., Ginsburg, H. P., & Balfanz, R. (2004). Big math for little kids. *Early Childhood Research Quarterly, 19*(1), 159–166.

Greenfield, P. M., & Cocking, R. R. (Eds.). (1994). *Cross-cultural roots of minority child development.* Hillsdale, NJ: Lawrence Erlbaum Associates.

Greenman, J. (2001). *What happened to the world? Helping children cope in turbulent times.* Cambridge, MA: Bright Horizons Family Solutions. Retrieved October 14, 2009, from http://www.brighthorizons.com/talktochildren/docs/whathapp.pdf

Greenman, J. (2005a). *Caring spaces, learning places.* Redmond, WA: Exchange Press.

Greenman, J. (2005b). Places for childhood in the 21st century. *Beyond the Journal, Young Children on the Web.* Retrieved July 26, 2008, from http://journal.naeyc.org/btj/200505/01Greenman.pdf

Greenman, J., & Stonehouse, A. (1994). Reality bites: Biting at the center, Part 1. *Child Care Information Exchange, 99,* 85–88.

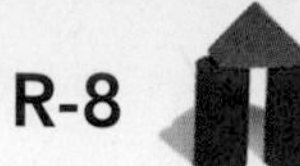

Greenspan, S. I. (1990). Emotional development in infants and toddlers. In J. R. Lally (Ed.), *Infant/toddler caregiving: A guide to social-emotional growth and socialization* (pp. 15–18). Sacramento: California State Department of Education.

Gregory, K. M., Kim, A. S., & Whiren, A. (2003). The effect of verbal scaffolding on the complexity of preschool children's block constructions. In D. E. Lytle (Ed.), *Play and educational theory and practice: Play and culture studies* (pp. 117–134). Westport, CT: Praeger.

Gresham, F. M., & Reschly, D. J. (1987). Dimensions of social competence: Method factors in the assessment of adaptive behavior, social skills, and peer acceptance. *Journal of School Psychology, 25*, 367–381.

Griffin, S. (2004). Number worlds: A research-based mathematical program for young children. In D. H. Clements & A.-M. DiBiase (Eds.), *Engaging young children in mathematics: Standards for early childhood mathematics education* (pp. 325–342). Mahwah, NJ: Lawrence Erlbaum Associates.

Grissom, J. B. (2005). Physical fitness and academic achievement. *Journal of Exercise Physiology Online, 8*(1), 11–25.

Gronlund, G. (2006). *Make early learning standards come alive: Connecting your practice and curriculum to state guidelines.* St. Paul, MN: Redleaf Press.

Gullo, D. F. (2006). Alternative means of assessing children's learning in early childhood classrooms. In B. Spodek & O. N. Saracho (Eds.), *Handbook of research on the education of young children* (2nd ed., pp. 443–455). Mahwah, NJ: Lawrence Erlbaum Associates.

Gullo, D. F. (2005). *Understanding assessment and evaluation in early childhood education* (2nd ed.). New York: Teachers College Press.

Hale, J. (1988). *Black children: Their roots, culture, and learning styles.* Baltimore: Johns Hopkins University Press.

Hale, J. E. (1994). *Unbank the fire: Visions for the education of African-American children.* Baltimore: Johns Hopkins University Press.

Halpern, D. F., & LaMay, L. M. (2000). The smarter sex: A critical review of sex differences in intelligence. *Educational Psychology Review, 12*, 229–246.

Hamre, B. K., & Pianta, R. C. (2001). Early teacher–child relationships and the trajectory of children's school outcomes through eighth grade. *Child Development, 72*, 625–638.

Hamre, B. K., & Pianta, R. C. (2005). Can instructional and emotional support in the first-grade classroom make a difference for children at risk of school failure? *Child Development, 76*(5), 949–967.

Hamre, B. K., & Pianta, R. C. (2007). Learning opportunities in preschool and early elementary classrooms. In R. C. Pianta, M. J. Cox, & K. Snow (Eds.), *School readiness, early learning, and the transition to kindergarten* (pp. 49–83). Baltimore: Paul H. Brookes.

Hannibal, M. A. Z., Vasiliev, R., & Lin, Q. (2002). Teaching young children basic concepts of geography: A literature-based approach. *Early Childhood Education Journal, 30*(2), 81–86.

Hannust, T., & Kikas, E. (2007). Children's knowledge of astronomy and its change in the course of learning. *Early Childhood Research Quarterly, 22*(1), 89–104.

Hanson, M. J. (2004). Ethnic, cultural, and language diversity in service settings. In E. W. Lynch & M. J. Hanson (Eds.), *Developing cross-cultural competence: A guide for working with children and their families* (3rd ed., pp. 1–18). Baltimore: Paul H. Brookes.

Hanson, M. J., & Lynch, E. W. (2004). *Understanding families: Approaches to diversity, disability, and risk.* Baltimore: Paul H. Brookes.

Hanson, M. J., & SooHoo, T. (2007). Cultural influences on young children's social competence. In W. Brown, S. Odom, & S. McConnell (Eds.), *Social competence of young children: Risk, disability, and intervention.* Baltimore: Paul H. Brookes.

Harms, T., Clifford, R. M., & Cryer, D. (2005). *Early childhood environment rating scale (ECERS-R)* (rev. ed.). New York: Teachers College Press.

Harris, K., Pretti-Frontczak, K., & Brown, J. (2009). Peer-mediated intervention: An effective, inclusive strategy. *Young Children, 64*(2), 43–51.

Harry, B., & Klingner, J. (2005). *Why are so many minority students in special education? Understanding race and disability in schools.* New York: Teachers College Press.

Hart, B., & Risley, T. R. (1995). *Meaningful differences in the everyday experience of young American children.* Baltimore: Paul H. Brookes.

Hart, B., & Risley, T. R. (1999). *The social world of learning to talk.* Baltimore: Paul H. Brookes.

Hart, C. H., Burts, D. C., Durland, M. A., Charlesworth, R., DeWolf, M., & Fleege, P. O. (1998). Stress behaviors and activity type participation of preschoolers in more and less developmentally appropriate classrooms. *Journal of Research in Childhood Education, 12*(2), 176–196.

Haugen, K. (2005, January/February). Learning materials for children of all abilities: Begin with universal design. *Exchange, 161*, 45–48.

Haugen, K. (n.d.). Steps for adapting materials for use by all children. Retrieved December 28, 2008, from http://www.childcareexchange.com/library/5016101.pdf

Haywood, K. M., & Gretchell, N. (2005). *Life span motor development* (4th ed.). Champaign, IL: Human Kinetics.

Head Start. (1998). *Head Start program performance standards.* Washington, DC: U.S. Department of Health and Human Services.

Head Start. (2003). *The Head Start leaders guide to positive child outcomes: Strategies to support positive child outcomes.* Washington, DC: U.S. Department of Health and Human Services.

Head Start. (2005, December 1). *Head Start bureau: Programs and services.* Washington, DC: U.S. Department of Health and Human Services.

Head Start. (2008a). *Dual language learning: What does it take? Head Start dual language report.* Washington, DC: U.S. Department of Health and Human Services.

Head Start. (2008b). *Head Start facts.* Retrieved December 19, 2008, from http://www.acf.gov/programs/ohs/about/fy2008.htm

Heath, S. B. (1983). *Ways with words: Language, life, and work in communities and classrooms.* Cambridge University Press.

Heath, S. B. (1989). Oral and literate traditions among Black Americans living in poverty. *American Psychologist, 44*, 367–373.

Hebbeler, K., Spiker, D., Bailey, D., Scarborough, A., Mallik, S., Simeonsson, R., et al. (2007). *Early intervention for infants and toddlers with disabilities and their families: Participants, services, and outcomes.* Palo Alto, CA: Stanford Research International.

Heckman, J. J. (2006). Skill formation and the economics of investing in disadvantaged children. *Science, 30,* 1900.

Helm, J. H., & Beneke, S. (Eds.). (2003). *The power of projects: Meeting contemporary challenges in early childhood classrooms: Strategies and solutions.* New York: Teachers College Press.

Helm, J. H., & Katz, L. G. (2001). *Young investigators: The project approach in the early years.* New York: Teachers College Press.

Hemmeter, M. L., Fox, L., Jack, S., & Broyles, L. (2007). A program wide model of positive behavior support in early childhood settings. *Journal of Early Intervention, 29*, 337–355.

Hemmeter, M. L., Joseph, G., Smith, B., & Sandall, S. (2001). *DEC recommended practices program assessment.* Longmont, CO: Sopris West.

Hemmeter, M. L., Ostrosky, M. M., & Fox, L. (2006). Social–emotional foundations for early learning: A conceptual model for intervention. *School Psychology Review, 35*, 583–601.

Henderson, H. T., & Mapp, K. L. (2002). *A new wave of evidence: The impact of school, family and community connections on student achievement.* Austin, TX: Southwest Educational Development Laboratory. Retrieved from http://www.sedl/org/connections/resources/evidence.pdf

Hendricks, C., & Smith, C. J. (1995). Transforming health curriculum. In S. Bredekamp & T. Rosegrant (Eds.), *Reaching potentials: Transforming early childhood curriculum and assessment* (Vol. 2, pp. 65–79). Washington, DC: National Association for the Education of Young Children.

Heroman, C., & Copple, C. (2006). Teaching in the kindergarten year. In D. F. Gullo (Ed.), *K today: Teaching and learning in the kindergarten year* (p. 66). Washington, DC: National Association for the Education of Young Children.

Heroman, C., & Jones, C. (2004). *Literacy: The creative curriculum approach.* Washington, DC: Teaching Strategies.

Hewes, D. W. (1976). Patty Smith Hill: Pioneer for Young Children. *Young Children, 31*(4), 297–306.

Hewes, D., & the NAEYC Organizational History and Archives Committee. (2001). NAEYC's first half-century: 1926–1976. In *National Association for the Education of Young Children (NAEYC), NAEYC at 75: 1926–2001* (pp. 35–52). Washington, DC: Author.

High/Scope Educational Research Foundation. (2003). *Preschool child observation record* (2nd ed.). Ypsilanti, MI: Author.

Hill, P. S. (1926/1987). The function of the kindergarten. *Young Children, 42*(5), 12–19.

Hilliard, A. G. (Baffour Amankwatia II). (2006). Aliens in the education matrix: Recovering freedom. *New Educator, 2,* 87–102.

Hills, T. W. (1992). Reaching potentials through appropriate assessment. In S. Bredekamp & T. Rosegrant (Eds.), *Reaching potentials: Appropriate curriculum and assessment for young children* (Vol. 1, pp. 43–63). Washington, DC: National Association for the Education of Young Children.

Hinitz, B. F. (2009). History of early childhood education in multicultural perspective. In J. L. Roopnarine & J. E. Johnson (Eds.), *Approaches to early childhood education* (5th ed., pp. 3–24). Upper Saddle River, NJ: Pearson Merrill Prentice Hall.

Hirsch, E. (1996). *The block book.* Washington DC: National Association for the Education of Young Children.

Hirsch, E. D. (2003). Reading comprehension requires knowledge—of words and the world: Scientific insights into the fourth-grade slump and the nation's stagnant comprehension score. *American Educator.* Retrieved October 15, 2009, from http://www.aft.org/pubs_reports/american_educator/spring2003/AE_SPRING.pdf

Hirsch, E. D. (2007a). *The knowledge deficit: Closing the shocking education gap for American children.* Boston: Mariner Books.

Hirsch, E. D., & Wiggins, A. K., Eds. (2009). *Preschool sequence and teacher handbook.* Charlottesville, VA: Core Knowledge Foundation.

Hirsh-Pasek, K., Golinkoff, R. M., Berk, L. E., & Singer, D. (Eds.). (2008). *A mandate for playful learning in preschool: Applying the scientific evidence.* New York: Oxford University Press.

Hoberman, M. A. (2004). *Whose garden is it?* Boston: Houghton Mifflin Harcourt.

Hohmann, M., & Weikart, D. P. (2002). *Educating young children: Active learning practices for preschool and child care programs* (2nd ed.). Ypsilanti, MI: High/Scope Press.

Horn, E., Lieber, J., Sandall, S., Schwartz, I., & Li, S. (2000). Supporting young children's IEP goals in inclusive settings through embedded learning opportunities. *Topics in Early Childhood Special Education, 20*(4), 208–223.

Horton, C., & Bowman, B. T. (2002). *Child assessment at the preprimary level: Expert opinion and state trends.* Chicago, IL: Erikson Institute.

Howes, C., Burchinal, M., Pianta, R., Bryant, D., Early, D., Clifford, R., et al. (2008). Ready to learn? Children's pre-academic achievement in pre-kindergarten programs. *Early Childhood Research Quarterly, 23*(1), 27–50.

Howes, C., & Ritchie, S. (2002). *A matter of trust: connecting teachers and learners in the early childhood curriculum.* New York: Teachers College Press.

Howes, C., & Smith, E. (1995). Children and their child care teachers: Profiles of relationships. *Social Development, 4,* 44–61.

Huffman, L. C., Mehlinger, S. L., Kerivan, A. S., Cavanugh, D. A., Lippitt, J., & Moyo, O. (2001). *Off to a good start: Research on the risk factors for early school problems and selected federal policies affecting children's social and emotional development and their readiness for school.* Washington, DC: Foundations and Agencies Workgroup.

Huffman, L., & Speer, P. W. (2000). Academic performance among at-risk children: The role of developmentally appropriate practices. *Early Childhood Research Quarterly, 15*(2), 167–184.

Hutchins, P. (1968). *Rosie's walk.* New York: Simon & Schuster.

Hyson, M. (Ed.). (2003). *Preparing early childhood professionals: National Association for the Education of Young Children's standards for programs. NAEYC's standards for initial licensure, advanced, and associate degree programs.* Washington, DC: National Association for the Education of Young Children.

Hyson, M. (2004). *The emotional development of young children: Building an emotion-centered curriculum.* New York: Teachers College Press.

Hyson, M. (2008). *Enthusiastic and engaged learners: Approaches to learning in the early childhood classroom.* New York: Teachers College Press.

Hyson, M., Copple, C., & Jones, J. (2006). Bringing developmental theory and research into the early childhood classroom: Thinking, emotions, and assessment. In W. Damon & R. M. Lerner (Series Eds.) & K. A. Renninger & I. E. Sigel (Vol. Eds.), *Handbook of child psychology: Vol. 4. Child psychology in practice* (6th ed., pp. 3–47). New York: Wiley.

Hyun, E. (1998). *Making sense of developmentally and culturally appropriate practice (DCAP) in early childhood education.* New York: Peter Lang.

Institute of Education Sciences. (2007, February). *Dialogic reading* (What Works Clearinghouse Intervention Report). Washington, DC: U.S. Department of Education. Retrieved September 2, 2009, from http://www.eric.ed.gov/ERICDocs/data/ericdocs2sql/content_storage_01/0000019b/80/29/e1/30.pdf

Institute of Education Sciences. (2009). *What Works Clearinghouse.* Washington, DC: U.S. Department of Education. Online at http://ies.ed.gov/ncee/wwc/reports

International Reading Association & National Association for the Education of Young Children. (1998). *Learning to read and write: Developmentally appropriate practices for young children: A joint position statement, adopted May 1998.* Retrieved October 14, 2009, from http://208.118.177.216/about/positions/pdf/PSREAD98.PDF

Isenberg, J. P., & Jalongo, M. R. (2006). *Creative expression and play in the early childhood curriculum.* Upper Saddle River, NJ: Merrill.

Jacklin, C. N. (1989). Female and male: Issues of gender. *American Psychologist, 44,* 127–133.

Jacobson Chernoff, J., Flanagan, K. D., McPhee, C., and Park, J. (2007). *Preschool: First findings from the preschool follow-up of the Early Childhood Longitudinal Study, Birth Cohort (ECLS-B)* (NCES 2008-025). Washington, DC: U.S. Department of Education, Institute of Education Sciences, National Center for Education Statistics.

Jalongo, M. R. (2004). *Young children and picture books* (2nd ed.). Washington, DC: National Association for the Education of Young Children.

Jalongo, M. R. (2008). *Learning to listen, listening to learn: Building essential skills in young children.* Washington, DC: National Association for the Education of Young Children.

Jarrett, O. S., Maxwell, D. M., Dickerson, C., Hoge, P., Davies, G., & Yetley, A. (1998). The impact of recess on classroom behavior: Group effects and individual differences. *Journal of Educational Research, 92*(2), 21–126.

Jensen, A. R. (1980). *Bias in mental testing.* New York: Free Press.

Johnson, B. (2001). *Cup cooking.* Beltsville, MD: Gryphon House.

Johnson, J. E., Christie, J. F., & Wardle, F. (2005). *Play, development, and early education.* Boston: Pearson Allyn & Bacon.

Johnson, M. H. (2005). *Developmental cognitive neuroscience* (2nd ed.). Oxford, UK: Blackwell.

Johnson, M. H. (2008). Developing verbal and visual literacy through experiences in the visual arts: 25 tips for teachers. *Young Children, 63*(1), 74–79.

Jones, E., & Nimmo, J. (1994). *Emergent curriculum.* Washington, DC: National Association for the Education of Young Children.

Jones, J. (2004). Framing the assessment discussion. *Young Children, 59*(1), 14–18.

Jordan, N. C., Huttenlocher, L., & Levine, S. C. (1994). Assessing early arithmetic abilities: Effects of verbal and nonverbal response types on the calculation performance of middle- and low-income children. *Learning and Individual Differences, 6*, 413–432.

Joseph, G. E. (2002). *If you're happy and you know it: The emotional literacy and social information processing scripts of young, at risk children.* Paper presented at Conference on Research Innovations in Early Intervention, San Diego, CA.

Joseph, G., & Strain, P. S. (2003a). Enhancing emotional vocabulary in young children. *Young Exceptional Children, 6*(4), 18–27.

Joseph, G., & Strain, P. S. (2003b). Helping young children control anger and handle disappointment. *Young Exceptional Children, 7*(1), 21–29.

Joseph, G., & Strain, P. S. (2004). Building positive relationships with young children. *Young Exceptional Children, 7*(4), 21–29.

Joseph, G., Strain, P. S., & Ostrosky, M. M. (2006). *Fostering emotional literacy in young children: Labeling emotions* (What Works Brief No. 21). Champaign, IL: Center on the Social and Emotional Foundations for Early Learning. Retrieved October 14, 2009, from http://www.vanderbilt.edu/csefel/briefs/wwb21.html

Joseph, G. E., Webster-Stratton, C., & Reid, J. (2006). *Fostering social and emotional competence: Implementing Dina Dinosaur's social skills and problem solving curriculum in inclusive early childhood programs.* Retrieved August 7, 2009, from http://www.incredibleyears.com/Library/items/fostering-social-emotional-curriculum_06.pdf

Juel, C. (1988). Learning to read and write: A longitudinal study of 54 children from first through fourth grade. *Journal of Educational Psychology, 80*(4), 437–447.

Juel, C. (2006). The impact of early school experiences on initial reading. In D. K. Dickinson & S. B. Neuman (Eds.), *Handbook of early literacy research* (Vol. 2, pp. 410–426). New York: Guilford Press.

Juel, C., Biancarosa, G., Coker, D., & Deffes, R. (2003). Walking with Rosie: A cautionary tale of early reading instruction. *Educational Leadership, 60*(7), 12–18.

Juel, C., Griffith, P. L., & Gough, P. (1986). Acquisition of literacy: A longitudinal study of children in first and second grade. *Journal of Educational Psychology, 78*, 243–255.

Justice, L. M., Pence, K., Bowles, R. B., & Wiggins, A. (2006). An investigation of four hypotheses concerning the order by which 4-year-old children learn the alphabet letters. *Early Childhood Research Quarterly, 21*(3), 374–389.

Kagan, S. L., Kauerz, K., & Tarrant, K. (2008). *The early care and education teaching workforce at the fulcrum: An agenda for reform.* New York: Teachers College Press.

Kaiser, B., & Rasminsky, J. S. (2003). Opening the culture door. *Young Children, 58*(4), 53–56.

Kaiser, B., & Rasminsky, J. S. (2007). *Challenging behavior in young children: Understanding, preventing, and responding effectively* (2nd ed.). Boston: Allyn & Bacon.

Karweit, N., & Wasik, B. (1996). The effects of story reading programs on literacy and language development of disadvantaged preschoolers. *Journal of Education for Students Placed At-Risk, 4*, 319–348.

Katz, L. G. (1994). *The project approach.* Champaign, IL: ERIC Clearinghouse on Elementary and Early Childhood Education.

Katz, L. G., & Chard, S. C. (2000). *Engaging children's minds: The project approach.* Norwood, NJ: Ablex.

Katz, L. G., & McClellan, D. E. (1997). *Fostering children's social competence: The teacher's role.* Washington, DC: National Association for the Education of Young Children.

Kauffman, D., Johnson, S. M., Kardos, S. M., Liu, E., & Peske, H. G. (2002). "Lost at sea": New teachers' experiences with curriculum and assessment. *Teachers College Record, 104*(2), 273–300.

Keeler, R. (2008). *Natural playscapes.* Redmond, WA: Exchange Press.

Keyser, J. (2006). *From parents to partners: Building a family-centered early childhood program.* St. Paul, MN: Redleaf Press.

Khairul, A. S., & Azniah, I. (2004). The improvement of mental rotation through computer-based multimedia tutor. *Malaysian Online Journal of Instructional Technology, 1*(2).

Kim, J. S. (2008). Research and the reading wars. *Phi Delta Kappan, 89*(5), 372–375.

King, M., with Gartrell, D. (2004). Guidance with boys. In D. Gartrell (Ed.), *The power of guidance: Teaching social-emotional skills in early childhood classrooms.* Clifton Park, NY: Delmar Learning.

Kirp, D. (2007). *The sandbox investment: The preschool movement and kids-first politics.* Cambridge: Harvard University Press.

Klein, L. G., & Knitzer, J. (2007). *Promoting effective early learning: What every policymaker and educator should know.* New York: National Center for Children in Poverty, Columbia University.

Klibanoff, R. S., Levine, S. C., Huttenlocher, J., Vasilyeva, M., & Hedges, L. V. (2006). Preschool children's mathematical knowledge: The effect of teacher "math talk." *Developmental Psychology, 42*(1), 59–69.

Kohn, A. (1999). *Punished by rewards: The trouble with gold stars, incentive plans, A's, praise and other bribes.* Boston: Houghton Mifflin.

Kostelnik, M. J., Soderman, A. K., & Whiren, A. P. (2006). *Developmentally appropriate curriculum: Best practices in early childhood education* (3rd ed.). Upper Saddle River, NJ: Prentice Hall.

Krashen, S. (1998). Bridging inequity with books. *Educational Leadership, 55*(4), 18–22.

Krauss, R. (1945). *The carrot seed.* New York: Harper Collins.

Kroll, V. (1997). *Masai and I.* New York: Aladdin.

Ladd, G. W. (1990). Having friends, keeping friends, making friends and being liked by peers in the classroom: Predictors of children's early school adjustment? *Child Development, 61*, 1081–1100.

Ladd, G. W., Birch, S. H., & Buhs, E. S. (1999). Children's social and scholastic lives in kindergarten: Related spheres of influence? *Child Development, 70*(6), 1373–1400.

Ladd, G. W., Herald, S. L., & Andrews, R. K. (2006). Young children's peer relations and social competence. In B. Spodek & O. N. Saracho (Eds.), *Handbook of research on the education of young children* (2nd ed., pp. 23–54). Mahwah, NJ: Lawrence Erlbaum Associates.

Ladson-Billings, G. (1994). *The dreamkeepers: Successful teachers of African-American children.* San Francisco: Jossey-Bass.

Lally, J. R., Mangione, P. L., & Greenwald, D. (Eds.). (2006). *Concepts for care: Essays on infant/toddler development and learning.* San Francisco: WestEd.

Land, K. C. (2008). *Special focus report: Trends in infant/early childhood and middle childhood well-being. 1994–2006.* New York: Child & Youth Well-Being Project, Index Project.

Landry, C. E., & Forman, G. (1999). Research on early science education. In C. Seefeldt (Ed.), *The early childhood curriculum: Current findings in theory and practice* (pp. 133–158). New York: Teachers College Press.

Landry, S. H. (2005a). *Effective early childhood programs: Turning knowledge into action.* Houston: University of Texas–Houston, Health Science Center.

Landry, S. H. (2005b). *Texas Early Education Model (TEEM): Improving school readiness and increasing access to child care for Texas—Year 2 findings.* Houston: University of Texas–Houston, Health Science Center.

Lawry, J., Danko, C., & Strain, P. (1999). Examining the role of the classroom environment in the prevention of problem behaviors. In S. Sandall & M. Ostrosky (Eds.), *Practical ideas for addressing challenging behaviors* (pp. 49–61). Denver, CO: Division for Early Childhood of the Council for Exceptional Children.

Layzer, J., Goodson, B., & Moss, M. (1993). *Life in preschool: Volume one of an observational study of early childhood programs for disadvantaged four-year-olds.* Cambridge, MA: Abt Associates.

Lee, R., Ramsey, P. G., & Sweeney, B. (2008). Engaging young children in activities and conversations about race and social class. *Young Children, 63*(6), 68–76.

Lee, V. E., & Burkam, D. T. (2002). *Inequality at the starting gate: Social background differences*

in achievement as children begin school. New York: Economic Policy Institute.

Leong, D., & Hensen, R. (2005). *Tools of the Mind research training manual* (2nd ed.). Denver, CO: Center for Improving Early Learning, Metropolitan State College.

Levin, D., & Kilbourne, J. (2008). *So sexy, so soon: The new sexualized childhood and what parents can do to protect kids.* New York: Ballantine Books.

Levine, S. C., Jordan, N. C., & Huttenlocher, J. (1992). Development of calculation abilities in young children. *Journal of Experimental Child Psychology, 53,* 72–103.

Levitt, P. (2008). Building brain architecture and chemistry: A primer for policymakers. In A. Tarlov & M. P. Debbink (Eds.), *Investing in early childhood development: Evidence to support a movement for educational change.* New York: Palgrave Macmillan.

Lillard, A. S. (2005). *Montessori: The science behind the genius.* New York: Oxford University Press.

Lillard, A. S., & Else-Quest, N. M. (2006). An evaluation of Montessori education. *Science, 313,* 1893–1894.

Linn, M. C., & Petersen, A. C. (1985). Emergence and characterization of sex differences in spatial ability: A meta-analysis. *Child Development, 56,* 1479–1498.

LoCasale-Crouch, J., Konold, T., Pianta, R., Howes, C., Burchinal, M., Bryant, D., et al. (2007). Observed classroom quality profiles in state-funded pre-kindergarten programs and associations with teacher, program, and classroom characteristics. *Early Childhood Research Quarterly, 22*(1), 3–17.

Locke, J. L. (1993). Learning to speak. *Journal of Phonetics, 21,* 141–146.

Loeber, R., & Hay, D. (1997). Key issues in the development of aggression and violence from childhood to early adulthood. *Annual Review of Psychology, 48,* 371–410.

Lonigan, C. J., & Whitehurst, G. J. (1998). Relative efficacy of parent and teacher involvement in a shared-reading intervention for preschool children from low-income backgrounds. *Early Childhood Research Quarterly, 13*(2), 263–290.

Louv, R. (2005). *Last child in the woods.* Chapel Hill, NC: Algonquin.

Love, J. M., Vogel, C., Raikes, H. H., Chazan-Cohen, R., Kisker, E. E., Constantine, J., et al. (2007, March). *Impacts of Early Head Start at the end of the program (age 3) and two years later when children were in prekindergarten.* Presentation at the SRCD Biennial Meeting, Boston, MA. Retrieved July 20, 2008, from http://www.mathematicampr.com/about%20us/srcd07abstracts.asp#impacts

Lynch, E. W. (2004). Developing cross-cultural competence. In E. W. Lynch & M. J. Hanson (Eds.), *Developing cross-cultural competence: A guide for working with children and their families* (3rd ed., pp. 41–77). Baltimore: Paul H. Brookes.

Lynch, E. W., & Hanson, M. J. (Eds.). (2004). *Developing cross-cultural competence: A guide for working with children and their families* (3rd ed.). Baltimore: Paul H. Brookes.

Lynch, R. G. (2004). *Exceptional returns: Economic, fiscal, and social benefits of investment in early childhood development.* Washington, DC: Economic Policy Institute.

Maccoby, E. (2002). Gender and group process: A developmental perspective. *Current Directions in Psychological Science, 11*(2), 54–58.

Maccoby, E., & Jacklin, C. N. (1974). *The psychology of sex differences.* Palo Alto, CA: Stanford University Press.

Mack, M. G., Hudson, S., & Thompson, D. (1997). A descriptive analysis of children's playground injuries in the United States 1990–2004. *Injury Prevention, 3,* 100–103.

Magnuson, K., & Waldfogel, J. (2005). Early childhood care and education, and ethnic and racial test score gaps at school entry. *The Future of Children, 15,* 169–196.

Main, M., & Solomon, J. (1990). Procedures for identifying infants as disorganized-disoriented during the Ainsworth strange situation. In M. Greenberg, D. Cicchetti, & E. M. Cummings (Eds.), *Attachment in the preschool years: Theory, research, and intervention* (pp. 161–184). Chicago: University of Chicago Press.

Malaguzzi, L. (1993). For an education based on relationships. *Young Children, 49*(1), 9–12.

Malaguzzi, L. (1998). History, ideas, and basic philosophy: An interview with Lella Gandini. In C. Edwards, L. Gandini, & G. Forman (Eds.), *The hundred languages of children: The Reggio Emilia approach—Advanced reflections* (2nd ed., 49–97). Greenwich, CT: Ablex.

Mallory, B. L., & New, R. S. (Eds.). (1994). *Diversity and developmentally appropriate practices: Challenges for early childhood education.* New York: Teachers College Press.

Malone, K., & Tranter, P. (2003). School grounds as sites for learning: Making the most of environmental opportunities. *Environmental Education Research, 9,* 282–303.

Manross, M. A. (1994). *What children think, feel, and know about the overhand throw.* Master's thesis, Virginia Tech University, Blacksburg, VA.

Manross, M. A. (2000). *Learning to throw in physical education class: Part 3. Teaching Elementary Physical Education.* New York: Oxford University Press.

Martin, B. (1996). *Brown bear, brown bear, what do you see?* New York: Henry Holt.

Marzano, R. J., Pickering, D. J., & Pollock, J. E. (2001). *Classroom instruction that works: Research-based strategies for increasing student achievement.* Alexandria, VA: Association for Supervision and Curriculum Development.

Mashburn, A. J., Pianta, R., Hamre, B. K., Downer, J. T., Barbarin, O., Bryant, D., et al. (2008). Measures of classroom quality in pre-kindergarten and children's development of academic, language and social skills. *Child Development, 79*(3), 732–749.

Maslow, A. H. (1954). *Towards a psychology of being.* New York: Van Nostrand.

Masten, A. S., & Powell, J. L. (2003). A resilience framework for research, policy and practice. In S. Luthar (Ed.), *Resilience and vulnerability: Adaptation in the context of childhood adversities.* Cambridge: Cambridge University Press.

Maxwell, K. L., & Clifford, R. M. (2004). Research in review: School readiness assessment. *Young Children, 59*(1), 42–46.

McAfee, O., & Leong, D. (2007). *Assessing and guiding young children's development and learning* (4th ed.). Boston: Pearson Allyn & Bacon.

McAfee, O., Leong, D. J., & Bodrova, E. (2004). *Basics of assessment: A primer for early childhood educators.* Washington, DC: National Association for the Education of Young Children.

McCabe, L. A., & Frede, E. C. (2007). *Challenging behaviors and the role of preschool education* (Policy Brief). New Brunswick, NJ: National Institute for Early Education Research.

McCardle, P., & Chhabra, V. (Eds.). (2004). *The voice of evidence in reading research.* Baltimore: Paul H. Brookes.

McClelland, M. M., Acock, A. C., & Morrison, F. J. (2006). The impact of kindergarten learning-related skills on academic trajectories at the end of elementary school. *Early Childhood Research Quarterly, 21*(4), 471–490.

McCollum, J., Yates, T., Ostrosky, M., & Halle, J. (2001). *Cross-cultural conceptions of child-rearing: Implications for reviewing/evaluating intervention practices* (Technical Report #14). Urbana-Champaign, IL: University of Illinois, Culturally and Linguistically Appropriate Services (CLAS). Retrieved October 3, 2007, from http://clas.uiuc.edu/techreport/tech14.html#4b

McConnell, S. R., & Odom, S. L. (1999). Performance-based assessment of social competence for young children with disabilities: Development and initial evaluation of a multi-measure approach. *Topics in Early Childhood Special Education, 19,* 67–74.

McGee, L., & Schickedanz, J. (2007). Repeated interactive read alouds in preschool and kindergarten. *The Reading Teacher, 60,* 542–551.

McGuire, M. (2007). What happened to social studies? The disappearing curriculum. *Phi Delta Kappan, 88*(8), 620–624.

McLaughlin, B., Blanchard, A. G., & Osanai, Y. (1995). *Assessing language development in bilingual preschool children.* Washington, DC: National Clearinghouse for Bilingual Education.

Mehigan, K. R. (2005). The strategy toolbox: A ladder to strategies teaching. *The Reading Teacher, 58*(6), 552–566.

Meisels, S. (1999). Assessing readiness. In R. C. Pianta & M. J. Cox (Eds.), *The transition to kindergarten* (pp. 39–66). Baltimore: Paul H. Brookes.

Meisels, S. (2007). Accountability in early childhood: No easy answers. In C. Pianta, M. J. Cox, & K. Snows (Eds.), *School readiness and the transition to kindergarten in the era of accountability* (pp. 31–47). Baltimore: Paul H. Brookes.

Meisels, S., & Atkins-Burnett, S. (2005). *Developmental screening in early childhood: A guide* (5th ed.). Washington, DC: National Association for the Education of Young Children.

Meisels, S. J., Jablon, J. R., Dichtelmiller, M. L., Dorfman, A. B., & Marsden, D. B. (2001). *The work sampling system*. Upper Saddle River, NJ: Pearson Early Learning.

Meisels, S. J., Marsden, D. B., Dombro, A. L., Weston, D. R., & Jewkes, A. M. (2003). *The ounce scale*. Upper Saddle River, NJ: Pearson Education.

MenTeach. (2009). *Data about men teachers*. Minneapolis, MN: Author. Retrieved August 19, 2009, from http://www.menteach.org/resources/data_about_men_teachers

Michaels, S., Shouse, A. W., & Schweingruber, H. A. (2008). *Ready, set, science! Putting research to work in K–8 science classrooms*. Washington, DC: National Academies Press.

Mid-Continent Regional Education Laboratory. (2009). *Compendium of content standards and benchmarks for K–12 education*. Denver, CO: Author. Retrieved October 14, 2009, from http://www.mcrel.org/Standards-benchmarks

Milbourne, S. A., & Campbell, P. H. (2007). *CARA's kit: Creating adaptations for routines and activities*. Philadelphia, PA: Child and Family Studies Research Programs, Thomas Jefferson University.

Miller, E., & Almon, J. (2009). *Crisis in the kindergarten: Why children need to play in school*. College Park, MD: Alliance for Childhood.

Miller, T. R., Douglass, J. B., Galbraith, M. S., et al. (1994). *Costs of head and neck injury and a benefit-cost analysis of bicycle helmets*. Landover, MD: Children's Safety Network, Economics and Insurance Resource Center, Society of Automotive Engineers.

Mindes, G. (2006). Social studies in today's early childhood curricula. In D. Koralek & G. Mindes (Eds.), *Spotlight on young children and social studies* (pp. 4–10). Washington, DC: National Association for the Education of Young Children.

Mindes, G. (2008). *Teaching young children social studies*. Lanham, MD: Rowman & Littlefield Education.

Mitchell, A., & David, J. (1992). Explorations with young children: A curriculum guide from the Bank Street College of Education. Mt. Rainier, MD: Gryphon House.

Mix, K. S., Huttenlocher, J., & Levine, S. C. (2002). *Quantitative development in infancy and early childhood*. New York: Oxford University Press.

Montessori, M. (1909/1964). *The Montessori method*. New York: Schocken.

Montie, J. E., Xiang, X., & Schweinhart, L. J. (2006). Preschool experience in 10 countries: Cognitive and language performance at age 7. *Early Childhood Research Quarterly, 21*(3), 313–331.

Moore, K. A. (2006). *Defining the term "at risk"* (Research to Results Briefs). Washington, DC: Child Trends.

Moore, K. A., Chalk, R., Scarpa, J., & Vandivere, S. (2002). *Family strengths: Often overlooked, but real* (Research Brief). Washington, DC: Child Trends.

Morris, A. (1993). *Bread, bread, bread* (Around the World Series). New York: Harper Collins.

Morrow, L. M. (1988). Young children's responses to one-to-one reading in school settings. *Reading Research Quarterly, 23*, 89–107.

Morrow, L. M. (1990). Preparing the classroom environment to promote literacy during play. *Early Childhood Research Quarterly, 5*, 537–554.

Mulligan, S. A. (2003, November). Assistive technology: Supporting the participation of children with disabilities. *Beyond the Journal: Young Children on the Web*, pp. 1–2. Retrieved October 14, 2009, from http://tyc.naeyc.org/articles/pdf/MulliganVol2No2NEXT.pdf

Mullis, I. V. S., Martin, M. O., & Foy, P. (2008). *TIMSS 2007 international report and technical report*. Chestnut Hill, MA: TIMSS & PIRLS International Study Center, Lynch School of Education, Boston College.

National Assessment of Educational Progress. (2005). *Reading assessment scores*. Retrieved from http://nces.ed.gov/nationsreportcard/reading

National Association for Music Education. (1995). Prekindergarten music education standards. Reston, VA: Author.

National Association for Sports and Physical Education. (2002). *Active start: A statement of physical activity guidelines for children birth to five years*. Reston, VA: Author.

National Association for Sports and Physical Education. (2004). *Moving into the future: National standards for physical education* (2nd ed.). Reston, VA: Author. Retrieved December 2, 2008, from http://www.aahperd.org/naspe/template.ctm?template+ns_active.html

National Association for the Education of Young Children (NAEYC). (1995). School readiness: A position statement of the National Association for the Education of Young Children, revised. Washington, DC: Author.

National Association for the Education of Young Children. (2001). *NAEYC at 75: Reflections on the past, challenges for the future*. Washington, DC: Author.

National Association for the Education of Young Children. (2005a). *Assessment of child progress: A guide to the NAEYC early childhood program standard and related accreditation criteria*. Washington, DC: Author.

National Association for the Education of Young Children. (2005b, April). *Code of ethical conduct and statement of commitment* (revised, p. 9). Retrieved September 21, 2009, from http://208.118.177.216/about/positions/pdf/PSETH05.pdf

National Association for the Education of Young Children. (2005c). *Curriculum: A guide to the NAEYC early childhood program standard and related accreditation criteria*. Washington, DC: Author.

National Association for the Education of Young Children. (2005d). *Families and community relationships: A guide to the NAEYC early childhood program standards and related accreditation criteria*. Washington, DC: Author.

National Association for the Education of Young Children. (2005e). *NAEYC Early childhood program standards and accreditation criteria: The mark of quality in early childhood education*. Washington, DC: Author.

National Association for the Education of Young Children. (2005f). *Relationships: A guide to the NAEYC early childhood program standard and related accreditation criteria*. Washington, DC: Author.

National Association for the Education of Young Children. (2005g). *Screening and assessment of young English-language learners: Supplement to the NAEYC and NAECS/SDE joint position statement on early childhood curriculum, assessment, and program evaluation*. Washington, DC: Author

National Association for the Education of Young Children. (2005h). *Teaching: A guide to the NAEYC early childhood program standard and related accreditation criteria*. Washington, DC: Author.

National Association for the Education of Young Children. (2009a). *Developmentally appropriate practice in early childhood programs serving children from birth through age 8: Position statement*. Washington, DC: Author. Retrieved August 23, 2009, from http://www.naeyc.org/files/naeyc/file/positions/position%20statement%20Web.pdf

National Association for the Education of Young Children. (2009b). *NAEYC standards for early childhood professional preparation: Initial licensure programs*. Retrieved September 19, 2009, from http://www.naeyc.org/positionstatements/prepstds_draft

National Association for the Education of Young Children & National Association of Early Childhood Specialists in State Departments of Education. (2002). *Early learning standards: Creating the conditions for success. A position statement*. Washington, DC:

National Association for the Education of Young Children.

National Association for the Education of Young Children & National Association of Early Childhood Specialists in State Departments of Education. (2003). *Early childhood curriculum, assessment, and program evaluation: Building an effective, accountable system in programs for children birth through age 8. Joint position statement.* Washington, DC: National Association for the Education of Young Children.

National Association for the Education of Young Children & National Council of Teachers of Mathematics. (2002). *Position statement: Early childhood mathematics: Promoting good beginnings.* Retrieved from http://www.naeyc.org/about/positions/psmath.asp

National Association for the Education of Young Children Technology and Young Children Interest Forum. (2008). Meaningful technology integration in early learning environments. *Young Children, 63*(5), 48–50.

National Association of Child Care Resource and Referral Agencies. (2008a). *Background issues papers: Working mothers need child care & quality child care makes a difference.* Retrieved January 3, 2009, from http://www.naccrra.org/policy/background_issues/working_mothers.php

National Association of Child Care Resource and Referral Agencies. (2008b). *Leaving children to chance: NACCRRA's ranking of state standards and oversight of small family child care homes.* Washington, DC: Author.

National Association of Child Care Resource and Referral Agencies. (2009). *We can do better: 2009 Update. NACCRRA's Ranking of state child care regulations and oversight.* Washington, DC: Author.

National Association of Early Childhood Specialists in State Departments of Education. (2000). *Still! Unacceptable trends in kindergarten entry and placement: A position statement.* Retrieved March, 2009 from http://naecs.crc.uiuc.edu/position/trends2000.html

National Association of Early Childhood Specialists in State Departments of Education. (2002). *Recess and the importance of play: A position statement on young children and recess.* Washington, DC: Author.

National Center for Children in Poverty. (2007). *Promoting effective early learning: What every policymaker and educator should know.* Columbia University, Mailman School of Public Health. Retrieved February 28, 2007, from http://nccp.org/pub_pes07a.html

National Center for Children in Poverty. (2009). *United States early childhood profile.* Retrieved October 14, 2009, from http://www.nccp.org/profiles/pdf/profile_early_childhood_US.pdf

National Child Care Information Center. (n.d.). *Costs and benefits of employer-sponsored child care.* Vienna, VA: Author. Retrieved from http://www.twc.state.tx.us/svcs/workfamch/nccic_costbenf.pdf

National Coalition for Parent Involvement in Education. (2006). *A new wave of evidence: The impact of school, family and community connections on student achievement.* Retrieved from http://www.ncpie.org/whatshappening/researchJanuary2006.html

National Council for Geographic Education. (1994). *Geography for life: The national geography standards.* Washington, DC: National Geography Society Committee on Research and Exploration. Retrieved October 1, 2009, from http://www.ncge.org/i4a/pages/index.cfm?pageid=3314

National Council for the Social Studies. (1994). Curriculum standards for social studies: Expectations of excellence. Silver Spring, MD: Author. Retrieved from http://www.socialstudies.org/standards/execsummary

National Council for the Social Studies. (1998). *Social studies for early childhood and elementary school children preparing for the 21st century: A report from the NCSS task force on early childhood/elementary social studies.* Silver Spring, MD: Author.

National Council of Teachers of Mathematics. (2000). *Principles and standards for school mathematics.* Reston, VA: Author. Retrieved from http://standards.nctm.org

National Council of Teachers of Mathematics. (2006). *Curriculum focal points.* Reston, VA: Author.

National Early Childhood Accountability Task Force. (2007). *Taking stock: Assessing and improving early childhood learning and program quality.* Washington, DC: Pew Charitable Trusts. Retrieved August 7, 2008, from http://www.policyforchildren.org/pdf/Task_Force_Report.pdf

National Early Literacy Panel. (2008). *Developing early literacy: Report of the National Early Literacy Panel. A scientific synthesis of early literacy development and implications for intervention.* Washington, DC: Author. Retrieved August 29, 2009, from http://www.nifl.gov/publications/pdf/NELPReport09.pdf

National Education Goals Panel. (1995). *Reconsidering children's early development and learning: Toward common views and vocabulary. Goal 1 Technical Planning Group.* Washington: DC: U.S. Government Printing Office.

National Institute of Child Health and Human Development. (2000). *Report of the National Reading Panel. Teaching children to read: An evidence-based assessment of the scientific research literature on reading and its implications for reading instruction.* Washington, DC: Author.

National Institute of Child Health and Human Development, Early Child Care Research Network. (2002). The relation of first grade classroom environment to structural classroom features, teacher, and student behaviors. *The Elementary School Journal, 102,* 367–387.

National Institute of Child Health and Human Development, Early Child Care Research Network. (2003). Social functioning in first grade: Prediction from home, child care and concurrent school experience. *Child Development, 74,* 1639–1662.

National Institute of Child Health and Human Development, Early Child Care Research Network. (2005). A day in third grade: A large-scale study of classroom quality and teacher and student behavior. *Elementary School Journal, 105,* 305–323.

National Professional Development Center on Inclusion. (2007). *Research synthesis points on early childhood inclusion.* Chapel Hill: The University of North Carolina, FPG Child Development Institute.

National Research Council. (1996). *National science education standards.* Washington, DC: National Academies Press.

National Research Council. (2000). *How people learn: Brain, mind, experience, and school* (exp. ed.). Washington, DC: National Academies Press.

National Research Council. (2001). *Adding it up: Helping children learn mathematics.* Washington, DC: National Academies Press.

National Research Council. (2008). *Early childhood assessment: Why, what, and how.* Washington, DC: National Academies Press.

National Research Council. (2009). *Mathematics learning in early childhood: Paths toward excellence and equity.* Washington, DC: National Academies Press.

National Research Council. (2007). *Rising above the gathering storm: Energizing and employing America for a brighter economic future.* Washington, DC: National Academies Press.

National Task Force on Early Childhood Education for Hispanics. (2007, March). *Para nuestros niños: Expanding and improving early education for Hispanic children in the United States.* Retrieved October 21, 2009, from http://www.ecehispanic.org/work/expand_MainReport.pdf

Neilsen, S. L., Olive, M. L., Donovan, A., & McEvoy, M. (1999). Challenging behaviors in your classroom? Don't react—Teach instead! In S. Sandall & M. Ostrosky (Eds.), *Practical ideas for addressing challenging behaviors* (pp. 5–15). Denver, CO: Division for Early Childhood of the Council for Exceptional Children.

Neisworth, J., & Bagnato, S. (2005). DEC recommended practices: Assessment. In S. Sandall, M. L. Hemmeter, M. McLean, & B. J. Smith (Eds.), *DEC recommended practices book: A comprehensive guide for practical application in early intervention/early childhood special education* (pp. 45–70). Longmont, CO: Sopris West.

Nelson, C. A., de Haan, M., & Thomas, K. M. (2006). *Neuroscience of cognitive development: The role of experience and the developing brain.* Hoboken, NJ: Wiley.

Neuman, S. B. (2006). The knowledge gap: Implications for early education. In D. K. Dickinson & S. B. Neuman (Eds.), *Handbook of early literacy research* (Vol. 2, pp. 29–40). New York: Guilford Press.

Neuman, S. B. (Ed.). (2008). *Educating the other America: Top experts tackle poverty, literacy, and achievement in our schools.* Baltimore: Paul H. Brookes.

Neuman, S. B., & Celano, D. (2002). Access to print in middle- and low-income communities: An ecological study of four neighborhoods. *Reading Research Quarterly, 36*, 8–26.

Neuman, S. B., Copple, C., & Bredekamp, S. (Eds.). (2000). *Learning to read and write: Developmentally appropriate practices for young children.* Washington, DC: National Association for the Education of Young Children.

Neuman, S. B., & Dickinson, D. K. (Eds.). (2001). *Handbook of early literacy research.* New York: Guilford Press.

Neuman, S. B., & Roskos, K. (1992). Literacy objects as cultural tools: Effects on children's literacy behaviors in play. *Reading Research Quarterly, 27*, 202–225.

Neuman, S. B., & Roskos, K. (1993). Access to print for children of poverty: Differential effects of adult mediation and literacy-enriched play settings on environmental and functional print tasks. *American Educational Research Journal, 30*, 95–122.

Neuman, S. B., & Roskos, K. (2005). The state of state pre-kindergarten standards. *Early Childhood Research Quarterly, 20*, 125–145.

New, R. S. (2007). Child-centered practice? In R. S. New & M. Cochran (Eds.), *Early childhood education: An international encyclopedia.* Westport, CT: Greenwood Publishing Group.

Newman, S., Brazelton, T. B., Ziegler, E., Sherman, L. W., Bratton, W., Sanders, J., & Christeson, W. (2000). *America's child care crisis: A crime prevention tragedy.* Washington, DC: Fight Crime: Invest in kids. www.fightcrime.org.

Nieto, S. (2004). *Affirming diversity: The sociopolitical context of multicultural education* (4th ed.). Boston: Allyn & Bacon.

Nourot, P. M. (2005). Historical perspectives on early childhood education. In J. L. Roopnarine & J. E. Johnson (Eds.), *Approaches to early childhood education* (5th ed., pp. 3–43). Upper Saddle River, NJ: Merrill Prentice Hall.

Odom, S. (2001). *Widening the circle.* New York: Teachers College Press.

Ogle, D. M. (1986). KWL: A teaching method that develops active reading of expository text. *The Reading Teacher, 39*(6), 564–570.

Oller, K. D., & Eilers, R. E. (Eds.). (2002). *Language and literacy in bilingual children.* New York: Multi-Lingual Matters.

Olsen, L., Bhattacharya, J., & Scharf, A. (2007). *Cultural competency: What it is and why it matters.* Sacramento: California Tomorrow. Retrieved October 14, 2009, from http://www.lpfch.org/informed/culturalcompetency.pdf

Olweus, D. (1993). *Bullying at school: What we know and what we can do.* Malden, MA: Blackwell.

Osborn, D. K. (1991). *Early childhood education in historical perspective* (3rd ed.). Athens, GA: Daye Press.

Ostrosky, M. O., Laumann, B. M., & Hsieh, W.-Y. (2006). Early childhood teachers' beliefs and attitudes about inclusion: What does the research tell us? In B. Spodek & O. N. Saracho (Eds.), *Handbook of research on the education of young children* (2nd ed., pp. 411–422). Mahwah, NJ: Lawrence Erlbaum Associates.

Paleremo, F., Hanish, L. D., Martin, C. L., Fabes, R. A., & Reiser, M. (2007). Preschoolers' academic readiness: What role does the teacher–child relationship play? *Early Childhood Research Quarterly, 22*(3), 401–422.

Papert, S. (1999, March 29). Time 100: Piaget. *Time* magazine. Retrieved October 9, 2009, from http://www.time.com/time/time100/scientist/profile/piaget.html

Parker, J. G., & Asher, S. R. (1987). Peer relations and later personal adjustment: Are low-accepted children at risk? *Psychology Bulletin, 102*(3), 357–389.

Parten, M. (1933). Social participation among preschool children. *Journal of Abnormal and Social Psychology, 27*, 243–269.

Patterson, D. L., & Van der Mars, H. (2008). Distant interactions and their affect on children's physical activity levels. *Physical Education Sports Pedagogy, 13*(3), 277–294.

Payton, J., Weissberg, R. P., Durlak, J. A., Dymnicki, A. B., Taylor, R. D., Schellinger, K. B., et al. (2008). *The positive impact of social and emotional learning for kindergarten to eighth-grade students: Findings from three scientific reviews.* Chicago, IL: Collaborative for Academic, Social, and Emotional Learning. Retrieved from http://www.casel.org or http://www.lpfch.org/sel

Pedulla, J. J. (2003). State-mandated testing: What do teachers think? *Educational Leadership, 61*(3), 42–46.

Peisner-Feinberg, E. S., Burchinal, M. R., Clifford, R. M., Culkin, M. L., Howes, C., Kagan, S. L., et al. (1999). *The children of the Cost, Quality, and Child Outcomes Study go to school.* Chapel Hill: University of North Carolina.

Pellegrini, A. (2005). *Recess: Its role in education and development.* Mahwah, NJ: Lawrence Erlbaum Associates.

Pellegrini, A. D., & Bohn, C. M. (2005, January/February). The role of recess in children's cognitive performance and school adjustment, *Educational Researcher*, pp. 13–17.

Pellegrini, A. D., & Holmes, R. M. (2006). The role of recess in primary school. In D. G. Singer, R. M. Golinkoff, & K. Hirsh-Pasek (Eds.), *Play = learning: How play motivates and enhances children's cognitive and social-emotional growth* (pp. 36–53). New York: Oxford University Press.

Pellegrini, A. D., & Smith, P. K. (1998). Physical activity play: The nature and function of a neglected aspect of play. *Child Development, 69*(3), 577–598.

Perry, T., Steele, C., & Hilliard, A. G. (2003). *Young, gifted, and black: Promoting high achievement among African-American students.* Boston: Beacon Press.

Pestalozzi, J. H. (1894 orig./2007 translation). How Gertrude teaches her children: An attempt to help mothers teach their own children and an account of the method. Whitefish, MT: Kessinger Publishing Co.

Phelan, K. J., Khoury, J., Kalkwarf, H. J., & Lanphear, B. P. (2001). Trends and patterns of playground injuries in United States children and adolescents. *Ambulatory Pediatrics, 1*(4), 227–233.

Phillips, C. B. (1991). *Culture as a process.* Unpublished paper.

Phillips, C. B. (1994). The movement of African-American children through sociocultural contexts: A case of conflict resolution. In B. L. Mallory & R. S. New (Eds.), *Diversity and developmentally appropriate practices: Challenges for early childhood education* (pp. 137–154). New York: Teachers College Press.

Phillips, C. B. (2003). Preparing teachers to use their voices for change. In C. Copple (Ed.), *A world of difference: Readings on teaching young children in a diverse society* (pp. 179–184). Washington, DC: National Association for the Education of Young Children.

Phillips, D., & Crowell, N. A. (Eds.). (1994). *Cultural diversity and early education: Report of a workshop.* Washington, DC: National Academies Press. Retrieved August 13, 2007, from http://www.nap.edu/readingroom/books/earlyed

Piaget, J. (1952). *The origins of intelligence in children.* New York: International Universities Press.

Piaget, J. (1955). *The language and thought of the child.* New York: Meridian Books.

Piaget, J. (1962). *Play, dreams, and imitation in childhood.* New York: Norton.

Pianta, R. C. (1997). Adult–child relationship processes and early schooling. *Early Education and Development, 8*(1), 11–26.

Pianta, R. C. (1999). *Enhancing relationships between children and teachers.* Washington, DC: American Psychological Association.

Pianta, R. C., Belsky, J., Houts, R., Morrison, F., & NICHD ECCRN. (2007). Opportunities to learn in America's elementary classrooms. *Science, 315*, 1795–1796. Retrieved March 19, 2009, from http://www.sciencemag.org/cgi/content/abstract/315/5820/1795?ijkey=09d80c0aad2b21db100d5ad6115fa1d36666bcdf&keytype2=tf_ipsecsha

Pianta, R., Howes, C., Burchinal, M., Bryant, D., Clifford, R., Early, D., et al. (2005). Features of pre-kindergarten programs, classrooms, and teachers: Do they predict observed classroom quality and child–teacher interactions? *Applied Developmental Science, 9*(3), 144–159.

Pianta, R. C., La Paro, K. M., & Hamre, B. K. (2008). *Classroom assessment scoring system (CLASS)*. Baltimore: Paul H. Brookes.

Pianta, R. C., & Stuhlman, M. W. (2003). Teacher–child relationships and children's success in the first years of school. *School Psychology Review, 33*(3), 444–458.

Pica, R. (1997). Beyond physical development: Why young children need to move. *Young Children, 52*(6), 4–11.

Pica, R. (2006). Physical fitness and the early childhood curriculum. *Young Children, 61*(3), 12–19.

Pikulski, J. J., & Chard, D. J. (2005). Fluency: Bridge between decoding and reading comprehension. *The Reading Teacher, 58*(6), 510–519.

Pollitt, E., Leibel, R., & Greenfield, D. (1991). Brief fasting, stress, and cognition in children. *American Journal of Clinical Nutrition, 34,* 1526–1533.

Powell, D. (1994). Parents, pluralism, and the NAEYC statement on developmentally appropriate practice. In B. Mallory & R. New (Eds.), *Diversity and developmentally appropriate practice: Challenges for early childhood education* (pp. 166–182). New York: Teachers College Press.

Powell, D., & Gerde, H. K. (2006). Considering kindergarten families. In D. F. Gullo (Ed.), *K today: teaching and learning in the kindergarten year* (pp. 26–35). Washington, DC: National Association for the Education of Young Children.

Powell, D. R., & O'Leary, P. M. (2009). Strengthening relations between parents and early childhood programs. In E. L. Essa & M. M. Burnham (Eds.), *Informing our practice: Useful research on young children's development* (pp. 193–202). Washington, DC: National Association for the Education of Young Children.

Preschool Curriculum Evaluation Research Consortium. (2008, July). *Effects of preschool curriculum programs on school readiness.* Washington, DC: U.S. Department of Education, Institute of Education Sciences, National Center for Education Research.

Pressley, M. J. (2003). A few things reading educators should know about instructional experiments. *The Reading Teacher, 57*(1), 64–71.

Puma, M., Bell, S., Cook, R., Heid, C., Lopez, M., Zill, N., et al. (2005). *Head Start impact study: First year findings*. Washington, DC: U.S. Department of Health and Human Services, Administration for Children and Families.

Putallaz, M., Grimes, C. L., Foster, K. J., Kupersmidt, J. B., & Coie, J. D. (2007). Overt and relational aggression and victimization: Multiple perspectives within the school setting. *Journal of School Psychology, 45,* 459–586.

Rae, P. (2008). *Physical education for young children: Movement ABCs for little ones.* Champaign, IL: Human Kinetics.

Raikes, H., & Whitmer, J. M. (2006). *Beautiful beginnings: A developmental curriculum for infants and toddlers.* Baltimore: Paul H. Brookes.

Ramey, C., Campbell, F., & Blair, C. (1998). Enhancing the life course for high-risk children. In J. Crane (Ed.), *Social programs that work* (pp. 184–199). New York: Russell Sage Foundation.

Ramming, P., Kyger, C. S., & Thompson, S. D. (2006). A new bit on toddler biting: The influence of food, oral motor development, and sensory activities. *Young Children, 61*(2), 17–23.

Ramsey, P. G. (2004). *Teaching and learning in a diverse world: Multicultural education for young children* (3rd ed.). New York: Teachers College Press.

Ramsey, P. G. (2006). Early childhood multicultural education. In B. Spodek & O. N. Saracho (Eds.), *Handbook of research on the education of young children* (2nd ed., pp. 279–301). Mahwah, NJ: Lawrence Erlbaum Associates.

Raver, C. C., Garner, P. W., & Smith-Donald, R. (2007). The roles of emotion regulation and emotional knowledge for children's academic readiness. In R. C. Pianta, M. J. Cox & K. L. Snow (Eds.), *School readiness and the transition to kindergarten in the era of accountability* (pp. 121–147). Baltimore: Paul H. Brookes.

Reggio Children. (1997). *Shoe and meter: Children and measurement.* Reggio Emilia, Italy: Reggio Children.

Reggio Children & Project Zero. (2001). *Making learning visible: Children as individual and group learners.* Reggio Emilia, Italy: Reggio Children.

Reineke, J., Sonsteng, K., & Gartrell, D. (2008). Nurturing mastery motivation: No need for rewards. *Young Children, 63*(6), 89.

Reynolds, A. J. (2000). *Success in early intervention: The Chicago Child–Parent Centers.* Lincoln: University of Nebraska Press.

Reynolds, A., Magnuson, K., & Ou, S.-R. (2006). *PK–3 education: Programs and practices that work in children's first decade* (FCD Working Paper: *Advancing PK–3,* No. 6). New York: Foundation for Child Development.

Richgels, D. J. (2001). Invented spelling, phonemic awareness, and reading and writing instruction. In S. B. Neuman & D. K. Dickinson (Eds.), *Handbook of early literacy research* (pp. 142–155). New York: Guilford Press.

Rightmyer, E. C. (2003). Democratic discipline in your classroom: A roadmap for beginners. *Young Children, 58*(4), 38–45.

Riley, D., San Juan, R. R., Klinkner, J., & Ramminger, A. (2008). *Social and emotional development: Connecting science and practice in early childhood settings.* St. Paul, MN: Redleaf Press.

Rimm-Kaufman, S. E., Early, D. M., and Cox, M. J. (2002). Early behavioral attributes and teachers' sensitivity as predictors of competent behavior in the kindergarten classroom. *Journal of Applied Developmental Psychology, 23*(4), 451–470.

Ritchie, S., Maxwell, K., & Bredekamp, S. (2009). Rethinking early schooling: Using developmental science to transform children's early school experiences. In O. A Barbarin (Ed.), *Handbook of child development and early education: Research to practice* (pp. 14–37). New York: Guilford Press.

Rivkin, M. S. (1995). *The great outdoors.* Washington, DC: National Association for the Education of Young Children.

Robin, A., Schneider, M., & Dolnick, M. (1976). The turtle technique: An extended case study of self-control in the classroom. *Psychology in the Schools, 13,* 449–453.

Robinson, A., & Stark, D. R. (2005). *Advocates in action: Making a difference for young children* (rev. ed.). Washington, DC: National Association for the Education of Young Children.

Rogoff, B. (1990). *Apprenticeship in thinking.* New York: Oxford University Press.

Rogoff, B. (2003). *The cultural nature of human development.* New York: Oxford University Press.

Roopnarine, J. L., & Johnson, J. (2008). *Approaches to early childhood education* (5th ed.). Upper Saddle River, NJ: Pearson Merrill.

Rosegrant, T., & Bredekamp, S. (1992). Reaching individual potentials through transformational curriculum. In S. Bredekamp & T. Rosegrant (Eds.), *Reaching potentials: Appropriate curriculum and assessment* (Vol. 1. pp. 68–73). Washington, DC: National Association for the Education of Young Children.

Roskos, K., & Neuman, S. (1993). Descriptive observations of adults' facilitation of literacy in play. *Early Childhood Research Quarterly, 8,* 77–97.

Roskos, K., & Neuman, S. B. (2001). Environment and its influences for early literacy teaching and learning. In S. B. Neuman & D. K. Dickinson (Eds.), *Handbook of early literacy research* (pp. 281–294). New York: Guilford Press.

Roskos, K. A., Tabors, P. O., & Lenhart, L. A. (2004). *Oral language and early literacy in preschool: talking, reading, and writing.* Newark, DE: International Reading Association.

Ross, T. (2000). *Wash your hands.* San Diego: Kane/Miller Book Publishers.

Rule, S. (1998). *Strategies for preschool intervention in everyday settings.* Logan, UT: Utah State University.

Rutter, M. (1987). Psychosocial resilience and protective mechanisms. *American Journal of Orthopsychiatry, 57,* 316–331.

Sacther, D. (2005). Healthy and ready to learn. *Educational Leadership, 63*(1), 26–30.

Sameroff, A. J. (1975). Early influences on development: Fact or fancy? *Merrill-Palmer Quarterly, 21*, 267–294.

Sameroff, A., & McDonough, S. (1994). Educational implications of developmental transitions: Revisiting the 5- to 7-year shift. *Phi Delta Kappan, 76*(3), 188–193.

Sammons, P., Sylva, K., Melhuish, E., Siraj-Blatchford, I., Taggart, B., Hunt, S., et al. (2008). *Effective pre-school and primary education 3–11 project (EPPE 3–11): Influences on children's cognitive and social development in year 6* (Department of Children, Schools and Families Research Brief). London: Institute of Education, University of London. Retrieved October 14, 2009, from http://eppe.ioe.ac.uk

Sandall, S., Hemmeter, M. L., Smith, B. J., & McLean, M. E. (Eds.). (2005). *DEC recommended practices: A comprehensive guide for practical application in early intervention/early childhood special education*. Longmont, CO: Sopris West, and Missoula, MT: Division for Early Childhood, Council for Exceptional Children.

Sandall, S.R., & Schwartz, I. S. (2008). *Building blocks for teaching preschoolers with special needs* (2nd ed.). Baltimore: Brookes Publishing Co.

Sandall, S., Schwartz, I., & Joseph, G. (2001). A building blocks model for effective instruction in inclusive early childhood settings. *Young Exceptional Children, 4*(3), 3–9.

Sandall, S., Schwartz, I., Joseph, G., Chou, H., Horn, E. M., Lieber, J., et al. (2002). *Building blocks for successful early childhood programs: Strategies for including all children*. Baltimore: Paul H. Brookes.

Sanders, K. E., Diehl, A., & Kyler, A. (2007). DAP in the 'hood: Perceptions of child care practices by African American child care directors caring for children of color. *Early Childhood Research Quarterly, 22*(3), 394–406.

Sanders, S. W. (2002). *Active for life*. Washington, DC: National Association for the Education of Young Children.

Sanders, S. W. (2006). Physical education in kindergarten. In D. Gullo (Ed.), *K today: Teaching and learning in the kindergarten year* (pp. 138–147). Washington, DC: National Association for the Education of Young Children.

Santos, R. M. (2004). Ensuring culturally and linguistically appropriate assessment of young children. *Young Children, 59*(1), 48–50.

Sarama, J. (2004). Technology in early childhood mathematics: Building blocks as an innovative technology-based curriculum. In D. H. Clements, J. Sarama, & A.-M. DiBiase (Eds.), *Engaging young children in mathematics: Findings of the 2000 National Conference on Standards for Preschool and Kindergarten Mathematics Education* (pp. 361–375). Mahwah, NJ: Lawrence Erlbaum Associates.

Sarama, J., & Clements, D. H. (2002). Learning and teaching with computers in early childhood education. In O. N. Saracho and B. Spodek (Eds.), *Contemporary perspectives on science and technology in early childhood education* (pp. 171–219). Greenwich, CT: Information Age Publishing.

Sarama, J., & Clements, D. H. (2004). Building blocks for early childhood mathematics. *Early Childhood Research Quarterly, 19*(1), 181–189.

Sarama, J., & Clements, D. H. (2007, March 12). *Manual for classroom observation of early mathematics—Environment and teaching (COEMET), Version 3.* See http://www.UBTRIAD.org

Sarama, J., & Clements, D. H. (2009a). *Early childhood mathematics education research: Learning trajectories for young children*. New York: Routledge.

Sarama, J. A., & Clements, D. H. (2009b). *Learning and teaching early math: The learning trajectories approach.* London: Routledge.

Say, A. (1993). *Grandfather's journey*. Boston: Houghton Mifflin.

Schechter, C., & Bye, B. (2007). Preliminary evidence for the impact of mixed-income preschools on low-income children's language growth. *Early Childhood Research Quarterly, 22*(1) 137–146.

Schickedanz, J. A. (1999). *Much more than the ABCs: The early stages of reading and writing.* Washington, DC: National Association for the Education of Young Children.

Schickedanz, J. A. (2008). *Increasing the power of instruction: Integration of language, literacy, and math across the preschool day.* Washington, DC: National Association for the Education of Young Children.

Schickedanz, J. A., & Casbergue, R. M. (2004). *Writing in preschool: Learning to orchestrate meaning and marks.* Newark, DE: International Reading Association.

Schneider, M. (1974). Turtle technique in the classroom. *Teaching Exceptional Children, 7*, 21–24.

Schultz, D., Izard, C. A., Ackerman, B. P., & Youngstrom, E. A. (2001). Emotion knowledge in economically disadvantaged children: Self-regulatory antecedents and relations to social difficulties and withdrawal. *Development and Psychopathology, 13*(1), 53–67.

Schwanenflugel, P. J., Hamilton, C. E., Bradley, B. A., Ruston, H. P., Neuharth-Pritchett, S., & Restrepo, M. A. (2005). Classroom practices for vocabulary enhancement in prekindergarten: Lesson from PAVEd for success. In E. H. Hiebert & M. Kamil (Eds.), *Bringing scientific research to practice: Vocabulary* (pp. 155–177). Hillsdale, NJ: Lawrence Erlbaum Associates.

Schweinhart, L. J., Barnes, H. V., & Weikart, D. P. (1993). *Significant benefits: The High/Scope Perry Preschool study through age 27.* Ypsilanti, MI: High/Scope Press.

Schweinhart, L. J., Montie, J., Xiang, Z., Barnett, W. S., Belfield, C. R., & Nores, M. (2005). *Lifetime effects: The High/Scope Perry Preschool study through age 40* (Monographs of the High/Scope Educational Research Foundation, 14). Ypsilanti, MI: High/Scope Press.

Schweinhart, L., Weikart, D., & Larner, M. (1986). Consequences of three preschool curriculum models through age 15. *Early Childhood Research Quarterly, 1*(1), 15–46.

Schwimmer, J., Burwinkle, T., & Varni, J. (2003). Health-related quality of life for severely obese children and adolescents. *Journal of the American Medical Association, 289*, 113–126.

Scott-Little, C., Lesko, J., Martella, J., & Milburn, P. (2007). Early learning standards: Results from a national survey to document trends in state-level policies and practices. *Early Childhood Research and Practice, 9*(10), 1–22.

Scott-Little, E., Kagan, S. L., & Frelow, V. S. (2006). Conceptualization of readiness and the content of early learning standards: The intersection of policy and research? *Early Childhood Research Quarterly, 21*(2), 153–173.

Scroufe, L. A. (1996). *Emotional development: The organization of emotional life in the early years*. New York: Cambridge University Press.

Seefeldt, C. (2005). *How to work with standards in the early childhood classroom*. New York: Teachers College Press.

Seefeldt, C., Castle, S., & Falconer, R. C. (2010). *Social studies for the preschool/primary child* (8th ed.). Upper Saddle River, NJ: Pearson.

Seefeldt, C., & Galper, A. (2007). *Active experiences for active children: Social studies* (2nd ed.). Upper Saddle River: NJ: Pearson Prentice Hall.

Seo, K.-H. (2003). What children's play tells us about teaching mathematics. In D. Koralek (Ed.), *Spotlight on young children and math* (pp. 19–24). Washington, DC: National Association for the Education of Young Children.

Seo, K.-H., & Ginsburg, H. P. (2004). What is developmentally appropriate in early childhood mathematics education? Lessons from new research. In D. H. Clements, J. Sarama, & A.-M. DiBiase (Eds.), *Engaging young children in mathematics: Standards for early childhood mathematics education* (pp. 91–104). Hillsdale, NJ: Lawrence Erlbaum Associates.

Shepard, L., Kagan, S. L., & Wurtz, E. (Eds.). (1998). *Principles and recommendations for early childhood assessments.* Washington, DC: National Education Goals Panel.

Shepard, L., & Smith, M. (1988). Escalating academic demand in kindergarten: Some nonsolutions. *Elementary School Journal, 89*(2), 135–146.

Shonkoff, J., & Phillips, D. A. (2000). *From neurons to neighborhoods: The science of early childhood development*. Washington, DC: National Academies Press.

Shure, M. B., & Spivack, G. (1982). Interpersonal problem-solving in young children: A cognitive approach to prevention. *American Journal of Community Psychology, 10*(3), 341–356.

Siegler, R. S., & Ramani, G. B. (2008). Playing board games promotes low-income children's numerical development. *Developmental Science, 11*(5), 655–661.

Simpson, W. J. (n.d.). A biographical study of Black educators in early childhood education. Unpublished dissertation, Fielding Institute.

Singer, D. G., Golinkoff, R. M., & Hirsh-Pasek, K. (Eds.). (2006). *Play = learning: How play motivates and enhances children's cognitive and social–emotional growth*. New York: Oxford University Press.

Siraj-Blatchford, I., Muttock, S., Sylva, K., Gilden, R., & Bell, D. (2003, January). *Researching effective pedagogy in the early years: Report of the effective provision of preschool project* (Research Report RR356). London: Institute of Education, University of London. Retrieved August 28, 2009, from http://www.dcsf.gov.uk/research/data/uploadfiles/RR356.pdf

Skinner, B. F. (1953). *Science and human behavior*. New York: Macmillan.

Skinner, B. F. (1968). *The technology of teaching*. New York: Appleton-Century-Crofts.

Slavin, R. (2006). *Educational psychology: Theory and practice* (4th ed.). Boston: Pearson Allyn & Bacon.

Slavin, R. E., & Cheung, A. (2005). A synthesis of research on language of reading instruction for English language learners. *Review of Educational Research, 75*(2), 247–281.

Smilansky, S. (1968). *The effects of sociodramatic play on disadvantaged preschool children*. New York: Wiley.

Smilansky, S., & Shefatya, L. (1990). *Facilitating play: A medium for promoting cognitive, socio-emotional, and academic development in young children*. Gaithersburg, MD: Psychological and Educational Publications.

Snow, C. E., Burns, M. S., & Griffin, P. (Eds.). (1998). *Preventing reading difficulties in young children*. Washington, DC: National Academies Press.

Snow, K. L. (2006). Measuring school readiness: Conceptual and practical considerations. *Early Education and Development, 17*(1), 7–41.

Snyder, A. (1972). *Dauntless women in early childhood education, 1856–1931*. Washington, DC: Association for Childhood Education International.

Soderman, A. K., Chikara, S., Hsiu-Ching, C., & Kuo, E. (1999). Gender differences that affect emerging literacy in first grade children: The U.S., India, and Taiwan. *International Journal of Early Childhood, 31*(2), 9–16.

Spodek, B., & Saracho, O. N. (Eds.). (2006). *Handbook of research on the education of young children* (2nd ed.). Mahwah, NJ: Lawrence Erlbaum Associates.

Sroufe, L. A., & Fleeson, J. (1986). Attachment and the construction of relationships. In W. Hartup & Z. Rubin (Eds.), *Relationships and development* (pp. 51–57). Hillsdale, NJ: Lawrence Erlbaum Associates.

Stahl, S. A. (2001). Teaching phonics and phonological awareness. In S. B. Neuman & D. K. Dickinson (Eds.), *Handbook of early literacy research* (pp. 333–347). New York: Guilford Press.

Stanovich, K. E. (1986). Matthew effects in early reading: Some consequences of individual differences in the acquisition of literacy. *Reading Research Quarterly, 24*, 402–433.

Starkey, P. (December 1, 2007). Presentation to the National Research Council Committee on Early Childhood Mathematics, Washington, DC.

Starkey, P., & Klein, A. (2008). Sociocultural influences on young children's mathematical knowledge. In O. N. Saracho & B. Spodek (Eds.), *Contemporary perspectives on mathematics in early childhood education* (pp. 253–276). Charlotte, NC: Information Age Publishing.

Starkey, P., Klein, A., Chang, I., Qi, D., Lijuan, P., & Yang, Z. (1999). *Environmental supports for young children's mathematical development in China and the United States*. Albuquerque, NM: Society for Research in Child Development.

Starkey, P., Klein, A., & Wakeley, A. (2004). Enhancing young children's mathematical knowledge through a pre-kindergarten mathematics intervention. *Early Childhood Research Quarterly, 19*(1), 99–120.

State of Washington. (2005). *Washington State early learning and development benchmarks*. Retrieved September 16, 2009, from http://www.k12.wa.us/EarlyLearning/Benchmarks.aspx

Stephens, K. (1993, July/August). A tree climbing advocate speaks out. *Exchange, 92*, 77–78.

Stewart, B. E. (2006). *Value-added modeling: The challenge of measuring educational outcomes*. New York: Carnegie Corporation of New York.

Stipek, D., Feller, R., Daniels, D., & Milburn, S. (1995). Effects of different instructional approaches on young children's achievement motivation. *Child Development, 66*, 209–233.

Stipek, D. J., Feller, R., Byler, P., Ryan, R., Milburn, S., & Salmon, J. M. (1998). Good beginnings: What difference does the program make in preparing young children for school? *Journal of Applied Developmental Psychology, 19*, 41–66.

Stoltz, L. M. H. (1977). An American child development pioneer: Lois Meek Stoltz (Interview by R. Takanishi, typescript). Washington, DC: National Archives.

Stork, S., & Sanders, S. W. (2008, January). Physical education in early childhood. *Elementary School Journal, 108*(3), 197–206.

Strain, P. S., & Hemmeter, M. L. (1999). Keys to being successful when confronted with challenging behaviors. In S. Sandall & M. Ostrosky (Eds.), *Practical ideas for addressing challenging behaviors* (pp. 17–25). Denver, CO: Division for Early Childhood of the Council for Exceptional Children.

Strain, P. S., & Hoyson, M. (2000). The need for longitudinal, intensive social skill intervention: LEAP follow-up outcomes for children with autism. *Topics in Early Childhood Special Education, 20*, 116–122.

Strain, P. S., & Joseph, G. E. (2006). *You've got to have friends* (Young Exceptional Children Monograph Series 8: Social Emotional Development). Longmont, CO: Sopris West.

Strain, P. S., & Schwartz, I. S. (2001). Applied behavior analysis and the development of meaningful social relations for young children with autism. *Focus on Autism and Developmental Disabilities, 16*, 120–128.

Strickland, D. S. (1998). *Teaching phonics today: A primer for educators*. Newark, DE: International Reading Association.

Sugai, G., Horner, R. H., Dunlap, G., Kieneman, M., Lewis, T. J., Nelson, C. M., et al. (2000). Applying positive behavior support and functional behavioral assessment in school. *Journal of Positive Behavior Interventions, 2*(3), 131–143.

Sutton-Smith, B. (1980). Children's play: Some sources of theorizing. In K. Rubin (Ed.), *Children's play*, (pp. 1–16). San Francisco, Jossey-Bass.

Swick, D. C., Head-Reeves, D., & Barbarin, O. (2006). Building relationships between diverse families and school personnel. In C. Franklin, M. B. Franklin, & P. Allen Meares (Eds.), *The school services sourcebook: A guide for school based professionals* (pp. 793–801). New York: Oxford University Press.

Sylva, K., Melhuish, E., Sammons, P., Siraj-Blatchford, I., & Taggart, B. (2004). *The effective provision of pre-school education (EPPE) project: Final report*. London: Institute of Education, University of London.

Tabors, P. O. (2008). *One child, two languages: A guide for preschool educators of children learning English as a second language*, 2nd ed. Baltimore: Paul H. Brookes.

Takanishi, R., & K. Kauerz. (2008). PK inclusion: Getting serious about a P–16 education system. *Phi Delta Kappan, 89*(7), 480–487.

Tarlov, A., & Debbink, M. P. (2008). *Investing in early childhood development: Evidence to support a movement for educational change*. New York: Palgrave Macmillan.

Taylor, A. F., Kuo, F. E., & Sullivan, W. C. (2001). Coping with ADD: The surprising connection to green play settings. *Environments and Behavior, 33*(1), 54–77.

Temple, J., & Reynolds, A. (2007). Benefits and costs of investments in preschool education: Evidence from the Child–Parent Centers and related programs. *Economics of Education Review, 26*, 126–144.

Tharp, R., & Entz, S. (2003). From high chair to high school: Research-based principles for teaching complex thinking. *Young Children, 58*(5), 38–44.

Tharp, R. G., Estrada, P., Dalton, S., & Yamachuchi, L. A. (2000). *Teaching transformed: Achieving excellence, fairness, inclusion and harmony*. Boulder, CO: Westview.

Tharp, R. G., Estrada, P., Dalton, S., & Yamachuchi, L. A. (2003, March). *Research evidence: Five standards for effective pedagogy and student outcomes* (Technical Report No. 1, March). Santa Cruz: University of California, Center for Research on Education, Diversity and Excellence.

The brain: A user's guide. (2007, January 29). *Time* (mind and body special issue).

Thomas, J. (2007, November/December). Early connections with nature support children's development of science understanding. *Exchange*, pp. 57–60.

Thomas, A., & Chess, S. (1984). Genesis and evolution of behavioral disorders: From infancy to early adult life. *American Journal of Psychiatry, 141*(1), 1–9.

Thompson, C. M. (1995). *The visual arts and early childhood learning*. Reston, VA: National Art Education Association.

Thompson, C. M. (2006). Repositioning the visual arts in early childhood education: A decade of reconsideration. In B. Spodek & O. N. Saracho (Eds.), *Handbook of research on early childhood education* (2nd ed., pp. 223–242). Mahwah, NJ: Lawrence Erlbaum Associates.

Thompson, R. A. (2002). The roots of school readiness in social and emotional development. In *Kauffman Early Education Exchange, 1*(1). Kansas City, MO: The Ewing Marion Kauffman Foundation. Retrieved October 20, 2005, from http://www.kauffman.org/pdf/eex_brochure.pdf

Thompson, R. A. (2008). *Connecting neurons, concepts, and people: Brain development and its implications* (Preschool Policy Brief, Issue 17). New Brunswick, NJ: National Institute for Early Education Research.

Tobin, K. (1987). The role of wait time in higher cognitive level learning. *Review of Educational Research, 57*, 69–95.

Tremblay, R. E., Mass, L. C., Pagani, L., & Vitaro, F. (1996). From childhood physical aggression to adolescent maladjustment: The Montreal prevention experiment. In R. D. Peters & R. J. MacMahon (Eds.), *Preventing childhood disorders, substance abuse and delinquency* (pp. 268–298). Thousand Oaks, CA: Sage.

Tucker, P. (2008). The physical activity levels of preschool-aged children: A systematic review. *Early Childhood Research Quarterly, 23*(4), 547–558.

U.S. Department of Agriculture. (2009). *Physical activity in 6 to 11 year olds*. Retrieved from http://www.mypyramid.gov

U.S. Department of Education. (2002). Leave No Child Behind Act of 2001. Retrieved from http://www.ed.gov/policy/elsec/leg/esea02/index.html

U.S. Department of Health and Human Services & U.S. Department of Agriculture. (2005). *The dietary guidelines for Americans, 2005* (6th ed.). Washington, DC: Authors.

Valencia, S. W., & Buly, M. R. (2004). Behind test scores: What struggling readers *really* need. *The Reading Teacher, 57*(6), 520–531.

Vance, E., & Weaver, P. J. (2002). *Class meetings: Young children solving problems together*. Washington, DC: National Association for the Education of Young Children.

Vaughn, S., Kim, A., Morris Sloan, C. V., Tejero Hughes, M., Elbaum, B., & Sridhar, D. (2003). Social skills interventions for young children with disabilities. *Remedial and Special Education, 24*(1), 2–15.

Vecchi, V. (2002). *Theater curtain: The ring of transformations*. Reggio Emilia, Italy: Reggio Children.

Verdick, E. (2006). *Germs are not for sharing*. Minneapolis: Free Spirit Publishing.

Voyer, D., Voyer, S., & Bryden, M. P. (1995). Magnitude of sex differences in spatial abilities: A meta-analysis and consideration of critical variables. *Psychological Bulletin, 117*, 250–270.

Vukelich, C., & Christie, J. (2004). *Building a foundation for preschool literacy: Effective instruction for children's reading and writing development*. Newark, DE: International Reading Association.

Vygotsky, L. S. (1962). *Thought and language*. Cambridge, MA: MIT Press.

Vygotsky, L. S. (1977). Play and its role in the mental development of the child. In M. Cole (Ed.), *Soviet developmental psychology* (pp. 76–99). Armonk, NY: M. E. Sharpe.

Vygotsky, L. S. (1978). *Mind in society*. Cambridge, MA: Harvard University Press.

Wallis, A. L., Cody, B. E., & Mickalide, A. (2003). *Report to the nation: Trends in unintentional childhood injury mortality*, 1987–2000. Washington, DC: National Safe Kids Campaign.

Ward, E. H. (1977). A code of ethics: The hallmark of a profession. In B. Spodek (Ed.), *Teaching practices: Reexamining assumptions* (pp. 57–69). Washington, DC: National Association for the Education of Young Children.

Wardle, F. (2008a, July 4). *Does race matter?* Retrieved October 14, 2009, from http://csbchome.org/?p=22

Wardle, F. (2008b, February 10). *Multicultural and multilingual education in early childhood (infants to age 8) programs*. Retrieved October 14, 2009, from http://csbchome.org/?p=20

Wardle, F. (2008c). *Responding to racial and ethnic diversity in schools and early childhood programs. Does race matter?* Retrieved October 14, 2009, from http://csbchome.org/?p=22

Wasik, B. A. (2001). Phonemic awareness and young children. *Childhood Education, 77*(3), 458–495.

Wasik, B. A., & Bond, M. A. (2001). Beyond the pages of a book: Interactive book reading and language development in preschool classrooms. *Journal of Educational Psychology, 93*(2), 243–250.

Wat, A. (2008, November). *The pre-K pinch: Early education and the middle class*. Washington, DC: Pre-K Now.

Watson, M. (2003). Attachment theory and challenging behaviors: Reconstructing the nature of relationships. *Young Children, 58*(4), 12–20.

Webster-Stratton, C. (1999). *How to promote children's social and emotional competence*. London: Paul Chapman Publishing.

Webster-Stratton, C., & Hammond, M. (1997). Treating children with early-onset conduct problems: A comparison of child and parent training interventions. *Journal of Consulting and Clinical Psychology, 65*(1), 93–109.

Weitzman, E., & J. Greenberg. (2002). *Learning language and loving it: A guide to promoting children's social, language, and literacy development in early childhood settings* (2nd ed.). Toronto: The Hanen Centre.

Welch, K. J. (2007). *Family life now: Conversation about marriages, families, and relationships*. Boston: Allyn & Bacon.

Wells, N. M., & Evans, G. W. (2003). Nearby nature: A buffer of life stress among rural children. *Environment and Behavior, 25*(3), 311–333.

Werner, E. E., & Smith, R. S. (1982). *Vulnerable but invincible: A longitudinal study of resilient children and youth*. New York: McGraw-Hill.

West, J., Denton, K., & Germino-Hausken, E. (2000). *America's kindergartners: Findings from the Early Childhood Longitudinal Study, kindergarten class of 1998–99*, Fall 1998. Washington, DC: U.S. Department of Education, National Center for Education Statistics.

Wien, C. A. (2004). *Negotiating standards in the primary classroom: The teacher's dilemma*. New York: Teachers College Press.

Whitebook, M. (2003). *Early education quality: Higher teacher qualifications for better learning environments—A review of the literature*. Berkeley: University of California, Institute of Industrial Relations, Center for the Study of Child Care Employment.

Whitehurst, G. J., Falco, F. L., Lonigan, C., Fischel, J. E., DeBaryshe, B. D., & Valdez-Menchaca, M. C., et al. (1988). Accelerating language development through picture-book reading. *Developmental Psychology, 24*, 552–558.

Whitehurst, G. J., & Lonigan, C. J. (1998). Child development and emergent literacy. *Child Development, 69*(3), 848–872.

Whitehurst, G. J., & Lonigan, C. J. (2001). Emergent literacy: Development from prereaders to readers. In S. B. Neuman & D. K. Dickinson (Eds.), *Handbook of early literacy research*. New York: Guilford Press.

Whoriskey, P. (2006, October 23). Political backlash builds over high-stakes testing: Public support wanes for tests seen as punitive. *Washington Post*, p. A3.

Williams, L. (1988). *The little old lady who was not afraid of anything*. New York: Harper Collins.

Williams, L. R. (1994). Developmentally appropriate practice and cultural values: A case in point. In B. L. Mallory & R. S. New (Eds.), *Diversity and developmentally appropriate practices: Challenges for early childhood education* (pp. 155–165). New York: Teachers College Press.

Wilson, D. M. (2008, November/December). A huge opportunity for middle-income children: An interview with Libby Doggett. *Harvard Education Letter, 24*(6). Retrieved October 16, 2009, from http://www.hepg.org/hel/article/183

Wiltz, N. W., & Klein, E. L. (2001). "What do you do in child care?" Children's perceptions of high and low quality classrooms. *Early Childhood Research Quarterly, 16*(2), 209–236.

Wolery, M., Bailey, D., & Sugai, G. (1988). *Effective teaching: Principles and procedures of applied behavior analysis with exceptional students*. Boston: Allyn & Bacon.

Wolery, M., Strain, P. S., & Bailey, D. (1992). Reaching potentials of children with special needs. In S. Bredekamp & T. Rosegrant (Eds.), *Reaching potentials: Appropriate curriculum and assessment for young children* (Vol. 1, pp. 92–111). Washington, DC: National Association for the Education of Young Children.

Wolery, M., & Wilbers, J. (1994). *Including children with special needs in early childhood programs*. Washington DC: National Association for the Education of Young Children.

Wolfe, J. (2000). *Learning from the past: Historical voices in early childhood education*. Mayerthorpe, Alberta: Piney Branch Press.

Wong Filmore, L. (1991). When learning a second language means losing the first. *Early Childhood Research Quarterly, 6*(3), 323–e47.

Wood, D., Bruner, J. S., & Ross, G. (1976). The role of tutoring in problem solving. *Journal of Child Psychology and Psychiatry, 17*, 89–100.

Worth, K., & Grollman, S. (2003). *Worms, shadows and whirlpools: Science in the early childhood classroom*. Portsmouth, NH: Heinemann.

Yamauchi, L. A., & Kuwahara, R. H. (2008). Research to practice. Joint productive activity: Collaboration that builds new understandings. *Young Children, 63*(6), 34–38.

Yopp, H. K., & Yopp, R. H. (2009). Phonological awareness is child's play. *Young Children, 64*(1), 12–17.

York, S. (2006). *Roots and wings: Affirming culture in early childhood programs*. Upper Saddle River, NJ: Pearson.

Zakriski, A., Wright, J., & Underwood, M. (2005). Gender similarities and differences in children's social behavior: Finding personality in contextualized patterns of adaptation. *Journal of Personality and Social Psychology, 88*(5), 844–855.

Zellman, G. L., & Johansen, A. S. (1998). *Examining the implementation and outcomes of the Military Child Care Act of 1989*. Santa Monica, CA: Rand Corp.

Zepeda, M., Rothstein-Fisch, C., Gonzalez-Mena, J., & Trumbull, E. (2006). *Bridging cultures in early care and education: A training module*. Mahwah, NJ: Lawrence Erlbaum Associates.

Zigler, E. F., & Bishop-Josef, S. J. (2004). Play under siege: A historical overview. In E. F. Zigler, D. G. Singer, & S. J. Bishop-Josef (Eds.). *Children's play: The roots of reading.* (pp. 1–13). Washington, DC: Zero to Three Press.

Zill, N., Sorongon, A., Kim, K., Clark, C., & Woolverton, M. (2006). *Children's outcomes and program quality in Head Start* (FACES 2003 Research Brief). Washington, DC: Head Start Bureau.

Zins, J. E., Bloodworth, M. R., Weissberg, R. P., & Walberg, H. (2004). The scientific base linking social and emotional learning to school success. In J. E. Zins, R. P. Weissberg, M. C. Wang, & H. J. Walberg (Eds.). *Building academic success on social and emotional learning: What does the research say?* New York: Teachers College Press.

Name Index

Subject Index